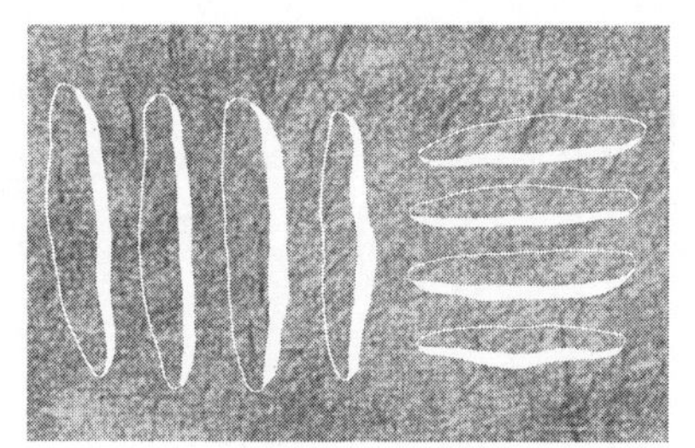

A DICTIONARY OF ARCHAEOLOGY

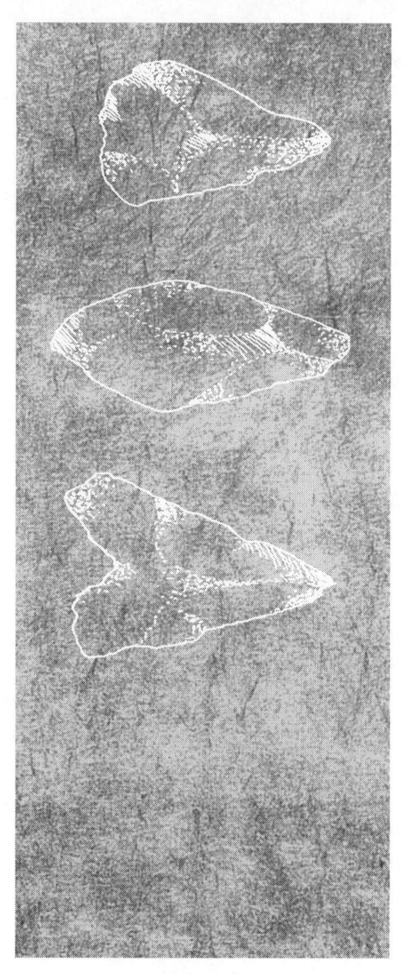

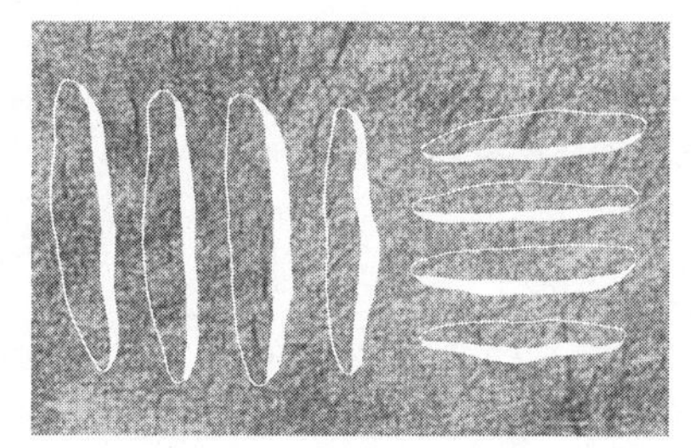

A DICTIONARY OF ARCHAEOLOGY

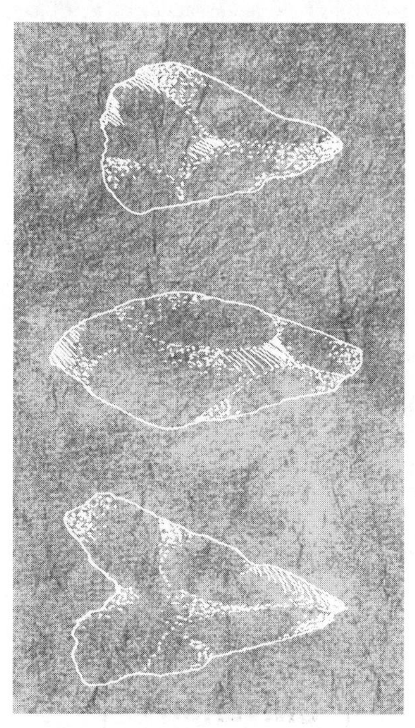

Edited by

IAN SHAW
AND
ROBERT JAMESON

First published 1999

2 4 6 8 10 9 7 5 3 1

Blackwell Publishers Ltd
108 Cowley Road
Oxford OX4 1JF
UK

Blackwell Publishers Inc.
350 Main Street
Malden, Massachusetts 02148
USA

British Library Cataloguing in Publication Data

A CIP catalogue record for this book is available from the British Library.

Library of Congress Cataloging-in-Publication Data

A dictionary of archaeology / edited by Ian Shaw and Robert Jameson.
p. cm.
Includes bibliographical references.
ISBN 0-631-17423-0 (alk. paper)
1. Archaeology—Dictionaries. I. Shaw, Ian, 1961–
II. Jameson, Robert.
CC70.D53 1999
930.1'03—dc21 98-5900
CIP

Typeset in Ehrhardt and Frutiger
by Grahame & Grahame Editorial, Brighton
Printed in Great Britain by TJ International, Padstow, Cornwall
This book is printed on acid-free paper

Contents

Illustrations

Figures

buried features may show either negatively (left) or positively (right). At first, a buried feature with fill of raised organic content may remain warmer than its surroundings (left), but after a prolonged cold spell it may become colder (right). *Source*: O. Braasch: *Luftbildarchäologie in Süddeutschland* (Stuttgart, 1983).

18 **Hallstatt** Selection of objects found in Tomb 507 at Hallstatt, *c*.7th century BC. *Source*: *Trésors des princes celtes*, exh. cat. (Paris, 1987), fig. 47a.

19 **Harappa** Plan of Harappa, type-site of the early Harappan civilization of the Indus Valley, showing the citadel mound, the mounds of the ruined lower town to the east, granaries and circular brick platforms (thought to be working areas for processing grain) to the north and, to the south, one of the few cemeteries known from the Harappan civilization (marked R37). *Source*: B. and R. Allchin: *The rise of civilization in India and Pakistan* (Cambridge, 1982), fig. 7.2.

20 **Hierakonpolis** The underlying map in this illustration shows areas of low density Predynastic settlement in the Hierakonpolis area, and the possible continuation of that settlement beneath the present floodplain. The tomb of a king of this period (inset A) is known as the 'Painted tomb' because of its striking murals (inset B). In the floodplain stands the walled town of Hierakonpolis, dating to the Dynastic period; this represents a smaller but denser form of settlement, exhibiting monumental architecture such as the Early Dynastic palace and gateway (inset C). *Source*: B.J. Kemp: *Ancient Egypt: anatomy of a civilization* (Cambridge University Press, 1989), fig.11.

21 **human evolution** Simplified chronological chart of the evolution of modern humans, together with a simplified chart of the first appearance of early humans in various regions around the world (drawn by Paul Graves-Brown).

22 **Ife** Ife culture, plan of the main artefact concentrations at the Obalara's Land site (labelled A–J), including terracotta heads modelled in naturalistic and schematic styles. *Source*: P.S. Garlake *WAJA* 4 (1974).

23 **Igbo-Ukwu** Igbo Ukwu, Igbo Richard: (A) schematic plan of the relative position of objects on or near the floor of the burial chamber, including numerous copper anklets, three tusks and (1) pectoral plate (2) skull (3) circle of spiral copper bosses set in wood (4) beaded armlets (5) copper handle for calabash (6) tanged copper fan-holder, (7) bronze horseman hilt and (8) crown (B) reconstruction showing the completed burial chamber as it was being roofed in (painting by Caroline Sassoon). *Source*: Thurstan Shaw.

24 **inductively coupled plasma-atomic emission spectrometry (ICP–AES)** Schematic diagram of an inductively coupled plasma-atomic (ICP) system. *Source*: M. Thompson, and J.N. Walsh: *A handbook of inductively coupled plasma spectrometry* (London: Blackie, 1983), fig. 1.2.

25 **Japan, 4** (a) Kofun-period bronze mirror found in the mounded tomb of Kannonyama No. 51, Hyogo prefecture, and map of mainland Japan showing the distribution of mirrors of the same type, as well as the location of Tsubai Otsukayama tomb which may well be the epicentre of the distribution, (b) contour plans of three typical examples of the characteristic 'keyhole shaped' tombs of the Kofun period in Japan, and map showing concentrations of keyhole-shaped tombs on the Japanese mainland. *Source*: A. Ono, H. Harunari and S. Oda, ed.: Zukai: Nihon no Jinrui Iseki (Tokyo University Press, 1992).

26 **Khafajeh** Reconstruction of the Temple Oval at Khafajeh (*c*.2750–2350), consisting of two concentric oval enclosure walls surrounding a platform approached by a flight of steps and surmounted by an inner sanctuary of an unknown deity (tentatively indicated here by the inner rectangular structure). *Source*: H. Crawford: Sumer and the Sumerians (Cambridge University Press, 1991), fig. 4.16.

27 **Kostenki-Borshevo** Upper Palaeolithic 'Venus figurine' from Kostenki-Borshevo, central Russia. *Source*: A. Velichko, ed.: *Arheolojia i paleogeografija pozdnego paleolita russkoi rauniny* (Moscow: Nauka, 1981).

28 **Linearbandkeramik** Longhouse 6 of the LBK culture at Olszanica, Poland. *Source*: S. Milisauskas and J. Kruk: 'Archaeological investigations on Neolithic and Bronze Age sites in south-eastern Poland', *Cave studies in European prehistory*, ed. D. Bogucki (Boca Raton, 1993), p.73, fig. 3.

29 **Maikop** Early 'landscape' design incised on a silver bowl of the 3rd millennium BC found at Maikop (now in the Hermitage, St Petersburg). *Source*: H. Frankfort: *The art and architecture of the ancient Orient*, 4th edn (Harmondsworth: Pelican, 1970), fig. 243.

30 **Maltese temples** The evolution of the 'Maltese temples': (A) a rock-cut tomb, Xemxija,

(B) lobed temple, Mgarr East, (C) trefoil temple, with later cross-wall, Skorba West, (D) 5-apse temple, Ggantija South, (E) 4-apse temple, Mnajdra Central, (F) 6-apse temple, Tarxien Central; the scale measures 3 m. *Source*: D. Trump: 'Megalithic architecture in Malta', *The megalithic monuments of western Europe*, ed. C. Renfrew (London, 1981), p. 65.

31 **Mari** Wall-painting from Mari known as 'The investiture of Zimri-Lin', showing the King before the goddess Ishtar and other deities. *Source*: J. Oates: *Babylon*, 2nd ed. (Thames and Hudson, 1986), fig. 42.

32 **Mask site** Spatial distribution of all item points over the Mask site, identified by cluster assignment in the 13-cluster solution (the shaded areas are hearths). *Source*: R. Whallon: 'Unconstrained clustering for the analysis of spatial distributions in archaeology', *Intrasite spatial analysis in archaeology*, ed. H. Hietala (Cambridge University Press, 1984), fig. 15.

33 **Mawaki** Late Jomon clay mask from the Mawaki site, Ishikawa prefecture, Japan (h. 128 mm). *Source*: K. Suzuki (ed.): *Jomonjin no seikatsu to bunka. Kodaishi Fukugen* (Tokyo: Kodansha, 1988), fig. 222.

34 **Maya** Intricate Maya carving on the side of Stele 31, Tikal, Guatemala. *Source*: W. Coe, Tikal Project, University Museum, University of Pennsylvania, Philadephia.

35 **Mohenjo-Daro** Plan of the citadel of Mohenjo-Daro. *Source*: B. and R. Allchin: *The rise of civilization in India and Pakistan* (Cambridge University Press, 1982), fig. 7.10.

36 **Nan Madol** Plan showing extent of platform structures at Nan Madol, Ponape, which supported houses, tombs and temples. *Source*: P. Bellwood: *Man's conquest of the Pacific* (New York: Oxford University Press, 1979).

37 **Nuri** Plan and cross-section drawing of the tomb of the 25th-dynasty ruler Taharqo, the earliest pyramid at Nuri, Nubia. *Source*: M. Lehner: *The complete pyramids* (London, 1997), p. 196.

38 **Old Bering Sea culture** Intricately carved harpoon head, Old Bering Sea culture, Alaska. *Source*: O.W. Geist and F.G. Rainey: *Archaeological excavations at Kukulik, St Lawrence Island, Alaska* (Washington D.C.: University of Alaska Publications, 1936), fig. 41.

39 **'oracle bones'** 'Oracle bones': a bovid shoulder blade (scapula) and a freshwater turtle under-shell (plastron) from ancient China, both incised with the queries of diviners. *Source*: G.L. Barnes: *China, Korea and Japan* (Thames and Hudson, 1993).

40 **Painted Grey Ware** Map showing the distribution of Painted Grey Ware in the Ganga Valley region of India. *Source*: M. Lal: 'The settlement pattern of the Painted Grey Ware culture of the Ganga valley', *Recent advances in Indo-Pacific prehistory*, ed. V.N. Misra and P. Bellwood (New Delhi, 1985), fig. 1.

41 **pit-and-comb culture** Rock carvings of (A) hunting and (B) fishing scenes, Karelian pit-and-comb culture, Lake Onega region, Russia.

42 **P'u-yang-shih** P'u-yang 'shaman tomb' (no. 45), China, showing how concentrations of shells were arranged in the shapes of animals. *Source*: *WW* 3 (1988), fig. 5.

43 **pyramid** Cross-sections of the major pyramids built during the 3rd and 4th dynasties in Egypt, drawn to the same scale. *Source*: M. Lehner: *The Complete Pyramids* (Thames and Hudson, 1997), p. 16.

44 **regression analysis** Graphs showing (A) best-fit linear regression line for the decrease in Oxford pottery with increasing distance from the kilns (the dotted line shows the decrease in New Forest Pottery away from the New Forest kilns); (B) decrease in Oxford pottery away from the kilns (filled circles indicate sites which may have been reached using water transport; open circles indicate sites not easily reached by water). *Source*: M.G. Fulford and I.R. Hodder: 'A regression analysis of some late Romano-British fine pottery: a case study', *Oxoniensia* 39 (1974), figs 1 and 3.

45 **Sarazm** Eneolithic–Bronze Age settlement at Sarazm, Tadjikistan: (1) walls of Sarazm III, (2) walls of Sarazm II, (3) walls of Sarazm I, (4) ditches, (5) hearths. *Source*: A. Isakov: 'Excavations of the Bronze Age settlement of Sarazm', *The Bronze age civilization of Central Asia*, ed. P. Kohl (Armonk, 1981), fig. 3.

46 **Seima–Turbino** Bronze celts of the Seima–Turbino tradition. *Source*: E.N. Chernykh and S.V. Kuz'minykh: 'Pamyatniki seiminsko-turbinskogo tipa v Evrazii', *Epoha bronzy lesnoi polosy SSSR*, ed. O.N. Bader (Moscow, 1987), fig. 42.

47 **Shang-ts'un-ling** Plan of one of the chariot burials from Shang-ts'un-ling and a reconstruction

drawing of the chariot, 1st millennium BC. *Source*: Anon.: *Shang-ts'un-ling Kuo-kuo mu-ti* (Peking, 1959).

48 **Sintiou-Bara** Long-distance trade contacts indicated by finds at Sintiou-Bara and the extent of the 'culture area' (drawn by Philip Allsworth-Jones).

49 **statistical cycle** Flow chart illustrating the concept of the statistical cycle (drawn by Clive Orton).

50 **statue-menhir** Corsican statue-menhirs: (A) Filitosa V, (B) Nativu, (C) Barbaggiu, (D) Filitosa IV (drawn by Philip Howard). *Source*: R. Whitehouse: 'Megaliths of the Central Mediterranean', *The megalithic monuments of Western Europe*, ed. C. Renfrew (London, 1981), fig. 9.

51 **Sumbar** Grave goods from the Sumbar cemetery. *Source*: I.N. Khlopin: *Jugo-zapadnaja Turkmenija v epohu pozdnei bronzy* (Leningrad, 1983).

52 **Swahili harbour towns** Stone buildings of the 14th- and 15th-century Swahili harbour town of Songo Mnara, part of the Kilwa group complex. The mosques can be identified by their *mihrab* projections in the *qibla* wall facing north to Mecca; the larger houses on the plan can be seen to contain interior courtyards; the small circles on the plan represent wells. *Source*: J.E.G. Sutton: *A thousand years of East Africa* (BIEA, 1990).

53 **Tărtăria** Inscribed clay tablets from Tărtăria, Transylvania, Romania. *Source*: A. Whittle: *Neolithic Europe: a survey* (Cambridge, 1985), fig. 3.15.

54 **Ta-wen-k'ou** Division of the Ta-wen-k'ou culture into three phases as reflected in the pottery styles. *Source*: Anon.: Ta-wen-k'ou (Peking, 1974), fig. 91.

55 **Teotihuacán** Isometric view of the ceremonial structures lining the main north-south axis of Teotihuacán, known as the Street of the Dead. *Source*: M.E. Miller: *The art of ancient Mesoamerica* (Thames and Hudson, 1986), fig. 41.

56 **Teshik-Tash** Reconstruction drawing of the head of a Neanderthal, based on the skull found at Teshik-Tash. *Source*: V.A. Ranov: *DA* 185 (1993).

57 **Tikal** Map of the central part of the Mayan city of Tikal, Guatemala; (1–5) Temples I–V, (6) Temple of Inscriptions, (7) Great Plaza, (8–14) Reservoirs. *Source*: M.D. Coe: *The Maya*, 2nd edn (Thames and Hudson, 1980), fig. 53.

58 **Tikopia** Paleogeographic reconstruction of the Tikopia environment at three points in time *Source*: P. Kirch and D.E. Yen: Tikopia: *The prehistory and ecology of a Polynesian outlier* (BMP, 1982), fig. 124.

59 **tomba di giganti** Plan of tomba di giganti, Li-Mizzani, Palau, Sardinia. *Source*: R. Joussaume: *Dolmens for the dead* (London, 1987), fig. 53.

60 **Ubaid** Male and female baked clay figurines of the Ubaid period (5th millennium BC) from Eridu and Ur (drawn by Tessa Rickards). *Source*: J. Black and A. Green: *Gods, demons and symbols of ancient Mesopotamia: an illustrated dictionary* (BMP, 1992), fig. 64.

61 **Yayoi** Yayoi period bronze bell-shaped *dotaku* from Sakuragaoka, Hyogo prefecture, Japan. *Source*: M. Komoto and S. Yamasaki: *Yayoi Jidai no Chisiki* (Tokyo: Tokyo Bijustsu Kokogaku Shirizu, 1984), fig. 28-1.

Maps

1 **Africa, 1: North** Some major sites in the region.

2 **Africa, 2: West** Major prehistoric sites in the region.

3 **Africa, 3: East** Major prehistoric sites in the region.

4 **Africa, 4: Southern** Some major prehistoric sites in the region.

5 **Africa, 5: Central** Some major prehistoric sites in the region.

6 **America, 1: Arctic North** Major sites in the region with individual entries in the Dictionary.

7 **America, 2: Western North** Major sites in the region with individual entries in the Dictionary.

8 **America, 2: Western North** Distribution of the four main cultural traditions in western North America (the Plateau Pithouse Tradition, the Pebble Tool Tradition, the Stemmed Point Tradition and the Fluted Point Tradition).

9 **America, 3: Southwestern North** Major sites in the region with individual entries in the Dictionary.

10 **America, 4: Eastern North** Major sites in the region with individual entries in the Dictionary.

11 **America, 5: Mesoamerica and Central** Archaeological sites and cultural areas.

Tables

Contributors

Consultant editors
Africa – Kevin McDonald
America – Dean Snow

Contributors

Philip Allsworth-Jones	PA-J
Graeme Barker	GB
Noel Barnard	NB
William Billeck	WB
Sheridan Bowman	SB
Karen Bruhns	KB
Roy Carlson	RC
Timothy Champion	TC
Mike Cowell	MC
David Crossley	DC
Pavel Dolukhanov	PD
David Gibbins	DG
Roberta Gilchrist	RG
Chris Gosden	CG
Paul Graves-Brown	PG-B
Frances Griffith	FG
Charles Higham	CH
Ian Hodder	IH
Richard Hodges	RH
Tom Huffman	TH
Ray Inskeep	RI
Robert Jameson	RJA
Richard Jefferies	RJE
Simon Kaner	SK
Geoffrey King	GK
Kevin McDonald	KM
F. Massagrande	FM
George Milner	GM
Peter Mitchell	PM
Steven Mithen	SM
Paul Nicholson	PTN
Clive Orton	CO
Marilyn Palmer	MP
Robert W. Park	RP
J. Jefferson Reid	JJR
Colin Renfrew	CR
Peter Reynolds	PRE
Prudence Rice	PRI
Ian Shaw	IS
Carla Sinopoli	CS
John Sutton	JS

Preface and Acknowledgements

The principal aim of this dictionary is to provide readers with a reference tool for the terms, techniques and major sites in archaeology, but it is also intended to reflect the constant state of flux in the discipline. This is a difficult balancing act in a concise volume. Presenting archaeology as a process rather than as a body of knowledge implies that particular sites, cultures, methodologies and conceptual models must also be described in a way that is in some sense 'provisional' and open to change. The degree to which the entries succeed in this varies from one subject area to another, but we hope that the book as a whole conveys a sense of the challenges, ambiguities and theoretical context of archaeology as well as the surveyed and excavated data.

We have attempted to make the contents of the dictionary as comprehensive and up-to-date as possible in terms of method and theory. As far as the historical coverage is concerned, the major omission is of classical Greek and Roman history and sites, except where these impinge on other areas (e.g. Roman colonies in North Africa). It is tempting to justify this in terms of the very thorough coverage of the archaeology of the classical world that can be found in recent reference works (e.g. Speake, 1994; Hornblower and Spawforth, 1996). Our real motivation, however, was to make room for a much more comprehensive coverage of previously neglected areas, such as the archaeology of China, Japan and Oceania, as well as longer articles on theory and methodology. To help readers gain an overview of the archaeology of the various geographical regions, many concise essays with regional site maps and cross-references to relevant sites are included in the dictionary (see selective list below).

Otherwise, readers will find little to surprise them in the way the dictionary is structured. It is arranged alphabetically, and adopts the usual conventions for a work of this kind (in the belief that very few readers read 'How To Use' pages in dictionary-style reference works, or remember them for long if they do). It is common for reference editors to argue that cross-references should only be used where they lead the reader to substantial further information about the entry that they are reading. This is certainly the most economical approach, but it does make it cumbersome to let readers know that, for example, a *comparable* site also has an entry in the dictionary, or that a discussion of the archaeology of the region exists (whether or not it greatly adds to the discussion of the individual site). We have therefore adopted a more flexible but inevitably more arbitrary approach, asking ourselves whether the reader might find it *useful* to be reminded that a related subject possesses its own entry in the dictionary.

As far as the dating of sites and artefacts is concerned, we have tried to ensure that the dates cited as BC or AD by contributors are best-estimates in calendar years. Where radiocarbon dating has been used to date a site, we encouraged authors to supply an educated guess as to the approximate calibrated (i.e. calendar) date, and wherever possible to avoid lengthy discussions of dating. This is clearly not ideal, but we felt that in a brief reference work such as this it was better than asking authors to select out or average radiocarbon dates, or to present these dates without the necessary date ranges and contextual qualifications – this would only have given a falsely 'scientific' impression. As some compensation, the site bibliographies can be used to locate more detailed discussions of the dating of sites.

The Wade–Giles method of romanization is used in the articles dealing with the archaeology of China. Despite increasing use, over the last decade, of the mainland Chinese *p'in-yin* system, the Wade–Giles system remains the standard by sheer weight of accumulated publication over the last century, and by virtue of its continuing use in current and forthcoming publications in English (including Chang Kwang-chi, 1986).

The bibliographies that follow virtually every entry are arranged in chronological order of publication, so that either the primary or the most recent sources can be readily found.

References
G. Speake: *A dictionary of ancient history* (Oxford, 1994); Chang Kwang-chi: *The archaeology of ancient China*, 4th edn (New Haven and London, 1986); S. Hornblower and A. Spawforth: *The Oxford Classical dictionary*, 3rd edn (Oxford, 1996).

Major entries on continents, countries and regions
Africa, America, Arabia (pre-Islamic), Asia, Axum, China, CIS and the Baltic States, Egypt, Europe (medieval and post-medieval), Japan, Lowland Maya, Nubia, Oceania, Persia

Major entries on archaeological theory
Annales, antiquarianism, behavioral archaeology, catastrophe theory, central place theory, chaos theory, cognitive archaeology, contextual archaeology, core–periphery models, covering laws, critical archaeology/theory, culture history, decision theory, diffusionism, ethnoarchaeology, ethnography, experimental archaeology, falsification, feminist archaeology, foraging theory, forensic archaeology, formal analysis, functionalism, gender archaeology, hydraulic despotism, inductive and deductive explanation, landscape archaeology, logical positivism, logicism, Marxist archaeology, middle-range theory, neo-evolutionism, nomads, nomothetic (generalizing) approaches, normative explanations, n-transforms, paradigm, phenomenology, post-processual archaeology, post-structuralism, processual archaeology, pulse theory, refuse deposition, secondary products revolution, sign and symbol, site catchment analysis, structuralism, symbolic archaeology, systems theory, theory and theory building, wave of advance, world systems theory.

Acknowledgements
We would like to thank Alyn Shipton, John Davey, Lorna Tunstall and Tessa Harvey for their support (and enormous patience) while waiting for this volume to emerge. We are also grateful to Louise Spencely and Brian Johnson for their hard work on the production and design of the book. The many archaeologists who have contributed to this volume have shown great perseverance during the seemingly everlasting process of commissioning and editing such a lengthy work. Above all we are grateful to Justyna, Ann, Nia and Elin whose lives have been intermittently disrupted by this book.

Ian Shaw
Robert Jameson

Bibliographical Abbreviations

AA	American Antiquity
AAR	African Archaeological Review
AE	Annales d'Ethiopie
AI	Ancient India
AJ	Antiquaries Journal
AJA	American Journal of Archaeology
AM	Ancient Mesoamerica
AO	Archiv für Orientforschung
AP	Ancient Pakistan
APAMNH	Anthropological Papers of the American Museum of Natural History
ARA	Annual Review of Anthropology
ARC	Archaeological Review from Cambridge
AS	Anatolian Studies
ASAE	Annales du Service des Antiquités de 'Egypte
Atlal	The Journal of South Arabian Archaeology
AWA	Advances in World Archaeology
BA	Biblical Archaeologist
BAR BS/IS	British Archaeological Reports (British Series/International Series)
BASOR	Bulletin of the American Schools of Oriental Research
BEFEO	Bulletin de l'Ecole Française d'Extrème Orient
BIE	Bulletin de l'Institut de l'Egypte
BIEA	British Institute in East Africa
BIFAN	Bulletin de l'Institute Française d'Archéologie Nordafricain
BIFAO	Bulletin de l'Institute Française d'Archéologie Oriental
BL	Boletín de Lima
BMFA	Bulletin of the Museum of Fine Arts
BMFEA	Bulletin of the Museum of Far Eastern Antiquities, Stockholm
BMM	Bulletin of the Metals Museum
BMMA	Bulletin of the Metropolitan Museum of Art, New York
BO	Bibliotheca Orientalis
BSEG	Bulletin de la Société d'Egyptologie de Genève
BSFE	Bulletin de la Société Française d'Egyptologie
BSGI	Bulletin de la Service Géologique d'Indochine
BSPF	Bulletin de la Société Préhistorique Française
CA	Current Anthropology
CAJ	Cambridge Archaeological Journal
CBA	Council for British Archaeology
CdE	Chronique d'Egypte
CRASP	Comptes Rendus de l'Académie des Sciences, Paris
CRIPEL	Cahier de Recherches de l'Institut de Papyrologie et d'Egyptologie de Lille
DA	Les Dossiers d'Archéologie
EA	Egyptian Archaeology: Bulletin of the Egypt Exploration Society
EC	Early China
EES	Egypt Exploration Society
EFEO	Ecole Française d'Extrème Orient
HA	Historical Archaeology
HJAS	Harvard Journal of Asian Studies
HKJCS	Hong Kong Journal of Chinese Studies
IA	Inventaria Archaeologica
IAR	Industrial Archaeology Review
IEJ	Israel Exploration Journal
IJNA	International Journal of Nautical Archaeology
JA	Journal Asiatique
JAA	Journal of Anthropological Archaeology
JAH	Journal of African History
JAI	Journal of the Anthropological Institute
JAOS	Journal of the American Oriental Society
JAR	Journal of Anthropological Research
JARCE	Journal of the American Research Center in Egypt
JAS	Journal of Archaeological Science
JASt	Journal of Asian Studies
JEA	Journal of Egyptian Archaeology

JESHO	Journal of the Economic and Social History of the Orient
JFA	Journal of Field Archaeology
JHSN	Journal of the Historical Society of Nigeria
JICS	Journal of the Institute of Chinese Studies
JJRS	Japanese Journal of Religious Studies
JMA	Journal of Mediterranean Archaeology
JNES	Journal of Near Eastern Studies
JOS	Journal of Oman Studies
JRAI	Journal of the Royal Anthropological Institute
JRAS	Journal of the Royal Asiatic Society
JSA	Journal de la Société des Américanistes
JSS	Journal of the Siam Society
JSSEA	Journal of the Society for the Study of Egyptian Antiquities
JWP	Journal of World Prehistory
KCH	Khao Co Hoc
KK	K'ao-ku
KKHP	K'ao-ku hsueh-pao
KSIA	Kratkiye soobshcheniya Institua Arkheologii akademiii nauk SSSR
LAA	Latin American Antiquity
LAAA	Liverpool Annals of Archaeology and Anthropology
LS	Libyan Studies
MASI	Memoirs of the Archaeological Survey of India
MDAIK	Mitteilungen des Deutschen Archäologischen Instituts, Abteilung Kairo
MDOG	Mitteilungen der Deutsche Orient-Gesellschaft
MIAS	Materialy i issledovanija po arheologii SSSR
MJA	Midcontinental Journal of Archaeology
MQRISA	Modern Quaternary Research in Southeast Asia
MS	Monumenta Serica
MSGI	Mémoires du Service Géologique de l'Indochine
NA	Nyame Akuma
NAR	Norwegian Archaeological Review
NARCE	Newsletter of the American Research Center in Egypt
NGM	National Geographic Magazine
NSSEA	Newsletter of the Society for the Study of Egyptian Antiquities
OAHSP	Ohio Archaeological and Historical Society Publication
OUSPA	Otago University Studies in Prehistoric Anthropology
PA	Pakistan Archaeology
PAnth	Plains Anthropologist
PEFEO	Publications de l'Ecole Française d'Extrème Orient
PEQ	Palestine Exploration Quarterly
PPS	Proceedings of the Prehistoric Society
PSAS	Proceedings of the Seminar for Arabian Studies
PSBA	Proceedings of the Society of Biblical Archaeologists
QAL	Quaderni di Archeologia della Libia
RCHME	Royal Commission on the Historical Monuments of England
SA	Scientific American
SAAB	South African Archaeological Bulletin
SAJS	South African Journal of Science
SCWW	Ssu-ch'uan wen-wu
SJA	Southwestern Journal of Anthropology
SMA	Suomen muinaismuistoydistyksen aikakauskrija
TAPS	Transactions of the American Philosophical Society
TLAPEPMO	Travaux du Laboratoire d'Anthropologie, de Préhistoire et d'Ethnologie des Pays de la Méditerranée Occidentale
TP	T'oung Pao
TSCYY	Ti-ssu-chi yen-chiu
UJ	Uganda Journal
WA	World Archaeology
WAJA	West African Journal of Archaeology
WW	Wen-wu
YCHP	Yen-ching hsüeh pao
YJSS	Yenching Journal of Sinological Studies
ZÄS	Zeitschrift für Ägyptische Sprache und Altertumskunde
ZDMG	Zeitschrift der Deutschen Morganländischen Gesellschaft

To
Justyna, Ann, Nia and Elin

A

AAS *see* ATOMIC ABSORPTION SPECTROPHOTOMETRY

Abadiya *see* HIW-SEMAINA REGION

Abkan *see* CATARACT TRADITION

Abri Pataud Large collapsed rock-shelter of the Upper Palaeolithic in the village of Les Eyzies, southwest France. From around 35,000 BC, the site was intermittently occupied over many thousands of years, providing evidence of tools, hearths and living areas from the early AURIGNACIAN through to the Proto-Magdelanian or later. Excavated in the 1950s and 1960s, the radiocarbon dating of the cultural sequence at Abri Pataud has greatly clarified the absolute chronology of the early Upper Palaeolithic. Various engraved and painted limestone plaques and a female figure in bas-relief were recovered from the Périgordian VI level.

Palaeolithic excavation techniques were significantly refined at Abri Pataud. First the excavator, Movius, developed a rigid suspended grid system to help control the excavation area. Second, the stratigraphy was determined by test trenches dug on either side of the edges of the main excavation. This allowed Movius to expose extensively and examine *in situ* the occupation layers in between the trenches. The analysis of the finds from Abri Pataud has been marked by an innovative and extensive use of attribute analysis (e.g. Bricker and David).

H.L. Movius Jr., ed.: 'Excavation of the Abri Pataud, Les Eyzies (Dordogne)', *American School of Prehistoric Research* 30/31 (1977); H. Bricker and N. David: 'Excavation of the Abri Pataud, Les Eyzies (Dordogne): the Périgordian VI (Level 3) assemblage', *American School of Prehistoric Research* 34 (1984).

RJA

Abu Ghurob Egyptian sun temple, 10 km southwest of Cairo, built by the 5th dynasty ruler Neuserra (*c.*2400 BC) and dedicated to the sun-god Ra. It consisted of an upper temple, including a stone-built obelisk and open courtyard with travertine altar, as well as a causeway and valley temple. Its plan must therefore have been similar to Old Kingdom pyramid complexes such as those at SAQQARA and ABUSIR. The excavation of Abu Ghurob, by the German archaeologists Ludwig Borchardt, Heinrich Schäfer and F.W. von Bissing (1898–1901), was a typical example of late 19th century 'clearance', designed primarily to recover choice relief blocks for European collections.

F.W. von Bissing et al.: *Das Re-Heiligtum des Königs Ne-Woser-Re*, 3 vols (Leipzig, 1905–28); D. Wildung: *Ni-User-Re: Sonnenkönig-Sonnengott* (Munich, 1985).

IS

Abu Habba *see* SIPPAR

Abu Hureyra, Tell Settlement site dating to the EPIPALAEOLITHIC, the ACERAMIC NEOLITHIC and the ceramic Neolithic (*c.*8000–5000 BC), which covers an area of 11.5 ha on the southern bank of the Euphrates in northern Syria. It was excavated in 1972–3 by Andrew Moore as part of the rescue work in advance of the construction of a new Euphrates dam (Moore 1975; Moore et al, forthcoming). The archaeological remains of Neolithic mud-brick houses at Abu Hureyra – like those at the roughly contemporaneous sites of Bouqras (in Syria) and AIN GHAZAL (in Jordan) – provide a foretaste of the more urbanized culture which was to emerge most strikingly at ÇATAL HÜYÜK in Anatolia.

A.M.T. Moore: 'The excavation of Tell Abu Hureyra in Syria: a preliminary report', *PPS* 41 (1975), 50–77; T. Molleson, G. Comerford and A.M.T. Moore: 'A Neolithic painted skull from Tell Abu Hureyra, northern Syria', *CAJ* 2/2 (1992), 230–33; A.M.T. Moore, G. Hillman and A. Legge: *Abu Hureyra on the Euphrates* (forthcoming).

IS

Abu Roash (Abu Rawash) Egyptian cemetery at the northern end of the Memphite necropolis, 10 km west of Cairo, which was excavated by Emile Chassinat in 1901. The earliest remains at the site are mud-brick mastaba-tombs, which contain

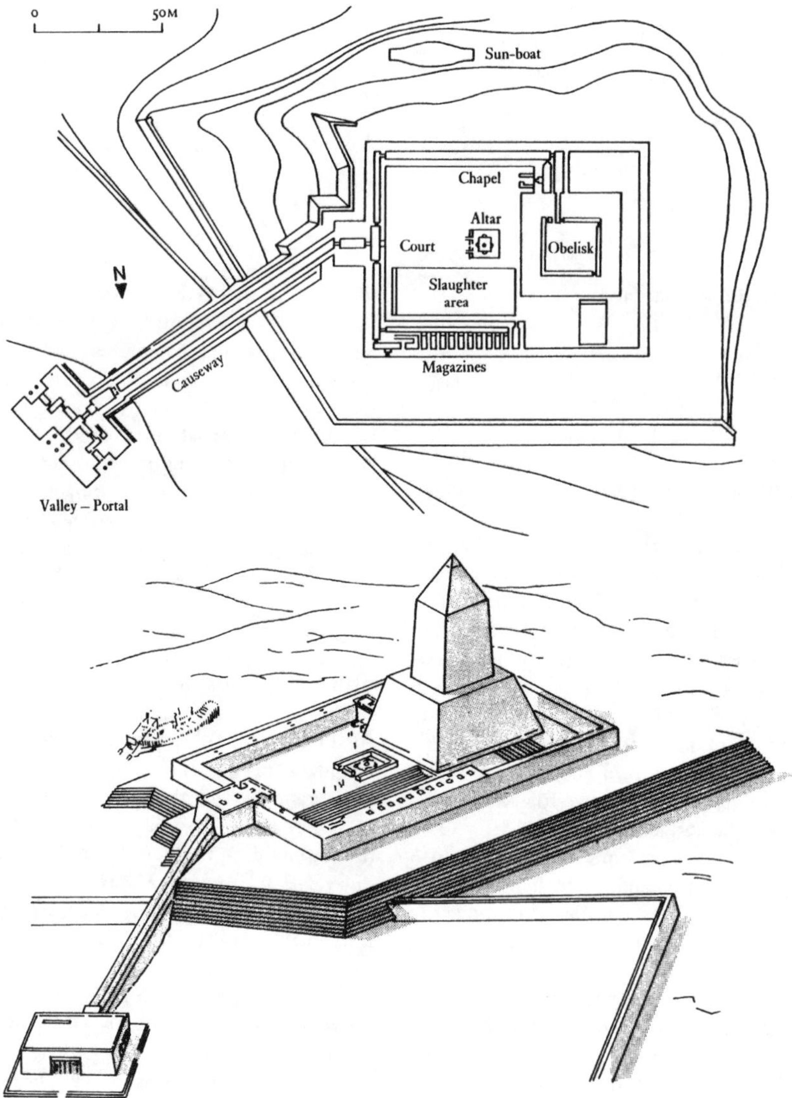

Figure 1 **Abu Ghurob** Plan and reconstruction drawing of the sun temple of Nyuserra at Abu Ghurob, Egypt. *Source*: W. Stevenson Smith: *The art and architecture of ancient Egypt*, 2nd edn (Harmondsworth: Pelican, 1981), figs 124, 125.

artefacts bearing the names of the 1st-dynasty kings Aha and Den (*c*.3000–2900 BC). The main surviving structure at the site is the 4th-dynasty unfinished pyramid of King Djedefra (*c*.2528–2520 BC), which was evidently originally intended to be cased in red granite. To the east of the pyramid Chassinat uncovered the remains of a mortuary temple, a trench intended to hold a solar boat (like those at GIZA), and a cemetery of Old Kingdom private tombs. In the mid-19th century, the German Egyptologist Lepsius noted the presence of a ruined mud-brick pyramid about 2 km to the south of the complex of Djedefra, but only its burial chamber has survived into modern times.

F. Bisson de la Roque: *Rapport sur les fouilles d'Abu-Roasch*, 3 vols (Cairo, 1924–5); V. Maragioglio and C. Rinaldi: *L'architettura della piramidi Menfite* V (Rapallo, 1966); C. Desroches Noblecourt, ed.: *Un siècle de fouilles françaises en Egypte, 1880–1980* (Paris, 1981), 44–53.

IS

Abu Salabikh Cluster of mounds comprising the site of a 4th–3rd millennium Sumerian town (the ancient name of which is uncertain) near the site of NIPPUR. The site was excavated by Nicholas Postgate mainly during the 1980s. One of the mounds consists of deposits dating to the Uruk period (*c*.4300–3100 BC) but the others date principally to the Early Dynastic phase (*c*.2900–2350 BC); the site was evidently occupied in the later periods, but the Sumerian remains are close to the modern ground-level. The survey and excavation at Abu Salabikh from the 1970s onwards has included a number of innovative techniques; on the West Mound, for instance, the whole Early Dynastic surface was investigated by scraping off the uppermost deposits, thus enabling the walls and features to be accurately planned over a wide area of the town (Postgate 1983). The exposure of large areas of mud-brick walling across the site has provided the excavators with an unusual opportunity to analyse large-scale settlement patterns within a Sumerian city (Matthews et al. 1994).

J.N. Postgate: 'Abu Salabikh', *Fifty years of Mesopotamian discovery*, ed. J. Curtis (London, 1982), 48–61; ——: *Abu Salabikh excavations I: The West Mound surface clearance* (London, 1983); ——: 'How many Sumerians per hectare? – probing the anatomy of an early city', *CAJ* 4/1 (1994), 47–65; W. Matthews et al.: 'The imprint of living in an early Mesopotamian city: questions and answers', *Whither environmental archaeology?*, ed. R. Luff and P. Rowley-Conwy (Oxford, 1994).

IS

Abu Shahrein *see* ERIDU

Abu Simbel Pair of Egyptian rock-temples, 280 km south of Aswan, built by Ramesses II (*c*.1290–1224 BC). The 'Great Temple' is dedicated to the king and the principal Egyptian deities, Amon-Ra, Ra-Horakhty and Ptah. Its sanctuary is precisely located so that the rays of the rising sun penetrate to the inner sanctum on two days of the year (22 February and 22 October), thus illuminating four statues in the inner sanctum. The 'Small Temple' is dedicated to the king's wife, Nefertari. Both temples were carved into the cliffs to the west of the Nile, with colossal statues of the king and queen sculpted along the outer façades. Abu Simbel was among the Nubian monuments saved from LAKE NASSER (the reservoir created by the construction of the Aswan High Dam). In the late 1960s, in an operation costing some $40 million, the temples were dismantled into separate blocks and then reassembled at a location 64 m higher and 200 m to the west of the original site. The alignment of the relocated Great Temple has been maintained so that the sanctuary is still illuminated twice a year.

W. MacQuitty: *Abu Simbel* (London, 1965); C. Desroches-Noblecourt and C. Kuentz: *Le petit temple d'Abou Simbel*, 2 vols (Cairo, 1968); T. Säve-Söderbergh, ed.: *Temples and tombs of ancient Nubia* (London, 1987).

IS

Abusir Egyptian royal necropolis and temple site, located 25 km west of Cairo. The major archaeological remains at Abusir are the pyramids of four of the 5th-dynasty kings (Sahura, Neferirkara, Neuserra and Neferefra (*c*.2458–2392 BC) and the sun temple of Userkaf (*c*. 2465–2458 BC), which were first scientifically excavated by Ludwig Borchardt. During the 1980s and 1990s other parts of the site, including the mastaba of Ptahshepses, the mortuary temple of Neferefra, the pyramid complex of Queen Khentkawes (mother of Sahura and Neferirkara) and several Late Period shaft tombs (including that of the chief physician Udjahorresnet), have been excavated by a Czechoslovakian team. The contents of papyrus archives discovered in the mortuary temple of Neferirkara have shed useful light on the structure and mechanisms of Egyptian Old Kingdom temple administration, especially when combined with archaeological evidence from sites such as DAHSHUR, GIZA and SAQQARA.

L. Borchardt: *Das Grabdenkmal des Königs Ne-user-Re* (Leipzig, 1907); ——: *Das Grabdenkmal des Königs Nefer-ir-ka-Re* (Leipzig, 1909); ——: *Das Grabdenkmal des Königs Sahu-Re* (Leipzig, 1910–13); H. Ricke: *Das Sonnenheiligtum des Königs Userkaf* (Cairo, 1965; Wiesbaden, 1969); P. Kaplony: 'Das Papyrus Archiv von Abusir', *Orientalia* 41 (1972), 180–244; P. Posener-Kriéger: *Les archives du temple funéraire de Neferirkare (Les papyrus d'Abousir)*, 2 vols (Cairo, 1976); M. Verner: Preliminary excavation reports in *ZÄS* (1982–).

IS

Abydos (anc. Abdjw) Pharaonic site on the west bank of the Nile, 50 km south of Sohag. Abydos was inhabited from the late predynastic to the Christian period (*c*.4000 BC–AD 641). As well as the Early Dynastic royal necropolis of Umm el-Qaʿab (dating to *c*.3000–2649 BC), the site includes the temple of the canine god Osiris-Khentimentiu (Kom el-Sultan), the temples of Seti I and Ramesses II, the Osireion (an archaizing 'dummy tomb' of Osiris), an extensive settlement and numerous graves and cenotaphs of humans and animals. During the second half of the 19th century the site was excavated by Auguste Mariette and Emile Amélineau, whose techniques amounted to little more than treasure hunting.

The scientific analysis of the site began with Flinders Petrie, who re-excavated the Early Dynastic royal tombs between 1899 and 1901. Peet's 1913 season included the excavation of a small circular area of settlement dating to the late predynastic period (Gerzean: *c*.3500–3000 BC), including an assemblage of over 300 stone tools, a midden and several hearths (discussed in Hoffman 1979). Although Peet simply dug two trenches through an area with a diameter of about 30 m, this was nevertheless the first scientific examination of an Egyptian settlement of the predynastic period, predating even Gertrude Caton-Thompson's pioneering work at the stratified settlement of Hammamia (*see* el-BADARI).

By re-analysing the results of the excavations of Petrie and Eric Peet, Barry Kemp (1967) has deduced that the Early Dynastic royal tombs were complemented by a row of 'funerary palaces' to the east, which may well have been the prototype of the mortuary temples in Old Kingdom pyramid complexes. In 1991 the excavations of David O'Connor revealed further support for this theory in the form of a number of Early Dynastic wooden boat graves near the Shunet el-Zebib, best surviving of the 'funerary palaces' (O'Connor 1991). Since 1973 German excavators have re-examined the Early Dynastic royal cemetery and its vicinity; their findings include conclusive proof of cultural continuity between the adjacent late pre-dynastic Cemetery U and the royal graves dated to 'Dynasty 0', the beginning of the Early Dynastic period (Dreyer 1992).

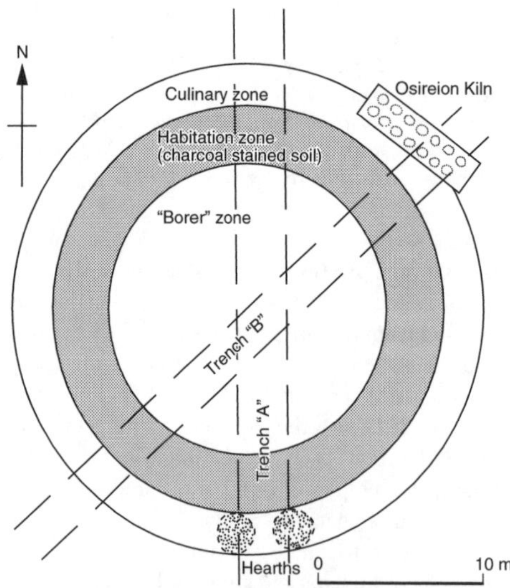

Figure 2 **Abydos** Schematic plan of the area of the late Gerzean settlement excavated by Eric Peet at Abydos, Egypt. *Source*: M.A. Hoffman: *Egypt before the pharaohs* (London: Ark, 1980), fig. 44.

A Mariette: *Abydos: description des fouilles exécutées sur l'emplacement de cette ville*, 2 vols (Paris, 1869–80); W.M.F. Petrie: *The royal tombs of the earliest dynasties*, 2 vols (London, 1900–1); B.J. Kemp: 'The Egyptian 1st dynasty royal cemetery', *Antiquity* 41 (1967), 22–32; M.A. Hoffman: *Egypt before the pharaohs* (New York, 1979), 150–4; D. O'Connor: 'Boat graves and pyramid origins: new discoveries at Abydos, Egypt', *Expedition* 33/3 (1991), 5–17; G. Dreyer: 'Recent discoveries at Abydos Cemetery U', *The Nile Delta in transition: 4th–3rd millennium BC*, ed. E.C.M. van den Brink (Tel Aviv, 1992), 293–9.

IS

accelerator mass spectrometry (AMS) As used in RADIOCARBON DATING, AMS selects and counts the ^{14}C atoms in the sample relative to the many orders of magnitude higher number of ^{13}C or ^{12}C atoms (*see* CONVENTIONAL RADIOCARBON DATING). Mass spectrometry differentiates between charged particles of very nearly the same mass, travelling at the same velocity, by subjecting them to a magnetic field. The heavier particles are deflected least. An accelerator, used in conjunction with mass spectrometry, increases the velocity of the particles which enhances differentiation. AMS needs only of the order of 1 mg of carbon (e.g. the amount that could be derived from about 0.5 g of bone) but precision is limited, typically ± 60 years at best.

J.A.J. Gowlett and R.E.M. Hedges, eds *Archaeological results from accelerator dating* (Oxford, 1986); H.E. Gove: 'The history of AMS, its advantages over decay counting: applications and prospects', *Radiocarbon after four decades: an interdisciplinary perspective*, ed. R.E. Taylor, A. Long and R.S. Kra (Berlin and New York, 1992).

SB

acllahuasi Houses in which INCA 'chosen women' (i.e. women removed from child-bearing to prepare beer and to weave for the state) lived and worked.

G. Gasparini and L. Margolis: *Inca architecture* (Indiana, 1980), 56, 67, 192, 264; B. Cobo: *Inca religion and customs*, trans. R. Hamilton (Texas, 1990), ch. 37.

KB

Açemhöyük (anc. Burushkhattum) Settlement mound in the central plain of Anatolia, which has been identified with the city of Burushkhattum (the HITTITE Purushkhanda). The site has been excavated since 1963 by Nimet Özgüç, revealing occupation levels stretching back to the 5th millennium BC. The city reached a peak of prosperity in stratum 5, dating to the Middle Bronze Age (*c*.2000–1500 BC), when the colonies of Old ASSYRIAN merchants were thriving at Kanesh (KÜLTEPE), Hattusas (BOGHAZKÖY) and Burushkattum itself. It is to this phase that Özgüç dates a massive Hittite palace complex, which is still only partially excavated.

N. Özgüç: 'Excavations at Açemhöyük', *Anadolu* 10 (1966), 1–52; J. Mellink: 'Archaeology in Asia Minor', *AJA* 71 (1967), 160–1 [section by Özgüç on the excavations at Açemhöyük]; N. Özgüç: 'An ivory box and a stone mould from Açemhöyük', *Turk Tarih Kurumu: Belleten* 40 (1976), 555–60.

IS

Aceramic Neolithic Phase of the Neolithic period in the ancient Near East preceding the introduction of pottery, which corresponds to Pre-Pottery Neolithic B and C in the Levant (*c*.8500–7000 BC). Some settlements during this period, such as AIN GHAZAL, JERICHO and ABU HUREYRA, reached a size of 10 hectares, but most were much smaller. The subsistence base combined cereal-crop cultivation and domestication of animals with a fairly high proportion of hunting and gathering. Some of the most important evidence for early food production and domestication has been excavated at Tell Aswad in Syria, but many other sites show that the transition from hunters and gatherers to settled agriculturalists was a slow and complex process. At Suberde and Çan Hasan, in southern Turkey, there has been considerable debate as to whether the many species of animals were wild or domesticated, while at Munhata in Israel there is ample evidence of cereal processing, in the form of sickles, querns and grindstones, but the botanical evidence suggests that only wild species of grain were being exploited.

Most of the earlier Aceramic communities were still living in the circular mud huts typical of the preceding NATUFIAN and Proto-Neolithic (Pre-Pottery Neolithic A) periods, but many later settlements, such as Beidha in Jordan and Bouqras in Syria, consisted of more elaborate rectilinear buildings. The stratigraphic sequence at MUREYBET, beside the Euphrates in Syria, shows the transition from the Natufian to the Proto-Neolithic and Aceramic Neolithic.

The technological advances of the period are best exemplified in the arid conditions of the Nahal Hemar cave site, where fragments of mats, basketry, wooden-handled sickles and lengths of cord have been preserved. In the absence of pottery, other vessels were carved from stone or moulded from 'white ware' (lime plaster). There is some evidence for metalworking, particularly at the anatolian site of ÇAYÖNÜ TEPESI, which is situated about 20 km from an abundant source of copper, but there is no evidence of smelting, suggesting that only naturally occurring copper was being used. There are already substantial indications of long-distance commerce, with obsidian trade-routes emanating from such sites as Asikli Hüyük, where abundant evidence of extraction and processing has been obtained.

At many Levantine sites of the Aceramic Neolithic, such as Jericho and Ain Ghazal, the rituals for the disposal of the dead involved burial of bodies beneath the living rooms of the houses (rather than in a separate cemetery), followed by the removal of the cranium and the burial of the scraped, painted or (more typically) plastered skulls. This behaviour has been interpreted as evidence of the veneration of dead ancestors.

O. Bar-Yosef: 'The pre-pottery period in the Southern Levant', *Préhistoire du Levant*, eds J. Cauvin and P. Sandaville (Paris, 1981); T. Watkins et al.: 'Qermez Dere and the early Aceramic Neolithic of northern Iraq', *Paléorient* 15 (1989), 19–24; H.-D. Bienert: 'Skull cult in the prehistoric Near East', *Journal of Prehistoric Religion* 5 (1991), 9–23.

IS

Achaemenid *see* PERSIA

Acheulean (Acheulian) Name given to a series of tool traditions of the Lower Palaeolithic linked by the presence of roughly symmetrical bifacial hand-axes and cleavers. Named after the site of Saint-Acheul in France, Acheulean-type assemblages are found widely across Africa (where they first evolved, and where they follow the simple Olduwan-type industries, *see* AFRICA 5.1), Europe and parts of Asia (from the Near East through to the Indian subcontinent); Acheulean assemblages are not present in the Far East. Some scholars have suggested that the wide regional spread of the Acheulean industries may be associated with the appearance and dispersion of *HOMO ERECTUS*. However, Acheulean-type industries are also associated with later *homo sapiens*, and were produced over such a range of time and region that it is best to regard the term simply as shorthand for Old World assemblages that exhibit very roughly the same level of technology. Acheulean assemblages vary considerably in terms of their exact constituents and the sophistication of the lithic technology, and may also include many simple tools based on flakes; in many regions, there are contemporary lithic traditions that lack handaxes and cleavers and are therefore not generally termed 'Acheulean'. Industries which contain Acheulean tool-types but which also show evidence of the LEVALLOIS TECHNIQUE, are sometimes badged as 'Evolved Acheulean'. *See also* HUMAN EVOLUTION *and* PALAEOLITHIC.

actualism, actualistic studies One of the principal interpretive techniques employed in modern historical sciences. Actualism has been defined by G.G. Simpson (1970: 84) as 'the confrontation of the [prehistoric] record with the knowledge of present processes'. Although the term is used relatively infrequently in archaeological literature, actualistic studies underlie such archaeological subdisciplines as ETHNOARCHAEOLOGY and EXPERIMENTAL ARCHAEOLOGY, and are undertaken particularly in association with MIDDLE RANGE THEORY.

G.G. Simpson: 'Uniformitarianism: an inquiry into principle, theory, and method in geohistory and biohistory', *Essays in evolution and genetics in honor of Theodosius Dobzhansky*, ed. M.K. Hecht and W.C. Steere (New York, 1970), 43–96; L.S. Binford: 'Middle-range research and the role of actualistic studies', *Bones: ancient men and modern myths* (New York, 1981), 21–30.

IS

Adamgarh Group of rock outcrops located 100 km south of the site of BHIMBETKA in the Vindhya Hills of Madhya Pradesh, India. Ramachandra V. Joshi excavated in 18 locales and identified a stratigraphic sequence spanning the Lower and Middle Palaeolithic periods, with the most significant remains being from later microlithic levels. The absolute dates of these levels are distinctly uncertain, as only two radiocarbon dates are available: a calibrated radiocarbon date of *c*.6410–5705 BC from a microlithic level, and an anomalous date of *c*.1100–805 BC from a 'Lower Palaeolithic' level (Possehl and Rissman 1991: 475–6). The early date for the microlithic level is comparable to dates from BAGOR in Rajasthan. In these levels, stone tools are found in association with domestic dog, sheep and goat, as well as wild cattle, buffalo, deer and pig. No evidence has been found for the cultivation of domestic plants. In higher strata, microliths are found in association with chalcolithic, Iron Age and even medieval ceramics, and may represent a technology with a very long duration.

G.L. Possehl and P. Rissman: 'The chronology of prehistoric India: From earliest times to the Iron Age', *Chronologies in Old World Archaeology* I, ed. R.W. Ehrich (Chicago, 1992), 465–90; R.V. Joshi: *Stone Age cultures of central India* (Pune, 1978).

CS

adaptionist Term sometimes used to describe an assumption that all change in the archaeological and human evolutionary record has come about as a physiological or behavioural adjustment to contemporary (particularly environmental) conditions. An archaeological example might be the tendency to try to relate the changes in material culture during the Mesolithic to the climate change at the beginning of the Holocene, rather than to internal cultural dynamics or the classic culture-historical explanations (i.e. migration and diffusion).

RJA

Addaura (Grotta Addaura, Monte Pellegrino, Addaura II) Small cave on Monte Pellegrino near Palermo, Sicily, that houses a series of engravings of animals (bovines, deer and horses) and a very fine and rare example of figurative cave art. One lightly incised set of engravings depicts horses, cattle and a woman. A more striking, and more boldly incised, set of engravings depicts a series of largely naked dancers, who seem to wear head-dresses and sometimes beak-like masks, surrounding two figures who seem to be tied by a cord stretching from their heads to their necks. This 'scene', beautifully drawn in a free and essentially naturalistic style, has been variously interpreted as a ritual dance, an endurance rite of initiation, an execution, and a re-enactment of the capturing of animals. There is no substantial archaeological context within the cave; similarities with the engravings at LEVANZO, and flints found in the locality, suggest a date in the 9th or 10th millennium BC, during the Epigravettian.

I. Marconi Bovio: *Bollettino di paletnologia Italiana* (1953), 5.

RJA

Addi Galamo (Azbi Dera; Haouli Assarou; Makalle) Ethiopian site of the pre-Axumite and Axumite periods, located about 100 km east of AXUM. A stone figure of a seated woman, similar to two pre-Axumite statues excavated at HAOULTI-MELAZO, was discovered at Addi Galamo in association with an altar dedicated to Almouqah, the moon-god worshipped both in northern Ethiopia and South Arabia.

A. Caquot and A.J. Drewes: 'Les monuments receuillis à Maqalle', *AE* 1 (1955), 17–51; A. Shiferacu: 'Rapport sur

la découverte d'antiquités trouvées dans les locaux du gouvernement général de Magallé', *AE* 1 (1955), 13–15.
IS

Adena Term used in North American archaeology to describe a group of sites in the middle Ohio River valley, particularly in southern Ohio and northern Kentucky, most of which date to the half-millennium following 500 BC. The best-known sites are earthen mounds, many of which have a distinctive conical shape, and other earthworks. Many mounds were built over places where one or more large, special-purpose structures were previously located. The mounds were built gradually through the addition of graves and layers of earth. They contain different kinds of graves, including log-lined tombs with skeletons and valued artefacts, such as copper bracelets. Adena mounds were often built in prominent places, presumably serving as important landmarks for nearby dispersed populations.

K.B. Farnsworth and T.E. Emerson, (eds): *Early Woodland archaeology* (Kampsville, 1986), 564–95.
GM

Adrar Bous One of about 25 'younger granite' volcanic ring complexes characteristic of the Air massif in the northwestern part of the Ténéré desert, northeastern Niger, consisting of a central granite upland, a discontinuous peripheral depression, an outer circle of low hills, and a dry lake bed to the southeast. The region was investigated by the Mission Berliet in 1959, by J.D. Clark and his colleagues in 1970, and by J.P. Roset from 1978 onwards. On the basis of various sites located in 1970, nine main lithostratigraphic units were distinguished, with three lacustrine phases of diminishing amplitude separated by two drier periods.

J.D. Clark et al.: 'The geomorphology and archaeology of Adrar Bous, Central Sahara: a preliminary report', *Quaternaria* 17 (1973), 245–97; J.P. Roset et al.: 'La faune de Tin Ouaffadene et d'Adrar Bous 10, deux gisements archéologiques de l'Holocène ancien au Niger nord-oriental', *Géodynamique* 5/1 (1990), 67–89; A.B. Smith: 'Terminal Palaeolithic industries of Sahara: a discussion of new data', *Studies in African Archaeology* IV, eds. L. Krzyzaniak et al. (Poznan, 1993), 69–75.
PA-J

Adulis (Zulla) Red Sea port, closely connected with the ancient city of AXUM. Located about 4 km inland from the Gulf of Zulla (or Annesley Bay) in the northeastern highlands of Ethiopia. In 1868 R. Holmes of the British Museum cleared a church, discovering a number of pieces of prefabricated ecclesiastical furniture imported from the eastern Mediterranean. The site was next excavated by Italian archaeologists, revealing considerable additional evidence of Axumite trade with the Mediterranean region as well as with India and Arabia (Paribeni 1907). No archaeological remains earlier than the 3rd century AD have yet been found at Adulis. There is, however, good reason to suppose that the port was in existence from a considerably earlier date, since it is mentioned by Pliny the Elder and other writers of the 1st and 2nd centuries AD. It was probably part of the same trade network as the port of HAFUN on the coast of Somalia. The port of Adulis eventually declined in the 7th century AD, when its role in international trade had diminished.

R. Paribeni: 'Richerche sul luogo dell'antica Adulis', *Monumenti Antichi, Reale Accademia dei Lincei* 18 (1907), 437–572; F. Anfray: 'Deux villes axoumites: Adoulis et Matara', *Atti del IV Congresso Internazionale de Studi Etiopici* (Rome, 1972), 752–65; ——: 'The civilization of Aksum from the first to the seventh century', *General history of Africa* II, ed. G. Mokhtar (Paris, Berkeley and London, 1981), 362–80; S. Munro-Hay: 'The foreign trade of the Aksumite port of Adulis', *Azania* 27 (1982), 107–25; ——: 'The British Museum excavations at Adulis, 1868', *AJ* 69/1 (1989), 43–52.
IS

Aegean Bronze Age *see* CYCLADIC; MINOAN; MYCENAEAN

aerial archaeology Term covering all applications of airborne reconnaissance for the purposes of archaeology, including AIRBORNE REMOTE SENSING. The photo-interpretation techniques used by archaeologists are closely related to those employed in geographical mapping, geological prospection and vegetation surveying (St Joseph 1977). The subject comprises two basic elements: (1) the *recovery* of archaeological information from air photographs, usually vertical and not necessarily taken for archaeological purposes, and (2) the *execution* of aerial reconnaissance, where the act of recognition of archaeological information is made by an airborne observer, usually flying in a normal light aircraft (preferably high-wing) using hand-held cameras to record the features recognised. The term also embraces the analysis and study of the resulting archaeological material.

Aerial photographs are used for the discovery of new sites (such as standing structures, shadow sites, CROPMARKS, SOILMARKS and dampmarks), the mapping of archaeological material, the illustration and comprehension of large or complex sites and landscapes, and the monitoring of the condition and use of known archaeological features or landscapes. This last is a powerful tool for the management and protection of the archaeological resource. Aerial photographs can also be used for the discovery, mapping, monitoring and illustration of underwater sites (*see* MARITIME ARCHAEOLOGY), where conditions of visibility permit.

Techniques of photo-interpretation are also used for broader environmental work, such as the identification and mapping of wetlands, palaeochannels (*see* OC EO), colluvial or alluvial deposits, land-use or vegetation patterns for predictive purposes, or the provision of information on the wider setting of an area of archaeological interest.

The impact of aerial archaeology has been substantial (Maxwell 1983). Its practice has permitted extensive surveys of inhospitable terrain; the mapping of complex archaeological landscapes; and, perhaps most fundamentally, the recognition of archaeological sites and landscapes the above-ground traces of which have been totally lost through cultivation or other causes. This has frequently revolutionized the perception of past settlement patterns and densities. Examples may be found in all countries where a programme of reconnaissance has been pursued, ranging from the transformation of the understanding of Roman Britain since the first Ordnance Survey Map of Roman Britain in 1928 to the great expansion of knowledge regarding sites of the Neolithic period in much of central and western Europe on soils that have long been cultivated, and the study of great areas of the American deserts. However, data recovered from the air are always subject to a range of distorting factors, which means that they should never be used uncritically or without a full appreciation of their inherent limitations and biases.

1. *The history of aerial archaeology*. The earliest air photographs date from the 19th century, and the first known archaeological air photograph was of Stonehenge, taken from a captive balloon in 1906. During the First World War the possibilities of airborne archaeology were appreciated by British and German fliers operating in the Near East, where well-preserved but unknown remains, particularly Roman, were observed and photographed (Beazeley 1919). The value of aerial photographs to archaeology was recognised almost as early as their utility for general geographical mapping. After the war, work continued in North Africa and the Near East, recording remote and extensive sites and frontier works whose mapping would have been difficult by other means (Beazeley 1919; Poidebard 1934). In America, the new techniques were also being applied to the mapping of extensive sites (Judd 1931). In Britain, during the 1920s and 1930s, aerial reconnaissance and photography were used to record both the earthworks of HILLFORTS and Celtic fields (Crawford and Keiller 1928) and the traces of sites surviving below ground, recognized through CROPMARKS (Crawford and Keiller 1928; Deuel 1971: 72–83; Allen 1984). All the principal means of identifying archaeological features from the air had been classified by Allen before 1940 (Riley 1946; Allen 1984).

In the Second World War the use of vertical photography for intelligence purposes provided a stimulus for its archaeological use, particularly as a number of archaeologists were employed in photo-interpretation. John Bradford examined wartime vertical photographs of the Mediterranean area and undertook his own photographic missions, achieving the identification, mapping and comprehension of very large areas of archaeological remains, notably in Tuscany and Apulia, and the identification of centuriation in a number of areas of Roman settlement (Bradford 1957; Jones 1987).

During the 1950s there was an increase in those undertaking reconnaissance for oblique photography, notably J.K.S. St Joseph in Britain and R. Agache in France, and the results of their more intensive researches greatly expanded the range of terrain to which the method was applied. More recently, numerous practitioners operate in Britain and most of western Europe, and since 1989 relaxations of airspace control over eastern Europe have permitted the beginning of civilian reconnaissance there. In some countries, such as Britain, France and Germany, work is now frequently undertaken on a regional basis, which allows both the rapid exploitation of suitable ground and meteorological conditions and the integration of aerial study with a detailed comprehension of the area's archaeology in general (Wilson 1975; Maxwell 1983; Léva 1990; Griffith 1990). For general discussions of the history of aerial archaeology see Crawford (1954), St Joseph (1951), Deuel (1971) and Riley (1987).

2. *Mapping*. Both vertical photographs and rectified oblique photographs can be used in mapping, and they may cover upstanding as well as buried features. Vertical photographs are taken in regular exposures by cameras mounted in the underside of an aircraft flown in a straight path. The exposures are timed to produce overlaps between the frames, so that two adjacent frames provide a three-dimensional effect (which can be scaled) when viewed through a stereoscope. Oblique photographs are taken individually using hand-held equipment, usually through the open window of a light aircraft banked toward the subject. If

taken at an appropriate interval, pairs of oblique photographs can also be used to provide a quasi-stereo effect.

Air photographs are used for mapping at all scales. Applications vary from extensive areas where other forms of mapping, or even site location, would be difficult, to detailed plotting of limited areas. Examples range from work to locate entire forts on the Near Eastern Roman *limes* (Poidebard 1934; Kennedy and Riley 1990) to the use of aerial photographs for the discovery and mapping of large numbers of defensive sites in the Rewa Delta, Fiji (Parry 1977), the use of AIRBORNE REMOTE SENSING and multispectral imagery in the American mid-west and the detailed photogrammetric plotting of purpose-flown vertical cover of Bodmin Moor, Cornwall (Johnson 1983; RCHME, forthcoming). The Bodmin Moor photography resulted in high quality mapping of 150 km^2 of a dense archaeological landscape, subsequently verified by ground survey. There have also been projects concerned with the systematic plotting of oblique photographs for one area taken over many years, such as the DANEBURY region (Palmer 1984). Aerial photography has been used in rescue-driven transcriptions of the archaeology of the English gravel terraces, as revealed by cropmarks, following the publication of *A matter of time* (RCHME 1960). Photography and subsequent transcription at single sites have permitted detailed study of buried features, as in the work concentrating on the Roman town of Wroxeter (Wilson 1984).

3. *Techniques*. Features may be transcribed from air photographs by a variety of techniques (Wilson 1982; Maxwell 1983; Riley 1987), such as photogrammetry (e.g. Lyons and Avery 1977, Avery and Lyons 1981), geometric transformation (Riley 1987: 66–72) and computer rectification. Sketch plotting is sometimes used for simple sites with good ground control. In computer rectification fixed points are identified on both photograph and map, and the detail is then plotted by transformation to map coordinates in either two or three dimensions. Image enhancement techniques can fruitfully be applied to digitized material (Becker 1990).

4. *Photo-interpretation, description and classification*. The archaeological interpretation of air photographs depends on the interpreter's appreciation of the potential causation of both archaeological and non-archaeological elements. (Wilson 1982; Riley 1987: 60–89). The description and classification of recorded features is complex, since it relies on largely two-dimensional evidence, not all familiar in the excavated archaeological record, and new classificatory systems may be needed to describe the results (Edis et al. 1989; Whimster 1989). Description and analysis alone may be the initial object, but frequently the results of aerial archaeology will be directly integrated with data from many other classes of study, from ground finds to placenames and documentary sources.

5. *Illustration and comprehension*. Air photographs are important for illustrative purposes. They may summarize the topography or morphology of a complex site, they may demonstrate its landscape or cultural context, or the relative siting of elements of a whole (a town and its siegeworks), or they can be the only way to present some inaccessible or very extensive sites, such as the NAZCA LINES in Peru. For tracing and illustrating surviving relict landscape elements such as boundary features, an air photograph may be more subtle than a map.

6. *Upstanding sites – standing structures or shadow sites*. Some archaeological sites are 'discovered' from the air because they have never been visited on the ground. Others may be visible on the ground only as low earthworks, either from inherent slightness or as a result of decay or destruction, including the effects of cultivation. Such earthworks are frequently recognized from the air through their accompanying vegetation variations: gorse, for instance, may outline field banks on moorland. Aerial photography is used in mapping large tracts of difficult terrain or in the recognition of slight or discontinuous earthwork features. The aerial archaeologist will seek to exploit unusual conditions. The low sunlight of winter, or of sunrise and sunset (two different angles), small variations in vegetation cover, slight flooding, the effects of driven snow lodging against or in features, or marks in frost or snow due to differential melting, may allow slight earthworks to be recorded clearly. Earthworks may show as parchmarks or differential vegetation growth in summer (for further discussion of the recognition of upstanding sites see Crawford and Keiller 1928; Wilson 1975: 27–39; Lyons and Avery 1977).

7. *Buried features*. Archaeological features surviving solely below modern ground-level can sometimes be identified from the air, as variation between buried features and the surrounding material can produce differential markings in surface vegetation. These are often only apparent either in extremes or points of change of climatic conditions. Depending on ground, crop and weather conditions, buried features may manifest themselves to the observer as dampmarks, CROPMARKS, SOILMARKS, or FROSTMARKS.

For case-study *see* SAMARRA.

G.A. Beazeley: 'Air photography in archaeology' *Geographical Journal* 55 (1919), 109–27; O.G.S. Crawford and A. Keiller: *Wessex from the air* (Oxford, 1928); N.M. Judd: 'Arizona's prehistoric canals from the air', *Explorations and fieldwork of the Smithsonian Institution in 1930* (Washington, D.C., 1931), 157–66; A. Poidebard: *La trace de Rome dans le désert de Syrie: le limes de Trajan à la conquète arabe; recherches aériennes (1925–1932)* (Paris, 1934); D.N. Riley: 'The technique of air-archaeology' *AJ* 101 (1946), 1–16; J.K.S. St Joseph: 'A survey of pioneering in air-photography past and future', *Aspects of archaeology in Britain and beyond: essays presented to O.G.S. Crawford*, ed. W.F. Grimes (London, 1951), 303–15; O.G.S. Crawford: 'A century of air-photography', *Antiquity* 112 (1954) 206–10; J. Bradford: *Ancient landscapes* (London, 1957); RCHME: *A matter of time* (London, 1960); R. Agache: *Détection aérienne de vestiges protohistoriques, gallo-romaines et médiévaux* (Amiens, 1970); L. Deuel: *Flights into yesterday* (London, 1971); R. Agache and B. Bréart: *Atlas d'archéologie aérienne de Picardie* (Amiens, 1975); R.J.A. Jones and R. Evans: 'Soil and crop marks in the recognition of archaeological sites by air photography', *Aerial reconnaissance for archaeology*, ed. D.R. Wilson (London, 1975), 1–11; D.R. Wilson, ed.: *Aerial reconnaissance for archaeology* (London, 1975); J.K.S. St Joseph, ed.: *The uses of air photography*, 2nd edn (London, 1977); T.R. Lyons and T.E. Avery: *Remote sensing: a handbook for archaeologists and cultural resource managers* (Washington, 1977); J.T. Parry: *Ring ditch fortifications in the Rewa Delta, Fiji: air photo interpretation and analysis* (Suva, 1977); R. Agache: *La Somme pre-Romaine et Romaine* (Amiens 1978); American Society of Photogrammetry: *Manual of Photographic Interpretation*, 4th edn (Washington, 1981); T.E. Avery and T.R. Lyons: *Remote sensing: aerial and terrestrial photography for archaeologists* (Washington, 1981); D.R. Wilson: *Air photo interpretation for archaeologists* (London, 1982); O. Braasch: *Luftbildarchäologie in Süddeutschland* (Stuttgart, 1983); N.D. Johnson: 'The results of air and ground survey of Bodmin Moor, Cornwall', *The impact of aerial reconnaissance on archaeology*, ed. G.S. Maxwell (London, 1983), 5–13; G.S. Maxwell, ed.: *The impact of aerial reconnaissance on archaeology* (London 1983); G.W.G. Allen: 'Discovery from the air', *Aerial Archaeology* 10 (1984) [whole issue]; R. Palmer: *Danebury, an Iron Age hillfort in Hampshire: an aerial photographic interpretation of its environs* (London, 1984); D.R. Wilson: 'The plan of Viroconium Cornoviorum', *Antiquity* 58 (1984), 17–20; G.D.B. Jones: *Apulia* I: *Neolithic settlement in the Tavoliere* (London, 1987); D.N. Riley: *Air photography and archaeology* (London, 1987); J. Edis, D. MacLeod and R. Bewley: 'An archaeologist's guide to classification of cropmarks and soilmarks', *Antiquity* 63 (1989), 112–26; R.P. Whimster: *The emerging past: air photography and the buried landscape* (London, 1989); H. Becker: 'Combination of aerial photography with ground magnetics in digital image processing', *Aerial photography and geophysical prospection in archaeology: proceedings of the second international symposium*, ed. C. Léva (Brussels, 1990), 25–36; F.M. Griffith: 'Aerial reconnaissance in Britain in 1989' *Antiquity* 64 (1990), 14–33; D. Kennedy and D. Riley: *Rome's desert frontier from the air* (London, 1990); C. Léva, ed.: *Aerial photography and geophysical prospection in archaeology: proceedings of the second international symposium* (Brussels, 1990); RCHME: *Air and ground survey of Bodmin Moor, Cornwall* (forthcoming).

FG

AES *See* AUGER ELECTRON SPECTROSCOPY

Africa

Sections: 1 North Africa; 2 West Africa; 3 East Africa; 4 Southern Africa; 5 Central Africa

1 North Africa

North Africa is a huge region measuring over 4000 km west to east from the Moroccan coast opposite the Canary Islands to the Egyptian border near the Nile, and over 2000 miles north to south from the Tangier/Tunis coast to the southern borders of the Sahara with the Sahel. There are three principal geographical features: the northern littoral zone, with its predominantly Mediterranean landscape and climate; the 'Maghreb' or north-western uplands – the Atlas mountains in Morocco rising over 3000 m above sea level, and the extension from them of hill country across northern Algeria into Tunisia (with the outlier of the Gebel Akhdar range in Cyrenaica); and the Saharan desert, an unforgiving expanse of rock, gravel and sand interspersed occasionally with upland 'islands', the highest of which, like the Hoggar and Tibesti, are almost as high as the Atlas mountains.

1.1. *Early prehistory*. In 1995, the mandible of an early hominid (*Australopithecus afarensis*), was found at Koro Toro in the Bahr-el-Ghazal region, providing evidence for the first inhabitants of the region, probably about 3–3.5 million years ago (Brunet et al. 1995). Before this find, the earliest remains of human activity in the region were Oldowan-style chopper (*see* OLDUVAI) and flake industries, such as those from Sidi Abderrahman on the Moroccan coast and AIN HANECH (McBurney 1960) in the Algerian uplands, as well as part of a human skull from YAYO in Chad (Coppens 1965), all of which date between about 1 and 1.5 million years BP. Sequences of ACHEULEAN industries follow, probably made by *Homo erectus* populations. During the arid phases of the Pleistocene, people retreated from the interior to the coastal areas, or to better-watered locations within the Sahara, whereas in cooler phases the hunter-gatherers were able to spread out across the interior as the Sahelian climate and environment spread from between 200 to as much as 500 km northwards (Van Campo 1975;

Clark 1980; Williams and Faure 1980). The period between 100,000 and 40,000 was one of the latter phases of settlement expansion, marked by Aterian industries broadly comparable with the European MOUSTERIAN; the most important stratigraphy is still that of HAUA FTEAH, a huge cave in Cyrenaica, northeast Libya (McBurney 1967).

Conditions of severe aridity returned between 40,000 and the end of the Pleistocene *c.*12000 years ago, forcing a major retreat from the Saharan zone. The Haua Fteah now was occupied by hunter-gatherers using Dabban backed-blade industries which developed in ways not dissimilar to the European Upper Palaeolithic sequence, ending with an industry characterized by numerous small backed bladelets termed the Eastern Oranian. Similar industries, termed IBEROMAURUSIAN, have been found across the rest of the North African coastal region from Tunis to Morocco (see TAFORALT). The system of subsistence included hunting animals such as Barbary sheep and cattle and collecting land and water molluscs (Saxon et al. 1974). The early Holocene brought a return to wetter conditions. On the coast, people developed more diversified systems of subsistence (Lubell 1984) and settlement expanded once more into the interior, the EPIPALAEOLITHIC people of this period with microlithic technologies (*c.* uncal 12,000–7000 BP) probably practising a broadly based system of subsistence involving fishing, fowling and plant gathering as well as hunting – much as in Egypt (Smith 1982). Typical sites are the Two Caves and Torha East Caves in the Tadrart Acacus mountains (Barich 1987), AMEKNI in southern Algeria (Camps 1969) and Tamaya Mellet in Niger (Smith 1980). Pottery was being used by these hunter-fisher-gatherers by uncal 7500–6500 BC.

1.2. *The transition to farming.* Twenty years ago, archaeologists characterized the change from hunting to farming in North Africa as a simple process of colonization, the movement from east to west of new people from the Nile valley, one stream along the coast around uncal 4500 BC (McBurney 1967) and the other across the Sahara around uncal 3500 BC (Hugot 1968; Camps 1969). Today it seems much more likely that the process mainly involved the adoption of new resources by the indigenous population. Domestic sheep may have spread along the Mediterranean littoral as prestige items of exchange among the hunter-fisher-gatherers (Lewthwaite 1986).

The hunter-fisher-gatherers of the Sahara began to specialize more on collecting plant foods and on hunting steppic animals perhaps as early as the 6th millennium BC (uncal). By the end of the 5th millennium BC (uncal) they were herding domestic cattle (probably for meat, milk and blood) in most of the Saharan uplands, for example in the Tassili-n-ajjer in Algeria (Aumassip 1981; Aumassip and Jacob 1976), Tadrart Acacus in Libya (Barich 1987) and Air in Niger (Roset 1981; 1983, *see* ADRAR BOUS), and in the TAOUDENNI BASIN in Mali (Petit-Maire and Riser 1983). Much of SAHARAN ROCK

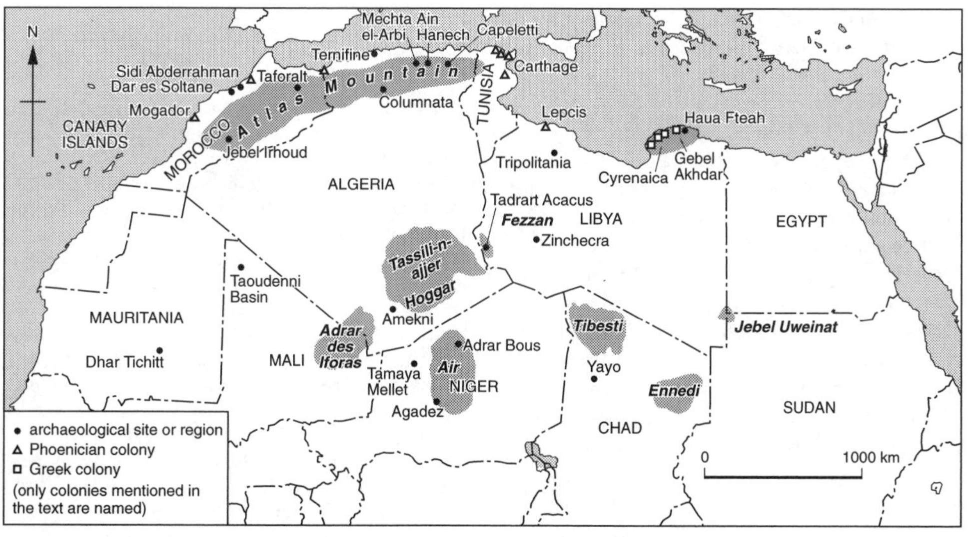

Map 1 **Africa, 1: North** Some major sites in the region.

ART may reflect the changing ideologies of Saharan societies during the transition from hunting to herding between about uncal 6000 and 3000 BC, though the precise correlations with climatic change are still unclear. It is generally agreed that significant aridity was established by about 2500 BC, but it is still debatable whether the early phase of cattle pastoralism correlated with the beginnings of the trend to aridity or, as Muzzolini, for example, argues, with an oscillation towards a moister climate, which he calls a 'Neolithic wet phase, between 4500 and 2500 BC (Muzzolini 1993). While the climatic context of early pastoralism therefore remains unclear, the increasing importance of sheep and goats over cattle in the 4th and 3rd millennia BC (Aumassip and Delibrias 1983; Barich 1987) suggests increasingly arid conditions.

The nature of settlement over the next 2000 years is unclear. The climate and environment of the modern Sahara had developed by *c.*2500 BC (Shaw 1976). Neolithic-style pottery continued in use in Cyrenaica long after it went out of use in the northern Mediterranean (Bacchielli 1979; Baldassarre 1987; Tiné 1987). Egyptian sources of this period indicate occasional contacts with the pastoralist 'Tjehenu' and 'Tjemehu' peoples in Libya (Leahy 1990), and there is archaeological evidence for predominantly pastoral societies further west in Algeria (Roubet 1979), the ancestors of the modern Berbers (Camps 1982). Cereal cultivation may not have begun in the Saharan oases until the later 2nd and early 1st millennia BC on the evidence of such sites as DHAR TICHITT in Mauritania (Munson 1976) and ZINCHECRA in the Libyan Fezzan (Van der Veen 1992), in both cases associated with sedentary competitive societies in fortified settlements; in the Fezzan, it may also have coincided with the construction of the first *foggaras* for channelling floodwaters to the fields.

1.3. *From Phoenician and Greek colonization to Romanization.* In the 8th and 7th centuries BC, the Phoenicians from the eastern Mediterranean established colonies on the North African coast from LEPCIS in Libya to MOGADOR in Morocco (Law 1978) and the Greeks settled in Cyrenaica soon afterwards (Boardman 1980). The colonies traded for raw materials with their hinterlands promoting the development of Berber client-kingdoms there, and several such as Carthage also became the endpoints for tans-Saharan trade: pottery, glass and metalwork went south in return for commodities such as salt, skins, ivory and slaves. The best evidence for indigenous settlement in the desert at this time is from Zinchecra in the Libyan Fezzan, the homeland of the Garamantes described by Herodotus (Daniels 1970; 1989).

By the 3rd century BC Carthaginian supremacy over the western Mediterranean was threatened by the expanding power of Rome, the bitter Punic Wars finally ending with the destruction of Carthage in 146 BC. Under Julius Caesar and Augustus direct Roman control was concentrated in Tunisia behind Carthage, but in the 1st and 2nd centuries Roman Africa extended from the former client-states of Mauritania and Numidia (roughly the western and eastern Maghreb respectively) eastwards across northern Libya to Cyrenaica (Fentress 1979, Raven 1993). The incorporation of the North African littoral and Maghreb into the Roman world also had a profound impact on the peoples living in the frontier zone to the south.

C.B.M. McBurney: *The Stone Age of northern Africa* (Harmondsworth, 1960); Y. Coppens: 'An early hominid from Chad', *CA* 7 (1965), 584–5; C.B.M. McBurney: *The Haua Fteah (Cyrenaica) and the Stone Age of the south-east Mediterranean* (Cambridge, 1967); H. Hugot: 'The origins of agriculture: the Sahara', *CA* 9 (1968), 483–9; G. Camps: *Amekni: Néolithique ancien du Hoggar* (Paris, 1969); M.C. Chamla: *Les hommes epipaléolithiques de Columnata, Algérie occidentale* (Paris, 1970); C. Daniels: *The Garamantes of southern Libya* (Cambridge, 1970); E.T. Saxon et al.: 'Results of recent investigations at Tamar hat', *Libyca* 22 (1974), 49–91; M. Van Campo: 'Pollen analyses in the Sahara', *Problems in prehistory – North Africa and the Levant*, ed. F. Wendorf and S. Marks (Dallas, 1975), 45–64; G. Aumassip and J.P. Jacob: 'Les grottes de Ti-n-Hanakaten au Tassili des Ajjers', *Archeologia* 94 (1976), 28–37; P.J. Munson: 'Archaeological data on the origins of cultivation in the southwestern Sahara and their implications for West Africa', *Origins of plant domestication*, ed. J.R. Harlan et al. (The Hague, 1976), 187–210; B.D. Shaw: 'Climate, environment and prehistory in the Sahara', *World Archaeology* 8 (1976), 133–48; M.C. Chamla: 'Le peuplement de l'Afrique du Nord de l'epipaléolithique à l'époque actuelle', *L'Anthropologie* 82 (1978), 385–430; R.C.C. Law: 'North Africa in the age of Phoenician and Greek colonization', *Cambridge History of Africa* II, ed. J.D. Fage (Cambridge, 1978), 87–147; L. Bacchielli: 'Contatti fra 'Libya' e mondo egeo nell'età del bronzo: una conferma', *Rendiconti Accademia Lincei* 34 (1979), 163–8; E. Fentress: *Numidia and the Roman army* (Oxford, 1979); C. Roubet: *Economic pastorale préagricolé en Algérie orientale: le Néolithique de tradition Capsienne* (Paris, 1979); J. Boardman: *The Greek overseas* (London 1980); J.D. Clark: 'Human populations and cultural adaptations in the Sahara and Nile during prehistoric times', *The Sahara and the Nile*, ed. M.A.J. Williams and H. Faure (Rotterdam, 1980), 527–82; A.B. Smith: 'The neolithic tradition in the Sahara', *The Sahara and the Nile*, ed. M.A.J. Williams and H. Faure (Rotterdam, 1980), 451–65; M.A.J. Williams and H. Faure, eds: *The Sahara and the Nile* (Rotterdam, 1980); G. Aumassip: 'Ti-n-Hanakaten (Tassili-n-Ajjers, Algérie): Bilan de 6 campagnes de fouilles', *Libyca* 28–9 (1981), 115–27; J.P. Roset: 'Les plus vieilles céramiques du Sahara', *Archéologie* (1981), 43–50; G. Camps: 'The beginnings of pastoralism and cultivation in northwest Africa and the Sahara: origins of the Berbers', *Cambridge History of Africa* I (Cambridge, 1982), 548–623; P.E.L. Smith: 'The late palaeolithic and epipalaeolithic of northern Africa', *History of West Africa* I, ed. J.F.A. Ajadi and M. Crowder (Cambridge, 1982), 342–409; G. Aumassip and G. Delibrias: 'Age des dépôts néolithiques du gisement de Ti-n-Hanakaten (Tassili-n-Ajjes, Algérie)', *Libyca* 30–31 (1983), 207–11; N. Petit-Maire and J. Riser: *Sahara ou Sahel? Quaternaire récent du Bassin de Taoudenni (Mali)* (Marseilles, 1983); J.P. Roset: 'Nouvelles données sur le problème de la Néolithisation du Sahara méridional: Air et Teneré, au Niger', *Cahiers ORSTOM* 13/2 (1983), 199–42; D. Lubell: 'The Capsian palaeoeconomy in the Maghreb', *Origins and early development of food-producing cultures in north-eastern Africa*, ed. L. Krzyzaniak and M. Kobusiewica (Poznan, 1984), 453–5; J. Lewthwaite: 'The transition to food production: a Mediterranean perspective', *Hunters in transition*, ed. M. Zvelebil (Cambridge, 1986), 53–66; I. Baldassarre: 'Tracce dell'abitato prebattiaco ad ovest dell'Agora di Cirene', *QAL* 12 (1987), 17–24; B. Barich: *Archaeology and environment in the Libyan Sahara* (Oxford, 1987); S. Tiné: 'Ceramica prebattiaca nell'area cirenea', *QAL* 12 (1987), 15–16; C. Daniels: 'Excavation and fieldwork among the Garamantes', *LS* 20 (1989), 45–61; A. Leahy, ed.: *Libya and Egypt c.1300–750* BC (London, 1990); M. Van der Veen: 'Garamantian agriculture: the plant remains from Zincechra, Fezzan', *LS* 23 (1992), 7–39; A. Muzzolini: 'The emergence of a food-producing economy in the Sahara', *The Archaeology of Africa: food, metals and towns*, ed. T. Shaw, P. Sinclair, B. Andah and A. Okpoko (London, 1993), 227–39; S. Raven: *Rome in Africa*, 3rd edn (London, 1993); M. Brunet et al.: 'The first Australopithecine 2,500 km west of the Rift Valley, Chad', *Nature* 378 (1995), 273–5.

GB

2 West Africa

Conventionally, West Africa is taken to be bounded on the north by the Tropic of Cancer and on the south and west by the Atlantic ocean; in modern political terms, its eastern boundary is often taken to coincide with the frontiers of Nigeria and Niger, but geographically and historically there are valid reasons to include Chad and Cameroun also. As Thurstan Shaw says, West Africa is a well-defined region which has its own historical 'personality'; perhaps because, as Mabogunje and Richards put it, a gradual dessication of the Sahara in recent millennia has given it an 'island-like character'. Contrasting vegetational zones have been recognised by both Francophone and Anglophone writers (A. Chevalier and R.W.J. Keay) trending broadly from west to east and reflecting decreasing annual rainfall from south to north (currently <1600 mm on the coast and >5 mm in some parts of the Sahara). Mangrove swamp and rain forest are succeeded by belts of Guinea, Sudan, and Sahel savanna, and then by the desert itself. Between the forest and Guinea savanna zones there is a belt of 'derived savanna', thought to have been brought about by human action (farming and fire). Savanna should be understood not as a tree-less plain but as a mixture of grass and woodland, the latter moister in the south and drier in the north. Sahel, as pointed out by Connah, is the Arabic word for 'shore'; the sea it faced was the desert, and the towns which eventually developed in this area were 'ports'. At one area on the south coast, the 'Dahomey Gap', the savanna comes down to the sea, and there are also patches of montane vegetation on the Fouta Djallon and Cameroun highlands. In West Africa generally high elevations are rare, but in the central Sahara the Adrar des Iforas, Hoggar, Tassili-n-Ajjer, Air, and Tibesti mountains all rise <1000 metres. Except for the lake Chad and river Niger drainage systems, most rivers flow more or less direct to the sea.

In terms of present-day political geography, West Africa is split into a number of nation states, the boundaries of which were established in colonial times, when French and English also came into use as official languages. These boundaries are certainly important, in this context because different Francophone and Anglophone traditions have had a marked effect on the development of archaeological research in the countries concerned, but there is no correspondence between them and other divisions which have been of historic significance in West Africa. Thus the number of major ethnic groups (some the centre of historic kingdoms such as the Yoruba, the Hausa, and the Ashanti) far exceeds the number of nation states and does not coincide with them, and the same is true of the major African languages. These can however be grouped into three large language families which are represented in this region: Nilo-Saharan, Afro-Asiatic, and Niger-Congo. Some tentative attempts have been made to link these language families to events in prehistory. Nilo-Saharan is the most internally diversified and the most fragmented geographically, hence it has been suggested that it is the most ancient; its speakers according to Sutton may have created an AQUATIC CIVILIZATION at the beginning of the Holocene. Niger-Congo is the most widespread, including many languages spoken in West Africa, as well as Bantu, and it is a popular hypothesis that the Bantu peoples spread to most of Central and Southern Africa from an original base in the Cameroon highlands. Since no words associated with cultivation can be securely reconstructed to Proto-Niger-Congo, it is inferred that the primary divisions in the phylum may have occurred before the development of agriculture, and the same is taken to be true of Afro-Asiatic. If this reconstruction is correct, then presumably the origins of these language families also go back to the early Holocene.

2.1. *Climatic change.* The climate of West Africa is in large part determined by the annual movement of the InterTropical Convergence Zone (ITCZ), from about 19° N in summer to 6° N in winter, reflecting the relative strength of the humid marine southwesterly (monsoon) and dry continental northeasterly (harmattan) trade winds. Marine and lacustrine cores have provided evidence (oxygen-isotope and pollen records, radiocarbon dates, and other environmental indicators such as diatoms and quartz grains) on the basis of which a succession of late Quaternary arid and humid phases has been recognised, corresponding to more southerly and more northerly positions of the ITCZ and broadly speaking to the glacials and interglacials of northern temperate latitudes.

The transition from the late Glacial to the early Holocene has been studied in particular detail. The late glacial maximum at 18,000 BP was marked by extreme aridity; general circulation models suggest that the climatic amelioration which followed was triggered by an increase in northern summer radiation peaking at 11,000 BP leading to stronger monsoon activity with a climax at 9000 BP. At that time precipitation is estimated to have been at least 25% greater than today, and the northern movement of the isohyets meant that areas (such as the TAOUDENNI BASIN and the Oyo depression in northwest Sudan) which now have >5 mm annual rainfall then had up to 400 mm. Deglaciation proceeded in two main 'steps', interrupted by a dry phase between 11,000 and 10,000 BP corresponding to the Younger Dryas event in northern temperate latitudes. Initial warming started at about 13,500 BP, when deposition of terrigenous material commenced in the Niger delta, and a montane-like wooded grassland suggesting mean temperatures 2–3°C lower than today was established around lake Bosumptwi in southern Ghana. The Holocene climatic optimum lasted from about 10,000 to 4000 BP, when many lakes including 'Megachad' were at a high stand and the West African vegetational zones were shifted 400–500 km to the north. Mean temperatures may have been up to 2.5°C higher than today. Following a regression, there are some signs of moderate climatic amelioration at about 3000 BP, for example at Kobadi in the 'dead delta'

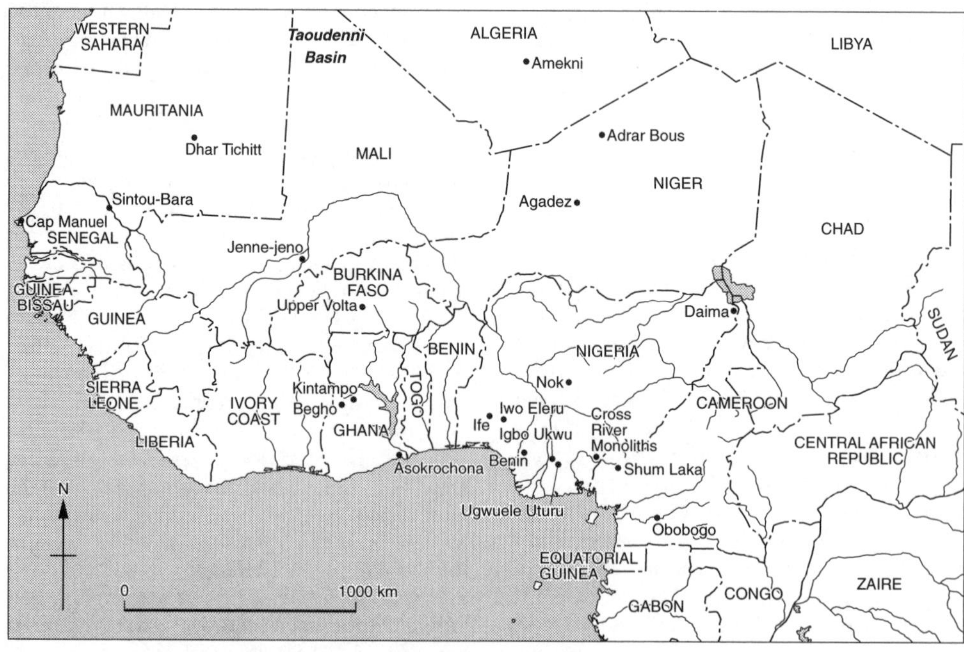

Map 2 **Africa, 2: West** Major prehistoric sites in the region.

of the Niger and at lake Bosumptwi, before another regression set in, but in the Sahara dessication had already taken hold and the present climatic regime had been established.

Even during the Holocene climatic optimum there were arid episodes which interrupted occupation at individual sites, for example in the Taoudenni basin and at ADRAR BOUS; indeed in the first of two general surveys of West African prehistory S.K. and R.J. McIntosh considered it possible to generalize the split between an earlier 'lacustrine tradition' and a later 'pastoralist period' at this site to apply to the whole region, but they subsequently took the view that it constituted no more than a 'regional anomaly'. Later movements of the ITCZ within the 'privileged area' of the Inland Niger Delta provided one of the essential ingredients of the PULSE THEORY developed by R.J. McIntosh.

2.2. *Earliest settlement.* In northern Chad an AUSTRALOPITHECUS mandible and upper premolar were discovered by a team under the direction of Michel Brunet in 1995–6 at a locality 45 km east of Koro Toro (*see* AFRICA 1). These finds were associated with apparently undisturbed fauna in a geological context which suggests that this was a lakeside environment. By comparison with analogous finds in East Africa, the fauna should date to the mid-Pliocene, about 3–3.5 million years ago. The hominid remains were at first compared to *A. Afarensis*, but are now recognized as a separate species '*Australopithecus bahrelghazali*'. Also in northern Chad, other hominid remains, with fauna but without artefacts, were discovered by F. and Y. Coppnes in 1961 at Angamma; at first themselves attributed to Australopithecus, they are now regarded as nearer to HOMO ERECTUS and would thus be comparable with those found at TERNIFINE in Algeria, in an Acheulean context.

ACHEULEAN sites are frequent in the region and (as at El-Beyyed in Mauritania) they are often associated with old lake deposits, suggesting that occupation at that time also took place during climatically favourable episodes, although so far there is only one absolute age determination (from Lagreich in Mali) where two burnt handaxes have a TL date of 282,000 ± 56,000 BP. Some well-known sites (such as those on and around the Jos Plateau in Nigeria) were discovered as a result of mining operations, but others (such as Sansandé in Senegal, Bilma and Blaka Kallia in Niger) have been excavated or investigated systematically in recent years. In the southern part of the region, as at ASOKROCHONA, other sites have been attributed to the Sangoan industrial complex, which J.D. Clark has suggested may have been a special forest adaptation.

The 'Middle Stone Age' is generally regarded as the equivalent of the MOUSTERIAN as recognized in North Africa at JEBEL IRHOUD and HAUA FTEAH. Again it is widely distributed throughout the region and usually takes the form of simple LEVALLOIS-based industries, for which there is a minimum radiocarbon date of uncal 33,400 ± 2500 BP at Bilma. At Adrar Bous and elsewhere in the Sahara the MSA is succeeded by the ATERIAN and this according to Tillet may have been associated with an Upper Ghazalian humid period immediately preceding the last glacial maximum at 18,000 BP. Since the Aterian at DAR ES-SOLTANE II and three other sites on the Moroccan coast is associated with anatomically modern man, it would be logical to assume that the same is true in the Sahara.

2.3. *Late Stone Age or 'Neolithic'?* Acute unresolved questions of terminology, in part arising from different Anglophone and Francophone approaches, abound in West African prehistory, particularly in regard to the 'Neolithic' and the artefactual or economic criteria regarded as sufficient for its recognition. Thus, in the Sahara, at AMEKNI and other sites, Gabriel Camps distinguished a 'Neolithic of Sudanese Tradition' on the basis of its pottery alone, in the absence of any trace of domestication. Although J.D. Clark was at one time inclined to accept this formulation as a 'pre-pastoral Neolithic', the majority of Anglophone writers have rejected the concept, and have sought other explanations for the lifestyle adopted by what Muzzolini now refers to as 'epipalaeolithic pottery-users'. Sutton's description of this lifestyle as an 'aquatic civilization' has been criticized on various grounds; less controversial is the McIntoshes' suggestion of a 'lacustrine tradition' within the overall framework of the LSA. Whatever framework is chosen, the early appearance of pottery in the Sahara and the wide geographical spread of what may be described at least as a 'horizon-style' is of undoubted importance. Originally, Camps claimed the pottery from Amekni at 8050 ± 80 BP was the oldest in the Sahara, and there were other sites in the same time bracket, which encouraged the idea of independent invention. More recently, J.P. Roset has located even older sites (none with evidence of domestication) in the vicinity of Adrar Bous, and also at Tagalagal 200 km to the southwest where pottery with dotted wavy line decoration is dated to 9370 ± 130 BP. Although the 'lacustrine tradition' is for the most part confined to the early Holocene, as in the Taoudenni basin, the McIntoshes emphasize that the 'old Saharan life-style' carried on later at some favourable localities, such as Kobadi and the lower levels at DAIMA, where however the inhabitants also kept domestic cattle.

South of the Sahara, Thurstan Shaw, following his excavations of the 1940s at Bosumpra cave, at one time proposed the creation of a 'Guinea Neolithic': 'a more or less homogeneous culture of post-Pleistocene date' characterized by the coexistence of microlithic quartz artefacts, ground stone axes, and pottery. Since, as he later said, this hypothesis was framed 'before any Childean thinking had reached him' he considered that the economy was 'probably based on hunting and collecting'. Subsequently he advocated the abandonment of this term and its replacement by Late Stone Age, which had, as his own excavations at IWO ELERU showed, both an aceramic and a ceramic phase. A similar succession has been demonstrated at a number of sites, including Bosumpra (re-excavated by A.B. Smith) and SHUM LAKA. The approximate dates for the introduction of pottery at these three sites are 5210 ± 100, 5570 ± 60, and 3810 ± 60 BP respectively. An earlier date of 6340 ± 250 BP for comb-stamped pottery comes from an open site near Konduga on the Bama ridge southwest of Lake Chad. Nevertheless, the fact that all these dates are significantly later than those in the Sahara, and that some decorative motifs are shared in common, suggests that a mechanism of diffusion (of ideas and techniques if not of people) was at work. Microliths (taken to imply the use of a bow and arrow) are still regarded by Shaw as a hunting and presumably savanna adaptation; by contrast, he draws attention to the fact that the stone inventories of certain sites in the presently forested southwestern part of the region (Kakimbon, Yengema, and Blandè) are non-microlithic. In the opinion of the McIntoshes, however, the significance of the dichotomy between microlithic industries and those characterized by 'hoes' or 'picks' remains difficult to evaluate.

Factory sites and shell middens constitute specialized occupations at this time. Examples of the former are CAP MANUEL, UGWUELE-UTURU, and Manianbugu near Bamako. Technically, Manianbugu is very similar to Cap Manuel and is likewise classified as 'Neolithic'; it has a few fragments of pottery and is only 2 km distant from another site (Sotuba) where its dolerite roughouts could well have been brought to a finished state. A shell midden with pottery and quartz artefacts on the coast of Ghana at the Gao lagoon has an age range from 5860 to 5510 BP, and a similar site with pottery and bone artefacts on the Senegalese coast at Khant has an age range from 5650 to 4220 BP. Shell middens as such of course continued in existence long after this, and it is known that they could build up quite rapidly, as in the case of Dioron Boumak, also on the Senegalese coast, where 10 m of deposits were accumulated in >500 years in the 1st and 2nd millennia AD.

A human burial described as 'proto-Negroid' was found at the base of the succession at Iwo Eleru with a date of 11200 ± 200 BP. The burials at Amekni associated with pottery at 8050 ± BP, and others at Saharan sites, have also been attributed to Negroids; but in the Taoudenni basin at Hassi el Abiod at 6970 ± 130 BP and at Kobadi as recently as 3335–2415 BP, a distinctive population of MECHTA-AFALOU type has been identified on the basis of large samples (89 and 97 skeletons respectively); so it will be for future research to work out what were the relations between these two different populations in the region during this period.

2.4. *Domestication and agriculture*. The most important domestic animals in West Africa, and the first to be introduced into the region, are cattle, sheep and goats. The latter are descended from wild Asian progenitors, not the Barbary sheep (*Ammotragus lervia*), and have been found as early as 6800 ± 350 BP at Haua Fteah in northeastern Libya. Gautier suggests that domestic cattle may also have been present, but so far there is no evidence of that. Sheep and/or goats have been found in large numbers from 6530 ± 250 BP onwards at CAPÉLETTI in northeastern Algeria, in levels attributed to the 'Neolithic of Capsian Tradition', thus forming the basis (in Roubet's words) of a 'pastoral pre-agricultural economy'. Bovids were also present and these, despite Gautier's doubts, are described by J. Clutton-Brock as the 'earliest securely dated finds' of cattle on the continent. Claims of older finds, going back to 9500 BP, have been made for Bir Kiseiba and NABTA PLAYA in the Egyptian desert, but the status of these 'exciting . . . troublesome large bovids' (Gautier 1987: 180) remains in doubt. Part of the problem lies in the difficulty of distinguishing cattle bones from those of their possible wild progenitor the aurochs (*Bos primigenius*) known to have been present both in the Nile valley and the Maghreb, where it was hunted by the CAPSIAN inhabitants.

There are also problems arising from the fact that different kinds of cattle are present in West Africa, some of which developed distinctive local characteristics. Humpless cattle (*Bos taurus*) both longhorn ('ndama'; shown in the rock paintings of the Sahara) and dwarf shorthorn ('muturu') are present in 'refuge areas', and the latter's natural immunity to trypanosomiasis indicates that it has long been living in the forests of the south. Dwarf cattle were identified by Carter and Flight at KINTAMPO and Gautier thinks they may have been present at Ntereso also, in the period from 3700 to 2770 BP. They were accompanied by dwarf goats of the trypano-tolerant type which also survives in the area today. Stahl's doubts about the dwarf cattle presumably arise from the difficulty (admitted by Carter and Flight) of distinguishing their bones from those of the forest buffalo (*Syncerus caffer nanus*) known to have been hunted for example by the inhabitants of Shum Laka. Humped zebu cattle (*Bos indicus*), now predominant in the region, probably constitute an independent domestication and were introduced from Asia within the last 2000 years, as illustrated artefactually by the changeover from humpless to humped forms among the clay figurines of phases II and III at Daima.

By plotting dated sites between Capéletti and Kintampo, Thurstan Shaw was able to present an 'isochronic diagram of the spread of cattle' from north to south over a 3000-year period. With the information available to him in 1975, this was as he said an 'artefact of the present state of research', but Gautier's revised map of 1987 does not differ in its essentials from this, except so far as the Nile valley is concerned. Shaw suggested that the movement would essentially have been in two phases, at first to take up the grazing grounds in the Sahara before 5000 BP, and then to move out of them as dessication set in after 4500 BP (when the southward movement of the tsetse fly along with the ITCZ would have opened up hitherto closed areas). This constitutes the 'pastoralist period' of the McIntoshes, as at Adrar Bous. Among the new dates listed by Gautier, perhaps the most interesting are those from the Tadrart Acacus in southwest Libya, which according to him now provides the 'most complete archaeozoological sequence' in the Central Sahara. It seems that both Uan Muhuggiag and Ti-n-Torha North were occupied by cattle, sheep and/or goat keepers after 7440 BP, and if so these sites clearly rival Haua Fteah, if not Bir Kiseiba and NABTA PLAYA.

None of the other domestic animals in West Africa can claim a comparable antiquity. Horses and donkeys (the latter descended from the African wild ass *Equus africanus*) are known from Egyptian pharaonic contexts, and Roger Blench claims that horses including dwarf varieties have been present in West Africa for 2500 years, but as J. Clutton-Brock points out there are problems in distinguishing their remains from those of other equids. Certainly in later times the horse played an unimportant role in West African prehistory, and at two relatively early sites (where osteological evidence is absent) there are artefactual indications of their presence: at IGBO-UKWU (*c.* 9th century AD) there is a bronze hilt in the form of a man on horseback, and at SINTIOU BARA (which is approximately contemporary) there are numerous horse trappings of copper and iron. The domestic chicken has been positively identified at JENNE-JENO prior to AD 850 and Kevin MacDonald has demonstrated that it can be distinguished from francolins and the helmeted guinea fowl (*Numida meleagris*), the latter being the only domestic species that certainly originated in the continent.

By contrast, the majority of the cultivated plants in West Africa are indigenous to the region, and there is every reason to think that they were domesticated locally. Unlike the Near East, as Harlan points out, there was no single nuclear area, and domestication is likely to have been a gradual process, involving protection, transplantation, and selection of certain species, the wild progenitors and relatives of which in many cases still exist and are also exploited in case of need. There is therefore no rigid dichotomy between wild and domesticated forms, certainly so far as the forest area is concerned. While the botanical and linguistic evidence for domestication in this region is good, however, the process is still poorly documented archaeologically, particularly in regard to dating.

In the savanna area, cereals are most important, notably bulrush millet (*Pennisetum glaucum*), guinea corn (*Sorghum bicolor*), African rice (*Oryza glaberrima*), and two species of *Digitaria* known as black and white acha or fonio. The latter grows on poor soils, particularly on the Jos Plateau and the Fouta Djallon, and is not widely known in the outside world, but besides being highly palatable it plays a crucial role in the belief systems of some peoples, particularly the Dogon. Cultivated millet is claimed at Amekni at 8050 ± 80 BP but the basis for this is slight, and its first definite reappearance is at DHAR TICHITT in Munson's phase 6 at 2947 ± 153 BP. The earliest proven occurrence of African rice is at JENNE-JENO in phase 2 of the settlement between 50 and 400 AD. In the forest area, tubers and oil-plants are particularly significant. There are many varieties of yams, of which the Guinea yam (*Dioscorea rotundata*) is the most important, and the many uses of the oil palm (*Elaeis guineensis*) are recognized world-wide. *Elaeis guineensis* is well documented in archaeological contexts at Bosumpra from 5210 ± 100 BP and at Kintampo and OBOBOGO from about 3700 BP onwards, and in non-archaeological contexts at Lake Bosumptwi and the Niger delta. It is, however, not the only oil-plant.

The shea butter tree (*Butyrospermum paradoxum*) is important today in the savanna area, and although the incense tree (*Canarium schweinfurthii*) is now less well known, it was in the past obviously much appreciated, since it has been found with *Elaeis* at Bosumpra, Kintampo, and Obobogo, and at the first of these sites a process can be discerned whereby *Elaeis* gradually displaced it. Cowpeas (*Vigna unguiculata*) may also have been present at Kintampo, and here as elsewhere including Amekni there was obviously much gathering of useful if non-domesticated plants such as the African nettle tree (*Celtis integrifolia*). In later times the importance of the trade in kolanuts (especially *Cola nitida*) is historically documented, as is that of spices such as *Afromomum melegueta*, the so-called 'grains of paradise' on account of which European sailors named Liberia the 'Grain Coast'.

Later, many crops were imported to West Africa, from America (maize, cassava, and sweet potatoes) and East Asia (cocoyams, bananas, and plantains – the latter perhaps as much as 3000 years ago), but still the most prestigious feast for a man from the forest area today might consist of 'grasscutter' (cane rat, as known at Shum Laka), pounded yam, and okra or egusi soup, washed down with 'palm wine' – indigenous products all.

2.5. *From stone to metal.* The sequence of technological stages in the Near East, whereby the working of native copper preceded copper smelting and was succeeded by iron smelting, has yet to be demonstrated in West Africa. A careful re-examination of the data from the AGADEZ region has shown no solid evidence for copper working there prior to 3000 BP, and the industry which was established between 2800 and 2040 BP produced a relatively small number of artefacts. The same is true of Akjoujt in Mauritania, although it has been estimated that 40 metric tons of malachite ore may have been mined at that site during the period of its existence between 2776 and 2350 BP.

Taruga, an iron working site belonging to the NOK culture with dates ranging from 2541 to 2042 BP, was long regarded as the earliest of its type, but it has now been equalled at Opi in southeastern Nigeria (2305–2080 BP) and at Obobogo in southern Cameroon (2310–2120 BP). The fact that there are similar dates from the Agadez region (2440–2010 BP) and also from the middle Ogooué river in Gabon (2480–2310 BP) indicates that this technology came into use at about the same time over a very wide area. A slightly earlier date of 2628 ± 120 BP from Do Dimmi southeast of the Air massif in Central Niger is not out of line with this, although it has been suggested that the same 'old wood' factor which affected the dates from Agadez may have been operative here too. The low shaft furnaces in use at these sites were of the non-slag-tapping variety, although at Lejja (near Opi) <500 cylindrical blocks at first thought to constitute a 'bloom bank' have been shown to consist of slag which was drawn off intermittently into pits. The normal product of these furnaces was low carbon content wrought iron, although on occasions medium carbon content steel and cast iron could be produced.

Iron smelting continued to be a vital part of the West African scene until well into the 20th century, when colonial importation of cheap steel, deforestation due to excessive demand for charcoal, and shortage of skilled labour finally put an end to it. Current research on iron working in the region has tended to move away from what Kense and Okoro describe as the 'vexing, and perhaps increasingly irrelevant, question' of its origin towards other themes, such as the impact of the technology on society, the place of the iron workers in that society, and associated myths and rituals, of which the celebrated Nok terracottas may be one of the first expressions.

The introduction of iron did not mean that other metals ceased to be used. There is some evidence that tin working was practised at sites of the Nok culture, and at the end of the 1st millennium AD remarkable virtuosity in metal working was shown both at IGBO-UKWU in southeastern Nigeria and at Sintiou Bara on the banks of the Senegal river. At Igbo-Ukwu both copper and bronze were employed and considerable reliance was placed on the lost wax (or lost latex) technique. At Sintiou Bara the emphasis was on brass, as well as alloys of copper and silver, and techniques included riveting, wire-drawing, and annealing to produce elaborate composite objects. Iron was produced in low shaft furnaces of the slag-tapping variety. 'Bronzes' (which are in fact mainly of brass) are of course characteristic of the well-known art works produced in IFE and BENIN in the first part of the 2nd millennium AD.

2.6. *Towns and trade.* Igbo-Ukwu, the dating of which aroused such controversy, no longer seems anomalous either chronologically or in any other way, in the light of evidence now available from elsewhere in the region. In 1904 Louis Desplagnes excavated a burial mound and wooden chamber at el-Oualadji in Mali which has now been dated to AD 1025 ± 70; the ritual indicated is reminiscent of Igbo-Ukwu, and parallels the description of the burial procedures for the kings of Ghana given by the Arabic traveller al-Bakri in 1068. At Tondidarou, not far away, burial mounds associated with megalithic alignments have been dated between AD 635 and 670, which perhaps makes the date of AD 170 claimed for some of the CROSS RIVER monoliths not altogether implausible. In overlapping areas of Senegambia about 1500 burial mounds and 1000 megalithic alignments with single or collective burials have been located and again an early date is indicated for some of them. Thus, the burial mounds at Ndalane and Rao have been dated at AD 793 ± 119 and AD 1199 ± 100, and the megalithic alignments at Tiékène-Boussoura and Sine-Ngayène at AD 790 ± 220 and 1083 ± 117, respectively. It is clear, as Calvocoressi and David (1979: 14) comment, that by AD 500 in this area 'large communities organised in complex societies were engaged in inter-regional and inter-areal trade'.

This evidence, together with that for the early growth of towns such as Jenne-jeno, has combined to undermine the 'external stimulus' model which for long maintained that the development of trade and urbanism in the region was dependent on impulses coming from the Islamic world. The evidence from Igbo-Ukwu argues in favour of its technological independence, and revised dates for BEGHO suggest that it and the other Akan kingdoms in the forest also grew up independently. The origins of Benin are considered to be 'still unclear', but early dates for Ife are now matched by those from Old Oyo where the 'Digoun phase' goes back to a period between AD 765 and 1140. This is not to deny that external trade had a role to play, and in the model proposed by Horton the rise and decline of Ife was much influenced by it. The status of Niani as a capital of the old state of Mali is still in dispute (in part because the radiocarbon dates fall into two disparate groups) but Koumbi Saleh (dated between AD 550 and 1720) is generally thought to correspond to the capital of Ghana and (not only in the latest phase) it shows clear signs of Arabic influence. The same is true of Tegdaoust, which has been tentatively identified as the town of Aoudaghost, known to have been destroyed by the Almoravids in AD 1054.

The reality of the trans-Saharan trade in raw materials was proved by Monod's discovery of a 'ship-wrecked' camel caravan at Ma'den Ijâfen in the desert of Majâbat al-Koubrâ which had been carrying cowries and <2000 brass rods south. The find was dated to AD 1130 ± 80 on the basis of material from the mats and ropes which had encircled them. It has also been demonstrated at Sintiou Bara, in the form of cowries, glass beads, non-ferrous metals (brass, copper and silver alloys, and tin), and enamelled pottery of a type which is well known in the Maghreb. The site has eight radiocarbon dates in the range AD 400–1050, which in Thilman's view form a coherent series, although the McIntoshes, following their recent work at Tioubalel and Siouré, are inclined to place reliance only on the more recent ones. These dates are paralleled at Saré Tioffi near Podor (AD 370–1384) and at Ogo (AD 930–1160) in the Sintiou Bara 'culture area'.

The 'Islamic contact' period, in Shaw's terminology, was followed by a 'coastal contact' and then by an 'inland contact' period in the years from 1475 onwards. He expects that during this time archaeology will only 'occasionally' have much to contribute. But even here, as Wesler has shown, it may have 'exciting potential', since the opportunity exists to merge 'traditionally disparate data and methodologies' to gain a coherent picture of a 'society in transition'.

2.7. *Conclusions.* There is no lack of theoretical issues relevant to 'mainstream' archaeology in the study of West Africa's past, and nor are these of the 'dry as dust' variety. Commenting on the controversy over the dating of the earliest pottery in the Sahara and the Nile valley, Posnansky and McIntosh remarked in 1976 that this was 'a complicated, and often emotional, problem'. Such problems are not rare, and the arguments advanced become emotionally loaded whenever any particular reconstruction of the past can be shown to favour either importation from outside the region or autochthonous development within it. These are not neutral issues. Even in the obtaining of radiocarbon dates, as Posnansky and McIntosh commented, there are 'underlying sampling biases of an ideological as well as of a geographical nature' and researchers tend to 'find what they are looking for'. Terminology is a perennial battleground, and one in which it is peculiarly difficult to reach anything resembling objectivity, even supposing the validity of that concept is granted. All this in a vast area where the data are still very sparse and the published data even more so. In 1979 Calvocoressi and David observed that there were 'less than 20 good monographic treatments of major sites from the whole of West Africa', and the situation has not much improved since then. But even when more data are available, rival interpretations will persist, and (unless human nature changes) will very likely tend to reflect the origins and assumptions of those who advance them, 'insiders' and 'outsiders', black and white, African and European.

General bibliography

J.M. Dalziel: *The useful plants of West Tropical Africa* (London, 1937) [new edition in preparation, H.M. Burkill, Royal Botanic Gardens, Kew]; G.W. Lawson: *Plant life in West Africa* (London, 1966); J.R.A. Harlan: 'Agricultural origins: centers and noncenters', *Science* 174 (1971), 468–74; C.T. Shaw: 'Holocene adaptations in West Africa: the Late Stone Age. *Early Man News* 3–4 (1978–9), 51–82; S.K. and R.J. McIntosh: 'West African prehistory', *American Scientist* 69 (1981), 602–13; J.F.A. Ajayi and M. Crowder, ed.: *History of West Africa* 1, 3rd edn (Harlow, 1985); P. Allsworth-Jones: 'The earliest human settlement in West Africa and the Sahara', *WAJA* 17 (1987), 87–128; G. Connah: *African civilizations, precolonial cities and states in tropical Africa: an archaeological perspective* (Cambridge, 1987); A. Gautier: 'Prehistoric men and cattle in North Africa: a dearth of data and a surfeit of models', *Prehistory of arid North Africa*, ed. A.E. Close (Dallas, 1987), 163–87; W.L. Prell and J.E. Kutzbach: 'Monsoon variability over the past 150,000 years', *Journal of Geophysical Research* 92 (1987), 8411–25; S.K. and R.J. McIntosh: 'From stone to metal: new perspectives on the later prehistory of West Africa', *JWP* 2 (1988), 89–133; A.M. Lézine: 'West African paleoclimates during the last climatic cycle inferred from an Atlantic deep-sea pollen record', *Quaternary Research* 35 (1991), 456–63; C.T. Shaw, P. Sinclair, B. Andah and A. Okpoko, ed.: *The archaeology of Africa: food, metals and towns* (London and New York, 1993).

Dating bibliography

The *Journal of African History* has produced some invaluable surveys summarizing new radiocarbon dates from West Africa and commenting on their significance. Authors, dates, volumes and page numbers are as follows: F. Willett, 12 (1971), 339–70; C. Flight 14 (1973), 531–54; M. Posnansky and R.J. McIntosh, 17 (1976), 161–95; D. Calvocoressi and N. David, 20 (1979), 1–29; J.E.G. Sutton 23 (1982), 291–313; S.K. and R.J. McIntosh, 27 (1986), 413–42. This series of articles also provides a unique account of the ebb and flow of research in West Africa over the last 25 years.

Specific bibliographical references (unless mentioned under individual site/culture entries)

R.W.J. Keay: 'Derived savanna – derived from what?', *BIFAN* 21/A (1959), 427–38; M. Brunet et al.: *Australopithecus bahrelghazali*, une nouvelle espèce d'hominid ancien de la région de Koro Toro (Tchad)', *CRASP*, série IIa, 322 (1966), 907–13; P.L. Carter and C. Flight: 'A report on the fauna from the sites of Ntereso and Kintampo rock shelter 6 in Ghana: with evidence for the practice of animal husbandry during the second millennium BC', *Man* 7 (1972), 277–82; A.B. Smith: 'Radiocarbon dates from Bosumpra cave, Abetifi, Ghana', *PPS* 41 (1975), 179–82; F.A. Street and A.T. Grove: 'Environmental and climatic implications of late Quaternary lake-level fluctuations in Africa', *Nature* 261 (1976), 385–90; L. Pastouret, H. Chamley, G. Delibrias, J.C. Duplessy and J. Thiede: 'Late Quaternary climatic changes in Western Tropical Africa deducted from deep-sea sedimentation off the Niger delta', *Oceanologica Acta* 1 (1978), 217–32; D. Calvocoressi and N. David: 'A new survey of radiocarbon and thermoluminescence dates for West Africa', *JAH* 20/1 (1979), 1–29; O. Davies: 'The Ntereso culture in Ghana', *West African culture dynamics: archaeological and historical perspectives*, ed. B.K. Swartz and R.E. Dumett (The Hague, Paris and New York, 1980), 205–22; J.F. Saliège et al.: 'Premières datations de tumulus pré-islamiques au Mali: site mégalithique de Tondidarou', *CRASP* 291/D (1980), 981–4; G. Thilmans and A. Ravisé: *Sintiou-Bara et les sites du fleuve* (Dakar, 1980); M.A. Sowunmi: 'Aspects of Late Quaternary vegetational changes in West Africa', *Journal of Biogeography* 8 (1981), 457–74; M. Raimbault and M. Dembélé: 'Les ateliers préhistoriques de Manianbugu (Bamako, Mali)', *BIFAN* 45/B (1983), 219–76; M.R. Talbot et al.: 'Preliminary results from sediment cores from Lake Bosumptwi, Ghana', *Palaeoecology of Africa and the Surrounding Islands* 16 (1984), 173–92; P.M. Fontes et al.: 'Prospection archéologique de tumulus et de buttes tumuliformes dans la région des lacs au Mali, Datations par le radiocarbone', *CRASP* 301/3 (1985), 207–12; J.C. Ritchie et al.: 'Sediment and pollen evidence for an early to mid-Holocene humid period in the eastern Sahara', *Nature* 314 (1985), 352–5; J.E. Kutzbach and F.A. Street-Perrott: 'Milankovitch forcing of fluctuations in the level of tropical lakes from 18 to 0 kyr BP', *Nature* 317 (1986), 130–4; F. Gasse et al.: 'The arid-humid transition in the Sahara and the Sahel during the last deglaciation', *Nature* 346 (1990), 141–6; M. Raimbault and O. Dutoru: 'Découverte de populations mechtoides dans le Néolithique du Sahel malien (gisement lacustre de Kobadi); implications paléoclimatiques et paléoanthropologiques', *CRASP* 310/III (1990), 631–8; P. Breunig et al.: 'Recent archaeological surveys in Borno, northeast Nigeria', *NA* 37 (1992), 10–17; K.C. MacDonald: 'The domestic chicken (*Gallus gallus*) in sub-Saharan Africa: a background to its introduction and its osteological differentiation from indigenous fowls (Numidinae and *Francolinus* sp.)', *Journal of Archaeological Science* 19 (1992), 303–18; S.K. and R.J. McIntosh and H. Bocoum: 'The Middle Senegal Valley Project: preliminary results from the 1990–91 field season', *NA* 38 (1992), 47–61; K.W. Wesler: 'The introduction of imported ceramics in Nigeria: an archaeological perspective', *WAJA* 22 (1993) 109–132; R.T. Loftus et al.: 'Evidence for two independent domestications of cattle', *Proceedings of the National Academy of Sciences of the USA* 91 (1994), 2757–61; M. Brunet et al.: 'The first australopithecine 2500 kilometres west of the Rift Valley (Chad)', *Nature* 378 (1995), 273–5.

PA-J

3 East Africa

Lying astride the Equator from the Western Rift Valley to the shores of the Indian Ocean, East Africa encompasses highly contrasting environments. These range from montane rain-forests to dry bushlands and semi-desert in the northeast bordering Somalia. Areas of cool high grasslands

Map 3 **Africa, 3: East** Major prehistoric sites in the region.

(notably in the regions of volcanic uplift bordering the two rifts) contrast with medium-altitude plateaus (both wooded and cleared) as well as humid lowlands and the coastal belt.

From the 1920s to 1950s the main archaeological emphasis was on the Stone Age which was considered in its pan-African, and indeed broader Old World context, and at the same time closely linked with the study of Pleistocene geology. Both Wayland in Uganda, working in the Western Rift and the Lake Victoria basin, and Louis Leakey in the Eastern Rift and adjacent highlands were concerned with constructing a chronology for East Africa, based on recognition of sequences of lake levels and volcanic activity, with the assistance of stratified mammalian fossils and broad classes of stone tools. In this way they endeavoured to establish a sequence of Stone Age cultures, distinguished in the traditional manner by tool types and flaking techniques and correlated with the European sequence – with the further attempt to correlate the succession of 'pluvial' and 'interpluvial' periods in East Africa with glacials and interglacials of higher latitudes.

From the mid-20th century, with the expansion of scientific interest and the development of new research methods (including radiometric dating), much of this geo-archaeological sequence and its theoretical base, has been refined or overturned (notably the supposed pluvial-glacial correspondences). Instrumental to these discussions and to generating fertile lines of field research – which placed East Africa in its continental context – was the Panafrican Congress on Prehistory and Quaternary Studies: this first met in Nairobi in 1947, on Louis Leakey's initiative, and has since regularly reconvened in different places in Africa (Francophone as well as Anglophone). At the same time the enhanced international interest in eastern Africa as the homeland of mankind (*see also* HUMAN EVOLUTION), especially following the sensational discoveries at OLDUVAI in 1959–60, stimulated a more sophisticated approach to both field methods and interpretation, and to the interdependence of archaeological and ecological studies. Such advances were by no means confined to the quest for earliest humans and their antecedents two and more million years ago, but were applied to the whole sequence of Early, Middle and Late Stone Age (as generally classified for convenience south of the Sahara). Here the leadership of Desmond Clark and his team of able students was influential in providing a modern scientific and intellectual context, to the exciting if somewhat erratic publicity which accompanied the discoveries of the Leakeys and the 'hominid gangs'. In many ways eastern Africa in the 1960s and 1970s took the centre-stage in field studies of human cultures (including those of existing hunter-gatherers). Work by specialist sub-teams set new models and directions for archaeology world-wide.

The achievement of independence by most African countries in the years around 1960 stimulated new intellectual directions in the continent, in particular demands for precolonial histories of the peoples of Africa. African studies, which had previously been oriented largely towards cultural and social anthropology, were redirected in the 1960s with a more avowedly historical purpose. This required the exploitation on a new scale of oral-historical, comparative-linguistic and especially archaeological approaches, in order to reconstruct the Iron Age and the development of African agricultural and pastoral populations. Since much of this stimulus came from the schools of History in the new African universities and African studies institutions world-wide (in contrast to the 'prehistoric' tradition of most Stone Age research), archaeologists working in Africa have become conscious of two 'camps'; and gatherings of Africanist archaeologists have in recent years witnessed an increasing Iron Age representation (with some of the contributions being of essentially local historical rather than continental interest, or else heavily concerned with demonstrating regional cultures, their ceramics and their dating by radiocarbon).

Nevertheless, the growing emphases on environmental understanding and other broad conceptual issues (as well as the organizational and logistical factors involved in field research) have ensured a fair maintenance of intellectual liaison, and some remarkable instances of specific co-operation, between the 'prehistoric' and the 'historical' wings of African archaeology. One of the prime concerns of African historians in the 1950s and 1960s was to vindicate the oral testimonies of kingdoms and their royal genealogies, sometimes claiming twenty or more generations. Accordingly, in the interlacustrine region of western Uganda and adjacent countries, considerable archaeological effort was put into locating and investigating former capitals of known kingdoms and sites associated with legendary rulers. While this line of research focused on the later Iron Age and recent centuries in particular districts, a broader historical concern (in south-central and west-equatorial as well as eastern Africa) has been the spread of Bantu languages, a phenomenon increasingly recognized as being associated with an expansion of early Iron

Age cultivators with distinctive ceramics around 2000 years ago (see discussion in EARLY IRON AGE). As both these subjects have developed, moving beyond mere concerns for oral-historical or linguistic correlations, they have encouraged a range of cultural, social, economic and technological considerations. The importance of agricultural history (and of an archaeological approach to it) is being increasingly reflected in excavations of settlement sites as well as studies of ancient field systems and their environments.

Similar ecological and techno-cultural concerns have been extended into Late Stone Age studies, and especially into what has been called (since Louis Leakey's first surveys) the 'Neolithic' of the high grasslands of Kenya and northern Tanzania. The term Neolithic has never been precisely or consistently defined in East Africa: some archaeologists emphasize pottery and stone bowls among the advanced aspects of pre-Iron Age technology, while others have supposed that the term refers to the introduction of food-production, i.e., pastoralism and even agriculture (perhaps deluding themselves with an exaggerated local dating, as with the 'PASTORAL NEOLITHIC'). However, these developments of the final millennia BC are gradually coming to be studied together with those of the Iron Age as part of the historical experience of the East African populations. An important concomitant has been the increasing amount of ethnographic recording, especially of rural industries such as iron-working, potting and house-building, and also of settlement spacing, resource catchment, cattle-herding strategies and hunter-gatherer societies and techniques. Ethnoarchaeological theory in the 1980s drew heavily on the East African experience (*see* ETHNOARCHAEOLOGY).

While some aspects of interior Iron-Age research have been rather narrowly conceived within local historical contexts, the study of the Swahili coast – which related very obviously between the 9th and 16th centuries AD to the Indian Ocean, the Islamic heartlands and the wider world – has been largely pursued as a separate subject (*see* SWAHILI HARBOUR TOWNS). Some East African scholars have tended to see the history and archaeology of the coast as somewhat foreign, and the pioneers of Swahili archaeology, Kirkman and Chittick, in particular, made little concession to the intellectual gulf between their work and that of other East African archaeologists, which manifested itself in the 1960s. This divergence derived partly from the different methods of study employed at the coastal sites and partly from the contrasting dating evidence, with coastal chronologies relying extensively on imported ceramics, as well as Islamic stone architectural styles and correlations with Arabic written sources. However, by the end of the 1980s, with more varied strands of studies of interior East Africa and the Indian Ocean, the relevance of historical and archaeological interests to each other has come to be better appreciated – as has the integration of East Africa into the study of the world as a whole.

S. Cole: *The prehistory of East Africa* (rev. edn, New York, 1963; London, 1964); *Azania* (1966–) [the annual journal of the British Institute in Eastern Africa]; J.D. Clark: *The prehistory of Africa* (London, 1970); R. Oliver and J.D. Fage, ed.: *Cambridge History of Africa* I–III (Cambridge, 1977–82); D.W. Phillipson: *The later prehistory of eastern and southern Africa* (London, 1977); UNESCO: *General History of Africa* I–II (1981); D.W. Phillipson: *African archaeology* (Cambridge, 1985); P.T. Robertshaw, ed.: *A history of African archaeology* (London, 1990); J.E.G. Sutton: *A thousand years of East Africa* (Nairobi, 1990).

JS

4 Southern Africa

Southern Africa is a subcontinent of contrasts. Climatically, rainfall is the most important factor, with a winter rainfall pattern dominant in its southwestern corner. Over the remaining western third of South Africa rainfall may fall all year round, but is high only along the coast; the rest of the subcontinent has a summer rainfall régime, with precipitation highest over its eastern half. Except for the Zambezi River and its tributaries, the westward-flowing Orange/Vaal system is the most extensive drainage system; most other rivers, including the Limpopo, drain into the Indian Ocean. Surface water is rare over the subcontinent's western half and much of Botswana and Namibia lack permanent rivers. Defining these drainage systems, the most important topographic feature is the Great Escarpment, of which the Drakensberg and the highlands of eastern Zimbabwe are the most prominent components, while the Cape Fold Belt is a further mountain range lying between the Escarpment and the southwestern coastline of South Africa. Running around all but the northern margin of the subcontinent, which is defined by the watershed between the Zambezi/Cunene rivers and those of the Congo Basin, it separates the lower-lying lands towards the coast from a higher interior plateau that trends gradually away towards the northwest, where it is occupied by the Kalahari; a southerly extension of the Rift Valley system is represented most obviously by Lake Malawi.

Ecologically, the northern half of southern Africa is a savanna region populated by browsing and mixed-feeding ungulates, with *miombo* and *mopane* woodland dominant in Zambia and Malawi. The east is mostly covered by grasslands suitable for large, gregarious grazers, while the west trends into sparsely vegetated scrub or (in southern Namibia and extending north along the coast) desert with a reduced diversity of large game; browsers are found in large numbers in a mostly heathland vegetation community (known locally as *fynbos*) along the subcontinent's southwestern margins.

The Khoisan peoples of the subcontinent hold a significance for archaeologists that goes far beyond a local or intrinsic interest. Viewed for decades as archetypal mobile foragers, they are now the focus of a major debate on the consequences of centuries of interaction between societies with widely different modes of production: hunting/gathering, pastoralism and mixed farming. As well, the subcontinent's rock-engravings and paintings form one of the best understood rock-art traditions anywhere in the world, and the area is seen by many as crucial to understanding the biological and perhaps also the cultural evolution of our own species: some of the oldest anatomically modern human fossils come from such local sites as KLASIES RIVER MOUTH and BORDER CAVE.

Map 4 **Africa, 4: Southern** Some major prehistoric sites in the region.

4.1. *The Middle and Later Stone Ages.* Southern African archaeologists distinguish two very generalized stone-working traditions within the last 150–200,000 years. The older of these, the Middle Stone Age (MSA), is characterized by the production of flakes and flake-blades, some of them retouched to form scrapers, knives, points or backed pieces. Prepared core technology is not as strongly developed a feature as it is of roughly contemporary Middle Palaeolithic technologies, but many flakes and flake-blades do have faceted platforms; true Levallois cores sometimes occur.

Although some regional industries have been identified (e.g. the Orangian Industry on South Africa's central plateau) detailed classification of Middle Stone Age assemblages is generally avoided: there are few long sequence sites and chronological controls, especially for open-air locations, are poor. Instead, four broadly successive stages are recognised. Dated by reference to the global oxygen isotope stage curve, they are: MSA 1 (stage 6); MSA 2 (stages 5e–5b, the Last Interglacial); the HOWIESON'S POORT (stages 5a/4); MSA 3 (stage 3). Within these stages assemblages vary widely in artefact morphology, core types and raw material. In broad terms the MSA 1 has very few retouched pieces with points completely absent; the MSA 2 features relatively large flake-blades, as well as scrapers and both unifacial and bifacial points (including those previously known as STILLBAY); the Howieson's Poort shows enhanced use of finegrained rocks and includes high frequencies of segments and other backed pieces, some of microlithic proportions; and the MSA 3 is highly variable, but clearly post-Howieson's Poort in age. While MSA 1 assemblages may have been produced by archaic hominids, anatomically modern human fossils have been found with more recent MSA assemblages at several sites in South Africa. However, still at issue is the extent to which this physical modernity necessarily implies similarities in cultural behaviour and potential, with unequivocal evidence for art and jewellery, for example, only found (e.g. at APOLLO 11 CAVE and BORDER CAVE respectively) after 40,000 BP.

For a long time debate has persisted on the date of the transition between Middle and Later Stone Age (LSA) technologies, but an emerging consensus, based on data from sites such as BOOMPLAAS, ROSE COTTAGE CAVE and SEHONGHONG, now locates this for the area south of the Limpopo to around 21,000 BP. Characteristic of most LSA assemblages is an emphasis on the production of microliths, but more significant in a behavioural sense are similarities with the material culture used by recent southern African hunter-gatherers. Examples found already in Pleistocene LSA contexts include ostrich eggshell and bone beads, bored stone digging stick weights, tortoiseshell bowls, ostrich eggshell containers (sometimes decorated with incised geometric designs) and bone (arrow?) points. Such similarities encourage archaeologists in their use of ethnographic data to interpret the archaeological record, though with a growing recognition of the value of looking beyond southern Africa for appropriate analogies.

Four or five broadly successive artefact traditions are generally recognized within the southern African Later Stone Age. Although the very earliest LSA assemblages are amorphous, quartz-dominated microlithic occurrences, between 19,000 and 12,000 BP the systematic production of unretouched bladelets from highly distinctive bladelet cores distinguishes Robberg assemblages, which are found across South Africa, Lesotho and Swaziland. These bladelets were used in a diverse range of tasks as the cutting edges of composite artefacts; those formally retouched tools (scrapers, adzes, backed microliths) that do occur are always rare. Broadly contemporary with the Robberg, the Maleme Industry of southwestern Zimbabwe retains some MSA features, while macrolithic assemblages are found at sites in Namibia.

Very different assemblages are found across the Pleistocene/Holocene boundary. Dating to roughly 12–8000 BP they are grouped within the OAKHURST Complex and cover a much wider area than the Robberg, extending north of the Limpopo to include sites in Zimbabwe and Namibia. Several regional industries are recognized, largely from differences in raw material usage: Kuruman in the Northern Cape Province, Lockshoek across much of South Africa's interior plateau, ALBANY in the Cape Fold Mountains and their adjacent coastlands, Pomongwan in Zimbabwe. The Oakhurst differs from the Robberg in that bladelets are extremely rare, coarser-grained rocks tend to be preferred and flakes and scrapers (virtually the only retouched tools) are larger. Much higher numbers of beads, other ornaments and bone tools are also found after 12,000 BP, perhaps signalling an increased role for exchange as a means of minimizing ecological risk and/or a transformation in social relations.

Zambia, Malawi and northern Zimbabwe fall into a different cultural province from the rest of the subcontinent. MSA assemblages, well documented at sites such as Mumbwa Cave, were replaced by 19,000 BP by microlithic traditions known locally as Nachikufan. Though similar to the Robberg in having evidence of bored stones, worked bone and jewellery, the Nachikufan is typified by the production of backed (as opposed to unmodified) bladelets and points. Once established this pattern of artefact manufacture also shows more continuity than is evident further south; there is no Zambian or Malawian equivalent of the Oakhurst Complex and Nachikufan-like assemblages continued to be produced in some areas, such as western Zambia, until recent centuries.

Beginning around 9500 years ago in Namibia and Zimbabwe, but occurring only from 8000 BP south of the Limpopo, a different technological tradition is found. This WILTON complex marks a return to a microlithic technology, but is only superficially similar to the Robberg. Both made extensive use of fine-grained rocks, but the Wilton was not a bladelet technology. Instead, it was geared to the systematic manufacture of a wide range of scrapers and backed microliths (especially segments in its earlier stages) generally made on small flakes. Microwear shows that scrapers were used to work skins, but perhaps mostly in finer, decorative work, with backed microliths used in a variety of cutting tasks as knives, and perhaps also as arrow armatures.

Holocene microlithic assemblages continued to be made in many parts of southern Africa until the nineteenth century, though with changes in the details of scraper design and the kinds of backed microliths produced. A general trend in many areas is for the frequency of adzes (widely interpreted as woodworking implements) to increase during the last 4000 years, a pattern linked in the Thukela Basin of KwaZulu-Natal and elsewhere to increased use of underground plant foods, for the exploitation of which wooden digging sticks would have been needed. Comparable developments are also observable in other parts of the subcontinent and may be linked to the development of more elaborate burials (as a means of establishing claims to local landscapes) and greater use of other small-sized food resources, such as fish, shellfish and ground game. At the same time the archaeological record exhibits an increasing regionalization of material culture, although only rarely is this formally recognized in archaeological nomenclature. One of the best examples of this regionalization is the distribution of pressure-flaked stone arrowheads and backed microliths across Lesotho, the Free State and the eastern Karoo: recent studies suggest this at least partly correlates with ostrich eggshell and seashell bead exchange networks and with the distribution of rock-paintings of fish belonging to the mormyrid family.

Despite growing social and economic complexity in some parts of the subcontinent, there is no evidence that any of the plant or animal resources indigenous to southern Africa were independently domesticated. However, for much of the last 2000 years the region's hunter-gatherers have been in close contact with food-producing societies. In the southwestern part of the sub-continent these contacts were with Khoi-speaking pastoralists, whose linguistic affiliations suggest an ultimate origin in north-central Botswana; sheep were presumably acquired here originally from Iron Age farmers. Recent accelerator dates show sheep present in the Cape Fold Belt *c.*1900 BP, though associations with the local introduction of pottery are not clearcut. As with recent dates suggesting that pottery appeared in southeastern southern Africa several hundred years before the oldest known Iron Age villages, this raises the possibility that ceramics were adopted ahead of, or by different means from, the local establishment of food-producing communities and encourages archaeologists to consider the active roles played by hunter-gatherers in the development of pastoralist and farming societies.

Side by side with pastoralists and Iron Age farmers, hunter-gatherer populations survived across most of southern Africa well into the colonial era, in some places (e.g. much of the eastern half of the subcontinent) gradually being assimilated into farming societies, in others (e.g. the Riet River Valley of South Africa) acquiring livestock of their own and elsewhere (e.g. the Caledon Valley) developing a range of exchange, ritual and economic ties with food-producers. Here and across much of the Karoo, hunter-gatherers made pottery of their own, with Smithfield ceramics (often associated with more macrolithic stone tool assemblages) a widespread tradition. South of the Limpopo, the nineteenth century saw the LSA end with the final displacement of hunter-gatherers and pastoralists and their incorporation into local Bantu-speaking communities or South Africa's emerging 'Coloured' population. In both Namibia and Botswana, however, thriving communities of Khoi-speaking pastoralists and Bushmen survive today.

4.2. *The history of Stone Age archaeological research in southern Africa.* The general trends in the study of the southern African Stone Age have broadly paralleled developments in other parts of the world. Beginning with essentially antiquarian observations in the mid-nineteenth century, the 1920s saw the emergence of a concern with the description and classification of stone tools and the interpretation of their spatial distributions, notably in terms of population movements and the effects of different raw materials on assemblage composition. The basic terminology (including the local 'Three Age System' of Early, Middle and Later Stone Ages) invented then by A.J.H. Goodwin and C. Van Riet Lowe continues in use today.

Beginning around 1959 when Desmond Clark argued that different environmental conditions had affected assemblage character in different parts of the subcontinent, a strongly ecological focus has prevailed in the region's research tradition. The work of Hilary Deacon, initially at Melkhoutboom and subsequently with a focus on Boomplaas and KLASIES RIVER MOUTH, along with the research of John Parkington and his colleagues in the Western Cape are two of several projects that have emphasized the study of prehistoric subsistence economies, adaptation to local ecologies and palaeoenvironmental reconstruction. More recently, there has been a partial shift from these people-to-nature focused studies to others that emphasize people-to-people approaches, especially the study of social and ideological change. This shift derives in part from the use of San ethnography in rock art interpretation and the impact of rock art research on other archaeological studies, notably in foregrounding questions of ideology and social relations.

Recent studies that place the study of social, rather than simply ecological, change at the top of their agenda include those of Lyn Wadley in Gauteng and the Free State and of Aron Mazel in the Thukela Basin of KwaZulu-Natal; the potential of rock art for understanding social change has been explored by David Lewis-Williams, Thomas Dowson and others.

PM

4.3. *The Iron Age*. Environmental data indicate that significant climatic shifts took place during the Iron Age, and wetter periods facilitated Iron Age expansion. Southern Africa has a somewhat varied environment; it lies south of the equator, therefore winters are dry and most rain falls in the summer, from November to March. Hunter–gatherers still lived throughout this diverse area in the Iron Age, but archaeologists consider this period to represent a cultural break with the past, since a new way of life and a fresh set of beliefs appear. Pole-and-daga houses, raised grain-bins and sunken storage pits represent settled agricultural villages, while bones of domestic small and large livestock, furnace, forge and metal slag, and pottery decorated in a distinctive set of styles are also characteristic.

Scholars commonly place these African Iron Age remains in two main phases: Early (AD 1–1000) and Late (AD 1000–1850). Some believe this new lifestyle emerged as the result of the diffusion of individual traits, but the archaeological evidence does not support this interpretation. As Robinson's excavations at MABVENI in Zimbabwe first showed in the 1960s, the diagnostic features occur together. Although there are pitfalls, archaeologists use ceramic styles in Central and Southern Africa to trace the origins and movements of Iron Age people. David Phillipson's Chifumbadze classification, somewhat modified by Thomas Huffman, identifies three principal divisions and therefore 'streams' of movement: (1) the UREWE Tradition, which contains firstly a KWALE Branch, including SILVER LEAVES/MATOLA in southern Africa and secondly an Nkope Branch, including Ziwa and Gokomere in Zimbabwe, and Kamnama and Kumadzulo (or the Dambwe group) in Zambia; (2) the Kalundu Tradition, which includes Benfica in Angola, KAPWIRIMBWE and Kulundu in Zambia, Sinoia in Zimbabwe and Matakoma, BROEDERSTROOM, Lydenburg and Msuluzi in South Africa. A direct cultural continuum in southern Africa from the Kalundu Tradition to modern Shona and from Kwale to Swahili in East Africa show that the Chifumbadze complex of styles was made by Eastern Bantu speakers. Other ceramic traditions are associated with Western Bantu speakers in the Congo basin. It is likely that Western Bantu speakers moved from the Nigeria/Cameroon homeland into the Congo Basin as rootcrop agriculturalists, perhaps by 1000 BC, before Eastern Bantu evolved.

A current debate concerns the movement of Eastern Bantu speakers into East, Central and Southern Africa and the nature of their society. Excavations at Broederstroom show that more cattle were herded than faunal samples indicate and that by this time (at least) settlement organization followed the 'CENTRAL CATTLE PATTERN' (i.e. a settlement pattern centred on a 'male domain' comprising a central cattle byre, elite burials and a 'men's court'). These people therefore valued hereditary leadership, a patrilineal ideology, cattle brideprice and a religion based on their ancestors.

The early presence of the central cattle pattern disproves a once commonly held theory that the Late Iron Age was heralded by the development of cattle rearing around AD 1000. The most significant event at this time was the evolution of the Zimbabwe culture at K2 and MAPUNGUBWE. The Indian Ocean trade with Swahili that was so important in this evolution began somewhat earlier, and glass beads are found throughout Zimbabwe in 9th-century contexts. Unrelated stimuli at the same time caused Western Bantu speakers with LUANGWA style pottery to move south across Zambia, ultimately forming the so-called 'matrilineal belt'. As a possible consequence, speakers of the Eastern Bantu, Sotho-Tswana and Nguni languages moved into southern Africa during the 13th century. Sotho-Tswana did not occupy the open highveld of the Transvaal and Orange Free State until the climate became warmer and wetter in the 16th century. Another warm episode in the mid- to late-18th century permitted the widespread cultivation of maize in Natal and the Transvaal.

Population increases followed by drought and famine contributed to the great military stress of the *difaqane* (a Sotho term meaning literally 'the hammering', used to refer to the violent period in the late 18th century AD, which led to the population movements of the 1820s and 1830s). In response, Sotho-Tswana in the interior aggregated into large towns of several thousand people (such as Olifantspoort and MOLOKWANE), and some Nguni moved as far away as Tanzania, Malawi, Zambia and Zimbabwe.

TH

Stone Age bibliography

R.R. Inskeep: *The peopling of southern Africa* (Cape Town, 1978); R.G. Klein, ed.: *Southern African prehistory and palaeoenvironments* (Rotterdam, 1984); J.E. Parkington and M. Hall, ed.: *Papers in the prehistory of the western Cape* (Oxford, 1987); L. Wadley: *The Later Stone Age of the southern Transvaal: social and ecological interpretations* (Oxford, 1987); J.D. Lewis-Williams and T.D. Dowson: *Images of power* (Johannesburg, 1989); A.D. Mazel: 'People making history: ten thousand years of hunter-gatherer history in the Thukela Basin', *Natal Museum Journal of Humanities* 1 (1989), 1–189; A.I. Thackeray: 'The Middle Stone Age south of the Limpopo River', *JWP* 6 (1990), 385–440; L. Wadley: 'The Pleistocene Later Stone Age south of the Limpopo River', *JWP* 7 (1993), 243–96; Journals: *South African Archaeological Bulletin*; *Southern African Field Archaeology*.

PM

Iron Age bibliography

K.R. Robinson: 'An Early Iron Age site in the Chibi District, Southern Rhodesia', *SAAB* 16 (1961), 95–102; T. Maggs: *Iron Age communities of the southern highveld* (Pietermaritzberg, 1976); D.W. Phillipson: *The later prehistory of eastern and southern Africa* (London, 1977); R.M. Gramly: 'Expansion of Bantu-speakers versus development of Bantu language and African culture in situ: an archaeologist's perspective', *SAAB* 33 (1978), 107–12; T. Maggs: 'Msuluzi confluence: a seventh century Early Iron Age site on the Tugela River', *Annals of the Natal Museum* 24 (1980), 111–45; T.M. Evers: Excavations at the Lydenburg Heads site, eastern Transvaal, South Africa', *SAAB* 37 (1982), 16–33; P.D. Tyson and J.A. Lindesay: 'The climate of the last 2000 years in southern Africa', *Holocene* 2 (1992), 271–8.

TH

5 Central Africa

Central Africa is usually defined geographically as the area lying between the Niger, Nile and Zambezi river basins, and south of the Lake Chad basin. For the purposes of this work it comprises the modern states of Zaire, Congo-Brazzaville, Gabon, Equatorial Guinea, the Central African Republic, as well as northern Angola and southern Cameroon. The most outstanding ecological feature of this zone is the presence of the Central African rainforest, filling the central depression of Africa and extending to the west African coastlands, and to the edge of the Central African lakes region. The prehistoric fluctuations of the rainforest's geographical coverage are uncertain, but evidence would suggest that its size has fluctuated substantially in response to arid and humid phases generated by the inter-tropical convergence zone. As its borders are savanna–forest mosaics, giving way to typical Sudanian savannas to the north and south, and montane grasslands and forests to the east and northwest. The heart of Central Africa is traversed by the powerful Zaire (Congo) River, which is the region's principal hydrological network.

Most of the modern inhabitants of Central Africa speak Bantu languages with some populations in the north of the region speaking other Niger–Congo languages, or languages of the Nilo–Saharan language phylum. However, it is likely that this linguistic uniformity over-printed a much greater linguistic diversity during the past few thousand years. It should be noted that the modern inhabitants of the Central African rainforest include both 'Bantu' and 'pygmy' populations, with the latter usually being in a client relationship to the former. It has been suggested that these Niger–Congo speaking pygmy populations are the acculturated remnants of the rainforest's original inhabitants, although the time depth of both the pygmoid physical type and the initial occupation of the rainforest environment remain uncertain.

5.1. *The earliest evidence for hominid occupations in Central Africa*. The existence of pre-Acheulean industries in Central Africa has long been a debated topic, with most finds coming from fluvially reworked contexts near principal channels in the Zaire basin and consisting mainly of heavily rolled 'choppers'. The most plausible pre-Acheulean sites are in the region of Lunda (northeast Angola), where a number of relatively unreworked assemblages have been found which lack bifaces and consist predominantly of core choppers and sidescrapers on flakes (Clark 1966). Other such assemblages in Zaire and the Central African Republic are not universally accepted.

Acheulean sites, particularly those of the evolved Acheulean, are much more widespread and easily confirmed. One of the most extensively and systematically excavated Acheulean sites in Central Africa is that of Kamoa (Zaire), which has supplied important spatial information on the stages of the stone knapping process represented at a main 'workshop' site and a 'living area' (Cahen 1976). The assemblages at Kamoa appear on typological grounds to belong to the Evolved Acheulean; being dominated by sidescrapers on flakes, possessing both handaxes and picks, and featuring rare examples of LEVALLOIS nuclei and flakes. Geological indications and a pollen core suggest that the locality was occupied during an arid period, when the area was open savanna. The site has not been directly dated, but on comparison with other

Map 5 **Africa, 5: Central** Some major prehistoric sites in the region.

assemblages should date to uncal *c*.200,000 BP. Other important Acheulean localities in Central Africa include the sites of the Sangha region in the Central African Republic, where assemblages comprising all stages of the Acheulean (lower, middle and upper) have been identified (Lanfranchi and Clist 1991). The Lunda region of Angola has likewise supplied lower and upper Acheulean industries.

SANGOAN localities are very numerous in Central Africa, although the best dated and most well-known occurrences are on its fringes. The original sequences for the post-Acheulean stone age industries of the region were built by J. Colette at GOMBE POINT (Zaire), however the stratigraphic integrity of these sequences are now in doubt (Cahen 1976). Regardless, macrolithic 'core tool' industries – sometimes with and sometimes without a Levallois component – occupy the period between *c*.200,000 and 40,000 years ago in Central Africa. Neither palaeoclimatic studies, nor archaeological research has allowed us to view with precision the environmental context of these early occupations, and particularly whether they were within or without the rainforest.

5.2. *The first microlithic industries*. Some of the earliest MICROLITHIC industries in the world are found in Central Africa. These include the important sites of MATUPI CAVE (Zaire) and SHUM LAKA (southern Cameroon), where microlithic quartz industries have been shown to date at or before the 'radiocarbon barrier' of uncal 40,000 BP.

Matupi Cave is located in eastern Zaire, almost on the Ugandan frontier. Palynological and faunal evidence suggests that the cave was surrounded by savanna vegetation, but in proximity to gallery or rain forest throughout its 'Late Stone Age' occupation. The earliest stone industry at Matupi (*c*.<40,700 to uncal 32,000 BP) is characterized by a fully microlithic reduction technique (bipolar cores with small flakes and bladelets), but lacking true geometric microliths. Geometric microliths, presumably used in making composite tools only begin to occur at uncal *c*.32,000 to 21,000 BP, coupled with substantial numbers of *pièces esquillées*, presumably for wood-working (Van Noten 1982).

Shum Laka is one of the most recently researched rockshelter sites in Central Africa, with fieldwork only being completed there by Pierre de Maret and his team in 1994. Preliminary information from palynological, faunal and macrobotanical analyses show that it, like Matupi, was probably situated on a savanna–forest ecotone for most of its occupation (an ecotone being an area bordering two different ecological zones). The lower sediments at Shum Laka have been dated to at least uncal 30,000 BP and contain three different quartz microlithic industries. From an Ash Member, overlying these lower sediments a group of human burials has been found dating to uncal *c*.7000 BP. These remains of at least 15 individuals, are associated with a microlithic quartz industry, and thus constitute the largest Late Stone Age mortuary population yet known from Central Africa. The future laboratory analyses of materials from the Shum Laka excavations have the potential to profoundly change our perception of ancient economy and populations at the edge of the rainforest.

It is interesting that all early microlithic occurrences in sub-Saharan Africa (Matupi, Shum Laka, HOWIESON'S POORT) seem to be associated with open savanna environments or savanna – forest ecotones. At their early stages at least, they are certainly not associated with deep forest environments, and indeed some authors (Ambrose and Lorenz 1990) have suggested that open environments, greater residential mobility (with greater information exchange), and the need for lighter (longer range) weapons and a more flexible toolkit may have conspired to stimulate the development of microlithic industries in Africa.

By uncal *c*.15,000 BP microlithic technology had become virtually universal in Central Africa. Indeed, the Central African microlithic techno-complex was to continue in Central Africa in some localities until uncal *c*.2000 BP.

5.3. *The 'Stone to Metal Age' and the 'Bantu expansion'*. The advent of ceramic technology was comparatively late in Africa south of the equator, considering that the first Saharan ceramics rank amongst some of the most ancient in the world. In most of the region ceramics appear along with polished stone tools only after uncal 4000 BP, however there are a few notable exceptions.

The coastal Sablières de Libreville (Gabon) hold within them several localities where ceramics and microliths have been found within discrete ash lens dated to between uncal 6450 and 4870 BP (Clist 1995). Many scholars have asserted that these ceramics might be somehow intrusive, due to high subsurface mobility in unconsolidated sand deposits. However, as further sites in coastal Gabon, such as Nzogobeyok and Rivière Denis, have been found to have similar associations at comparable dates, the integrity of these finds is becoming more probable. If these datings are accurate, they indicate that in at least some instances pottery was appropriated or developed by Central African hunter-gatherers well before the 'Bantu Expansion'.

The beginnings of the expansion of Niger–Congo speakers of the Bantu Super-Family into Central Africa has been placed by historical linguists at around uncal 4000 BP. The current consensus is that the core area for this expansion may be found in the Cameroon grassfields. It would seem that the first Bantu-speaking immigrants into Central Africa arrived before the beginnings of metallurgy, but with ceramics, polished stone tools and small livestock. The initial population movements could have been encouraged by the beginnings of the recent arid phase around uncal 4500 BP – opening savanna corridors into the rainforest. Additionally, it would seem that some migration was maritime (between southern Cameroon, Equatorial Guinea, and Gabon), since the island of Bioko was occupied by local seafarers around uncal 4000 BP (Vansina 1990; Clist 1995).

As research has progressed over the past few decades, it has become evident that it is no longer possible to trace a clean line in Central Africa between one period when groups were using stone tools and another in which iron implements were employed. Thus, to alleviate confusion, de Maret (1995) has suggested the use of Stone to Metal Age (or SMA) as a term for this technologically transitional period (*c.*4,000–2,000 uncal BP). Within the Central African SMA there would appear to be a wide diversity of local ceramic traditions and associated technologies and economies.

The sites of OBOBOGO and Nkang (Cameroon) provide us with some of our clearest economic evidence for this period. At Obobogo, ceramics, oil palm endocarps and the fruits of the tree *Canarium schweinfurthii* have been associated in disposal or storage pits with dates of between uncal 3625 and 2120 BP while at Nkang domesticated ovicaprines are present at around uncal 2,500 BP (de Maret 1995). These sites seem to mark the first documented occurrences of a vegecultural and small livestock management economy which appears to have slowly expanded within the Central African forests around uncal, 2000 BP potentially along river corridors.

Also in the 3rd millennium BP (uncal) interesting developments were taking place in the savanna of the Central African republic. There, in the Bouar region, numerous megalithic monuments (called locally *tazunu*) were being constructed. These *tazunu*, which number in the hundreds, consist primarily of stone aggregations of approximately 10 m in diameter and 1 to 2 m in height, with a series of monoliths placed at or around their summit. Six *tazunu* have been excavated and dated, providing absolutely no evidence for inhumations, but featuring dates on associated charcoal falling between uncal 2800 and 2000 BP. Associated material culture from excavations has been rather sparse but includes some ceramics, ground stone and lithics (David 1982). In terms of function, these monuments have usually been viewed as territorial or group lineage markers.

The expansion of ceramic-using groups into the Central African forest and the Zaire Basin has been studied in recent years by the German River Reconnaissance Project (Eggert 1993). Their work established the existence of three cultural groups in the river basin on the basis of ceramic analysis. These included: the Imbonga Group (uncal 2400–2000 BP, no associated iron or stone tools), the Batalimo Group (uncal 2100–1600 BP, no associated iron, but associated polished stone axes common at the 'type site' of Batalimo, Central African Republic) and the Pikunda–Munda Group (uncal 2000–1700 BP, clearly associated with iron artefacts). It is unclear at this point whether or not the technological variability encountered in these groups is simply an artefact of sampling. Unfortunately no economic evidence for these groups is yet available.

The earliest indications of iron metallurgy in Central Africa come from Gabon in the Ogooué basin. There, certain localities at Otoumbi (Middle Ogooué) and Moanda (Upper Ogooué) have supplied some of the earliest dates for iron furnaces yet known in Africa (Otoumbi 2: 2640 ± 70 and 2400 ± 50 uncal BP; Moanda 1: 2350 ± 140 uncal BP and Moanda 2: 2330 ± 90 uncal BP). There is some controversy surrounding these dates since contemporary occupations in the same region are still essentially 'Neolithic' in material culture (Clist 1995). However, it should be remembered that the transfer to iron technology everywhere in Africa was a gradual process, with little immediate change in material culture and only a slow proliferation of metal artefacts. Indeed, by uncal 2000 BP iron technology was very widespread in central Africa.

5.4. *Complex societies: the case of the Luba kingdom and its antecedents.* It would seem that by the late 1st millennium AD several complex societies were in existence along the Zaire basin. Certainly by the time of European contact in the 15th century, the impressive, urbanized kingdom of Kongo already controlled the mouth of the Zaire river and the kingdom of Teke occupied much of what is now Congo-Brazzaville. However, archaeological evidence for the background to these polities is rather scarce when compared with that for the kingdom of Luba.

The historic kingdom of Luba existed during the

18th and 19th centuries in and around the riverine Upemba Depression of eastern Zaire. However, the Luba kingdom has important antecedents which are only attested by the archaeological record (de Maret 1991). Between *c.*AD 700 and 900, the Upemba Depression was already occupied by an apparently stratified society, featuring graves of differential status and including symbols of wealth and power (non-functional 'ceremonial' axes and cylindrical anvils) which would still have been recognizable as legitimation symbols at the time of the Luba Kingdom. This cultural phase, termed the Early Kisalian, was followed by a more sophisticated expression of the same cultural tradition, the Classic Kisalian (*c.*AD 900–1300). The graves of the Classic Kisalian reached a level of unparalleled richness, often holding in excess of 20 finely made Kisalian pots and quantities of copper bangles, necklaces, bracelets, fishhooks and spearheads, as well as objects in ivory and iron. Subsequently grave-goods decreased in quantity and diversity being replaced in the following Kabambian cultural phases (*c.*AD 1300–1700) by collections of copper croissettes (cross-shaped ingots which seem to have acted as a currency in parts of Central Africa at that time).

The wealth of the Kisalian period in the Upemba Depression seems to have been based upon two factors: first the abundance of freshwater fish resources in the region which allowed the formation of large sedentary settlements and even the export of dried fish, and secondly a proximity to the 'copperbelt' of southern Zaire and northern Zambia which allowed local elites to participate in the distribution web of copper to the coast and the interior. Interestingly, a contemporary polity at the southern end of the Upemba Depression – the Katotian – whilst featuring similar pottery and grave goods to the Kisalian, also possessed cowries, *Conus* shells and glass beads as tangible markers of connection with the Indian Ocean trade.

J.D. Clark: *The distribution of prehistoric culture in Angola* (Diamang, 1966); D. Cahen: 'Nouvelles fouilles à la Pointe de la Gombe (ex-Pointe de Kalina), Kinshasa, Zaire', *L'Anthropologie* 80 (1976), 573–602; N. David: 'Tazunu: megalithic monuments of Central Africa', *Azania* 17 (1982), 43–8; F. Van Noten, ed.: *The archaeology of Central Africa* (Graz, 1982); S.H. Ambrose and K.G. Lorenz: 'Social and Ecological Models for the Middle Stone Age in Southern Africa', *The emergence of modern humans: an archaeological perspective*, ed. P. Mellars (Edinburgh, 1990), 3–33; J. Vansina: *Paths in the rainforests: toward a history of political tradition in equatorial Africa* (London, 1990); R. Lanfranchi and B. Clist: *Aux origines de l'Afrique Centrale* (Libreville, 1991); P. de Maret: 'L'archéologie du royaume Luba', *Aux origines de l'Afrique Centrale*, ed. R. Lanfranchi and B. Clist (Libreville, 1991), 234–41; M. Eggert: 'Central Africa and the archaeology of the equatorial rainforest: reflections on some major topics', *The archaeology of Africa: food, metals and towns*, eds. T. Shaw, P. Sinclair, B. Andah and A. Okpoko (London, 1993), 289–33; B. Clist: *Gabon: 1000,000 ans d'Histoire* (Libreville, 1995); P. de Maret: 'Pits, pots and far-west streams', *The growth of farming communities in Africa from the Equator southwards*, ed. J.E.G. Sutton [*Azania* special volume 29–30] (Nairobi, 1995), 318–23.

KM

Agade *see* AKKADIAN

Agadez Region situated southwest of the Air massif, central Niger, which was investigated by Danilo Grébénart in 1978–81; it contains abundant remains, both above and below the Tigidit scarp, attributed to the Neolithic, Copper and Iron Ages, and the medieval period; most interest has centred on the early Copper Age, because of Grébénart's claim that 'an autonomous centre for the working of native copper' developed here at that time. A total of 42 radiocarbon dates from 17 sites belonging to four phases of settlement is summarized as follows: [*Phase*: number of sites; number of dates; date range BP]: *Neolithic* (6; 8; 3390 ± 100–2795 ± 105). *Copper I* (3; 15; 4140 ± 90–2900 ± 100). *Copper II* (5; 15; 2800 ± 90–2040 ± 90). *Iron I* (3; 4; 2440 ± 90–2010 ± 90).

The scheme implies that the early Copper Age in the Agadez region preceded and ran parallel with the Neolithic and that the late Copper Age was likewise largely contemporaneous with the early Iron Age. Some copper slag was analysed by J.R. Bourhis and R.F. Tylecote, but they did not agree in their interpretation, and a third opinion was therefore sought from N.J. van der Merwe, who with his colleagues has provided a complete reassessment of the sites attributed to the Copper Age, particularly Afunfun 175, where according to Grébénart more than 100 furnaces representative of the early period have been identified. Of the 18 structures excavated at this site, only furnace 1 produced a large quantity of fused material, and two samples of this were shown to consist of fayalitic iron-smelting slag, directly dated by accelerator mass spectrometry to 1510 ± 100 BP. The structure itself was identified as a burnt-out tree stump, and, as van der Merwe comments, 'a span of more than two millennia' therefore separates the formation of this structure from 'its use as an iron-smelting furnace'. Only four of the other structures attributed to the early Copper Age are considered to be definitely furnaces of some kind, and there are only four samples of fayalitic copper-smelting slag, most of them being no more than partially vitrified soils. Only furnace 8 has both a radiocarbon date (3660 ± 110 BP) and a residue containing 1% copper, but because of the proven use of fossil charcoal at the site, van der Merwe warns, even this date cannot be taken at face value until it is supported by a thermoluminescence date on the fired lining of the furnace. All in all, therefore, the evidence for metallurgy in Niger prior to 3000 BP 'must remain in doubt' (Killick et al. 1988: 390).

The same doubts do not apply to the late Copper Age, characterized by standard non-tapping shaft furnaces and distinctive red melilite slag, the product of a true smelting process. Grébénart emphasizes that only 85 m^3 of slag has been recovered and that over a thousand year period the mean annual production of copper will have been no more than 8.5–17 kg. The smelters therefore were itinerant craftsmen and the manufacture of metal was only an occasional activity. The small artefacts produced were hot-hammered, and the lost-wax technique was unknown, although there were some moulded ingots, and some bronze and brass alloys were used mainly for jewellery.

Iron- and copper-working continued in this region during the medieval period, at Marandet and Azelik respectively, the latter probably being equivalent to the town of Takedda visited by Ibn Battuta in AD 1354.

D. Grébénart: 'Characteristics of the final Neolithic and Metal ages in the region of Agadez (Niger)', *Prehistory of arid North Africa*, ed. A.E. Close (Dallas, 1987), 287–316; D. Killick et al.: 'Reassessment of the evidence for early metallurgy in Niger, West Africa', *JAS*, 15 (1988), 367–94; D. Grébénart: 'L'âge du cuivre au Sahara central et occidental', *Sahara* 5 (1992–3), 49–58.

PA-J

Agordat Set of four small settlement sites in western Eritrea, Ethiopia, none of which have yet been excavated or properly dated, although surface finds of ground stone tools and figurines suggest that they may have been connected with the Nubian C GROUP of the late 3rd millennium BC. This would indicate possible links between the cereal-based Neolithic cultures of northern Ethiopia and the Nile Valley.

A.J. Arkell: 'Four occupation sites at Agordat', *Kush* 2 (1954), 33–62.

IS

Agrab, Tell *see* DIYALA REGION

A Group, A Horizon Semi-nomadic Neolithic culture, characterized by black-polished and 'eggshell' handmade pottery, which flourished in Lower Nubia from the mid-4th millennium BC until at least 2800 BC (i.e. roughly contemporary with the Egyptian late predynastic period and 1st dynasty). The term 'A Group' was first used by George Reisner (1961). W.Y. Adams later attempted (unsuccessfully) to replace it with the term 'A Horizon' in order to tone down the migrationist implications of Reisner's designation (*see* DIFFUSIONISM). A-Group cemeteries have been excavated at a number of sites, including Qustul and Sayala.

G. Reisner and A.J. Arkell: *A history of the Sudan*, 2nd edn (London, 1961), 37–45; H. Nordström: *Neolithic and A-group sites* (Stockholm, 1972), 17–32; W.Y. Adams: *Nubia: corridor to Africa*, 2nd edn (Princeton, 1984), 118–32; H.S. Smith: 'The development of the A-Group "culture" in northern Lower Nubia', *Egypt and Africa*, ed. W.V. Davies (London, 1991), 92–111.

IS

Agua Blanca Village in the Manabí province of Ecuador, which provides a prime example of a grass-roots approach to archaeological education and site preservation. An intense drought in Manabí in the 1970s led to intensified logging as an alternative to the failing agricultural system. In addition to destroying the forest, the local people looted the archaeological sites they encountered, selling the artefacts to a local dealer for much-needed cash. In 1979 the Machalilla National Park was created to preserve the forest and fauna of the Ecuadorian coast. No provision was made for communities such as Agua Blanca which were within the park boundaries. In the same year an archaeological project was inaugurated, with the aim of surveying the valley, including a large, important Manteño-culture (AD 1300–1500) site.

The head of the project, Colin McEwan, moved into the village hall in 1980; this made the project highly visible, and interested local people were able to ask about the project and about archaeology in general. This interest led to impromptu classes in archaeology, and as the project grew to include excavation, more members of the community were incorporated and trained in archaeological methodologies by María Isabel Silva. Both the visibility of all parts of the project and the direct involvement of some community members brought the past directly into the community and it became a source of interest and community pride – something that belonged to them, as well as a source of income for some. A small exhibit organized in the town led to an interest in building a more permanent one, and funds were obtained for a local museum and cultural hall. The entire town participated in the construction of these buildings; discussions and outside speakers were organized; and a site exhibit was installed.

The Agua Blanca project was based on respect for local people and on a recognition of their expressed needs and wishes; the project has increased community solidarity, giving members the strength and the skills to deal with outside planners who do not normally consider country peoples' needs in their projects. Looting has ceased, as short-term gains are passed up for long-term advantages, including employment within the park, the building and maintenance of tourist facilities, and work as guides.

C. Hudson and C. McEwan: 'Focussing pride in the past: Agua Blanca, Equador', *Museum* 154/2 (1987), 125–8; M.I. Silva and C. McEwan: 'Machalilla: el camino de integración', *Colibrí* 2/5 (1989), 71–5; P. Norton, ed.: *5000 años de ocupación: Parque Nacional Machalilla* (Quito, 1992).

KB

Aguada Site in northwestern Argentina, dating to *c*.AD 600–1200, best known for its elaborate bronze ornaments and ceramics decorated with supernatural feline or 'draconian' motifs which have inspired considerable interest in the diffusion of motifs and/or mythic themes throughout the Andes.

A.R. Gonzalez: *Las placas metálicas de los Andes del Sur* (Mainz am Rhein, 1992).

KB

Ahar *see* BANAS

ahu Sacred stone structures found in central and eastern Polynesia, but also in New Zealand. *Ahu* took the form of lines of stones or, more commonly, a platform. The most famous are the *ahu* of EASTER ISLAND, which acted as a platform on which the famous statues were placed. Thor Heyerdahl considered the Easter Island *ahu* to have a South American derivation, but their widespread occurrence throughout Polynesia demonstrate their Pacific origin.

P. Bellwood: *Man's conquest of the Pacific* (New York, 1978), 329–30; P.V. Kirch: *The evolution of Polynesian chiefdoms* (Cambridge, 1984), 264–78.

CG

Aihole Town-site of the 6th–12th centuries AD (Chalukya and Rastrakuta periods), in Mysore, India, consisting of a large fortified hill in the south-east, at the foot of which lay a walled settlement containing many elaborately sculpted Hindu and Jain stone temples. Some of the latter are free-standing structures while others are CAVE TEMPLES carved into the surrounding hills.

R.S. Gupte: *The art and architecture of Aihole* (Bombay, 1962); S. Rajasekhara: *Early Chalukya art at Aihole* (New Delhi, 1985).

CS

Ain Ghazal Very large Pre-Pottery Neolithic (*see* ACERAMIC NEOLITHIC) and Yarmukian (ceramic Neolithic) settlement-site adjacent to Amman in Jordan, which was occupied during the 8th, 7th and 6th millennia BC. Gary Rollefson's excavations (from 1983 onwards) uncovered two pits containing sets of anthropomorphic statues dating to the Pre-Pottery Neolithic B period, as well as a third pit containing fragments of plaster from a plastered skull. The statues range from 35 cm to 90 cm in height and are made up of lime plaster modelled around armatures of reed and twine, the eyes being applied in the form of a bituminous substance. Similar statues, perhaps used in religious ceremonies, were also found at JERICHO and Nahal Hemar, a cave to the southwest of the Dead Sea.

G.O. Rollefson: 'Ritual and ceremony at Neolithic Ain Ghazal', *Paleorient* 9/2 (1983), 29–38; ——: 'Early Neolithic statuary from Ain Ghazal (Jordan)', *MDOG* 116 (1984), 185–92; A.H. Simmons and G.O. Rollefson: 'Neolithic Ain Ghazal (Jordan): interim report on the first two seasons, 1982–1983', *JFA* 11 (1984), 387–95; G.O. Rollefson et al.: 'Neolithic cultures at Ain Ghazal, Jordan', *JFA* 19 (1992), 443–70.

IS

Ain Hanech *see* AFRICA 1

Ain Mallaha *see* NATUFIAN

Ainu Term used to describe former fisher-hunter-gatherers who also practised some millet cultivation and occupied the islands of Hokkaido in Japan and Sakhalin in the Russian Federation. Ainu culture developed out of the SATSUMON and OKHOTSK cultures. Historically formulated ethnic groups first documented in the 16th–17th centuries AD, they have long been mistakenly identified as the direct successors to the Jomon populations of Japan (*see* JAPAN 2–3).

H. Watanabe: *The Ainu ecosystem: environment and group structure* (Seattle, 1973); Y. Fukasawa: 'Emishi and the Ainu: from an archaeological point of view', Paper presented at 'Japanese archaeology in protohistoric and early historic period: Yamato and its relations to surrounding populations': international symposium at the University

of Bonn, 1992; H. Utagawa: 'The "sending back" rite in Ainu culture', *JJRS* 19/2–3 (1992), 255–70.
SK

Air *see* AFRICA 1; SAHARAN ROCK ART

airborne remote sensing Term used for the aerial recording of data in wavelengths outside the visible range. The necessary equipment may be borne by satellites or by aircraft flying in systematic patterns – as in normal vertical photography.

The only form of extra-visible photography used in conventional archaeological reconnaissance is the use of infra-red photographic film, either black and white or false colour, where in some conditions the data recorded in the near infra-red waveband can enhance the information visible to the naked eye. Infra-red photography is used by some aerial archaeologists as a valuable ancillary to other films. The other forms of electromagnetic energy (of which the visible range forms a small part) recorded either through photography or digital imaging include the ultra-violet, the near, middle and thermal infra-red, and the microwave. Imaging from aircraft can provide direct evidence of archaeological features, as well as a wide range of information on geology, vegetation, climate, land-use, hydrology etc. Information from airborne remote-sensing is often enhanced by recording different wavelengths simultaneously – this is known as multispectral imaging and may be combined with conventional photography. Although the resolution of satellite material available for civilian use is not yet good enough for the recognition of most archaeological features, it is already valuable for predictive purposes.

P.J. Curran: *Principles of remote sensing* (New York, 1985); S.A. Drury: *A guide to remote sensing: interpreting images of the earth* (Oxford, 1990); J. Allsop and D. Greenbaum: 'Airborne remote sensing of alluvial deposits in the reconnaissance of potential archaeological sites', *Proceedings of the Third National Archaeological Sciences Conference 1991*, ed. J. Szymnaski.
FG

Ajanta *see* CAVE TEMPLE

Ajdabiya Site on the coast of Libya, which is one of several Fatimid settlements of the 10th century AD that were established during the revival of the coastal region for the first time since the Islamic conquest. A mosque and a fortress (*qasr*) were among the buildings constructed at Ajdabiya as a result of the ambition of the Fatimid Caliphs in Tunisia (Ifriqiya) to expand eastwards. This ambition culminated in their seizure of Egypt and the foundation of Cairo in AD 969. Sites such as Ajdabiya mark the first important Islamic foundations in Libya after the Islamic conquest. Beyond their intrinsic interest, the Fatimid sites in Libya provide a background against which to set the subsequent 'efflorescence regime' after it had been subsumed by the cultural vitality of Egypt. The ceramics from Ajdabiya and other Libyan sites form a corpus that generally precedes the eclipse of north African after 1051 when the Fatimid Caliph al-Mustansir sent the Bani Hilal and the Bani Sulaym nomads to attack his former supporters in North Africa.

A. Abdussaid: 'Early Islamic monuments at Ajdabiyah', *Libya Antiqua* I (1964), 115–19; D. Whitehouse: 'The excavations at Ajdabiyah: an interim report', *LS* 3–4 (1972–3) [interim reports]; G.R.D. King: 'Islamic archaeology in Libya, 1969–1989', *LS* 20 (1989), 193–207.
GK

Akhetaten *see* AMARNA, (TELL) EL-

Akhmim (anc. Ipu, Khent-Mim) Egyptian site on the east bank of the Nile opposite the modern city of Sohag. Akhmim has been occupied continuously from the Early Dynastic period to the present day. The pharaonic settlement at Akhmim was the centre of the 9th nome (province) of Upper Egypt, but because of extensive quarrying of the buildings in the 14th century AD, little has survived either of the pharaonic town or of the temples of Min, the god of fertility. The Old and Middle Kingdom rock-tombs and a well-preserved 18th-dynasty rock-cut chapel were examined by Percy Newberry in 1910, and the former were re-examined by Naguib Kanawati during the 1980s. Colossal statues of Ramesses II and his wife Meritamun were excavated in the 1990s by Egyptian archaeologists.

P.E. Newberry: 'The inscribed tombs of Ekhmim', *LAAA* 4 (1912), 101–20; K.P. Kuhlmann: 'Der Felstempel des Eje bei Akhmim', *MDAIK* 35 (1979), 165–88; N. Kanawati: *Rock tombs of El-Hawawish: the cemetery of Akhmim*, 6 vols (Sydney, 1980–); K.P. Kuhlmann: *Materialen zur Archäologie und Geschichte des Raumes von Achmim* (Mainz, 1983); E.J. Brovarski: *Akhmim in the Old Kingdom and First Intermediate Period* (Cairo, 1985).
IS

Akkad, Akkadian The term Akkadian was used from the early 3rd millennium BC to refer to the Semitic-speaking people who gradually supplanted the non-Semitic SUMERIANS in central Mesopotamia. Sargon the Great (*sharru-kin*: 'the true king') established the Akkadian dynasty (*c*.2317–2150 BC), the first Semitic-speaking empire in Mesopotamia, which eventually disintegrated as a result of the incursions of nomads such as the AMORITES and GUTIANS. The location of Akkad (or Agade), the Akkadian capital city, remains uncertain, although various sites have been suggested; it is thought most likely to be in the region of KISH OR BABYLON. From the time of Sargon onwards the CUNEIFORM script was used to record the Akkadian language, and the Sumerian tongue was preserved only in certain names and archaisms.

H. Weiss: 'Kish, Akkad and Agade', *JAOS* 95 (1975), 434–53; J. Oates: *Babylon*, 2nd edn (London, 1986), 22–59; G. Roux: *Ancient Iraq*, 3rd edn (Harmondsworth, 1992), 146–60.

IS

Ak-Kaya (Zaskal'naya) Group of Palaeolithic shelters in the Red Ravine near the village of Vishennoye in the Crimea, 50 km east of Simferopol. The group, which includes 13 sites, was discovered in 1964 by V.F. Petrun and excavated in the 1970s and 1980s by Y.G. Kolosov. The site of Zaskal'naya 5 comprises eight MOUSTERIAN levels with abundant faunal remains, numerous hearths and a rich flint inventory similar to that of the upper level of KIIK-KOBA CAVE (also in the Crimea). A fragment of a human skull (occipital bone), found in a trench pit further down the slope beneath the main concentration of finds, may belong to a female Neanderthal. Zaskal'naya 6, 70 m uphill from Zaskal'naya 5, consists of five Mousterian levels. Level 3 contained the remains of burials of five children, aged 8–12 years old, classed as *Homo sapiens neanderthalensis*. The skeletal evidence is morphologically similar to that from Kiik-Koba, TESHIK TASH in Uzbekistan and some Palestinian NEANDERTHALS (*see* AMUD, MOUNT CARMEL). Sedimentation and pollen evidence suggests that the Mousterian sequence of Ak-Kaya belongs to the early stages of the Würm glacial.

Yu.G. Kolosov: 'Akkaiskie must'erskie stoyanki i nekotorye itogi ih izučenija' [The Ak-Kaya Mousterian sites and some results of their studies], *Issledovanie paleolita v Krymu* [Palaeolithic studies in the Crimea], ed. Yu.G. Kolosov (Kiev 1979), 33–55.

PD

Akrotiri *see* THERA

Aksum *see* AXUM

al- The prefix al- is disregarded in the alphabetical sequence of this dictionary. For example, al-KUFA.

Alaca Hüyük *see* HITTITES

Alalakh *see* ATCHANA, TELL

Albany industry (Oakhurst industry) Term applied to a group of southern African Stone Age assemblages found south of the Zambezi River, but known mostly from sites south of the Limpopo River. The industry is characterized by the presence of large scrapers (L< 20 mm), but bladelets, bladelet cores and backed microliths tend to be either absent or extremely rare. Other formal tools in stone are rare. In coastal sites bone is used for points (probable fish gorges), spatulas, and beads. Rare bored stones (digging-stick weights) are recorded, and engraved stones are known from two sites. It is sometimes referred to as the Oakhurst industry after the site of OAKHURST (Sampson 1974); assemblages generally fall between uncal 12,000 and 8000 BP, and intervene stratigraphically between the Late Pleistocene microlithic Robberg Industry and the Holocene microlithic WILTON INDUSTRY. Mitchell (1988: 247) has argued that the shift from the Robberg to the Albany reflects the adoption of the bow and arrow. See also AFRICA 4.1.

R.G. Klein: 'Environment and subsistence of prehistoric man in the southern Cape Province, South Africa', *WA* 5 (1974), 249–84; C.G. Sampson: *The Stone Age archaeology of southern Africa*. (New York, 1974); J. Deacon: *The Later Stone Age settlement of southernmost Africa* (Oxford, 1984); P. Mitchell: *The early microlithic industries of southern Africa* (Oxford, 1988).

RI

Aleutian tradition Distinctive tradition of the Aleutian Islands and the westernmost Alaska Peninsula, which dates from 2500 BC through to historic times. The assemblages are characterized by flaked stone implements, including knives and stemmed points.

D.E. Dumond: *The Eskimos and Aleuts* (London, 1987).

RP

Alexandria Greco-Roman city on the Mediterranean coast of Egypt which was founded by Alexander the Great on the site of an earlier Egyptian settlement called Raqote. The latter has survived only in the form of the pre-Ptolemaic sea-walls to the north and west of the island of Pharos. Alexandria was a cultural melting pot, particularly during the Ptolemaic and Roman periods (*c*.332 BC–AD 395), when the population gradually expanded, reaching about half a million by the middle of the 1st century BC. The major Greco-Roman monuments were the Library, the Museum, the Serapeum (a temple of the god Sarapis, which may have incorporated part of the Alexandrian library), the Caesarium, a Roman stadium and Kom el-Shugafa (funerary catacomb dating to the first two centuries AD). On a peninsula about 1.5 km off the coast of Alexandria was the early Ptolemaic multi-storey *pharos*, which was the first known lighthouse in the world. It appears to have collapsed in the 12th century AD, but in 1995 French marine archaeologists, working on the sea-bed near the Qait Bey Islamic-period fortress, lifted a number of fragments of stone believed to derive from it (Empereur 1996).

P.M. Fraser: *Ptolemaic Alexandria*, 3 vols (Oxford, 1972); A.K. Bowman: *Egypt after the pharaohs* (London, 1986), 204–33; J.-Y. Empereur: 'Alexandria: the underwater site near Qaitbay fort', *EA* 8 (1996), 7–10.

IS

alignment In its strictest sense, the term 'alignment' refers to a class of simple prehistoric monuments that consist either of two or more stones marking a straight line, or a single marker set up to form a line in conjunction with a natural feature such as a mountain top. Alignments are often assumed to mark some astronomically or mythically significant point on the horizon.

Some of the greatest concentrations of stone alignments are found in Britain (such as the numerous small alignments found on Dartmoor) and Brittany (the most famous alignments in the world are found at CARNAC), where the majority seem to date from the 3rd or early second millennium BC. However, simple alignments are present in regions all around the world, notably India (North Karnataka), Indonesia and Malaysia. In the remoter regions of the world, alignments continue to be discovered; for example, the alignments recently surveyed at the Old Kingdom quarry site of Hatnub in the Eastern desert of Egypt, where simple rows of small monoliths seem to have been erected by the visiting quarriers as temporary shrines.

Apart from defining a specific class of monuments, the term alignment is used widely in the sub-discipline of archaeoastronomy to indicate any astronomically significant line incorporated in more complex monuments. These alignments often take the form of a selection of the very large number of possible 'lines' that can be drawn between the stones of complex megalithic structures such as STONE CIRCLES; the difficulty of proving that such alignments were intentional on the part of the builder is discussed in Heggie (1981). The term alignment is also used to describe the creation of astronomical alignments in the architectural elements of sophisticated monumental buildings; two famous examples are the passage alignments at the main temple of ABU SIMBEL, Egypt, and the passage grave of KNOWTH, Ireland.

S. Heggie: *Megalithic science* (London, 1981); C.L.N. Ruggles: *Megalithic astronomy*, BAR BS 123 (Oxford 1984); A Ghosh, ed.: *an encyclopaedia of Indian archaeology* (New Delhi, 1989).

RJA

Aligrama *see* GANDHARA GRAVE CULTURE

Ali Kosh, Tepe Mound in the Deh Luran valley of southwestern Iran (LURISTAN); it consists of a sequence of Epipalaeolithic occupation remains similar to those at the nearby site of TEPE SABZ, the earliest of which (the 'Bus Mordeh phase') date to *c*.8000–7000 BC. During this first phase the settlement was already made up of small mud-brick houses and the subsistence base included a combination of goat-herding and hunting. The principal strata at the site comprise the 'Ali Kosh phase' (*c*.7000–6000 BC), during which cultivated emmer and barley began to be used, and the repertoire of artefacts expanded to include a new range of butchery tools. The excavations of Hole and Flannery at Ali Kosh and other sites of similar date in the Deh Luran region have produced a great deal of information on the origins of food production in the Near East (Hole et al. 1965; 1969).

F. Hole and K.V. Flannery: 'Excavations at Alikosh, Iran, 1961', *Iranica antiqua* 2 (1962), 97–148; F. Hole, K.V. Flannery and J.A. Neely: 'Early agriculture and animal husbandry in Deh Luran, Iran', *CA* 6 (1965), 105–6; F. Hole et al.: *Prehistory and human ecology in the Deh Luran plain: an early village sequence from Khuzistan, Iran* (Ann Arbor, 1969).

IS

Alişar Hüyük (anc. Ankuwa?) Hittite city site in Cappadocia, about 200 km from Ankara, the ceramic sequence from which forms part of the basis for the Bronze Age chronology of Anatolia from the mid-3rd millennium onwards. The site was excavated by Hans von der Osten and Erich Schmidt in 1927–32. In level II (*c*.2300–1900 BC) they found distinctive 'Cappadocian' painted pottery as well as cuneiform tablets from a *karum* (settlement of Old Assyrian merchants) like that at KANESH. Later levels at Alişar (III–VII) corresponded to the Hittite empire and successive phases of Phrygian, Achaemenid, Seleucid, Parthian, Roman and Seljuk domination.

H. von der Osten: *Alishar Hüyük*, 3 vols (Chicago, 1937).

IS

allées couvertes French archaeological term related to the English archaeological term 'gallery grave', which describes a set of Neolithic and Chalcolithic monumental tombs that lack a well-defined entrance passage (i.e. are not PASSAGE GRAVES) and which have elongated (up to 20 m long) rectangular chambers (sometimes with vestibules), and which are often constructed of parallel rows of orthostats. The classic regions in the study of *allées couvertes* are Britanny and, especially, the Paris Basin, where they are associated with the late Neolithic SOM CULTURE and date largely to the later 3rd millennium BC and after. In Brittany, the chambers are often above ground, and covered with an oval mound. In the Paris Basin, most chambers are cut into the earth or rock (up to 2 m deep), and were often roofed with timber at ground-level; there may be no mound at all. The chambers usually possess ante-chambers, and the main chamber is commonly entered via a roundish opening cut through a transverse slab. Many *allées couvertes* are decorated with a repeated set of schematic motifs, notably reliefs of two breasts, sometimes with a necklace, and hafted axes. The SOM culture also disposed of its dead in hypogeés, typically rectangular, sometimes with an ante-chamber, hollowed out of solid chalk, and in pits. All of these tomb types tend to be associated with the practice of collective burial (of up to 350 individuals).

J. Howell: 'The later Neolithic of the Paris Basin', *Ancient France 6000–2000 BC*, ed. C. Scarre (Edinburgh, 1983), 64–8; C. Masset and P. Soulier: *Alleés couvertes et autres monuments funéraires du néolithique dans la France* (Paris, 1995).

RJA

alpha recoil dating Scientific dating technique used on the minerals in ceramics or lava flows. The process is similar to FISSION TRACK DATING, but using the much more frequent alpha decay of the naturally occurring ^{238}U, ^{235}U and ^{232}Th chains. When a nucleus emits an alpha particle, it recoils and creates a damage track. If the various decay chains are present in known concentrations and each is in equilibrium (or the disequilibrium is quantified), then the number of tracks per unit of time can be calculated. Heating anneals any previous damage. In principle, the number of tracks present since the last heating of the material can be counted after suitable etching of a prepared surface, thus allowing the age of minerals to be inferred.

Although alpha recoil tracks are much more numerous than fission tracks, they are also much shorter because the recoil is less energetic than spontaneous fission fragment emission. Alpha recoil tracks are thus more difficult to identify reliably and the technique has found little application in archaeology.

W.H. Huang and T.E.R.M. Walker: 'Fossil alpha particle recoil tracks', *Science* 155 (1967), 1103–4; E.G. Garrison et al.: 'Alpha-recoil tracks in archaeological ceramic dating', *Archaeometry* 20 (1978), 39–46.

SB

Altamira Principal example of Upper Palaeolithic (Magdelanian/Solutrean) cave art in Cantabrian Spain, near the town of Santillana del Mar, decorated from perhaps 16,000 BP onwards. Of the animals depicted, bison and red deer are the most numerous with about 50 representations of each. (The faunal remains in the Solutrean and Magdalenian stratigraphic levels associated with the art are dominated by red deer, with bison and horse second and third). The Great Hall or Hall of Bison, a chamber *c.*10 by 20 m, is impressively decorated with large engraved and brightly coloured polychrome images of 16–19 bison up to 2 m long, a horse and a large red deer (hind). The bison, which may have been painted as a composition by a single artist, may represent a herd in the rutting season or being driven together by hunters; the care with which the bison are depicted may reflect the prestige of the bison as hunting prey. In a terminal chamber, Altamira presents a series of enigmatic masks and signs. There are also stencilled hands and painted hands. Together with EL CASTILLO, Altamira has produced the finest series of mobiliary art plaques in Cantabria – especially scapulae engraved with red deer.

H. Breuil and H. Obermaier: *The cave of Altamira at Santillana del Mar, Spain* (Madrid, 1935); M.A. García Guinea: *Altamira* (Madrid, 1979); L.G. Freeman et al.: *Altamira revisited* (Chicago, 1987).

RJA

Altyn-depe (Altintepe) Large settlement of Eneolithic/Bronze Age in Southern Turkmenistan, located in the interfluve of the Meana and Chaacha rivers. The first settlement dates to the NAMAZGA I period in the 5th millennium BC; by the end of the 4th millennium the site was a large centre, with ceramics dominated by the 'GEOKSYUR style' and rich burials that suggest social stratification. In the mid-3rd millennium BC, the introduction of the potter's wheel and other social and cultural changes mark the gradual transformation of the site into a proto-urban centre – the most significant in Central Asia – with a large cult building and a number of smaller sanctuaries and temples. The highest degree of urbanization was attained during the Middle Bronze Age (end of the 3rd and early 2nd millennia BC). Social differentiation and craft specialization were marked, the site layout revealing isolated elite and craftsmen quarters as well as a cult centre in the form of a ZIGGURAT-type structure on a stepped platform. *See also* ASIA 1.1/1.2 for a discussion of urbanization at Altyn-depe within a regional context.

V.M. Masson: *Pervye civilizacii* (Leningrad, 1989); ——: *Altyn-depe: Raskopki goroda bronzovogo veka v Juzhnom Turkmenistane* (Leningrad, 1991).

PD

Amara Nubian site 180 km south of Wadi Halfa, consisting of two separate archaeological zones to the east and west of the Nile: Amara West and East. In the Ramessid period (*c*.1307–1070 BC) Amara West probably replaced SOLEB as the seat of the Deputy of Kush (Upper Nubia), and the town may also have served as a staging post for gold-mining expeditions and a centre for trade with the Selima Oasis. There are extensive urban remains as well as cemeteries of the New Kingdom and the Ballana period (*c*.AD 400–543). The pharaonic walled town – described by its excavator H.W. Fairman as one of the best preserved settlements in the Nile valley – covered an area of about 60,000 square metres and was occupied between about 1400 and 1070 BC. It incorporated a stone-built temple of Ramesses II, a set of vaulted store-rooms and an extensive area of extra-mural house remains. Amara East is the site of a town and temple of the MEROITIC period (*c*.300 BC–AD 350).

Figure 3 **Altyn-depe** Plan of the mound at Altyn-depe, Southern Turkmenistan, showing the main features of the Eneolithic–Bronze Age settlement. *Source*: V.M. Masson: *Altyn-depe: Raskopki goroda bronzovogo veka v Juzhnom Turkmenistane* (Leningrad, 1991).

H.W. Fairman: Preliminary excavation reports in *JEA* 24, 25, 34 (1938, 1939, 1948); B.J. Kemp: 'Fortified towns in Nubia', *Man, settlement and urbanism*, ed. P.J. Ucko et al. (London, 1972), 651–6; P.A. Spencer: *Amara West* (London, 1997).
IS

Amarna, (Tell) el- (anc. Akhetaten) Ancient Egyptian city, located about 280 km south of Cairo, founded by the pharaoh Akhenaten (*c*.1353–1335 BC). It is the best-preserved Egyptian settlement of the New Kingdom, including several temples, palaces and other public buildings, as well as large numbers of mud-brick private houses. The city was abandoned soon after Akhenaten's death, having been occupied for only about 25–30 years; this unusually brief period of occupation has made the site ideal for spatial and statistical analyses (Kemp 1984–95, Shaw 1992, Kemp and Garfi 1993), providing an important body of socio-economic data. Although much of the western side of the city has been covered by modern cultivation, enough of the ceremonial centre and surrounding residential quarters has survived to enable the site to serve as an example of town planning and social patterning in 18th-dynasty Egypt. The original population of the city has been estimated at about 20,000, most of whom would have lived in the so-called 'south suburb', stretching between the central city and the modern village of Hagg Qandil. There are two groups of nobles' rock-tombs at the northern and southern ends of the semi-circular bay of cliffs to the east of the city. The remains of the tombs of Akhenaten and his family, located several kilometres to the east of the cliffs, were rediscovered in the late 1880s (Martin 1974–89), but they have suffered greatly from vandalization.

In the centre of the city a cache of cuneiform tablets was discovered in and around a building identified as the House of Correspondence; these texts, all but three of which were written in AKKADIAN, consisted of letters sent between the late 18th-dynasty pharaohs and the rulers of cities and states in Syria-Palestine, Mesopotamia and Anatolia. The 'Amarna Letters' have provided a great deal of evidence concerning Egypt's political influence and foreign policy in the New Kingdom (Moran 1992).

N. de G. Davies: *The rock tombs of El Amarna*, 6 vols (London, 1903–8); T.E. Peet et al.: *The city of Akhenaten*, 3 vols (London, 1923–51); G.T. Martin: *The royal tomb at el-Amarna*, 2 vols (London, 1974–89); B.J. Kemp, ed.: *Amarna reports* I–VI (London, 1984–95); W. Moran: *The Amarna letters* (Baltimore, 1992); I. Shaw: 'Ideal homes in ancient Egypt: the archaeology of social aspiration', *CAJ* 2/2 (1992), 147–66; B.J. Kemp and S. Garfi: *A survey of the ancient city of el-'Amarna* (London, 1993).
IS

Amarna Letters *see* AMARNA (TELL) EL-

Amekni Rock outcrop site 40 km west–northwest of Tamanrasset, southern Algeria, excavated by Gabriel Camps in 1965 and 1968. Ashy deposits up to 1.65 m thick, between boulders on the eastern side of the site, produced an occupation characterized as 'Neolithic of Sudanese Tradition', largely on the basis of the pottery, which consisted of simple round-bottomed vessels extensively decorated with comb impressions including dotted wavy line motifs. There were no polished stone axes or bone harpoons. Three human burials (two children and one adult) were described as 'negroid', and there was an exclusively wild mammalian fauna dominated by dorcas gazelle, bohor reedbuck, and giant buffalo. The presence of fish (*Clarias* and *Lates*) and freshwater bivalves indicates that the climate was significantly more humid than at present, with rivers which flowed all the year round. Besides *Celtis* sp., the abundant pollen analysed produced 263 examples of *Gramineae*, of which two (at a depth of 1.4 m) were identified as cultivated bulrush millet (*Pennisetum* sp.), although this attribution is not now generally accepted. Four radiocarbon dates span the period from 8670 to 5500 BP. The early occurrence of pottery (with which the human burials at the site were associated) encouraged Camps to claim that pottery vessels had been independently invented in the Saharan region by at least 8050 ± 80 BP.

G. Camps: *Amekni, Néolithique ancien du Hoggar* (Paris, 1969); A. Gautier: 'Prehistoric men and cattle in North Africa: a dearth of data and a surfeit of models', *Prehistory of arid North Africa*, ed. A.E. Close (Dallas, 1987), 163–87.
PA-J

America

Sections: 1 Arctic North America; 2 Western North America; 3 Southwestern North America; 4 Eastern North America; 5 Mesoamerica and Central America; 6 South America

1 Arctic North America

The extreme conditions in the Arctic region of the North American continent have led to some of the most fascinating adaptations of human life anywhere on earth. The region is delimited to the south by the tree line (which also marks the southernmost edge of the tundra), and extends some 11,000 km from the Aleutian Islands in the west to Greenland and Labrador in the east.

In terms of geomorphology, the Arctic includes high mountains, sedimentary plain, exposed bedrock and lowlands, most of it with little or no soil development. For humans, the winter landscape also includes the frozen sea ice. In Alaska, Greenland and Labrador this is often a wide strip of landfast ice along the coast, while in the Canadian Arctic Archipelago the channels between the islands freeze completely for much of the year. The Arctic is also characterized by the persistence of cold (long winters and short cool summers); permafrost (year-round frozen ground); large seasonal differences in the amount of sunlight; and by the paucity of plant foods suitable for humans.

Human populations in the Arctic have, of necessity, relied on animal resources to a far greater extent than foraging populations elsewhere. The most important terrestrial species are caribou, musk-ox, arctic fox and arctic hare, while the most important marine resources include seal, walrus, whale, polar bear and arctic char. Economically, most communities have made use of both terrestrial and marine resources, either through migrating through an 'annual round', encompassing land and sea, or through trade. Over time, the INUIT developed a complex technology to deal with their environment, including snowhouses, toggling harpoons, large and small watercraft, drag floats and dog traction.

During the last glaciation, the westernmost part of the Arctic formed the uplands of BERINGIA, the first part of the Americas occupied by humans. However, most authorities agree that the earliest sites found in Alaska are somewhat later, and may be assigned to the PALEO-ARCTIC TRADITION. This is succeeded by the ARCTIC SMALL TOOL TRADITION (or ASTt), whose bearers also became the first humans to occupy the Canadian Arctic and Greenland. In Alaska, the ASTt is followed by the NORTON TRADITION, while in the Eastern Arctic it is followed by the DORSET CULTURE. The cultures of the THULE TRADITION developed in the area around the Bering Strait and subsequently spread, in part through population movement, throughout the entire Arctic region except the Aleutian Islands. The present-day Inuit peoples (i.e. the people formerly described as Eskimos) are the cultural and biological descendants of the Thule.

Despite the fact that archaeological research in the Arctic presents a number of unique challenges (including excavation into permafrost, short field seasons and immense logistical problems), it has made a number of valuable contributions to archaeology generally. The majority of Arctic research until the mid-1980s focused on filling gaps in its

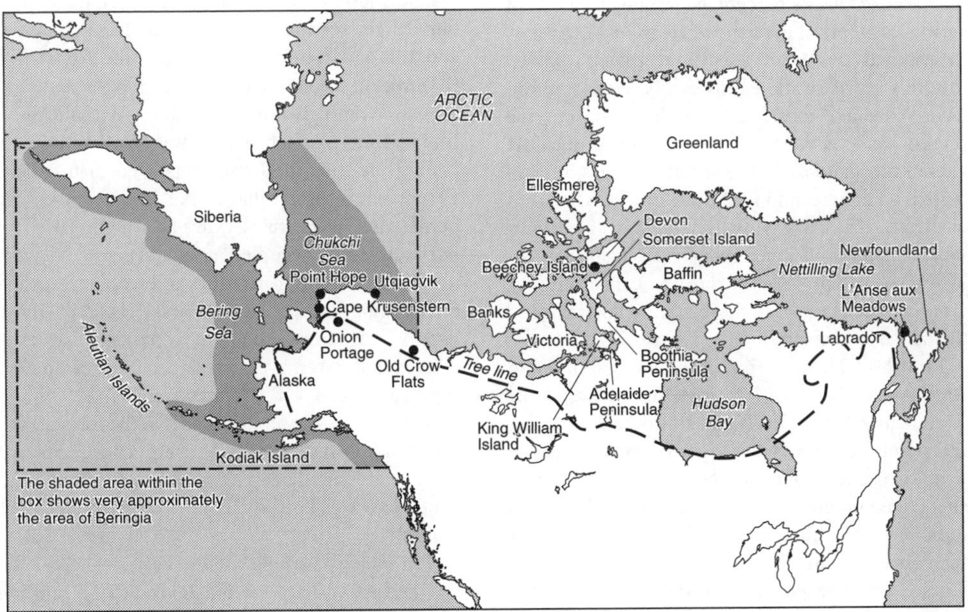

Map 6 **America, 1: Arctic North** Major sites in the region with individual entries in the Dictionary.

culture history, but the extensive ethnographic literature documenting Inuit ways of life in the recent past has proved invaluable in interpreting the data recovered through archaeology, and in providing a basis for constructing models that can be tested utilizing the archaeological record. Human adaptations to the Arctic have generally employed a much more complex technology than that of foragers in lower latitudes, and at many sites the large material culture component of this technology has been preserved due to burial in permafrost. Given the rich ethnographic record, we can generally employ analogy with some confidence to understand the functions of the many artefact types and, by inference, the ecological significance of changes in technology over time. For these reasons, material culture has long been – and continues to be – an important focus of Arctic archaeological research.

The North American Arctic has also provided an important context for ethnoarchaeology, perhaps the most influential example being Lewis Binford's work in Alaska (e.g. MASK SITE). His studies of caribou hunting and butchering by the Nunamiut led him to develop his MIDDLE RANGE THEORY, which has the potential for linking patterns of archaeological findings with patterns of prehistoric behaviour. Specifically, Binford developed a method of analysing faunal remains based on a particular species' 'economic anatomy', which is essentially a measure of the differential utility (such as nutritional value or percentage of bone to meat) of various anatomical portions of an animal carcass as determined by 'ACTUALISTIC STUDIES'. Given that this set of relationships can be considered to have remained constant from the past into the present (as long as evolution has not significantly altered the anatomy of the species in question and basic human perceptions of these portions have not changed), the analysis of the anatomical portions represented in the faunal remains from an archaeological site can provide information concerning the economic behaviour of the people who produced the faunal assemblage.

Probably the most important contribution of Arctic archaeology derives from the nature of the Arctic environment itself and from the constraints that it imposes on human adaptations to this region. The extreme cold imposes unusually high energy requirements on humans living there, and these requirements were met almost exclusively by the consumption of meat obtained from hunting. These facts have led Moreau Maxwell (1985: 3) to argue that the archaeological data recovered from the Arctic provide 'abundant materials for testing hypotheses and propositions focused on the economies of ecology, that is, the way in which the energy is cycled through the food chain'. Thus, concepts like optimal FORAGING THEORY have proven particularly amenable to testing in the Arctic environment using both ethnographic and archaeological data.

L.R. Binford: *Nunamiut ethnoarchaeology* (New York, 1978); D. Damas, ed.: *Handbook of North American Indians*, V: *Arctic* (Washington, D.C., 1984); M.S. Maxwell: *Prehistory of the Eastern Arctic* (Orlando, 1985).
RP

2 Western North America

Western North America comprises an area of 2,577,000 sq. km west of the Rocky Mountains, south of the Yukon, and north of southern California. It was the home of an estimated 413,000 aboriginal peoples in the early 19th century (Kroeber 1939: table 18), by which time introduced diseases may have already reduced the size of the population. Population density per 100 sq. km varied from as little as one person in the desert regions of the Great Basin to as high as 95 in the Queen Charlotte Islands on the northern coast. Coniferous forests typify the coast from northern California to Alaska, and woodworking was highly developed. In the higher parts of the interior, pines predominated, whereas in low-lying areas vegetation varied from grass to sagebrush to desert. Seeds in the Great Basin and acorns in California were vital to subsistence. Major rivers breach the mountain ranges separating the interior from the coast and the anadromous salmon was the basic food resource on the coast and the interior plateaux.

The common feature of the aboriginal cultures in this area was that subsistence was based entirely on fishing, hunting, and gathering wild plant foods. Permanent winter villages (i.e. settlements with permanent structures serving as a home-base but normally fully occupied only during the winter months) with storage facilities and seasonal hunting or foraging camps were characteristic of those regions with large salmon runs or acorn harvests, whereas short-term seasonally occupied camp sites typified the less well endowed regions. The village was the basic socio-political unit in the former, and the band in the latter. Kinship and reciprocal obligations united people from adjacent villages and bands into social networks frequently referred to as 'tribes'.

Technology varied, but the basic tool kit – the bow and arrow, harpoon, fish hook, nets for hunting or fishing, and the digging stick – was used everywhere. Stone-grinding tools were important in seed-rich areas. Wood and basketry containers were widely used. The highest achievements in the arts and crafts were the monumental wood sculptures of northern coastal peoples, and the superb basketry of the central Californians. Spirit power and SHAMANISM typified the religious system. Archaeological research indicates that these ethnographic patterns extended far back into prehistory. Relative dating methods such as superposition and association and the comparative method underlie the chronologies and CULTURE HISTORY syntheses of this area. SYSTEMS THEORY, particularly cultural-environmental-demographic interactions, has been used to guide some explanations of culture change, although models based on DIFFUSIONISM and migration are also employed. ETHNOGRAPHIC ANALOGY is widely used.

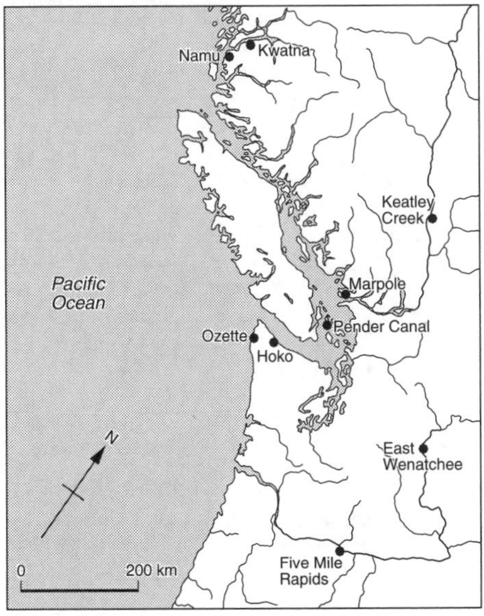

Map 7 **America, 2: Western North** Major sites in the region with individual entries in the Dictionary.

2.1. *Cultural taxonomy*. There are four culturally defined areas: the Northwest Coast, the Columbia-Fraser Plateau, the Great Basin, and Central California. A method of cultural classification based on propinquity and degree of similarity of artefact assemblages (Willey and Phillips 1958) is widely used. The concept of the 'cultural tradition', implying continuity of whole cultures through time, is the largest unit of synthesis and is applied both regionally and across western North America as a whole. Cultures are frequently subdivided into a number of chronological phases defined on the basis of some aspect of culture content – styles or frequencies of projectile points, burial types, houses etc. – which vary in one or more aspect from phase to phase. The term 'component' is widely used to refer to the expression of a phase at a particular site. For example, there are 18 components of the MARPOLE phase, which means that there are 18 spatially discrete assemblages assignable to the Marpole phase. Such components are usually from different sites, and the term 'multiple component site' means that there are components of more than one phase at the site.

2.2. *Early period*. The generally accepted chronology in all regions (except the Northwest Coast north of the Canada–United States border) places the western FLUTED POINT TRADITION at the beginning of the sequence. There is some debate as to whether this tradition is earlier or later than the intermontane STEMMED POINT TRADITION. The Fluted Point Tradition has estimated dates of 9500 to 9000 BC, based on CROSS-DATING with sites in eastern and southwestern North America. The majority of radiocarbon dates for the Stemmed Point Tradition, on the other hand, are between 8500 and 6000 BC, but there are dates from two sites, FORT ROCK CAVE (Bedwell 1973) and Smith Creek Cave (Bryan 1988: 53–72) which if correct would place the beginning of this tradition earlier than 9500 BC. On the coast north of the United States–Canada border the PEBBLE TOOL TRADITION is the earliest, first attested at NAMU in *c*.7700 BC (Carlson 1991: 85–95). Further north in southeast Alaska the MICROBLADE TRADITION radiocarbon-dated at HIDDEN FALLS to 7060 BC is the best-documented early cultural tradition (Davis 1989).

2.3. *Middle period*. From about 6000 BC to AD 1 was a time of cultural growth, technological exchange among the earlier cultural traditions, increased efficiency in exploiting local environments, regional divergence, and growth of nuclear areas of cultural elaboration. During this time the atlatl remained in use, while atlatl projectile points notched for hafting superseded earlier fluted, stemmed, and foliate forms in most regions. Microblade technology spread south as far as the Columbia River by 4800 BC. The Namu data indicate that by 4000 BC salmon had become the staple item of subsistence on the Northwest Coast. The evidence from PENDER CANAL shows that by 1500 BC the Northwest Coast art style, the memorial potlatch, and advanced woodworking and social ranking had developed. In the Columbia-Fraser Plateau, permanent winter villages emerged by 3000 BC and by 2000 BC they became the norm with the development of the PLATEAU PITHOUSE TRADITION. In the Great Basin seasonal transhumance and exploitation of varied ecological niches with emphasis on seed gathering and hunting became the standard way of life. In California acorn processing with hopper-mortars began, leading to the development of permanent villages and a considerable increase in population.

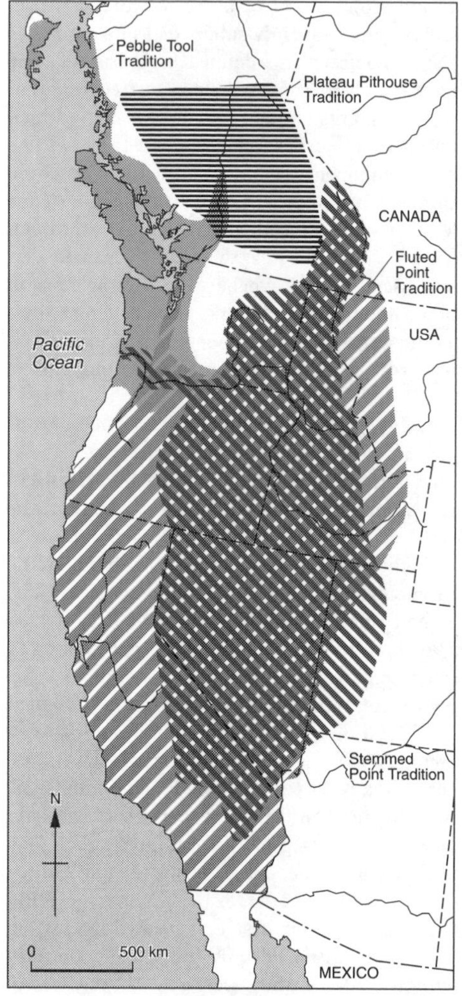

Map 8 **America, 2: Western North** Distribution of the four main cultural traditions in western North America (the Plateau Pithouse Tradition, the Pebble Tool Tradition, the Stemmed Point Tradition and the Fluted Point Tradition.

2.4. *Late period.* The late period, from AD 1 to European contact at about AD 1800, was characterized by further elaboration of the cultural patterns developed earlier, and the chief technological change was the replacement of the atlatl by the bow and arrow. Simple pottery vessels began to be made in the Great Basin, while ceramic figurines were produced both in the Great Basin and the lower Columbia River. Increased warfare and probably slavery occurred on the Northwest Coast. The cultures of the late period in western North America are typified by localized styles of artefacts such as arrow points, harpoon heads, seed-grinding tools and celts.

A.L. Kroeber: *Cultural and natural areas of native North America* (Berkeley, 1939); G. Willey and P. Phillips: *Method and theory in American archaeology* (Chicago, 1958); S.F. Bedwell: *Fort Rock Basin prehistory and environment* (Eugene, 1973); M.J. Moratto, ed.: *California archaeology* (London, 1984); W.L. d'Azevedo, ed.: *Handbook of North American Indians* II: *Great Basin* (Washington, 1986); T.H. Richards and M.K. Rousseau: *Late prehistoric cultural horizons on the Canadian plateau* (Burnaby, B.C., 1987); A.L. Bryan: 'The relationship of the stemmed point and fluted point traditions in the Great Basin', *Early human occupation in far western North America: the Colvis-Archaic interface*, ed. J.A. Willig, C.M. Aitkens and J.L. Fagan (Carson City, 1988); S.D. Davis: *The Hidden Falls site, Baranof Island, Alaska*, Alaska Anthropological Association Monographs Series (Fairbanks, 1989); W. Suttles, ed.: *Handbook of North American Indians* VII: *Northwest Coast* (Washington, 1990); R.L. Carlson: 'Namu periodization and C-14 chronology', *The economic prehistory of Namu*, ed. A. Cannon (Burnaby, B.C., 1991).

RC

3 Southwestern North America

The geographical 'Greater Southwest' region of North America lies within the area defined by 104°–115° west longitude and 29°–39° north latitude. A more informal and southern-oriented region is bounded by Las Vegas, New Mexico to Las Vegas, Nevada and Durango, Colorado to Durango, Mexico. The United States portion of the Southwest, consisting of Arizona, most of New Mexico, southern Utah and southern Colorado, has received most archaeological attention and is the area usually meant by the term American Southwest in discussions of prehistory.

Desert precipitation and temperature regimes, differential distribution and seasonal availability of surface water, and extremes of elevation all set severe constraints on prehistoric human adaptation. Three broad adaptations are recognized: (1) hunting and gathering augmented by gardening according to local, mountain conditions, (2) rainfall and runoff agriculture on the Colorado Plateau and (3) irrigation farming along desert rivers.

PALEOINDIAN big-game hunters and gatherers of the CLOVIS culture (*c*.9,500–9000 BC) had shifted to small-game hunting and gathering by the end of the Pleistocene and the beginning of the Archaic period (*c*.9000 BC–AD 1), while big-game bison hunting continued on the Plains beyond the eastern border of the Southwest. The appearance of maize between 1200 and 500 BC led to the development of ANASAZI (AD 1–1540) and SINAGUA (AD 700–1450) villages based on rainfall and runoff agriculture on the Colorado Plateau and to the establishment of long-term HOHOKAM communities (AD 200–1450) dependent on irrigation farming of Sonoran Desert river valleys and basins. The mountain-adapted MOGOLLON (AD 200–1400) pursued a semi-sedentary hunter-gatherer way of life augmented by gardening. The poorly known PATAYAN (AD 800–1450) practised

Map 9 **America, 3: Southwestern North** Major sites in the region with individual entries in the Dictionary.

floodwater farming along the lower Colorado River and hunter-gatherer in the surrounding desert.

Prehistoric cultures become less distinct in the 1400s prior to the close of prehistory with the Spanish expedition of Francisco Vasquez de Coronado in 1540. Historic PUEBLO peoples of the northern Southwest are descendants of the Anasazi, and probably also the Mogollon, although the assignment of specific languages to prehistoric regional groups is complicated and uncertain. The relationship between the Hohokam and the river Pima and desert Tohono O'odham (Papago) remains unclear, while most scholars accept that Colorado River Yumans are descendants of the Patayan.

L.S. Cordell: *Prehistory of the Southwest* (New York, 1984); J.J. Reid and D.E. Doyel, eds: *Emil W. Haury's prehistory of the American Southwest* (Tucson, 1986); L.S. Cordell and G.J. Gumerman, eds: *Dynamics of Southwest prehistory* (Washington, D.C., 1989).

JJR

4 Eastern North America

Many different cultures over the past 12,000 or more years occupied the part of North America that stretches from the high, rugged western mountains eastwards to the Atlantic Ocean. During that long period Native American populations increased, and in most places gradually shifted from mobile hunting-and-gathering to settled agricultural ways of life. While villagers late in prehistory grew crops such as maize, beans, squash, and several native cultigens, they never completely gave up collecting wild plants, fishing, and hunting game, especially white-tailed deer.

Tributaries of the Mississippi River drain much of this region. Several major rivers flow eastwards before joining the Mississippi River, the mightiest being the Missouri. The largest of the eastern tributaries is the Ohio River with headwaters in the Appalachian mountains. Numerous shorter rivers flowing directly into the Gulf of Mexico, Atlantic Ocean, or Hudson Bay drain the rest of this region, including the Great Lakes. This vast region is more arid towards the west and colder to the north. Vegetation patterns vary accordingly. In the vicinity of the Mississippi River, typically west of it, dense eastern forests are replaced by grasslands, first tall-grass and then short-grass prairies as the land becomes drier. Continental climatic conditions are to some extent ameliorated near the Atlantic Coast and Great Lakes. Modern vegetation patterns were established several millennia after humans first appeared in this region. Climate changes since that time continued to exert strong influences on the ways people lived. They include a warmer and dryer interval *c*.6500–3000 BC, the Hypsithermal, and a four-century-long colder period starting about AD 1400, the Little Ice Age.

The earliest people, called PALEOINDIANS, were hunters who possessed the distinctive lanceolate, fluted projectiles of the FLUTED POINT TRADITION. Those west of the Mississippi River hunted big game, particularly bison, for at least part of their diet. To the east, which is where the majority of fluted points have been found, they pursued more generalized hunting and gathering. A highly mobile way of life is indicated by short-term occupation sites and numerous projectile points fashioned from stones derived from distant sources. Roughly contemporaneous points have different geographical distributions, all covering vast areas.

By *c*.8000 BC fluted points were replaced by other kinds of points, the sizes and shapes of which varied greatly over time and space (it should be noted that dates for archaeological units in Eastern North America vary from one region to another; the ones used here pertain most closely to the mid-western and southeastern parts of the Eastern Woodlands). From *c*. 8000 BC onwards, regional traditions defined by various kinds of artefacts tended to get smaller as populations increased, people focused on more restricted areas, and ways of life became more sedentary.

Archaic hunting and gathering ways of life varied according to the opportunities and constraints of different environmental settings. Early Archaic

Map 10 **America, 4: Eastern North** Major sites in the region with individual entries in the Dictionary.

(*c*.8000–6000 BC) groups moved frequently, and their sites were correspondingly ephemeral with few features such as hearths and shallow pits. By the Middle Archaic (*c*.6000–3000 BC), some groups were living for much of the year in particularly favourable resource-rich spots. Thick middens heavily laden with cultural debris developed along the banks of some midcontinental rivers and shallow lakes. The onset of the Hypsithermal, marked by an eastward expansion of grasslands through the Midwest, caused some populations to aggregate alongside wetlands. In what is now Kentucky and Tennessee, people often settled where mussels were plentiful. These sites, which gradually developed into great piles of shell, continued to be used into the Late Archaic (*c*.3000–1000 BC). Shell heaps dating to this time also developed near ocean shorelines, particularly along the south Atlantic and Gulf coasts, through the repeated use of especially favourable places.

Archaic diets varied according to the resources locally available. In the midcontinent in particular, people increasingly came to rely on several native plants that yield great numbers of starchy and oily seeds. These weedy species grow well in disturbed habitats, and they would have thrived in the nutrient enriched soils of human encampments. By the 2nd millennium BC, several of these plants displayed morphological features indicating that they had been domesticated. Changes in life were accompanied by alterations in artefact assemblages. Ground-stone tools such as grooved axes, plummets (net weights), and spearthrower weights (bannerstones) were common by the Middle Archaic. During the Late Archaic, vessels were being carved from steatite that outcrops in the Appalachian mountains. Pottery first appeared by *c*.2500 BC at sites along the south Atlantic coast.

Some interregional exchange of non-local raw materials and items such as decorated bone pins took place during the Middle Archaic. Such interactions consisted of down-the-line reciprocal exchanges, and they increased in Late Archaic times. The POVERTY POINT mound group in northeastern Louisiana and related sites, dated to *c*.1000 BC, were unusually well supplied with non-local raw materials that were fashioned into objects used for utilitarian and other purposes.

By *c*.500 BC, pottery had become common across much of this broad geographical region. Archaeologists often use pottery as the principal defining characteristic of variously dated Early WOODLAND cultures. People at this time were living increasingly sedentary ways of life. In many parts of the Eastern Woodlands they placed greater emphasis on growing plants. Burials in mounds referred to as ADENA (*c*.500 BC–AD 1) in the middle Ohio River valley indicate that important people in local communities enjoyed greater access to exotic goods, including mica and copper bracelets, than most members of their societies.

Native cultigens were an important component of Middle Woodland diets (*c*.150 BC–AD 500). These people tended to live in small villages or dispersed communities, although in some places deep middens developed from repeated occupations of particularly attractive spots. People who had achieved high status in their local communities were buried in mounds. They were interred with finely crafted artefacts including pottery and objects made of nonlocal materials such as copper, marine shell, mica, and obsidian. Many of the largest Middle Woodland mounds and the most impressive earthworks consisting of circular and square embankments were built in the middle Ohio River valley, particularly in southern Ohio. The mounds and artefacts, known collectively as HOPEWELL after a site in Ohio, were associated with many, but not all, societies of this period. They were distributed across much of the Eastern Woodlands, as well as up the Missouri River into the eastern Plains.

The subsequent Late Woodland period, beginning *c*.AD 500, was a time of more limited interregional exchange, greater regionalism in cultural complexes, and population growth. Late in the 1st millennium AD the bow-and-arrow spread throughout this broad geographical region, and intergroup conflicts increased. At this time many, but not all, groups placed more reliance on maize, which soon became a critical staple of diets.

The Late Woodland period is said to extend to the time of contact with Europeans in the Great Lakes, Northeast, and mid-Atlantic regions, and localized archaeological complexes are given names such as Monongahela and Iroquois. Regional traditions distributed across the Plains into the Midwest after *c*.AD 1000 are referred to by other names, such as Plains Village, Middle Missouri, Oneota, and FORT ANCIENT. These tribally organized, sedentary villagers lived along the major rivers of the Plains and in the resource-rich parts of the northern Eastern Woodlands. Villages were often enclosed by defensive palisades after *c*.AD 1000. Inter-group conflicts intensified several centuries later, sometimes with devastating effects on individual villages, such as a 14th-century massacre at Crow Creek on the Missouri River. Throughout the late prehistoric period, small constellations of villages linked by unstable alliances jockeyed for advantageous positions, which often entailed movement from one place to another. These people relied on mixed subsistence strategies based in large part on maize, although there was considerable regional variability. In the western part of this area bison hunting was an important part of the annual cycle. Wild rice was collected by people in the Great Lakes area. Fish, typically caught with nets, varied in importance depending on their availability.

In the southern Midwest and Southeast, Late Woodland is followed at *c.*1000 by the MISSISSIPPIAN period. These societies, as well as contemporaneous Caddoan groups west of the Mississippi, included the most populous and organizationally complex sociopolitical systems to exist in this broad region during pre-Columbian times. These agricultural peoples tended to live in chiefdoms consisting of one or more principal settlements surrounded by closely affiliated small communities. The most important settlements were often marked by flat-topped earthen mounds that supported buildings used by high-ranking people. The largest of these sites was CAHOKIA in southwestern Illinois. Individuals of high status inherited their positions, often lived in large houses, and were buried with highly valued artefacts indicative of their prestigious positions. Warfare among these societies was common, and large sites in particular were frequently defended by palisades, which were often reinforced by stout bastions and deep ditches.

Throughout this area, Native American cultures with roots extending back thousands of years changed quickly following the arrival of Europeans in the 16th century AD. Groups were decimated by new diseases and most of them were displaced, generally in a westward direction. Ways of life were transformed through access to horses and various valued trade goods, especially guns, and by the incorporation of Native Americans into the expanding political and economic spheres of Euroamerican powers. Currently popular images of Native Americans are more closely related to conditions in these turbulent years than they are to life in more distant times.

K.B. Farnsworth and T.E. Emerson, eds.: *Early Woodland archaeology* (Kampsville, 1986); B.D. Smith: 'The archaeology of the southeastern United States: from Dalton to de Soto, 10,500–500 BP', *Advances in world archaeology*, ed. F. Wendorf and A.E. Close (Orlando, 1986), 1–92; ——: *Rivers of change: essays on early agriculture in eastern North America* (Washington, D.C., 1992); D.G. Anderson: *The Savannah River chiefdoms: political change in the late prehistoric Southeast* (Tuscaloosa, 1994); K.H. Schlesier, ed.: *Plains Indians, AD 500–1500* (Norman, 1994).

GM

5 Mesoamerica and Central America

Mesoamerica is a 'culture area', a geographical region in which a number of individual societies, prehistoric and contemporary, share marked cultural similarities despite being differentiated by political, linguistic, religious, and other distinctions (see Kirchoff 1943). The northern boundary of the Mesoamerican culture area stretches east–west across the vast arid lands of northern and north-central Mexico, while its southern boundary, more difficult to define, runs generally north–south through tropical forests of central Honduras and western Nicaragua. In terms of today's political boundaries, the culture area includes most of modern Mexico and most or all of the Central American countries of Guatemala, Belize, El Salvador, western Honduras, western Nicaragua and northwestern Costa Rica. The prehistoric cultures of the eastern portions of Honduras, Nicaragua and Costa Rica, plus all of Panama, are grouped together and are known collectively either as the 'Intermediate Area' (i.e. intermediate between the civilizations of Mesoamerica and the Andes of South America) or by the region's modern political designation, Central America.

In terms of geology, topography, climate, flora and fauna, the lands of Mesoamerica display a great deal of variability, from snow-covered mountains to arid desert to lush tropical forest to coastal swamps. Dramatic differences in elevation, soils, mean temperatures and rainfall often occur within relatively small areas, creating a complex mosaic of ecological settings, patterns of resource distribution and agricultural potential for the prehistoric societies of Mesoamerica. Mesoamerican environments are most broadly distinguished as highland and lowland. The highlands are formed by the Sierra Madre mountain chain running north–south through Mexico and eastward into southern Guatemala and then south through western Central America. The mountainous region is tectonically active, and OBSIDIAN from its many volcanoes was a valued resource for stone tools. The principal lowland area lies in eastern Mesoamerica, where the limestone shelf of the Yucatán peninsula comprises parts of Mexico, northern Guatemala and Belize. Another important lowland region is the coastal plain along the western and southern Gulf of Mexico.

Prehistoric Mesoamerica falls into two main parts: eastern Mesoamerica, occupied by speakers of Mayan languages (*see* LOWLAND MAYA) and western Mesoamerica, or Mexico west of the Isthmus of Tehuantepec, occupied by diverse cultures (*see* AZTECS, MIXTECS, TEOTIHUACAN *and*

ZAPOTECS) speaking a great variety of languages. In each of these areas further subregional distinctions are made, often on the basis of cultural similarities and differences coinciding roughly with physiographic divisions (e.g. Gulf coast cultures, highland and lowland Maya cultures, BASIN OF MEXICO, valley of Oaxaca, trans-isthmian cultures, etc.).

Mesoamerica has a long history of human occupation, with several sites dating back 10,000 or more years. These have yielded remains of late Pleistocene fauna and/or artefacts typical of PALEOINDIAN hunters elsewhere in the New World. The ARCHAIC or Preceramic period, dating roughly 7000–2500 BC in Mesoamerica, is a period of cultural adaptations to changing Holocene environments in the New World. While there has been relatively little archaeological attention to this period in eastern Mesoamerica (cf. MacNeish 1983), in highland Mexico a number of scholars have investigated the beginnings of agriculture and sedentary settlement during these millennia (*see* TEHUACAN). The principal cultigens of Mesoamerica – corn (*Zea mays*), several varieties of beans (*Phaseolus*) and squash (*Cucurbits*), peppers (*Capiscum*), tomatoes and avocados, as well as non-food cultigens such as cotton – were domesticated during this time. Mesoamerican peoples domesticated dogs and turkeys, but they lacked domesticated animals for milk, hides, meat and transportation; they also lacked wheeled transport vehicles, although wheeled toys have been found.

The development, florescence and decline of large, complex societies in Mesoamerica took place during three broad time periods known as the

Radiocarbon Years	Major Mesoamerican Period	Valley of Mexico: Ceramic Phases	Valley of Mexico: Neutral Terminology	Valley of Oaxaca Ceramic Phases	Eastern Lowlands Major Archaeological Periods
1500					
1400	Late Postclassic	Late Aztec	Late Horizon		Mayapan
1300				Monte Albán V	
1200		Early Aztec			
1100	Early Postclassic	Mazapan	Second Intermediate		Chichén Itsá
1000					
900		Coyotlatelco		Monte Albán IV	Puuc
800	Late Classic				
700		Metepec		Monte Albán IIIB	Tepeu
600		Xolalpan			
500	Early Classic		Middle Horizon		
400		Tlamimilolpa		Monte Albán IIIA	Tzakol
300					
200		Miccaotli			Floral Park
100		Tzacualli		Monte Albán II	
AD/BC	Late Preclassic or Formative				
100		Patlachique			Chicánel
200					
300			First Intermediate	Monte Albán Late I	
400		Ticoman			
500	Middle Preclassic or Formative			Monte Albán Early I	Mamom
600				Rosario	
700		Zacatenco			
800				Guadalupe	
900					Xé
1000				San José	
1100		Ixtapaluca	Early Horizon		
1200	Early Preclassic or Formative				
1300				Tierras Largas	
1400					Swasey
1500			Initial Ceramic		
1600					

Table 1 **America, 5: Mesoamerica and Central** Mesoamerica: the relationship of the three regional Mesoamerican chronologies to the overall Mesoamerican chronology. *Source*: R.E. Blanton et al.: *Ancient Mesoamerica: a comparison of change in three regions* (Cambridge University Press, 1981).

Preclassic (or Formative), Classic and Postclassic. The dating of each of these intervals varies in eastern vs. western Mesoamerica and each period has numerous subdivisions in which archaeologists have traced events and processes specific to particular sites or regions. Nonetheless, some broad features are shared throughout the culture area.

The Preclassic or Formative period, dating from *c.*2500 BC to AD 0/200, was characterized by the beginnings of most of the major characteristics of Mesoamerican civilizations. These include: monumental architecture of stone, with temple-pyramids arranged at the cardinal directions around open plazas; hieroglyphic writing systems used to record celestial/calendrical observations and the achievements of rulers; art systems characterized by sculpted stone, slipped and painted pottery, and portable objects of carved jade; and elaborate systems of status symboling for elite individuals and lineages through local and imported goods (such as jade, shells, feathers), evidenced most dramatically in mortuary ritual (*see* CHALCHUAPA, IZAPA, LOWLAND MAYA, OLMEC *and* SAN JOSÉ MOGOTE).

The Classic period, dating to *c.*AD 0–700 in central Mexico (e.g. MONTE ALBAN; TEOTIHUACAN) and AD 200–900 in the lowland Maya area, is characterized by the full development and expression of these evolving characteristics. However, features of settlement layout, population density, regional integration, rulership and polity, agricultural organization and productivity and economic interaction varied considerably from area to area.

The Postclassic period in Mesoamerica is often described in terms of a contrast with the Classic, the differences being seen in greater emphasis on (or evidence for) militarism, mercantile activity (especially maritime) and a more 'secular' character of rulership. The period is usually divided around AD 1200 into Early and Late subdivisions. The Early Postclassic period in central Mexico is best known from the TOLTEC site of TULA, and in the Maya lowlands by sites such as CHICHÉN ITZÁ. The Late Postclassic period in central Mexico is dominated by the Triple Alliance 'empire' of the AZTECS, and their relations with other regional states (*see* MIXTECS, TARASCANS, *and* ZAPOTECS).

In the Maya region a number of relatively small sites are important as capitals of regional kingdoms in the highlands (IXIMCHE, UTATLAN *and* Zaculeu) or confederacies in the lowlands (e.g. MAYAPAN). Much of what we know about Late Postclassic society and economy comes from indigenous writings, such as tribute or king lists (*see* CODICES; HIEROGLYPHIC WRITING), as well as documents written by the first Spaniards to visit the area.

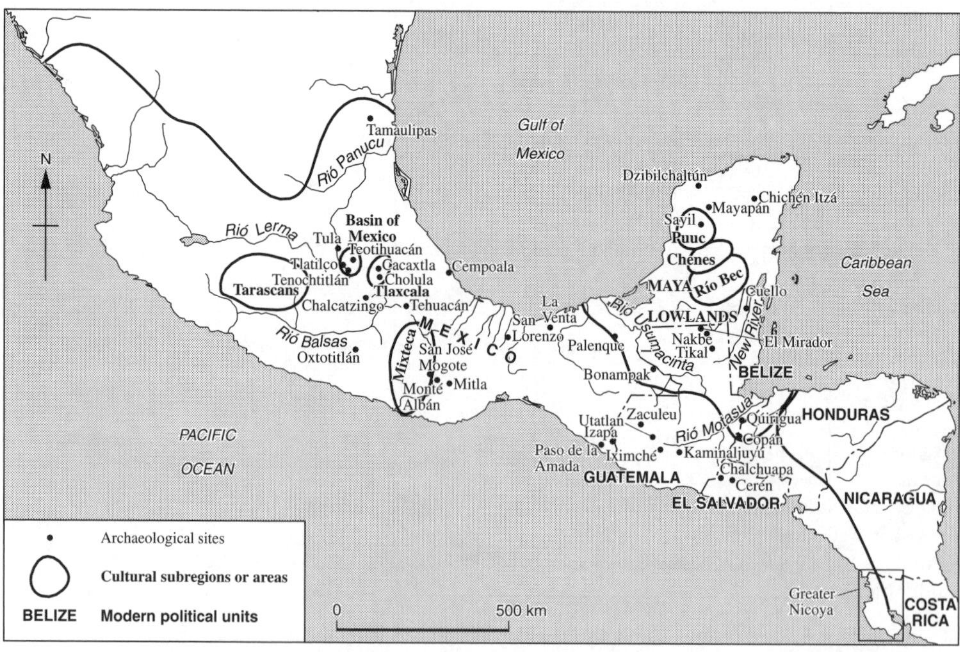

Map 11 **America, 5: Mesoamerica and Central** Archaeological sites and cultural areas.

The contact and Spanish colonial periods in Mesoamerica began with the fall of TENOCHTITLAN, the Aztec capital, to Hernan Cortés in 1521. Subsequent European conquest and conversion of native peoples to Catholicism throughout Mesoamerica and Central America involved not only subjugation and relocation, but also a massive decline in population due to introduced diseases.

P. Kirchoff: 'Mesoamerica', *Acta Americana* 1 (1943) 92–107; R.E. Blanton, S.A. Kowalewski, G. Feinman and J. Appel: *Ancient Mesoamerica, a comparison of change in three regions*, 2nd edn (Cambridge, 1993); R.S. MacNeish: 'Mesoamerica', *Early man in the New world*, ed. R. Shutler, Jr. (Beverly Hills, 1983) 125–35; R.E.W. Adams: *Prehistoric Mesoamerica* (Norman; 1991); M. Porter Weaver: *The Aztecs, Maya and their predecessors*, 3rd edn (New York, 1993).

PRI

6 South America

There are six principal regions in South America: the Central Andes (Peru, Bolivia, Northwest Argentina, northern Chile), the Northern Andes (Ecuador and Colombia), Venezuela, the Amazon (including the Guianas and the upper Paranä/La Plata system), the Planalto (southeastern Brazil, including the Planalto proper, parts of the Chaco, and the coastal strip) and the Southern Cone (southern and eastern Argentina, including the Pampas and Patagonia, southern Chile and Tierra del Fuego). The Central Andes region encompasses three very different environmental zones: coastal desert and oases, montane basins and valleys, forested eastern Andes. There are no macro-schemes in common use for the Amazon region; in the western Amazon sites are usually dated/classified according to the scheme in the adjacent Andean country. The same is true for the eastern Caribbean littoral, the Planalto, the Southern Cone and southern Chile. Sites and cultural traditions are dated through chronometric methods, usually radiocarbon dating, or by rough comparison with dated sites of the same tradition. The reliance upon few or poorly associated radiocarbon dates is one of the major problems in South American archaeology.

Human occupation in most areas of south America began in the PALEOINDIAN period; the Archaic (nomadic to semisedentary foraging cultures) is well developed in the Planalto and is beginning to be explored elsewhere. Agricultural communities begin as early as the 4th millennium BC in Brazil, whereas in the southern cone the Paleoindian adaptation gave way to variations on the Fuegian/Patagonian tradition of coastal hunting/foraging and inland hunting. In all areas there are beginning to be local sequences, and some researchers use named periods (often the same as those of the Northern Andes, as 'evolutionary' schemes fit local ideologies), but there are few, if any, agreed upon general organizations of time and culture aside from the recognition of a Paleoindian, and perhaps an Archaic, horizon.

Central Andes (Peru, Bolivia, Northwest Argentina, Northern Chile)

Paleoindian Period	?12,000 – ?6000 BC
Preceramic (Archaic)	
(Early or Non-Cotton)	6000 – 3000 BC
Late (Cotton)	3000 – 2000 BC
Initial Period	2300 – 1200 BC
Early Horizon (Chavin expansion)	1200 – 400 BC
Early Intermediate Period	c.400 BC – c.AD 500
Middle Horizon (Huari	
expansion or empire)	AD 550 – 900
Late Intermediate Period	AD 900 – 1438
Late Horizon	
(Inca empire)	AD 1438 – Spanish Conquest

Northern Andes (Ecuador and Colombia)

Paleoindian	?12,000 – ?6000 BC
Archaic	6000 – 3000 BC
Formative	3000 – 500 BC
Regional Development	500 BC – AD 500
Integration (in Colombia,	
Chiefdoms)	AD 500 – c.1450
Inca (only in Ecuador)	c.1450 – Spanish Conquest

Venezuela

Paleoindian	?12,000 – ?6000 BC
Mesoindian	?6,000 – 5000 BC
Neoindian I	c.5000 – 1000 BC
Neoindian II	1000 BC – AD 300
Neoindian III	AD 300 – 1000
Neoindian IV	AD 1000 – 1500
Neoindian V	AD 1500 – 1600

Note:
There are no macro-schemes in common use for the Amazon region; in the western Amazon, sites are usually dated/classified according to the scheme in the adjacent Andean country. The same is true for the eastern Caribbean littoral (the scheme given above for Venezuela is debated), the Planalto, the Southern Cone and southern Chile. Sites and cultural traditions are dated through chronometric methods, usually radiocarbon, or by rough comparison with dated sites of the same tradition. The reliance upon few or poorly associated radiocarbon dates is one of the major problems in South American archaeology.

Table 2 **America, 6: South** Chronologies of the principal regions of South America.

Map 12 **America, 6: South** Major sites in the region with individual entries in the Dictionary.

6.1. *Prehistory*. South American archaeology has not been noted for innovation in the areas of method or theory. Sadly, many projects are so underfunded that a radiocarbon date is cause for rejoicing. In terms of theory, diffusion (often intercontinental), variations on themes of cultural ecology (such as maritime theories of the development of complex societies), or various evolutionary schemes have been the commonest frameworks on which the scanty data are displayed. In recent years the major advances have been in building a more reliable, and larger, data base, in ETHNOARCHAEOLOGY (such as CUEVA IGLESIA and MAPUCHE), in EXPERIMENTAL ARCHAEOLOGY (such as the study of INCA stone masonry) and in projects which integrate archaeological investigation into the local community (e.g. AGUA BLANCA).

A general vision of the prehistory of the continent is possible, although there are major gaps in knowledge, as well as considerable debates concerning the meaning of the archaeological data. Despite recurrent claims of very ancient sites in the Americas (e.g. PEDRA FURADA), the best evidence suggests an initial Paleoindian occupation of South America no earlier than *c*.12,000 BC. The evidence from the currently earliest known site, MONTE VERDE, indicates that there must be earlier sites north of Chile and, with the PAIJÀN sites (Peru), it suggests that there was a mixed economy among these earliest immigrants.

	Peru						Bolivia	
Years	North Coast		Central Coast	South Coast	Northern Sierra	Southern Sierra	Lowlands	Sierra
– 1600								
– 1500	Inca		Inca	Inca	Inca	Inca		Inca
– 1400								
– 1300	Late Sicán							Mollo and Iskanwaya
– 1200							?	
– 1100	Middle Sicán		*oracle only*		Gran Pajatén	Killke		
– 1000		Chan Chan					Upper Mound Velarde	
– 900								
– 800	Early Sicán				?			
– 700								
– 600			Pachacamac				Lower Mound Velarde	
– 500						Huari		
– 400	Sipán							Tiahuanaco
– 300				Nazca culture				
– 200				?				
– 100								
– AD BC	Vicús					Pucara		
– 100				Paracas				
– 200								
– 300				?				
– 400								
– 500								
– 600					Chavín de Huántar			
– 700								
– 800								
– 900								
– 1000	Cerro Sechín							
– 2000			El Paraíso					
– 3000								
– 4000								
– 5000								
– 6000	Paiján							
– 7000								
– 8000								

Table 3 **America, 6: South** Chart showing the approximate dates of the major sites and cultural traditions in Peru and Bolivia.

Hunting/foraging cultures continued in the Southern Cone from the terminal Pleistocene until the modern era at sites such as FELL'S CAVE. The move towards an archaic/incipience agricultural pattern began earliest in the equatorial regions; LAS VEGAS (Ecuador) shows the utilization of the paramount cultigen of the Americas, *Zea mays*, as early as 5500 BC. By 3000 BC, nearby VALDIVIA had well-established agriculture and the same site includes evidence that ceramics had entered the Andean world (ceramics are earlier on the Caribbean littoral at PUERTO HORMIGIA, MONSÚ and SAN JACINTO, although in non-agricultural contexts).

Precocious in terms of ceramics and sedentary life, the northern Andean cultures were extremely late to develop state formations. What may be chiefdoms appear in Ecuador with CHORRERA, and long-distance trade procuring luxury goods for the emerging elite is seen at Pirincay, on a major access route to the Amazon. Later coastal Ecuadorian cultures, especially BAHIA/JAMA COAQUE and La Tolita, are more noteworthy for the quality of their representational ceramics and the sophistication of their metallurgy than for any complex political developments. Virtually nothing is known of the contemporary tropical lowland sites, such as HUAPULA (previously known as Sangay) save that they have impressive earthworks and were involved in exchange with the highlands. In addi-

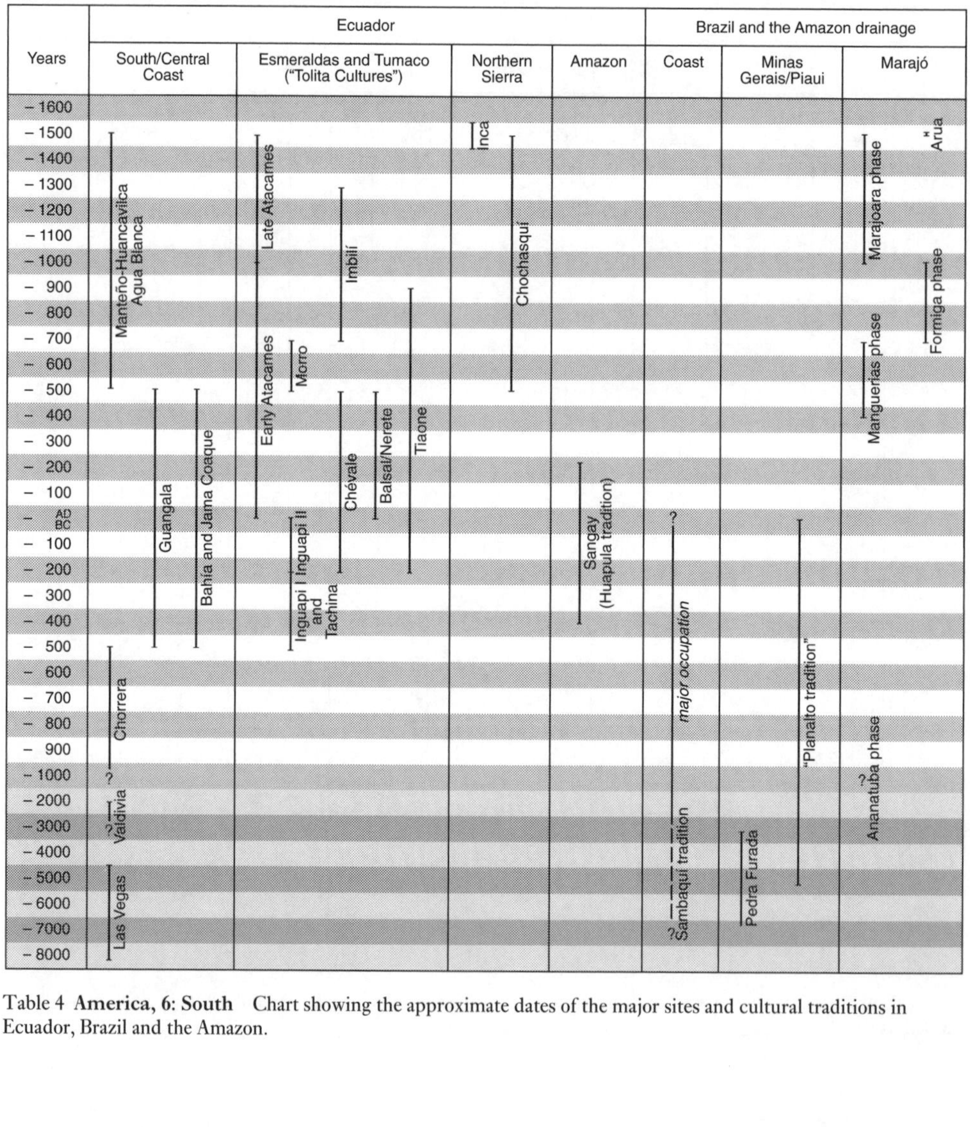

Years	Ecuador				Brazil and the Amazon drainage		
	South/Central Coast	Esmeraldas and Tumaco ("Tolita Cultures")	Northern Sierra	Amazon	Coast	Minas Gerais/Piaui	Marajó
– 1600							
– 1500	Manteño-Huancavilca Agua Blanca	Late Atacames	Inca; Chochasquí				Marajoara phase; Arua
– 1400							
– 1300		Imbilí					
– 1200							
– 1100							
– 1000		Early Atacames					Formiga phase
– 900		Tiaone					
– 800							Manguerias phase
– 700		Morro					
– 600							
– 500	Guangala; Bahía and Jama Coaque	Chévale; Balsal/Nerete					
– 400							
– 300							
– 200				Sangay (Huapula tradition)			
– 100							
– AD/BC		Inguapi I and Tachina; Inguapi II			? major occupation	"Planalto tradition"	
– 100							
– 200							
– 300							
– 400							
– 500	Chorrera						
– 600							
– 700							
– 800							
– 900							
– 1000	?						? Ananatuba phase
– 2000	? Valdivia						
– 3000					? Sambaquí tradition	Pedra Furada	
– 4000							
– 5000	Las Vegas						
– 6000							
– 7000					?		
– 8000							

Table 4 **America, 6: South** Chart showing the approximate dates of the major sites and cultural traditions in Ecuador, Brazil and the Amazon.

tion, relatively small political units are found in Colombia, where SAN AGUSTÍN exemplifies the elaboration of mortuary rituals and shamanistic practices in a setting of small, independent political units. To the north, the Ilama and CALIMA cultures show elaborate ceramics, metalworking, and communal undertakings, such as drained field systems, but without a centralized political power. Immense raised field systems are found in the SINÚ region of Colombia, in Barinas in western Venezuela (where they are likewise attached to populous, but quite small, ranked social groups) and in the Llanos de Mojos of eastern Bolivia, where the relatively early site of MOUND VELARDE and related areas attest to dense populations modifying the landscape to support their numbers.

In the southern Andes, SAN PEDRO DE ATACAMA formed an important element of northern procurement systems because of its proximity to copper and turquoise sources, and its grazing facilities for llama caravans. The region supported sedentary villages that produced fine ceramics and textiles, but were receivers, not donors, in terms of religious practices and the iconography associated with them. The uniqueness of southern Andean cultures is exemplified by CHINCHORRO, with its elaborate techniques of artificial mummification. The Chinchorro culture is found as far south as southern Peru, but it seems to have had no impact on Peruvian groups, which were already embarking on

Years	Venezuela			Argentina	Chile			Colombia		
	Maracaibo-Coro	Lower Orinoco	Barinas	Valleserrana	Arica Coast and Pisagua	Tierra del Fuego	Araucania	Magdalena	Cauca	Caribbean Coast
1600, 1500, 1400, 1300, 1200, 1100, 1000, 900, 800, 700, 600, 500, 400, 300, 200, 100, AD BC, 100, 200, 300, 400, 500, 600, 700, 800, 900, 1000, 2000, 3000, 4000, 5000, 6000, 7000, 8000	Dabajuro tradition	Los Barrancos; Barrancas	drained fields; La Betania; Cueva Iglesia	Inca; Aguada	Inca; ? Chinchorro ?	? Fell's Cave	Mapuche; pottery ?	Sombrillas; San Agustín Phases; Isnos; Primavera; Hurqueta	Sonso; Yotoco; Ilama	Sinú; San Jacinto; Puerto Hormiga

Table 5 **America, 6: South** Chart showing the approximate dates of the major sites and cultural traditions in Argentina, Chile, Colombia and Venezuela.

the process of cultural intensification that led to state formation in the 1st millennium BC. Argentina was likewise culturally and politically peripheral: the decorative arts are highly developed in AGUADA and its ancestral cultures, but large urban centres, ceremonial architecture and state organization were unknown.

It was in the central Andean region of Peru and highland Bolivia that complex societies, often urban and often forming large territorial units, emerged. Late preceramic sites such as EL PARAÍSO indicate considerable population growth and, perhaps, some central authority, while CERRO SECHÍN shows that warfare was an early element in the formation of political units. CHAVÍN, the characteristic religion, art style and technologies of which spread widely through the central Andes, was the first international culture of this region; its influence on contemporary and future cultures was tremendous. On the south coast, PARACAS utilized Chavín images in ceramics (although not in the elaborate embroidered textiles) and echoes of Chavín are seen in the religious art of PUCARA, the first of the *altiplano* states. The Early Intermediate Period Nazca culture shows an early development of the Andean pilgrimage tradition at the ceremonial centre of CAHUACHI; the NAZCA LINES are concerned with ceremonial processions and lineage rituals. On the north coast the centralization of power and wealth can be seen in the SIPÁN burials. This period ended in considerable disruption and population movement; the QUELCCAYA ICE CAP suggests that a major drought was a causal factor in these political realignments (since the annual ice layers – rather like tree rings – indicate severe disruptions of normal highland winter rains), although the growing power of the Middle Horizon HUARI state was contributory.

Under the Huari, the oracle of PACHACAMAC became powerful; it survived the empire's collapse to continue as an advisor to rulers under the Inca. In the *altiplano*, TIAHUANACO succeeded Pucara as the major political power, establishing a large state whose urban capital was supported by large systems of raised fields throughout the Titicaca Basin. The religion of both Tiahuanaco and Huari show iconographic evidence of a Chavín heritage. With the slow collapse of Tiahuanaco, the political scene in the *altiplano* changed to multiple small kingdoms, such as Mollo, whose major site was the planned town of Iskanwaya. By the 15th century tropical forest sites such as Gran Pajatén were flourishing. The tropical forest regions, whether western Andean slope (NAMBILLO) or the Amazon proper (MARAJÓ) may have developed fairly large chiefdoms, but no political unification is visible and cultural unification is not outstanding.

In coastal Peru at this time a number of larger states arose, notable among them the Sicán of Lambayeque who were key players in the *SPONDYLUS* SHELL trade with Ecuador and who buried their elite at BATAN GRANDE. The slightly later Chimu kingdom with its capital at the peculiar city of CHAN CHAN, expanded over much of the north coast until they too fell to the military expansion of the Inca Empire under Topa Inca – the man whose father Pachacuti had founded the empire and built one of its best known sites, MACHU PICCHU. The Inca expansion continued into Ecuador where small highland chiefdoms such as Cochasquí fell amidst considerable bloodshed. The Inca were encircling the large Manteño kingdoms, such as that at AGUA BLANCA, which controlled the lucrative distribution of the *Spondylus* shell. The Spanish invasions, heralded by an epidemic of smallpox or measles which entered western South America via the spanish colony at Buenos Aires, stopped the Inca conquests and ultimately put an end to the unique series of indigenous cultures of the South American continent.

G. Reichel-Dolmatoff: *Goldwork and shamanism* (Bogotá, 1988); R.L. Burger: *Chavín and the origins of Andean civilization* (New York and London, 1992); A.R. Gonzales: *2000 años de arte precolombino en la Argentina* (Buenos Aires, 1992); M.E. Moseley: *The Incas and their ancestors: the archaeology of Peru* (London and New York, 1992); A. Prouse: *Arqueologia Brasileria* (Brasilia, 1992); W. Alva and C.B. Donnan: *Royal tombs of Sipán* (Los Angeles, 1993); M. Malpass, ed.: *The provincial Inca: archaeological and ethnohistorical assessment of the impact of the Inca state* (Iowa, 1993); R.F. Townsend, ed.: *The ancient Americas: art from sacred landscapes* (Chicago, 1993); K.O. Bruhns: *Ancient South America* (Cambridge, 1994); T.D. Dillehay, ed.: *Tombs for the living: Andean mortuary practices* (Washington, D.C., 1995); T. Heyerdahl et al.: *The pyramids of Tucumé: the quest for Peru's forgotten city* (New York, 1995); D. Levine, ed.: 'Les derniers Incas: civilizations précolombiennes en Equateur', *DA* 214 (1996); A. Oyuela-Caycedo: 'The study of collector variability in the transition to sedentary society in northern Columbia', *JWP* 10 (1996), 49–92; H. Silverman: 'The formative period in the south coast of Peru: a critical review', *JWP* 10 (1996), 95–146.

KB

amino acid dating Scientific method used by archaeologists to date such faunal remains as bones, teeth and shells. Amino acids are the building blocks of proteins; a particular amino acid can exist in more than one form (L & D isomers) depending on the three-dimensional arrangement of the molecules about the central carbon atom. If, rather than one carbon atom (the chiral carbon), there are two at the centre of the asymmetry then four forms can exist (e.g. L-isoleucine D-isoleucine, L-alloisoleucine and D-alloisoleucine). Living organisms produce proteins containing only L-isomers. Racemization is the conversion of the L-form of an amino acid to a D-form. The reaction is reversible, leading ultimately to an equilibrium between the proportions of L- and D-forms. Strictly the term epimerization is used when the conversion involves only one of the possible chiral carbon atoms (e.g. L-isoleucine to D-alloisoleucine), but racemization is often used to describe all interconversions.

Racemization begins after death or, for example in tooth enamel, once the protein is formed and is no longer being renewed. If the rate constant of the racemization is known, then measurement of the D/L amino acid ratio will enable the time since death to be calculated. The interconversions used in dating are L to D aspartic acid and L-isoleucine (L-Ile) to D-alloisoleucine (D-aIle). Techniques such as high performance liquid chromatography enable these D/L ratios to be determined with reasonable precision. The so-called racemization rate constant is in fact highly temperature-dependent, increasing exponentially with temperature, thus there is typically an increase of two orders of magnitude in the rate for a temperature increase from 0 to 25°C (it is also species-dependent). In theory the rate constant can be determined from experiments at elevated temperature, but to convert a D/L ratio to a date also requires an *effective* temperature over the period of burial to be assumed: this affects the accuracy of the technique i.e. whether the result is biased.

In the 'calibrated' method, the rate constant is found using a sample the age of which is known by other means and the temperature history of which parallels that of the samples to be dated. However, the accuracy of this method depends on the specific circumstances and, particularly, on how accurately the calibration sample is dated and reflects the thermal history of the unknowns.

The equilibrium ratio and the racemization rate (and hence temperature) determine the upper age limit; for aspartic acid this is of the order of 100,000 years and for L-Ile to D-aIle is several million years. The materials most often dated are teeth and mollusc shell. Amino acid dates on bone tend to be unreliable; because of its more open structure, there is the risk of contamination by amino acids from ground water, and there is evidence to suggest that the kinetics of the racemization process are not straightforward. Much work has been done on mollusc shells in determining aminostratigraphy and aminozones; given common thermal histories, the D/L ratios are used to link strata or regions of similar age. Teeth can also be used to determine age at death; in certain circumstances racemization at body temperature during the life-time of the individual can be significant relative to that *post mortem*. Amino acid ratios can also be used to determine effective palaeotemperature if the age of the sample is known.

P.M. Masters: 'Amino acid racemisation dating – a review', *Dating and age determination of biological materials*, ed. M.R. Zimmerman and J.L. Angel (London, 1986), 39–58; G. Sykes: 'Amino acid dating', *Quaternary dating methods – a user's guide*, ed. P.L. Smart and P.D. Frances (Cambridge, 1991), 161–76.

SB

Amlash *see* MARLIK, TEPE

Amman Islamic-period site in the modern capital of Jordan. The citadel of Amman (Qalʿa) is the only administrative building of the early Islamic period to have been excavated extensively, apart from the palaces at AL-KUFA and JERUSALEM (and the latter has yet to be published). The Umayyad structures were built within the walled Roman citadel of the 2nd century AD, which had been reused in the Byzantine period. In the Umayyad period it became the administrative centre for al-Urdunn (Jordan and northern Palestine). The resulting Umayyad reconstruction of *c.*AD 735 included an axial street system leading to a formal reception chamber, built in the SASANIAN manner with four *iwâns* and stone carved decoration. The excavations by Spanish and British teams conclusively demonstrated that this structure was in fact Umayyad and overturned earlier stylistic analysis that had suggested that the four-*iwân* structure was a product of the Sasanian occupation after the fall of Jerusalem in 614. The citadel was destroyed by earthquake in 747–8 but it continued to be used during Abbasid and Fatimid times until the 11th and 12th centuries. It was reoccupied in the Ayyubid period but fell out of use in the 14th century.

A. Almagro: *El palacio Omeya de Amman I: la arquitectura* (Madrid, 1983); A. Northedge, ed.: *Studies on Roman and Islamic ʿAmmân I: history, site, architecture* (Oxford, 1992).

GK

Amorites Ancient Near Eastern people first attested in the mid-3rd millennium BC; they were initially nomadic but eventually settled in large numbers throughout Mesopotamia and the Levant during the 2nd millennium BC. Their name comes from the Akkadian word *Amurrum* which in turn derives from the Sumerian term *Martu* ('west'), used to describe both the western desert and the tribes who emanated from that area. The Amorites first appear in texts of the Early Dynastic III period (*c*.2600–2350 BC) either as the despised Bedouin in the desert to the west of the Euphrates or as foreign labourers or mercenaries living in the Sumerian city-states of Mesopotamia. The Amorite language (a west Semitic dialect) has survived only in the form of personal names, since the Amorites themselves wrote in AKKADIAN, the language of the first Semitic-speaking empire in Mesopotamia.

After the fall of the Ur III dynasty (*c*.2150–2000 BC), the Amorites not only seized power in most of the existing cities of Sumer and Akkad but also established powerful new settlements. At the same time they spread into the Levant, where they dominated most of the Middle Bronze Age Syro-Palestinian polities, e.g. Yamhad (*see* ATCHANA, TELL), until the arrival of another nomadic West Semitic group, the ARAMAEANS, in the late 2nd millennium BC.

The widespread establishment of Amorite and Elamite kingdoms, replacing the earlier city-states, appears to have had a lasting (and revitalizing) effect on the socio-economic development of Mesopotamia and the Levant, significantly reducing the power of the temples and gradually transferring the ownership of the land into the hands of individuals. The integration of nomadic tribes into sedentary life is clearly a complex process (see Postgate 1992; Kamp and Yoffee 1980; *see also* NOMADS), and the history of the Amorites is more easily discernible in the textual evidence than in surviving archaeological traces of their material culture. As with the later influx of Aramaeans into Mesopotamia, the more settled Amorites of the 2nd millennium BC appear to have adopted most of the cultural attributes of the peoples whom they supplanted, thus reducing their own impact on the archaeological record. Postgate (1992: 86) points out that 'in Mesopotamia the Amorites are integrated so completely into society that no trace of them survives the fall of the 1st Dynasty of Babylon'.

J.R. Kupper: *Les nomades en Mésopotamie au temps des rois de Mari* (Paris, 1957); G. Buccellati: *The Amorites of the Ur III period* (Naples, 1963); A. Haldar: *Who were the Amorites?* (Leiden, 1971); K.A. Kamp and N. Yoffee: 'Ethnicity in ancient Western Asia during the early second millennium BC: archaeological assessments and ethnoarchaeological perspectives', *Bulletin of the American Schools of Oriental Research* 237 (1980), 85–104; N. Weeks: 'The Old Babylonian Amorites: nomads or mercenaries?', *Orientalia Lovaniensia Periodica* 16 (1985), 49–57; J.N. Postgate: *Early Mesopotamia: society and economy at the dawn of history* (London, 1992), 82–7.

IS

el-Amra Egyptian predynastic site, 60 km south of modern Sohag, which is the type-site for the 'Amratian' cultural phase or NAQADA I period (4000–3500 BC; *see* EGYPT 1). Amratian cemeteries have been excavated at several sites in the Nile Valley, stretching from Khor Bahan in Lower Nubia up to Matmar in Middle Egypt.

D. Randall MacIver and A.C. Mace: *El Amrah and Abydos, 1899–1901* (London, 1902).

IS

Amratian period *see* EGYPT 1

Amri Settlement site of the INDUS CIVILIZATION, consisting of two mounds near the edge of the alluvial plain of the Lower Indus valley, Pakistan. The excavations of Nani Gopal Majumdar in 1929 first revealed that the valley was occupied during the Early Indus period. The excavations of Jean-Marie Casal in 1959–62 enabled the occupation to be divided into two main periods, Ia–d (*c*.3700–3000 BC) and II (not yet accurately dated), followed by a phase of decline (period III).

Period Ic, the best documented Early Indus level at Amri, is characterized by distinctive cellular structures built of stone and mud brick, that appear to have been used for grain storage, as well as chert blades, bone tools and wheel-made ceramics decorated with painted motifs. Period-II Amrian sherds were mixed with HARAPPAN ceramics, but by period III the local forms had disappeared and the site had begun to diminish in size, with a Mature Indus ceramic style dominating. Several other sites with local Amrian ceramics have been identified in the Lower Indus region, including Gazi Shah and the fortified sites of Tharro and Kohtras Buti.

Amri's long chronological sequence provides evidence for local pre-Indus developments, with affinities to KOT DIJI and Kili Ghul Muhammad (*see* QUETTA), with a gradual introduction of mature Indus material culture, and eventual replacement of local material forms by characteristic Indus goods. The recognition of the interaction of local and regional processes highlights the complex historical processes of the 4th–3rd millennia BC in Pakistan, as local traditions are incorporated into the pan-regional traditions of the Indus Civilization.

N.G. Majumdar: *Explorations in Sind* (Delhi, 1934); J.-M. Casal: *Fouilles d'Amri*, 2 vols (Paris, 1964); ——: 'Amri: An introduction to the history of the Indus civilization',

Essays in Indian Protohistory, ed. D.P. Agrawal and D.K. Chakrabarti (New Delhi, 1979), 99–112.
CS

AMS *see* ACCELERATOR MASS SPECTROMETRY

Amuq Roughly triangular region of north-western Syria and southern Turkey, watered by the River Orontes and covering an area of some 500 sq. km. An American expedition conducted a survey of the Amuq plain, identifying nearly 200 individual sites, a third of which (including Tell Judeida and ÇATAL HÜYÜK) contained prehistoric ceramics. The combined results of this survey and several subsequent excavations have allowed a continuous but crude sequence to be constructed for the Amuq plain as a whole from *c.*7000 BC onwards; this enables the late Neolithic and Early Bronze Age phases of Anatolia, Mesopotamia and Syria to be knitted together to some extent, with Amuq phases C–D, for instance, corresponding to the HALAF phase in Mesopotamia, and Amuq H–I relating to the EARLY TRANSCAUCASIAN CULTURE in eastern Anatolia. The ceramics from phase E in the Amuq plain – contemporary with the UBAID period – show various unusual local adaptations and variations on the basic Ubaid styles. The results have been refined somewhat by more recent projects such as the surveys in the Qoueiq river valley (Matthers 1981).

R.J. Braidwood: *Mounds in the Plain of Antioch: an archaeological survey* (Chicago, 1937); R.J. and L.S. Braidwood: *Excavations in the Plain of Antioch* (Chicago, 1960); M.E.L. Mallowan: 'The ʿAmuq plain', *Antiquity* 37 (1963), 185–92; M. Tadmor: 'Contacts between the ʿAmuq and Syria-Palestine', *IEJ* 14 (1964), 253–69; J. Matthers, ed.: *The river Qoueiq, northern Syria and its catchment: studies arising from the Tell Rifaʿat survey, 1977–9* (Oxford, 1981).
IS

Amurru *see* AMORITES

analogy *see* CROSS-CULTURAL LAWS AND ANALOGIES; ETHNOARCHAEOLOGY; ETHNOGRAPHY

analytical archaeology An information-systems approach to archaeology, developed by the British archaeologist David Clarke in the mid-1960s. Clarke's manifesto for the theory and practice of archaeology was essentially spelled out in a single published volume, *Analytical archaeology* (1968), described by Ian Hodder (1991: 189) as 'the most significant attempt to develop a peculiarly archaeological methodology based on archaeological objects and their associations and affinities in archaeological contexts'. It employed techniques of quantitative and systems analysis (*see* SYSTEMS THEORY) that were largely borrowed from other subjects such as biology, the New Geography and sociology, and which allowed artefacts to be classified and interpreted in terms of social and ecological systems and processes of cultural change, rather than simply being used as the basis for historical narratives. The approach taken by Clarke lacked the anthropological slant of many other early proponents of processual archaeology such as Lewis Binford or Kent Flannery.

D.L. Clarke: *Analytical archaeology* (London, 1968); S. Shennan: 'Archaeology as archaeology or anthropology? Clarke's *Analytical archaeology* and the Binfords' *New perspectives in archaeology* 21 years on', *Antiquity* 63/241 (1989), 831–5; I. Hodder: *Reading the past*, 2nd edn (Cambridge, 1991).
IS

Anasazi Major prehistoric culture of the American Southwest, which flourished in Colorado Plateau country between the end of the Archaic period and the arrival of the Spanish in AD 1540. In 1924 Alfred Vincent Kidder defined the Basketmaker-Pueblo culture; three years later he synthesized it into the Pecos classification, and in 1936 he renamed it Anasazi (the Navajo word for 'enemy ancestors'). The Anasazi are the best-known of the Southwestern cultures because of (1) the highly visible ruins of pueblo masonry, for example, the remarkable ruins of Chaco Canyon (New Mexico), (2) the preservation of perishable materials in dry caves and on surface sites, (3) the applicability of DENDROCHRONOLOGY and (4) the extensive archaeological research due to climate, large cultural resource management projects and historical connections with the contemporary Pueblo Indians.

The characteristics distinguishing Anasazi from MOGOLLON and HOHOKAM on the most general level include: directional pueblo village layout (storage rooms–habitation rooms–ceremonial

Chronology of the Anasazi culture

Basketmaker II	AD 1 – 400
Basketmaker III	AD 400 – 700
Pueblo I	AD 700 – 900
Pueblo II	AD 900 – 1150
Pueblo III	AD 1150 – 1300
Pueblo IV	AD 1300 – 1540

Table 6 **Anasazi** Chronology of the Anasazi cultures.

rooms–burial and trash areas); curvilinear kivas (circular, D-shaped and keyhole-shaped ceremonial chambers); primary flexed inhumation of the deceased; lamboidal head deformation; use of full-grooved axes; and black-on-grey utility pottery thinned by coil-and-scrape and fired in a non-oxidizing atmosphere.

There are also regional variants, or 'branches', of the Anasazi, which are distinguished by ceramic and architectural differences. The western Anasazi branches (Kayenta, Virgin, Fremont and Winslow) are often grouped together under the term Kayenta branch, while the eastern Anasazi branches (Chaco, Mesa Verde and Rio Grande) are more distinct both in space and time. Finer subdivisions of the Anasazi, known as 'provinces' are also recognized.

The Anasazi sequence from Basketmaker to Pueblo (see Table 6), which is framed in the Pecos classification, is used to label overall phases and periods, but these are not coincident throughout the various branches of the culture. The span of about 200 years for each period, which was even more pronounced in the original 1927 formulation, influenced the perception of gradual cultural change throughout the Southwest.

The Anasazi were dependent on maize cultivation from the earliest period (Basketmaker II) onwards; they developed dry- and runoff-farming techniques to permit the expansion of farmsteads throughout much of the Colorado Plateau, while more complicated water-control systems supported the large populations and rituals of the Pueblo II period Chaco expansion. The abandonment of the upper San Juan River drainage by AD 1300 is attributed to agricultural problems caused by the effects of drought, erosion and lowered water tables. The expansion of Numic speakers into the region may also have contributed to its desertion. This contraction of Anasazi territory led ultimately to the historic settlement pattern of the Pueblos – Hopi, Zuni, Acoma and Rio Grande villages – which were encountered by Vasquez de Coronado's expedition in 1540.

The major Anasazi sites in the state of Arizona are Allentown, Antelope House, Awat'ovi, Betatakin, Homol'ovi, Kiatuthlanna, Kiet Siel. Awat'ovi (a Hopi pueblo on the southern edge of Antelope Meas, Hopi Reservation) consists of about 1300 ground-floor rooms and about 25 rectangular kivas. Homol'ovi comprises six sites (Homol'ovi I–IV, Chevelon and Cottonwood Creek ruins), dated between AD 1250 and 1400, and the region as a whole figures prominently in the migration legends of the Hopi. Kiet Siel is a cliff dwelling in Tsegi Canyon, which was occupied during the Tsegi phase (AD 1250–1400) and consists of 154 rooms. The analysis of the site (Dean 1969), including comparison with the nearby Betatakin cliff dwelling, is one of the most influential studies in Southwestern American archaeology.

Anasazi sites in New Mexico include Arroyo Hondo, Aztec, Chetro Ketl, Grab Quivira, Hawikuh, Pecos, PUEBLO BONITO, Salmon and Shabik'eshchee, and those in Colorado include CLIFF PALACE, Sand Canyon and Yellow Jacket. Arroyo Hondo, a 1100-room site located in the northern Rio Grande region, is one of the largest of the Anasazi pueblos; it was excavated in 1971–4 (see Schwarz 1979–93).

R.G. Montgomery et al.: *Franciscan Awatovi* (Harvard, 1939); A.V. Kidder: *An introduction to the study of Southwestern Archaeology* (New Haven, 1962); J.S. Dean: *Chronological analysis of Tsegi phase sites in northeastern Arizona* (Tucson, 1969); W. Smith: *Painted ceramics of the western mound at Awatovi* (Harvard, 1971); D.W. Schwartz, ed.: *Arroyo Hondo archaeological series*, 8 vols (Santa Fe, 1979–93); G.J. Gumerman and J.S. Dean: 'Prehistoric cooperation and competition in the western Anasazi area', *Dynamics of Southwestern prehistory*, ed. L.S. Cordell and G.J. Gumerman (Washington, D.C., 1989), 99–148; R.G. Vivian: *The Chacoan prehistory of the San Juan Basin* (New York, 1990); E.C. Adams and K.A. Hays: *Homol'ovi II: archaeology of an ancestral Hopi village, Arizona* (Tucson, 1991).

JJR

Anatolia The modern region of Anatolia in Turkey corresponds to the area described by Classical writers as Asia Minor, but in pre-Classical times it was by no means a discrete political unit, and parts of it were dominated at different times by several different civilizations, from the HITTITES and CIMMERIANS to the kingdoms of URARTU and PHRYGIA (table 7). In purely geographical terms, Anatolia is sometimes defined as a wide 'land-bridge' between Europe and Asia, effectively linking together the northern and southern coasts of the Mediterranean. See map, opposite, for principal sites.

J. Mellaart: *The archaeology of ancient Turkey* (Oxford, 1978); O.R. Gurney: *The Hittites*, 2nd edn (Harmondsworth, 1981); S. Lloyd: *Ancient Turkey: a traveller's history of Anatolia* (London, 1989); M. Roaf: *Cultural atlas of Mesopotamia and the Ancient Near East* (New York and Oxford, 1990).

'anatomically modern' humans (AMH) Term used to describe the first hominids in the line of HUMAN EVOLUTION that, in anatomical terms, resemble modern humans and belong to the subspecies *Homo sapiens sapiens*. It is a somewhat confusing term since, like other hominid species,

Neolithic	8000 – 4500 BC
Chalcolithic	4500 – 3000 BC
Early Bronze Age	3000 – 2000 BC
Middle Bronze Age	2000 – 1500 BC
Hittite Old Kingdom	1700 – 1500 BC
Late Bronze Age	1500 – 1200 BC
Hittite Empire	1400 – 1200 BC
Iron Age	1200 – 546 BC
Dark Age	1200 – 1000 BC
Neo-Hittite (Luwian) period	1000 – 700 BC
Urartian Kingdom	900 – 600 BC
Achaemenid period	546 – 330 BC
Macedonian period	330 – 307 BC
Seleucid period	305 – 64 BC
Parthian period	250 BC – AD 224
Attalids of Pergamum	230 – 133 BC
Roman Empire	133 BC – AD 395

Table 7 **Anatolia** Chronology of Anatolia.

the early representatives are in fact markedly different from the later examples (such as ourselves). For instance, the examples from QAFZEH AND SKHUL preserve to some extent the brow ridges and larger teeth of more archaic fossils.

The earliest fossil examples of modern human anatomy date from the 130–90,000 BP range, probably the earliest being the Omo-Kibish fossil (*see* OMO). However, these species attributions depend upon cranial remains; post-cranial skeletal material is rare. Nevertheless several specimens, including those from KLASIES RIVER MOUTH and BORDER CAVE, are said to conform with the theory that all living humans are of relatively recent descent from populations living in Africa, as predicted by genetic research and particularly by mitochondrial DNA studies. (Although there is still some uncertainty over the reliability of the microbiological techniques and the theory is not yet proven, *see* DNA ANALYSIS.)

It is clear from sites such as Qafzeh and Skhul that the earlier anatomically modern humans are not always associated with the superior technology that we find with anatomically modern humans in the Upper Palaeolithic. While early anatomically modern humans *may* have been as intelligent and adept as modern man, it is only when their remains are found associated with the kind of advances and art seen in the European Upper Palaeolithic that we can be reasonably *sure* that humans had attained a modern level of intelligence.

P. Mellars and C.B. Stringer, eds: *The human revolution: Behavioural and biological perspectives on the origin of modern humans* (Edinburgh, 1989); R. Foley: *Another unique species* (London, 1987); G. Richards: *Human evolution: an introduction for the behavioural sciences* (London, 1987); C.S. Gamble: *Timewalkers: The prehistory of global colonization* (London, 1993).

PG-B

Anau Central Asian site consisting of two mounds (northern and southern), now within the city of Ashgabad, containing Eneolithic and Bronze Age deposits. First excavated by General Komarov, and later in 1904 by R. Pumpelly, it served as the

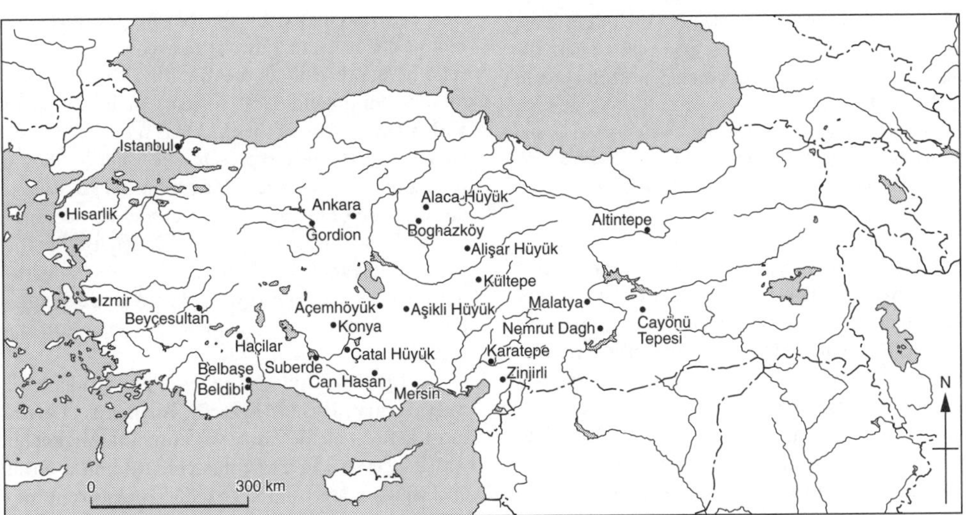

Map 13 **Anatolia** Major sites in the region with individual entries in the Dictionary.

basis for the initial stratigraphic division of Eneolithic to Bronze Age assemblages in the region (Anau I–IV). The lower stratigraphic unit (Anau I) first identified at the northern mound was later subdivided into two sub-units (A and B). The pottery of this stage quite distinct from that of the other early type site in the region, JEITUN, and consists of thin-walled drinking vessels, often with concave bases, with painted geometric decorations. Later this pottery was identified at a number of sites in southern Turkmenistan (Koushut, Mondjukly and Chakmali), and also in Iranian Khorassan, in the upper Atrek valley. The age of Anau IA is estimated by Kohl (1984) as 5200–4800 BC.

P.L. Kohl: *Central Asia: Palaeolithic beginnings to the Iron Age* (Paris, 1984); V.M. Masson: *Pervye civilizacii* (Leningrad, 1989).

PD

Ancient Near East *see* ANATOLIA; MESOPOTAMIA; SYRIA-PALESTINE

Anghelu Ruju Largest rock-cut cemetery of the Sardinian Copper Age. The tombs, entered via a shaft or along a ramp, consist of a main oval or rectangular chamber with smaller secondary and sometimes tertiary chambers. Some of the main chambers are decorated with relief carving, for example framing the doorways or depicting horned bulls' heads. Tombs in other related cemeteries are also provided with striking architectural details: at Sant' Andrea Priu-Bonorva carving imitates raftered roofs, while at Mandra Antine-Thiesi a roof is painted with a red rafter pattern and with a decoration of white spirals on black. Bell-beakers and material of the Ozieri culture – including some schematic female figurines – recovered from the tombs of Anghelu Ruju suggest a date at the end of the 3rd millennium BC.

A. Taramelli: *Alghero: nuovo scavi nella necropole preistorica, Anghelu Ruju*, Monumenta Antichi 19 (1908), col. 397; M. Guido: *Sardinia* (London, 1963), 49–51.

RJA

Angkor Complex of over 250 stone monuments in northwest Cambodia, which formed the centre of the Khmer state from the late 9th century AD until its destruction in 1431. The site's name derives from the Sanskrit term *nagara*, or holy city, but it was originally known as Yasodharapura after its founder, Yasovarman I. Established by the ruling dynasty of Jayavarman II in AD 802, the Khmer state was based on a major change in political organization in which central authority over provinces replaced the previous system of numerous court centres vying for supremacy. This centralization focused on the person of the overlord, manifested in the royal cult of the 'God who is king'. Angkor grew as successive rulers instituted extensive building programmes. These included palaces, reservoirs for water storage and reticulation, and temple mausolea (such as the Bayon mausoleum at Angkor Thom). The last served as burial places for rulers and their close kin, and as temples for worshipping the dead ruler. The Khmer overlords embraced Hinduism and, less often, Buddhism. A network of roads radiated from Angkor, and surplus produce from the provinces was assigned to the maintenance of the numerous temples and their functionaries. With time, a complex hierarchy of offices developed, and, from 1181 onwards, under Jayavarman VII, building programmes reached such a scale that the sustaining area became exhausted. Angkor began as a ceremonial centre, but in later stages must have incorporated a large secular population. There followed a decline in central power and ultimately Angkor fell to a Thai invasion.

1. *Angkor Thom.* At the heart of the city was a massive square-walled precinct known as Angkor Thom. It consisted of an area of 9 sq. km surrounded by 8-metre high walls and a 100 m wide moat. The walls and moat represent the mountain range and ocean which bounds the cosmos. Outside each main gate there is a stone representation of a battle between the heavenly and underworld gods over a serpent; these depict gods and demons churning the ocean to extract the liquor of immortality. The enclosed area, which was more a sacred precinct than a residential area, contains the Phimeanakas or royal palace, while the centre is dominated by the Bayon, Jayavarman's temple mausoleum. Jayavarman considered himself the apotheosis of the Buddha, therefore the mausoleum includes 50 towers, each decorated with a huge image of the Buddha. Wheatley (1983) contends that these represent the Buddha multiplying himself to confuse his enemies. Fish carved on the exterior walls indicate the netherworld below the oceans, portraying the Bayon itself as the home of the gods. The building was erected without the care of the nearby Angkor Wat, during the building frenzy which characterized Jayavarman's reign.

2. *Angkor Wat.* Built as the temple mausoleum of Suryavarman II (AD 1113–50), Angkor Wat is the most famous of the many structures at Angkor. It was conceived on a giant scale, the outer moat enclosing an area of 195 ha. The enclosure incorporates a series of square walled precincts which culminate with five central sandstone towers in the

form of lotus buds – the tallest such 'TEMPLE MOUNTAIN', rising to a height of 65 m. The walls were decorated with bas reliefs, the longest ever recorded. Thus, the outer terrace incorporates over 800 m of reliefs to a height of 2 m. These portray scenes from Indian epics and the life of the king himself, whose posthumous name, Paramavisnuloka, means 'one who has gone to the supreme world of Visnu'.

Cosmic imagery permeates the structure of Angkor Wat. The length of the central raised precinct measures 365.37 *hat* (the Khmer unit of measurement), thus symbolizing the number of days in the year. The four major axial distances of the great causeway correspond to the four eras in the Hindu conception of time. The layout of the temple mountain permitted the prediction of eclipses and as the sun progresses on its annual round so, in the earlier part of the year, it illuminates the bas reliefs of the creation, while during the autumn equinox it highlights scenes from the Battle of Kurukshetra. This link with the sun is reflected also in the King's name, for Suryavarman, a Sanskrit name, means 'protegé of the sun'.

L.P. Briggs: 'The ancient Khmer empire', *TAPS* 4/1 (1951); B.P. Groslier: *Angkor: art and civilization* (London, 1966); P. Wheatley: *The pivot of the four quarters* (Chicago, 1971), 437–8; R. Stencel et al.: 'Astronomy and cosmology at Angkor Wat' *Science* 193 (1976), 281–7; P. Wheatley: *Nagara and commandery* (Chicago, 1983); C.F.W. Highman: *The archaeology of mainland Southeast Asia* (Cambridge, 1989).

CH

Angkor Borei *see* FUNAN

Angkor Thom *see* ANGKOR

Angkor Wat *see* ANGKOR

Angles-sur-l'Anglin (Le Roc-aux-sorciers)

Two cave-shelter sites exhibiting Upper Palaeolithic art, situated in Vienne, France. Part of the very fine low-relief (and originally painted) friezes which decorated the walls and ceiling remain *in situ*, while fallen fragments are stored in the Musée des Antiquités Nationales, St Germain-en-Laye. The friezes depict bison, horses (including remarkable horse heads), ibex and other animals; there is also a famous deep engraving of three 'Venuses' – in fact, female thighs and pubic triangles in half-profile, quarter profile and full view – and an engraved and painted male head. The sculptures were sealed in a 'Final Magdelanian' layer just above a Magdalenian III deposit containing picks, pigment, ochre and spatulas, and may date to *c*.13,000–14,000 BC.

S. de Saint-Mathurin and D. Garrod: 'La frise sculptée du Roc-aux-sorciers à Angles-sur-l'Anglin (Vienne)', *L'Anthropologie* 55 (1951), 413–23; S. de Saint-Mathurin: 'Les sculptures rupestres du Roc-aux-Sorciers', *Dossiers d'Histoire et Archéologie* 131 (1988), 42–9.

RJA

Annales

Influential French school of historians (linked to the journal *Annales: économies, sociétés, civilizations*, published from 1929) which gained currency among Anglophone historians and geographers in the 1970s. The first important example of the Annaliste approach in history (also known as 'structural history' or 'total history') was Ferdinand Braudel's study of the Mediterranean region in the 16th century AD, published in 1949, which was divided into three sections, each corresponding to a kind of temporal 'wave-length': (1) analysis of the interaction between physical geography and cultural change during what he described as the *longue durée* (the 'long term', i.e. very long periods of time such as centuries and perhaps even millennia); (2) the study of the forces (or *conjonctures*) which affect culture and society in the *moyenne durée* (medium term, i.e. decades or generations); (3) the study of the world of the *évenements* (events) or incidents within the lifetimes of individuals, i.e. traditional narrative-style political history.

Within the medium- and long-term frames, Braudel sought to understand the *mentalités* (world-views or ideologies) that characterized different social, geographical or ethnic groupings over very long periods of time. He was then able to study the more ephemeral *évenements* within the explanatory context of the long-term *mentalités*. John Bintliff (1991:8) argues that 'as a theory of how the world works, and how we can reconcile in a single methodology the general and the particular, the event and the general trend, the individual and the community or society, Braudel's Structural History is a landmark with inexhaustible potential', although he notes that Braudel ultimately fails to solve the problem of properly linking long-term change with rapid short-term events. Emmanuel Le Roy Ladurie's description of medieval life in the 14th-century village of Montaillou (Ladurie 1975) is somewhat more successful in terms of linking events with long-term cycles in such areas as economics and demography.

The original Annales approach is defined by Stoianovitch (1976: 19) as 'the attempt by French scholars to adapt economic, linguistic, sociological, geographic, anthropological, psychological, and natural-science notions to the study of history and to infuse an historical orientation into the social and human sciences'. In practice, this meant that Annales school historians turned away from treating history as a chronology of political events, and instead used a much wider, multidisciplinary approach to explain social change over extended periods of time.

The Annales school was applied to archaeological data from the 1980s onwards, partly as a means of encouraging a more multidisciplinary approach to archaeological data, but partly also as a means of dealing with an archaeological dilemma: how to harmonize the analysis of the archaeological remains of the activities of individuals with the study of long-term trends of social, cultural and economic change. The Annales school also offers some possible solutions to the difficulty of reconciling textual and archaeological sources employed by protohistoric and historical archaeologists. In comparing Annaliste historians with Annaliste archaeologists, the American prehistorian Patricia Galloway notes that both tend to be concerned primarily with a similar form of data, whether 'censuses, ledgers, baptismal records, and customs declarations' or 'potsherd counts, records of burial layouts, and distribution of sites over a landscape' (quoted in Bintliff 1991: 115). Archaeologists, however, have encountered some difficulties in agreeing on the lengths of time to which Braudel's three temporalities correspond, e.g. is the *longue durée* a period of centuries or millennia, and is something like the Neolithic Revolution an *évenement*?

James Lewthwaite (1987: 31) has taken a Braudelian stance on the BEAKER PHENOMENON of the European Chalcolithic period (*c*.2500–1800 BC), arguing that 'it is possible to recognise the Beaker *conjoncture* proper (the introduction of west-central European cultural traits into the western Mediterranean) as immediately consequent upon a previous *conjoncture* of intensified interaction throughout the Mediterranean'. He envisages the Beaker phenomenon as a *conjoncture* taking place amid various long-term processes of the Neolithic–Bronze Age *longue durée*, such as 'high pressure, pan-Mediterranean innovation and interaction' (e.g. the commercial and colonial achievements of the Phoenicians, Greeks and Carthaginians), 'low pressure situations of continental impingement on the Mediterranean' (e.g. the erruptions of the Celts and Galatians and, in later times, the Crusades). The Beaker phenomenon would thus arguably be (1) a *conjoncture* within the process of 'continental impingement', and (2) an 'epochal turning point' between the centripetality of the Mediterranean region in the Neolithic period and its centrifugality in the Bronze Age and later.

In one of the most impressive applications of the approach, John Bintliff (1991: 19–26) combines (1) anecdotal evidence of incidents (*évenements*) of famine and debt in the Boeotian region of central Greece in the late 3rd and early 2nd century BC, with (2) the 2nd-century Greek historian Polybius' accounts of trends of economic decline in Boeotia in the *moyenne durée*, and (3) archaeological evidence indicating the gradual depopulation of the landscape and reduction in the size of settlements, as a result of a long-term agricultural cycle that appears to be operating in successive phases of four or five centuries.

The early Annales school set out by Braudel complements the PROCESSUAL ARCHAEOLOGY later championed by Lewis Binford and Colin Renfrew, in that both are concerned with POSITIVIST analysis of long-term, anonymous processes of change (and Braudel's *mentalités* are in some respects similar to Binford's 'laws' of cultural dynamics), as opposed to the more particularist aspects of traditional political history. Ironically, the more recent exponents of the Annales approach (e.g. Ladurie) have moved away from positivism and environmental determinism towards a concern with symbols, individuals and *évenements* that aligns them more closely with the POST-PROCESSUAL archaeologists. However, Bintliff (1991: 1–6) suggests that the Annales style of archaeological analysis and interpretation can be very effective precisely *because* it combines complementary aspects of both processual and post-processual approaches.

F. Braudel: *La Méditerranée et le monde méditerranéen à l'époque de Philippe II* (Paris, 1949) [trans. S. Reynolds, London, 1972]; E.L. Ladurie: *Montaillou* (Paris, 1975); T. Stoianovitch: *French historical method: the Annales paradigm* (Ithaca, 1976); C.C. Lamberg-Karlovsky: 'The longue durée of the Ancient Near East', *De l'Indus aux Balkans, receuil Jean Deshayes*, ed. J.-L. Huot, M. Yon and Y. Calvet (Paris, 1985), 55–72; I. Hodder: *Archaeology of the long term* (Cambridge, 1987); J. Lewthwaite: 'The Braudelian beaker: a Chalcolithic conjuncture in western Mediterranean prehistory', *Bell beakers of the western Mediterranean*, ed. W.H. Waldren and R.C. Kennard (Oxford, 1987), 31–60; J. Bintliff, ed.: *The Annales school and archaeology* (Leicester and London, 1991); A.B. Knapp, ed.: *Archaeology, Annales and ethnohistory* (Cambridge, 1992) [reviewed by G.L. Barnes, *JESHO* 37/4 (1994), 328–31].

IS

Anshan *see* PERSIA; *and* TAL-I MALYAN

Antequera Group of passage graves of the 3rd millennium BC near the town of Antequera, about 40 km north of Malaga, Spain. Some of the finest monuments of their type in Iberia, the most interesting architecturally is the Cueva de Romeral, the circular mound (90 m diam.) of which covers a dry-stone passage roofed with megaliths and two round dry-stone chambers. The larger chamber (4.5 m diam.) is connected to the smaller one, which contains a supposed 'altar' slab, by a short secondary passage. Both chambers have domed corbelled roofs – topped with a slab – and the tomb is thus sometimes described as a 'THOLOS'-type construction, after the (otherwise unrelated) beehive-shaped tombs of the Aegean. Underneath the mound (*c.*50 m diam.) of the Cueva de la Menga a short passage leads to an exceptionally large, oval (6.5 m wide) megalithic chamber roofed with huge capstones supported by three pillars. An orthostat in the passage is decorated with anthropomorphic figures and a star-like design. The long (originally *c.*30 m) passage of the Cueva de la Viera, under a mound of 60 m diameter, is lined and roofed with megaliths; the passage, the chamber, and an additional space beyond the small slab-built chamber are all entered via porthole slabs.

C. de Mergelina: 'La necrópolis tartesia de Antequera', *Actas y memórias de la Sociedad Español de Antropología, Etnografía y Prehistoria* 1 (1922), 37–90; R. Joussaume: *Dolmens for the Dead*, trans. A. and C. Chippendale (London, 1988), 188–94.

RJA

antiquarianism Term used to refer to the study of the ancient world before archaeology emerged as a discipline. Antiquarianism first appeared in the 15th century as a historical branch of Renaissance humanism. Perhaps the earliest writer to be specifically described as an 'antiquario' was the Italian epigrapher Felice Feliciano (1433–80), but there were many other European scholars in the early 15th century who were studying 'antiquities' (although the word 'antiquity' was not used in its modern sense until Andrea Fulvio's *Antiquitates urbis* of 1527).

Most of the early antiquaries were more historians than proto-archaeologists or prehistorians, although the archetypal antiquary was increasingly distinguished from the historian by his supposed obsession with ancient objects, particularly in the form of the so-called 'cabinet of curiosities' (typically consisting of coins, medals and flint arrowheads); these were often disparaged by contemporaries in comparison with collections of sculpture or paintings. The overriding link between the antiquary and the early archaeologist was therefore the concern with physical antiquities as opposed to ancient texts. The key difference is that antiquaries tended to be interested in antiquities alone rather than their archaeological and cultural contexts.

The best-known of the 17th-century antiquaries was John Aubrey (1626–97), whose studies of Stonehenge and Avebury, published in his *Monumenta Britannica* (*c.*1675), led him to identify them as the temples of the druids (see Hunter 1975). However, the scholar who probably brought the world of antiquarianism closest to the brink of early archaeology was William Stukeley (1687–1785), whose theodolite surveys and perspective drawings of STONEHENGE and AVEBURY, as well as his recognition of prehistoric field systems, lead Piggott to describe him as a 'field archaeologist'.

T.D. Kendrick: *British Antiquity* (London, 1950); M. Hunter: *John Aubrey and the realm of learning* (London, 1975); S. Piggott: *William Stukeley* (London, 1985); J.M. Levine: *Humanism and history* (Cornell, 1987); S. Piggott: *Ancient Britons and the antiquarian imagination: ideas from the Renaissance to the Regency* (London, 1989); B.G. Trigger: *A history of archaeological thought* (Cambridge, 1989), 27–72.

IS

Antrea Find-site of early Mesolithic objects near the hamlet of Antrea-Korpilahti, 15 km east of Viborg. The site is now in Russia, about 20 km southeast of the Russo-Finish border, and it was first reported by Pälsi in 1920. The finds included a fishing net, which consisted of double-threaded cord, made from the bast of willow bark, with 18 oblong pine-bark floats and sink stones. The stone implements included adzes and a chisel with its working edge hollowed by polishing to a gouge-like form. Among the bone and antler implements was a knife handle made from a pointed piece of elk shin-bone; a hollow chisel made from a tubular bone; a short stout point; a knife-like tool with traces of engraved lines. Samples of the net and the bark float presented uncalibrated dates of 9230 ± 210 BP (Hel-269) and 9310 ± 140 BP (Hel-1301).

S. Pälsi: 'Ein steinzeitlicher Moorfund', *SMA* 28 (1920), 1–19; V. Luho: 'Die Suomusjärvi-Kultur', *SMA* 66 (1967), 1–120; D.L. Clarke: *The earlier Stone Age settlement in Scandinavia* (Cambridge, 1975).

PD

Anuradhapura Ancient capital of Sri Lanka (*c.*AD 200–1000), located on the Aruvi river, 170 km northeast of Colombo. The walled core (citadel area) of the city and its surrounding Buddhist monasteries extended over an area of about

40 sq. km. Architectural remains include palaces, stupas and a rock-cut temple.

J. Uduwara: *Illustrated guide to the Museum of Archaeology, Anuradhapura* (Anuradhapura, 1962); S.U. Deraniyagala: 'The citadel of Anuradhapura 1969: excavations in the Gedige area', *Ancient Ceylon* 2 (1972), 48–169; C. Wikramgange: *Abhayagiri Vihara Project, Anuradhapura: first report of excavations* (Colombo, 1984).

CS

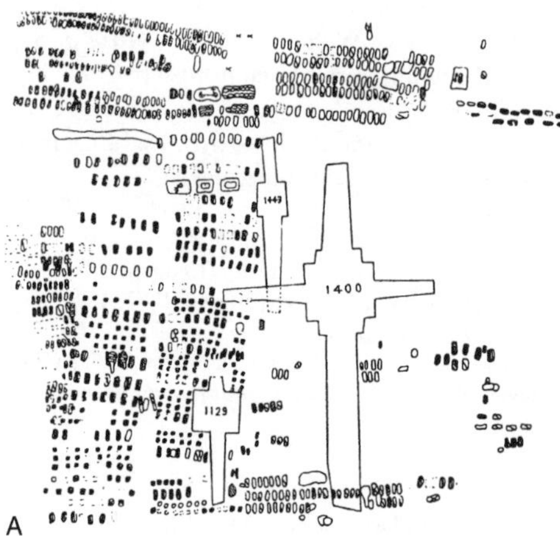

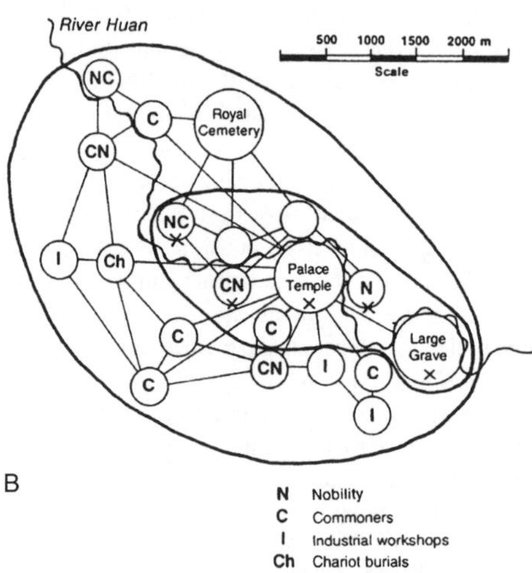

Figure 4 **An-yang** (A) Plan of typical royal burials (M1129, M1400 and M1422) at Hsi-pei-kang, An-yang, with long ramps leading down to the tombs, and numerous single and multiple burials arranged alongside; (B) structural model of the An-yang urban network during the Shang period, based on archaeological foci. *Source*: Chang Kwang-chih: *Shang China* (New Haven and London, 1980), p. 130.

An-yang (Anyang: 'ruins of Yin') Area of settlement and funerary sites in the province of Ho-nan, China, which was both the last capital of the SHANG dynasty (*c.*1400–1122 BC, *see* CHINA 2) and the first major region of China to be subjected to intensive modern excavation. The earliest excavations took place between 1928 and 1937, in and around the village of Hsiao-t'un and in the major 'royal' tomb area at Hsi-pei-kang (also known by the names of nearby villages such as Wu-kuan-ts'un-pei-ti and Hou-chia-chuang). The work was directed by Li Chi and scholars of the Academia Sinica, Peking, and included the recovery of some 17,000 inscribed ORACLE BONES and turtle *plastrons* from the storage pit, YH 127, during the winter of 1936–7; they were carefully lifted out of the ground as a solid mass of material, thus allowing a precise record of each fragment's original placement to be made during the cleaning process. A similar find of some 5000 inscribed oracle bones in 1972 at the Hsiao-t'un Nan-ti site has added to the considerable volume of these invaluable primary documents (*see* CHINA 3).

The principal tombs at Hsi-pei-kang are mainly of a characteristic cross-shape with ramps leading from the original ground level to the floor of the tomb pit (figure 4A). The occupant (presumably royal) was laid in a wooden chamber built to a height of about 3 m together with a large quantity of grave goods of which only a small number remains because of robbery in recent and earlier times. Outside the chamber, and along the ramps, further goods were placed and sacrificial victims (human as well as animal) were interred.

Nearby in this funerary area, and possibly related to the royal tombs, are many small burials (single and multiple – some with skulls only, others with bodies only), horse-burials, pits with elephants and other animals, and chariots. Settlement sites include appreciably large foundations of many layers of rammed earth (*hang-t'u*) in the Hsiao-t'un Locus North sector which have been classed as 'palace foundations'. Sufficient evidence remained to show that wooden structures comprising posts resting on stone supports, with wattle-and-daub walls, and thatched roofs had been built on these. Elsewhere the dwelling remains of the general populace consisted mainly of semi-subterranean structures of round shape which appear to have differed little from the pit-houses of the late Neolithic period. Workshop areas were evident and the various industrial activities in which much of the populace was engaged seem to have been concentrated in areas of specialized manufacturing: large quantities of stone knives were found in one sector, bone arrowheads in another, shell and jade working remains in another. In at least two areas, a few ingots of copper and tin, hundreds of clay moulds and crucible fragments demonstrated the extent of bronze manufacturing.

Excavations have continued at the site and in its vicinity since the 1950s; finds of considerable importance have been reported, among which the Fu Hao tomb ranks supreme. The finds include numerous bronze vessels and other bronze artefacts: helmets, chariot fittings, weapons, ornaments, etc., together with stone sculptures, carved ivory and bone, jade, lacquer, sacrificial burials of chariots and horses, all illustrating many aspects of Shang culture and daily life. It has thus been possible to reconstruct from the archaeological loci and associated evidence a model of the urban network which constituted the Shang capital (figure 4B).

Cheng Te-k'un: *Archaeology in China* II: *Shang China* (Cambridge, 1960); D.N. Keightley: *Sources of Shang history: the oracle-bone inscriptions of Bronze Age China* (Berkeley, 1978); Chang Kwang-chih: *Shang China* (New Haven and London, 1980); D.N. Keightley, ed.: *The origins of Chinese civilization* (Berkeley, 1983); Chang Kwang-chih: *The archaeology of ancient China*, 4th edn (New Haven and London, 1986); Chang Kwang-chih, ed.: *Studies of Shang civilization* (New Haven, 1986).

NB

apadana Persian term for the reception hall in the palaces of the Achaemenid rulers (*c*.538–331 BC), such as those at PASARGADAE, PERSEPOLIS and SUSA. It usually consisted of a vast rectangular building with its roof supported by dozens of columns, often built on a terrace and surrounded by columned porticoes. The Persepolis *apadana* had porticoes on three sides and towers at each corner; its 36 stone columns were each almost 20 m in height and were surmounted by impressive capitals in the form of bulls. The architectural antecedents of the *apadana* are perhaps to be found in the square columned halls at pre-Achaemenid sites such as HASANLU, and perhaps even in Urartian structures, such as the palace building at ALTINTEPE.

E.F. Schmidt: *Persepolis* I (Chicago, 1953), 70–90; R. Ghirshman: 'L'apadana de Suse', *IA* 3 (1963), 148–60; H. Frankfort: *The art and architecture of the ancient Orient*, 4th edn (Harmondsworth, 1970), 351–5.

IS

Apis Rock (Nasera) Inselberg incorporating a large rock-shelter, located on the high eastern side of the Serengeti plain in northern Tanzania. Apis Rock was first investigated by Louis Leakey in 1932, who identified a sequence running through 'Developed Levalloisian', 'Proto-Stillbay' and 'STILLBAY' proper to 'MAGOSIAN' and 'WILTON', the last being microlithic (Leakey 1936). The site was more thoroughly excavated by Michael Mehlman in 1975–6; his excavation of nine metres of deposits yielded vast quantities of lithic artefacts and animal bones, as well as pottery in the upper layers, thus providing confirmation of a long (if punctuated) sequence encompassing much of what is informally called the African Middle and Late Stone Age, and spanning the Upper Pleistocene and Holocene. Much of Leakey's nomenclature – together with the theories concerning the evolution of cultures to which it is related – is now redundant; and some of the 'intermediate' categories, such as 'Magosian', may result from the mixing of deposits (as at MAGOSI itself).

L.S.B. Leakey: *Stone Age Africa* (Oxford, 1936), 59–67; M.J. Mehlman: 'Excavations at Nasera Rock', *Azania* 12 (1977), 111–18.

JS

Apollo 11 Cave Large cave-site in the Huns Mountains, south-west Namibia, which presents evidence for some of the earliest art in Africa. Four distinct levels of MSA (Middle Stone Age) assemblages include one showing affinities with the HOWIESON'S POORT industry, radiocarbon-dated to uncal >48,000 BP, and including worked ostrich eggshell and a pebble with faint traces of red paint. Above the MSA (Middle Stone Age) level there is an early LSA (Later Stone Age) level (uncal 19,760–12,510 BP) which may be a local (and early) expression of the ALBANY INDUSTRY, with ostrich eggshell beads, bone beads, bone tools and ostrich eggshell containers. Later levels contain typical Holocene microlithic assemblages (WILTON INDUSTRY) with an early commencing date of uncal 10,420 BP. The cave is most notable for a group of seven painted tablets of stone recovered as a group from an horizon dating to between uncal 25,500 and 27,500 BP, associated with MSA artefacts. The paintings include an animal thought to be a feline, but with human hind legs, suggesting a direct link with therianthropic paintings of Holocene age.

E. Wendt: '"Art Mobilier" from Apollo 11 Cave, South West Africa: Africa's oldest dated works of art', *SAAB*, 31 (1976), 5–11.

RI

Aqar Quf *see* KASSITES

Aquatic civilization (or 'aqualithic') Term coined by John Sutton to describe 'communities whose livelihood and outlook on life revolved around lakes and rivers'. The aqualithic sites occupied a belt or arc in 'Middle Africa' (much of it now very dry) from Senegal in the west to Kenya in the east, in the period of 10,000–4000 BP. The culture was characterized archaeologically by bone harpoons and by independently invented pottery decorated with wavy and dotted wavy line motifs, of the type first recognized by A.J. Arkell at Khartoum (*see* EARLY KHARTOUM). Created by a Negroid population probably bearing some relation to the present-day speakers of J.H. Greenberg's Nilo–Saharan language family, it was a 'non-Neolithic' culture, i.e. not associated with either agriculture or domestication, but with a pottery-based 'new gastronomy' constituting a 'soup, porridge, and fish-stew revolution'. According to Sutton, the success of the aquatic lifestyle may have hampered the spread of the 'Neolithic' in Africa, but nonetheless under its impact the aquatic cultural complex began to break up from around 7000 BP onwards. What followed were no more than late 'regional revivals' such as that characterized by KANSYORE ware in Kenya. 'In the long run the aquatic way of life was unable to compete with the food-producing one'.

Subsequent modifications to, or criticisms of, Sutton's model relate to its chronology, archaeological content and philosophical basis: (1) A.B. Smith points out that, following the appearance of domestic cattle, sheep and/or goats in the Sahara at about 7000 BP, the region was dominated by pastoralists, and it is difficult to be certain that these were the same people as the preceding lake dwellers. Kansyore ware in Kenya (if indeed it can be connected to that in the rest of the area) also turns out not to be so late after all, according to Peter Robertshaw. Hence Sutton's 'lacustrine tradition' may be confined to the early Holocene. (2) The cultural unity of the area, which is supposed to belong to the Neolithic of Sudanese Tradition, has been much exaggerated, according to T.R. Hays. There may have been a Khartoum 'horizon-style' in the pottery, but otherwise there is little to link the disparate settlements of the Sahara in the early Holocene. (3) B.W. Andah takes issue with the 'non-Neolithic' emphasis of Sutton's work, since he believes it distracts attention from the possibilities and processes of indigenous African development of agriculture, and in his view tends to portray the early Holocene inhabitants of the area as mere passive reactors to their environment.

J.E.G. Sutton: 'The aquatic civilization of Middle Africa', *JAH* 15 (1974), 527–46; T.R. Hays: 'An examination of the Sudanese Neolithic', *Proceedings of the Panafrican Congress of Prehistory and Quaternary Studies VIIth session Addis Ababa 1971*, ed. Abebe Berhanou, J. Chavaillon and J.E.G. Sutton (Addis Ababa, 1976), 85–92; J.E.G. Sutton: 'The African aqualithic' *Antiquity*, 51 (1977), 25–34; A.B. Smith: 'The Neolithic tradition in the Sahara', *The Sahara and the Nile*, ed. M.A.J. Williams and H. Faure (Rotterdam, 1980), 451–65; B.W. Andah: 'Early food producing societies and antecedents in Middle Africa', *WAJA* 17 (1987), 129–70; P. Robertshaw: 'Gogo Falls, excavations at a complex archaeological site east of Lake Victoria', *Azania* 26 (1991) 63–195.

PA-J

Arabia, pre-Islamic The pre-Islamic archaeological remains of the Arabian peninsula are still poorly known, owing to a relative dearth of excavation in Yemen and Saudi Arabia, although a great deal of evidence is beginning to emerge concerning the pre-Islamic Gulf region. There were earlier European explorers in the region, such as Johann Wild, Carsten Niebuhr and Joseph Pitts in the early 17th century, but the first to examine the antiquities in any detail were the late 19th-century travellers, Charles Doughty (who particularly studied the NABATAEAN city of Madain Salih), Charles Huber and Sir Richard Burton. The archaeological remains of Central Arabia, particularly the rock carvings (some possibly dating as early as 10,000 BC), were investigated by Harry St John Philby in the 1930s and 1950s. Most modern researches have concentrated along the Gulf coast, including excavations on the islands of BAHRAIN, FAILAKA and UMM AN-NAR. The first genuine stratigraphic excavation of a pre-Islamic site in Arabia was undertaken in 1950–1 at Hajar Bin Humeid, uncovering at least 19 major phases of occupation (*c*.1000 BC–AD 500) and providing an extremely useful chronological sequence of southwest Arabian ceramics (Van Beek 1969).

The survey of the site of Dosariyah, in eastern Saudi Arabia, has revealed UBAID (*c*.5000–3800 BC) ceramics imported from Mesopotamia, as well as faunal remains probably indicating early domestication of sheep and goats. Evidence of early contacts with Mesopotamia has also survived at a number of other sites, such as Hafit, a mountain ridge in southeastern Arabia, where JEMDET NASR (*c*.3100–2900 BC) pottery and beads (as well as locally produced artefacts) were excavated in a number of burial-cairns. A much later Arabian site with strong Mesopotamian connections is Tayma (or Teima), a settlement in the Hejaz area of northwestern Arabia, which assumed surprising importance in the mid-6th century BC, when the neo-Babylonian ruler Nabonidus chose to spend about a decade there in preference to his capital, BABYLON (perhaps as part of an attempt to forge an alliance with the Arabs against the PERSIANS). The

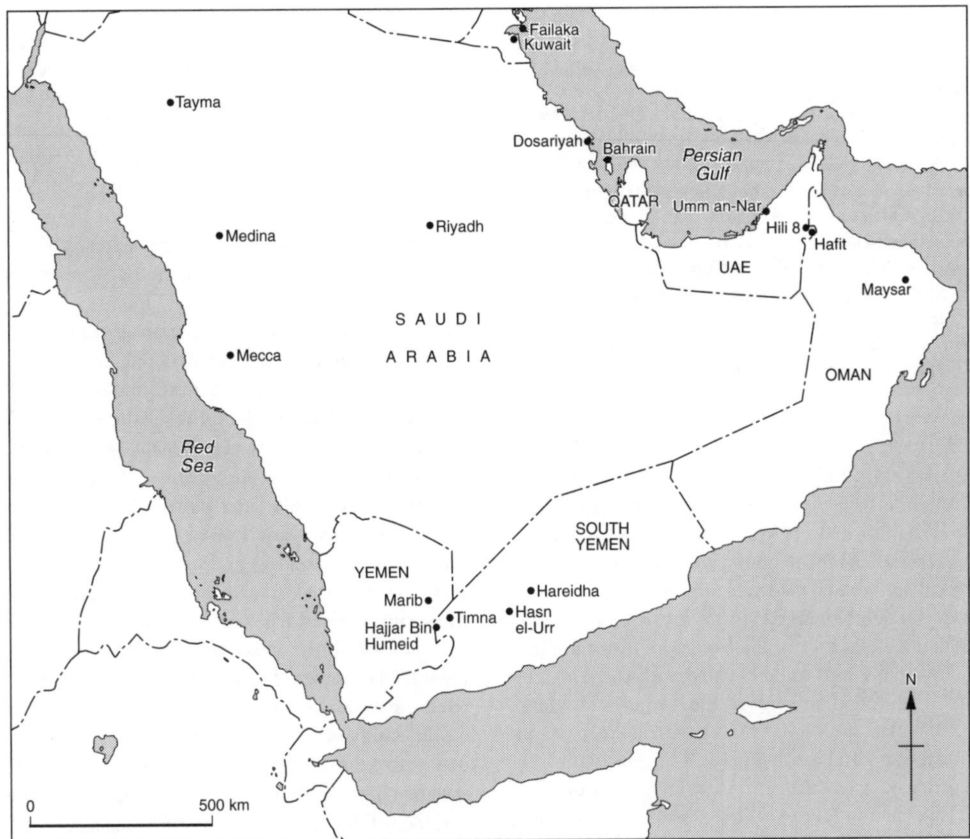

Map 14 **Arabia, pre-Islamic** Some major sites in the region.

excavation of Tayma has revealed continued links with Mesopotamia after the time of Nabonidus, in the form of a set of stone reliefs incorporating Achaemenid-style motifs.

The site of Hili 8, excavated by S. Cleuziou, is one of several settlements of the 3rd to early 2nd millennium BC in southeastern Arabia. The excavation of Hili 8 has enabled the material culture of Bronze Age Arabia to be arranged into a coherent sequence, with regard to pottery and architecture, as well as demonstrating the use of oasis farming, including very early exploitation of sorghum, possibly pre-dating its use in Africa. Both Hili 8 and Maysar, a Bronze-Age site in Oman, are associated with the Umm an-Nar cultural phase. The evidence of copper processing at Maysar is of some significance in that copper appears to have been the primary material exported from the district of Magan (a Mesopotamian term which probably referred to the whole of Oman).

During the 1st millennium BC southern Arabia was dominated by the Qatabanaeans, Minaeans and Sabaeans, as well as the kingdom of Hadramaut. The Qatabanaeans had their capital at Timnaʿ (Hajar Kohlan); this was a walled city occupied continuously from the mid-1st millennium BC until its destruction after defeat by the people of Hadramaut in the 1st century AD. About 2 km to the north of the walled city of Timnaʿ was a cemetery in which rich grave goods, including items of statue and jewellery, were found. The Minaeans' capital was Qarnawu.

The Sabaeans have left behind an extensive corpus of texts (von Wissmann 1975–82; Kitchen 1994: 80–111, 190–222). Their capital city, Marib, was a 15-hectare site in the Wadi Dhana in northern Yemen, excavated in the 1950s and 1970s. Facing the city, on the opposite side of the wadi, was the temple of Haram Bilqis, while the wadi itself was the site of a large dam, contemporary with the city. *See also* HATRA, ISLAMIC ARCHAEOLOGY *and* AL-RABADHA.

E. Anati: *Rock art in central Arabia* (Louvain, 1968); G.W. van Beek: *Hajar Bin Humeid: investigations at a pre-Islamic site in South Arabia* (Baltimore, 1969); D. O'Leary: *Arabia before Muhammad* (New York, 1973); H. von Wissmann: *Die Geschichte von Saba'*, 2 vols (Vienna, 1975–82); ——: *Die Mauer der Sabäerhauptstadt Maryab* (Istanbul, 1976); J.F.A. Sawyer and D.J.A. Clines, ed.: *Midia, Moab and Edom* (Sheffield, 1983); D.T. Potts, ed.: *Araby the blest: studies in Arabian archaeology* (Copenhagen, 1988); D.T. Potts: *The Arabian Gulf in antiquity*, 2 vols (Oxford, 1990); A. Invernizzi and J.-F. Salles, ed.: *Arabia antiqua: Hellenistic centres around Arabia* (Rome, 1993); K.A. Kitchen: *Documentation for ancient Arabia* I (Liverpool, 1994).

IS

Aramaeans Cultural group of the Ancient Near East whose origins are a matter of some debate: their West Semitic dialect (Aramaic), resembling Arabic, suggests an Arabian homeland, but the archaeological and textual evidence appear to indicate that they initially emerged from the region of the FERTILE CRESCENT in the late 2nd millennium BC. They are perhaps to be equated with the Ahlamu, first mentioned in one of the 'Amarna Letters' (*c.*1350 BC; *see* EL-AMARNA), particularly as an inscription of Tiglath-Pileser I in the late 12th century BC uses the term 'Ahlamu-Aramaeans'.

Like their predecessors the AMORITES, they were clearly originally bedouins, but by the 12th century BC they had begun to settle over an increasing area, arranging themselves into territories dominated by particular tribal groups. The tribal names each consisted of the word *bit* ('house') followed by the name of their principal ancestor, such as Bit-Adini. Nicholas Postgate (1974) has argued that – in north Mesopotamia at least – the Aramaeans may have been restricted to particular fortified towns, since there is little archaeological evidence for small rural settlements in the surrounding areas during the Middle Assyrian period. Indeed the fertile land of north Mesopotamia appears to have been under-used during the period of Aramaean incursions, and correspondingly there seems to be considerable evidence for a deliberate programme of resettlement in the area during the Neo-Babylonian period (*c.*625–539 BC).

In Syria the Aramaeans took control of a number of AMORITE and CANAANITE areas, including Hama and Damascus, and posed a persistent threat to the kingdom of Israel during the reigns of David and Solomon (*c.*1044–974 BC). In the 10th century BC they appear to have occupied several other cities in the Levant, including ZINJIRLI and Til Barsip, as well as settling in the region to the east of the northern Euphrates, which became known as 'Aram of the rivers'. They also began to make incursions into Mesopotamia, settling in the KHABUR valley at the ancient site of HALAF, renamed Guzana, and establishing numerous kingdoms within Babylonia. By the 8th century BC, however, the resurgent Assyrians were apparently able to profit from discord between the various Aramaean states, perhaps even temporarily uniting with the Babylonians in order to drive them out of many of their Mesopotamian and northern Syrian strongholds.

In terms of religion and material culture, the Aramaeans often appear to have integrated with the local populations where they settled, although at Tell Halaf there are the remains of a temple usually interpreted as a specifically Aramaean foundation. Undoubtedly their most enduring impact on the Near East was achieved through the spread of the Aramaic language and script. Their language gradually replaced Akkadian in Babylonia, while the script, derived from the PHOENICIAN alphabet and ancestral to modern Arabic, eventually completely replaced the cuneiform script in Mesopotamia.

The study of the archaeological and textual evidence for the Aramaeans presents an intriguing instance of the difficulties encountered in defining and identifying the material culture of a group with essentially nomadic origins and traditions. This problem also contributes to the general uncertainty as to the means by which the Aramaeans apparently spread so effectively across the Near East – as with the HYKSOS in Egypt, their eventual military defeats are well documented, but it is not clear whether they had originally gained control through invasion or simply through gradual infiltration (see Dupont-Sommer 1949; Postgate 1974).

S. Schiffer: *Die Aramäer* (Leipzig, 1911); A. Dupont-Sommer: *Les Araméens* (Paris, 1949); A Malamat: 'The Aramaeans', *Peoples of Old Testament Times*, ed. D.J. Wiseman (London, 1973), 134–55; J.N. Postgate: 'Some remarks on conditions in the Assyrian countryside', *JESHO* 17 (1974), 225–43; H. Tadmor: 'The aramaization of Assyria: aspects of western impact', *Mesopotamien und seine Nachbaren*, ed. H.J. Nissen and J. Renger (Berlin, 1982), 449–70.

IS

Aramaic *see* ARAMAEANS

Ar-Ar *see* ARGON-ARGON DATING

Ararat *see* URARTU

Araya Late Palaeolithic (30,000 BP–10,000 BC) site in Niigata prefecture, Japan, radiocarbon-dated to 13,200 BP. It is famous as the typesite for Araya burins (made on the ends of large broad flakes which had been previously blunted by abrupt and direct retouch), which are widely distributed throughout northeast Asia.

C. Serizawa: 'Niigata-ken Araya iseki ni okeru saisekkijin bunka to Araya-gata chokokuto ni tsuite', [A new micro-blade industry discovered at the Araya site, and the Araya-type graver] *Dai Yonki Kenkyu* 1/5 (1959), 174–81 [English abstract]; C.M. Aikens and T. Higuchi: *The prehistory of Japan* (London 1982), 74–8.

SK

L'Arbreda Cave in Catalonia, which – together with that of El Castillo near Santander – has produced the earliest dates for Aurignacian UPPER PALAEOLITHIC artefacts in Western Europe. With accelerated radiocarbon dates in the uncal 38,000–40,000 BP range, these sites are significantly earlier than those of the classic French Perigordian sequence, largely dated from ABRI PATAUD. The L'Arbreda dates are much closer to those of 43,000–40,000 BP known for Eastern Europe (e.g. Bacho Kiro cave in Bulgaria). It is claimed that L'Arbreda shows a rapid transition from MOUSTERIAN to Aurignacian, perhaps implying a rapid replacement of indigenous populations.

J.L. Bischoff et al.: 'Abrupt Mousterian/Aurignacian Boundary at c. 40 ka bp: Accelerator ^{14}C dates from L'Arbreda cave (Catalunya, Spain)', *JAS* 16 (1989), 563–76.

PG-B

archaeomagnetic dating Scientific dating technique based on changes in the intensity and direction of the earth's magnetic field with time (*secular variation*). Since the time dependence is not predictable, the measurements need to be calibrated with reference to material of known age.

The earth's magnetic field has two components, dipole and non-dipole. The dipole component arises from electric currents in the fluid part of the core and the non-dipole from the boundary region between the mantle and the core. The field is characterized by its intensity and direction, both of which vary, but the rate of intensity variation is relatively small. Direction is defined by *declination* (the angle between magnetic north and true geographic north) and *inclination* (or angle of dip: the angle from horizontal at which a freely suspended compass needle would lie). The majority of archaeological applications of archaeomagnetism use thermoremanent magnetism (TRM) of ferrimagnetic iron oxide grains in clay. These grains are usually very small and each behaves in effect like a magnet; under normal circumstances they are randomly oriented and there is no net magnetization. If, however, the clay is heated sufficiently, the thermal energy enables partial re-arrangement and alignment with the earth's magnetic field to occur. When the clay cools there is a net, albeit weak, magnetization reflecting both the direction and intensity of the prevailing field of the earth.

The temperatures required are typically 500–700 °C, depending on the size, shape and mineralogy of the grains. Temperatures above about 300 °C lead to TRM that is stable over periods of the order of 100,000 years. Magnetization of grains acquired at significantly lower temperatures is unstable and there is a tendency to re-align with the earth's field as it changes; this component of the magnetization is referred to as *viscous*.

In principle, both intensity and directional changes can be used for dating. However, intensity variation does not have the sensitivity of directional, although it does have the advantage of being usable on samples no longer *in situ*, such as sherds of pottery. It has also occasionally been used to good effect in authenticity testing. Using direction changes requires *in situ* samples, for example, kilns or hearths, and sample orientation must be known. This is now often done by attaching a plastic disc which is levelled and marked with the direction of geographic north. To avoid distortion of the ancient field direction by the magnetism of the structure itself, it is usual to select 12 to 16 sampling positions on a structure such as a kiln. Accurate measurements can be achieved with sample sizes of typically 1 cubic cm in modern magnetometers. Using inclination measurements only, it may be possible to date other ceramics if their function or shape dictate which way up they would have been standing when fired, for example, tiles stacked on end.

In addition to TRM, ferrimagnetic grains can align with the earth's magnetic field through deposition (as in lake sediment), and, provided there is no bioturbation or turbulence, a continuous magnetic record is recorded with depth (*depositional remnant magnetism*: the study of which is one aspect of PALEOMAGNETIC DATING). Samples are extracted by coring. Lake sediment sequences, the organic content of which has been dated by radiocarbon, provide the basis of many of the archaeomagnetic calibration curves but the accuracy and precision of the archaeomagnetic dates derived are then limited by those of RADIOCARBON DATING, and in particular by the problems of radiocarbon calibration. Reference data using TRM on structures dated historically or my dendrochronology clearly have the advantage.

The variation in the earth's magnetic field is cyclical but not predictable. Hence a particular combination of declination and inclination may not be unique, and other broad chronology indicators may be needed to resolve the problem. Nevertheless, where reference curves exist for a region, accuracies of a few decades may be possible. The size of the region over which a calibration curve can be used is typically 50 to 100 km, because of the localized variation in the non-dipole component of field.

D.H. Tarling: *Palaeomagnetism* (London, 1983); A.J. Clark, D.H. Tarling and M. Noel: 'Developments in archaeomagnetic dating in Britain', *JAS* 15 (1988), 645–68; M.J. Aitken: *Science-based dating in archaeology* (London, 1990), 225–61.

SB

Archaic *see* AMERICA 4

Arctic Small Tool tradition (ASTt) Widespread tradition of the North American Arctic, which has been dated to between *c*.2200 and 800 BC. It is characterized by finely made microblades, spalled burins, small side and end scrapers, and side and end blades. The tradition as a whole incorporates a number of other cultural entities, including the Denbigh Flint complex in northern Alaska, the Independence I and Pre-DORSET CULTURES in Arctic Canada, and the Sarqaq culture in Greenland. The ASTt does not appear to be related to the preceding PALEO-ARCTIC TRADITION, and its most likely source is Eastern Siberia. ASTt peoples were the first humans to occupy the Canadian Arctic archipelago and Greenland, apparently entering those regions from Alaska in a rapid population movement around 2000 BC.

D. Damas, ed.: *Handbook of North American Indians* V: *Arctic* (Washington, D.C., 1984).

RP

Arcy-sur-Cure Series of caves/rock shelters on a river terrace in the Yonne region, France, which is one of the most important early Upper Palaeolithic sites in Europe. Each cave or shelter has yielded MOUSTERIAN and CHÂTELPERRONIAN artefacts dating to *c*.35,000–34,000 and 33,000–34,000 BP respectively, making Arcy one of the latest known Châtelperronian sites. Moreover, the material culture of these caves is particularly unusual. In the Grotte du Renne, and possibly in other caves, evidence of structures with central hearths has been excavated. Like some Russian sites, these structures utilised mammoth tusks in their construction. Among Châtelperronian assemblages, Arcy is unique for the presence of bone points and pierced tooth pendants – no bone tools are known from other Châtelperronian sites. If the Châtelperronian is indeed the work of NEANDERTHALS, Arcy represents crucial evidence for the development of an indigenous Upper Palaeolithic tradition alongside the AURIGNACIAN.

C. Farizy, ed.: *Paléolithique moyen récent et paléolithique supérieur ancien en europe* (Nemours, 1990).

PG-B

ard marks Linear scoring of ancient land surfaces caused by an early form of plough (the 'ard'), which broke the ground surface but did not turn the sod. Ard marks usually consist of a series of roughly parallel lines in one direction, with another series forming the 'criss-cross' necessary to thoroughly break up the ground. The marks are most often preserved under European Neolithic barrows, and there is a continuing debate as to whether they occur in this context simply because barrows act to preserve a small part of the ancient landscape (the most likely reason in most cases, see Kristiansen 1990), or whether they represent a 'ploughing ritual' performed to consecrate the area of the funerary monument.

K. Kristiansen: 'Ard marks under barrows: a response to Peter Rowley-Conwy', *Antiquity* 64 (1990), 332–7.

RJA

Arene Candide Cave on the western Ligurian coast, Italy, which has provided an important series of cultural sequences and human and animal bone assemblages dating from the Epigravettian to the Middle Neolithic. The bones of about 20 individuals of the Epigravettian period buried in graves at the site were contemporary with the remains of deer, wild boar, bear, birds and plentiful mollusc shells. Molluscs and wild animals remained an important part of the diet during the early Neolithic, after which there was an increase in the importance of domesticated animals (goats and sheep) and grain; many querns and some milk strainers have been found. The earliest Neolithic levels at Arene Candide provided an interesting collection of CARDIAL pottery, where the design is limited to wide horizontal or zig-zag bands. The cardial pottery levels are followed by a much more developed ceramic assemblage, including typical Ligurian square-mouthed pots decorated with scratched and red and white encrusted designs.

These are followed by layers that yielded Lagozza-style pottery.

L. Bernabo Brea: 'Le Culture preistoriche della Francia meridionale e della Catalogna e la successione stratigrafica della Arene Candide', *Revista di Studi Liguri* 15 (1949), 149–56; P. Francalacci: 'Dietary reconstruction at Arene Candide cave (Liguria, Italy) by means of trace element analysis', *JAS* 16 (1989), 109–24.

RJA

Argin *see* ARKIN

Argissa Settlement mound near Larisa in Thessaly, northern Greece. Excavations by V. Milojcic (1955–8) revealed an important cultural sequence for the region, running from an early 'pre-ceramic' phase (which may, in fact, show evidence of pottery) through Proto-Sesklo, Dimini and Mycenaean phases. The earliest Neolithic evidence at Argissa is associated with ill-defined structures and earth hollows; dwellings later in the Neolithic were timber-framed mudwall constructions. At Argissa, as in other Greek sites of the early Neolithic such as NEA NIKOMEDIA, sheep/goats tend to be more strongly represented in faunal evidence than cattle/pig.

V. Milojcic et al.: *Die deutschen Ausgrabungen auf der Argissa-Magula in Thessalien* (Bonn, 1962).

RJA

argon-argon (Ar-Ar) dating Scientific dating technique related to POTASSIUM-ARGON (K-Ar) dating but offering significant advantages. The basis of the two techniques is the same, but in Ar-Ar dating the ^{40}K content is determined by converting some of it to ^{39}Ar by neutron activation (standards of known K-Ar age determine the neutron flux). This enables the ratio of ^{40}Ar to ^{39}Ar (and hence ^{40}Ar to ^{40}K) to be determined by mass spectrometry on the same sample, thus avoiding sample inhomogeneity. Indeed ^{40}Ar/^{39}Ar measurement can now be made on single mineral grains of about 1 mm diameter (equivalent to a sample weight of about 1 mg) using argon laser fusion to release the gas. Furthermore, by measuring the isotopic ratio of the gas released by the sample during stepped heating to progressively higher temperatures, the reliability of the 'closed system' assumption (*see* POTASSIUM-ARGON DATING) can be assessed: the age should be constant with temperature.

As in K-Ar dating, measurement of ^{36}Ar allows a correction to be made for atmospheric ^{40}Ar incorporated in the mineral on cooling. However, if the initial ^{40}Ar is of non-atmospheric origin (e.g. from nearby outgassing rocks) a K-Ar age in excess of the true age of cooling will result. In Ar-Ar dating, use of an ISOCHRON plot allows other sources of contaminating ^{40}Ar to be detected and circumvented in the age evaluation (for example, the slope of a plot of ^{40}Ar/^{36}Ar *vs.* ^{39}Ar/^{36}Ar will be related by known constants to age and the ^{40}Ar/^{36}Ar intercept will indicate the origin of the initial ^{40}Ar (the atmospheric ^{40}Ar/^{36}Ar ratio is 295.5). The isochron plot requires that the different minerals measured have the same crystallization times (i.e. age), are 'closed systems' and have the same initial ^{40}Ar/^{36}Ar ratio. Deviation from linearity can indicate incorporation of older detrital material.

For bibliography *see* POTASSIUM-ARGON DATING.

SB

Arikamedu Harbour town of the 1st and 2nd centuries AD, located on the Indian Ocean in Tamil Nadu, southeast India. Excavations at Arikamedu by Mortimer Wheeler yielded not only local glass and ceramics but also significant quantities of Mediterranean artefacts, including Roman amphorae, terra sigillata, raw glass, glass beads and vessels.

R.E.M. Wheeler: 'Arikamedu: an Indo-roman trading-station on the east coast of India', *AI* 2 (1946), 17–24; V. Begley and R.D. De Puma, eds: *Rome and India: the ancient sea trade* (Madison, 1991), 125–56.

CS

Arkin, Arkinian A group of Palaeolithic sites near the village of Arkin (3 km from Wadi Halfa) in northern Sudan, incorporating Arkin 8 and 5. Arkin 8 is a late ACHEULEAN encampment with traces of some of the earliest known domestic structures in Egypt and Sudan. Arkin 5 is a Middle Palaeolithic site with distinct clusters of MOUSTERIAN artefacts. Because of its low percentage of finished tools Arkin 5 has been identified as a manufacturing site, but Hoffman (1979) suggests that the inhabitants might have simply been re-using ostensibly unfinished tools. The region of Arkin is also the type-site for one of the two earliest microlithic industries of the EPIPALAEOLITHIC (or Final Palaeolithic) period in northern Sudan, known primarily from DIBEIRA West 1 (DIW 1) near Arkin. Both Arkinian and SHAMARKIAN sites consist of groups of stone tools and appear to have been the seasonal encampments of small groups of hunters and foragers.

W. Chmielewski: 'Early and Middle Palaeolithic sites near Arkin, Sudan', *The prehistory of Nubia* I, ed. F. Wendorf (Dallas, 1968), 110–47; R. Schild, M. Chmielewska and H. Wieckowska: 'The Arkinian and Shamarkian industries', *The Prehistory of Nubia* II, ed. F. Wendorf (Dallas, 1968), 651–767; M.A. Hoffman: *Egypt before the pharaohs* (New York, 1979); W. Wetterstrom: 'Foraging and farming in

Egypt', *The archaeology of Africa: food, metals and towns*, ed. T. Shaw, P. Sinclair, B. Andah and A. Okpoko (London, 1993), 165–226 [184–5].
IS

Armant (anc. Iunu-Montu) Egyptian site located on the west bank of the Nile, 9 km southwest of Luxor, which was excavated by Robert Mond and Oliver Myers in the early 1930s. The principal features of Armant are its extensive predynastic and A-GROUP cemeteries, a small area of predynastic settlement, and a stone-built temple of Montu, the god of war. The latter dates from the 11th dynasty to the Roman period (*c.*2040 BC–AD 200), but it was largely destroyed in the late 19th century. The so-called Bucheum, at the northern end of the site, is the necropolis of the sacred *bekh*-bulls and the 'Mother of buchis'-cows, dating from *c.*350 BC to AD 305.

Seriation. By the excavation standards of the time (i.e. the early decades of the 20th century), the necropolis at Armant is probably one of the most assiduously documented predynastic sites. Werner von Kaiser and Kathryn Bard have therefore been able to analyse the cemeteries statistically in modern times, in order to study the chronology (Kaiser 1957) and socio-economic structure (Bard 1988) of the late predynastic period (*c.*4000–3000 BC). The excavated predynastic remains at Armant consist of a small area of settlement (Area 1000) and about 250 graves (Areas 1400–1500), all located on the desert edges. Although they clearly date to the Naqada I–III periods (*see* EGYPT 1), neither the settlement nor the cemeteries were excavated in a proper stratigraphic manner, and it follows that the pottery cannot be automatically arranged in a vertical (i.e. chronological) sequence.

Kaiser identified three basic groups of ceramics, the distribution of which acts as a guide to the temporal and spatial growth of the cemeteries. Kaiser's work at Armant, as well as at other predynastic sites, such as Naqada, Mahasna and el-Amra, demonstrated that the middle dates in Petrie's 'sequence dating' system (a method of relative dating based on typological trends in funerary vessels, *see* SERIATION) were partially inaccurate. Archaeological support for Kaiser's new sequence was provided by Caton-Thompson's stratigraphic excavation of the late predynastic settlement at Hammamia. His new method of seriation has resulted in a revised relative chronology dividing the late predynastic period into three basic phases. He has also called into question Petrie's hypothesized stylistic progression for the 'W-ware' (wavy-handled vessels) at Armant, thus casting some doubt on Petrie's sequence dates 40–80.

Cluster analysis. On the basis of Kaiser's ceramic studies and the evidence of changing size and spatial distribution of graves, the Armant cemeteries can be seen to have spread gradually northwards. In order to build up a more detailed picture of socio-economic differentiation over time, Bard (1988) has used CLUSTER ANALYSIS to examine the patterning of the Armant funerary assemblages. Since many of the Armant graves had been plundered or incompletely recorded, Bard used BMDP K-means cluster analysis with Euclidean distance, since this is the best type of cluster analysis for situations where there are cases with missing values in the VARIABLES. The specific variables used for the analysis were the totals of decorated and undecorated pots, quantities of 'W-ware', grave size and artefacts made from 'new materials' (e.g. agate, carnelian and ivory).

This cluster analysis showed that there were two relatively clear groups of richer and poorer burials throughout most of the predynastic period at Armant, which Bard interprets as an indication of a relatively unchanging two-tiered social system, rather than the process of increasing social complexity which is usually associated with the gradual move towards urbanization. Bard suggests that the situation at Armant is not necessarily typical of the Egyptian late predynastic as a whole, since the types of burial goods found in the Armant graves appear to be characteristic of a small farming village, showing little tendency towards the kind of increasing social stratification found in the cemeteries of the early town at NAQADA. Bard points out, however, that the interpretation of the cluster analysis might be undermined if the elite graves of the final predynastic phase at Armant had simply been located elsewhere (perhaps on the floodplain rather than the desert, as Fekri Hassan has shown for Naqada).

R. Mond and O.H. Myers: *The Bucheum*, 3 vols (London, 1934); ——: *Cemeteries of Armant* I (London, 1937); ——: *Temples of Armant: a preliminary survey* (London, 1940); W. Kaiser: 'Zur inneren Chronologie der Naqadakultur', *Archaeologia Geographica* 6 (1957), 69–77; K. Bard: 'A quantitative analysis of the predynastic burials in Armant cemetery 1400–1500', *JEA* 74 (1988), 39–55.
IS

Armorican First and Second Series graves Two series of rich tumuli of the Early Bronze Age in Brittany, France, divided by Cogné and Giot (1951) with reference to the grave-goods. The first group tends to present high quality flint arrowheads, bronze daggers and sometimes axes (e.g. KERNONEN); the second group tends to contain a pottery vessel (especially a four-handled jar), sometimes with a bronze dagger. Both groups of tumuli are large, the First Series producing most of the exceptionally sized examples; the First Series tombs are concentrated in Finestère and Morbihan near the coast, while the Second Series graves tend to occur inland. First Series tombs tend to be earlier, although the chronological relationship is complex and as yet not fully resolved. The flint arrowheads, bronze daggers and occasional stone wristguards found in the First Series can be compared to the 'prestige item' assemblages found with Beaker pottery elsewhere in Europe, though Beakers themselves are not present.

Armorican series and Wessex. The Armorican graves – particularly the First Series – are comparable to the barrows in southern Britain produced by the WESSEX CULTURE. The most important differences in the material assemblages are that the Wessex graves lack the emphasis on elaborate arrowheads and the long 'sword' daggers found in Brittany, do not tend to show such accumulations of axes and other weaponry, and are accompanied by Beakers; the most important assemblage similarities are the shared Armorico-British daggers and, at the level of individual sites, the hilt decoration of gold pins at Kernonen and BUSH BARROW.

J. Cogné and P.-R. Giot: 'L'âge de bronze ancien en Bretagne', *L'Anthropolgie* 55 (1951), 425–44; J. Briard: *Les tumulus d'Armorique* (Paris, 1984); D.V. Clarke et al.: *Symbols of power at the time of Stonehenge* (Edinburgh, 1985), 128–40.

RJA

Arpachiyah, Tell Prehistoric site dating to the 5th and 6th millennia BC, located 6 km northeast of the site of Nineveh in the Mosul region of northern Iraq. It was excavated by Max Mallowan in 1933, his attention having been drawn to the site by Campbell Thompson's discovery of surface finds of HALAF pottery in 1928. Mallowan hoped that by excavating the easily accessible Halafian strata at Arpachiyah he would shed further light on the context of the Halaf pottery which he had discovered in the deepest strata at Nineveh in 1932. At Arpachiyah he identified ten building phases (TT1–10): the four uppermost of which (TT1–4) contained the distinctive painted pottery of the UBAID period (*c*.5000–3800 BC), while the six lower phases were Halafian in date (*c*.5500–4500 BC). In levels TT7–10 he discovered a large group of unusual circular (perhaps domed) structures, which he described as *tholoi* because their shape resembled that of a Mycenaean THOLOS tomb.

In 1976 the excavations of Ismail Hijara demonstrated that there were six further Halafian levels below Mallowan's lowest stratum. Hijara distinguished three broad ceramic phases of the Halafian period at Arpachiyah, the earliest of which was built directly on the natural soil and consisted of rectangular mud-brick buildings rather than the circular *tholoi* of the later levels. In the latest Halafian strata (i.e. Mallowan's TT7–10), Hijara also identified a wall separating the *tholoi* from the rest of the Halafian settlement, perhaps indicating that the buildings served a religious rather than domestic function.

M.E.L. Mallowan and C. Rose: 'Prehistoric Assyria: the excavations at Tell Arpachiyah, 1933', *Iraq* 2 (1935), 1–178; T.E. Davidson and H. McKerrell: 'The neutron activation analysis of Halaf and 'Ubaid pottery from Tell Arpachiyah and Tepe Gawra', *Iraq* 42 (1980), 155–67; J. Curtis: 'Arpachiya', *Fifty years of Mesopotamian discovery*, ed. J. Curtis (London, 1982), 30–6.

IS

Arras culture Iron Age culture (4th–1st centuries BC) of eastern Yorkshire, England, known largely from its barrows with pit burials. Some burials contain elaborate cart burials, as at the type site of Arras, and at Wetwang Slack and Garton Slack (Dent 1985). At the latter site, four cart burials outside the main cemetery contained dismantled two-wheeled carts with iron tyres and hubs laid underneath a flexed skeleton; grave goods included iron swords in iron and bronze scabbards with circular open chapes characteristic of the earlier La Tène, iron horse-bits and an iron mirror and bronze container. Because the barrows and the cart burials are similar to La Tène burials found in the Seine valley and north France around the 5th century BC, the Arras culture is often cited as an example of immigration into, or invasion of, the British Isles (at least, by an aristocratic elite) during the later 1st millennium BC.

J. Dent: 'Three cart burials from Wetwang, Yorkshire', *Antiquity* 59 (1985), 85–92.

RJA

arrow straightener Prehistoric stone plaques characterized by a carved and worn groove, which are thought to have been used to smooth arrowshafts.

Arroyo Hondo *see* ANASAZI

Arslantepe *see* MALATYA

Arzawa *see* BEYÇESULTAN

Arzhan Large barrow of around the 8th to 7th centuries BC located in the valley of the Uyuk river, Republic of Tuva (southern Siberia), Russia. Discovered and excavated by M.P. Gryaznov in 1971–4, the chamber contained burials of a 'king' and 'queen', the skeletons of 15 human attendants and 160 horses. Grave goods included horse gear, weapons and works of art in the SCYTHIAN tradition.

M.P. Gryaznov: *Aržan: carskii kurgan ranne-skifskogo vremeni* [Arzhan: a royal kurgan from early Scythian times] (Leningrad, 1970).

PD

Ashdod *see* PHILISTINES

Ashkelon *see* PHILISTINES

ash-mound sites Characteristic sites of the south Indian Neolithic period in modern Karnataka (*c*.2800–1500 BC), consisting of low mounds of burnt cattle dung and associated faunal remains and artefacts. They have been interpreted by Allchin (1963: 162–7) as the remains of series of cattle pens which were repeatedly burnt and rebuilt over several phases. The precise reasons for burning remain unknown, whether accidental, for hygienic reasons, or for ritual purposes (Allchin 1963: 76). Associated materials include domestic cattle bones, hand-made ceramics, chipped stone blades and cores, ground stone axes and grinding stones.

F.R. Allchin: *Neolithic cattle keepers of the Deccan* (Cambridge, 1963).

CS

Asia

Sections: 1 Central Asia; 2 South Asia; 3 Southeast Asia. The archaeology of Western Asia is discussed in the following articles: ANATOLIA; ARABIA; ISLAMIC ARCHAEOLOGY; MESOPOTAMIA; SYRIA-PALESTINE.

1 Central Asia

The prehistory and archaeology of this vast area is to some extent dependent upon its diverse geography. The larger part of Central Asia is taken up by the Turanian Lowland: a huge trough filled with clastic deposits. An impressive belt of folded mountains separates this region from the Iranian and Indian lowlands to the south. This mountainous belt, oriented roughly northwest to southeast, comprises the Kopet Dag (or Koppeh Dagh, the northern ridge of the Khorassan Mountains), Pamir, Alai and Tien Shan. The northern fringe of the Kopet Dag forms 'piedmont foothills': a cluster of alluvial fans shaped by numerous streams. The climate is continental and very dry (mostly under 250 mm of rainfall annually). The wettest areas are found on the northern slopes of folded mountain belts (350–450 mm), while the foothills of the Kopet Dag are very rich in groundwater. Central Asia drains inwards: its major basins (the Caspian Sea, the Aral Sea) have no outlet to the oceans.

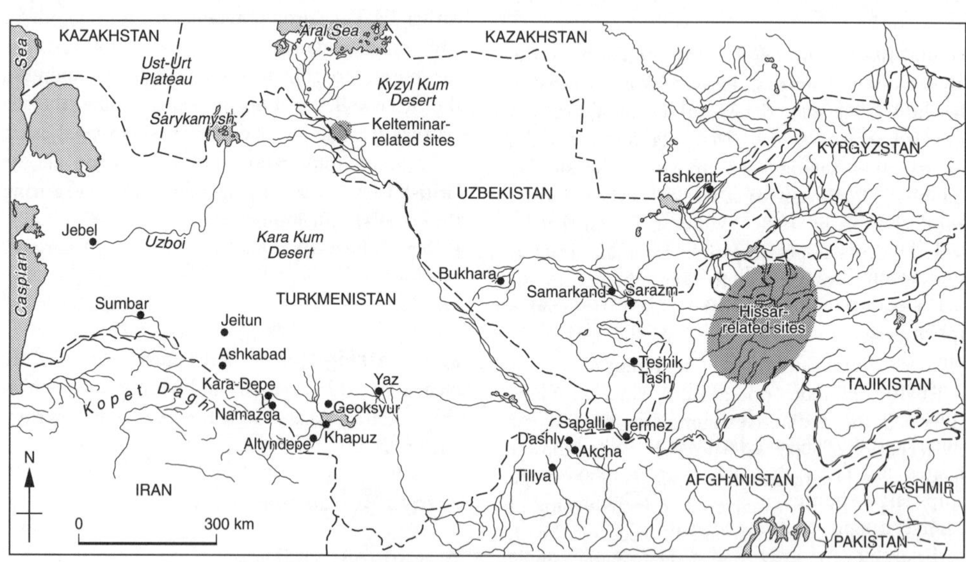

Map 15 **Asia, 1: Central** Major sites in the region mentioned in the main text or with individual entries in the Dictionary.

The southern part of Turanian Lowland is occupied by the two huge deserts of Kara Kum and Kyzyl Kum. The coarse clay and sand deposits found here were deposited by the Amy-Darya (Oxus) and Syr Darya rivers, which repeatedly changed their course during the Pleistocene and Holocene. The scarce desert vegetation of much of this area contrasts with rich *tugai* forests (poplar, willow, tamarisk etc.) restricted to river valleys. The northern part of the Turanian Lowland forms an undulating plain covered by steppe-like vegetation. Until comparatively recently, the now-barren slopes of the mountains were covered by deciduous forests offering a great variety of wild fruit trees; the foothills of Kopet Dag still support a wide variety of wild cereals.

1.1 *Cultural sequence*. The earliest evidence of hominids in the region comes from the long loess sequences in the Southern Tadjik depression. At one of the sites, KULDURA, archaic choppers were found in fossil soils exhibiting a reverse polarity, suggesting an age of *c*.800,000 years (Ranov 1993). A sequence of loess deposits in southwest Tadjikistan suggests an uninterrupted settlement of that area throughout the entire Pleistocene. Sites in other areas allegedly belong to Lower Palaeolithic: the cave of Sel Ungur in Fergana valley, and Kul'bulak, southeast of Tashkent. Several finds of bifacial tools have been reported from southern Kazakhstan.

More than 100 Mousterian sites, apparently belonging to the early stadials of the last glaciation (radiocarbon dates from the sites of Ogzi-Lichik and Khoudji suggest an age of 40–30,000 years) demonstrate a degree of cultural diversity in the Middle Palaeolithic: artefacts can be grouped into at least four typologies (Ranov 1993). The deliberate burial of a Neanderthal child at TESHIK-TASH suggests some kind of 'religious' beliefs.

The stratified site of Shugou was found in Tadjikistan, at an altitude of *c*.2000 m above sea-level. The site consists of five levels which yielded radiocarbon dates from 35,000 to 10,000 years BP. The stone industries include Mousterian and Upper Palaeolithic tools, end-scrapers and points being the most numerous. This combination of Mousterian and Upper Paleolithic artefacts is also typical of another site, found in the city of Samarkand, Uzbekistan. Judging from the location of sites and faunal remains, these were seasonal camps left by hunters procuring wild animals such as horse, camel, red deer and goat.

Mesolithic sites are found almost exclusively in the mountainous regions – notably, the cave sites Jebel and Dam-Dam-Cheshma 1 and 2 in the Greater Balkans, the northwestern off-shoot of the Kopet Dag. A third cave, Kaylyu, lies in a cliff of the Caspian Sea in the Krasnovodsk peninsula (Okladnikov 1955: 1966). A number of Mesolithic sites have also been discovered in the eastern part of Central Asia: the cave of Machai (Islamov 1975); Obishir 1 and 5 in the southern Fergana valley; Tut-Kaul, Sai-Sayod, Oshkhona and others in the western Pamir (Ranov 1993).

Around 6000 BC, judging from a series of AMS datings for the site of Jeitun in Turkmenistan, the earliest farming settlements in Central Asia began to appear in the foothills of the Kopet Dag, and especially the northern foothills of the Khorassan Mountains. They belong to the JEITUN culture, and were predominantly agricultural (especially einkorn wheat), with stock-breeding (mostly sheep and goats) supplemented by hunting (Masson 1971; Harris et al. 1993).

The next stage in the early agricultural sequence of Central Asia is referred to as Anau IA and dates to 5200–4800 BC (Kohl 1984). Several clusters of Anau IA sites are distinguishable: the western group (west of Ashgabad), the central group (near Kaakhka), and a group in the eastern part of the 'piedmont foothills' (the Meana-Chaacha interfluve). Local differences in stock-breeding become apparent: pig being the most numerous in the western group, with either sheep/goat, or cattle, dominating elsewhere. Domestic architecture became technically more sophisticated: complexes of houses built of mud-bricks of a standard size and separated by narrow alleys.

In the subsequent stage in the cultural sequence, referred to as NAMAZGA I and dating from 4800 to 4000 BC (Kohl 1984), the number and size of settlements (and presumably population levels) increase particularly in the central foothills (Namazga 50 ha, and Kara-depe, 6–8 ha). The settlements usually consisted of a large number of one-roomed houses without marked social distinctions; towards the end of the period, the houses tend to form denser clusters but there are no obvious defensive walls. Smaller agricultural settlements appeared further east in the Tedjen delta. The intensification of agriculture depended upon the development of irrigation, which is clear around the settlement of Namazga and, particularly, in the Tedjen delta.

The first half of the 4th millennium BC, corresponding to the Middle Eneolithic, is known locally as Namazga II. Sites cluster around Ashgabad and in the northeast piedmont foothills, notably Namazga, Kara-depe and ALTYN-DEPE. The proto-urban nature of these settlements is particularly striking in the northeastern sector, where there is a marked settlement hierarchy (Masson 1989). At least two settlements, Altyn-depe and Ingynly-depe, exceeded 15 hectares; the former was encircled by a wall 1.5 m thick with rectangular towers. A network of settlements based on irrigated agriculture evolved in the Tedjen delta (Khlopin 1964).

The Namazga III stage (or Late Eneolithic) corresponds to the second half of the 4th millennium BC. There was remarkable increase in urbanization, particularly in the central and north-eastern sectors of the Kopet Dag piedmont. Namazga and Altyn-depe grew to 30 ha each – while smaller sites tended to diminish or to disappear. Agricultural settlements also emerged further east in Central Asia in the Murghab delta (Margiana) (Masimov 1981).

The Namazga IV stage, or Early Bronze Age, corresponds to the first half of the third millennium BC. Settlements continued to grow: Namazga and Altyn-depe reached *c.*50 and 25 ha, respectively (Mason 1991). Yet the general settlement pattern changed considerably: settlements totally disappear from the Tedjen delta, although they are still present in the Murghab delta (Masimov 1981). Agricultural settlements spread into the intermontane valleys of the Kopet Dag; settlements and cemeteries appeared in the SUMBAR valley of western Kopet Dag (Khlopin 1983).

During the Middle Bronze Age, or Namazga V stage, of the second half of the 2nd millennium BC, the development of proto-urban civilization in the south of Central Asia reached a climax. The excavation of Altyn-depe (Masson 1991) revealed advanced social stratification and craft specialization: the settlement included an elite quarter, a potter's area, a sanctuary and a priest's house. There is clear evidence for monumental architecture in the form of a 'ziggurat'-like structure on a high stepped platform, and for long-distance trade in prestige goods.

Agricultural settlements continued to develop in the Murghab delta, and there is evidence for agricultural expansion further east, into the area of historic Bactria. Agricultural settlements north and south of Oxus Sapalli-tepe in southern Tadjikistan and the Dashly group in northern Afghanistan (Askarov 1973; Sarianidi 1977) show a cultural development similar to that of Margiana in the Murghab delta. The agricultural communities of the intermontane valleys of the western Kopet Dag (Khlopin 1983) developed rather differently, and a particular cultural tradition of catacomb graves developed.

At the same time, a totally different line of socio-cultural development emerged in the north of Central Asia, on the Turanian Lowland. In conditions of increased rainfall (the 'Lyavlyakan pluvial'), a network of settlements based entirely on foraging strategies emerged along numerous waterways – and especially along the Amu Darya river, which flowed directly to the Caspian Sea, via Sarykamysh lake and Uzboi. A large cluster of sites is located in the ancient deltas of Amu-Darya, notably Akcha-Darya, and along the Zerafshan further south. Numerous sites are also situated in the Amu-Darya–Syr-Darya interfluve, in the proximity of the fresh-water lakes of that area (Vinogradov and Mamedov 1975; Vinogradov 1981).

The faunal remains at these sites consist of wild animals adapted to *tugai* forests, open steppes and desert mountains (red deer, fallow deer, boar, saiga, gazelle, camel etc.). Hunting waterfowl and fishing were also important. Food-gathering included a wide spectrum of plants (pomegranate, apricots, wild olives), small animals (e.g. tortoise) and molluscs (Okladnikov 1955; Vinogradov 1981). The stone inventories include grinding stones, mortars and pestles as well as blades with sickle gloss (Korobkova 1969). Vinogradov (1981: 139) describes a sophisticated technology for harvesting and processing wild plants. The remains of rectangular houses, with the roof supported by posts, were identified at a number of sites. Some of the sites, particularly in the Akcha-Darya delta, are of a considerable size and of a permanent character.

In the mountain valleys of western Tadjikistan numerous food-gathering groups, known collectively as the 'HISSAR culture', survived over a considerable period of time (7000 to around 2000 BC) (Amosova et al., 1993). The sites are of a considerable size (0.75–0.5 ha) and include stone floors and hearths.

The development of early metal-working communities, based on the cultural contacts with the Geojksyur and other agricultural areas and on rich local metallurgical resources, is exemplified at the site of SARAZM in the Middle Zerafshan Valley, dated to 3250–2750 BC (Isakov 1981).

The environment of Central Asia changed dramatically between 3200 BC and 2500 BC, as levels of rainfall dropped. The Sarykamysh lake, and numerous other lakes in the Kyzyl-Kum, gradually dried up; the Uzboi river ceased to exist soon after. This may be connected to a contemporary change in settlement pattern in the Kopet Dag foothills further south. Over a short time-span – *c.*2170–2050 BC (Dolukhanov et al. 1985) – the large proto-urban settlements (notably, Altyn-depe and

Namazga) disappeared. Numerous small villages (less than 2 ha) emerged in their place, and stock-breeding became much more important.

At the same time, in the northern part of Central Asia, there was gradual but fundamental shift to a predominantly stock-breeding economy. Yet even in areas with a semi-desert environment, large permanent settlements emerged. The economy of the site of Batai in northern Kazakhstan, dated using radiocarbon to around 2900 BC (Zaibert 1993), was entirely based on horse-breeding (99.9% of the faunal remains). However, the remains of numerous dwellings, workshops and storage pits leave no doubt that this was an established settlement.

In the same period, sites appeared in some areas of western Central Asia that exhibit marked similarities to the steppe cultures of the north (Andronovo, TIMBER GRAVE CULTURE); the cemetery of Kokcha-3 in the delta of Amu-Darya contained bronze objects that have analogies with those from sites in northern Kazakhstan and further to the west. Several sites in the Akcha Darya delta yielded imported Andronovo wares.

The contemporary Tazabagiab settlements present evidence of developed stock-breeding combined with irrigated agriculture (in river deltas). Andronovo-influenced local variants of a similar subsistence pattern can be identified in the Tashkent oasis, in eastern and central Kazakhstan, northern Kirghizia and Fergana Valley.

The interesting 'Yaz I' complex of the Namazga-Anau area of southeast Turkmenistan developed during the early 1st millennium BC (the early site of Tillya 1 has been dated using radiocarbon to 1140–940 BC). Combining stock-breeding (showing an ever-increasing amount of horse bones) with irrigated agriculture, Yaz I-type sites exhibit impressive fortifications ('citadels') often built on thick brick platforms. The predominance of hand-made ware, and the style of certain bronze artefacts, suggest that this culture resulted from an invasion of the area by 'steppe' groups from the north.

The 'Chust culture' which emerged in the Fergana Valley during the late second to early first millennia BC may have had a more agricultural economy, although the evidence is not clear. It has been suggested (Kohl 1984), that the culture resulted from the contact of local pastoral groups with agricultural newcomers; there is also evidence of cultural contacts with Eastern Turkestan (Xinjiang). The earlier sites have been radiocarbon dated to *c.*1500–1100 BC, but the later sites are not yet securely dated. The largest settlements (Dalversin, Ashkal-depe) were in excess of 25 ha, while other were of a medium (Chust: 4 ha) and small (under 1 ha) size. There is no clear evidence of fortifications.

During the middle of the 1st millennium BC, the greater part of Central Asia became the eastern satrapies of the Achaemenid empire. Achaemenid sources mention several Central Asian tribes (the Bactrians, the Sacae and the Choresmians) in connection with military expeditions mounted against Egypt and Greece. By this time (the 6th to 4th centuries BC) major cities existed in all the principal regions of Central Asia: Gyaur-Kala (Merv), Kakaly-Gir (Khorezmia), Afrosiab (Sogdiana) etc. After the conquest of Alexander (329–327 BC), and until 130 BC, a major Greco-Bactrian kingdom dominated cultural developments in Central Asia. The impressive urban centres of that time combine local cultural traditions with Hellenistic influences.

The involvement of central Asia in trans-continental trade (it occupied a central position along the 'Great Silk Road') further enhanced the urban economies and culture. In the first and second centuries AD, Central Asia became part of the Kushan Kingdom, the establishment of which coincided with the spread of Buddhism.

The SASSANIAN (i.e. Iranian) offensive against Kushan, combined with pressure from nomadic groups in the north, eventually destroyed the kingdom in the 4th century. Between the downfall of the Kushan Kingdom and the Arab conquest of the 8th century a number of independent cultural centres developed in various parts of the Central Asia. Perhaps the most interesting example is the urban site of Pendjikent, east of Samarkand, which has provided outstanding examples of early medieval art and architecture in Central Asia in the 5th to early 6th centuries AD (Belenitsky 1969).

1.2 *Growth and decline of proto-urban cultures in Central Asia: analysis.* The large land-locked area of Central Asia had limited contacts with the outer world, so that internal and external developments are relatively easy to distinguish. Agriculture can be first identified in the better watered 'piedmont strip' of the Turkmeno-Khorassan mountains in the late 5th to early 4th millennia BC. This area is particularly suited to early forms of agriculture: wild varieties of barley and wheat still form considerable stands on the mountain slopes. Vavilov (1926) considered this area as the 'Turkmeno-Khorassan sub-centre' of the West Asian centre of origin of cultivated plants.

The earliest agricultural settlements here belong to the 'Jeitun culture', and are found on both sides of the Khorassan Mountains, in southern

Turkmenistan and northern Iran. In spite of the rich local resources, early agriculture in the central Asia clearly resulted from the contacts between local Mesolithic groups and early farmers in the agricultural heartland further south in the Zagros foothills.

The further spread of agriculture during the next stage (Namazga I), east into the Tedjen delta, is seen by Khlopin (1964) as resulting from the outflow of surplus population from the Kopet Dag foothills. Subsequently, a dense network of agricultural settlements arose in these foothills and the deltaic plains, some of which reached impressive dimensions (e.g. Namazga). The settlement network was bound together by multiple trade and social links. At the same time, there is an increasing evidence of long-distance trade with the areas in the south, particularly in prestige items intended for the emerging elite e.g. lapis-lazuli and alabaster imported from Afghanistan and Iran.

Contacts with the outside world became yet more intense during the first half of the 4th millennium BC (Namazga II period). Typical Namazga II ceramics and terracottas have been identified in the Quetta assemblage in northern Baluchistan, while strong cultural parallels in pottery styles, anthropomorphic figurines, stamp steals and burial rites can be seen in distant sites such as Mundihgak (Afghanistan) and Shahr-i-Sokhta (Sistan, eastern Iran).

During the second half of the 4th millennium BC (Late Eneolithic, or Namazga III stage), when a remarkable phase of urbanization took hold in the central and northeastern sectors of the Kopet Dag, and agricultural settlements emerged in the Murghab delta (Margiana) further east (Masimov 1981), the cultural influence of Central Asia is clear throughout northern Iran. This is demonstrated in pottery assemblages from Khorassan, the Gorgan Plain and the northern fringes of the Iranian plateau (including Tepe Hissar). Again, Central Asian styles appear further south at Quetta in Baluchistan, Mundighak in Afghanistan and Shahr-i-Sokhta in Sistan. At the latter site, Namazga III-related pottery comprises 40% of the corpus of painted pottery.

During the Middle Bronze Age, or Namazga V (later 2nd millennium BC), proto-urban civilization developed strongly in the south of Central Asia. As described above, the excavation of Altyn-depe (Masson 1991) revealed a social elite and indications of the long-distance trade in prestige goods (e.g. ivory). Two seals with the signs in the Proto-Indus script prove the presence of individuals (presumably merchants) from the Indus Valley.

Eventually, the entire area north and south of the Khorassan Mountains was incorporated into a major socio-cultural network that exhibited most of the common features of 'civilization': a hierarchy of sedentary settlements; craft specialization and an increasingly regulated the work force; wide distribution of material goods; and emerging social stratification. This network, referred to as 'prehistoric Turan' by Biscone and Tosi (1979) and as 'l'Iran exterieur' by Amiet (1988), was linked by multiple ties with the main trade centres in the Indus Valley, eastern Iran and Elam. Kohl (1989) has even suggested a Bronze Age 'world system' of interconnected civilised areas which embraced the entire Middle East and included the Caucasus, Central Asia and the Indus Valley. This system consisted of localized areas bound together by trade links and by a constant movement of people, ideas and symbols.

At the same time, as described above, a different network was formed to the north, in the plains of the Turanian Plateau, by foraging communities. Thus two major socio-cultural networks are identifiable in the Central Asia during the wetter period: the agricultural network, restricted mainly to the Kopet Dag foothills and the deltaic plains in the south and linked by numerous ties with the centres of agricultural civilization in the Middle East and Indus Valley; and the foraging network, situated predominantly along the waterways of the otherwise desert-like Turanian lowland. Yet, the artefactual assemblages leave one in no doubt that the two networks were bound together by intensive social, economic and cultural contacts. The spread of pottery production may be viewed as an adoption of the southern technological innovation by the northern 'Mesolithic' groups, and the continuing similarity in the ornamental patterns on the pottery is proof of constant cultural contacts. Korobkova (1969: 146–8) stresses the similarity in the technique of manufacture of sickle blades in the Jeitunian and Zerafshan groups.

As described above, the environment of Central Asia dramatically changed around 3200–2500 BC. The proto-urban settlements in the south (notably, Altyn-depe and Namazga) gave way to numerous small villages leading to what has been termed a 'crisis of urbanization' around 2170–2050 BC (Biscone 1977; Dolukhanov et al. 1985). Spectacular changes also occurred in the semi-desert and steppe areas to the north, where the entire hydrological system of Amu-Darya-Sarykamysh-Uzboi gradually collapsed. The pastoral economy became the dominant strategy of survival throughout the entire steppe belt of Eurasia.

In the south, the small village economy was gradually absorbed into the world of 'aggressive pastoralism'. This process manifested itself in the spread of new ideological symbols: the catacomb burial ritual is often viewed as an incursion from the steppe cultures of the north, and has suggested to many authorities the complete collapse of proto-urban civilization and even a barbarian occupation (Kohl 1984). However, given the aridization of the climate, the transition to a pastoral economy may instead have been a response to acute ecological crisis. Heightened competition for scarce resources can lead to a sharpened sense of group identity and the maintenance of group boundaries (Hodder 1982: 193). Perhaps this ecological crisis undermined the economic, cultural and economic system that incorporated the agricultural south into the greater network of early Middle Eastern civilization, and caused its replacement by a very different network of pastoral chiefdoms – a network that eventually dominated the greater part of the semi-desert and steppe area of Eurasia.

Two distinct processes of social integration are thus distinguishable in prehistoric Central Asia. The first consisted of a large social network consisting of the centres of early agricultural civilization and a linked, if distinctive, 'foraging periphery'. The unity of this network was based on the circulation of goods, ideas and symbols. The second process, generated by a quite different ecology and economy, manifested itself as a multitude of localized powerbases emitting strong symbolic signals of cohesive group identity.

1.3 *History of archaeology in Central Asia*. Archaeological investigation of Central Asia started soon after the Russian conquest of the region in the mid to late 19th century. P.I. Lerch was one of the first to conduct excavations in the lower Amu Darya, in 1867. The excavations of Old Samarkand (Afrosiab), initiated by the Russian military in 1875, were conducted by N.I. Veselovsky later that century and still later by V.L. Vyatkin. In the 1880s, General Komarov started exploring the first prehistoric site: he opened up two mounds at ANAU, near Ashkhabad. The first archaeological museum was opened in Samarkand in 1896, where an Archaeological Society was set up soon after.

The excavations of Anau were resumed in 1904 by an American multi-disciplinary team led by R. Pumpelly. These excavations established the first cultural sequence in Central Asia, covering the Eneolithic, Bronze and Iron Ages. Important discoveries (including the site of NAMAZGA) were made in 1916–26 by D.D. Bukinich, an irrigation engineer, and the intensity of archaeological investigations increased in the 1930s. At first, most work was carried out by archeological institutions based in Moscow and Leningrad, but local bodies soon started to appear. Long-term projects were set up, notably the Zerafshan Expedition led by A. Yakubovsky, and the Termez Expedition headed by M.E. Masson. The Khorezmian Archaeological and Ethnographic Expedition led by S.P. Tolstov in 1937 was the most ambitious project, and remains an important milestone in archaeology of Central Asia. This project, which included Uzbekistan and Turkmenistan, pioneered sophisticated field techniques, including air reconnaissance, and concentrated on the study of the socio-economic development, irrigation and ethnoarchaeology of various prehistoric and historic groups. Perhaps the most spectacular single find was made by A.P. Okladinkov in 1937, when he discovered a Neanderthal burial at TESHIK-TASH in Uzbekistan.

In the 1940s and early 1950s local archaeological institutions were set up by the newly constituted Academies of Sciences of the Central Asian republics. The South Turkmenistan Complex Archaeological Expedition, attached to the Turkmenistan Academy of Sciences, was organized by M.E. Masson in 1946. Several important projects developed under this organizational umbrella, including the study of Mesolithic sites (including JEBEL) by A. Okladnikov in 1947–52; systematic excavations of Eneolithic and Bronze Age sites by Kuftin in the 1940s–1950s; the study of Neolithic sites including Jeitun and a large group of prehistoric sites in the GEOKSYUR oasis by V.M. Masson, I.N. Khlopin and Sarianidi in 1955–62; the excavations of Bronze Age sites including ALTYN-DEPE by V.M. Masson and others since 1965; the investigations of prehistoric economies and irrigation systems by G.N. Lisitsyna; explorations in SUMBAR Valley by Khlopin in 1977–92; and many other projects.

After 1971, archaeological investigations in Uzbekistan were coordinated by the Institute of Archaeology based in Samarkand, and were attached to the Uzbek Academy of Sciences. Highlights during the 1970s and 1980s included the excavation of Mesolithic sites in the Fergana Valley by U. Islamov; the exploration of the complex Bronze Age site of Sapalli-tepe by A. Askarov; and the investigation of the 2nd millennium BC Chust culture (described below) in the eastern Fergana Valley by A. Zadneprovsky.

In Tadjikistan, the most spectacular achievements include the exploration of the Sakae kurgans by A.N. Bershtam in the 1940s and 1950s; the excavation of the early medieval city of Penjikent by

A.M. Belenitsky since 1951; the investigations of Bronze Age barrows by B.A. Litvinsky in the 1960s; the discovery of early Palaeolithic sites by V.A. Ranov; and the exploration of the HISSAR culture by Ranov et al. In recent years, A.I. Isakov, in collaboration with French scholars, has excavated the Eneolithic-Bronze Age site of Sarazm in the Zerafshan valley. British archaeologists are active in several major archaeological projects in the Central Asia, including environmental and archaeological investigations on and around the site of JEITUN (Harris et al. 1993).

N.I. Vavilov: *Studies on the origin of cultivated plants* (Leningrad, 1926); A.P. Okladnikov: 'Peshchera Djebel – pamjatnik drevnei kul'tury prikaspiiskih plemjon Turkmenii', *Trudy Yutake* 7 (1955), 11–219; I.N. Khlopin: *Geoksjurskaja gruppa poselenii epohi eneolita* (Leningrad, 1964); G.N. Lisitzyna: *Oroshaemoe zemledelie epohi neolita na juge Turkmenii* (Moscow, 1965); A.P. Okladnikov: 'Paleolit i mezolit Srednei Azii' in V.M. Masson, ed., *Srednjaja Azija v epohu kamnja i bronzy* (Moscow and Leningrad, 1966); A.M. Belenitsky: *Central Asia* (London, 1969); G.F. Korobkova: 'Orudija truda i hozjaistvo neoliticheskih plemjon Srednei Azii', *Materialy i issledovaniya po arheologii SSSR* 158 (Leningrad, 1969); V.M. Masson: *Poselenie Djeitun* (Leningrad, 1971); A. Askarov: *Sapallitepa* (Tashkent, 1973); U. Islamov: *Peshchera Machai* (Tashkent, 1975); A.V. Vinigradov and E.D. Mamedov: *Pervobytnyi Ljavljakan* (Moscow, 1975); R. Biscione: 'The crisis of Central Asian urbanization in the 2nd millennium BC and villages as an alternative system' in *Le Plateau Iranien et l'Asie centrale des Origines à la Conquête Islamique* (1977), Colloques Internationaux du CNRS; V.I. Sarianidi: *Drevnie zemledel'cy Afganistana* (Moscow, 1977); R. Biscione and M. Tosi: 'Protoistoria degli Stati Iuranici', *Annali dell ' Istituto Universitario Orientale*, 1979, Supplement no. 20; A. Isakov: 'Excavations of the Bronze Age settlement of Sarazm' in P.L. Kohl, ed., *The Bronze Age civilization of Central Asia* (Armonk, 1981), 273–86; I.S. Masimov: 'The study of Bronze Age sites in the Lower Murhgab' *The Bronze Age civilizations of Central Asia*, ed. P.L. Kohl (Armonk, 1981), 104–20; A.V. Vinogradov: *Drevnie ohotniki i rybolovy Sredneaziatskogo Mezhdurech'ja* (Moscow, 1981); I. Hodder: *The present past* (London, 1982); I.N. Khlopin: *Jugo-zapadnaja Turkmenija v epohu pozdnei bronzy* (Leningrad, 1983); P.L. Kohl: *Central Asia: Palaeolithic beginnings to the Iron Age* (Paris, 1984); P.M. Dolukhanov et al.: 'Serija radiouglerodnyh datirovok poselenii epohi bronzy na Namazga-depe', *Sovetskaya arheologiya* 4 (1985), 118–24; J.-F. Jarrige: 'Les styles de Geoksyur et de Quetta et la question des rapports entre les régions au nord et au sud de l'Hindu Kush à la fin du 4e et au début du 3e millénaires', *L'Asie centrale et ses rapports avec les civilization orientales, des origines à l'âge du fer* (Paris, 1985), 95–102; P. Amiet: 'Elam et Bactrianne', *L'Asie centrale et ses rapports avec les civilization orientales, des origines à l'âge du fer* (Paris, 1988), 27–30; P.L. Kohl: 'The use and abuse of world system theory: the case of the "pristine" west asian state', *Archaeological thought in America*, ed. C.C. Lamberg-Karlovsky (Cambridge, 1989), 218–40; V.M. Masson: *Pervye civilizacii* (Leningrad, 1989); V.M. Masson: *Altyn-depe: Raskopki goroda bronzovogo veka v Juzhnom Turkmenistane* (Leningrad, 1991); A.G. Amosova et al.: 'Les énigmes de la culture de Hissar', *DA* 183 (1993), 14–21; P.M. Dolukhanov: *Environment and ethnicity in the ancient Middle East* (Avebury, 1993); D.R. Harris, V.M. Masson et al.: 'Investigating early agriculture in Central Asia: new research at Jeitun, Turkmenistan', *Antiquity* 67 (1993), 324–38; V.A. Ranov: 'Tout commence au Paléolithique', *DA* 185 (1993), 4–13; V.F. Zaibert: *Eneolit Uralo-Irtyshskogo mezhdurech'ja* (Petropavlovsk, 1993).

PD

2 South Asia

The modern countries of Pakistan, India, Nepal, Bangladesh, and Sri Lanka incorporate significant environmental, cultural, and historic diversity. From north to south, major geographic zones include: the Himalayas, the broad alluvial plains of the Indus River and its tributaries, and the Ganges and Yamuna Rivers, and the now-extinct Ghaggar-Hakra River located to the east of the Indus; the Vindhya and Aravalli Hills that define the northern boundary of central India and are crossed by the Narbada and Tapti rivers; and peninsular India, consisting of a central plateau and narrow coastal plains. Although some degree of interaction and

Pakistan/Northwest India	
Early agricultural communities	*c.*6500 – 4000 BC
Early Indus	4000 – 2600 BC
Mature Indus	2600 – 1900 BC
Late Indus	1900 – 1300 BC
Ganges Valley	
Ochre coloured pottery	1800 – 1400 BC
Painted grey ware	1300 – 600 BC
Northern black polished ware	600 – 50 BC
Deccan plateau and Southern India	
Early agricultural villages	*c.*3000 – 2000 BC
Malwa	1800 – 1400 BC
Jorwe – early	1400 – 1000 BC
Jorwe – late	1000 – 700 BC
Iron Age	*c.*800 BC ?
Early Historic India	
Mauryan empire	324 – 184 BC
Sunga dynasty	184 – 73 BC
Kanva dynasty	73 – 28 BC
Satavahana dynasty	50 BC – 225 AD
Gupta period	AD 320 – 647

Table 8 **Asia, 2: South** Chronology of the four principal regions of Southern Asia.

population movement occurred throughout prehistoric and historic periods, the South Asian past is best viewed as a complex mosaic, with considerable variation in ethnic groups, ways of life, and the pace and nature of cultural and technological change.

2.1 *Prehistory*. Knowledge of the South Asian Palaeolithic has been hampered by the paucity of primary sites and a reliance on surface finds and typological parallels to stone tool traditions in Africa and Europe to develop chronological frameworks. Recent work on important sites such as RIWAT, BHIMBETKA, SANGHAO, and sites in the HUNSGI VALLEY of Karnataka, the Palaeolithic traditions of Rajasthan, and the Potwar Plateau of Pakistan is providing evidence for a long sequence of occupation from the Lower Palaeolithic through the Mesolithic period.

The transition to an agricultural economy occurred at widely different times in the different regions of South Asia. The earliest agricultural settlement is the site of MEHRGARH in western Pakistan, with domesticated sheep, goat, cattle, barley and wheat from the 7th millennium BC.

Map 16 **Asia, 2: South** Some major archaeological sites in the region.

BURZAHOM in Kashmir contains domesticates from *c*.2900 BC; while in the southern Indian Deccan domesticated cattle are associated with the ASH MOUND sites of the 3rd millennium BC. In many areas, hunting and gathering communities persisted alongside and in interaction with agricultural and even urban settlements.

2.2. *History*. The recognition of the 3rd millennium urban settlements of the Indus Valley in the 1920s radically altered understandings of South Asian prehistory. Since then, more than 1000 sites of the Indus civilization have been identified, over an area of more than half a million sq km, and the Indus sequence has been refined into three main phases: the Early Indus (*c*.4000–2600 BC), the Mature or Urban Indus period (*c*.2600–1900 BC), and the Late Indus (1900–1300 BC); precise dates of these phases vary somewhat from region to region. Although the Mature Indus or Harappan period is best known for the large urban settlements of MOHENJO-DARO, HARAPPA, and GANWERIWALA, most sites of the Indus Civilization are small villages, towns and specialized production locales. Characteristic artefacts of the Mature Indus include standardized stone weights, copper tools, ceramic figurines and painted ceramic vessels, and steatite seals, inscribed with an, as yet, untranslated script.

The 2nd and early 1st millennia BC were characterized by the re-emergence of localized traditions in areas where Indus sites were known, and the expansion and development of copper using agricultural communities elsewhere throughout peninsular India. PIRAK in the Kachi Plain of Pakistan was a 9 ha settlement with evidence of considerable contact with Central Asia and Eastern Iran; in the Ganges Basin, the OCHRE COLOURED POTTERY (1800–1400 BC) and PAINTED GREY WARE (1300–600 BC) periods are the antecedents to the GANGES CIVILIZATION, the second period of South Asian state formation.

Contact with Central Asian pastoral nomads, and their movement into South Asia, significantly affected South Asian developments, especially in the north and the Ganges Basin. Although the traditional view of a massive Central Asian Aryan 'invasion' is not supported by archaeological data, it is also clear that developments in South Asia cannot be treated in isolation, and that population movements and broad inter-regional reaction were important to historical developments. South of the Ganges, agricultural settlements of the BANAS tradition (Rajasthan), and the Deccani MALWA (1800–1400 BC), and JORWE (1400–700 BC) are known, while in the south ASH MOUND sites and small agricultural settlements such as TEKKALAKOTA are found.

In the early first millennium BC, iron appeared. In the northwest, cemetery sites of the GANDHARA GRAVE CULTURE are of this period, and the centres of CHARSADA and TAXILA arose; the impact of Achaeminid, Parthian, Scythian, and Greek civilizations were also evident in this region. In southern India, the 1st millennium BC is characterized by the appearance of megalithic tombs, such as those from Brahmagiri.

In the Ganges River Basin, the GANGES CIVILIZATION emerged, first as a network of small competing city states centred at sites such as KAUSAMBI, ATRANJIKHERA, HASTINAPURA, RAJGHAT, Mathura and Noh. During this dynamic period the Buddha and Mahavira (the founder of JAINISM) preached and many of South Asia's historic religious and cultural traditions emerged. In 324 BC, the Ganges region and much of India and Pakistan were united into a single polity, the MAURYAN empire, which lasted until 184 BC. Following the decline of the Mauryans, South Asian history is characterized by the rise and fall of countless historic states and empires, formed through cycles of conquest and collapse.

2.3 *Archaeological research*. The earliest archaeological work in south Asia was initiated by the British in the 18th century and formalized through the founding of the Asiatic Society in 1784 and the Archaeological Survey of India in 1854. In the 1920s the INDUZ CIVILIZATION was discovered and large-scale excavations were conducted at HARAPPA, MOHENJO-DARO and related sites. Following independence in 1947, archaeological work in the different nation states of south Asia proceeded under the authority of national and local departments of archaeology and in university contexts. Research has been most intensive within India and Pakistan.

A considerable amount of descriptive data has been accumulated in the two centuries of archaeological research in South Asia; however, it is only within the last two to three decades that significant attempts have been made to synthesize these data into broader understandings of regional developments and cultural traditions.

D.P. Agrawal and D.K. Chakrabarti: *Essays in Indian protohistory* (Delhi, 1979); D.P. Agrawal: *The archaeology of India* (Copenhagen, 1982); B. and R. Allchin: *The rise of civilization in India and Pakistan* (Cambridge, 1982); G.L. Possehl, ed.: *Harappan civilization* (Delhi, 1982); K.A.R. Kennedy and G.L. Possehl, eds: *Studies in the archaeology and palaeoanthropology of South Asia* (New Delhi, 1984); B.B. Lal and S.P. Gupta, eds: *Frontiers of the Indus*

Civilization (Delhi, 1984); V.N. Misra and P. Bellwood, eds: *Indo-Pacific prehistory* (New Delhi, 1985); M.L. Kenoyer, ed.: *Old problems and new perspectives in the archaeology of South Asia* (Madison, 1989).
CS

3 Southeast Asia

The physical relief of the region of southeast Asia offers a sharp contrast between the floodplains of the Chao Phraya, Mekong and Red rivers and the intervening uplands. The climate is monsoonal, with a dry season which lasts from November to April, and rains which commence in May. The most significant environmental change in the Holocene involved the drowning of extensive continental shelves by a rising sea, and the formation of shorelines higher than the present sea level.

3.1 *Prehistory*. The drowning of the continental shelves has prevented the consideration of maritime adaptation before 4000–5000 BC, when raised beaches with prehistoric settlements are encountered, but it is clear that the inland, forested uplands were occupied by small bands of transitory foragers. Numerous rock shelters are known, particularly in the karst uplands of northern Vietnam, and these are often ascribed to the Hoabinhian technocomplex. The material culture included flaked river cobbles and, with time, edge-ground and polished adzeheads and pottery sherds. These sites have been dated from 11000 BC, and some late contexts in northern Thailand lasted into the 3rd millennium BC or even later. The material culture corresponds to that found in the lowest levels of thick coastal shell middens found on raised

Date	Period	Principal events and sites
AD 1500 – AD 200	General period D	The rise of states or *mandalas* in the lower Mekong valley, coastal Viet Nam, Northeast Thailand and Chao Phraya valley. Increased centralisation in court centres, Indian inspired religion, statecraft and the Sanskrit language. Angkorian *Mandala* founded in AD 802 and attracted widespread loyalty. Han Chinese set up commanderies in Bac Bo.
500 BC	General period C	Iron-working, centralisation and formation of chiefdoms. Initial contact with Indian traders and Han Chinese armies and increased exchange, social ranking and agriculture. Specialist bronze-workers produce ceremonial drinking vessels, decorative body plaques, bowls and great decorated drums. Chiefly burials in boat coffins.
2000 – 500 BC	General period B	Bronze-working spread among autonomous iowland communities. Ores mined in hills, ingots traded and implements cast in lowlands. Increase in ranking within small communities. Some family groups had high rank signified by jewellery and bronze implements. Subsistence wide-ranging and included rice which was probably cultivated.
3000 BC	General period A	Settlement expansion into the tributary streams of the Khorat plateau, middle country of Bac Bo, the Tonle Sap plains, margins of the Mekong delta and Chao Phraya valley. Settlements small, and social organisation weakly ranked. Stone implements and shell were exchanged between communities which probably cultivated rice in swamp margins.
5000 – 1500 BC	Coastal Settlement	Sea level rose sharply from about 7000-4000 BC; probably drowned coastal settlements. At 4000 BC, sea level stabilised at a higher level than today. Evidence for rich sedentary coastal settlement involving ranking, exchange and elaborate mortuary ritual at Khok Phanom Di. Pollen evidence for settlement by 4700 BC. Marine resources important, rice consumed. Latter may have been harvested from natural stands in freshwater swampland.
10,000 BC	Early Hunter-Gatherers	Sea level began much lower than today, rose to about 3m higher than at present. Former coastal settlements now drowned under sea. Main surviving sites inland rock shelters. Limited range of stone tools, wooden implements for hunting and gathering probably important. Small, mobile groups collected wild plants and shellfish. Evidence for hunting, fishing and trapping.

Table 9 **Asia, 3: Southeast** Chronology of Southeast Asia.

beaches in Vietnam. These midden sites, which have been assigned to several regional cultures (Ha Van Tan 1980) can be in excess of 10 m deep, and sometimes contain inhumation cemeteries. Due to their rich material culture, which includes pottery, polished stone implements and a stone and bone industry, they are often referred to as a coastal Neolithic, but there is as yet no biological evidence for agriculture.

The earliest evidence for rice cultivation within village communities belongs to the 3rd millennium BC, when settlements were established in the

Map 17 **Asia, 3: Southeast** Major archaeological sites in the region.

tributary stream valleys of the major rivers. Over 50 sites of the PHUNG NGUYEN culture above the confluence of the Red and Black rivers in Vietnam have been identified. In northeast Thailand, there are such early contexts at BAN CHIANG and BAN PHAK TOP, while several sites are known in central Thailand, for example BAN KAO, Non Pa Wai and KHOK PHANOM DI. All incorporated a sophisticated ceramic industry, inhumation burials and grave goods which include pottery vessels and jewellery often exotic to the region. A widespread feature was the decoration of pottery with parallel incised lines infilled with impressions. Rice was often used as a ceramic temper, but it is not possible to deduce whether such chaff was from a wild or cultivated variety. The only firm evidence for the latter comes from Khok Phanom Di, an estuarine site with a mortuary sequence revealing about 20 successive generations of the same family groups. The associated grave offerings suggest that status was obtained through personal achievement rather than kinship.

By the mid-2nd millennium BC, copper-based metallurgy was widespread. Southeast Asia is rich in copper, tin and lead, and two mining complexes in the Khao Wong Prachan valley of central Thailand and the PHU LON hill in northeast Thailand have been examined. The earliest mining and smelting activity at both has been dated to about 1500 BC. At Khao Wong Prachan the ores contain significant quantities of arsenic, and tin was not used. The smelting sites there reveal the production of circular ingots, as well as socketed axes and projectile points. Away from the ore sources, there are several village sites within which bronze socketed axes, spearheads and arrowheads were cast in bivalve clay or sandstone moulds, while bracelets were cast using the lost-wax technique.

Until the mid-1st millennium BC, metallurgy was undertaken in small-scale enterprises, perhaps even as a dry season activity. Copper and bronze artefacts were included as grave offerings alongside stone, ivory, ceramic and shell items. But from about 500 BC, a number of major cultural changes took place. In the Khao Wong Prachan valley, there is evidence for iron smelting and forging. Use of this metal spread rapidly. Indian mercantile expansion led to a two-way exchange, particularly with strategically placed coastal or riverine communities, such as BAN DON TA PHET. Bronze bowls, ladles, decorative plaques, and above all drums, reveal the establishment of specialized workshops. The DONG SON CULTURE in northern Vietnam, which best exemplifies these changes, became increasingly exposed to Chinese expansion, and by the 1st century AD it had been incorporated into the Han empire.

The rest of mainland Southeast Asia, however, saw the development of indigenous states which drew heavily on Indian religious and political notions of leadership and statehood. These influences involved Hinduism and Buddhism. The former was particularly popular in Cambodia, and the latter in central Thailand where early indications of contact with India are known from Ban Don Tha Phet and Chausen. From about 200 AD, such polities are known from the lower Mekong area, where they have been subsumed under the name FUNAN. The best-known site is OC EO, a rectangular area of about 450 ha which lies at the centre of a web of canals linking it with other sites. Subsequent polities developed in central Cambodia (Vickery 1986), and inscriptions in Sanskrit and archaic Khmer provide the names of the overlords and stress the worship of Siva. Analagous polities (Higham 1989: 297–306) are found on the coast of Vietnam, where Cham was spoken. This is an Austronesian language, probably brought from island Southeast Asia in the late prehistoric period.

In Central Thailand, the polities characterized by the DVARAVATI CULTURE developed, and here the language spoken was Mon, a close relative of Khmer. The most successful and powerful state, however, was established at ANGKOR on the northern shore of the Tonle Sap (Great Lake) of Central Cambodia in the early 9th century AD. The rulers, responsible for such monuments as Angkor Wat and the Bayon (*see* ANGKOR), exerted their influence over much of the mainland until the fifteenth century AD, when Angkor was sacked by an invading Thai army.

In 1983, Bayard proposed four successive cultural periods to describe the prehistoric sequence in northeast Thailand. General Period A antedated metallurgy, and saw weak social ranking. Period B involved the use of copper-based metallurgy associated with increased social ranking, but still within small, autonomous communities. The next period witnessed the use of iron as well as bronze, and the development of chiefdoms based on large, moated centres. Finally, General Period D involved the development of states. This scheme has since been more widely applied to other parts of lowland Southeast Asia. The dating of these phases is tentatively: A: 21500–1500 BC; B: 1500–600 BC; C: 600 BC–AD 200; and D: from AD 200. The scheme has been applied more widely by Charles Higham (1989).

3.2 *Archaeological research.* The archaeology of mainland Southeast Asia effectively began after the incorporation of Vietnam, Cambodia and Laos into the French colonial empire, and was stimulated by the foundation of the École Française d'Extrême Orient in 1898. Early excavations were undertaken under the auspices of the French colonial administration, with particular encouragement from the École Française and the Geological Service of Indo-China. Coastal shell-midden sites, inland rock shelters, and large settlements, such as Dong Son, were used to establish an archaeological sequence, although most energy was directed to the large historic sites, particularly Angkor.

Such efforts were effectively terminated by the Second World War and the Vietnamese–French conflict. From the 1960s, Western archaeologists began research in Thailand, and the Vietnamese inaugurated their own programme. The former introduced the full range of Western methodology and interpretative structures, while the latter largely remained within the pre-war French paradigm, with some Soviet influence.

O.R.T. Jause: *Archaeological research in Indo-China* III: *The ancient dwelling site of Dong-S'on (Thanh-Hoa, Annam)* (Cambridge, MA, 1958); Nguyen Phuc Long: 'Les nouvelles recherches archéologiques au Vietnam', *Arts Asiatiques* 31 (1975) [entire issue]; Ha Van Tan: 'Nouvelles recherches préhistoriques et protohistoriques au Viet Nam', *BEFEO* 68 (1980), 113–54; J.C. White: *Ban Chiang* (Philadelphia, 1982); D.T. Bayard: 'Rank and wealth at Non Nok Tha', *Southeast Asian archaeology at the XV Pacific Science Congress*, ed. D.T. Bayard (Otago, 1984), 87–128; ——: 'A tentative regional phase chronology for northeast Thailand', *Southeast Asian Archaeology at the XV Pacific Science Congress*, ed. D.T. Bayard (Otago, 1984), 161–8; M. Vickery: 'Some remarks on early state formation in Cambodia', *Southeast Asia in the 9th to 14th centuries*, ed. D.G. Marr and A.C. Milner (Canberra and Singapore, 1986), 95–115; I.C. Glover: *Early trade between India and Southeast Asia* (Hull, 1989); C.F.W. Higham: *The archaeology of mainland Southeast Asia* (Cambridge, 1989); ——: *Khok Phanom Di* (Fort Worth, 1993).

CH

Askut Island Upper Nubian site at the southern tip of LAKE NASSER, primarily consisting of an Egyptian fortress of the Middle Kingdom (*c*.2040–1640 BC) and a Nubian settlement of the Christian period (*c*.AD 550–1500), both excavated by the University of California during the early 1960s. Since a high percentage of the interior of the 12th-dynasty fortress is occupied by the remains of mud-brick granaries, it has been suggested that Askut may have been an emergency supply depot for the Egyptian army rather than a straightforward garrison.

A. Badawy: 'Preliminary report on the excavations by the University of California at Askut', *Kush* 12 (1964), 47–53; ——: 'Archaeological problems relating to the Egyptian fortress at Askut', *JARCE* 5 (1966), 23–7; S. Tyson Smith: *Askut in Nubia: the economics and ideology of Egyptian imperialism in the second millennium BC* (London, 1995).

IS

Asmar, Tell (anc. Eshnunna) Site of a SUMERIAN city-state to the north-east of modern Baghdad, Iraq. The cult-centre at the site has yielded an extraordinary series of religious statues (see figure 5). See DIYALA REGION for further discussion.

Asokrochona Site of a Stone Age lithic workshop near the coast east of Accra, Ghana. The site was located by Oliver Davies in 1958 and excavated by S.E. Nygaard and M.R. Talbot, and by B.W. Andah, in 1972–4. The principal archaeological horizon occurs on or at the top of what Nygaard and Talbot call an ironstone gravel of well-rounded laterite fragments (the Asokrochona Formation) said to have been formed under semi-arid conditions, beneath red aeolian sand (the Nungua Formation) which contains a few Middle Stone Age artefacts. The main archaeological occurrence has

Figure 5 **Asmar, Tell** Limestone statues of worshippers, 0.34 m high, with eyeballs of inlaid shell, found buried in the shrine of an Early Dynastic temple at Tell Asmar. *Source*: J. Black and A. Green: *Gods, demons and symbols of ancient Mesopotamia: an illustrated dictionary* (BMP, 1992), fig. 1.

commonly been regarded as SANGOAN (although local names for it have also been proposed) and it is the most extensively excavated and most fully published site representative of this entity in West Africa. There are over 20,000 artefacts, of which around 2500 are tools and cores, the remainder consisting principally of flakes, manuports, chips and chunks. The tools include a few handaxes, picks, and core-axes, as well as other heavy and light duty components, mainly of quartz and quartzite. There is no fauna, and the dating of the site remains hypothetical.

O. Davies: *The Quaternary in the Coastlands of Guinea* (Glasgow, 1964); S.E. Nygaard and M.R. Talbot: 'Interim report on excavation at Asokrochona, Ghana', *WAJA* 6 (1976), 13–19; B.W. Andah: 'The early palaeolithic in West Africa: the case of Asokrochona coastal region of Accra, Ghana', *WAJA* 9 (1979), 47–85; S.E. Nygaard and M.R. Talbot: 'Stone age archaeology and environment on the southern Accra plains, Ghana', *NAR* 17 (1984), 19–38; P. Allsworth-Jones: 'The earliest human settlement in West Africa and the Sahara', *WAJA* 17 (1987), 87–128.

PA-J

assemblage Set of artefacts, not necessarily of the same type, recovered from a specific archaeological context. Distinct groups of artefacts (for instance, flints that have been manufactured using a particular technique) from different assemblages may be categorized as an INDUSTRY. Distinctive assemblages or industries whch recur in different contexts are often taken as indicators of a specific culture; however, archaeologists have become increasingly wary of assuming that distinctive assemblages of material culture necessarily indicate wider linguistic and social groupings (*see* CULTURE HISTORY).

The term 'assemblage' is sometimes used more loosely to describe artefacts grouped together for the purposes of argument or analysis, or in a particular collection.

RJA

Assiut *see* ASYUT

associated, association *see* CONTINGENCY TABLE

Assur *see* ASSYRIA

Assyria, Assyrians Semitic state and people whose origins perhaps lay in the desert surrounding the upper Tigris; they first appeared in northern Mesopotamia in the 3rd millennium BC, and their name derives from the city of Assur which they established in northern Mesopotamia. The tell-site of Qalat Shergat (ancient Assur), located beside the Tigris, midway between modern Mosul and Baghdad, appears to date back at least to the Early Dynastic II period (*c*.2750–2600 BC), but it remained a relatively obscure settlement until the 19th century BC, when colonies of merchants from Assur began to establish profitable colonies beside some of the major Anatolian cities, hundreds of miles to the north of Assur itself (*see* KÜLTEPE). Under the successful AMORITE ruler Shamshi Adad I (*c*.1813–1781 BC) an Assyrian empire was established, with its capital initially at Shubat-Enlil (Tell Leilan) and later at Assur. The political machinations and administrative structure of the Old Assyrian empire are recorded in an archive of more than 20,000 cuneiform tablets excavated from the Syrian city of MARI. For over 400 years after the rise of the Babylonian ruler Hammurabi (who sacked Mari in 1757 BC), the Assyrians were overshadowed by BABYLON to the south and MITANNI to the north, but eventually – under Ashuruballit I (c.1363–1328 BC) – they regained their independence. It was, however, not until the late 10th century BC that the Assyrians regained control of northern Mesopotamia in the reign of Adad-Nirari II (*c*.911–891 BC). The Late Assyrian empire, which was centred on the three major cities of Kalhu (NIMRUD), NINEVEH (Tell Kuyunjik) and Dur-Sharrukin (KHORSABAD), expanded rapidly over an area stretching from modern Iran to the Mediterranean. At Maltaï, about 60 km from Mosul, there are three rock-carved reliefs of the reign of Sennacherib (*c*. 704–681 BC) depicting processions of Assyrian deities (Bachmann 1927).

Although Esarhaddon (*c*.680–669 BC) succeeded in conquering Egypt, the Assyrian heartland was under increasing attack from the Medes and the Babylonians; ultimately, in 612 BC the whole empire crumbled and Nineveh itself was destroyed. For a few years after the sack of Nineveh the Assyrians appear to have fought a rearguard action from the Syrian city of Harran (Sultantepe), which had previously been an important commercial centre of the empire, but overall control of Mesopotamia had by then been irretrievably ceded to the neo-Babylonian rulers.

D. Oates: *Studies in the ancient history of northern Iraq* (London, 1968), 19–41 [early development of Assyria]; W. Andrae: *Das wiedererstandene Assur*, 2nd edn (Munich, 1977) [the German excavations at Assur, 1903–14]; J. Reade: *Assyrian sculpture* (London, 1983); J. Curtis and J. Reade, eds: *Art and empire: treasures from Assyria in the British Museum* (London, 1995).

IS

ASTt *see* ARCTIC SMALL TOOL TRADITION

Asturian Mesolithic stone and bone industry linked to the shell-midden sites or *concheros* of northern Spain. The Asturian lithic industry is crude and has a high proportion of heavy duty tools, including a unifacial pick; compared to the AZILIAN it exhibits a relatively high proportion of serrated artefacts and a relatively low proportion of backed bladelets. The Asturian was identified as a distinct 'culture' after excavations by the Count of Vega del Sella at the cave of El Penicial (Asturias) in 1914. Strauss and Clark have more recently argued against this, suggesting that the *concheros* should be viewed as the middens of specialized exploitation sites which operated within an integrated Azilian-Asturian Mesolithic economy. However, the contemporaneity of the Azilian and Asturian is not yet quite proven, and González Morales has criticized this FUNCTIONALIST interpretation.

G.A. Clark: 'Site functional complementarity in the Mesolithic of northern Spain', *The mesolithic in Europe*, Papers presented at the Third International Symposium, Edinburgh, ed. Clive Bonsall (Edinburgh, 1985), 589–603; M.R. González Morales: 'Asturian resource exploitation: recent perspectives', *The mesolithic in Europe*; L.G. Strauss: *Iberia before the Iberians* (Albuquerque, 1992), 217–29.

RJA

Asuka District in Nara prefecture, Japan, which was the centre of the introduction of Buddhism from the Asian continent in the 6th–7th centuries AD. Early palace sites and temples, including the site of Asuka-dera, the first Buddhist temple in Japan and Kawahara-dera, are now protected as part of a special historical district. The Fujiwara Palace site has also been excavated. The region was the centre of the Ritsuryo state until the capital was moved to HEIJO in AD 710.

K. Tsuboi: 'The excavation of ancient palaces and capitals', *Acta Asiatica* 63 (1992), 87–98.

SK

Aswad, Tell *see* ACERAMIC NEOLITHIC

Aswan (anc. Swnt, Syene) Pharaonic site in Upper Egypt at the northern end of LAKE NASSER. On the eastern bank of the Nile are the town, temples and granite quarries of Aswan itself, while the Old and Middle Kingdom rock-cut tombs of Qubbet el-Hawa are situated on the opposite bank. In the centre of the Nile at Aswan are the town and temples of the island of Elephantine. Apart from two small Ptolemaic and Roman temples there are few surviving remains of the city of Aswan itself since the area has continued to be occupied up to modern times. The tombs of Qubbet el-Hawa, which date mainly to the Old and Middle Kingdoms (*c*.2649–1640 BC), contain important reliefs and inscriptions, including the 'funerary biographies' of important officials such as the 6th-dynasty provincial governor Harkhuf. Elephantine has been excavated by a German team since the 1970s (Kaiser et al. 1972–95). It has proved possible to trace the gradual enlargement of the town of Elephantine from the early Dynastic period to the Roman period (*c*.2900 BC–AD 395), thus contributing to the understanding of processes of urbanization in pharaonic Egypt.

E. Edel: *Die Felsengräber der Qubbet el-Hawa bei Assuan* (Wiesbaden, 1967–); W. Kaiser, G. Dreyer and S. Seidlmayer: Regular preliminary reports on Elephantine excavations in *MDAIK* 28–51 (1972–95); E. Bresciani and S. Pernigotti: *Assuan: il tempio tolemaico di Isi. I blocchi decorati e iscritti* (Pisa, 1978).

IS

Aswan High Dam *see* LAKE NASSER

Asyut (anc. Djawty) Site in Egypt, roughly midway between Cairo and Aswan, which was the ancient capital of the 13th Upper Egyptian *nome* (province), where, according to many surviving texts, the principal cult-centre of the wolf-god Wepwawet was located. The archaeological remains consist primarily of the rock tombs of the local elite, dating from the 9th dynasty to the Ramessid period (*c*.2134–1070 BC). The so-called 'biographical' inscriptions on the walls of the tombs of the 1st Intermediate Period and Middle Kingdom (*c*.2134–1640 BC) provide historical information on the struggle between the rulers of HERAKLEOPOLIS MAGNA and THEBES.

F.L. Griffith: *The inscriptions of Siut and Der Rifeh* (London, 1889); G.A. Reisner, 'The tomb of Hepzefa, nomarch of Siñt', *JEA* 5 (1919), 79–98; H. Thompson, *A family archive from Siut* (Oxford, 1934).

IS

Atchana, Tell (Açana; anc. Alalakh) Settlement mound by the River Orontes in northwestern Syria, which was the site of Alalakh, the capital of a small kingdom in the 2nd millennium BC. It appears to have particularly prospered in *c*.1550–1400 BC, when it was one of the westernmost vassals of the HURRIAN kingdom of MITANNI. It was excavated by Leonard Woolley in 1937–9 and 1946–9, revealing an unusual temple of the 24th century BC, and the palaces of two of its rulers, Yarim-Lim (*c*.1750 BC) and Niqmepa (*c*.1500 BC), the former including a *BIT-HILANI*. Woolley also explored the neighbouring port of el-Mina, at the mouth of the Orontes, which was used primarily during the Achaemenid period (*c*.538–331 BC).

The site of Alalakh consisted of 17 strata in all, stretching from the Chalcolithic period (*c*.3500 BC) until the early 12th century BC, when it may have been destroyed by the SEA PEOPLES. Stratum VII, dating to the 18th century BC, when the city was part of the AMORITE kingdom of Yamhad, included a cache of cuneiform tablets, inscribed in Akkadian, which first enabled Woolley to identify the site as Alalakh. Another archive, discovered in stratum IV and dating to the 15th and 16th centuries BC, has shed a great deal of light on the society and administration of Mitanni and its relations with the HITTITES, providing a useful comparison with the slightly later diplomatic correspondence from EL-AMARNA (Wiseman 1953). Sidney Smith (1940) was able to use the Alalakh stratigraphy and textual evidence to construct a general chronology for the northern Levant in the 2nd millennium BC.

A group of carved ivory objects excavated from the same stratum show the same mixture of external influences as the wall-paintings at NUZI, one of the easternmost cities of Mitanni. The style of palace architecture at Alalakh, both before and after the Hurrian domination, is part of a local tradition, using stone foundations, basalt orthostats and a great deal of plaster-clad timber. The maintenance of different local architectural traditions at Alalakh and Nuzi suggests that there was no overall Mitannian palatial style.

S. Smith: *Alalakh and chronology* (London, 1940); D.J. Wiseman: *The Alalakh tablets* (London, 1953); C.L. Woolley: *Alalakh: an account of the excavations at Tell Atchana in the Hatay, 1937–49* (London, 1955).

IS

Aterian Palaeolithic industrial complex, named by Maurice Reygasse in the 1920s, after the site of Bir el-Ater in the Oued Djebbana, eastern Algeria, at first on the basis of a distinctive 'fossile directeur', the tanged point. The industry as a whole was later defined by Jacques Tixier as a LEVALLOIS facies of the MOUSTERIAN, in which tanged tools of various kinds (not only points) constituted up to one quarter of the retouched artefacts. François Bordes observed that the many technological and typological elements common to both Mousterian and Aterian suggested that the second derived from the first. This is supported by stratigraphic superposition of these industries at Témara, northwestern Morocco, and at Taforalt and Rhafas, eastern Morocco. Apart from the Maghreb, the Aterian has a very wide extension in North Africa and the Sahara, as far as Cyrenaica and the Egyptian desert in the east (HAUA FTEAH and the oases of Kharga and Bir Tarfawi) and the TAOUDENNI and Northern Chad basins in the south (including ADRAR BOUS).

J.D. Clark suggests that within the Aterian as a whole various 'culture areas' or 'traditions' may be distinguished, characterized by distinctive artefact forms, such as bifacially worked foliate points, which are particularly numerous southeast of the Hoggar mountains. Tanged points (implying hafting) in his view constitute the first unequivocal evidence for simple compound tools in the palaeolithic record. Chronologically, the Aterian in the Maghreb is commonly regarded as falling in the interval 40,000–20,000 years ago, and there are a number of finite radiocarbon dates in this range; as well as OSL (optically stimulated luminescence) and TL (thermoluminescence) dates now available from Chaperon Rouge in northwestern Morocco indicative of an occupation at 28,200 ± 3300 BP. Nevertheless, minimum or infinite radiocarbon dates for Taforalt suggest that the Aterian there may be >40,000 years old, and the finding of Aterian artefacts in or above Tyrrhenian beach deposits in the vicinity of Oran, western Algeria, would be consonant with this.

At HAUA FTEAH, Charles McBurney detected possibly tanged pieces and a 'strong hint of Aterian affinities' in layers XXXII–XXXI, corresponding to a period >43,400 BP, and at Bir Tarfawi the tanged pieces originally identified as Aterian are likely to date to the end of the sequence around 60,000 years ago. The Aterian in the Sahara is generally considered to be relatively late, corresponding to the Upper Ghazalian humid period *c*.30–20,000 years ago. An upper limit is provided by a date of 18,600 ± 400 BP from Ekouloulef in the Air mountains. At Adrar Bous and Bilma the Aterian is preceded by Middle Stone Age industries which Tillet places in the Lower Ghazalian humid period *c*.40–35,000 years ago; while 'probably comparable to the Mousterian in the Maghreb' such industries in his view might represent a local origin for the Aterian and constitute its early phase in this area. The Aterian is associated with anatomically modern man at DAR-ES-SOLTANE II and three other sites on the Moroccan coast.

J. Tixier: 'Procédés d'analyse et questions de terminologie conçernant l' étude des ensembles industriels du paléolithique récent et de l'epipaléolithique dans l'Afrique du Nord-ouest', *Background to evolution in Africa*, ed. W.W. Bishop and J.D. Clark (Chicago, 1967), 771–820;

C.R. Ferring: 'The Aterian in North African prehistory', *Problems in Prehistory: North Africa and the Levant*, ed. F. Wendorf and A.E. Marks (Dallas, 1975), 113–26; F. Bordes: 'Moustérien et Atérien', *Quaternaria* 19 (1976–7), 19–34; J.D. Clark: 'Human populations and cultural adaptations in the Sahara and Nile during prehistoric times', *The Sahara and the Nile*, ed. M.A.J. Williams and H. Faure (Rotterdam, 1980), 527–82; A.E. Close: 'Current research and recent radiocarbon dates from Northern Africa', *JAH* 21 (1980), 145–67; G. Delibrias et al.: 'Gif natural radiocarbon measurements IX', *Radiocarbon* 24 (1982), 291–343; T. Tillet: 'The palaeolithic and its environment in the northern part of the Chad basin', *AAR* 3 (1985), 163–77; A. Debénath et al.: 'Stratigraphie, habitat, typologie et devenir de l'Atérien marocain: données récentes', *L'Anthropologie* 90 (1986), 233–46; L. Wengler: 'Position géochronologique et modalités du passage Moustérien–Atérien en Afrique du Nord, L'exemple de la grotte du Rhafas au Maroc oriental', *CRASP*, Série II 303 (1986), 1153–6; J.P. Tixier et al.: 'Nouvelles données sur la situation chronologique de l'Atérien du Maroc et leurs implications', *CRASP*, Série II, 307 (1988), 827–32; F. Wendorf et al.: *Egypt during the Last Interglacial: the Middle Palaeolithic of Bir Tarfawi and Bir Sahara East* (New York and London, 1993).
PA-J

Atestine culture *see* ESTE

atomic absorption spectrophotometry (AAS) Quantitative technique of chemical analysis applicable to metals, ceramics, glass and lithics for major, minor and trace element analysis. The technique relies on the principle that electron energy level changes in atoms may be stimulated by the absorption of light at element-specific wavelengths. A small sample is required, typically 10 mg when applied to metals, and usually this must be in solution.

The basic instrument consists of a light source emitting the spectrum for the element being measured (e.g. copper), a flame through which the light is directed and sample atomized, and a monochromator measuring the intensity of light transmitted through the flame at a specific wavelength characteristic of the element. Solutions are introduced into the flame via a nebulizer with a capillary uptake tube. While the sample solution is sprayed into the flame, any atoms of the element being measured will respond by absorbing some of the light from the lamp. The absorbance recorded is proportional to the quantity of the element in the flame and hence in the solution. Standard solutions of known concentration are measured initially to calibrate for each element.

The technique is sequential for each element, although one solution is normally used to measure all elements in a given sample. The precision and accuracy are high (1–2% for major components) and a very wide range of elements can be quantified but this does not include certain non-metals such as, for example, oxygen, carbon, nitrogen or chlorine.

The sensitivity may be increased, and detection limits lowered to the ultra-trace level, by using electrothermal instead of flame atomization. This uses a graphite tube, into which the sample is injected and through which the light is directed, that is electrically heated to about 3000°C which atomizes the sample and generates a transient absorption signal.

AAS – first applied in the early 1970s – has been used extensively to analyse a wide range of archaeological materials such as copper-based alloys of all periods, flint, slag, pottery and glass. Applications include artefact characterization, technology and provenance investigations. AAS is beginning to be challenged by ICP-AES (INDUCTIVELY COUPLED PLASMA-ATOMIC EMISSION SPECTROMETRY) as an alternative technique for chemical analysis of sampleable inorganic materials.

M.J. Hughes et al.: 'Atomic absorption techniques in archaeology', *Archaeometry* 18 (1976), 19–37; W.J. Price: *Spectrochemical analysis by atomic absorption* (Wiley, 1979).
MC

Atranjikhera Multi-period site on the Kali Nanga tributary of the Ganges in Uttar Pradesh, India, consisting of a single mound (about 40 ha in area). Excavations in the 1960s and 1970s showed that there were seven phases of the site, the first four of which – OCHRE COLOURED POTTERY, BLACK AND RED WARE, PAINTED GREY WARE and NORTHERN BLACK POLISHED WARE – date to late prehistoric and early historic periods (*c*.1800–50 BC). Twenty-three coins of the Nanda, MAURYAN and Sunga dynasties were recovered from the levels dating to the Northern Black Polished Ware period (*c*.600–50 BC), when the site reached its maximum extent, with densely packed mud-brick and fired brick buildings and a massive defensive wall. *See also* GANGES CIVILIZATION.

R.C. Gaur: *Excavations at Atranjikhera* (Delhi, 1983).
CS

Atrib, Tell (anc. Hwt-Heryib, Athribis) Egyptian settlement site located in the central Delta region near the modern town of Benha, 40 km north of Cairo. The principal surviving features of Tell Atrib are a temple dating to the time of Amasis (*c*.570–526 BC), the tomb of Queen Takhut (*c*.590 BC) and extensive urban, religious and funerary remains of the Greco-Roman period (*c*.332 BC–AD

395). The site as a whole has been severely damaged by the activities of *sabbakhin* (farmers plundering ancient mud-brick for use as fertilizer), one of whom discovered a large cache of Late Period (*c*.712–332 BC) jewellery in 1924. During the 1980s and 1990s a team of Polish archaeologists have concentrated on the excavation of the Greco-Roman town.

A. Rowe, 'Short report on the excavation of the Institute of Archaeology Liverpool at Athribis (Tell Atrib)', *ASAE* 38 (1938), 523–32; P. Vernus: *Athribis* (Cairo, 1978); K. Mysliwiec and T. Herbich: 'Polish archaeological activities at Tell Atrib in 1985', *The Archaeology of the Nile Delta: problems and priorities*, ed. E.C.M. van den Brink (Amsterdam, 1988), 177–203.

IS

attribute/attribute state *see* VARIABLE

auger electron spectroscopy (AES) Qualitative and quantitative non-destructive surface technique particularly suited to light-element chemical analysis. In principle, the technique is related to energy dispersive X-ray analysis using a scanning electron microscope (SEM EDX). Electron excitation causes ionization of atoms in the specimen but, instead of the re-arrangement which would cause a fluorescent X-ray photon to be emitted, there is an internal conversion which results in the release of low-energy electrons. The electron energy is specific to a particular element and is subject to small changes due to chemical effects, specifically the valance state of the element. The technique is therefore capable of detecting the presence of compounds, such as oxides, on metal surfaces and has been applied to the analysis of patinas. The surface layer analysed is of the order of 10–2 μm in depth.

M. Polak et al.: 'Auger electron spectroscopy applied to archaeological artefacts', *Archaeometry* 25 (1983), 59–67.

MC

Aurignacian Early Upper Palaeolithic industry (*c*.38000–28000 BC) that presents a full blade technology and a wide range of tools, including carinate (thick) scrapers, burins, endscrapers, and blades with a distinctive 'scalar' (or 'Aurignacian') retouch around their margins. The Aurignacian, named after the Aurignac shelter in the French Pyrenees, is also characterized by a rich bone industry that includes bone points and awls (*see also* MOBILIARY ART). It seems highly probable, if not quite certain, that Aurignacian assemblages were produced solely by *Homo sapiens sapiens*. In France and Spain, the Aurignacian is strongly associated with the early stages of CAVE ART.

The Aurignacian industry was first recognized in the Périgord region of France, where it succeeds the MOUSTERIAN rather before 35,000 BP. However, the industry seems to appear rather earlier in Central Europe, where it is associated with well-crafted MOBILIARY ART. The oldest Aurignacian in Europe (*c*.40,000 BP) has been identified in the Middle Danube and the Balkans. It seems probable that the Aurignacian is intrusive in both Central and Western Europe, and that its appearance is associated with the replacement in Europe of the NEANDERTHALS by ANATOMICALLY MODERN HUMANS. *See* UPPER PALAEOLITHIC for further discussion.

Aurignacian assemblages are traditionally divided into different stages (I–V) according to the typology of their bone tools. Stages I and perhaps II may still be useful classifications, but controlled excavation at sites such as ABRI PATAUD has suggested the need for more subtle schemes defined by the comparative *frequency* of different kinds of tool and tool attribute.

C. Gamble: *The Palaeolithic settlement of Europe* (Cambridge, 1986); J.F. Hoffecker and C.A. Wolf, eds: *The early Upper Palaeolithic*, BAR IS 437 (Oxford, 1988).

RJA

Australia *see* OCEANIA

Australian core tool and scraper tradition Traditionally, archaeologists have assigned to this single tradition all tools dating from before about 5000 years ago from across the Australian continent: 'horsehoof' cores and steep-edged scrapers are the most characteristic elements. However, the similarity of assemblages across the continent may simply be due to common functions, such as shaping wood and hides and cutting meat, rather than any sort of cultural or stylistic cohesion. The homogeneity has anyway been over-emphasized, and recently archaeologists have begun to stress that regional tool types exist (such as the thumbnail scrapers in Tasmania, and the edge-ground axes of northern Australia and Papua New Guinea). *See also* OCEANIA 1.

J.P. White and J.F. O'Connell: *A prehistory of Australia, New Guinea and Sahul* (Sydney, 1982), 64–70.

CG

Australian small tool tradition Generic term used to describe the blade tools, delicately retouched to make a variety of points and backed blades, produced across the continent from about

5000 years ago to the present day. The regional variations of the tradition derive from a variety of techniques: Kimberley points, for instance, are bifacially flaked, while Bondi points, a type of backed blade first found on Bondi beach, are unifacially flaked. There are geographical differences in the distributions of these types – backed blades, for example, occur less commonly in tropical Australia – but these regional variations are presently inadequately researched.

D.J. Mulvaney: *The prehistory of Australia* (Melbourne, 1975), 210; J.P. White and J.F. O'Connell: *A prehistory of Australia, New Guinea and Sahul* (Sydney, 1982), 106–25.
CG

Australopithecus Originally discovered by Raymond Dart in 1925, the inappropriately named *Australopithecus* – 'Southern Ape' – was not recognized as a human ancestor until the PILTDOWN HOAX was unmasked in the 1950s. Since the 1970s, it has become clear that Australopithecines were the progenitors of modern humans, but that there were a number of species at different times and in different parts of Africa, not all of which were ancestral to our own lineage.

The earliest known hominids belong to the species *Australopithecus afarensis*, discovered at HADAR and later also represented by fossils from LAETOLI. While *Afarensis* was a full biped, its mode of walking was somewhat different to modern humans and its forelimbs retained adaptation for climbing. It was a relatively small-brained hominid (*c*.450–500 cm^3), although calculated body weights range from 30 to 80 kg. These wide differences have led to controversy as to whether the large and small *afarensis* are sexual dimorphs of the same species, or members of different species. In all, one might view *Australopithecus* as a bipedal ape similar to other modern great apes.

Some time around 3 million years ago, the basal species of Australopithecines began to diverge into distinct species/subspecies. Just how these relate to the origin of genus *Homo*, in the shape of *HOMO HABILIS*, is not at all certain. But it is clear that Australopiths did diverge between the gracile *Australopithecus africanus* and the more robust *A. aethiopicus* (represented by the WT 17 000 fossil from WEST TURKANA). This latter branch then led to other robust, small-brained species (*A. robustus* and *A. boisei*) whilst the gracile form probably led to the genus *Homo*. Nevertheless, it is clear that for some considerable time between 1.8 and 1.1 million years ago, robust and gracile Australopithecines coexisted with both *Homo habilis* and *HOMO ERECTUS*.

Archaeologically, it is unclear whether Australopithecines made tools of any kind. Although some possible examples have been proposed, it is probable that the earliest OLDOWAN tools, dating to *c*.2.3 million years ago, were in fact made by the larger brained *HOMO HABILIS*.

R. Foley: *Another unique species* (London, 1987); G. Richards: *Human evolution: an introduction for the behavioural sciences* (London, 1987); C.S. Gamble: *Timewalkers: The prehistory of global colonization* (London, 1993), 47–73.
PG-B

Austrasia *see* KEMPEN PROJECT

Avaris *see* DAB'A, TELL EL-

Avebury Late Neolithic ceremonial complex, including a massive HENGE and stone circles, situated in Wiltshire, England near the contemporary earthwork at Silbury Hill. Sherds of Windmill Hill, PETERBOROUGH and GROOVED WARE were excavated from the bottom of the henge ditch; this, and comparison with other large Wessex henges (e.g. Durrington Walls), suggests that construction may have begun soon after 2600 BC. The main henge consists of a massive ditch (originally 9 m deep) with external bank, breached by four entrances, two of which were originally approached via stone processional avenues. The roughly circular great stone ring (*c*.330 m in diameter) is erected along the inner edge of the ditch. Inside the great ring are the remains of two precisely laid-out smaller stone circles (*c*.100 m in diameter). In the centre of the northern inner circle three large stones originally formed a simple open-ended enclosure (The Cove); the centre of the southern ring was marked by a very large stone (The Obelisk) and an enigmatic, roughly triangular arrangement of smaller stones. One of the (restored) stone avenues follows a curving route to a terminal ritual site, known as The Sanctuary, where excavation has revealed three successive circular arrangements of posts. Whether the posts supported roofs or formed free-standing timber circles is unclear, but they were eventually replaced by two small concentric rings of stones.

Recent surveys and excavations indicate that the area between the West Kennet Avenue and West Kennet Long Barrow once contained two roughly circular enclosures, the larger one concentric, ringed by palisades of oak timbers set in trenches about 2 m deep. The enclosures are of uncertain function, perhaps comparable to the palisade enclosure at Mount Pleasant henge in Dorset; they may represent a relatively late ritual phase at Avebury, a few centuries after the construction of the main megalithic structures.

A. Burl: *Prehistoric Avebury* (London, 1979); A. Whittle: 'A late Neolithic complex at West Kennet, Wiltshire, England', *Antiquity* 65 (1991), 256–62.

RJA

Awat'ovi *see* ANASAZI

axe-money Small bronze artefacts, apparently manufactured in northern Peru beginning *c.*AD 900 and traded to Ecuador for *Spondylus* shells.

D. Hosler et al.: *Axe-monies and their relatives* (Dumbarton Oaks, 1990).

KB

Axum City in the Ethiopian highlands, founded in the 3rd century AD, perhaps by migrants from southern Arabia. It was the capital and type-site of the Axumite culture. The remains include several groups of tall, narrow, stone stelae (up to 33 m in height), as well as tombs, monolithic platforms and urban material. The sites of three monumental multi-roomed buildings, known as Enda Mika'el, Enda Semon and Ta'akha Mariam, were excavated by a German expedition (Littmann et al. 1913). These massive structures, each standing on a masonry podium and consisting of up to three storeys, were identified by the excavators as the residences of the rulers of Axum. In 1966–8, a fourth structure, the 'Dongur Mansion', was excavated (Anfray 1972); this 40-room complex, covering an area of about 3000 square metres and dating to the 7th century AD, was interpreted as an elite 'villa' rather than a royal palace. Excavations elsewhere at Axum have revealed a number of smaller stone buildings, suggesting that it was an extensive urban site throughout the 1st millennium AD.

In the early 1970s a geoarchaeological study (Butzer 1981) and a settlement pattern survey (Michels 1979: 22-4) were conducted across a wide area around Axum. Both suggested that natural resources were unequally distributed in north-eastern Ethiopia during the 1st millennium AD, leading to a distinct clustering of sites. Graham Connah (1987: 91) argues that population pressure brought about by differential access to resources in Axumite Ethiopia could have been a crucial influence on the course of Ethiopian history.

In the 1990s, the excavations of the British Institute of East Africa, directed by David Phillipson (1994), concentrated on the examination of the archaeological context of Stele 1, showing that the investigation of the impressive stone-built funerary remains at Axum can contribute to the understanding of the function and symbolism of the Axumite stelae. Phillipson argues that the stelae served as grave-markers, representing a tradition which was modified after the people of Axum had adopted Christianity in the 4th century AD. He

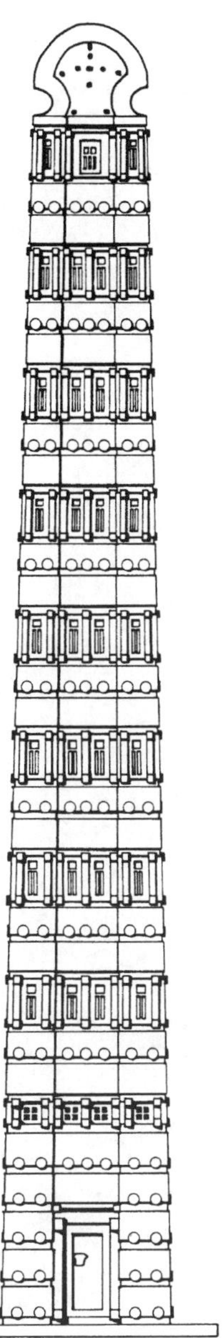

Figure 6 **Axum** Granite stele, Axum, Ethiopia. *Source*: G. Connah: *African civilizations* (Cambridge University Press, 1987), fig. 4.2.

points out that, as the Axumite rulers were gradually Christianized, 'erection of storeyed stelae was abandoned, but certain features of earlier graves and markers were retained, implying some continuity in underlying tradition'. *See also* ADULIS, MATARA *and* YEHA.

E. Littmann et al.: *Deutsche Aksum Expedition*, 2 vols (Berlin, 1913); H. Monneret de Villard: *Aksum: richerche di topografia generale* (Rome, 1938); F. Anfray: 'L'archéologie d'Axoum en 1972', *Paideuma* 18 (1972), 60–78; J.W. Michels: 'Axumite archaeology: an introductory essay', *Aksum*, ed. Y.M. Kobishchanov (Philadelphia, 1979), 1–34; K. Butzer: 'Rise and fall of Axum, Ethiopia: a geoarchaeological interpretation', *AA* 46/3 (1981), 471–95; G. Connah: *African civilizations, Precolonial cities and states in tropical Africa: an archaeological perspective* (Cambridge, 1987), 76–84; S. Munro-Hay: *Aksum: an African civilization of Late Antiquity* (Edinburgh, 1991); D. Phillipson: 'The significance and symbolism of Aksumite stelae', *CAJ* 4/2 (1994), 189–210.

IS

Ayla/al-Aqaba Islamic urban site which was the port of Palestine and formed the link with the Red Sea as well as serving as a strategic point on the pilgrim road from Egypt to the Hijaz. Although urban remains had not been suspected at the site before excavations commenced in 1986, Ayla must now be regarded as comparable with such better-known foundations as al-FUSTAT, al-KUFA and al-Basra in terms of its archaeological importance for the understanding of early Islamic settlements.

The town was fortified, and such features as its

Map 18 **Axum** Prehistoric and Axumite sites in Ethiopia and Eritrea.

towers, the organization of its gates and its central terapylon all recall Roman legionary camps in southern Jordan and Egypt. The site has been attributed to the reign of the third Caliph Uthman in about AD 650. Rising water has prevented the excavations reaching virgin soil, but there can be no doubt that the site's discovery transforms the understanding of Umayyad and even pre-Umayyad activity in southern Palestine and Jordan. It also provides a focus for the study of the early Islamic period in the Red Sea, an area that has been neglected by archaeologists.

D. Whitcomb: 'Excavations in Aqaba: first preliminary report', *ADAJ* 31 (1987), 247–66; ——: 'A Fatimid residence in Aqaba, Jordan', *ADAJ* 32 (1987), 207–24; ——: 'The *Misr* of Ayla: settlement of al-ʿAqaba in the early Islamic period', *The Byzantine and early Islamic Near East II: land use and settlement patterns*, ed. G.R.D. King and A. Cameron (Princeton, 1994), 155–70.

GK

Ayn Asil *see* DAKHLA OASIS

Ayutthaya Capital of the Thai kingdom, founded by King U-Thong or Ramathibodi in AD 1351, and sacked by the Burmese in 1767. Located on the Chao Phraya River, 50 km north of Bangkok, it was the centre of Thai power and culture for four centuries. It was, however, prone to attacks by the Burmese, suffering a major setback when it was destroyed and sacked in 1569. Under King Narai (1656–88), however, the Thais entered a period of strong diplomatic and trade relationships with the West. A 17th-century plan prepared by de la Loubére, a member of a French diplomatic mission, shows the location of the royal palace, the arsenal, port, market and area occupied by the populace. There were also buildings of the Dutch, Portuguese and French missions. After its final destruction in 1767, the Thai leadership retreated to the marshy delta of the Chao Phraya river in the vicinity of Bangkok.

D.K. Wyatt: *Thailand, a short history* (New Haven, 1984), 61–9.

CH

Azania *see* HAFUN; RHAPTA

Azilian Industry or 'culture' transitional between the Upper Palaeolithic (Magdalenian) and Mesolithic, *c.*10,000–7000 BC. Because the Azilian appears at the end of the last glaciation it has traditionally been regarded as marking the beginning of cultural and technological adaptions to a post-glacial environment. The Azilian was first excavated in 1874 at Abri Duruthy in France (Landes), but MAS D'AZIL (Ariège) and La Tourasse (Haute-Garonne) are regarded as its type-sites. The character of an Azilian assemblage has never been strictly defined; many definitions are essentially negative, stressing the poverty of Azilian lithic industries in comparison to the Magdalenian (which may be partly due to a tendency to use lower-grade flint) and the paucity of its art. The strongest positive indicators are flat single-row Azilian harpoons (often with button-hole perforations) and curious painted AZILIAN PEBBLES. Where these indicators are absent Azilian assemblages are identified by their high proportion of backed bladelets and small end-scrapers; a low (but variable) proportion of burins; and the presence of Azilian points (double-pointed backed blades). Because the character of the Azilian is indistinct at both chronological ends, there has been a proliferation of terms such as 'Azilian-like' or 'epi-Azilian'. 'Azilian' points and even flat harpoons are found in Magdalenian contexts (Bahn), while a probable chronological overlap with 'true' Mesolithic entities such as the Asturian has led to suggestions of a complex relationship (see ASTURIAN).

P. Bahn: *Pyrenean prehistory* (Warminster, 1984), 45; J.A. Fernández-Tresguerres Velasco: 'Thoughts on the transition from the Magdalenian to the Azilian in Cantabria: evidence from the Cueva de Los Azules, Asturias', *The mesolithic in Europe*, Papers presented at the Third International Symposium, Edinburgh, ed. Clive Bonsall (Edinburgh, 1985), 582–8; L.G. Strauss: *Iberia before the Iberians* (Albuquerque, 1992), 194–216, 227–9.

RJA

Azilian pebbles The AZILIAN is characterized by the replacement of the rich naturalistic mobiliary and parietal art of the preceding Magdalenian with a rather limited art of a much simpler geometric style. This art is occasionally manifested on bone tools, but most characteristically on the famous painted and occasionally engraved Azilian pebbles found in great concentrations at MAS D'AZIL and Rochdane in France; examples are also known from another 35 sites in France, Spain, Switzerland and Italy. Single and multiple dots and strokes running across the width of the pebbles are the most common motifs; more complex designs include crosses, wavy lines, and longitudinal lines hatched with short strokes. The motifs are usually painted in red, or occasionally black, but some are engraved. D'Errico's examination of engraved pebbles has cast doubt on suggestions that the dots and strokes represent some kind of hunting tally or lunar cycle notation; however the repeated combinations of motifs does seem to some extent to be ordered, which may suggest a simple syntax.

C. Couraud and P. Bahn: 'Azilian pebbles in British collections: a re-examination', *PPS* 48 (1982), 45–52; C. Couraud: *L'art Azilien: origine, survivance*, XXe supplément à Gallia Préhistoire (Paris, 1985); F. D'Errico: 'Palaeolithic lunar calendars: a case of wishful thinking?', *CA* 30/1 (1989), 117–18; ——: *L'art gravé Azilien: de la technique à la signification* (Paris, 1994).

RJA

Azmak, Tell Settlement mound 6 km east of Stara Zagora in Bulgaria, formed between the 5th and 3rd millennium BC. Excavations between 1960 and 1963 by Georgi Georgiev provided a vital cultural sequence for the Neolithic and the Eneolithic of Bulgaria. Georgiev identifies the Azmak phases as equivalent to KARANOVO phases I, III, V, VI and VII. The earliest houses were rectangular and square in plan, and made of clay-covered wicker supported by posts; the inner walls of houses from Azmak Neolithic II and Azmak Eneolithic IV were painted with geometric patterns. The pottery from most of the Neolithic period is polished with mainly white geometric decoration on a red ground (Karanovo I), while the sides of some of the later Neolithic vessels were enlivened with small figures in relief. Schematic figurines in bone, clay and marble were discovered in all levels, including one particularly fine marble example from Neolithic I.

G. Georgiev: 'The Azmak mound in southern Bulgaria', *Antiquity* 39 (1965), 6–8.

RJA

Aztalan Late prehistoric 'mound center' located on the bank of the Crawfish River in southern Wisconsin, eastern North America. An embankment and a strong wooden palisade with regularly spaced bastions once encompassed an area of about 9 ha, several earthen mounds, a plaza and living areas. Additional mounds are located on high ground near the site, but outside the palisade. At its peak, in about AD 1100–1300, Aztalan had strong ties to more southerly MISSISSIPPIAN sites, particularly CAHOKIA. It has long been regarded as an outlier in the overall geographical distribution of Mississippian sites.

L.G. Goldstein and J.D. Richards: 'Ancient Aztalan: the cultural and ecological context of a late prehistoric site in the Midwest', *Cahokia and the hinterlands: Middle Mississippian cultures of the Midwest*, ed. T.E. Emerson and R.B. Lewis (Urbana, 1991).

GM

Aztecs More properly known as the Mexica, the Aztecs were late migrants into central Mexico and came to dominate much of western Mesoamerica during the Late Postclassic period (AD 1200–1521). According to Mexica myth and history, which emphasize their humble CHICHIMEC origins, they left their home of Aztlán (whence the name Aztec) and arrived in the BASIN OF MEXICO at some time in the late 13th or early 14th century. A despised, nomadic group, led by their patron deity Huitzilopochtli and serving as mercenaries for the more powerful indigenous city-states in the basin, the Mexica finally (*c.*AD 1325) settled successfully on an island in the western part of Lake Texcoco and established what would become their capital, Tenochtitlán. It covered an area of approximately 12 sq. km, with a population estimated at 125,000–200,000. Likened by early European visitors to Venice, the island was criss-crossed by a system of canals that facilitated easy canoe-transport on the lake and throughout the basin. There were two main ceremonial precincts on the island, the largest having some 72 buildings, including temples, priests' quarters, ball-courts (*see* BALLGAME), COATEPANTLI ('serpent-walls') and *tzompantli* ('skull-racks'). The principal temple, known today as the 'Templo Mayor', had twin structures dedicated to the gods Huitzilopochtli and Tlaloc; it was rediscovered by accident in 1978 during subway construction in central Mexico city. During the following five years the multidisciplinary investigations of Mexican archaeologists, biologists and geologists at the Templo Mayor (Matos Moctezuma 1988) revealed a great complex of buildings including a *tzompantli*, a CHACMOOL, sculptures, ceramics and several smaller temples.

During the 14th and 15th centuries the Aztecs developed political and marital ties with their more powerful neighbours. In 1430 the NAHUATL-speaking Mexica became part of and eventually dominated an alliance with two of these polities, the Acolhua of Texcoco and the Tepanecs of Tlacopan. This 'Triple Alliance' was the core of the 'Aztec empire' which expanded throughout western Mesoamerica during the following century.

The area dominated by the Triple Alliance included some 50–60 city-states in central Mexico, with an estimated total population of 1–2.5 million people. In addition, the 'empire' incorporated about 40 conquered tributary provinces in the hinterland, representing approximately 5–6 million people. There is considerable argument about the degree to which this can truly be considered an empire (Conrad and Demarest 1984: 11–83; Smith 1986), for Triple Alliance control of these distant areas was weak, provincial rebellions were frequent and there was no standing imperial army. In addition, local dynasties were usually allowed to maintain their position after marriage to a member of one of the royal families of the Triple Alliance. The primary objective of imperial expansion seemed to be the incorporation of new populations from which to draw regular payments of tribute. This expansion was aided by regular reports, from *pochteca*, or long-distance traders, who some scholars claim acted as state agents in their travels throughout Mesoamerica and provided estimates of the tribute-paying potential of distant regions. Tribute coming in from the conquered provinces was itemized in lists, such as the Codex Mendoza, which reveal that Triple Alliance demands were staggering: literally tons of corn, beans, amaranth, CACAO and countless other goods poured into Tenochtitlan as part of annual assessments.

Among the most famous – or infamous – features of Aztec society were the practices of human sacrifice and cannibalism. Although argued by some to be strategies for adding protein to an otherwise meat-deficient diet (see Harner 1977), there is broader agreement that human sacrifice and cannibalism were ritual practices. Aztec religion demanded regular offerings of blood to nourish the sun god and maintain the universe, and the sacrifice of brave warriors was the offering of choice. Warriors and other sacrificial victims were sanctified through this act and it was a special privilege for the living to consume their flesh. Although the Aztecs apparently suffered several famines, during which they consumed all the grain stored in their storehouses, there is virtually no evidence supporting protein deficiency given the ready availability of fish, game and domesticated dogs.

Hernán Cortés and his army, accompanied by the enemies of the Aztecs, the people of Tlaxcala, arrived in the Basin of Mexico in 1519. After a series of skirmishes and retreats, the Spaniards conquered the Aztecs in 1521 by attacking the island capital from a boat and maintaining siege for 90 days.

G.C. Vaillant: *Aztecs of Mexico* (New York, 1966); N. Davies: *The Aztecs, a history* (Norman, 1973); E.E. Calnek: 'The internal structure of Tenochtitlan', *The valley of Mexico*, ed. E.R. Wolf (Albuquerque, 1976) 287–302; M. Harner: 'The ecological basis for Aztec sacrifice', *American Ethnologist* 4 (1977) 117–35; F.E. Berdan: *The Aztecs of central Mexico, an imperial society* (New York, 1982); G.W. Conrad and A. Demarest: *Religion and empire* (Cambridge, MA, 1984); M. Smith: 'The role of social stratification in the Aztec empire: a view from the provinces', *American Anthropologist* 88 (1986) 70–91; E. Matos Moctezuma: *The great temple of the Aztecs: treasures of Tenochtitlan* (London, 1988); S.D. Gillespie: *The Aztec kings: The construction of rulership in Mexica history* (Tucson, 1989); I. Clendinnen: *Aztecs* (Cambridge, MA, 1991).

PRI

Azykh Cave Stratified cave site with early Palaeolithic sequence, situated on the southern slopes of the Little Caucasus, in the Nagorno–Karabakh region (Azerbaidjan/Armenia). Pebble-based industries, reminiscent of the Oldowan in Eastern Africa (*see* OLDUVAI), were discovered in the lower levels; these have shown the inverse magnetic polarity identified as the Matuyama palaeomagnetic epoch (before 735,000 BP). The overlaying strata contained ACHEULEAN- and MOUSTERIAN-type industries. In 1968, a fragment of a mandible of a hominid (*Azykhanthropus*) was found in the Acheulean layer of the Azykh Cave; it is generally viewed as belonging to a 'PRE-NEANDERTHAL' species.

A.A. Velichko et al.: 'Paleogeografija stojanki Azyh – drevneišego poselenija pervobytnogo čeloveka na territorii SSSR' ['Palaeogeography of the Azykh site – the oldest dwelling site in the territory of the USSR'], *Izvestiya AN SSSR.* ser. geograf., (1980/3), 20–35; V.P. Lyubin: 'Paleolit Kavkaza' [The Palaeolithic of the Caucasus], *Paleolit Kavkaza i Severnoi Azii* [The Palaeolithic of the Caucasus and Northern Asia], ed. P.I. Boriskovsky (Leningrad, 1988), 9–142.

PD

B

Babadan A One of a series of Early Palaeolithic sites in Miyagi prefecture. The oldest well-dated site in Japan, it ended the long-standing controversy over the dating of the Japanese Early Palaeolithic (pre-30,000 BP). Circular scrapers, awls, knife-shape tools and gravers of agate and chalcedony were found on a surface overlain by a pumice layer dated by TEPHROCHRONOLOGY to *c.*130,000 BP.

M. Okamura: 'Babadan A', *Ancient Japan*, ed. R. Pearson (Washington, D.C., 1992).

SK

Babel, Tower of *see* BABYLON

Babylon (Hilla) The ancient site of Babylon (Akkadian: 'gate of the gods'), located in southern Iraq 80 km south of Baghdad, was initially only a provincial city during the Ur III period (*c.*2150–2000 BC), but it flourished from the reign of Hammurabi (*c.*1792–50 BC) until Sasanian times (*c.*AD 224–651). At about 850 ha, Babylon was the largest ancient Mesopotamian city; it was first identified correctly by Claudius James Rich and then excavated by Austin Henry Layard in 1850. The most significant excavations were undertaken by Robert Koldewey in 1899–1917 and by German and Iraqi archaeologists from 1958 onwards. The height of the water-table has tended to restrict most excavation to the Neo-Babylonian (CHALDAEAN) dynasty (*c.*625–539 BC), when the political power of the Babylonians probably reached its greatest height.

For the First Dynasty of Babylon (*c.*1894–1595 BC) other sites have proved more informative, particularly MARI, Tell Shimshara and Tell el-Rimah, where both excavation of houses and temples and the translation of surviving royal archives of thousands of cuneiform tablets have provided invaluable evidence concerning the society, economy, administration and religion of the Old Babylonian period. Although the Babylonian elite arrived in Mesopotamia as late as the end of the 3rd millennium BC (probably originating in the desert to the west of Babylon), they were Semitic speaking and readily adopted the customs of the indigenous peoples: the art, architecture and writings of Babylonia are therefore very much within the Mesopotamian tradition.

In the Neo-Babylonian period, the city of Babylon was surrounded by a large, baked-brick inner wall as well as an extremely long outer wall with a circumference of some 8 km, which is described by Herodotus. The inner city, divided into eastern and western sectors by the Euphrates, was entered via eight gates, each named after a deity, the most elaborate of which was the Ishtar Gate, with its facade of coloured glazed bricks. Immediately to the west of this gate was the southern palace, built by the neo-Babylonian ruler Nebuchadnezzar II (*c.*604–562 BC) and possibly the site of the Hanging Gardens. It was in this building that Belshazzar (*c.*550 BC) may perhaps have witnessed the Biblical 'writing on the wall', and where Alexander the Great is supposed to have died. The principal buildings in the city would originally have been the ziggurat and temple dedicated to Marduk, the most important Babylonian deity, although ironically the ziggurat – which was called Etemenanki but was almost certainly the original 'Tower of Babel' – has now been reduced to a shapeless pit.

R. Koldewey: *The excavations at Babylon* (London, 1914); H. Figulla and W.J. Martin: *Letters and documents of the Old Babylonian period* (London and Philadelphia, 1953); J. Oates: *Babylon*, 2nd edn, (London, 1986); H.W.F. Saggs: *The Babylonians* (London, 1995).

IS

Babylonia *see* BABYLON

backed blade Flint blade with at least one edge blunted by secondary retouch, apparently to allow the tool to be handled more comfortably. Backed blades were first produced in the early Upper Palaeolithic, and curved backed blades (Châtelperron points) are diagnostic of the CHÂTELPERRONIAN (Lower Périgordian).

RJA

Bacsonian Culture identified in the province of Bac Son in north Vietnam in the 1920s by the French archaeologist Henri Mansuy. The sites, comprising small rock shelters from which both forest and aquatic resources were exploited by mobile foragers, were located in the limestone uplands on the northern border of the Red River delta, and have been dated to *c.*5000–8000 BC. They were distinguished from the contemporary HOABINHIAN culture by the greater incidence of edge-ground stone artefacts – an innovation which preceded the first evidence for the use of pottery. The rock shelters contrast with the larger, permanent settlements of farmers found in coastal locations from about 4000 BC (e.g. Quynh Van), once the sea level – which had risen rapidly in the Holocene period – stabilized (*see* COASTAL NEOLITHIC).

H. Mansuy: 'Stations préhistoriques dans les cavernes du massif calcaire de Bac-Son (Tonkin)', *BSGI* 11/2 (1924).

CH

el-Badari Area of Upper Egypt stretching for about 30 km between Matmar and Qau, where numerous predynastic cemeteries are located. These include Mostagedda, Deir Tasa and the cemetery of el-Badari itself, as well as at least one early settlement at Hammamia. The region was first investigated by Guy Brunton and Gertrude Caton-Thompson between 1922 and 1931. Many of the finds from this region constitute the original basis for the 'Badarian period', the earliest phase of the Upper Egyptian predynastic sequence (*c.*5500–4000 BC; *see* EGYPT 1). The Badarian graves have yielded distinctive pottery vessels (particularly red-polished ware with blackened tops), as well as terracotta and ivory anthropomorphic figures, slate palettes, stone vases and flint tools. The assemblages of funerary equipment from the predynastic cemeteries at el-Badari have been subjected to a number of statistical analyses attempting to clarify the chronology and social history of the Badarian period (e.g. Kaiser 1985).

The Badarian settlement of Hammamia was first examined by Gertrude Caton-Thompson in the 1920s. Her pioneering approach to the site involved a wide survey area across the surrounding desert, which amounted to an early form of SITE CATCHMENT ANALYSIS (not usually supposed to have been introduced until the work of Higgs and Vita-Finzi in the late 1960s). Her excavation of about half of the area of stratified predynastic settlement remains at Hammamia was unusually meticulous and systematic; she divided the site into strips of 5 × 10 m squares and excavated them in arbitrary 30 cm levels. She provided the first stratigraphic confirmation of Petrie's cemetery-based predynastic 'sequence dates' (*see* SERIATION).

In 1989 Diane Holmes and Renée Friedman re-examined the predynastic sites in the el-Badari region, finding that 50% of them were being affected by modern activities, some having been completely destroyed. This project, which also included a number of small test excavations, is a rare instance of the application of a CRM (cultural resource management) approach to an Egyptian site. Caton-Thompson had suggested that the small quantities of Amratian pottery found at Hammamia, deriving from strata amounting to only about 5% of the total depth of deposits, were an indication that the site had gone into temporary decline during the Amratian period (*c.*4000–3500 BC). Holmes and Friedman (1989), however, argue (on the basis of two test-pits in Caton-Thompson's strip 'H') that the relative dearth of Amratian ceramics may actually be an indication that the Badarian ceramics were more of a regional tradition and that the Badarian period may therefore have overlapped chronologically with the Amratian.

G. Brunton et al.: *Qau and Badari*, 3 vols (London, 1927–30); G. Brunton and G. Caton-Thompson: *The Badarian civilization and prehistoric remains near Badari* (London, 1928); ——: *Mostagedda and the Tasian culture* (London, 1937); ——: *Matmar* (London, 1948); G. Caton-Thompson and E.H. Whittle: 'Thermoluminescence dating of the Badarian', *Antiquity* 49 (1975), 89–97; W. Kaiser: 'Zur südausdehnung der vorgeschi-chtlichen Deltakulturen und zur frühen Entwicklung Oberägyptens', *MDAIK* 41 (1985), 61–87; D.L. Holmes and R.F. Friedman: 'The Badari region revisited', *Nyame Akuma* 31 (1989), 15–18; D.L. Holmes: 'Archaeological cultural resources and modern land-use activities: some observations made during a recent survey in the Badari region, Egypt', *JARCE* 29 (1992), 67–80.

IS

Badarian *see* EL-BADARI; EGYPT: PREHISTORIC

baetyls *see* LOS MILLARES

Baghdad *see* ISLAMIC ARCHAEOLOGY

Bagor Open-air site located on an ancient sand dune along the Kothari River in eastern Rajasthan, India, excavated by V.N. Misra. Three chronological phases were defined. In Phase I, radiocarbon dated to *c.*5300–3800 BC, chert microlithic tools were associated with domestic sheep/goat, and wild fauna, providing early evidence for animal domestication in Rajasthan. Structural remains include stone pavements and circular stone alignments, perhaps hut foundations. In Phase II, MICROLITHIC tools continued, handmade pottery appeared, and copper arrowheads with affinities to artefacts of the contemporary INDUS CIVILIZATION have been found, perhaps implying trade or contact. Two radiocarbon dates are available from this period: *c*.3395–3160 BC and *c*.2645–2310 BC (Possehl and Rissman 1992:477). Phase III is characterized by historic pottery and iron fragments, dated (on the basis of artefact form) to *c*.600 BC–AD 200. Burials are found from all three phases, associated with the habitation area.

V.N. Misra: 'Bagor: A late Mesolithic settlement in northwest India', *WA* 5 (1973), 92–100; G.L. Possehl and P. Rissman: 'The chronology of prehistoric India: from earliest times to the Iron Age', *Chronologies in Old World archaeology* I, ed. R.W. Ehrich (Chicago, 1992).

CS

Bahariya Oasis Fertile depression in the Libyan Desert, located about 200 km west of the Nile, which was occupied by Egyptians from at least as early as New Kingdom until the Roman period (*c*.1500 BC–AD 395). One of the most significant sites in the region is a group of tombs of 26th-dynasty (*c*.600 BC) Egyptian governors of the oasis situated near the modern town of Bawit. The site of el-Hayz, at the southern end of the oasis, consists of a Roman garrison, a basilica and a small settlement dating to the Roman and Christian periods (*c*.30 BC–AD 641). In the immediate vicinity of Bawit are a number of other sites, including the 19th-dynasty tomb of the provincial governor Amenhotpe Huy (*c*.1250 BC), a necropolis of sacred birds associated with the worship of the gods Thoth and Horus (dating to the 26th dynasty and Ptolemaic and Roman periods), the remains of a Roman triumphal arch and two temples dating to the 6th and 4th centuries BC respectively.

A. Fakhry: *Bahria oasis*, 2 vols (Cairo, 1942–50); ——: *The oases of Egypt* II (Cairo, 1974); L. Giddy: *Egyptian oases: Bahariya, Dakhla, Farafra and Kharga during pharaonic times* (Warminster, 1987).

IS

Bahia and Jama-Coaque Two closely related cultures on the central coast of Ecuador, dating to the Regional Development Period (500 BC–AD 500). They are best known from their elaborate figurines of musicians, dancers and members of the elite with exotic costumes and a wealth of jewellery. High tides at Los Esteros near Manta uncovered a pyramid with a large number of these figures arranged along the stages, looking out to sea; otherwise, little is known of the contexts of the figures or of other aspects of these cultures. They do, however, present the most detailed evidence of costume, ornament, and the gender and occupational associations of these to be found in the northern Andes. Regional surveys in the Jama Valley combined with site testing and paleobotanical investigations are slowly adding a cultural setting to the figurines.

T. Cummins: 'La tradición en el arte prehispanico Ecuatoriano: la cerámica de Chorrera y Jama-Coaque', *Signos Amerindios: 5000 años de arte precolombino en Ecuador*, ed. F. Valdez and D. Veintimilla (Paris, 1992), 63–81; T. Zeidler and D. Pearsall, ed.: *Regional archaeology in northern Manabí, Ecuador I: Environment, cultural chronology, and agricultural production* (Pittsburgh, 1993).

KB

Bahrain (anc. Dilmun) Island in the Persian Gulf where remains dating from the Palaeolithic to the Islamic period have been excavated. From the late Uruk period (*c*.3500–3100 BC) onwards the name Dilmun was used in southern Babylonian cuneiform texts to refer to the eastern Arabian mainland, where goods from the east were obtained by trade. By the late 3rd millennium BC, however, the term was applied to Bahrain alone, since it had apparently become the most convenient entrepot for trade-goods from the Oman peninsula, Iran and the INDUS CIVILIZATION. The principal pre-Islamic sites on Bahrain include the temple at Barbar dating to *c*.2200–1500 BC; the fortified city at Ra'ʾs al-Qalʾat; a 'well-temple' at Diraz; the burial mounds at Rifaʾa dating to the late 3rd millennium BC (the earliest major cemetery on the island), and a town with central temple as well as cemeteries in the region of Sar (thousands of burial mounds dating from the late 3rd millennium BC to the 3rd century AD).

T.-G. Bibby: *Looking for Dilmun* (New York, 1970); D.T. Potts, ed.: *Dilmun: new studies in the archaeology and early history of Bahrain* (Berlin, 1983); H.A. al-Khalifa Shaika and M. Rice, eds: *Bahrain through the ages: the archaeology* (London, 1986); H. Crawford: 'Dilmun reconsidered', *Antiquity* 71 (1997), 701–8.

IS

Balambai *see* GANDHARA GRAVE CULTURE

Balat *see* DAKHLA OASIS

Balawat, Tell (anc. Imgur-Enlil) Assyrian city site in northern Iraq, 16 km north of TELL NIMRUD. The site is best known for the 16 embossed bronze bands surviving from the massive gates erected by the late Assyrian ruler Shalmaneser III (*c*.858–824 BC), each leaf of which measured 4 × 2 m; the figurative designs accompanied by cuneiform inscriptions depict Shalmaneser's major exploits, including a journey to the 'source' of the Tigris (i.e. a point where it disappears underground for several kilometres) and the campaigns against the Urartians and Chaldaeans. The first unprovenanced fragments of the gate appeared on the art market in 1876, and in 1877–8 Hormuzd Rassam excavated at Tell Balawat, discovering further fragments as well as the remains of another gate erected by Shalmaneser's father, Ashurnasirpal II. However, doubt was unjustifiably cast on Rassam's work, and it was not until fragments of another bronze gate, again dating to the time of Ashurnasirpal II, were excavated, that the origins of the gates of Shalmaneser were placed beyond any question (see Lloyd 1980).

H. Rassam: *Asshur and the land of Nimrod* (New York, 1897), 207–8; L.W. King: *Bronze reliefs from the Gates of Shalmaneser* (London, 1915); M. Mallowan: *Twenty-five years of Mesopotamian discovery* (London, 1956), 79; S. Lloyd: *Foundations in the dust: the story of Mesopotamian exploration*, 2nd edn (London, 1980), 150–4; J. Curtis: 'Balawat', *Fifty years of Mesopotamian discovery*, ed. J. Curtis (London, 1982), 113–19.

IS

Ballana Post-Meroitic Nubian cemetery located some 15 km south of ABU SIMBEL, Egypt. It is the type-site of the Ballana (or X-Group) period, which lasted from the decline of the MEROITIC empire in *c*.AD 350 to the arrival of Christianity in Nubia in *c*.AD 550. Both Ballana and the nearby contemporary cemetery of Qustul were excavated in the 1930s (Emery and Kirwan 1938) but they are now submerged under LAKE NASSER. Many of the distinctive tumulus burials at Ballana and Qustul, nearly 200 of which were excavated, contain evidence of human sacrifice in the form of the bodies of retainers buried alongside the pre-Christian rulers of Lower Nubia. The drift sand and low scrub covering the tumuli at Ballana has helped to preserve the graves from the widespread plundering that affected the earlier elite Kushite cemeteries of MEROE and NAPATA.

W.B. Emery and L.P. Kirwan: *The royal tombs of Ballana and Qustul* (Cairo, 1938); B.G. Trigger: 'The Ballana culture and the coming of Christianity', *Africa in Antiquity: the arts of ancient Nubia and the Sudan* I, ed. S. Wenig (New York, 1978), 107–11; W.Y. Adams: *Nubia: corridor to Africa*, 2nd edn (Princeton, 1984), 404–13; B. Williams: *Excavations between Abu Simbel and the Sudan frontier IX: Noubadian X-Group remains from royal cemeteries*, (Chicago, 1991).

IS

ballgame Ritual game played with a rubber ball throughout Mesoamerica from the Preclassic period (*c*.2500 BC) until recent times. Variants of the game spread southward as far as Costa Rica, northward into the southwestern United States and eastward into the Caribbean. In prehispanic Mesoamerica the game was played in rectangular fields or courts with vertical or sloping walls, usually of masonry at the larger sites. In some areas the architecture was elaborated with goal-like rings on the walls and carved markers in the playing floor. Depictions of the ballgame on ceramic vessels show players wearing elaborate ornamental and/or protective paraphernalia on the head, waist and limbs. Many variants of the soccer-like game existed in terms of numbers of players, rules of play, scoring and consequences of loss or victory (which often involved human sacrifices). All of these characteristics suggest that the Mesoamerican ballgame was a ceremonial activity carried out by elites. While it is occasionally considered to have been pure sport, more common interpretations focus on such phenomena as celestial/calendrical ritual, cycles of death and renewal (especially agricultural), symbolic warfare and dynastic celebrations.

V.L. Scarborough and D.R. Wilcox, eds: *The Mesoamerican ballgame* (Tucson, 1991); L. Schele and Mary Ellen Miller: *The blood of kings: Dynasty and ritual in Maya art* (London, 1992).

PRI

Balof Cave Limestone doline (sink-hole) on northern New Ireland, Papua New Guinea, with occupation horizons from 15,000 years ago through to the present. The site probably represents a campsite, and reveals the changing range of animals that were hunted; it also provides evidence for the introduction of animals, such as the cuscus (Flannery and White 1991). The raw material for the tools may have been obtained some distance from the site: the obsidian certainly derives from TALASEA.

T.F. Flannery and J.P. White: 'Animal translocations', *National Geographic Research and Exploration* 7 (1991), 96–113; J.P. White et al.: 'The Balof shelters, New Ireland', *Report of the Lapita Homeland Project*, ed. J. Allen and C. Gosden (Canberra, 1991), 46–58.

CG

balsa South American log raft generally made of the very light-weight wood of *Ochromo piscatoria*, a tree found in coastal Ecuador. Balsas were first developed for river transport, but in late prehistory became very large and were utilized in trade passing along the coast from southern Colombia to northern Peru and, perhaps, further afield.

J. Estrada: *La balsa en la historia de la navegación Ecuatoriana* (Guayaquil, 1990).

KB

Bambandyanalo Part of a complex of Iron Age sites (Mapungubwe, Bambandyanalo, K1 and K2), which are perhaps more correctly referred to as K2, located on the farm Greefswald in the northwestern Transvaal, South Africa, just south of the confluence of the Shashi and Limpopo Rivers. K2 is the oldest of the localities, being settled by *c.* AD 950 and abandoned by *c.*1070, although K2-type occupation continued on the southern terrace of MAPUNGUBWE HILL. In its earliest stages the K2 settlement covered a very large area, surrounding a large central cattle kraal. Later, the cattle were kraaled elsewhere and an enormous ash heap accumulated over the old kraal area, to a depth of 6 m. Sanga and Afrikander cattle, sheep and goats were important, and the domestic dog was present. Agriculture was practised from the beginning. Iron and copper were smelted and ivory was both traded (to Arabs in exchange for beads) and used extensively for personal adornment. Human burials and several cattle burials were found in the ash mound. Trade beads were re-processed on the site, to make large cylindrical beads.

G.A. Gardner: *Mapungubwe* II (Pretoria, 1963); E.A. Voigt: 'Iron Age herders of the northern Transvaal, South Africa, in the first millennium AD', *Animals and archaeology 3: early herders and their flocks*, ed. J. Clutton-Brock and C. Grigson (Oxford, 1984).

RI

Bambata pottery Thin, extensively decorated pottery first found overlying WILTON deposits in Bambata Cave in the Matopos hills of Zimbabwe. Later excavations yielded a caprine tooth and a date of 90 BC, although the association is not secure. Archaeologists have found Bambata pottery with Late Stone Age material in open sites around the Makadikadi pans in Botswana and in rock shelters with post-classic Wilton in the Waterberg and Magliesberg mountains of the Transvaal. As a rule the stone industries remain unchanged and the style lacks local antecedents; the pottery is therefore a 'trait intrusion'. Consequently Bambata figures in debates about moving frontiers and the origins of pastoralism in southern Africa. Huffman places it within the Kalundu Tradition (*see* AFRICA 4) and believes it is part of BENFICA rather than a style of its own. A village site dated at AD 150 at Toteng in Botswana yielded domestic cattle as well as small stock. Independent climatic evidence suggests it was drier at this time, and cattle may have been brought through open savanna along the Congo coast from Cameroon.

J.F. Schofield: 'A report on the pottery from Bambata Cave', *SAJS* 37 (1941), 361–72; N.J. Walker: 'The significance of an early date for pottery and sheep in Zimbabwe', *SAAB* 38 (1983), 88–92; J. Denbow: 'A new look at the later prehistory of the Kalahari', *JAH* 27 (1986), 3–28; T.N. Huffman: *Iron Age migrations: the ceramic sequence in southern Zambia* (Johannesburg, 1989).

TH

Bamboo Annals (Chu-shu-chi-nien, Zhushujinian) Chronological list of Chinese rulers with brief records of major events concerning each reign. These annals originally comprised brush-written tablets of split bamboo found among the plunder of a tomb which, at the time (*c.* AD 280), was thought to have been that of Hsiang Wang of Wei, who died in 295 BC. There was no other such reign list extant apart from the dynastic list (San-tai shih-piao) in Ssu-ma Ch'ien's *Shih-chi* ('memoirs of the historian'), which was the first comprehensive history of China, compiled between 104 and 87 BC. Contemporary descriptions of the discovery of the Bamboo Annals show that the tablets had been partly destroyed, disarranged, and offered ancient scholars considerable difficulties in the transcription/interpretation of the ancient characters. The original version of the resultant form of the Annals was lost before Sung times, but has been reconstructed in part from citations (deriving from one or more of the earlier copies) which have been assembled from pre-Sung compilations (i.e. the *Ku-pen*: 'ancient text' reconstruction).

A version of the Annals of highly doubtful authenticity has been extant since Sung times (the *Chin-pen*: 'current text'); this version has been rather uncritically used as a basis, in recent attempts by several American scholars, to establish the chronology of Shang and Western Chou (i.e. with the Chou conquest of Shang fluctuating in and around 1045 BC). In China, since the 1950s, the favoured chronological system (in which the conquest is dated to 1027 BC) has been established. Based on the *Ku-pen* version, it is essentially dependent upon a single sentence deriving from the text of a commentary; this interpretation was originally proposed by Ch'en Meng-chia and introduced to the West by Bernard Karlgren (1945).

B. Karlgren: 'Some weapons and tools of the Yin Dynasty', *BMFEA* 17 (1945), 101–44; Fang Shih-ming and Wang Hsiu-ling: *Ku-pen Chu-shu-chi-nien chi-cheng* (Shanghai, 1981); D.N. Keightley: 'The Bamboo Annals and Shang-Chou chronology', *HJAS* 38/2 (1978), 423–38; D.S. Nivison: *The dates of Western Chou* (1981); E.L. Shaughnessy: 'The "Current" Bamboo Annals and the date of the Zhou conquest of Shang', *HJAS* 46/1 (1986), 149–80; N. Barnard: 'Astronomical data from ancient Chinese records and the requirements of histori-

cal research methodology', *East Asian History* 6 (1993), 47–74.
NB

Ban Ang Mortuary complex, located on the Plain of Jars in upland Laos, which was excavated in the 1930s by Madeleine Colani. The central part of the site incorporates a hill in which Colani identified a crematorium associated with two groups of stone jar burials. The smaller, which stood on a slightly raised area, was interpreted as the burial area of the ruling group. Grave goods included glass and carnelian beads, cowrie shells, bronze bells and bracelets and knives, arrowheads and spearheads of iron. There were also fragments of clay moulds used in bronze casting. The parallels of these artefacts in the lowlands to the south date to the later 1st millennium BC. Colani has suggested that sites such as Ban Ang represent communities which prospered on the exchange of goods, such as salt, between Yunnan and the Khorat Plateau.
M. Colani: 'Mégalithes du Haut-Laos', *PEFEO* (1935) 25–6.
CH

Banas Chalcolithic culture of southeast Rajasthan, India, dating from the late 3rd to early 2nd millennium BC. More than 50 sites are known from surface remains, but only a small number (including Ahar, Gilund and Kayatha) have been excavated. Banas-culture settlements are agriculturally based with evidence of domesticated cattle, fowl, sheep, goats and pigs, as well as remains of rice, sorghum and possibly millet. The sites are also characterized by wide ceramic diversity, with seven major ware categories and 290 distinct vessel forms defined. These include storage jars, pedestalled vessels and small BLACK AND RED WARE bowls. Banas sites are also characterized by terracotta figurines, copper tools and metalworking debris. The type-site, Ahar, is a large mound comprising two main phases (Chalcolithic and Iron Age), lasting from the mid-3rd to early 2nd millennium BC. Hasmukh Dhirjlal Sankalia's excavations of Chalcolithic levels (*c*.2580–1500 BC) revealed a number of rectangular, north-south oriented, stone-footed, mud-brick houses. The strata of period I (the Chalcolithic) included copper artefacts and traces of copper smelting.
H.D. Sankalia et al.: *Excavations at Ahar* (Pune, 1969), 215–24.
CS

Ban Chiang Site in the upper Songkhram valley of northeast Thailand which has yielded an unparalleled sequence of archaeological deposits dating from the 3rd millennium BC to the early 1st millennium AD. Since the 1960s, when complete pottery vessels bearing curvilinear red-painted designs were discovered (see figure 7), there have been numerous excavations – most recently in 1992. Two major excavations in 1974–5, directed by Chester Gorman and Pisit Charoenwongsa, revealed a stratigraphic sequence up to 4 m deep which incorporated a large sample of inhumation burials. Individuals were interred with a range of grave goods which included pottery vessels, artefacts of shell, bone, stone, bronze and iron. Early graves were accompanied by burnished black pottery vessels with incised decoration, but the style of vessels changed markedly with time, the red-on-buff pottery being late in a sequence which probably began in the late 3rd or 2nd millennia BC and terminated in the early 1st millennium AD.

There has been much controversy over the date of bronze at this site, but it probably appeared by the mid-2nd millennium BC and iron by about 500 BC. Bronzes included socketed axes and spearheads, and bracelets cast in a wide variety of shapes. A casting area, comprising a clay furnace, crucibles and mould fragments was found in 1975. Two composite iron-bladed spears with bronze hafts were recovered, and represent an early phase in the use of iron which has parallels in Vietnam and Yunnan.

From initial settlement, the inhabitants consumed rice and maintained domestic cattle and pigs. A detailed statistical analysis of the dog remains has revealed probable descent from the Chinese wolf (Higham et al. 1980). They also fished, collected shellfish and trapped or hunted wild animals. The area occupied at Bang Chiang has not been defined, and would have varied markedly over time, but it probably never exceeded 5 ha. Surveys in the area show that it was one of many such settlements, but none has revealed a longer cultural sequence.
C.F. Higham et al.: 'An analysis of prehistoric canid remains from Thailand', *JASt* 7/2 (1980), 149–66; J.C. White: *Ban Chiang: the discovery of a lost Bronze Age* (Philadelphia, 1982).
CH

Ban Chiang Hian Moated settlement in the Chi valley, northeast Thailand, which formed the focus of a survey undertaken by Higham and Kijngam in 1981. Aerial photographs have revealed that both the moats, which enclose about 38 ha, and an associated circular reservoir, were filled by means of a diverted watercourse. Small canals issued from the moats, and probably reticulated water to rice fields between the site and the Chi River to the north. Few such large moated sites have been excavated, and a limited sounding made near the centre of this settlement usefully revealed a 6 m deep cultural sequence, with basal layers containing red-on-buff painted pottery dated to the late 2nd millennium BC, together with crucible fragments indicating local bronze casting. A group of inhumation burials, associated with shell and stone jewellery, dated from this early period. There was a break in the ceramic tradition *c.*500 BC, after which

Figure 7 **Ban Chiang** Late Period painted pottery from Ban Chiang, southeast Asia, showing the great variety of decorative motifs. *Source*: C.F.W. Higham: *The archaeology of mainland Southeast Asia* (Cambridge, 1989), fig. 4.25.

the first evidence for iron forging and the domestic water buffalo was found. The extensive earthworks which ring the site have not been dated directly, but may belong to the later 1st millennium BC. Such sites, which are thickly distributed in the Mun and to a lesser extent the Chi valleys, are usually seen as evidence for the development of local chiefdoms.

P. Chantaratiyakarn: 'The Middle Chi research programme', *Prehistoric investigations in northeast Thailand*, ed. C.F.W. Higham and A. Kijngam (Oxford, 1984), 565–643.

CH

Ban Don Ta Phet Cemetery site of the late 1st millennium BC, located on the western margins of the Chao Phraya lowlands in central Thailand, which has furnished an unparalleled body of evidence for early exchange between this area and India. Its strategic position at the eastern end of a historic exchange route to Burma may well account for the wealth of the grave goods. The inhumations, ringed by a ditch and probably reinterred from elsewhere, were discovered in 1975 and excavated by first Chin You-di and then Ian Glover. The grave goods include many pottery vessels, iron tools and weapons and, most significantly, a range of bronze bowls bearing incised decoration that includes scenes of houses and people. These bowls were made of a very high tin bronze requiring considerable technical expertise; similar bronze bowls have been found in Indian contexts, for example at the Bhir mound at TAXILA. There are also beads of agate, carnelian and glass, some of which match those known from India in the 2nd and 3rd centuries BC, as well as a splendid lion in carnelian. The radiocarbon dates confirm that the site was occupied in the 4th–3rd centuries BC. Glover has stressed that this site reveals the nature and early date of the exchange of ideas and goods between India and Southeast Asia, an ingredient often cited as contributing to the local development of complex societies.

I.C. Glover et al.: 'The cemetery of Ban Don Ta Phet, Thailand. Results from the 1980–1 season' *South Asian Archaeology 1981*, ed. B. Allchin and M. Sidell (Cambridge, 1984), 319–30; I.C. Glover: *Early trade between India and Southeast Asia* (Hull, 1989).

CH

Ban Kao Site of the first major excavation of a prehistoric cemetery in Thailand. In 1961–2, Per Sørensen uncovered 44 inhumations, which he divided into three mortuary phases. The earliest included a distinctive variety of unpainted pottery with parallels in Malaysia and peninsula Thailand, but the range of vessel forms is considerable, and their complexity indicates a mastery of the medium. The second phase saw a change to red or black burnished pottery. The two most recent graves contained iron implements. Radiocarbon dating suggests that the graves of the first and second phases date to 2500–1500 BC; as bronze was not present Sørensen labelled these phases Early and Late Neolithic. The grave goods included many polished stone adzeheads and a small quantity of shell jewellery, both indicating the existence of exchange networks.

P. Sørensen and T. Hatting: *Archaeological investigations in Thailand II: Ban Kao* I: *The archaeological material from the burials* (Copenhagen 1967).

CH

Ban Muang Phruk Settlement of the later 1st millennium BC located close to the eastern dry-season shore of Lake Kumphawapi, Thailand. The site was identified in 1980 during a survey by Higham and Kijngam that was designed to document the settlement pattern of village communities as it related to the long sequence then known from BAN CHIANG. A small excavation revealed that the site was first occupied from about 500 BC; it may therefore be an example of the way in which settlements dating from relatively late in the prehistoric sequence of northeast Thailand expanded onto the heavier clayey soils near the lake edge in contrast to an earlier preference for soils of the low terrace. Some sites of the General Period C (*c*.600 BC–AD 200) were large and moated (*see* BAN CHIANG HIAN) but most, like Ban Muang Phruk, remained small and undefended.

C.F.W. Higham and A. Kijngam: 'The test excavation at Ban Muang Phruk', *Prehistoric investigations in northeast Thailand*, ed. C.F.W. Higham and A. Kijngam (Oxford, 1984), 34–5.

CH

Ban Na Di One of the few prehistoric sites in northeast Thailand to have been examined extensively (1981), this settlement and cemetery site is located adjacent to a stream which flows into Lake Kumphawapi. The lowest layer, dated to the late 2nd millennium BC by radiocarbon, included occupation evidence in the form of pits, hearths and fragments of bronze. This was followed by a cemetery phase, manifested in at least two clusters of inhumations, which probably ended in the second half of the 2nd millennium BC. The graves yielded a common range of pottery vessels, mostly of local manufacture. One cluster, however, contained the majority of exotic grave goods, including most of the bronze artefacts, all the clay figurines of cattle, elephant, deer and humans, most shell beads, all the exotic stone bracelets and, at the end of the sequence, the only iron implements from this mortuary phase. This suggests that one social group consistently secured access to exotic goods obtained by exchange. A clay-lined pit for heating copper and tin was contemporary with the graves.

C.F.W. Higham and A. Kijngam, eds: *Prehistoric investigations in northeast Thailand* (Oxford, 1984).

CH

Ban Phak Top Settlement mound, radiocarbon-dated to the 2nd millennium BC, located 15 km west of BAN NA DI in northeast Thailand. It was systematically looted during the 1970s, leaving parts of the modern village littered with prehistoric human remains, broken pottery vessels, clay figurines and ivory bracelet fragments. In 1976 Schauffler excavated a small area on the edge of the mound – the only undisturbed area he could find – but discovered no burials. The pottery is black, burnished and covered with curvilinear parallel bands infilled with punctate impressions which match the style of the early ceramics from BAN CHIANG.

W. Schauffler: 'Archaeological survey and excavation of Ban Chiang culture sites in northeast Thailand', *Expedition* 18 (1976), 27–37.

CH

Ban Tamyae Settlement site discovered during a survey of the Phimai region, which was a major Khmer centre in the upper reaches of the Mun valley of northeast Thailand. The lowest of nine layers contained bronze remains, while layer 7 provided the earliest evidence for iron working at this site. Cattle and pig remains were recovered, and the earliest bones of the water buffalo appeared in layer 4; no burials were found. The large pottery sample was used to divide the sequence into four phases. The first, named after Ban Tamyae itself, was dated 1000–600 BC (layers 8–9) and represents the period immediately prior to the marked social changes associated with the development of chiefdoms in Southeast Asia (*see* ASIA 3; BAN CHIANG HIAN; CO LOA; DONG SON CULTURE *and* NON DUA). At Ban Tamyae this change is recognized by first the Prasat period (600–200 BC) and then the Classic Phimai phase (200 BC–AD 300).

D. Welch: 'Settlement pattern as an indicator of socio-political complexity in the Phimai region', in *Southeast Asian archaeology at the XV Pacific Science Congress*, ed. D.T. Bayard (Otago, 1984), 129–51.

CH

Banteay Chmar Temple mausoleum in northwest Cambodia, constructed for the deified crown prince Srindrakumara by the Angkorean overlord Jayavarman VII (1181–1219 AD). One of the largest such monuments, Banteay Chmar is surrounded by a substantial wall and is associated with a reservoir. The walls are richly ornamented in bas-reliefs, including a well-known naval battle between the Khmer of ANGKOR and the invading CHAMS which took place shortly before the accession of Jayavarman.

L.P. Briggs: 'The ancient Khmer empire', *TAPS* 4/1 (1951), 1–295.

CH

Ban Tha Kae Large settlement (1200 × 800 m) located 15 km southwest of the copper deposits of the KHAO WONG PRACHAN VALLEY in central Thailand. In the face of the systematic removal of the mound by civil contractors and looting, excavation has elucidated a three-phase cultural sequence. The first probably belongs to the latter half of the 2nd millennium BC, a period when the copper mines to the northeast were being exploited, and is represented by a cemetery in which bronze bracelets, pottery vessels and shell and stone jewellery were found as grave goods. Phase 1 also saw the local manufacture of shell bracelets from *tridacna*, a marine species. The second phase, dating from about 500 BC, saw the first use of iron, and the presence of imported glass beads, while the final phase represents the DVARAVATI CULTURE. The remains of a small early and a large later moat have not yet been related to the cultural sequence.

S. Natapintu: 'Ancient settlement at Ban Tha Kae in Lopburi', *Muang Boran* 10/4 (1984).

CH

Bantu *see* AFRICA 5

Banyan Valley Cave *see* HOABINHIAN

Baradostian *see* SHANIDAR

Barinas Culture in Venezuela dating from the 6th or 7th century AD to the Conquest. Investigations in the western Orinoco plains and the adjacent Andean piedmont have been dedicated to the study of the origins and development of chiefdoms. Such evidence as immense earthworks, including pyramidal mounds, a three-level settlement pattern with a regional centre at Gaván, status differentiation in household and grave goods, and long-distance trade appearing *c.*AD 500 suggest that growing populations had led to the establishment of chiefdoms whose descendants were the Conquest period Caquetó Nation.

C. Spenser and E. Redmond: 'Pre-Hispanic chiefdoms of the Western Venezuelan Llanos', *WA* 24/1 (1992), 135–57.

KB

Barnenez Perhaps the most famous of the complex Neolithic chambered tombs of Brittany, Barnenez is also among the earliest, having been radiocarbon dated to around 5750 ± 150 BP uncal. The trapezoidal monument (over 70 m long) was built of drystone and megaliths in two stages: the earliest cairn covers five passage graves, while the secondary cairn, built onto the first, conceals a further six; the passages are arranged side by side and vary from 5–12 m in length. Excavations by Giot et al. from 1955 revealed that tiers of drystone revetments were used to strengthen the body of the cairn; the round and polygonal chambers were constructed using combinations of drystone and/or orthostats, and are roofed with false corbelling or capstones. The megaliths of certain of the chambers are decorated with megalithic art; those of Chamber H, which was the central and most monumental chamber in the primary cairn, exhibit wavy lines, axes and curves.

P.R. Giot: *Barnenez, Carn, Guennoc* (Rennes, 1987).

RJA

barrow (tumulus) Generic term for the variously shaped earth and rubble mounds used to cover and mark burials in prehistoric Europe; where the covering is of heaped stones it is more precise to use the term cairn, while 'tumulus', although sometimes interpreted as synonymous with barrow, is best used to embrace both categories of monument as well as the occasional ancient mound with no apparent burial (such as the greatest European tumulus, Silbury Hill, near Avebury in Wiltshire, southern England). Barrow building in prehistoric Europe may be broadly divided into three phases:

(1) The large barrows of the Early to Middle Neolithic, which follow various regional styles. These mounds usually covered a wooden mortuary house or megalithic chambers, housing the remains of multiple bodies. The barrows are often subrectangular, such as the KUJAVIAN barrows of Poland or the earthern long barrows of southern Britain; however, many circular examples also exist. Barrows and cairns covered many tombs of MEGALITHIC construction.

(2) The numerous, and usually smaller, circular barrows of the Bronze Age, which usually housed individual primary burials and accompanying grave goods (e.g. BUSH BARROW), although secondary burials were often later dug into the mound. In Britain, barrows were constructed in a variety of shapes: simple bowl barrows are the most common shape, often with a ditch and/or bank; bell barrows, often associated with the richer barrows of the WESSEX CULTURE, have a berm between the mound and the ditch surrounding it; disc, pond and saucer barrows occur more rarely. In Central Europe, there is a limited number of very rich burials in the Early Bronze Age, while the TUMULUS COMPLEX of the Middle Bronze Age is characterized by barrow construction. In Eastern Europe, the Bronze Age was marked by a series of mound (or 'kurgan') building cultural complexes known as the PIT GRAVE, CATACOMB GRAVE and TIMBER GRAVE CULTURES.

(3) A smaller number of large and richly furnished princely tumuli, usually circular, began to be constructed in the Iron Age (such as the late Hallstatt tombs of VIX and HOCHDORF), and barrows continued to be erected in the early medieval period – for example, burials of the SUTTON HOO type.

RJA

Barsippa *see* BORSIPPA

Barumini (Su Nuraxi) The site of Su Nuraxi, near Barumini, is the pre-eminent example of the Sardinian NURAGHE form of fortification; largely built in the 2nd millennium BC, it was excavated from 1940 by Giovanni Lilliu. The construction sequence is not quite certain, but it seems the first part of the fortress to be built was a tower of basalt blocks about 19 m tall, in the first half of the 2nd millennium BC. Some centuries later, possibly in the later 2nd millennium or early 1st millennium BC, this tower was strengthened and its shape altered, and four massive round towers were built abutting it. Like the early tower, these were multistoried and contained skilfully vaulted rooms. This whole core fortification was finally encircled with seven further smaller towers linked by straight sections of walling. Outside this wall is a settlement of about 60 round huts built of the same massive blocks. Barumini was partly destroyed and rebuilt at least once in its history, before being abandoned in the 7th century BC.

G. Lilliu: 'Il nuraghe di Barumini e la stratigrafia nuragica', *Studi Sardi*, xii–xiii, part 1 (1952–4), 90–469; ——: *La civiltà nuragica* (Milan, 1982); G. Webster: *The prehistory of Sardinia* (1996).

RJA

Bascomb Down *see* BUTSER ANCIENT FARM

Bashu *see* PA-SHU

Basin of Mexico Interior highland valley or structural basin in central Mexico, which was a favoured location of human settlement from Formative times (*c*.2500 BC) onwards. It is now the site of Mexico City (*see also* AZTECS; TENOCHTITLAN; TEOTIHUACAN). Located at an average altitude of 2200 m (about 7000 feet), the basin originally held a series of interconnected lakes, the largest of which is known as Lake Texcoco; the Spaniards began draining the lake after the Conquest.

E.R. Wolf, ed.: *The valley of Mexico. Studies in pre-hispanic ecology and society* (Albuquerque, 1976); W.T. Sanders et al.: *The basin of Mexico: ecological processes in the evolution of a civilization* (New York, 1979).

PRI

Basta, Tell (anc. Per-Bastet, Bubastis) Temple and town in the eastern Nile Delta, 80 km northeast of Cairo, which flourished from the 4th dynasty to the late Roman period (*c*.2649 BC–AD 395). The main excavated features of the site are the red granite temple of the cat-goddess Bastet, the *ka*-temples of Teti and Pepy I (*c*.2323–2255 BC), the temples of Atum and Mihos and the 'jubilee chapels' of Amenemhat III and Amenhotep III, as well as a series of vaulted mud-brick cat cemeteries and adjacent ateliers to the north of the city. Bubastis reached its peak when it became the capital of Egypt in the 22nd dynasty (*c*.945–712 BC). The site provides a particularly satisfying instance of the successful combination of textual and archaeological data in that some of the details of Herodotus' architectural description of the temple of the cat-goddess Bastet (*History* II, 59–60) were confirmed by the excavations of Edouard Naville (1891).

E. Naville: *Bubastis (1887–1889)* (London, 1891); L. Habachi: *Tell Basta* (Cairo, 1957); C.C. Van Siclen III: 'The city of Basta: an interim report', *NARCE* 128 (1984), 28–39.

IS

Batan Grande Immense site of the Sicán culture, in the Lambayeque Valley of Peru, dating to the Middle Horizon and Late Intermediate Period (*c*.AD 550–1438). It consists of a ceremonial precinct of some eight large adobe pyramid complexes, most of which are apparently mortuary structures. A long-term archaeological project in this precinct (and in adjacent habitation and production areas) has delineated the familial organization of metallurgical production and state-directed trade in a network that covered much of western South America; the development and organization of industrial level ceramics production; and the existence of a four-tier social organization among the Sicán elite. An unlooted 'royal' tomb discovered in 1991 provided a context for the elaborate gold work, including the huge mummy masks, characteristic of this culture.

I. Shimada: 'The Batan-Grande-La Leche archaeological project: the first two seasons', *JFA* 8:4 (1981), 405–46; ——: 'Perception, procurement and management of resources: archaeological perspectives', *Andean civilization and ecology*, ed. S. Masudo et al. (Tokyo, 1985), 357–99; I. Shimada and J. Merkel: 'A Sicán tomb in Peru', *Minerva* 4/1 (1993), 18–25; Y. Masuda, T. Yamaqudi and I. Shimada, ed.: *Shikan Hakkutsoten – Ogen no Miyako* [Exhibition of Sicán excavation – golden capitol] (Tokyo, 1994); I. Shimada and J.A. Griffin: 'Precious metal objects of the Middle Sicán', *SA* 270 (1994), 82–9.

KB

Bat Cave Set of adjacent rockshelters on the southern margin of the San Agustin Plains in west-central New Mexico. The initial excavation of the site by Herbert Dick in 1948 and 1950 yielded the earliest maize in North America, radiocarbon dated to *c*.6000 BP. The re-excavation of Bat Cave by W.H. Wills in 1981 and 1983 led to a reassessment of the data, setting the appearance of maize and squash in North America at *c*.1200 BC.

W.H. Wills: *Early prehistoric agriculture in the American Southwest* (Santa Fe, 1988).

JJR

bâton de commandement *see* BATÔN PERCÉ

bâton percé Antler tool-type of unknown function that forms part of the Magdalenian (and occasionally Aurignacian) industry in the Upper Palaeolithic, for example at La Madeleine in the Dordogne. Often decorated, they consist of a length of reindeer antler with a hole drilled through, and may have served as arrow straighteners. When this artefact type was first recognized it was given the misleading name of *bâton de commandement*, and this is the name used in the earlier literature.

RJA

baulk (balk) Unexcavated strips deliberately preserved by archaeologists between excavated trenches. Baulks are useful for a number of practical reasons (access, photography, survey stations), but primarily because they allow the excavator to see a vertical section of stratigraphy at the edge of

the excavated area. When sites have very complex or confused stratigraphies, the trenching strategy often makes use of multiple baulks, while sites with simpler stratigraphies tend to be excavated extensively using few or no baulks (*see* OPEN-AREA EXCAVATION).
RJA

Bawit *see* BAHARIYA OASIS

Bayesian approach, Bayesian statistics Approach to statistics which allows previous results or experience to be taken into account and to influence future results; for this reason it is sometimes called subjective analysis, in contrast to classical (or objective, or frequentist, statistics). At its heart lies Bayes' Theorem, which enables prior PROBABILITIES to be combined with data to yield posterior probabilities, that express a researcher's degree of belief about a subject in the light of both the data and previous experience. The approach makes heavy demands on computer time, but developments in statistical theory and computer hardware are reducing this problem. Buck et al. (1996) have applied the approach to RADIOCARBON DATING, SPATIAL ANALYSIS, provenancing, SERIATION and DENDROCHRONOLOGY, and further uses can be expected.
T.R. Bayes: 'An essay towards solving a problem in the doctrine of chances', *Philosophical Transactions of the Royal Society* 53 (1763), 370–418; C.E. Buck et al.: 'Combining archaeological and radiocarbon information: a Bayesian approach to calibration', *Antiquity* 65 (1991) 808–21; D.A. Berry: *Statistics: a Bayesian perspective* (Belmont, 1995); C.E. Buck et al.: *Bayesian approach to interpreting archaeological data* (Chichester and New York, 1996).
CO

Bayon *see* ANGKOR

beakers In its generic sense, this term can be used to describe any flat-based (and usually handleless) drinking cup, made of any material. Archaeologists tend to use the term more particularly to describe the tall, decorated, pottery drinking vessels that are a distinctive element in various late Neolithic and Copper Age cultural assemblages in Europe such as the CORDED WARE COMPLEX and the later bell beakers of the 'BEAKER PHENOMENON'. Well-fired, and usually boldly decorated with simple repeated geometric ornament within zones, beakers are most often found as grave-goods; the stylistic evolution of bell beakers in the Low Countries and Britain is described in Clarke (1970) and reinterpreted in Lanting and van der Waals (1972).
D.L. Clarke: *Beaker pottery of Great Britain and Ireland* (Cambridge, 1970); J.N. Lanting and J.D. Van Der Waals: 'British beakers as seen from the Continent', *Helenium* 12 (1972), 20–46; R.J. Harrison: *The beaker folk: Copper Age archaeology in Western Europe* (London, 1980); W.H. Waldren and R.C. Kennard, eds: *Bell Beakers of the West Mediterranean* (Oxford, 1987).
RJA

'beaker phenomenon' Term used to describe the spread and adoption of a set of similar material culture, notably pottery beakers, across broad areas of Europe, especially Atlantic Europe, during the later 3rd millennium BC. The beaker phenomenon is recognized largely from burials, where the richer interments are characterized by gravegoods such as daggers (at first flint, then copper), archery equipment (especially stone wristguards), jewellery made of exotic materials such as jet and gold and in characteristic shapes such as the 'V-perforated button' – and, of course, the characteristic 'bell-shaped' pottery beaker. The earliest bell beaker assemblages in northern European contexts are truly 'Neolithic' – there is no sign of metallurgy. Later assemblages boast early tanged copper daggers and metal beads and other jewellery and are usually classified as 'Copper Age' or 'Early Bronze Age'.

Regions exhibiting beaker material include areas bordering the Atlantic and North Sea such as the Low Countries, Britain, Brittany, southwest and southern France, Spain and Portugal (the southern countries exhibiting some of the earliest forms of beaker); beaker assemblages and traits also appear along the upper Rhine, along the Rhône, and on some of the Mediterranean islands. In the past, archaeologists (e.g. Abercromby 1902) regarded the spread of beakers and their associated material culture as evidence for the movement of people (as invaders, traders or colonizers); it was often assumed that they travelled by sea, as the areas first and most characteristically affected appeared to be maritime or accessible by great rivers such as the Rhône or Rhine. It became clear, however, that different elements of the beaker material culture originated in different regions of Europe. For example, despite the fact that very early styles of beaker can be identified in Iberia (the Maritime-style beaker), the bell beaker form itself seems to have derived from earlier beaker forms in the Rhine delta area (where an important early decorated variant is known as the All-Over Ornamented or AOO beaker), and is perhaps ultimately derived from the earlier CORDED WARE beakers; metallurgy and some styles associated with it seem more likely to have spread from Iberia, where they are known in an earlier period from centres such as LOS MILLARES. Furthermore, styles and influences seemed to flow back to supposed 'originating' areas as well as forward to 'invaded' areas, and there seemed to be some regions where elements of the beaker cultural complex were adopted while other elements were ignored. For all these reasons, the idea of a single colonizing or itinerant 'beaker folk' as an explanation of the phenomenon has fallen out of favour.

While it still seems possible that in some areas movements of people were involved in the spread of the beaker cultural assemblage, archaeologists now prefer to view it as primarily a social phenomenon. According to this interpretation, the beaker phenomenon represents a 'package' of elite material culture, probably associated with particular practices (e.g. warrior drinking rituals) and perhaps with a radical change in social organization. Much has been made of the fact that traces of pollen found in some beakers suggest it may have been associated with the drinking of mead or other forms of alcohol; the importance of daggers and archery equipment in beaker burials suggests a cult of the warrior, while the richness of some of the jewellery has been termed 'individualizing'. The fact that beaker burials are generally single male inhumations, often under round barrows, contrasts sharply with the more 'collective' burials of the early and middle Neolithic (although single burials in round barrows are now recognized in a few regions before the beaker assemblages arrived). Andrew Sherratt traces the origin of the dynamic underlying the bell-beaker phenomenon in northwest Europe as far back as the introduction of specialized 'liquid handling' and drinking vessels in southeast and central Europe from the 4th millennium onwards. He associates the spread of beakers with the spread of other novelties from the east (horses, woolly sheep) and perhaps the export from the west of metals. Most authorities now accept that the explanation for the spread of the beaker material culture package lies in its symbolic strength and in the changing nature of societies in Early Bronze Age Europe. *See* BEAKER for further bibliography.

J. Abercromby: 'The oldest Bronze-Age ceramic type in Britain', *Journal of the Royal Anthropological Institute* 32 (1902), 373–97; A. Sherratt: 'The emergence of elites: Earlier Bronze Age Europe', *The Oxford Illustrated Prehistory of Europe*, ed. B. Cunliffe (Oxford, 1994), 244–77.

RJA

Beechey Island Site where Sir John Franklin's ships *Erebus* and *Terror* wintered in 1845/6 during their attempt to navigate the Northwest Passage. Three sailors died that winter and were buried on the island. In 1984 and 1986 Owen Beattie temporarily exhumed from the permafrost the perfectly preserved bodies and autopsied them. Hair samples later confirmed the hypothesis that lead poisoning, probably from food sealed in cans with lead solder, was already affecting the crews during that first winter and may have contributed to the eventual death of the remaining 126 sailors by the summer of 1848.

O. Beattie and J. Geiger: *Frozen in time* (Saskatoon, 1987).

RP

Begarawiya *see* MEROE

Begho Site of a market town in the Brong Ahafo region of western Ghana, made up of four quarters 1–2 km from each other. On the basis of six radiocarbon dates obtained from the Brong quarter, the excavator, Merrick Posnansky, concluded that the town was occupied from around AD 1430 to 1710 (520–240 BP) and that it attained a peak of prosperity towards the beginning of the 17th century. Local manufactures included objects of iron and ivory, beads, ceramics and textiles, and Posnansky considered that there was a continuity in material culture between the ancient inhabitants and their modern descendants. Notable finds included two ivory side-blown trumpets, still important in ceremonials today, and Posnansky (1976: 56) suggested that this instrument 'spread south from Mali, together with a knowledge of brass-working, systems of weights, building methods and ceramic forms'. These items were transmitted in turn from forest fringe states such as Bono Manso to Asante, which was the most important of the Akan kingdoms in the forest, and subsequently a centre of the gold trade. It is now known, however, that the town is older than previously suspected. Two radiocarbon dates obtained by L.B. Crossland in 1975 from the Nyarko quarter indicate an occupation in the 11th and 12th centuries AD (905 ± 80 and 830 ± 80 BP). The view hitherto accepted that Begho and similar towns grew up in response to traders coming down from JENNE may therefore be, as Posnansky and McIntosh (1976: 166) comment, 'in need of some alteration'.

M. Posnansky: 'Archaeology and the origins of the Akan society in Ghana', *Problems in economic and social anthropology*, ed. G. de G. Sieveking et al. (London, 1976), 49–59; M. Posnansky and R. McIntosh: 'New radiocarbon

dates for Northern and Western Africa', *JAH* 17 (1976), 161–95.
PA-J

behavioral archaeology, behaviorism Form of PROCESSUAL ARCHAEOLOGY devised by the American archaeologist Michael Schiffer in the 1970s. Schiffer's ideas, set out in the book *Behavioral archaeology*, were concerned with the diversity of human behaviour in the past, and the dialogue between behaviour and the environmental context. His body of method and theory was based on the premise that cultural and natural 'transforms' (C-TRANSFORMS and N-TRANSFORMS) converted the 'systemic context' (i.e. the original set of dynamic relationships within ancient material culture and society) into the 'archaeological context' (the 'distorted' form of the cultural material examined by archaeologists). Behavioral archaeology is therefore primarily concerned with SITE FORMATION PROCESSES. He suggested that many archaeological projects, such as Robert Whallon's SPATIAL ANALYSIS of occupation floors (1974), were deeply flawed because they failed to distinguish between systemic and archaeological contexts.

Lewis Binford (1981) argued that Schiffer's approach was based on a dubious 'Pompeii premise'. That is, just as the Roman city of Pompeii was preserved by volcanic ash without being abandoned or allowed to deteriorate, so the original behavioural systems were envisaged by Schiffer as perfect frozen systems. 'What Schiffer has described is . . . not a picture of a cultural system but a slice of "history" in the literal sense of the word'. Whereas Schiffer defined practices such as the cleaning out of hearths as C-transforms, Binford argued that these were part of the archaeological record itself, not 'distortions' of some original perfect system. Despite such criticism, Schiffer's behavioral archaeology has permanently affected perceptions of the archaeological record. Indeed, it might be argued that it is precisely by means of the distinction between systemic and archaeological contexts that the 'Pompeii premise' can be avoided.

See GRASSHOPPER PUEBLO for a discussion of the application of behavioral archaeology to the study of complexity.

M.B. Schiffer: 'Archaeological context and systemic context', *AA* 37/2 (1972), 156–65; R. Whallon: 'Spatial analysis of occupation floors II: the application of nearest neighbour analysis', *AA* 39 (1974), 16–34; M.B. Schiffer: *Behavioral archaeology* (New York, 1976); L.S. Binford: 'Behavioral archaeology and the "Pompeii premise"', *Journal of Anthropological Research* 37/3 (1981), 195–208; M.B. Schiffer: *Formation processes of the archaeological record* (Albuquerque, 1987).
IS

Behistun *see* BISITUN

Beidha *see* ACERAMIC NEOLITHIC

Belbaşe Rock-shelter on the coast of southern Turkey which was excavated by Envor Bostanci in the early 1960s. It has given its name to an Upper Palaeolithic regional culture typified by a combination of rock engravings and a distinctive microlithic assemblage consisting of points, tanged arrowheads and blades. Although Belbase itself is the type-site, the most impressive collection of Belbase material has been excavated from the lower strata at the Beldibi rock-shelter, which is itself the typesite for the succeeding MESOLITHIC 'Beldibi culture' (characterized by a hunting and fishing subsistence pattern and early pottery production).

E.Y. Bostanci: 'The Belbasi industry', *Belleten* 26 (1962), 253–72; ——: 'The Mesolithic of Beldibi and Belbasi', *Antropoloji* 3 (1965), 91–134.
IS

Beldibi *see* BELBAŞE

Bellows Beach One of the earliest Hawaiian sites on the island of O'ahu, this beach site lies near a permanent stream. The site shows evidence of house structures, cooking facilities and evidence of subsistence, as well as burials. The site may date to 1700 BP, although this early date has been questioned by Spriggs and Anderson (1993), who feel there is no evidence for the settlement of Hawaii prior to 1400 BP.

P.V. Kirch: *The evolution of Polynesian chiefdoms* (Cambridge, 1984), 244–5; M. Spriggs and A. Anderson: 'Late colonization of East Polynesia', *Antiquity* 67 (1993), 200–17.
CG

Bender, Tell el- *see* KISH

Benfica Site on the coast of Angola, a little south of Luanda, the chief interest of which lies in the occurrence of a small sample of pottery considered to have Early Iron Age affinities in a shell midden with Later Stone Age artefacts, and with radiocarbon dates of uncal 1810 and 1770 BP. The date would be very early for Iron Age in such a locality, and the possibility cannot be ignored that the affinities may lie with older pottery traditions of the equatorial forest region to the northeast, not necessarily associated with the 'Iron Age'.

J.R. dos Santos Junior and C.M.N. Everdosa: 'A estacao arqueologica de Benfica, Luanda', *Revista da Faculdade de Çiençias da Universidaed de Luanda* 5 (1970), 33–51; C. Everdosa: *Arqueologia Angolana* (Lisbon, 1980).

RI

Beni Hasan Egyptian necropolis located in the cliffs to the east of the Nile about 23 km north of modern el-Minya. The site dates from the 6th to 12th dynasties (*c.*2323–1783 BC) and is best known for the rock-cut tombs of the Middle Kingdom provincial governors of the 'oryx' *nome* (province). The walls of several of these tomb-chapels are decorated with painted scenes from daily life (such as trading, warfare and wrestling) and episodes from funerals. At the southern end of the site is a New Kingdom rock-cut temple (the Speos Artemidos) dedicated to the lioness-goddess Pakhet and dating to the 15th century BC.

P.E. Newberry et al.: *Beni Hassan*, 4 vols (London, 1893–1900); J. Garstang: *Burial customs of ancient Egypt* (London, 1907); S. Bickel and J.-L. Chappaz: 'Missions épigraphiques du Fonds de l'Egyptologie de Genève au Speos Artemidos', *BSEG* 12 (1988), 9–24.

IS

Benin City in southern Nigeria, well-known internationally on account of the 4,000–7,000 'bronze' artefacts seized and transported to Europe by a British expeditionary force in 1897 (now in the British Museum). The city was surrounded by an earthen wall and ditch, with a total vertical height of 16–17 m and a circumference of 11.5 km, which was sectioned by Graham Connah during his excavations of 1961–4 and found to post-date 610 ± 105 BP (AD 1340). In his view this did not contradict the oral tradition which attributes the building of the wall to Oba Ewuare at around AD 1450. Connah contrasted the city wall with a network of linear earthworks surrounding it: the former had a defensive purpose, whereas the latter – the result of many different events spread over a long period of time – did not. This interpretation has been confirmed by Patrick Darling, who has surveyed about 1500 km of the network, which he estimates to have a total length of >16,000 km and an average total vertical height of nearly 3 m. The network stretches in an ellipse for about 100 km to the northeast of Benin, which is in fact on its periphery. Darling suggests that the earthwork (or 'iya') builders, the ancestors of the present Bini and Ishan Edo-speaking peoples, came as sedentary rotational bush-fallow farmers in a 'migratory wave front' from the savanna country to the north around the middle of the 1st millennium AD. The available radiocarbon dates for the moment however relate only to the later stages of this process, at Ohovbe 650 ± 50 and at Idu 530 ± 80 BP (AD 1300 and 1420). Within the city, Connah found some evidence for early settlement at the Clerks' Quarters site, where a well-like cistern extending to a depth 18 m below present ground surface contained the remains of at least 41 young women (with bracelets, finger-rings, and beads) who had apparently been sacrificed. Charcoal associated with the mass burial produced radiocarbon dates of 770 ± 105 and 640 ± 90 BP (AD 1180 and 1310). At the Benin Museum site, Connah found some lumps of edge-laid potsherd pavement beneath charcoal with a radiocarbon date of 645 ± 105 BP (AD 1305); but he suggested that these were not necessarily connected with IFE, where a similar technique was employed. He argues that, in general, the origins of the city are 'still unclear'; and, as Thurstan Shaw comments, excavations to date 'have not thrown light' on the relative validity of the various chronological schemes which have been proposed for its 'bronze' artefacts. An analysis of the metal objects found associated with the mass burial at the Clerks' Quarters site showed that they did consist of tin bronze, but the more recent works of art for which the city is famous are in fact of leaded brass. In terms of their TRACE ELEMENTS (nickel, arsenic, and antimony) and lead isotope ratios these artefacts are distinct from those of IFE and IGBO-UKWU, suggesting that they formed a separate tradition. On the other hand, a TL date of 530 ± 60 BP (AD 1420) has been obtained on the clay core of a 'bronze' casting generally believed to portray an Oni of Ife and to provide good evidence of a link between these two cities. Three more Benin 'bronzes' TL-dated to the 16th century AD are also said to show evidence of the same stylistic connection.

G. Connah: *The archaeology of Benin* (Oxford, 1975); F. Willett and S.J. Fleming: 'A catalogue of important Nigerian copper-alloy castings dated by thermoluminescence', *Archaeometry* 18/2 (1976), 135–46; T. Shaw: *Nigeria: its archaeology and early history* (London, 1978); P.J. Darling: *Archaeology and history in Southern Nigeria: the ancient linear earthworks of Benin and Ishan* (Oxford, 1984); G. Connah: *African civilizations, precolonial cities and states in tropical Africa: an archaeological perspective* (Cambridge, 1987).

PA-J

Bering land bridge *see* BERINGIA

Beringia Widely believed to be the route by which humans populated the Americas, Beringia was a massive landmass periodically exposed during the last glaciation due to lowered sea levels in the shallow Bering and Chukchi seas between Siberia and Alaska. This vast plain, sometimes called the Bering land bridge, appears to have been a steppe–tundra environment that supported herds of large mammals. It was drowned for the last time approximately 14,000 years ago, taking with it any archaeological sites that would have documented this important human migration.

B.M. Fagan: *The great journey* (London, 1987).

RP

Beth Shan *see* SCYTHOPOLIS

Beth Yerah *see* KHIRBET KERAK

Beyçesultan Anatolian Bronze Age site consisting of two settlement mounds located in the upper reaches of the Meander river valley, near Civril in southwestern Turkey. The excavations of Seton Lloyd and James Mellaart in 1954–9 revealed a long stratigraphic sequence of 40 occupation levels, stretching from the late Chalcolithic to the late Bronze Age (*c*.4750–1200 BC), which has served as a linchpin for the early chronology of southwestern Anatolia. The lowest levels include a number of unusual mud-brick shrines dating to the 5th millennium BC; more elaborate versions of the same type of shrine were excavated from Middle and Late Bronze Age strata at the site.

The Middle Bronze Age phase incorporates the remains of a vast colonnaded palace with state-rooms on an upper floor (a *piano nobile* like that in the palace of Yarimlim at TELL ATCHANA), which was pillaged and burnt to the ground in *c*.1750 BC. The late Bronze Age settlement includes numerous 'MEGARON'-style houses (consisting of rectangular halls with open porticoes along their long sides). At this time Beyçesultan may have been part of the kingdom of Arzawa, which was contemporary with the MYCENAEANS and HITTITES, but there is no written evidence to confirm this hypothesis (Mellink 1967).

S. Lloyd and J. Mellaart: *Beyçesultan*, 3 vols (London, 1961–72); S. Lloyd: 'Bronze Age architecture of Anatolia', *Proceedings of the British Academy* 49 (1963), 153–76; M.J. Mellink: 'Beyçesultan: a Bronze Age site in southwestern Turkey', *BO* 24 (1967), 3–9; J. Mellaart and A. Murray: *Beyçesultan III/2: Late Bronze Age and Phrygian pottery* (London, 1995).

IS

B Group Term coined by George Reisner to describe the latter stages of the Neolithic A GROUP in Nubia from *c*.2800 to 2300 BC. The B-Group culture was intended to fill a supposed chronological gap between the end of the A Group and the beginning of the C Group, but most archaeologists are now agreed that the B Group never existed. When Smith (1966: 95–6) reanalysed the excavations undertaken by Reisner and Firth in Cemetery 7 at Shellal, which formed the original basis for the B Group, he was able to demonstrate that most of the graves identified by the excavators as 'B-Group' were either completely devoid of artefacts, too disturbed to be properly recorded or more characteristic of the preceding A group or succeeding C Group.

G. Reisner: *Archaeological survey of Nubia: report for 1907–8*, I (Cairo, 1910), 18–52; H.S. Smith: 'The Nubian B-group', *Kush* 14 (1966), 69–124; ——: 'The development of the A-Group "culture" in northern Lower Nubia', *Egypt and Africa*, ed. W.V. Davies (London, 1991), 92–111.

IS

Bhimbetka Hill containing a cluster of prehistoric cave sites located in the Vindhya Hills of Madhya Pradesh, India. Excavations in more than a dozen caves were conducted by V.N. Misra, Vishnu S. Wakankar and Susanne Haas in 1972–7. The most significant of these sites, Cave III F-23, yielded a 4 m thick deposit divided into eight major stratigraphic levels. Levels 6–8 contained ACHEULEAN artefacts, including cleavers, handaxes, scrapers and flake tools; some LEVALLOIS flaking was evident. Level 5 (radiocarbon-dated to *c*.16,000–14,000 BC) was defined as Middle Palaeolithic: flake and blade tools increased in this period, and cleavers and handaxes declined in frequency. In Upper Palaeolithic Level 4, flake and blade tools again increased in frequency and decreased in size. Artefacts from Levels 4–8 were predominantly made of quartzite, with infrequent use of chalcedony or chert.

The tools from levels 1–3 were dramatically different from those found in the earlier levels: chert and chalcedony tools predominated and the technology was primarily microlithic. Groundstone artefacts, bone tools and burials also appeared during levels 1–3, and calibrated radiocarbon dates range from *c*.5000 BC to 1000 AD, thus providing evidence of the long continuity of microlithic traditions in Central India.

Over 500 caves in the Bhimbetka region contained paintings dating from late prehistoric ('microlithic') until comparatively recent times.

The subject-matter of the prehistoric paintings included hunting and dancing scenes, with depictions of a wide range of animals including rhinoceros, bison, elephant, tiger, fish and fowl.

V.N. Misra: 'The Acheulian succession at Bhimbetka, Central India', *Recent advances in Indo-Pacific prehistory*, ed. V.N. Misra and P. Bellwood (New Delhi, 1985), 35–47; V.S. Wakanakar: 'Bhimbetka: The stone tool industries and rock paintings', *Recent advances in Indo-Pacific prehistory*, ed. V.N. Misra and P. Bellwood (New Delhi, 1985), 176–7; Y. Mathpal: *Prehistoric rock paintings of Bhimbetka* (New Delhi, 1984).

CS

Bhir *see* TAXILA

Big Game Hunting Tradition Outdated and inaccurate term referring to the subsistence strategies of late Pleistocene PALEOINDIAN hunter-gatherers of North and South America. The derivation of this term was based on the alleged focus of the Paleoindian hunters of *c.*12,000 BP on large Pleistocene megafauna such as mammoth and mastodon. The widespread focus on 'big game' was commonly used to explain the generally similar kinds of Paleoindian artefacts found throughout much of the western hemisphere. In contrast, recent research focuses on recognition of the temporal and regional variation in the diet and other cultural characteristics of late Pleistocene hunter-gatherers.

D. Dragoo: 'Some aspects of Eastern North American prehistory', *AA* 41 (1926), 3–27; D. Meltzer and B. Smith: 'Paleoindian and early Archaic subsistence strategies in Eastern North America', *Foraging, collecting, and harvesting*, ed. S.W. Neusius (Carbondale, 1986), 3–31; J. Stoltman and D. Baerries: 'The evolution of human ecosystems in the eastern United States', *Late-Quaternary environments of the United States* II: *The Holocene*, ed. H. Wright (Minneapolis, 1983), 252–368.

RJE

'big house' *see* CASA GRANDE

'big man' Term adopted by anthropologists after *c.*1935 to describe the leading figures of Melanesian society. The term was coined to replace the potentially misleading 'chief', with its connotations of extensive, formally recognized, and inherited power. In contrast, anthropologists noted that Melanesian leaders seemed obliged to achieve and continually maintain their influence through strength of character, exchange of shell valuables, economic success (in pig production etc.), sponsorship of feasts, and consensus leadership. In doing so, it has been claimed, the chiefs act both as an economic stimulus and as a social strata able to form political and economic relationships between the individual units of a segmentary society. The concept of the 'big man' has become familiar to many archaeologists through the work of Marshall Sahlins (especially Sahlins 1963). As a result, a loosely defined term in social anthropology has come to be associated in archaeology with Sahlins's redistributive model. This model is not universally accepted by social anthropologists, and has been sharply criticized (see Binford 1983). Van der Velde (1990) represents an interesting attempt to distinguish 'big men' from chiefs in the archaeological record.

M.D. Sahlins: 'Poor man, rich man, big man, chief: political types in Melanesia and Polynesia', *Comparative studies in society and history* 5 (1963), 285–303; ——: *Stone age economics* (London, 1974); L. Lindstrom: '"Big man": a short terminological history', *American Anthropologist* 83 (1981), 900–5; L. Binford: *In pursuit of the past* (London, 1983), 216–20; P. van der Velde: 'Bandkeramik social inequality – a case study', *Germania* 68/1 (1990), 21.

RJA

Bigo Largest of several bank-and-ditch complexes in the undulating cattle country of western Uganda, dating to the mid-Iron Age (*c.*13th–15th centuries AD). The earthworks consist of a central set of enclosures on a rise overlooking the papyrus-choked swamps of the Katonga river, and an outer work which, with a secondary extension, encloses over 300 ha. With various additions the earthworks measure altogether some 10 km; the V-shaped ditches were cut 3–5 metres into the rock. The banks of upcast material inside the ditches have considerably eroded. Excavations by Shinnie in 1957 and Posnansky in 1960 confirmed that the central earthworks of Bigo contained a settlement, one related, by its distinctive roulette-decorated pottery, to the bigger agricultural-pastoral settlement of Ntusi nearby. In the mid-Iron Age, cattle became the main source of wealth, power and patronage in the interlacustrine region.

P.L. Shinnie: 'Excavations at Bigo, 1957', *UJ* 24 (1960), 16–28; M. Posnansky: 'Bigo bya Mugenyi', *UJ* 33 (1969), 125–50; J.E.G. Sutton: 'The antecedents of the interlacustrine kingdoms', *JAH* 34 (1993), 33–64.

JS

billes *see* CHASSÉEN

Bim Son Cemetery of the Chinese HAN DYNASTY located in northern Vietnam. From the 1st century AD, the valleys of the Red and Ma rivers were incorporated forcibly into the Han Empire. The rich indigenous culture of DONG SON withered, and a Chinese system of provincial government was imposed. Archaeologically, this is best expressed in the Chinese burial grounds, of which Bim Son is one of the best known. Burials were placed in brick structures comprising a number of rooms. The dead were interred with rich grave goods, including iron weapons and bronze ornaments, mirrors and bowls.

O.R.T. Janse: *Archaeological research in Indo-China*, I (Cambridge, MA, 1947).

CH

binary opposition *see* STRUCTURALISM

Birka The island of Bjork lies in Lake Malaren, 30 km west of Stockholm in the parish of Adels. Since the Middle Ages the island has been associated with the Viking-age centre called Birka in 9th-century written sources. Ansgar, a Frankish monk, journeyed here by sea in the 820s, and was given permission to preach Christianity. Modern excavations were launched in 1872 by Hjalmar Stolpe, a natural scientist and entomologist. Stolpe trenched the Black Earth site in the western bay, and then from 1874, on the occasion of a visit by the World Archaeological Congress, he began 20 years of systematic excavations of about 1100 burial mounds. Stolpe's excavations were remarkable for his scale field drawings made on graph paper. These revealed the richness of the Viking Age archaeology, and the far-flung connections maintained by the islanders between the 9th and 10th centuries. Stolpe's records were eventually catalogued and published by Holger Arbman in the 1940s. There followed small-scale excavations in the Black Earth site in 1969–71, and the large 1990–4 open-area excavation in the same place. These show that Birka was first settled in the early to mid-8th century, when the first jetties were made beside the harbour. Craftsmen gathered around the jetties who had trading connections from the later 8th to mid-9th centuries primarily with the Franks (probably via DORESTAD). By the 10th century, new jetties had been made overlying the earlier ones. Birka's principle connections were now with the eastern Baltic and, to a lesser extent, Byzantium. By the 11th century Birka had been eclipsed by other settlements around the lake. Birka appears to have been a winter fair as well as a proto-urban site serving the kings of central Sweden whose estate centre was on the adjacent island of Adelso.

H. Arbman: *Schweden und das Karolingische Reich* (Stockholm, 1937); ——: *Birka* I, *Die Graber* (Stockholm, 1940–3); B. Ambrosiani and H. Clark, eds: *Early investigations and future plans* (Stockholm, 1992).

RH

Bir Tarfawi *see* ATERIAN

Birs Nimrod *see* BORSIPPA

birth house *see MAMMISI*

Bishapur *see* SASANIAN

Bisitun (Behistun) The so-called Rock of Bisitun, situated about 30 km east of Kermanshah in western Iran, is decorated with a stele of the Achaemenid ruler Darius I (522–486 BC). The stele was carved into a carefully prepared and polished surface at a height of 122 m above ground-level; it consists of a scene depicting the king himself, under the protection of the god Ahuramazda, and a trilingual CUNEIFORM inscription in Elamite, Persian and Babylonian. This inscription was copied by the intrepid Sir Henry Rawlinson in 1835–47, providing him with the first real breakthrough in the decipherment of the cuneiform script.

H.C. Rawlinson: 'The Persian cuneiform inscription at Bisitun', *Journal of the Royal Asiatic Society* 10 (1847), i–lxxi.

IS

Biskupin Fortified lakeside settlement of the early Iron Age, 75 km north of Poznań in Poland. Discovered in 1933, on a peninsula in Lake Biskupin, this water-logged and well-preserved site dates from the 7th–8th century BC and is associated with the Lusatian culture (manifest across much of central Europe from the end of the 2nd millennium BC to *c*.400 BC). The settlement was surrounded by a breakwater of rows of oak and pine stakes. Within this was a rampart 6 m high, built of a system of interlocking log 'boxes' filled with earth/sand and then plastered with clay. A gateway through the rampart was guarded by a watchtower. Occupied by up to 1000 people, the oval settlement was encircled by a road and dissected by 11 further roads which gave access to rows of two-roomed houses. The houses were again built of logs, typically measured 9 × 8 m; the roads of the settlement were paved with clay-covered logs. Finds include incised vessels encrusted with white or painted with red, numerous bronze and many iron tools, ornaments and weapons, as well as a simple wooden plough and a solid wheel. The site is now a major tourist centre and has been partly reconstructed.

J. Kostrewski: 'Biskupin: an early Iron Age village in Western Poland', *Antiquity* 12 (1938), 311–17; W. Niewiarowski et al.: 'Biskupin fortified settlement and its environment in the light of new environmental and

archaeological studies', *The Wetland Revolution in Prehistory*, ed. B. Coles (Exeter, 1992), 81–92.
RJA

bit-hilani (Hittite: 'gate-house'?) Type of palatial structure which has been excavated at various sites in the Mesopotamia and the Levant, *c.*1400–600 BC. It consisted of one or two parallel rectangular rooms with a pillared portico in front (consisting of one to three wooden columns on elaborate stone bases) and sometimes a set of small rooms to the rear, as well as a staircase adjoining the portico which would probably have led to an upper storey consisting of living quarters. In its original form, at north Syrian sites such as TELL ATCHANA, ZINJIRLI, TELL HALAF and Tell Tayanat, the *bit-hilani* was an independent structure, and an even earlier example may even have been found in the palace of Yarim-Lim at Tell Atchana, dating to the 18th century BC. Much later, at the Assyrian cities of KHORSABAD and NINEVEH in the 9th–8th centuries BC, a simplified form of the portico was used as a kind of gate-house attached to the front of palatial complexes. Although there are clearly strong similarities between the north Syrian and Assyrian styles of porticoed palatial buildings, Frankfort (1970: 283–4) argues that they were essentially separate architectural traditions, not deriving from a common prototype.

H. Frankfort: 'The origin of the bit-hilani', *Iraq* 14 (1952), 120–31; ——: *The art and architecture of the ancient Orient*, 4th edn (Harmondsworth, 1970), 151–2, 282–9.
IS

Black-and-Red Ware Widespread ceramic style found at sites throughout India during the 1st and 2nd millennia BC. Black-and-Red Ware vessels tend to be similar in terms of surface colour and treatment (with black interiors and red burnished exteriors with blackened upper portions), but they vary greatly in form, and cannot be attributed to a single cultural tradition. Three interpretations of the firing technology have been proposed (see Singh 1982: 57–65). The origin of this widespread ware is controversial, and its diverse chronological and spatial context precludes a simple explanation. Singh (1982: 424–5) has proposed that the ware may first have developed in LOTHAL where some of the earliest dated vessels have been recovered, and then expanded in a process of 'multi-directional diffusion and multi-dimensional proliferation'.

H.N. Singh: 'Black-and-Red Ware: a cultural study', *Essays in Indian protohistory*, ed. D.P. Agrawal and D.K. Chakrabarti (New Delhi, 1979), 267–83; S. Gurumurthy: *Ceramic traditions in south India* (Madras, 1981); H.N. Singh: *History and archaeology of Black-and-Red Ware* (Delhi, 1982).
CS

Blackdog Cemetery Eastern or Santee Sioux cemetery site of the mid-19th century AD, located on a sandy river terrace in Dakota County, Minnesota, North America. The cultural designation 'Sioux' is used to refer to a large association of related tribes – including the Dakota – which once inhabited the woodlands and plains from western Wisconsin to the Rocky Mountains. Ethnohistoric sources suggest that the 19th-century Dakota people were egalitarian, hunter-gatherer horticulturalists who occupied large villages during the summer and divided into smaller, mobile family groups during the rest of the year. The cemeteries were associated with the villages, often positioned above them on high terraces.

The period during which the Blackdog burial site was in use (AD 1830–60) has been indicated both by a documented reference to the village in 1835 and by the presence of datable artefacts, including beads, medals, buttons, a coin and Euro-American ceramics. A total of 39 individuals were interred in 24 different burials, aligned in linear fashion along the river terrace, including 20 coffin burials and two wrapped in birch bark or cloth. Roughly equal numbers of male and female were recovered, with approximately equal representation of adult and juvenile.

Distinguishing sex and gender in the Blackdog Cemetery M.K. Whelan (1991) has examined the documentary and burial data from the Blackdog burial site. She considers historical archaeology to be important in revealing the ways in which gender is represented in archaeological deposits. Because of the range of additional sources available for correlation she believes that the study of gender in prehistory will be able to draw upon historical studies as a source of MIDDLE-RANGE THEORY.

As the first stage of her analysis of the Blackdog cemetery, Whelan stresses that sex and gender must be distinguished analytically. She suggest that non-western definitions of gender can only be perceived archaeologically if we reject any biological equation for gender. In addition, she refers to ethnographic investigations of Native American groups which have identified *berdache*, individuals who in entering adulthood elect to change the gender ascription of their youth. In such societies multiple genders are present. Biological sex is not the determinant factor in creating gender, but rather personal preference, or supernatural visions can be the shaping factors.

Skeletal remains from the Blackdog site were analysed independently of artefacts associated with each burial, using multivariate sexing and ageing methods where possible. The following results were obtained: 6 men, 6 women, 27–9 sex indeterminate; 16 adults, 16 juveniles and 7–9 indeterminate age. No absolute age or sex artefact correlates were found, and no artefacts related to subsistence activities were present in the grave goods. When gender was examined without reference to sex, certain artefacts appeared to suggest gender categories. Artefacts with documented ritual associations (pipestone pipes, mirrors, pouches) were associated with seven people; when compared with evidence for biological sex, six of this group were male. The predominance of male sex in this group suggests a gender category because sex played an important, although not exclusive, role in defining membership. The woman in this group was young (20–25 years) and associated with more artefacts of more types than any other in the cemetery. This woman's burial may be indicative of a *berdache* who elected to change gender ascription. Whelan also suggests that gender categories may have been signalled by dress, and in particular that the size and colour of wampum beads were used to distinguish masculine and feminine dress. In contrast, little artefact correlation was present in juvenile burials, leading Whelan to suggest that children were considered as a separate gender. Status of burial was considered according to the number of artefacts and types accompanying a burial. Male and female status was revealed to be comparable, in keeping with the egalitarian descriptions provided by ethnographic and ethnohistoric sources.

Whelan's study is important in a number of respects. First she concludes that a gendered division of labour cannot be observed from Dakota burials, possibly indicating that burial was reserved to signal more symbolic gender differences. Second, the status of children's burials suggests that three or more gender categories may exist. Finally, she demonstrates that ritual status among the Blackdog people may have been a category of gender more often held by men, but not exclusive to them. The occurrence of a young female skeleton accompanied by artefacts found more commonly with men seems to suggest that it was possible for individuals to transcend categories of gender based partly on biological differences, in order to be accepted into a social category not linked to their biological sex.

M.K. Whelan: 'Gender and historical archaeology: Eastern Dakota patterns in the 19th century', *HA* 25/4 (1991), 17–32.

RG

Black Pottery Culture *see* LUNG-SHAN

Blackwater Draw Former small pond in eastern New Mexico, USA, which was a favoured hunting location during the LLANO and FOLSOM cultures of the PALEOINDIAN period. Many separate kills of small numbers of mammoths and extinct species of bison occurred in and on the edges of the pond, suggesting that the animals were killed when their legs became mired in the sediments on the pond bottom. In addition, temporary camp sites have been found near the pond margins. The site is primarily known for several CLOVIS kill-and-butchery locations of mammoths, but there are also bison kills. Folsom kills were limited to bison. The site is of special importance in that the Clovis to Folsom sequence was first demonstrated here with reference to the stratigraphy of the kill localities.

J. Hester: 'Blackwater, Locality No. 1: a stratified, early man site in eastern New Mexico', *Publications of the Fort Burgwin Research Centre 8* (Dallas, 1972); A Boldurian: 'Lithic technology at the Mitchell locality of Blackwater Draw: a stratified Folsom site in eastern New Mexico', *PAnth* 35 (1990), 1–115.

WB

blade Long, thin flakes of hard stone such as flint or obsidian. Conventionally, a blade is differentiated from a simple flake in that it is at least twice as long as it is wide and has roughly parallel sides. In Palaeolithic stone industries, blade production predominates after about 35,000 BC and helps define the Middle to Upper Palaeolithic transition. Typically, blades are produced in batches from carefully prepared cores; they often served as projectile points.

RJA

Blemmyes Nomadic group in the Eastern Desert of Lower Nubia who flourished during the BALLANA, or X-Group, phase (*c*.AD 350–550). They are generally identified as the ancestors of the modern Beja people of Sudan. Along with the Nobatae (the inhabitants of Lower Nubia during the late Meroitic and Ballana periods), the Blemmyes are mentioned by such ancient historians as Olympiodorus of Thebes (early 5th century AD) and Procopius (6th century AD).

A. Paul: *A history of the Beja tribes of the Sudan*, 2nd edn (London, 1971); W.Y. Adams: *Nubia: corridor to Africa*, 2nd edn (Princeton, 1984), 382–429; P. Rose: *The aftermath of the Roman frontier in Lower Nubia* (unpublished Ph.D. thesis, Cambridge, 1993).

IS

blood residue analysis *see* RESIDUES

Bluff Village MOGOLLON pithouse village in the Forestdale Valley, east-central Arizona, which was excavated by Emil W. Haury in 1941 and 1944. The Mogollon is a major prehistoric culture of the American Southwest characterized by pithouses and coil-and-scraped pottery. DENDROCHRONOLOGICAL dates of *c.*AD 300 from the Bluff Village site supported the notion that the Mogollan culture was of great antiquity and was culturally independent of the ANASAZI – a thesis first put forward by Haury in 1936.

E.W. Haury: *Mogollon culture in the Forestdale Valley, East-Central Arizona* (Tucson, 1985).

JJR

boat ethnography *see* MARITIME ARCHAEOLOGY

Bodh Gaya Sacred Buddhist site about 100 km south of modern Patna, in Uttar Pradesh, India, where the Buddha received enlightenment beneath the *bodhi*-tree. Construction at the site occurred from the death of Buddha in the 5th century BC until the 15th century AD. The principal feature of Bodh Gaya is the Mahahbodhi complex dating to the 7th century AD and consisting of a massive brick temple.

D. Mitra: *Buddhist monuments* (Calcutta, 1971), 60–6.

CS

Boghazköy (anc. Hattusas) *see* HITTITES

bolas South American weapon for hunting in open grassland consisting of two or more weights connected by cords or thongs. The *bolas* is thrown at the legs of the fleeing prey, felling it for dispatch with another weapon.

Bonampak (Mayan: 'painted wall') A small LOWLAND MAYA centre located along the Usumacinta River, in Chiapas, Mexico. Bonampak is particularly known for its spectacular Late Classic (*c.*AD 600–900) murals on the walls of three rooms in a single structure. Room 1 shows a scene of ritual preparations, with a richly costumed ruler and attendants, including an orchestra; Room 2 shows a raid and the judgment of captives on the stairs of a structure; and Room 3 shows a dance and bloodletting ceremony. Thought to represent the record of an actual event occurring around AD 790, the murals are painted in an unusual naturalistic style and provide a wealth of detail on royal costuming.

R.E.W. Adams and R.C. Aldrich: 'A re-evaluation of the Bonampak murals: a preliminary statement on the paintings and texts', *Third Palenque Round Table, 1978, Part 2*, ed. M.G. Robertson (Austin, 1980), 45–59; M.E. Miller: *The murals of Bonampak* (Princeton, 1986).

PRI

Bondi point *see* AUSTRALIAN SMALL TOOL TRADITION

Bonfire Shelter Stratified bison-jump site in southern Texas Great Plains which has three major bone deposits. The bone beds resulted from bison that were driven over the cliff edge above the shelter. Bone Bed 1 contains extinct Late Pleistocene animals, and based on the presence of charcoal and bone breakage patterns is suspected to be the result of human activity. Bone Bed 2 contains the remains of 120 bison and several Plainview and a FOLSOM point of the PALEOINDIAN period, and is radiocarbon dated to 8000 BC. The most recent bone bed contains the remains of 800 bison and projectile points of the Archaic period and is radiocarbon dated to 650 BC.

D. Dibble: 'On the significance of additional radiocarbon dates from Bonfire Shelter, Texas', *PAnth* 15 (1970), 251–4; —— and D. Lorrain: 'Bonfire Shelter: a stratified bison kill site, Val Verde County, Texas', *Miscellaneous Papers 1*, Texas Memorial Museum (Austin, 1968).

WB

Boomplaas Cave Stone Age cave in the Cape Folded Mountain Range, a few miles west of Oudtshoorn, in the southern Cape, South Africa. The cave has a succession of archaeological layers spanning the past 80,000 years. A HOWIESON'S POORT variant of the MSA (Middle Stone Age) is overlain by 'typical' MSA dated to uncal 32,000 BP. Above this are levels containing Late Pleistocene microblade (Robberg) assemblages, macrolithic (ALBANY) assemblages from the end of the Pleistocene, microlithic assemblages dating to the Holocene (WILTON), and an early sheep-herding occupation dated to uncal 1700 BP. Associated with a late part of the Wilton occupation were over 60 small storage pits evidently used to store the oil-rich fruits of *Pappea capensis*. Combined charcoal and faunal studies trace clear environmental changes through the Last Glacial Maximum and into the Holocene.

H.J. Deacon: 'Excavations at Boomplaas Cave – a sequence through the Upper Pleistocene and Holocene in South Africa', *WA* 10/3 (1970), 241–57; ——: 'Late Pleistocene palaeoecology and archaeology in the southern Cape, South Africa', *The human revolution*,

ed. P. Mellars and C. Stringer (Cambridge, 1989), 547–64.
RI

Border Cave Middle Stone Age site in South Africa, high on the west-facing scarp of the Lebombo Mountains, overlooking the Swaziland lowveld. The site is important both for its long MSA (Middle Stone Age) succession (capped by an early Later Stone Age level currently dated to uncal 38,000 BP) and for a number of fossils of anatomically modern humans, some of which date to between uncal 70,000 and 90,000 BP. The early Middle Stone Age deposits, with unifacial and bifacial points, were followed by a HOWIESON'S POORT-like industry with various forms of backed blades and slender, punch-struck bladelets dated to between uncal 45,000 and 75,000 BP by the ELECTRON SPIN RESONANCE method. In the overlying Middle Stone Age levels, backed pieces are few and are limited to trapezoids, and points with bulbar reduction occur.

P.B. Beaumont et al.: 'Modern man in sub-Saharan Africa prior to 49,000 BP: a review and evaluation with particular reference to Border Cave', *SAJS* 74 (1978), 409–19; R. Grün and C.B. Stringer: 'Electron spin resonance dating and the evolution of modern humans', *Archaeometry* 33 (1991), 153–99.
RI

Borsippa (anc. Barziba; now Birs Nimrud) Settlement site in Iraq, often erroneously described by early travellers as the Biblical Tower of Babel, which flourished during the Neo-Babylonian period (*c*.625–539 BC). Situated close to the ruins of BABYLON itself, it was visited in the mid-19th century by Henry Rawlinson, who identified it as the city of Barziba, on the basis of foundation cylinders. It was occupied as early as the Ur III period (*c*.2150–2000 BC), according to inscriptions, but the surviving remains are dominated by the ziggurat and temple of Nabu, the god of writing, erected by Nebuchadnezzar in the 6th century BC. It was excavated by Hormuzd Rassam in 1879, Robert Koldewey in 1902 and Helga Trenkwalder in the 1980s.

R. Koldewey: 'Die Tempel von Babylon and Borsippa', *Wissenschaftliche Veröffentlichungen Deutschen Orient-Gesellschaft* 15 (1911), 50–9; T. Baqir: *Babylon and Borsippa* (Baghdad, 1959).
IS

Bouqras *see* ACERAMIC NEOLITHIC

Boyne valley tombs (Brugh na Bóinne) Concentration of imposing MEGALITHIC passage graves situated in a bend of the River Boyne in County Meath in east-central Eire. The cemetery contains at least 30 mounds, which cluster around the three huge monuments of NEWGRANGE, KNOWTH and Dowth. The larger tombs have cruciform chambers and circular mounds, but the smaller, and in some instances probably older, monuments sometimes have rectangular or trapezoidal coverings. The Boyne valley group is especially noted for its megalithic art.
RJA

Boxgrove Probably the most important Lower Palaeolithic site in Britain, and one of the most important in Western Europe. Situated on the Slindon raised beach deposit in the English county of Sussex, Boxgrove is also one of the most extensive areas of *in situ* fauna and flintwork yet discovered in Britain. Dated by faunal remains to the middle Pleistocene, towards the latter part of an interglacial or an interstadial period, the material was found in a complex sequence of sediments which hold knapping floors in extremely good conditions of preservation. The site, excavated by the Field Archaeology Unit of the Institute of Archaeology (University College London) since 1983, is not only important for its early date (probably shared with sites such as High Lodge, Suffolk), but also for the detailed evidence of knapping practices.

In 1994 a hominid shin-bone – one of the earliest known human fossils in Europe – was discovered in a context dated to *c*.500,000 BP. It appears that the individual in question was well over 1.8 m high, an observation which would accord with early HOMO ERECTUS fossils from Africa (e.g. WT15,000, *see* WEST TURKANA). In 1995, in a slightly earlier

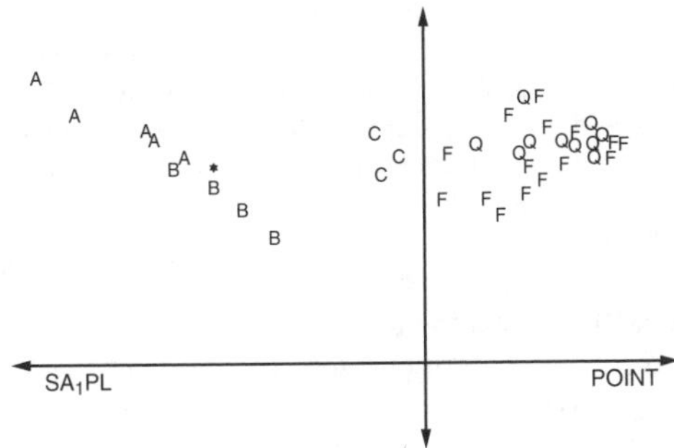

Figure 8 **Boxgrove** Plot of the results of a discriminant analysis, showing two distinct groups of percussors. *Source*: F. Wenban-Smith: *JAS* 16 (1989), fig. 3.

context, a human tooth was found in association with over one hundred flint hand-axes and the butchered bones of a rhinoceros.

Experimental archaeology and statistical analysis at Boxgrove. Wenban-Smith used a combination of EXPERIMENTAL ARCHAEOLOGY and canonical variates analysis (CVA, a form of DISCRIMINANT ANALYSIS) to suggest the most likely material used as percussors in flint-knapping at Boxgrove. He replicated bifaces made at the site, using a variety of materials as percussors, both 'hard-hammer' (flint, cortical flint and quartzite) and 'soft-hammer' (animal bone and antler). The waste flakes from this exercise were kept and 13 variables were recorded on each. The data, consisting of the average values of these variables for each of 50 batches of flakes produced by each method, were subjected to CVA to discover which variables contributed to the differences between the flakes produced by the different methods. It was found that over 80% of the differences between batches was accounted for by the first two axes, and that when plotted the data separated into two distinct groups, 'soft-hammer' to the left and 'hard-hammer' to the right along the first axis.

At this stage, the position of a sample of 'real' flakes from the site was plotted against the axes defined by the replicated flakes. They fell clearly into the 'soft-hammer' area of the plot, strongly suggesting that the bifaces at Boxgrove had been made in this way. This suggestion, if true, has considerable implications for the level of organization of the occupants of the site. Although the analysis can be criticized for using variables of different types and scales (which is almost inevitable, given the need to use more than just metrical characteristics), the technique does seemed to have coped with this and to have produced useful results.

M.B. Roberts: 'Excavation of the lower paleolithic site at Amey's Eartham Pit, Boxgrove, West Sussex: a preliminary report' *PPS* 52 (1986), 215–45; F. Wenban-Smith: 'The use of canonical variates for determination of biface manufacturing technology at Boxgrove Lower Palaeolithic site and the behavioural implications of this technology', *JAS* 16 (1989), 17–26.

CO/PG-B

BP, bp The convention BP indicates years 'before present', in contrast to years BC or AD. Thus *c*.2000 BP indicates a date at around the start of the Christian era.

The convention bp is used by the British journal *Antiquity*, and many of its readers, to indicate a date measured in 'radiocarbon years' before present i.e. a date that has *not* been calibrated so as to give true calendar dates. For consistency, 'present' is defined as AD 1950. *See* RADIOCARBON DATING for a discussion of the alternative international conventions.

Brahmagiri Cemetery and settlement site located in the Indian Deccan region (in modern Karnataka) and dating to the South Indian Iron Age of the 1st millennium BC, although the precise chronology of the site remains controversial (McIntosh 1983). Excavated features include 10 domestic structures assigned by Mortimer Wheeler (1947) to three phases/cultures – Brahmagiri Stone Axe, Megalithic and Andhra. There are also about 300 tombs dating to the Megalithic period; the burials include rectangular cists, 'cist-circles' (granite-slab cists surrounded by stone circles) and pit-circles. The inhumations were multiple and often included secondary burials, with a variety of associated artefacts, including BLACK-AND-RED WARE vessels (many with graffiti), stone beads and iron and copper tools.

R.E.M. Wheeler: 'Brahmagiri and Chandravalli 1947: Megalithic and other cultures in Chitaldurg District, Mysore State', *AI* 4 (1947–8), 181–310; A. Sundara: *The early chamber tombs of South India* (Delhi, 1975); J. McIntosh: 'Dating the South Indian megaliths', *South Asian Archaeology 1983*, eds J. Schotsmans and M. Taddei (Naples, 1985), 467–93.

Brak, Tell Mesopotamian urban site located at the southern end of the Khabur basin in northeastern Syria, about 30 km northeast of the modern town of Hasseke. The tell was occupied from *c*.6000 to 1500 BC and covers an area of about 40 ha, making it the largest surviving settlement site in the Khabur region. It was first excavated in 1937–8 by Max Mallowan (1947), who discovered a series of temples of the URUK period (*c*.4300–3100 BC) and a large public building dating to the AKKADIAN and UR III periods (*c*.2317–2000 BC). The latter was initially identified as a 'palace' of the Akkadian ruler Naram-Sin, but is now interpreted as a massive storehouse (Crawford 1991: 89–90).

From 1976 onwards, the excavations of David and Joan Oates (Oates 1977, 1982; Oates and Oates 1994) have revealed that Brak was already the site of a substantial city (surrounded by smaller satellite towns) during the Uruk period and maintained its importance well into the 2nd millennium BC. The significance of the site may have derived partially from its location on the route between Sumer and the Anatolian copper mines of Ergani Maden. Oates (1982: 71) therefore suggests that the gradual diminution of the settlement after the Agade period might relate to the Babylonians' exploitation of new sources of copper.

M.E.L. Mallowan: 'Excavations at Brak and Chagar Bazar', *Iraq* 9 (1947), 1–258; D. Oates: 'The excavations at Tell Brak, 1976', *Iraq* 39 (1977), 233–44; ——: 'Tell Brak', *Fifty years of Mesopotamian discovery*, ed. J. Curtis (London, 1982), 62–71; H. Crawford: *Sumer and the Sumerians* (Cambridge, 1991); D. Oates and J. Oates: 'Tell Brak: a stratigraphic summary, 1976–93', *Iraq* 56 (1994), 167–76.

IS

broch Round dry-stone defensive structure of the 1st millennium BC, examples of which are concentrated in Shetland, Orkney, Caithness and the Western Isles in Scotland. Traditionally the term 'broch' has been restricted to the more elaborate circular examples of a diverse family of compact fortified buildings erected in the Scottish Iron Age; the famous broch of MOUSA forms, in effect, a type site. Mackie has attempted to regularize the term by selecting the technically sophisticated high hollow-built wall, which often contains chambers and a staircase to an upper floor, as a principal defining feature (Mackie 1965). However, Hedges (Hedges and Bell 1980) and others have argued that simpler round fortified structures such as the early (*c*.600 BC) Bu Broch, Stomness, are also true brochs. A solution to this, partly semantic, problem is provided by Armit who argues that Mackie's elaborate brochs are best classified as 'tower brochs' within a wider category of round houses, thus freeing the term 'broch' to be used more loosely (Armit 1990).

Traditionally, brochs have been consigned to a relatively brief interval after the 1st century BC. However, modern excavations have made this late dating seem unlikely, and even the developed 'tower brochs' may have been emerging a century or so earlier. Recent explanations of the origins of the broch (e.g. Armit 1990) have discarded the idea of migrants from the south, preferring to stress local prototypes and the broch's functional and symbolic importance in the negotiation of power.

E. Mackie: 'The origin and development of the broch and wheelhouse building cultures of the Scottish Iron Age', *PPS* 31 (1965), 93–146; J. Hedges and B. Bell: 'That tower of Scottish prehistory – the broch', *Antiquity* 54 (1980), 87–94; I. Armit: 'Broch building in northern Scotland', *WA* 21 3 (1990), 435–45.

RJA

Broederstroom Type-site of the first phase of Early Iron Age (EIA) occupation in the central Transvaal, dated to between the 4th and 7th centuries AD. Situated west of Pretoria, the site was excavated by Mason, revealing Negro skeletons, metal slag, storage pits, pole-and-daga houses and grainbins, characteristic Kwale pottery and the bones of domesticated animals. The low proportion of cattle to small stock (1:42) is similar to other EIA sites and has led to the mistaken belief that cattle-based bridewealth and economic dominance did not develop until herds naturally increased after AD 800. Renewed excavations, SOIL PHOSPHOROUS ANALYSIS and PHYTOLITH (silica residue in grasses and sedges) studies show that there were at least five homestead centres containing small stock or cattle byres, prestige burials in a cattle byre, grain storage pits smeared with cow dung and storage pits with washed-in cattle dung. This evidence for the 'CENTRAL CATTLE PATTERN' shows that faunal remains do not directly indicate the economic and social importance of livestock. Phytolith counts indicate the climate was warmer and wetter than today.

R.J. Mason: 'Early Iron Age settlement at Broederstroom 24/73, Transvaal, South Africa', *SAJS* 77 (1981), 401–16; T.N. Huffman: 'Broederstroom and the origins of cattle-keeping in southern Africa', *African Studies* 49 (1990), 1–12; ——: 'Broederstroom and the Central Cattle Pattern', *SAJS* 89 (1993), 220–6.

TH

Bubastis *see* BASTA, TELL

Bucheum *see* ARMANT

Bug-Dniestrian Late Mesolithic and early Neolithic cultural tradition identified at sites on the rivers Dniestr and Southern Bug in Moldova and Ukraine, and principally investigated by V.N. Danilenko and V.I. Markevich. The fullest cultural sequence was established at a group of sites near the town of Soroca (Soroki), on the narrow flood-plain of the river Dniestr (Moldovia). The aceramic levels (3 and 2) of Soroki 1 have been radiocarbon dated, and this suggests respective calendar dates of *c*.6500 and *c*.6400 BC. The remains of two oval-shaped semi-subterranean dwellings were found. The stone inventory, of Mesolithic character, included end-scrapers trapezes, triangles and retouched blades. The faunal remains belong largely (80–90%) to wild animals (especially roe deer and red deer), plus a few bones of domesticates including pig and cattle. The deposits contained numerous fish bones (e.g. roach, pike, sturgeon and catfish) and several hundred shells of molluscs.

The pottery-bearing levels at Soroki 2 and Soroki 5 have been radiocarbon dated, suggesting calendar dates of 5800–5500 BC. The ratio of domesticates among the faunal remains increased, reaching in several cases 50% (pig, cattle); the wild animals were still largely roe deer and red deer. The number of wild animals represented in the faunal analysis was much greater (over 90%) at the sites on the Southern Bug. Impressions of emmer, einkorn and spelt wheat were identified on potsherds. Oval semi-subterranean dwellings were constructed at several sites. The lithic industry retained a Mesolithic character. The coarse pottery, made with an admixture of sand, crushed shells or organic matter, is dominated by spherical and biconical bowls decorated by rows of wavy lines, shell impressions and finger-nail impressions. These ceramics reveal similarities with the 'barbotine' type pottery of the Balkan early Neolithic. At the sites of Soroki 5 and Baz'kov Island (the Southern Bug), fragments of imported LINEARBANDKERAMIK pottery have been found.

Foraging to farming transition. Danilenko (1969) and V.I. Markevich (1974) argue that the Bug-Dniestrian reflects a gradual transition from foraging to agriculture, citing the impressions of cereals on the potsherds; the occurrence of blades with sickle-gloss; hoe-like implements made of red-deer antler, and querns; and the gradual increase of the rate of domesticates in the faunal remains from the earlier to the later phase. However, P.M. Dolukhanov (1979) argues that the situation of the Soroki and other Bugo-Dniestrian sites makes agriculture very unlikely. The sites were located on a narrow stony flood-plain, covered with meadow soils poor in humus; the nearest arable land lies 5 km away, cut off from the settlement by almost impassable slopes. Thin archaeological deposits, and the lack of permanent dwelling structures, suggests that the sites were occupied seasonally by small groups of foragers; the 'farming' evidence may be explained by intensive cultural and economic contacts with nearby communities of farmers. It seems likely that the grain, pigs and cattle (which, in number, never exceeded eight individuals) were procured in exchange for the products of hunting and food-gathering. The blades with sickle gloss, the querns, and the hoe-like implements could all have been used for harvesting and processing wild plants. The occurrence of cultural contacts with farmers is further substantiated by the resemblance between the pottery, as well as by the direct import of Linearbandkeramik ware in the later stages. The Bugo-Dniestrian sites may thus be viewed as belonging to the 'availability phase' of the proto-Neolithic, as described by Zvelebil and Dolukhanov (1991).

V.N. Danilenko: *Neolit Ukrainy* [The Neolithic of the Ukraine] (Kiev, 1969); V.I. Markevich: *Bugo-Dnestrovskaya kul'tura na territorii Moldavii* [The Bug-Dniestrian culture on the territory of Moldavia] (Kishinev, 1974); P.M. Dolukhanov: *Ecology and economy in neolithic Eastern Europe* (London, 1979); M. Zvelebil and P. Dolukhanov: 'The transition to farming in Eastern and Northern Europe', *JWP*/III (1991), 233–78.

PD

Buhen Egyptian urban site in Lower Nubia, which was first examined in 1819 but mainly excavated at the time of the UNESCO Nubian Campaign, between 1957 and 1964 (Emery et al. 1979). The settlement was founded in the Old Kingdom (*c*.2649–2150 BC) or perhaps even in the Early Dynastic period (*c*.3000–2649 BC), probably as a centre for Egyptian mining and quarrying expeditions in Nubia. An impressive array of mud-brick fortifications were constructed around the settlement in the 12th dynasty (*c*.1991–1783 BC), enabling it to serve as a military garrison dominating the area to the north of the second Nile cataract. The settlement had a basic grid-iron plan, comprising a number of rectangular blocks separated by six major streets. The subsequent New Kingdom town was much more of a 'colony' than a fortress, since the southern frontier of Egypt had by then been pushed further south than the fourth Nile cataract, leaving Buhen in comparatively safe territory.

R.A. Caminos: *The New Kingdom temples of Buhen*, 2 vols (London, 1974); H.S. Smith: *The fortress of Buhen: The inscriptions* (London, 1976); W.B. Emery et al.: *The fortress of Buhen: The archaeological report* (London, 1979).

IS

Bükk culture Regional successor culture to the LINEARBANDKERAMIK, centered on the Bükk mountains of northeast Hungary and east Slovakia, with some sites in south Poland. Bükk pottery is made of a fine alluvial clay, generally globular in shape, thin walled and well fired. Typically, it is decorated with bands of incised ornament forming spirals and wavy, sometimes geometric, patterns. The decoration may be encrusted with white or yellow paste; some vessels have painted motifs. Settlements associated with Bükk pottery include large and small open-air sites, as well as a large proportion of caves in upland areas – a mixture of settlement type that may indicate transhumance.

J. Lichardus: *Studien zur Bükker Kultur*, Saabrücker Beiträge zur Altertumskunde 12 (Bonn, 1974).

RJA

Bur Gavo *see* SWAHILI HARBOUR TOWNS

Burial Mound Period Term used in North American archaeology to refer to a chronological phase stretching from *c.*1000 BC to AD 700, which roughly corresponds to the WOODLAND period. The expression – rarely used now – first appeared in a synthesis of Eastern North American prehistory published by Ford and Willey in 1941. Later, Willey (1966) used the term as a period designator in *An introduction to North American archaeology*, subdividing it into two phases. Burial Mound I (1000 to 300 BC) included Tchefuncte, Deptford, Candy Creek and ADENA cultures, now classified as Early Woodland. Burial Mound II (300 BC–AD 700) included Marksville, HOPEWELL, and Weeden Island, now classified as Middle and/or Late Woodland. Cultural traits associated with the Burial Mound Period include pottery, burial mounds and agriculture (Stoltman 1978).

J. Stoltman: 'Temporal models in prehistory: an example from eastern North America', *CA* 19 (1978), 703–46; G. Willey: *An introduction to American archaeology* I: *North and Middle America* (Englewood Cliffs, 1966).

RJE

burin Multi-purpose blade tool, usually made of flint, which presents a gouging or chisel-like working edge formed by removing a distinctive flake or 'burin spall'. Burins are one of the tool types that appear in the richer assemblages of the Upper Palaeolithic, helping to differentiate them from the Middle Palaeolithic.

burin spall *see* BURIN

burnishing Process of smoothing and polishing hardened, but not yet fired, clay vessels with a rounded tool such as a pebble or smooth bone. By compacting the clay, the permeability of the pot surface is reduced and a high shine (sometimes slightly facetted from the burnisher's strokes) is produced. The term is distinct from 'polish', which should strictly be reserved for the buffing-up of pottery surfaces *after* firing.

RJA

Burushkhattum *see* AÇEMHÖYÜK

Burzahom Settlement and cemetery site in the Srinigar Valley of Kashmir, dating to the Kashmiri Neolithic of the 3rd millennium BC. Located by De Terra and Patterson in 1935, Burzahom was excavated by the Indian government from 1960 to 1971. Four chronological phases have been defined, ranging from the Neolithic (periods I–II) to the early historic period (IV: 324 BC–AD 347). The remains dating to Period I include pit-dwellings, handmade ceramics, ground stone axes and a wide array of bone and antler tools. Period II is characterized by mud-brick and wooden structures, one containing a stone slab engraved with a hunting scene, and many incorporating primary and secondary burials, some with dogs, wolves and ibex in association with human inhumations. In Period III a rough semi-circle of large standing stones was erected, and wheel-made pottery began to be used. Unfortunately, few indications of subsistence patterns have survived.

R.N. Kaw: 'The Neolithic culture of Kashmir', *Essays in Indian protohistory*, ed. D.P. Agrawal and D.K. Chakrabarti (New Delhi, 1979), 219–28; U. Sant: *Neolithic settlement pattern of northeastern and northern India* (Delhi, 1991), 154–69.

CS

Bush Barrow (Wilsford G5) Bronze Age round barrow in Wiltshire, England, close to Stonehenge, which covered one of the richest burials of the WESSEX CULTURE. Dug into in 1808, the grave-goods included some of the finest and richest

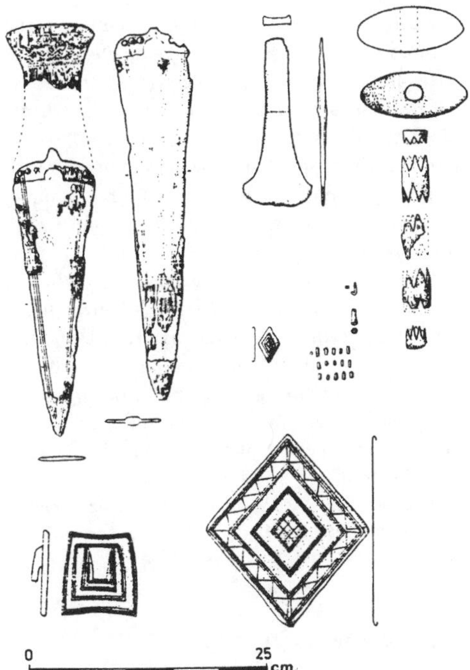

Figure 9 **Bush Barrow** Grave goods from rich 'Wessex' tradition graves dating to the mid-2nd millennium BC at Bush Barrow, Wiltshire. *Source*: T. Darvill: *Prehistoric Britain* (London, 1987), fig. 55a.

examples of Bronze Age metalwork: sheet-gold ornamental lozenges finely incised with bands of lines; a gold belt-hook similarly incised; daggers (Armorico-British type) including one with a hilt decorated by hammering into it numerous tiny gold pins. The gravegoods also included a flanged axe, a polished stone macehead and 'serrated' bone mounts for a staff – often assumed to be a symbol of status of some kind. The staff mounts resemble grave-goods recovered from MYCENAE – though there are also parallels in gold objects found in Brittany – and have provoked continuing debate as to whether the Wessex elite responsible for Bush Barrow were in some sort of contact with the Mycenaean culture of the Mediterranean. However, while the Mycenaean material dates to around 1600 BC, the Bush barrow burial probably dates from a few centuries earlier.

S. Piggott: 'The early Bronze Age in Wessex', *PPS* 4 (1938), 52–106; J.J. Taylor: *Bronze Age goldwork of the British Isles* (Cambridge, 1980), 45; D.V. Clarke, et al.: *Symbols of power at the time of Stonehenge* (Edinburgh, 1985); I.A. Kinnes et al.: 'Bush Barrow gold', *Antiquity* 62 (1988), 24–39.

RJA

Butmir Late Neolithic typesite, situated near Sarajevo, Bosnia, of the 'Butmir culture'; the culture itself extends from the Middle Neolithic to Chalcolithic (5th and 4th millennium BC). Butmir culture vessels tend to be of a globular shape, elaborately decorated with the incised and painted (red and white) spiral and meander motifs; unlike the pottery of most contemporary cultures in south-east Europe paint was applied to ceramics after firing, rather than before. Butmir itself has provided a great number of figurines, the bodies of which tend to be quite crudely fashioned, while some of the heads are relatively naturalistic and full of expression. Phase II of the more recently excavated site of Obre, near Sarajevo, has provided significantly greater information about the development and settlements of the Butmir culture than the type-site itself.

M. Hoernes et al.: *Die Neolithische Station von Butmir*, 2 vols (Vienna, 1895, 1898); M. Gimbutas: *The Goddesses and Gods of Old Europe* (London, 1982).

RJA

Buto *see* FARA'IN, TELL EL-

Butser Ancient Farm Site of one of the first major projects in EXPERIMENTAL ARCHAEOLOGY, which was established in 1972 by Peter Reynolds in order to provide an experimental means of studying the agriculture and domestic economy of the late Iron Age and early Roman period in Britain (*c*.400 BC–AD 300). Its overall objective was to create practical working research programmes based directly upon the archaeological evidence as interpreted from excavations. The design included the construction of a working farm, dating to *c*.300 BC and provided with appropriate livestock and plantstock, as well as a working Roman villa similarly fitted with all accoutrements.

During the period between 1972 and 1995 the Ancient Farm has actually occupied three locations. The first site, from which the farm draws its name, was a northerly spur of Butser Hill in the county of Hampshire; from 1976, a second site, with deeper soil cover, was developed in the valley bottom on Hillhampton Down on the southern slopes of Butser Hill. It was operated as a research site in conjunction with Little Butser, but it served primarily as an open-air museum and an educational resource for schoolchildren. On both of these sites the infrastructure comprised research fields, animal paddocks and an enclosure within which were built 'constructs' (*see discussion in* EXPERIMENTAL ARCHAEOLOGY) based upon specific archaeological data. The livestock maintained at the Ancient Farm comprised five breeds of sheep (Moufflon, Soay, Manx Loughtan, Hebridean and Shetland), Old English goats, Dexter cattle and Old English game fowl. Occasionally Tamworth pigs and European wild boars were also kept. The differing natures of the two sites allowed direct comparisons to be made between the two bioclimatic zones. However, at the beginning of 1991, both of these sites were vacated, and a new site developed at Bascomb Copse near Chalton, Hampshire, where the underlying geology (upper chalk with a loamy soil averaging 350 mm deep) offered an agricultural setting more typical of the chalk downlands of southern England.

P.J. Reynolds: *Iron Age farm: the Butser experiment* (London, 1979); ——: *Ancient farming* (Princes Risborough, 1987).

PRE

Byblos Syro-Palestinian coastal site (now in Lebanon), which was occupied from the Neolithic period onwards. The prosperous Bronze Age port had strong political and economic connections with pharaonic Egypt, to the extent that Egyptian hieroglyphs were sometimes employed. However, the site appears to have gone into a relative decline from the late 2nd millennium BC onwards (although the Iron Age PHOENICIAN city may lie beneath the modern town of Jubeil). The surviving remains of a *nymphaeum*, temple and theatre suggest that Byblos was still of some importance during the time of the Roman empire.

P. Montet: *Byblos et l'Egypte*, 2 vols (Paris, 1928); M. Dunand: *Fouilles de Byblos* (Paris, 1939–58); J.-F. Salles: *La nécropole "k" de Byblos* (Paris, 1980).

IS

Bylany One of the principal early (1953–4) excavations of a Linearbandkeramik or LBK culture site, this early farming settlement near Prague in central Bohemia in the Czech Republic consisted of longhouses (up to 45 m in length) built of posts, with possible grain stores and pits. The economy was based upon emmer wheat and the raising of cattle. *See* LINEARBANDKERAMIK *for further discussion and bibliography*.

RJA

C

^{14}C *see* RADIOCARBON DATING

Caban *see* CHAM

cacao The pod-like fruits of the cacao tree (*Theobroma cacao*) contain large oval seeds, which the pre-hispanic inhabitants of Mesoamerica ground into a powder and mixed with water and chiles – and/or honey and maize gruel – to create a beverage. Cacao seeds or beans were also used as a medium of exchange by the Aztecs and perhaps by earlier Mesoamerican societies. The pods and seeds often appear as decorative motifs on pottery and other art; residue analysis has confirmed the presence of cacao in a ceramic vessel found in an Early Classic (*c.*AD 200–600) burial at the LOWLAND MAYA site of Río Azul. Cacao trees were cultivated in limited areas of rich, fertile lowland soils.

J.E.S. Thompson: 'Notes on the use of cacao in Middle America', *Notes on Middle American Archaeology and Ethnology* 128 (1956), 95–116; D. Stuart: 'The Rio-Azul cacao pot: epigraphic observations on the function of a Maya ceramic vessel', *Antiquity* 62 (1988), 153–7; A. Gómez-Pompa et al.: 'The sacred cacao groves of the Maya', *LAA* 1 (1990), 247–57.

PRI

Cacaxtla Fortified site in southwest Tlaxcala, Mexico, dating to the 8th–10th centuries AD, known for its mural paintings. The style and content of the paintings are similar to those of the lowland Maya site of BONAMPAK; they depict a battle scene between elaborately attired (and vanquished) lowland Maya(?) and victorious highland (Teotihuacano?) peoples, as well as winged images of patron deities.

M. Foncerrada de Molina: 'Mural painting in Cacaxtla and Teotihuacán cosmopolitanism', *Third Palenque Round Table, 1978, Part 2*, ed. M.G. Robertson (Austin, 1980), 183–98.

PRI

Cahokia Major MISSISSIPPIAN 'mound center' located in the Mississippi River floodplain in Illinois, eastern North America. The site covered 13 sq. km and consisted of residential areas, plazas and over 100 mounds, widely scattered over bottomland ridges, with the most heavily occupied areas located on high ground alongside an abandoned river channel. The central focus of the site is a large, rectangular plaza surrounded by mounds, including Monks Mound, the largest prehistoric mound in the United States. Cahokia was occupied for many hundreds of years, rising to regional prominence in about AD 1000. The site and surrounding region were virtually abandoned by 1400.

M.L. Fowler: *The Cahokia atlas* (Springfield 1989); G.R. Milner: 'The late prehistoric Cahokia cultural system of the Mississippi River valley: foundations, fluorescence, and fragmentation', *JWP* 4 (1990), 1–43.

GM

Cahuachi The largest known site of the Nazca culture, situated in the Nazca Valley, Peru, and dating to the Early Intermediate Period (*c.*400 BC–AD 500). It consists of a large number of large platforms, built on cores of existing hills, with associated walled spaces. Cahuachi was a pilgrimage centre, uninhabited for much of the time but connected by geoglyphs across the high desert with the urban 'Site 165'. Comparisons to modern pilgrimage patterns and Andean concepts of space suggest that Cahuachi and Site 165 may have been lower and upper (*hatun* and *hurin*). Cahuachi is associated with strange-shaped hills, later modified into platforms and walled areas for temporary occupation, perennial water sources, and with an echoing phenomenon, being the sacred half of the dual organization typical of Andean sociopolitical constructs.

H. Silverman: *Cahuachi in the ancient Nasca world* (Ames, 1993).

KB

Caihouluan *see* TS'AI HOU LUAN

caitya Structure built to house a sacred Buddhist relic, such as a notable image of the Buddha.

calcite banding Layers in stalagmitic calcite giving luminescence due to humic and fulvic acids derived from soil. These layers appear to be annual and thus could provide a high resolution climatic indicator (e.g. calcite growth is rainfall-dependent and stable isotope analysis provides temperature information).

A. Baker et al.: 'Annual growth banding in a cave stalagmite', *Nature* 364 (1993), 518–20.

SB

calcium-41 dating *see* RADIOCALCIUM DATING

calendars, Mesoamerican Mesoamerican peoples recorded time and history by means of several calendars that counted days and also multiples of days roughly analogous to months, years and larger units of time. Two primary calendars were in use throughout Mesoamerica and both recorded cycles of time by day or month names and numbers. One was a very ancient calendar, known to the AZTECS as Tonalpohualli, which was composed of 20 day names or signs prefixed by a number from 1 to 13 (e.g. 5 Cimi or 9 Xochitl). The same names and numbers coincided every 260 days. The other was a 365-day calendar, approximating our solar year, which consisted of 18 named 'months' of 20 days each, counted from 0 to 19 (as 0 Pop, 1 Pop, 2 Pop, etc.); the last five days of the year (known as *Uayeb* among the Maya and *Nemontemi* among the Aztecs) were considered unlucky. Most Mesoamerican peoples used both calendars simultaneously to record time. The Maya, for example, recorded time on their STELAE by means of the simultaneous cycling of the two calendars and also by use of the 'long count' (itself an absolute method of recording time from a given starting date, rather than a calendar).

The cycling of the two calendars defined another important interval of time for Mesoamerican peoples. For any particular numbered day in the 260-day calendar to coincide with any particular day and month in the 365-day calendar, the calendars had to cycle through 18,980 days, or 52 years. The beginning and ending of this 52-year cycle, known by archaeologists as the 'Calendar Round', was celebrated widely throughout Mesoamerica, as, for example, in the Aztec new fire ceremony.

M.S. Edmonson: The *book of the year: Middle American calendrical systems* (Salt Lake City, 1989); M.E. Miller and K. Taube: *The gods and symbols of ancient Mexico and the Maya: an illustrated dictionary of Mesoamerican religion* (London, 1993), 48–54.

PRI

Calico Hills Controversial lithic site located in an alluvial fan deposit in southeastern California. Assemblages consist of surface finds and flaked objects excavated from a depth of over 5 m. Bifaces found on the surface are part of the Manix Lake complex and are clearly artefactual. The subsurface finds consist of thousands of pieces of flaked chert, some of which resemble struck flakes and simple stone tools. These few objects are a highly selected sample sorted by archaeologists from thousands of pieces of fractured chert and are considered by many archaeologists to be GEOFACTS. This has led to investigations of how to differentiate quarry debris from early primitive industries (Glennan 1976: 43–61) and distinguish pseudo-artefacts produced by natural forces from real artefacts (Haynes, 1973). Dates range from 500,000 BP, based on the geology (Haynes 1973), to about 80,000–125,000 BP for the site surface and 200,000 BP at its base, determined by uranium-thorium assays of $CaCO^3$ (*see* URANIUM-SERIES DATING).

C.V. Haynes: 'The Calico site: artefacts or geofacts?', *Science* 181 (1973), 305–10; W.S. Glennan: 'The Manix Lake lithic industry: early lithic tradition or workshop refuse?' *Journal of New World Archaeology* 1 (1976), 43–62; W.C. Schuiling, ed.: *Pleistocene man at Calico* (Redlands, 1979).

RC

Calima Region of southwestern Colombia with a long cultural tradition (*c*.1000 BC –Conquest; see AMERICA 6) beginning with the Ilama Phase (Early Calima, 1st millennium BC), whose finely incised and painted ceramics and hammered gold work show an elaborate development of shamanistic beliefs, the ritual use of coca, and an appreciation of the animal life around them. Ilama is ancestral to Yotoco (Calima, AD 100–7/1100)), known for its large hammered gold ornaments. These can now be related to distinctive modelled and organic resist-painted pottery as well as habitation sites consisting of series of artificial terraces which had rectangular houses on them. The Calima culture was also characterized by large-scale drained field and road systems, and the burial of the dead in shaft-and-chamber tombs. A terminal pre-Conquest phase, Sonso, has also been identified.

M. Cardale de Schrimpff et al.: *Calima: trois cultures pré-colombiennes dans le sud-oueste de la Colombie* (Lausanne, 1991).

KB

Canaanites Term used to describe the people occupying Palestine and southwestern Syria from at least the beginning of the Middle Bronze Age (*c*.2000 BC) onwards. The geographical term Canaan is much easier to define than the cultural or ethnic traits of its Bronze Age inhabitants. Numerous Egyptian and Mesopotamian texts refer to the Canaanites from the 15th century BC onwards and the beginning of the Iron Age (*c*.750 BC) is usually considered to represent the end of the Canaanite culture, but there are major problems in attempting either to assess the origins of the Canaanites or to correlate the written references with archaeological sites. Kenyon (1966) argued that the Canaanites emerged during the period of AMORITE incursions into Syria-Palestine at the end of the 3rd millennium BC, and were in fact 'urbanized Amorites', whereas Millard (1973: 38) suggests that the situation was much more complex: 'Palestine received a motley array of peoples and influences. Should the amalgam be designated Canaanite? . . . If the name was used by the natives of the area, then either they survived the various invasions, retaining some sense of identity . . . or the name was assumed by their conquerors, or simply applied to any denizens or products of the region.'

If the term is taken to refer simply to the inhabitants of Palestine in the 2nd and early 1st millennia BC then the major Canaanite cities would include Hazor, BETH SHAN and MEGIDDO. Canaanite personal names in the AMARNA letters and the UGARIT archives suggest that the population was a mixture of Semites, Hurrians and Indo-Europeans. In *c*.1600 BC the West-Semitic speaking Canaanites began to write texts using an alphabet of 32 letters, which was perhaps derived partly from the Egyptian HIERATIC script. The Canaanite alphabet evolved into the PHOENICIAN script and was eventually to form the basis for the Greek, Hebrew and Arabian alphabets.

T. Bauer: *Die Ostkanaanäer* (Leipzig, 1926); J. Gray: *The Canaanites* (London, 1964); K. Kenyon: *Amorites and Canaanites* (Oxford, 1996); A.R. Millard: 'The Canaanites', *Peoples of Old Testament times*, ed. D.J. Wiseman (Oxford, 1973), 29–52.

IS

Can Hasan *see* ACERAMIC NEOLITHIC

canonical variates analysis *see* DISCRIMINANT ANALYSIS

canopic jar Egyptian stone or ceramic funerary vessel containing the entrails extracted from a mummified body; four canopic jars were commonly placed in the tomb alongside the sarcophagus. The shapes of the lids of the four jars developed from a basic convex form in the Old Kingdom (*c*.2649–2150 BC) to a human head in the Middle Kingdom (*c*.2040–1640 BC). From the 19th dynasty (*c*.1307–1196 BC) onwards the lids took the form of the heads of the mythical Sons of Horus. The last surviving set of royal canopic equipment was made for the Late Period ruler Apries (589–570 BC). The term 'canopic' (an Egyptological term derived from the misconception that human-headed jars were worshipped at the town of Canopus in the Egyptian Delta) was also applied to a type of Etruscan cinerary urn in the form of a sculpture of the deceased, the head serving as the lid and the arms as the handles. Many Etruscan canopics were found at the Italian site of Clusium and date to between the 6th and 3rd centuries BC.

R. Gempeler: *Die Etruskischen Kanopen* (Einsiedeln, 1974); C. Dolzani: *Vasi Canopi* (Milan, 1982); A. Dodson: *The canopic equipment of the kings of Egypt* (London, 1994).

IS

Cape Gelidonya *see* GELIDONYA

Cape Krusenstern One of the richest site localities in the North American Arctic, located on Kotzebue Sound, Alaska. Here, clearly separated by an impressive horizontal stratigraphy produced by the accumulation over thousands of years of 114 separate beach ridges (see map 19), there are remains deriving from the Denbigh Flint complex, Old Whaling, Choris, NORTON TRADITION, IPIUTAK, Birnirk, THULE and more recent occupations.

J.L. Giddings: *Ancient men of the Arctic* (New York, 1967); —— and D.D. Anderson: *Beach ridge archaeology of Cape Krusenstern* (Washington, 1986).

RP

Capéletti Cave at an altitude of 1580 m above sea level on the northern slopes of the Aurès mountains south of Constantine in northeastern Algeria. It was excavated by Colette Roubet in 1968, and four distinct occupation horizons attributed to the 'Neolithic of Capsian Tradition' have produced 7 radiocarbon dates ranging from 6530 to 4340 BP. The mammalian fauna is dominated by domestic sheep and/or goat which account for 70–90% of the identified bones and which must have been introduced into the area. Bovids are important in the uppermost horizon only, where their bones constitute 25% of the total. According to Achilles Gautier, it is not completely clear whether they were domesticated or not. In Roubert's interpretation, the inhabitants (who also relied on seasonal collection of plant resources and land snails) practised a 'pastoral, pre-agricultural' transhumant

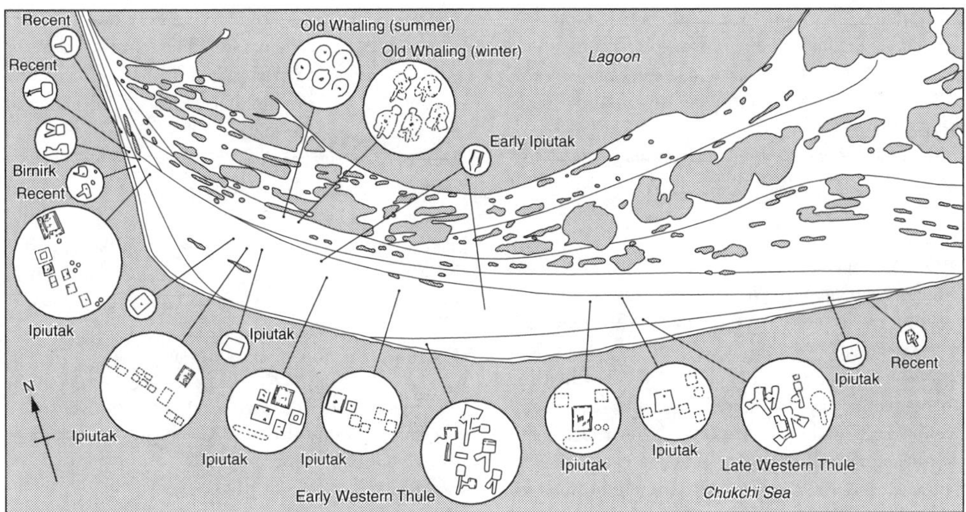

Map 19 **Cape Krusenstern** Plan of Cape Krusenstern, showing excavated settlements from various periods (after J.L. Giddings and D.D. Anderson: *Beach ridge archaeology of Cape Krusenstern* (Washington, D.C., 1986), fig. 6).

economy, retreating to the lower slopes during the winter. It is suggested that the system of animal husbandry in force until recently among the Berbers of the area differed little from that of their Neolithic predecessors

C. Roubet: 'Une économie pastorale, pré-agricole en Algérie orientale: le néolithique de tradition Capsienne', *L'Anthropologie* 82 (1978), 583–6; —— and P.L. Carter: 'La domestication au Maghreb: état de la question', *Origin and early development of food-producing cultures in north-eastern Africa*, ed. L. Krzyzaniak and M. Kobusiewicz (Poznan, 1984), 437–51; A. Gautier: 'Prehistoric men and cattle in North Africa: a dearth of data and a surfeit of models', *Prehistory of arid North Africa*, ed. A.E. Close (Dallas, 1987), 163–87.

PA-J

Cap Manuel Stone workshop site at the southern extremity of the Cape Verde peninsula, on a promontory within the city of Dakar, Senegal; discovered in 1942 and excavated by C. Descamps in 1967–8. The site is on the eastern sheltered side of the promontory; the numerous finds are concentrated over an area up to 100 m from the shore at the foot of a 30 m cliff of ankaratrite, the volcanic rock of which the promontory consists. The stratigraphy and chronology of the site were established principally by means of a 6 m^2 trench excavated to a depth of 2.80 m starting at a point 3.50 m above sea level. Beneath recent colluvial and storm beach deposits, layer III contained traces of a shell midden with some rolled artefacts; *in situ* archaeological material was found in layer II amid large ankaratrite boulders, which also constituted the basal beach deposit. The great majority of the industry is made of ankaratrite, and because of the presence of a number of bifacially worked tools it was in the past variously classified by different authors as either 'Toumbian' or 'Sangoan'. Descamps eliminated many misunderstandings by his careful study of these artefacts, establishing their characteristic breakage patterns by refitting, and lumping them all together as one broad category ('pièces allongées'). These and what he termed pushplanes ('rabots') made up the great majority of the retouched tools; but the context and significance of this industry were made much clearer by the other elements found *in situ* in layer II, including one polished stone axe and 130 fragments of potsherds, as well as a number of fishbones (some of them in anatomical connection). He therefore unambiguously defined the industry as a specialized facies of the Neolithic. A *terminus ante quem* was provided by two radiocarbon dates on shells from layer III of 2880 ± 80 and 2839 ± 127 BP, and by relying on the radiocarbon dates from AMEKNI to provide a maximum starting point, Descamps considered that the site most probably dated to a period between 4000 and 8000 BP. As a hypothesis he suggested that the tools were used for woodworking and that – since the use of boats is indicated not only by the fishbones but also by the presence of similar artefacts on the Ile aux Serpents, 4 km out to sea – the site served as a kind of 'naval dockyard'. This explanation, however, could not apply to Diack, a site otherwise very similar to Cap Manuel, but lying well inland 30 km east of Thiès.

C. Descamps: *Contribution à la préhistoire de l'ouest Sénégalais* (Dakar, 1979).

PA-J

Capsian Palaeolithic industry, named by Jacques de Morgan in 1909 after the town of Gafsa in southern Tunisia, and with a chronological range of *c*.10,000–6,500 BP. Generally regarded as 'EPIPALAEOLITHIC', it is conventionally divided into two units: Typical and Upper Capsian; both have backed bladelets, but the Typical Capsian has a heavier component including large numbers of burins, and the Upper Capsian a lighter component including geometric microliths of various kinds.

Geographically, the Capsian is concentrated on the High Constantine Plains of northeastern Algeria and in adjacent parts of Tunisia. The technology and typology of this industry have been intensively studied since its first identification, and successive models have been proposed to chart its development: at first a unilinear scheme proposed by Raymond Vaufrey in 1935, then a binary scheme in which the Capsian was seen to develop in parallel with the IBEROMAURUSIAN proposed by Lionel Balout in 1955, and then a scheme inspired by the concept of 'branching evolution' espoused by Gabriel Camps in 1974. In all these schemes, the Capsian led on to a 'Neolithic of Capsian Tradition' as at CAPÉLETTI. All were rejected on epistemological grounds by David Lubell and his colleagues, who recognize instead two major 'regional traditions' in the eastern and western parts of the Maghreb, both developing from the Iberomaurusian and therefore not intrusive to the area. The Capsian is particularly well known for its open-air sites, in which land snails form a prominent part of the occupational debris, often referred to as 'escargotières'. One such site was partially excavated by Lubell and his colleagues at Ain Misteheyia southwest of Tébessa in eastern Algeria, as a result of which he estimated that snails in fact accounted for probably no more than one sixth of the animal protein consumed. The majority was provided by large vertebrates such as horse, gazelle, aurochs, and hartebeest. A general pattern of rotating settlement was discerned, with intermittent residency at any one site, and the likely Capsian diet is described as 'a stew containing meat, snails, and some plants, perhaps accompanied by a gruel made from boiled grasses, garnished with nuts, and perhaps seasoned with wild herbs and shallots' (Lubell et al. 1976: 919). According to Chamla, 24 individuals have so far been found in eastern Algerian Capsian contexts, of which 10 are of MECHTA-AFALOU and 14 of 'Proto-Mediterranean' type, the latter being regarded as immigrant. This scenario is disputed by Lubell and his colleagues, who emphasize population continuity in this area and therefore development *in situ* from the Iberomaurusian onwards. *See also* KENYA CAPSIAN.

G. Camps: *Les civilizations préhistoriques de l'Afrique du Nord et du Sahara* (Paris, 1974); D. Lubell et al.: 'The Capsian escargotières', *Science* 191 (1976), 910–20; M.C. Chamla: 'Le peuplement de l'Afrique du Nord de l'épipaléolithique à l'époque actuelle', *L'Anthropologie* 82 (1978), 385–430; D. Lubell et al.: 'Continuity in the Epipaleolithic of Northern Africa with emphasis on the Maghreb'. *AWA* 3 (1984), 143–91.

PA-J

carbon isotope analysis Carbon exists in three isotopes of which two, ^{12}C and ^{13}C, are stable; the latter has a natural abundance of about 1%. Variations in the abundances of these, and other, light element stable isotopes can arise through physical and chemical factors which fractionate between lighter and heavier isotopes leading to changes in the isotopic ratio. The ratio ($^{13}C/^{12}C$) is usually measured by gas source mass spectrometry on samples converted to carbon dioxide. Results are expressed in the form $\delta^{13}C$, which is the difference in the ratio in 'parts per mil' (parts per thousand) from the carbonate reference material Pee Dee belemnite (PDB, ratio 0.0112372). The $\delta^{13}C$ value may be positive, enriched in ^{13}C relative to the reference, or negative, depleted in ^{13}C.

The $\delta^{13}C$ value of archaeological material is of interest for several reasons. It is, for example, essential to measure the $^{13}C/^{12}C$ ratio of radiocarbon samples in order to correct for the likely natural fractionation of ^{14}C relative to ^{12}C (*see* RADIOCARBON DATING). The $\delta^{13}C$ value is also used, in conjunction with that of $\delta^{18}O$ (OXYGEN ISOTOPE ANALYSIS), as a means of characterizing and provenancing carbonates, particularly the marble used for Classical sculpture and building construction. Carbon isotopes are also exploited in studies of ancient diet because the fractionation effects of the two plant photosynthesis pathways, C3 and C4, lead to differences in $\delta^{13}C$ value. Herbivores take on a $\delta^{13}C$ value related to the plant groups consumed and thus their dietary source may be deduced. This approach has been used, for example, to show the spread in consumption of maize (a C4 plant) through parts of North America in areas where consumption of C3 plants had previously predominated.

N. Herz and M. Waelkens: *Classical marble: geochemistry, technology, trade* (Dordrecht, 1988); N.J. van der Merwe: 'Light stable isotopes and the reconstruction of prehistoric diets', *New developments in archaeological science*, ed. A.M. Pollard (Oxford, 1992), 247–64.

MC

Carchemish (Djerablus) City in northern Syria, 125 km northeast of Aleppo, located at a crucial crossing-point on the Euphrates. Occupied from the Neolithic period until the Roman empire, it prospered particularly during the Bronze Age, both as a major HITTITE town during the Old Kingdom and Empire (*c*.1680–1205) and as an important post-Hittite centre in the 1st millennium BC, with impressive fortifications similar to those at the contemporary (though slightly larger) site of ZINJIRLI. The post-Hittite phase of the site is characterized by a considerable number of sculpted basalt reliefs carved with Hittite hieroglyphs, as well as rare examples of neo-Hittite statuary, which were excavated by Leonard Woolley.

D.G. Hogarth et al.: *Carchemish*, 3 vols (London, 1914–52); H.G. Güterbock: 'Carchemish', *JNES* 13 (1954), 102–14; M.E.L. Mallowan: 'Carchemish: reflections on the chronology of the sculpture', *AS* 22 (1972), 63–85.

IS

cardial ware Form of impressed ware that comprises the earliest type of pottery (7th–5th millennium BC) in the coastal regions of the central and west Mediterranean. Cardial ware vessels are decorated by pressing the serrated edge of the *Cardium* shell into the clay. Cardial ware is found in Liguria (e.g. ARENE CANDIDE), southern France, Spain, Sardinia and Corsica. A few examples of cardial ware are now known from west-central France (Charente-Maritime), outside the Mediterranean region. Early cardial ware may have functioned as a prestige object in exchange – a suggestion supported by the fact that in many contexts the earliest cardial ware is noticeably finer than the later cardial ware (the so-called 'epicardial ware').

RJA

carination Term used to describe the angle formed when the surface of a pottery vessel changes direction, usually forming a shoulder or creating a distinct rim. The use, placing and angle of carination help to give many pots their distinctive profile, and it is thus an important visual identifier in pottery classification.

RJA

Carmel *see* MOUNT CARMEL

Carnac region Neolithic funerary and megalithic ceremonial complex, including the largest set of ALIGNMENTS in the world, situated near the town of Carnac in Morbihan, Brittany. Near the hamlet of Le Menec, 11 rows of stones lead away from a large oval ring of stones. Close by are the Kermario alignments (seven main rows of over 1000 stones), which are associated with a large earth mound originally topped with a standing stone. The nearby Kerlescan alignments (13 rows of *c*.540 stones) are associated with an arrangement of megaliths in a rounded square. The smaller alignments at Petit Menec, a walk away, contain about 100 stones.

Despite clumsy restoration in the 19th century, the Carnac alignments share a number of features: they seem not to have been intended as straight lines (as a whole the rows curve gently and some individual lines wander badly); the gaps between the rows tend to be wider in the middle of the lines; the heights of the megaliths become lower as one walks along them, and then may rise again at the end. It also seems likely that at least the Le Menec and Kermario alignments originally had rings of megaliths at both ends. There has been an attempt by Thom and others (Thom and Thom 1971, 1972) to prove that the alignments have an astronomical significance. While there is evidence for concern with the major solar events, and possibly some major lunar events, claims that the alignments contain sophisticated astronomical alignments and subtle geometry are not yet generally accepted by archaeologists.

The Carnac area also boasts huge, early standing stones – notably the fallen Grand Menhir Brisé at Locmariaquer (originally Europe's tallest menhir, at over 20 m). There are also a series of distinctive long mounds known as 'Carnac mounds' (e.g. Er Grah, 120m long with megalithic chamber) that contain particularly rich grave goods, notably the jadeite polished stone axes found within the massive Tumulus de Saint-Michel. In terms of relative chronology, the Carnac mounds and large standing stones seem to be the earliest major monuments in the Carnac region (late 5th millennium onwards), the passage graves rather later (late 4th millennium onwards), while the major alignments seem to date from the 3rd millennium.

A. Thom and A.S. Thom: *Journal for History of Astronomy* II (1971), 147; III (1972), 11, 151; P.R. Giot et al.: *Préhistoire de la Bretagne* (Rennes, 1979); D. Heggie: *Megalithic science* (London, 1981); A. Burl: *From Carnac to Callanish* (London, 1993).

RJA

'cart burials' *see* KISH

Carter Ranch Pueblo Pueblo of 39 rooms located in the Hay Hollow Valley, east-central Arizona, occupied between AD 1100 and 1225. Domestic rooms were built of stone masonry around a plaza containing a D-shaped kiva. A detached circular great kiva was located 10 m northwest of the PUEBLO.

The birth of processual archaeology. Carter Ranch Pueblo was excavated by Paul S. Martin and John B. Rinaldo of the Southwest Expedition of the Chicago Field Museum of Natural History, and the ceramics were analysed by W.A. Longacre, effectively marking the beginning of contemporary American archaeological research into social organization. During this critical time, Lewis R. Binford arrived at the University of Chicago to fuse additional theoretical and methodological elements, especially an ecological focus, with indigenous sociological concerns to form the initial paradigmatic statement of PROCESSUAL ARCHAEOLOGY.

The University of Chicago had long been a bastion of social anthropology, and in the late 1940s Paul Martin and John Rinaldo were inspired by Fred Eggan's seminar on social structures to speculate on features of prehistoric social organization in Sites of the Reserve phase, Pine Lawn Valley, western New Mexico (Martin and Rinaldo 1950). George Peter Murdock's *Social structure* and Fred Eggan's *Social organization of the western pueblos*, published in 1949 and 1950 respectively, provided comparative and historical support to archaeological investigations in the American Southwest. During the 1950s, Martin directed his interest in social organization into settlement pattern research, which was the prevailing analytical problem of the period (*see* SPATIAL ANALYSIS). Together, Paul Martin and the University of Chicago team laid the foundations for the emergence of processual archaeology.

In 1959, William Longacre was hired by Martin to conduct an archaeological survey in east-central Arizona during the summer, and that autumn he became a graduate student in the Department of Social Anthropology at the University of Chicago. In the following year he continued his survey work. During the 1960–1 academic year, Constance Cronin, another social anthropology graduate student, analysed black-on-white ceramics from a number of sites investigated by Martin, discovering that design elements of different pottery types at a single site were more similar than the design elements on the same type at different sites. The implications for the transmission of design information – and thus for the inferring of features of social organization – were immediately apparent.

The first season of excavation at Carter Ranch, in the summer of 1961, was designed to test the proposition that analysis of ceramic decoration could provide access to prehistoric social organization. It was afterwards, in the autumn of 1961, that Lewis Binford joined the Chicago faculty. The 1962 season at Carter Ranch clearly shows Binford's influence on fieldwork in the use of SAMPLING STRATEGIES and in the investigation of room function.

Proceeding from Cronin's original insight, Longacre interpreted the spatial clustering of ceramic design elements in different sections of the pueblo as an indication of the localization of female potters maintained over several generations by matrilocal residence and matrilineal descent. His doctoral dissertation (*Archaeology as anthropology: a case study*), which was presented in 1963 and published in 1970, embodies Martin's long-term interest in social organization and Binford's theoretical concerns; its methodological flaws, such as the assumption that pots were locally made and Longacre's general inattention to SITE FORMATION PROCESSES, were to characterize processual archaeology as a whole.

The component of processual archaeology relating to social organization was thus nurtured by Paul Martin in the laboratories of the University of Chicago and the Field Museum, as well as in the prehistoric sites of the American Southwest such as Carter Ranch.

G.P. Murdock: *Social structure* (New York, 1949); F. Eggan: *Social organization of the Western Pueblos* (Chicago, 1950); P.S. Martin and J.B. Rinaldo: *Sites of the Reserve Phase* (Chicago, 1950); L.R. Binford: 'Archaeology as anthropology', *AA* 28 (1962), 217–25; W.A. Longacre: *Archaeology as anthropology: a case study* (Tucson, 1970).

JJR

Carthage *see* AFRICA 1

Casa Grande Late Classic period HOHOKAM site on the Gila River near Coolidge, Arizona, dating to *c*.AD 1300–1400, which was visited by Father Eusebio Kino in 1694. It contains the only extant Hohokam 'big house': a four-storey adobe building with astronomical alignments set in an adobe-walled compound. Other walled compounds at the site enclose platform mounds (flat-topped mounds of earth) and residential structures.

D.R. Wilcox and L.O. Shenk: *The architecture of the Casa Grande and its interpretation* (Tucson, 1977).

JJR

Casas Grandes (Paquime) Prehistoric site covering an area of about 36 ha in northern Chihuahua, Mexico, excavated in 1959–61 by the Amerind Foundation, under the direction of Charles Di Peso. Both the excavated artefacts and the architectural features of the site, such as blocks of adobe rooms, plazas, platform mounds and ball-courts (*see* BALLGAME), show pronounced Mesoamerican affiliation, interpreted by Di Peso as evidence of a mercantile (*pochteca*) network operating throughout the American Southwest with Casas Grandes as the trading centre. The abandonment of the site, once thought to have taken place in *c.*AD 1340 at the end of the Diablo phase of the Medio period, is now placed in the early 15th century AD.

C.C. Di Peso et al.: *Casas Grandes: a fallen trading center of the Gran Chichimeca*, 8 vols (Dragoon, 1974); D.I. Woosley and J.C. Ravesloot, eds: *Culture and contact; Charles Di Peso's Gran Chichimeca* (Albuquerque, 1993).

JJR

Castelluccian culture Sicilian culture of the Early Bronze Age, dating to the second half of the 3rd and the early 2nd millennium BC and defined after the investigation of the site of Castelluccio by Paolo Orsi in 1892–3. The distinctive pottery is a slipped red ware of vessels such as handled cups, bowls and amphorae painted in black (sometimes edged in white) with complex and often dense fields of geometric patterning; there is also an incised dark ware. At Castelluccio, *c.* 25 km inland from Noto in southeast Sicily, there are numerous rock-cut tombs with single and double chambers, and porticos carved to give the effect of pillars flanking the entrance. Castelluccian settlement seems to have varied from small farmsteads and hamlets to more substantial villages such as that at Melilli, the latter sometimes displaying defensive walls with semi-circular bastions in a manner that parallels certain settlements elsewhere in the Mediterranean (e.g. Lerna, Greece). Another trait which reveals Mediterranean contacts is the production of embossed bone plaques (e.g. Cava della Signora, Castelluccio) which may be schematic representations of deities; these finely decorated items are of uncertain function but have also been found in Malta, Greece (Lerna) and Turkey (Troy).

P. Orsi: 'La necropoli sicula di Castelluccio (Siracusa)', *Boll. di Paletnologia Italiana* 18 (1892); L. Bernabo Brea: *Sicily before the Greeks* (London, 1966), 103; P.E. Arias: 'Monumenti funerari della prima e media età del bronzo nella Sicilia centro meridionale', *Sicilia Archeologica* 46–7 (1981), 73–86.

RJA

Catacomb-grave culture Bronze Age culture of the beginning of the 2nd millennium BC, represented primarily by kurgans (burial mounds) in the steppe regions of Ukraine and southern Russia; it was first identified by V.A. Gorodtsov in 1901–3 in the Seversi Donets river area. The so-called 'catacomb' graves consist of mounds covering rectangular or oval shafts leading to a burial chamber, or 'pit-grave'; the chamber usually contains only one or, rarely, two or three skeletons, laid in a contracted posture on their sides. The burials include red ochre. The grave-goods consist of pottery, stone maceheads, and flint spearheads and arrowheads. Bronze implements are common and include shaft-hole axes, adzes, chisels and ornaments (temple rings, spirals, rings, beads, pendants); their typology reflects the influence of the northern Caucasus (e.g. MAIKOP). The tools were manufactured from arsenic-rich copper ores, presumably obtained from the Donets Basin. Several burials (e.g. Malaya Ternovka in the Lower Dniepr area) contain copper slag, ingots and sets of foundry and casting tools; they are thought to be the graves of metalsmiths. Silver rings and amber pendants have been found in several catacomb graves near Donetsk. In another grave, near the village of Bolotnoe in the Crimea, the remains of a woven bag with wheat-ears have been found; the same grave contained four wheels and the wheel axis of a cart. Settlements belonging to the same culture have been found in the catchment area of the river Ingul and along the lower stretches of the Southern Bug; they are situated on promontories of the upper river terraces, and some houses have stone foundations. The faunal remains consist mainly of the bones of cattle and sheep/goat.

S.N. Bratchenko and O.G. Shaposhnikova: 'Katakombnaja kul'turno-istoričeskaja obščnost' [The Catacomb cultural-historical entity], *Arheologiya Ukrainskoi SSR* [The archaeology of the Ukrainian SSR], ed. D.Ya. Telegin (Kiev, 1985), 403–19.

PD

Çatal Hüyük One of the largest known Neolithic sites in the Near East, located in the Konya plain of southern Anatolia, about 11 km from modern Çumra. A section of the 32-acre site was excavated by James Mellaart in the 1960s (1967; 1975), revealing 14 building phases radiocarbon-dated to the period 6250–5400 BC, roughly contemporary with the Levantine Pre-pottery Neolithic B or AMUQ A-B periods (*see* ACERAMIC NEOLITHIC). The subsistence at Çatal Hüyük was based on cattle domestication and irrigation agriculture, with crops including emmer, einkorn and barley, as well as field peas, acorns, pistachios and almonds. Mellaart's study of the carbonized organic remains from the site as well as the evidence for early metallurgy were both exceptional achievements for an excavation in the 1960s.

The site is perhaps best known for the paintings, ox skulls and relief sculptures decorating the internal walls of many of the houses, including protuberances interpreted as female breasts (sometimes incorporating boar-tusks and vulture-beaks) and figures of women apparently giving birth to wild beasts, as well as paintings of humans dressed as vultures apparently engaged in funeral rites. As at many other Near Eastern Neolithic sites, the corpses were buried beneath the floors of houses. At Çatal Hüyük, however, the burial customs also involved the deliberate excarnation of the bodies and the removal of the skulls, which were placed in baskets on the floors of some of the houses.

Ian Hodder has re-examined the GENDER distinctions and symbolic relationships of the house decoration, deducing that 'early material symbolism is involved in the celebration and control of the wild, and that the control relates to social power through the representation of male and female and through the organization of space' (Hodder 1990: 10–11). This study of the Çatal Hüyük house decoration forms part of the basic thesis of *The domestication of Europe*, in which he interprets the emergence of the European Neolithic as 'a social-symbolic process' in which 'animals, plants, clay, death, and perhaps reproduction are all "natural" phenomena which are "cultured" and brought within the control of a social and cultural system' (Hodder 1990: 18–19). Beginning in the 1990s, Hodder undertook new excavations at the site, partly in order to address the question of whether, as Mellaart had suggested, craftwork was undertaken in a specialized area of the site rather than within the individual houses.

J. Mellaart: *Çatal Hüyük: a Neolithic town in Anatolia* (London, 1967); ——: *The Neolithic of the Near East* (London, 1975), 98–111; I. Todd: *Çatal Hüyük* (Menlo Park, 1976); I. Hodder: 'Contextual archaeology: an interpretation of Çatal Hüyük and a discussion of the origins of agriculture', *Bulletin of the Institute of Archaeology* (University College London) 24 (1987), 43–56; ——: *The domestication of Europe* (Oxford, 1990), 3–21; ——, ed.: *On the surface: Çatalhöyük 1993–95* (Cambridge, 1997).

IS

'cataract tradition' Group of three Nubian Neolithic 'industries' – the Gemaian, Qadan and Abkan – located primarily in the area of the second Nile cataract and dating to *c*.4000–3000 BC (see Shiner 1968: 535). The Abkan, first identified by O.H. Myers at Abka, was roughly contemporary with the KHARTOUM NEOLITHIC and SHAMARKIAN cultures. The assemblages are characterized mainly by flake tools, with high proportions of denticulates, lightly retouched scrapers, borers and groovers. Abkan lithics and ceramics – reddish-brown open bowls – are stylistically similar to those of the BADARIAN culture, and there is also evidence of contact with the Khartoum Variant culture (*see* KHARTOUM NEOLITHIC). Abkan groups appear to have relied primarily on fishing and herding for their subsistence; evidence of hunting or gathering is sparse. The Qadan (*c*.15000 to 11,000 BP, roughly contemporary with the ARKINIAN), is characterized by a strong degree of variability in the proportions of types of microlithic tools; this appears to indicate a very diverse subsistence base comprising fishing, hunting and gathering. The processing of wild grain is attested by the presence of SICKLE-SHEEN on many Qadan microliths (Unger-Hamilton 1988). Cemeteries of Qadan graves, consisting of shallow pits covered by stone slabs, have been excavated at JEBEL SAHABA and Tushka.

O.H. Myers: 'Abka re-excavated', *Kush* 6 (1958), 131–41; J. Shiner: 'The cataract tradition', *The prehistory of Nubia* II, ed. F. Wendorf (Dallas, 1968), 535–629 (611–29); M. Hoffman: *Egypt before the pharaohs* (New York, 1979), 85–98; R. Unger-Hamilton: *Method in microwear analysis: prehistoric sickles and other stone tools from Arjoune, Syria* (Oxford, 1988).

IS

catastrophe theory Mathematical theory that can be used to explain sudden change and collapse in systems that seem otherwise relatively stable, without relying upon a single major cause. Essentially, the mathematical relationships described in catastrophe theory show how even small changes in a variable (i.e. a factor governing change) can lead to very rapid system overloads. Invented by the French mathematician René Thom (1975), the theory was first adapted to analyse processes of change in the archaeological record by Colin Renfrew (1978). With the mathematician

Kenneth Cooke, Renfrew went on to develop applications of catastrophe theory to archaeology (Renfrew and Cooke 1979); one of the chapters in this volume is a study of changes in settlement pattern, in which Renfrew and the theoretical physicist Tim Poston examine whether changes in settlement pattern (e.g. from scattered farmsteads to nucleated villages) might be induced by such local factors as changes in soil fertility or agricultural techniques, rather than by external influences (e.g. conquest or sudden environmental change). This hypothesis, however, is explored in terms of the more abstract mathematical notion that – as catastrophe theory would suggest – 'discontinuous behaviour arising from continuous change in the variables in one of these frameworks can radically affect the variables in the other' (Renfrew and Cooke 1979: 459). Radical socio-economic changes, such as those reflected in the archaeological record of the Cyclades in the late 3rd millennium BC might therefore be ascribed not to 'external agencies' but to 'a cascade of catastrophes, the state variables of one acting as control variables of the next so as to produce a sequence of changes – a domino effect, to use the political jargon of the 1960s'.

As well as explaining cultural collapse, catastrophe theory can be used to explain sudden change and innovation in societies, when there does not seem to be any single major cause. However, the ability of the theory to cope with the complexity of social systems is compromised by the fact that Thom's mathematics can only deal with four variables at once. Renfrew himself comments that 'such a procedure can in itself allow us to define more closely the special or unique features of the individual process, but it will never predict the infinite complexity and variety of each individual case' (Renfrew and Cooke 1979: 505), while Thom points out: 'It is tempting to see the history of nations as a sequence of catastrophes between metabolic forms . . . But in a subject like mankind itself, one can see only the surface of things' (Thom 1975: 320).

R. Thom: *Structural stability and morphogenesis* (Reading, MA, 1975); A.C. Renfrew: 'Trajectory discontinuity and morphogensis', *AA* 43 (1978), 203–22; —— and K.L. Cooke, eds: *Transformations: mathematical approaches to cultural change* (New York, 1979), 418–506; P.T. Saunders: *An introduction to catastrophe theory* (Cambridge, 1980); A.C. Renfrew et al., eds: *Theory and explanation in archaeology* (New York, 1982).

IS

catchment analysis *see* SITE CATCHMENT ANALYSIS

cation-ratio dating Dating technique applied to rock varnish on stone artefacts and petroglyphs, based on differences in the rate at which cations (positively charged ions) such as K^+ and Ca^{2+} are leached out relative to the less soluble Ti^{4+}. For absolute dating, a cation leaching curve must be established using independently dated rocks from the region of interest. The methodology of the technique is not without controversy.

R.I. Dorn: 'Cation-ratio dating: a new rock varnish age-determination technique', *Quaternary Research* 20 (1983), 49–73; P.R. Bierman and A.R. Gillespie: 'Accuracy of rock-varnish chemical analyses: implications for cation-ratio dating', *Geology* 19 (1991), 196–9 [see also various comments and replies in *Geology* 20 (1992), 469–72].

SB

causewayed camp (causewayed enclosure) Type of sub-circular early Neolithic enclosure demarcated by one to four concentric rings of 'interrupted ditches' – that is, ditches with long sections left undug to form apparent 'causeways'. The camp at WINDMILL HILL (late 4th millennium BC) is the type-site, while those at Crickley Hill in Gloucestershire, Hambledon Hill in Dorset, and Haddenham in Cambridgeshire are the most recently and thoroughly excavated. Since their identification there has been much discussion over whether causewayed camps functioned as defensive structures or as livestock enclosures (both ideas undermined by the incompleteness of the ditches, though the material dug from these may have formed continuous banks at some sites); permanent settlements or temporary meeting and trading places; or even as religious monuments. The mystery is heightened by an apparent lack of evidence at Windmill Hill for permanent structures (although pottery and other debris show that the site was regularly frequented), and by the discovery there of human bones deposited in the ditches that had apparently been taken from the nearby chamber tomb of WEST KENNET; more recently human bones and skulls and two complete burials were excavated from the ditches at Hambledon Hill. It is often suggested that the causewayed camps signal the evolution of chiefdoms and the formation of larger and more complex population groups than are generally recognized at the very beginning of the Neolithic. However, as more sites have been excavated there has also been an increasing tendency to try to treat these complex sites individually, rather than as a homogenous class.

I.F. Smith: *Windmill Hill and Avebury – excavations by Alexander Keiller 1925–39* (Cambridge, 1965); ——:

'Causewayed enclosures', *Economy and settlement in Neolithic and Early Bronze Age Britain and Europe*, ed. D.D.A. Simpson (1971), 89–112; R.J. Mercer: *Hambledon Hill: a neolithic landscape* (Edinburgh, 1980); C. Evans: 'Excavations at Haddenham, Cambs: a "planned" enclosure and its regional affinities', *Enclosures and defences in the Neolithic of Western Europe*, ed. C. Burgess et al. (Oxford, 1988), BAR IS 403; I. Hodder: 'The Haddenham causewayed enclosure', *Theory and practice in archaeology* (London, 1992), 213–40.

RJA

cave art Term used to describe the art of the Upper Palaeolithic, especially the paintings and engravings on the walls of caves and rockshelters (the parietal art) rather than the smaller figurines and carvings (the MOBILIARY ART). To begin with, many authorities doubted the authenticity of the images, most notoriously in the case of the important cave of ALTAMIRA in Spain, discovered in 1879 but not accepted as genuine until the early years of this century. Since then a series of caves have been opened up and recorded, from LASCAUX in 1940 to CHAUVET CAVE, discovered as recently as December 1994.

The techniques adopted by Palaeolithic artists include drawing and painting with fingers and sticks in red (often ochre) and/or black (often charcoal, sometimes manganese dioxide); engraving and incision; low relief in the living rock or clay; and mixtures of all these approaches. Sometimes the surface of the rock is lightly cleaned or prepared before the work is executed, and artists often made use of naturally smoother areas of wall and natural alcoves or 'panels'. Some works make use of natural bulges in the rock, or the line of cracks or crevices, as part of the composition or to accentuate a feature.

Two characteristics of cave art stand out. The first is that the subjects of Palaeolithic art are primarily individual animals, particularly the larger mammals of the Palaeolithic environment. There are virtually no depictions of vegetation or landscape, and only a few and rather dubious depictions of insects; there are relatively few depictions of smaller mammals, fish and birds. The second characteristic is that, with some famous exceptions, the art is a collection of depictions of individual animals. The depictions on any given panel may be gathered together in loose composition, or panels may be arranged in a way that seems to be deliberately balanced; but 'scenes' in which there is an attempt to associate animals with each other, to relate them by perspective or scale, or to introduce any sense of narrative, are rare. Famous exceptions to this generalization include the scene of 'swimming deer' at Lascaux.

Attempts to analyse the contents of cave art in more detail have tended to focus on the following issues: the style of the art, and what this can tell us about the relative chronology of the works; the subjects of the art, and what this can tell us about the concerns of Palaeolithic hunters; the relationship between the different works of art within any one cave, and what we can deduce from this about Palaeolithic society.

Henri Breuil, the leading figure in French cave art studies in the first part of this century, was the first to put forward a widely accepted scheme for the evolution of different styles of cave art. He described two evolutionary schemes, one for art that he interpreted as belonging to the Aurignacian and Perigordian periods (as defined from tools found within archaeological deposits) and one for the later and apparently more sophisticated art of the Solutrean and Magdalenian periods. In both schemes, Breuil tended to date the simpler, cruder or more schematic examples of art as earlier than the more naturalistic (life-like), complex or detailed examples.

In Breuil's time, one popular explanation for the art was that creativity was a natural human desire once human intellect had fully evolved – usually summed up as the 'art for art's sake' argument. However, it was increasingly recognized that much cave art is executed deep into cave systems, not near the cave entrance where hunters might be living or camping in the area lit by natural light. It therefore seemed more likely to some authorities that the art was linked to religious or superstitious rituals. The first attempts to specify the nature of these rituals linked them to the idea of 'sympathetic magic': hunters painted the animals as a way of gaining a greater understanding and control over their prey.

André Leroi-Gourhan, arguably the second great theorist of cave art after Breuil, formally defined a series of stages in Palaeolithic art (Styles I–IV), which again assumed that the art evolved through a series of steps from the relatively stiff hieratic art of his Style I in the Aurignacian and Gravettian through to the graceful naturalistic art of his Style IV in the later Magdalenian. Leroi-Gourhan's scheme was not universally accepted, although as a widely-read attempt to categorize cave art styles it gained a descriptive currency of its own. Some prehistorians felt that it was dangerous to try to fit the corpus of Palaeolithic art into rigid evolutionary schema, given the huge range of the art, the vast length of the tradition (at the most conservative estimate, 15,000 years) and – above all – the lack of reliable independent dating. Ucko and Rosenfeld (1967) represented a more cautious and less systematizing approach to understanding cave art.

Prehistorians also attempted to put forward more sophisticated arguments concerning the motivation of the cave artists. Quantitative and spatial analysis of the species of animals represented seemed to show a discrepancy between the animals that were actually being hunted (as reflected in faunal analysis of the bones of animals in the archaeological layers in some of the caves) and the animals that were being painted. This seemed to undermine the argument that the paintings in some way facilitated hunting. If the paintings did not relate directly to hunting, might they represent mythologies, or totems of clans or lineages, or even some more complex symbolism? Leroi-Gourhan constructed an involved theory, related to STRUCTURALIST analysis, which explained the groupings of the animals and signs in terms of male/female symbolism.

One of the problems with such complex explanations is that they rarely seem to hold true for more than the sample of art used in their formulation; another is that any detailed interpretation of the spatio-symbolic nature of a body of art depends upon the art having been executed in the same period. This is often a difficult assumption to make. In the past, cave art could only be dated indirectly by one of three means: by assigning it to the same broad period as the tool types found in the archaeological layers associated with the art; by dating organic remains found within the archaeological layers; or by comparison with art of similar styles. The first two approaches can only give the broadest indication of the age of a body of cave art (rather than demonstrating how individual works relate to one another chronologically), while the last approach leads almost inevitably to circular arguments.

More recently, the new technique of ACCELERATOR MASS SPECTROMETRY (which can analyse very tiny amounts of organic material) has begun to be used to radiocarbon date the charcoal used in the paintings themselves. This offers archaeologists their first chance to date individual drawings directly, and it is probably only after a prolonged campaign of AMS dating that we will be able to build up a reliable picture of the stylistic and chronological relationships of cave art as a whole. Already, AMS dates are beginning to suggest that cave art may have begun much earlier than expected; that some caves will represent a much more complex and episodic picture than is presently realized; and that, while particularly brilliant 'schools' or epochs of art are identifiable, it is wrong to try and string these together into a stylistic hierarchy (*see* CHAUVET CAVE).

Difficulties with the more fashionable social explanations have led some archaeologists back to neo-economic or utilitarian interpretations. Strauss (1992), for example, points out that rejection of the 'hunting magic' hypothesis may have been hasty. It is true that while red deer are economically important in Cantabria, and reindeer predominate in the faunal assemblages of the French Pyrenees and Dordogne, neither animal is represented as often or as dramatically as the bison (e.g. Altamira) or horse (e.g. LASCAUX) in those areas respectively. But what if bison and horse represented vital, and challenging, prey in times of scarcity? Might the art not have focused on the critical, rather than the staple, hunted species? Mithen (1990) goes further, suggesting that the art could have acted as a sort of mnemonic or teaching aid for the bison/horse hunting strategies precisely because they were more difficult and more rarely applied.

The complex variety of explanations offered to ethnographers by modern cave artists such as Australian aborigines and the San of southern Africa suggests that there is unlikely to be a single 'interpretation' of cave art that holds true for all sites and over the millennia in which the art was produced. While the vitality of cave art in the particular region of southern France and northern Spain may well be explicable in palaeoeconomic terms (i.e., an optimal regional climate concentrated populations of hunters), reducing the complex internal dynamics (style, subject) of this cultural tradition to single neo-FUNCTIONALIST social or economic 'explanations' seems less and less plausible. *See also* EL CASTILLO, LES COMBARELLES, LES TROIS FRÈRES *and* LE TUC D'AUDOUBERT.

P. Ucko and A. Rosenfeld: *Palaeolithic cave art* (London, 1967); N.K. Sandars: *Prehistoric art in Europe* (London, 1968), 72–140; H. Laville et al.: *Rockshelters of the Périgord* (New York, 1980); A. Lerois-Gourhan: *The dawn of European art* (Cambridge, 1982); P. Bahn and Jean Vertut: *Images of the Ice Age* (London, 1988); J.D. Lewis-Williams et al.: 'The signs of all times: entoptic phenomena in Upper Palaeolithic art', *CA* 24 (1988), 201–45; S. Mithen: 'Looking and learning: Upper Palaeolithic art and information gathering', *WA* 19 (1988), 297–327; ——: *Thoughtful foragers* (Cambridge, 1990); C. Gamble: 'The social context for European Palaeolithic art', *PPS* 57 (1991), 3–15; L.G. Strauss: *Iberia before the Iberians: the Stone Age prehistory of Cantabrian Spain* (Albuquerque, 1992); R. Layton: *Australian rock art: a new synthesis* (Cambridge, 1994); Jean-Marie Chauvet et al.: *Chauvet*

Cave: The discovery of the world's oldest paintings, trans. P. Bahn (London, 1996).
RJA

Cave of Hearths Site in the Transvaal, South Africa, in the Makapan valley, 10 km east of Potgietersrus, which has yielded important hominid remains. The cave is notable for the discovery of a fragment of juvenile mandible, generally described as archaic *HOMO SAPIENS*, in association with Late ACHEULEAN artefacts. The sequence includes three levels of Acheulean material and six levels of MSA (Middle Stone Age), LSA (Later Stone Age) and Iron Age deposits. The name refers to a thick bed of ash in the lowest levels of the cave, which, in fact, represented naturally ignited bat guano. True hearths, however, occur in the uppermost Acheulean layers.

R.J. Mason: *Prehistory of the Transvaal* (Johannesburg, 1962).
RI

cave temple Type of temple or monastery carved into the rock outcrops common in the western Deccan region of India (in Maharashtra and northern Andra Pradesh) and dating to the period between the 2nd century BC and the 8th century AD. Among the best-known of Buddhist or Hindu cave-temple sites are Ajanta, Ellora, AIHOLE, Karli, Elephanta, Bedsa and Bhaja. The earliest examples imitated the forms of wooden temples, particularly the apsidal-ended Buddhist *chaitya*-hall.

Ajanta comprises 28 Buddhist temples and monasteries carved into the cliffs of a deep basalt gorge near Aurangabad in the Deccan plateau of western India. Built in two phases (the 2nd and 5th centuries AD respectively), the cave temples contain elaborately sculpted columns, ceilings and Buddhist stupas and images. Several of the temples incorporate elaborate murals depicting scenes from the life of the Buddha, portrayed in the idiom of courtly life as experienced by the 5th-century Gupta sponsors of the most elaborate shrines. Ellora, located about 30 km northwest of the city of Aurangabad, consists of a long sequence of cave temples extending for 2 km along the face of a basalt escarpment. The southern cluster of 12 temples, dating to the 7th and 8th centuries AD and dedicated to Buddhist deities, are the earliest at the site. There are also 17 Hindu temples dating from the 7th–9th centuries AD and five 9th-century Jain temples. The most elaborate of the cave temples incorporates the monolithic Kailasa Hindu temple within an enormous rock-hewn chamber with a two-storeyed entranceway.

R.S. Gupte and B.D. Mahajan: *Ajanta, Ellora and Aurangabad caves* (Bombay, 1962), 32–106; W. Spink: *Ajanta to Ellora* (Bombay, 1967); T.V. Pathy: *Ellora, art and culture* (New Delhi, 1980); R. Parimoo et al., ed.: *The art of Ajanta: new perspectives* (New Delhi, 1991); G.H. Malandra: *Unfolding a mandala: the Buddhist cave temples at Ellora* (Albany, 1993).
CS

Çayönü Tepesi Tell-site dating to the Prepottery Neolithic B period (*see* ACERAMIC NEOLITHIC) and located in southeastern Turkey beside a tributary of the Tigris, about 20 km from the ancient copper and malachite mines of Ergani Madem. The oval mound, excavated by Çambel and Braidwood (1970), comprises five major strata radiocarbon-dated to *c*.7500–6800 BC. The surviving faunal remains from the lower strata show that animals were being hunted (only the dog had been domesticated) and wild emmer, einkorn, pistachio, almond and vetch were being exploited. The two upper strata (IV–V), however, contain evidence of the domestication of sheep, goat and pigs, alongside continued hunting of deer and aurochs. The site also presents exceptional evidence for the spatial organization of architecture and the differentiation of areas of activity.

H. Çambel and R.J. Braidwood: 'An early farming village in Turkey', *Scientific American* 222 (1970), 50–6.
IS

Celts, Celtic Terms used to describe a loosely defined prehistoric linguistic and ethnic group in Iron Age Europe, as well as the related (historical and modern) Welsh, Irish and Scots Gaelic ethnic and linguistic communities. The term carries with it a confusing bundle of meanings, depending on whether it is being used by archaeologists, historians or linguists.

To linguists, Celtic is a branch of the archaic Indo-European language family. Its earliest form ('common' or 'proto-' Celtic) is identifiable as a distinct language from the 5th century BC in south-central Europe, though it surely existed prior to this. In the 1st millennium, or before, Celtic speakers spread through much of Europe, notably into France (the Galli, or Gauls), Spain (the Celtiberi), and the Balkans and Asia Minor (the Galatae). Historians first learn about the early Celts, or *keltoi*, from the accounts of classical authors, notably Herodotus (*c*.450 BC). Soon after, the movement of Celtic warriors and tribal migrations brought them into conflict with the classical world, most infamously in the sack of

Rome in the early 4th century BC and the later sack of Delphi (279 BC).

Later authorities (notably Caesar in his description of the conquest of Gaul), paint a broad picture of Celtic society as the classical world perceived it: tribal, war-like, obsessed with personal valour and honour, with important kinship relationships but a rather fluid power structure based upon standing within the tribe. 'Standing' seems to have depended on an admixture of lineage, deeds, wealth, and number and standing of followers – reinforced by oratory skills and control of craftsmen. The religion of the early Celts is dimly understood, partly through the iconography in CELTIC ART and the importance of votive offering places such as SOURCES DE LA SEINE, partly through late and atypical shrines and cult art such as those found at ENTREMONT, and partly through myths and legends recorded much later in the Irish and Welsh early medieval period.

On the Continent, the Celtic language family died out completely (Celtic Breton is a re-introduction from southern England in the 5th century AD). The surviving Celtic languages are thus all derivatives of the common Celtic introduced into the British Isles before the Roman Conquest. Debate continues as to when Celtic groups first settled in Britain. Conservative estimates suggest they arrived in Ireland in the 4th century BC, where common Celtic then developed into Goidelic or Gaelic Celtic (known to linguists as Q-Celtic), later spreading to the Isle of Man and Scotland. Other Celtic groups entered mainland Britain (e.g. *see* ARRAS) in the later 1st millennium, where the British Celtic dialect (known to linguists as P-Celtic) developed. This linguistic group was later pushed west and north by the Anglo-Saxon invasions of the 5th century AD, leading to the division between Cornish and Welsh dialects.

Although modern Celtic ethnicity is sharply defined by contrast with Anglo-Saxon or English linguistic and cultural groups, the ethnic identity of prehistoric speakers of Celtic languages is much more obscure. It is not absolutely certain that all the groups labelled as Celtic by ancient historians actually spoke common Celtic, and still less certain that they regarded themselves as members of a distinct cultural family. Because language is archaeologically invisible in prehistoric peoples, the classic indicator of 'Celtic' identity to the archaeologist studying the prehistory of continental Europe is the production of decorative art in the curvilinear LA TÈNE art style, popularly known as 'CELTIC ART'. This style, which developed from the earlier HALLSTATT art style, was certainly produced in the Celtic linguistic area, and is closely associated with peoples identified in ancient sources as Celtic, but it is by no means certain that all Celtic-speaking peoples produced Celtic art, or that Celtic art was produced exclusively by peoples speaking Celtic languages.

T.G.E. Powell: *The Celts* (London, 1958); B. Cunliffe: *The Celtic world* (London, 1979); P.S. Wells: *Culture contact and culture change* (Cambridge, 1980); David Crystal: *The Cambridge Encyclopedia of Language* (Cambridge 1987), 302–3; B. Cunliffe: *Greeks, Romans and Barbarians: spheres of interaction* (London, 1988).

RJA

Celtic art Popular name for the distinctive art-style of the late Iron Age LA TÈNE culture, which evolved from about 480 BC. Celtic art is largely a decorative art, manifest on metal weaponry, jewellery, horse equipment, and serving vessels, though with some significant bronze and stone statuary. It is known mainly from burials and votive offerings. The extent to which the La Tène style of art can be equated with a distinct Celtic ethnicity is uncertain (*see* CELTS, CELTIC). The origins of La Tène art lie to some extent with the motifs and decorated metalwork of the earlier Iron Age (the HALLSTATT period). Throughout the La Tène, local elites obtained objects from the Mediterranean world, just as the Hallstatt chieftains had done. But to a far greater extent they encouraged the production of local craft, reinterpreting a range of objects – some of imported type (e.g. copies of Etruscan wine flagons) and some of purely Central European origin (bronze horse fittings etc.). The local elites of the Marne–Moselle region seem to have especially strong connections with the Etruscans, manifested in the distribution of imported beaked bronze wine flagons.

The La Tène art-style was described by its most famous historian, Paul Jacobstahl, as emerging from three roots: the art of contemporary classical societies of the Mediterranean; the art of east (the animal art style of the Scythian tribes, but also iconography of Persian civilization); and local native styles (principally the style of the early Iron Age in central Europe, the HALLSTATT). The classical influence is most obvious, with Celtic metalworkers taking motifs such as the palmette and lotus bud, but reworking and often transforming them.

Following Jacobstahl, the art can be divided up into five styles, although the relationships are complex. The 'Early Style' of the 5th/early 4th century BC is largely known from objects taken from chieftains' graves in the western Celtic region such as

KLEIN ASPERGLE (Württemburg), and includes a famous series of flagons (e.g. Basse-Yutz, Lorraine and Dürrnberg-bei-Hallein, Austria) decorated with heads and fantastic animals. It employs decorative designs and friezes made up of quite tightly controlled repeated motifs as well as bold and relatively naturalistic figurative work. The influence of Etruscan, Greek and Near Eastern art is clear – most obviously in the form of the vessels.

The 'Waldalgesheim' of the 4th century develops from this into a much less naturalistic, curvilinear style. It is named after a female aristocrat's grave of about 330 BC in the Hunsrück-Eifel, which contained a gold neck-ring, arm-rings and other jewellery and horse fittings decorated with plant motifs flowing into each other in a continuous and very characteristic manner (sometimes termed 'continuous vegetal'). Elements of human and animal faces and bodies are subtly incorporated into the art. Although the Waldalgesheim burial is a late barrow, the style is more characteristically found in objects from the flat cemeteries of southern Germany, Italy, Switzerland and central and south-east Europe.

The 'Plastic' style, perhaps from the late 4th century on, used raised motifs in a distinctively three-dimensional, almost sculptural, style – notably on a series of heavy armrings. The characteristic of Plastic objects is that, rather than having two-dimensional decoration placed on the surface of an artefact, the shape of the object is made a part of the decorative scheme. In contrast to the Plastic style the 'Sword Style', known largely from swords and scabbards left as votive offerings at sites in Hungary and Switzerland (including LA TÈNE itself), is based on two-dimensional engraving. It includes some figurative scenes, but is characterized largely by delicate abstract designs of curvilinear interlacing, or geometric interlocking, lines. Like the other Celtic styles, the triskel, lotus bud, palmette and tendril-like motifs are recurring devices.

Monumental Celtic art can be divided into rare examples of large stone pillars decorated with curvilinear, abstracted designs using floral motifs and triskels (notably Pfalzfeld, Rhineland and the later Turoe Stone, County Galway, Ireland) that are very much like the metalwork designs translated into stone, and a Mediterranean-influenced series of religious statues and architectural elements from sites such as Roquepertuse and ENTREMONT in southern France.

It should be stressed that all the styles described above are artificial impositions upon a complex set of regional and stylistic relationships. Celtic art was multi-faceted, and does not form an easily bounded corpus: at the one end of Europe it fades into regional traditions that relate more closely to Eastern and classical predecessors (IBERIAN ART), while at the other it evolves into the Insular La Tène style (the name given to Celtic art in Britain before the Roman Conquest). Although Brittany and Britain are strongly associated with the later survival of 'Celtic' culture into the early medieval period, these more westerly regions were originally peripheral to the heartland of La Tène Celtic culture. It was only in the last couple of centuries BC, when certain regions may have received an immigrant elite (*see* ARRAS CULTURE), that Britain developed a strong tradition based on imported art objects.

The fact that much Celtic art, for all its styles and regional traits, remains recognizably 'Celtic' despite such different manifestations is probably the result of the widespread elite and chiefdom networks of Celtic society – most La Tène art is found in elite burials – and because of the migration of peoples in the period, as recorded by classical authors.

P. Jacobstahl: *Early Celtic art* (Oxford, 1944); N.K. Sandars: *Prehistoric art in Europe* (Harmondsworth 1968), 346–431; J. Driehaus: 'Zum Grabfund von Waldalgesheim', *Hamburger Beitrage zure Archäologie*, 1 (1971), 100–13; R. Megaw and J.V.S. Megaw: *Celtic art* (London, 1989).

'Celtic field' Misnomer commonly applied to prehistoric fields in Britain of any period. Some of these do indeed date to the Iron Age, but many date to the Bronze Age. *See* FIELD SYSTEMS.

Cempoala The site of a large Totonacan-speaking community of the Postclassic period (*c.*AD 900–1521) on the Gulf coastal plain of Veracruz, Mexico, Cempoala was a tributary province of the AZTEC empire. Visited by Hernán Cortés and his men in 1519, it was the first major Mesoamerican city to be seen by the Spaniards. The Cempoala region was the subject of archaeological research in the late 19th century and in more recent years the site has undergone major excavation and reconstruction as a tourist site but no English-language publication has yet appeared.

I. Kelly and A. Palerm: *The Tajin Totonac* (Washington, D.C., 1952).

PRI

cenotaph burial Although deliberately grave-like in form and/or contents, cenotaph 'burials' do not contain human remains. Usually identified by the presence of characteristic grave goods – some of the richest gold objects from the cemetery at VARNA were recovered from cenotaphs – they are often assumed to act as symbolic memorials for individuals whose bodies could not be recovered for reasons such as warfare or natural disaster.

RJA

cenote Hispanicization of the Yucatec Mayan *dz'onot*, a cenote is a sinkhole, a natural well formed by dissolution of limestone bedrock. Because cenotes were important sources of water, they were a focus for human settlement in the water-deficient Yucatán peninsula; they were also centres of ritual and sacrifice (*see* CHICHÉN ITZÁ, DZIBILCHALTUN).

C.C. Coggins and O.C. Shane III: *Cenote of sacrifice. Maya treasures from the sacred well at Chichén Itzá* (Austin, 1984).

PRI

Central Andes *see* AMERICA 6

central cattle pattern Form of settlement organization in Iron Age Central Africa that was characterized by a central cattle byre containing grain storage pits and elite burials and a men's court nearby, together forming a 'male domain'. Outer areas of houses and grain-bins, associated with women, are arranged according to some pattern of seniority expressed through left and right, starting with a principal house upslope of the court and byre. In parallel with this idiom of status the main house contains a right-male/left-female distinction. At right angles another distinction between front-secular and back-sacred activities informs behaviour not only in the main house but also the household and whole settlement. According to ethnographic evidence, this specific pattern is associated only with Eastern Bantu speakers who have hereditary leaders, brideprice in cattle, a belief in the daily influence of ancestors and a patrilineal ideology concerning biological descent (i.e. blood from the father).

T.N. Huffman: 'Archaeology and ethnohistory of the African Iron Age', *ARA* 11 (1982) 133–50; A. Kuper: *Wives for cattle: bridewealth and marriage in southern Africa* (London, 1982).

TH

central place theory Theoretical model for the spatial ordering of sites, based on the ideas published by German geographer Walter Christaller in 1935 (translated into English in 1966). Central place theory was particularly popular among archaeologists in the 1970s, at the height of the New Archaeology (*see* PROCESSUAL ARCHAEOLOGY).

Christaller was interested in the geography of southern Germany in the 1930s, and he sought to provide a general theory to explain the variations in the size and distribution of towns. He put forward three initial premises: that settlements performed economic or service functions; that there was a human tendency to centralization; and that the supply of goods was the reason for the existence of towns. In any region, certain goods and services will be provided, and efficiency means that their supply will concentrate in particular sites called 'central places'. Not all services or goods will be available in all centres, and people will be prepared to travel different distances for different goods; there will therefore be a hierarchy of levels of central places, so that the larger the range of goods or services offered, the smaller the number of sites providing them.

The theory assumes that all people in the region will require access to at least one centre of each level of the hierarchy, and that the resulting pattern of centres and hinterlands will be efficiently organized. In purely geometrical terms, the most efficient method of dividing a landscape into a pattern of such equal areas is by packing it with hexagonal territories, each with the central place at its centre; the central places themselves are thus distributed in a regular network at the points of a pattern of equilateral triangles. The different levels of the hierarchy would in turn be distributed in such a way that a centre at one level would have a hexagonal pattern of six centres of the next order down dependent on it, and so on down through the levels. There are a number of different geometrical ways in which this relationship between one order and the next order down can be structured, which Christaller suggested were associated with principles of marketing, transport or administration.

Christaller's particular concern with the urban geography of southern Germany in the 1930s led him to suggest that the principle of marketing was the determining factor in structuring the spatial relationship between central places.

However, as Christaller himself recognized, social and economic formations other than modern capitalism might generate very different structuring principles. Germany in the 1930s was a money-based economy with a highly organized system of state financing. In other societies, settlement systems may have been equally determined by the demands of exchange, but the *modes* of exchange such as tribute collection, especially of bulky staple commodities rather than prestige valuables, may have resulted in very different patterns. Christaller emphasized the economic or service function of settlements; in pre-capitalist societies, however, such functions were only weakly developed and should more properly be seen as facets of social relationships. Other assumptions include a deference to 'efficiency' and 'rationality' and an expectation of a regular system of sites. Pedlars and carriers, periodic markets and fairs provide alternative models of distribution, while the peripatetic migrations of some medieval European rulers show that the state could be financed in other ways than from a single central place.

For archaeologists, the theory seems to provide a way of using settlement data (often available in considerable quantities and to a high standard, particularly from modern surveys) to answer questions about the nature of the social organization of past societies. However, there are particular operational problems in applying the theory to archaeological data, such as the recognition of the functions performed at putative central places. It has sometimes been assumed that size of site is a good indication of the range of functions performed, but the justification for this assumption has seldom been examined. So far, the most successful applications of the theory have been to societies which shared at least some of the characteristics of the modern capitalist world, such as the towns of the Roman provinces, where a market distribution system and territorially organized government prevailed, or to settlement patterns where exchange systems are assumed to have played a prominent role in the determination of settlement locations, as in the DIYALA REGION in Iraq. Occasionally, as in a study of the settlement system around MOUNDVILLE (Alabama, USA), the underlying assumptions have been questioned and alternative patterns tested.

W. Christaller: *Central places in southern Germany*, trans. C.W. Baskin (Englewood Cliffs, 1966); I. Hodder and C. Orton: *Spatial analysis in archaeology* (Cambridge, 1976); C.A. Smith: *Regional analysis* (London and New York, 1976).

TC

Cerén (Joya de Cerén) Town-site of the Mesoamerican Classic period located in west-central El Salvador. The excavators of the site used geophysical detection methods (ground penetrating radar and RESISTIVITY SURVEY) to determine the location of residential structures buried by 5 m of volcanic ash (tephra) from the eruption of Laguna Caldera volcano, which took place suddenly (i.e. while the settlement was still occupied) around AD 600. Removal of roughly 5000 cubic metres of ash by power shovel allowed the excavation of several households of the early Classic period (*c*.AD 300–600). On an interior bench in one of the houses was the remains of what has tentatively been identified as a painted codex (*see* CODICES), preserved by the ash.

P.D. Sheets, ed.: *Archaeology and volcanism in Central America* (Austin, 1983); ——, H.F. Beaubien and M. Beaudry: 'Household archaeology at Cerén, El Salvador', *AM* 1 (1990) 81–90.

PRI

Cernavodă Archaeological complex situated in the lower Danube valley near the Black Sea coast in east Romania, the most significant part of which consists of the largest cemetery of the Neolithic Hamangia culture, excavated in the 1950s by D. Berciu; a later settlement forms the type-site of the Eneolithic Cernavodă culture. The 400 or so extended inhumations of the Hamangia cemetery date to the late 5th and 4th millennium BC; typical gravegoods are a black burnished pot and jewellery in the form of stone and *Spondylus* shell beads. Stylized pottery figurines are also relatively common, and represent an unusual instance in southeast Europe of figurines recovered from a funerary context. They include two exceptionally carefully conceived and well-made seated figures (Berciu 1960), apparently of a man and woman; the man sits on a low stool, his face resting on his hands, while the woman sits on the floor, her arms on one knee that is bent up towards her body.

D. Berciu: 'Neolithic figurines from Rumania', *Antiquity* 34 (1960), 283–4; ——: *Cultura Hamangia* (Bucharest, 1966); M. Gimbutas: *The goddesses and gods of old Europe* (London, 1982); N. Sandars: *Prehistoric art in Europe* (London, 1985; 1st edn 1968), 184–6.

RJA

Cerro Sechín Large platform temple and room complex in the Casma Valley, Peru, dating to the Initial Period (*c*.2300–1200 BC). The complex is decorated with more than 300 stone reliefs showing warriors, trophy heads, and disarticulated human body parts, an indication that warfare had early become an activity considered worthy of commemoration in public architecture.

L. Samaniego et al.: 'New evidence on Cerro Sechín, Casma Valley, Peru', *Early ceremonial architecture in the Andes*, ed. C.B. Donnan (Washington, D.C., 1985), 165–90.

KB

C Group (C Horizon) Lower Nubian cultural phase lasting about 700 years and roughly contemporary with the Egyptian Old and Middle Kingdoms and 1st and 2nd Intermediate Periods (*c*.2300–1500 BC) as well as with KERMA in Upper Nubia. The term C Group essentially refers to the material culture at a number of archaeological sites in Lower Nubia which are later than the A GROUP and earlier than the towns and temples of the Egyptian New Kingdom. C-Group assemblages are particularly characterized by black-topped hand-made pottery bearing incised white decoration. The archaeological entity probably corresponds to the geographical zone of Wawat, which is frequently mentioned in contemporary Egyptian texts. Unfortunately, most of the physical evidence concerning the C-Group culture derives from cemeteries such as those at Aniba, FARAS and Dakka, rather than from settlements. It has therefore proved difficult, despite the extensive archaeological survey undertaken during the UNESCO Nubian campaign of the 1960s, to identify the overall C-Group settlement pattern. Similarly, such factors as their social and political organization (probably tribal), their economy (probably based on cattle-herding) and their commercial and religious links with Egypt tend to be primarily deduced from funerary data. It has been suggested that the Egyptian domination of Lower Nubia from the early 12th dynasty onwards may have prevented the C Group from establishing closer links with the Kushite kingdom of Kerma.

M. Bietak: *Studien zur Chronologie der Nubischen C-Gruppe* (Vienna, 1968); T. Säve-Söderbergh, ed.: Middle *Nubian sites: Scandinavian Joint Expedition to Nubia* 4/1 (Uddevalla, 1989), 6–14; D. O'Connor: 'Early states along the Nubian Nile', *Egypt and Africa*, ed. W.V. Davies (London, 1991), 145–65.

IS

chacmool Type of stone sculpture representing a reclining human figure with a bowl or plate held on its stomach, usually found at the entrance to Postclassic temples in Mesoamerica, such as CHICHÉN ITZÁ, QUIRIGUA, TENOCHTITLAN and Tula (*see* TOLTECS).

M.E. Miller: 'A re-examination of the Mesoamerican chacmool', *Art Bulletin* 67 (1985), 7–17.

PRI

Chaco Canyon *see* ANASAZI; PUEBLO BONITO

Chagar Bazar Extensive settlement of the prehistoric HALAF period (*c*.5500–4500 BC) located in northern Mesopotamia, about 30 km northwest of TELL BRAK in Syria. The site was excavated by Max Mallowan during the 1930s, revealing deep Halaf stratigraphy, with a number of painted sherds of the SAMARRA period (*c*.5600–5000 BC) in the lowest levels. The settlement appears to have been abandoned for about 1500 years between the end of the Halaf period and the first phase of the Early Dynastic. By the reign of the AMORITE ruler Shamshi Adad I (*c*.1813–1781 BC), the construction of an impressive ceremonial centre suggests that Chagar Bazar had become an important administrative centre in the Old ASSYRIAN empire.

M.E.L. Mallowan: 'Excavations at Tell Chagar Bazar and an archaeological survey of the Habur region, 1934–5', *Iraq* 3 (1936), 1–86; ——: 'Excavations at Tell Chagar Bazar and the archaeological survey of the Habur region, second campaign, 1936', *Iraq* 4 (1937), 91–117; ——: 'Excavations at Braq and Chagar Bazar', *Iraq* 9 (1947), 1–258.

IS

Chalcatzingo Site of the Early-to-Middle Formative period (*c*.2000–1000 BC), located in Morelos, Mexico. The town of Chalcatzingo, incorporating early public architecture built of stone and earth, played an important role in trade between the Gulf coast and highland Mexico. Monument 1, a petroglyph showing an elaborately attired person seated in a cave, has been compared to OLMEC art from LA VENTA.

D.C. Grove, ed.: *Ancient Chalcatzingo* (Austin, 1987).

PRI

Chalchuapa Sizable Maya site of the Middle and Late Preclassic periods (*c*.800 BC–AD 300), located in the highlands of El Salvador. The growth of the settlement was truncated by the eruption of Ilopango volcano in the 3rd century AD.

R.J. Sharer, ed.: *The prehistory of Chalchuapa*, El Salvador, 3 vols (Philadelphia, 1978).

PRI

Chaldaeans (Akkadian: Kaldu) Ancient Near Eastern people who, like the ARAMAEANS, were originally nomadic. Since they also spoke a West Semitic dialect similar to Aramaic, there has been some debate as to whether they may simply have been a southern branch of the Aramaeans (Dietrich 1970). They are first mentioned in the ASSYRIAN annals of the 9th century BC, when Shalmaneser III waged war against three Chaldaean tribes in southern Iraq (Bit-Amukani, Bit-Dakuri and Bit-Yakin). Their origins are uncertain: by the time they appeared in the late Assyrian texts of the 9th century BC, however, they were settled in the area of southern Mesopotamia surrounding the lower courses of the Tigris and Euphrates, roughly corresponding to SUMER. Although they were still organized in tribes ruled by sheikhs, they led sedentary lives, owning herds of cattle and horses, and controlling the profitable trade-routes with the Gulf.

In the 8th century BC, Chaldaean sheikhs took control of BABYLONIA. Merodach-Baladan II, the sheikh of Bit-Yakin (*c*.721–710 BC), appears to have temporarily succeeded in uniting the various Chaldaean tribes, but eventually the Assyrian rulers Sargon II and Sennacherib recaptured Babylonia and the SEALAND in the early 7th century BC. The second period of Chaldaean domination came after the death of the Assyrian king Ashurbanipal, when the sheikh Nabopolassar regained control of Babylon and established the Neo-Babylonian dynasty (*c*.625–539 BC). It is a measure of the Chaldaeans' political and economic abilities that his illustrious successor, Nebuchadnezzar II, was able to raise Babylon to its greatest period of prosperity.

M. Dietrich: *Die Aramäer Südbabyloniens in der Sargonidenzeit* (700–648) (Neukirchen-Vluyn, 1970); J. Oates: *Babylon*, 2nd edn (London, 1986), 110–35.

IS

Cham Austronesian language spoken in the powerful polities which developed in coastal Vietnam in the 1st millennium AD. The language has its closest parallels in island Southeast Asia, and some uncertainty surrounds the timing and nature of the initial settlement of Austronesian speakers in an area otherwise dominated by speakers of Austroasiatic languages.

The Cham ceremonial centre of Caban, located near Qui Nhon in Vietnam, was probably occupied between AD 800 and 1200 (although there are no inscriptions therefore the dating is uncertain). According to their own inscriptions, the Cham-speaking occupants of the coastal tract of central Vietnam divided themselves into at least four regional polities: Amaravati, Vijaya, Kauthara and Panduranga. Each polity constructed major temple sanctuaries as well as walled enclosures. Caban, strategically located beside the confluence of two streams, may have been the centre of Vijaya. The site consists of a rectangular enclosure (1400 × 1100 m), orientated on the cardinal points of the compass, the centre of which is dominated by a large sanctuary structure.

Po Nagar was a Cham ceremonial centre within the polity of Kauthara, south Vietnam. The six surviving sanctuaries at Po Nagar were built between the 7th century AD and AD 1256 as foci for the worship of Siva. Like other Cham polities, Kauthara succumbed in the 13th century AD to the southward expansion of the Vietnamese.

Chau Xa, a small (*c*.25 ha) rectangular Cham settlement in the area of Amaravati, Vietnam, is surrounded by brick walls, a berm and moat, with traces of an extension wall to the south. Another fortified Cham centre in the Amaravati region was Tra Kieu, dating to the 1st millennium AD; it was excavated in the 1920s by J.Y. Claeys, who uncovered sanctuary foundations and a defensive wall. It has been suggested that Tra Kieu was the historic centre of Simhapura.

M.H. Parmentier: *Inventaire descriptif de monuments Cams de l'Annam* (Paris, 1918); J.Y. Claeys: 'Configuration du site de Tra-Kieu', *BEFEO* 27 (1927), 469–82.

CH

chamber tomb General term for all those collective tombs of the Neolithic and early Bronze Age period in Europe that have extant stone or rock-cut chambers. In fact, many earthen long barrows also originally had chambers, but these were of wood – recent excavations suggest that posts of monumental size were sometimes used – and have long since decayed. The usual features of a built chamber tomb include: the chamber(s) itself, with drystone or MEGALITHIC walls that support capstone(s) or

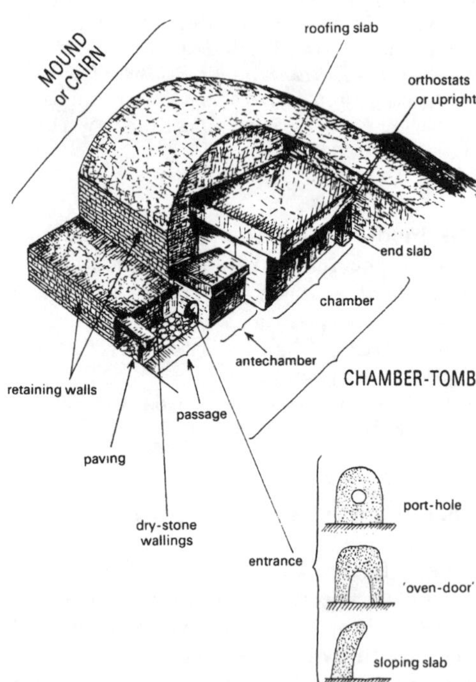

Figure 10 **chamber tomb** Archetypal three-dimensional reconstruction showing the different elements of a chamber tomb under its mound. *Source*: R. Joussaume: *Dolmens for the dead* (London, 1987), fig. 1.

corbelled roofs; an entrance, which may lead directly into the chamber or into a connecting passage; a covering mound of stone or earth, sometimes strengthened or retained with drystone walling; embellishments to the exterior of the tomb, such as a façade of megaliths, a forecourt in front of the entrance,or a kerb of stone slabs around the base of the mound. Chamber tombs in Europe, which in the main housed collective burials, are commonly divided into two main groups: GALLERY GRAVES and PASSAGE GRAVES.

R. Joussaume: *Dolmens for the Dead*, trans. A. and C. Chippindale (London, 1988).

RJA

Chan Chan Capital of the protohistoric Chimu kingdom, located in the Moche Valley, northern Peru, and dating to the Late Intermediate Period (AD 900–1438). The city consists of 11 huge walled enclosures (*ciudadelas*) which contain elaborate meeting, living, and storage facilities, and multi-roomed, platform-like burial structures, which originally contained huge quantities of sacrifices and goods. The *ciudadelas* are surrounded by smaller walled compounds, large areas of humble dwellings where craftworkers, farmers, labourers, and others lived, walk-in wells, sunken fields, and cemeteries, protected by a large wall on the north.

M.E. Moseley and K. Day, eds: *Chan Chan: Andean desert city* (Albuquerque, 1982); M.E. Moseley and A. Cordy-Collins eds: *The northern dynasties: kingship and statecraft in Chimor* (Washington, D.C., 1990).

KB

Ch'ang-sha (Changsha) *see* CH'U

Chanhu-Daro Three mounds dating to the 3rd millennium BC, located on the Indus river, 130 km south of MOHENJO-DARO in Pakistan. Excavated by Mackay in the 1930s, the site has been divided into three phases: Mature HARAPPAN and two post-Harappan periods (Jhukar and Jhangar). The Harappan architectural remains include rectangular structures built on mud-brick platforms and oriented with regard to a major street. Although the site had been much disturbed by brick robbing, excavations and surface survey have revealed extensive traces of Harappan manufacturing processes. Vidale (1989: 171, 181) has suggested that Chanhu-Daro was a small regional centre of the Harappan civilization whose inhabitants were involved in the manufacture of a number of important commodities, many of which were then transferred to Mohenjo-Daro and other urban centres of the INDUS CIVILIZATION.

E.J.H. Mackay: *Chanhu-Daro excavations 1935–36* (New Haven, 1943); M. Vidale: 'Specialized producers and urban elites: on the role of craft industries in Mature Harappan urban contexts', *Old problems and new perspectives in the archaeology of South Asia*, ed. J.M. Kenoyer (Madison, 1989), 171–81.

CS

Chansen Substantial moated site of the 1st millennia BC and AD, located in the Central Plain of Thailand. The cultural sequence has been divided into six phases, the first two of which are late prehistoric (800 BC–200 AD). The second has yielded an ivory comb decorated with a goose, two horses and Buddhist symbols reflecting early contact with India. The material from the second and third phases (200–650 AD) includes tin amulets, pottery stamps, decorated bronze bells and the stone moulds used to cast jewellery. These correspond to the finds from many other sites of a similar date which were in exchange contact with Indian merchants. This is further confirmed at Chansen by the presence of pottery which originated in Sri Lanka. In phase 5, a moat was constructed round the site, with a diameter of 640 m, associated with a rectangular reservoir. The increased quantity of pottery, and its parallels with sites of the DVARAVATI CULTURE, suggests that in its final two phases, the population grew and the site took its place as one of many large moated sites ascribed to the first civilization in the valley of the Chao Phraya River.

B. Bronson and G.F. Dales: 'Excavations at Chansen, Thailand, 1968, 1969: a preliminary report', *Asian Perspectives* 15/1 (1973) 15–46.

CH

chaos theory, chaology Branch of mathematics and science concerned with systems whose diachronic development (although governed by such deterministic equations as Newton's Law of Motion) is essentially unpredictable. A key characteristic of chaos theory is that it can help us to explain how major systemic changes can be sparked off by apparently minor changes in system variables. The term chaos was first used, in its scientific sense, by T.-Y. Li and J.A. Yorke (1975). Chaos theory is neither a scientific 'law' nor one particular view of the world – rather it is a collection of mathematical, numerical and geometrical techniques, which, according to Ali Çambel (1993: 16) manages to combine both determinism and chance within the same paradigm.

'Chaos' means the condition of 'unpredictability', in that complex systems of the type described above may quickly develop in unpredictable ways, although some features of the system can be statistically defined. An alternative means of defining and analysing complex systems is CATASTROPHE THEORY, which was developed by the French mathematician René Thom in 1972, and utilized as a means of explanation by some archaeologists in the late 1970s (particularly Colin Renfrew).

Archaeological applications of chaos theory have tended to revolve around environmental change. T.K. Park (1992), for instance, argues that relatively minor changes in weather may have resulted in the major social change apparent in the Nile valley during the late 4th and early 3rd millennia BC, and in the Jordan Rift in the 9th millennium BC. He points out that many early civilizations appear to have developed within the context of 'flood recession agriculture', with its 'potential for high returns per unit of labour', but that the emergence of social and economic stratification might be ultimately determined by 'the chaotic pattern of the floods'. Thus the inherent uncertainties of flood recession agriculture (i.e. the tendency for there to be occasional disastrously high or low floods) do not promote stability but instead encourage the development of both socio-economic stratification and diversification into other means of subsistence, such as foraging or pastoralism. Park (1992: 107) therefore suggests that the 'model of harmonious and balanced ecosystems' should be replaced by a model of 'continuously changing adaptations to a more chaotic environment'.

T.-Y. Li and J.A. Yorke: 'Period three implies chaos', *American Mathematical Monthly* 82 (1975), 985–92; J. Gleick: *Chaos: making a new science* (New York, 1987); T.K. Park: 'Early trends towards class stratification: chaos, common property, and flood recession agriculture', *American Anthropologist* 94 (1992), 90–117; A.B. Çambel: *Applied chaos theory: a paradigm for complexity* (San Diego and London, 1993).

IS

Charavines Neolithic village of the earlier 3rd millennium BC, situated on the edge of Lake Paladru in Isère, France. The site is now underwater and has yielded some of the best-preserved organic evidence of the French Neolithic. The village was occupied in two phases from about 2800 BC, and consisted of rectangular houses grouped together in rows. The approach to the settlement from the landward side was closed by a palisade. The structural timbers of the houses were remarkably well-preserved underwater, as were a range of wooden implements.

A. Bocquet and A. Houot: 'La vie au Néolithiques: Charavines, un village au bord d'un lac il y a 5000 ans', *Histoire et Archéologie, Les Dossiers*, vol. 64 (1982).

RJA

chariot pit-burials (China) *see* SHANG-TS'UN-LING

Charsada (anc. Pushkalavati, Peukolaotis) Multi-mound urban site dating from the 6th century BC to the 7th century AD, located along the Swat river near modern Peshawar, Pakistan. Charsada was excavated in 1958 by Mortimer Wheeler. Its four phases – pre-Alexander, Alexander, NORTHERN BLACK POLISHED WARE (NBPW) and Gandharan – include abundant evidence of international contacts, such as links with the Persian empire in the pre-Alexander period (*c*.530–327 BC). In the late 4th century BC, as the local capital of a small polity, Charsada was heavily fortified with ditches and ramparts. However, in 327 BC it was conquered by Alexander the Great and occupied for a brief time by Greek armies. In the ensuing NBPW period (300–150 BC) a local ceramic form, the 'lotus bowl', emerged.

R.E.M. Wheeler: *Charsada* (Oxford, 1962).

CS

Chasséen Cultural complex of the Middle Neolithic of France, broadly contemporary with – and related to – the other major cultural complexes of west-central Europe in the mid Neolithic, the MICHELSBERG and the CORTAILLOD. In the north of France it succeeds the first farming culture, the LINEARBANDKERAMIK, while in the south it succeeds groups transitional from the first pottery-using CARDIAL WARE cultures.

The Chasséen is named after the type-site Chassey-le-Camp (Cote-d'Or), and most authorities recognize the following cultural traits: fine, smooth-surfaced pottery, commonly round-based pottery with carinated rims, that is usually undecorated, except for a special class of highly decorated ritual ceramics called VASE SUPPORTS; a lithic industry that emphasizes blade technology; the use of honey-coloured flint over a wide area and the frequent occurrence of obsidian (implying extensive exchange networks); the occurrence of small polished stone balls or *billes*; association with ditched enclosures; in the south of France, the replacement of largely cave and rock-shelter sites with open-air settlements; the increasing use of interfluvials and plateau regions for farming, in contrast to earlier LBK valley bottom sites, and an apparent emphasis on wheat and barley crop growing with concomitant increase in the number of sickles and querns.

Culture or material culture complex? The Chasséen was first closely defined as a culture by Arnal (1950), and though the finer points of Arnal's subdivision of the Chasséen were quickly discarded as unworkable, the concept of a distinct and unitary Chassey culture took root. In many ways this was a logical way of interpreting the evidence: apart from the similarities between the material cultures evidenced in different regions, the middle Neolithic also saw the first evidence for prolonged contact between northeast France (the initial Neolithic of which was associated with an offshoot of the LBK phenomena) and the south and west, which developed their first farming communities more slowly and in contact with the other first farming cardial or Impressed Ware cultures of the Mediterranean. As the concept of the Chasséen became central to the understanding of the French Neolithic, archaeologists began to give the concept universal core features, and to assume that the material culture similarities implied a deeper ethnic homogeneity (an approach now characterized as the CULTURE HISTORY approach to archaeology). A central question in early discussions of the Chasséen culture was therefore where the 'culture' came from, or which region of France it formed in. Some authorities pointed to the similarity between some Chasséen decorative motifs and those on the square-mouthed pottery tradition in North Italy, others suspected local evolution in Languedoc.

More recently, however, there has been a shift of emphasis in understanding the Chasséen. Like other cultural phenomenon in prehistory (e.g. the BEAKER PHENOMENON) it is now seen as an agglomeration of cultural traits over time, which may not have been invented in the same region or in the same period, and which do not necessarily imply an ethnic identity. It is clear, for example, that the most distinctive ceramic manifestation of the Chasséen, the vase supports, are concentrated in certain areas (particularly Languedoc and Brittany), occur less frequently in other 'Chasséen' areas, and may not occur at all in other regions. Furthermore, in northern France the Chasséen at many sites is now recognized as having features of the Michelsberg cultural complex – at Jonquières there are both repoussé buttons and baking plates (Michelsberg) and vase supports (Chasséen) – which suggests that the term 'Chasséo-Michelsberg' might be more accurate than a term suggesting a single culture. Furthermore, research has begun to identify assemblages of an early Middle Neolithic character that do not seem to belong to the full Chasséen: Guilane (1970) has identified one such in western Languedoc, while Escalon de Fonton (1980) has identified another at Fontbrégoua in the Var.

J. Arnal: 'A propos de la "néolithisation" de l'Europe occidentale', *Zephyrus* 1 (1950), 23–7; J.P. Thévenot: 'Eléments Chasséens de la céramique de Chassey', *Revue Archéologique de l'Est*, 20 (1969), 7–95; J. Guilane, ed.: *Les civilizations Néolithiques du Midi de la France* (Carcassonne, 1970); A. Gallay: *Le néolithique moyen du Jura et des plaines de la Saône: contribution à L'etude des relations Chassey-Cortaillod-Michelsberg* (1977); M. Escalon de Fonton: 'Circonscription de Provence-Alpes-Côte-d'Azur', *Gallia Préhistoire* 23 (1980), 525–47.

RJA

'Chasséo-Michelsberg' *see* CHASSÉEN

Châtelperronian (Lower Périgordian) Stone industry of the Upper Palaeolithic, distinguished by the presence of curved BACKED BLADES (Châtelperron points), found in central and southwest France. The status of the Châtelperronian industry has formed a key debate in Upper Palaeolithic studies. Although technologically it is a blade-based industry, and therefore Upper Palaeolithic in nature, it has many characteristics of the MOUSTERIAN assemblages of the Middle Palaeolithic that in Europe are closely associated with Neanderthal populations. Though not yet certain, it seems likely that the Châtelperronian (like the SZELETIAN of central Europe and the ULUZZIAN of Italy) was produced by local Neanderthal populations acculturated by contemporary anatomically modern humans who were responsible for the AURIGNACIAN cultural assemblage. At certain key sites (e.g. ROC DE COMBES) this contemporaneity is attested by the inter-stratification of Aurignacian and Châtelperronian layers. In some of the literature, the Châtelperronian is called the 'Lower Périgoridan' and linked with a later industry characterized by backed blades, the GRAVETTIAN or 'Upper Périgordian'.

RJA

Chau Can *see* DONG SON CULTURE

Chauvet Cave Cave with mural art of the Upper Palaeolithic, located in the gorges of the Ardèche in south-east France. Discovered as recently as December 1994 by Jean-Marie Chauvet (after whom the cave is named) and others, the cave consists of a series of galleries and caverns over half a kilometre long decorated with single and grouped examples of paintings (red and, predominantly, black) and carvings of animals, and some hand stencils and signs. The cave will not be fully surveyed for some years, but estimates suggest Chauvet contains much higher concentrations of rhinoceroses and carnivores than most Upper Palaeolithic galleries: rhinos (provisional estimate of 22%), lions (17%), mammoths (16%), horses (12%), bison (9%), bears (5.5%) and reindeer (5%). There are also some interesting oddities: an anthropomorphic bison figure, recalling the anthropomorphized figure of the 'Sorceror' at LES TROIS-FRÈRES, and the first known Palaeolithic depiction of an owl. The technique at Chauvet is also surprising, with greater use of shading and infill than at comparable sites. Perspective is attempted in a number of drawings and, although the general effect is naturalistic, there seems a stronger than usual tendency to exaggerate or embolden an animal feature (especially horns) to strengthen the design; animal groups seem to be more strongly related to one another than at other sites, and may in some instances form compositions. Some of the panels also seem to be consciously balanced into two or three groupings of animals.

The first radiocarbon dates for Chauvet suggest a date for some of the art of around 30,000 BC (though the cave was revisited over thousands of years); this cuts across conventional understanding of the chronology of Upper Palaeolithic art – which would have placed the paintings after about 20,000 BC. If these dates are confirmed, Upper Palaeolithic mural art in a form as developed as that found at Lascaux must have been produced as early as some of the earliest mobiliary art and VENUS FIGURINES. As well as suggesting that still earlier examples of Palaeolithic art await discovery (perhaps among known but wrongly dated examples), such an early dating would deal a final blow to any simplistic evolutionary scheme of how the various styles in cave art developed across the millennia (*see* CAVE ART).

Jean-Marie Chauvet et al.: *Chauvet Cave: The discovery of the world's oldest paintings*, trans. P. Bahn (London, 1996).

RJA

Chavez Pass *see* GRASSHOPPER PUEBLO

Chavín Site located in the Mosna Valley (north central highlands, Peru), dating from 1000 to 400 BC. The centre of the first widespread religion and art style in Peru, Chavín has a series of large cut-stone constructions decorated with reliefs of supernatural felines, birds, and other associates of the deities, the Smiling God and the Staff God, whose cults spread over Peru, carrying with them the heddle loom, gold metallurgy, agriculture, hallucinogen use, and other traits.

R.L. Burger: *Chavín and the origins of Andean civilization* (London, 1992).

KB

Chemagel Late Iron Age site in the Sotik region of the south-western Kenyan highlands, incorporating a group of large 'SIRIKWA HOLES' identified as unroofed cattle-pens with attached houses.

JS

Chenes *see* RIO BEC/CHENES

Chibuene *see* MANEKWENI

Chichén Itzá Large Terminal Classic and Early Postclassic Maya site (dating *c.*AD 800–1200) in the north-central Yucatan Peninsula, one of the largest

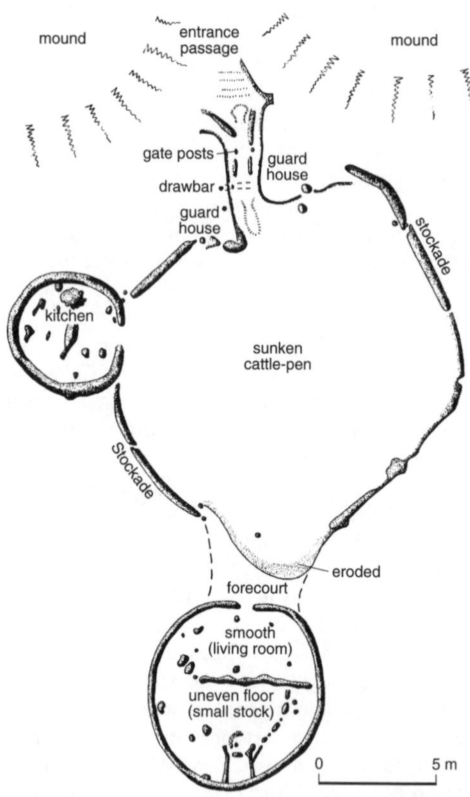

Figure 11 **Chemagel** Chemagel, an east African Iron Age settlement of the 'Sirikwa hole' type, as excavated in 1964. *Source*: J.E.G. Sutton: *A thousand years of East Africa* (BIEA, 1990), p. 44.

and wealthiest in Mesoamerica, perhaps best known for its complex architecture, its CENOTE and its huge ballcourt (*see* BALLGAME). The Chichén Itzá ballcourt is the largest in Mesoamerica, with a 'playing field' measuring some 146 m long and 36 m wide. The vertical sides of the court, 8 m in height, rise above a sloping, sculptured basal apron showing two teams of elaborately dressed players facing each other. The central figure is a decapitated player, with serpents of blood gushing from the headless neck. A large ball in front of the figure is decorated with a skull.

Chichén Itzá has often been called 'Toltec-Maya', because its architecture is a blend of Mexican and Maya traits. Some buildings are constructed in the PUUC Maya style, while others are built in what has been considered the TOLTEC style, with distinctive serpent columns, colonnades, CHACMOOL sculptures and benches with atlantean figures. Still other structures, such as the TZOMPANTLI (or 'skull racks'), show more general similarities with central Mexican architecture.

Chichén Itzá was the site of one of the earliest major archaeological projects in the Maya lowlands from 1923 to 1937, under the sponsorship of the Carnegie Institution of Washington and directed by the famous Maya archaeologist Sylvanus G. Morley. Despite this long period of excavations, the chronological position of Chichén Itzá – especially the relation of the Mexican and Maya architectural phases – is still poorly understood. The traditional interpretation of the site (Tozzer 1957) is strongly based on Mesoamerican legends telling of the flight of QUETZALCOATL from Tula, and Chichén Itzá was thought to have had two sequential (and ethnically distinct) building occupation periods: Maya and then intrusive Toltec. More recent analyses (Lincoln 1986) have argued for a much greater 'overlap' or even contemporaneity between the two episodes of the site, forcing a still-incomplete reconsideration of the Early Postclassic period in the northern lowlands.

A.M. Tozzer: *Chichén Itzá and its cenote of sacrifice: a comparative study of contemporaneous Maya and Toltec* (Cambridge, MA, 1957); C.E. Lincoln: 'The chronology of Chichén Itzá: a review of the literature', *Late lowland Maya civilization: classic to postclassic*, ed. J.A. Sabloff and E.W. Andrews V (Albuquerque, 1986) 141–96.

PRI

Ch'i-chia culture (Qijia) Early Neolithic culture in China, named after the type site at Ch'i-chia-p'ing, Kuang-ho-hsien, Kan-su. When Johan G. Andersson first reported it in 1923, he regarded it as the earliest of the Neolithic cultures, but this view was later demonstrated to be incorrect, since Chi'i-chia culture has generally been found stratigraphically later than the YANG-SHAO culture. Several hundred sites have been excavated, yielding pottery with some characteristic types, such as the flat-bottomed narrow-necked *kuan*-jar, and occasional finds of copper artefacts. Some of the latter may actually be intrusive from the Chung-Yüan culture.

J.G. Andersson: 'Researches into the prehistory of the Chinese', *BMFEA* 15 (1943); Chang Kwang-chih: *The archaeology of ancient China*, 4th edn (New Haven, 1986), 280–6.

NB

Chichimecs Semi-nomadic hunting and horticultural peoples living on the northwestern fringes of ancient Mesoamerica. The Chichimecs were generally regarded as 'barbarians' by the settled peoples to the south. A series of migrations during the epi-Classic and Postclassic (*c*.AD 700–1521) periods brought the Chichimecs into the BASIN OF MEXICO, where they gradually integrated and intermarried with urban, farming peoples of the basin. Many Postclassic peoples, including the TOLTECS, the Mexica or AZTECS and the TARASCANS, claim to have had their origins among the Chichimecs.

P. Kirchoff et al., eds: *Historia Tolteca-Chichimeca* (Mexico, 1976).

PRI

Ch'in (Qin) Ancient state located in the west of China (Shen-hsi and Kan-su) which was enfeoffed as one of the *chu-hou*, a princely state the rulers of which were given the title *kung* ('duke') by the Chou king, P'ing Wang. The honour was in return for services during the crucial period ultimately leading to the removal of the Chou capital in 771 BC to the east at Lo-yi (Lo-yang) – whence commences EASTERN CHOU. The Ch'in state was then established in the homeland of the Chou (*see* CHINA 2). As a consequence, the still extant styles of Late WESTERN CHOU in both pottery and bronze strongly influenced Ch'in art and design in the ensuing centuries; but concurrently, local Ch'in art merged with the adopted forms so giving rise to the sometimes rather crude castings, particularly in such vessels as *ting* and *kuei*, so characteristic of Ch'in bronzes during Ch'un-ch'iu times (771–481 BC). The innovative TUI appears in this period, while in Chan-kuo times (480–255 BC) such distinctive vessels as the *Mou*-vase and *Hu-Hu*-flask made their debut.

Archaeologically, early Ch'in is known for the

major bronze manufacturing sites around HOU-MA-CHEN, and the vast number of brush-written jade tablets (datable *c*.490 BC) containing 'oaths of allegiance' discovered among a complex of some 400 pits in which were buried 'sacrificial' animals (mainly sheep, some horses and cattle).

The distribution of characteristic tomb structures of Ch'in, many hundreds of which have been discovered throughout China, provide valuable evidence for the study of the rise and expansion of this state, including the ultimate subjugation of the other Chinese polities and their unification under Shih-huang-ti. This expansion of the Ch'in began during the 4th century BC with the annexation of the Sichuan region, and culminated in the period between their destruction of the decaying Chou dynasty in 256 BC and the assumption of the title 'First Emperor' (Shih-huang-ti) by the triumphant Ch'in king in 221 BC. The tomb of Shih-huang-ti, at Mount Li near Xian, contained vast amounts of funerary equipment, including 1400 life-size human figures, the so-called 'terracotta warriors' (see Cotterrell 1981; Li Hsüeh-ch'in 1988). Although the Ch'in empire was short-lived (221–207 BC), it decisively established the imperial theme that prevailed in China from the Han period (206BC–AD 220) practically up to the present day. In addition, the Ch'in empire unified key governmental and economic units (script, systems of measurement, currency etc) and introduced many aspects of Chinese officialdom and central government.

Anon.: *Hou-ma ming-shu* [The Hou-ma oaths of allegiance jade tablets] (Shanghai, 1976); M.K. Hearn: 'The terracotta army of the First Emperor of Qin (221–206 BC)', *The Great Bronze Age of China*, ed. Wen Fong (London, 1980), 351–68; A. Cotterrell: *The first emperor of China* (London, 1981); Li Hsüeh-ch'in: *Eastern Zhou and Qin civilization*, trans. Chang Kwang-chih (New Haven, 1985); ——: *Ch'in-shih-huang-ling ping-ma yung-k'ang* [The terracotta army of Ch'in Shih-huang-ti], 2 vols (Peking, 1988).

NB

Pre Shang	
Early Shang	2000 – 1650 BC
Middle Shang	1650 – 1400 BC
Late Shang	1400 – 1123 BC
Early Western Chou	**1122** – 1001 BC
Middle Western Chou	1000 – 878 BC
Late Western Chou	877 – 772 BC
Early Ch'un-ch'iu	**771** – 670 BC
Middle Ch'un-ch'iu	669 – 570 BC
Late Ch'un-ch'iu	569 – 482 BC
Early Chan-kuo	**481** – 395 BC
Middle Chan-kuo	394 – 310 BC
Late Chan-kuo	309 – 221 BC
Ch'in Shih Huang Ti	221 – 210 BC
Erh Shih Huang Ti	209 – 208 BC
San Shih Huang Ti	207 BC
Western Han	206 BC – 24 AD
Eastern Han	25 – 220 AD
Three Kingdoms	221 – 264 AD
Western Chin	265 – 316 AD
Eastern Chin	317 – 419 AD
Northern & Southern Dynasties	420 – 581 AD
Sui	581 – 617 AD
T'ang	618 – 906 AD
Five Dynasties	907 – 960 AD
(Liao 907 – 168)	
(Chin 1115 – 1234)	
Sung	960 – 1126 AD
(Southern Sung 1127 – 1280)	
Yuan	1280 – 1368 AD
Ming	1368 – 1644 AD
Ch'ing	1644 – 1911 AD

Note:
The chronology presented in the above table is generally based upon the orthodox system. Note that there is no Hsia period; this could be considered to lie somewhere in the 'Pre-Shang' section, while Shang comprises essentially the archaeological eras: Erh-li-t'ou, Erh-li-kang, and An-yang. These three sub-divisions of Shang are assessed with reference to both radiocarbon and orthodox dates, and then 'rounded-off' mathematically. Orthodox dates from the Chou conquest of Shang onwards are highlighted by bold figures. Each of the periods: Western Chou, Ch'un-ch'iu, and Chan-kuo, are mathematically sub-divided into equal parts. From Ch'in onwards, the dynastic divisions are highly simplified.

Table 10 **China** Chronology of China from the Shang period to modern times.

China The present-day boundaries of China cover an area of about 9,600,000 sq. km: slightly less than Europe, slightly more than the USA. There is considerable variation in the topography, climate and vegetation, including the subarctic *taiga* of Manchuria, the arid deserts and steppes of Mongolia, the cold inhospitable wastes of the Tibetan plateau, the highly fertile Red Basin of Ssu-ch'uan, the temperate alluvial plains of the Yellow River Valley, the river-dissected tablelands of the southeast and the semi-tropical hill-country of the Liang-kuang.

The major rivers flow more or less 'horizontally' across to the Pacific in a west–east direction, only to a small extent running through different major climatic and vegetational zones. There are various detailed geographical and cultural subdivisions of

China, although the country can be demarcated simply into Northern, Central and Southern China. The Yellow River Valley played a special role in the establishment of the formative eras of the Chinese civilization, following the advent of metallurgy and then writing (*see* EASTERN CHOU, WESTERN CHOU *and* SHANG.) Chang Kwang-chih (1986) has therefore made the useful proposal that China should be divided into three ecological areas: the Yellow River Valley, the 'southern deciduous zone', and the 'northern forests and steppes zone'.

1. *Prehistory*. As a result of tremendous advances in archaeological discovery over the last few decades, the concept of the Chung-yüan (the central plains of the Yellow River Valley) as the fountainhead of Chinese civilization and culture has been challenged, and its significance will doubtless be open to some further degree of modification, but probably not in its entirety. The debate hinges on the question of what constitutes a 'civilization' and what is to be accepted as the starting point thereof. Neolithic cultures, and their Palaeolithic antecedents, throughout continental China are now seen to have contributed appreciably towards the ultimate development of civilization in the Chung-yüan, no less than the comparable contributions of their counterparts have in other cultural regions of the ancient world.

By *c*.5000 BC several distinct regional Neolithic cultures had crystallized: YANG-SHAO, TA-WEN-K'OU, MA-CHIA-PANG, HO-MU-TU and TA-P'EN-KENG; during the ensuing two millennia, interconnections gradually developed between them (see map 20, showing the diagrammatic distribution of the principal Neolithic cultures). Foci of research and interpretation in Chinese archaeology now tend towards appraisals of the settlement patterns, the nature of building construction, social organization, religious practices, and various other aspects of daily life that can be determined from archaeological context, such as the extent of agriculture and domestication of animals, the variety of prey hunted or fished, and the technical levels of lithic and ceramic industries. Much of the better-preserved data naturally derive from funerary goods and are systematically studied in terms of the site stratigraphy, particularly with reference to ceramics, which offer significant variations in the materials employed, developments in mode of manufacture (in particular, the increasing use of the potters' wheel), and developments in design and decoration. SERIATION of such site data, often allied with the results of radiocarbon (and occasionally thermoluminescence) dating, have provided chronological frameworks – of varying levels of dependability – which form the bases for comparisons between one

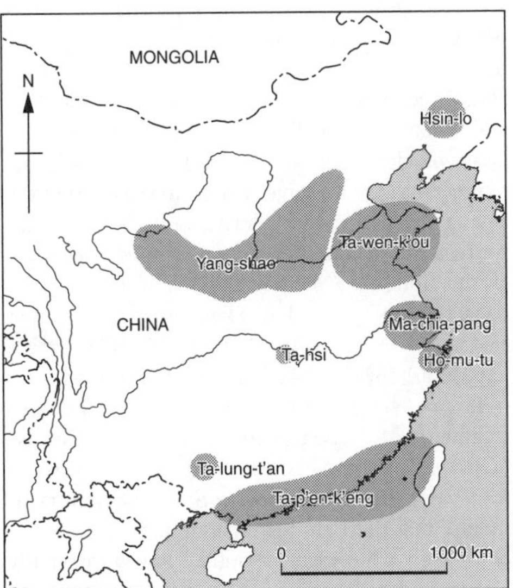

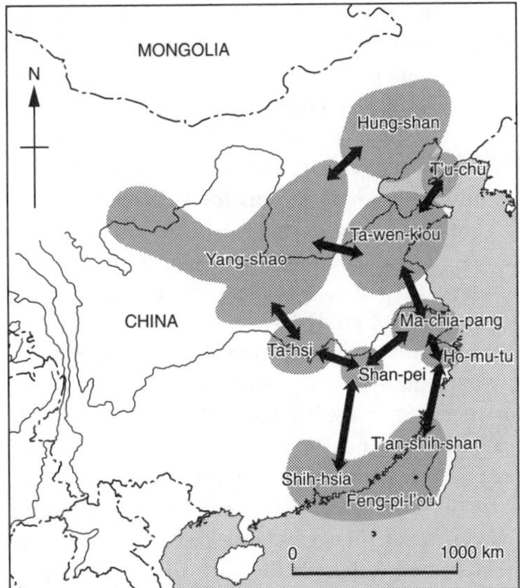

Map 20 **China** The distribution of the main Neolithic cultures of China, c.5000 BC (left) and *c*.4000–3000 BC (right). The arrows on the right indicate interactions between the various later cultures. *Source*: Chang Kwang-chih: *The archaeology of ancient China*, 4th ed. (New Haven and London, 1986).

site-area and another, or one cultural region and another.

Current research is now gradually being influenced by the proposed division of China into seven or eight cultural regions (see Su Ping-ch'i and Yin Wei-chang 1981), but most of these investigations have so far been concerned with Neolithic antecedents. Towards the close of the Neolithic era (i.e. at the advent of the various LUNG-SHAN and CH'I-CHIA cultures), with the loom of the 'historical' era embracing traditional text accounts of the San-tai (the 'Three Dynasties': HSAI, SHANG, and Chou) on the horizon, there has arisen considerable debate regarding the alleged existence of the Hsia dynasty as detailed in literary accounts. Many arguments have been advanced which seek to identify the early 2nd millennium ERH-LI-T'OU culture of the Chung-yüan as Hsia, and the following ERH-LI-KANG culture as either Hsia or Early Shang.

The earliest dependable evidence of metallurgical production that has come to light derives from Lung-shan sites in the Chung-yüan, such as T'AO-SSU. The current excavations of sophisticated copper mining complexes at T'UNG-LING, sections of which have been radiocarbon dated to *c.*1500 BC, have provided supplementary evidence relevant to the beginnings of metallurgy in China, now assessed to have been somewhat earlier than 2000 BC.

In recent years, further investigations into the nature of the centrifugal diffusion of metallurgical technology from the Chung-yüan into the peripheral 'barbarian' regions has been rewarding. In these regions both technological and artistic adaptations and modifications of the Chung-yüan bronze casting methods were in progress. At the same time, there was also an intermingling of the local foundry practices with alien technologies and art infiltrating these regions from cultural spheres far outside the modern boundaries of China. A reverse flow of the new technologies towards the Chung-yüan was to take place late in Chou times. This avenue of study has thrown further light on the independent nature of the origins of metallurgy in the Chung-yüan. However, it has also provided instructive commentary on the way in which several of the non-metal-using cultures in these regions were later to achieve the level of 'states' and, in their development of local bronze founding industries, sought to emulate aspects of the Chung-yüan culture (often on the basis of long outdated art-forms).

G.B. Cressey: *China's geographic foundations* (New York, 1951); Su Ping-ch'i and Yin Wei-chang: 'Kwan-yü k'ao-ku-hsüeh wen-hua ti chü-hsi-lei-hsing wen-t'i' [Problems regarding the classification of archaeological cultural regions], *WW* 5 (1981), 10–17; Chang Kwang-chih: *The archaeology of ancient China*, 4th edn (New Haven, 1986); N. Barnard: 'Thoughts on the emergence of metallurgy in pre-Shang and Early Shang China and a technical appraisal of relevant bronze artifacts of the time', *BMM* 19 (1993), 3–48.

2 *History: Shang and Chou.* The Shang dynasty comprised about 30 kings whose seats of power were located variously in the eastern and northern parts of northern Ho-nan, northern An-hui, and western Shan-tung; the capital is said to have been shifted five times in this general area. Traditional literary accounts show that the rule of Shang lasted from 1766 to 1122 BC, and that the last move of the capital, in *c.*1375 BC, was to Yin (now AN-YANG). This move was instigated by P'an-keng, the 24th king of the dynasty. Sometimes the term Yin is applied to the ensuing period, although the name does not actually appear with reference to Shang until after the Chou conquest (1122 BC).

The Shang people of the ORACLE BONE INSCRIPTIONS actually refer to themselves as Shang, and reference is also made to Ta-yi-Shang ('the great city, Shang'), and T'ien-yi-Shang (the 'heavenly city, Shang') which some believe to have been a major city located elsewhere, prior to the move. This period, conventionally rounded off as 1400–1122 BC, constitutes the archaeo-historical era of Late Shang. Most of what is known about Early Shang (2000–1650 BC) and Middle Shang (1650–1400 BC), over and above the results of archaeological discovery, derives from the less dependable traditional literature. The exotic picture of the Shang period presented by the literary sources is of Arthurian proportions and validity, and it contrasts vividly with the extensive array of archaeological evidence. It should be realized, too, that even the reign-lengths used to reconstruct the Shang dynastic tables, derive only from literary sources compiled a millennium or more later, such as the Shih-chi ('memoirs of the historian'), the BAMBOO ANNALS, and the Han-shu, a situation that also holds largely for WESTERN CHOU. These reign lengths are therefore no less open to question.

It is evident from the content of the 100,000 or so fragments of incised ORACLE BONE, and tortoise *plastrons*, that have come to light since 1899 (when they were first recognized as Shang period documents) that the Late Shang administration system comprised a 'network' of walled towns under the Shang king's suzerainty. The imposition of his suzerainty was apparently effected by a combination of military might and, possibly, the manifold varieties of ritual ceremonies. Oracle-bone entries record numerous military and punitive expeditions, while the role of the hunt (which is one of the most frequently mentioned royal activities) may well be significant. The numerous place-names recorded in connection with both military and hunting expeditions offer plenty of opportunity for academic argument among those who attempt to identify the archaic names with present-day geographical features and similarly named localities.

Such documents as the records of expeditions to Ch'iang-fang ('the Ch'iang regions') for the capture of Ch'iang peoples as well as for sacrificial and menial purposes, have been eagerly cited by Marxist-inspired writers in an effort to follow the Marxist model of history. (The nature of the *chung* ('the multitudes') would need to be defined without bias, as a step towards clarification of the status and role of peasants, craftsmen, and soldiers in Shang society.) Thus the 'approved' periodization of Chinese history since 1949 follows the evolutionary stages of human society according to Marx and Engels (and Kuo Mo-jo's interpretations thereof): primitive society, slave society, feudal society, and capitalistic society (see Kuo Mo-jo 1954). Much has been written on the problems of 'periodization' since 1945 (when Kuo changed his earlier interpretation of Shang as a 'primitive society' to that of a 'slave society'). There are more than a score of 'systems' which attempt to establish the date of the Chou conquest of Shang which, in both the archaeological literature (inscribed bronze ritual vessels) and the traditional literary sources, is ascribed to Wu Wang, the first king of the newly established dynasty. These systems disagree on the date of the conquest (which ranges from 1122 BC – the orthodox date used here – to 1111, 1110, 1088, 1078, 1075, 1066, 1063, 1050, 1045, 1027 and 1018 BC), and there is also conflict among the historico-literary sources with regard to the reign-lengths of individual kings.

The Bamboo Annals have exerted a considerable influence on the chronological problem but the value of this semi-archaeological document as an historical source is very much open to question. Attempts to establish the chronology have further sought to employ astronomical data as recorded in the traditional literature along with reign-years and event-dates recorded in the bronze inscriptions, but these generally lack the names of the kings in question, and only occasionally record the year of reign, while there are numerous problems attending the interpretation of the events recorded. Art-historical assessments of vessel typology and decoration are often cited in support of one favoured chronology or another. To sum up, however, unless some major find of unambiguous purport turns up, the problem of Shang and Chou chronology will remain unsolved and continue to fuel academic exercises of debatable value.

The Chou dynasty, comprising 35 rulers, was originally located in the area of present-day Chou-yuan. It established its hegemony over Shang and most of the then 'civilized' (as opposed to 'barbarian') areas of China, instituting an administrative system similar to Western-style feudalism. The first half of the period is termed WESTERN CHOU (1122–771 BC), which ends with the transfer of the ROYAL DOMAIN eastwards from Hao and Feng (near present-day Hsi-an) to Lo-yi (near Lo-yang). This is followed by the EASTERN CHOU period (770–255 BC), which in turn is divided into the Ch'un-ch'iu and Chan-kuo phases (770–482 BC and 481–221 BC respectively). With the ascendancy of CH'IN towards the close of the Chan-kuo period, the last decades of this phase are sometimes classed as falling within the Ch'in period.

Since the establishment of the modern political regime in China, the Chinese use of the term 'feudalism' (rendered as *feng-chien*) has been influenced by ideology. The so-called feudal institutions in China are actually quite different to those of the late 9th to early 13th centuries AD in western and central Europe, from which the term feudalism (*feodalus*, *feodalité*) derives. However, because of the preoccupation of Chinese writers with the existence of a 'slave society' during Shang, the concept of a 'feudal society' has been extended from Chou to Ch'ing.

The Western Chou period, at its inception and for several centuries thereafter, manifests many of the characteristics of feudalism as detailed by Ch'i Ssu-ho (1948) and further elaborated by Creel (1970). However, the latter's working definition of feudalism, as 'a system of government in which the ruler personally delegates limited sovereignty over portions of his territory to vassals' (Creel 1970: 320), is, like most others, open to debate. Nevertheless, there exist a remarkable number of similar features, so much so that it is as well to recollect Marc Bloch's observation: 'it is by no means impossible that societies different from our own should have passed through a phase closely resembling that which has just been defined. If so, it is legitimate to call them feudal during that phase' (Bloch 1961: 446).

During Eastern Chou (771–255 BC) the power of the Chou kings reached a low ebb and with the rise of the 'Five Hegemons' (*wu-pa*), powerful rulers of states who, one after the other, practically usurped the royal functions and authority, the Chou kings became little more than figureheads. In the Chan-kuo period a picture of internecine warfare emerged. It was during this phase that the rulers of such states as WU, YÜEH, LU and CH'U, which came into prominence early in Eastern Chou times, generally adopted feudal titles and even the title of 'king'. They also claimed lineage, or inter-marriages, with the Chi-surnamed royal family of the Chou dynasty, and records of their forebears having assisted the founder kings Wen and Wu in the conquest of Shang abound in the traditional literature.

From the close of the Ch'un-ch'iu period, the traditional texts which are considered to have been compiled during this period, present a wealth of information on many aspects of contemporary Chinese administration, society, thought, warfare and history in general. The form in which we now know them, however, is mainly the result of Han period recensions: contemporary archaeological versions are limited, since recent finds mainly derive from Han-period burials.

There is a vast literature in Chinese emanating from such scholars as Tung Tso-pin, Ch'en Meng-chia, Hu Hou-hsuan and Chang Cheng-lan. These works are based on the oracle bones and cover many aspects of the Shang period (see Keightley 1978).

Ch'i Ssu-ho: 'Chou-tai hsi-ming-li k'ao' [An investigation into the investiture ceremony of the Chou Period], *YCHP* 23 (1947), 197–226; ——: 'A comparison between Chinese and European feudal institutions', *YJSS* 4 (1948): 1–13; Kuo Mo-jo: Chung-kuo ku-tai she-hiu yen-chiu (Peking, 1954); N. Barnard: 'A recently excavated bronze of Western Chou date' *MS* 17 (1958), 12–46; M. Bloch: *Feudal society* (London, 1961); H.G. Creel: *The origins of statecraft in China* (Chicago, 1970); N. Barnard: 'The Nieh Ling Yi', *JICS* 9 (1978), 585–628; D.N. Keightley: *Sources of Shang history: the oracle-bone inscriptions of Bronze Age China* (Berkeley, 1978); ——: 'The Bamboo Annals and Shang-Chou chronology', *HJAS* 38/2 (1978), 423–38; Chang Kwang-chih: *Shang civilization* (New Haven, 1980); D.W. Pankenier: 'Astronomical dates in Shang and Western Chou' *EC* 7 (1981/2), 2–37; D.N. Keightley, ed.: *The origins of Chinese civilization* (Berkeley, 1983); Chang Kwang-chih, ed.: *Studies of Shang archaeology* (New Haven, 1986); D.N. Keightley: *The archaeology of ancient China*, 4th edn (New Haven, 1986); E.L. Shaughnessy: 'The "Current" Bamboo Annals and the date of the Zhou conquest of Shang', *HJAS* 46/1 (1986), 149–80; N. Barnard: 'Astronomical data from ancient Chinese records and the requirements of historical research methodology', *East Asian History* 6 (1993), 47–74.

3 *Writing and texts.* The Chinese script employed throughout the vast literary heritage of China, from Han times up to the latest issue of such archaeological journals as *Wen-wu* ('cultural relics') and *K'ao-ku* ('archaeology'), is very close in principle to that preserved in the oracle bones, inscriptions on bronze and other artefacts. Many extant characters in common use today are directly descended from those used in pre-Han times. There are, of course, numerous obsolete characters to be noted throughout the archaeological documents; these create some difficulties in interpretation. Nevertheless, the links between the culture of 'modern China' and that of the past two millennia ('imperial China', from Han to Ch'ing i.e. 220 BC–AD 1911), and the preceding two millennia (the 'era of cultural foundations', from early Shang to Ch'in: *c.*2000–221 BC) constitute a unique cultural continuum spanning four millennia.

Incised graphs on ceramics of pre-Shang date comprise some of the earliest examples of Chinese 'characters'. Although many are of uncertain significance, many recent studies are devoted to the important role that these ceramic markings appear to have played in the development towards true characters. There is, however, no evidence to suggest that the markings were combined to form sentences. It was not until Middle to Late Shang times that a written language developed. Systematic study of the ceramic symbols has resulted in the interesting discovery, however, that quite a few signs are repeated over a wide geographical range of sites – a situation that may well be relevant to the development of the Chinese character (Cheung 1983: 323–91); not unexpectedly, too, those markings which appear fairly certainly to be numerals have the greater incidence. Strings of 'characters' such as those incised on pottery in the Wu-ch'eng-ts'un find are – like the bronze artefacts found there – probably local emulations of the contemporary Shang script, made without an actual understanding of 'writing'.

The practice from Late Shang to Chou times of incorporating records of contemporary significance cast in bronze (as opposed to being incised into the metal, which does not occur until the late Ch'un-ch'iu period) has resulted in the gradual recovery of a large corpus of bronze 'documents'. Publications of numerous repositories of bronze inscriptions have appeared over the last 900 years; these texts (excluding repeated inscriptions) amount to almost 10,000 items. Most are unprovenanced, and a large number of doubtful materials are present. However, the gradual increase in archaeological exploration in China from the 1920s, and especially the tremendous momentum since the 1950s, has resulted in the controlled excavation of some 3300 new bronze inscriptions. This corpus of well-provenanced historical documents is now available as a means of control. Inscriptions range from large documents of 500 or so characters to groups of as few as five or six characters. Inscriptions of less than five characters are generally of the 'clan-sign' type (i.e. the phrase 'X has cast this vessel' followed by a clan-sign). Interpretations of the archaeological documents still tend to be influenced too strongly by long-established concepts engendered by the traditional literature. Nevertheless, studies over the last century, and particularly over the last few decades, have succeeded in clarifying the nature of the culture and civilization of Shang and Chou (*see* CHINA 2 *above*). The bronze documents, however, being the products of the ruling classes, naturally require supplementary evidence from the widest possible range of archaeological data to obtain a reasonably reliable and more general view of the society of the time.

The earliest examples of brush-written characters are on Shang oracle bones and ceramics. Presumably, during Late Shang and Western Chou bamboo, wood, and perhaps even silk, provided the ground for the writing of substantial amounts of text. It was not until Late Ch'un-ch'iu (*c*.600 BC), however, that writings on these materials entered the archaeological context. The most common surviving brush-written texts are INVENTORIES OF TOMB FURNISHINGS, usually recorded on wooden or bamboo strips. Other subjects include writings on fortune-telling, laws and ordinances, lists of punishments and state annals.

As far as writings on silk are concerned, the longest surviving single text is the Ch'u silk manuscript, which was the product of tomb robbery in Ch'ang-sha in the 1930s and is about 950 characters in length. From Han tombs, however, there are particularly impressive finds of archaeological documents such as those from WU-WEI (Mo-chui-tzu), Kan-su; Yün-meng (Shui-hu-ti), Hu-pei; Lin-yi-hsien (Yin-chüeh-shan), Shan-tung; HSIN-YANG, Ho-nan; Ch'ang-sha, and Pao-shan, Hu-pei. The subject-matter comprises tomb inventories, astrological works, maps, medical works, contemporary versions of the transmitted traditional literature, and lost texts of various kinds. The documents are often of substantial size; many are written on strips of bamboo or wood and bound together with cord, while others are written on scrolls of silk.

Recovery of textual data from ancient burials has invariably been heralded in China as an event of special importance. There has been a tradition of palaeographic studies, literary, philosophical, and historical writing, and textual criticism for 2000 years. Since Han times, these efforts have been directed towards (and in turn strongly tempered by) the traditional literature. The accumulated background of archival and intellectual activity, which is embodied in a vast volume of publications, many of the extant original printings of which date back to Sung times (*c*.AD 1100), is now receiving renewed attention from a variety of directions.

Research devoted to the newly discovered archaeological documents is gradually being published. Studies of the new materials have led to intensive researches into the traditional literature and have already resulted in revisions, modifications, and confirmations of age-old concepts. There is a constant process of review concerning the interpretations of individual characters, phrases, and even whole passages of text, as preserved throughout numerous commentaries from Han times. A renaissance in the age-old study of the traditional literature has thus been in progress over the last few decades, and has exerted a considerable influence over interpretations of archaeological data.

Tsien Tsuen-Hsuin: *Written on bamboo and silk: the beginnings of Chinese books and inscriptions* (Chicago and London, 1963); M. Loewe: *Records of Han administration*, 2 vols (Cambridge, 1967); N. Barnard: *The Ch'u silk manuscript: translation and commentary* (Canberra, 1973); Cheung Kwong-yue: 'Recent archaeological evidence relating to the origin of Chinese characters', *Origins of Chinese civilization*, ed. D.N. Keightley (Berkeley, 1983), 323–91.

4. The history of the archaeology of China. Two major features have characterized research and writing since the beginnings of modern archaeology in China over 60 years ago. First, there has been widespread use of western-style approaches in fieldwork, as well as the adoption (and adaptions) of western-style interpretational assessments of the data unearthed. Where these activities are directed to pre-Shang Neolithic contexts, the approach differs little from that of archaeology in other prehistoric cultural spheres. There are, however, fewer applications of the mathematical and statistical approaches of 'NEW ARCHAEOLOGY', the nature of which has only recently begun to be discussed in China (e.g. Huo Wei 1992).

Not unexpectedly, the more impressive excavations which relate so closely to the formative eras of Chinese culture, from Early Shang to Ch'in (*c*.2000–221 BC) occupy much the larger proportion of the published reports and associated studies. This is largely because of the vast quantity of textual documentation unearthed: oracle bone texts, inscribed bronzes, bamboo tablets, and silk manuscripts. We have already noted the marked effect of the traditional literature (and also, since 1949, that of 19th- and 20th-century ideological influences) upon the manner in which the overall archaeological context is assessed.

The influx of western influences is to be noted mainly in the conduct of fieldwork (since the late 1920s), museum conservation (from the 1950s), applications of science (from the 1970s), systematic methods in the study of archaeological data (gradually, but with increasing acumen, over the whole period), and, over the last decade a welcome tendency among some writers to break away from the ideological restraints imposed since 1949. The importance of archaeological data to the historian has, of course, long been realized. Indeed, we should recall that before the modern era China had already developed critical approaches to history, notably in the 17th and 18th centuries, although these unfortunately languished until the late 19th century. Revivals of historical criticism thence stemmed from the works of K'ang Yu-wei, Hu Shih, Ku Chieh-kang, Liang Chi-ch'ao, and others who were strongly influenced by (or had studied in) the West. In the realm of archaeology, however, it was mainly through the persuasive expositions of the theoretical evolutionary models of Marx and Engels by Kuo Mo-jo in the 1930s, that these politically acceptable (albeit somewhat antiquated and materialistic) approaches were to come into their own after the events of 1949. They still remain an issue to be weighed carefully by users of Chinese archaeological reports and secondary writings.

Considerable time and effort is spent on the reconstruction and repair of archaeological artefacts but, unfortunately, often without subjecting the materials to thorough scientific scrutiny beforehand so as to elicit all data of possible significance. Much of the reconstruction work, however, is of a high standard – especially where materials of exceptional significance are concerned, e.g. the bronze chariot and horses (No. 2) found in a pit burial to the west of the tomb mound of Shih-huang-ti, the 'terracotta army' to the east of the mound, numerous individual items ranging from Neolithic pottery through textiles, brush-written bamboo tablets, lacquer-ware, to gold, silver, bronze and iron artefacts. Owing to the ravages of time and burial conditions, restoration work is also occupied with the production of facsimile representations of the original artefacts; the results are usually excellent. Possibly, these activities might seem to savour of the financial aspects of 'making the past work for the present'. The preparation of major archaeological sites as tourist attractions, some with especially constructed buildings to house them (and museums to display the treasures unearthed), and, of course, the organization of overseas exhibitions, are all excellent money-making investments.

This contrasts with the rudimentary level of preservation of archaeological artefacts characteristic of numerous provincial and lesser museums, despite the continual appearance of articles relating to conservation techniques in the archaeological journals. The frequent instances of untreated 'bronze disease' among items on display is but one indication of this. Few such museums have proper conservation facilities let alone staff with adequate expertise to engage even in stop-gap measures. There are, of course, exceptions to be observed among the comparatively few better-endowed museums where conservation activities and laboratory research have progressed appreciably – often the latter is conducted in co-operation with outside research laboratories.

Scientific examination of the materials unearthed has progressed well in several archaeological institutes and museums, but there is an appreciable lack of equipment and qualified staff, while a considerable quantity of potentially valuable data remains unexamined, or incompletely examined, in many institutes and museums throughout the country – much of it lying dormant in store-rooms where access is limited. Generally, however, this situation has been balanced by the extensive publication of detailed and exact measurements of site areas, building foundations, kilns, skeletal remains, and of the vast quantities of artefacts unearthed; as well as the considerable proportion of fine quality drawings, décor rubbings, adequate and gradually improving photographic coverage, and quite detailed descriptive notes on individual artefacts. Along with these data, radiocarbon assessments, elemental analyses, microscopic examinations, and other such laboratory-derived information are occasionally incorporated where the institutes concerned have been fortunate enough to obtain the interest of outside laboratories to undertake such work.

Because of the comparative paucity of scientifically derived information, and the lack of experience of many of the report compilers in the use of such data (when it does become available), misleading interpretations occur at times. One has to turn to the reports on major finds to discover examples of the more extensive and reliable applications of laboratory examination, or to such periodic publications as *Tzu-jan k'o-hsüeh-shih yen-chiu* [Studies in the History of Natural Science], Peking, and *Wen-wu pao-hu yü k'ao-ku k'o-hsüeh*

[Sciences of Conservation and Archaeology], Shanghai. Although techniques of dating archaeological remains such as thermoluminescence are in use, radiocarbon assessments have played the major role to date. Dendrochronological conversions still continue to follow the DLW (Damon, Long and Wallick) tables of 1972. In using the radiocarbon data, care is required. Sampled materials and their site associations are not always clear, while risky materials such as shell and bone are usually allowed the same status as more reliable charcoal, wood, etc. In the case of wood, however, it is seldom indicated specifically where the sample has been taken (e.g. from heart-wood or sap-wood). Radiocarbon-dated sites that have been reported with merely a single dated sample are treated in the archaeological literature on much the same level as sites with multiple dates, and clusters thereof. Far too often 'mid-point dates' are regarded as the actual date! Secondary studies using these data require careful assessment at practically all stages of reading. However, improvements have steadily been taking root: An Chi-min's recent assessment of the nature of the anomalies attending the Neolithic periodization in South China on the basis of radiocarbon dates (An Chin-min 1989: 123–33), is an indication of current trends towards more cautious interpretative approaches.

Replication experiments involving the reconstructions of kilns, the baking of pottery, reconstructions of smelting furnaces, the casting of bronze vessels of various types in mould-assemblies following known ancient approaches, and other such experimental investigations, employing where possible comparable raw materials, have been conducted in both Mainland China and Taiwan. Very useful information at the technical level has resulted and this has allowed more effective assessments of the archaeological data.

Since the 1950s, and especially in the 1990s, the variety and rate of publication of Chinese archaeological reports has been phenomenal. In this dictionary, only a minute proportion of the available materials is cited directly – precedence has been given to English language sources (translations and secondary works) to enable the general reader to follow up on the thumbnail sketches offered here; of these, one or more items have been chosen – among other considerations – because of the extensive lists of reference materials consulted and recorded in them. For Chinese and Japanese language publications a free translation of titles is given. In the case of mainland Chinese reports where the authorship comprises one or more institutes – a most awkward custom when it comes to the compilation of bibliographies – the practice adopted here is simply to use the term 'Anon.'.

Kuo Mo-jo: *Chung-kuo ku-tai she-hui yen-chiu* [Researches into Ancient Chinese Society] (Peking, 1930); A.W. Hummel: *The autobiography of a Chinese historian* (Leiden, 1931); C.S. Gardner: *Chinese traditional historiography* (Cambridge, MA, 1938); Li Chi and Wan Chia-pao: *Ku-ch'i-wu yen-chiu chuan-k'an* [Researches into ancient vessels], 5 vols (Taipei, 1964–72); Chang Ching-hsien: *Chung-kuo nu-li she-hui* [Chinese slave society] (Peking, 1974); Chang Kwang-chih: *Shang civilization* (New Haven, 1980); Lu Pen-shan and Hua Chüeh-ming: 'T'ung-lü-shan Ch'un-ch'iu lien-t'ung shu-lu ti fu-yüan yen-chiu' [Reconstructional researches into the Ch'un-ch'iu period smelting furnaces of T'ung-lü-shang], *WW* 8 (1981), 40–5; Anon.: *Ch'in-ling erh-hao t'ung-ch'e-ma* [The bronze horse and chariot No. 2 of the Ch'in Mound] (Peking, 1983); Anon.: *Ch'in-shih-huang-ling ping-ma yung-k'ang* [The terracotta warriors pit of the Ch'in-shih-huang-ti mound], 2 vols (Peking, 1988); An Chih-min: 'Hua-nan tsao-ch'i Hsin-shih-ch'i te ^{14}C tuan-tai ho wen-t'i' [Problems attending the early Neolithic periodization in South China on the basis of radiocarbon dates], *TSCYY* (1989), 123–33; Huo Wei: 'P'ing Ao Mi'Hsin k'ao-ku-chia-p'ai' [A critical assessment of the New Archaeology school in Europe and America], *SCWW* 1 (1992), 8–13.

NB

chinampa Aztec term for a highly productive system of raised-field intensive agriculture practised along the shallow lakeshore in central Mexico (and elsewhere), whereby rich organic muck from the lake bottom was dug up to build a network of rectangular plots. Canals between the plots provided drainage and allowed access by canoe. Chinampas were primarily associated with the AZTECS (in the Postclassic period) but may also have been constructed in TEOTIHUACAN times (the Classic period).

P. Armillas: 'Gardens in swamps', *Science* 174 (1971) 653–704.

PRI

Chinchorro Culture of northern coastal Chile and far southern coastal Peru, between *c.*4000 and 1000 BC. These were the only South American people to develop artificial MUMMIFICATION: internal organs were removed, sticks inserted along the limbs to make a rigid body, the muscles plumped out with grass; the body was then covered with clay, painted and given a mask of human hair. Not all Chinchorro bodies were given this treatment, but males, females and children in roughly equal numbers were mummified in this way.

B. Bittman: 'Revision del problema Chinchorro', Chungara-Arica 9 (1982), 46–79; B.T. Arriaza: *Beyond*

death: the Chinchorro mummies of ancient Chile (Washington, D.C., 1995).
KB

Ch'ing-lien-kang (Qingliangang) *see* TA-WEN-K'OU

Ch'i-shan (Qishan) *see* WESTERN CHOU

chi-squared test One of a number of ways of examining the 'fit' between two or more sets of DATA, or one set and a theoretical MODEL, when the data consist of the numbers of objects that fall into various categories, for example the numbers of artefacts of different types on two or more sites. Tests of a dataset against a model are known as GOODNESS-OF-FIT tests; comparisons of datasets give rise to CONTINGENCY TABLES.
S. Shennan: *Quantifying archaeology* (Edinburgh, 1988), 70–6; M. Fletcher and G.R. Lock: *Digging numbers* (Oxford, 1991), 115–25.
CO

Choga Mami Prehistoric site in eastern central Iraq, at the edge of the Mesopotamian plain. Excavations during the 1960s revealed strata of the late SAMARRA period (*c*.5000 BC) containing ceramics known as Choga Mami Transitional; this discovery is important since the upper strata at TELL ES-SAWWAN, the classic Samarra site, have been eroded away. The 'Transitional' ceramics resemble early UBAID pottery from sites in southern Iraq, such as Eridu and Hajji Muhammed, perhaps indicating that the origins of the Ubaid culture are to be found in the Samarra period. The late Samarra settlement at Choga Mami, as at Tell Songor in the Hamrin Basin, consists primarily of grid-planned multi-room buildings; like Tell es-Sawwan, it was contained within an enclosure wall.
Preliminary reports by J. Oates in *Sumer* 22/25 (1966, 1969) and *Iraq* 31/34 (1969, 1972); J. Oates: 'Choga Mami', *Fifty years of Mesopotamian discovery*, ed. J. Curtis (London, 1982), 22–9.
IS

Choga Mami Transitional *see* SAMARRA

Choga Zanbil *see* ELAM

Cholula Large site in Puebla, Mexico, occupied since Preclassic times but best known for the role it played in the Postclassic period (*c*.AD 900–1521). Cholula has been identified as a centre of the QUETZALCOATL cult, and its enormous main temple-pyramid, with episodes of Classic-period TALUD-TABLERO construction, is now surmounted by a Catholic church. Postclassic Cholula is also associated with the manufacture and wide distribution of a brightly-coloured, polychrome ceramic known as the 'Mixteca-Puebla' style.
I. Marquina, co-ord.: *Proyecto Cholula, Serie Investigaciones* 19 (Mexico, 1970).
PRI

Choris culture *see* NORTON TRADITION

Chorrera Series of related fishing and agricultural village cultures in coastal Ecuador during the Formative Period (*c*.3000–500 BC) whose ceramic style was traded and copied throughout Ecuador and may have influenced early ceramic styles, including the coastal CHAVÍN ones, of northern Peru. These cultures were instrumental in the development of long-distance trade networks to procure exotic stones and other items (including metal) for the emerging elites.
C. Zevallos Mendez: 'Informe preliminar sobre el Cementerio Chorrera, Bahia de Santa Elena, Ecuador', *Revista del Museo Nacional* 34 (1965–6), 20–7; K.O. Bruhns: 'Intercambio entre la costa y la sierra en el Formativo Tardío: nuevas evidencias del Azuay', *Relaciones culturales en el area ecuatorial del Pácifico durante la Epoca Precolombina*, ed. J.-F. Bouchard and M. Guinea (Oxford, 1989), 57–74.
KB

Chou dynasty (Zhou dynasty) *see* CHINA 2; EASTERN CHOU; WESTERN CHOU

Choukoutien Complex cave site near Beijing, China, where in 1927 Davidson Black found hominid fossils which he named *Sinanthropus Pekinensis* ('Peking Man'). The fossils have more recently been identified with HOMO ERECTUS although they differ from the early African examples. The lower deposits are now thought to date from *c*.4–500,000 BP. Unfortunately many of the original fossils were destroyed during the Second World War and only casts remain. The associated archaeological remains for this period resemble the developed Oldowan (*see* OLDUVAI) chopper/flake industries, although the ACHEULEAN, biface-based technology had by that point existed for nearly one million years in Africa.

Choukoutien is also noted for early evidence of the use of fire, although no identifiable hearths have been found, unlike those claimed for the roughly contemporary site of Terra Amata in France. The Upper Cave has yielded fossil hominids dating from 20–30,000 BP, which, whilst clearly modern, are said not to resemble modern Chinese.

H.L. Shapiro: *Peking man* (London, 1976); Jia Lanpo and Huang Weiwan: *The story of Peking man* (Oxford, 1990).
PG-B

Chou-yüan (Zhouyuan: 'the plains of Chou') Archaeologically rich area in China, *c.*70 km (east–west) by 20 km (north–south), which embraces mainly modern Fu-feng, Chi'-shan, Feng-hsiang and Wu-kung. Large numbers of inscribed bronzes (many from storage pit burials) figure prominently among the various finds from numerous sites in the area. However, the name 'Chou-yüan' has become associated with the excavations around Feng-ch'ü-ts'un, near Ch'i-shan-hsien, where two pits in the precincts of palace (or, temple?) remains radiocarbon dated to 1295–1241 BC have yielded over 17,000 ORACLE BONES, 292 of which were inscribed. These artefacts not only indicate the practice of SCAPULIMANCY by the Chou people but also shed light upon the nature of Chou civilization before it subjugated the SHANG city-state in 1122 BC. *See also* CHINA 2 *and* WESTERN CHOU.

Ch'en ch'uan-fang: *Chou-yüan yü Chou-wen-hua* [Chou-yüan and the Chou culture] (Shanghai, 1988).
NB

chron *see* PALAEOMAGNETIC DATING

Ch'u (Chu) Major Chinese state which flourished in the EASTERN CHOU period (771–255 BC), the legendary origins of which are ascribed to the reign of Ch'eng Wang of Chou (*c.*1100 BC), at which time it was named Ching. It was eventually extinguished by the CH'IN polity in 253 BC. At the height of its power, the state of Ch'u extended from eastern Shen-hsi to the lower Yangtze Valley and from the north well into Ho-nan and northern An-hui thence southwards as far as the Tung-t'ing Lake region in southern Hu-pei and northern Hu-nan.

Ch'u, along with WUR and YÜEH, was regarded as a more or less 'barbarian' entity outside the pale of the MIDDLE STATES. In terms of material culture, however, it was a highly cultured region with very advanced levels in mining technology, metallurgy, weaving and embroidery, woodworking and joinery, lacquerware, music, calligraphy, various writings and poetry. The bulk of Eastern Chou literary remains have been unearthed from various Ch'u sites. Poetry (rhymed metric verse) plays a leading role in the compilation of many of the bronze inscriptions (especially those from the state of Ts'ai under Ch'u suzerainty); while the Ch'u silk manuscript from Ch'ang-sha, includes sections of rhymed text which are among the longest unearthed to date. Very impressive finds such as the TS'AI HOU LUAN tomb, the TSENG HOU YI tomb, the HSI-CH'UAN, HSIA-SSU tombs, the Pao-shan Tomb No. 2, and the well-known Western Han period MA-WANG-TUI Tomb No. 1, along with such recent discoveries of the mining complexes at T'UNG-LÜ-SHAN, JUI-CH'ANG, and Nan-Ling, demonstrate the fact that Ch'u and several of the states under its control, comprised one of the most highly cultured regions of Ch'un-ch'iu and Chan-kuo times.

N. Barnard: 'The origin and nature of the art of Ch'u – a necessary prelude to assessments of influences from the Chinese sphere into the Pacific', *Proceedings of the First New Zealand International Conference on Chinese Studies* (Hamilton, 1972), 1–47; Li Hsüeh-ch'in: *Hou-ma ming-shu* [The Hou-ma oaths of allegiance texts] (Shanghai, 1976); ——: *Eastern Zhou and Qin civilizations*, trans. Chang Kwang-chih (New Haven, 1985).
NB

Ch'ü-fu (Qufu) Ancient city site in Shan-tung, China, which was the capital of LU, the territory enfeoffed to Po-ch'in, son of Tan, Duke of Chou, who, as tradition tells us, acted as regent during the

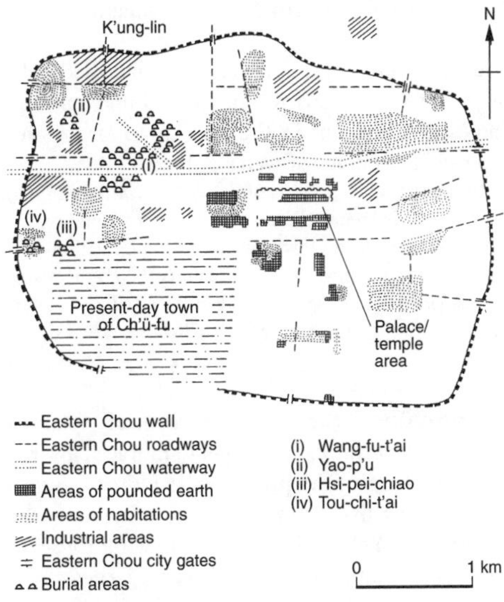

Figure 12 **Ch'ü-fu** Eastern Chou walled city of Ch'ü-fu (the capital of the kingdom of Lu), showing features of the city revealed in the 1977-8 excavations. *Source*: T.F. Munford: *Burial patterns of the Chou period: the location and arrangement of cemeteries in North China, 1000-200 BC* (Ph.D. thesis, Australian National University, 1985), fig. 6.

minority of Ch'eng Wang, the second king of the newly-established feudal kingdom of Chou which followed upon the SHANG conquest (1122 BC). Ch'ü-fu was also the birthplace of Confucius, who was supposedly also buried here. According to the Shih-chi [The memoirs of the historian], the burial of Confucius was to the north of Lu-ch'eng [Ch'ü-fu]; the tumulus still marked as his tomb lies several hundred metres north of the ancient wall. The site-area is centred around the villages of Chou-kung-miao and Hsiao-pei-kuan; the latter two having been the loci of earlier excavations.

The excavators seek to date some burials (M44, M57, and M35) in the Wang-fu-t'ai cemetery area in the western side of the ancient city from as early as Early Western Chou (1122–1001 BC) but, as well demonstrated by T.F. Munford (1985: 41–55), among other factors, the close similarities of the burials and funerary furnishings generally with those of the SHANG-TS'UN-LING cemetery site do not allow a dating much earlier than Ch'un-ch'iu times (771–481 BC).

Anon.: *Ch'ü-fu Lu-kuo-ch'eng* [The ancient city of Ch'ü-fu of the state of Lu] (Ch'i-nan, 1982); T.F. Munford: *Burial patterns of the Chou period: the location and arrangement of cemeteries in North China, 1000–200 BC* (Ph.D. thesis, Australian National University, 1985).

chullpa Burial house or tower, characteristic of the central and southern Andean highlands.

chultun Underground cistern, usually bell-shaped with a narrow mouth, found around domestic settlement in the LOWLAND MAYA area and used for storage of water or food.

D. Puleston: 'The chultuns of Tikal', *Expedition* 7 (1965) 24–9; P.A. McAnany: 'Water storage in the Puuc region of the northern Maya lowlands: a key to population estimates and architectural variability', *Precolumbian population history in the Maya lowlands*, ed. T.P. Culbert and D.S. Rice (Albuquerque, 1990) 263–84.

PRI

Chung-yüan (Zhongyuan; 'central plains') Region in central China largely embraced by the adjoining areas of the provinces of Ho-nan, Shen-hsi, and Shan-hsi; comprising the confluence of the Huang-ho ('Yellow River') Basin with those of the Wei-shui and the Fen-ho. Long regarded as the very cradle of Chinese civilization, it has also been referred to as the 'nuclear area' and roughly co-incides with the territories of the MIDDLE STATES of Chou times. With the rapid and extensive rate of archaeological discovery over the last three decades, however, and the application of radio-carbon dating (see CHINA 2), this concept has been modified. It now seems that in the earliest periods the Chung-yüan was only one of several major cultural regions each with indigenous roots extending appreciably into high antiquity. Some, such as TZ'U-SHAN and related cultures in southern Ho-pei, PEI-LI-KANG in Ho-nan, HO-MU-TU, in Shang-tung, TA-P'EN-K'ENG, Taiwan (incorporating also the southeast coastal areas of China), variously date back to at least 5000 BC, a few even earlier. Thus up to the historical level (*c*.2000–1500 BC), increasing attention has been given to the regional developments of the several major Neolithic cultural regions and the variant characteristics of each, while the nature and extent of cultural interplay between them is gradually being clarified. However, from historical times in China, essentially the age of metallurgy and writing, the centrifugal nature of the development of Chinese civilization with its spread from the MIDDLE STATES (i.e. the major states under Chou suzerainty centred in the Chung-yüan) outwards into the peripheral 'barbarian' regions, where regional modifications embodying local cultural concepts intermingled with the incoming Chung-yüan influences, has become much clearer. At the same time, the entry of alien influences into the outermost of the peripheral 'barbarian' regions is to be noted.

Su Ping-ch'i and Yin Wei-chang: 'Kwang-yu k'ao-ku-hsueh wen-hua ti chu-hsi-lei-hsing wen-t'i' [Problems regarding the classification of archaeological cultural regions] *WW* 5 (1981), 10–17; Chang Kwang-chih: *The archaeology of ancient China*, 4th edn (New Haven, 1986).

NB

Chu-shu-chi-nien (Zhushujinian) *see* BAMBOO ANNALS.

Ch'u silk manuscript (Ch'u-tseng-shu, Chuzengshu) *see* CHINA 3

'Cimmerians' *see* TIMBER-GRAVE CULTURE

circumscription theory Theory that explains how cultural development is influenced by environmental constraints. The theory was first put forward by Robert Carneiro (1970) in an attempt to explain the origins of the state in the Andes. He argued that communities relying on the farming of narrow valleys for their subsistence were effectively 'circumscribed', i.e. a point could easily be reached at which no further land was available for exploitation. This circumscription, combined with population growth, generates conflict between different settlements and thus encourages the development of chiefdoms and subordinate, tribute-paying communities. According to Carneiro's theory, the process of territorial conflict provided a continuous stimulus to the development of the state in coastal Peru.

In collaboration with the Egyptologist Kathryn Bard, Carneiro takes a similar approach to the question of the rise of the state in the Nile valley (Bard and Carneiro 1989). They suggest that five principal factors were involved: a concentration of food resources (both in the earlier Predynastic for hunting and fishing and in the late Predynastic for cereal crops); the circumscription of the Nile valley by the desert on either side; increasing population pressure; gradual change in society; and the development of warfare. A sixth crucial factor produced a situation somewhat different to that in the Andes – the concept of the Egyptian divine ruler, which Carneiro believes to have contributed to the final integration of a set of chiefdoms which might otherwise have been continually at war.

R.L. Carneiro: 'A theory of the origin of the state', *Science* 169 (1970), 733–8; ——: 'Political expansion as an expression of the principle of competitive exclusion', *Origins of the state: the anthropology of political evolution*, ed. R. Cohen and E.R. Service (Philadelphia, 1978), 205–23; K. Bard and R.L. Carneiro: 'Patterns of predynastic settlement: location, social evolution, and the circumscription theory', *CRIPEL* 11 (1989), 15–23.

IS

Cîrna Mid-second millennium Bronze Age cremation cemetery near the Danube in Oltenia, Romania, consisting of *c.*500 urns buried in about 200 pits about 1m deep. Many of the urns and accompanying vessels (bowls and cups), are impressed and incised with tendril-like designs and arcade or swag-like motifs, often terminating in spirals. Associated with the urns were a series of similarly decorated schematic bell-shaped figurines (*c.*20cm high), apparently of women wearing dresses.

V. Dumitrescu: *Necropola de incineratie din epoca bronzului de la Cîrna* (Bucharest, 1961).

RJA

CIS and the Baltic states This region, essentially the European part of the ex-USSR plus Siberia, presents a huge range of archaeological sites, cultures and natural landscapes. Two huge plains – the Russian (East European) and West Siberian, separated by the Ural mountains – make up the western part of the Russian territory. The Altai mountains flank the West Siberian plain in the south. The eastern part consists of the Central Siberian Plateau, Central Yakut Plain and the system of mountain ridges, plateaux and uplands in southern and eastern Siberia and the far east. The region includes the largest rivers of Eurasia draining to the Arctic Ocean (the Lena, Ob/Irtysh, Northern Dvina); Pacific Ocean (the Amur); Caspian Sea (the Volga); Black Sea (the Dniepr) and Baltic Sea (the Western Dvina, Neva). The climate is markedly continental, with cold winters (below 50°C in Yakutia) and mild or warm summers. The greater part of Russian territory is taken up by the tundra and forest vegetation zones. A treeless steppe corridor stretches from Southern Russia via Northern Caucasus and South Urals into southern Siberia.

1 Prehistory. The earliest evidence of hominids in the region is provided by the lower levels of AZYKH CAVE in the Caucasus, palaeomagnetically dated to >735,000 years ago. The archaic stone assemblages at the site of KOROLEVO (on the upper Tisza River in the Western Ukraine) are geologically dated to the Mindel-Günz interglacial (780–730,000 years ago). A group of sites with archaic stone inventories, including pebble tools and scrapers, have been discovered in the loess sections in the south Tadjikistan. The oldest site (Kouldoura) has been found in a buried soil below the Brunhes-Matuyama geomagnetic boundary, *c.*735,000 years ago (Ranov 1993).

The Caucasus was intensively settled during the MOUSTERIAN epoch (*c.*110,000–40,000 BP), as is clear from the cave-sites of Azykh, KUDARO and many others. Mousterian sites are also located near Volgograd (Sukhaya Mechetka), near Kursk (Khotylevo) and in a few other areas of European Russia, as well as in Moldova and in the Ukraine (the Crimean cave sites of KIIK-KOBA, AK-KAYA and others). At the site of STAROSL'YE the skeleton of an anatomically modern human was found within the Mousterian layer.

During the Upper Palaeolithic (*c.*40,000–15,000 BP), a network of dwelling sites developed in European Russia, Ukraine and Moldova, notably in the basins of the Middle Don, Middle Dniepr and Dniestr. The earliest sites of the KOSTENKI-BORSHEVO group on the River Don (belonging to the Streletskian tradition) retain elements of the Mousterian. A fully developed Upper Palaeolithic tradition (Kostenkian) emerged between 24,000 and 21,000 BP.

In the 1930s, Russian archaeologists identified substantial structures made of mammoth bones at a number of Upper Palaeolithic sites in the Russian Plain: Kostenki 1, stratum 1, Kostenki 11 stratum 1, Kostenki 4 and others. The quality of evidence at these sites invites sophisticated analysis; for

Millennia BC/AD	Epochs	W.-C. Europe	South Russia	Lith.	ZDvin	N–E Peri-Baltic	C Russ
1			Prag-P.	Kurg		Spk	Diakov.
0		Przew	Sa, C, Za, Sc, ScA	Stroked Pottery	Upper D	Textile	
1	IA / Halls	Laus	Tim G				Pozn
	BA	Tr	Cata	LBA	LBA	LBA	Fa
2		CoW	Pit-G	Rzucz	N-B	Cord W	V
					Usviaty	S / P	PrV
3		TBK	Tripolye / Str-G Dn-Don	Dubit.		Narva / CW	Ly
4	Neolithic	LP	B-D			Sperrings	Up. Vol
5		E Balkan Neolithic					
6							
7	Mesolithic						
8							
9		Swiderian					
10							
11							
12	Epipalaeolithic						
13							
14							
15		Yudinovian					
16							
17							
18							
19		Kostenkian					
20							
21							
21							
23							
24		Gorodtsovian					
25							
26							
27							
28							
29							
30	Upper Palaeolithic						
31							
32		Streletzkian				Spitzinian	
33							
34							
35							
36							
37							
38							
39							
40		Mousterian					

instance Olga Soffer (1985) has used faunal analysis in an attempt to distinguish the sites in terms of seasonality and social hierarchy. Complicated burials indicative of social stratification were found at the site of SUNGHIR in Central Russia, while the cave of KAPOVA in the Southern Urals proves the existence of Palaeolithic cave art basically similar to that of the Franco-Cantabria region.

Upper Palaeolithic sites first appeared in Siberia no later than 30,000 years BP (Tseitlin 1979). At that time, the Palaeolithic complex spread north of the Polar Circle, as is evidenced by the sites on the Pechera River (Konivets 1976). After about 15,000 BP, large dwelling-sites practically disappeared from central and southern Russia. However, from *c.*11,000–10,000 BP there are numerous seasonal camps of reindeer hunters in the ice-free areas of northern and northwestern Russia, notably in the catchments of Upper Dniepr, Upper Volga, and Western Dvina – for example, Nobel, Pribor.

Between 10,000 and 6000 BP various groups of hunter-gatherers can be defined in the region, and these are traditionally classified as MESOLITHIC. In Russian archaeology the term 'Mesolithic' implies cultural assemblages left by groups of foragers in an environment of post-glacial forests and steppes. The lithic inventories suggest a degree of cultural continuity with regard to the Late Palaeolithic – the main innovations concerned settlement and subsistence. The sites tend to gravitate to the inshore lagoons in the coastal area and to lakes further afield, reflecting the exploitation of a wide variety of forest, lake and estuarine wild-life resources. Some of the sites (e.g. KUNDA) were of considerable size and were used on a permanent or semi-permanent basis. Large Mesolithic cemeteries were discovered

Table 11 **CIS and the Baltic states** Chronological table for the Upper Palaeolithic to Iron Age.

Key

BA = Bronze Age; B-D = Bug-Dniestrian; C = Cherniakhov Culture; Cata = Catacomb Grave Culture; CW = Comb Ware; CoW = Corded Ware; Dn-Don = Dniepr-Donetsian; Fa = Fatyanovo: Rzucz-Rzuczewo; Gu = Huns; Halls = Hallstatt; IA = Iron Age; Kurg = Kurgans; Laus. = Lausitzian; LBA = Late Bronze Age; LP = Linear Pottery; Ly = Lyalovo; N-B = North Bielorussian Culture; P = Piestina; Pit-G = Pit-Grave Culture; Ponz. = Pozniakov Culture; Prag-P. = Prag-type Pottery; PrV = Protovolosovo; Przew = Przeworsk Culture; S = Sarnate; Sa = Sarmatians; Sc = Scythians; ScA = Agricultural Scythians; Spk = Sopki; Str-G. = Strumel-Gastyatin; TBK = Funnel Beaker Culture; TimG = Timber Grave Culture; Tr = Trzciniec Culture; Up Vol = Upper Volga Culture; V = Volosovo; Za = Zarubincy Culture

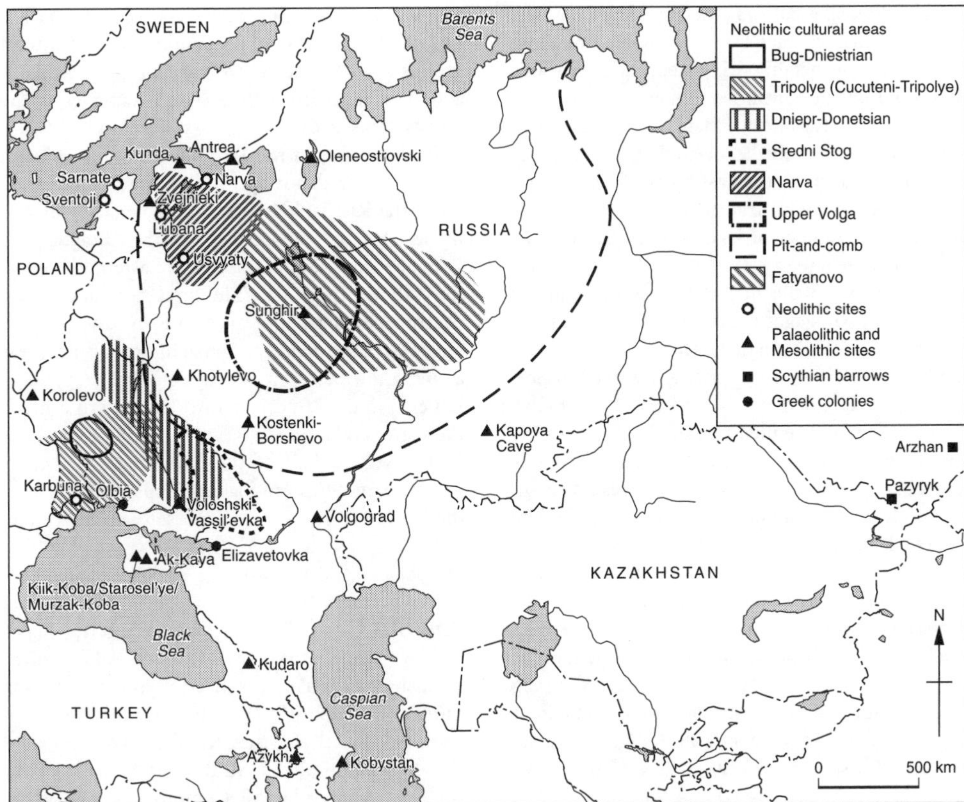

Map 21 **CIS and the Baltic states** Some major Palaeolithic, Mesolithic and Neolithic sites in the CIS and the Baltic states, as well as selected Greek colonies and Scythian barrows.

in north Russia (OLENEOSTROVSKI), Latvia (ZVEJNIEKI) and the Ukraine (VOLOSHSKI-VASSIL'EVKA), and the evidence from these sites suggests both inter-group conflicts and a degree of social stratification.

Around 6500–6000 BP, pottery began to be produced on a large scale throughout much of European Russia, but many of the local economies retained a foraging character. The sites in the river valleys of Moldova and Ukraine (BUG-DNIESTRIAN, DNIEPR-DONETSIAN) contained a limited number of domesticated animal bones. This, and the imprints of cereals on the pottery, indicates contact with groups of farmers. However, sites belonging to cultural groups in central Russia (UPPER VOLGA) and the Eastern Baltic (NARVA) suggest a purely foraging economy.

In Azerbaidjan, south of Baku, Kobystan presents an impressive assemblage of paintings and engravings on the surface of rock outcrops on the coast of the Caspian Sea. The earliest group, presumed to have been executed during the early Mesolithic, consists of elongated (up to 1.5 m high) human figures. A later group, attributed to a time-span from the late Mesolithic to Neolithic, features hunting scenes with archers, dancing human figures, and 'solar boats'. (The latest group, presumed to be Bronze Age, consists of stylized human and animal figures; amongst the latter, wild goats may be recognized.)

Around 4000 BC (6000 BP), Tripolye (*see* TRIPOLYE-CUCUTENI) groups emerged in Moldova and southwestern Ukraine, later spreading into the Middle Dniepr area. Initially, the Tripolye economy mixed farming with foraging, but by *c*.3500 BC it had become strongly agricultural; metallurgy and metal-working began to develop even in the early stages of the Tripolye culture (e.g. at KARBUNA). Simultaneously, GUMELNIŢA sites appeared in southern Moldova and the northwestern Pontic area. Concurrently with the Middle/Late Tripolye 5600–4800 BP

(4500–3400 BC), a cultural tradition known as the SREDNI STOG, characterized by horse-breeding, developed in the neighbouring steppe area. Various groups of foragers continued to live in the forested areas of East-European Plain. PIT-AND-COMB POTTERY, exclusively associated with foraging economies, spread across vast areas of central and northern Russia. The tradition of 'pile dwelling' emerged at a number of lake sites in the Western Dvina catchment (e.g. USVYATY).

From about 3000 BC, the Tripolye culture entered its final stage, characterized by a gradual disintegration of the single cultural tradition into a number of differently oriented metallurgical centres (e.g. Usatovo and Sofievka). The Tripolye complex ultimately ended in a total collapse of the agricultural economy: from 2800 BC, the predominantly pastoral PIT-GRAVE tradition spread through the South Russian steppes. At about the same time (*c*.3000–2300 BC), the Corded Ware tradition emerged, comprised of several local groups, widely spread across northwestern and central Russia. One of these groups (Fatyanovo) spread far to the east. Stock-breeding became an important element in the economy of many of these groups, but foraging remained the dominant strategy in a number of areas (North Belorussian sites in the Usyvaty area, late Neolithic sites in the Lubana area of Latvia, the sites belonging to the 'coastal tradition' in ŠVENTOJI and elsewhere).

In the forested area of European Russia, from the late 2nd to early 1st millennium BC, there seems to have been a gradual increase in the importance of stock-breeding as well as the development of local metallurgical and metal-working tradition. The main source of copper ores for these groups were the Uralian and South Siberian deposits. At some stage, the influence of Uralian groups which controlled the production and distribution of bronze tools became apparent in a wider area from Finland to Lake Baikal (e.g. the SEIMA-TURBINO complex).

2 Iron Age. Agriculture, allegedly of a swidden type (Petrov 1968), spread through the forested area of European Russia during the early Iron Age (1st millennium BC). A number of fortified settlements (GORODIŠCE) emerged, and several cultural groups are identifiable, e.g. STROKED POTTERY, DNIEPR-DVINIAN, MILOGRADIAN and others (Sedov 1982).

The predominantly nomadic SCYTHIANS left numerous barrows in the 'steppe corridor' of southern Russia and Ukraine. The Scythian groups developed political and economic relationships with the Greek colonies and city-states on the Black Sea (e.g. OLBIA, Elizavetovka). Their cultural influence extended far to the east, as evidenced by the 'royal tombs' in the Southern Siberia (PAZYRYK, ARZHAN). A number of predominantly agricultural groups – sometime called 'agricultural Scythians' and often regarded as 'pre-Slavs' – emerged in the forest-steppe area.

In the course of the 1st millennium AD, plough agriculture gradually spread into the forested areas of central Russia. The first archaeologically identifiable Slavic antiquities (with 'Prague-type pottery') emerged in Central and Eastern Europe in the 6th century AD. The first Slavonic urban centres (Ladoga, Novgorod, Kiev and others) emerged in the densely populated agricultural areas along the major waterways (Volkhov, Ilmen, Dniepr) in the 8th century AD. In the 9th century these areas became the target of Viking intrusions. In the second half of the 10th century AD, the greater part of Eastern Slavic groups united to form the Kievan Rus: the first major state in the region.

3 The history of archaeology in the region. The first archaeological excavations in Russia were made in Russia in the early 18th century during the reign of Peter the Great. The excavations of the Slavic barrows near Ladoga (Brandenburg 1985) and the acquisition of gold objects from Scythian barrows in Siberia (Rudenko 1962) are typical of this phase of enquiry. In 1846, the Russian Archaeological Society was founded in St. Petersburg. In 1859, the Imperial Archaeological Commission was set up within the Ministry of the Imperial Court. During the 19th century, Russian archaeologists concentrated on the excavation of classical sites: Greek colonies on the Black Sea coast (where the excavators included L. Stefani, V.V. Latyshev and M.I. Rostovtseff), SCYTHIAN sites (I.E. Zabelin and S.A. Zhebelev), Bronze Age sites in the Southern Russia, including the famous MAIKOP barrow (N.I. Veselovsky), and the PIT-GRAVE, CATACOMB and TIMBER-GRAVE tumuli (V.A. Gorodtsov); and the Slavic antiquities of Central and Northern Russia (N.E. Brandenburg, A.A. Samokvasov and D.Y. Spitsyn).

From the 1870s onwards, Russian scholars carried out the excavations of Palaeolithic sites at KOSTENKI-BORSHEVO (I.S. Polyakov) as well as in the Ukraine and in Siberia. During these years, Neolithic sites were discovered south of Ladoga Lake (A.A. Inostrantsev), as was the Fatyanovo cemetery (A.S. Uvarov), and the Bronze Age Volosovo site (I.S. Polyakov).

At a methodological level, V.A. Gorodtsov (1908) outlined the principles of typological classification of prehistoric materials. At the same time, Gorodtsov was one of the first to introduce the concept of an 'archaeological culture' to the Russian discipline (Gorodtsov 1908). Both he and A.A. Spitsyn (Spitsyn 1899) adhered to the cultural-ethnic theory which equated 'archaeological culture' with ethnicity. On 18 April 1919, Lenin signed a decree establishing the Russian Academy for the History of Material Culture (RAIMK), which replaced the Imperial Archaeological Commission. The establishment of this centralized archaeological structure in the new Communist state was instigated by Nikolai Y. Marr (1865–1934), a Marxist linguist and archaeologist.

The structure of Soviet archaeology was repeatedly modified until the 1970s, when at least three hierarchical levels could be distinguished: All-Union; Republic; and regional. All-Union institutions were entitled to carry out archaeological investigations on the whole territory of the USSR; they included the Research Institutes of the Academy of Sciences of the USSR in Moscow, St. Petersburg (earlier Leningrad) and Novosibirsk. Each Soviet republic had either its own Institute of Archaeology (as in Ukraine and Georgia) or Departments of Archaeology within the Institutes of History (as in the Baltic republics, Belarus and elsewhere). Archaeological investigations were also carried out by major universities, and national (e.g. the State Museum of History, Moscow) and local museums.

The excavation techniques adopted in the USSR encouraged the large-scale exposure and stripping of archaeological layers. Great attention was attached to the identification of various types of structures, and to the distribution of artefacts within these structures. The minute application of this technique resulted in some outstanding achievements, such as the identification of Palaeolithic dwellings in the 1930s.

At a theoretical level, MARXIST historical materialism was the dominant epistemology in the Soviet archaeology. In accordance with this, archaeology was viewed as a part of history and was oriented towards the study of the evolution of society and culture. The Marxist approach greatly encouraged interpretations of a 'sociological' kind, and Soviet archaeology focused on the identification of three paramount elements in ancient cultures: technology, social organization and ideology. In the 1930s, Soviet archaeologists (e.g. Ravdonikas 1930) promoted the 'stadial concept' of prehistory, which viewed prehistory as a sequence of 'socio-economic formations' (a concept which greatly influenced V. Gordon Childe). In the 1930s and 1940s, P.P. Efimenko (1938a) and P.I. Boriskovsky (1950) advanced a theory according to which the basic social structure, characterizing the Lower and Middle Palaeolithic, was an egalitarian 'primitive herd'. This was replaced by a matriarchal 'clan society' at the transition to the Upper Palaeolithic. The remains of Palaeolithic 'long houses' were cited as one piece of evidence for this change. This theory was later much criticized: G.P. Grogor'ev (1968) convincingly argued that no major social differences are detectable through the Palaeolithic, that the nuclear family had already existed in the Lower Palaeolithic, and that there was no evidence for clan organization in the Upper Palaeolithic.

In the period after the Second World War, the Marxist approach took the form of a 'sociological archaeology' based on the early agricultural civilizations of Central Asia (e.g. Masson 1976; Alyokshin 1986). A different strand in Soviet archaeology concentrated on the analysis of prehistoric technology, and culminated in the works of S.A. Semenov, G.F. Korobkova and their disciples who pioneered the technique of USE-WEAR ANALYSIS (Semenov 1964; Semenov and Korobkova 1983). Like their counterparts in the West, Soviet archaeologists continually debated the proper aims of archaeology. According to one school of thought, e.g. Yu.N. Zakharuk (Zakharuk 1969) and V.F. Henning (Henning 1983) the prime objective of archaeology is to isolate an 'ideal' social model of human society – the 'archaeological sources' (such as artefacts) providing the means to discover this.

Another school of thought, often referred to as 'strict archaeology' and exemplified by L.S. Klejn (1991), G.S. Lebedev (1992) and their followers, focused their attention on the development of the theoretical base of archaeology and on the strict definition of basic concepts. This approach, similar in some ways to the ideas advanced by David Clarke in his 'ANALYTICAL ARCHAEOLOGY', examines the relations between artefact, attribute, type and culture. For example, 'type' in these schemes is often viewed as a 'system of attributes' (Lebedev 1979). Proponents of this school argue that only after completing an 'internal synthesis' can archaeologists proceed to 'historical synthesis', i.e. to the interpretation of archaeological entities in terms of social, economic, ethnic and cultural processes.

The dual approach of Soviet archaeologists to archaeological entities was particularly clear in their treatment of archaeological 'cultures' – 'culture' being universally recognized as the basic archaeological concept. The approach that stemmed from the theories of Spitsyn and Gorotsov, assuming a direct equation of archaeological cultures with ethnicities, remains the leading paradigm among many Russian and Ukrainian archaeologists, such as A.Y. Bryusov (1956), Y.N. Zakharuk (1964), M.Yu Braichevsky (1965). This approach, in particular, informed those Soviet archaeologists who developed theories related to the origin of the Slavs (e.g. Tretyakov 1966; Lyapushkin 1961; Sedov 1982) and the SCYTHIANS (e.g. Artamonov 1974). However, another group of scholars (e.g. Zhukov 1929; Sorokin 1966; Grogir'ev 1972) tended to view archaeological cultures as purely taxonomic units.

General

P.P. Efimenko: *Dorodovoe obščestvo: Očerki po istorii pervobytnogo obščestva* [Pre-clan society: essays on the history of primitive society] (Leningrad, 1938a); V.P. Petrov: *Podsečnoe zemledelie* [Swidden cultivation] (Kiev, 1968); V.I. Konivets: *Paleolit Krainego Severo-Vostoka Evropy* [Palaeolithic of the extreme northeast of Europe] (Moscow, 1976); S.M. Tseitlin: *Geologija paleolila Severnoi Azii*, [Geology of the Palaeolithic of Northern Asia] (Moscow, 1979); L.L. Zaliznjak: *Ohotniki na severnogo olenja Ukrainskogo Polesja epohi final'nogo paleolita.* [Final Palaeolithic reindeer hunters of the Ukrainian Polesye] (Kiev, 1981); V.V. Sedov: *Vostočnye slavjane v VI–XIII vekah* [The Eastern Slavs in the 6th–13th centuries AD] (Moscow, 1982); O. Soffer: The *Upper Palaeolithic of the Central Russian Plain* (Orlando, 1985); V. Ranov: 'Tout commence au Paléolithique', *DA* 185 (1993), 4–13.

History of archaeology in the region

A.A. Spitsyn: 'Rasselenie drevne-russkih plemën po arheologičeskim dannym' [The settlement of early Slavic tribes according to archaeological evidence]. *Žurnal ministerstva prosveščenija* (St. Petersburg, 1898/9), 301–40; V.A. Gorodtsov: *Russkaja doistoričeskaja keramika* [Russian prehistoric pottery], Transactions of the 11th Russian Archaeological Congress (Kiev, 1901); ——: *Pervobytnaja arheologija* [Prehistoric archaeology] (Moscow, 1908); V.S. Zhukov: 'Voprosy metodologii vydelenija kul'turnyh elementov i grupp' [On the methodology of the identification of cultural elements and groups], *Kul'tura i byt neselenija Central'no-Promyšlennoi oblasti* [Culture and mode of life of the population of the Central Industrial District] (Moscow, 1929); V.I. Ravdonikas: 'Za marksistskuju istoriju material'noi kul'tury' [Marxist history of material culture], *Izvestija GAIMK* (1930/7), 3–4; P.P. Efimenko: *Pervobytnoe obščestvo: Ocerki po istorii paleolithiceskogo vremeni* [Primitive society: essays on the history of Palaeolithic epoch] (Leningrad, 1938b); P.I. Boriskovsky: *Načalnyi etap pervobytnogo obščestva* [The initial stage of primitive society] (Leningrad, 1950); A.Ya. Bryusov: 'Arheologičeski kul'tury i etničeski obščnosti' [Archaeological culture and ethnic entities], *Sovetskaja arheologija* 26 (1956), 5–27; I.I. Lyapushkin: 'Dneprovskoe lesostepnoe levoberež'e v epohu železa' [The forest-steppe Dniepr left-bank in the Iron Age], *MIAS* 104 [Materials on the archaeology of the USSR] (Moscow and Leningrad, 1961); S.I. Rudenko: *Sibirskaja kollekcija Petra I* [The Siberian Collection of Peter I], Svod arheologicheskih istochnikov [Collection of Archaeological Records], D 3–9 (Moscow, 1962); S.A. Semenov: *Prehistoric technology*, trans. N.W. Thomson (Bath, 1964); Yu. N. Zakharuk: 'Problemy arheologičeskoi kul'tury' [The problems of archaeological culture], *Arheologija* 17 (1964), 12–42; V.Yu. Braichevsky: 'Teoretičny osnovy doslidžen' etnogenezu' [Theoretical basis of ethnogenetic studies], *Arheologija* 2 (1965), 46–56; V.S. Sorokin: *Andronovskaja kul'tura* [The Andronovo Culture], Svod arheologičeskih istochnikov [Collection of Archaeological Records], 133/2 (Moscow, 1966); P.P. Tretyakov: '*Finno-ugry, balty i slavjane na Dnepre i Volge* [The Finno-Ugrians, Balts and Slavs on the Dniepr and Volga] (Moscow and Leningrad, 1966); G.P. Grigor'ev: *Naččalo verhnego paleolita i proiskhoždenie Homo sapiens* [The beginnings of the Upper Palaeolithic and the origin of Homo sapiens] (Leningrad, 1968); Yu.N. Zakharuk: 'O metodologii sovetskoi arheologii I eë problemah' [On the methodology of Soviet archaeology and its problems], *Sovetskaja arheologija* 3 (1969), 11–20; G.P. Grigor'ev: 'Kul'tura i tip v arheologii: kategorii analiza ili real'nost?' [Culture and type in archaeology: analytical units or realities?], *Transaction of the All-Union Session on the Results of Archaeological and Ethnographic Field Investigations in 1971* (Baku, 1972), 5–9; M.I. Artamonov: *Kimmeriitsy i skify* [The Cimmerians and Scythians] (Leningrad, 1974); V.M. Masson: Ekonomika i social'nyi stroi drevnih obščestv [Economy and social pattern in ancient societies] (Leningrad, 1976); G.S. Lebedev: 'Arheologičeskii tip kak sistema priznakov' [The archaeological type as a system of attributes], *Tipy v kul'ture* [Types in culture], ed. L.S. Klejn (Leningrad, 1979), 74–87; V.V. Sedov: *Vostočnye slavyane v VI–XIII vekah* [The Eastern Slavs in the 6th–13th centuries AD], Arheologija SSSR (Moscow, 1982); V.F. Henning: *Predmet i ob'jekt nauki arheologii* [The subject-matter of archaeology] (Kiev, 1983); S.A. Semenov and G.F. Korobkova: *Tehnologija drevnih proizvodstv* [Technology of prehistoric production] (Leningrad, 1983); N.E. Brandenburg: *Kurgany Juznogo Priladoz'ja* [Barrows of the south Ladoga area], Materialy po arheologii Rossii [Materials on the archaeology of Russia] (St. Petersburg, 1985); V.A. Alyokshin: *Social'naja struktura i pogrebal'nyi obrjad drevnezemledel'ceskih obscesty Srednei Azii i Bliznego Vostoka* [The social structure and burial rites of early agricultural societies in Middle Asia and the Near East] (Leningrad, 1986); L.S. Klejn: *Arheologičeskaja tipologija* [An archaeological typology] (Leningrad, 1991); G.S. Lebedev: Istorija otečestvennoi arheologii 1700–1917 [History of Russian archaeology, 1700–1917] (St. Petersburg, 1992).

PD

Cishan *see* TZ'U-SHAN

Cliff Palace Largest cliff dwelling in the American Southwest, consisting of 217 rooms and 33 kivas, occupied by the ANASAZI in the 13th century AD. It was discovered in 1888 by Richard Whetherill, a local cowboy and explorer of Southwestern prehistoric sites, while he was looking for stray cattle on Mesa Verde (now a National Park) in southwestern Colorado.

F. McNitt: *Richard Wetherill: Anasazi* (Albuquerque, 1957).

JJR

Clogg's Cave Limestone cave and rock shelter in the Buchan region of Victoria, Australia. The basal deposits contain extinct megafauna, with no human associations, dating back to 23,000 BP. The earliest occupation is associated with the AUSTRALIAN CORE TOOL AND SCRAPER TRADITION dating to 17,000 BP; increasing use of the cave between 13,000 and 9000 BP is associated with backed blades on chert, quartz and jasper. The cave is one of the few Pleistocene sites dug in Victoria.

J. Flood: 'Pleistocene man at Clogg's Cave: his tool kit and environment', *Mankind* 9 (1974), 175–88; ——: *Archaeology of the dreamtime* (Sydney, 1983), 23–8.

CG

Clovis PALEOINDIAN culture, dating from *c*.10,000 to 9,000 BC, evidence of which occurs throughout much of North America. Clovis sites are identified by the presence of the distinctive Clovis fluted projectile point; these lanceolate bifaces are distinguished from later projectile points by a shallow flake scar or 'flute' that extends from the point's base, approximately one-third up each face of the tool. Clovis is the earliest Paleoindian, big-game hunting culture of North America and is one of the complexes making up the LLANO tradition. On the basis of linguistic, dental and genetic evidence, Clovis is hypothesized to have been the New World 'founding culture'. Traits shared with Palaeolithic sites in eastern Europe include large blades, end-scrapers, burins, unifacial flake tools, shaft wrenches, cylindrical bone points, flaked bone, red ochre and worked tusks. Examples of major sites are Naco, LEHNER and MURRAY SPRING (Arizona), BLACKWATER DRAW (New Mexico), Dent (Colorado) and EAST WENATCHEE (Washington state). Clovis people hunted a wide variety of Late Pleistocene animals, including now-extinct forms of mammoth and bison, as well as smaller animals like deer. Although poorly represented in the archaeological record, plant foods were undoubtedly important as well.

E.W. Haury et al.: 'The Lehner mammoth site, southeastern Arizona', *AA* 25 (1959), 2–34; G. Frison: *Prehistoric hunters of the High Plains* (New York, 1991); D. Stanford: 'Clovis origins and adaptations: an introductory perspective', *Clovis: origins and adaptations*, ed. R. Bonnichsen and K. Turnmire (Corvallis, 1991), 1–13; D. Meltzer: 'Is there a Clovis adaptation?', *From Kostenki to Clovis: Upper Palaeolithic Paleo-Indian adaptations*, ed. O. Soffer and N. Praslov (New York, 1993), 293–310.

RJE/JJR

cluster analysis Techniques of MULTIVARIATE STATISTICS, with the common aim of dividing a collection of objects into groups or clusters on the basis of the similarity between each pair of objects. 'Similarity' can be regarded as the statistical equivalent of the spatial proximity of objects (*see* MULTIVARIATE STATISTICS); groups should ideally consist of objects which are close to each other but further from objects in other groups. There are many measures of distance; for continuous data the most common is Euclidean distance (the multivariate equivalent of a 'crow-fly' distance on a map, in contrast to, for example, distances measured along roads). Archaeologists experimented with various techniques in the 1960s and 1970s; the most commonly used now are k-means cluster analysis and Ward's method. The main criticisms of cluster analysis are that it creates clusters whether any exist naturally in the data or not, and that the choice of the number of clusters is often arbitrary. The k-means method partly meets these objections by providing diagnostic statistics which can be used to suggest the best number of clusters in a DATASET. For case-studies *see* ARMANT *and* MASK SITE.

R.M. Cormack: 'A review of classification', *Journal of the Royal Statistical Society* Series A, 134 (1971), 321–67; J.E. Doran and F.R. Hodson: *Mathematics and computers in archaeology* (Edinburgh, 1975), 173–86, 180–4 [K-means]; B.S. Everitt: *Cluster analysis*, 2nd edn (London, 1980), 16–7 [Ward's method]; C.R. Orton: *Mathematics in archaeology* (Glasgow, 1980), 46–55; S. Shennan: *Quantifying archaeology* (Edinburgh, 1988), 196–208; M.J. Baxter: *Exploratory multivariate analysis in archaeology* (Edinburgh, 1993).

CO

'Coastal Neolithic' (Vietnam) Many coastal regions of Southeast Asia incorporate the remains of raised shorelines on which are located prehistoric settlements. These sites, dating from after *c*.4000 BC, were sited to take advantage of rich coastal resources, and excavations reveal the remains of shellfish and fish, as well as pottery vessels, polished stone artefacts including large hoes, and inhumation cemeteries. In Vietnam, these sites are referred to as 'coastal Neolithic', but to date there appear to be no surviving biological remains to indicate the presence of agriculture or stock raising. It might be that the inhabitants cultivated root crops, such as yam or taro, but equally they could have been sedentary hunter-gatherers. The best-known 'coastal Neolithic' cultures in Vietnam are called after the sites of Da But, Cai Beo, Hoa Loc, Bau Tro and Quynh Van. Thac Lac (in central Vietnam), probably dating to *c*.3000–2000 BC, incorporates ceramics richly ornamented with parallel bands infilled with impressions recalling those found at PHUNG NGUYEN sites.

Two radiocarbon dates suggest that the upper layers of the six-metre-deep midden at Quynh Van (in northern Vietnam) belong to the mid-4th millennium BC. Excavations have uncovered 31 inhumation graves; unusually, for a site of this date, there were no polished stone implements. Although usually ascribed to the 'Coastal Neolithic', Quynh Van might just as well have been a sedentary settlement whose inhabitants exploited the wealth of the marine habitat rather than practising agriculture.

Ha Van Tan: 'Nouvelles récherches prehistoriques et protohistoriques au Viet Nam', *BEFEO* 68 (1980) 113–54.

CH

coatepantli (Nahuatl: 'serpent-wall') Mesoamerican structure of the Postclassic period (*c*.AD 900–1521) consisting of a long stone wall placed within or surrounding a ceremonial precinct, decorated with relief carvings of serpents and/or sacrifice. There are surviving examples at TENOCHTITLAN and Tula (*see* TOLTECS).

PRI

Cochasquí Residential site of the so-called Cara Phase peoples in northern Ecuador during the Integration Period (*c*.AD 500–1450), consisting of 15 rectangular earthen pyramids with ramps and a large number of circular funerary platforms covering shaft-and-chamber tombs. Each of the pyramids had one or more perishable structures on their tops. Cochasquí was the residence of the chiefly and noble families of one of the small kingdoms that characterized late period highland Ecuador.

U. Oberem: *Cochasquí: estudios arqueologicos, Colección Pendoneros*, 3 vols (Otavalo, 1981); S.J. Athens: 'Ethnicity and adaptation: the Late Period-Cara occupation in Northern Highland Ecuador', *Resources, power, and interregional interaction*, ed. E. Schortman and P. Urban (New York, 1992), 93–219.

KB

Cochise Archaic, pre-ceramic hunter-gatherer culture of the southern American Southwest from the early Holocene until the appearance of pottery in *c*.AD 1–200. Cochise was defined in 1941 by Edwin Sayles and the geologist Ernst Antevs, on the basis of buried sites in the Whitewater Draw region of southeastern Arizona. The developmental sequence is divided into three stratigraphically distinct stages: Sulphur Spring (*c*.10,000–8000 BP), Chiricahua (up to 3500 BP) and San Pedro (*c*.3500–2000 BP). The relationship with CLOVIS remains unclear, although chronometric evidence does not support contemporaneity. The discontinuity between Sulphur Spring and Chiricahua is less than current stratigraphic and chronometric evidence indicates. The validity of Sayles' 'Cazador stage', transitional between Sulphur Spring and Chiricahua, has been seriously questioned following the re-examination of deposits at the Whitewater Draw localities. Reinvestigation of BAT CAVE reliably dates the introduction of maize and squash to *c*.1200 BC. Cochise, long thought to have been ancestral to the MOGOLLON culture, is considered by many to have a similar link with the HOHOKAM. The major sites of the culture are VENTANA CAVE and Cienega Creek in Arizona, and Bat Cave and Tularosa Cave in New Mexico.

E.W. Haury: *The stratigraphy and archaeology of Ventan Cave* (Tucson, 1950); E.B. Sayles: *The Cochise cultural sequence in southeastern Arizona* (Tucson, 1983); N.H. Wills: *Early prehistoric agriculture in the American Southwest* (Santa Fe, 1988).

JJR

Coclé Culture which flourished between AD 500 and 1100 in the south-central Panama province of the same name. It is known primarily for its gold objects and polychrome pottery decorated with crested birds, dogs, reptiles, marine creatures and insects. The typically small Coclé sites, such as SITIO CONTE and Río Cano, are located along rivers; they appear to be the centres of chiefdoms. The structural remains are built of earth, and sites typically lack stone masonry; lines of stone pillars or columns in association with 'altar'-like boulders are often found.

S.K. Lothrop: *Coclé: an archaeological study of central Panama*, Memoirs of the Peabody Museum, Harvard University 8 (Cambridge, 1942); O.F. Linares: *Studies in Pre-columbian art and archaeology* 17 (Washington, D.C., 1977) [section on 'Ecology and the arts in ancient Panama'].

PRI

codices (sing. codex) Mesoamerican 'books' made from the beaten bark of the fig tree or deer skin. They were usually sized and coated with lime plaster, painted with HIEROGLYPHIC texts and then folded like a screen.

F.B. de Sahagún: *The Florentine Codex: general history of the things of New Spain*, 12 books in 13 vols, trans. A.J.O. Anderson and C. Dibble (Santa Fe, 1950–82); J.E.S. Thompson: *The Dresden Codex* (Philadelphia, 1972); K. Ross: *Codex Mendoza: Aztec manuscript* (Fribourg, 1978); 'Special section: rethinking Mixtec codices', *AM* 1/1 (1990).

PRI

Cody Complex One of several complexes of the PLANO culture of the PALEOINDIAN period in the northern Great Plains of the United States. The tool assemblage consists of projectile points, flake tools, scrapers, gravers, wedges, choppers, bifaces, hammer stones, and bone tools that are often found with bison kill and processing sites. Diagnostic tools are both Eden and Scottsbluff projectile points types as well as Cody knives. The Horner site in northwestern Wyoming is the type site for the Cody Complex, and is estimated to date between 8000–5500 BC. The Cody Complex lies stratigraphically between the Alberta and Frederick complexes at the HELL GAP site.

C. Irwin-Williams et al.: 'Hell Gap: Paleo-Indian occupation on the High Plains', *PAnth* 18 (1973), 40–53; G. Frison and L. Todd: *The Horner site: the type site of the Cody cultural complex*. (New York, 1983).

WB

cognitive archaeology Study of the ways of thought of past societies (and sometimes of individuals in those societies), as inferred from surviving material remains. Cognitive archaeology, or the archaeology of the human mind, can be recognized as a theme in the New Archaeology of the 1960s and 1970s, but it did not gain a distinct identity until the early 1990s. Like environmental archaeology, however, it is very much part of a wider enterprise of archaeology: the study of the whole human past. In humans, thought and action (or at least sustained action) are inseparable. For that reason Marcus and Flannery, for instance, prefer to speak of 'holistic' rather than 'cognitive' archaeology, in their approach to the study of Zapotec ritual at the Mesoamerican site of SAN JOSE MOGOTE (Marcus and Flannery 1994: 55).

Whereas the so-called POST-PROCESSUAL ARCHAEOLOGY of the late 1980s and early 1990s was largely *anti-processual* in its aims and rhetoric, cognitive archaeology developed directly and without hiatus from the functional-processual archaeology of earlier decades. It represented a change of emphasis towards cognitive issues, which had been somewhat neglected after a few initial and programmatic statements in the first writings of the New Archaeology.

Certainly Kent Flannery in his early overview of Mesoamerican prehistory offered an early example of what he termed 'contextual analysis' (Flannery 1976), applied in the cognitive sphere, and in the same volume Robert Drennan considered the role of religion in social evolution, working very much in the functional-processual tradition. Flannery and Marcus have gone on to produce innovatory work on ritual and religion (Flannery and Marcus 1983; Marcus and Flannery 1994). Another early and significant contribution was Martin Wobst's pioneering study of style and communication (Wobst 1977).

Cognitive-processual archaeology went beyond its functional-processual predecessor, however, by attempting to apply valid generalizations not only to material aspects of culture but also to the cognitive sphere. This undertaking recognized that ideology is an active force within societies and must be given a role in explanations – as Marxist and neo-Marxist thinkers have long argued. However, if generalizations about human cognitive behaviour are to be made, this must be on the basis of research, not through the formation and application of some a priori principle, in the manner of many MARXIST ARCHAEOLOGISTS.

Cognitive archaeology, although working in the processual tradition, does not overlook the role of the individual. The notion of the 'cognitive map' is a useful one (Renfrew 1987), making explicit the world view which each individual carries in the mind's eye. The shared beliefs and concepts of the community are in some ways the aggregate of those of the individuals who constitute it. This approach, which is termed by some philosophers 'methodological individualism' (Bell 1994), is common enough in the systematic social sciences. For instance the economic decisions of the individual are considered in the field of microeconomics, and their aggregate effects in macroeconomics. The philosophy of science has its own contributions to make to the understanding of the role of the individual in society.

Cognitive archaeology acknowledged, too, that material culture is to be seen as an active force in constituting the world in which we live. As Hodder (1986) has argued, individuals and societies construct their own realities, and material culture has an integral place within that construction. The scope of cognitive archaeology can be outlined in several ways (see Renfrew and Bahn 1991: 339–70). For instance, it may be divided into two very broad fields: pre-sapient and sapient. It is now well documented that about 100,000 years ago our own species, *Homo sapiens sapiens*, became established in parts of Africa, and that by 40,000 years ago it had dispersed over much of the globe. The development of the cognitive faculties of the earlier hominids, which formed a crucial part in the processes leading to the emergence of *Homo sapiens*, constitutes the 'pre-sapient' area of cognitive archaeology. What, for instance, is the relationship between tool-making and cognitive abilities? When and how did language emerge?

The sapient field of cognitive studies, on the other hand, is concerned with the human story over the past 40,000 years. The hardware (i.e. our brain power) may have changed little over this time-span, but the changes in our 'software' (i.e. 'culture') have brought about radical transformations. Organized hunting requires the deployment of sophisticated cognitive faculties (Mithen 1990), and it has been suggested that Palaeolithic CAVE ART was used as part of an educational process by which the young were initiated into and introduced to the society and social store of knowledge and experience which this necessitated. The emergence of settled village life and then of cities, the use of writing and of developing technologies such as metallurgy, the rise of organized religion and of widely influential ideologies, the development of states and empires: all of these have their cognitive aspects, as indeed do farming origins (see Hodder 1990). Moreover, although some of these developments may be traced in quite different parts of the world, each area followed its own trajectory of development: the 'software' was independently generated. Part of the challenge of cognitive archaeology is to analyse the ways in which the formation of symbolic systems, in each particular case, moulded and conditioned later developments.

The focus of cognitive archaeology is the special human ability to construct and use symbols (*see also* SIGN AND SYMBOL). A symbol is something which stands for, or represents, something else: 'a visible sign of an idea or quality or of another object' (*Webster's Collegiate Dictionary* 1925: 974 'symbol'). The word derives from the Greek 'to place together', and the notions of juxtaposition (of X by Y) and of metaphor (where X is equated with Y) are closely related. The cognitive-processual archaeologist focuses on the ways in which symbols were *used*. This may be contrasted with the attempt to seek the 'meaning' of symbols, which would generally be the object of the anti-processual or interpretive archaeologist (*see* CONTEXTUAL ARCHAEOLOGY). The distinction is an important one. As we shall see, both approaches inevitably rely upon the insights and intuitions of the modern investigator: the creative, and in that sense subjective, aspects of scientific enquiry are not in doubt. It is a common misconception of the scientific method, deriving largely from the polemic of Bourdieu, that it is somehow inhuman, mechanistic or lacking in creativity. On the contrary, the role of the individual, as noted above, has to be considered systematically, as the approach of methodological individualism allows (Bell 1994). For the cognitive-processual archaeologist, it is enough that this approach should generate insights into how ancient minds worked, and into the manner in which that working shaped their actions.

For the interpretive archaeologist, working in the grand tradition of idealists like Collingwood, this is not enough. One seeks, instead, to 'enter the mind' of early individuals through some effort of active empathy. This experience of 'being' that other, long-dead person, or at least undergoing an experience to be compared with theirs, is what characterizes the subjective, idealist and interpretationist approach of the anti-processual and 'post-modern' archaeologist (*see* POST-PROCESSUAL ARCHAEOLOGY). The cognitive-processual archaeologist is sceptical of the validity of this empathetic experience, and sceptical too of the privileged status which must inevitably be claimed by the idealist. As in the conduct of all scientific enquiry, it is not the source of the insight which validates the claim, but the explicit nature of the reasoning which sustains it and the means by which the available data can be brought into relationship with it. As Popper (1968) long ago emphasized, validation rests not upon authority but on testability and on the explicitness of the argumentation, even if testing is not always, in practice, an easy undertaking.

The scope of cognitive archaeology roughly coincides with the various ways in which humans use symbols:

1 design, in the sense of coherently structured, purposive behaviour;
2 planning, involving time scheduling and sometimes the production of a schema prior to carrying out the planned work;
3 measurement, involving devices for measuring, and units of measure;
4 social relations, with the use of symbols to structure and regulate inter-personal behaviour;
5 the supernatural, with the use of symbols to commune with the other world, and to mediate between the human and the world beyond;

6 representation, with the production and use of depictions or other iconic embodiments of reality.

The distinction between planning and design is not always a clear one, since so much human behaviour involves both. For instance the builders of the MALTESE TEMPLES of the 3rd millennium BC produced small models in limestone of the structures which they had built or were to build. It is difficult now to know whether the model preceded or succeeded the construction of the building itself. In either case, however, the model is a representation of the relevant part of the cognitive map in the mind of the modeller, and such material representations help to make more concrete the concept of the cognitive map itself. Of course cognitive maps are involved in all planning and design: in such cases they are models for the future. But if the former were the case (i.e. model before construction), this is a good example of both planning and design. In some cases, however, it is useful to emphasize the distinction between the two. For instance, in the production of stone tools (Gowlett 1984; Davidson and Noble 1989; Wynn 1991), raw material may have had to be acquired from some distant source. There is no doubt that the use of the material in some cases entails a deliberate journey undertaken at least in part to secure its acquisition. That implies planning, in the sense of time-structuring of a more complex kind. Comparable structuring of manufacturing processes has been considered in terms of the '*chaîne opératoire*' (the ordered chain of actions etc., leading towards the transformation of a given material towards the manufacture of a product (Karlin and Julien 1994), and time structuring has been emphasized by Marshack (1991) in his consideration of Palaeolithic mobiliary art. In a different sense it was involved in the solar and lunar alignments of some of the European MEGALITHIC monuments and STONE CIRCLES (Heggie 1981).

The cognitive issues involved in tool production are often subsumed under the term 'design'. It has long been assumed that the production of most artefacts, for instance of such stone tools as Acheulean handaxes, involves the use of a mental template, which serves to guide the person producing the artefact. But, as one example of cognitive archaeological investigation has shown, the production of an artefact type need not depend upon any sophisticated conceptualizing, nor need it presume the use of language (Bloch 1991). 'Representation', the sixth symbolic category in the list, comes very close to the literal meaning of the term 'symbol', as defined above. Of course not all symbols are visible or material – spoken words may reasonably be regarded as symbols – but no-one could doubt that all representations are symbols. We have perhaps not yet sufficiently considered the momentous nature of the step taken when clay was first modelled to produce, for instance, a small representation of the human form, or when a sharp implement was first used to carve the outline of an animal on a piece of bone. The creation and preservation of representations offers us great potential for considering a number of important cognitive steps, from the first application of pigment in some ice age cave to the great fresco cycles of the Italian Renaissance.

It is in the archaeology of historic periods, where written texts are available, that the most rapid progress in cognitive archaeology can perhaps be made. The problem in periods when such records are available is generally one of relating the archaeological and the textual evidence (for if elucidation of the material evidence carries pitfalls, that of the written text is still more perilous, as the critical theorists have so effectively shown). (It seems unnecessary, by the way, to follow the post-modernist fashion of regarding everything, including the archaeological record, as 'text': the archaeological record is usually a palimpsest, and the notion of 'reading a text' can hardly be applied to the randomly accumulated detritus of the centuries.) A message, if it is to be decoded, has to have been encoded in the first place. Here there is need for much further research on the semiotics of non-verbal communication. For the historical archaeologist (along with the Near Eastern specialist, the Classicist or the Mayanist) the challenge is to use the available texts in such a way that they can be applied to the inferences drawn from the material remains. The theoretical problems in reconciling such disparate bodies of evidence have yet to be systematically addressed.

There are numerous published case-studies of cognitive archaeology, ranging from research into the specific cognitive changes that characterized the emergence of modern humans (Mellars 1991) to the analysis of the symbolism of Classical Greek portraiture (Tanner 1992). The adoption of a cognitive approach often forces archaeologists to address fundamental questions which would previously have been ignored or avoided, such as 'How religious were the ancient Egyptians?' (Kemp 1995), 'Is there a place for aesthetics in archaeology?' (Taylor et al. 1994) and 'How did ancient people perceive the landscapes in which they lived?' (Bradley 1994).

E. Cassirer: *An essay on man* (New Haven, 1944); L.A.

White: *The science of culture* (New York, 1949); K.R. Popper: *Conjectures and refutations* (New York, 1968); R. Drennan: 'Religion and social evolution in Formative Mesoamerica', *The early Mesoamerican village*, ed. K.V. Flannery (New York 1976), 345–68; K.V. Flannery: 'Contextual analysis of ritual paraphernalia from Formative Oaxaca', *The early Mesoamerican village*, ed. K.V. Flannery (New York, 1976), 333–45; M. Wobst: 'Stylistic behaviour and information exchange', *For the Director: essays in honor of James B. Griffin*, ed. C.E. Cleland (Ann Arbor, 1977), 317–42; D.C. Heggie: *Megalithic science, ancient mathematics and astronomy in Northwest Europe* (London, 1981); C. Renfrew: *Towards an archaeology of mind* (Cambridge, 1982); K.V. Flannery and J. Marcus, eds: *The Cloud People: divergent evolution of the Zapotec and Mixtec civilizations* (New York, 1983); J.A. Gowlett: 'Mental abilities in early man: a look at some hard evidence', *Hominid evolution and community ecology*, ed. R.A. Foley (London, 1984), 167–92; I. Hodder: *Reading the past*, 1st edn (Cambridge, 1986); C. Renfrew: 'Problems in the modelling of socio-cultural systems', *European Journal of Operational Research* 30 (1987), 179–92; I. Davidson and W. Noble: 'The archaeology of perception: traces of depiction and language', *CA* 30 (1989), 125–56; I. Hodder: *The domestication of Europe* (Cambridge, 1990); S. Mithen: *Thoughtful foragers: a study of prehistoric decision making* (Cambridge, 1990); M. Bloch: 'Language, anthropology and cognitive science', *Man* 26 (1991), 183–98; M. Donald: *Origins of the modern mind* (Cambridge, 1991); A. Marshack: 'The Taï plaque and calendrical notation in the Upper Palaeolithic', *CAJ* 1/1 (1991), 25–61; P. Mellars: 'Cognitive changes and the emergence of modern humans', *CAJ* 1/1 (1991), 63–76; C. Renfrew and P. Bahn: *Archaeology, theories, methods and practice* (London, 1991), 339–70; T. Wynn: 'Tools, grammar and the archaeology of cognition', *CAJ* 1/2 (1991), 191–206; J.J. Tanner: 'Art as expressive symbolism: civic portraits in Classical Athens', *CAJ* 2/2 (1992), 167–90; C. Renfrew et al.: 'What is cognitive archaeology?', *CAJ* 3/2 (1993), 247–70; J.A. Bell: *Reconstructing prehistory, scientific method in Archaeology* (Philadelphia, 1994); R. Bradley, 'Symbols and signposts – understanding the prehistoric petroglyphs of the British Isles', *The ancient mind: elements of cognitive archaeology*, ed. C. Renfrew and E. Zubrow (Cambridge, 1994), 95–106; C. Karlin and M. Julien, 'Prehistoric technology: a cognitive science?', *The ancient mind: elements of cognitive archaeology*, ed. C. Renfrew and E. Zubrow (Cambridge, 1994), 152–64; J. Marcus and K.V. Flannery: 'Ancient Zapotec ritual and religion', *The ancient mind: elements of cognitive archaeology*, ed. C. Renfrew and E. Zubrow (Cambridge, 1994), 55–74; C. Renfrew and E. Zubrow, eds: *The ancient mind: elements of cognitive archaeology* (Cambridge, 1994); M. Taylor, T. Vickers, H. Morphy and C. Renfrew: 'Is there a place for aesthetics in archaeology?', *CAJ* 4/2 (1994), 249–69; B.J. Kemp: 'How religious were the ancient Egyptians?', *CAJ* 5/1 (1995), 25–54.

CR

cognitive-processual approach *see* COGNITIVE ARCHAEOLOGY

collapse, Lowland Maya *see* COPÁN; LOWLAND MAYA

Co Loa *see* DONG SON CULTURE

colorimetric analysis Method of quantitative chemical analysis relying on the formation of a coloured compound in solution. The coloured compound is specific to the element being measured and it absorbs in the uv/visible region with an intensity proportional to concentration.

MC

Columnata *see* AFRICA 1

Commagene *see* NEMRUT DAGH

cone mosaics *see* STIFTMOSAIK

confidence interval Term used in statistical analysis to describe a range of values between which the value of a particular PARAMETER is thought to lie, together with a percentage representing the level of confidence with which this can be expressed (*see* PARAMETER ESTIMATION). In BAYESIAN STATISTICS this figure expresses a level or strength of belief; in classical statistics it represents the frequency with which repeated SAMPLES can be expected to include the true value of the parameter within their confidence interval, e.g. with a 90% confidence interval, 90% of samples would include the true value.

S. Shennan: *Quantifying archaeology* (Edinburgh, 1988), 301–9; M. Fletcher and G.R. Lock: *Digging numbers* (Oxford, 1991), 70–3.

CO

confirmatory data analysis (CDA) Term used to describe such classical approaches to statistical analysis as HYPOTHESIS TESTING, as opposed to the more open-minded techniques of EXPLORATORY DATA ANALYSIS (EDA).

Confucius (K'ung-tzu; Kongzi) *see* CH'U-FU; LU

Con Moong Cave located on the Cuc Phuong massif, south of the Red River Delta in Vietnam. It has an unusually long stratigraphic sequence, beginning with the late Pleistocene SON VI culture and terminating in a layer ascribed to the HOABINHIAN. The early stone industry was dominated by a flaked technology, but in the succeeding Hoabinhian layer 3, we find the first evidence of edge grinding and polishing. The cave was the focus of hunting and gathering, and the faunal remains include wild cattle and water buffalo, rhinoceros, forest birds and the water turtle.

Ha Van Tan: 'The Hoabinhian in the context of Viet Nam', *Vietnamese Studies* 46 (1976) 127–97.

CH

contextual archaeology Influential epistemological approach defined and promoted by the Cambridge theoretician Ian Hodder during the 1980s. Building upon a sustained critique of PROCESSUAL ARCHAEOLOGY, Hodder attempted to draw archaeologists away from a methodology based on the natural sciences and back towards a methodology rooted in the historical tradition.

An explanation of contextual archaeology is best preceded by a brief survey of Hodder's general theoretical position. Hodder particularly criticized SYSTEMS THEORY, which he regarded as having been applied with a materialist bias that denied the formative (as opposed to justificatory or concealing) power of IDEOLOGY. He also believed that systems theory assigned an overly passive role to the individual and offered an inadequate explanation of change through time. According to Hodder, adaptive mechanisms that regulate systems do not properly explain change because they cannot explain how societies 'choose' between a great variety of actions that possess the same potential systemic value. Hodder also disputed the claim that hypothetico-deductive methods ought to replace inductive reasoning, and asserted that MIDDLE-RANGE THEORY was unlikely to provide a platform for truly objective analysis of archaeological evidence. Hodder accepted that theories should be validated by a continuing examination of coherence and correspondence with the basic data, but insisted that the hypothetico-deductive method must be supplemented by intuitive insights arising from personal experience and from an attempt to get 'inside' past events and imagine the motives of the individuals concerned. He admitted the usefulness of general theory (not laws) and ETHNOGRAPHIC ANALOGY, but only when these are grounded in proper 'contextual' explanation. He also admitted certain 'universal principals of meaning' (such as the organization by contrasts, identified in STRUCTURALIST analysis). In the context of the 1980s, his ideas may be summarized as an attempt to redress the balance between contextual and cross-cultural interpretations; idealist and materialist explanations; inductive and hypothetico-deductive investigation; individual action and systemic adaptation; and historical and ahistorical perspectives.

Hodder's advocacy of a contextual archaeology sprang from a belief that the relationship between material culture and society is complex and interactive. In particular, material culture has a symbolic value that is not only important in itself, but also liable to distort the interpretation of more obvious technical, economic and social functions. Furthermore, this symbolic value varies not only from culture to culture, but even from situation to situation. To understand societies via their material culture, archaeologists must be able to interpret how the symbolic meaning of material culture is manipulated within a specific context by individuals and groups in pursuit of disparate social strategies (*see* SYMBOLIC ARCHAEOLOGY).

Within archaeology, 'context' is traditionally used to indicate either the depositional or cultural environment of an artefact. Contextual archaeology extends the term to include the whole network of relationships that give symbolic meaning to an object. In addition to being more extensive, 'context' in this sense is also more specific: it is the unique location of each element within the network that defines its meaning, just as the position of words within a sentence determines meaning in language. Hodder has stressed that contextual analysis includes examination of materialist as well as symbolic functions, of an object's place within a MODE OF PRODUCTION as well as within a symbolic code. He has also stretched the term to include a probing of the 'context of the archaeologist' (*see also* LOGICISM). However, when used by other archaeologists, the term tends to focus on the *contextually defined symbolic use of material culture*.

The two main criticisms of contextual archaeology seem paradoxical: that it simply describes what archaeologists do anyway, and that it makes archaeology impossible because it demands full contextual evidence. Hodder's response to the first criticism was that he simply sought to make explicit and to extend certain existing procedures; to the second he replied that, in some instances, proper analysis *would* be impossible. We should, he argued, accept that the symbols on a cave wall will remain scarcely readable if they cannot be related to evidence from different types of site – that is, if they lack a context. Contextual archaeology has been accused of being full of contradictions: it was born of anthropological research but denies cross-cultural laws; it stresses the unique contextual meaning of evidence, but recommends interpretation through a whole network of contexts; it searches for coherence and correspondences in a way that comes very close to PROCESSUAL ARCHAEOLOGY, but at the same time it promotes subjective understanding through 'insight'. Finally, it argues for the importance of individual action and complete contextual evidence within a discipline that is largely unsuited to these concerns – certainly, the more convincing studies explicitly adopting Hodder's approach have tended to make use of detailed ethnographic or ethnohistorical, evidence.

Despite these flaws, 'contextual' analysis proved a founding and influential strand within POST-PROCESSUAL ARCHAEOLOGY. Recapitulated and somewhat redefined by its originator in a collected series of essays (Hodder 1992), it occupies the centre ground of the theoretical debate when compared to more recent and extreme relativist positions within the post-processual movement.

I. Hodder: *The present past* (London, 1982); ——: *The archaeology of contextual meanings* (Cambridge, 1987); B. Trigger: *History of archaeological thought* (Cambridge, 1989), 348–57; I Hodder: *The domestication of Europe* (Oxford, 1990); ——: *Reading the past*, 2nd edn (Cambridge, 1991), 121–55; ——: *Theory and practice in archaeology* (London, 1992).

RJA

contingency table A table used in the statistical analysis of archaeological DATA to show the numbers of objects which take certain values of two (or more) VARIABLES, which are usually discrete but may be grouped values of continuous variables. The aim is to discover whether variables are associated, i.e. whether certain values of one occur more (or less) frequently with certain values of another than would be expected if there were no relationship between them. For example, one might investigate whether certain types of finds occur particularly on certain types of site. Analysis is most commonly carried out by use of the CHI-SQUARED TEST; modern methods include log-linear analysis and CORRESPONDENCE ANALYSIS.

Y.M.M. Bishop, S.E. Fienberg and P.W. Holland: *Discrete multivariate analysis* (Cambridge, 1975) [log-linear analysis]; J.E. Doran and F.R. Hodson: *Mathematics and computers in archaeology* (Edinburgh, 1975), 54–6; S. Shennan: *Quantifying archaeology* (Edinburgh, 1988), 70–4, 89–99; K. Barclay, M. Biddle and C. Orton: 'The chronological and spatial distribution of the objects', *Object and economy in medieval Winchester*, ed. M. Biddle (Oxford, 1990), 42–73 [Winchester]; M. Fletcher and G.R. Lock: *Digging numbers* (Oxford, 1991), 115–25 [general].

CO

continuous variable *see* VARIABLE

conventional radiocarbon dating RADIOCARBON DATING methods in which the beta particles from the decay of the ^{14}C atoms are counted using either liquid scintillation or gas counting (*see* ACCELERATOR MASS SPECTROMETRY). Only 1% of the ^{14}C atoms present decay every 80 years, hence about 3–5 g of carbon (equivalent to about 200 g of bone) are needed. Not to be confused with the convention for quoting radiocarbon dates.

SB

Copán Site in northwestern Honduras in the 'southeastern periphery' of the LOWLAND MAYA area, known for its extraordinary stelae (*see* STELE, MESOAMERICAN) and architecture, including a large ballcourt (*see* BALLGAME) and HIEROGLYPHIC stairway. A long-term, multi-disciplinary, international research project has focused on the elite architecture, inscriptions and dynastic history, and burial patterns of Copán, as well as on settlement patterns, population change and land use in the large Copán valley area. This project has led to revision of many long-standing interpretations of the site's history.

Like many Maya sites, Copán is best known for its architecture and monuments dating to the Classic period (*c*.AD 300–900). Nevertheless, the Copán region clearly had a long settlement history going back to the late Early Preclassic period (*c*.1000–800 BC). A small rectangular house with associated domestic artefacts was found in excavations, deeply buried under a later residential compound. In the same area a series of Middle Preclassic (*c*.800–300 BC) burials were uncovered, richly furnished with jade beads and other items and ceramics with incised motifs typical of OLMEC culture. Occupation in the Late Preclassic period (*c*.300 BC–AD 300) was not substantial, a situation Fash (1991: 71) describes as an 'anomaly' given the striking developments during this period at places like KAMINALJUYU to the southwest and in the lowlands to the north.

Copán's participation in Classic period Maya culture was traditionally believed to have been the result of colonization of the area by elite settlers from the Petén region to the north, who brought with them the lowland Maya STELE cult. The first stele with a 'long count' date at Copán dates to AD 485. Recent investigations, however, have revised this view, leading to the conclusion that the stele cult with its associated HIEROGLYPHIC WRITING and 'long count' dating, typical Maya architecture, polychrome pottery, divine kingship and other characteristics of Maya civilization, developed locally (Fash 1991).

Copán has also contributed to our understanding of the complex patterns of the Classic LOWLAND MAYA collapse. Fash (1991) sees the political collapse as a consequence of inter-elite competition and possibly inter-ethnic conflict, while acknowledging the role of population growth and the consequent stresses on agricultural productivity. Regardless of the causes, the more refined chronologies afforded by OBSIDIAN HYDRATION DATING (Webster and Freter 1990) from residential construction have indicated that the 'collapse' at Copán was a prolonged process, rather than a sudden event, with the closing stages of the Late Classic (Coner phase) occupation of the site extending until perhaps as late as AD 1200. The last centuries of the Late Classic period were accompanied by population movements away from the civic-ceremonial centre into more peripheral areas of the valley.

D. Webster and A. Freter: 'Settlement history and the classic collapse at Copan: a redefined chronological perspective', *LAA* 1 (1990) 66–85; W.L. Fash: *Scribes, warriors and kings. The city of Copán and the ancient Maya* (London, 1991); 'The archaeology of ancient Copan', *AM* 3 (Spring, 1992) [several authors].

PRI

Coppergate (York) The Coppergate excavations in York, which took place between 1976 and 1981, revealed the remains of the wattle-built workshops at the back of a line of four 10th-century tenements. The remains are the main feature of the Jorvik Centre, an influential 'Viking experience' in which the modern visitor takes a train – a type of time-capsule – back through the ages to Anglo-Scandinavian York in the age of King Eric Bloodaxe. Statuesque figures among the ruins speak a Viking dialect, and smells add to the atmosphere. The visitor passes through a reconstruction of the museum before entering a traditional museum. The 'experience' illustrates Viking urbanism and industrial productivity, and lays emphasis upon archaeology as a technologically-based science.

Richard Hall: *The Viking dig* (London, 1984).

RH

'Copper Hoard Culture' *see* OCHRE COLOURED POTTERY (OCP)

coprolites (palaeofaeces) Ancient copralites, sometimes called palaeofaeces, are the preserved remains of human or animal defecation. Their survival is usually as a result of dessication, waterlogging, mineralization or charring. Coprolites are particularly valuable as direct evidence of prehistoric diet, though they are generally not preserved with sufficient regularity to form an independent test for the vagaries of faunal and botanical analysis. Perhaps the most remarkable concentrations of well-preserved human coprolites have been found in cave-sites in the American south-west (e.g. Bryant 1974).

V.M. Bryant: 'Prehistoric diet in south-west Texas: the coprolite evidence', *AA* 39 (1974), 407–20; V.M. Bryant and G. Williams-Dean: 'The coprolites of man', *SA* 232 (1975), 100–9; G. Hillman: 'Plant foods in ancient diet: the archaeological role of palaeofaeces in general and Lindow Man's gut in particular', *Lindow Man: the body in the bog* (London, 1986), 99–115.

RJA

Coptic Term used to describe the Christian period in Egypt, lasting from the end of the Roman domination to the Islamic conquest (*c.*AD 400–641), which is broadly contemporary with the Byzantine period elsewhere in the Near East. The art historical definition of 'Coptic' is somewhat vague, since the term is often applied not only to the material culture of the Christian period but also to material from the late Roman period in the 3rd and 4th centuries AD ('proto-Coptic') and the early medieval period (*c.*AD 700–1200). The Coptic language and alphabet, which combines Greek letters with six signs taken from DEMOTIC, were used throughout the Christian period in Egypt. The liturgies and Biblical texts of the Coptic church are still written and spoken in the Coptic language. The archaeology of the Coptic period has been comparatively neglected, compared with the excavation of pharaonic and Greco-Roman sites, but a few expeditions in the late 20th century (such as the German study of the pilgrimage centre of Abu Mina at Maryut, to the west of Alexandria, see Grossman 1986), have begun to address this yawning gap. In addition, examples of early Coptic art and monumental architecture have survived at such isolated and still-flourishing Coptic monasteries as St Anthony's in the Eastern Desert and St Catherine's in the Sinai peninsula.

C.C. Walters: *Monastic archaeology in Egypt* (Warminster, 1974); P. Grossmann: *Abu Mina: a guide to the ancient pilgrimage center* (Cairo, 1986); J. Kamil: *Coptic Egypt* (Cairo, 1987); G. Gabra: *Cairo, the Coptic Museum and old churches* (Cairo, 1993).

IS

corbelled arch The 'false' or cantilevered arch used in LOWLAND MAYA construction, having the form of an inverted 'V' and topped with a flat capstone rather than a fitted keystone. Compared to the true arch it is much weaker and this limitation contributed to the typically thick walls and narrow rooms of Classic Maya buildings.

E.H. Thompson: 'The genesis of the Maya arch', *American Anthropologist* 13 (1911), 501–16; A.L. Smith: 'The corbelled arch in the New World', *The Maya and their neighbours*, ed. C.L. Hay et al. (New York, 1977), 202–21.

PRI

corbelling Simple roofing technique involving the creation of dome or beehive-shaped roofs by laying over-lapping courses of masonry closer and closer to the centre of the space to be covered. Fine examples of early corbelling can be seen in the Neolithic chambered tombs of ANTEQUERA in Spain; the Mycenaean THOLOS tombs of Greece in the later 2nd millennium represent the most sophisticated use of the technique.

RJA

Corded Ware complex Cultural complex of northern Europe in the earlier 3rd millennium BC (*c*.2900–2500 BC) characterized by the production of beakers (tall handle-less vessels with everted rims) decorated on their upper half with impressions of cords; polished stone axes with bored shaft-holes and curving 'battle-axe' type blades; and individual male burials covered by circular mounds. There are also occasional finds of small items made of copper in Corded Ware contexts, identifying it as a Late Neolithic/Copper Age transitional culture.

Manifested across much of the North European plain from Scandinavia and the Rhineland and Switzerland through into Russia, the Corded Ware complex, like the BELL BEAKER PHENOMENON to which it is in some senses a predecessor, has in the past been taken to represent a movement of specific peoples through Europe in the 3rd millennium BC (most often, nomadic pastoralists from the Russian steppe lands to the east). However, many scholars now interpret the presence of the complex as indicating the adoption of a cultural 'package' by local populations. Because the funerary rite tends to be individual rather than communal, and because the most notable gravegood has been interpreted as a battleaxe (there is also some evidence to link the decorated beakers to the use of alcohol in drinking ceremonies), the advent of the Corded Ware culture is sometimes taken as indicating the spread of an aggressive, individualizing male warrior culture (a view summarized in Sherratt 1994). It is not yet clear where this package of material culture was first adopted, although a set of early male burials set in pits under low mounds (rather than laid on the ground under mounds) can be identified in a broad region stretching between Denmark and the Ukraine. In the earlier 3rd millennium, across much of the area manifesting the Corded Ware, the settlement pattern seems to become more dispersed, with settlement units tending to consist of small hamlets and farmsteads; this has been interpreted as indicating a general shift in subsistence strategies towards 'expansive' (rather than intensive) farming with the adoption of the plough in agriculture, and a greater emphasis on stock-breeding (*see* SECONDARY PRODUCTS REVOLUTION). *See also* FATYANOVO *for description of the eastern European variant of the Corded Ware complex.*

A. Sherratt: 'The transformation of early agrarian Europe: the later Neolithic and Copper Ages 4500–2500 BC', *The Oxford illustrated prehistory of Europe*, ed. B. Cunliffe (Oxford, 1994), 190–3.

RJA

core-periphery models Theoretical models concerned with how social, economic, cultural and political relationships between societies bring about change. Like PEER-POLITY INTERACTION models, they emphasize the importance of relationships with external societies for the understanding of social change, rather than purely internal factors or interaction with the environment; in this case, however, the relationships are essentially unequal. The most detailed example of such a model is the historian Immanuel Wallerstein's analysis of the emergence of European world domination in the early modern period (*see* WORLD SYSTEMS THEORY). Although Wallerstein was not concerned with pre-capitalist societies, the potential application of his ideas to earlier societies has attracted archaeological attention.

The models envisage a contrast between a core, or centre, and a periphery. The core may comprise more than one political entity, but has a broadly common culture, characterized as technologically, economically and politically more developed than the periphery. The periphery may be very extensive, and is typically a supplier of labour or raw materials. The relationship between core and periphery is asymmetric in the sense that the economic advantages flow to the centre from the periphery, but also in the sense that social, economic and political conditions at the centre affect, or even determine, those at the periphery, but not vice versa. The model as originally developed was specifically economic, and needs reinterpretation for pre-capitalist societies. In prehistory, economic activity can seldom be entirely isolated from the social sphere. Core–periphery models in archaeology concentrate on long-distance connections, identified particularly through exchange of exotic goods, and the role they play in the social reproduction of the societies concerned. Examples include the relationship between Mesoamerica and the cultures of the Mexican American West, described with other case studies in Champion (1989).

M. Rowlands et al.: *Centre and periphery in the ancient world* (Cambridge, 1987); T. Champion, ed.: *Centre and periphery: comparative studies in archaeology* (London, 1989).

TC

core tool and scraper tradition *see* AUSTRALIAN CORE TOOL AND SCRAPER TRADITION

correspondence analysis Technique of MULTIVARIATE ANALYSIS which was originally a French technique but made its way into the English-speaking world via Scandinavia and South Africa. It is similar in some ways to PRINCIPAL COMPONENTS ANALYSIS (PCA), but designed for use on two-way tables of discrete DATA (*see* CONTINGENCY TABLES). Like PCA, it extracts axes of maximum variability (here called inertia), against which objects can be plotted. It differs from PCA in its metric (measure of distance); the distance between two rows (or columns) of a table is the CHI-SQUARED STATISTIC that would be derived from a comparison of the two.

J.-P. Benzecri et al.: *L'analyse des donnees*, 2: *L'analyse des correspondances* (Paris, 1973); E. Bolviken et al.: 'Correspondence analysis: an alternative to principal components analysis', *WA* 14 (1982) 41–60; M.J. Greenacre: *Theory and applications of correspondence analysis* (New York, 1984); T. Madsen, ed.: *Multivariate archaeology* (Aarhus, 1988); M.J. Baxter: *Exploratory multivariate analysis in archaeology* (Edinburgh, 1993).

CO

corrosion product Chemical compound, or usually a mixture of compounds, formed through the natural chemical reaction of a metal artefact with its environment. Although most obvious on the surface of the metal it is also likely to be present internally. Most corrosion products are mixtures including oxides, hydroxides, carbonates or chlorides.

MC

Cortaillod Cultural complex of the Middle Neolithic in Switzerland, identified by Emil Vogt in 1934 and known largely from lakeside villages, especially around Lake Neuchâtel (the location of the typesite, Cortaillod). The Neuchâtel lakeside villages also include numerous well-preserved sites from the Bronze Age.

The Neolithic Cortaillod cultural complex succeeds the Egolzwil in Switzerland, and is broadly contemporary with – and related to – the other major cultural complexes of west-central Europe in the Middle Neolithic, the Michelsberg and the Chasséen. Typical features of Cortaillod pottery assemblages are lugs, cordons and high 'S-profile' jars; the presence of lamps, large numbers of antler beakers and the use of birchbark appliqué decoration help distinguish the material culture of the Cortaillod from that of the Chasséen. Although there is no evidence for metalworking in the Cortaillod, a few metal objects (beads and flat axes) are found, probably imported from the neighbouring Pfyn or Michelsberg regions. Typically, Cortaillod villages comprised 15–25 houses, built on a wooden frame fixed into soft ground, with sloping roofs and walls made of firm poles and plaster.

There are also various Late Bronze Age sites along the Neuchâtel shoreline, known and planned from aerial surveys. In the early 1980s, ambitious underwater rescue excavations took place at the site of Cortaillod-Este, revealing a settlement that grew into a cluster of around 17 houses and which was associated with a series of dams and pallisades. Like most of the Swiss prehistoric 'lake villages' the settlement was located on soft ground near the edge of the lake, rather than being built on piles in the water itself as early interpreters tended to surmise. The original oak posts of the basic house structures are well preserved, revealing houses *c*.8–15m long in regular, dense narrow rows oriented north-west by south-east. Dendrochronology has allowed the development of the settlement (1009–955 BC) to be minutely charted, although given the small size of the village (estimated population: 150–400), the claim that the planning was in some sense 'proto-urban' seems enthusiastic.

B. Arnold: *Cortaillod-Este et les villages du lac de Neuchâtel au Bronze final*, Archéologie neuchâteloise 6 (Sainte-Blaise, 1990).

RJA

cost-benefit analysis *see* DECISION THEORY

Cotswold-Severn (Severn-Cotswold) tombs Regional group of megalithic and/or drystone tombs constructed in south-west Britain from the early 4th millennium BC; they are concentrated to the east of the River Severn in the Cotswold hills, but also occur more sporadically in southeast Wales, from Brecon to the Gower Peninsula. The group was traditionally defined morphologically and culturally within a geographical framework (e.g. Daniel 1950), but recent researchers have preferred a simple geographic definition (Darvill 1982). The chambers are usually covered by long wedge-shaped mounds, which may have indented or concave façades or well-developed 'horned' fore-courts. The most impressive Cotswold–Severn monument is that of WEST KENNET, which forms something of a type-site, while the laterally chambered tomb at Hazleton near Cheltenham is the most recently and painstakingly excavated (Saville 1990). Useful guides to the extensive literature may be found in Daniel (1970) and Darvill (1982).

G. Daniel: *The prehistoric chambertombs of England and Wales* (Cambridge, 1950); ——: 'Megalithic answers', *Antiquity* 44 (1970), 260–9; T.C. Darvill: *The megalithic chambered tombs of the Cotswold–Severn region* (Highworth, 1982); A. Saville et al.: *Hazleton North* (London, 1990).

RJA

covering laws In archaeology, as in other sciences, an attempt to explain a phenomenon may consist of an attempt to show that it falls under a law 'covering' similar phenomena – a law which suggests a particular outcome or a particular relationship between two sets of evidence. A covering law does not have to be sophisticated or answer an important question, but it does have to be general and to be formulated so as to be true in every situation where the stated conditions hold. A covering law is not the only way to forge a relationship between data and different levels of theory explaining that data (*see* THEORY AND THEORY BUILDING), but the approach lies at the centre of certain key debates in the philosophy of science and has played an important role in the continuing debate about the merits of PROCESSUAL ARCHAEOLOGY.

The belief in the centrality of covering, or general, laws in philosophical and scientific enquiry formed the dominant strand of the LOGICAL POSITIVIST movement from the late 1940s. In this movement, the covering law approach to describing and explaining events in the world was taken to its extreme. It was assumed that the only true or useful kind of explanation was the strictly logical result of a combination of covering (general) laws and initial (starting) conditions. Because the outcome is governed by logic, it is predictable – providing the starting conditions are true and the law has been proved empirically. In the logical positivist project, covering laws themselves were to be discovered by rigorously formulating *hypotheses* which could then be tested empirically. The relationship between the covering law, starting conditions and outcome is *deduced* logically. Thus, this use of covering laws falls into the more general hypothetico-deductive means of scientific enquiry (*see* INDUCTIVE AND DEDUCTIVE EXPLANATION).

One key developer of the approach was the philosopher of science, Carl Hempel. Hempel differentiated the kind of covering law argument in which the conclusion is logically certain (deductive-nomological explanations) from the kind of scientific argument that employs the laws of probability to suggest how *likely* a conclusion is (statistical, or inductive probabilistic, explanations). Statistical explanations are not deduced, but they still make use of covering laws, together with laws of probability and sometimes logic, to generate meaningful statements about the world. Hempel maintained that these two covering law or generalizing means of enquiry – deductive-nomological explanation and inductive probabilistic explanation – described most valid routes of enquiry. *See also* NOMOTHETIC ARGUMENTS.

This general approach hugely influenced the New Archaeology of the 1960s. It implied that a principal *aim* of archaeologists should be the discovery and confirmation of laws, through a process of formulating hypotheses that could be tested against archaeological data. This seemed likely to shift the discipline towards the formulation of general theories of the kind seen in geography and anthropology, as opposed to the more traditional particularist, historical approach. It also suggested that archaeological practice should be slanted toward problem solving and theory testing, rather than the 'theory neutral' collection of evidence to be evaluated later on. As a network of tested theory evolved, and became accepted as generalizing (covering) laws and law-like propositions, it was hoped that it would become possible to interpret individual sites with more certainty and to test higher-level theories concerning social dynamics.

In practice, the formulation and verification of universal laws proved elusive. There was a continuing debate about the most useful definition and application of an archaeological 'law', and in particular how to discover whether a law was simply descriptive or contained within it the 'cause' of a relationship between statements (a much more ambitious project). There was also disagreement about whether the aim of archaeology was to use covering laws to elucidate archaeological cultures, or whether it was to use archaeological cultures to identify covering laws. In practice, it proved difficult to put observations of archaeological phenomena into language that facilitated logical deduction or testing without instantaneously interpreting the phenomena in such a way as to compromise the exercise. It was also not clear that a laborious statement of definitions and assumptions increased the value, or acceptance, of an archaeological statement. Gibbon (1989) suggests that most processual archaeologists side-stepped the problem of stating definitions and assumptions in such a way as to make their hypothesis testable; they did this by offering up preliminary ideas that were subsequently rarely pursued in any systematic way. Reviewing the New Archaeology project twenty years after its inception, he concludes: 'no non-trivial general laws of cultural process were ever systematically tested and formally confirmed or falsified: no formal covering-law model explanations were ever presented except in "they would look like this" illustrative examples; no deductive theory nets were ever formally proposed' (1989: 91).

However, the failure of the more dogmatically 'scientific' New Archaeologists to produce a varied and useful body of tested and useful covering laws does not mean that the New Archaeology project – in its wider definition – failed. The more pragmatic search for covering laws that would provide a robust link between archaeological evidence and human behaviour in the form of MIDDLE-RANGE THEORY stimulated excellent and novel research: even critics of the covering law approach in archaeology recognize great value in the better studies of SITE FORMATION PROCESSES. It may also be that the covering law approach in the discipline has left a useful legacy in the relatively more explicit formulation and assessing of hypotheses – whether or not this assessment leads to formal testing and the positing of a covering law. On a more abstract level, many of the arguments about the validity of the covering law approach continue to be revisited in the ongoing debate in archaeology about the usefulness and validity of cross-cultural and ETHNOGRAPHIC ANALOGIES and law-like statements, and the relationship between the aims of archaeology and those of the other social sciences.

C.G. Hempel: 'Studies in the logic of explanation', *Philosophy of Science* 15 (1948), 135–75; ——: 'Deductive–nomological vs statistical explanation', *Minnesota Studies in the Philosophy of Science*, vol. 3, ed. H. Feigl and G. Maxwell (Minneapolis, 1962); ——: *Aspects of scientific explanation* (New York, 1965); L. Binford: 'Smudge pits and hide smoking: the use of analogy in archaeological reasoning', *AA* 32 (1967), 1–12; ——: 'Some comments on historical versus processual archaeology', *SJA*, 24 (1968), 267–75; J.M. Fritz and F.T. Plog: 'The nature of archaeological explanation', *AA* 35 (1970), 405–12; D.W. Read and S.A. LeBlanc: 'Descriptive statements, covering laws, and theories in archaeology', *CA* 19 (1978), 307–35; P.J. Watson, S.A. LeBlanc and C.L. Redman: *Explanation in archaeology: an explicitly scientific approach* (New York and London, 1971); G. Gibbon: *Explanation in archaeology* (Oxford, 1989), 86–7.

RJA

Craig Mound *see* SPIRO

Criş culture *see* STARCEVO-KÖRÖS-CRIŞ CULTURE

critical archaeology A primarily American school of archaeological theory, which closely resembles POST-PROCESSUAL ARCHAEOLOGY in that it comprises a rather eclectic mixture of approaches, drawing on Marxism, STRUCTURALISM and CRITICAL THEORY, being united primarily by the rejection of POSITIVISM and PROCESSUAL ARCHAEOLOGY. Most 'critical archaeologists' have also been heavily influenced by the view that archaeology has an active, politicized role to play in the presentation of the past to the public, whether through museum displays, degree programmes or other media (see, for instance, Leone 1986; Potter 1990). Despite such demonstrable similarities to post-processualism, the more Marxist-inspired proponents of the critical approach have been criticized by the post-processualists Michael Shanks and Chris Tilley (1987) for crusading against ideological (particularly capitalist) bias in archaeology, instead of adopting the kind of radical pluralist, hyper-relativist approach which assumes that there are many equally defensible views of the same set of archaeological data.

M.P. Leone: 'Symbolic, structural and critical archaeology', *American archaeology: past and future*, eds D.J. Meltzer et al. (Washington, D.C., 1986), 415–38; M. Shanks and C. Tilley: *Archaeology and social theory* (Cambridge, 1987); V. Pinskie and A. Wylie, eds: *Critical traditions in contemporary archaeology* (Cambridge, 1989); B.P. Potter, Jr.: 'The "what" and "why" of public relations for archaeology: a postscript to DeCicco's public relations primer', *AA* 55/3 (1990), 608–13.

IS

critical theory Anti-POSITIVIST, anti-modernist theory espoused by the academic, intellectual proponents of western MARXISM, who react to the pervasive and dominant nature of capitalism by stressing that empirical, logical positivist analysis is not truly objective but heavily biased and value-laden by the IDEOLOGIES of scientists. The movement, inaugurated by Max Horkheimer, the director of the Frankfurt Institute for Social Research in the 1920s (hence the term 'Frankfurt School', which is sometimes applied to the earliest phase of critical theory), also stresses the early (Hegelian) writings of Marx and avoids the economic determinism of orthodox Marxism – focusing instead on analysis of the role of the superstructure, and ideology in particular. The approach was adopted by many anthropologists from the 1970s onwards, and by a number of American archaeologists in the 1980s and 1990s (*see* CRITICAL ARCHAEOLOGY). Critical theorists argue that even their own analyses are indissociable from the social and ideological context in which they take place (hence the anti-positivist stance); they therefore concentrate on the hermeneutics of their subject (i.e. the process of interpretation itself), attempting, by discriminating between the various possible versions of the past, to emancipate people from dominant ideologies. Hodder (1991: 178) argues that critical theory is fatally flawed by the fact that it is itself a value-laden and ideologically biased phenomenon: 'If the past is ideology, how can we presume to argue that only certain intellectuals [i.e. critical theorists and critical archaeologists] can see through ideology to identify the social reality?'

M. Horkheimer and T. Adorno: *Dialectic of enlightenment* (New York, 1972); D. Held: *Introduction to critical theory: Horkheimer to Habermas* (Berkeley, 1980); I. Hodder: *Reading the past*, 2nd edn, (Cambridge, 1991), 174–80.

IS

Crô Magnon Rock-shelter site at Les Eyzies, France, where the first ANATOMICALLY MODERN HUMAN (AMH) human remains were discovered in the 19th century. It became the type-site for AMH populations, often known in the older literature as 'Cro-Magnon man', in contrast to NEANDERTHAL populations.

RJA

cromlech This term has fallen out of use in Britain, but like the term 'dolmen' it was once used to indicate a simple megalithic structure consisting of uprights supporting a capstone – especially when there was no extant covering mound. In France and Iberia, the term *cromlech* is used to identify a quite different class of megalithic structure: rings of free-standing stones such as those found in the CARNAC REGION of France and the Evora region of Portugal.

RJA

cropmarks Non-upstanding features, archaeological or otherwise, can often be distinguished from the air as 'cropmarks', where differential growth reveals their presence below growing crops. The study of cropmarks has revealed that areas where archaeological features are now least readily apparent as surviving structures may be those where past activity has been most intense. These are often the lighter soils, such as those on gravels, which are often under almost constant cultivation over millennia. The archaeological record is otherwise biased toward areas with abundant stone, those which have not been subject to significant later cultivation and land-use change, and marginal or upland areas, whether in the deserts of the American mid-west or the upland moors of Britain.

Aerial reconnaissance, combined with modern intensive fieldwalking techniques, partially redresses the balance. However, the identification of 'sites' as cropmarks depends not only on the highly variable effects of climate, crops, soil types and agricultural regimes, but also on the character of the archaeology. It provides an effective means of recognition for some site types such as ditched enclosures, but if enclosure were by a hedge, its cropmark visibility would be almost non-existent. Unenclosed settlement can usually only be recognized where substantial pits or structural foundations survive, and many classes of site, including virtually all of the pre-Neolithic archaeological record of Europe, offer little susceptibility to this technique. Thus, while the results of aerial reconnaissance in filling out the understanding of the rich archaeological resources of some areas have been immense, the limitations must be remembered. Cropmarks are most common when soil moisture deficit in a particular soil affects a crop during its peak moisture demand. This varies from crop to crop: while the phenomenon is commonest in cereals in summer, cropmarks may be recorded in maize in September, or roots in autumn or winter. Although not regularly producing cropmarks, grass can sometimes produce very clear marks ('grassmarks' or 'parchmarks'). Non crop plants – weeds – may also grow differentially, picking out features.

Cropmarks occur in either positive or negative form, depending on the relationship of feature and surrounding material. Normally, positive cropmarks manifest themselves as stronger, denser or taller growth in the maturing crop, or as a slightly later ripening, evident as colour variation. These types of marks are produced by such features as ditches and pits. Negative cropmarks (in grass, parchmarks), where the buried features are less moisture-retentive than their surroundings, such as walls or road surfaces, appear as stunting, parching or early ripening. Sites revealed in relief may be recorded in oblique lighting conditions. There is also a wide diversity of 'abnormal' types of cropmark, including reversal.

Cropmarks may have other causes than those described above: if germination marks are seen in a developing crop, this may relate to moisture content (particularly where either the buried feature or the surrounding subsoil is waterlogged), or it may derive from variation in the warmth-retaining characteristics, through factors such as moisture-retention or humic or stone content, allowing earlier sprouting of seed; FROSTMARKS are products of a similar process. Cropmarks can derive from SOILMARKS, where variation in soil colour affects the reflectance and heat-retaining capacity of the soil, and hence crop growth.

R.J.A. Jones and R. Evans: 'Soil and crop marks in the recognition of archaeological sites by air photography', *Aerial reconnaissance for archaeology*, ed. D.R. Wilson (London, 1975): 1–11; D.R. Wilson; *Air photo interpretation for archaeologists* (London, 1982), 53–70; G.W.G. Allen: 'Discovery from the air', *Aerial Archaeology* 10 (1984) [whole issue].

FG

cross-cultural laws and analogies When archaeologists attempt to explain archaeological data and build plausible theories, they often try to relate archaeological evidence to the evidence seen in other cultures (past or present). These analogies may relate to low-level theorizing, such as how a particular implement was used, or to higher level theories such as those concerning the emergence of agriculture or the reasons for a cultural collapse. Analogies are often constructed very loosely – for example, an attempt to increase the plausibility of a particular explanation by showing that a similar set of evidence can be linked to a similar kind of behaviour or event in another culture. Sometimes, however, archaeologists try to make the link between the analogy and the archaeological phenomena under investigation more rigorous (see discussion of formal and relational analogy in ETHNOARCHAEOLOGY), either to increase the plausibility of the analogy in that particular instance, or as an attempt to build a COVERING LAW – that is, a law that is held to be true in all equivalent instances.

RJA

cross dating A method of relative dating from artefacts, whereby the occurrence of a foreign object of culture x found in association with objects of culture y is taken to mean that y must be contemporary with or later than x. Where the date of the import from culture x is known, culture y can sometimes be dated. Before the advent of absolute dating methods elaborate chronologies were constructed using the cross-dating method, often relying on similarities between objects in two cultures as well as actual imports from one culture to another. This comparison of similarities made the technique one of the key elements in the diffusionism of Childe and others, as well as in the hyper-diffusionism of Elliot-Smith and his school. Re-assessment by radiocarbon showed that many of these supposed links based on similarities were invalid.

V.G. Childe: *The dawn of European civilization* (London, 1925); C. Renfrew: *Before civilization* (London, 1973), 30–2.

PTN

Cross River Monoliths Set of 295 carved boulders, recorded by P.A. Allison in 1961–2 and described by him as a 'remarkably isolated phenomenon', located at 39 sites in a 900 sq. km area northwest of Ikom in southeastern Nigeria. They occur mostly in groups, of which 10 are circular, but there are some single stones on the periphery. Most are of basalt, although some are of shelly limestone, and they vary in height from less than 0.5 m to 2 m. The present Ekoi-speaking inhabitants of the area know them as 'Akwanshi', memorials for the ancestors. The Ekoi are divided into seven main clans, traditionally forming two antagonistic groups, each headed by a chief priest or Ntoon. According to Allison (1968: 26), recognizably different styles coincide with present clan boundaries, suggesting that the carvings were made by their predecessors: 'the decorations on the figures probably represent tribal marks, tattooing or body painting'. He considered that the monoliths of the Nta clan were the prototype for all the others, since they show the greatest variety of styles (from the phallic columns at Oyengi onwards) and the traditions about them are better preserved. Relying on information about the succession of the 39 Ntoons of the Nta, and assuming that the art of stone carving developed only after the establishment of their line, Allison argued that the carvings had probably been made from the early 16th century AD onwards. The only excavation conducted in the area, that by Ekpo Eyo at the Nnam clan site of Emangabe in 1983, produced a radiocarbon date of considerably greater antiquity 1780 ± 50 BP (AD 170); but he warns that this seems 'rather early' and 'must be viewed with great caution' (Eyo 1986).

P.A. Allison: *Cross River monoliths* (Lagos, 1968); E. Eyo: 'Alok and Emangabe stone monoliths: Ikom, Cross River

State of Nigeria', *Art in Africa – reality and perspectives in a study of the history of African arts*, ed. E. Bassani (Modena, 1986), 101–4.
PA-J

Crystal River North American site located near the mouth of Crystal River on Florida's north central peninsular Gulf Coast. It consists of a complex of sand and shell burial – and PLATFORM-MOUNDS, earthworks and midden heaps that were constructed and used over several hundred years. The lower portion of the centrally-located burial mound appears to be associated with the Deptford (Yent Complex) occupation (AD 100–500). Exotic artefacts from this part of the mound (copper ear-spools, sheet mica, quartz crystals) indicate ties to HOPEWELLIAN-affiliated groups elsewhere in the southeastern or mid-western United States. The upper parts of the burial mound and an associated platform-mound and enclosure appear to have been built during the 'Weeden Island' period (AD 400–800).
G. Willey: 'Archaeology of the Florida Gulf Coast', *Smithsonian Miscellaneous Collections* 113 (Washington, D.C., 1962); J. Milanich: *Archaeology of Precolumbian Florida* (Gainesville, 1994), 215–21; B. Weisman: *Crystal River: a ceremonial mound center on the Florida Gulf Coast* (Tallahassee, 1995).
RJE

Ctesiphon *see* PARTHIANS; SASANIANS

c-transforms Abbreviation for 'cultural formation processes', a term coined by the American archaeologist Michael Schiffer (e.g. 1976, 1987) to describe the ways in which human activities (such as burial practices or treatment of refuse) affect archaeological remains. C-transforms and N-TRANSFORMS were the two distinct types of 'SITE FORMATION PROCESSES' outlined by Schiffer in his description of BEHAVIORAL ARCHAEOLOGY. The term 'c-transforms', in addition to referring to the cultural influences on the original formation of the archaeological record, was also applied by Schiffer to such post-depositional activities as ploughing, looting or even the act of archaeological excavation itself.
M.B. Schiffer: *Behavioral archaeology* (New York, 1976); L.S. Binford: 'Behavioural archaeology and the "Pompeii premise"', *JAR* 37/3 (1981), 195–208; M.B. Schiffer: *Formation processes of the archaeological record* (Albuquerque, 1987).
IS

Cucuteni-Tripolye *see* TRIPOLYE

Cuello Site in northern Belize, which is the most extensively excavated Middle Formative village in the Maya lowlands, although occupation extends considerably later. The first suite of radiocarbon dates associated with early Swasey-phase pottery from the site suggested extremely – perhaps unbelievably – early dates for the establishment of a farming village in the lowlands in the late 3rd millennium BC (Hammond 1977). These dates were associated with pottery, corn and other domesticated plant remains and vestiges of perishable houses on low stone platforms. Assays of new carbon samples (Andrews and Hammond 1990), however, argue for a more orthodox revised dating for this material in the early 1st millennium BC. The burial evidence suggests that social ranking began as early as the 7th century BC.
N. Hammond: 'The earliest Maya', *SA* 236 (1977) 116–33; E.W. Andrews and N. Hammond: 'Redefinition of the Swasey phase at Cuello, Belize', *AA* 55 (1990) 570–84.
PRI

Cuevo Iglesia One of some 40 caves in the southwestern Bolivar state of Western Venezuela, dating from about 1000 BC to the present day. The cave contains pictographs and is the only known example with over a hundred motifs. Work with shamans of the local Piaroa Indians (who still use the cave as a cemetery) has enabled an understanding of the significance of the rock art to the present-day indigenous peoples.
F. Scaramelli: *Las pinturas rupestres del Parguaza: mito y representación* (Ph.D. thesis, Universidad Central de Venezuela, Caracas).
KB

cultural lag Term used particularly in the field of Chinese archaeology to refer to the time element involved in the passage of technical, artistic, and other cultural influences from the source of origin to distant cultures. The concept, as applied to Chinese metallurgy, takes into account not only the period of passage of technical 'know-how', but also that which followed its assimilation after arrival, i.e. the ensuing period of experiment and modification, the search for metals (the development of mining and smelting operations, and/or trade for metals), the manufacture of simple artefacts from two-piece mould-assemblies developing in time to more complex core-cast artefacts, articulated joinery, thence the casting of containers (generally in two-piece mould-assemblies). While it is not always easy to state precisely the length of this 'cultural lag', the important point is that the process was not instantaneous.

N. Barnard and Satö Tamotsu: *Metallurgical remains of ancient China* (Tokyo, 1975); ——: 'Bronze casting technology in the peripheral "barbarian" regions', *BMM* 12 (1987), 3–37.

NB

culture-historical theories *see* CULTURE HISTORY

culture history Term used to describe a broad range of archaeological approaches that use historical explanatory principles to examine changes in culture. The origins of cultural-historical archaeology are to be found in the late 18th century, when the word culture (which had once been applied simply to the practice of agriculture) began to be used by German ethnologists to describe rural or tribal ways of life in contrast to the 'civilized' socio-economic activities of city-dwellers (e.g. Klemm 1843–52). By the late 19th century, scholars such as E.B. Tylor (1871) and Eduard Meyer (1884–1902) were writing about culture in its broader, more modern sense of 'a particular form, stage or type of intellectual development or civilization'.

Trigger (1989: 163) argues that the systematic definition of a whole sequence of interacting groups of 'archaeological cultures', such as the CYCLADIC or TRIPOLYE cultures, did not fully emerge until the nationalistically-motivated attempts of the German archaeologist Gustaf Kossinna (1911) to establish the origins of the INDO-EUROPEAN peoples. From this point until the emergence of NEW ARCHAEOLOGY, the idea of prehistory and history as long sequences of spatial and temporal mosaics of cultures was firmly established. Whereas 19th-century scholars had primarily viewed cultural change in terms of an evolution from primitive to advanced forms of culture and technology, the cultural-historical archaeologists of the early 20th century began to describe and analyse changes in the archaeological record in terms of the emergence and movement of different (but not necessarily more 'advanced') cultural groupings. Needless to say, such archaeologists did not self-consciously proclaim any programmatic 'culture history' approach to archaeology – the term itself was rarely used until the advent of New Archaeology (see below).

The work of such pioneering archaeologists as Gordon Childe (1925), James Ford and Gordon Willey (1941), working within the culture history framework, did a great deal to establish meaningful chronological foundations for European and American archaeology. There were, however, also numerous misuses and abuses of the idea of culture-history, such as the work of hyper-diffusionists (*see* DIFFUSIONISM) and nationalists (including Kossinna). Culture historians are also sometimes accused of assuming the dominance of cultural norms (shared sets of rules and expectations; *see* NORMATIVE EXPLANATIONS). It is of course via norms, expressed through material culture, that archaeologists are able to identify distinct cultures in the archaeological record in the first place – but in some cultural-historical explanations this can lead to a down-playing of cultural dissention, cultural dynamics and the actions of individuals. It can also lead to an unwarranted equating of material culture with non-material culture facies such as language, religion and ritual, and political structure (as an example of the dangers of this approach, *see* 'BEAKER PHENOMENON').

In the 1960s, the term 'culture history' began to be employed in a more derogatory manner to describe 'traditional' attitudes that were in direct opposition to the study of 'culture process' as espoused by New Archaeology (or PROCESSUAL ARCHAEOLOGY). New Archaeologists argued that scientific and anthropological principles should be applied to archaeological evidence in the search for an understanding of how past societies functioned – often in terms of SYSTEMS THEORY. This allowed them to downplay the traditional cultural historian's favoured mechanisms of cultural change and diversity (i.e. cultural and technological invention, migration of peoples, diffusion) in favour of concepts such as the multiplier effect and systemic adaption to environmental change (*see* SYSTEMS THEORY). Certain proponents of the New Archaeology also emphasized the search for universal laws of culture process over and above the importance of cultural diversity and difference – although some scholars (e.g. Hogarth 1972) continued to argue that archaeology was essentially a culture-historical discipline.

The reaction against processual archaeology from the late 1970s led some archaeological theorists to re-examine the culture-historical tradition. For example, CONTEXTUAL ARCHAEOLOGY returned to a more historical and 'particularist' stance, although it attempted to understand the relationship between culture and the material culture of the archaeological record in a more sophisticated fashion than in traditional culture-historical studies (e.g. Hodder 1982).

G.F. Klemm: *Allgemeine Cultur-Geschichte der Menschheit*, 10 vols (Leipzig, 1843–52); E.B. Tylor: *Primitive culture* (London, 1871); E. Meyer: *Geschichte des*

Alterthums, 5 vols (Stuttgart, 1884–1902); G. Kossinna: *Die Herkunft der Germanen* (Leipzig, 1911); V.G. Childe: *The dawn of European civilization* (London, 1925); J.A. Ford and G.R. Willey: 'An interpretation of the prehistory of the eastern United States', *American Anthropologist* 43 (1941), 325–63; A.C. Hogarth: 'Common sense in archaeology', *Antiquity* 46 (1972), 301–4; I. Hodder: *The present past: an introduction to anthropology for archaeologists* (London, 1982); B.G. Trigger: *A history of archaeological thought* (Cambridge, 1989), 148–205.

IS

culture process *see* PROCESSUAL ARCHAEOLOGY

cuneiform Earliest known writing system, which emerged in SUMER during the early 3rd millennium BC. Probably evolving originally from simple tokens, the cuneiform script rapidly established itself as the principal medium for diplomatic communication and economic transactions throughout the Ancient Near East, until it was eventually replaced by the alphabetic Aramaic script (*see* ARAMAEANS). The initial breakthrough in the decipherment of the cuneiform script was made in the 1830s when Henry Rawlinson studied Darius I's trilingual inscriptions at BISITUN.

D. Schmandt-Besserat: 'From tokens to tablets', *Visible Language* 15 (1981), 321–44; J.N. Postgate: 'Cuneiform catalysis: the first information revolution', *ARC* 3 (1984), 4–18; J. Oates and S.A. Jasim: 'Early tokens and tablets in Mesopotamia: new information from Tell Abada and Tell Brak', WA 17 (1986), 348–62; C. Walker: *Cuneiform* (London, 1987); J.N. Postgate: *Early Mesopotamia: society and economy at the dawn of history* (London and New York, 1992), 51–70; D. Schmandt-Besserat: *Before writing* (Austin, 1992); H.J. Nissen: *Archaic book-keeping: early writing and techniques of the economic administration in the Ancient Near East* (Chicago, 1993).

IS

cup marks Simple cup-shaped depressions that were pecked out on megaliths, natural boulders and outcrops in northern Britain and certain other areas of Europe. When the cup mark is enclosed by one or more concentric circles the motifs are known as 'cup-and-ring' marks. In these cases, the concentric circles are sometimes traversed by a radial groove, often referred to in the literature as a 'gutter', or may be incomplete. Cup marks are difficult to date, but seem to have been made during the later Neolithic, the Bronze Age (especially) and possibly the Iron Age.

RJA

cursus Neolithic monuments consisting of two parallel linear banks with external ditches, forming ceremonial 'avenues'. The avenues are often closed at both ends by a continuation of the bank and ditch. Over 30 British examples are now known, the longest being the Dorset Cursus in southern England which extends about 9 km across the chalk downlands. The banks of the Dorset Cursus are about 90 m apart and incorporate two long barrows. The other cursus monuments vary greatly in size (typically under 1 km in length and below 45 m in width), but often incorporate or seem related to other Neolithic ritual enclosures (henges, square 'mortuary enclosures') or funerary monuments. The term 'cursus' derives from 18th-century speculation that they may be the remains of racetracks; modern interpretations tend to favour the idea of processional avenues, perhaps linking up complex ritual landscapes. Excavation suggests that they were built from around 3000 BC onwards (the Dorset Cursus is associated with PETERBOROUGH ware); not all were built in one phase – excavations have shown that some have been extended, while others are composed of a series of separately constructed sections.

R.J.C. Atkinson: 'The Dorset Cursus', *Antiquity* 29 (1955), 4–9; R. Bradley: *The Dorset cursus* (London, 1986).

RJA

Cuzco Capital of the INCA empire, located in a high valley in the Peruvian Andes. Although there had been an occupation in the city area since the Early Horizon, imperial Cuzco was defined as the sacred centre of the Inca realm by Pachacuti Inca Yupanki (crowned AD 1438), the founder of the Inca empire. Pachacuti sponsored a major building programme and many of the remaining Inca buildings can be ascribed to his architects. Inca Cuzco was laid out in the form of a puma and was a sacred place where ordinary people were not permitted to live. Among the most notable structures were the Coricancha (the Temple of the Sun, now under the church of Santo Domingo), with its garden of gold and silver plants and animals; the Haucaypata, the huge central square where the ruler watched public rituals and made (public) solar observations from a stone platform (an *usnu*); and the 'fortress' of Sacsayhuaman above the city, with its famous cyclopean walls. Most of these buildings and spaces are now much destroyed and modern construction tops the much finer Inca foundations.

J. Rowe: *An introduction to the archaeology of Cuzco* (Washington, D.C., 1944); S. Niles: *Callachaca: style and status in an Inca community* (Iowa, 1987).

KB

cybernetics Body of scientific theory that attempts to understand and measure the control mechanisms that regulate and characterize mechanical, electronic, biological and other systems. A core feature of cybernetics is the analysis of communication and information flows between different elements within a system. Although the term cybernetics is used rarely in archaeology, certain core concepts have been imported as part of SYSTEMS THEORY.

RJA

Cycladic culture Culture which developed on the Cyclades Islands in the southern Aegean during the phase known as the Early Bronze Age or Early Cycladic (*c*.3300–2000), characterized by a series of fine figurines made from the local marble. Most of the evidence of the culture is from its – much looted – cemeteries, which are relatively small and which suggest a degree of social differentiation: the richest graves may contain more than one figurine and multiple marble bowls, together with painted pottery or even special items such as the silver diadem found at Dokathismata.

Throughout their history the cultures of the islands seem to have been linked culturally and to some extent economically, at first by canoe traffic – canoes are shown on early pottery – and later by sailing ships. The islands also offered the mainland important sources of obsidian (Melos) in the Neolithic and, later, metals. The Early Cycladic cultural assemblage seems to have evolved out of the local Neolithic, as expressed at SALIAGOS and KEPHALA. The Early Cycladic is generally divided into at least two phases: the Early Cycladic I (ECI) or Grotta-Pelos culture (3300–2700) and the Early Cycladic II (ECII) or Keros-Syros culture (2700–2300). Many scholars recognize an Early Cycladic III or Kastri phase (ECIII), lasting a few centuries after the end of the ECII.

The known ECI settlements are generally small and unfortified. There was only limited use of metal during the ECI, and obsidian continued to provide many of the tools. The phase is characterized by a form of cylindrical lidded vessel (or *pyxis*) with finely incised decoration, by fine marble bowls and ornaments, and especially by a series of very simple but finely made schematic marble figurines. These 'violin' or 'fiddle' figurines (so-called after their shape) are flat, headless and largely plain except for the incised lines that occasionally delineate the pubic region etc. Most of the marble-work has been recovered from the cemeteries of simple slab-built cist-tombs. A particularly rich set of burials, assumed to date from near the end of ECI and known as the 'Plaistos group', presents a distinctive assemblage of grave-goods: marble collared vases (or kandela) with a bulbous body and pedestal, marble bowls, and a form of figurine that is more three-dimensional and detailed than usual.

During ECII settlements seem to be located in more defensible positions, and they gain fortifications. From the middle of the 3rd millennium the Cycladic culture began to influence sites on the Greek mainland, and Cycladic material is found in Early Minoan II and III contexts. There are developments across the whole range of material culture (summarized in Renfrew 1991), but the most dramatic is the development of the marble figurines described below. In the late Early Cycladic settlements developed in coastal locations, and during the succeeding Middle Bronze Age phase these became the sites of true ports and towns – an example is the site of Akrotiri on THERA. From the Middle Bronze Age, the influence of Minoan, and subsequently Mycenaean, civilizations increased – illustrated most dramatically by the Theran wall-paintings. After these early Mediterranean civilizations disappeared, the Cyclades became absorbed in the wider Mediterranean cultural world and lost their early cultural and artistic distinctiveness.

Cycladic figurines. The classic expression of the early Cycladic culture is a series of figurines produced during ECII, simple but not schematic like the ECI examples. Most are less than 50 cm in height, though there are monumental examples (e.g. Renfrew 1991, pl 103). The figurines conform to strict conventions: carved facial detail is restricted to the prominent nose (eyes and hair were sometimes painted on); the arms are folded over stomach/chest; the legs are defined by a groove or full incision rather than being fully separated; there is little attempt to convey volume by carving fully in the round. Many of the sculptures may also follow a convention of proportion (Renfrew 1991, ch. XI).

C. Renfrew: *The emergence of civilization: the Cyclades and the Aegean in the third millennium BC* (London, 1972);
——: *The Cycladic spirit* (London, 1991).

RJA

Cyclopean masonry Type of walling that consists of large polygonal blocks of stone, either shaped or in their natural form, carefully fitted together to provide a continuous – but not necessarily smooth – wall. (By contrast, MEGALITHIC architecture is composed of large unshaped or only slightly shaped stones which may rest against or on top of each other, but which rarely give a continuous surface without the aid of drystone infilling). Cyclopean masonry is named after Cyclops, the mythical one-eyed giant of Greek legend, whom the ancient Greeks supposed to have constructed the massive MYCENAEAN fortifications in the Cyclopean style. The term is now applied elsewhere in the world – for instance, to describe the walls of Inca sites such as CUZCO.

RJA

Figure 13 **cylinder seal** Banqueting scenes depicted on a Sumerian cylinder seal of the Early Dynastic Period. *Source*: H. Crawford: *Sumer and the Sumerians* (Cambridge University Press, 1991), fig. 6.6.

cylinder seal Stone cylinder carved with relief decoration, which was rolled across wet clay items (particularly cuneiform documents or jar-stoppers) in order to indicate their genuineness or prove their ownership. Developed as an alternative to stamp seals, particularly in Mesopotamia during the late 4th to 1st millennia BC, it was eventually replaced by the increasing use of stamp-seals and ring-bezels. The complex variations in size, style and design make cylinder seals extremely useful in terms of iconographic analysis and the dating of the archaeological features in which they are found.

A.M. Gibson and R.D. Biggs: *Seals and sealing in the Ancient Near East* (Malibu, 1977); B. Teissier: *Ancient Near Eastern cylinder seals from the Marcopoli collection* (Berkeley, 1984); D. Collon: *First impressions: cylinder seals in the Ancient Near East* (London, 1987).

IS

Cyrenaica *see* AFRICA 1

D

Dabʿa, Tell el- (anc. Avaris) Egyptian settlement site in the eastern Delta, immediately to the south of modern QANTIR, where the Ramessid city of Piramesse grew up from the late 14th century BC onwards. The ancient town, temples and cemeteries of Avaris, covering an area of about two square kilometres on a natural mound partly surrounded by a lake, have been excavated by the Austrian archaeologist Manfred Bietak since 1966. The work has been spread over a number of different sites within the region of Tell el-Dabʿa, comprising a complex series of phases of occupation ranging from the 1st Intermediate Period to the 2nd Intermediate Period (*c*.2150–1532 BC). The deep stratigraphy at Tell el-Dabʿa has allowed the changing settlement patterns of a large Bronze Age community to be observed over a period of many generations. Bietak's excavations indicate that the Egyptian settlement at Avaris was transformed into the capital of the HYKSOS in the 2nd Intermediate Period (1640–1550 BC), when it effectively became the centre of a Syro-Palestinian colony within the Delta.

In the early 1990s the principal focus of attention in Bietak's work was the substructure of a substantial building (probably a palace) of the Hyksos period, located at Ezbet Helmi at the western side of Tell el-Dabʿa. The site has achieved particular prominence because of the discovery, in 1991, of numerous fragments of early 18th-dynasty wall-paintings in the ancient gardens adjoining the structure. These depictions include scenes of 'bull-leaping' closely resembling those excavated from the Middle Bronze Age palace at Knossos as well as from two sites in the Levant (Kabri and Alalakh). The paintings may indicate that people of Aegean origins were living within Avaris itself.

M. Bietak: *Avaris and Piramesse: archaeological exploration in the eastern Nile delta* (London and Oxford, 1981); W.V. Davies and L. Schofield, eds: *Egypt, the Aegean and the Levant: interconnections in the second millennium* BC (London, 1995); M. Bietak: *Avaris* (London, 1996).

IS

Dabar Kot Large settlement mound, about 70 ha in area, located in the Thal river in the Loralai valley of northern Pakistan. Limited excavations were conducted by Aurel Stein in 1929, followed by the surface surveys of Walter Fairservis and Sadurdin Khan in the 1950s. The site incorporates evidence for a very long occupation, from the 3rd millennium BC to the 1st millennium AD. Artefacts from the site include pre-Harappan and Mature Harappan material (*see* INDUS CIVILIZATION), including such painted ceramics as pre-Harappan Kili Ghul Muhammad (*see* QUETTA) and Periano wares and Mature Harappan black-on-red pottery. Other artefacts from pre-Harappan and Mature Harappan levels include terracotta figurines and copper and flint tools. Materials from early historic levels include iron tools and Buddhist figurines; a large unexcavated structure in the upper levels of the site may be the remains of a Buddhist religious complex.

W.A. Fairservis: 'Archaeological surveys in the Zhob and Loralai District, West Pakistan', *Anthropological Papers of the American Museum of Natural History* 47 (1959), 277–478.

CS

Dabban *see* AFRICA 1

Dabenarti *see* MIRGISSA

Dahshur Egyptian cemetery of pyramids and mastaba-tombs, forming part of the southern end of the Memphite necropolis, which was used for royal burials during the Old and Middle Kingdoms (*c*.2649–1640 BC). The two earliest attempts at true pyramids (the Red Pyramid and the Bent Pyramid) were built at Dahshur by Sneferu (*c*.2575–2551 BC); the Bent Pyramid has retained more of its stone outer casing than any other pyramid. There are also three Middle Kingdom pyramids at Dahshur, belonging to Amenemhat II, Senusret III and Amenemhat III; these make up the northern extension of the royal cemetery that grew up around the 12th-dynasty capital, Itj-tawy, probably located near EL-LISHT about 25 km to the south.

J. de Morgan: *Fouilles à Dahchour*, 2 vols (Vienna, 1895–1903); A. Fakhry: *The monuments of Sneferu at*

Dahshur, 2 vols (Cairo, 1959–61); D. Arnold: *Der Pyramidenbezirk des Königs Amenemhet III in Dahschur* I (Mainz, 1987).
IS

Daima Settlement mound 5 km from the Nigeria–Cameroon frontier and 45 km south of the shore of Lake Chad in northeastern Nigeria, excavated by Graham Connah in 1965–6. The site is located on flat clay plains subject to annual flooding and known as 'firki' from their propensity to crack during the dry season. The mound, 250 × 170 m in size, was sectioned by means of main cutting VIII, which was 50 × 6 m at ground level and 11.5 m deep. The sequence produced eight radiocarbon dates in the range 2520–890 BP, but they are in part problematical because of stratigraphic inversions and imperfect agreement between results based on charcoal and those based on animal bones. A division of the apparently continuous occupation into three phases (I: 550 BC–AD 50, II: AD 50–700, and III: AD 700–1150) is suggested by plotting all the dates against depth and drawing a best-fit curve through them. In Graham Connah's opinion, phase III represents a more affluent society with a more complex culture; nonetheless it continued the same distinctive exploitation pattern as before. Adopting an explicitly ecological model, he has labelled this 'the firki response'. Very probably those who put it into effect (the 'So' people) were Chadic speakers, who only gradually came under Kanuri control from the 14th century AD onwards.
G. Connah: *Three thousand years in Africa: man and his environment in the Lake Chad region of Nigeria* (Cambridge, 1981).
PA-J

Daimabad Chalcolithic mound, about 50 ha in size, located on a tributary of the Godavari river in Maharashtra, India. The excavations of Deshpande (1958–9), Nagaraja Rao (1974) and S.A. Sali (1975–7) have documented five main phases: Savalda (*c*.2200–2000 BC), a locally defined Late HARAPPAN phase (*c*.2000–1800 BC), Daimabad (*c*.1800–1600 BC), MALWA (*c*.1600–1400 BC) and JORWE (*c*.1400–1000 BC), each distinguished by changes in ceramic styles, architecture and funerary remains. The most dramatic discovery from Daimabad was a unique undated hoard found by a local farmer in 1974. This consisted of four massive bronze sculptures: an elephant, a rhinoceros, a buffalo and an ox-drawn cart with human occupant. Dhavalikar (1982: 366) has suggested that these bronzes probably date to the Late Harappan period and may have been imported.

Figure 14 **Daimabad** Copper buffalo from the Daimabad hoard (Prince of Wales Museum, Bombay).

M.K. Dhavalikar: 'Daimabad bronzes', *Harappan civilization*, ed. by G.L. Possehl (New Delhi, 1982) 361–6; S.A. Sali: *Daimabad 1976–79* (New Delhi, 1986).
CS

Dakhla Oasis Fertile region in the Libyan Desert, about 300 km to the west of modern Luxor, where the remains of circular stone huts indicate that the area was settled by sedentary groups as early as the EPIPALAEOLITHIC period (*c*.9000–8500 BP; McDonald 1991). A village of the Old Kingdom (*c*.2649–2150 BC) and a group of associated 6th-dynasty mastaba-tombs have been excavated near the modern village of Balat (Giddy and Jeffreys 1980; Giddy 1987), and a cemetery of the 1st Intermediate Period (*c*.2150–2040 BC) has been discovered near the village of Amhada. These remains suggest that the pharaohs had already gained control of areas beyond the confines of the Nile valley by the end of the Early Dynastic period. Later ruins include a Ramessid temple of the goddess Mut (*c*.1130 BC), near Azbat Bashindi, a Greco-Roman necropolis (*c*.332 BC–AD 395), a temple of the Theban triad (Amun, Mut and Khonsu) at Deir el-Hagar, a temple of Thoth at el-Qasr, Roman tombs at Qaret el-Muzawwaqa, and a Roman settlement and temple at Ismant el-Kharab (Hope 1994).
H.E. Winlock, ed.: *Dakhleh Oasis* (New York, 1936); L.L.

Giddy and D.G. Jeffreys: 'Balat: rapport préliminaire des fouilles à 'Ayn Asil, 1979–80', *BIFAO* 80 (1980), 257–69; ——: *Egyptian oases: Bahariya, Dakhla, Farafra and Kharga during pharaonic times* (Warminster, 1987); M.M.A. McDonald: 'Technological organization and sedentism in the epipalaeolithic of Dakhleh Oasis, Egypt', *AAR* 9 (1991), 81–109; C. Hope: 'Excavations at Ismant el-Kharab in the Dakhleh Oasis', *EA* 5 (1994), 17–18.

IS

Dalton Tradition dating from *c*.8500 to 7900 BC, evidence of which has been found throughout much of the southeastern United States, with particularly dense concentrations of sites in the central Mississippi River valley. Dalton toolkits are characterized by distinctive, nonfluted projectile points which are lanceolate in outline with a concave base. Also represented are hafted, bifacially flaked Dalton adzes. Differences between Dalton toolkits and those of earlier PALEOINDIAN cultures are probably attributable first to the transition from Late Pleistocene to Holocene environmental conditions and secondly to the exploitation of different kinds of plants and animals.

A. Goodyear: 'The chronological position of the Dalton Horizon in the southeastern United States', *AA* 47 (1982), 382–95; D. and P. Morse: *Archaeology of the central Mississippi Valley* (New York, 1983) 71–97.

RJE

Damascus *see* ISLAMIC ARCHAEOLOGY

Damb Sadaat Pre-Harappan mound site located near modern Quetta in northern Pakistan near the strategic Bolan Pass linking South to Central Asia. In the 1950s Walter Fairservis identified three chronological phases stretching from *c*.3400 to 2500 BC, according to calibrated radiocarbon dates. The first phase (Period I), comprising remains of mud-brick architecture, painted ceramics, including Kechi Beg polychrome and red paint wares and QUETTA black-on-buff ware, bone implements and a stone-blade industry, shows affinities with the earlier site of Kili Ghul Muhammad. In period II, plain and painted Quetta wares dominated the ceramic assemblage; a ceramic seal, and copper dagger and fragments were also recovered. Quetta wares declined in period III and were replaced by Sadaat black-on-red or buff wares.

W.A. Fairservis: 'Excavations in the Quetta Valley, West Pakistan', *APAMNH* 45 (1956), 169–402; S. Asthana: *Pre-Harappan cultures of India and the Borderlands* (New Delhi, 1985).

CS

dampmarks *see* SOILMARKS; AERIAL ARCHAEOLOGY

Danangombe (Dhlo Dhlo) Large Khami-period settlement, with a population in excess of 5000, which was the capital of the ruling Rozwi dynasty in Zimbabwe from the 1690s onwards. The first ruler was the famous Changamire Dombolakonachingwango who is credited with destroying the PORTUGUESE TRADING *FEIRA* of Dambarare and forcing the Portuguese to retreat to the Zambezi. The ruling dynasty in Venda today were originally Rozwi, or closely related to them, and they moved south of the Limpopo River in the 1690s during this initial Rozwi expansion. Danangombe was mentioned in a Portuguese document in 1831, but it may have been abandoned shortly before then. Because it continued well into the historic period, Danangombe forms an important bridge between archaeological data and Shona and Venda ethnography. The settlement organization found here serves as a model that can be applied to older sites such as GREAT ZIMBABWE.

D.R. MacIver: *Mediaeval Rhodesia* (London, 1906); G. Caton-Thompson: *The Zimbabwe culture: ruins and reactions* (Oxford, 1931); D. Beach: *The Shona and Zimbabwe 900–1850* (Gwelo, 1980); T.N. Huffman: *Snakes and crocodiles: power and symbolism in ancient Zimbabwe* (Johannesburg, 1996).

TH

Danebury Iron Age hillfort of *c*.550–100 BC located in Hampshire, England, which from 1969 was subjected to an intensive series of excavations led by Barry Cunliffe. The defences consisted of a massive timber-revetted inner rampart and ditch encircled by a later and slighter rampart and ditch, and an outer ditch – giving a total area of 16.2 ha. The excavations revealed a heavily used and to some extent planned interior filled by: a central road running across the fort between the two entrances, and later subsidiary roads; circular 'houses' (6–9 m diameter), either built of stakes and wattle and daub, or of continuous plank walls; concentrations of storage pits; and small shrines. Like other Wessex hillforts, Danebury was found to contain numerous settings of four or six posts, which are usually interpreted as raised granaries. The low ratio of houses to storage facilities suggests that Danebury may have functioned more as a form of regional storehouse than as a settlement; this interpretation is supported by the analysis of the plant remains, which suggests that the grain was collected from a number of different growing environments. (The complex question of the control of this 'storehouse'

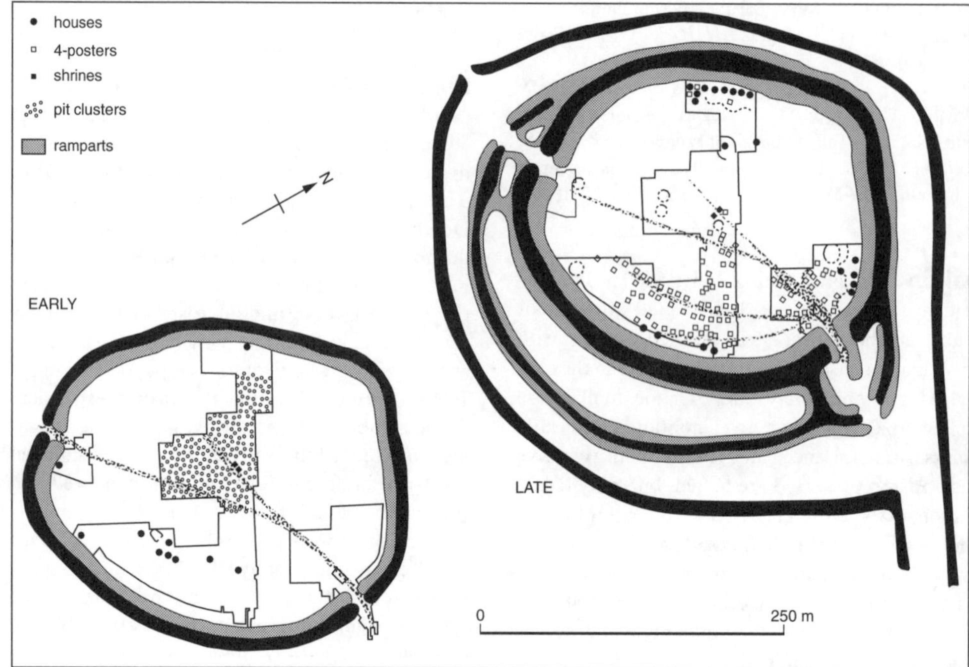

Figure 15 **Danebury** Plans of the two major phases of the Danebury hillfort: the 6th century BC (left) and the 4th century BC (right). *Source*: B. Cunliffe: *Anatomy of an Iron-Age hillfort* (London, 1983), figs 29–31.

is critically addressed in Bradley, 1984.) At the same time Danebury seems to have been in use throughout much of its history – contradicting a model for Iron Age hillforts as temporary refuges in times of crisis.

R. Bradley: *The social foundations of prehistoric Britain* (London, 1984), 135–9; B.Cunliffe: *Danebury: an Iron Age Hillfort in Hampshire* (London, 1984–91), 5 vols; critical review of vols 1 and 2 by J. Collis in *PPS* 51 (1985), 348–9; B. Cunliffe: 'Danebury: the anatomy of a hillfort exposed', *Case studies in European prehistory*, ed. P. Bogucki (Boca Raton, 1993), 259–85.

RJA

Danger Cave Site near Great Salt Lake, Utah, in western North America, which provided a 10,000-year sequence of short-term occupations, forming the basis for the so-called Desert Culture, a way of life limited by and adapted to the extreme environmental conditions of the Great Basin. Based partly on ethnographic analogy with the Shoshone and partly on inference from the artefactual and contextual data derived from the excavation of Danger Cave, this long-stable lifestyle of small nomadic bands intensively exploiting a desert environment provides a sharp contrast with the BIG GAME HUNTING TRADITION of the earlier period.

J.D. Jennings: *Danger Cave*, Memoirs of the Society for American Archaeology 14, (1957).

RC

Danzantes *see* MONTE ALBAN

Dapenkang *see* TA-P'EN-K'ENG

Dar es-Soltane II Cave on the Moroccan coast 6 km southwest of Rabat (excavated by André Debénath from 1969 onwards), 200 m from the cave of Dar-es-Soltane I (excavated by Armand Ruhlmann in 1937–8). Five metres of deposit at the front of the cave produced traces of human occupation in layers 2 (Neolithic), 3 (Epipalaeolithic) and 6 (ATERIAN). The remains of at least three hominids (one adult partial skull and mandible, one adolescent mandible, and one juvenile calvaria) were found over a quarter-square-metre area beneath a sandstone block in layer 7 (marine sands resting on bedrock) and are regarded as being associated with the Aterian. The skull was studied by Denise Ferembach, who came to the conclusion that it represented a robust *HOMO SAPIENS*

SAPIENS with characteristics intermediate between those of JEBEL IRHOUD and the MECHTA-AFALOU population associated with the IBEROMAURUSIAN. In her view, therefore, the remains from this cave testify to a local evolutionary transformation from archaic to anatomically modern man in northwest Africa. R.G. Klein comments that 'the skull exhibits no features that distinguish it significantly from most modern human skulls, yet the population it represents inhabited Morocco at the same time that Neanderthals occupied Europe'. Five more individuals of the same type (four adult and one juvenile) are known from Aterian layers at three other sites on the Moroccan coast: El Harhoura I (Grotte Zouhrah), Témara (Grotte des Contrebandiers), and Tangier (Mugharet el-Aliya). The remains from the last two sites were originally identified as pre-Neanderthal or Neanderthal; but, as J.J. Hublin comments, these hominids always display a 'very robust masticatory apparatus and a pronounced megadonty' and such features could explain why the first discoveries were considered to be 'more primitive than they actually are'.

A. Debénath: 'Découverte de restes humains probablement atériens à Dar es Soltane (Maroc)', *CRASP*, série D, 281 (1975), 875–6; D. Ferembach: 'Les restes humains de la grotte de Dar-es-Soltane 2 (Maroc) campagne 1975', *Bulletins et Mémoires de la Société d'Anthropologie de Paris* 3 (1976), 183–93; K.P. Oakley et al.: *Catalogue of fossil hominids, Part 1: Africa*, 2nd edn (London, 1977); A Debénath et al.: 'Position stratigraphique des restes humains paléolithiques marocains sur la base des travaux récents', *CRASP*, série II, 294 (1982), 1247–50; A. Debénath et al.: 'Stratigraphie, habitat, typologie et devenir de l'Atérien marocain: données récentes', *L'Anthropologie* 90 (1986), 233–46; R.G. Klein: *The human career* (Chicago and London, 1989); A. Debénath: 'Les Atériens du Maghreb', *DA* 161 (1991), 52–7; J.J. Hublin:

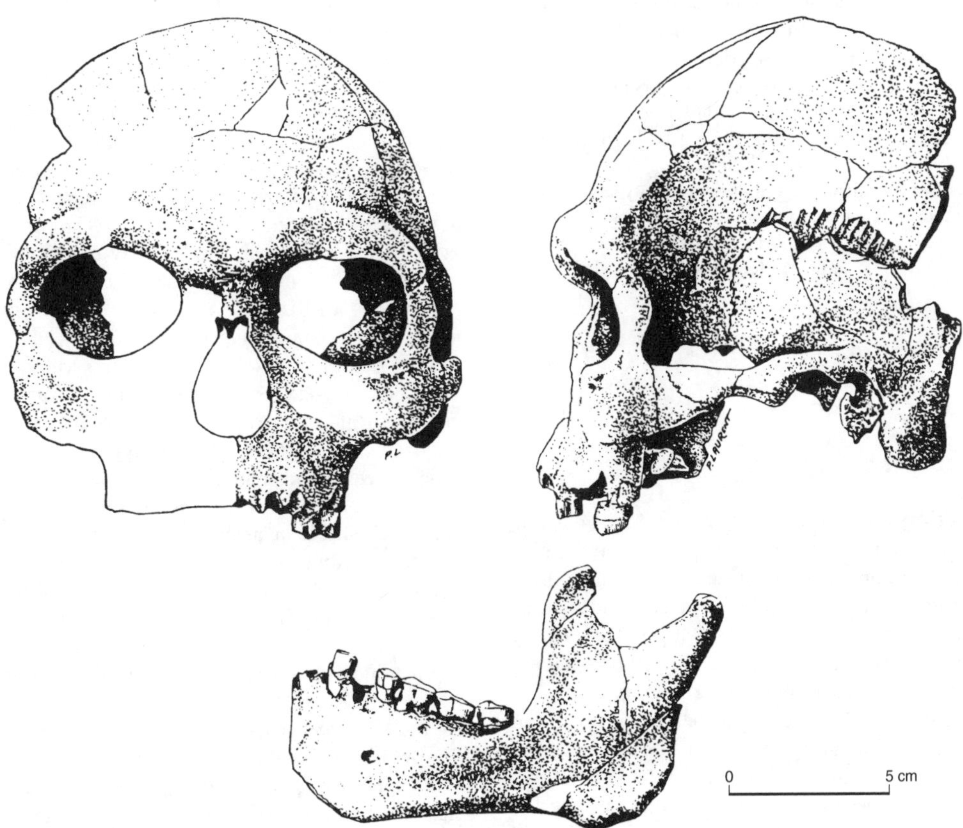

Figure 16 **Dar-es-Soltane II** The partial skull and mandible of an adult hominid found in layer 7 at Dar-es-Soltane II (drawing by P. Laurent). *Source*: A. Debénath et al.: *L'Anthropologie* 90 (1986), fig. 2.

'Recent human evolution in northwestern Africa' *Philosophical Transactions of the Royal Society of London*, series B, 337/1280 (1992), 185–91.

PA-J

data Archaeological data consist of measurements made on archaeological objects (using the term in the widest possible sense, to include for example artefacts, features, assemblages, sites), as well as counts of such objects. Measurements include physical measurements (e.g. lengths and weights), scientific determinations (e.g. chemical analyses), other descriptive characteristics (e.g. colour), and assignments of objects to categories (i.e. types). Each measurement or characteristic is known as a VARIABLE; a set of variables measured on a collection of objects is known as a dataset. A dataset in tabular form, usually with rows representing objects and columns representing variables, is called a data matrix. The fundamental problem of using statistics in archaeology is QUANTIFICATION, i.e. the reduction of collections of objects to datasets. Some objects, such as building plans, are so complex that their data must take account of internal relationships (e.g. between rooms) as well as measurements and counts.

J.E. Doran and F.R. Hodson: *Mathematics and computers in archaeology* (Edinburgh, 1975), 93–114; S. Shennan: *Quantifying archaeology* (Edinburgh, 1988), 8–21; C. Dallas: 'Relational description, similarity and classification of complex archaeological entities', *Computer applications and quantitative methods in archaeology 1991*, ed. G.R. Lock and J. Moffett (Oxford, 1992), 167–78.

CO

data matrix *see* DATA

data reduction *see* REDUCTION OF DATA

data set *see* DATA

dating techniques Scientifically-based dating techniques have a number of prerequisites. There must be a time-dependent variable, which ideally is accurately and precisely measureable and its time dependence must be well-known (e.g. the quantity of ^{40}Ar relative to ^{40}K in POTASSIUM-ARGON DATING defined by radioactive decay and hence the half-life of ^{40}K). There must be a point which can be defined as being 'time zero' (for example, the point of death of an animal in RADIOCARBON DATING, the firing of a pot in THERMOLUMINESCENCE, or the solidification of a lava flow in POTASSIUM-ARGON DATING). This time zero and the sample dated must be relatable to the archaeological event for which the age is actually required. In radiocarbon dating, for example, an articulated bone in a grave can readily be associated with the burial event, but mature wood charcoal fragments in the fill of a ditch are of little or no value in dating the cutting of the ditch. Similarly a piece of volcanic rock in an archaeological level will provide a date only for the formation of the rock, not its incorporation within the sediment, but archeological finds sandwiched between two volcanic layers must lie within the limits defined by these *terminus* results: whether these provide a sufficiently detailed chronology will depend on the circumstances. One further prerequisite is that no factor affects the intrinsic value of the time-dependent variable, other than the time dependence itself. In URANIUM-SERIES DATING of calcite, for example, the sample must be a *closed system*, preventing migration of uranium in or out of the calcite once it has formed, and in RADIOCARBON DATING pre-treatment techniques are used to remove any contaminating carbon acquired *post mortem*.

The techniques used in archaeological dating can be broadly categorized as based on radioactive decay or spontaneous fission (ALPHA RECOIL, FISSION TRACK, POTASSIUM-ARGON, RADIOCALCIUM, RADIOCARBON, URANIUM-SERIES); based on climatic change (CALCITE BANDING, DENDROCHRONOLOGY, ICE CORES, OXYGEN ISOTOPE, CHRONOSTRATIGRAPHY, VARVES); based on particular properties of materials (AMINO ACID RACEMIZATION, ARCHAEOMAGNETISM, CATION-RATIO, ELECTRON SPIN RESONANCE, FLUORINE UPTAKE, NITROGEN LOSS IN BONE, PALAEOMAGNETISM, OPTICALLY STIMULATED LUMINESCENCE, TEPHROCHRONOLOGY, THERMOLUMINESCENCE), and based on diffusion processes (OBSIDIAN HYDRATION, NITROGEN PROFILING AND SODIUM PROFILING). Not all of these in fact have an inherent time-dependence; some (e.g. ARCHAEOMAGNETISM) require calibration by other techniques, or at best provide only a very rough indication of chronology (e.g. flourine uptake). A number of other techniques (not listed here) have time ranges applicable to geological problems.

Scientific dating techniques quote an error term which is the *precision* (reproducibility) at the 1 level i.e. there is a 68% chance, if the result is *accurate* (i.e. unbiased), that the true age will lie between –1 and +1 of that quoted. Equally there is a 32% chance (i.e. nearly 1 in 3) that it will not. The probability increases to 95% for the range –2 to +2.

G. Faure: *Principles of isotope geology*, 2nd edn (New York, 1986); M.J. Aitken: *Science-based dating in archaeology*

(London, 1990); P.L. Smart and P.D. Frances, eds: *Quaternary dating methods – a user's guide* (Cambridge, 1991).
SB

Dawenkou *see* TA-WEN-K'OU

'dawn man' *see* PILTDOWN MAN HOAX

Dead Sea Scrolls *see* QUMRAN

Debeira *see* DIBEIRA

Debra Damo Site in the northern Ethiopian highlands dating primarily to the post-Axumite period (*c*.AD 1000–1500), and including a 10th- or 11th-century monastic church. The walls and windows of the church, which is stone-built rather than rock-hewn as at LALIBELA, incorporate many of the characteristics of the monolithic Axumite stelae (*see* AXUM). The town of Debra Damo appears to have been part of an extensive medieval commercial network, and excavated trade items include a hoard of over a hundred Indian coins dating to the 3rd century AD, as well as textiles imported from Coptic and Islamic Egypt between the 6th and 12th centuries.

D.H. Matthews and A. Mordini: 'The monastery of Debra Damo, Ethiopia', *Archaeologia* 97 (1959); D. Buxton: *The Abyssinians* (London, 1970), 97–102.
IS

decision theory Body of theory used by archaeologists to understand the nature of ancient processes of decision making. Since the 1970s, archaeologists have become increasingly interested in attempting to understand the short-term decisions made by people in the past. Such work often sees long-term cultural evolution as no more than the accumulated consequences of short-term decisions made by individuals throughout prehistory.

In fact, 'decision theory' represents a whole range of theories, which share concepts but also exhibit unique elements due to the particular disciplines in which they were developed. For instance a very quantitative approach to decision making has been developed in economics which focuses on maximizing benefits to costs, while in psychology several approaches, such as 'social judgement theory', have been explored, laying greater stress on the use of cues from the natural environment in forming judgements about how to act (e.g. Hammond et al. 1980).

Several aspects of these approaches have been adopted in archaeological studies. First is the notion of the 'decision tree'. This is a representation of the sequence of sub-decisions one must pass through to reach a final decision as to how to behave. For instance the manufacture of an arrow with a stone point involves decisions about raw materials, knapping methods, arrowhead form, hafting methods and so on. As each sub-decision is made, certain options are opened and others closed to the decision maker. In analysing a prehistoric artefact such as an arrowhead or a pottery vessel, one might attempt to recreate the path taken through a decision tree and contrast this with the paths taken to produce a similar, but significantly different, artefact. Some of the most effective uses of decision trees have been found in computer simulation models. For instance Aldenderfer (1978) used this as a framework for simulating the manufacture, use and discard of stone tools by Australian aborigines. Decision trees have also been used in anthropological studies of farming, concerning choices about which crops to plant (e.g. Barlett 1980) and this approach could be effectively applied to the study of prehistoric agriculture.

The choices made at each node in the decision tree are often the result of a conscious process of weighing up the costs and benefits of following each of the alternative paths. This cost-benefit analysis is a very important element in a wide range of theories concerning decision making, especially those deriving from economics and ecology. Often these approaches rely on the development of models which have explicitly defined goals for the decision maker, such as the maximization of net utility gain, as in FORAGING THEORY.

Further aspects of decision theory that have been applied to archaeology include the distinction between the acquisition of information and the processing of information. The first of these may be from numerous different sources, such as personal experience and the experiences of others. Such information may be passed between individuals in various media, such as talking in formal (teaching) or informal contexts, or by means of material culture. For instance, Palaeolithic CAVE ART has been interpreted as a means of storing and transmitting information (e.g. Pfeiffer 1982: Mithen 1988). Information processing is the means by which all the different bits of information are compared and evaluated so that a final decision can be made. This can be usefully studied with simplified mathematical MODELS of decision rules. For instance, Mithen (1990) used simple algorithms to define the probability of particular types of game being hunted by Mesolithic foragers, taking into account different hunting goals as well as the processes by which information about such phenomena as past hunting success are processed. Parameters within Mithen's equations controlled the strength of past experience over current decisions in the form of a 'memory' factor.

Meta-decision making, i.e. deciding how a particular decision should be made, is a further important concept in decision theory. There is a large body of theory developed for group decision-making. This explores how a consensus is reached and how the views of certain individuals may emerge as more or less prominent within the group.

The study of foraging behaviour has benefited most from the use of decision theory, in the form of foraging theory. Similarly, our understanding of early technology is being developed by greater attention to the costs and benefits of particular manufacturing methods. For instance, Bleed (1986) has drawn a distinction between 'maintainable' and 'reliable' hunting weapons, each having different sets of costs and benefits, while Torrence (1983, 1989) employed the efficient use of time and energy as the critical variable for explaining the design of hunter-gatherer tool kits in different environments.

M. Aldenderfer: 'Creating assemblages by computer simulation: the development and uses of ABSIM', *Simulations in archaeology*, ed. J. Sabloff (Albuquerque, 1978), 67–117; P. Barlett, ed.: *Agricultural decision making* (New York, 1980); K. Hammond, G. McClelland and J. Mumpower: *Human judgement and decision making: theories, methods and procedures* (New York, 1980); J. Pfeiffer: *The creative explosion: an inquiry into the origins of art and religion* (New York, 1982); R. Torrence: 'Time-budgeting and hunter-gatherer technology', *Hunter-gatherer economy in prehistory*, ed. G.N. Bailey (Cambridge, 1983), 11–22; P. Bleed: 'The optimal design of hunting weapons: maintainability or reliability', *AA* 51 (1986), 737–47; S. Mithen: 'Looking and learning: information gathering and Upper Palaeolithic art', *WA* 19 (1988), 297–327; R. Torrence, ed.: *Time, energy and stone tools* (Cambridge, 1989); S. Mithen: *Thoughtful foragers: A study of prehistoric decision making* (Cambridge, 1990).

SM

decision tree *see* DECISION THEORY

deductive-nomological explanations *see* COVERING LAWS

deductive statistical explanation *see* INDUCTIVE AND DEDUCTIVE EXPLANATION

deep sea cores *see* OXYGEN ISOTOPE CHRONOSTRATIGRAPHY

deffufa *see* KERMA

Deh Luran *see* TEPE ALI KOSH, TEPE SABZ

Deir el-Bahari Egyptian site on the west bank of the Nile opposite Luxor, comprising temples and tombs dating from the early Middle Kingdom to the Ptolemaic Period. The site consists of a deep bay in the cliffs containing the remains of the temples of Nebhepetra Mentuhotep II (*c*.2035 BC), Hatshepsut (*c*.1460 BC) and Thutmose III (*c*.1440 BC), as well as private tombs contemporary with each of these pharaohs. The temple of Hatshepsut is the best-preserved of the three, consisting of three colonnaded terraces incorporating chapels to Hathor, Anubis and Amun. An 11th-dynasty shaft tomb at the southern end of Deir el-Bahari (plundered in 1875 and excavated in 1881) yielded a cache of some 40 royal mummies from the Valley of the Kings, reinterred there by 21st-dynasty priests. Another mummy cache (consisting of more than one hundred and fifty 21st-dynasty priests) was discovered in 1891.

E. Naville: *The temple of Deir el-Bahari*, 7 vols (London, 1894–1908); H.E. Winlock: *Excavations at Deir el-Bahari, 1911–31* (New York, 1942); ——: *The slain soldiers of Nebhepetre Mentuhotep* (New York, 1945); J. Lipinska: *Deir el-Bahari* II: *The temple of Tuthmosis III* (Warsaw, 1974); D. Arnold: *The temple of Mentuhotep at Deir el-Bahari* (New York, 1979).

IS

Deir el-Ballas Egyptian settlement site on the west bank of the Nile some 45 km north of modern Luxor, which was probably originally a staging post in the reconquest of northern Egypt by Kamose and Ahmose (*c*.1600–1500 BC). Peter Lacovara (1985) interprets the early New Kingdom phase of Ballas as a prototype of the 'royal city', foreshadowing such later settlements as GUROB, MALKATA and EL-AMARNA.

W. Stevenson Smith: *The art and architecture of Ancient Egypt* (Harmondsworth, 1958, rev. 1981), 278–81; P. Lacovara: *Survey at Deir el-Ballas* (Malibu, 1985).

IS

Deir el-Bersha Egyptian site on the east bank of the Nile 40 km south of el-Minya, which dates from the Old Kingdom to the Christian period (*c*.2649 BC–AD 641). Deir el-Bersha is known primarily for a row of tomb chapels in the cliffs, most of which were constructed for 12th-dynasty provincial governors (*c*.1991–1783 BC). Closer to the river are a church and monastery (Deir Anba Bishuy) which were at their peak during the 6th and 7th centuries AD.

P.E. Newberry and F.L. Griffith: *El-Bersheh*, 2 vols

(London, 1892); E. Brovarski et al.: *Bersheh reports* I (Boston, 1992).
IS

Deir el-Medina Egyptian site on the west bank of the Nile opposite Luxor, situated in a bay in the cliffs midway between the RAMESSEUM and MEDINET HABU, excavated primarily by Ernesto Schiaparelli (1905–9) and Bernard Bruyère (1917–47). The settlement now known as Deir el-Medina was called the Place of Truth in the New Kingdom; it was inhabited by the workmen who built the royal tombs in the VALLEY OF THE KINGS between the early 18th dynasty and the end of the Ramessid period (*c.*1550–1070 BC). Nearby are the remains of the tombs of many of the workmen as well as a temple dedicated to various gods, which was founded in the reign of Amenhotep III (*c.*1370 BC) and almost completely rebuilt in the reign of Ptolemy IV (*c.*210 BC).

B. Bruyère: *Rapport sur les fouilles de Deir el Medineh*, 17 vols (Cairo, 1924–53); E. Schiaparelli: *Relazione sui lavori della missione archaeologica italiana in Egitto* II (Turin, 1927); J.J. Janssen: *Commodity prices from the Ramessid period* (Leiden, 1975); M.L. Bierbrier: *The tomb-builders of the pharaohs* (London, 1982); L. Meskell: 'Deir el-Medina in hyperreality: seeking the people of pharaonic Egypt', *JMA* 7/2 (1994), 193–216.
IS

Deloraine Iron Age site located in an area of modern farm land in the elevated stretch of the Kenya Rift Valley. The site first came to archaeological attention in the 1960s when rich deposits of cattle bones and a unique type of pottery were observed in the farm tracks, together with obsidian tools and flakes and iron-working waste. The results of four separate sets of excavations between the 1960s and 1980s (by Mark Cohen, Neville Chittick, Stanley Ambrose and John Sutton), together with several radiocarbon tests, confirm a dating late in the 1st millennium AD, and help fill the gap in the local archaeological sequence between the final Late Stone Age ('PASTORAL NEOLITHIC') and the later Iron Age Sirikwa period (*see* SIRIKWA HOLES). Indeed the pottery has certain elements in common with that of the preceding ELMENTEITAN facies of the 'Neolithic'; and, while Deloraine is indisputably an Iron Age site, the presence of obsidian may argue for its being transitional. As an early Iron Age manifestation in the high grasslands, it is very distinct culturally (especially in its ceramics) from the better known Early Iron Age of the Bantu regions of eastern Africa. The plentiful cattle bones indicate a strong – but not exclusively – pastoral base to the economy, one less specialized than in the following Sirikwa period. The choice of site was determined by the presence of springs, frequented by wild animals as well as by cattle and their herders, at the foot of Londiani mountain.

S.H. Ambrose: 'Excavations at Deloraine, Rongai, 1978', *Azania* 19 (1984), 79–104; J.E.G. Sutton: 'Deloraine: further excavations and the Iron Age sequence of the Central Rift', *Azania* 28 (1993).
JS

DEM (Digital Elevation Model) *see* GIS

demic diffusion The spread of an innovation or cultural trait as a result of the cumulative effect of multiple small-scale movements of people. By contrast, 'colonization' implies an organized and often large-scale movement of people, and 'cultural diffusion' need not imply any physical movement of populations at all. Ammerman and Cavalli-Sforza hypothesized that demic diffusion provided the mechanism behind their WAVE OF ADVANCE model for the spread of farming.
RJA

demotic Ancient Egyptian writing system which developed out of the HIERATIC script and eventually replaced the latter by the 26th dynasty (*c.*600 BC).

Denbigh Flint complex *see* ARCTIC SMALL TOOL TRADITION

Dendera (anc. Iunet, Tentyris) Site of a well-preserved temple of the goddess Hathor, situated in Upper Egypt and built and decorated between 125 BC and AD 60. There are only a few remaining traces of the pre-Ptolemaic temple, which was founded at least as early as the 6th dynasty (*c.*2280 BC). The neighbouring necropolis dates back to the Early Dynastic period (*c.*3000–2649 BC).

A. Mariette: *Denderah*, 4 vols (Paris, 1870–3); E. Chassinat and F. Daumas: *Le temple de Dendara*, 6 vols (Cairo, 1934–52); H.G. Fischer: *Dendera in the 3rd millennium BC* (New York, 1968); F. Daumas: *Dendera et le temple d'Hathor* (Cairo, 1969).
IS

dendrochronology Dating technique based on tree rings. In temperate climates, where there is a contrast between the seasons, trees usually grow by the addition of an annual ring. The growth region is a thin band of cells (the cambium), which lies between the bark and the sapwood. Division of these cells adds new bark to the outer side of the cambium and new sapwood to the inside. The rings are usually well-defined due to differences in the cells produced at different times of the year. For some species, but not all, the width of each ring depends largely on prevailing climatic conditions, such as temperature and rainfall. Thus, for a living tree, counting backwards from the cambium layer gives the age of a particular ring, and its relative thickness indicates whether the growing season was good or bad in that year and locality. Trees of a single species growing in the same locality should have a similar pattern of ring widths, uniquely defined by their common history. This is the basis of dendrochronological cross-dating: being able to associate a tree-ring sequence of unknown age with one of known age by matching one pattern with another.

Long chronologies ('master curves') are established starting with living trees, or timbers where the 'zero age' ring is present and the year of felling known. The timescale is then extended by using large felled timbers which have patterns sufficiently overlapping the existing chronology to be certain of a unique match (for example from early buildings and archaeological excavations). Relative ring width patterns for several timbers are averaged to avoid the idiosyncracies of any individual tree, and to verify the validity of the linkages. In the process of establishing a master chronology, it is not uncommon to have a ring width pattern, the time span of which is inherently known, but which has not yet been linked to the sequence: this is a 'floating chronology'.

For an archaeological sample, accurate dendrochronological dating requires that three criteria be satisfied: there must be a master chronology for the given species and region; there must be sufficient rings present to ensure a unique match is found with the master chronology; and the sapwood rings must be present. Typically about 100 rings are needed. The presence of sapwood is often the most stringent criterion. The heartwood of a living tree is itself no longer alive, and chemical changes have occurred which help to preserve the timber. The sapwood on the other hand is softer and, because it transports the sap, is prone to insect attack and decay; furthermore, woodworking techniques will often remove the sapwood prior to usage of the timber. If all of the sapwood is present, a precise date for the last year of growth is possible, and sometimes even the season of felling. If only some of the sapwood is present, a sapwood correction can be made and a likely age range determined. However, if the sapwood–heartwood boundary is missing, the date of the last ring provides only a *terminus post quem* for the felling of the tree which could have been centuries after the formation of that ring. Sapwood corrections are based on typical sapwood ring numbers. For oak in Britain, 95% of mature trees have between 19 and 50 sapwood rings, with the number also increasing the higher up the trunk: an average figure of 30 is therefore used. The value, however, varies geographically.

Measurement of relative ring widths requires a radial section and ideally a full cross-section of the wood, as this will help to identify missing rings (years of little or no growth) and false rings (years where growth is arrested and then restarts) which may not appear the same around the whole circumference (oak is less prone to these effects than conifers: a ring is unlikely to be missing for more than a short section of circumference). For less destructive sampling, coring can be used, but this usually destroys the sapwood and a wedge sample is also required of the sapwood and sapwood—heartwood boundary. Panels for panel paintings were cut radially to avoid warping: a small amount of planing or sanding of an edge therefore exposes the radial sequence.

Long chronologies have been built up for a number of areas of the world e.g. nearly 7000 years for bristlecone pines in California, some 7500 years on oak in northern Ireland and a combined oak and pine chronology extends 11,000 years in Germany. For the Mediterranean area, linkage of a number of floating chronologies (using oak, cedar of Lebanon, pine and juniper) is near and will provide a sequence stretching back at least 5000 years. Apart from this last, each of the long chronologies has been used to provide the accurate calendar scale for a RADIOCARBON DATING calibration curve.

The study of tree-rings started in climatology, and this aspect of their use has received something of a revival, not least because narrow rings in the Irish oak sequence appear to correlate with climatic deterioration as a result of volcanic eruptions such as that of Santorini (Thera), the island in the Cyclades, where a volcano erupted in *c*.1500 BC, burying the settlement of Akrotiri.

M.G.L. Baillie: *Tree-ring dating and archaeology* (London, 1982); D. Eckstein: *Dendrochronological dating* (Strasbourg, 1984); M.G.L. Baillie and M.A.R. Munro: 'Irish tree rings, Santorini and volcanic dust veils', *Nature* 332 (1988) 344–6.

SB

depositional remnant magnetism *see* ARCHAEOMAGNETIC DATING

Der, Tell ed- *see* SIPPAR

Dereivka *see* SREDNI STOG

descriptive statistics *see* REDUCTION OF DATA

Deverel-Rimbury Bronze Age pottery style of southern England (Wiltshire, Dorset etc.) associated with the development of urnfield cremation burials in Britain in the middle to late 2nd millennium BC. Deverel Rimbury pottery is characterized by a distinctive set of large urns (the main types are 'bucket', 'barrel' and 'globular' urns) found with cremation burials in large flat cemeteries and at settlement sites. The settlements associated with Deverel-Rimbury pottery are sometimes open, but often consist of rectilinear banked enclosures with circular huts inside; they are often linked to extensive systems of CELTIC FIELDS.

RJA

Devil's Lair This site helped to show that the southwest of Australia was populated prior to 30,000 years ago. Situated in the extreme southwest of Western Australia, the lowest artefactual levels date back to 33,000 years ago and intensive occupation ceased around 12,000 BP. The site is especially remarkable for its early bone tools (29,000 BP), and bone beads made from kangaroo long bone dating to 12,000 to 15,000 years ago.

C. Dortch: 'Devil's Lair: an example of prolonged cave use in south-western Australia', *WA* 10 (1979), 258–79.

CG

Dhar Tichitt Southward-facing 60 m high sandstone plateau and cliff overlooking a sandy plain with interdunal depressions in the presently desertic south central part of Mauritania. The site covers an area of 44 × 15 km and contains 46 'Neolithic' sites, 43 on the plateau, with elaborate drystone walled enclosures, and 3 on the plain, without such features. Investigations by Patrick J. Munson in 1967–8 and by Augustin Holl in 1980–1 have led to contrasting interpretations of the subsistence economy and settlement history of the area. Munson distinguishes eight separate phases of occupation, extending, on the basis of 15 radiocarbon dates which he considers reliable, from 3365 ± 114 to 2465 ± 135 BP. With increasing dessication, the focus of settlement moved from the plain to the plateau, and the inhabitants, who were at first predominantly hunters and fishers, became mainly herders and cultivators. Domestic animals include goats and/or sheep and cattle. Munson obtained 593 latex casts of identifiable grain impressions on potsherds from sites in the area, of which 400 were recognized as cultivated bulrush millet (*Pennisetum* sp.), the remainder belonging to wild species such as cram-cram (*Cenchrus biflorus*). Millet became increasingly important from phase 6 onwards, although Munson did not believe that there was an independent *in situ* development of plant domestication in this area.

By contrast, Holl considers that the sites on the plateau and the plain were contemporary, forming a single complex system, and he lists 24 radiocarbon dates (including some rejected by Munson) to demonstrate this point; they stretch from 3850 ± 250 to 2170 ± 105 BP. According to this interpretation, the agro-pastoralists occupied the plateau, where almost all the grain impressions of millet have been found, during the rainy season and moved to the plain during the dry season, when they were obliged to collect 'emergency foods' such as cram-cram. A new model has therefore transformed the data by realigning them along a geographical rather than a chronological axis.

P.J. Munson: 'Archaeological data on the origins of cultivation in the southwestern Sahara and their implications for West Africa', *Origins of African plant domestication*, ed. J.R. Harlan, J.M.J. de Wet and A.B.L. Stemler (The Hague and Paris, 1976), 187–209; A. Holl: 'Subsistence patterns of the Dhar Tichitt Neolithic, Mauritania', *AAR* 3 (1985), 151–62; ——: 'Habitat et sociétés préhistoriques au Dhar Tichitt (Mauritanie)', *Sahara* 2 (1989), 49–60 [comment by P.J. Munson: 106–8].

PA-J

Dian *see* SHIH-CHAI-SHAN

Diana ware Expertly fired late Neolithic red ware, identified following excavations near the Lipari 'acropolis' on the Aeolian Islands, but also common through Sicily and southern Italy from the early 4th millennium BC. Diana ware is quite distinct from earlier wares in the region in both its colour and form; the vessels exhibit angular profiles and cylinder ('trumpet') lugs. It seems to be a little later than, or overlapping with, SERRA D'ALTO ware.

RJA

Dibeira Nubian site 20 km north of the second Nile cataract, which has now been submerged under LAKE NASSER. Dibeira West (on the western bank of the Nile) included the principal site of the ARKINIAN period: DIW 1. This consists of 13 oval concentrations of burnt stones, chipped artefacts (including microlithic flakes, blades and double-platform cores) and a few bones of fish and animals: the remains of a seasonal encampment of hunters and fishers occupied annually during the Nile flood. There were also remains of a substantial settlement dating to the Nubian Christian period (*c.*AD 550–1500), where the population is estimated at about 200–400, as in the contemporary towns of Meinarti and Arminna. At Dibeira East (on the eastern bank of the Nile) there was a C-GROUP-style cemetery of shaft-graves (lined with flat stone slabs and covered with rough stone ring-shaped superstructures) but the sherds derive from Egyptian pottery of New Kingdom date (*c.*1550–1070 BC).

P. Shinnie: Preliminary excavation reports in *Kush* 11–13 (1963–5); R. Schild et al.: 'The Arkinian and Sharmarkian industries', *The Prehistory of Nubia* II, ed. F. Wendorf (Dallas, 1968), 651–767.

IS

diet breadth *see* FORAGING THEORY

Dietz Multiple-component surface site found on a series of pluvial lake terraces in eastern Oregon (*c.*9500–5000 BC), western North America. Spatial analysis of the horizontal location and elevation of each artefact has permitted reconstruction of FLUTED POINT and STEMMED POINT TRADITION occupation surfaces across the paleo-landscape. The discrete two-level distribution of point types has been correlated with the two successive shorelines. The superimposition of shoreline deposits in parts of the lake basin shows that the shoreline relating to the Stemmed Point Tradition artefacts, dated by radiocarbon to 7660 ± 100 BP (AA-3932), is younger than the shoreline associated with artefacts of the Fluted Point Tradition, which has been cross-dated to *c.*9500–9000 BC by typological comparison with Fluted Point sites outside the area.

J.A. Willig et al., eds: *Early human occupation in far western North America: the Clovis-Archaic interface* (Carson City, 1988); J.A. Willig: *Broad spectrum adaptations at the Pleistocene-Holocene boundary in far western North America* (unpublished Ph.D. thesis, Department of Anthropology, University of Oregon, Eugene, 1989).

RC

diffusionism Tendency to explain cultural change and cultural similarities in terms of the adoption of technologies and stylistic traits from neighbouring or trading-partner cultures. Diffusion differs from migration in that it does not imply the physical movement (or replacement of) peoples. Together with migration, cultural diffusion was the favoured mechanism of change for many CULTURAL HISTORIANS writing about prehistoric peoples before the advent of PROCESSUAL ARCHAEOLOGY. This was particularly true from the later 19th century, when ethnologists such as Friedrich Ratzel and, later, Franz Boas, began to argue that independent invention of significant technological advances was highly unlikely to have happened more than once, implying that diffusion or migration would have to be disproved by archaeologists if they were to convincingly substantiate the independent origin or evolution of an (already known) idea in any given region.

In the most extreme form, 'hyper-diffusionists' argued that there was a single point of origin for all cultural innovations. W.J. Perry (1923) and Grafton Elliot Smith (1923, 1933), for instance, promoted the idea that ancient Egypt was the ultimate source of human civilization. For decades, various archaeologists continued to argue that the design of MEGALITHIC monuments spread originally from the Near East via various regions of Europe. Even after it became clear that a Near Eastern origin was unlikely, diffusionist studies built up an elaborate family tree of megalithic tomb styles describing various waves of tomb-style spreading from southern Europe into western and northern regions.

Gordon Childe, and many other archaeologists of his generation, continued to lean on the mechanism of diffusion to explain how complex technologies (notably, the development of farming, but also metallurgy etc) spread from the Near East to western Europe, although in Childe's accounts there is an increasing emphasis on the economic environment in which diffusion acted. As Marxist thought influenced his belief, he laid greater stress on the internal evolution of social relations as the prime mover of change, rather than the simple introduction of technological advance. However, for many Western archaeologists, diffusion remained the principal explanation for cultural change until the development of radiocarbon dating dealt some diffusionist explanations a death blow. In his revolutionary study of prehistoric Europe, *Before civilization*, Colin Renfrew (1973) used new and controversial radiocarbon dating to suggest that the MEGALITHIC tradition may have been invented in several different areas at once and could not have followed the diffusionist path mapped out in previous decades. Later, Renfrew's writings also highlighted the fact that metallurgy seemed to have developed independently in southeastern Europe and could not have diffused from the Near East.

In the same period, proponents of PROCESSUAL ARCHAEOLOGY began to put forward new ways in which change and cultural innovation could arise out of the disposition of social systems, using SYSTEMS THEORY. It became 'too easy' to argue that change was simply introduced from outside – even where the key features of change made it clear that diffusion had indeed operated, the focus of the archaeologist was now to be the reason why change was accepted and the effect that change in one (e.g. the technology) subsystem had on another (e.g. the political). In the case of domesticates and farming, for example – which, in the broadest sense, certainly did diffuse from east to west – the focus of enquiry is now the complex reasons for acceptance (and rejection) of various elements of the farming revolution and their rate of acceptance. The diffusion of knowledge and technologies remains a key concept – but the idea of diffusion as the primary, necessary and sufficient cause of change has sunk forever.

F. Ratzel: *Anthropogeographie* (Stuttgart, 1882–91); G.A. Reisner: *Archaeological survey of Nubia, Bulletin no. 3* (Cairo, 1909); W.J. Perry: *The children of the sun* (London, 1923); G.E. Smith: *The ancient Egyptians and the origin of civilization* (London, 1923); ——: *The diffusion of culture* (London, 1933); A.C. Renfrew: *Before civilization: The radiocarbon revolution and prehistoric Europe* (London, 1973); B.G. Trigger: *A history of archaeological thought* (Cambridge, 1989), 150–5.

RJA

Dilmun *see* BAHRAIN

Diospolis Parva *see* HIW-SEMAINA REGION

disc core *see* LEVALLOIS TECHNIQUE

discrete variable *see* VARIABLE

discriminant analysis (canonical variates analysis) A technique of MULTIVARIATE STATISTICS concerned with discovering which VARIABLE, or combination of variables, best distinguish ('discriminate') between predefined groups of objects. This problem can be visualised as choosing the angle from which to view a group of clouds, so that one sees as much 'air' between them, and as little overlap, as possible. Also called canonical variates analysis (CVA), these techniques can be used to clarify the outcome of a CLUSTER ANALYSIS, or to probe a typology handed down by a specialist. The groups should in theory have the same internal variability, but the technique seems to be ROBUST, and good results can be obtained even when this requirement is not met. For a case-study *see* BOXGROVE.

J.E. Doran and F.R. Hodson: *Mathematics and computers in archaeology* (Edinburgh, 1975), 209–13; S. Shennan: *Quantifying archaeology* (Edinburgh, 1988), 286–8.

CO

distribution-free statistics *see* NON-PARAMETRIC STATISTICS

diversity Term that can be used to signify either 'richness', i.e. the number of different types of artefact in an assemblage, or the related concept of 'evenness', which deals instead with the relative proportions of each different type. The concept of diversity is invariably complicated by the problem of sample-size. The clear statistical relationship between quantity of artefacts and diversity of types is so strong and overriding that it tends to obscure the more subtle reasons for variations in diversity. This problem was encountered in several case-studies published in the early 1980s, such as an analysis of hunter-gatherer 'aggregation sites' in prehistoric Iberia (Conkey 1980). Margaret Conkey attempted to overcome the effect of differences in sample size by using 'indices' of diversity (similar to those used by plant scientists, see Pielou 1977: 292).

In 1984, Keith Kintigh argued that this kind of 'information-theoretic' index of diversity was an inadequate measure, since it attempted to combine both quantity and diversity in a single number, whereas the two aspects of quantification should be treated separately. He suggested that a better method of assessing the significance of different levels of diversity was to use a computer program which creates a SIMULATION of the process of diversification itself, thus producing an 'expected diversity' for each sample size, which can then provide a meaningful comparison with the actual diversity.

The basic principles of Kintigh's method have been criticized, particularly in the work of Schlanger and Orcutt in the Dolores river valley, in southwest Colorado. Schlanger and Orcutt (1986) suggest first that there is a problem of circularity (when the same data that are used to simulate expected diversity for different sample sizes are also then compared with that expected diversity), and second that the use of Kintigh's simulation program constitutes an assumption that 'assemblages contain items chosen at random in accordance with some unchanging, culturally determined probability' and therefore ignores SITE FORMATION PROCESSES.

E.C. Pielou: *Mathematical ecology* (New York, 1977); M.W. Conkey: 'The identification of prehistoric hunter-gatherer aggregation sites: the case of Altamira', *CA* 21 (1980), 609–30; K.W. Kintigh: 'Measuring archaeological diversity by comparison with simulated assemblages', *AA* 49 (1984), 44–54; S.H. Schlanger and J.D. Orcutt: 'Site surface characteristics and functional inferences', *AA* 51 (1986), 296–312.

IS

Divuyu Settlement site of the 7th and 8th centuries AD in the Tsodilo Hills of northern Botswana. Faunal remains indicate an emphasis on fishing and small stock herding rather than cattle (in a ratio of 160:8). The analysis of the iron and copper objects at the site offers a useful archaeometallurgical study and lays the groundwork for future comparisons. Denbow associates the ceramics with the 'Western Stream' (i.e. Kalundu Tradition) in South Africa and Mandingo Keyes near the Congo River mouth. A MULTIDIMENSIONAL ANALYSIS, however, shows that Divuyu belongs to a new 'tradition' that includes Naviundu near Lumbabashi as well as Mandigo Keyes. The locations and styles of the ceramics indicate that Western Bantu-speaking peoples produced this second tradition. The population of Divuyu thus shared a linguistic and cultural background with a broad arc of people around the southern fringes of the equatorial forest.

J. Denbow: 'Congo to Kalahari: data and hypotheses about the political economy of the western stream of the early Iron Age', *AAR* 8 (1990), 139–76.

TH

Diyala region Large basin of cultivable land covering an area of about 1000 sq. km around the confluence of the rivers Tigris and Diyala in northern Iraq, to the northeast of modern Baghdad. Five major SUMERIAN city-states – Tell Asmar (Eshnunna), KHAFAJEH, Tell Agrab, Ischali and TELL HARMAL – are located in the Diyala plains. All five towns were established at least as early as the Protoliterate phase and flourished during the Early Dynastic period (*c*.2900–2350 BC). Much of the perceived character of the Early Dynastic period is based on data from these towns, although ironically they were probably relatively peripheral sites (Crawford 1991: 65). The deep and detailed stratigraphy excavated at these sites by Henri Frankfort, Thorkild Jacobsen and Seton Lloyd has enabled artefacts from Sumerian sites elsewhere in southern Mesopotamia to be assigned to the three main phases of the Early Dynastic period. By the Isin-Larsa period (*c*.2025–1763 BC) the Diyala region had become a definite political grouping, which was known collectively as the kingdom of Eshnunna; its main cult centres were at Tell Asmar and Ischali.

In the first phase of the Early Dynastic period the nucleus of Tell Asmar appears to have consisted of an amorphous one-roomed shrine surrounded by houses. During the second phase this shrine was transformed into the Square Temple (a complex consisting of three sanctuaries and resembling an Early Dynastic house in plan), in which a cache of 12 Sumerian sculptures – representing worshippers rather than the god himself – were discovered. Although the deity traditionally associated with Eshnunna in later periods was Tishpak, an inscription from the nearby 'palace'-building suggests that the god worshipped in the Square Temple may have been Abu, god of vegetation. A seal found in the immediate vicinity of the temple provides evidence of links with the INDUS CIVILIZATION.

From the point of view of the history of archaeology in Mesopotamia, the overwhelming significance of the Diyala basin lies in Robert Adams' choice of the region for the first of his surveys in the early 1960s. Adams (1965) effectively revolutionized the discipline by transferring the focus from individual excavated sites to overall settlement patterns and contexts, borrowing such ideas as settlement-ranking from geography, and using newly-available statistical and computerized methods to avoid the flaws and biases that were inherent in earlier distribution maps.

Case-study: central place theory. Intensive field survey in the Diyala region revealed evidence for the development of the prehistoric settlement pattern. The Early Dynastic I (early 3rd millennium BC) pattern in particular has been analysed to test the utility of CENTRAL PLACE THEORY. The settlements vary considerably in size, and can be grouped into a range of sizes from large towns down to hamlets. There is little direct evidence for site function, and surface area is therefore taken as a measure of the range of services offered by a site; this assumption is critical to the analysis, and needs further investigation.

The analysis of the distribution of the settlements in the various size classes in the Diyala region shows some degree of correspondence with expectations derived from the theory, in particular a measure of regularity of spacing between sites of the same size and some nesting of smaller sites around larger ones. The hexagonal latticing predicted by the classic theory is not found, however, and the pattern is more rectangular, possibly due to the importance of water and the effect of the parallel orientation of the local water-courses. Sites in the smaller size groups are located on lines between larger sites, suggesting a locational principle based on the importance of transport, although this is not reflected in the contemporary documentary evidence. The analysis would suggest that a centrally organized settlement system was emerging in which exchange and transport were significant determining factors.

H. Frankfort and T. Jacobsen: *The Gimilsin temple and the palace of the rulers of Tell Asmar* (Chicago, 1940); P.

Delougaz and S. Lloyd: *Presargonic temples in the Diyala region* (Chicago, 1942); P. Delougaz: *Pottery from the Diyala region* (Chicago, 1952); R.M. Adams: *Land behind Baghdad: a history of settlement on the Diyala Plains* (Chicago and London, 1965); P. Delougaz et al. *Private houses and graves in the Diyala region* (Chicago, 1967); G.A. Johnson: 'A test of central place theory in archaeology', *Man, settlement and urbanism*, ed. P.J. Ucko, R. Tringham and G.W. Dimbleby (London, 1972), 769–85; S. Lloyd: *The archaeology of Mesopotamia* (London, 1978), 93–134; H. Crawford: *Sumer and the Sumerians* (Cambridge, 1991), 29–47, 65–9.
TC

D/L ratio *see* AMINO ACID DATING

DNA analysis Extraction and characterization of ancient DNA (deoxyribonucleic acid) in order to study genetic change. This area of archaeology has experienced considerable growth in the 1990s, with the application of newly developed techniques in microbiology to ancient human and faunal remains. The majority of genetic information is stored in the nuclei of human body cells, but some DNA is also contained in the cells known as mitochondria, which are only inherited from mothers – unlike nuclear DNA, this so-called mitichondrial DNA (mtDNA) preserves a better record of the genetic make-up of human ancestors.

The Swedish biologist Svante Pääbo has made many pioneering contributions to DNA analysis, especially in his early work on extraction and cloning of DNA from Egyptian mummies and Archaic-period American Indians. The development of techniques such as polymerase chain reaction, enabling the extraction of very small quantities of DNA from bones and teeth, as opposed to soft tissues, has opened the way to studying the genetic relationships between the fossil remains of early hominids. Rebecca Cann and others (see Cann et al. 1987; Stoneking and Cann 1989) put forward the controversial hypothesis, on the basis of mtDNA extracted from 147 modern women, that all humans may be descended from a single woman who lived in Africa in *c.*200,000 BP. Milford Wolpoff (Wolpoff et al. 1984, 1989) offers the alternative view that modern humans may have emerged roughly simultaneously in several different regions of the world. More recently, Pääbo may have proved that NEANDERTHALS were not ancestral to modern *Homo sapiens* by establishing clear genetic differences between the two.

M. Wolpoff et al.: 'Modern Homo sapiens origins: a general theory of hominid evolution involving the fossil evidence from East Asia', *The origins of modern humans: a world survey of the fossil evidence*, ed. F.H. Smith and F. Spencer (New York, 1984), 411–83; R.L. Cann et al.: 'Mitochondrial DNA and human evolution', *Nature* 325 (1987), 31–6; M. Stoneking and R.L. Cann: 'African origin of human mitochondrial DNA', *The human revolution*, ed. P. Mellars and C. Stringer (Edinburgh, 1989), 17–30; S. Pääbo: 'Ancient DNA: extraction, characterisation, molecular cloning, and enzymatic amplification', *Proceedings of the National Academy of Sciences of the USA* 86 (1989), 1939–43; M.H. Wolpoff: 'Multi-regional evolution: the fossil alternative to Eden', *The human revolution*, ed. P. Mellars and C. Stringer (Edinburgh, 1989), 62–108; C. Cataneo et al.: 'Identification of ancient blood and tissue – ELISA and DNA analysis', *Antiquity* 65 (1991), 878–81; G. Eglinton and G.B. Curry, eds: *Molecules through time: fossil molecules and biological systematics* (London, 1991); M. Hoss et al.: 'DNA damage and DNA sequence retrieval from ancient tissues', *Nucleic Acids Research* 24/7 (1996), 1304–7; A.C. Stone et al.: 'Sex determination of ancient human skeletons using DNA', *American Journal of Physical Anthropology* 99/2 (1996), 231–8.
IS

Dniepr-Donetsian Neolithic cultural tradition identified from dwelling sites and cemeteries found mainly in the river basins of the Dniepr and Severski Donets (in Ukraine and Belarus), and dating from perhaps 5000 to 3000 BC. The culture was identified in 1927–33 and was intensively studied in the 1950s and 1960s by D. Ya. Telegin (1961, 1968). The sites are usually located on the river flood-plains. In rare cases, the remains of small oval-shaped semi-subterranean dwellings can be identified. The economy was based predominantly on hunting (aurochs, red deer, wild board, elk), fishing and food-collecting. Rarely, and only at the later sites, the bones of domesticated animals are found (cattle, pig, sheep/goat). An impression of barley (*Hordeum sativum*) was identified on a potsherd at the site of Vita Litovskaya near Kiev.

The stone inventory includes geometric microliths of Mesolithic type, bifacially retouched arrowheads and spearheads, and large polished axes.

The earliest stage of the cultural tradition, which is often viewed as an independent cultural unit, is represented by the Strumel-Gastyatin group of sites near Kiev. The sites yielded fragments of large conical vessels decorated with rows of comb impressions. The following types of ceramics are typical of the Dniepr-Donetsian proper: (1) egg-shaped wide-mouthed pots with pointed base and a straight or slightly flaring rim; (2) wide-mouthed pots with a pointed base and a straight rim; (3) spherical bowls with a pointed bottom, a short cylindrical neck and a straight or everted rim; (4) hemispherical bowls with a flat bottom and a straight rim. The ornament consists of rows of comb impressions, incised lines, geometric patterns (triangles, rhombi, rectangles) formed using closely-set strokes. The patterns are generally similar to those of the BUG-DNIESTR ceramics, while the practice of using strokes to make geometric patterns is similar to the stroke-ornamented ware of the Funnel Beaker tradition in Central Europe.

The Dniepr-Donetsian tradition produced several large cemeteries, which feature at least two types of burial rite. Burials belonging to an earlier stage were made in deep oval ditches. Later burials were made in rectangular graves filled in with earth mixed with red ochre. The richer graves of the latter type contained prestige ornaments, in copper and gold, and stone mace-heads. The cemeteries of Yasinovatski, Osipovski and Nikol'ski have been radiocarbon dated, and in calendar years date to between 5200–4500 BC.

D.Ya. Telegin: 'K voprosu o dnepro-donetskoi neolitičeskoi kul'ture' [On the problem of the Dniepr-Donetsian neolithic culture], *Sovetskaja arheologija* 4 (1961), 26–40; ——: *Dnipro-Donec'ka kul'tura* [The Dniepr-Donetsian culture] (Kiev, 1968); P.M. Dolukhanov: *Ecology and economy in Neolithic Eastern Europe* (London, 1979).

PD

Dniepr-Dvinian Iron-Age culture identified in the catchment areas of the upper western Dvina and Dniepr, in northwest Russia, northeast Belarus and northern Ukraine during the 1st millennium BC. The hillfort settlements are usually located on morainic hills, close to lakes and river valleys. In the early stages (7th–2nd centuries BC) there were no artificial fortifications, but turf walls and ditches appeared during the 2nd–1st centuries BC. The size of the hillforts varies from 400 to 3,000 sq. m. (usually 800–1,500 sq. m). Two types of houses are distinguishable: small (3.0 to 3.2 m) and long (3.0 to 10–14 m). Both had hearths in the middle of the living space, and wooden posts supporting the roof and walls. The material remains included numerous ceramics (flat-bottomed red-grey pots) and iron implements, including sickles, daggers, axes, spear- and arrowheads and ornaments (brooches, rings and bracelets). Bronze implements were manufactured from the ingots imported from the area west of the Urals; at a site near Nakvasino on the upper Dniepr there was a remarkable find of a mould for a Scandinavian type of celt. The bone tools are similar to those of central Russia. Several specialized smelting and forging sites have been found (e.g. Chernaya Gora near the town of Sebezh on the Russian-Latvian border). The rate of domesticates in the faunal remains varies between 40–80%: pigs make up about a third of the assemblage; cattle around 24%; sheep/goat around 20–23%; horse around 15% (Sedov 1970). The crops included bread and spelt wheats; naked and hulled barley (Krasnov 1971).

V.F. Isaenko et al.: *Očerki po arheologii Belorussii* [Essays on the archaeology of Belarus] (Minsk, 1970); V.V. Sedov: *Salvjane Verhnego Podeprov'ja i Podvin'ja* [The Slavs of the Upper Dniepr and Dvina area] (Moscow, 1970); Yu.A. Krasnov: *Rannee zemledelie i životnovodstvo v lesnoi polose Vostočnoi Evropy* [Early stock-breeding and agriculture in the forest belt of Eastern Europe] (Moscow, 1971).

PD

Doc Chua Located on the edge of the Be River to the east of the Mekong Delta, Vietnam, this site yielded 50 bivalve sandstone or clay moulds when excavated in 1976–7. The moulds were used for casting bronze bells, tanged arrowheads, socketed spearheads, harpoons and chisels. Several of the moulds had been rejected due to imperfections. The typology of the bronzes is closely matched in north-east Thailand at NON NOK THA, BAN CHIANG and BAN NA DI, and the calibrated radiocarbon dates of 1420 and 608 BC are well within the expected range. The distance of this site from the nearest likely copper and tin sources (200 km to the north and west) reveals the distance over which ingots were exchanged.

Le Xuan Diem: 'Ancient moulds for casting bronze artefacts from the Dong Nai basin', *Khao Co Hoc* [Archaeology] 24 (1977), 44–8 [in Vietnamese].

CH

Doian Term applied to Late Stone Age assemblages in south-western Ethiopia and adjacent parts of Somalia, following Desmond Clark's work in the 1940s. These assemblages are distinguished from the broad category of WILTON industries by being less markedly microlithic and containing more delicately flaked pieces, including leaf-shaped and hollow-based points. Some late facies are said to occur with pottery.

J.D. Clark: *The prehistoric cultures of the Horn of Africa* (Cambridge, 1954), esp. 226 ff.

JS

Doigahama An Early to Middle Yayoi community cemetery in Yamaguchi prefecture, Japan (*c*.300–100 BC). Analysis of 300+ bodies supports the model of immigration at the beginning of the Yayoi period (*see* JAPAN 3). There was considerable variation in burial form, including multiple, partly crouched and extended inhumation. Most Yayoi burials have heads oriented eastwards.

T. Kanaseki et al.: 'Yamaguchi-ken Doigahama iseki' [Doigahama site, Yamaguchi prefecture], *Nihon noko bunka no seisei*, ed. Nihon Kokogaku Kyokai (Tokyo, 1961), 223–61 [in Japanese]; C.M. Aikens and T. Higuchi: *The prehistory of Japan* (London, 1982), 204–6.

SK

dolmen *see* CROMLECH

Dong Dau Prehistoric settlement site covering 3 hectares, located just north of the Red River, which forms the type-site for the Dong Dau phase of the Vietnamese prehistoric sequence in the Red River valley. Excavations in 1965 and 1967–8 revealed a stratigraphy 5–6 m thick, the earliest phase belonging to the PHUNG NGUYEN culture. Such sites are rarely deeply stratified, and at Dong Dau it was possible to trace the development of the Phung Nguyen pottery tradition into the cultural phase named after Dong Dau itself. The Phung Nguyen tradition of ornamenting pottery with incised designs continued into this phase, and there was a vigorous bone industry, including the production of harpoons. Stone jewellery, such as pierced ear ornaments, were fashioned, and rice remains reveal an agricultural subsistence base.

Whereas the Phung Nguyen sites have very little evidence for copper-based technology, there is no doubt that metal casting became fully established in northern Vietnam during the Dong Dau culture, the sandstone and clay moulds as well as the cast axeheads and fishhooks being closely paralleled in northeast Thailand and at DOC CHUA. Towards the end of the 2nd millennium BC, the Dong Dau developed into the GO MUN culture, a period which saw a further increase in the number of bronze implements cast in the Red River valley.

Ha Van Tan: 'Nouvelles recherches préhistoriques et protohistoriques au Viet Nam', *BEFEO* 68 (1980), 113–54.

CH

Dongodien *see* EAST TURKANA; NDERIT

Dong Son culture One of the most complex manifestations of centralized chiefdoms in mainland Southeast Asia, originating in the 1st millennium BC in the lower valley of the Red River, Vietnam. The culture is characterized by its inhumation cemeteries, which contain an impressive range of bronze artefacts such as the famous Dong Son bronze drums.

In a handful of Dong Son cemeteries, the dead were interred in wooden boat coffins. Eight such burials have been found at Chau Can, in the Red River valley of Vietnam, where the coffin wood has been radiocarbon-dated to the unexpectedly early date of 1000–400 BC, although this may simply reflect the age of trees used to make the coffins. Apart from the human skeletons, much organic material has survived at Chau Can, including the wooden haft of a bronze axe, a bamboo ladle and a spear handle. In the Viet Khe burial, on the northern margins of the Red River delta, the boat coffin is 4.5 m long and contained over 100 artefacts, mainly of bronze. Calibrated radiocarbon dating suggests that this burial took place in about 400 BC, and may be compared to the burials at Chau Can, although in this case no primary interment was found.

Although most Dong Son archaeological sites comprise cemeteries, investigations at Co Loa (a moated settlement of the later 1st millennium BC located on the Red River floodplain, 15 km northwest of Hanoi) confirm the historic sources in revealing at least one large, central, defended site which has been widely interpreted as a chiefly centre. The moat at Co Loa surrounds three sets of ramparts, which have been dated by literary and archaeological evidence to at least the 3rd century BC. In 1982, excavations uncovered a Heger 1 bronze drum (one of four basic types of southeast Asian bronze drums, according to a descriptive system suggested by the Austrian F. Heger in 1902). The drum, like others of the Heger 1 type, was richly decorated with scenes showing warriors with feathered head-dresses, war canoes, houses and a set of four drums being played from a wooden platform. Co Loa also contained over 100 bronze socketed ploughshares or hoes, and a cache of several thousand bronze arrowheads was found outside the defended area. Other similar sites probably existed in other parts of the Red River delta area and the Ma valley (Higham 1989: 190–209).

Dong Son, the type-site of the culture, is located on the southern bank of the Ma River in northern Vietnam. It was first examined in 1924 by the French customs official Pajot, who encountered inhumation graves associated with bronze spearheads, decorated axes, ornamented plaques and drums. More recently, Vietnamese excavations have shown that there was a rapid transition from the Go Mun to the early Dong Son culture at this site. Decoration on the drums indicates that the people were given to ceremony and display in which the drums themselves played a significant part. It was formerly thought that the Dong Son bronze industry had its origins in China or even eastern

Europe, but research on the DONG DAU and GO MUN cultures has provided clear evidence that it had local origins.

F. Heger: *Alte Metalltrommeln aus Südost-Asien* (Leipzig, 1902); O.R.T. Janse: *Archaeological research in Indo-China* III: *The ancient dwelling site of Dong-S'on (Thanh-Hoa, Annam)* (Cambridge, MA, 1958); Luu Tran Tieu: *Khu Mo Co Chau Can* (Hanoi 1977) [Vietnamese-language description of the excavation of Chau Can]; Ha Van Tan: 'Nouvelles recherches préhistoriques et protohistoriques au Viet Nam', *BEFEO* 68 (1980), 113–54; P. Wheatley: *Nagara and commandery* (Chicago, 1983), 91–3; C.F.W. Higham: *The archaeology of mainland Southeast Asia* (Cambridge, 1989).

CH

Dongzhou *see* EASTERN CHOU

Dorestad Urban site in the Netherlands, the archaeological investigations of which constitute perhaps the most ambitious open-area study of a medieval site in Europe. L.J.F. Janssen carried out the first excavations in 1842 for the Rijksmuseum van Oudheden at Leiden; by 1859 Janssen was convinced that this was the site of the celebrated Carolingian port of Dorestad. Further campaigns were led by J.H. Holwerda in the 1920s. From a methodological standpoint, the massive 30 ha excavations from 1967 by W.A. van Es for the Dutch State Archaeological Service remain a remarkable undertaking.

Van Es, a Roman archaeologist by training, was faced with the destruction of the site by a new housing development. Convinced that the tradition of trenching early medieval emporia (e.g. BIRKA, Haithabu, IPSWICH and Kaupang) failed to provide any topographical data which, in turn, might demonstrate the function and political character of the site, he adopted mechanical means to expose as much of the settlement as possible. This controversial decision was not uniformly accepted at the 1972 Göttingen conference on early medieval towns, but the results affirmed van Es' decision.

Dorestad lies beneath the modern small town of Wijk bij Duurstede where the most northerly branch of the Rhine splits into the river Lek and the Kromme Rijn. The 7th- to 9th-century written sources indicate that it was located within the bifurcation of the rivers. The sources indicate that as early as the mid-7th century it was a mint for the gold trientes of the Frankish moneyer Madelinus. At this time it lay within Frisia, although it may have been under Merovingian dominance. By the early 8th century the centre lay in territory disputed between Radbod of Frisia and his Merovingian neighbours. By 720 it was finally in Merovingian hands, and from then on served intermittently for the Franks. Throughout this period it is mentioned as a port at which Anglo-Saxon monks disembarked. Its role was undoubtedly developed under the Carolingians when it became one of the greatest centres in Europe.

Coins bearing a distinctive symbol of a ship were minted at Dorestad in the early 9th century, and its status as a toll station is mentioned in numerous sources. The coin evidence suggests that Dorestad's economic decline had begun by 830, when its mint ceased to function. This coincided with the first recorded Viking attack of 834. From 841 or 850 it was actually in Viking hands. After this the raids continued, and by the 860s a combination of raids and the silting up of the river brought about its final abandonment. Its functions thereafter were taken over by Tiel and Deventer.

Van Es' investigations indicate that Dorestad covered at least 40 hectares by the 9th century. It appears to have been composed of several zones. Alongside the river lay the harbour. Only part of this was excavated, showing that this consisted of plank walkways (each about 8 m wide) which were supported on wooden piles and extended out into the Kromme Rijn. Behind these lay a road approximately 3 m wide which ran along the original river bank.

On the other side of the road lay a line of buildings with their longitudinal axes towards the river. Each building would appear to have had its own walkway, an extension of the plot of land in which it lay. Possibly each building occupied an enclosed yard. Behind these buildings lay a cemetery at De Heul containing as many as 2350 individuals. In the centre of the cemetery was found a rectangular wooden building, about 8 × 15 m, which has been interpreted as a church.

North of the cemetery, beyond the riverbank settlement, lay a complex of farms, identified by their accompanying granaries. Each farm was situated in its own farmyard with its own well. The buildings themselves were bow-shaped, post-built structures similar to rural dwellings known from this region. Most buildings were internally divided into two sections of unequal length with opposing entrances in each side wall. Roads also ran through this part of Dorestad. To the south (i.e. to the west of the de Heul cemetery) lay another sector of the settlement. This contained another cemetery (De Engk) comprising a further 1000 inhumations. The surrounding sector remains undefined. South of this, occupying Middelweg, it has been proposed that there lay a Roman fort, from which the earliest

Merovingian trading settlement would have evolved.

Dorestad was pre-eminently a trading settlement founded about 630, which, to judge from the dendrochronological dates obtained from the wooden piles found in the river, was significantly enlarged in *c*.675. The influx of coins found in the excavations, many of them minted at Dorestad, indicates that its economic boom occurred between *c*.775 and *c*.825. The range of objects found at Dorestad indicates that it served the central Rhineland as an entrepot. Wooden barrels for transporting wine (re-used as the linings of wells) have been provenanced to the central Rhineland as has a huge proportion of the pottery (made either at Mayen or at production sites in the Vorgebirge Hills). Mill-stones, glass vessels and a range of minor stone objects were produced in the same region. Most scholars believe that these goods were shipped on via the Dutch archipelago and via the Frisian port of Medemblik, to places along the north German littoral, and as far north as the port of Ribe in western Jutland.

Products brought southwards remain a mystery. Only Baltic amber attests a two-way traffic. However, goods like slaves, furs, salt, honey, wax and possibly precious metals (to judge from the written sources) passed through the settlement en route for Merovingian and Carolingian centres to the south. Van Es' decision means that Dorestad represents a key site in North Sea archaeology; it is a measure of economic and political activity in a formative age for the European community. In addition, its material culture is a well-dated point of reference for the archaeology of post-classical northwestern Europe.

W.A. van Es and W.J.H. Verwers: *Excavations at Dorestad 1, the harbour: Hoogstraat* I (Amersfoort, 1980); ——: 'Dorestad centred', *Medieval archaeology in the Netherlands*, ed. J.C. Besteman, J.M. Bos and H.A. Heidinga (Maastricht, 1990), 151–82.

RH

Dorset culture Culture that occupied the Canadian Arctic from 550 BC until at least AD 1000. Best known for exquisite miniature carvings – perhaps the paraphernalia of SHAMANS – the Dorset culture appears to have been a more successful adaptation to the conditions of this region than the preceding ARCTIC SMALL TOOL TRADITION cultures (from which it developed). This is demonstrated by the huge area occupied by Dorset groups, and by evidence that they had perfected winter hunting on the sea ice. However, by the time the THULE culture spread across the Canadian Arctic around AD 1000, the Dorset had largely or entirely disappeared for reasons that are not well understood.

M.S. Maxwell: *Prehistory of the Eastern Arctic* (Orlando, 1985).

RP

Dosariyah *see* ARABIA; PRE-ISLAMIC

Dotawo, Kingdom of, *see* GEBEL ADDA

double spout and bridge bottle Type of closed vessel common in much of Andean South America in which two spouts on the top of the vessel are connected by a handle.

dromos *see* THOLOS

Dura Europus *see* PARTHIANS

Dur Kurigalzu *see* KASSITES

Dur-Sharrukin *see* KHORSABAD

Dur-Untash-Napirisha *see* ELAM

Duweir, Tell ed- *see* LACHISH

Dvaravati culture Complex polity which emerged in the central plain of Thailand between about AD 200 and 950. The name derives from two silver medallions found under a sanctuary at Nakhon Pathom in central Thailand, which proclaim that the building was the meritorious work of the King of Sri Dvaravati. Nakhon Pathom and U Thong are the best known of several large moated settlements; such sites contain substantial religious buildings which reveal a preference for Buddhism, although Hindu gods such as Siva were also worshipped.

U Thong was occupied at least from the beginning of the first millennium AD; the moats enclose an area of about 1690 by 840 m, and numerous foundations for Buddhist buildings have been uncovered. Excavations by J. Boisselier have revealed the foundations of an assembly hall and 3 octagonal *STUPA* bases. An inscription on copper, dated stylistically to the mid-7th century AD, records the accession of Harsavarman to the lion throne. It is feasible to see U Thong and other large moated sites, such as Nakhon Pathom, as competing centres within the polity of the Dvaravati culture. Excavations at Nakhon Pathom, the largest of the moated ceremonial centres, have concentrated on Buddhist buildings, and the nature of any secular structures remains to be clarified. Covering an area of 3700 × 2000 m, the site is dominated by a number of Buddhist sanctuaries.

At the site of Ku Bua, the moats and ramparts, which follow a roughly rectangular outline, cover an area of 2000 × 800 m, and are dominated by a central Buddhist temple; several other ruined structures are visible within the moats. The Buddhist temple and other buildings were decorated in stucco. Some representations show upper-class individuals or prisoners being chastised; the depiction of Semitic merchants stresses the importance of exchange to the Dvaravati economy.

The few inscriptions which have survived show that the vernacular language of the Dvaravati culture was Mon. The presence of an upper stratum in Dvaravati society is shown by the two terracotta 'toilet trays' from Nakhon Pathom, which bear numerous symbols of royalty. Early in the 11th century AD, the area came under strong influence from the expansionary and powerful rulers of ANGKOR, who probably exerted political control over the occupants of the Chao Phraya valley thereafter.

The early phases of the Dvaravati culture correspond to the FUNAN polities in the lower Mekong and trans-Bassac area of Vietnam, but the full development was contemporary with the ZHENLA CULTURE and the early period of Angkor. A series of competing polities centred on the large moated sites, rather than a single state, is the more likely interpretation of the political organization of the Dvaravati (*see also MANDALA*).

P. Dupont: *L'archéologie Mi Mone de Dvaravati* (Paris 1959); E. Lyons: 'The traders of Ku Bua', *Archives of the Chinese Art Society of America* 19 (1965), 52–6; J. Boisselier: *Nouvelles connaissances archéologiques de la ville d'U-T'ong* (Bangkok 1968); P. Wheatley: *Nagara and Commandery* (Chicago, 1983), 199–219.

CH

Dzibilchaltún Large LOWLAND MAYA city located in the dry northwestern corner of the Yucatán peninsula. Occupation extended from Middle Preclassic times into the Late Postclassic (i.e. *c*.1000 BC–AD 1400). The population declined in the Early Classic, peaking at about 25,000 during the Late Classic period, and dropped again in the Early Postclassic. With a large CENOTE at its centre, Dzibilchaltún consists of about 8000 structures arranged in numerous groupings, some joined by SACBES; many buildings of the Late Classic period (*c*.AD 600–900) feature PUUC-style architecture. The structural remains of the site cover nearly 20 sq. km, with rural agricultural populations living in the surrounding 100 sq. km. Located near the salt-producing regions of coastal Yucatán, Dzibilchaltún probably played an important role in the Maya salt trade.

E.W. Andrews IV: 'Dzibilchaltun, a northern Maya metropolis', *Archaeology* 21 (1968) 36–47; E.B. Kurjack: *Prehistoric lowland Maya community and social organization: a case study at Dzibilchaltun, Yucatan, Mexico* (New Orleans, 1974); E.W. Andrews V: 'Dzibilchaltun', *Supplement to the Handbook of Middle American Indians* I, ed. V.R. Bricker and J.A. Sabloff (Austin 1981), 313–41.

PRI

dzimbahwe *see* GREAT ZIMBABWE

E

Early Dynastic (Mesopotamia) One of the earliest periods of the Sumerian civilization (*see* SUMER), which was divided into three phases (ED I–III: *c*.2900–2350 BC) defined primarily by excavations in the DIYALA REGION. Also known as the 'pre-Sargonic period'.

Early Dynastic (Egypt) The first two (or, according to some chronologies, the first three) dynasties of pharaonic Egypt, *c*.3000–2649 BC. Also known as the Archaic period.

Early Historical periods *see* JAPAN 5

early ('archaic') *Homo sapiens* The species *Homo sapiens* has its origins some 400,000 years ago, although the first fossils attributed to our species are not actually 'anatomically modern', this being true only of the later subspecies *Homo sapiens sapiens* (*see* ANATOMICALLY MODERN HUMANS). Early *Homo sapiens* fossils from Petralona in Greece, Swanscombe in Kent, Heidelburg, Broken Hill/Kabwe (central Africa *see* SANGOAN) and the Dali skull from China exhibit a high cranial vault with associated reduction of the facial bones and teeth which sets them apart from *HOMO ERECTUS*. Brain sizes for these hominids fall within the modern human range at 1100–1400 cm^3. Given their African and European distribution, it has been suggested that early *Homo sapiens* constituted the ancestors of both anatomically modern humans and NEANDERTHALS. Others wish to classify the Neanderthals separately as *Homo neanderthalensis*.

C.B. Stringer: 'Human evolution and biological adaptation in the Pleistocene', *Hominid evolution and community ecology*, ed. R. Foley (London, 1984), 55–84; G. Richards: *Human evolution: an introduction for the behavioural sciences* (London, 1987); C.S. Gamble: *Timewalkers: The prehistory of global colonization* (London, 1993).

PG-B

Early Iron Age (East Africa) Widespread cultural complex with a related set of distinctive pottery wares most of which date to the early and mid-1st millennium AD, although those in the region west of Lake Victoria date back as early as the latter part of the 1st millennium BC. The distribution excludes the drier, more northerly parts of East Africa and the Eastern Rift Valley and flanking high grasslands; it fits remarkably closely with that of Bantu languages in south-central as well as eastern Africa. Following the arguments of Posnansky, Oliver and Fagan in the early 1960s and the research thus provoked (see Soper 1971), it is generally held that this Early Iron Age ('EIA') complex indicates the rapid expansion of speakers of eastern Bantu with a new iron-based and agricultural economy. Its emergence from the older, pre-Iron Age western Bantu in the forest zone remains a subject of debate.

The East African Early Iron Age has several known regional variants, one of the most important of which is Urewe, found at sites around Lake Victoria and westwards to Rwanda, Burundi, the Western Rift Valley and the forest edge in Zaire. The type-site of Urewe (the exact location of which is more correctly called Ulore) is close to the Lake in western Kenya, where collections were made by Archdeacon W.E. Owen in the 1940s. Some occurrences of Urewe ironwork and pottery (formerly described as 'dimple-based') are about 2000 years old, but claims for much earlier dates, such as 500 BC or earlier, have generally been discounted. Apart from their 'dimpled' bases, Urewe and related Early Iron Age pottery vessels are distinguished by bevelled rims and decoration in patterns of grooves and scrolls.

Beyond the Eastern Rift Valley, towards the coast and extending southwards, the Early Iron Age is represented by the related Kwale pottery, beginning in about the 2nd and 3rd centuries AD. Kwale pottery was first recognized and defined by Robert Soper (1967), the type-site being in the Kwale hills behind Mombasa. Other derivatives of Urewe further south in Tanzania and beyond have comparable dating in the early-mid 1st millennium AD (e.g. UVINZA and KALAMBO). The term 'Mwitu tradition' has been proposed recently for much of this widespread early Iron Age phenomenon. Before the end of the 1st millennium AD, however, as these agricultural and iron-using communities adjusted, stabilized and differentiated as regional Bantu-speaking groupings in their various local environments across sub-equatorial Africa, the ceramic continuity also broke up. Pottery groups of the later Iron Age and recent times vary from one region to another and generally contrast with those of the Early Iron Age.

M.D. Leakey et al.: *Dimple-based pottery from Central Kavirondo*, Coryndon Memorial Museum Occasional Papers 2 (Coryndon, 1948); R.C. Soper: 'Kwale', *Azania* 2 (1967), 1–17; ——: 'Early Iron Age sites in north-eastern Tanzania', *Azania* 2 (1967), 19–36; ——: 'Radiocarbon dating of "dimple-based ware" in western Kenya', *Azania* 4 (1969), 148–53; —— ed.: 'The Iron Age in eastern Africa', *Azania* 6 (1971) [whole volume]; D.W. Phillipson: *The later prehistory of Eastern and Southern Africa* (London, 1977).

JS

Early Khartoum *see* KHARTOUM MESOLITHIC

Early Transcaucasian culture *see* KURA-ARAXIAN

Easter Island Easternmost Polynesian island, first settled around 1400 BP from central eastern Polynesia. Easter Island presents one of the poorest terrestrial and marine floras and faunas in the Pacific. Its prehistory is divided into three phases: early (1400–1000 BP), Ahu Moai phase (1000–500 BP) and the Huri Ahu phase (500 BP to European contact in AD 1722). The famous statues, *AHU* and temple complexes were constructed in the middle phase and may have been destroyed in the wars of the last phase.

P. McCoy: 'Easter Island', *The prehistory of Polynesia*, ed. J. Jennings (Canberra, 1979), 135–66; P.V. Kirch: *The evolution of Polynesian chiefdoms* (Cambridge, 1984), 264–78.

CG

Eastern Anatolian Bronze Age *see* KURA-ARAXIAN

Eastern Chou (Tung-Chou; Dongzhou) Chinese cultural phase lasting from 771 to 255 BC, which was in many respects the most formative era in the history of China. It occupies the latter half of the Chou dynasty (1122–220 BC, *see* CHINA 2) which followed the shift of the ROYAL DOMAIN from its WESTERN CHOU location near Hsi-an to that of Lo-yang.

The period is divided into two main eras: the Chu'un-ch'iu period (770–481 BC) and the Chan-kuo period (480–255 BC). The former coincides with *Ch'un-ch'iu Tso-chuan* [The Tso commentary on the Ch'un-ch'iu], a literary source with detailed accounts of that era which, in the form we know now, has been transmitted from Han times. The latter period coincides with similarly transmitted literary sources such as the *Chan-kuo-ts'e* ['Intrigues' of the Warring States] and the *Kuo-yü* [Discourses of the States].

It was during the Eastern Chou period that sovereignty of the Chou kings gradually came to an end, while the major states were largely occupied with internecine warfare; one or another briefly gaining ascendency. Yet, at the same time, there was marked progress towards the foundation of the historico-literary culture together with the development of philosophical concepts that were to mould the future two millennia of 'imperial' China's culture. Much of this cultural development was proscribed during the CH'IN dynasty (Ch'in from 255 BC had rapidly conquered the remaining states and established in 221 BC the short-lived Empire under its name), but then restored under the Han dynasty (206 BC–AD 220).

Very valuable finds relating to the cultures of the various MIDDLE STATES and to such 'barbarian' states as CH'U, WU, YÜEH, PA, SHU and TIEN have shed considerable light upon the manner in which both technological and artistic influences from the Middle States were adapted and modified by the 'barbarian' states. These peripheral regions, however, also influenced certain technological and artistic developments in the Middle States (Barnard 1987). The discovery of iron casting and the development of malleable cast-iron technology emerged early in the Eastern Chou period.

M. Hsiao: 'Shih-lun Chiang-nan Wu-kuo ch'ing-t'ung-ch'i' [Thoughts on the bronzes of the State of Wu from Chiang-nan], *WW* 5 (1984), 11–15; Li Hsüeh-ch'in: *Eastern Zhou and Qin civilizations*, trans. Chang Kwang-chih (New Haven, 1985); Chang Kwang-chih: *The archaeology of ancient China*, 4th edn (New Haven, 1986), 394–9; N. Barnard: 'Bronze casting technology in the peripheral "barbarian" regions', *BMM* 12 (1987), 3–37; D.B. Wagner: 'Toward the reconstruction of ancient Chinese techniques for the production of malleable cast iron', *East Asian Institute Occasional Papers* 4 (1989), 1–72; ——: *Iron and steel in ancient China* (Leiden, 1993).

NB

East Turkana Area east of Lake Turkana (Rudolf) in northern Kenya, which has been celebrated since the 1960s for its volcanic-ash and lake beds containing Early Stone Age materials and Lower Pleistocene and Plio-Pleistocene fossils. With regard to the history of the discovery of early hominid remains, the finds made in this region – at Koobi Fora and other sites – by Richard Leakey and Glynn Isaac followed up those at OLDUVAI (Tanzania) and in the OMO valley (Ethiopia). Apart from the controversy over the classification and dating of the remarkable '1470' skull, generally held now to be a representative of *HOMO HABILIS* dated at about 1.75 million years old (see Reader 1988), this region has produced other *Homo habilis* and *HOMO ERECTUS* specimens (the latter from 1.5 million years), as well as both robust and gracile australopithecines (*see AUSTRALOPITHECUS*), some well over 2 million years old.

Y. Coppens et al., eds: *Earliest man and environments in the Lake Rudolf basin* (Chicago, 1976); G. Meave and R.E. Leakey, eds: *Koobi Fora Research Project* I: *The fossil hominids and an introduction to their context, 1968–74* (Oxford, 1978); J. Reader: *Missing links: the hunt for earliest man*, 2nd edn (London, 1988).

JS

East Wenatchee Single component câche site on the upper Columbia River in eastern Washington state, western North America, which contained the largest CLOVIS fluted points ever found, as well as 'preforms', and bevelled bone artefacts. TEPHROCHRONOLOGY was used to date the câche: grains of volcanic ash from the eruption of Glacier Peak in the nearby Cascade Mountains dated at 9300 BC adhering to the lower face of the points indicate a date of deposition shortly after this eruption.

P.J. Mehringer, Jr.: 'Clovis cache found – weapons of ancient Americans', *NGM* (1988), 500–3; —— and F.F. Foit, Jr.: 'Volcanic ash dating of the Clovis cache at East Wenatchee, Washington', *National Geographic Society Research* 6/4 (1990), 495–503.

RC

Eberdingen-Hochdorf *see* HOCHDORF

Ebla (Tell Mardikh) Town-site 55 km southwest of Aleppo in northern Syria, which flourished in the Early to Late Bronze Age. In its earliest phase Tell Mardikh was the site of a protohistoric village of the late 4th millennium BC, followed by an early proto-Syrian settlement containing substantial remains of KHIRBET KERAK ware. The Bronze Age city, with an estimated population of many thousands, was divided into four main quarters, as well as an acropolis including palaces and administrative structures.

Between 1974 and 1976 Italian archaeologists excavated an archive of about 6000 fragmentary clay tablets, incised with texts written in a cuneiform script similar to that used in the roughly contemporary Sumerian town of KISH, identifying Tell Mardikh as Ebla and casting light for the first time on the history of northern Syria during the late 3rd millennium BC (Pettinato 1981). The archive, written in both Sumerian and 'Eblaite', a previously unknown form of the Semitic family of languages (i.e. similar to Ugaritic and Hebrew), was found in the ruins of Palace G, dating to *c*.2400–2250 BC. Until the discovery of the archive very little was known about northern Syria before the 2nd millennium BC, and it had not been suspected that there were such powerful 3rd-millennium Syrian city-states interacting with the Early Dynastic cities of SUMER and northern Mesopotamia (e.g. LAGASH and MARI).

In the 23rd century BC the Bronze Age city was sacked by the early Akkadian ruler Naram-Sin, and by *c*.2000 BC it appears to have been completely destroyed. The city nevertheless continued to thrive in the Middle Bronze Age until it was sacked by the HITTITES in *c*.1600 BC, and there are numerous subsequent settlement strata, including traces of occupation as late as the 7th century AD.

C. Bermant and M. Weitzmann: *Ebla: an archaeological enigma* (London, 1979); P. Matthiae: *Ebla: an empire rediscovered*, trans. C. Holme (London, 1980); G. Pettinato: *The archives of Ebla: an empire inscribed on clay* (New York, 1981).

IS

eboulis (*éboulis*) Fragments of naturally fallen rock which often form the bulk of the archaeological deposit in caves and rock shelters. The rate and type of eboulis deposition, and its subsequent alteration by natural processes, are often used as indicators of climate in the archaeology of the Upper Palaeolithic in Europe.

F. Bordes: *A tale of two caves* (New York, 1972), 11, 28–36; H. Laville et al.: *Rock shelters of the Périgord* (London, 1980), 51–73.

RJA

Eburran *see* KENYA CAPSIAN

Ecbatana *see* MEDES

Eda *see* EXPLORATORY DATA ANALYSIS

Edfu (anc. Djeb, Apollonis Magna) Egyptian site consisting of a large stone temple complex, dating to the period between the reigns of Ptolemy III and XII (*c*.237–57 BC), and the adjacent ruins of a city inhabited from the early pharaonic period until the Christian (Byzantine) and Islamic periods. The earliest remains at Edfu have made it the type-site for the 'Edfuan', a group of non-microlithic Palaeolithic industries in Upper Egypt, which are roughly contemporary with the HALFAN industry (the latter being found further to the south, in the Wadi Halfa area of Nubia). The temple of Horus at Edfu is the best-preserved major Ptolemaic religious structure in Egypt. The study of the inscriptions has enabled Egyptologists to reconstruct many of the details of the daily rituals within the temple, including the feeding, bathing and clothing of the cult-image of the god in his sanctuary (Fairman 1954).

M. de Rochemonteix and E. Chassinat: *Le Temple d'Edfou* (Paris, 1892; Cairo, 1918–); K. Michalowski et al.: *Tell Edfou*, 4 vols (Cairo, 1937–50); H.W. Fairman: 'Worship and festivals in an Egyptian temple', *Bulletin of the John Rylands Library*, Manchester 37 (1954), 165–203; B.J. Kemp: 'The early development of towns in Egypt', *Antiquity* 51 (1977), 185–200; S. Cauville: *Edfou* (Cairo, 1984).

IS

Edfuan *see* EDFU

edge effects *see* NEAREST NEIGHBOUR ANALYSIS

EDXRF *see* X-RAY FLUORESCENCE SPECTROMETRY

Effigy Mound Culture Late WOODLAND peoples who lived in what is now Wisconsin (and parts of neighbouring states) in eastern North America from *c.*AD 600 to 1200. They built variously shaped mounds, and the name Effigy Mound Culture comes from the animal shapes of many mounds, although conical and linear mounds also occur. Burials and hearths are frequently found in these low, often large mounds. The mounds are usually clustered together in groups, typically in locally prominent places. They perhaps served as the focus of group activities for widely distributed, semi-sedentary populations.

W.M. Hurley: 'The Late Woodland stage: effigy mound culture', *The Wisconsin Archeologist* 67 (1986), 283–301; L.G. Goldstein: 'Landscapes and mortuary practices: a case for regional perspectives', *Regional approaches to mortuary analysis*, ed. L.A. Beck (New York, 1995), 101–21.

GM

Egypt (Arab Republic of Egypt; anc. Kemet, Aegyptus) The Egyptian section of the Nile Valley descends for 800 km from the Sudan border to Cairo, then continues for a further 240 km along each of the major Delta branches down to the Mediterranean coast. The modern country of Egypt, consisting of the Nile Valley, the Delta, the oases and the eastern and western deserts, is in an unusual geographical position at the junction of three continents. Its northern border faces towards Europe (across the Mediterranean), its southern and western borders are in Africa and its eastern border is separated from Western Asia only by the Sinai desert and the Red Sea.

1 *Prehistory*. Egypt's earliest inhabitants appeared during the Palaeolithic period in the grasslands of northeastern Africa (*c.*700,000 BC). With the onset of a drier climate (*c.*25,000 BC) the Eastern and Western Deserts began to form, evidently forcing the early Egyptians to move into the Nile Valley. There is evidence at some terminal Palaeolithic sites in Egypt (e.g. WADI KUBBANIYA and TUSHKA) for an unexpectedly early phase of experimentation with plant domestication. In the EPIPALAEOLITHIC period (*c.*10,000–7000 BC) several semi-nomadic, hunting and fishing cultures emerged in the Western Desert (*see* NABTA PLAYA) and the Nile valley (*see* ELKAB *and* FAIYUM REGION). By about 5300 BC, as the climate moistened, numerous

Palaeolithic	**700,000 – 5000 BC**
Lower Palaeolithic	700,000 – 100,000 BC
Middle Palaeolithic	100,000 – 30,000 BC
Upper Palaeolithic	30,000 – 10,000 BC
Epipalaeolithic (Elkabian, Faiyum B)	10,000 – 5500 BC
Predynastic	**5500 – 3000 BC**
Badarian (Faiyum A, Merimda)	5500 – 4000 BC
Amratian (Merimda, el-Omari A)	4000 – 3500 BC
Early Gerzean (el-Omari B)	3500 – 3200 BC
Late Gerzean (protodynastic, Ma^{c}adi)	3200 – 3000 BC
Dynastic period	**3000 – 332 BC**
Early Dynastic period (Dynasty 1–2)	3000 – 2649 BC
Old Kingdom (Dynasty 3–6)	2649 – 2150 BC
1st Intermediate period (Dynasty 7–11)	2150 – 2040 BC
Middle Kingdom (Dynasty 11–13)	2040 – 1640 BC
2nd Intermediate period (Dynasty 14–17)	1640 – 1550 BC
New Kingdom (Dynasty 18–20)	1550 – 1070 BC
3rd Intermediate period (Dynasty 21–25)	1070 – 712 BC
Late period (Dynasty 25–30)	712 – 332 BC
Greco-Roman period	**332 BC – AD 395**
Macedonian period	332 – 304 BC
Ptolemaic period	304 – 30 BC
Roman period	30 BC – AD 395
Christian period ('Coptic')	**AD 395 – 641**
Islamic period	**AD 641 –**

Table 12 **Egypt** Chronology of Egypt.

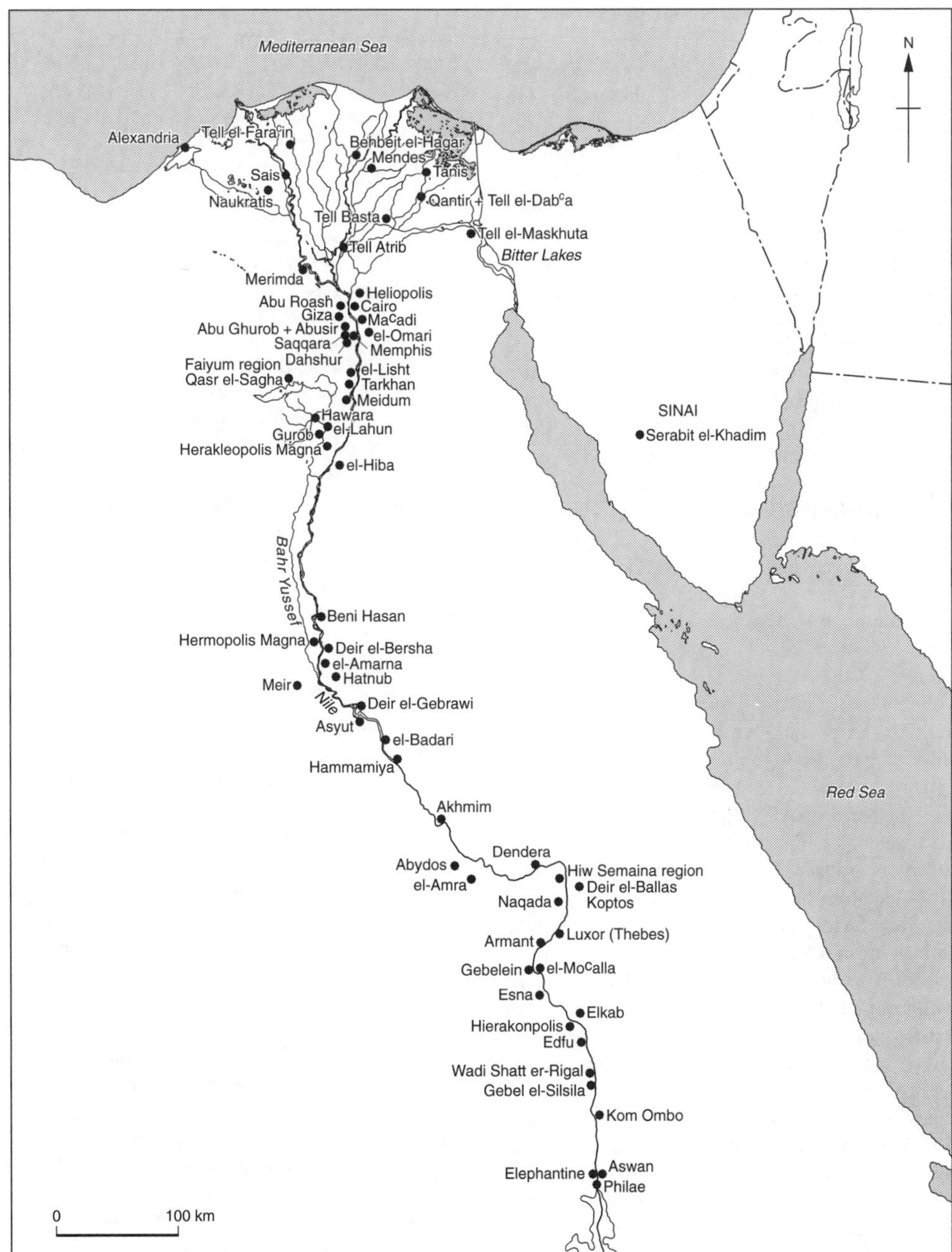

Map 22 **Egypt** Major sites in the region mentioned in the main text or with individual entries in the Dictionary.

Neolithic communities had begun to settle along the course of the Nile.

The late Neolithic period in Egypt, generally described as the 'predynastic', began in the late 6th millennium BC. A relative chronology for the Upper Egyptian predynastic period (i.e. the AMRATIAN and GERZEAN periods), was first created by Flinders Petrie in the early 1900s (*see* SERIATION). When Caton-Thompson and Brunton excavated in the el-Badari region (1924–6), they found stratigraphic confirmation of Petrie's dating system (at Hammamia) and considerable evidence of the earliest Upper Egyptian phase, the Badarian period (see el-BADARI; *c*.5500-4000 BC). Petrie's sequence dates 1 to 30 – which he had been careful to leave unallocated – were duly assigned to the various phases of the Badarian. Although radiocarbon and thermoluminescence dates from el-Badari suggest that the period stretched back at least as early as 5500 BC, Brunton's pre-Badarian – or 'Tasian' – phase has been discredited since the 1960s (Hoffman 1979: 142). It has proved somewhat difficult to make direct comparisons between the culture of northern and southern regions of Egypt, since the sites in Upper (southern) Egypt are mainly cemeteries while those in Lower Egypt are mainly settlement remains. Excavations from the 1970s onwards, however, have begun to obtain more information on Upper Egyptian settlements and Delta cemeteries (see van den Brink 1992).

Cemeteries dating to the Amratian phase (also known as Naqada I; *c*.4000–3500 BC) have been excavated at several sites in Upper Egypt, stretching from Deir Tasa in the north to the Lower Nubian site of Khor Bahan. A rectangular Amratian house has been excavated at Hierakonpolis (Hoffman 1980) and small areas of late Gerzean settlement were excavated at ABYDOS (Peet 1914: 2) and el-Badari (Baumgartel 1970: 484). The earliest Neolithic remains in Lower Egypt are the Faiyum A encampments excavated by Caton-Thompson (1926). The Faiyum A culture was followed by that of MERIMDA BENI SALAMA, the latest phase of which was roughly synchronous with the settlements and cemeteries of EL-OMARI, south of Cairo. The next phase in the Lower Egyptian predynastic is attested at MA'ADI, a settlement and cemetery dating from the early to mid-4th millennium BC. Excavations during the 1980s at Minshat Abu Omar and TELL EL-FARA'IN have begun to provide crucial new evidence for the transition to the Early Dynastic period.

T.E. Peet: 'The year's work at Abydos', *JEA* 1 (1914), 37–39; G. Caton-Thompson: 'The Neolithic industry of the Northern Faiyum Desert', *JRAI* 56 (1926), 309–23; E.J. Baumgartel: *The cultures of prehistoric Egypt*, 2 vols (Oxford, 1955–60); W.B. Emery: *Archaic Egypt* (Harmondsworth, 1961), 30–1; E.J. Baumgartel: *Petrie's Naqada excavation: a supplement* (London, 1970); A.J. Arkell: *The prehistory of the Nile valley* (Leiden, 1975); M.A. Hoffman: *Egypt before the pharaohs* (New York, 1979); ——: 'A rectangular Amratian house from Hierakonpolis', *JNES* 39 (1980), 119–37; B.G. Trigger: 'The rise of Egyptian civilization', *Ancient Egypt: a social history*, ed. B.G. Trigger et al. Cambridge, 1983), 1–70; E.C.M. Van den Brink, ed.: *The Nile Delta in transition: 4th–3rd millennium BC* (Tel Aviv, 1992); B. Midant-Reynes: *Préhistoire de l'Egypte: des premiers hommes aux premiers pharaons* (Paris, 1992); A.J. Spencer: *Early Egypt* (London, 1993); K. Bard: 'The Egyptian predynastic: a review of the evidence', *JFA* 21 (1994), 265–88.

2 *Pharaonic period.* The historical period in Egypt began with the unification of the country into a single state in *c*.3000 BC, which appears to have coincided with the appearance of many of the accepted components of the state: urbanization, literacy and bureaucracy. Whereas the chronology of the prehistoric and predynastic periods is based primarily on stratigraphy, seriation and radiometric methods of dating, the historical period (usually divided into thirty 'dynasties' in accordance with the History compiled by the Egyptian historian Manetho in the 3rd century BC) relies primarily on an elaborate framework of textual evidence.

During the Early Dynastic period (*c*.3000–2649 BC) the fundamental elements of pharaonic civilization took shape, from the development of the elaborate funerary architecture of the elite to the codification of temple rituals and the evolution of complex systems of taxation and government. The Old Kingdom (*c*.2649–2150 BC) was characterized archaeologically by the appearance of stone architecture, particularly in the form of royal PYRAMID complexes such as the Step Pyramid of Djoser (*c*.2620 BC) at SAQQARA and the Great Pyramid of Khufu (*c*.2540 BC) at GIZA. Only a few traces of Old Kingdom settlements have survived, therefore the evidence for daily life and socio-political change derives primarily from religious and funerary contexts. A general decline in royal architecture is observable by the 6th dynasty (*c*.2323–2150 BC). The proliferation of funerary monuments among the provincial elite of the 6th–8th dynasties has been interpreted as evidence of a gradual decentralization of power, leading to the social instability of the 1st Intermediate Period (*c*.2150–2040 BC).

At the height of the Middle Kingdom (*c*.2040–1640 BC) the pharaohs of the 12th dynasty (mostly called Amenemhat or Senusret) re-established the traditional political hierarchy and built royal pyramid complexes at DAHSHUR, EL-LAHUN and EL-LISHT. The southward extension of the political border into Lower Nubia is indicated by the archaeological remains of large mud-brick fortresses (such as BUHEN, MIRGISSA and SEMNA) stretching down to the 3rd Nile cataract (Kemp 1989: 166–80). Both the material remains and the historical records show that numerous commercial and political links with the Near East and the Aegean were being established. The Delta region was gradually infiltrated by Asiatic peoples, leading eventually to the establishment of a series of foreign ('HYKSOS') dynasties in Lower Egypt during the 2nd Intermediate Period (*c*.1640–1550 BC).

The New Kingdom (*c*.1550–1070 BC) began with the expulsion of the Hyksos, as the rulers of the Theban region once more extended their rule across the whole country. The pharaohs of the 18th–20th dynasties included Thutmose III and Ramesses II, whose policies of expansion in Nubia and the Levant brought them into direct conflict with the empires of the MITANNI and the HITTITES. The New Kingdom ended in economic and political decline, as Egypt temporarily disintegrated into a number of principalities vying for the kingship of the country as a whole. During the 3rd Intermediate Period (*c*.1070–712 BC) and the Late Period (*c*.712–332 BC) the reigns of native pharaohs were interspersed with dynasties of Libyan and Nubian rulers, and Egypt was conquered first by the Assyrians and then by the Persians. Opinions differ as to whether acculturation took place during the two periods of Persian domination (525–404 BC and 343–332 BC), but it seems clear that Egypt had effectively become a 'satrapy', politically and economically absorbed into the Persian empire (for discussion of Egypt as part of the Achaemenid empire see Sancisi-Weerdenburg and Kuhrt 1991).

In 332 BC the Egyptians were ostensibly 'liberated' by Alexander the Great, and subsequently ruled by his two Macedonian successors (323–304 BC). During the ensuing Ptolemaic period (304–30 BC) the archeological and historical evidence seem increasingly to indicate fundamental socio-economic continuity with the dynastic period, although – as with the Persian periods – the Ptolemaic administrative and economic structure has not yet been properly researched. Nevertheless, the Ptolemaic rulers clearly continued to construct temples dedicated to Egyptian deities (*see* EDFU, DENDERA *and* PHILAE). Even after the country's absorption into the Roman empire (30 BC–AD 395), the material culture of Egypt appears to have retained much of its native character, in terms of social and religious customs as well as artistic and architectural conventions.

See also COPTIC *and* ISLAMIC ARCHAEOLOGY.

J. Baines and J. Malek: *Atlas of ancient Egypt* (Oxford, 1980); B.G. Trigger et al.: *Ancient Egypt: a social history* (Cambridge, 1983); A.K. Bowman: *Egypt after the pharaohs* (London, 1986); B.J. Kemp *Ancient Egypt: anatomy of a civilization* (London, 1989); H. Sancisi-Weerdenburg and A. Kuhrt: *Achaemenid History* IV: *Asia Minor and Egypt: old cultures in a new empire* (Leiden, 1991); J. Malek, ed.: *Cradles of civilization: Egypt* (Sydney, 1992).

IS

Ekron *see* PHILISTINES

el- The prefix el- is disregarded in the alphabetical sequence of this dictionary. For example, el-BADARI.

Elam, Elamite Earliest known kingdom in the region of modern Khuzistan, southwestern Iran. The 'proto-Elamite' phase is known from the excavations of strata of the late 4th millennium BC at such sites as SUSA, SHAHR-I SOKHTA and Tepe Yahya, although it has been suggested that the Elamites began to arrive in Iran during the 5th millennium BC. Elam is the Biblical version of *Hamalti* ('land of god'), the name given to their homeland by the early Bronze Age inhabitants of the alluvial southwestern Iranian plateau. The Elamite language, recorded both in the proto-Elamite script and Babylonian CUNEIFORM, was probably originally related to the Dravidian languages of the southern Indian subcontinent. Although the proto-Elamite script was gradually replaced by cuneiform, the language continued to be used in the Achaemenid period (*c*.538–331 BC), when many royal inscriptions were trilingual (Old Persian, Babylonian and Elamite), and it effectively survived into medieval times in the form of the Khozi language.

The kingdom of Elam essentially emerged out of the fusion of the neighbouring polities of Susa and Anshan, and the cultural development of Elam during the 3rd millennium BC is largely known from the excavations at these two sites. Positioned astride the main land-routes between the INDUS CIVILIZATION, the Gulf and Mesopotamia, the Elamites were able to profit from the trade in such commodities as silver, tin and diorite. They also periodically invaded Mesopotamia, contributing to the fall of certain dynasties (including UR III) and posing a constant threat to the stability of the region. At Haft Tepe, about 15 km south of Susa, are the remains of another important city, Kabnak, which was built by the Elamite ruler Tepti-Ahar in the mid-14th century BC. Although the size of the whole city, including several ziggurats, palaces and vaulted royal burials, has been estimated at some 30 ha, only a small part of the site has so far been excavated (Negahban 1969).

In the reign of Untash-Napirisha (*c.*1260–1235 BC) a new capital city, Dur-Untash-Napirisha, was constructed at Choga Zanbil, about 40 km to the southeast of Susa; the population was supplied with water from the River Kharkheh via a canal 50 km in length. The site included a distinctively Elamite style of ZIGGURAT, the first three stages of which have survived into modern times, and it has been suggested that this palace/temple complex, like the ziggurat and palace at the Kassite city of DUR-KURIGALZU, may have formed a large royal funerary temple. At the eastern side of the city the remains of the so-called Funeral Palace have been excavated – this building contained five subterranean tombs in which the cremated remains of certain members of the Elamite royal family may have been buried, as at Kabnak and Susa. The town went into a comparative decline after Untash-Napirisha's death and it was eventually sacked by the ASSYRIANS in the mid-7th century BC. By the late 6th century BC both Elam and Mesopotamia had been absorbed into the Achaemenid empire (*see* PERSIA).

R. de Mecquenem and J. Michalon: *Recherches à Tchoga Zanbil* (Paris, 1953); P. Amiet: *Elam* (Auvers-sur-Oise, 1966); R. Ghirshman: *Tchoga Zanbil* I–II (Paris, 1966–8); E.O. Negahban: 'Haft Tepe', *Iran* 7 (1969), 173–7; P. Meriggi: *La scrittura proto-elamica* (Rome, 1971); C.C. Lamberg-Karlovsky: 'The proto-Elamites on the Iranian plateau', *Antiquity* 52 (1978), 114–20; E. Carter and M.W. Stolper: *Elam: surveys of political history and archaeology* (Berkeley, 1984); F. Hole, ed.: *The archaeology of western Iran* (Washington D.C. and London, 1987).

IS

Elands Bay Cave Coastal cave located 200 km north of Cape Town, in a headland immediately south of the outlet of Verloren Vlei (a coastal lake occupying the last 14 km of the seasonal river of the same name). The history of occupation at Elands Bay Cave and a dozen Holocene sites in the vicinity comprises a series of 'pulses' of occupation spanning an estimated 100,000 years, from the Middle to Late Stone Age. These pulses are shown, in a major research programme, to be intimately tied to changing patterns of resource availability, with the encroachment of the shoreline following the low sea level of the Last Glacial Maximum low and the climatic changes extending through the Holocene. At times the coastal niche was virtually abandoned, probably in favour of the mountains 50 km to the east.

J. Parkington and M. Hall: *Papers in the prehistory of the western Cape, South Africa* (Oxford, 1987); J. Parkington et al.: 'Holocene coastal settlement patterns in the western Cape', *The archaeology of prehistoric coastlines*, ed. G. Bailey and J. Parkington (Cambridge, 1988), 22–41.

RI

Elandsfontein Farm close to Hopefield, 100 km north of Cape Town, South Africa, where wind erosion of the thick sand deposits of the countryside has exposed a rich fossil horizon in bays between dunes, over an area of some 5 sq. km. Associated with the fossils are numerous ACHEULEAN artefacts, and a fossil human skull-cap and fragmentary mandible. On faunal grounds the artefacts and human remains (archaic *HOMO SAPIENS*) are assigned to some part of the Middle Pleistocene.

R. Singer and J. Wymer: 'Archaeological investigations at the Saldahna skull site in South Africa', *SAAB* 25 (1968), 63–74.

RI

El Castillo Cave site in the Santander region of north Spain with an important Palaeolithic culture sequence and a rich inventory of cave art. The site was excavated before the First World War, but was not fully published until 1984 (Cabrera). Excavations at the cave entrance revealed one of the most complete culture-stratigraphic sequences in Cantabria, including one or more horizons of Acheulean, Mousterian, Aurignacian, Gravettian, Solutrean, Magdalenian, Azilian, Bronze Age and Medieval. The cave art at the site, in both red and black pigments, includes over 150 images of bison, horse, ibex, deer etc. There is an unusually large concentration of stencilled hands (in red), sometimes clustered together, and dots and signs. There are also some polychrome paintings of bison that are often compared to those at ALTAMIRA, and which recent radiocarbon dating suggests may date to about 11,000 BC.

H. Alcalde del Rio, H. Breuil and L. Sierra: *Les cavernes de la région cantabrique* (Monaco, 1911); V. Cabrera: *El Yacimiento de la Cueva de 'El Castillo'* (Madrid, 1984).

RJA

electron probe microanalysis (EPMA) Quantitative surface analysis technique combining some of the principles of X-RAY FLUORESCENCE SPECTROMETRY (XRF) with those of the scanning electron microscope (SEM). The technique uses a focused electron beam, comparable to that employed in SEM, to analyse small areas or spots, about 0.1 to 1 μm across, on the surface of a specimen. The electrons excite X-ray emission in the material by a process analogous to XRF and with similar restrictions on the depth of analysis. The X-rays are detected and quantified by energy dispersive or wavelength dispersive XRF procedures. Although the measurement itself is non-destructive, the material being analysed must be polished flat and must be small enough to fit inside the evacuated chamber below the electron column. Hence, it is usual to work with small, sectioned, polished and mounted samples – although small artefacts such as coins have been analysed in situ on a prepared edge. Locating the spot to be analysed is achieved using an integral optical microscope, or by an SEM type image, and precision adjustments of the stage supporting the specimen.

Since the material is analysed in a vacuum (a requirement of the electron beam) the X-rays of the light elements (e.g. below silicon) are readily quantifiable in addition to heavier elements. The technique is therefore suitable for the examination of silicate-based materials, and in this context has been applied to glass and slags, but is also applicable to metals. Examples include work on copper-based alloys, coins and slag inclusions in iron artefacts. Since the analysis of very small areas is involved, EPMA excels in the study of specific phases or inclusions in materials. For bulk or large area analysis it is necessary to analyse a number of points on the specimen, a process which can usually be automated, and combine or average the results. The technique is primarily for major and minor element analysis although with WDXRF detection some trace analysis is possible (*see* X-RAY FLUORESCENCE SPECTROMETRY). Hence applications are usually directed at identification and technical studies rather than, for example, provenance.

P.J. Potts: *A handbook of silicate rock analysis* (Glasgow, 1992).

MC

electron spin resonance (ESR) dating

Scientific dating technique the basic principles of which are the same as for THERMOLUMINESCENCE (TL) dating, where the age is the ratio of the total radiation dose received and the effective radiation dose-rate: similar methodology is used to determine these factors as in TL dating. In ESR, however, the trapped electrons are detected by their paramagnetic (i.e. normally magnetic, as opposed to diamagnetic) properties. In a strong and slowly varying magnetic field, microwaves of a given frequency passing through the sample will be absorbed. Maximum, or resonance, absorption for a given microwave frequency occurs at a field strength characteristic of the particular paramagnetic centre.

ESR signals are referred to by their 'g-values': the g-value is proportional to the ratio of microwave frequency to magnetic field strength and is always near to 2, the free electron value. The strength of the signal reflects the trapped electron population and therefore age.

In principle, the same range of materials is datable as for TL, provided they produce an appropriate radiation-induced ESR signal. ESR can also be used for other materials that cannot be heated e.g. aragonite, which dissociates on heating, and materials with an organic component which will burn on heating, such as bone and tooth. In practice, bone cannot, in fact, be dated because its degree of crystallinity changes with time, and the technique has largely been used for dating calcite and tooth enamel from Palaeolithic sites (for both, the ESR age evaluated is the time since crystal formation when the initial ESR signal was negligible). Application to burnt flint and other stone is still under development.

Evaluation of the radiation dose-rate in tooth enamel is complex. Although a thin layer (about 100 μm) can be removed to simplify the alpha dosimetry, the enamel is not sufficiently thick to allow removal of all of the layer (about 2 mm) affected by beta radiation from the soil. This complicates the dosimetry calculation but also requires that the sediment *directly* in contact with the tooth must be collected. Furthermore, any adhering dentine or cement must be considered, particularly as this has typically up to 100 times more uranium than the enamel itself. Uranium is also the dominant contribution from the enamel, and, as in the other tooth components, this is acquired during burial, thus disequilibrium must be considered and a model for uranium uptake with time must be assumed (*early uptake* or *linear uptake*; *see also* URANIUM SERIES DATING): this affects the accuracy of the date (i.e. the degree to which the ESR date is biased). The dosimetry is simplest for big teeth (e.g. of a mammoth); because the uranium concentration profile across the enamel is U-shaped, use of only the inner portion would remove not only the external beta contribution but also most of the internal uranium thereby minimizing the dependence on the uptake model. When such large teeth are not available, bovid and horse teeth are suitable, but those with thin enamel layers, such as deer, are avoided. Dependence of the ESR age on the uptake model is also a function of relative levels of internal dose-rate to gamma dose-rate from the sediment.

In ESR dating of calcitic cave deposits, the radiation dose (as in TL dating) is dominated by the gamma dose from the cave environment which can be very non-uniform. Travertine from open-air sites has also been dated by ESR; its organic content generally makes it unsuitable for TL dating.

Typical precision of the technique is ± 10% of the age, based on dating several samples from the same context. Its upper age range is similar to that of TL dating, being influenced by similar factors i.e. signal saturation, signal stability and radiation dose-rate. The technique has recently been applied to the Palaeolithic cave site of Pech de L'Azé (see Grün et al. 1991).

R. Grün: 'Electron spin resonance (ESR) dating', *Quaternary International* 1 (1989), 65–109; —— and C.B. Stringer: 'Electron spin resonance dating and the evolution of modern humans', *Archaeometry* 33 (1991), 153–99; R. Grün et al.: 'ESR chronology of a 100,000-year archaeological sequence at Pech de L'Azé II, France', *Antiquity* 65 (1991), 544–51.

SB

Elephantine *see* ASWAN

Elkab (anc. Nekheb) Site in Egypt on the east bank of the Nile, about 80 km south of Luxor, consisting of prehistoric and pharaonic settlements, early 18th-dynasty rock-tombs, remains of temples dating from the Early Dynastic period to the Ptolemaic period, as well as part of the walls of a monastery. The rock-tombs include that of Ahmose son of Ibana, an admiral in the Theban war against the HYKSOS rulers, *c*.1550 BC. A number of well-stratified EPIPALAEOLITHIC campsites, radiocarbon-dated to *c*.6400–5980 BC, were discovered in 1967; these are the type-sites of the Elkabian microlithic industry.

J.E. Quibell: *El-Kab* (London, 1898); P. Vermeersch: 'Les Fouilles d'Elkab', *ZDMG* 17 (1969), 32–8; ——: 'L'Elkabien. Une nouvelle industrie epipaléolithique à Elkab en Haute Egypte: sa stratigraphie, sa typologie', *CdE* 45 (1970), 45–68; P. Derchain and P. Vermeersch: *Elkab*, 2 vols (Brussels and Louvain, 1971–8).

IS

Elkabian *see* ELKAB; EPIPALAEOLITHIC

Ellora *see* CAVE TEMPLE

Elmenteitan One of the best defined 'advanced' Late Stone Age (or 'Neolithic') cultures of the East African highlands and Rift Valley. The Elmenteitan dates to the 1st millennium BC, probably extending into the 1st millennium AD and continuing alongside the earliest iron-using communities in the broader region. It is defined by its pottery types, long two-edged blades and other tools made from local obsidian, which distinguish it from other cultures of this region and period. Certain features may derive from the older 'KENYA CAPSIAN'. As a specialization, the Elmenteitan is fairly restricted to the elevated central part of the Rift and the plateau grasslands to the west, and is associated with the herding of cattle and goats (and/or sheep). Attempts have been made to reconstruct the Elmenteitan economy and ecology through ethnoarchaeological studies of Maasai now inhabiting the same region (Robertshaw 1990: esp. chapters 3 and 13) and by reference to the pre-Maasai Sirikwa people of the late Iron Age (*see* SIRIKWA HOLES). *See also* GAMBLE'S CAVE *and* NGAMURIAK.

P.T. Robertshaw: 'The Elmenteitan: an early food-producing culture in East Africa', *WA* 20 (1988), 57–69; —— ed.: *Early pastoralists of south-western Kenya* (Nairobi 1990).

JS

El Mirador LOWLAND MAYA city of the Late Preclassic period (*c*.300 BC–AD 300), located in northern Petén, Guatemala, with perhaps the most monumental public architecture in the Maya area. The site covers approximately 16 sq. km and the mapped structures, numbering about 200, include three enormous building complexes, an acropolis, causeways, reservoirs and a wall enclosing the sacred precinct. Very little of the site was occupied during the Classic period (*c*.AD 300–900).

R.T. Matheny: 'Investigations at El Mirador, Petén, Guatemala', *National Geographic Research* 2 (1986) 332–53.

PRI

El Paraíso The largest of the terminal Preceramic sites of Peru, located on the central Peruvian coast and dating to *c*.1600 BC. The 11 architectural units, huge complexes of rooms and platforms used as residences, workshops and perhaps for ceremonial purposes, cover over 58 ha along the Chillón River. The giant platforms were constructed of bags of stones filling rooms; their uniform nature may indicate that some sort of labour tax was already in existence.

J. Quilter et al.: 'Subsistence economy of el Paraíso: an early Peruvian site', *Science* 251 (January 1991), 277–88.

KB

Elsloo Settlement and cemetery of the LINEARBANDKERAMIK culture, located in the Dutch province of Limburg. Successive hamlets of about 5–15 longhouses (up to 37 m long) were erected; the remains of about 95 houses have been excavated. The houses were built of substantial posts supporting wooden and wattle-and-daub walls. Over 70 inhumations and around 40 cremations were excavated from the cemetery, the inhumations attracting the most grave goods (pottery, adzes, flints etc.).

P.J.R. Modderman: *Linearbandkeramik aus Elsloo and Stein*, 3 vols (Leiden, 1970); ——: 'Elsloo, a Neolithic farming community in the Netherlands', *Recent archaeological excavations in Europe*, ed. R. Bruce-Mitford (London, 1975), 260–87.

RJA

emblem glyph A Mesoamerican glyph (see HIEROGLYPHS, MESOAMERICAN) that serves as a name or 'emblem' of a particular LOWLAND MAYA site, its ruling dynasty, or the territorial polity controlled by the site or dynasty. First identified by Heinrich Berlin in 1958, emblem glyphs began to be used by the Maya in the Early Classic period (c.AD 200–500).

H. Berlin: 'El glifo "emblema" en las inscripciones mayas', *JSA* n.s. 47 (1958) 111–19; J. Marcus: *Emblem and State in the Classic Maya Lowlands* (Washington D.C., 1976).

PRI

Emerald Mound Site of the Plaquemine culture of the MISSISSIPPIAN tradition on the lower Mississippi River. The site dates to AD 1250–1600 and was occupied by Indians ancestral to the Natchez. The second largest ceremonial mound in the United States, it is a natural hill that has been modified into a flat-top mound that covers 8 acres and is 35 feet tall. A 30-ft and a 10-ft mound stand atop the large mound, perhaps supporting temples or the residence of chiefs. Descriptions of Natchez culture and social organization described by French traders in the early 18th century have been used as models of Mississippian society. Natchez society was a chiefdom that had two basic classes: commoners and nobles. Nobles were further divided into 'suns', 'nobles', and 'honoureds', with the person who occupied the position of Great Sun being the highest ranking individual.

J. Cotter: 'Stratigraphy and area tests at the Emerald and Anna mound sites', *AA* 17 (1951), 18–32; C. Hudson: *The Southeastern Indians* (Knoxville, 1976); I. Brown: 'Plaquemine architectural patterns in the Natchez Bluffs and surrounding regions of the lower Mississippi valley', *MJA* 10/2 (1985), 251–305.

WB

empiricism Approach to science and the social sciences which maintains that useful knowledge can only be obtained by observing scientific and social phenomena as manifested empirically (i.e. in the external or 'real' world), rather than by abstract or conceptual formulations. Explanations based on intuition, faith or complex concepts not securely linked to real-world phenomena, are rejected or classified as inferior.

Empiricism as a means of discovering truths about the world was born out of the mode of scientific enquiry, based on physical observation and experimentation, developed from the 17th century onwards in the natural sciences. In the philosophy of science, empiricism informs the POSITIVIST approach. It reached its most extreme form in the LOGICAL POSITIVIST (or logical empiricist) movement that centred on the University of Vienna in the 1920s and 1930s. This movement, which included mathematicians, philosophers and social scientists, denied the usefulness of any statement that could not be *proved* empirically – a stance sometimes labelled as 'verificationism' (*see also* VERIFICATION *and* FALSIFICATION).

In archaeology, the term 'empirical research' is sometimes used to describe research that centres on the collection of 'hard' archaeological data or (more loosely) that emphasizes the primacy of such data. As an extension, empirical generalisations include fields such as taxonomy and classificatory schemes. The term 'empiricist', on the other hand, usually implies a value judgement. Thus Shanks and Tilley (1987: 10–11) argue that, in empiricism, 'theoretical reflection is always systematically discouraged in favour of the primacy of facts or methodologies geared to producing such facts'. Empirical approaches and empiricism therefore form the backdrop to much of the argument in archaeological theory concerning the usefulness and likelihood of gaining 'objective' truth about the past from archaeological evidence (*see also* THEORY AND THEORY BUILDING).

P.J. Watson, S.A. LeBlanc and C.L. Redman: *Explanation in archaeology: an explicitly scientific approach* (New York and London, 1971); M. Shanks and C. Tilley: *Archaeology and social theory* (Cambridge, 1987).

RJA

energy dispersive X-ray fluorescence *see* X-RAY FLUORESCENCE SPECTROMETRY

Engaruka Site located at the foot of the Rift Valley escarpment in northern Tanzania, which is renowned in African archaeology as one of the very few instances of sub-Saharan Iron Age fields that can be discerned in the landscape. Along with the terraced hillsides of Nyanga in Zimbabwe, it contributes to the reconstruction of African agricultural and settlement history. Together with associated nucleated villages, the Engaruka field system belongs to the later Iron Age, about three to six centuries ago. When the Engaruka 'ruin field' came to notice early in the century it was hailed as 'a lost metropolis'; and Louis Leakey's brief investigation in 1935, while noting its likely agricultural significance, did not dispel the romantic notion of a 'city' with a population numbering '30–40 thousand at least' (Leakey 1936). Later excavations by Hamo Sassoon in the 1960s and Peter Robertshaw in 1982 in the villages, together with John Sutton's study of the fields and recognition of the complex irrigation system (Sutton 1978; 1986), show that at its height Engaruka's population would have reached 5–10,000 people intensively cultivating a minimum of 2000 ha.

L.S.B. Leakey: 'Preliminary report on examination of the Engaruka ruins', *Tanganyika Notes and Records* 1 (1936), 57–60; H. Sassoon: 'New views on Engaruka', *JAH* 8 (1967), 201–17; J.E.G. Sutton: 'Engaruka and its waters', *Azania* 13 (1978), 37–70; P.T. Robertshaw: 'Engaruka revisited', *Azania* 21 (1986), 1–26; J.E.G. Sutton: 'The irrigation and manuring of the Engaruka field system', *Azania* 21 (1986), 27–51; —— ed.: 'History of African agricultural technology and field systems', *Azania* 24 (1989) [whole volume]; ——: *A thousand years of East Africa* (Nairobi, 1990), 32–41.

JS

Engedi (Ayn Gedi) Settlement site in Israel, located in the Judaean Desert near the west bank of the Dead Sea. It was occupied from the CHALCOLITHIC to the Byzantine period, reaching its greatest prosperity in the 3rd century BC (stratum III), when a Hellenistic fortress was constructed at the summit of the tell. The main part of the site (Tell el-Jurn) was excavated by B. Mazar and I. Dunayevski between 1949 and 1964. In 1962, excavations to the west of the town revealed a late Chalcolithic sacred enclosure entered by two gateways and incorporating a 20 m long sanctuary which may have been the principal religious centre for the Judaean district, and it has been suggested that the enormous hoard of copper objects at NAHAL MISHMAR may have derived from the Engedi sanctuary. The pottery from the area of the shrine was roughly contemporary with that of TELEILAT EL-GHASSUL (*c*.3300–3200 BC).

B. Mazar: 'Excavations at the oasis of Engedi', *Archaeology* 16 (1963), 99–107; D. Ussishkin: 'The "Ghassulian temple" in Ein Gedi and the origin of the hoard from Nahal Mishmar', *BA* 34 (1971), 23–39; A. Kempinski: 'The Sin temple at Khafajeh and the En-Gedi temple', *IEJ* 22 (1972), 10–15.

IS

Entremont Iron Age oppida strategically situated in Provence, France, on both the inland route to the Alpine passes and the route between Italy and Spain. Taken by the Romans in 123 BC, it was the capital of the Ligurian Celtic tribe the Saluvii. The hillfort is a triangular hilltop enclosure, with ramparts and drystone walls and towers, containing small blocks of single-room houses, evidence of food-processing including an olive press, and slag heaps of iron and copper ore. Near the centre of the settlement was a sanctuary, within which were fragmentary skulls and evidence that skulls – probably war trophies, perhaps of Roman soldiers – had been nailed to posts. Entremont is the richest find-site of Celtic stone statuary, an art-form adopted by the Celts under the influence of the Mediterranean civilizations. Examples occur at other south Gaul centres, especially Roquepertuse; in southern France, such statuary was produced from about 250–100 BC. At Entremont the largest group of sculptures is of seated 'gods' or warriors, though there are standing figures and a smaller equestrian statue. In the seated figures, the legs are crossed beneath the body, and a hand may touch a carving of a decapitated head with half-closed eyes, while the other hand originally held some iron symbol, perhaps a thunderbolt. The sculptural style is relatively naturalistic, with some stylization of the face. There are also carved architectural elements, notably a pillar depicting a pile of skulls.

F. Benoît: *Entremont capitale celto-ligure des Salyens de Provence* (Aix-en-Provence, 1957); ——: 'The Celtic oppidum of Entremont, Provence', *Recent archaeological excavations in Europe*, ed. R. Bruce-Mitford (London, 1975), 227–60.

RJA

Eoanthropus *see* PILTDOWN MAN HOAX

eolith Naturally formed pieces of stone found in deposits in Europe ranging in date from the early Pleistocene back to the Miocene. When they were first identified by archaeologists in the 1860s, they were thought to be very crude pre-Palaeolithic tools (e.g. de Mortillet 1897). By the early 20th century, however, many experiments concerning the appearance of natural and human types of flaking (e.g. Warren 1905) were beginning to demonstrate that eoliths were not artefacts.

G. de Mortillet: *Formation de la nation française* (Paris, 1897); S.H. Warren: 'On the origin of eolithic flints by

natural causes, especially by the foundering of drifts', *Journal of the Royal Anthropological Institute* 35 (1905), 337–64; A.S. Barnes: 'The differences between natural and human flaking on prehistoric flint implements', *American Anthropologist* 41 (1939), 99–112; D.K. Grayson: 'Eoliths, archaeological ambiguity, and the generation of "middle-range" research', *American archaeology, past and future*, ed. D.J. Meltzer et al. (Washington D.C., 1986), 77–133.
IS

epigraphy Practice of recording and copying ancient texts and pictures, which is employed at archaeological sites throughout the world but most frequently in Egypt, the Near East, Greece, Rome, China and Mesoamerica. The earliest known epigraphers were the Chinese scholars of the Song dynasty (AD 960–1279) who produced drawings and transcriptions of inscribed bronze and jade objects dating from the SHANG dynasty (*c*.1500–1027 BC). In the 15th century AD Cyriacus of Ancona, an Italian merchant and perhaps the first European archaeologist worthy of the name, established the western tradition of epigraphy with his copies of monuments in Greece. The earliest systematic epigraphic expedition was the team of savants sent to Egypt by Napoleon to compile detailed hand-copies of the major decorated monuments of the pharaonic period (published in 1809–22 as the *Description de l'Egypte*).

One of the most common 19th-century epigraphic practices was the taking of 'squeezes', obtained by pressing wet paper against the decorated surface, but this technique is now rarely used since it can sometimes damage the surface of the monument. Modern epigraphers use a combination of simple tracing (on polythene or acetate film) and photogrammetry to obtain accurate and comprehensive copies, whether of petroglyphs, tomb-paintings or temple reliefs.

R. Weiss: *The Renaissance discovery of classical antiquity* (Oxford, 1969); R. Caminos and H.G. Fischer: *Ancient Egyptian epigraphy and palaeography* (New York, 1976); B.K. Swartz: 'Recording standards for petroglyphs and pictographs', *JFA* 8 (1981), 118–9; C. Ogleby and L.J. Rivett: *Handbook of heritage photogrammetry* (Canberra, 1985); D. Elisseeff: *China: treasures and splendors* (Paris, 1986).
IS

Epipalaeolithic Loosely defined chronological/cultural classification applied in some regions of the world to the last phase of the Palaeolithic period. In the past, researchers of European prehistory have sometimes used the term to describe the period between the Palaeolithic and the MESOLITHIC (*c*.9500–7500 BC). During this interval the material culture complexes in Europe, such as the AZILIAN, exhibit certain aspects of MAGDALENIAN technology and subsistence (and make use of many of the same sites) but lack key cultural indicators of the Upper Palaeolithic such as developed art; at the same time these cultures lack microlithic technology, and so have fallen outside the traditional classification of the 'Mesolithic'. Confusingly, the term is also occasionally used, in the European context, to denote the entire interval between the Magdalenian and the farming cultures of the first NEOLITHIC phase (i.e. including the Mesolithic).

In north Africa and the Ancient Near East the term is applied to the final phase of the Palaeolithic. Like the European Mesolithic, the Egyptian and Lower Nubian Epipalaeolithic is characterized mainly by its innovative lithic technology (microlithic flake tools) and its chronological position, neatly filling the gap between the Nilotic Upper Palaeolithic and Neolithic phases (i.e. *c*.10,000–5500 BC). The Lower Egyptian Faiyum B (or Qarunian) culture was an Epipalaeolithic phase preceding the Faiyum A Neolithic. The manufacture of backed and truncated blades at the Faiyum B sites shows that some Upper Palaeolithic techniques were still used, while the presence of hollow-base arrowheads like those at Faiyum A and Merimden sites provides a technological link with the lithic industries of the early Neolithic. The first Upper Egyptian Epipalaeolithic site was discovered at ELKAB by the Belgian archaeologist Pierre Vermeersch (1970). The well-stratified settlement remains, radiocarbon-dated to 6400–5980 BC and including over 4000 geometric microlithic tools, formed the basis of a new cultural phase: the Elkabian. The deposits at Elkab were seasonal riverside encampments dependent on fishing for subsistence, as were the ARKINIAN and SHAMARKIAN industries of the Lower Nubian Epipalaeolithic.

P. Vermeersch: 'L'Elkabien: une nouvelle industrie epipaléolithique Elkab en Haute Egypte: sa stratigraphie, sa typologie', *CdE* 45/89 (1970), 45–68; B.J. Trigger: 'The late Palaeolithic and Epi-Palaeolithic of northern Africa', *Cambridge history of Africa* I, ed. J.D. Clark (Cambridge, 1982), 342–409.
IS/RJ

equilibrium theory *see* SYSTEMS THEORY

Erebuni *see* URARTU

Erech *see* URUK

Erh-li-kang (Erligang) Early phase of the Shang culture of CHINA (sometimes referred to as Middle Shang), *c*.1650–1400 BC, pre-dating the levels at AN-YANG (Late Shang: *c*.1400–1122 BC), found in an extensive area, much of which lies beneath the modern city of Cheng-chou. Its main period of occupation was earlier than that of An-yang, and has been identified with the traditional record of a city of Ao which was one of the seven changes of capital traditionally supposed to have occurred in Shang times. Evidence suggesting a highly stratified and specialized society, with associated variations in areas of domicile, has gradually come to light despite the fact that much of the excavation is of a salvage nature. The picture of the Erh-li-kang city which emerges is, in many ways, close to that of the far better excavated An-yang sites; but the appreciable advances in metallurgy here had not as yet, apparently, been accompanied by any form of succinctly written records, let alone an embryo literature.

Chang Kwang-chih: *Shang civilization* (New Haven, 1980); An Chin-huai: 'The Shang city at Cheng-chou and related problems', *Studies of Shang archaeology*, ed. Chang Kwang-chih (New Haven, 1986), 15–48; Chang Kwang-chih: *The archaeology of ancient China*, 4th edn (New Haven, 1986).

NB

Erh-li-t'ou (Erlitou) Name assigned to the Early Shang city site south of the village of Erh-li-t'ou near Yen-shih, in Ho-nan, China. There has been considerable controversy as to whether the Erh-li-t'ou culture, or the lower two (of the four distinct) levels thereof, is that of traditional HSIA; or whether it should be classed as Early Shang. It is stratigraphically intermediate between LUNG-SHAN and ERH-LI-KANG – the latter more generally accepted as a Shang phase. Radiocarbon datings suggest a range of *c*.2100–1800 BC. Foundations of palatial buildings originally of timber frames, with wattle-and-daub walls, and gabled roofs, constructed upon rectangular stamped earth platforms, some tombs with remnants of lacquered coffins, a small number of bronze *chia*- and *chüeh*-wine cups (and recently also a *ting*-cauldron and a *ku*-beaker) and other bronze implements, turquoise 'inlaid' bronze plaques, and carved jades serve to indicate the appreciable qualitative advances attained over the earlier Lung-shan levels. The size of the larger of two extensive 'palace' foundations in Level III located at the centre of the site, is 108 m in length and 100 m in width, upon which other structures were built, and constitutes one of the earliest such structures excavated to date. However, the bulk of the artefactual context comprises stone, shell, and bone implements and a rich inventory of pottery utensils – several of these adapted currently, and others later, in the design of bronze vessels. Decoration on the bronze vessels was quite rudimentary. Other than symbols incised in ceramics, no signs of a written script appear. The status of the site would seem to be one generally comparable to other Shang city-state complexes as at Erh-li-kang and AN-YANG.

Chang Kwang-chih: *The archaeology of ancient China*, 4th edn (New Haven, 1986); Yin Wei-chang: 'A re-examination of Erh-li-t'ou culture', *Studies of Shang archaeology*, ed. Chang Kwang-chih (New Haven, 1986), 1–13.

NB

Eridu (Abu Shahrein) Sumerian town-site located near the marshes of southern Iraq, which flourished during the Ubaid period (*c*.5000–3800 BC) and the Early Dynastic period (*c*.2900–2350 BC). The town was once located on the River Euphrates, which now runs some distance to the north. One of the oldest cities in the world, the excavations of Fuad Safar and Seton Lloyd between 1946 and 1950 have revealed some 14 m of occupation dating to the UBAID culture (*c*.5000–3800 BC). It was the cult-centre of the river-god Enki, and a temple dedicated to this deity has survived from the Ubaid 4 period (*c*.4000 BC), roughly contemporary with similar temples at URUK and TEPE GAWRA. The site is now dominated by a mud-brick ZIGGURAT dating to the UR III period (*c*.2150–2000 BC). One of the earliest 'palaces' in Mesopotamia was discovered in Early Dynastic III strata at Eridu.

R.C. Thompson: 'Abu Shahrain in Mesopotamia in 1918', *Archaeologia* 70 (1918–20), 101–44; A. Jalil Jawad: 'The Eridu material and its implications', *Sumer* 30 (1974), 11–46; F. Safar, M.A. Mustafa and S. Lloyd: *Eridu* (Baghdad, 1981).

IS

Erligang *see* ERH-LI-KANG

Erlitou *see* ERH-LI-T'OU

Ertebølle culture Late Mesolithic culture of southern Scandinavia, principally known from a series of large SHELL MIDDEN sites and dated 4500–3200 BC. The Ertebølle is particularly interesting as a culture with a hunting and gathering economy that also used pottery. Like earlier Mesolithic communities, the lithic technology is characterized by microliths (trapeze and rhomboid shaped), but there are also groundstone implements; the pottery is characterized by plain jars with pointed bases, and oval bowls. The economy seems to have been a sophisticated exploitation of maritime and riverine resources, including shellfish (particularly oysters) and sea mammals such as seals. In comparison to other Mesolithic economies, the range of sites used by the Ertebølle is quite comprehensively studied, and apparently included semi-sedentary sites as well as specialized hunting sites for particular species. While the site of Ertebølle, a large shell midden site in north Denmark, reveals a range of fauna and long-term exploitation, the remains at Aggersund in the same region are dominated by the whooper swan – suggesting that this site acted as a winter swan hunting station. The Danish site of Ringkloster also seems to have been a specialist station, this time for hunting wild pig and pine marten. It has been suggested that the degree of specialization in exploitation of resources increased markedly in the Ertebølle, as compared to earlier cultures in the Scandinavian Mesolithic (the Maglemose and the Kongemose). As a procurement strategy, it is perhaps best explained by FORAGING THEORY, which attempts to understand and model the decision-making strategies of hunters and gatherers. The increase in specialization may also be related to an increase in population. Some Ertebølle sites exhibit excellent preservation of organic remains. Tybrind Vig yielded fish hooks with line attached, made by weaving plant fibres together; two canoes with wooden paddles carved with decorations were also found.

P. Rowley-Conwy: 'Sedentary hunters: the Ertebølle example', *Hunter-Gatherer Economy in Prehistory*, ed. G. Bailey (Cambridge, 1983), 111–30.

RJA

Eshnunna *see* TELL ASMAR

Eskimo *see* AMERICA 1; INUIT; MASK SITE

Esna (anc. Iunyt, Ta-senet, Latopolis) Upper Egyptian site located on the west bank of the Nile, 50 km south of Luxor, where important late Palaeolithic remains have been found. The 'Esnan' lithic industry flourished alongside the QADAN, Afian and SEBILLIAN industries during the Sahaba-Darau period (a phase of high seasonal flooding, *c*.13,000–10,000 BC). The principal archaeological remains from later periods are the sacred necropolis of the Nile perch (*Lates niloticus*) and the Ptolemaic and Roman temple of Khnum (*c*.180 BC–AD 249), which, according to textual evidence, was built on the site of a temple of Thutmose III (*c*.1479–1425 BC).

S. Sauneron: *Esna*, 5 vols (Cairo, 1959–67); D. Downes: *The excavations at Esna 1905–1906* (Warminster, 1974); F. Wendorf and R. Schild, eds: *Prehistory of the Nile valley* (New York, 1976), 289–911.

IS

Esnan *see* ESNA

ESR *see* ELECTRON SPIN RESONANCE DATING

Este (anc. Ateste) From about 650 BC this town in the region of Padua, northeast Italy became the centre of a rich Iron Age culture which produced a distinctive style of art. Manifested especially on beaten and chased bronzework belts, ornaments and vessels (situlae), and also on ceramic vessels, the art is influenced by that of the Etruscans and the classical Greeks, and employs a series of animal and 'orientalizing' motifs (winged gryphons, sphinxes) derived from the civilizations of the ancient Near East. These objects were probably largely made in Este itself, and have been recovered from many tombs in the area, but they were traded across a wider region. Este artefacts influenced a later phase of decorated bronzework and situlae found in the wide region of north Italy, Austria and Slovenia (*see* SITULA ART).

RJA

estimated vessel equivalent (eve) *see* QUANTIFICATION

estimation *see* PARAMETER ESTIMATION

Ethiopia, pre-Axumite and Axumite *see* ADULIS, AXUM, MATARA; YEHA

Ethiopia, medieval *see* DEBRA DAMO; LALIBELA

Ethiopia, post-medieval *see* GONDAR

ethnoarchaeology Term used to describe studies of contemporary societies undertaken in order to see how material culture relates to other aspects of society (social, ideological, economic, environmental, technical). Whereas modern material culture studies often straddle many disciplines from anthropology and sociology to folklore, media and subculture studies, ethnoarchaeology differs in that it is specifically directed towards the asking of archaeological questions about the interpretation of material remains, thus linking archaeology and ETHNOGRAPHY as integral parts of the same subdiscipline.

Although the word 'ethnoarchaeology' had been used by J.W. Fewkes as early as the turn of the century, it was not until the rise of the New Archaeology (*see* PROCESSUAL ARCHAEOLOGY) and the increased application of more rigorous scientific procedures in the 1960s that the subdiscipline of ethnoarchaeology expanded. By this time, the questions that were being asked of ethnography by archaeologists were becoming too specific for ethnographers to provide the answers. Ethnographers had often failed to provide detailed descriptions of material culture, detailed maps and plans, or detailed accounts of residues and discard processes.

Ethnographic analogies are used in archaeology in two very different ways. In the first, the ethnographic information is used to support or 'test' an archaeological hypothesis. Thus, archaeologists might often have ideas that seem unlikely until supported by ethnographic examples. The underlying claim is that an hypothesis can be supported by showing that it is an example of widely found relationships. The more cross-cultural examples that are found, the more plausible is the archaeological hypothesis. Thus, much effort has been directed towards demonstrating that in small-scale societies women are involved in gathering plants or arable farming and in domestic pottery production (Balfet 1965; Watson and Kennedy 1991). It is very difficult, on archaeological evidence alone, to demonstrate that women gathered plants or made pots (*see also* GENDER ARCHAEOLOGY). The difficulty with such uses of ethnography to support archaeological hypotheses is that the widespread nature of certain cultural features does not prove their existence in a particular case in the past.

In a second, and very different use of ethnographic analogies, the ethnographic information is used as a source of ideas which then have to be tested against the archaeological data. Lewis Binford (1967) argued that ethnography should be used to suggest hypotheses from which deductions could be drawn (the HYPOTHETICO-DEDUCTIVE METHOD) and tested against the archaeological data. Such testing depends on having some independent yardsticks so that the past can be measured. During the 1970s and 1980s, especially in North America, the use of ethnography intensified in order to develop 'MIDDLE-RANGE THEORY' (Raab and Goodyear 1984). These theories are claimed to be of a general nature, and to be independent of the specific hypothesis (which might often be based on ethnographic analogy) that is being tested. Considerable success was claimed in relation to what Michael Schiffer (1976) termed N-TRANSFORMS, the natural transformations of materials and archaeological data. Bone TAPHONOMY, ceramic breakage and abrasion, USE-WEAR TRACES all proved susceptible to generalization. Indeed, the boundary between ethnoarchaeology and EXPERIMENTAL ARCHAEOLOGY became blurred, as both in the ethnographic and laboratory contexts, archaeologists tried to understand the natural processes which formed the archaeological record (Schiffer 1987). More detailed ethnoarchaeological fieldwork was conducted, for example by Binford (1978) among the North American Nunamiut in his attempt to understand hunter-gatherer carcass use and discard behaviour (*see* REFUSE DEPOSITION).

In the 1980s and 1990s archaeologists became increasingly concerned with Schiffer's C-TRANSFORMS – the cultural processes which lead to the formation of the archaeological record (Schiffer 1976). Here there has been ethnographic work directed towards an understanding of the symbolism of material culture (e.g. Hodder 1982b) and the social use of space (e.g. Moore 1986). But there has been a lack of consensus about how these cultural transformations should be understood. On the one hand, some uses of ethnography have placed their observations within general ecological or evolutionary models; thus Binford's Nunamiut work explored the relationship between hunter-gatherer strategies of resource procurement and ecological parameters. On the other hand, ethnography has been used to demonstrate the historical specificity of material practices. For example, burial practices can be related to attitudes to death which are historically contingent (e.g. Parker Pearson 1982). Discard practices too can be understood as socially constructed and as manipulated in specific historical contexts (Moore 1986). Rather than emphasizing the cross-cultural nature of archaeological dependence on ethnography, such studies tend to lead to a recognition of the importance of direct historical analogy. In the latter case, instances of cultural continuity between past and present are used as the basis for the transfer of information from ethnographic or ethnohistoric groups into the past. Thus, in many parts of the world outside Europe, and to some extent in Europe, ethnographic information concerning local groups can be used to aid the interpretation of archaeological evidence of presumed ancestral groups (e.g. Flannery and Marcus 1983). Where such continuities cannot be demonstrated, the problem becomes one of evaluating the relevance of ethnographic information to past archaeological contexts. For an extended example, see IGBO-UKWU.

A distinction can be made between *formal* and *relational* analogies (Wylie 1985). In using formal analogies, similarities between past and present contexts are sought, and differences are identified but deemed irrelevant to the transfer of information from past to present concerning unknown issues. For example, similarities in the form of present and past post-hole arrangements might lead to the transfer of information concerning the use of those arrangements in the construction of houses (Hodder 1982a). Such formal arguments are supported by demonstrating the closeness of the similarities and/or their widespread cross-cultural occurrence.

Relational analogies, on the other hand, are more concerned with the causal relations between the items deemed similar, different or unknown within the two contexts being compared. The relevance of the analogy has to be demonstrated by showing not only similarities in form, but also in meaning or function within determinant historical situations. The emphasis can again be cross-cultural, emphasizing the generality of certain links between material residues and the behaviour which produced them. However, few non-trivial generalizations have been identified concerning c-transforms. Alternatively, emphasis is placed on in-depth understanding (or 'thick' description) of the specific contexts being compared and of the regularity of behaviour within historical trajectories. Even when direct historical analogy cannot be demonstrated, relational analogies can be used to enhance the understanding of specific societies in the distant past (e.g. Tilley 1993) – given careful contextual consideration of all types of data within the societies being compared.

J.W. Fewkes: 'The prehistoric culture of Tusayan', *American Anthropologist* 9 (1896), 151–73; H. Balfet: 'Ethnographic observations in North Africa and archaeological interpretation: the pottery of the Maghreb', *Ceramics and man*, ed. F.R. Matson (Chicago, 1965), 161–77; L.R. Binford: 'Smudge pits and hide smoking: the use of analogy in archaeological reasoning', *AA* 32 (1967), 1–12; M.B. Schiffer: *Behavioral archaeology* (New York, 1976); L.R. Binford: *Nunamiut ethnoarchaeology* (New York, 1978); R. Gould and M.B. Schiffer, eds: *Modern material culture* (New York, 1981); B. Orme: *Anthropology for archaeologists* (London, 1981); I. Hodder: *The present past* (London, 1982a); ——: *Symbols in action* (Cambridge, 1982b); M. Parker Pearson: 'Mortuary practice, society and ideology: an ethnoarchaeological study', *Symbolic and structural archaeology*, ed. I. Hodder (Cambridge, 1982); K. Flannery and J. Marcus: *The cloud people* (New York, 1983); L.M. Raab and A.C. Goodyear: 'Middle range theory in archaeology: a critical review of origins and applications', *AA* 49 (1984), 255–68; A. Wiley: 'The reaction against analogy', *Advances in archaeological method and theory*, ed. M. Schiffer (New York, 1985); H. Moore: *Space, text and gender* (Cambridge, 1986); M.B. Schiffer: *Formation processes of the archaeological record* (Albuquerque, 1987); D. Miller: *Material culture and mass consumption* (Oxford, 1989); P.J. Watson and M.C. Kennedy: 'The development of horticulture in the Eastern Woodlands of North America: women's role', *Engendering archaeology*, ed. J.M. Gero and M.W. Conkey (Oxford, 1991), 255–75; C. Tilley: *Material culture as text: the art of ambiguity* (London, 1993).

IH

ethnographic analogy *see* ETHNOARCHAEOLOGY

ethnography The anthropological observation and study of contemporary societies and cultures. For many archaeologists, particularly in the New World, their discipline is indissolubly linked with anthropology in that it contributes to a general comparative understanding of human beings and their culture. In the Old World, archaeology has closest ties with history; without the broader umbrella of anthropology, ethnography has been identified as a specific source for ideas about the past. At times archaeologists in Europe have been suspicious of drawing ethnographic parallels, wary of transferring information between specific historical contexts. But the dependence of archaeology on analogies with the present is too pervasive to undermine the general close relationship between archaeology and ethnography.

By the 16th century AD, travels to North America had led to the emergence of an image of native peoples which was used in the reconstruction of the lives of ancient Britons (Orme 1981: 3–12). In the 18th century, Thomas Pownall compared the culture of North American Indians with the antiquities of the British Isles and developed the uniformitarian principle, some version of which is at the basis of all use of ethnography in archaeology: 'Man is, in the natural course of his being, always the same thing under the same circumstances' (Pownall 1795, quoted by Orme 1981: 13). In 1865, John Lubbock interpreted ancient remains by drawing parallels with what he termed 'modern savages'.

It was General Pitt Rivers' ethnographic knowledge, as well as his military interest in firearms, which allowed him to develop archaeological approaches to stylistic variation and change through time. In the United States at the end of the 19th century, the Moundbuilder controversy was settled when John W. Powell and Cyrus Thomas demonstrated similarities between archaeological material concerning mound sites and contemporary Indian material culture in the same areas (Hodder 1982: 35). Throughout the early 20th century a cautious acceptance of the need for drawing ethnographic parallels in archaeology was widespread, if little theorized. Archaeology remained separate from, but closely related to, ethnography. The term ETHNOARCHAEOLOGY is used to describe ethnographic studies that are undertaken specifically in order to solve archaeological problems. For an ethnographic case-study *see* IGBO-UKWU.

J. Lubbock: *Pre-historic times, as illustrated by ancient remains, and the manners and customs of modern savages* (London, 1865); B. Orme: *Anthropology for archaeologists* (London, 1981); I. Hodder: *The present past* (London, 1982).

For further bibliography *see* ETHNOARCHAEOLOGY.

IH

Etowah Major MISSISSIPPIAN 'mound center' located along the Etowah River in northwestern Georgia, eastern North America. Etowah was occupied for several centuries and for much of this period it was one of the most important sites in the region. Three large mounds and several smaller ones, along with plaza and habitation areas, were constructed within a 21 ha area. The site was protected by a strong palisade with bastions and a deep ditch. Excavations in one of the large mounds uncovered many burials with ornate SOUTHERN CULT artefacts, as well as lines of postmoulds from fences which once screened the mortuary area from view.

L.H. Larson: 'Archaeological implications of social stratification at the Etowah site, Georgia', *AA Memoir* 25 (1971), 58–67; ——: 'Functional considerations of warfare in the Southeast during the Mississippi period', *AA* 37 (1972), 383–92.

GM

Europe, medieval and post-medieval

1 Medieval Europe; 2 Post-Medieval Europe

1 Medieval Europe

The origins of medieval archaeology – the study of the material culture of the period from *c.*AD 400 to 1500 in Europe – lie in the mid- to later 19th century as amateur archaeologists excavated burial mounds of all periods and as the scope of architectural history was enlarged to encompass small churches. The discovery of post-classical artefacts in British, French and Scandinavian burial mounds, in particular, demonstrated the material wealth of the early medieval period. A significant development was Hjalmar Stolpe's excavations of the Viking-period cemetery at BIRKA, Sweden (Ambrosiani and Clarke 1992). Stolpe, a natural scientist, made scale drawings of his excavations. He took a keen interest in the historical importance of the cemetery which led to a series of major publications by Holger Arbman in the 1930s and 1940s; the most notable of these was *Schweden und das Karolingische Reich* (Arbman 1937) which illustrated how the material culture located early medieval Sweden within the Carolingian economic sphere. By contrast, the study of church architecture has evolved slowly as a subdiscipline of art history. Major studies of Early Christian churches in the later 19th century, for example, by G.B. De Rossi (1864–77) in Italy or G. Baldwin Brown in the case of Anglo-Saxon churches in England (1903), led to major studies such as Richard Krautheimer's *Corpus basilicarum christianarum Romae* (1937–77) of the major early medieval churches of Rome.

In the early 20th century the discipline developed slowly. While Roman towns became the subject of large-scale exavations, medieval occupation levels were literally shovelled away. Nevertheless, museum curators actively promoted the collection of medieval objects. E.T. Leeds at the Ashmolean Museum, Oxford, for example, encouraged the young T.E. Lawrence to search building sites for medieval objects. By the 1930s such incidental finds were being rigorously catalogued by British, German and Scandinavian museum directors. R.E.M. Wheeler in London supported G.C. Dunning to make a systematic survey of finds from London (Hurst 1982), and later commissioned John Ward-Perkins to prepare a catalogue of medieval finds. Urban archaeology before 1939 was also advanced by Herbert Jankuhn's excavations at Haithabu, financed by the Nazi party to demonstrate the early commercial prowess of German merchants in Slavic areas (see Arnold 1990). Jankuhn's important excavations showed the need for adopting prehistoric methodologies which in turn might provide new sources of information for the historian.

The obliteration of many European towns during the Second World War provided the opportunity for systematic urban excavations. From medieval Cologne to Anglo-Saxon Southampton, a new school of rescue archaeologist came to the fore. These excavations provoked an interest among historians in post-classical remains, giving rise to investigations of deserted rural sites. Large-scale excavations of early medieval coastal villages in

Frisia had begun in the 1930s under the direction of A.E. van Giffen; after the war excavations at Feddersen Wierde and later on, at Wijster revealed hitherto unexpected data on domestic architecture, production and, indeed, agrarian life in general.

Similarly, the archaeology of villages was recognized by economic historians like M.W. Beresford and W.G. Hoskins as a vital new source of data about the peasantry. The excavations at WHARRAM PERCY, North Yorkshire, started in 1952 gave rise to deserted village excavations and to the study of rural sites throughout Europe (Hurst 1971). The systematic recording of churches, as major village buildings, much influenced by West German detailed studies emulating the recording of classical monuments, evolved in parallel with rural excavations. Such systems led effectively to the re-calibration of churches hitherto dated by architectural historians on the bases of their stylistic features.

With stratigraphic excavations came the opportunity to date material culture. Major studies of Late Roman pottery (Hayes 1972) and of medieval pottery by scholars throughout western Europe made it possible by 1980 to reconstruct regional settlement history from south Etruria, north of Rome (Potter 1979) to the Eifel mountains (Janssen 1975), the Dutch polders (Besteman 1990) and East Anglia (Hurst 1976). Such patterns, when integrated with the evidence from rescue excavations made in towns, provided a historical geography for the post-classical period. From 1980 onwards, the scope of this evidence was enlarged, as the open-area excavation techniques introduced in the 1960s by Martin Biddle in his excavations at Winchester (*see* OLD MINSTER) have been adopted throughout western Europe.

New topographic insights derived from, for example, the excavations at the Cripta Balbi, Rome (Manacorda and Zanini 1989), Marseilles, DORESTAD and Birka, provide the measured contextual information on which to hang patterns of production, distribution and consumption. A popular illustration of this development is the Jorvik Centre at York where the York Archaeological Trust have reconstructed a 10th-century street frontage of workshops found during rescue excavations (*see* COPPERGATE). Perhaps the most provocative illustration of this trend was Charles L. Redman's excavations of the later medieval port of QSAR-ES-SEGHIR in Morocco (Redman 1986), where probability and judgement sampling strategies were employed to examine the patterning of material within the town.

With such data, post-classical archaeology has developed far beyond the scope of classifying churches and burial mounds (note Carver's research design at SUTTON HOO: Carver 1992) to become a historical instrument of singular importance because it sheds light on the peasantry as well as elites. In the late 20th century, medieval archaeology probably accounts for the greater share of public monies spent on archaeology in western Europe. However, while its academic place has been safeguarded by teaching posts in most European universities, it is still poorly represented in research terms. Its future appears to rest firstly upon collaboration between archaeologists and all branches of history, and secondly upon regionally based professional archaeologists in local government concerned with curating the past.

See also HUSTERKNUPP, IPSWICH, KEMPEN PROJECT, RABITA DE GUARDAMAR, ROCCA SAN SILVESTRO, ST GALL PLAN, SAN VINCENZO AL VOLTURNO, SARÇHANE, SERÇE LIMAN, TINTAGEL *and* VORBASSE.

G.B. de Rossi: *Roma Sotterranea Cristiana* (Rome, 1864–77); G. Baldwin Brown: *The arts in early England* (London, 1903); H. Arbman: *Schweden und das Karolingische Reich* (Stockholm, 1937); J.G. Hurst: 'A review of archaeological work', M.W. Beresford and J.G. Hurst, eds, *Deserted medieval village studies* (London, 1971), 76–89; J.W. Hayes: *Late Roman pottery* (London, 1972); W. Janssen: *Studien zur Wustungsfrage im frankischenzwischen Rhein, Mosel und Eifelnordrand* (Cologne, 1975); J.G. Hurst: 'The pottery', *The archaeology of Anglo-Saxon England*, ed. D.M. Wilson (London, 1976), 283–348; T.W. Potter: *The changing landscape of south Etruria* (London, 1979); J.G. Hurst: 'Gerald Dunning and his contribution to Medieval Archaeology', *Medieval Ceramics* 6 (1982), 3–20; C.L. Redman: *Qsar es-Seghir, an archaeological view of medieval life* (Orlando, 1986); D. Manacorda and E. Zanini: 'The first millennium AD in Rome: from the Porticus Minucia to the Via delle Botteghe Oscure', *The birth of Europe*, ed. K. Randsborg (Rome, 1989), 25–32; B. Arnold: 'The past as propaganda in Nazi Germany', *Antiquity* 64 (1990), 464–78; J.C. Besteman: 'North Holland AD 400–1200: turning tide or tide turned?', *Medieval archaeology in the Netherlands*, ed. J.C. Besteman, J.M. Bos and H.A. Heidinga (Assen, 1990), 91–120; B. Ambrosiani and H. Clarke: *Early investigations and future plans* (Stockholm, 1992); M. Carver, ed.: *The age of Sutton Hoo* (Woodbridge, 1992).

RH

2 Post-medieval Europe

Term used to describe research into the archaeology of Europe during the centuries since 1500. This subdiscipline has developed in the past 30 years, as a result of the increasing realization that physical evidence has a significant contribution to make to the understanding of the economic history of the post-medieval period. The impetus for the development of post-medieval archaeology has arisen not only from the need to provide complementary evidence in answering historical questions but also from archaeological and conservational interest in the post-medieval monuments themselves.

Archaeological effort has been devoted to topics for which archives are sparse, for despite the growth of record-keeping in the 16th century and after, many activities generated little written material or, where anything was set down, it was unlikely to be preserved. Even where archives are at first sight substantial, they are essentially quantitative, and there is rarely description or comment, apart from some aspects of land surveys, or depositions in legal cases. Correspondence on economic as opposed to political matters is relatively rare. Practice, of course, varied over Europe. In Britain, for example, written evidence for property transfer survives unevenly until (and in many regions well beyond) the beginnings of deed registration in the 18th century. In France, by contrast, notarial registers are an important surviving source from the Middle Ages onwards. Where the qualitative emphasis is absent from the written record, valuable evidence can frequently be derived from the archaeology of structures, standing or buried, the land which surrounded them, the possessions of their occupants, or the products or residues of crafts and industries.

Over Europe as a whole there is a basic context of economic change into which the archaeological evidence can be fitted. Population growth, after the epidemics of the later middle ages, led to new settlement, more intensive agriculture, employment in urban and rural industries which fed new markets, and the growth of towns, whether centres of trade or of government. In many areas successive development has left relict landscapes which illustrate these changes, and overlie features of the Middle Ages (as in the case of post-medieval enclosed fields overlying medieval ridge and furrow).

One facet of landscape history is of particular importance in the period between the 15th and the 19th centuries: industry. Before the growth which characterizes the Industrial Revolution period, industry was predominantly rural. All over Europe there can be found examples of communities where individuals combined industrial and agricultural work, and this is recognized as a key to the understanding of many post-medieval landscapes.

There are valleys where industries have made intensive use of water power, mining areas linked to managed woodlands which provided fuel for smelting, metalworking by farmer-smiths whose fuel came from new coal-mines as well as from woodlands, areas of pastoral farming where textile production developed from a by-employment to become the driving force of local economies (*see* RCHME 1985). These combinations of occupations leave characteristic traces; they also gave rise to signs of wealth in the form of improved domestic buildings: the study of vernacular architecture, and of the houses and grounds of the better-off, is linked to the relict-landscapes which result from industrial activities, as well as to the growing productivity of agriculture, spurred on by the demands of a rising population.

The identification of landscapes in which multiple occupations have been practised has been enhanced by excavation and field survey which has led to an understanding of technological change in early industry. The iron industry has been the subject of many excavations, particularly in Britain, where bloomeries, blast furnaces and forges have been examined. In Spain, field and archive work has demonstrated the key features of the Catalan forges of the Basque country, while in France, the work of the Inventaire National has provided high-quality published surveys of ironworking districts in the regions of Châteaubriant, Ardennes, Normandy and the French Alps (*see* Ministère de la Culture 1991, 1992). Some progress has been made in Italy with the study of the characteristic *bergamasque* blast furnaces of Tuscany and the Alpine regions.

The glass industry has been the subject of increasing interest: this is another occupation which in most areas was dependent on the management of woodlands for fuel. Excavations carried out on post-medieval furnace-sites include examples in England, Finland, France, Germany, Italy, Switzerland and the Czech and Slovak republics.

The field archaeology of the post-medieval period is assisted by the precision with which many artefacts found on excavations and during field-walking can be dated. Of particular importance is the occurrence of clay-tobacco-pipes, found in post-1600 deposits, and datable to narrow limits as a result of close studies of types and makers' marks (Oswald 1975). The study of post-medieval ceramics is of great importance, for many types of pottery were traded over considerable distances (*see* Hurst et al. 1986), and regional decoration and design were influenced by exotic items. Of particular importance were far-eastern imports of porcelain and the extent to which they inspired imitation amongst the makers of tin-glazed earthenware in the Mediterranean region and in northwest Europe.

Not to be underestimated is the extent to which research in the post-medieval archaeology of Europe and the historical archaeology of colonial regions outside Europe are inter-linked. This is particularly true of work in the lands bordering the north Atlantic: many artefacts produced in Europe are found in north America, often in closely-dated contexts which in turn help to confirm the chronology of production and trade. *See also* INDUSTRIAL ARCHAEOLOGY.

A. Oswald: *Clay pipes for the archaeologist* (Oxford, 1975); T.S. Reynolds: *Stronger than a hundred men: a history of the vertical water wheel* (Baltimore, 1983); Ministère de la Culture: *Les forges du pays de Châteaubriant* (Paris, 1984); H.F. Cleere and D.W. Crossley: *The iron industry of the Weald* (Leicester, 1985); Royal Commission on the Historical Monuments of England (RCHME): *Rural houses of the Lancashire Pennines* (London, 1985); J.G. Hurst et al.: *Pottery produced and traded in North-West Europe 1350–1650* (Rotterdam, 1986); Royal Commission on the Historical Monuments of England: *Houses of the North York moors* (London, 1987); Ministère de la Culture: *La Métallurgie du fer dans les Ardennes (XVIe–XIXe)* (Paris, 1988); F. Verhaeghe and M. Otte: *Archéologie des temps modernes* (Liege, 1988); D.W. Crossley: *Post-medieval archaeology in Britain* (Leicester, 1990); H. Horat: *Der Glasschmelzofen des Priesters Theophilus* (Bern, 1991); M. Mendera: *Archeologia e storia della produzione del vetro preindustriale* (Siena, 1991); Ministère de la Culture: *La Métallurgie Normande* (Caen, 1991); ——: *Fonte, fer, acier: Rhine-Alpes* (Lyon, 1992).

DC

experimental archaeology Archaeological approach that seeks to explore and test interpretations, theories and hypotheses by practical experimentation. Although experimentation has long been used by archaeologists, the subdiscipline was fundamentally changed from the 1960s onwards, with the inauguration of several large-scale projects, including the OVERTON DOWN earthwork, the BUTSER ANCIENT FARM (both in England) and the Experimental Centre at Lejre in Denmark.

Experimental archaeology can be divided into five distinct categories: construct, process and function, simulation, probability trials and technological innovation. The 'construct' is perhaps the simplest type of experiment to explain, not least because it has the greatest visual and physical impact. The term 'construct' is deliberately used here to differentiate an experimental building from a 'reconstruction', the latter being those buildings for which sufficient material evidence has survived to allow their accurate reconstruction, as in open-air museums devoted to the preservation and reconstruction of buildings from earlier historical periods. Prehistoric buildings, on the other hand, are usually known only through patterns of post and stake holes and often very little else. Creating a superstructure based on this kind of data often requires artistic licence or even pure imagination. However, the attempt can focus the attention of excavators on explaining why such a structural interpretation is right or wrong. At the very least, a construct can provide an idea of the space contained by a building and the material requirements for its construction.

At Butser Ancient Farm, a construct of a late Iron Age house was created on the basis of the archaeological data from Pimperne Down in Dorset, where two double ring houses (one built immediately after the other in the same location) were excavated, each taking the form of an outer ring of stakeholes with a diameter of 12.9 m and an inner ring of postholes with a diameter of 9.9 m (see Reynolds 1994: 4–10). The sheer quantity of materials required for the Butser construct was remarkable: over 200 mature trees, mostly oak averaging 0.3 m at the butt, some ten tonnes of clay to make the daub (for the wattle-and-daub outer wall) and twelve tonnes of thatching straw to cover the roof.

The second category of experiment is 'process and function': this involves the examination of the ways in which things actually work. It embraces trials with ards (such as the ways in which they stir the soil and the effect of the soil on the ard itself), the manufacture of ancient tools such as the vallus (and the testing of their efficiency or otherwise), as well as the building of kilns and the study of their use in firing pottery.

One of the most significant process-and-function experiments was carried out at Butser Ancient Farm with regard to the creation of underground grain storage silos. Although excavations have often demonstrated the use of underground silos at all periods, there is very little documentary evidence for the practice (Tacitus, *Germania*, 16 and Pliny, *Natural History* 18, 306) and many archaeologists in the 1970s began to express doubts as to whether the large pits typically found on Iron Age sites could have been used for this purpose. Experimental pits dug into a number of different rock types at Butser, however, indicated that it was perfectly feasible to store grain in this way in England for a period of at least 18 years. It was demonstrated that the same pit could be used over and over again without any deleterious effect on the grain. These experiments also examined different types of lining for which there was putative archaeological evidence. A basketry-lined pit proved unusable after the first year, since the wood became an ideal substrate for concentrating micro-organisms; a clay-lined pit, on the other hand, worked extremely well for many years. The clay simply acted as a barrier against any further penetration of water, although its own humidity accelerated germination of the grain and slightly increased the loss rate.

The third category of experiment – the simulation trial – is best exemplified by the experimental earthwork, such as those constructed at Overton Down in 1962 and Wareham Down in 1963. These were both massive replicas of ditch-and-bank earthworks containing various deliberately buried artefacts, which have been excavated at various intervals in order to investigate the processes of deterioration and change in the archaeological record. An experimental earthwork was also constructed at Butser Ancient Farm in 1976 as a simulation of the typical ditch and bank which surrounded small settlements of the Bronze and Iron Ages, thus allowing the examination of erosion patterns in so far as they created specific layers in the ditch profile when excavated. The Butser earthwork, based on an actual Iron Age example at East Castle in Dorset, showed the remarkable speed at which vegetation began to encroach, generally serving to stabilize the structure as a whole. In 1984, a series of sections were cut across the ditch on the east, south and north sides of the enclosure with totally unexpected results. It is normal to find on archaeological ditches that the layers are not evenly distributed in the sense that one side always seems to have a greater quantity of material than the other. This has often been used to argue that the side with the greatest deposit is the side where the bank was located. However, the experimental ditch showed exactly the opposite. The reason is not difficult to isolate. It seems that the skewed deposition of material is caused directly by the pattern of vegetative growth on the inner elements of the ditch and bank.

As a result of the pilot scheme at Butser, a major experimental design was implemented, involving the construction of much more complex octagonal earthworks at three sites in Britain: the National Science Museum Reserve Collection at Wroughton, near Swindon (in 1985); the grounds of Fishbourne Roman Palace at Chichester (also in 1985); and Bascomb Down, the new site of the Butser Ancient Farm, in Hampshire (in 1992). Each of these is accompanied by a meteorological station and each one is monitored annually to record the vegetation cover.

The fourth category of experiment is the probability trial, which is a combination of the first three categories with the added component of seeking and outcome. The ideal example of this type of experiment is the long series of agricultural trials carried out at the Butser Ancient Farm since 1972. Any agricultural trial is subject to the five basic criteria of farming: climate, soil, crop or cereal type, the nature of treatment and finally pests and pestilences. The probability trial is extremely complex in terms of recording all of these variables and presenting the results within the strict parameters of the experiment. In order that the results are acceptable to the agriculturalist/agronomist, experimental design must take account of modern agricultural research design and sampling technique. For example, the area cultivated has to be large enough to allow the sample to completely ignore a metre-wide perimeter band around the crop, in order to avoid an 'edge effect'.

The final category of experiment, technological innovation, covers attempts to improve or enhance archaeological practice (whether excavation technique or methods of prospection). For example, the initial use of RESISTIVITY SURVEY was an experiment, and its adoption as an archaeological tool only came after a series of trials.

Experiment is central to the practice of archaeology, forcing reappraisal and focusing on anomalies and absurdities; it is no more than the application of deductive logic reinforced by physical testing: without experiment, archaeology would stagnate into endless repetition and unquestioned typologies. The use of experiment has increasingly brought scientific discipline to bear upon a subject steeped in a more traditional, humanistic way of thinking.

For a non-European case-study *see* INCA and TIAHUANACO.

J. Coles: *Experimental archaeology* (London, 1979); P.J. Reynolds: *Iron Age farm: the Butser experiment* (London, 1979); ——: *Ancient farming* (Princes Risborough, 1987); D.W. Harding et al.: *An Iron Age settlement in Dorset* (Edinburgh, 1993); P.J. Reynolds: *Experimental archaeology: a perspective for the future* (Leiden, 1994); M. Bell et al.: *The experimental earthwork project 1960–1992* (London, 1996).

PRE

exploratory data analysis (EDA) An approach to statistical analysis advocated by Tukey (1977), which explores archaeological DATASETS in an open-minded way and looks for patterns in them. It is contrasted with classical methods such as HYPOTHESIS TESTING and PARAMETER ESTIMATION, sometimes called confirmatory data analysis, which seek to prove or disprove a particular point of view. EDA is of most value in

MULTIVARIATE STATISTICS, in which a confirmatory approach is both difficult and unrealistic, and the data are difficult to visualize. It therefore makes extensive use of VISUAL DISPLAY OF DATA.

J.W. Tukey: *Exploratory data analysis* (Reading, MA, 1977); S. Shennan: *Quantifying archaeology* (Edinburgh, 1988), 22–3.

CO

Eynan *see* AIN MALLAHA

F

Failaka Small island in the northern Arabian/Persian Gulf, 20km from the coast of Kuwait. A settlement dating to the 2nd millennium BC has been excavated in the south-western corner, as well as the remains of a Hellenistic town. The Danish and French excavations since the early 1960s have dated the 2nd-millennium architectural sequence by identifying seven phases of ceramics between 2000 and 1200 BC, although there are also a few isolated earlier finds, such as Early Dynastic stamp and cylinder seals. In the section of the island designated F6 the Danish expedition uncovered a large elite building containing a columned court resembling that in the Sinkashid temple at URUK, with which it seems to have been roughly contemporary. X-RAY FLUORESCENCE analysis for the distinctive glazed pottery and faience vessels on Failaka has suggested that they may be locally made, since the ratio of magnesium to calcium is unparalleled elsewhere in the pre-Islamic Near East (Pollard and Hõjlund 1983).

Failaka's extensive contacts with Mesopotamia and Bahrain are indicated by the discovery of large numbers of cuneiform documents and seals, suggesting that the island was first colonized by Mesopotamia during the Isin-Larsa period (*c.*2025–1763 BC). Potts (1990: 291–2) argues that the population of Failaka has consistently been multi-ethnic, citing the presence of Old Babylonian inscriptions and KASSITE ceramic forms as well as Dilmun seals (*see* BAHRAIN), imported pottery from the Iran and the Oman peninsula, an inscribed sherd bearing AMORITE names, and one seal bearing an Indus inscription (*see* INDUS CIVILIZATION). There are important Seleucid and early Islamic settlements on the island, the latter with a so-called 'Sasanian' church in its centre.

A. Pollard and F. Hõjlund: 'High-magnesium glazed sherds from Bronze Age tells on Failaka, Kuwait', *Archaeometry* 25 (1983), 196–200; J.-F. Salles, ed.: *Failaka: fouilles françaises 1983* (Lyons, 1984); Y. Calvet and J.-F. Salles, ed.: *Failaka: fouilles françaises 1984–1985* (Lyons, 1986); P. Kjaerum: 'Architecture and settlement patterns in 2nd millennium Failaka', *Proceedings of the Seminar for Arabian Studies* 16 (1986), 77–88; D.T. Potts: *The Arabian Gulf in antiquity*, 2 vols (Oxford, 1990), I, 261–97, II, 154–96.

IS

Faiyum region (anc. She-reshy, Moeris) Large fertile depression in the Egyptian Western Desert about 60 km to the southwest of Cairo, covering an area of some 12,000 sq. km. Before the Palaeolithic period it had a huge salt-water lake at its centre, but this eventually became linked to the river Nile by the Bahr Yusef canal, thus transforming it into the fresh-water Lake Moeris. The earliest inhabitants of the Faiyum were the EPIPALAEOLITHIC 'Faiyum B' people, who were succeeded by the Neolithic 'Faiyum A' culture in *c.*5500 BC (Caton-Thompson and Gardner 1934). Although the Faiyum gained a degree of importance in the Middle Kingdom (*c.*2040–1640 BC), the surviving remains are dominated by Greco-Roman towns such as Bacchias (Kom el-Atl), Karanis (Kom Aushim) and Tebtunis (Tell Umm el-Breigat).

G. Caton-Thompson and E.O. Gardner: *The Desert Fayum* (London, 1934); H. Geremek: *Karanis, communauté rurale de l'Egypte romaine au IIe–IIIe siècle de notre ére* (Warsaw, 1969); E. Husselman: *Karanis: excavations of the University of Michigan in Egypt, 1928–35* (Michigan, 1979); A.K. Bowman: *Egypt after the pharaohs* (London, 1986), 142–55.

IS

Fakhariya, Tell *see* MITANNI

falsification Process of attempting to disprove a theory or hypothesis by testing it against the empirical evidence (via observation or experiment). A sustained but unsuccessful attempt to falsify any given theory thus increases that theory's plausibility – although it can never prove the universality of the theory. Falsification is the opposite process to VERIFICATION, which presents the evidence for believing that a statement or theory is true. Karl Popper, one of the most influential philosophers of science this century, advanced falsification, rather than verification, as the key activity of science. This seemed to answer a paradox in the philosophy of science: how could the *universal* truth of laws ever be established from the verification of their truth in a *finite* number of instances? Popper's approach seemed to answer this paradox without reducing scientific endeavour to logically certain, but drastically limited, statements in the way that the more extreme positivist approaches threatened to (*see* LOGICAL POSITIVISM).

In essence, Popper argued that advances in science did not arise out of linear generalizations from the particular at all. Instead, scientists invented theory using existing theory and reasoning that often could not be justified logically. The rigour of science arose out of the determined attempt to find an instance in the real world that did not conform to the theory as formulated (and which would thus falsify it). In that both stress the importance of scientific methodology, the positivist approach and the falsification approach may seem quite similar. Yet taken to the extreme, positivism discounts the usefulness of any statement that cannot be verified. Whereas philosophies of science that stress falsification are able to accept as meaningful and useful a variety of frameworks and approaches that lead to theories, providing these theories lead to useful (non-obvious, clear and unambiguous) hypotheses formulated in such a way that they are open to falsification in the real world.

(*see also* INDUCTIVE AND DEDUCTIVE EXPLANATION; VERIFICATION; THEORY AND THEORY BUILDING.)

K. Popper: *Conjectures and refutations: the growth of scientific knowledge* (London, 1963; 4th edn, 1985); P.J. Watson, S.A. LeBlanc and C.L. Redman: *Explanation in archaeology: an explicitly scientific approach* (New York and London, 1971).

RJA

Fara, Tell (anc. Shuruppak) Tell-site comprising the remains of the Sumerian city of Shuruppak, located in the Mesopotamian alluvial plain midway between Baghdad and the Gulf. The city originally lay on the banks of the western branch of the Euphrates, but the river has moved gradually westwards. The earliest settlement remains date to the Jemdet Nasr period (*c.*3200–2900 BC). The city grew rapidly, reaching a size of some 100 hectares by the Early Dynastic period (*c.*2900–2350 BC), but it appears to have been abandoned at the end of the 3rd millennium BC. The site was excavated by a German expedition in 1902–3 and an American expedition in 1931. The term 'Fara period/style' is used to describe distinctive cuneiform tablets of the Early Dynastic IIIa period and CYLINDER SEALS of Early Dynastic II, large numbers of which were found in the course of the excavations. Harriet Martin (1988: 127) argues that the findspots of the cuneiform archives at Shurrupak, primarily in large houses on the central and southern rises of the mound, support Diakonov's assertion that the Early Dynastic economic system consisted of 'household' units controlling large numbers of workers (Diakonov 1963).

E. Heinrich and W. Andrae, ed.: *Fara, Ergebnisse der Ausgrabungen der Deutschen Orient-Gesellschaft in Fara und Abu Hatab 1902/3* (Berlin, 1931); I.M. Diakonov: 'The commune in the Ancient Near East as treated in the works of Soviet researchers', *Soviet Anthropology and Archaeology* 2 (1963), 32–46; H. Martin: *Fara: a reconstruction of the ancient Mesopotamian city of Shuruppak* (Birmingham, 1988).

IS

Farafra Oasis (anc. Ta-iht) Fertile depression located in the Egyptian Western Desert, about 300 km west of Asyut. The smallest of the major Egyptian oases, it is first mentioned in texts dating to the Old Kingdom (*c.*2649–2150 BC), but the earliest known sites are the Roman-period settlements and cemeteries at Ain el-Wadi and Wadi Abu Hinnis (*c.*30 BC–AD 395) and the remains of an Early Christian town (*c.*AD 450 BC).

H.J.L. Beadnell: *Farafra Oasis* (Cairo, 1901); L. Giddy: *Egyptian oases: Bahariya, Dakhla, Farafra and Kharga during pharaonic times* (Warminster, 1987).

IS

Far'ah, Tell el- (southern Palestine) *see* PHILISTINES

Far'ah, Tell el- (Biblical Tirshah) Settlement site near modern Nablus in northern Palestine, which was occupied from the Pre-pottery Neolithic period (*see* ACERAMIC NEOLITHIC) to the 8th century BC, when the town was destroyed by the Assyrians. The Chalcolithic levels at the site contain sherds of Ghassulian pottery (*see* TELEILAT EL-GHASSUL) as well as flint and basalt artefacts.

R. de Vaux: 'The excavations at Tell el-Farah and the site of the ancient Tirzah', *PEQ* (1956), 125–40; J. Mallet: *Tell-el-Far'ah* (Paris, 1973).

IS

Fara'in, Tell el- (anc. Pe and Dep, Per-Wadjet, Buto) Cluster of three mounds in the northwestern Delta of Egypt. The site comprises a temple complex and the remains of two towns occupied from late predynastic times until the Roman period (*c.*3300 BC–AD 395). Textual sources have identified Buto with 'Pe and Dep', the semi-mythical predynastic twin-capitals of Lower Egypt, but the predynastic strata were not located until the 1980s (von der Way 1992). Von der Way's excavations appear to have revealed a cultural sequence in which Lower Egyptian predynastic pottery types were gradually being replaced by Upper Egyptian Early Dynastic wares.

W.M.F. Petrie and C.T. Currelly: *Ehnasya* (Cairo, 1904); M.V. Seton-Williams and D. Charlesworth: Preliminary reports in *JEA* 51–3, 55 (1965–7, 1969); T. von der Way: 'Excavations at Tell el-Faraʿin/Buto in 1987–1989', *The Nile Delta in transition: 4th–3rd millennium* BC, ed. E.C.M. van den Brink (Tel Aviv, 1992), 1–10.

IS

Faras (anc. Pachoras) Site located on the border between modern Egypt and Sudan, which was initially a small Egyptian fortress dating from the Middle Kingdom (*c.*2040–1640) to the 18th–19th dynasties (*c.*1550–1196 BC) when five Egyptian temples were built. It continued to function as a religious centre after the departure of the Egyptians, and during the Christian period (*c.*AD 550–1500) it was one of the most important bishoprics in Nubia, the cathedral and bishop's palace having survived very well (Michalowski 1962–74). The stratified pottery from the site, as well as the paint-layers and stylistic development of the cathedral murals, have contributed significantly to the development of a chronological framework for Christian Nubia. Polish archaeologists saved 169 painted murals from the cathedral (now in the national museums at Warsaw and Khartoum) before it was flooded by LAKE NASSER.

K. Michaelowski, S. Jakobielski and J. Kubinska: *Faras*, 4 vols (Warsaw, 1962–74); ——: *Faras: Centre artistique de la Nubie chrétienne* (Leiden, 1966); W.Y. Adams: *Nubia: corridor to Africa*, 2nd edn (Princeton, 1984), 226, 472–84.

IS

Fatyanovo Fatyanovo sites – almost exclusively cemeteries – are spread over vast areas of northeastern Europe, from the Ilmen Lake in the west to the Middle Volga in the east, and are generally viewed as the eastern variant of the CORDED WARE culture. The culture was first identified by A.S. Uvarov, A.A. Spitsyn, and V.A. Gorodtsov in the late 19th–early 20th centuries and was thoroughly investigated by D.A. Krainov from the 1940s onwards (Krainov 1972).

Based on the typology of the distinctive battle-axes and pottery, Krainov distinguished several local variants: Dvina-Ilmen; Moskva-Klyazma; Upper Volga; Oka-Desna and Sura-Sviyaga (or Balanovo group, often regarded as an independent cultural tradition). The cemeteries are usually on elevated sites, close to river valleys or lakes. The number of flat graves varies from two to ten in the early stage, to perhaps 125 in the later stages. The dead were usually interred in a contracted posture (males laid on their right side, head to the west; females on their left side, head to the east); burial goods included stone, bone and metal implements, ceramics and animal bones.

Shaft-hole axes were usually found near the head in the male graves; in the juvenile graves they were put at the feet. Copper battle-axes, usually in bark cases, were found exclusively in the richer graves. Female graves contained numerous ornaments made of animal bones and teeth and, in rare cases, metal (bracelets, rings, pendants) or amber. The metal objects were manufactured predominantly from the local ore (copper sandstone of the Middle Volga). Pottery consists mainly of beakers and amphorae, ornamented with rows of cord impressions, incised lines and geometric patterns.

The animal bones belonged largely to domestic pig and sheep/goat. The bones of wild animals (e.g. brown bear, reindeer, elk, wild board, roe deer, fox) are less numerous; fish bones and the shells of river molluscs are also present.

Radiocarbon dates obtained from Turginivi cemetery (Moskva-Klyazma) and Volosovo-Danilovo cemetery (Upper Volga) suggest a calendar date range of 2300–2000 BC, although settlements with Corded Ware assemblages in the Eastern Baltic (e.g. ŠVENTOJI and USVYATY) have yielded earlier dates of *c.*2800–2300 BC.

D.A. Krainov: *Drevneišaja istorija Volgo-Okskogo meždurečja: Fatjanovskaja Kul'tura II tysjač-eletie do n.e.* [The ancient history of the Volga-Oka interfluve: Fatyanovo culture of the 2nd millennium BC] (Moscow, 1972).

PD

Fauresmith Proposed variant of the South African ACHEULEAN, named in 1926 after a town in the Orange Free State, South Africa. The industry is characterized by the small size and refined finish of its handaxes. It seems, however, that it may simply be a raw material variant (lydianite) of the normal Acheulean of the region. A URANIUM SERIES DATING of uncal 200,000 BP at Rooidam indicates a likely date for a 'Fauresmith' site.

A.J.B. Humphreys: 'The role of raw material and the concept of the Fauresmith', *SAAB* 25 (1970), 139–44; B.J. Szabo and K.W. Butzer: 'Uranium-series dating of lacustrine limestones from pan deposits with final Acheulian assemblage at Rooidam, Kimberley District, South Africa', *Quaternary Research* 11 (New York, 1979), 257–60.

RI

feedback *see* SYSTEMS THEORY

feira *see* PORTUGUESE TRADING *FEIRAS*

Fell's Cave Site in Tierra del Fuego, Chile, dating from PALEOINDIAN times (*c.*12000–6000 BC) to the historic period. Fell's Cave and Palli Aike Cave were discovered in the 1930s and were the first Paleoindian sites to be investigated in South America. They are still among the very few sites with a long stratigraphic sequence showing the transition from Paleoindian hunters of megafauna to hunters of modern animals and from prehistoric to historic (the latest occupation at the cave being the historic Ona culture).

J.B. Bird and M. Bird: *Travels and archaeology in South Chile*, ed. J. Hyslop (Iowa, 1988).

KB

feminist archaeology Term used to encompass the concerns of feminists in archaeology. Feminists acknowledge that structured inequalities exist between men and women, and they are committed to challenging and transforming these structures. Within archaeology, feminists seek to expose and remedy male-bias in archaeological interpretation and education, inequalities in professional employment, male-bias in the presentation of archaeology to the public, and to consider issues of female agency as part of a broader programme of GENDER ARCHEOLOGY.

In common with the wider feminist movement, feminist archaeology consists of diverse political and theoretical interest groups. The majority of feminists in archaeology might be described as 'empiricist' feminists who work largely within the accepted academic standards of the discipline. More radical 'standpoint' feminists question the structures within which archaeological knowledge is constructed, sometimes suggesting a greater validity for explicitly feminist research. Because of its critical approach, feminist archaeology has sometimes been viewed as allied to CRITICAL ARCHAEOLOGY or POST-PROCESSUAL ARCHAEOLOGY. Few feminist archaeologists support intuitive interpretations of the past based on the subjectivity of being a woman. Moreover, feminist archaeologists have largely resisted the view that an 'essential' category of woman can be studied in the past, proposing instead that gender is socially constructed and culturally specific.

While feminism has been influential in anthropology for some 20 years, its impact has been apparent in archaeology only from the 1980s. In its primary phase, feminist archaeology consisted mainly of critique. The first published works exposed androcentrism, or male-bias, in archaeological interpretation (Conkey and Spector 1984). Subsequent discussions included the problems of male-bias in the language of archaeology (e.g. 'mankind'), the invisibility of women in the historiography of the discipline, and stereotyped images of men and women in popular books and museum presentation (e.g. Jones and Pay 1990). Like other disciplines, within archaeology the feminist critique of androcentrism was followed by 'remedial' research on women, predominantly concerned with identifying women in archaeological contexts, and finally by a broader reconceptualization of existing subject fields as gender archaeology (Wylie 1991).

The initial criticisms of male-bias in archaeological education and employment have been followed up with extensive surveys of the archaeological profession in America, Australia, Britain, Germany and Scandinavia, and new syllabi have been proposed for incorporating gender into archaeological teaching (Spector and Whelan 1989). A survey of the profession in Britain has shown that while women are relatively well-represented numerically in archaeology (35%), they are discriminated against in a number of ways. Despite holding equal academic qualifications they are less likely to hold management positions or to achieve professional qualifications; they are concentrated in the lower salary bands and levels of responsibility, and they specialize in particular areas of archaeological competence, especially finds, post-excavation research and environmental archaeology; they are least likely to be employed in university teaching and archaeological administration (Morris 1992).

To date, the major contribution of feminist archaeology to academic research has been its critique of the mainstream discipline and its challenge to existing methodologies and research priorities. However, the results of reinterpretations and theory-building have recently come to fruition through contributions to gender archaeology. Feminist concerns with the origins of sexual inequality that dominated early studies have been superseded by issues such as female agency, the cultural construction of the category of 'woman', and the role of women in cultural transformations related to technology, agriculture, religion and social formations (Gero and Conkey 1991; Seifert 1991). The feminist critique continues to unmask male-bias in the definition of academic research, but the male agenda is now replaced with new analyses and interpretations (e.g. Gilchrist 1993). Recent feminist archaeology has integrated a more humanistic approach to the past, seeking to illuminate 'the interpersonal and intimate aspects of social settings' (Gero and Conkey 1991: 15) and to present more 'inclusive' archaeological interpretations (Spector 1991: 389) which will engage audiences of different genders, classes, ethnicities and ages.

M.W. Conkey and J.D. Spector: 'Archaeology and the study of gender', *Advances in Archaeological Method and Theory* 7 (1984), 1–38; J.D. Spector and M.K. Whelan: 'Incorporating gender in archaeology courses', *Gender and anthropology: critical reviews for research and teaching*, ed. S. Morgan (Washington D.C., 1989), 65–94; S. Jones and S. Pay: 'The legacy of Eve', *The politics of the past*, ed. P. Gathercole and D. Lowenthal (London, 1990), 160–71; D.J. Seifert, ed.: 'Gender in historical archaeology', *HA* 25/4 (1991) [whole issue]; J.M. Gero and M.W. Conkey, eds: *Engendering archaeology: women in prehistory* (Oxford, 1991); J.D. Spector: 'What this awl means: towards a feminist archaeology', *Engendering archaeology: women in prehistory*, ed. J.M. Gero and M.W. Conkey (Oxford, 1991), 388–406; A. Wylie: 'Gender theory and the archaeological record. Why is there no archaeology of gender?', *Engendering archaeology: women in prehistory*, ed. J.M. Gero and M.W. Conkey (Oxford, 1991), 31–54: E. Morris, ed.: *Women in British archaeology*, *IFA* Occasional Paper 4 (London, 1992); R. Gilchrist: *Gender and medieval monasticism: the archaeology of religious women* (London, 1993).

RG

Ferrières Late neolithic culture of southern France, the type site of which is the dolmen of Ferrières-les-Verreries in Hérault, near Montpellier. Ferrières pottery is distinctively decorated with incised lines and motifs such as chevrons and 'garlands'. The culture is known mainly from excavations within caves, although it is also found associated with late Neolithic dolmens (as at the type site) and open-air sites towards the east are known.

X. Gutherz: 'Le groupe de Ferrières', *Le Groupe de Véraza et la Fin des Temps Néolithiques dans le Sud de la France et la Catalogne*, ed. J. Guilane (Toulouse, 1980), 217–21.

RJA

Fertile Crescent Crescent-shaped region, the geographical extent of which was originally defined as stretching from the Levant (its 'western horn') to the Mesopotamian river basin (its 'eastern horn'), although later fieldwork on the peripheries has extended the term to include Anatolia and Eastern Arabia. It is traditionally regarded as the region in which the earliest civilizations arose. There is some evidence to suggest that certain important early plants, such as emmer wheat, barley and grapes, may have originally been cultivated in the central part of the Fertile Crescent.

H. Holbaek: 'Domestication of food plants in the Old World', *Science* 130 (1959), 365–72.

IS

fibula (pl. fibulae) Metal and metal composite clothes pins, consisting of a bow, pin and catch, which were used throughout Europe in the 1st millennium BC. Proto-type fibulae seem to have developed in the late 2nd millennium BC, and during the 1st millennium BC these evolved into such a variety of designs that they have proved a useful adjunct to pottery as chronological indicators.

J. Alexander: 'The history of the fibula', *Archaeological theory and practice*, ed. D.E. Strong (London, 1973), 217–30; J. Alexander and S. Hopkin: 'The origins and early development of European fibulae', *PPS* 48 (1982), 401–16.

RJA

field systems Substantial evidence of prehistoric land systems survives in areas of north-west Europe, and particularly in moorland and upland areas of western and northern Britain. The land systems fall into two main classes: extensive linear banks and ditches that are usually supposed to have been constructed to control livestock, and which are often called RANCH BOUNDARIES; and 'field systems', which delineate cultivated areas. The shape of these cultivated areas is made apparent through surviving LYNCHETS and dykes, or through low stone walls or lines of stone and boulder clearance. In Britain, extensive field systems of square, or more often rectangular, fields seems to have been laid out from the early 2nd millennium BC. They are especially well preserved in moorland and downland areas, such as Dartmoor and Shetland, since these have often not been used for intensive agriculture since the prehistoric period; in these areas field systems are often associated with hut circles and other enclosures, and the size of the fields and their proximity to the settlements often suggests a division into hoe plots, ard-ploughed fields, and livestock enclosures. Fleming (1978) provides a classic regional survey in his analysis of the parallel reaves (stone-built walls) of Dartmoor. The marking out of fields seems to represent a move toward a more organized and possibly more intensive use of viable land, and may be a symptom of pressure on existing land resources; it has also been suggested that the climate became warmer and milder in the late 2nd millennium BC, making upland regions more agriculturally viable. (For comparison, ENGARUKA offers an example of a recently studied field system in sub-Saharan Africa.)

J.G. Evans et al., eds: *The effect of man on the landscape*, CBA Research Reports xi and xxi (London, 1975, 1978); A. Fleming: 'The prehistoric landscape of Dartmoor: part 1', *PPS* 44 (1978), 97–123; J.C. Barrett and R.J. Bradley, eds: *Settlement and society in the British Later Bronze Age*, BAR BS 83 (Oxford, 1980); G. Wainwright and K. Smith: 'The Shaugh Moor project: second report – the enclosure', *PPS* 46 (1980), 65–122; G. Barker, ed.: *Prehistoric communities in northern England* (Sheffield, 1981). R. Mercer: *Farming practice in British prehistory* (Edinburgh, 1981).

RJA

Fiji *see* OCEANIA 2

Filitosa Situated on a small hill in the Taravo Valley of southern Corsica, this Bronze Age site consists of a circuit of Cyclopean masonry – built around rocky outcrops – enclosing tower structures of the TORRE type that have been radiocarbon dated to about 1750–1500 BC. One of these was built partly of re-used statue menhirs, and other statue-menhirs have been found in the area. As well as many fragments, at least 13 complete anthropomorphic menhirs have now been located, making Filitosa the most prolific site of its kind. The statues seem to be schematic representations of the warriors of the period: most have either a dagger or a long sword, and some have holes bored in their heads that may have been used to attach horns. The statue-menhirs must predate the tower structures, but possibly not by more than a few centuries.

R. Grosjean: *Filitosa, haut lieu de la Corse préhistorique* (Sartène, 1975); R. Whitehouse: 'Megaliths of the Central Mediterranean' in *The megalithic monuments of Western Europe*, ed. C. Renfrew (London, 1981), 55–9.

RJA

Fine Orange Ware Fine-textured orange-paste pottery manufactured in a variety of forms and widely traded throughout the MAYA LOWLANDS during the Postclassic period (*c.*AD 900–1521). NEUTRON ACTIVATION ANALYSES indicate that the vessels were manufactured in the western Maya lowlands at various still-undetermined locations in the drainage of the Usumacinta River, on the western periphery of the lowlands.

J.A. Sabloff et al.: 'Analyses of fine paste ceramics', *Excavations at Seibal, Department of Petén, Guatemala*, Peabody Museum of Archaeology and Ethnology, Memoirs 15/2, (Cambridge, MA, 1982).

PRI

fire-altars *see* KALIBANGAN

fire altar, fire temple From at least the time of the MEDES onwards, some of the people living in the geographical area now occupied by Iran worshipped a single deity, Ahuramazda. Much later, their religion, Zoroastrianism, was to become the state religion under the Sasanians. Open-air altars on which a sacred fire was burnt formed a focus of worship. Such altars are depicted on rock carvings at Achaemenid sites such as Naqsh-i Rustam, while the earliest surviving 'fire temple' – containing a square mud-brick altar covered in white stucco – was constructed in the 8th century BC at Tepe Nush-i Jan. More controversial are claims that the origins of Zoroastrianism can be traced back to the late 3rd or early 2nd millennium BC in central Asia (Sarianidi 1994).

K. Schippmann: *Die Iranischen Feuerheiligtumer* (Berlin, 1971); R. Boucharlat: 'Monuments religieux de la Perse achémenide, état des questions', *Temples et sanctuaires: séminaire de recherche 1981–1983* (Lyons, 1984), 119–37; V. Sarianidi: 'Temples of Bronze Age Margiana: traditions of ritual architecture', *Antiquity* 68 (1994), 388–97.

IS

First Series *see* ARMORICAN FIRST AND SECOND SERIES GRAVES

First Temperate Neolithic Term occasionally used to describe the first fully formed neolithic (ie farming) cultures of temperate southeast Europe. It includes cultures such as STARCEVO, KÖRÖS, CRIŞ *and* KARANOVO I.

Firuzabad *see* SASANIAN

fish tail point Projectile point characteristic of the period 6000–5000 BC in much of South and Central America. It has a wide tang with a convex end which somewhat resembles a fish's tail.

fission track dating Scientific dating technique used more in geology than archaeology. It is based on the infrequent spontaneous fission of ^{238}U into two roughly equal nuclei, the fission fragments, which are ejected in opposite directions. These nuclei are large, charged and have high energies. As they pass through the matrix they ionize atoms along their path; in an insulating material, to neutralize the charge, these atoms displace and there is a resultant track of damage, some 10–20μm long and a few angstroms wide, which can be made visible by suitable chemical etching. Under the microscope, the number of tracks per unit area is counted. The ^{238}U content is determined by inducing fission, by exposure to thermal neutrons, in ^{235}U, the natural abundance ratio of ^{235}U to ^{238}U is 1:138. The induced number of fission tracks is then counted. Heating the material to a sufficiently high temperature restores order to the matrix, so that recently formed glass, for example, has no fission tracks but they build up with time. It is assumed that the tracks, once formed, are stable. Track size is an indicator of stability and whether the material was initially heated to a sufficiently high temperature to anneal all tracks not of archaeological relevance.

The probability of ^{238}U fission is extremely low (approximately 8×10^{-17} per year). Thus the number of tracks is small (and difficult to identify reliably) unless the uranium content is high or the material is very old. For zircon, the uranium content is typically between 100 and 1000 ppm, and ages as low as a few hundred years are measurable in theory. The random errors depend on the number of tracks counted, but systematic errors are more critical and depend on the value used for the ^{238}U fission probability (which is not well known) and track stability. In archaeology the technique has largely been used for dating volcanic glass and minerals (usually zircon) associated with deposits containing hominid remains.

A.J. Hurford: 'Fission track dating', *Quaternary dating methods – a user's guide*, ed. P.L. Smart and P.D. Frances (Cambridge, 1991), 84–107; G.A. Wagner and P. van der Haute: *Fission-track dating* (Dordrecht, Borton and London, 1992).

SB

Five Mile Rapids Locality on the Columbia River near the Dalles, Oregon, western North America, where two sites (35-WS-1, 35-WS-4) provided the first long sequence of local prehistory (dating from *c.*7800 BC to contact), as well as evidence of the importance of salmon fishing by 5700 BC (Cressman et al. 1960). SERIATION of assemblages from the non-contiguous excavation units was achieved by comparison of percentage frequencies of points, blades, blade fragments, end scrapers, and peripherally flaked cobbles. The cultural-historical model tested was that the Oregon Coast was first populated from the continental interior. The initial early component lacks both salmon bones and diagnostic artefacts, but is generally assigned to the Windust phase (Rice 1972: 164; Cressman 1978: 134), a local variant of the STEMMED POINT TRADITION. The succeeding component, characterized by foliate bifaces, pebble tools, and salmon remains, belongs to the PEBBLE TOOL TRADITION.

L.S. Cressman et al.: *Cultural sequences at the Dalles, Oregon* (Philadelphia, 1960); D.G. Rice: *The Windust phase in lower Snake River region prehistory* (Pullman, 1972); L.S. Cressman: *Prehistory of the Far West* (Salt Lake City, 1978).

RC

Florisbad Warm springs on the South African highveld, close to Bloemfontein, Orange Free State, where an important human fossil skull was discovered in 1932. The skull was assigned to the group of archaic HOMO SAPIENS and estimated to be between 100,000 and 200,000 years old. The complicated sequence of spring deposits contains various MSA (Middle Stone Age) horizons.

T.F. Dreyer: 'The archaeology of the Florisbad deposits', *Argeologiese Navorsing van die Nasionale Museum*, Bloemfontein 1/15 (1938), 183–90; K. Kuman and R.J. Clarke: 'Florisbad – new investigations at a Middle Stone Age hominid site in South Africa', *Geoarchaeology* 1/2 (1986), 103–25.

RI

fluorine uptake Like uranium, fluorine is taken up both by the inorganic (hydroxyapatite) part of bone and by teeth *post mortem* and its concentration level with distance into the bone (*fluorine profile*) gives an indication of age. The concentration of fluorine in the bone differs depending on the burial environment and its use is limited to relative dating. It was used to expose the PILTDOWN MAN forgery (*see also* URANIUM SERIES DATING *and* NITROGEN IN BONE).

K.P. Oakley: 'Analytical methods of dating bones', *Science and Archaeology*, ed. D. Brothwell and E. Higgs (London, 1969), 35–45; G. Coote and S. Holdway: 'Radial profiles of fluorine in archaeological bone and teeth: a review of recent developments', *Archaeometry: an Australian perspective*, ed. W. Ambrose and P. Duerden (Canberra, 1982), 251–62.

SB

Fluted Point Tradition A cultural tradition found throughout North America, except in the coastal regions of Canada north of the United States border and in the far north. In the west many sites simply consist of undated surface finds of distinctive CLOVIS fluted points (Davis and Shutler 1969; Carlson 1983). The most important sites are EAST WENATCHEE, DIETZ, and China Lake (Davis 1978). There are no accepted radiocarbon dates and date estimates of 9500–9000 BC are based on cross-dating with sites in the Southwest and with associated tephra at EAST WENATCHEE. The subsistence pattern of people associated with fluted points is usually that of the BIG GAME HUNTING TRADITION; however, some researchers now believe that megafauna may only have been part of a more diverse subsistence strategy that is less easily discernible within the archaeological record.

E.L. Davis and R. Shutler, Jr.: *Recent discoveries of fluted points in California and Nevada* (Carson City, 1969), 154–69; ——, ed.: *The ancient Californians: Rancholabrean hunters of the Mojave Lakes country* (Los Angeles, 1978); R.L. Carlson: 'The far west', *Early man in the New World*, ed. R.S. Shutler (Beverly Hills, 1983), 73–96; R. Bonnischsen and K.L. Turnmire, eds: *Clovis origins and adaptations* (Corvallis, 1991).

RC

Folsom Late PALEOINDIAN tradition (*c.*9000–8500 BC) which followed the LLANO tradition on the Great Plains and in other parts of western North America. The type-site, located eight miles west of modern Folsom in New Mexico, was discovered by George McJunkin, a black cowboy. It was excavated in 1926–7 by Jesse Figgins of the Denver Museum of Natural History, revealing the first North American instance of a clear association between the undisturbed remains of human activity in the Pleistocene and the articulated bones of an extinct animal (*Bison antiquus*). Folsom-tradition hunters heavily exploited the large herds of bison that roamed the Great Plains at this time, using new hunting strategies, such as the cul-de-sac technique, to kill many bison at one time. Much of what is known about Folsom culture comes from the excavation of such bison-kill sites (thus probably giving undue emphasis to this aspect of the Folsom way of life). The Lindenmeier site in Colorado, however, appears to have been a Folsom campsite. Folsom projectile points are fluted like CLOVIS points, but smaller, thinner and with the flute extending almost to the tip of the point.

E. Wilmsen: *Lindenmeier: a Pleistocene hunting society* (New York, 1978); —— and F.H.H. Roberts: *Lindenmeier, 1934–1974: concluding report on investigation* (Washington D.C., 1978).

RJE/JJR

Fontbouisse culture Late Neolithic to Chalcolithic culture of southern France. Fontbouisse pottery is finely finished in a variety of forms, decorated with complicated incised motifs ('garland' patterns, chessboard patterns etc.). The distribution of the culture is similar to that of the FERRIÈRES culture, but is concentrated in open-air settlements (rather than cave sites). Fontbouisse settlements typically comprise small numbers of huts (5–15) built rather closely together, but without much evidence of planning. Huts often show evidence of hearths and large storage vessels. There are a few more complex Fontbouisse settlements, notably the enclosed and (arguably) fortified sites of Lébous and Boussargues (Hérault), which exhibit a drystone enclosure wall, built onto which are a series of round drystone structures. The excavator (Arnal) has interpreted Lébous as a settlement defended by a bastioned wall. This would invite analogies with other Mediterranean cultures with bastioned defended enclosures of the same date (such as the LOS MILLARES culture) – however, other authorities have suggested that the circular wall structures are shepherds huts and that the walling is too insubstantial to justify calling Lébous 'fortified'.

J. Arnal: 'Le Lébous: un château préhistorique', *Archéologia* 58 (1973).

RJA

Font de Gaume Palaeolithic painted and engraved cave, 2 km from Les Eyzies, France. About 200 animals are depicted, often superimposed upon each other. Most of the art is thought to date to the Magdalenian (from *c.*15,000 to 10,000 BC); the superimposition and the various styles have inspired various schemes of relative dating. Discovered in 1901 by Denis Peyrony, analysis by Henri Breuil in 1910 identified around 80 bison, 40 horses, 23 mammoths, and 17 reindeer or deer; polychrome friezes of the bison in the Main Gallery are particularly remarkable.

L. Capitan, H. Breuil and D. Peyrony: *La caverne de Font-de-Gaume aux Eyzies* (Dordogne) (Monaco, 1910); P. Daubisse et al.: *La grotte de Font-de-Gaume* (Périgueux, 1984).

RJA

foraging theory Body of theory used to explain variability in the foraging behaviour of individuals and groups. Developed in evolutionary ecology during the 1960s, it has been used in anthropology and archaeology since the 1970s. Foraging models specifically address the issues of 'patch choice', diet breadth and group size. In archaeology, one of the most promising applications is to explain variability in the contents of faunal assemblages across space and time; of course, one must also take into account the many and complex effects of assemblage formation and SITE FORMATION PROCESSES. Archaeological applications of foraging theory may take the form of quantitative models, or may simply use concepts drawn from foraging theory without explicit modelling.

The underlying assumption behind foraging theory is that the decision rules used by predators have been shaped by natural selection to result in 'efficient' foraging, and thus reproductive success. The models and applications are not concerned with the question of whether behaviour is in any sense 'optimal', but with identifying the efficiency criteria (or 'foraging goals') of a particular forager. Goals may include: the maximization of the rate of energy gain; the minimization of time spent foraging (and hence exposure time for predation); the minimization in the variance of the food supply. Human foragers are likely to use a combination of such goals and to frequently switch goals.

Two of the most important models are the diet breadth (prey choice) model and the patch-use model. The first concerns the number and character of prey items within the diet. Assuming a random encounter with prey types, which of these should be exploited by the forager, and which ignored, if he/she is to achieve the foraging goal? Appropriate applications of this model might be with carcass scavenging in the Lower Palaeolithic (e.g. Lake 1994) or Mesolithic hunting in the forests of northern Europe (see case-study below).

The patch-use model is applicable when prey types are heterogeneously distributed and a 'patch' refers to a discrete resource or set of resources. It is concerned with two questions: which patch to choose and how long to remain within it. For the latter, the 'marginal value' theorem has been developed. This states that one should remain within a patch until its marginal rate of energetic gain falls below that of the average for the environment as a whole. The patch-use model is appropriate for studying Upper Palaeolithic economies in south-west Europe for which we can think of foragers as choosing between different patches, either in terms of biomes (e.g. coastal, mountain) or resources (e.g. red deer, salmon or ibex). Patch-use models have been used in the analysis of the foraging behaviour of modern hunter-gatherers such as the Alyawara aborigines of Australia (O'Connell and Hawkes 1984).

In building such models it is necessary to define the costs, benefits and risks acting upon a forager with a hypothesized foraging goal. Costs may be measured in time, energetic requirements or raw materials – or some combination of these. For hunting, costs are often divided between search and handling times, i.e. the time spent in locating a prey item and that spent killing, butchering and preparing it for consumption. Benefits may similarly be measured in terms of the material acquisition and energetic gain, while the risks relate to the unpredictable fluctuations in these. The constraints acting on a forager when making decisions must also be considered. These may be various but the most important is the information with which a forager has to make his or her decisions.

The aim of foraging models which use a cost-benefit analysis is to set up templates against which the observed/inferred behaviour of real foragers can be compared. By this means an attempt can be made to assess whether the correct efficiency criteria and set of constraints have been identified. Often the modelling process is one of gradual refinement as particular variables are included or excluded from the model, and as the model becomes more complex and realistic. In this respect, one of the most important benefits from the development of foraging models is derived from the modelling process itself which encourages clear, explicit thinking about past foraging behaviour.

The application of foraging theory to ecology and anthropology/archaeology has taken place in two stages. The early models tended to be rather crude and deterministic: the efficiency criterion was almost always the rate of energetic gain, and limited constraints on foragers' behaviour were included. Foragers were often assumed to have complete information about available resources. Since the late 1970s, more sophisticated and interesting models have been developed (e.g. Winterhalder and Smith 1981). In these, greater emphasis is placed on variability within the natural environment, the role of stochastic factors during foraging activity and the minimization of risk as a foraging goal. Information flow and the lack of knowledge about the environment play a critical role in these models. The problem with such models is that they become mathematically complex.

A complementary approach has been to try to model the proximate decision-making itself, i.e. the psychological processes people actually use to make decisions (see Mithen 1989), rather than to derive optimal foraging strategies for use as templates. In this case, we become more concerned with the 'rules of thumb' that may lead decision makers *towards* optimal strategies, i.e. ones that are meliorizing.

Case Study: Mesolithic foraging in Southern Scandinavia. The later Mesolithic period of southern Scandinavia (*c.*7500–5000 BP) is characterized by a large series of settlements with well-preserved faunal remains. Considerable inter-site variability has been identified, in terms of the frequency of different species and the season of year when they were exploited. Concepts and models drawn from foraging theory (and DECISION THEORY) can be used to explain such patterning.

The analysis of faunal assemblages by specialists such as Peter Rowley-Conwy (1983, 1987) has resulted in sophisticated models for the Mesolithic settlement pattern involving the use of base camps, some of which may have been occupied for long periods if not on a sedentary basis, and a wide range of specialist task-specific sites. Such models are simply descriptive of Mesolithic foraging; to actually explain it we need to turn to foraging theory.

Rowley-Conwy has suggested that Danish sites such as ERTEBØLLE, Bjørnsholm and Meilgaard are likely to have been large base camps and possibly permanent settlements. These are found in 'generalized' locations that give access to coastal, terrestrial and freshwater resources. Often the faunal remains from these sites indicate that they were occupied at all seasons of the year. Complementing these large settlements are a range of smaller sites with smaller faunal assemblages marking locations where specialized hunting activities were undertaken in particular seasons. For instance Åggersund contains very high frequencies of Whooper swan, and the evidence indicates winter occupation, while Vaengo Sø, located on a small islet a few metres from the shore, has an assemblage of whale bones and is likely to have been a location where stranded whales were exploited.

A similar range of sites is found in southern Sweden. Here the large multi-phase settlement-cemetery site of Skateholm has a remarkably diverse faunal assemblage indicating hunting in all biomes and all seasons of the year. Other sites, such as Segebro, may also have been large base camps, while sites such as Agerod 1:D and Agerod V, with assemblages dominated by red deer, appear to be small-scale hunting camps probably used in specific seasons.

Foraging theory can be drawn upon to help explain the nature of these faunal assemblages. In essence, they represent the results of choices made by Mesolithic foragers, such as the decision to hunt swans at Åggersund in the winter or to hunt red deer from Agerod V. To explain the variability in the archaeological record it is necessary to try to understand why such choices were made. In this light we might consider the different resources or biomes as 'patches' and use notions from the patch-use model. To do so, we would need to estimate the costs, benefits and risks of exploiting each of the alternative patches at any particular moment. For this, it would be necessary to draw on an understanding of the ecology of these species and the nature of Mesolithic technology. On the basis of these estimates and an assumed foraging goal and set of constraints for the Mesolithic hunters, a foraging strategy (i.e. a series of choices made at each time of the year) could be predicted. From this strategy certain expectations for the character of the archaeological record could be established on the basis of simple mathematical equations. These, and expectations derived from the use of alternative foraging goals, could be compared against the real data to examine which provides the best fit. The 'best-fit' model would then supply a useful indication of the probable foraging strategy.

The prey-choice model might be used to explore the exploitation of one particular patch in more detail. For instance, a recent study (Mithen 1990: chs 4–6) has built a model for the exploitation of large terrestrial game (such as red deer, wild pig and roe deer) by Mesolithic foragers. These animals were exploited by 'encounter foraging' in the forests of Denmark and Sweden. By drawing on literature concerning the behaviour of these species and ethnographic studies of hunting, it was possible to estimate the probability of encounter, the utility, pursuit time, processing costs and the risk involved for each species. By using computer SIMULATION methods various different foraging goals were explored for the Mesolithic foragers and it was found that when the goal of increasing the rate of energetic gain was adopted, the resulting archaeological record had significant similarities to that from southern Sweden. The foraging patterns arising from this goal involved considerable variation in the opportunities to acquire game (i.e. they involved high risk), and the study suggested that such risk was ameliorated by the exploitation of other resources in other patches, such as plants and freshwater fish.

B. Winterhalder and E.A. Smith: *Hunter-gatherer foraging strategies: ethnographic and archaeological analysis* (Chicago, 1981); P. Rowley-Conwy: 'Sedentary hunters: the Ertebølle example', *Hunter-gatherer economy in prehistory*, ed. G.N. Bailey (Cambridge, 1983), 111–26; E.A. Smith: 'Anthropological applications of optimal foraging theory: a critical review', *CA* 24 (1983), 625–51; J. O'Connell and K. Hawkes: 'Food choice and foraging sites among the Alyawara', *Jar* 40 (1984), 504–35; B. Winterhalder: 'Diet choice, risk and food sharing in a stochastic environment', *JAA* 5 (1986), 369–92; P. Rowley-Conwy: 'Animal bones in Mesolithic studies: recent progress and hopes for the future', *Mesolithic northwest Europe: recent trends*, ed. P. Rowley-Conwy, M. Zvelebil and H.-P. Blankholm (Sheffield, 1987), 74–89; S. Mithen: 'Modelling hunter-gatherer decision making: complementing optimal foraging theory', *Journal of Human Ecology* 17/1 (1989), 43–89; L. Larson: 'The Mesolithic of southern Scandinavia', *JWP* 4 (1990),

257–309; S. Mithen: *Thoughtful foragers: a study of prehistoric decision making* (Cambridge, 1990); M. Lake: *Simulating early hominid foraging behaviour* (unpublished Ph.D. thesis, University of Cambridge, 1994).

SM

forces of production *see* MARXIST ARCHAEOLOGY; MODE OF PRODUCTION

forensic archaeology Form of archaeology in which the data is examined and interpreted within a legal context, usually with the aim of assisting criminal investigations. As Hunter et al. (1996: 11) point out: 'There is a theme common to the work of archaeologists and the work of investigating police officers; both endeavour to understand the nature, sequence, and underlying reasons for certain events in past time.'

The origins of forensic archaeology as a subdiscipline may be traced back either to the 18th-century origins of forensic science itself or to the emergence of forensic anthropology in the USA from the 19th century onwards. It has been suggested that George Dorsey, an anthropologist based in Chicago in the late 19th century, may have been the earliest genuine forensic scientist: Adolf Luetgert, a sausage manufacturer, was arrested for the murder of his wife, and Dorsey was able to identify her remains among the bones from a vat in Luetgert's factory. In 1971, the physical anthropology section of the American Academy of Forensic Sciences was established, and five years later a course in forensic anthropology began to be taught at Florida State University (see Snow 1982). When forensic anthropologists are called in to examine a set of remains, they usually attempt to answer the following five questions: (1) Are the remains human? (2) How many individuals are represented? (3) What was the interval of time since death? (4) Can the individual(s) be identified? (5) What was the cause and manner of death?

The growth of forensic archaeology in Britain is a relatively modern phenomenon, compared with its long history in the USA. As recently as 1983, outrage was expressed by some professional archaeologists at the relatively crude nature of a police excavation of a garden in north London where a multiple murderer had buried the remains of his victims. After this event, closer co-operation between the British police and archaeologists led to a gradual adaptation of archaeological techniques to the very specific demands of forensic examination. Thus, as Hunter et al. (1996: 16) point out, forensic archaeologists have to operate within a set of stringent legal parameters if they are to ensure that their evidence is admissable in a court of law: 'Appropriate authority has to be received before removal or disturbance; access routes have to be defined; and the handling of the material via a defined and logged chain of custody is critical.'

T.D. Stewart: *Essentials of forensic anthropology* (Springfield, 1979); C.C. Snow: 'Forensic anthropology', *ARA* 11 (1982), 97–131; D. Morse et al.: *Handbook of forensic archaeology and anthropology* (Tallahassee, 1983); A. Boddington et al., eds: *Death, decay and reconstruction: approaches to archaeology and forensic science* (Manchester, 1987); J. Hunter, C. Roberts and A. Martin: *Forensic archaeology* (London, 1996); W.D. Haglund and M.H. Sorg, eds: *Forensic taphonomy: the postmortem fate of human remains* (Boca Raton, New York and London, 1997).

IS

formal analogy *see* ETHNOARCHAEOLOGY

formal analysis Approach to archaeological data that concentrates on the form of the data rather than the content, the aim being to analyse patterns and to try to understand the cultural or environmental rules according to which they were constructed. Dorothy Washburn (1983), for example, focuses on the arrangement of design motifs decorating pottery vessels, rather than analysing the *meaning* of the individual motifs. She thus attempts to define the nature of the societies producing the pottery through their adherence to certain principles of design. Formal analysis also often places little emphasis, in the first instance, on the cultural context in which artefacts were produced. It can be applied not only to pottery decoration but also to architecture, site planning and any other arranged body of data.

Shanks and Tilley (1987: 98–9) point out that it is possible to explore the formal structure of material culture by treating the archaeological data as if it were a written text, arguing that objects in the archaeological record are connected with one another by a system of connections similar to the grammars, codes and syntax of language (*see* COGNITIVE ARCHAEOLOGY for a related discussion). Bill Hillier (1996) uses a similar linguistic approach as the basis for his formal analysis of the 'syntax of space', i.e. the way in which space is manipulated and divided up by humans as they impose themselves on their environment. *See also* POST-STRUCTURALISM, STRUCTURALISM *and* SYSTEMS THEORY.

B. Hillier et al.: 'Space syntax', *Environment and Planning*, Series B3 (1976), 147–85; R. Fletcher: 'Settlement studies (micro and semi-micro)', *Spatial archaeology*, ed. D.L. Clarke (New York, 1977); D. Washburn, ed.: *Structure and*

cognition in art (Cambridge, 1983); M. Shanks and C. Tilley: *Social theory and archaeology* (Oxford, 1987), 98–105; I. Hodder: *Reading the past*, 2nd edn (Cambridge, 1991), 37–41; B. Hillier: *Space is the machine* (New York, 1996).
IS

formation processes *see* SITE FORMATION PROCESSES

Fort Ancient Late Prehistoric cultural tradition (*c.* AD 1000–1700) in North America, instances of which have been found throughout the middle Ohio River valley including portions of extreme southern Indiana, southern Ohio, central and eastern Kentucky, and western West Virginia. Important Fort Ancient sites include Madisonville, Anderson and Hardin Village. Through time, Fort Ancient communities increased in size and complexity, although never developing chiefdom-level societies like their MISSISSIPPIAN contemporaries who lived to the south and west. Fort Ancient diet was based on a combination of cultivated plants (maize, beans, squash), nuts and wild game (elk, bear, white-tailed deer, turkey).

P.S. Essenpreis: 'Fort Ancient settlement: differential response at a Mississippian-Late Woodland interface', *Mississippian settlement patterns*, ed. B.D. Smith (New York, 1978), 141–67; D. Pollack and A.G. Henderson: 'Toward a model of Fort Ancient society', *Fort Ancient cultural dynamics in the Middle Ohio Valley*, ed. A.G. Henderson (Madison, 1992), 218–94.
RJE

Fort Rock Cave Site in the pluvial lakes region of eastern Oregon, in western North America, which was first excavated in 1938 by Luther Cressman. Finds included woven sandals of the early 7th millennium BC, which were among the first samples to be dated by RADIOCARBON analysis (Cressman 1942; 1951). It was also at Fort Rock Cave that TEPHROCHRONOLOGY was first employed in western North America, with subsequent dating of the Mount Mazama tephra at about 4800 BC. Another series of excavations took place at the site in 1966–7 (Bedwell 1973), when quantitative analyses using CHI-SQUARED TESTS and an F-test to analyse variance were employed. The earliest radiocarbon date of 11250–720 BC (Gak 1738) is from Bedwell's excavations. This is suspect because of the large standard deviation and the associated artefact types which, at other sites, are dated about 2000 years younger. The earliest component at Fort Rock Cave belongs to the intermontane STEMMED POINT TRADITION.

L.S. Cressman: *Archaeological researches in the northern Great Basin* (Washington D.C., 1942); ——: 'Western prehistory in the light of carbon 14 dating', *Southwestern Journal of Anthropology* 7 (1951), 289–313; D.G. Rice: *The Windust phase in lower Snake River region prehistory* (Pullman, 1972); S.F. Bedwell: *Fort Rock Basin prehistory and environment* (Eugene, 1973).
RC

Franchthi cave Cave site northwest of Porto Kheli on the coast of the southern Argolid peninsula, Greece. Excavations at the site (1967–79) have produced a unique stratigraphic sequence from *c.*18,000–4000 BC that is helping to clarify the region's transition from hunting and gathering to an economy based upon agriculture and domesticated animals. The seasonal use of Franchthi may have begun in the Upper Palaeolithic, possibly at the time of the final Würm glaciation *c.*18,000 BC. The faunal remains in the earlier periods are dominated by horse, giving way to red deer and bison by the early Mesolithic. Lentils, vetches, almonds, wild oats and barley were gathered in this period. The later Mesolithic, in the 8th millennium BC, is marked by the use of obsidian (apparently brought by sea 150 km from the island of Melos) and by the exploitation of large fish such as tunny. About 7000 BC, after a possible gap in occupation, domesticated sheep and goats were suddenly introduced, together with emmer wheat and two-row hulled barley. Their introduction is associated with polished stone axes, flint sickles and millstones. At about the same time pottery appears and a new occupation area was established just to the northwest of the cave (named 'Paralia' by the excavators). It has been suggested (e.g. Whittle 1994) – but not yet proven – that Franchti represents an example of the adoption of agriculture and animal husbandry by a native Mesolithic population that was in touch by sea with early farming communities of the eastern Mediterranean. Paralia was occupied for much of the Greek Neolithic (i.e. until *c.*4000BC) and its excavation has provided usefully controlled examples of Neolithic pottery, figurines and obsidian.

T.W. Jacobsen, general ed.: *Excavations at Franchthi Cave, Greece, Fascicles 1–* (Bloomington and Indianopolis, 1987–); A. Whittle: 'The first farmers', *The Oxford Illustrated Prehistory of Europe*, ed. B. Cunliffe (Oxford, 1994), 138.
RJA

frostmarks/snowmarks These marks are formed in the same way as dampmarks (*see* SOILMARKS), but may be seen in aerial photographs of bare soil or, less usually, low vegetation. They are formed by the differential melting – either positive

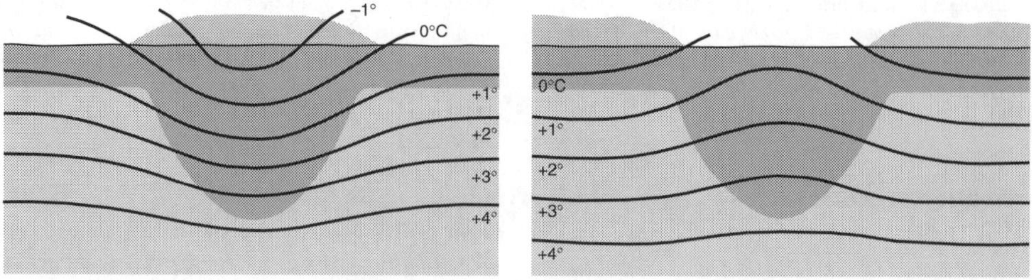

Figure 17 **frostmarks** Frost and snowmarks over buried features may show either negatively (left) or positively (right). At first, a buried feature with fill of raised organic content may remain warmer than its surroundings (left), but after a prolonged cold spell it may become colder (right). *Source*: O. Braasch: *Luftbildarchäologie in Süddeutschland* (Stuttgart, 1983).

or negative – of frost or snow over buried features, caused by their different heat-retaining properties. The same feature may produce either positive or negative marks, as the cause is the variation in the coefficient of heating between the buried feature and the surrounding subsoil. These marks have been a key source of information in much Central European flying in recent years (Braasch 1983). In addition, the visibility of low earthworks may be increased in conditions of frost and snow (*see* AERIAL ARCHAEOLOGY for general discussion).

O. Braasch: *Luftbildarchäologie in Süddeutschland* (Stuttgart, 1983).

FG

Fufeng (Fu-feng) *see* WESTERN CHOU

Fu-hao *see* AN-YANG

Fukui Cave Site in Nagasaki prefecture, Japan, which has yielded sherds from the oldest dated ceramic vessels in the world. Radiocarbon-dated to 12,700 BP, the earliest sherds were thin-walled and decorated with thin appliqué strips of clay and were associated with typical Late Palaeolithic obsidian microliths, indicating continuity between the non-ceramic Palaeolithic and the Jomon period (*see* JAPAN 1–2).

Y. Kamaki and C. Serizawa: 'Nagasaki-ken Fukui doketsu' [Fukui Cave, Nagasakai Prefecture], *Nihon no Doketsu Iseki* [Cave sites in Japan] (Tokyo, 1967); C.M. Aikens and T. Higuchi: *The prehistory of Japan* (London, 1982), 99–104.

SK

Funan The earliest known state in Southeast Asia, which dates to AD 100–550 and was centred on the flat and low-lying land west of the Bassac River in southern Vietnam. Some scholars prefer the Sanskrit term *MANDALA*, meaning a circle, rather than the word 'state' when describing Funan; the former brings with it the notion of a polity with fluid boundaries ringed by like entities, and centred on the overlord and his ability to attract and retain followers. Inscriptions reveal the adoption of Sanskrit names for rulers, while archaeology has confirmed the presence of moated cities such as the coastal settlement of OC EO, substantial brick buildings and intensive trade contacts with both India and the Mekong hinterland.

It seems likely that the capital of the Funan polity was the site of Angkor Borei, 70 km south of Phnom Pehn. Two Chinese visitors in the mid-3rd century AD described the area as Funan, noting walled settlements, palaces, taxation and a writing system (evidently of Indian origin). Angkor Borei is a nodal centre within the canal system, lying at the northern end of a 90 km canal linking it to OC EO. Coinage of Roman and Iranian origin shows that the Funan region was itself a nodal point in a trade route connecting the Roman and Chinese empires. Centres were linked by a network of canals, which would have been used in the moving of goods and as a means of draining the flat lowlands of floodwater. By the middle of the 6th century AD, the centre of political power had moved to the middle Mekong, with the establishment of the *mandalas* of the ZHENLA CULTURE (AD 550–800).

C. Jacques: ' "Funan", "Zhenla": the reality concealed by these Chinese views of Indochina', *Early South East Asia*, ed. R.B. Smith and W. Watson (Oxford, 1979), 371–9; P. Wheatley: *Nagara and Commandery* (Chicago, 1983).

CH

functionalist argument, functionalism In its widest sense, an approach to describing and explaining societies and cultures that recognizes a functional relationship between different elements within society, or a functional relationship between society as a whole and its wider environment. Functionalist arguments often explain the nature of a particular social phenomenon by reference to the contribution it makes to the continuation of a society of a particular character. Functional descriptions of the internal workings of societies and cultures tend to assume that *all* significant elements of societies serve describable functions or purposes, and are interdependent – which implies that change in one element or institution leads to change in society as a whole. In this sense, a functionalist paradigm underlies many classic explanations of the growth of complexity in civilizations, such as Wittfogel's theory of HYDRAULIC DESPOTISM. Functionalist assumptions also underlie the descriptive and explanatory approach known as SYSTEMS THEORY, as well as much MARXIST theory and interpretation.

Although functionalist explanations do not really form a systematized body of thought, the functionalist approach to explaining the internal workings of a society can be traced back to the works of Émile Durkheim (1858–1917), a founder of modern sociology. Durkheim developed the concept of a social system composed of functionally related parts – he often used the analogy of the organs of the body – in opposition to contemporary explanations for the existence of social institutions based on the random circumstances of history and cultural environment (essentially, the CULTURE HISTORY approach). Although Durkheim recognized the importance of historical analysis, his work focused on the mechanisms which held society together at any one time. This relative disinterest in the mechanisms of change can also be seen in the work of later 'functionalist' anthropologists such as Radcliffe-Brown (e.g. Radcliffe-Brown 1922) or Bronislaw Malinowski (e.g. Malinowski 1939). In sociology, functionalist explanation reached a peak in elaboration with the work of Talcott Parsons (1902–79) who developed a school of 'structural-functionalism'. This was based on the idea that systems and subsystems functioned in various ways to achieve four things: adaptation to the physical environment; goal attainment; integration (i.e. social cohesion and orderliness); and latency (i.e. system stability). However, functionalist explanations were heavily criticized in sociology from the 1960s onwards because they tended to ignore change over time. This has also proved to be a weakness in archaeological applications of systems theory, though mitigated by concepts such as the 'multiplier effect' and catastrophe theory.

In archaeology, there has also been a tendency to give primacy to economic or materialist functions. An example might be the argument put forward by Lewis and Sally Binford (1969) that MOUSTERIAN assemblages excavated in southwestern France were different toolkits, used for different functional tasks, rather than being the equipment used by different ethnic groups as Francois Bordes had proposed (Bordes and de Sonneville-Bordes 1970; Mellars 1970).

Trigger (1989, 247) uses the term 'environmental functionalism' as a catch-all to describe those accounts of cultures, written from the 19th century on, that give environmental circumstance or change (for example, the distribution of LINEARBANDKERAMIK settlement in relation to LOESS soil) a primary role in the explanation of culture and cultural change. Here the environment is seen as precipitating a functional response in a whole society. While often offering an explanation for social change over time, such explanations tend to be deterministic: that is, they tend to assume that the functionalist response manifest by a society is the only possible response.

A.R. Radcliffe-Brown: *The Andaman Islanders* (Cambridge 1922); B. Malinowski: 'The group and the individual in functional analysis', *American Journal of Sociology* 44 (1939), 938–64; S.R. and L.R. Binford: 'A preliminary analysis of functional variability in the Mousterian of Levallois facies', *American Anthropologist* 68 (1969), 238–95; F. Bordes and D. de Sonneville-Bordes: 'The significance of variability in Palaeolithic assemblages', *WA* 2 (1970), 61–73; P.A. Mellars: 'Some comments on the notion of "functional variability" in stone tool assemblages', *WA* 2 (1970), 74–89; G.R. Willey and J.A. Sabloff: *A history of American archaeology*, 2nd edn (San Francisco, 1980), 130–80; R. Dunnell: 'Five decades of American archaeology', *American archaeology: past and future*, ed. D. Meltzer et al. (Washington D.C., 1986), 23–49; G. Clark: *Economic prehistory: papers on archaeology* (Cambridge, 1988); B.G. Trigger: *A history of archaeological thought* (Cambridge, 1989), 244–88.

RJA

al-Fustat Site on the edge of Cairo in Egypt, which is one of the most extensively excavated of the great urban sites of the Islamic period. The extent of its ruin fields and the depth of medieval overburden is so vast that relatively little of the site has been exposed. Resources to clear such great areas have always been limited; had they been available, the site may have been revealed as an Islamic Pompeii. A particular problem at al-Fustat, however, is the tendency of builders in all periods to strike down to bedrock when digging foundations. This has disrupted the traces of the earliest occupation on the site. Based on texts and archaeology, W. Kubiak (1987) has produced a masterly interpretation of the planning and evolution of early al-Fustat. In the early period, fuelled by immigration from Arabia and Syria and the revenue of taxation, al-Fustat sucked technical skills from Alexandria that allowed rapid development of its industries in the fields of glass, ceramic and textile production.

The excavations of George Scanlon (1994) have lent support to the textual evidence suggesting that the city was given a coherent street plan in about AD 700. Scanlon's work also attests to the complexity of the water and sewage system of the town. Final publication is still awaited, but Kubiak's study is a model of what can be achieved with the synthesis of texts and archaeological results.

R. Guest: 'The foundation of Fustat and the Khittahs of that town', *JRAS* (1907), 49–83; J.-C. Garcin: 'Toponomie et topographie urbaines médiévales au Fustat et au Claire', *JESHO* 37 (1984), 113–55; W.B. Kubiak: *Al-Fustat: its foundation and early development* (Cairo, 1987); G.T. Scanlon: 'Al-Fustât: the riddle of the earliest settlement', *The Byzantine and early Islamic Near East II: land use and settlement patterns*, ed. G.R.D. King and A. Cameron (Princeton, 1994), 171–9.

GK

Funnel Beaker culture (Funnel Neck Beaker) *see* TRB

G

gallery grave One of the two main types of Neolithic chambered tomb (the other being the PASSAGE GRAVE), defined by an elongated chamber or 'gallery' that is entered directly – rather than via a passage. In some examples the galleries make a 'dog's leg'. The more complex examples have side chambers and an end chamber opening off the main gallery, in which case the main gallery effectively functions as a passage; this can make the distinction between a gallery grave and a passage grave confusing, the essential difference being that in a complex gallery grave the central gallery is nearly always as high and wide as the subsidiary chambers, whereas in a passage grave the passage is of markedly inferior dimensions and the chamber is designed as the focal point of the tomb. As a general rule gallery graves are covered by a sub-rectangular (often wedge-shaped) mound, while passage graves have round tumuli. The SEVERN-COTSWOLD tombs are perhaps the most well-researched group of gallery graves in Britain. Variants of the gallery grave design include the 'segmented gallery graves', such as the Clyde group, in which the gallery is subdivided by slabs.

RJA

Gamble's Cave One of two adjacent rockshelters with substantial internal and external Stone Age deposits. The site, overlooking Lake Elmenteita in the Eastern Rift Valley in Kenya, was formed by wave action in the wet period of the early Holocene when the level of Lake Elmenteita rose to combine with Lake Nakuru, forming a vast expanse of water that overflowed into the Nile basin. The archaeological potential of Gamble's Cave was appreciated in the 1920s by Louis Leakey (1931) who thus undertook one of the first excavations of note in East Africa. The upper deposits contained 'ELMENTEITAN' lithics and pottery; below were encountered various stages of a blade tradition which Leakey at first called 'Kenya Aurignacian', and later 'KENYA CAPSIAN'. The lowest levels of the site lie on a beach sand and are now dated to *c.*7000–5000 BC (much later than Leakey had imagined); finds here include a bone harpoon fragment of Nile basin type and a few sherds of pottery also of the Nilotic and Saharan 'AQUALITHIC' (or 'Khartoum horizon' style) of the early Holocene.

L.S.B. Leakey: *The Stone Age cultures of Kenya colony* (Cambridge, 1931), 90–175; J.E.G. Sutton: 'New radiocarbon dates for eastern and southern Africa', *JAH* 13 (1972), 3–4.

JS

game theory Mathematical formalization of the processes of making decisions and formulating strategies (*see also* DECISION THEORY) which was first developed in the 1940s by the American mathematician John von Neumann (see Neumann and Morgenstern 1964). It has subsequently been applied to many areas of study, such as evolutionary biology, philosophy, psychology and economics. The application of game theory to archaeological data involves the assessment and quantification of the probabilities and values of various outcomes of action which might be chosen in particular cultural and environmental contexts. In the field of human evolution, John Maynard Smith (1988) introduced the concept of an ESS (evolutionarily stable strategy), i.e. a strategy which dominates the human population in question, and therefore has to be able to compete successfully against other similar strategies. As Richard Dawkins (1989: 282) puts it: 'An ESS is a strategy that does well against copies of itself.'

J. von Neumann and O. Morgenstern: *The theory of games and economic behaviour*, 3rd edn (New York, 1964); J. Maynard Smith: *Games, sex and evolution* (London, 1988); R. Dawkins: *The selfish gene*, 2nd edn (Oxford, 1989).

IS

Gandhara The Gandhara period is a distinctive stylistic phase in South Asian Buddhist art, dating to the 1st–3rd centuries AD. The period is named after its geographic centre, the Gandhara region (comprising the Peshawar Valley in northwest Pakistan and Afghanistan) and corresponds to the period of Central Asian rule known as the Kushana period (late 1st to mid-3rd century AD). The

Gandhara period is also frequently described as the Indo-Greek period of Buddhist sculpture, since clear Greek and Roman influence can be seen in the facial features and draped robes of the numerous stone sculptures of the Buddha that characterize this period.

V.A. Smith: *The Oxford History of India*, 4th edn (Delhi, 1981), 151, 154–5; S.J. Czuma: *Kushan sculpture: images from early India* (Cleveland, 1985), 18–25.

CS

Gandhara grave culture Characteristic protohistoric cemetery sites in the region of Swat, Pakistan. According to calibrated radiocarbon dates, these sites range from the late 2nd millennium to the end of the 1st millennium BC. Important cemetery sites include Katelai, Loebanr and Timargarha; little is known of settlement sites from this period, though some small test excavations have been conducted at Balambai and Aligrama.

The Gandharan graves are rectangular pits, sometimes enclosed within stone circles and covered by stone slabs. Most contain primary inhumations of one or two individuals, but there are also remains of cremations and secondary burials. Two horse burials are known from Katelai, and an iron bit was recovered at Timargarha. The graves contain large quantities of undecorated wheel-made pottery, including tall, slender jars and beakers and pedestal vessels; throughout the material culture there are strong parallels with sites in eastern Iran. It has been suggested that the cemeteries may contain remains of peoples from diverse ethnic backgrounds, with the cremation graves most strongly associated with populations who originated to the west of the Swat region. Terracotta female figurines and pins of copper and bronze are commonly found at Gandhara sites, but iron artefacts are rare until after 400 BC.

A.H. Dani et al.: 'Timargarha and the Gandhara grave culture', *AP* 3 (1967), 1–407; C. Silva Antonini and G. Stacul: *The proto-historic graveyards of Swat*, 2 vols (Rome, 1972); ——: 'Inhumation and cremation in Northwest Pakistan at the end of the second millennium BC, *South Asian archaeology*, ed N. Hammond (Cambridge, 1973). 197–201.

CS

Ganges civilization The second phase of urbanization in South Asia, which emerged in the mid-1st millennium BC, more than a thousand years after the collapse of the INDUS CIVILIZATION; it corresponds with the origins of historic Indian philosophical, religious and historic traditions. Urban settlements of the Ganges civilization are found over a wide area in the fertile valleys of the Ganges and Yamuna rivers. Important sites include ATRANJIKHERA, Ahicchatra, HASTINAPURA, KAUSAMBI, Mathura, Noh, Patilaputra and Ujjain. The importance of the Ganges region has been recognized since the start of the 20th century but substantial archaeological research did not begin until the 1940s and 1950s, with the excavations of Ahicchatra, Hastinapura and Kausambi (only the work at Hastinapura and Kausambi having been fully published). Excavations have in general been small in scale, and little is known of the overall plans of sites. Regional settlement pattern surveys have been conducted in the Kanpur district by Makhan Lal (1984) and around Kausambi by George Erdosy (1985).

A. Ghosh: *The city in early historical India* (Simla, 1973); M. Lal: *Settlement history and rise of civilization in Ganga-Yamuna Doab* (Delhi, 1984); R. Thapar: *From lineage to state: social formations in the mid-first millennium BC in the Ganga valley* (Bombay, 1984); G. Erdosy: 'Settlement archaeology of the Kausambi region', *Man and Environment* 9 (1985), 66–79.

CS

Gangetic hoards About seventy-five copper hoards, most with very poor provenances, are known from a variety of regions in late prehistoric India, including the Ganges Basin, Chota Nagpur and northern Rajasthan, but little is known of their function or the circumstances of their deposition. The Ganges Basin hoards are the best-known, and copper finds there are often associated with the problematic OCHRE COLOURED POTTERY of the 2nd millennium BC. The copper artefacts include flat and shouldered celts, double-axes, swords, harpoons, lance-heads, bracelets and anthropomorphic figures. The Gangetic hoards probably dated to the 2nd millennium BC, but it is important to note that none of them have been dated and no radiocarbon dates are available. A range of interpretations concerning the producers of these hoards have been raised, including such suggestions as Western Asian influence, Indo-Aryans, displaced Harappans, and local tribal populations (Agrawal 1982: 210). Agrawal, however, has cautioned against accepting any of these views without improved spatial and chronological control.

D.P. Agrawal: *The Copper-Bronze Age in India* (Delhi, 1971); ——: *The archaeology of India* (Copenhagen 1982), 203–10; P. Yule: 'On the function of the prehistoric copper hoards of the Indian subcontinent', *South Asian archaeology, 1983*, ed. J. Schotsmands and M. Taddei (Naples, 1985), 495–508.

CS

Ganweriwala Large unexcavated urban site of the Harappan culture located in the Cholistan region of Pakistan. Identified by M. Rafique Mughal in a regional survey along the ancient course of the Hakra river (1974–7), it is one of 174 sites dating to the Mature Harappan period (*see* INDUS CIVILIZATION), out of a total of 377 protohistoric sites recorded in the region. The extent of surviving surface remains suggests that the site originally covered an area of about 85.5 ha, roughly comparable with the mounded areas of MOHENJO-DARO and HARAPPA.

M.R. Mughal: *Archaeological explorations in Cholistan* (Islamabad, 1989); ——: 'The protohistoric settlement patterns in the Cholistan Desert', *South Asian archaeology, 1987*, ed. M. Taddei (Rome, 1990), 143–56.

CS

Gaochengxian *see* KAO-CH'ENG-HSIEN

garbage *see* REFUSE DEPOSITION

Gath *see* PHILISTINES

Gavrinis Neolithic passage-grave situated on an island in the Morbihan gulf off Brittany, France. Gavrinis, which was constructed towards the end of the 4th millennium BC, is exceptional in the density and quality of the MEGALITHIC art that decorates the orthostats of its passage and chamber. The motifs include concentric arcs, U-shapes, spirals, crook-shapes and repeated axe-heads, and on some stones the designs are carefully arranged in panels in a way that is very unusual in Neolithic art.

C.T. Le Roux: *Gavrinis et les îles du Morbihan* (Paris, 1985)

RJA

Gawra, Tepe Tell-site in northern Iraq, north-east of modern Mosul, which flourished particularly during the Ubaid and Uruk periods (*c*.5000–3100 BC). It is the only site in northern Mesopotamia where pre-Uruk monumental architecture has been excavated. The excavations of E. Speiser and Charles Bache (1927–38), which revealed 20 stratified levels, were originally intended to expose the entire site but the financial support ultimately proved unequal to the task. The earliest known strata at Gawra date to the HALAF period (*c*.5500–4500 BC), which include pottery suggested by NEUTRON ACTIVATION ANALYSIS to have been imported from workshops at TELL ARPACHIYAH (Davidson and McKerrell 1980).

E.A. Speiser: *Excavations at Tepe Gawra* I (Philadelphia, 1935); A.L. Perkins: *The comparative stratigraphy of early Mesopotamia* (Chicago, 1949); A.J. Tobler: *Excavations at Tepe Gawra* II (Philadelphia, 1950); T.E. Davidson and H. McKerrell: 'The neutron activation analysis of Halaf and 'Ubaid pottery from Tell Arpachiyah and Tepe Gawra', *Iraq* 42 (1980), 155–67; J.-D. Forest: *Les pratiques funéraires en Mésopotamie du Vème millenaire au début du IIIème* (Paris, 1983).

IS

Gawra period *see* TEPE GAWRA

Gaza *see* PHILISTINES

Gebel Adda Hilltop fortress in Nubia, 5 km south of Abu Simbel, now submerged by LAKE NASSER. Like QASR IBRIM, Gebel Adda was a major urban centre in Lower Nubia from the late MEROITIC period to medieval times (*c*.AD 100–1600). The remains include a large BALLANA-period cemetery (*c*.AD 350–550) and a complex of large brick-built domestic structures identified as the palace of the rulers of Dotawo, a Christian kingdom which is thought to have lasted from about AD 1144 to 1484 (Millet 1967: 61–2). Adams (1984: 535) agrees that Gebel Adda must have been important during the Dotawo phase but dismisses the identification of the palace as pure conjecture.

N. Millet: Preliminary reports in *JARCE* 3/6 (1964,1967); W.Y. Adams: *Nubia: corridor to Africa*, 2nd edn (Princeton, 1984), 349–51, 532–5.

IS

Gebel Barkal *see* NAPATA

Gebel Moya *see* JEBEL MOYA

Gebel Sahaba *see* JEBEL SAHABA

Gebel el-Silsila (anc. Khenw, Kheny) Egyptian site consisting of sandstone quarries and rock-cut shrines and stelae located on either side of the Nile some 65 km north of Aswan. The quarries were in use from the 18th dynasty to the Roman period (*c*.1550 BC–AD 395), while the shrines date mainly to the New Kingdom (*c*.1550–1070 BC). There are also rock-carved drawings and graffiti in the cliffs dating back to the late predynastic period (*c*.3400–3000).

R.A. Caminos and T.G.H. James: *Gebel el Silsilah* I (London, 1963).

IS

Gebel Uweinat *see* JEBEL UWEINAT

Gedi Best-known of the SWAHILI HARBOUR TOWNS, located near Malindi, a short distance inland from the Kenyan coast. Although it is unexceptional in terms of the history of Swahili harbour towns, it is of paramount importance for the study of East African stone architecture (domestic, mortuary and religious) of the 14th–15th centuries AD, since the ruins of coral-rag buildings are unusually well preserved and readily accessible. The mosques, houses and presumed palace were excavated and cleared by James Kirkman and studied architecturally by Peter Garlake. Chinese ceramics, which were traded indirectly across the Indian Ocean, have been instrumental in dating the site, which was probably still occupied in the 16th century.

J.S. Kirkman: *Men and monuments on the East African coast* (London, 1964).

JS

Gelidonya Cape on the coast of southwestern Turkey where a Bronze Age wreck, dating to *c.*1200 BC and located at a depth of 27 m, was excavated by George Bass in 1960 and again in 1987–8. The cargo comprised at least 34 'oxhide' copper ingots, as well as disc-shaped and oval copper ingots, tin ingots, and broken bronze tools (probably scrap). Other finds included a swage block, whetstones, a jar of glass beads, stone maceheads and polishers, an oil lamp, five scarabs, a cylinder seal, polished stone balance-pan weights and a sword.

In 1982 a similar but more opulent wreck dating to *c.*1325 BC was reported at a depth of 44–51 m at Ulu Burun, where excavations have been conducted since 1984 by Bass and Cemal Pulak from the Institute of Nautical Archaeology at Texas A & M University. The estimated 12 tonnes of cargo include 250+ ingots, mainly copper oxhide (but also disk and bun), and several tin; 100 'Canaanite' amphorae (many containing turpentine); seven pithoi (one containing Cypriot pottery); 100 kg of cobalt-blue glass ingots, the earliest known; murex shells; ostrich egg-shells; ebony logs; and ivory (elephant tusk and hippopotamus teeth). The extensive catalogue of small finds includes musical instruments (five tortoise-shell sound-boxes), the earliest known diptych (wooden writing tablet), a gold cup, jewellery, rock-cut seals (one a gold scarab of the Egyptian Queen Nefertiti), fishing equipment, tools, and a câche of weapons. The ship was equipped with at least 24 stone anchors and was constructed by pegged mortise-and-tenon, the technique preferred by later Greco-Roman shipwrights in which the shell rather than the frames provided the hull's integral strength (*see* MARITIME ARCHAEOLOGY).

These wrecks have fuelled debate over whether late Bronze Age maritime transport in the Eastern Mediterranean was primarily in the hands of Mycenaean Greeks, Egyptians, or Cannanites (Syro-Palestinians), the last being favoured by Bass. What seems clear is the role of Cyprus, both in trans-shipment and for its own produce, since TRACE ELEMENT ANALYSIS has indicated a Cypriot origin for the copper. The wider issue of the mechanism of transport also remains unresolved, although the presence of mercantile equipment and some relatively humble goods suggests some commerce. The possibility that the Ulu Burun ship contained a 'royal' consignment accords with a primitivist model of the Bronze Age economy in which socially-embedded mechanisms such as reciprocity and redistribution are paramount; Anthony Snodgrass, for instance, has stressed the evidence for Mycenaean bronze-working being under close centralized control, and has shown that the Ulu Burun ingots would have provided enough bronze to equip the army of an average Mycenaean kingdom (Snodgrass 1991: 15–20).

Underwater archaeological techniques. The excavation of the Gelidonya wreck in 1960 was the first compelling demonstration of archaeology underwater. Bass showed both that archaeologists could dive and that an adequately funded, equipped and staffed expedition could survey and excavate to the same standards as land archaeology. Tools pioneered at that and subsequent excavations include the 'vacuum airlift', for clearing spoil, and the underwater communications booth. Equally important was the discovery that standard techniques of measuring and recording on land required only slight modification, including baseline triangulation, PLANE-TABLE LEVELLING and note-taking. More recent technical developments have included computer-linked acoustic and electronic devices for site survey. Bass has also set the standard for wreck publication (e.g. Bass 1967; Bass and Van Doorninck 1982).

G.F. Bass: *Cape Gelidonya: a Bronze Age shipwreck* (Philadelphia, 1967); G.F. Bass and F.H. Van Doorninck, Jr.: *Yassi Ada 1: a seventh century Byzantine shipwreck* (College Station, 1982); C. Pulak: 'The Bronze Age shipwreck at Ulu Burun, Turkey: 1985 campaign', *AJA* 92 (1988), 1–37; G.F. Bass, C. Pulak, D. Collon and J. Weinstein: 'The Bronze Age shipwreck at Ulu Burun: 1986 campaign', *AJA* 93 (1989), 1–29; G.F. Bass: 'Evidence of trade from Bronze Age shipwrecks', *Bronze Age trade in the Mediterranean*, ed. N.H. Gale (Jonsered, 1991), 69–82; A. Snodgrass: 'Bronze Age exchange: a minimalist position', *Bronze Age trade in the Mediterranean*, ed. N.H. Gale (Jonsered, 1991); 15–20.

DG

gender archaeology A term encompassing varied approaches to the archaeological study of gender in past societies. Gender is defined as a socially and culturally constructed category of difference between men and women, as distinct from the fixed categories of biological sex. Gender archaeology emerged during the 1980s in American, British and Scandinavian archaeology, in response to feminist critiques which declared mainstream archaeology to be male-biased in its chosen topics and methods of analysis (*see* FEMINIST ARCHAEOLOGY).

Gender is considered to be a major structuring principle of all societies. It classifies male and female roles, informs attitudes and relations between the sexes and constructs social identity through an imagery of gender. While not synonymous with biological sex, gender can be viewed as the social construction of values invested in the sexual differences between men and women. The proponents of gender archaeology view gender as a social relationship subject to constant negotiation and change, and therefore specific to each time and place. This social (as opposed to biological) definition of gender is used to challenge previous interpretations which accepted present-day gender stereotypes as timeless, objective and 'natural'.

At first the concept of gender was found to be difficult to test archaeologically. In contrast to biological sex, which is easily approached through skeletal evidence, the social definition of gender seemed to offer no empirical evidence. The earliest studies sought to identify material correlates indicative of the presence of men and women in excavated material. Such correlates might take the form of particular artefacts, tools or grave goods, which when recovered through excavation would suggest the activities of men or women. This approach is still prevalent in many studies which seek to identify from ethnographic and ethnohistoric sources artefacts representative of women's activities. Once such correlates have been established, archaeological evidence is scrutinised for the presence of women (e.g. McEwan 1991). While important for redressing the imbalance of earlier male-dominated narratives, such studies may be more correctly termed the archaeology of women.

In contrast to approaches which seek to identify women, gender archaeology takes as its starting point the relationship between men and women and the changing definitions of masculinity and femininity. Material correlates for gender are problematic in a number of ways. Often their identification requires an exclusive sexual division of labour, when in most cases a degree of task-sharing can be expected. In addition, the approach adopts a static and descriptive definition of gender. To date, empirical studies of gender archaeology remain somewhat controversial. Disagreement exists over the forms of analogy on which to base archaeological interpretations, in particular whether ethnographic or ethnohistoric sources should be used, and whether a methodology exists which will unlock gender in archaeological assemblages.

Gender archaeology developed initially from within the American tradition of PROCESSUAL ARCHAEOLOGY (Conkey and Spector 1984), and shared with it a primary concern with methodological issues. The first studies sought to make gender visible in the archaeological record by identifying men's and women's work and their attendant activity areas. In the 'task differentiation' methodology proposed by Janet Spector, links are sought between the social definitions of gender and its material aspects. Spector began with ethnographically well-documented examples in which men's and women's tasks could be examined according to the social composition of task groups, the frequency, duration and season of task performance, the environment and community (or site) location of various tasks, and the artefacts, structures and facilities associated with tasks. From this she suggested that it would be possible to extrapolate to undocumented groups. However, in applying this methodology to archaeological assemblages associated with the Wahpeton people of East Dakota, Spector concluded that the method provided only a means for organising data. She suggested that the full interpretation of this data could be fulfilled by moving to a more narrative way of writing about native Americans (Spector 1991). Gender archaeologists have come to agree that gendered interpretations cannot be delivered according to a particular methodology, but rather as the result of asking new questions of archaeological data.

While American gender archaeology first concentrated on the relationship of gender to the organisation of production, European approaches were influenced by a long-standing tradition which studied gender as a descriptive category of material culture linked to biological sex, explored particularly in relation to Anglo-Saxon grave goods (e.g. Pader 1982).

Approaches influenced by STRUCTURALIST ARCHAEOLOGY gave greater emphasis to the symbolic dimensions of gender, characterizing it as a system of signification composed of series of binary oppositions expressed through material culture. Artefacts and forms of decoration were viewed as being organized according to opposites such as decorated: undecorated, raw: cooked, male: female, and so on. Some of these studies considered forms of material culture as a means of mediating tensions between men and women, so that objects ordered according to binary oppositions could maintain gender relations or facilitate strategies for their change (Braithwaite 1982; Sorensen 1987). Although such binary oppositions were generally viewed as having been socially constructed, they nevertheless implied a universal contradiction between male and female cultural categories. Such universals are contradictory to the social definition of gender, in which gender relations and imagery are culturally specific and constantly changing. Moreover the concept of binary oppositions insists that gender is always dualistic, constructed of male and female categories. More recently gender archaeologists have suggested that alternative structures may be anticipated in the gender relations of past societies, in which three, four or any number of genders may have existed (Gilchrist 1991) e.g. BLACKDOG CEMETERY.

Gender studies influenced by CONTEXTUAL ARCHAEOLOGY sought to explore the potential meanings of gender derived from archaeological context. For example, representations of women depicted in a range of data types from Bronze Age Denmark were explored in order to comment on long-term changes in gender relations (Gibbs 1987) and archaeological deposits have been used to suggest gender domains within settlements in Iron Age Noord-Holland (Therkorn 1987).

More recently, gender archaeology has been approached through the adoption of gender as an analytical category in organizing archaeological data and enquiries (Gero and Conkey 1991; Seifert 1991). Much of this work highlights the role of women, but does so within a critical framework which seeks to evaluate female agency in major cultural transformations, such as state formation and the development of forms of agriculture and new technologies. Gender is employed as the basis of a conceptual framework which challenges existing interpretations and reclaims women as subjects active in the formation of the archaeological record. The primary concern is no longer the need to find empirical methods of testing for gender in archaeological data. Indeed, American gender archaeology now challenges the positivist tradition in which it was initially based, arguing that gendered interpretations can be achieved from a strongly developed theoretical position that focuses on gender as agency (Gero and Conkey 1991). Gender archaeology has developed into a new phase in which its proponents demonstrate the invalidity of traditional methodologies and interpretations and provide alternatives. For example, in her study of 19th-century American ceramic assemblages, Anne Yentsch has moved away from previous methods of artefact pattern analysis, which enumerate artefacts primarily according to a description of their materials (*see* SPATIAL ANALYSIS), to a gendered approach which considers the functions of vessels and the activities of men and women which they represent (Yentsch 1991).

This more mature gender archaeology considers the cultural formulation of constructs such as the household, family and gender domains, considering for example the role of differential male and female mobility in constructing domesticity and household in the 19th-century American West (Purser 1991). The active nature of gender and material culture is explored through case-studies of changing male and female space (for example in medieval monasticism, Gilchrist 1993) and women's choices in consumer goods in maintaining gender roles and social values in 19th-century New York (Wall 1991). Many studies now emphasize the fluid nature of gender and examine the mechanisms through which change is enacted. In American gender archaeology a great deal of emphasis has been placed on transitions brought about through European colonialism and colonization of North and South America.

No single approach or method dominates gender archaeology, but its proponents are united in defining gender as a socially created and historically specific force. The majority link its practice with the resolution of feminist aims to reinterpret the past through the reclamation of women as subjects. Problems remain surrounding the use of ethnographic and ethnohistorical analogies and in resolving the gulf between gender theory and archaeological data. Few fully developed case studies have been published, and the majority of successful examples rely heavily on documentary and ethnographic evidence as a starting point for analysis.

Case study: gender archaeology and the domestication of plants in the Eastern Woodlands of North America. Watson and Kennedy (1991) explore the assumptions of gender implicit in explanations of the domestication of plants, proposing a more active role for women in this process. Before the feminist critique, characterisations of the sexual division of labour suggested men to be strong, dominant hunters and women to be weaker, more passive beings hampered by their reproductive responsibilities and therefore confined to plant gathering. This study combines archaeological and ethnohistoric data to review explanations for the origins and early development of plant cultivation and domestication in the Eastern WOODLAND of North America, 7000–2000 years before present. Three phases have been suggested to date: 7000 BP gourd-like cucurbits and bottle gourds appear in archaeological deposits in Eastern USA; 3500 BP domesticated forms of native cultigens, the weedy plants sump weed, chenopod and sunflower, begin to appear; 2000–1000 BP maize varieties begin to be developed.

Explanations for the domestication of native cultigens are often 'co-evolutionary', that is plants are thought to have gradually domesticated themselves alongside human habitations (Smith 1987). On the basis of ethnographically documented associations between women and horticulture, Watson and Kennedy propose that plants were domesticated by intentional soil disturbance and repeated introduction of seeds by women. They suggest that this process would have accompanied everyday activities: the construction of houses, windbreaks, storage and refuse pits, drying racks, earth ovens and hearths. From ethnographic and ethnohistoric accounts, they are confident that such activities can be associated primarily with women. Nevertheless, they conclude that where the role of women in such co-evolutionary schemes is recognized it is still accorded a passive status.

In contrast, the introduction of the cucurbita gourd and bottle gourd is considered to have been a deliberate introduction through trade with tropical areas (Prentice 1986). It is assumed that an intentional act of domestication, or any major innovation, can only take place when introduced by a person of high status, such as a specialist or SHAMAN. In this interpretation, gourd domestication was linked to trade and ceremony and was therefore a male innovation. When viewed as a high status act of innovation, Watson and Kennedy note that typically androcentric interpretations no longer consider plant domestication to be connected with women.

In relation to maize agriculture, they suggest that it was purposefully cultivated in hospitable climates, such as that around Lake Erie, in the southern Great Lakes, from AD 800–900. They infer from this deliberate acclimatisation of a new species that the women gardeners of the native cultigens in Middle and Late Woodland communities must have been responsible for the successful introduction of maize agriculture.

They conclude that some, if not all, of the species would have required special, self-conscious, and deliberate treatment to convert them to garden crops, and, on the basis of ethnographic comparisons, suggest that plant domestication was carried out by Late Archaic women acting intentionally and drawing from an accumulated body of knowledge. Watson and Kennedy acknowledge that we may never know exactly who domesticated plants in the Eastern Woodlands, and that their preferred explanation relies only on ethnographic evidence. However, in contrast with previous androcentric approaches, assumptions on the sexual division of labour are made explicit in their interpretation and the sources of analogy on which they base their conclusions are made clear. Despite its ethnographic basis, their explanation of plant domestication is no less valid or testable than other interpretations. It challenges existing perceptions in that it attributes a major cultural transformation to deliberate female agency, and raises the status of women in hunter-gatherer societies from passive to active.

See also BLACKDOG CEMETERY.

M. Braithwaite: 'Decoration as ritual symbol: a theoretical proposal and an ethnographic study in Southern Sudan', *Symbolic and structural archaeology*, ed. I. Hodder (Cambridge, 1982), 80–8; E.J. Pader: *Symbolism, social relations and the interpretation of mortuary remains* (Oxford, 1982); M.W. Conkey and J.D. Spector: 'Archaeology and the study of gender', *Advances in Archaeological Method and Theory* 7 (1984), 1–38; G. Prentice: 'Origins of plant domestication in the Eastern United States: promoting the individual in archaeological theory', *Southeastern Archaeology* 5 (1986), 103–19; L. Gibbs: 'Identifying gender representations in the archaeological record: a contextual study', *The archaeology of contextual meanings*, ed. I. Hodder (Cambridge, 1987), 79–87; B.D. Smith: 'The independent domestication of the indigenous seed-bearing plants in Eastern North America', *Emergent horticultural economies of the Eastern Woodlands*, ed. W. Keegan (Carbondale, 1987), 3–47; M.L.S. Sorensen: 'Material order and cultural classification: the role of bronze objects in the transition from Bronze Age to Iron Age Scandinavia', *The archaeology of contextual meanings*, ed. I. Hodder (Cambridge, 1987), 90–101; L. Therkorn: 'The interrelationships of materials and meanings: some suggestions on housing concerns within Iron Age Noord-Holland', *The archaeology of contextual meanings*, ed. I. Hodder (Cambridge, 1987), 102–10; 'Women and archaeology', *ARC* 7.1 (1988) [whole issue]; J.M. Gero and M.W. Conkey, eds: *Engendering archaeology: women in prehistory* (Oxford, 1991); R. Gilchrist: 'Women's archaeology? Political feminism, gender theory and historical revision', *Antiquity* 65 (1991), 495–501; B.G. McEwan: 'The archaeology of women in the Spanish New

World', *HA* 25/4 (1991), 33–41; M. Purser: '"Several Paradise Ladies are visiting in town": gender strategies in the Early Industrial West', *HA* 25/4 (1991), 6–16; D.J. Seifert, ed.: 'Gender in historical archaeology', *HA* 25/4 (1991) [whole issue]; J.D. Spector: 'What this awl means: towards a feminist archaeology?', *Engendering archaeology: women in prehistory*, ed. J.M. Gero and M.W. Conkey (Oxford, 1991), 388–406; D.D. Wall: 'Sacred dinners and secular teas: constructing domesticity in mid-19th century New York', *HA* 25/4 (1991), 69–81; P.J. Watson and M.C. Kennedy: 'The development of horticulture in the Eastern Woodlands of North America: women's role', *Engendering archaeology: women in prehistory*, ed. J.M. Gero and M.W. Conkey (Oxford, 1991), 255–75; A. Yentsch: 'Engendering visible and invisible ceramic artifacts, especially diary vessels', *HA* 25/4 (1991), 132–55; R. Gilchrist: *Gender and medieval monasticism: the archaeology of religious women* (London, 1993); R.P. Wright, ed.: *Gender and archaeology* (Philadelphia, 1996); S.M. Nelson: *Gender in archaeology* (Walnut Creek, 1997).

RG

general laws *see* COVERING LAWS

General Periods A–D *see* ASIA 3

geofacts Term used to describe objects, particularly lithics, that have been created by natural geological processes rather than human activity (*see*, for instance, CALICO HILLS).

Geographical Information Systems *see* GIS

Geoksyur Agricultural oasis in the Tedjen delta, Southern Turkmenistan, containing a number of early Neolithic and Bronze Age sites excavated in the 1950s and 1960s. The initial settlement occurred during the NAMAZGA I stage, in the 6th to 5th millennium BC, and seems to have been the result of influx from the overpopulated foothills of the Kopet Dag and the deltaic plains (ie the Namazga region).

The settlements of this period (e.g. Dashlijidepe) consisted of rectangular houses; larger rectangular buildings, thought to belong to the social elite, offer some evidence for social stratification. The irrigation system developed in this period consisted of several canals drawing water from the main branch of the delta. The number of sites considerably increased during the subsequent Yalangach and Mullali periods (which correspond to Namazga II), the largest settlement, Geoksyur I reaching 25 ha. The settlement of Yalangach-depe, which contained a central structure built upon a platform, was surrounded by a wall.

The following Geoksyur period, which parallels Namazga III, is represented by at least two settlements: Geoksyur I with a settled area of 10–12 ha, and the much smaller Chong-depe in the north. A canal 5 km long was constructed north of the site of Geoksyur I, a considerable feat of irrigation. The first half of the 3rd millennium BC saw a collapse of agricultural settlement in the Geoksyur oasis. The only site attributed to this period, Khapuz, was located south of the delta.

I.N. Khlopin: *Geoksjurskaja gruppa poselenii epohi eneolita* (Leningrad, 1964).

PD

Geometric and Protogeometric Terms used to describe phases in the pottery, and by extension cultural, sequence of ancient Greece in the early 1st millennium BC. The phases are defined largely with reference to artefacts recovered from burials in the region of Athens. The Protogeometric (*c.*1050–900 BC) developed from the 'Sub-Mycenaean' style – itself a very simple geometric style – that prevailed in the centuries immediately following the collapse of the MYCENAEAN civilization. Protogeometric pottery is characterised by wheel-made fine wares decorated with carefully executed but quite plain geometric designs. In the Geometric (*c.*900–750 BC) phase, these designs grew more elaborate and cross-hatching and other more detailed decoration was adopted; towards the end of this period stylized animals started to be used in bands of decoration on exceptional vessels. The Late Geometric (*c.*750–700 BC) describes the final period of the Geometric during which a fine series of vessels – especially large funerary urns – began to be produced with much more complicated scenes including narrative art. The style is still geometrized and schematic, often with bodies represented by triangles, but this art is the predecessor of the figurative art of archaic classical Greece.

A.M. Snodgrass: *The Dark Age of Greece* (Edinburgh, 1971); N. Coldstream: *Geometric Greece* (London, 1977); A.M. Snodgrass: *Archaic Greece: the age of experiment* (London, 1980).

RJA

geometric pottery (China) Type of pottery of the late Neolithic and Bronze Age in China, bearing paddle-impressed decoration including geometric designs such as circles, parallel lines, wavy lines, cross-hatches, spirals, chevrons. This decorative form developed from the Late Neolithic onwards and reached a peak of production during the Shang and Chou periods, persisting into Han and later. It is found largely at sites in the lower

Yangtze valley, southern Chiang-su, northern Che-chiang, Chiang-hsi (e.g. Wu-ch'eng-ts'un), and throughout much of eastern South China and coastal areas.

Chang Kwang-chih: *The archaeology of ancient China*, 4th edn (New Haven, 1986), 195.

NB

geophysical survey Technically, any survey designed to investigate the physical structure of the soils and geology of a region or site. In archaeology, a geophysical survey almost always refers to the use of non-invasive surveying techniques such as the RESISTIVITY SURVEY or MAGNETIC SURVEY.

Gerzean *see* EGYPT 1; NAQADA

Gezer (Tell el-Jezari) Settlement site in Israel, midway between Tel Aviv and Jerusalem, which was occupied continuously from before the Middle Bronze Age (*c*.2000–1600 BC) until the time of the Crusades. The town of Gezer was well-placed to benefit from the principal commercial routes along the Levantine coast, although its defences – comprising thick fortified walls and glacis – clearly indicate the disadvantages of its strategic location. The excavations of 1902–9 and 1964–73 have revealed nearly 30 major strata containing evidence not only of the local Canaanite population but also of cultural contact with the Egyptians, Philistines and Persians.

R.A.S. Macalister: *Excavation of Gezer*, 3 vols (London, 1912); W.G. Dever et al.: *Gezer*, 2 vols (Jerusalem, 1970–4).

IS

Ghassul, Teleilat el- Type-site of the Ghassulian culture (*c*.4500–3400 BC), consisting of a cluster of three small Chalcolithic tell-sites located on the plain to the north of the Dead Sea in Jordan. The site as a whole is characterized by four major phases, the most recent of which (stratum IV) contains evidence of agriculture (including sickle blades and silos), early metalworking (copper artefacts), weaving and pottery, as well as substantial stone-built and mud-brick houses, some decorated with unusual painted wall-plaster bearing geometric and figurative designs. A large cemetery, consisting of CIST burials and micro-dolmens, has been excavated at 'Adeima, several kilometres to the east, although it is not clear whether this was directly connected with the settlement at Ghassul.

The 'Ghassulian' is one of the most distinctive and widespread Chalcolithic assemblages in Palestine. The discovery of similar sites in the Beersheba region has led to the use of the term 'Beersheba-Ghassul civilization' to refer to the southern Palestinian Chalcolithic phase, although there are 'Beersheba' sites both earlier and later than those of the Ghassulian, and the early stages of the Beersheba culture are characterized by subterranean housing. The rich hoard of copper artefacts found at the Ghassulian cave-site of NAHAL MISHMAR is an indication of the sophistication of metalworking during this phase.

A. Mallon et al.: *Teleilat Ghassul* I (Rome, 1934); R. Koeppel: 'Ma'adi und Ghassul', *Biblica* 18 (1937), 443–50; ——: *Teleilat Ghassul* II (Rome, 1940); J. Perrot; 'A propos du Ghassoulien', *Syria* 29 (1952), 403–5; R. de Vaux: 'Palestine during the Neolithic and Chalcolithic periods', *Cambridge Ancient History*, eds I.E.S. Edwards et al., 3rd edn (Cambridge, 1970), 499–538 [522–31].

IS

Ghassulian *see* GHASSUL, TELEILAT EL-

giant's grave *see* TOMBA DI GIGANTI

Girsu *see* TELLOH

GIS (Geographical Information Systems) Computer technique consisting of a set of tools for the storage, manipulation, retrieval, transformation, display and analysis of geographical, environmental and spatial data (such as site or artefact distribution in the landscape). The basic geographical elements that are dealt with in GIS are the point, the line and the polygon (area). Data in GIS can be organized either in 'raster format' (a line being represented by a series of contiguous cells with the same value in a grid) or in 'vector format' (a line being represented by a series of points joined together in a reference system).

The raster format is suitable for the storage of continuous data, such as elevation or distance from given points, and discrete data, such as soil types, while the vector format is suitable for the storage of linear data, such as road systems, hydrology, coastlines. Raster-based systems generalize the data into a grid with a loss of precision, but they allow boolean and algebraic operations to be carried out.

Vector-based systems are considerably more precise than raster-based systems in storing the data, but the operations that can be performed on the data are limited. The way the data is organized dictates the type of analysis that can be carried out: SPATIAL ANALYSIS and MULTIVARIATE ANALYSIS are only possible on raster data (e.g. multiple REGRESSION of site location with regard to elevation, orientation, soil type and distance from water), while network analysis is only possible on vector data (e.g. speed and the best way to reach point A from point B along the local Roman roads).

As each cell in a raster-based system can only contain one number, each variable must be kept in a separate map called an *overlay*. All overlays with information about one region must be referenced on the same coordinate system and must cover exactly the same area on the ground. Anything that can be quantified on the nominal scale or above can be used as a variable in a GIS overlay. The possibility of combining variables of a different nature facilitates the creation of predictive models. These models work by identifying all of the points in the area under analysis in which the sum of the values of all the variables reaches a certain threshold. By giving different weights to the variables it is possible to determine their relative importance.

Starting from a set of altitude contours or points, a GIS package can interpolate a continuous surface, thus reducing the error due to the gap between two contour lines on a map. An interpolated elevation surface is known as a DEM (Digital Elevation Model) and can be used to calculate the slope and orientation of the area.

P.A. Burrough: *Principles of Geographical Information Systems for land resources assessment* (Oxford, 1986); K.M. Allen et al.: *Interpreting space: GIS and archaeology* (London, 1990); V. Gaffney and Z. Stančič: *GIS approaches to regional analysis: a case study of the Island of Hvar* (Ljubljana, 1991).

FM

Giyan, Tepe *see* LURISTAN

Giza The Giza plateau, on the very edge of modern Cairo, is the site of one of the royal necropolises of the Old Kingdom, incorporating the Great Pyramid of Khufu (*c.*2540 BC), as well as the pyramid complexes of his successors Chephren (*c.*2500 BC) and Mycerinus (*c.*2480 BC), the Great Sphinx (*see* SPHINX) and the MASTABA-TOMBS of important members of the nobility. In the New Kingdom the Spinx became the focal point of the cult of the sun-god Horemakhet. Although it is one of the most well-known archaeological sites in the world, surveyed and excavated by countless archaeologists from Flinders Petrie to George Reisner, the first systematic survey of the plateau as a whole was not undertaken until the 1980s (Lehner 1985).

W.M.F. Petrie: *The pyramids and temples of Gizeh* (London, 1883); H. Junker: *Giza*, 12 vols (Vienna, 1929–55); G.A. Reisner and W. Stevenson Smith: *A history of the Giza necropolis*, 2 vols (Cambridge, MA, 1942–55); I.E.S. Edwards: *The pyramids of Egypt*, 5th edn (Harmondsworth, 1993); M. Lehner: 'A contextual approach to the Giza pyramids', *AO* 32 (1985), 136–58.

IS

Gla Mycenaean fortress in the northeast of the Copais plain, Greece. With walls stretching for over 2 km, and four gateways including a double-gate, this is one of the most impressively fortified Mycenaean sites, although the walls are not as thick as at the other great Mycenaean fortresses of MYCENAE and Tiryns. Although there is fragmentary evidence of frescoes, and the buildings in the inner enclosure are often referred to as a palace, Gla's main function may have been as a strategically important stronghold. From the gates, roads once led out across the plain, while around the Lake Copais region there is evidence for a system of Mycenaean dykes that may once have turned extensive areas of marsh into productive farmland.

RJA

Gladysvale Ancient cavern/fissure system containing rich deposits of fossils suggestive of an age of around 2.5 million years BP, lying a few miles east of Johannesburg, South Africa. The site has been the subject of several (unpublished) investigations, but acquired new interest in 1992 with the discovery of two hominid teeth thought to represent *AUSTRALOPITHECUS AFRICANUS*.

L.R. Berger, A.E. Keyser and P.V. Tobias: 'Gladysvale: first early hominid site discovered in South Africa since 1948', *American Journal of Physical Anthropology* 92 (1993), 107–11.

RI

glass weathering layers Layers within the weathered crust of glasses which are produced at an approximately constant rate, but which cannot reliably be used to date the glass.

R.G. Newton: 'The enigma of the layered crusts on some weathered glasses, a chronological account of the investigations', *Archaeometry* 13 (1971), 1–9.

SB

glyphs *see* HIEROGLYPHS, MESOAMERICAN

Goat's Hole *see* PAVILAND

Gobedra Palaeolithic/Neolithic rockshelter near AXUM in the highlands of Tigre, Ethiopia, where excavations have revealed deeply stratified Stone Age remains dating back to *c.*10,000 BC, including both blade (Clark's 'mode 4', i.e. long parallel-sided blades produced from prismatic cores) and backed microlithic industries. Ceramics and a camel-tooth were found in the microlithic levels, indicating the earliest Ethiopian evidence for the transition to the Neolithic, *c.*4500–3000 BC, although the seeds of cultivated finger millet (*Eleusine coracana*) initially reported by Phillipson (1977) were subsequently radiocarbon-dated and found to be recent intrusions. Later levels at the site contain evidence for domesticated cattle in the 1st millennium BC.

D.W. Phillipson: 'The excavation of Gobedra rock-shelter, Axum: an early occurrence of cultivated finger millet in Northern Ethiopia', *Azania* 12 (1977), 53–82.

IS

Godin Tepe *see* MEDES

Gogo Falls Rich and complex late Holocene site located on the Kuja river, near to Lake Victoria in south-western Kenya. The three distinct cultural traditions at Gogo Falls were revealed by Peter Robertshaw in the early 1980s. Represented are (1) KANSYORE pottery and lithics, dating probably to the final millennia BC, which are frequently associated with lakes, rivers and their fish resources; (2) 'pastoral Neolithic' ELMENTEITAN occupation of around 2000 years ago, previously identified only in higher and more open grasslands to the east; and (3) EARLY IRON AGE remains of the Urewe variety, probably dating to about the 2nd–6th centuries AD.

P.T. Robertshaw: 'Gogo Falls: a complex site east of Lake Victoria', *Azania* 26 (1991), 63–195.

JS

Gombe Point (formerly Kalina Point) Stone Age site at Kinshasa, Zaire, which was first excavated in 1925. The 3–5 metres of silty sand were long thought to contain a sequence of post-ACHEULEAN industries representative of the whole of the southern Zaire Basin. Re-excavation in 1973 and 1974, however, showed that the assemblages were in fact mixed, with numerous conjoins, often separated vertically by more than a metre.

J.R.F. Colette: 'Complèxes et convergences en préhistoire', *Bulletin de la Société royaume belge d'Anthropologie et de Préhistoire* 50 (1935), 49–192; D. Cahen and J. Moeyersons: 'Subsurface movements of stone artefacts and their implications for the prehistory of central Africa', *Nature*, 266 (1977), 812–5.

RI

Go Mun Cultural phase of the Bronze Age in Vietnam, dated to *c.*1000–600 BC, and thus immediately preceding the rich DONG SON bronze culture of the Red River valley. The type-site is located above the junction of the Red and Black rivers, and was excavated over a ten-year period from 1961. The range of implements cast in bronze included socketed axeheads, chisels, spear and arrowheads and bracelets. A single sickle has also been recovered, together with a human figure cast with the lost-wax method.

Ha Van Phung and Nguyen Duy Ti: *Di Chi Khao Co Hoc Go Mun* [The excavation of the archaeological site of Go Mun] (Ha Nôi 1982) [in Vietnamese].

CH

Gondar The most impressive of the surviving post-medieval sites in the northern Ethiopian highlands, located just to the north of Lake Tana. For the first few hundred years after the decline of the Axumite civilization the medieval 'emperors' of northern Ethiopia were semi-nomadic, ruling the country from a succession of temporary camps. But from about 1500 onwards a number of more permanent capital cities were established. During the 17th-18th centuries AD, the village of Gondar was transformed into the first capital city of post-medieval Ethiopia, with the earliest 'castle-palace' at its centre.

D. Buxton: *The Abyssinians* (London, 1970), 52–4.

IS

Gondwanaland *see* OCEANIA

goodness-of-fit In statistical analysis this term is used by archaeologists to describe a measure of how well a DATASET can be represented, or 'fitted', by a specified DISTRIBUTION. The null hypothesis (see HYPOTHESIS TESTING) that it does not fit can be tested by a goodness-of-fit test. The most common test, appropriate for discrete DATA, i.e. data that can take only certain specified values, is the chi-squared test; for continuous data the Kolmogorov-Smirnov test is preferable. Examination of the 'residuals' (the difference between the actual and the fitted values) often yield valuable insights into the problem being studied.

J.E. Doran and F.R. Hodson: *Mathematics and computers in archaeology* (Edinburgh, 1975), 292–5; S. Shennan: *Quantifying archaeology* (Edinburgh, 1988), 65–70; M. Fletcher and G.R. Lock: *Digging numbers* (Oxford, 1991), 91–102.

CO

Gordion *see* PHRYGIANS

Grächwil One of a group of Hallstatt tumulii close to the hamlet of Grächwill, near Berne in Switzerland. Roughly excavated in the mid-19th century, the tomb was found to contain, among other bronze objects and pottery, an extraordinary

Greek bronze 'hydria' dating from about 570 BC. The vessel, now held in the Musée d'Histoire de Berne, sported a detailed representation of the 'Mistress of the animals' – an icon derived from the Near East – with an eagle on her head and surrounded by lions grasping hares. Like the cauldron from VIX in eastern France, the piece is a dramatic manifestation of the trade that grew up between the Mediterranean civilizations and the Hallstatt 'chieftains' in the mid-1st millennium BC.

K. Zimmerman: 'Grächwil', *Trésors des princes celtes*, ed. J.-P. Mohen et al., exh. cat. (Paris, 1987), 244–6.

RJA

grammars, generative *see* STRUCTURALISM

Grand Pressigny flint Distinctive honey-coloured iron-rich flint dug from the valleys of the Claise and Creuse at Grand Pressigny (Indre-et-Loire), France, during the Neolithic. It was used to make daggers, sickles and other fine implements. Some of the daggers are over 10 cm in length, carefully pressure-flaked along the cutting edge, and were probably prestige rather than functional objects. Although there have been claims of Grand Pressigny flint in middle Neolithic contexts, it is really a late Neolithic material, and is often the only exotic material found in *allées couvertes* of the late Neolithic SOM CULTURE of the Paris basin. It is also found in the Midi and in Switzerland in the same period (the 3rd millennium BC).

RJA

Gran Pajatén Site in Amazonian Peru dating to the Late Intermediate Period (AD 900–1438) and the Late Horizon (AD 1438–Conquest). Also known as Abiseo, this is perhaps the largest and most elaborate site in the montaña (the precipitous forest on the eastern side of the Andes). It has been the focus of numerous 'discoveries' by explorers, travellers, and other passers-by. It consists of a number of large circular masonry buildings, some with mosaics depicting humans or birds, on platforms.

D. Bonavia: *Las ruinas de Abiseo: informe presentado al Museo Nacional de Antropología y Arqueología de Lima* (Lima, 1968); G.A. Savoy: *The search for the lost cities of the Amazon* (New York, 1970); T. Lennon: 'Investigaciones arqueológicals en el Parque Nacional Río Abiseo, San Martín', *BL* 62 (1989), 43–56.

KB

Grasshopper Pueblo Pueblo of 500 rooms on the White Mountain Apache Reservation, east-central Arizona, which was occupied by people of the MOGOLLON culture from AD 1275 to 1400. The site made a significant contribution to the development of BEHAVIORAL ARCHAEOLOGY during its excavation as part of the University of Arizona Field School between 1963 and 1992.

There was a small population at Grasshopper during the Great Drought (AD 1276–1299), but it grew exponentially during the ensuing period of high rainfall (1300–1330), through the aggregation of local inhabitants and immigration from as far away as the Colorado Plateau. The extent of the immigration has been deduced from compositional analysis of ceramics and TRACE-ELEMENT analysis of tooth enamel. The abandonment of the pueblo was gradual, perhaps beginning as early as 1325, with movement to satellite communities during a time of reduced rainfall ending in 1355. The latest tree-ring date of AD 1373 accords with an estimated abandonment of the pueblo and surrounding region by 1400.

The long-term mountain Mogollon subsistence strategy of hunting (mule deer, turkey, rabbit and squirrel), gathering (pinyon, acorn, walnut, agave and cactus) and gardening (maize, beans and squash) shifted rapidly with the population increase of the early 1300s to a total reliance on maize agriculture. Community organization comprised individual households, groups of households sharing religious rooms, and four male societies, which provided community leaders. At least two ethnic groups – Mogollon and Anasazi – lived together at Grasshopper in apparent harmony.

Behavioral archaeology and the 'complexity debate'. The research at Grasshopper was initially guided by the questions and aims of the CULTURE HISTORY approach to archaeology, but in 1966 it began to be influenced significantly by PROCESSUAL ARCHAEOLOGY. By the mid-1970s it was clear that a research programme based on processual archaeology lacked the necessary conceptual tools to unite explanatory goals with the realities of prehistoric remains. Eventually processual theorists were to fill this void with MIDDLE RANGE THEORY, but in the interim behavioral archaeology emerged to provide a comprehensive approach to the archaeological record. Behavioral archaeology is best-known from Michael Schiffer's work on SITE FORMATION PROCESSES. This research focus aimed to provide a sharp scientific edge and a strong POSITIVIST character to the understanding of the formation of the archaeological record, the first step in a sequence of research objectives that include the reconstruction and explanation of human behaviour (where, when, what and why). The programme provides a conceptual framework and procedures for generating authentic, verifiable reconstructions of past behaviour that can form the basis of explanatory models.

During the early 1980s, a debate emerged between the two groups of researchers studying 14th century pueblo ruins at Grasshopper and Chavez Pass respectively. These two sites are situated only about 75 km apart, in the mountains of east-central Arizona. Chavez Pass is interpreted as representing a level of social complexity bordering on statehood and characterized by stratification, social inequality and coercive decision making by an elite class managing the trade and allocation of scarce commodities. Grasshopper, on the other hand, is considered to be similar to a generalized ethnographic model of Western Pueblo organization, structured by kinship, ritual and non-kin-based societies (sodalities). The Grasshopper research, beginning with a thorough consideration of formation processes, proved able to provide credible accounts of variability in the archaeological record in terms of human behaviour rather than extraneous natural or cultural processes.

J.J. Reid, M.B. Schiffer and W.L. Rathje: 'Behavioural archaeology: four strategies', *American Anthropologist* 77 (1975), 864–9; M.B. Schiffer: *Behavioral archaeology* (New York, 1976); W.A. Longacre, S.J. Holbrook and M.W. Graves: *Multidisciplinary research at Grasshopper Pueblo* (Tucson, 1982); M.B. Schiffer: *Formation processes of the archaeological record* (Albuquerque, 1987); J.J. Reid: 'A Grasshopper Perspective on the Mogollon of the Arizona Mountains', *Dynamics of Southwest Prehistory*, ed. L.S. Cordell and G.J. Gumerman (Washington D.C., 1989), 65–97; G. Brown, ed.: *Technological change in the Chavez Pass region, north-central Arizona* (Tempe, 1990).

JJR

Gravettian (Upper Périgordian) Upper Palaeolithic industry dating from perhaps 26,000 BC or earlier to around 19,000 BC, traditionally regarded as successive to the AURIGNACIAN, the first industry of the Upper Palaeolithic – although it is now known to be interstratified or mixed with the Aurignacian at a number of sites and must therefore be to some extent contemporary with the later Aurignacian. The Gravettian lithic industry is characterised by backed blades, end scapers and distinctive points, including shouldered points; it has various regional expressions, some of which include Noailles burins. The 'eastern Gravettian' is the expression of the industry in Central Europe at very rich sites such as Pavlov and Dolní Věstonice and in Russia at sites such as SUNGHIR and KOSTENKI-BORSHEVO, and is characterized by some distinctive tool types such as Kostenki-type shouldered points. The eastern Gravettian is associated with some of the finest figurines and ornaments known from the earlier Upper Palaeolithic, notably the eastern Gravettian of the later layers at Willendorf which yielded the famous figurine from that site (*see* VENUS FIGURINES), the baked clay figurines of Dolní Věstonice and the many art objects found at Kostenki; there are also relatively elaborate burials (*see* SUNGHIR).

RJA

Great Langdale Neolithic quarry and 'axe factory' in the Lake District of England. Since the site's discovery by Brian Bunch in 1947, numerous subsidiary quarry, scree exploitation and working floor areas have been identified in the vicinity of Langdale and nearby Scafell Pike. Finished axes made from the fine-grained Langdale tuffs seem to have been manufactured over a considerable period, from the Early Neolithic to the Beaker period.

Great Langdale axe distribution Great Langdale is the most prolific stone-source for axes in Britain. The handaxes (categorized at a national level as Group VI) were roughed out at the site itself; their distribution is concentrated in Yorkshire and Lincolnshire, and to a lesser extent in the Midlands and in eastern and southern Britain. It has been suggested that as Langdale axes cluster around Humberside, the Humberside area might be a distributional centre to which the axes were transported in bulk – which would imply directional trade. However, the concentrations can be accounted for more simply by village-to-village reciprocal exchange, and this seems to have been confirmed by Chappell's detailed analysis of spatial patterning and morphological variability.

B. Bunch and C. Fell: 'A stone-axe factory at Pike of Stickle, Great Langdale, Westmorland', *PPS 15* (1949), 1–20; S. Chappell: *Stone axe morphology and distribution in Neolithic Britain*, BAR BS 177; 2 vols (Oxford, 1987); P. Claris and J. Quartermaine: 'The Neolithic quarries and axe-factory sites of Great Langdale and Scafell Pike: a new field survey', *PPS* 55 (1989), 1–25.

RJA

Great Wall of China (*wan-li-ch'eng*) *see* HSIUNG-NU

Great Zimbabwe Large stone-walled complex which has given its name to Zimbabwe, the Central African country in which it is located. Many scholars used to believe that the PHOENICIANS or SABAEANS built the town, but archaeologists have shown that it is the product of a Shona-speaking society. Period Ia at Great Zimbabwe is now well-dated as a 5th-century AD occupation by agro-pastoralists (with BAMBATA or Gokomere pottery) several metres below the first stone walls. Period Ib is an 8th century Zhizo occupation. Period II (AD 1150–1220) encompasses the first occupation by proto-Shona people with Gumanye pottery; the deposit is still several metres below the stone walling. Great Zimbabwe could not, therefore, have been built before the 13th century AD, eliminating completely any question of construction by ancient Egyptians, Phoenicians, Sabaeans and Pre-Muslim Arabs.

During Period III (AD 1220–1275), MAPUNGUBWE to the south became important, and Gumanye pottery incorporated some Mapungubwe elements. Period IV (AD 1275–1420/50) brackets the rise and florescence of Great Zimbabwe: Period IVa (AD 1275–1300) is a transitional stage in the ceramic sequence (Keith Robinson's 'Class 3 influenced by Class 4') and marks the first stone walling, large population and control over long-distance trade. Period IVb (AD 1300–1450) encompasses characteristic Zimbabwe pottery and the main occupation, while IVc (AD 1450–1550) covers a small occupation in the lower valley, after the town had been largely abandoned.

Archaeologists use three types of free-standing stone walls at Great Zimbabwe (defined by Anthony Whitty) to date individual buildings or features. P-coursing (uneven granite blocks laid in uneven and short courses) dates from AD 1275 to about 1350, and Q-coursing (regular blocks laid in even and long courses with a systematic batter) dates from its evolution in the Great Enclosure at about 1350 to the end of Great Zimbabwe. Terrace walls with P- and Q-coursing encircle the north and west sides of the central hill.

Whitty placed his third type, R-coursing (poorly fitted, irregular stones wedged together into a rough vertical face), at the end of his P/Q sequence, but subsequent research shows that R-coursing was in use at the same time as both P- and Q-coursing. Generally, Zimbabwe builders used P- and Q-coursing for important structures, such as the Hill Ruin and the Great Enclosure, while R--coursing was employed for perimeter walls and outlying structures.

The distribution of ruins with similar architecture demarcates the Zimbabwe culture area. Some 300 of these *dzimbahwe* are known in present-day Zimbabwe, eastern Botswana, northern Transvaal and Mozambique. Archaeologists divide these settlements into two phases: Zimbabwe (AD 1275–1450) and Khami (AD 1450–1830). Portuguese records and Shona tradition show that the principal social dynamic of the Zimbabwe culture was class distinction and sacred leadership. To function, each *dzimbahwe* had to have five components: a raised palace at the back (the Hill Ruin at Great Zimbabwe), providing ritual seclusion for the sacred leader; a place for followers in front (high-density housing units around the bottom of the Hill Ruin); a public court for equal justice; an area for royal wives, who were indispensable to political alliances (Lower Valley enclosures); and a circle of soldiers and medicine to guard against physical and magical danger. According to a more controversial interpretation, some *dzimbahwe* also contained special enclosures (like the Great Enclosure at Great Zimbabwe) that appear to have been schools for large-scale initiations. Commoner homesteads in rural areas followed the 'CENTRAL CATTLE PATTERN' (*see* VUMBA). The elite Zimbabwe spatial pattern, generated by class distinction and sacred leadership, evolved at K2 and Mapungubwe, as the Shona society there was transformed by the tremendous wealth from the East Coast gold and ivory trade (*see* SWAHILI HARBOUR-TOWNS). *Dzimbahwe* and their leaders were ranked in a political hierarchy that archaeologists can reconstruct by comparing settlement sizes. During the Zimbabwe phase, Great Zimbabwe was the largest, sheltering an estimated 18,000 people. As the supreme capital, it controlled a vast network of trade and tribute involving metals, cattle, grain and other items. It was probably abandoned because control over the hinterland collapsed, rather than because of ecological degradation. Several small chiefdoms were established at this time south of the Limpopo River and north into Mashanoland. The historically known Torwa dynasty based at Khami near present-day Bulawayo was the principal successor.

R.N. Hall: *Great Zimbabwe* (London, 1905); D.R. MacIver: *Mediaeval Rhodesia* (London, 1906); G. Caton-Thompson: *The Zimbabwe culture: ruins and reactions* (Oxford, 1931); R. Summers, K.R. Robinson and A. Whitty: 'Zimbabwe excavations, 1958', *Occasional Papers National Museums of Southern Rhodesia* 3/23A (1961), 157–332; P.S. Garlake: *Great Zimbabwe* (London, 1973); C.K. Brain: 'Human food remains from the Iron Age of Zimbabwe', *SAJS* 70 (1974), 303–9; C. Thorp: *Faunal remains as evidence of social stratification at Great Zimbabwe*, MA thesis (Johannesburg, 1984); T.N. Huffman: 'Iron Age settlement patterns and the origins of class distinction in southern Africa', *AWA* 5 (1986), 291–338; T.N. Huffman and J.O. Vogel: 'The chronology of Great Zimbabwe', *SAAB* 46 (1991), 61–70.

TH

Grimaldi Group of caves and rockshelters on the north Italian coast near Ventimiglia, near the French frontier, notable for its Upper Palaeolithic evidence. The industries, which prehistorians variously relate to the Gravettian or the Noillian/ Perigordian V, are sometimes termed 'Grimaldian'. They are associated with a series of Upper Palaeolithic burials, the earliest of which exhibit a prognathism that may suggest a part-Neanderthal ancestry. Grimaldi is the source of a series of important, mainly steatite, Upper Palaeolithic figurines retrieved in mysterious circumstances in the late 19th century. Most of the figurines are featureless with bulbous breasts and buttocks; the legs of the more complete examples join to form a point which may have been used to plant the figurines in the ground. One detached and finely detailed head has a hairstyle marked by incisions. Many of the figurines, which may relate to the 'Gravettian' levels, are now known only through brief descriptions or poor illustrations.

D. Collins: 'The Palaeolithic of Italy in its European context', *Italian Archaeology I*, BAR S41 (Oxford), 61; H. Delporte: *L'image de la femme dans l'art préhistorique* (Paris, 1979), 96–109, 315.

RJA

Grimes Graves Late Neolithic flint mining complex in Norfolk, England, dating in its principal phase from about 2100 BC. The site, which consists of perhaps 500 galleried shafts, represents one of the most developed early extractive industries in Britain. The main phase of mining is strongly associated with Grooved Ware pottery and seems to have come to an end in the first part of the 2nd millennium BC. The shafts were sunk to exploit a particularly fine seam of black flint that occurs at a depth of around 12 m. Around 90 antler picks used by the miners were recovered from a shaft with two galleries excavated by Roger Mercer in 1971, and it is estimated that this shaft alone would have yielded eight tons of flint.

R.J. Mercer: *Grimes Graves, Norfolk 1971–72* (London, 1981), 2 vols; Ian Longworth et al.: 'Excavations at Grimes Graves, Norfolk 1972–1976', Fascicule 2: 'The Neolithic, Bronze Age and Later Pottery' (London, 1988).

RJA

Grooved Ware (Rinyo-Clacton) Characterized by profuse grooved ornament in repeated geometric patterns, this fine pottery was produced in Britain during the 3rd millennium BC. The shape of the vessels is also distinctive, being either splay-sided bowls or flat-bottomed bucket, barrel and flowerpot forms; it is thus possible to identify the occasional undecorated 'Grooved Ware' vessels. Grooved Ware was first identified at Rinyo in Orkney and Clacton in Essex, and although it is no longer referred to as the Rinyo-Clacton style, this earlier name emphasizes the wide but patchy distribution of the type across the British Isles and Ireland; in fact, it forms an important part of pottery assemblages in Orkney, Wessex, Yorkshire and Essex. In these regions, Grooved Ware has been recorded at most types of site: domestic (Skara Brae), funerary (Boyne Valley tombs) and ceremonial (the henges of Wessex). However, its representation within assemblages can be idiosyncratic: it is very rare at the great henge of Avebury, but abundant at nearby Marden. The traditional 'first option' in the explanation of a distinctive form of pottery – that it represents the expression of a definable cultural entity – is precluded in the case of Grooved Ware by the geographically sporadic distribution. Instead, Bradley (1984) has suggested that Grooved Ware was adopted asynchronously, as a part of a system of 'prestige items', in those regions of Britain that show evidence of relative economic dynamism and social complexity. As the ware seems to occur earliest in the north of Britain, this may be its area of origin, although there are no obvious ceramic precedents for its form or decorative style; it has also often been remarked that certain motifs that occur occasionally on Grooved Ware vessels, such as spirals, seem to be derived from the megalithic art found in the Boyne Valley tombs (and on associated maceheads etc.), which is also present in the Orkney tombs and villages.

G. Wainwright and I. Longworth: *Durrington Walls: excavations 1966–1968* (London, 1971), 234–306; R. Bradley: *The social foundations of prehistoric Britain* (London, 1984), 46–67; G. Wainwright: *The henge monuments* (London, 1989), 32–41; A. Gibson and A. Woods: *Prehistoric pottery for the archaeologist* (Leicester, 1990), 64–6, 173–6.

RJA

Guanghan *see* KUANG-HAN

Gumban *see* PASTORAL NEOLITHIC

Gumelniţa (Gumelnitsa) Chalcolithic culture spread across areas of Romania, Bulgaria, southern Moldova and southwestern Ukraine (Odessa district), identified by V. Dumitrescu (1924). Gumleniţa sites, usually unfortified tells, are located on river terraces (e.g. the Danube and Prut) and on the shores of fresh-water lakes. Their economy was based on agriculture and stock-breeding; domestic cattle, sheep/goat, pig and horse, in that order of importance, make up about 90% of the faunal assemblage. Crops included einkorn, emmer and spelt wheats; hulled and naked barley; and millet. Remains of two-storeyed dwellings, 13 to 7 m in size, have been found at the site of Ozyornoe in the Danube-Dniestr interfluve. Three ritual burials have been identified at the site of Bolgrad in the same area, comprised of two burials of skulls, and a burial of a child in a contracted posture on a stone pavement with a polished beaker at its feet. The radiocarbon dates suggest a calendar date of around 4700–4200BC.

V. Dumitrescu: 'Découvertes de Gumelniţa', *Dacia*, n.s. (1924/1), 407–23; S.N. Bibikov: 'Pam-jatki kul'turi Gumel'nitsja n territorii URSR' [Gumelniţa sites in the territory of the Ukrainian SRS], *Arheologija Ukrains'koi RSR* [Archaeology of the Ukrainian SSR], ed. D. Ya. Telegin (Kiev, 1971), 210–13; E. Comsa: 'Querques remarques sur l'évolution de la culture Gumelniţa', *Balcanica* VII (Beograd, 1976), 14–43; L.V. Subbotin: 'O sinhronizacii pamjatnikov kul'tury Gumelnica n nižnem Poduvav'je' [On the synchronization of the Gumelniţa sites in the Lower Danube area], *Arheologičeski issledovanija Severo-Zapadnogo Pročernomor'ja* [Archaeological investigations in the Northwestern Pontic area] (Kiev, 1978), 29-40.

PD

Gundestrup cauldron Partly gilded silver vessel composed of a simple basin and side-wall plaques decorated in repoussé in Animal Style, found disassembled in the Gundestrup peat bog in Jutland, Denmark in Jutland in 1891. The superb workmanship is paralleled in Thracian work from the 4th century BC on, and the most recent analysis of its origins suggests that it may be a southeast European work of the 2nd century BC – possibly carried north as war booty – although Gaul *c.*100 BC–AD 200 has also been suggested. Certain parts of the complex iconography (particularly an antlered god or shaman figure) seem to be Celtic-influenced; others derive from Greek and even Indian mythology.

A. Berquist and T. Taylor: 'The origin of the Gundestrup Cauldron', *Antiquity* 61 (1987), 10–24.

RJA

Guran, Tepe *see* LURISTAN

Gurob (Medinet el-Ghurob; anc. Mi-wer) Egyptian site at the southeastern end of the Faiyum region, which was excavated between 1888 and 1920. The principal settlement at Gurob is identified with the textually-attested town of Mi-wer, which was established by Thutmose III (*c.*1479–1425 BC) as a royal 'harim', and appears to have flourished in the reign of Amenhotep III (*c.*1391–1353 BC). Kemp (1978) has synthesized the results of the various excavations to gain an impression of the New Kingdom harim-town which must have superseded an early 18th-dynasty village.

W.M.F. Petrie: *Kahun, Gurob and Hawara* (London, 1890); ——: *Illahun, Kahun and Gurob* (London, 1891); W.L.S. Loat: *Gurob* (London, 1905); G. Brunton and R. Engelbach: *Gurob* (London, 1927); B.J. Kemp: 'The harim-palace at Medinet el-Ghurab', *ZÄS* 15 (1978), 122–33; A.P. Thomas: *Gurob: a New Kingdom town*, 2 vols (Warminster, 1981).

IS

Gutians Ancient Near Eastern people of the late 3rd millennium BC whose origins were perhaps in the northern ZAGROS region of Mesopotamia. Along with the AMORITES and ELAMITES, the Gutians appear to have made a significant contribution to the decline of the AKKADIAN dynasty in the mid-22nd century BC, and texts from Hammurapi's reign indicate that they also troubled the emerging First Dynasty of Babylon in the early 19th century BC. The king-lists suggest that there was a single Gutian dynasty consisting of 21 rulers and lasting for approximately 80 years (*c.*2200–2120 BC), but there is little evidence – whether archaeological or textual – to suggest that the Gutians made any enduring cultural impact on Mesopotamia.

J. Gadd: 'The dynasty of Agade and the Gutian invasion', *Cambridge Ancient History* I/2, ed. I.E.S. Edwards et al., 3rd edn (Cambridge, 1971), 417–63 [457–63]; W.W. Hallo: 'Gutium', *Reallexikon der Assyriologie* 3 (1971), 708–20.

IS

Guzana *see* TELL HALAF

Gwisho Group of mounds located on the south flank of the Kafue River, 80 miles southwest of Lusaka, Zambia, where a set of hot springs lie along the margin of the wooded uplands and the grassy lowlands of the Kafue valley bottom. Three hot-spring mounds have been excavated, revealing intermittent occupation over a period of 400 years, from around uncal 4,700 BP onwards. The excellent preservation of plant and animal remains provides a vivid picture of material culture and diet. The material includes both winter and summer indicators and the sites were evidently used at all seasons for the exploitation of both adjacent eco-zones. Thirty-five burials indicate a population described as 'Large Khoisan'.

C. Gabel: *Stone Age hunters of the Kafue: the Gwisho A site* (Boston, 1965); B.M. Fagan and F.L. van Noten: *The hunter-gatherers of Gwisho* (Tervuren, 1971).

RI

H

Habuba Kebira (including Tell Qannas) Site of an important settlement of the late URUK period (*c.*3300–3100 BC), located on the right bank of the Euphrates in northern Syria. Excavated during the 1970s by Dietrich Sürenhagen and Eva Strommenger, Habuba is one of the best surviving examples of town planning from the 4th millennium BC. The 18-hectare city was surrounded on three sides by a huge mud-brick buttressed wall, while its eastern side was protected by the river. There are two fortified gateways in the western wall, and at the southern end of the city is an acropolis (Tell Qannas) surmounted by a series of temples. The settlement is divided in two along its north-south axis by a wide potsherd-paved road, and the southern side (still unexcavated) incorporates a harbour area. Harvey Weiss (1985: 81–2) suggests that colonies in Syria, such as Habuba and the nearby Jebel Aruda, were established in order to supply the cities of the Mesopotamian heartland with certain commodities unavailable in the south, such as mineral resources or animal skins.

E. Strommenger: *Habuba Kabira: ein Stadt vor 5000 Jahren* (Mainz, 1980); H. Weiss: 'Protohistoric Syria and the origins of cities and civilization', *Ebla to Damascus: art and archaeology of ancient Syria*, ed. H. Weiss (Seattle, 1985) 77–83; G. Algaze: *The Uruk world system* (Chicago, 1993).

IS

Habur *see* KHABUR

Haçilar Southwestern Anatolian Neolithic settlement, the earliest strata of which contain ACERAMIC NEOLITHIC architectural remains dating to at least as early as the 7th millennium BC. The surviving evidence of flora and fauna indicates that the inhabitants relied on a combination of hunting and farming. Little artefactual material has survived in these deposits; James Mellaart (1970: 309) suggests that more objects would have been left on the floors if the early Neolithic settlement had been destroyed abruptly by fire rather than gradually abandoned. The next major phase, the 'Late Neolithic' (levels IX–VI), has been radiocarbon-dated to *c.*5750–5600 BC (Mellaart 1970: 313), and the material culture indicates a move away from the earlier subsistence base to a purely agricultural diet. The final phase, the early Chalcolithic (*c.*5600–4700 BC), includes a totally excavated fortified village (levels I–II) which is larger than the similar fortress constructed at Mersin almost a millennium later. The Haçilar fortress is a typical example of a Western Asiatic Chalcolithic settlement, with its two-storey mud-brick houses, potters' workshops and communal well. The Chalcolithic sequence at Haçilar ends in a conflagration which seems to have destroyed the entire village.

Preliminary excavation reports by James Mellaart in *AS* 8–11 (1958–61); ——: *Excavations at Haçilar*, 2 vols (Edinburgh, 1970).

IS

Hadar Early hominid site in the Afar depression of northeastern Ethiopia, about 300 km north of Addis Ababa. Numerous postcranial Australopithecine remains, dating to about 3.5 million years ago, were discovered at Hadar, including almost half of an *Australopithecus africanus* (or *afarensis*) skeleton, nicknamed 'Lucy' (Johanson and Edey 1981). Acheulean tools were found in the upper layers, while flaked-cobble artefacts were found at levels dated to about 2.6 million years ago (Roche and Tiercelin 1980), too late to have been associated with the Australopithecine remains. As at OMO, the site has been dated by PALAEOMAGNETISM and POTASSIUM ARGON DATING, as well as by the study of several thousand fossilized bones of mammals found throughout Pliocene and Pleistocene levels (White et al. 1984).

D.C. Johanson and M. Taieb: 'Plio-Pleistocene hominid discoveries in Hadar, Ethiopia', *Nature* 260 (1976), 293–7; H. Roche and J.J. Tiercelin: 'Industries lithiques de la formation plio-pleistocène d'Hadar, Ethiope', *Proceedings, 8th Panafrican Congress of Prehistory*, ed. R.E. Leakey and B.A. Ogot (Nairobi, 1980), 194–9; D.C. Johanson and M.A. Edey: *Lucy: the beginnings of humankind* (London, 1981); T.D. White et al.: 'Hadar biostratigraphy and

hominid evolution', *Journal of Vertebrate Paleontology* 4 (1984), 575–83.
IS

el-Hadr *see* HATRA

Hafit *see* ARABIA; PRE-ISLAMIC

Haft Tepe *see* ELAM

Hafun (Opone) Site of an early maritime trading settlement on the coast of Somalia, at the easternmost point of the African continent. Investigations by the British Institute in Eastern Africa have revealed two principal periods of activity at Hafun: the 1st century BC and the 3rd–5th centuries AD. Ras Hafun appears to have served as a stopping point for ships plying between the Red Sea and India, and also as a link for the trade of Azania (East Africa) as far as the port of RHAPTA. *The Periplus of the Erythraean Sea*, a Greek document of the 1st century AD, refers to Hafun as Opone.
H.N. Chittick: 'An archaeological reconnaissance in the Horn: the British-Somali expedition 1975', *Azania* 11 (1976), 117–33; M.C. Smith and H.T. Wright: 'The ceramics from Ras Hafun in Somalia: notes on a classical maritime site', *Azania* 23 (1988), 115–46.
JS

Hajar bin Humeid *see* ARABIA, PRE-ISLAMIC

Hajji Muhammed *see* UBAID

Halaf, Tell (anc. Guzana) Type-site of the Halaf period of protohistoric northern and eastern Mesopotamia (*c.*5500–4500 BC) which was roughly contemporary with the early UBAID culture in southern Mesopotamia. Tell Halaf, a large settlement mound situated by the Khabur river on the border between Turkey and Syria, was excavated by Baron Max Freiherr von Oppenheim in 1899–1929. He concentrated mainly on the remains of the ARAMAEAN town of Guzana, dating to the 1st millennium BC, although his excavations below the floor-level of the palace revealed earlier strata of exquisite hand-made, black and red painted pottery. It was not until the excavation of Halaf–period strata at other sites, such as NINEVEH and TELL ARPACHIYAH, that this 'Halaf ware' was recognized as one of the essential characteristics of material culture in Mesopotamia overlapping with the SAMARRA and UBAID periods. The Halaf phase was, as a matter of geographical necessity, characterized by a 'dry farming' subsistence pattern (i.e. based on rainfall rather than irrigation) and settlements consisting of a mixture of rectilinear architecture and small mud-brick beehive-shaped huts or storerooms (known as *tholoi* by analogy with the Mycenaean tomb-type), rather than the large multi-roomed houses of the preceding HASSUNA and Samarra cultures. Typical Halaf artefacts included flint and obsidian tools, female terracotta figurines, and amulets in the form of gabled houses or double-axes, but it was the pottery, fired in two-chamber kilns, that was the most distinctive (and widely traded) aspect of the assemblage. More recently excavated Halaf-period strata at YARIM TEPE and various sites in the Hamrin basin (Watson 1983) have helped to refine the perception of the Halaf culture.
M.F. von Oppenheim: *Tell Halaf: A new culture in oldest Mesopotamia* (London, 1933); H. Schmidt: *Tell Halaf I: Die prähistorischen Funde* (Berlin, 1943); D. Frankel: *Archaeologists at work: studies on Halaf pottery* (Worcester, 1979); T.E. Davidson and H. McKerrell: 'The neutron activation analysis of Halaf and Ubaid pottery from Tell Arpachiyah and Tepe Gawra', *Iraq* 42 (1980), 155–67; P.J. Watson: 'The Halafian culture: a review and synthesis', *The hilly flanks and beyond*, ed. T.C. Young et al. (Chicago, 1983), 231–50; G. Roux: *Ancient Iraq*, 3rd edn (Harmondsworth, 1992), 55–9.
IS

Halaf period, Halaf culture *see* TELL HALAF

Halawa Valley On eastern Moloka'i in the Hawaiian Islands, Halawa is a broad deep valley with a permanent stream, and is one of a number of Hawaiian valleys to be surveyed archaeologically (Kirch 1984). Permanent settlement was established around 1400 BP, when it was restricted to the mouth of the valley. From 650 BP there was a major extension of settlement into the interior of the valley, and rectangular buildings were erected on stone-faced terraces; agricultural terraces were also built at this time, as well as irrigation systems. These were considerably extended from 300 BP onwards, as was the amount of public architecture in the valley, demonstrating the links between the intensification of agriculture and the intensification of social interactions.
P.V. Kirch and M. Kelly, eds: *Prehistory and human ecology in a windward Hawaiian valley: Halawa valley, Moloka'i* (Honolulu, 1975); P.V. Kirch: *The evolution of Polynesian chiefdoms* (Cambridge, 1984), 243–63.
CG

Halfan Late Palaeolithic industry in Sudan and Egypt, characterized primarily by the lithic assemblages found at hunting and fishing encampments along a 360 km stretch of the Nile Valley, from the second cataract northwards up to the region of KOM OMBO. Dated to the period between about 18,000 and 15,000 BC, the Halfan assemblages include some unusually small tool types, manufactured with an unusual LEVALLOIS technique and used to produce compound tools such as harpoons and arrows. The encampments generally appear to be smaller than those of their KHORMUSAN predecessors.

A.E. Marks: 'The Halfan industry', *The prehistory of Nubia* I, ed. F. Wendorf (Dallas, 1968), 392–460.

IS

half-life The time taken for half of a given number of atoms of a radioactive isotope to decay e.g. the half-life of ^{14}C (*see* RADIOCARBON DATING) is 5730 years.

Hallstatt Cultural phase of the late Bronze Age and the first part of the Iron Age in central Europe, named after a site close to Lake Hallstatt near Salzburg in the Austrian Alps. The site itself consists of the remains of a large cemetery, in an area made rich from the Bronze Age onwards by salt-mining – there are many ancient mine galleries in the locality. The inhumations and cremations (over 2000 burials have been found) are associated with numerous grave-goods, including pottery, finely made swords and other weaponry, horse fittings, and ornaments such as FIBULAE.

Following the German archaeologist Paul Reinecke, who first classified the material from Hallstatt, it is conventional to divide the Hallstatt period into Hallstatt A (1200–1000BC) and Hallstatt B (1000–800/750 BC) in the later Bronze Age; and Hallstatt C (800/750–600 BC) and Hallstatt D (600–450 BC) in the early Iron Age. The Hallstatt is also often broken up geographically into an 'east' Hallstatt (Austria, Poland etc) and 'west' Hallstatt (south Germany, east France).

Hallstatt A and B belong to the period of the URNFIELD COMPLEX of the later Bronze Age. This era is characterised by cremation burial in large pottery urns, often with short cylindrical necks and wide bodies. Grave goods include swords in range of standardized shapes – those discovered at the site of Hallstatt, as elsewhere, were often extremely finely made and decorated (e.g. amber pommels) – and a range of bronze pins and other ornaments. Although urnfield burials are not much differentiated in terms of grave structure, the number and richness of grave goods varies greatly and presumably reflects a social elite. A quite specific range of symbols was used in bronze decoration, including sun symbols, waterfowl and wagons. Unlike the cemeteries, settlements are not well documented but seem to consist largely of groups of farmsteads; excavations at one site at Hascherkeller in Lower Bavaria indicate that a range of crafts (weaving, bronze ornament casting, potting) were carried out even at smaller settlements (Wells 1993).

Hallstatt C marks the beginning of the Iron Age, during which iron implements and weaponry

Figure 18 **Hallstatt** Selection of objects found in Tomb 507 at Hallstatt, *c.*7th century BC. *Source*: *Trésors des princes celtes*, exh. cat. (Paris, 1987), fig. 47a.

gradually replace bronzes, and central Europe begins to reveal contact with Italy, perhaps facilitated by earlier trade in salt. Inhumation burial under barrows replaces cremation burial, and burials are more strongly differentiated by wealth. Hallstatt D is the period of the great Hallstatt princely burials, which present extremely rich inventories of gravegoods as well as four-wheeled funerary carts – an especially elaborate example is the HOCHDORF cart, covered in iron sheeting. However, many decorative objects continue to use the typically Hallstatt motifs of the waterbird, sun and wagon; Reinecke contrasted this early Iron Age Hallstatt material culture with the material in the succeeding LA TÈNE style (the classic period of CELTIC ART), which evolved after *c.*450BC and gives its name to the second half of the Iron Age.

Mediterranean trade and the growth of social complexity. The archaeology of the early Iron Age (Hallstatt D) in central and central-western Europe is dominated by a series of massive hillfort settlements, such as the famous HEUNEBURG and MONT LASSOIS hillforts, associated with a sequence of extremely rich princely burials such as those of KLEIN ASPERGLE or VIX. The hillforts of this period represent a complexity of organization in economy and society that outstrips anything seen before the 6th century BC; they are often regarded as 'proto-urban' in the sense that they demonstrate a concentration of population, a degree of planning in their layout or architecture, and specialised craft production centres. It is also during Hallstatt D (i.e. *c.*600–475 BC) that direct trading with the Mediterranean region and Mediterranean entrepots such as Massalia in southern France develops. The richer Hallstatt sites (e.g. Vix, Heuneberg) are often located near important river valley trading routes, particularly those that link northern and central Europe to the Mediterranean. The material culture of these sites is characterized by imports from the Mediterranean region, and by Mediterranean-influenced local production; in one of its building phases, the Heuneburg fortifications were rebuilt in mudbrick in a Mediterranean-influenced style. Much of the discussion of the early Hallstatt archaeological record centres on the question of whether the particularly rich and powerful chiefdoms of Hallstatt D arose as a direct result of trading relationships with the civilised world (e.g. Frankenstein and Rowlands 1978).

The prime example of an early Greek trading entrepôt, Massalia (or Massilia, now Marseilles) in southern France, was founded in the 6th century BC. The establishment of Massalia followed a Greek pattern of settling colonies and entrepots on the coast near trading river systems – a pattern begun with the establishment of Al Mina on the Orontes in Syria before 800 BC, Naucratis on the Nile Delta in Egypt in the 7th century BC etc. Unlike these early colonies, but like other colonies established on the Spanish and Black Sea coasts in the 7th and 6th centuries, the contacts Massalia established with its non-urban hinterland had a fundamental impact on the political and economic structure of the region. In the case of Massalia, 'luxury' goods such as decorated bronzes, fine pottery and wine flowed north; archaeological evidence for the goods obtained by the Greeks is lacking, but perhaps they secured slaves, furs, salt and iron.

Many of the imported goods are connected with wine consumption (Greek painted cups, Etruscan flagons, bowls and kraters), and seem to have formed prestige goods for the local elites. It may be that this form of 'conspicuous consumption' reflects the importance of feasting and gift exchange between elites at such meetings in the establishment of social dominance. In one developed version of this argument (summarised in Nicholson 1989), it is posited that the Greeks initiated the 'trade' by presenting local chieftains with elaborate presents in exchange for access to raw materials. The local leaders then used these exotic gifts to enhance their prestige and passed on the material as gifts to subordinate leaders. It is argued, though impossible to prove, that the gift-giving and receiving became intensely competitive, leading to an inflationary spiral in the exchange economy, with local leaders demanding ever more costly items to gather and permit passage of goods. As they developed trading relationships with the region north of the Black Sea, and elsewhere in Europe, it is possible that the Greeks discovered a cheaper or less problematic source of goods. Whatever the cause, the trading/exchange relationship between the Greek world and the early Celtic chiefdoms ended in crisis: at the end of Hallstatt D centres such as the Heuneburg are destroyed or quickly decline. As the established prestige-goods economy of the west Hallstatt region sank in importance, elites of adjacent regions grew in strength and inventiveness: the Hallstatt/La Tène transition seems to mark a shift in regional power as well as a cultural and artistic evolution.

S. Frankenstein and M.J. Rowlands: 'The internal structure and regional context of early Iron Age society in south-western Germany', *Institute of Archaeology Bulletin* 15 (1978), 73–112; P.S. Wells: *Culture contact and culture change: Early Iron Age Central Europe and the Mediterranean world* (Cambridge, 1980); N. Freidin: *The early Iron Age in the Paris Basin*, BAR IS 131 (Oxford,

1982); P. Nicholson: *Iron Age pottery production in the Hunsrück-Eifel-Kulture*, BAR IS 501 (Oxford, 1989); M.L.S. Sorensen and R. Thomas: *The Bronze Age-Iron Age transition in Europe*, BAR IS 483 (Oxford, 1989); P.S. Wells: 'Investigating the origins of temperate Europe's first towns: Excavations at Hascherkeller, 1978 to 1981, *Case studies in European prehistory*, ed. P. Bogucki (Ann Arbor, 1993), 181–203.
RJA

Hallur Prehistoric settlement on the Tungabhadra river in Karnataka, India, which was excavated by Nagaraja Rao in 1965. It consists of two phases: the Neolithic-Chalcolithic (early 2nd millennium BC) and the early Iron Age (BLACK-AND-RED WARE period; late 2nd millennium BC). Circular houses with earthen floors and interior hearths were found in the earlier phase, along with food remains dominated by cattle and domesticated millet. The iron artefacts recovered from the second phase have been identified as the earliest iron implements in southern India (Nagaraja Rao 1971: 139–41).
M.S. Nagaraja Rao: *Protohistoric cultures of the Tungahadra valley* (Dharwar, 1971).
CS

Hama (pre-Islamic) *see* ARAMAEANS

Hama (Islamic) Ayyubid and Mamluk citadel (11th–14th centuries AD), excavated in 1931–8. Still one of the most important Syrian TELLS so far studied, the Hama citadel – like other fortifications on the Islamic side of the frontier with the Crusaders – was rebuilt in the 12th century. The ceramics recovered were somewhat imprecisely recorded in terms of stratigraphy, but the excavation remains a central point of reference for the studies of Syrian ceramics of the 12th–14th centuries. The chronology of these ceramics is now being revised in the light of excavations at AL-RAQQA, ʿAna, Qalʿat Jabar and other Syrian sites.
V. Poulsen: 'Les Poteries médiévales', *Hama: fouilles et recherches de la Fondation Carlsberg 1931–38* IV/2 (Copenhagen, 1957), 115–283; D. Sourdel: 'Hamât', *Encyclopedia of Islam*, 2nd edn (Leiden, 1971); A. Northedge et al.: *Excavations at ʿÂna* (Warminster, 1988); C. Tonghini: *Qalʿat Jaʿbar: a study of a Syrian fortified site of the late 11th–14th century* (unpublished Ph.D. thesis, University of London, 1995).
GK

Hamadan *see* MEDES

Hamangia culture Late Neolithic culture of the lower Danube Black Sea region (Romania and Bulgaria) of the late 5th/early 4th millennium BC. Makers of a dark-coloured impressed and burnished pottery, the most famous site of the Hamangia culture is the cemetery of CERNAVODĂ where 400 or so extended inhumations are accompanied by stone jewellery, *Spondylus* shell beads and stylized pottery figurines.
D. Berciu: *Cultura Hamangia* (Bucharest, 1966).
RJA

Hammamia *see* EL-BADARI

Han dynasty Chinese chronological phase dating from 206 BC to AD 220. Following the downfall of the short-lived empire of CH'IN, and the unsuccessful attempt of the aristocratic Hsiang Y to re-establish the old Chou form of federalism (*see* CHINA 2), Liu Pang (of peasant origin) finally defeated the former, and so established the empire of Han. The new centralized imperial form of government was gradually to take shape, with its marked emphasis on the roles of scholars and officials, and with the Confucian doctrine suitably applied to the exigencies of the new regime (*see* LU for brief discussion of Confucius). This general pattern persisted over the next two millennia. It was also during Han that the empire expanded over most of the area of present-day China, overland contacts with the civilizations of the West (including Rome) were first recorded, and tremendous progress was made in the arts, science, technology and commerce.
H.H. Dubbs: *The history of the former Han dynasty*, 3 vols (Baltimore, 1938–55); M. Loewe: *Records of Han administration*, 2 vols (Cambridge, 1967); Y Ying-shih: *Trade and expansion in Han China* (Berkeley, 1967); M. Loewe: *Everyday life in early imperial China* (London, 1968); H. Bielenstein: *The bureaucracy of Han times* (Cambridge, 1980).
NB

Hang Gon Settlement site in the Dong Nai valley, southern Vietnam. The site was disturbed by a bulldozer and subsequently examined by Saurin in 1960, when the surface finds recovered included three sandstone moulds for casting an axe and ring-headed pins. A late 3rd millennium BC radiocarbon date from the organic crust on the surface of potsherd has been used to support an early date for bronze metallurgy in Southeast Asia, but there was no stratigraphic relationship between the dated material and the moulds.
E. Saurin: 'Station préhistorique à Hang-Gon près Xuan Loc', *BEFEO* 51 (1963), 433–52.
CH

Haoulti-Melazo Axumite site in the Ethiopian highlands, located about 10 km southwest of the city of AXUM itself, which was excavated by Jean Leclant and Henri de Contenson during the 1950s. The principal building is a stone-built sanctuary in which numerous votive deposits have been found, including figurines representing domesticated animals and women. The pre-Axumite phase of the site has yielded South Arabian stelae, a pair of unusual limestone statues of seated women and an elaborate limestone throne, all of which indicate the cultural influence of South Arabia on the early development of the site.

J. Leclant: 'Haoulti-Mélazo 1955–1956', *AE* 3 (1959), 43–81; H. de Contenson: 'Les monuments d'art Sud-Arabe découverts sur le site de Haoulti (Ethiopie) en 1959', *Syria* 39 (1962), 64–87; ——: 'Les fouilles à Haoulti-Mélazo en 1958', *AE* 5 (1963), 1–52.

IS

Harappa Large urban site of the INDUS CIVILIZATION, dating to the 3rd millennium BC and located along the ancient course of the river Ravi, a tributary of the Indus, Pakistan. The total area covered by Harappa is about 150 ha, almost half of which is taken up by two principal mounds (AB and E) and a number of smaller ones.

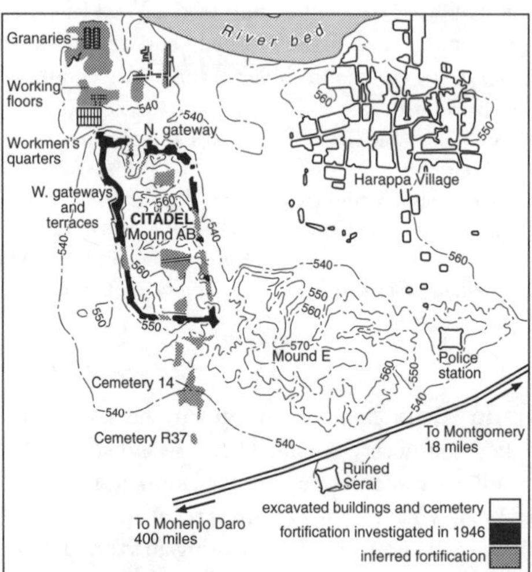

Figure 19 **Harappa** Plan of Harappa, type-site of the early Harappan civilization of the Indus Valley, showing the citadel mound, the mounds of the ruined lower town to the east, granaries and circular brick platforms (thought to be working areas for processing grain) to the north and, to the south, one of the few cemeteries known from the Harappan civilization (marked R37). *Source*: B. and R. Allchin: *The rise of civilization in India and Pakistan* (Cambridge, 1982), fig. 7.2.

The site has been excavated by Rai Bahadur Daya Ram Sahni (1920–25), Madho Sarup Vats (1925–34), Sastri (1937–41), Mortimer Wheeler (1946) and M.R. Mughal (1966). The current excavations (Meadow 1991) indicate continuous occupation from pre-urban Early Harappan to the post-urban Late Harappan period. Brick quarrying by 19th-century British railway builders resulted in disturbances of archaeological deposits and little is known of the original urban plan and architectural style. The architectural fragments that have been excavated provide evidence for multi-roomed rectangular structures built on unbaked brick platforms.

The structures and platforms at Harappa, constructed of standardized unbaked or fired bricks in the typical Indus 1:2:4 size ratio, were arranged along streets, and evidence for an extensive system of drains and wells also exists. The 'citadel mound' (AB), 18m high, consisted of massive mud-brick platforms and revetment walls, containing numerous wells, drains and fragmentary structural remains. Recent excavations on the eastern mound (E) have revealed an enclosure wall and gateway, structures of baked and unbaked brick arranged into streets, and several superimposed pottery kilns. Evidence for production of a range of other specialized craft goods has been identified from surface remains. The excavations on Mound F uncovered circular fired-brick platforms interpreted by Wheeler (1947: 77–8) as threshing floors, and a large structure often construed as a granary.

Two distinct areas of burials have been excavated – the Mature Harappan Cemetery R37, with more than 200 graves, and the post-urban Cemetery H. Artefacts from the Early Harappan levels include painted ceramics similar to KOT DIJI style ceramic vessels, as well as ceramic bangles, and animal and human figurines. Typical Mature Harappan artefacts include steatite seals, terracotta figurines, FAIENCE, shell, stone and ceramic ornaments and a wide range of wheel-made ceramic vessels. The types of pottery range from undecorated wares to black painted red ware storage and serving vessels, including the characteristic dish on stand, painted in naturalistic motifs including leaves, birds, fish, and herbivorous mammals, and trees. Late Harappan artefacts include the distinctive Cemetery H ceramic burial urns, painted in black, with common motifs including the peacock, bull, stars, leaves, and trees, within parallel black bands.

M.S. Vats: *Excavations at Harappa* (Delhi, 1940); R.E.M. Wheeler: 'Harappa 1946: the defences and Cemetery

R37', *AI* 3 (1947), 58–130; R.H. Meadow, ed.: *Harappa excavations, 1986–1990* (Madison, 1991).
CS

Hargeisan Term used to describe the Late Stone Age industries of the Holocene in northern Somalia (Somaliland) and bordering Ethiopia. Like KENYA CAPSIAN, the Hargeisan industries are distinguished from the general run of the East African Late Stone Age (*see* WILTON) by the marked blade-and-burin element, the variety of types of point and, conversely, a less pronounced microlithic tendency.
J.D. Clark: *The prehistoric cultures of the Horn of Africa* (Cambridge, 1954), 218–9.
JS

Hariri, Tell *see* MARI

Harmal, Tell (anc. Shaduppum) Small townsite of the Early Dynastic period (*c.*2900–2350 BC) at the eastern edge of modern Baghdad, which was excavated in 1946 by the Iraqi archaeologist Taha Baqir. It was a small but well fortified town incorporating three temples. Cuneiform tablets found at the site identify it as the ancient city of Shaduppum ('the treasury'), a peripheral administrative centre of the Sumerian state of ESHNUNNA in the DIYALA REGION.
T. Baqir: *Tell Harmal* (Baghdad, 1959).
IS

Harness (Edwin Harness Mound) The largest of 14 earthen mounds comprising the Liberty Earthworks, Ross County, Ohio (USA). It is associated with the Middle WOODLAND period (*c.*200 BC–AD 400, *see* HOPEWELL) cultural manifestation. Mound investigations began in the early 19th century and continued, intermittently, until the 1970s. The presence of numerous human burials, many containing exotic materials (such as copper, mica and galena), indicates that the Harness mound was a Hopewell mortuary facility. Archaeological investigations conducted in 1976–7 revealed the remains of a Hopewell civic-ceremonial building at the base of the mound. Radiocarbon dates suggest that this building was constructed in about AD 300.
N. Greber: 'A comparative study of site morphology and burial patterns at Edwin Harness and Seip Mounds 1 and 2', *Hopewell archaeology: the Chillicothe conference*, ed. D. Brose and N. Greber (Kent, OH, 1979), 27–38; N. Greber: *Recent excavations at the Edwin Harness Mound, Liberty Works, Ross County, Ohio*, MJA Special Paper No. 5 (Kent, OH, 1983).
RJE

Harran (pre-Islamic) *see* ASSYRIA

Harran (Islamic) Islamic site which is one of the few in the Turkish part of Jazira to have been excavated, although the results have never been properly published. The excavations mainly had the effect of clarifying K.A.C. Creswell's studies of the Great Mosque, but had they been completed they would have been far more significant, since the site had survived very well, having avoided obliteration by Crusader period fortifications or modern settlement. Harran is far older than the Islamic period, but it is especially interesting as a site where paganism survived as late as the Caliph al-Maʿmun's visit in AD 830. It was the last capital of the Umayyads under Marwan II (744–750) who built a mosque. Under Salah al-Din (Saladin), much of the Umayyad mosque was rebuilt between 1171 and 1184 and in this later period the site relates to Ayyubid and Mamluk sites in northern Syria and Seljuk sites in Anatolia.
D.S. Rice: 'Mediaeval Harrân', *AS* 2 (1952), 36–84; K.A.C. Creswell: *Early Muslim architecture* I/2 (Oxford, 1969), 644–8; G. Fehérvari: 'Harrân', *Encyclopedia of Islam*. 2nd edn (Leiden, 1971).
GK

Hasanlu Bronze Age to Iron Age settlement site located to the south of Lake Urmia in northwestern Iran, which was first excavated by Aurel Stein in 1936. The site was occupied from the early 3rd millennium BC onwards, and the artefactual record of the second half of the 2nd millennium BC was characterized by a distinctive style of burnished black or grey pottery. However, it was during the 11th–9th centuries BC that the settlement flourished, when it was the principal city of the Manneans, a non-Indo-European people whose territory surrounded Lake Urmia. Stratum IV, the Mannean phase, includes the remains of a large palace complex. The site was eventually destroyed in *c.*800 BC, probably at the hands of the rulers of URARTU. The American excavations between 1959 and 1977 have revealed the bodies of the city's last defenders as well as weaponry, jewellery and metalwork. Among the metalwork, was a unique gold bowl decorated with motifs including deities, chariots and animals thought to be connected with HURRIAN mythology; the bowl is thought to be some centuries earlier in date than the phase of destruction.
A. Stein: *Old routes of western Iran* (London, 1940), 390–404; M.J. Mellink: 'The Hasanlu Bowl in Anatolian perspective', *IA* 6 (1966), 72–87; O.W. Muscarella: 'Hasanlu in the 9th century', *AJA* 75 (1971), 263–6;

——: *The catalogue of ivories from Hasanlu* (Philadelphia, 1980).
IS

Hassuna, Tell Type-site of the Hassuna cultural phase of the 6th millennium BC, which has been found at a number of sites in northern Mesopotamia. The sequence of three Neolithic camp sites in the lowest excavated strata at Tell Hassuna, a few kilometres to the south of Mosul, constitute the earliest traces of settled life in the plains of northern Mesopotamia. The next phase in the site's history is Hassuna Ib, which is probably contemporary with stratum I at the more southerly site of TELL ES-SAWWAN. The beginnings of the Hassuna culture (including elaborate mud-brick buildings and carved stone artefacts) have in fact been found at Tell es-Sawwan, rather than at the type-site itself. The people of the Hassuna phase typically relied on the cultivation of a variety of forms of grain (emmer, einkorn, bread wheat and barley) and built settlements consisting of streets of multi-room mud-brick houses with plastered walls; some of the dead (particularly children and adolescents) were buried, along with grave-goods (pottery and stone vessels and alabaster statuettes), under the floors of houses, although unidentified extramural cemeteries must also exist. There are two phases of Hassuna ceramics: 'archaic' and 'standard', the latter being more skilfully decorated and painted in a thicker brown paint. Tell Shemshara, a settlement in the lower Zab valley, is an aceramic version of the Hassuna culture, with no evidence of pottery until the onset of the Samarra phase in *c.*5600BC.

S. Lloyd and F. Safar: 'Tell Hassuna', *JNES* 4 (1945), 255–89; C.S. Coon: 'Three skulls from Hassuna', *Sumer* 4 (1950), 93–6; T. Dabagh: 'Hassuna pottery', *Sumer* 21 (1965), 93–111; P. Mortensen: *Tell Shimshara: the Hassuna period* (Copenhagen, 1970).
IS

Hassuna period *see* HASSUNA, TELL

Hastinapura Large multi-mounded site, located along an ancient course of the Ganges river in modern Uttar Pradesh, India, which may have been the site of the capital of the Kaurava kingdom. It dates from the early 2nd millennium BC to *c.*AD 300 and is mentioned in the Mahabharata. A few features in the lowest excavated levels may date to the OCHRE COLOURED POTTERY period (pre-1200 BC). The site was reoccupied from *c.*200 BC until *c.*AD 300, with the construction of fired brick buildings oriented along cardinal directions; materials from this period include wheel-made grey ware pottery vessels and Buddhist figurines.

B.B. Lal: 'Excavations at Hastinapur and other explorations in the upper Ganga and Sutlej Basin, 1950–52', *AI* 14 (1958), 4–48; T.N. Roy: *The Ganges civilization* (New Delhi, 1983), 30–3, 84–6.
CS

Hathial *see* TAXILA

Hatnub Ancient name for the site of a set of travertine quarries situated 18 km southeast of el-Amarna, on the eastern side of the Nile in Middle Egypt. The inscriptions, graffiti and archaeological remains of the workers' settlements show that it was intermittently exploited for about 3000 years, from the reign of Khufu (*c.*2551–2528 BC) until the Roman period.

R. Anthes: *Die Felseninschriften von Hatnub* (Leipzig, 1928); I.M.E. Shaw: 'A survey at Hatnub', *Amarna reports* III, ed. B.J. Kemp (London, 1986), 189–212; ——: 'Pharaonic quarrying and mining: settlement and procurement in Egypt's marginal regions', *Antiquity* 68 (1994), 108–19.
IS

Hatra (el-Hadr) Pre-Islamic town-site in the central Jazira steppe about 250 km northwest of Baghdad, which emerged during the SELEUCID period (*c.*250 BC) as a small caravan town and meeting place. By the end of the 1st century BC it had become the capital of the kingdom of Araba, which lay at the edge of the PARTHIAN empire. The fortified town, covering an area of over 300 ha, became a centre of Parthian resistance to the Romans as well as an important cult centre, but in AD 233 it was captured by the Roman army. A few years later the town was sacked by the SASANIANS (some of whose siege equipment was excavated in the surrounding region) and was then effectively abandoned.

W.I. al-Salihi: *Hatra* (Baghdad, 1973); J.K. Ibrahim: *Pre-Islamic settlement in Jazirah* (Baghdad, 1986).
IS

Hattusas (Boghazköy) *see* HITTITES

Haua Fteah Large cave site, forming the roofed portion of an oval, sediment-filled limestone dissolution shaft (120 × 70 metres in size) not far from the coast on the northern slopes of the Gebel el Akhdar in Cyrenaica, northeastern Libya. In 1951–5, Charles McBurney excavated a 14 m deep trench inside the cave, consisting of a main cutting (11 × 9 m) and a basal deep sounding (2.5 × 1.5 m), still without reaching bedrock. In analysing this single stratigraphic column, McBurney concentrated on questions of chronology and long-term culture change, as reflected above all in the lithic artefacts, particularly their metrical attributes. Eighteen radiocarbon dates were obtained for the upper part of the sequence, but for the lower part McBurney relied upon a combination of other methods, and in doing so he pioneered approaches later to be tested and tried at sites such as KLASIES RIVER MOUTH and BORDER CAVE. Interpolating and extrapolating from the radiocarbon dates, and making use of estimated rates of sedimentation, McBurney calculated the age of the basal deposits at about 90–100,000 years BP; within the sequence there were warmer and colder episodes (as shown by sedimentological and faunal analyses) which he equated with the last interglacial, the last glacial, and the current interglacial periods respectively. The occurrence throughout the sequence of molluscs used for food (*Patella coerula* and *Trocus turbinatus*) permitted a palaeo-temperature analysis of their shells and the comparison of these results with those obtained on Mediterranean DEEP-SEA CORES where the foraminifera showed similar fluctuations; these in turn could be compared with Caribbean cores for which absolute dates had been obtained by the Pa/Th method (*see* URANIUM SERIES DATING).

In McBurney's view, the 'industrial traditions' at the Haua could be seen 'growing and developing', subject to 'sudden outbursts or mutations' and also to 'decay and atrophy', 'in a manner strangely similar to the evolutionary history of organisms' (McBurney 1967: 14). The various changes in the cultural sequence were almost invariably interpreted as evidence of migration and/or population replacement, although the ultimate origins for such movements usually remained unknown. Whatever imperfections or limitations may be detected in the excavator's methods and theoretical assumptions, however, it remains true (as recognised by P.E.L. Smith) that the Haua is 'the most important Upper Pleistocene site known in North Africa.'

C.B.M. McBurney: *The Haua Fteah (Cyrenaica) and the Stone Age of the Southeast Mediterranean* (Cambridge, 1967); P.E.L. Smith: 'A key site on the Mediterranean', *Science* 164 (1969), 705–8; C.B.M. McBurney: *Archaeology and the* Homo sapiens sapiens *problem in Northern Africa. Lecture in honour of Gerrit Heinrich Kroom* (Amsterdam–Harlem, 1977); A.E. Close: 'The place of the Haua Fteah in the late palaeolithic of North Africa', *Stone Age prehistory*, ed. G.N. Bailey and P. Callow (Cambridge, 1986), 169–80.

PA-J

Hawara Egyptian royal necropolis in the south-east corner of the Faiyum region, dominated by the 12th-dynasty pyramid complex of Amenemhat III (*c.*1800 BC), which was excavated by Flinders Petrie in 1888–9 and 1910–11. The mortuary temple immediately to the south of the pyramid may originally have been similar to the complex surrounding the Step Pyramid of Djoser (*c.*2620 BC) at SAQQARA. Known to Classical authors as the 'Labyrinth', the temple was visited by Herodotus, who gave an account of a complex of 3000 rooms and many winding passages. In the surrounding cemetery Petrie found some of the most impressive Faiyum mummy-portraits dating to the Roman period (*c.*30 BC–AD 395).

W.M.F. Petrie: *Hawara, Biahmu and Arsinoe* (London, 1889); ——: *Kahun, Gurob and Hawara* (London, 1890); ——, G.A. Wainwright and E. Mackay: *The Labyrinth, Gerzeh and Mazguneh* (London, 1912); A.B. Lloyd: 'The Egyptian Labyrinth', *JEA* 56 (1970), 81–100; D. Arnold: 'Das Labyrinth und seine Vorbilder', *MDAIK* 35 (1979), 1–9.

IS

Hazleton *see* COTSWOLD-SEVERN TOMBS

Hazor *see* CANAANITES

heavy mineral analysis Destructive analytical technique used in pottery studies, whereby heavy minerals (specific gravity >2.9) are separated from the lighter fraction by flotation of the crushed sample in a liquid of known specific gravity, such as Bromoform. The heavy minerals sink in this liquid and can then be examined using a polarizing microscope. The technique is mainly applied to sandy fabrics which may not lend themselves to examination in thin section since the heavy minerals are present in low concentrations relative to the mass of undiagnostic quartz. The heavy mineral suite (e.g. kyanite, zircon etc.) can be compared to the heavy mineral assemblage in sands from known localities and thus helps to provenance the pottery.

D.P.S. Peacock: 'The heavy mineral analysis of pottery: a preliminary report', *Archaeometry* 10 (1967), 97–100; D.F. Williams: 'The Romano-British black-burnished industry: an essay on characterisation by heavy mineral analysis', *Pottery and early commerce*, ed. D.P.S. Peacock (London, 1977), 163–220.

PTN

Hebrews *see* ISRAEL, ISRAELITES

Heijo Site of the palace and capital of the Ritsuryo state in Nara prefecture Japan from AD 710 to 784. The capital was laid out on a grid-plan after the design of the Chinese capital of Chang-an and measured 4.3 × 4.8 km. The palace site was excavated from 1952 onwards, and was bought by the government to protect it from development in 1961. Plans of excavated palace buildings are reproduced in surface landscaping and some of the buildings and parts of the wall have been reconstructed using a combination of traditional and modern building techniques.

K. Tsuboi and M. Tanaka: *The historic city of Nara: an archaeological approach* (Paris and Tokyo, 1991).

SK

Heliopolis (Tell Hisn; anc. Iwnw) Egyptian site of the pharaonic period which is now largely covered by the northwestern suburb of Cairo. It was the site of the first known sun temple, dedicated to the god Ra-Horakhty and probably dating back to the early Old Kingdom (*c.*2600 BC). Excavations have also revealed a Predynastic cemetery, the tombs of the 6th-dynasty chief priests of Heliopolis, and a necropolis of 'Mnevis-bulls' dating to the late New Kingdom (*c.*1300–1070 BC). The only major monument still *in situ* is a pink granite OBELISK from the reign of Senusret I (*c.*1971–1926 BC). The obelisks now in New York and London (Cleopatra's Needles) both date to the New Kingdom phase of the site (*c.*1550–1070 BC).

W.M.F. Petrie and E. Mackay: *Heliopolis, Kafr Ammar and Shurafa* (London, 1915); F. Debono: *The predynastic cemetery at Heliopolis* (Cairo, 1988).

IS

Helladic Term used to describe the Bronze Age of central and southern Greece, just as Cycladic and Minoan describe the Bronze Age cultural sequences of the Aegean islands and Crete, respectively. The Helladic is divided into Early (3000–2000BC), Middle (2000–1550BC) and Late (1550–1050BC), with Late Helladic corresponding to the MYCENAEAN period.

RJA

Hell Gap Site in southeastern Wyoming which has given its name to a type of PALEOINDIAN projectile point and also to a complex of the PLANO Culture. The Hell Gap site consists of a stratified series of short-term campsites where bison was the predominant animal represented. Stratigraphy and point types at the Hell Gap site firmly established the Paleoindian sequence of Goshen, FOLSOM, Midland, Agate Basin, Hell Gap, Alberta, CODY, and Frederick complexes. Possible dwellings are represented by post-mould patterns at the Midland and Agate Basin levels and a circular arrangement of rocks that were weights for a *tipi* in the Frederick level.

C. Irwin-Williams et al.: 'Hell Gap: Paleo-Indian occupation on the High Plains', *PAnth* 18 (1973), 40–53.

WB

Hembury (or Southwestern) ware Type of early Neolithic pottery of the very end of the 5th millennium and earlier 4th millennium BC, named after a causewayed enclosure in Devon, and found throughout southwest England (and as far east as Wiltshire). Hembury ware is in the form of round-based open and rimmed bowls, often with lugs in a variety of shapes (and sometimes perforated). Peacock (1969) demonstrated that the gabbroic clay from which most Hembury ware is made comes from the Lizard Peninsular at the tip of Cornwall; it appears to have been a prestige ware, made by skilled potters and traded or exchanged over considerable distances.

D.P.S. Peacock: 'Neolithic pottery production in Cornwall', *Antiquity* 43 (1969), 145–9.

RJA

Hemmamieh (Hammamia) *see* EL-BADARI

Hemudo *see* HO-MU-TU

henge Ditched and banked circular and subcircular ritual enclosures of the British Neolithic and Bronze Age. The ditch is usually internal to the bank (unlike most historic defensive enclosures), although there are exceptions to this rule (notably Stonehenge); occasionally there is a bank both inside and outside the ditch. Henges can be as small as 10 m or less in diameter, while the most massive examples (e.g. the later examples in Wessex, notably DURRINGTON WALLS, Mount Pleasant, Marden, AVEBURY and Dorchester) can be over 400 m in diameter. There is usually one entrance (a 'Class I' henge), or two (a 'Class II' henge), most often opposed, entrances. Exceptional sites, such as Avebury, have up to four entrances. Class I henges seem to be the earliest, with examples dating from the late 4th millennium BC onwards, with Class II henges dating from the mid-3rd millennium into the late 2nd millennium. The Class II henges are also more likely to enclose major stone circles, and are often associated with GROOVED WARE pottery.

When excavated, many henges have revealed features such as internal settings of wooden posts. Exceptionally, at Durrington Walls and other major Wessex henges, these settings are concentric and massive and have been interpreted as the posts of huge wooden buildings, lying within the banks of the henge. There may also be pits, cists and burials or associated standing stones. A relatively small number of henges enclose stone circles; where this is so, the ditch and bank of the henge may remain an imposing element of the site, as at Avebury, or become a relatively minor boundary marker as at STONEHENGE. (Slightly confusingly, the term henge is derived from the name of Stonehenge – 'hanging stone' – which as a site is by no means a typical example of the henge class of monument.) Henges occasionally have bank-and-ditch ceremonial avenues leading up to their entrances, as at Stonehenge, and are sometimes also associated with another class of enigmatic ritual monument, the CURSUS.

Henges occur across much of Britain, although there are marked regional concentrations – notably in southern Britain (Wessex) and the Orkneys (e.g. the Stones of Stenness and Brodgar). They seem to have replaced the CAUSEWAYED ENCLOSURES of the earlier Neolithic in providing a ritual focus for communities. Although they are generally classed as ritual (i.e. non-domestic, non-utilitarian) structures, henges are so varied in their size, development over time, and the internal structures they exhibit, that the nature of that ritual must have varied considerably.

R.J.C. Atkinson et al.: *Excavations at Dorchester, Oxon* (Oxford, 1951); A. Burl: *Stone circles of the British Isles* (Yale, 1976); A.F. Harding and G.E. Lee: *Henge monuments and related sites of Great Britain: Air photographic evidence and catalogue*, BAR BS 175 (Oxford, 1987).

RJA

Herakleopolis Magna (Ihnasya el-Medina; anc. Henen-nesut) Egyptian town 15 km west of modern Beni Suef, which reached its peak as the capital of the 9th and 10th dynasties during the 1st Intermediate Period. The surviving remains include two New Kingdom temples (one dedicated to the ram-god Harsaphes) and the nearby necropolis of Sedment el-Gebel incorporating a cemetery of the 1st Intermediate Period and Greco-Roman rock-tombs. There are also a settlement, cemetery and temple of the Third Intermediate Period (1070–712 BC), which have been excavated during the 1980s.

E. Naville: *Ahnas el Medineh (Heracleopolis Magna)* (London, 1894); W.M.F. Petrie: *Ehnasya 1904* (London, 1905); J. Padro and M. Pérez-Die: 'Travaux récents de la mission archéologique espagnole à Hérakleopolis Magna', *Atken München 1985* II, ed. S. Schoske (Hamburg, 1989), 229–37; M. Pérez-Die: 'Discoveries at Heracleopolis Magna', *EA* 6 (1995), 23–5.

IS

Hermopolis Magna (el-Ashmunein; anc. Khmun) Egyptian site located close to the modern town of Mallawi, which was the cult-centre of the god Thoth and capital of the 15th Upper Egyptian province. It was subject to extensive plundering in the early Islamic period, but there are still many remains of temples dating to the Middle and New Kingdoms, including a pylon (ceremonial gateway) constructed by Ramesses II (*c*.1290–1224 BC). The latter contained stone blocks quarried from the abandoned temples at the nearby site of EL-AMARNA (*c*.1353–1335 BC). There is also a comparatively well-preserved COPTIC basilica built entirely in a Greek architectural style and reusing stone blocks from a Ptolemaic temple.

G. Roeder: *Hermopolis 1929–39* (Hildesheim, 1959); J.D. Cooney: *Amarna reliefs from Hermopolis in American collections* (Brooklyn, 1965); G. Roeder and R. Hanke: *Amarna-reliefs aus Hermopolis*, 2 vols (Hildesheim, 1969–78); A.J. Spencer: *Excavations at el-Ashmunein*, 4 vols (London, 1983–93).

IS

Heshbon *see* HISBÂN

Hesy, Tell el- Settlement site on the southern Palestinian coastal plain, 26 km northeast of Gaza. The deepest strata date to the Early Bronze Age (*c*.3000–2100 BC) and the most recent archaeological remains comprise a Muslim cemetery of the 17th and 18th centuries AD. Flinders Petrie argued that the site was that of ancient LACHISH (now identified with Tell ed-Duweir), while William Albright suggested that it was the CANAANITE city-state of Eglon mentioned in the Bible (Joshua 10: 34–7), a theory which has still been neither proved nor disproved.

Investigated by Petrie in 1890, this tell-site was the first in the Palestinian region to be excavated using scientific stratigraphic techniques. The fortunate exposure of a large number of strata, as a result of floodwater erosion, enabled Petrie to establish an evolutionary typology (or SERIATION) of pottery types that could then be applied to the sections of stratigraphy in other parts of the site. He also used CROSS DATING, based on stratified Egyptian imports, to link the local chronology with that of Egypt. The site was subsequently excavated by Frederick Bliss, whose methods involved the pioneering use of a site GRID system involving a network of 5-foot squares. In 1892, Bliss's excavations in one of the Late Bronze Age strata ('City III') unearthed a cuneiform tablet bearing a letter written in Akkadian by an Egyptian colonial official called Pa'pu. This document, roughly contemporary with the 'AMARNA letters', was the first item of Egyptian diplomatic correspondence to be excavated outside Egypt.

From 1969 onwards the site has been surveyed and excavated by the American Schools of Oriental Research (Fargo and O'Connell 1978; Blakely et al. 1980–93), with the principal aim of re-evaluating the stratigraphy described by Petrie and Bliss. In addition to clarifying many details of the site's history, the American expedition has studied the changing climate and landscape of the coastal plain, in order to view the settlement in its full environmental and geomorphological context.

W.M.F. Petrie: *Tell el-Hesy* (London, 1891); F.J. Bliss: *A mound of many cities* (London, 1894); V.M. Fargo and K.G. O'Connell: 'Five seasons of excavation at Tell el-Hesy', *BA* 41 (1978), 165–92; J.N. Tubb and R. Chapman: *Archaeology and the Bible* (London, 1990), 26–9; J.A. Blakely et al., eds: *Tell el-Hesi*, 5 vols (Winona Lake, 1980–93).

IS

Heuneburg, the Early Iron Age (Hallstatt) hillfort near the upper reaches of the Danube in Baden-Württemberg, southern Germany. In most of its phases defended with timber and rubble fortifications, in the late 6th century BC the hilltop of the Heuneburg was (uniquely for Iron Age northern Europe) partly encircled with mud-brick walling on stone foundations and given projecting rectangular bastions. This is perhaps the most striking archaeological manifestation of the way in which the HALLSTATT elites copied Mediterranean inventions and styles, also shown in the imported items and artistic motifs and styles revealed in the princely burials of the period – e.g. HOCHDORF. (It seems doubtful whether mudbrick defences were suited to the wetter northern European climate, and it has been argued that the bastions were not usefully arranged – the innovations were abandoned in the next phase of building.) The Heuneburg settlement evidence includes amphorae, perhaps originally filled with wine, sherds of black-figure Greek vases (imported from the Greek trading centre of Massalia in southern France, founded *c.*600 BC) and other exotic items and materials such as coral. The Heuneburg may itself may have been a centre for the manufacture of elite items, including high quality wheel-made ceramics, and evidence of metal-working shops.

The Heuneburg is surrounded by a series of rich princely wagon graves, notably the 13m-high Hohmichele. The burials of this barrow (probably 6th century BC) were robbed, but fragments suggest a rich set of gravegoods and include a very rare find of silk cloth. This Heuneburg-Hohmichele pattern of a defended settlement with rich satellite burials is repeated at other chiefly residences of the period such as the Hohenasperg near Stuttgart (the richest grave here is KLEINASPERGLE) and MONT LASSOIS in eastern France (associated with the VIX burial).

E. Gersbach: 'Heuneburg – Aussensiedlung-Jüngere Adelsnekropole: Eine historische studie', *Marburger Beiträge zur Archäologie der kelten*, 1 (1969), 29; W. Kimmig: 'Early Celts on the Upper Danube: the excavations at the Heuneburg', *Recent archaeological excavations in Europe*, ed. R. Bruce-Mitford (London, 1975), 32–65.

RJA

el-Hiba (anc. Teudjoi, Ancyronpolis) Ancient Egyptian settlement and necropolis comprising remains dating from the late New Kingdom to the Greco-Roman period (*c.*1100 BC–AD 395). The date of the foundation of the pharaonic town of Teudjoi is not known – the range of ceramics and depth of stratigraphy revealed by excavations in 1980 suggest that it was founded during the New Kingdom or earlier. In the 21st and 22nd dynasties (*c.*1070–712 BC) Teudjoi became an important frontier settlement between the two areas controlled by the cities of HERAKLEOPOLIS MAGNA and HERMOPOLIS MAGNA respectively. It was during this period that the large temple of Shoshenq I was built. After a period of decline the town regained its importance under the name of Ancyronpolis in the Greco-Roman period (*c.*304 BC–AD 395), when it developed into a military settlement.

Surface survey and sampling strategies. The earliest excavators at el-Hiba tended to focus either on the Greco-Roman settlement (Ranke 1926; Paribeni 1935) or on the cemeteries, where a number of caches of Greek and demotic papyri were found (Grenfell and Hunt 1906; Turner 1955). In 1980, Robert Wenke undertook a surface survey of the whole site and a set of test excavations among the settlement remains. This procedure involved the use of surface sampling, which was initially intended to take the form of a series of randomly selected transects (i.e. a form of 'probabilistic sampling', *see* SAMPLING STRATEGIES) from which deductions about the site as a whole might be made by statistical means. However, the ancient construction methods at el-Hiba had involved the movement of debris across the site and, in the post-depositional phase, varying degrees of looting and disturbance had taken place in different locations.

Wenke was therefore forced to adopt a more pragmatic non-probabilistic sampling design in which artefacts were collected from relatively undisturbed parts of the site or from locations intuitively considered to be more 'informative'. Because this design was not sufficiently comprehensive or systematic, it proved impossible to transform the samples into a computerized interpolation map of artefact-densities, as Wenke had originally intended. The samples instead formed the basis for interpretation of specific locations within the site (such as exposed surfaces below the foundations of the town enclosure wall, where stratigraphic layers predating the 21st dynasty were identified) and 'somewhat general observations about el-Hiba, none of which could be rigorously tested and confirmed' (Wenke 1984: 12). While these results were less satisfactory than originally hoped, they show that even severely disturbed Nilotic sites such as el-Hiba can provide new information with the use of non-probabilistic sampling designs specifically adapted to the site.

B. Grenfell and A. Hunt: *The Hibeh papyri* I (London, 1906); H. Ranke: *Koptische Friedhofe bei Karara und der Amontempel Scheschonks I. bei el Hibe* (Berlin, 1926); E. Paribeni: 'Rapporto preliminare su gli scavi di Hibeh', *Aegyptus* 15 (1935), 385–404; E.G. Turner: *The Hibeh papyri* II (London, 1955); R.J. Wenke: *Archaeological investigations at el-Hibeh 1980: Preliminary report* (Malibu, 1984).

IS

Hiba, Tell el- *see* LAGASH

Hierakonpolis (Kom el-Ahmar) Egyptian settlement and necropolis, some 80 km to the south of modern Luxor, which flourished during the late predynastic and Early Dynastic periods (*c*.4000–2649 BC). The walls of the Gerzean-period Tomb 100, now lost, were decorated with important late predynastic paintings (making this the first Egyptian tomb to have decorated interior walls); see figure 20 overleaf. It was during the work of James Quibell and Frederick Green on the town-site of Hierakonpolis that a number of protodynastic ceremonial artefacts, including the Narmer Palette (Egyptian Museum, Cairo) and Scorpion Macehead (Oxford, Ashmolean), were discovered in the so-called 'Main Deposit', between two walls connected with the Old Kingdom temple. Unfortunately the report of Quibell and Green's publication of this find was lacking in accurate plans and stratigraphic sections, therefore the original archaeological context of the assemblage is uncertain.

A new phase of survey and excavation in the Hierakonpolis region has been underway since the 1970s. The results of this more recent work have ranged from the identification of further predynastic sites (including a probable shrine, see Hoffman et al. 1986) to the analysis of social and economic differentiation in the early town (Hoffman 1974).

J.E. Quibell and F.W. Green: *Hierakonpolis*, 2 vols (London, 1900–2); B.J. Kemp: 'Photographs of the decorated tomb at Hierakonpolis', *JEA* 59 (1973), 36–43; B. Adams: *Ancient Hierakonpolis* (Warminster, 1974); M.A. Hoffman: 'The social context of trash disposal in the Early Dynastic Egyptian town', *AA* 39 (1974), 35–50; M.A. Hoffman et al.: 'A model of urban development for the Hierakonpolis region from predynastic through Old Kingdom times', JARCE 23 (1986), 175–87; B. Adams: *The fort cemetery at Hierakonpolis (excavated by John Garstang)* (London, 1988); ——: *Ancient Nekhen: Garstang in the city of Hierakonpolis* (New Malden, 1995).

IS

hieratic Ancient Egyptian script which was introduced by the end of the Early Dynastic period (*c*.2649 BC). Unlike the more elaborate HIEROGLYPHS, from which it presumably evolved, it was basically a cursive script (but should not be confused with 'cursive hieroglyphs'). The earliest surviving hieratic documents date to the 4th dynasty (*c*.2500 BC). Scribes were able to use hieratic for more rapid writing on papyri and ostraca, and their education was in hieratic rather than hieroglyphs.

R.J. Williams: 'Scribal training in ancient Egypt', *JAOS* 92 (1972), 214–21; W.V. Davies: *Egyptian hieroglyphs* (London, 1987), 21–3.

IS

hieroglyphs (Greek: 'sacred carved [letters]')
Sections: 1 Egyptian; 2 Mesoamerican

1 Egyptian

Egyptian writing system dating from the late predynastic period (*c*.3200 BC) to the 4th century AD. The hieroglyphic script, which comprised rows or columns of pictograms, ideograms and phonograms, was deciphered by Jean-François Champollion in 1822. The key to Champollion's success lay in his knowledge of the COPTIC language and his detailed study of the ROSETTA STONE, which was inscribed with a decree of Ptolemy V Epiphanes (196 BC) written out three times in different scripts (Greek, DEMOTIC and hieroglyphs), thus enabling both hieroglyphs and demotic to be compared directly with a known ancient language. Because hieroglyphs were mainly employed to decorate religious or funerary artefacts and architecture, they were essentially somewhat inflexible and conservative. Not unexpectedly,

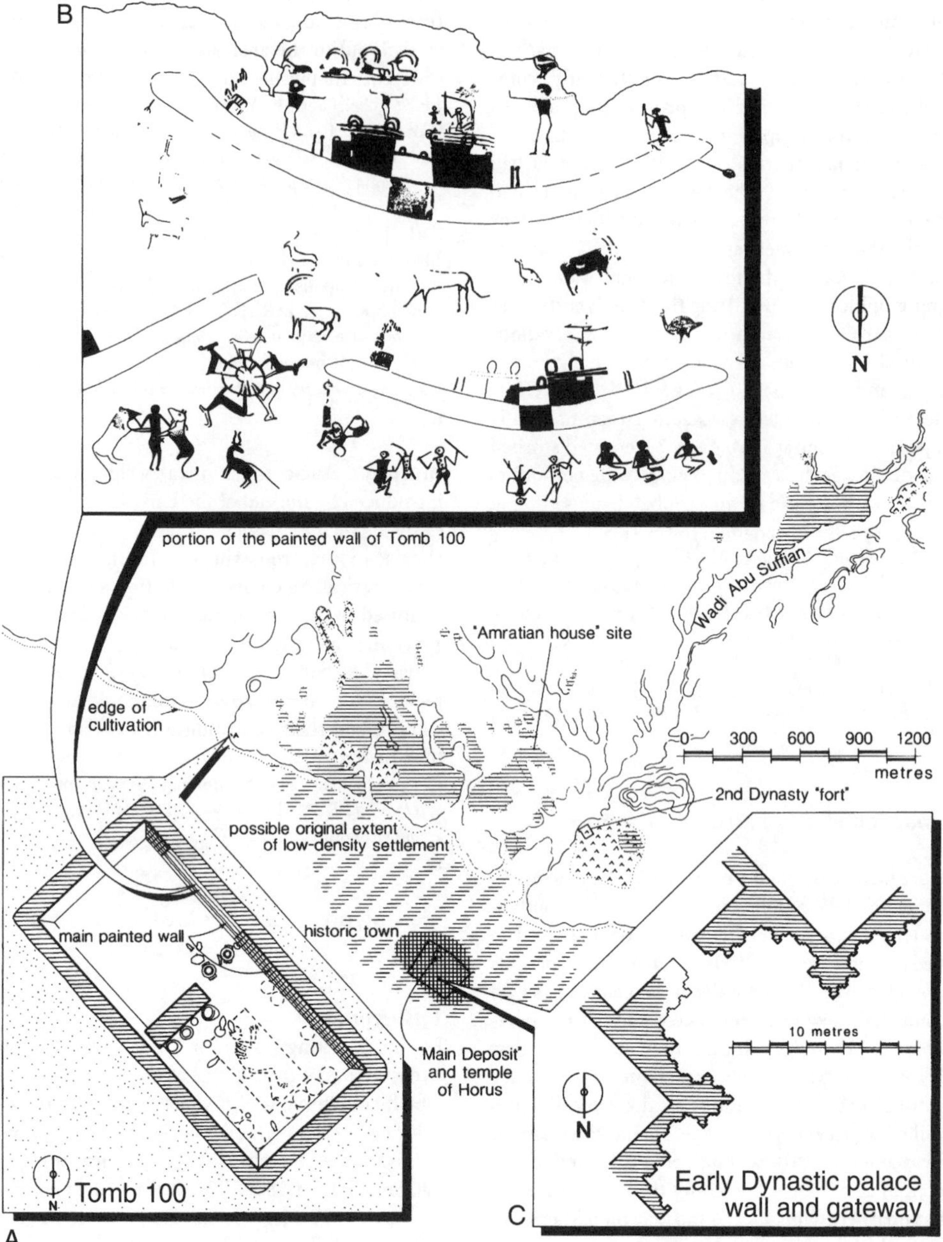

Figure 20 **Hierakonpolis** The underlying map in this illustration shows areas of low density Predynastic settlement in the Hierakonpolis area, and the possible continuation of that settlement beneath the present floodplain. The tomb of a king of this period (inset A) is known as the 'Painted tomb' because of its striking murals (inset B). In the floodplain stands the walled town of Hierakonpolis, dating to the Dynastic period; this represents a smaller but denser form of settlement, exhibiting monumental architecture such as the Early Dynastic palace and gateway (inset C). *Source*: B.J. Kemp: *Ancient Egypt: anatomy of a civilization* (Cambridge University Press, 1989), fig.11.

therefore, the vocabulary and syntax of the script appears always to have been somewhat antiquated compared with the spoken version of Egyptian. Nevertheless, the written language itself went through three fundamental phases: early, middle and late.

C.A. Andrews: *The Rosetta Stone* (London, 1981); J.R. Baines: 'Literacy and ancient Egyptian society', *Man* 18 (1983), 572–99; J.D. Ray: 'The emergence of writing in Egypt', *WA* 17/3 (1986), 390–8; W.V. Davies: *Egyptian hieroglyphs* (London, 1987).

IS

2 Mesoamerican

From Preclassic times onward, various Mesoamerican civilizations used symbols (called glyphs, or hieroglyphs) to record language. The earliest Mesoamerican writing is thought to be the name signs associated with the Danzantes at MONTE ALBAN in Oaxaca, Mexico, in the Late Preclassic period. Later, painted or carved glyphic texts appear on a variety of media, including stelae (*see* STELE), CODICES, building elements such as lintels or murals and portable objects of pottery, jade, bone, or carved stone. Relatively few examples of Classic-period Mesoamerican books (codices) are known, partly because they were perishable, but also because the Spaniards destroyed many of them as examples of 'idolatry' and 'heathenism' practiced by the indigenous Mesoamerican peoples they encountered in the 16th century AD.

In eastern Mesoamerica, Mayan writing is believed to be derived from a poorly understood tradition in the isthmian region of Mesoamerica. It is first found among the LOWLAND MAYA as brief inscriptions on portable objects and later appears in extensive texts on stelae or building elements. The writing style is syllabic and highly pictorial, consisting of glyphs representing ideas (ideographs), words (logographs) and phonetic signs. Texts are read from top to bottom and left to right. It was long thought that texts and images were impersonal references to deities (e.g. Thompson 1960). However in the late 1950s, the identification of EMBLEM GLYPHS, plus Tatiana Proskouriakoff's (1960) determination that some of the stelae at the site of Piedras Negras recorded the birth and accession of rulers, provided compelling evidence for interpreting the texts as history. Archaeologists then began to realize that most Maya texts are political, ritual, or calendrical, recording dynastic histories, genealogies and events in the lives of their rulers, as well as astronomical observations and calendrical rituals (see CALENDARS, MESOAMERICAN). Great advances have been made recently in deciphering Mayan glyphic texts through an increased understanding of individual elements (e.g. verbs) and syntax. Nonetheless, there is still some disagreement among epigraphers and archaeologists as to how much of the content is 'factual' political history as opposed to dynastic propaganda.

In Mexico, few if any texts are known from the large site of TEOTIHUACAN, although glyphs – often shared with other Mesoamerican languages – appear on murals, pottery and in other contexts. Because of the lack of evidence for readable texts, we know little about Teotihuacan's system of government, and apparently the site's administrators relied on oral histories or other methods for record-keeping. By contrast, MIXTEC codices from Postclassic (*c.*AD 900–1521) Oaxaca, like those of the Maya, reveal much about dynastic histories, genealogies and marital alliances, as well as providing territorial 'maps'. ZAPOTEC writing has a long history beginning roughly 600 BC and similarly records political events, conflicts and alliances, in addition to genealogical information, tribute records and 'maps' of lands. No large corpus of codices exists for the Zapotecs, unfortunately. AZTEC glyphic writing systems, like Zapotec, are more pictorial and less phonetic as compared to Mayan writing and relied heavily on contextual details to convey much of the information. Many of the surviving Aztec codices are tribute lists written after the conquests and have notations on them in Spanish.

The knowledge of how to 'write' (or inscribe) glyphic texts was probably fairly limited in Mesoamerica, and perhaps restricted to elite/priestly sectors of society. It is not known to what degree Mesoamerican peoples could read the texts, although the strong pictorial quality of most of the signs and the public placement of many of the texts (e.g. on stelae) suggests a minimal level of comprehension. Many texts may have been 'scripts' performed or chanted with musical accompaniment, rather than simply read.

T. Proskouriakoff: 'Historical implications of a pattern of dates at Piedras Negras', *AA* 25 (1960), 454–75; J.E.S. Thompson: *Maya hieroglyphic writing* (Norman, 1960); T.P. Culbert, ed.: *Classic Maya political history: hieroglyphic and archaeological evidence* (Cambridge, MA, 1991); Michael D. Coe: *Breaking the Maya code* (London, 1992); J. Marcus: *Mesoamerican writing systems: propaganda, myth and history in four ancient civilizations* (Princeton, 1992).

PRI

hilani *see BIT-HILANI*

Hili *see* ARABIA, PRE-ISLAMIC

hillfort Loosely-defined term used to group together a range of prehistoric sites. (Not all sites known as 'forts' were built primarily for defence, and not all fortifications occupy hill-tops – though this is certainly true of most.) Although defended hilltop sites are now known from the Neolithic (see CAUSEWAYED CAMP) and the earlier Bronze Age, significant numbers of massively defended sites appear only from the Late Bronze Age in the 1st millennium BC. A variety of constructional techniques were used, most commonly timber framework or lacing with an earth or rubble core, or drystone, though with occasional departures such as the mudbrick of the 6th-century phase at the HEUNEBERG in southern Germany. With regard to design, the simpler enclosures of the Bronze Age gave way to complex defences in the last few centuries BC, for example the elaborate, winding, heavily defended gateways at Maiden Castle, southern England. In southern England, the forts may be divided into an early group, often containing round houses and probable grain stores, and a more elaborate group constructed in the last few centuries of the first millennium that show planned interiors, including a division between grain and residential areas (Cunliffe 1978), and which are distant relations of the more sophisticated continental OPPIDA. Though many of the structures in this period are self-evidently defensive, they surely also acted as expressions of 'tribal' identity and power, and perhaps as centres of ritual. While the continental oppida (e.g. MANCHING) and a few of the later British forts may have been permanently occupied, and show evidence for manufacturing and as centres of trade, most hillforts probably acted only as temporary defensive or gathering points for people, livestock and stored produce. The complexities of understanding the function and history of one Iron Age hillfort are illustrated by the extensive excavations at DANEBURY in southern England.

B. Cunliffe: *Iron Age communities in Britain* (London, 1978).

RJA

Hirschlanden Tumulus of the 6th century BC, situated in Baden-Württemberg, Germany, which consisted of a central burial and secondary inhumations under a slab- and stone-bordered round mound. The mound was probably originally crowned by an imposing sculpture of a phallic warrior (ht. 1.5 m), found at the site in three pieces, who wears a conical helmet, belt and collar, and grasps a dagger. The hat is particularly interesting in that it resembles an actual hat made of birch-bark recovered from the contemporary burial at HOCHDORF. The Hirschlanden sculpture is especially important as the earliest large-scale figurative sculpture found in prehistoric Europe; this and certain parallels in the stiff pose suggest that its sculptor may have been influenced by the *kouroi* of Greece.

J.-P. Mohen: 'Hirschlanden', *Trésors des princes celtes*, eds. J.-P. Mohen et al., exh. cat. (Paris, 1987); W. Kimmig: 'Eisenzeitliche Grabstelen in Mitteleuropa', *Studi de Paletnologia in onore di Salvatore M. Puglisi* (Rome, 1985), 591–615.

RJA

Hisarlik (anc. Troy) Fortified Bronze Age settlement site on the western coast of Turkey which has been identified with the Homeric city of Troy. Excavated by Heinrich Schliemann and Wilhelm Dörpfeld between 1871 and 1890, the site presents a multi-phase fortress in a geographical location closely resembling that described in the *Iliad*. Schliemann and Dörpfeld were pioneering in their use of scientific stratigraphic excavation on a tell-site (see Daniel 1950: 166–9). However, the stratum which Schliemann identified as that corresponding to the period of the Trojan War (*c.*1250–1200 BC) eventually turned out – when the site was re-excavated by Carl Blegen in 1932–8 – to belong to a much earlier stage in the site's history (*c.*2000 BC). Until the early 1990s there was also great uncertainty regarding the present whereabouts of a hoard of 259 items of jewellery of the 3rd millennium BC, which Schliemann excavated from this erroneously dated stratum (therefore romantically described as 'Priam's Treasure'), but it is now known that the objects are in the Pushkin Museum in Moscow, having been removed from Berlin at the end of the Second World War.

H. Schliemann: *Troy and its remains* (London, 1875); ——: *Ilios, the city and country of the Trojans* (London, 1880); C.W. Blegen et al.: *Troy*, 4 vols (Princeton, 1950–8); G. Daniel: *A hundred years of archaeology* (London, 1950), 166–9; C.W. Blegen: *Troy and the Trojans* (London, 1963); J.M. Cook: *The Troad: an archaeological and topographical study* (London, 1973); J. Yakar: 'Troy and Anatolian Early Bronze Age chronology', *AS* 29 (1979), 51–68; C. Moorehead: *The lost treasures of Troy* (London, 1994); H. Duchêne: *The golden treasures of Troy* (London, 1996); I. Antonova et al.: *The gold of Troy: searching for Homer's fabled city* (London, 1996).

IS

Hisban (Heshbon) Islamic-period site in Jordan which, although not a key site in its own right, has considerable historical significance with regard to the study of early Islamic ceramics in Jordan and the neighbouring territories. It was on the basis of the excavated material from Hisban that a chronology for unglazed wares in the area was proposed by James Sauer (1971, 1986). Until this point, the study of Islamic ceramics was principally based on glazed wares and tended to ignore unglazed wares. Hisban placed these ceramics from Jordan within a chronology that embraced the Late Hellenistic, Roman, Byzantine, Umayyad and Ayyubid/Mamluk periods. The Hisban chronology and typology was subsequently refined by work at other sites (as the bibliography below reflects), with studies based on ceramics from Caesaraea, AMMAN, Pella, Bayt Ra'ṣ, AYLA and elsewhere.

J.A. Sauer: *Heshbon pottery 1971: a preliminary report on the pottery from the 1971 excavations at Tell Hesbân* (Berrien Springs, 1971); ——: 'Umayyad pottery from sites in Jordan', *The archaeology of Jordan and other sites*, ed. L. Geraty and L. Herr (Berrien Springs, 1986), 301–30; A. Walmsley: 'Architecture and artefacts from Abbasid Fihl: implications for the cultural history of Jordan', *The fifth conference on the history of Bilâd al-Shâm during the Abbasid period* II, ed. M.A. Bakhit and R. Schick (Amman, 1991), 135–59; D. Whitcomb: 'Reassessing the archaeology of Jordan in the Abbasid period', *Studies on the history and archaeology of Jordan* IV (Amman, 1992), 385–90.

GK

Hissar Group of sites in the mountain valleys of southeastern Tadjikistan, first discovered by A.P. Okladnikov in the 1940s and 1950s, and intensively studied by V.A. Ranov and others since the mid-1960s. Some of the sites were of a considerable size and consisted of several cultural layers (e.g. Tutkaul and Sai-Sayed). Subsistence strategies were predominantly hunting and food-collecting; stock-breeding appeared only at a later stage. Certain sites contained permanent dwellings with hearths, while others were seasonal hunting-camps. The lithic industry combined polished tools with microliths and archaic choppers and chopping tools. The lower level of Tutkaul has been dated to *c.*7100–7000 BC in calendar years. At some sites, the late Hissar levels are directly overlain by Bronze Age deposits dated to *c.*2000 BC.

A.G. Amosova et al.: 'Les enigmes de la culture de Hissar', *DA* 185 (1993), 14–21.

PD

Hissar, Tepe This site, located near Damghan in Iran, was identified in the 1920s as the illicit source of a particular style of painted pottery that had begun to appear on the art market. Excavated by Eric Schmidt in 1931–2, the earliest strata at the site (Hissar I), dating to the late Chalcolithic period (*c.*5000–4000 BC), consisted of mud-brick buildings accompanied by quantities of this distinctive ware, decorated with geometrical motifs. The next stratigraphic layer (Hissar II) appears to have strong connections with the proto-ELAMITE culture and incorporates a large number of lapis lazuli beads, suggesting that the city was playing an important role in the Mesopotamian trade with the quarries at Badakshan. However, the settlement reached its peak of prosperity in the Hissar III phase (*c.*2000–1550 BC, although see Gordon 1951 for a discussion of the dating problems), when a number of large public/ceremonial buildings were constructed. Among these was the 'Burnt Building'; its function is still a matter of some debate, but a season of further excavation in 1976 seems to have provided confirmation that it was a cult-place or sanctuary rather than a fortification, as the original excavators had suggested (Dyson 1977).

E.F. Schmidt: *Excavations at Tepe Hissar* (Philadelphia, 1937); D.H. Gordon: 'The chronology of the third cultural period at Tepe Hissar', *Iraq* 18 (1951), 40–61; R.H. Dyson: 'Tepe Hissar: Iran revisited', *Archaeology* 30 (1977), 418–30; —— and S.M. Howard, eds: *Tappeh Hesar* (Florence, 1989).

IS

Hittites Indo-European people who are initially encountered in the archaeological record of Anatolia during the late 3rd millennium BC, when they are probably to be identified with the early LUWIANS. Two further 'waves' of Hittite migration, probably emanating from the area of the Black Sea, culminated in the domination of the central Anatolian plateau, which was already known as Hatti; eventually the invaders took on the name of their new homeland, becoming known as Hatti or Hittites. At central Anatolian settlement sites such Alaca Hüyük the phases of pre-Hittite (or 'Hattian') occupation are followed immediately by the remains of typical Hittite structures, often using a CYCLOPEAN style of stone architecture.

Hattusas (now Boghazköy), was an important Hittite settlement from the late 3rd millennium onwards, and – like KANESH and many other Cappadocian sites – it incorporated a small satelite settlement of Old Assyrian merchants during the early 2nd millennium BC. By the mid-17th century BC it had become the Hittite capital, and the Boghazköy archive of cuneiform tablets has provided the principal basis for the reconstruction of their history, particularly after Bedrich Hrozny's decipherment of the Hittite language (Hrozný

1915). The sacred site of Yazilikaya – a series of rock-carved images of Hittite deities – is located about 2 km to the northeast of Hattusas.

There were two principal phases in Hittite history: the Old Kingdom (*c.*1680–1420 BC), when they consolidated their control over central Anatolia, and the 'Empire' (*c.*1420–1205 BC), during which they came into conflict – and diplomatic contact – with the other major powers in the region: Egypt, Assyria and Mitanni. The invasion of the SEA PEOPLES in the early 12th century BC appears to have instigated their decline. In the ensuing five centuries the 'neo-Hittites' (or Syro-Hittites) dominated part of eastern Anatolia and northern Syria, notably at Karatepe, CARCHEMISH and ZINJIRLI, but their political influence was considerably diminished. It was in the neo-Hittite phase that the 'Hittite hieroglyphs' came into use – the discovery of a bilingual Phoenician/Hittite hieroglyph text at Karatepe has helped greatly in the slow process of their decipherment (although it appears that most of the hundred or so texts consist simply of names and titles).

B. Hrozný: 'Die Lösung des hethitischen Problems', *MDOG* 56 (1915), 17–50; K. Bittel et al.: *Bogazköy-Hattusa*, 14 vols (Berlin, 1952–87); E. Akurgal: *The art of the Hittites* (London, 1962); K. Bittel: *Hattusha: the capital of the Hittites* (New York, 1970); I.J. Winter: 'On the problems of Karatepe: the reliefs and their context', *AS* 29 (1979), 115—51; J.G. Macqueen: *The Hittites and their contemporaries in Asia Minor*, 2nd edn (London, 1986); O.R. Gurney: *The Hittites*, 2nd edn (Harmondsworth, 1990).

IS

Hiw-Semaina region (Diospolis Parva) Group of Egyptian sites dating from the predynastic period to the Roman period, situated on the east bank of the Nile in Upper Egypt. The 15 km region was surveyed and excavated by Flinders Petrie in 1898–9, and it was his excavation report on the predynastic cemeteries of Abadiya and Hiw (Petrie 1901) that provided him with the necessary data to create the first relative chronology of the late predynastic period (*see* SERIATION). In 1989 Kathryn Bard conducted a fresh survey of the area; although she discovered that the predynastic Cemeteries U and R and the Old Kingdom mastaba at Cemetery A had been destroyed, she was able to re-examine a few surviving patches of predynastic settlement, of which Petrie had made only cursory mention in his report. Bard (1989: 4) notes that the range of pottery from the settlement-sites HG and SH differs in a number of respects from that found in the associated cemeteries.

W.M.F. Petrie: *Diospolis Parva: the cemeteries of Abadiyeh and Hu* (London, 1901); K. Bard: 'Predynastic settlement patterns in the Hiw-Semaineh region, Upper Egypt', *Nyame Akuma* 32 (1989), 2–4.

IS

Hoabinhian Stone Age culture in Southeast Asia, named after the Hoa Binh province of northern Vietnam, south of the Red River delta, where Madeleine Colani identified and excavated a number of rock shelters in the 1920s. The cultural remains included a flaked stone industry, with edge-ground implements and pottery in the upper layers of some sites. Animal bones included extant species, and there was much evidence for fishing and shellfish collecting. Radiocarbon dates from this region fall between 9000–5000 BC. Subsequent research in island as well as mainland Southeast Asia has identified other sites, mainly rockshelters, with a similar material culture and chronology, and these too have been labelled Hoabinhian. Solheim (1972) has sought the origins of agriculture in these sites, but so far with no convincing evidence.

Hoabinhian-style material dated to the 4th millennium BC and later is documented at sites such as the Banyan Valley Cave, a set of large caves located next to a stream in precipitous karst country in northern Thailand. Excavations in 1972–3 revealed a material culture based on flaked stone implements, associated with animal and plant remains that indicted exploitation of the surrounding forest and stream margins. The upper layers at Banyan Valley Cave contained pottery remains, small slate knives and edge-ground adzes as well as 110 rice husks. Yen (1977) has concluded that the husks were probably harvested from wild stands. The basal layers have been radiocarbon-dated to the 4th millennium BC, but the upper contexts date as late as the 1st millennium AD, long after rice was a cultivated crop in the lowlands of Southeast Asia. This late context for the upper layers at Banyan Valley Cave is most unusual, and a detailed report on the material dated is required before its affinities (if any) with the Hoabinhian can be assessed.

M. Colani: 'L'âge de la pierre dans la province de Hoa Binh', *MSGI* 13/1 (1927); W.G. Solheim: 'An earlier agricultural revolution', *SA* 206/4 (1972), 34–41; D.E. Yen: 'Hoabinhian horticulture: the evidence and the questions from Northwest Thailand', *Sunda and Sahul*, eds J. Allen et al. (New York and London, 1977), 567–99; T.E.G. Reynolds: 'Excavations at Banyan Valley Cave, northern Thailand. A report on the 1972 season', *Asian Perspectives* 31/1 (1992), 38–66.

CH

el-Hobagi *see* MEROITIC

Hochdorf (Eberdingen-Hochdorf) Rich barrow burial of the Celtic HALLSTATT period, associated with the fortified settlement of Hohenasperg in Baden-Württemberg, Germany. The barrow, which was constructed between *c.*550–500 BC, covered a wood-lined chamber hung with patterned woollen and linen coverings; the organic grave-goods at Hochdorf are preserved to an unusual extent, and include a shallowly conical hat, made of birch-bark, of the type worn by the contemporary HIRSCHLANDEN figure. Within the chamber the remains of a Celtic chieftain lay on a unique bronze couch that was decorated with horse-drawn wagons and sword-dancers. The grave goods included a four-wheeled wagon and drinking horns, while pieces of sheet gold-work (such as shoe-coverings) had apparently been manufactured at the site specifically to dress the corpse. The richness of the burial and the presence of an imported Greek cauldron encourage comparison with the roughly contemporary burial at VIX in eastern France.

J. Biel: 'The late Hallstatt chieftain's grave at Hochdorf', *Antiquity* 55 (1981), 16–18; ——: *Der Keltenfürst von Hochdorf* (Stuttgart, 1985); —— et al: 'Hochdorf', *Trésors des princes celtes*, exh. cat., ed. J.P. Mohen et al. (Paris, 1987), 95–188.

RJA

Hohokam Major prehistoric culture of the American Southwest, which lasted from the end of the Archaic period to the arrival of the Spanish in AD 1540. The Hohokam were peasant farmers who practised irrigation along the major rivers of the Sonoran desert of southern Arizona and northern Mexico. They cultivated corn, beans, squash, agave and cotton, and exploited Sonoran desert wild plant resources, especially cactus and legumes. During the Classic period, the Hohokam participated in the 'Mexican' expansionism that spread the temple mound/plaza complex throughout the agriculturally based societies of North America.

The Hohokam culture was defined by Harold S. Gladwin and Emil W. Haury in the 1930s on the basis of (1) extensive surveys to assess the extent of red-on-buff pottery (2) the excavation of two sites: Roosevelt 9:6 in 1931 and Snaketown in 1934–5, and (3) Haury's dissertation of 1934 in which he analysed Frank H. Cushing's excavation of Los Muertos.

Snaketown, a large multi-component site on the Gila river, south-central Arizona, served as the type-site and as the centre for debates concerning Hohokam chronology, which comprised three periods: Pioneer, Colonial and Sedentary (*c.*AD 1–1150). Unlike other cultural traditions of the Southwest, there are no DENDROCHRONOLOGICAL dates for the Hohokam; instead, its chronology is based on a combination of ceramic SERIATION and CROSS-DATING, as well as radiocarbon and ARCHAEOMAGNETIC DATING. Haury returned to Snaketown in 1964–5 to resolve questions of chronology, and this further galvanized the single-site focus of Hohokam studies. However, during the 1970s and 1980s, urban expansion and federally funded water projects necessitated extensive survey and excavation in Hohokam territory, the results of which have begun to form the basis for a broader regional picture.

The Hohokam cultural sequence is most conveniently divided into a Preclassic period (*c.*AD 200–1150), and a Classic period (*c.*AD 1150–1450), with the former encompassing the Pioneer, Colonial and Sedentary periods devised by Haury and Gladwin. The distinctive artefacts and behavioural characteristics of the Preclassic period include pottery thinned by paddle and anvil; red-on-buff decorated pottery with simple repetitive designs of people, desert animals and geometric shapes; clay figurines and effigy vessels; palettes, censers and other ceremonial items made of stone; brush houses arranged in extended family clusters dispersed in villages along major water courses; ballcourts (*see* BALLGAME) serving a public/ritual function; and cremation of the dead.

The Classic period is marked by a decrease in red-on-buff pottery and the appearance of distinctive Roosevelt Red Ware (SALADO) ceramics; adobe construction of houses and brush structures within adobe-walled compounds; extensive irrigation systems; public/ritual architecture of adobe 'great houses' and platform mounds; funerary practices including both inhumation and cremation. Throughout the Hohokam sequence, the material culture indicates that there was a strong and continuing connection with the agricultural peoples to the south, in modern northern Mexico.

The historical occupants of the southern Arizona desert – Tohono, O'odham (Papago) and Pima – are considered by many to be descendants of the Hohokam, but the evidence is more circumstantial than conclusive. The major sites of the Hohokam culture are CASA GRANDE, Hodges, La Ciudad, Las Colinas, Los Muertos, MARANA, Pueblo Grande, Roosevelt 9:6, Snaketown and VENTANA CAVE.

E.W. Haury: *The Hohokam* (Tucson, 1976); P.L. Crown and W.J. Judge, eds: *Chaco and Hohokam* (Santa Fe, 1991); G.P. Gumerman, ed.: *Exploring the Hohokam* (Albuquerque, 1991); V.L. Scarborough and D.R.

Wilcox, eds: *The Mesoamerican ballgame* (Tucson, 1991); S.K. Fish, P.R. Fish and J.H. Madsen: *The Marana community in the Hohokam world* (Tucson, 1992).
JJR

Hoko Waterlogged site with perishables (*c.*1000 BC–AD 250) and adjacent rock shelter (*c.*AD 1000–1850) at the mouth of the Hoko River on the Strait of Juan de Fuca in northwest Washington state, USA. Numerous wooden fish hooks, cordage, basketry, woodworking tools, hafted microliths and several wood carvings depicting stylized birds were found in the waterlogged component. The rock shelter contained 1300 separately analysed layers/features in 3.5 m of vertical shell midden deposit. The overall contents of the site served as the basis for a model of local prehistory based on economic decision-making involving exponential population growth, territorial circumscription, and critical resource stress.
D.R. Croes and E. Blinman, eds: *Hoko River: a 2500 year old fishing camp on the Northwest Coast of North America* (Pullman, 1980); —— and S. Hackenberger: 'Hoko River archaeological complex: modeling prehistoric Northwest Coast economic evolution', *Research in economic anthropology*, ed. B.L. Isaac (London, 1988), 19–87.
RC

Homo erectus Early species of hominid, although increasingly controversial as a species definition since fossils attributed to *erectus* span more than one million years between 1.8 and 0.3 million years. It may well be that the early specimens, such as OLDUVAI hominid 9 or WT 15000 are not of the same species as later examples from JAVA and China. All are, however, characterised by heavy brow ridges and a low cranial vault, in contrast to specimens from the succeeding stage in human evolution (known as EARLY *HOMO SAPIENS*). All appear to have an essentially modern, if robust, skeleton – the evidence from the virtually complete skeleton of a boy (WT 15 000) from WEST TURKANA indicates that these hominids matured much more rapidly than modern humans (at *c.*12 years old the boy was already 1.68 m tall). In terms of intelligence, *Homo erectus* has a brain size of between 850–1000 cm^3, considerably larger than the earlier *HOMO HABILIS* and approaching the low end of the modern range. They made and developed the ACHEULEAN technology (bifaces and flakes) and colonized large areas of Europe and Asia. Isernia la Piretta, the earliest site of hominid occupation in Europe at *c.*730,000 BP, is assumed to be the product of *Homo erectus*. The location has produced chopper and flake implements, but as yet no fossils. The site of Vallonnet in France may be still earlier at *c.*9000,00 BP. See also HUMAN EVOLUTION.
R. Foley: *Another unique species* (London, 1987); G. Richards: *Human evolution: an introduction for the behavioural sciences* (London, 1987); C.S. Gamble: *Timewalkers: The prehistory of global colonization* (London, 1993).
PG-B

Homo habilis Discovered by Louis Leakey in the OLDUVAI deposits of East Africa, *Homo habilis* appears to be the link between the AUSTRALOPITHECINES and HOMO ERECTUS. With a brain size of *c.*750 cm^3, and as the probable maker of OLDOWAN flake and core tools, *habilis* seems to have been considerably more 'human-like' than the Australopithecines, although anatomically it retained climbing adaptations in the structure of its arm and hand. Although initially considered one species, *H. habilis*, like *Australopithecus*, now appears to have had a gracile form (represented by the 1470 skull from KOOBI FORA) and a more robust form (as represented by OH 62 from Olduvai and the 1813 skull from Koobi Fora). It is thus argued that a distinct species *H. rudolfensis* should be named for the gracile habilines, and that the robust examples are more closely related to the Australopithecenes. See also HUMAN EVOLUTION.
G. Richards: *Human evolution: an introduction for the behavioural sciences* (London, 1987).
PG-B

Homol'ovi *see* ANASAZI

Homo sapiens *see* EARLY ('ARCHAIC') *HOMO SAPIENS*

Ho-mu-tu (Hemudu) Prehistoric Chinese culture that was more or less contemporary with the Ma-chia-pang culture and datable from *c.*5000 to 3500 BC, on the basis of a long series of calibrated radiocarbon dates. Traces of the Ho-mu-tu culture were first found in 1973 near Ho-mu-tu village, Yu-yao-hsien, Che-chiang, China, but it has since been identified at more than 20 sites around Hang-chou Bay.
Anon.: 'Ho-mu-tu ye-chih ti-yi chi'i fa-chüeh pao-kao' [Report on the excavations of Level 1 at the Ho-mu-tu site], *KKHP* 1 (1978), 39–94: Chang Kwang-chih: *The archeology of ancient China*, 4th edn (New Haven, 1986), 208–12.
NB

Hongshanhou *see* HUNG-SHAN-HOU

Hopefield *see* ELANDSFONTEIN

Hopewell Large Middle WOODLAND site (*c.*200 BC–AD 400) located in the central Scioto region of Ross County, Ohio, which is the type site for the Ohio Hopewell 'culture'. The site consists of a large two-part earth and stone enclosure (the Great Enclosure), two smaller enclosures, and more than 40 mounds, the largest of which, Mound 25, was described in the 19th century as consisting of three conjoined mounds measuring 10 m high, 152 m long, and 55 m wide. Excavations yielded large quantities of exotic Hopewell artefacts including obsidian bifaces, copper geometric and zoomorphic figures, axes, adzes, plates, ear ornaments and bracelets, and copper, silver and meteoric iron beads.

W. Moorehead: *The Hopewell mound group of Ohio* (Chicago, 1922); N. Greber and K. Ruhl: *The Hopewell site; a contemporary analysis on the work of Charles C. Willoughby* (Boulder, 1989).

RJE

Horgen culture Late Neolithic culture of the mid- to late-3rd millennium BC, identified by Vogt in 1938 at lake-edge sites across Switzerland, especially in the north and east. It succeeds the Swiss PFYN and CORTAILLOD cultural complexes at many sites and seems to be contemporary with, and may in some sense be derived from, the SOM CULTURE of the Paris basin. Like the SOM, the ceramic assemblages are of poor quality, largely consisting of large flat-based tubs with steep and thick walls. Burial rites are not as developed as in the SOM, although Horgen material is sometimes found associated with dolmens; surprisingly, metal objects are apparently scarcer even than in earlier Pfyn and Cortaillod contexts.

J. Winiger: *Das Neolithikum der Schweiz* (Basle, 1981); ——: *Feldmeilen Vorderfeld: Der Ubergang von der Pfyner zur Horgener Kultur*, Antiqua 8, Publications de la Société Suisse de Préhistoire et d'Archéologie (Verlag Huber, Frauenfeld, 1981).

RJA

horsehoof core Tapered cores, part of the AUSTRALIAN CORE TOOL AND SCRAPER TRADITION, in which the edge overhangs the narrow end of the core. Their shape is either due to heavy use or resharpening, or because these cores had flakes removed until further flaking became impossible without re-sharpening. Horse hoof cores are distributed widely over the continent.

D.J. Mulvaney: *The prehistory of Australia* (Melbourne, 1975), 175; J.P. White and J.F. O'Connell: *A prehistory of Australia, New Guinea and Sahul* (Sydney, 1982), 65.

CG

Hou-ma-chen (Houmazhen) Bronze casting foundry site excavated at Niu-ts'un-ku-ch'eng, Hou-ma-shih, Shan-hsi, China, of Late Ch'un-ch'iu–Early Chan-kuo date (*c.*600–400 BC), located in the area traditionally ascribed to the ancient city, Hsin-t'ien, to which CH'IN moved the state capital *c.*583 BC. In and around Hou-ma are the remains of at least five ancient cities – all once within the boundaries of the ancient state of Ch'in. Valuable light has been thrown on the highly advanced foundry technology of the period, particularly the complex nature of ceramic models, moulds, pattern-blocks and cores (see Barnard and Satö 1975). Several well-known bronzes in Western collections (Weber 1973) exhibit decor closely matching that in the Hou-ma pattern-blocks and moulds.

Site reports in *KK* 5 (1959), 222–8 and *WW* 8/9 (1960), 11–14; N. Barnard: *Bronze alloys and bronze casting in ancient China* (Tokyo, 1961); G.W. Weber, Jr.: *The ornaments of late Chou bronzes, a method of analysis* (New Brunswick, 1973); N. Barnard and Satö Tamotsu: *Metallurgical remains of ancient China* (Tokyo, 1975); B.W. Keyser: 'Décor replication in two late Chou bronze Chien', *Ars Orientalis* 11 (1979), 127-62.

NB

Houmazhen *see* HOU-MA-CHEN

Howieson's Poort Middle Stone Age (MSA) cave-site near Grahamstown, E. Cape, South Africa, which is the type site for the Howieson's Poort industry (formerly a 'culture'). This is a variant MSA industry with backed blades of various forms (obliquely blunted, trapezes, segments etc.). Four radiocarbon dates of uncal 11,120 to 19,600 BP exist for the type-site, but are inexplicable in relation to the indications of age from other sites, especially KLASIES RIVER MOUTH, where an age in the order of uncal 70,000 BP is indicated.

P. Stapleton and J. Hewitt: 'Stone implements from a rock-shelter at Howieson's Poort near Grahamstown', *SAJS*, 24 (1927), 574–87; ——: 'Stone implements from Howieson's Poort, near Grahamstown', *SAJS*, 25 (1928), 399–409.

RI

Hrazany Celtic oppidum of *c.*75 acres built on a spur about 50 km south of Prague in the Czech Republic. The fortifications, pierced by four gates, consist of a stone wall and a clay and gravel fill. Timbers were spaced vertically along the stone wall and transversely through the fill as a way of strengthening the structure. Two phases of construction have been identified, both of which burnt down; the older structure was destroyed *c.*100–50 BC; the more recent structure later in the 1st century BC.

L. Jansová: 'Celtic oppida in Bohemia', *Recent archaeological finds in Czechoslovakia*, ed. J. Filip (Prague, 1966); ——: *Hrazany: das keltische oppidum in Böhmen* (Prague, 1986).

RJA

Hsia (Xia) Name of a mythical Chinese dynasty supposedly preceding the SHANG period. Archaeologists sometimes apply the term 'Hsia' to certain sites of the essentially Neolithic era before Shang. The term is even applied to ERH-LI-T'OU sites whose labelling as 'Early Shang' is equally uncertain.

Ts'ao Heng Hsia: *Shang, Chou k'ao-ku-hsüeh lun-wen-chi* (Peking, 1980); Chang Kwang-chih: *The archaeology of ancient China*, 4th edn (New Haven, 1986), 305–16.

NB

Hsiao-t'un (Xiaotun) *see* AN-YANG

Hsi-ch'uan, Hsia-ssu (Xichuan, Xiasi) Site in the southwestern Ho-nan province of China, consisting of 30 or so Ch'u tombs of Ch'un-ch'iu-Han date (*c.*600–200 BC), located along the ridge of Lung-shan. Both the ridge and a Buddhist temple (known as Hsia-ssu) at the foot of the hill were submerged under the waters of the Tan-chiang Reservoir but were partly exposed when the waters subsided in October, 1977. During the following two years, 24 tombs and five chariot burials were excavated. It is clear from the inscriptions that these were royal burials, and one of the tombs (M2, the largest) has been associated with Kung-tzu Wu (son of Chuang Wang of Ch'u) known to have died in 552 BC.

Anon.: *Hsi-ch'uan Hsia-ssu Ch'un-ch'iu Ch'u-mu* [The Ch'un-ch'iu period tombs of Hsia-ssu, Hsi-ch'uan] (Peking, 1991).

NB

Hsin-kan, Ta-yang-chou-hsiang (Xingan, Dayangzhou-xiang) Site in Chiang-hsi, China, where, in September 1989, a large rectangular tomb was discovered lying 2.15 m below the present urface level. The suggested dating to the Late Shang period (*c.*1400–1122 BC) was later seemingly confirmed by radiocarbon dating of rotted wood remants of part of the tomb structure which comprised a *kuo*-chamber (8.22 × 3.6 m) with the *kuan*-coffin (2.34 × 0.85 m) lying in the centre. At both ends of the burial pit were a number of *erh-tsang-t'ai* ('second-level platforms'), each measuring 2.5 m in length. These wooden and originally lacquered structures had almost completely disintegrated, and the only surviving human remains were 24 teeth apparently deriving from three individuals. The 1900+ items of funerary equipment have generated great interest, particularly the group of over 480 bronzes, which, in both structural design and decor, are markedly influenced by Shang and Western Chou stylistic elements, combined with obviously local aspects.

Anon.: 'Chiang-hsi Hsin-kan Ta-yang-chou Shang-mu fa-chüeh chien-pao' [Report on the excavation of the Shang Period tomb at Ta-yang-chou, Hsin-kan, Chiang-hsi], *WW* 19 (1991), 1–2.

NB

Hsin-yang (Xinyang) Site of CH'U culture finds in Ho-nan, China, noted especially for the rich funerary furnishings: fine quality lacquer-ware, musical instruments, cabinet-making wood sculptures, intricate bronze castings and inlay work, deriving from Tombs 1 and 2 of Early–Middle Chan-kuo date (*c.*480–300 BC), excavated at Ch'ang-t'ai-kuan 20 km north of Hsin-yang, between 1957 and 1958. The two tombs comprised massive rectangular wooden structures forming the seven-divisions' mausoleum (*kuo*).

Anon.: *Ho-nan Hsin-yang Ch'u-mu ch'u-t'u wen-wu* [Relics excavated from the Ch'u tombs at Hsin-yang] (Chengchou 1959); Anon.: *Hsin-yang Ch'u-mu* [The Ch'u Tombs at Hsin-yang] (Peking, 1986).

NB

Hsiung-nu (Xiongnu) General term applied to certain of the tribal peoples of ancient China who inhabited the Northern Regions (*pei-fang*) i.e. north of the Great Wall, which was built gradually from Late Western Chou times to withstand their incursions into the MIDDLE STATES. The Great Wall was made into a unified structure by the ruler of CH'IN, who became known as Shih-huang-ti, the 'First Emperor' of China. This protective structure of pounded earth, stone and brick, stretches across some 6000 km of mountainous terrain, grasslands and deserts; and in succeeding dynasties has been rebuilt time and again at an enormous cost in human life and effort.

The Hsiung-nu rose to prominence during the Late Chan-kuo period (*c.*3rd century BC) and began to decline during the Eastern Han period (*c.*1st - century AD). Later they were also referred to as the Shen-yu. The geographical and ethnographical situation, past history, and the later rise to power of one, or other, of the various tribal peoples of the Northern Regions is complex; many of the names applied to these peoples are recorded throughout both the archaeological documents and traditional literature (*see* CHINA 3).

Lin Kan: *Hsiung-nu-shih lun-wen hsuan-chi* [A selection of studies on the Hsiung-nu] (Peking, 1983); Cheng Dalin: *The Great Wall of China* (Hong Kong, 1984) [excellent illustrations].

NB

Hu *see* HIW-SEMAINA REGION

huaca Word used by the INCA to refer to a sacred place and, by extension, now often used to indicate an archaeological monument or site. Hence also *huaco*, an ancient artefact (usually a ceramic vessel), *huaquería*, clandestine excavation of archaeological sites and *huaquero*, a looter.

Huang-niang-niang-t'ai (Huangniangniangtai) Site of the CH'I-CHIA culture, near Wu-wei-hsien, Kan-su, China. It was first excavated in 1957–9 and has been regarded as an important site because of the finds of 30 or more copper artefacts (two of which were analysed spectroscopically) among an otherwise Neolithic context. The reporters of the site believe that evidence of metalworking is present. Similarly, finds of copper artefacts in other Kan-su sites (Ta-ho-chuang, Yung-ching-hsien, Ch'in-wei-chia and Yung-ching-hsien) with calibrated radiocarbon assessments dating from as early as *c.*2000 BC have given rise to the opinion that a COPPER AGE preceded the Chinese Bronze Age. However, in recent years, the gradual appearance of the more sophisticated alloy, bronze (albeit, in some instances, probably to be classed as a 'high copper' alloy) in the direct casting of artefacts in sectional moulds of even earlier date unearthed from such Ho-nan sites as Mei-shan, Lin-ju-hsien, WANG-CH'ENG-KANG, Teng-fung-hsien, P'ING-LIANG-T'AI, Huai-yang-hsien, and T'AO-SSU, Hsiang-fen-hsien, continue to support the working hypothesis that in China metallurgy originated in the CHUNG-YÜAN area, independent of other metallurgical cultures elsewhere in the ancient world (Barnard 1961; Barnard and Satö 1975).

N. Barnard: *Bronze alloys and bronze casting in ancient China* (Tokyo, 1961); —— and Satö Tamotsu: *Metallurgical remains of ancient China* (Tokyo, 1975); An Chih-min: 'Several problems relating to bronze vessels of the early periods in China', *EC* 8 (1982–3), 53–75; Sun Shu-Yün and Han Ju-pin: 'Preliminary studies of bronze vessels of the early periods in China', *EC* 9/10 (1983–5), 261–89.

NB

Huapula (previously Sangay) Series of immense earthworks in the southern Ecuadorian Amazon, dating from 400 BC onwards. The long platforms are arranged in geometric patterns and one platform has a 'feline' geoglyph. Related sites also have huge earthworks, including terrace systems and flattened ridge tops with architectural remains. Material in the fill of these sites is related to imported ceramics found in adjacent highland sites, an indicator of the early importance of highland-lowland exchange in the Andean region.

G. Porras and I. Pedro: *Investigaciones arquelógicas a las faldas del Sangay: tradición Upano* (Quito, 1987); E. Salazar: 'The Sangay complex revisited', *The Ecuadorian Formative*, ed. J. Raymond and R. Burger (Washington, D.C., in press).

KB

Huari Immense urban site in the Central Peruvian highlands dating to the Early Intermediate Period and Middle Horizon (*c.*400 BC–AD 900). It has a peculiar architectural style of high-walled compounds with multi-storey long narrow rooms. The unique art style, expressed in polychrome ceramics and woollen tapestry, features supernatural beings related to those of CHAVÍN and TIAHUANACO. Huari established a short-lived but very large empire in Peru and profoundly influenced later events in the central Andes.

W.H. Isbell and G.F. McEwan, eds: *Huari administrative structure: prehistoric monumental architecture and state government* (Washington, D.C., 1991); K. Schreiber: *Wari imperialism in Middle Horizon Peru* (Ann Arbor, 1992).

KB

human evolution The study of human evolution has always been riven by controversy, partly because of the extremely patchy data upon which it relies. The primate origin of humanity, in itself undisputed, is a good example of this. Humans belong to the 'hominoid' family which includes the 'great apes'. Originating in the Miocene period (23–25 million years ago), the fossil record illustrates hominoid divergence from Old World Monkeys. However, the record is particularly poor for the late Miocene (*c.*8-5 million years ago), and no fossils directly demonstrate the divergence of modern African apes from the hominid lineage.

It is now accepted that *Proconsul* and other early Miocene 'apes' represent common ancestors of all living primates, but that their anatomy was substantially different from living primates. The long-armed 'suspensory' locomotion typified by the Gibbon only developed later in the Miocene.

Contrary to earlier theory, the late Miocene *Sivapithecus* (known from Africa and Asia *c.*10–15 million years ago) was the ancestor not of humans, but of the orang-utan. Whilst the relationship of other middle and late Miocene apes to living apes remains unclear, research using microbiological techniques has recently filled some of the gaps in our knowledge of ape evolution. Protein and DNA comparisons indicate that the African apes (including humans) diverged from Asian orang-utans around 15 million years ago. Ape and human lineages diverged between 4 and 6 million years ago. Here again, however, controversy continues; the validity of some analytical techniques has been questioned and any firm dating by 'molecular clocks' remains a distant prospect (see below).

1 *Climate*. Many new sources of data, such as ICE CORES and deep-sea cores (*see* OXYGEN ISOTOPE CHRONOSTRATIGRAPHY) have produced a detailed picture of the history of Earth's climate. It is clear that human evolution took place within a complex pattern of climatic and vegetational change, particularly during the Pleistocene (the last two million years). Late 19th-century research established four major glacial cycles during the Pleistocene, but it now appears that there were at least 16. Moreover, the coldest 'stadial' periods were relatively short, beginning and ending very suddenly, whereas, for the most part, climates maintained an intermediate level that was neither glacial nor interglacial. This pattern has major implications for our understanding of the colonization of higher latitudes, and is complicated by the fact that, as a result of tectonic movements in the earth's crust, no two glacial-interglacial cycles have been the same. One reason, then, for the haphazard evidence for human evolution lies with climatic change. The late Miocene, for example, witnessed extreme aridity in North Africa and the Near East, limiting fossil evidence for African Primates.

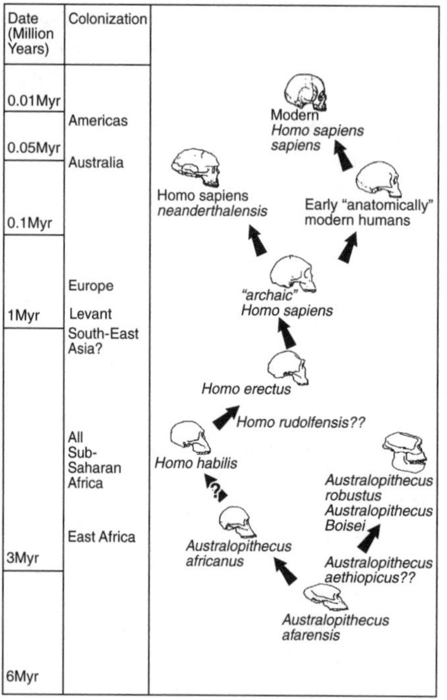

Figure 21 **human evolution** Simplified chronological chart of the evolution of modern humans, together with a simplified chart of the first appearance of early humans in various regions around the world (drawn by Paul Graves-Brown).

2 *Bipedalism*. Above all other characteristics, bipedalism distinguishes the *hominid* (human) lineage from those of other apes. We and our ancestors are the only apes whose hind limb, pelvis, spinal column and skull are specifically adapted for upright locomotion. Apart from the relatively complete fossils of AUSTRALOPITHECUS from HADAR, the now famous fossil footprints from LAETOLI prove that our ancestors have been bipeds for at least 3.7 million years. However, the bipedalism of early hominids differed from our own; their arm and hand appearing to retain an adaptation for tree climbing, and even the pelvic structure of NEANDERTHALS differs from that of modern humans (*see* KEBARA).

The reasons for the origins of bipedalism remain obscure, but attempts to explain it are a feature of the study of human origins. Like science in general, studies of human origins are presented as narratives, as stories. In recent years a more reflexive awareness has promoted study of narrative structure in accounts of human evolution. In particular, Landau suggests that accounts of human origins share narrative structures with folklore and myth. Most models involve a vital gift (like many a talisman in folklore) and hominids, like folk-tale heroes, are generally represented as the underdog, facing the terrors of savannah life with only their magic gift, be it fire, technology or intelligence, to aid them.

While Landau's account may seem too fanciful in some respects, the general desire to present coherent accounts of human origins has tended to distort the evidence. Bipedalism is one example of this tendency, and is often represented as the essential gift which enabled humans to rise (literally and metaphorically) above nature. Freed hands make tools and carry food or children; an upright body remains cooler in tropical climates or thus enables the development of a larger brain. And yet, the fossil record confirms that bipedal locomotion evolved several million years before the appearance of stone tools or significant increases in hominid intelligence.

Similarly, it has often been assumed that human intelligence itself evolved to facilitate tool making and associated subsistence adaptations. Yet, again, we know that the major changes in human brain size took place over a period of two million years and had virtually ceased by the time rapid technological change took place in the Upper Palaeolithic. In each case, the need to create a causal account has led to the teleological connection of (possibly) unrelated events and processes. The need to tell a coherent story has led many to overlook the essential lesson of Darwinism – that evolutionary processes are haphazard and never progress towards a pre-ordained objective.

3 *Origins of tool use*. Undisputed evidence of stone tool making dates from at least 2.3 million years ago in both East and South Africa (*see* HADAR, OMO *and* OLDUVAI GORGE). The earliest stone industries consist only of crude flakes and choppers, the latter being, quite possibly, only cores. Bifacial stone tools, or 'handaxes', appear in their crudest form around 1.6 million years ago, and persist in progressively refined forms until only 30–40,000 years ago. By around 200,000 years ago the first LEVALLOIS tools appear – flake-based implements struck from a prepared, 'tortoise shaped' core. The refined Levallois '*recourante*' produced more, and more blade-like flakes, eventually being replaced by blade/core techniques around 40,000 years ago. Blade-based tools are struck from a prismatic shaped core, exploiting the volume of the material, rather than simply its surface.

The authorship of stone tools is a controversial topic. Whilst most assume that the earliest stone tools were the work of genus *Homo* (*see HOMO HABILIS*), there is some suggestion that early flake tools were made by *Australopithecus*. Similarly there is some dispute about the authorship of blade-based 'Upper Palaeolithic' tools. Traditionally, these have been regarded as the exclusive work of 'modern' humans, but evidence from Neanderthal sites such as St Césaire seems to contradict this.

4 *Intelligence and social life*. Evidence of early hominid intelligence is, of necessity, indirect. Brain size can give some indication, but here it must be remembered that the brain is scaled to body size, and that modern human brain size is extremely variable (*c*.1000–2000 cm^3). Australopithecines appear to have been no more encephalized than modern apes (brain sizes *c*.500 cm^3), but their relative body size is hotly disputed. The earliest members of genus *Homo* had brain sizes of *c*.800 cm^3 and their appearance coincides with the first stone tools (*see* PALAEOLITHIC). But the connection is not necessarily causal. With the appearance of *HOMO ERECTUS*, around 1.6 million years ago, brain sizes already approached the lower end of the modern range at about 900–1000 cm^3.

Meanwhile, attempts to correlate intelligence with developments in technology have proved problematic (see Mithen 1996). Human technology before 40,000 years ago was simple, and changed very slowly, despite changes in brain size and the colonization of new habitats. In any case, those modern peoples who are known to possess simple technologies are demonstrably as intelligent as anyone else! More recent theories stress social interaction, social grooming and deception as driving forces in increasing intelligence. However, evidence to support 'collegiate' models of hominid social life is elusive.

5 *Origin of modern humans*. The origin of 'anatomically modern' humans is probably the most interesting and controversial aspect of human evolution studies. A few years ago, genetic studies led to the proposal of an African genetic 'Eve' from whom all modern humans were meant to have descended. Anatomical evidence conformed to this view, but the archaeological data had to be contorted to fit the theory. The studies were criticized for technical reasons and more recent work suggests that a larger, but still relatively small, number of females contributed to the modern human gene pool. Whatever the truth of this, the early 'modern' fossils seem to show that our ancestors originated in Africa around 100–200,000 years ago (*see* ANATOMICALLY MODERN HUMANS, QAFZEH, SKHUL, MOUNT CARMEL), colonizing Europe and Asia between 50–40,000 years ago. Not all palaeoanthropologists accept this 'out of Africa' hypothesis, some arguing that archaic humans present in many regions of the world evolved into modern humans, and that gene flows between these populations later on account for the relative similarity of human populations, rather than a single 'original' population from Africa or the Near East. However, there is now a considerable weight of evidence against this view (*see* QAFZEH, SKHUL *and* KEBARA).

That said, the fate of 'archaic' hominids (e.g. in Europe, NEANDERTHALS) is debatable. Proponents of the 'out of Africa' origin of the modern human population have sometimes claimed that 'modern' humans replaced 'archaic' humans because of more complex social, intellectual and technical abilities. However, Neanderthals at least could perform many of the complex tasks supposedly reserved for 'modern' humans; making Upper Palaeolithic types of stone tools (the Châtelperronian industry – *see* ARCY-SUR-CURE *and* ROC DE COMBE) and probably bone tools as well. It also seems probable that 'archaic' humans buried their dead and cared for the injured and disabled.

'Archaic' and 'modern' appear to have coexisted for some time (*see* ROC DE COMBE), but did the populations intermix? Strenuous efforts to discount the humanity of Neanderthals have not succeeded in obscuring their essentially human qualities. But at the same time they were certainly very different from any living human beings. Ultimately, the encounter between 'archaic' and 'modern' humans may prove too have been too ephemeral an event to have left a discernible trace, and this problem is compounded by climatic conditions in the early part of the last glacial which were not favourable to the deposition of archaeological remains.

6 *Colonization*. As discussed above, it is now widely accepted that hominids originated in Africa, although other locations (particularly Europe and South East Asia) and multiple locations have been suggested. On current evidence, the earliest hominids, Australopithecines, evolved in East Africa and subsequently spread throughout sub-Saharan Africa. *Homo habilis* is also known only from Africa, and hence the first phase of 'out of Africa' colonization began with *Homo erectus*, perhaps around 1 million years ago (given dates from ISERNIA and JAVA). Whether EARLY *HOMO SAPIENS*, as represented by the Swanscombe or Petralona skulls, constituted a distinct wave of colonists is a moot point – these hominids might have evolved indigenously from *Homo erectus*. African 'anatomically modern' humans, NEANDERTHALS, and perhaps East Asian *Homo* (e.g. CHOUKOUTIEN), seem likely to have evolved *in situ* from the *Homo erectus/* early *Homo sapiens* population.

However, the evolution of European modern humans from Neanderthals seems highly unlikely. Although the Asian situation could turn out to be different, it seems reasonable to attribute the very rapid phase of colonization in the late Pleistocene, represented in many places by changes in fossil types and material culture, to the dispersal of a single population of 'modern' humans. Increasingly detailed data for this dispersal have emerged in the last ten years. For example, it is clear that Australia and New Guinea were colonized at least 40,000 years ago. Meanwhile, in the Western Pacific, dates of *c*.30,000 years BP for the New Hebrides confirm that sea travel was possible in the Upper Palaeolithic.

The colonization of America is, and always has been, controversial. Although dates as early as 30,000 years BP have been claimed for sites in Brazil, a colonization across the Bering Strait land bridge probably occurred around 14–15,000 years ago, as the Wisconsin ice sheet retreated across North America (*see* BERINGIA *and* PALEOINDIANS). Extant dates indicate a relatively rapid exploration of the continent with dates of *c*.11,000 BP for Fells cave in Tierra del Fuego. However, hominid colonization of the globe was not complete until around AD 1100 if not later still – New Zealand, for example, was not discovered by humans until AD 1000 (see OCEANIA).

7 *Gender in human evolution*. It is only within the last 15 years or so that gender has become a focus in the study of human origins (see Dahlberg 1981: Conkey and Gero, 1991). The customary image of 'Man the Hunter' has survived, despite some evidence to the contrary; the dominant role of men as providers of meat continues to be assumed in contemporary theories of human origins.

Although a number of sources exist for inference of gender relations during evolution, many are controversial. Large differences in body size between Australopithecines have been interpreted as evidence for sexual dimorphism, whereby female hominids, like other primates, would be smaller than their male counterparts. This would have dietary consequences and would imply a radically different social structure from that of modern humans. However, evidence for a large degree of sexual size difference in early hominids is controversial since skeletal variation may, in fact, represent the existence of different species.

Most other inferences about gender relations tend to be drawn from modern human and primate analogies. The particularities of human sexual behaviour and anatomy have been co-opted into a variety of theories. In particular, sexual characteristics have been linked with the origin of a monogamous pair bond between male and female. Such a pair bond would, it is argued, enable females to obtain food from male hunting activities and protection for their offspring. In return, males would be sure of their paternity. However, this idea, which has appeared in many forms, is often contradicted by the evidence. It has been difficult to establish that human sexual characteristics are commensurate with monogamy, and this ambiguity has been underlined by ethnographic evidence for widespread polygamy of various kinds.

Moreover, it has become clear that in modern

hunter-gatherer and agrarian societies, males are far from being the only providers of nutrition. Indeed, it may be argued that the role of 'Woman the Gatherer' is more important than that of 'Man the Hunter'. This situation has tended to be obscured by the symbolic and social importance accorded to hunting and its products – an importance usually promoted by men.

In summary, whilst gender is undoubtedly a key factor in understanding human evolution, reliable evidence for differences in gender roles, or for practices of mating and parental investment, is hard to find. This is particularly true of archaeological evidence, since it is virtually impossible to ascribe gender roles to the material culture of Palaeolithic sites without perpetuating the unjustified assumptions that men hunt whilst women remain in the domestic sphere.

R.B. Lee and I. DeVore: *Man the hunter* (Chicago, 1968); F. Dahlberg, ed.: *Woman the gatherer* (New Haven, 1981); N.M. Tanner: *On becoming human* (Cambridge, 1981); G. Beer: *Darwin's plots: evolutionary narrative in Darwin, George Eliot and nineteenth century fiction* (London, 1983); R. Foley: *Another unique species* (London, 1987); G. Richards: *Human evolution: an introduction for the behavioural sciences* (London, 1987); J. Diamond: 'Island occupation', *Nature* 339 (1989), 605–6; D. Haraway: *Primate visions* (London, 1989); P. Mellars and C.B. Stringer, eds: *The human revolution: behavioural and biological perspectives on the origin of modern humans* (Edinburgh, 1989); M. Conkey and J. Gero: *Engendering archaeology: women and prehistory* (London, 1991); P.M. Graves: 'New models and metaphors for the neanderthal debate', *CA* 32/5 (1991), 513–42; M. Landau: *Narratives of human evolution* (London, 1991); C.S. Gamble: *Timewalkers: The prehistory of global colonization* (London, 1993); S. Mithen: *The prehistory of the mind: a search for the origins of art, religion and science* (London, 1996).

PG-B

hunebed (pl. *hunebedden*) Distinctive form of megalithic chamber tomb, constructed from large and often roundish glacial erratics, examples of which are concentrated in northern Holland (Drenthe). The rectangular chambers, often entered through one of the long sides via a short roofed or unroofed passage, are commonly built of pairs of orthostats supporting capstones; perhaps for this reason the chambers of the more spectacular examples tend to be elongated rather than widened. The oval mound covering the chamber is usually edged around the whole of its perimeter with large boulders. The *hunebedden* were constructed in the 4th millennium BC and are associated with the early and middle Neolithic TRB CULTURE.

R. Klok: *Hunebedden in Nederland* (Haarlem, 1979); R. Joussaume: *Dolmens for the Dead*, trans. A. and C. Chippindale (London, 1988), 43–6.

RJA

Hung-shan-hou (Hongshanhou) Chinese culture named after a settlement-site in Liao-ning, northeast China, which was discovered in 1908 by Japanese archaeologists. The nature of the culture has been more clearly defined as a result of the excavation of stratified sites throughout the surrounding area since the 1970s. It is distributed along river valleys in the highlands of southeastern Inner Mongolia and western Liao-ning and probably dates to *c*.4000–2500 BC. There seems to have been some contact with the Yang-shou culture in the Yen-shan Mountains east of Peking.

The Hung-shan-hou culture is remarkable for its sophisticated kiln structures – some with double firing chambers and chimney structures; the pottery was handmade, mostly plain but some decorated with comb incisions, rocker-stamped, appliqués, or painting (red and black pigments). There are also small clay 'venus' figurines of apparently pregnant women, jade ornaments of fine workmanship, and a variety of stone implements: axes, hoes, knives, mortars and pestles, arrow-heads, have been recovered. Of particular importance are the large-scale ceremonial stone mounds and burials, and open-air altars of circular and rectangular shape, and the 'Goddess temple' (*nü-shen-miao*) excavated at Niu-ho-liang, Liao-ning. The temple site yielded a ceramic head and shoulders from a life-size statue of a 'fertility goddess' which, along with other statues of varying sizes, has been the source of great debate among Chinese scholars. It has been suggested that the origin of the later traditional text references to Hou-t'u ('sovereign mother earth') might have some kind of association with this cultural complex, while the 'pig-dragon' jade artefacts may represent supplementary deities (see Childs-Johnson 1991).

Anon.: *Hung-shan-hou, Ch'ih-feng – prehistoric sites at Hung-shan-hou, Chi'in-feng, in the province of Jehol, Manchukuo* (Tokyo, 1938); Chang Kwang-chih: *The archaeology of ancient China*, 4th edn (New Haven, 1986), 181–8; E. Childs-Johnson: 'Jades of the Hongshan culture: the dragon and fertility cult worship', *Arts Asiatiques* (1991), 82–95.

NB

Hunsgi Valley in the Gulbarga district of Karnataka, India, that has been the focus of intensive survey by K. Paddaya (1982), along with the adjacent Baichbal Valley (Paddaya 1991). Paddaya's research has focused on Palaeolithic remains and the palaeoenvironmental context. About one hundred

ACHEULIAN sites were identified in eight seasons of survey (Paddaya 1991: 118), most in primary undisturbed contexts, with 12 secondary sites (i.e. resulting from water transport). Sites were located through surface survey. Surface distributions range in area from only a few square meters to 50–60 sq. ms, and Paddaya has divided the sites into four size-categories on the basis of spatial extent and artefacts (1991: 118–19). On the basis of site size, distribution and their topographic and environmental context, he has proposed that the Hunsgi sites constitute the remains of seasonal camps, with movement occurring between large dry-season occupations and smaller wet-season sites.

K. Paddaya: *The Acheulian culture of the Hunsgi Valley* (Pune, 1982); B.J. Szabo, T.S. McKinney, T.S. Dalbey and K. Paddaya: 'On the age of the Acheulian culture of the Hunsgi-Baichbal valleys, Peninsular India', *Bulletin of the Deccan College Post-Graduate and Research Institute* 50 (1990), 317–21; K. Paddaya: 'The Acheulian culture of the Hunsgi-Baichbal Valleys, Peninsular India: a processual study', *Quartar* 41 (1991), 111–38.

CS

Huo-shao-kou (Huoshaogao) Cemetery site near Yu-men-shi, Kan-su, China, which was excavated in 1976, but has not yet been reported in sufficient detail to allow a full assessment of its significance. From 312 burials surveyed, more than 200 metal artefacts were obtained from 106 burials (a remarkably high proportion for a CH'I-CHIA site); 66 of the artefacts have been examined in the laboratory. Dating of this cemetery is based upon calibrated radiocarbon assessments from the nearby settlement area; these range from *c.*2000 to 1600 BC. This part of Kan-su is known to have been the region, Ch'iang-fang, into which the Shang made frequent incursions as evidenced in the oracle bone prognostications (*see* CHINA 3) to obtain human sacrificial victims. The Ch'iang were mainly sheep-herders, and their burials often include the bones of dogs, pigs and oxen, as well as great quantities of sheep, together with rams' horns in pairs and of varying sizes.

An Chih-min: 'Some problems concerning China's early copper and bronze artifacts', *EC* 8 (1982–3), 53–75; S.Y. Sun and J.P. Han: 'A preliminary study of early Chinese copper and bronze artifacts', *EC* 9/10 (1983–5), 261–89; N. Barnard: 'Thoughts on the emergence of metallurgy in pre-Shang and early Shang China and a technical appraisal of relevant bronze artefacts of the time', *BMM, Sendai* (1993), 3–48.

NB

Hurrians Non-Semitic people of the Ancient Near East, whose ethnic and geographical origins are uncertain, although they are sometimes linked with the Early Transcaucasian Culture of the 3rd millennium BC (*see* KURA-ARAXIAN). Like the MEDES and PERSIANS, the Hurrians may have been the distant descendants of the Indo-Aryan peoples who gradually moved from Central Asia down into Iran and the Indian subcontinent. The agglutinative Hurrian language, preserved in the form of cuneiform texts (including horse-training manuals), belongs to the 'Asianic' group of languages, like that of URARTU. Their material culture is typified by grey pottery goblets decorated with buff-painted floral and geometrical motifs (known variously as Hurrian, Atchana or Billa ware), which are clearly distinguishable from the plainer pottery of their contemporaries in Syria and northern Iraq. However, apart from the distinctive Mitannian CYLINDER SEALS (see Frankfort 1939: 273–84), it has proved difficult to distinguish a specifically Hurrian style of art or architecture.

Hurrian place names and personal names begin to feature in cuneiform texts during the Akkadian and Ur III periods (*c.*2317–2000 BC). In terms of archaeological remains, they appear at the far northern edges of Mesopotamia during the 3rd millennium BC, but by the early 2nd millennium BC they had spread over a wide area of the region between northern Syria (*see* TELL ATCHANA) and northeastern Iraq (*see* NUZI). Eventually, in *c.*1500 BC, several small Hurrian states banded together to form the polities of Hanigalbat and MITANNI, which flourished during the 15th and 14th centuries BC between the Zagros mountains and the coast of the northern Levant, severely curtailing the expansion of the Egyptian and KASSITE empires.

H. Frankfort: *Cylinder seals: a documentary essay on the art and religion of the Ancient Near East* (London, 1939); I.J. Gelb: *Hurrians and Subarians* (Chicago, 1944); F. Imparati: *I Hurriti* (Florence, 1964); H. Frankfort: *The art and architecture of the ancient Orient*, 4th edn (Harmondsworth, 1970), 248–62; M.A. Morrison and D.I. Owen et al. ed., *Studies on the civilization and culture of Nuzi and the Hurrians*, 6 vols (Winona Lake, 1981–94); G. Wilhelm: *The Hurrians* (Warminster, 1989).

IS

Hu-shu (Hushu) Chinese culture first discovered in the early 1950s and named after the type-site, near Chiang-ning-hsien, Chiang-su, China. It now appears to have been concentrated in areas around Nanking and Chen-chiang, and is characterized by dwelling sites located on raised mounds, houses with baked floors and walls, stone implements including sickles, adzes, knives, hoes hammers, etc., and also arrow-heads and net-sinkers. Domestic animals included cattle, sheep, pigs, and dogs; pottery was of a hand-made sandy red ware and also a fine paste black-skinned polished type with geometric designs. Signs of small-scale bronze-casting operations and scapulimancy appear in the early stages. Comparatively late-arriving influences from Late Shang and Chou may be traced among the locally produced bronze wares; and there are some intrusions of Chung-yüan bronzes (a few inscribed). Impressive local bronze castings with obvious attempts to emulate the latter (but without inscriptions) have been excavated within the boundaries of the ancient state of WU which gradually rose to prominence in the area in Late Ch'un-ch'iu and Chan-kuo times (i.e. from *c.*600 BC onwards). Recent study of casting technology and methods of incorporating décor among bronzes from Tan-t'u-hsien, Yen-tun-shan, and Tan-yang-hsien have shown interesting aspects of local adaptations of CHUNG-YÜAN technology as well as vessel design.

Chang Kwang-chih: *The archaeology of ancient China*, 4th edn (New Haven, 1986), 394–9; N. Barnard 'Bronze casting technology in the peripheral "barbarian" regions', *BMM* 12 (1987), 3–37.

NB

Husterknupp The first major motte-and-bailey castle excavation made in 1934, and 1949–51, this site lay in the Erft valley close to Cologne. As a type-site it illustrated the complex evolution of private fortifications from the later Carolingian age. Excavations showed four major periods: first, a 9th- to 10th-century sub-rectangular fortified area in the bend of the river; second, over the demolished first phase, a low mound was raised; in phase three a true motte (an earthen mound) was created with a crescent-shaped bailey to the east: this probably dates to the 11th century; finally, a brick-built castle dated to *c.*1244 replaced the timber structures.

A. Herrnbrodt: *Der Husterknupp, eine niederrheinische Burganlage des frühen Mittelalters-Cologne* (Böhlau, 1958).

RH

hüyük *see* TELL

hydraulic despotism In 1957 Karl Wittfogel put forward a FUNCTIONALIST theory to relate the evolution of despotic Chinese society to the highly centralized management of the massive Chinese irrigation system. At the heart of his theory of 'hydraulic despotism' was the contention that the organizational needs of large-scale irrigation systems necessitated or facilitated the creation of coercive political systems (part of Wittfogel's motivation in putting forward this theory being a post-World War II desire to explain the origins of authoritarianism). He differentiated between primitive hydraulic societies, and state-centred hydraulic societies distinguished by a professional bureaucracy.

Although the theory was grounded in study of early Chinese civilization, Wittfogel himself pointed to his theory's applicability to irrigated civilizations in the Near East, Mesoamerica and elsewhere. While Wittfogel's argument has proved attractive to many of those searching for a 'prime mover' in the development of early civilizations, it has also been heavily criticized: 1 It is unclear (both within the theory, as originally stated, and from the archaeological data) whether large-scale irrigation systems are a *cause* or an *effect* of a centralized political system. 2 Wittfogel is imprecise in his separation of primitive and state-centred systems. 3 Many of his archaeologically identified irrigation systems, even those associated with advanced civilizations, are of a simple type. Yet even quite complex irrigation systems do not seem to *require* centralized or specialized management systems (e.g. Hunt and Hunt 1974: 3). 4 It is difficult to separate Wittfogel's managerial prime mover from other possible effects of irrigation that might also promote the development of hierarchies (e.g. increased productivity and population; differential yields). 5 The association of elites with water control often appears to be opportunistic, or even simply justificatory, rather than managerial in any economically beneficial sense.

K. Wittfogel: *Oriental despotism: a comparative study of total power* (New Haven, 1957); ——: 'Chinese society: an historical survey', *JASt* 16 (1967), 343–64; E. and R. Hunt: 'Irrigation, conflict and politics: a Mexican case', *Irrigation's impact on society*, ed. T. Downing and McGuire Gibson (Tucson, 1974), 129–57; K.W. Butzer: *Early hydraulic civilization in Egypt* (Chicago, 1976); M. Hoffman *Egypt before the pharaohs* (New York, 1979), 312–17.

RJA

Hyksos (*heka-khaswt*, 'rulers of foreign lands') Term commonly used to refer to the Asiatic rulers (and, by extension, their subjects) who gradually moved into the Nile Delta during the late Middle Kingdom (*c.*1800–1640 BC), apparently gaining control of at least part of Lower Egypt during the 2nd Intermediate Period (*c.*1640–1550 BC). Although the settlements, cemeteries and temples at eastern Delta sites of this era (e.g. TELL EL-DABʿA and TELL EL-YAHUDIYA) are dominated by artefacts characteristic of Syro-Palestinian Middle

Bronze Age II culture, the sculptures apparently commissioned by the Hyksos rulers are characterized by the style and iconography of Middle Kingdom Egyptian rulers.

J. von Beckerath: *Untersuchungen zur politischen Geschichte der zweiten Zwischenzeit in Ägypten* (Glückstadt and New York, 1965); J. Van Seters: *The Hyksos, a new investigation* (New Haven, 1966); B.J. Kemp: 'Old Kingdom, Middle Kingdom and Second Intermediate Period', *Ancient Egypt: a social history*, ed. B.G. Trigger et al. (Cambridge, 1983), 71–182; M. Bietak: *Avaris* (London, 1996); E.D. Oren, ed.: *The Hyksos: new historical and archaeological perspectives* (Philadelphia, 1997).

IS

hypercoherence *see* SYSTEMS THEORY

hyper-diffusionism *see* DIFFUSIONISM

hypostyle hall Type of large columned hall which was one of the most characteristic elements of Egyptian temples, e.g. EDFU and LUXOR. The great Hypostyle Hall in the Temple of Amun at KARNAK is the largest ever built, comprising 134 columns, each reaching a height of about 20 m.

hypothesis testing (statistical) A branch of statistical analysis concerned with the verification or rejection of statistical hypotheses about the values of PARAMETERS. For example, an archaeologist studying changes in cooking practices over a period may choose as a parameter the change in the capacity of cooking pots over the period. A certain value (called the null hypothesis, and reflecting the simplest possible situation, e.g. no change in the capacity of cooking pots) is chosen in advance and compared with the estimated value of the parameter based on data from a sample. If the PROBABILITY of the difference between the two being greater than observed is less than a pre-specified level (known as the size, or SIGNIFICANCE LEVEL, of the test), then the null hypothesis is rejected, otherwise it is accepted. The procedure is conservative, in that the evidence has to be strongly against the null hypothesis before it can be rejected. It has been criticized on the grounds that the critical value (the smallest difference between null hypothesis and observed value that would lead to rejection) decreases indefinitely as the sample size increases.

J.E. Doran and F.R. Hodson: *Mathematics and computers in archaeology* (Edinburgh, 1975), 51–4; C.R. Orton *Mathematics in archaeology* (Glasgow, 1980), 200–14; S. Shennan: *Quantifying archaeology* (Edinburgh, 1988), 50–61; M. Fletcher and G.R. Lock: *Digging numbers* (Oxford, 1991), 60–2.

CO

hypothetico-deductive method *see* INDUCTIVE AND DEDUCTIVE EXPLANATION

Hyrax Hill Neolithic and Iron Age site, located on a small rocky eminence at the eastern edge of Nakuru town in the elevated stretch of the Eastern Rift Valley in Kenya. The site is central to the study of the later archaeology of the East African highlands and Rift Valley. Its archaeological potential was first recognized by Louis Leakey in the 1920s and later confirmed by Mary Leakey's excavations on both sides of the hill (Sites I and II) in 1937–8, which revealed a pre-Iron Age ('Neolithic') phase and two late Iron Age occupations including a series of SIRIKWA HOLES. Further excavations between 1964 and 1990, including those of the British Institute in Eastern Africa on Site II (Sirikwa), have refined the dating and cultural associations in the context of later regional research (Sutton 1987).

Excavations at Hyrax Hill II in 1985–6 have enhanced knowledge of the Sirikwa (pre-Maasai) pastoral culture. During the Maasai period, probably in the 18th or 19th century AD, there was renewed occupation of Site I by people with a derived Sirikwa style of pottery; this was possibly a camp (with burial place) of a specialized iron-working and hunting/ivory-trading community.

M.D. Leakey: 'Report on the excavations at Hyrax Hill, Nakuru, Kenya Colony, 1937–1938', *Transactions of the Royal Society of South Africa* 30/4 (1945) [whole volume]; J.E.G. Sutton: 'Hyrax Hill and the Sirikwa', *Azania* 22 (1987), 1–36.

JS

I

'Iberian art' Term used to describe the material culture – in particular, sculptural and decorative art – of indigenous peoples of the Iberian peninsular as it developed under the successive influences of eastern Mediterranean civilizations from the 7th century BC. The first such 'Iberian art' was produced under the influence of the Phoenicians – the earliest colonists and traders with Iberia – who established 'Tartessos' at the end of the 7th century BC, probably at the mouth of the River Guadalquivir in southern Spain. One of the earliest eastern Mediterannean intrusions into the west, Classical authors refer to Tartessos as both a region and as a specific place or city; it has not been identified with any individual archaeological site, but was apparently established to gain access to tin, bronze, silver and copper from Iberia and perhaps Brittany and the Scilly Isles.

The trading relationships that the Phoenicians of Tartessos and other eastern Mediterraneans established with local elites, and the objects and craftsmen introduced into the area, profoundly affected indigenous traditions – and transformed the economy and social development of the region (*see* HALLSTATT *for a parallel phenomenon in contemporary central Europe*). Adopting some of the basic forms (e.g. carved funerary monuments etc.) and motifs (e.g. mythical animals such as the sphinx) of the eastern Mediterranean, craftsmen working for local chieftains – apparently sometimes within specific workshops or schools – established their own artistic language. Their most distinctive products were jewellery made using new techniques (granulation, filigree etc.) and sculptural carving in soft sandstone. The finest monumental work of this early period is the (funerary?) monument of Pozo Moro (Albacete), built before 500 BC, which consisted of a stepped base and monumental sculpture including lions at each corner.

From the middle of the 6th century BC, Greek influence in Iberia began to weigh more heavily than Phoenician influence. This is reflected in the almost life-size carvings of mythical animals and humans produced during the later 6th and 5th centuries, including sphinxes, griffins, lions and armed warriors. From the early 5th to the 4th century BC a series of remarkable sculptural works were produced, often as part of elite funerary architecture or sanctuary sculptures – the most famous and complete being the so-called 'Lady of Elche', dating to *c.*450 BC and discovered in Alicante in the mid-19th century. This essentially naturalistic sculpture depicts a goddess in a severe figurative style, but elaborately dressed and adorned in a manner quite distinct from Classical models. Iberian art of the later centuries BC is particularly manifest in decorative art, including silver dishes and elaborate jewellery. As the region fell under Roman domination, Iberian art faded as a distinct material culture.

RJA

Iberomaurusian Palaeolithic industry, named by Paul Pallary in 1909, on the basis of material from La Mouillah, southwest of Oran, western Algeria. The 'baroque' name (as Gabriel Camps calls it) was chosen in order to indicate the industry's supposed occurrence in southern Spain as well as the Maghreb. The name has continued to be used, despite the fact that this supposition was shown to be false, and that an alternative name of 'Oranian' (as employed by Charles McBurney at HAUA FTEAH) was proposed in the 1930s. Generally regarded as 'EPIPALAEOLITHIC', the industry is dominated by backed bladelets, although there is a macrolithic component, and some bone tools, the most characteristic of which is an oblique bevel-edged knife. Geographically, the industry is concentrated along the shores of the Maghreb, although it does also extend inland, and sites with analagous occurrences have been shown to exist not only in Cyrenaica but also in the Nile valley. Since there is no technological or typological continuity between the Iberomaurusian and the preceding ATERIAN industrial complex, and there is also a chronological hiatus between them, Camps and his predecessors have tended to regard the industry as intrusive to the Maghreb. He and his colleagues have also tended to emphasize its distinctiveness from the CAPSIAN and other 'hypermicrolithic' industries such as those at Columnata, Koudiat Kifène Lahda, and Kef el-Kerem.

The earliest radiocarbon dates for the industry now known are 21,900 ± 400 and 20,600 ± 500 BP from Taforalt and Tamar Hat, and the latest is 8220 ± 820 BP from el-Haouita. If Close (1986) is right, the Oranian at Haua Fteah may go back to 18,620 ± 150 BP. Both open-air and cave sites are known, and Camps emphasizes the great thickness of deposits which may exist in the latter. The Iberomaurusian is associated exclusively with a population of MECHTA-AFALOU type. A total of 282 individuals so far have been found in Iberomaurusian contexts in the Maghreb, 183 of these having been found in a cemetery at Taforalt and 50 in another at Afalou.

G. Camps: *Les civilizations préhistoriques de l'Afrique du Nord et du Sahara* (Paris, 1974); D. Lubell, et al.: 'Continuity in the Epipaleolithic of Northern Africa with emphasis on the Maghreb', *AWA* 3 (1984), 143–91; A.E. Close: 'The place of the Haua Fteah in the late palaeolithic of North Africa', *Stone Age prehistory*, ed. G.N. Bailey and P. Callow (Cambridge, 1986), 169–80; M. Raimbault: 'Les cultures cromagnoides africaines', *DA* 161 (1991), 58–67.

PA-J

Iblis, Tall-i Settlement site located in the central Zagros mountains of Iran, roughly contemporary with Tepe Yahya and Tall-i Bakun as well as the UBAID period of Mesopotamia. The distinctive mud-brick single-storeyed houses of the second-earliest stratum at Iblis ('level 1') each consisted of a central group of storerooms surrounded by living rooms with red-plastered floors. The faunal remains from the lowest stratum ('level O') upwards indicate that goats and dogs, as well as possibly sheep and cattle, were domesticated, while such animals as the aurochs and gazelle were still being hunted. The cultivation of bread and wheat also dates back to the earliest phase. The economic activities of the inhabitants of Iblis also appear to have included the procurement and trading of copper and steatite.

J. Caldwell: *Investigations at Tal-i Iblis* (Chicago, 1967).

IS

ice cores In polar glaciers, annual ice layers, defined by variations in dust content and acidity, have been counted back some 14,000 years in long cores (errors are typically a few years per thousand). There is also variation in O^{18} (*see* OXYGEN ISOTOPE ANALYSIS *and* OXYGEN ISOTOPE CHRONOSTRATIGRAPHY) with depth, but its relationship to past climate is complex. Very high dust and acidity in ice cores can be the result of volcanic eruptions; assumed correlations have been used indirectly to date important eruptions such as that of Santorini (Thera).

C.U. Hammer et al.: 'Dating of Greenland ice cores by flow methods, isotopes, volcanic debris, and continental dust', *Journal of Glaciology* 20 (1978), 3–26; D.J. Schove and R.W. Fairbridge: *Ice-cores, varves and tree-rings* (Rotterdam, 1984).

SB

ideology The notion of ideology originated in the work of Karl Marx, who identified bodies of ideas and beliefs that promoted the interests of the ruling class while hiding or obscuring the concerns of the working classes. For Marx, 'ideology' was essentially determined by, and supportive of, the existing economic and political structure, although what he meant by the term often has to be inferred from his writings on other Marxist themes.

Since Marx, various thinkers have used the notion of ideology in a wider sense, to describe the tendency of individuals or groups to manipulate cultural symbols in order to achieve political or social aims. The characteristics of all ideologies are therefore derived from the cultures in which they are embedded. Particular sectors of societies use ideology for their own ends; thus, in highly stratified class-based societies (such as pharaonic EGYPT or medieval Europe), different ideologies are used by particular classes. In more egalitarian societies (such as that of the Aboriginal Australians), ideology appears to develop along gender- or age-based lines.

See also CRITICAL ARCHAEOLOGY, CRITICAL THEORY, MARXIST ARCHAEOLOGY, POST-PROCESSUAL ARCHAEOLOGY *and* THEORY AND THEORY BUILDING *for a discussion of the impact of modern ideologies on the practice and theory of archaology.*

K. Kristiansen: 'Ideology and material culture: an archaeological perspective', *Marxist perspectives in archaeology*, ed. M. Spriggs (Cambridge, 1984); D. Miller and C. Tilley, eds: *Ideology, power and prehistory* (Cambridge, 1984); R.H. McGuire and R. Paynter, eds: *The archaeology of inequality* (Oxford, 1991); [see also review: C. Tilley, *Antiquity* 67 (1993), 178–9].

IS

Ife City in southwestern Nigeria, widely reputed to be the 'spiritual capital' of the Yoruba people; this status, while it has helped to focus attention on Ife, also has attendant dangers, since, as Robin Horton (1979: 139) remarks, 'the scholar attempting to delve into the city's past is entering a sensitive,

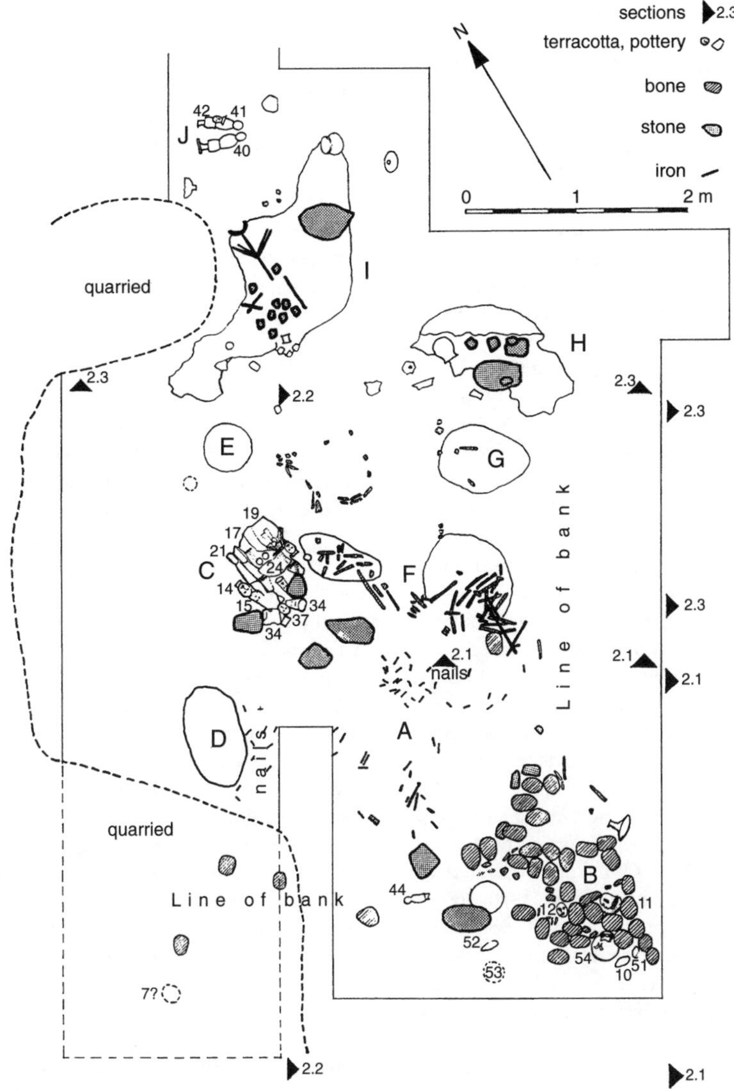

Figure 22 **Ife** Ife culture, plan of the main artefact concentrations at the Obalara's Land site (labelled A–J), including terracotta heads modelled in naturalistic and schematic styles. *Source*: P.S. Garlake *WAJA* 4 (1974).

emotionally charged area' subject to 'extra-academic pressures and sanctions'. It is said to be home to 401 deities, the last being the ruler or Oni, who claims descent from Oduduwa the founder of the dynasty. In 1943, Kenneth Murray established that there were at least 120 shrines in the city, most of them originally situated in groves, small patches of forest often with sacred 'peregun' trees. Many of the groves have been destroyed by modern urban development, one of the few to survive being at Obameri, excavated by Oliver Myers in the 1960s. At that time the grove measured 60 m^2 and the shrine 25 m^2; it is typical of many in Ife, in that the fragments of terracotta found were judged to have been 'dug up and reburied' annually as part of the festivities for the god, and a radiocarbon date of 220 ± 100 BP (AD 1730) confirmed that some of these activities were quite recent. Something of an archaeologist's nightmare, the practice of deliberate reburial renders the distinction between primary and secondary contexts more than usually difficult and necessary. Thus, at a site on Odo Ogbe street, where there are also much older deposits, Ekpo Eyo found that a terracotta head in a 'scoop' of earth with a radiocarbon date of 320 ± 95 BP (AD 1630) had itself been reburied. The 'artefact concentrations' excavated by Peter Garlake at Obalara's Land, 'an extra-ordinarily diverse range of objects to a considerable extent purposefully arranged' (Garlake 1974: 143), included a group of already damaged terracottas covered with red clay. They are interpreted as part of a shrine, with four radiocarbon dates in the range 760–480 BP (AD 1190–1470). The practice of 'burial and reburial' therefore goes back to what has been termed the 'Classical' period of Ife.

By the term 'Classical', W.B. Fagg and Frank Willett, who first coined it, meant to refer to a 'type period' in the history of the city characterized by 'naturalistic bronzes' and terracottas, but it has subsequently been taken to include edge-laid potsherd pavements, and it is now more usual to refer to the 'potsherd pavement' period as marking the high point of the city's early development. Thurstan Shaw and Garlake list 25 radiocarbon dates currently available from seven excavated sites in Ife, of which Shaw attributes 13 to this period, with in addition 10 pre- and two post-pavement dates (Shaw 1981: figs 2–4). Most important of the pre-pavement sites is Orun Oba Ado, excavated by Willett, with five dates in the range 1390–960 BP (AD 560–990). Pavement period 'one component' sites, apart from Obalara's Land, include Woye Asiri and Lafogido, excavated by Garlake and Ekpo Eyo respectively. Excluding one anomalous result, there are four dates from Woye Asiri in the range 815–545 BP (AD 1135–1405) and one from Lafogido of 840 ± 95 BP (AD 1110). Also important is Ita Yemoo, excavated by Willett in 1957–63, but here, as Garlake puts it, the dates cover a long period and are 'not internally consistent': three underlie pavements and two (associated with terracotta sculptures) overlie them, whereas two came from 'pit or well fills'. Taking all the dates together and calibrating them, Shaw concluded that the 'potsherd pavement period' in Ife extended from about AD 1100 to 1450.

The nature of the potsherd pavements can be most clearly discerned at Obalara's Land and Woye Asiri (Garlake 1974: figs 3–4; 1977: figs 4–8) – not an accident, if we accept the author's claim that, apart from his own work, 'not a single comprehensive or detailed report on any excavation in Ife' has up to now been published. The pavements were frequently constructed around complete buried pots (interpreted by Garlake as libation jars) and semicircular cut-aways were convincingly shown to represent altars. The overall orientation of the pavements at the two sites was consistent enough to justify the claim that they represented deliberate urban planning. At Lafogido 15 pots surmounted by terracotta animal heads were arranged in a rectangular formation around a potsherd pavement, which suggested to Ekpo Eyo that this was a primary occurrence, a royal temple or tomb. A primary context has also been claimed for the terracotta sculptures overlying the potsherd pavements at Ita Yemoo. Two of the pavements were found underlying the town wall sectioned by Willett, suggesting that the walled city encompassed a much smaller area than that occupied when the 'potsherd pavement period' was at its height. A date of 600 ± 100 BP (AD 1350) for one of the pits beneath the wall provides a *terminus post quem* for its construction.

Among the elements making up the corpus of 'Classical' Ife art, it is the terracotta sculptures and 'naturalistic bronzes' that have attracted the most attention, ever since Léo Frobenius unearthed them at the Olokun grove in 1910–11. The terracottas are more numerous and varied, including a composite group from the Iwinrin grove which is claimed to be the 'largest single' such object ever made in Africa. The majority of terracottas are naturalistic, but there is no doubt that schematic representations were made at the same time, since both have been found together at Obalara's Land and are shown side by side on one of the libation jars from the site (Garlake 1974: fig. 6 and pl.xlvi). As Shaw emphasizes, the 'naturalistic bronzes' (which are actually of copper or leaded brass) are few in number, < 30, of which 18 were recovered from the Wunmonije compound in 1938–9 and seven from Ita Yemoo in 1957. Fagg and Willett suggested that they represent royal or chiefly personages and that they were made for a 'royal ancestor cult, probably associated with some form of divine kingship' (Fagg and Willett 1962: 361). They may have been used in connection with second burial ('ako') ceremonies. In view of their stylistic homogenity, Shaw (1981: 112) expressed the opinion that they might be 'the work of one generation, even perhaps of a single great artist'. It is now possible to test this proposition, and to assess the relationship between the 'bronzes' and the other elements making up the 'Classical' Ife complex, because seven TL dates have been obtained on their clay cores at Ita Yemoo and Wunmonije (Shaw 1981: fig 5). The dates from

Wunmonije are in the range 510–415 BP (AD 1440–1535), whereas two pieces from Ita Yemoo come to 585 ± 70 and 530 ± 50 BP (AD 1365 and 1420) respectively. Taken together the dates suggest that the 'bronzes' occur towards the end of the 'Classical' period in Ife. By contrast, the earliest casting in Ife style is now known to occur at Tada on the Niger > 200 km north of the city, where the so-called 'seated figure' has a TL date of 625 ± 60 BP (AD 1325). A 'standing figure' from the same site has a date of 585 ± 55 BP (AD 1365) but whereas its affinities are uncertain the seated figure has been described as the 'supreme masterpiece of Ife founding' (Willett and Fleming 1976: 139).

Other elements of material culture associated with the 'Classical' period include tubular blue glass beads ('segi'), manufactured locally as shown by numerous fragments of crucibles found in excavated contexts and widely exported to other parts of West Africa, and quartz stools. Horton indeed suggests (1979: 88, 107–8) that the symbolic role of these items – particularly the beads which form an essential component of Yoruba royal crowns ('*ade*') – may have been greater than that of the naturalistic sculptures. Iron working also played an important role, as shown by its ritual representation in the form of a > 50 kg pear-shaped lump in the shrine of Ogun Ladin, artefacts excavated at Obalara's Land, and slag and tuyères found at Woye Asiri. The evidence of local manufacture at the last site contrasts sharply with the fact that up to now no such positive indications have been found for the 'bronzes' for which the city is justly famous. Research questions arising from the still fragmentary record of Ife's archaeological and historical past include the following:

Reasons for Ife's rise and decline. In the model proposed by Horton (in which 'causal priority' is given to geographic, technological, and economic factors rather than to politics and religion), Ife's rise to power in the period from AD 900 to 1450 and its subsequent decline are due to changing patterns of trade between the forest and coastal areas on the one hand and the Sahara and savanna on the other. Ife originally controlled a 'central trade route' but was subsequently cut off and bypassed by the successor states of Benin and Oyo. The Tada 'bronzes' mentioned above are relics of the once flourishing trade route from Ife to Gao. Graham Connah (1987: 148–9) warns however that the 'external stimulus hypothesis remains untested . . . until we know far more about the archaeology of the first millennium AD within the forest'.

Continuity and discontinuity in Ife's history. The early centuries of Ife's history have been termed the 'pre-Oduduwa' period by Ade Obayemi ('prince of iconoclasts' as Horton calls him) in an attempt to downgrade the role of the Oduduwa dynasty in the history of the city. If this period is considered to extend up to the time of the building of the town wall, as Obayemi suggests, then clearly it would embrace all the years of Ife's greatness. Whatever might be thought of this controversial suggestion, the results of the excavations at Obalara's Land and Woye Asiri have tended to confirm that there are indeed elements of continuity between the early city and the Yoruba 'spiritual capital' of today. Thus, the pottery wares recovered include bowls of 'isasun' and 'agbada' type; two iron artefacts from Obalara's Land are similar to 'ogboni staves' used by 'Ifa' diviners (Garlake 1974: fig. 10); and 'ogboni' motifs can also be discerned on certain pottery vessels from this site (Garlake 1974; fig. 6). The same vessels also show gagged heads and decapitated bodies, a reminder that human sacrifice at Ife was not forbidden until 1886 (Fagg and Willett 1962: 362).

Ife's relationship with Nok and Benin. Willett stressed the African-ness of Ife's artistic achievements (shown in the characteristic body proportions of the 'bronzes' and terracottas) in part no doubt as an antidote to Frobenius's suggestion that the city was a lost Greek Atlantis, and he endeavoured to trace its roots to the NOK culture on stylistic grounds. In view of the chronological gap, others have doubted whether there are adequate reasons for linking the two except 'in a remote and very generalized way'. There are much stronger grounds in local tradition to link Ife and BENIN. It is said that as late as AD 1888 the heads of the Obas of Benin were brought for burial at Orun Oba Ado, in recognition of the fact that the dynasty sprang from there. Willett's excavations failed to provide confirmation of this point, but at Obalara's Land and Woye Asiri a surprisingly large number of artistic motifs were found which did connect them: leopards' heads, human heads with snakes issuing from the nostrils, 'cat's whiskers' and keloid scarifications, snakes, and rectangular panels behind the altars. The available radiocarbon and TL dates are not inconsistent with the tradition of a link between the two cities, but this and all other aspects of Ife's early development await further investigation.

F. Willett: 'Ife and its archaeology', *JAH* 1 (1960), 231–48; W. Fagg and F. Willett: 'Ancient Ife: an ethnographical summary', *Actes du IV Congrès Panafricain de Préhistoire et de l'Etude du Quaternaire, section III, pré- et protohistoire* (Tervuren, 1962), 357–73; O.Myers: 'Excavations at Ife, Nigeria', *The West African Archaeological Newsletter* 6

(1967), 6–11; 7 (1967), 4–6; M.A. Fabunmi: *Ife shrines* (Ife, 1969); F. Willett: 'A survey of recent results in the radiocarbon chronology of Western and Northern Africa', *JAH* 12 (1971), 339–70; F. Willett: 'Archaeology: chapter VIII', *Sources of Yoruba history*, ed. S.O. Biobaku (Oxford, 1973), 111–39; E. Eyo: 'Odo Ogbe Street and Lafogido: contrasting archaeological sites in Ile-Ife, Western Nigeria', *WAJA* 4 (1974), 99–109; P.S. Garlake: 'Excavations at Obalara's Land, Ife: an interim report', *WAJA* 4 (1974), 111–48; F. Willett and S.J. Fleming: 'A catalogue of important Nigerian copper-alloy castings dated by thermoluminescence', *Archaeometry* 18/2 (1976) 135–46; P.S. Garlake: 'Excavations on the Woye Asiri family land in Ife, Western Nigeria', *WAJA* 7 (1977), 57–95; R. Horton: 'Ancient Ife: a reassessment', *JHSN* 9/4 (1979), 69–149; A. Obayemi: 'Ancient Ile-Ife: another cultural reinterpretation', *JHSN* 9/4 (1979), 151–85; T. Shaw: 'Ife and Raymond Mauny', *Le sol, la parole et l'écrit: mélanges en hommage à Raymond Mauny* (Paris, 1981), 109–35; G. Connah: *African civilizations, precolonial cities and states in tropical Africa: an archaeological perspective* (Cambridge, 1987).

PA-J

Igbo-Ukwu Town 40 km southeast of Onitsha, southeastern Nigeria, where excavations carried out by Thurstan Shaw in 1959–60 (on behalf of the Nigerian Federal Department of Antiquities) and in 1964 (on behalf of the Institute of African Studies, University of Ibadan) identified a cultural complex associated with a series of fine coppers and bronzes. The excavations were at three sites, all on land owned by a local family called Anozie, which in order to distinguish them have been christened Igbo Isaiah, Igbo Richard, and Igbo Jonah. Public attention was first drawn to this area in 1938, when Isaiah Anozie recovered a number of bronze artefacts while digging a cistern in his compound, although it subsequently became clear that finds had been made at the other two sites as far back as 1922. Shaw established that the three sites were functionally distinct but also shared many traits in common; hence he regarded them all as belonging to what he termed the 'Igbo-Ukwu culture'. The results of his excavations were published in meticulous detail in two large volumes in 1970, thanks to a subvention from the Ford and Rockefeller Foundations. His principal objective, as he said, was to make the primary data available to others, and his philosophy was to 'keep separate what is description and observation and what is interpretation' (Shaw 1977: 109). He published a shorter and more popular account in 1977, and these two works (as well as Shaw's later papers) provide the essential baseline for any consideration of the finds at Igbo-Ukwu and the controversies which have subsequently surrounded them.

All the sites together produced 685 artefacts of copper and bronze (weighing > 74 kg) of which 110 are counted as major pieces: > 165,000 beads of glass and stone; and 21,784 potsherds, the majority consisting of characteristic ancient 'Igbo-Ukwu ware' with deep grooving, protuberant bosses, and patterns reminiscent of basketwork; and other objects, including some iron artefacts and iron slag, three ivory tusks, and fragments of textiles and calabashes. It is the metalwork which has attracted the most attention, on account of what W.B. Fagg called its 'strange rococo, almost Fabergé-like virtuosity'. Whereas the copper was worked by smithing and chasing, the bronze (actually, leaded bronze with on average 6.5% tin and 8% lead) was cast using a 'lost wax' (or, more probably, a 'lost latex') technique. The resulting products have seemed to many, as Denis Williams has put it, to constitute 'an exquisite explosion without antecedent or issue' (Williams 1974: 119). Apart from the question of the raw materials employed for metalworking and their implications in terms of indigenous versus imported technology, controversy has centred around two topics arising directly from Thurstan Shaw's work: (1) dating and (2) the possible ethnographic interpretation of these finds.

Dating. Shaw originally obtained five radiocarbon dates on the following materials: wood from the stool in Igbo Richard 1100 ± 120 BP; charcoal from Igbo Jonah pit VI 1075 ± 130 BP; charcoal from Igbo Jonah pit IV 1110 ± 110, 505 ± 70, and 1110 ± 145BP. Four of these dates therefore fell in the 9th century AD and one (an 'odd man out') in the 15th. Shaw explained that the younger date might well be due to contamination from the modern clay pit above pit IV, and indicated that the balance of probability was very much in favour of a 9th century date. In his view, none of the other evidence contradicted this conclusion; the most difficult point concerned the beads, many of which, in the opinion of Alex du Toit and W.G.N. van der Sleen, must have had an Indian or Venetian origin and been imported, perhaps via Egypt. In the ensuing controversy, summarized by Shaw in 1975, there were both those who defended a younger and an older date (in particular because the latter seemed to confirm the antiquity of the Ibo people) and he himself was 'caught in the cross-fire between the contending parties'. At the Pan-African Congress in 1983 he was able to announce that he had obtained three more dates from the British Museum, but these were subsequently revised, as follows: wood from the stool in Igbo Richard 940 ± 370BP; charcoal from Igbo Jonah pit IV 1260 ± 310 and 1100 ± 260BP (Shaw 1995a:

1995b). Calibrating the results according to the dendrochronological calender, Shaw concludes that seven of the eight dates indicate that the finds belong to a period between the 8th and 11th centuries AD. Both old and new dates are in very close agreement, and Shaw has expressed the hope that this controversy can now be allowed to 'die down' so that attention can be focused on other problems.

Ethnographic interpretation. In his original report, Shaw drew attention to the fact that the finds at Igbo-Ukwu might be interpreted by reference to the 'Eze Nri' institution first investigated by M.D.W. Jeffreys in the 1930s. This idea has been taken up and expanded by M.A. Onwuejeogwu and K. Ray. The institution exists both at Agukwu and at Oreri, immediately north of Igbo-Ukwu, and in fact Shaw ascertained that the land on which the sites are located had originally belonged to Oreri. The repository at Igbo Isaiah is therefore interpreted as having been an 'obu' or lineage temple used in connection with the title system, and the burial as that of a priest king or 'ozo' titled man. Ray, emphasizing what he calls the 'communicative uses of material culture . . . within a culturally and historically determined structure of meaning', suggests that the symbols of lineage authority at Igbo Isaiah served to reinforce the strategy of social control practised by the elders and title-holders, whereas the 'material metaphor' of the snake as divine messenger appearing on the copper crown of the 'Eze Nri' at Igbo Richard underlined his role as divine representative. The 'historical metaphor' of the 'children of Nri' (male and female, each bearing characteristic 'ichi' scarification marks) is clearly seen on the 'altar stand' from Igbo Isaiah. Not everyone is convinced of the utility of these parallels. John Sutton (1991: 149) considers that this line of enquiry 'encourages a synchronic and on

Crown, IR 337 and IR 343
Pectoral plate, IR 407
Circle of spiral copper bosses set in wood, IR 454
Copper handle for calabash, IR 464
Skull
Tanged copper fan-holder IR 432
Beaded armlets, IR 416 and IR 417
Bronze horseman hilt, IR 350
0
1
metre

Figure 23 **Igbo-Ukwu** Igbo Ukwu, Igbo Richard: (A) schematic plan of the relative position of objects on or near the floor of the burial chamber, including numerous copper anklets, three tusks and (1) pectoral plate (2) skull (3) circle of spiral copper bosses set in wood (4) beaded armlets (5) copper handle for calabash (6) tanged copper fan-holder, (7) bronze horseman hilt and (8) crown (B) reconstruction showing the completed burial chamber as it was being roofed in (painting by Caroline Sassoon). *Source*: Thurstan Shaw.

occasion a sentimental approach' which 'tends to emphasize the ritual and ceremonial aspects of art and wealth at the expense of addressing squarely the question of how that wealth would have been amassed'. He therefore opposes 'the supposition of timeless continuity' as likely to hinder further progress in understanding Igbo-Ukwu. This discordant note suggest that the ability of these sites to generate controversy is far from exhausted.

T. Shaw: *Igbo-Ukwu: an account of archaeological discoveries in eastern Nigeria*, 2 vols (London, 1970); D. Williams: *Icon and image* (New York, 1974); T. Shaw: 'Those Igbo-Ukwu radiocarbon dates: facts, fictions and probabilities', *JAH* 16/4 (1975), 503–17; ——: *Unearthing Igbo-Ukwu: archaeological discoveries in eastern Nigeria* (Ibadan, 1977); K. Ray: 'Material metaphor, social interaction and historical reconstructions: exploring patterns of association and symbolism in the Igbo-Ukwu corpus', *The archaeology of contextual meanings*, ed. I. Hodder (Cambridge, 1987), 66–77; V.E. Chikwendu et al.: 'Nigerian sources of copper, lead and tin for the Igbo-Ukwu bronzes', *Archaeometry* 31/1 (1989), 27–36; P. Craddock: 'Man and metal in ancient Nigeria', *British Museum Magazine* 6 (1919), 9; J.E.G. Sutton: 'The international factor at Igbo-Ukwu', *AAR* 9 (1991), 145–60; T. Shaw: 'Further light on Igbo-Ukwu, including new radiocarbon dates', *Proceedings of the 9th Congress of the Pan-African Association of Prehistory and Related Studies, Jos, 1983*, ed. B. Andah, P. de Maret and R. Soper (Ibadan, 1995a), 79–83; ——: 'Those Igbo-Ukwu dates again', *NA* 44 (1995b), 43.

PA-J

Ihnasya el-Medina *see* HERAKLEOPOLIS MAGNA

Impressed ware *see* CARDIAL WARE

Inamgaon Large Chalcolithic site on the Bhima river in Maharashtra, India, consisting of five mounds spanning the MALWA and early and late JORWE periods (*c*.1800–700 BC). Excavations have uncovered over 130 structures and 260 burials, as well as evidence for pottery kilns and substantial constructions relating to defence and irrigation, including a large embankment of the early Jorwe period. Domesticates known from the site include rice, wheat, barley, lentil, pea and millets, as well as humped cattle, dog, sheep and goat, and domestic horse. Wild fauna including deer, antelope, mongoose, hare, turtle, and fish were also recovered.

M.K. Dhavalikar et al.: *Excavations at Inamgaon*, 2 vols (Pune, 1988).

CS

Inca South American cultural group whose empire represents the last great expansionist state in the Andean region. The Incas were originally one of many small, warring tribes found in the Peruvian highlands after the collapse of HUARI. Under their ninth ruler, who renamed himself Pachacuti ('earthquake') when a series of military victories over local rulers led him to usurp the throne, the Inca rapidly expanded across the highlands and then the coast, eventually controlling most of the central and south Andean area and the Ecuadorian highlands. Throughout this area, the Inca introduced their own peculiar ceramic and architectural styles and their official religion, itself invented by Pachacuti to serve the ideological needs of his new empire. Inca architecture, especially the finely-cut stone architecture that typifies many important buildings, has long entranced the western world.

Inca stone working The very fine fitting and often immense stones used in important Inca constructions has been a subject of considerable speculation, much of it risible (i.e. extra-terrestrials or travelling Asians, Africans and Europeans), over the years. A combination of experimental archaeology and architectural analysis has allowed researchers to reconstruct the methods and procedures used in Inca stone work, and to better understand the conceptualization of projects and the organization of labour in the Inca state.

In 1979 Jean-Pierre Protzen, an architect at the University of California, became interested in the subject, and began fieldwork aimed at reconstructing the process from quarrying methodologies to working the stones and erecting structures (buildings, terrace walls, etc.). Work at the largely destroyed Sacsahuaman (the stones from which were moved downhill to reconstruct Cuzco in a European mode) and at unfinished parts of Ollantaytambo indicated that the Inca characteristically worked the top of a block when the block was in place, fitting the stones by a trial and error method and using stone dust as an indication of when to work a block down. Transport of the stones was accomplished by means of chutes, and by dragging stones with the help of wooden sleepers (perhaps), although the huge stones of terrace walls seem to have been quarried on site and moved very little. Protzen's work indicates that the Inca, like other South American peoples, used relatively simple technologies pushed to their utmost. It reinforces ideas concerning the value of time put into the manufacture of luxury goods, in this case the finely worked stone walls of royal and religious buildings.

J.H. Rowe: 'Inca culture at the time of the Spanish conquest', *Handbook of South American Indians* 2 (1946), 183–330; ——: 'The origins of creator worship among the

Inca', *Culture in history: essays in honour of Paul Radin*, ed. S. Diamond (New York, 1960); E. Guillén: 'El enigma de las momias Incas', *BL* 5/28 (1983), 29–42; J. Hyslop: *Inca settlement planning* (Austin, 1990); J. Idrovo: 'Arquitectura y urbanismo en Tomebamba, Ecuador', *Beiträge zu Allgemeinen Verlagleichenden Archäologi* 13 (1993), 254–330; J.-P. Protzen: *Inca architecture and construction at Ollantaytambo* (Oxford and New York, 1993).

KB

incensario (incense burner, censer) Pottery vessel used to burn incense, usually some kind of tree resin (e.g. *Protium copal*), and found throughout Mesoamerica in all periods. There are many different varieties and they are often elaborately modelled and painted with figures of costumed deities.

M. Goldstein: 'The ceremonial role of the Maya flanged censer', *Man* 12 (1977), 402–20; J.C. Berlo: 'Artistic specialization at Teotihuacan: the ceramic incense burner', *Precolumbian art history: selected readings*, ed. A. Cordy-Collins (Palo Alto, 1982), 83–100.

PRI

India *see* ASIA, SOUTH

Indo-European Indo-European is the name given by linguists to a family of languages found across a broad area from northern India and Iran to western Europe, including the Germanic and Romance tongues. These languages can be shown to share certain words, especially the names of certain trees and the words for 'horse' and 'wheeled vehicles'. The way in which these modern languages are related is best explained by their having had a common root language, which at some unknown point spread throughout the 'Indo-European' area. Various attempts have been made to identify the likely original homeland of the speakers of this archaic Indo-European language – the so-called Proto-Indo-Europeans – although linking linguistic and archaeological evidence is notoriously difficult. One approach to the problem seemed to be to identify the earliest cultures to domesticate horses and to use wheeled vehicles. Partly because the early Bronze Age KURGAN cultures of the Pontic-Caspian steppe qualify on both counts, and, as mobile pastoralists are assumed to have had a propensity for migration or invasion, they have traditionally been regarded as strong contenders.

However, there is no direct evidence that these peoples spoke an Indo-European language, or that they invaded central or western Europe, and this traditional interpretation (fully described and discussed in Mallory 1989), was challenged in 1987 by Colin Renfrew. In a controversial analysis Renfrew suggested instead that the first agriculturalists in the Near East were Indo-Europeans, and that the Indo-European language accompanied the spread of farming from Anatolia, across Europe, after *c*.6500 BC; a related hypothesis has been advanced by Krantz (1988).

C. Renfrew: *Archaeology and language: the puzzle of the Indo-European origins* (Cambridge, 1987); critically reviewed in *Quarterly Review of Archaeology* 9, 1988, by C.C. Lamberg-Karlovsky and M. Gimbutas; G. Krantz: *Geographical development of European languages* (New York, 1988); J.P. Mallory: *In search of the Indo-Europeans: language, archaeology and myth* (London, 1989); C. Renfrew: 'They ride horses, don't they?: Mallory on the Indo-Europeans', *Antiquity* 63 (1989), 43–7.

RJA

inductive and deductive explanation Philosophers of science identify two fundamental ways of generating and validating descriptive and explanatory theories about phenomena in the world: inductive explanation and deductive explanation.

Inductive explanations begin with particular observations about the real world. These observations are then used to build the generalizations and links that constitute theories. Archaeologists often use inductive thinking when trying to interpret the evidence that they are gathering from an individual site. For example, archaeologists may notice that an unusual kind of pottery seems to occur repeatedly in a ritual context; they may move from this series of real-world observations to suggest that the pottery is 'ritual pottery'.

In contrast, *deductive explanation* begins with theory-building. A series of premises are built up, from which, logically, a particular conclusion *must* be deduced. From this theory, the archaeologist can derive various hypotheses that must be true if the theory is valid (given that a hypothesis is simply an untested assertion of the relationship between certain aspects of a theory). At this point, the archaeologist can turn to the real world and try to substantiate his or her theory by testing the associated hypotheses against the evidence. If the evidence contradicts the hypothesis, then both the hypothesis and (if the logic is correct) the theory *as formulated* must be untrue. Because this approach depends upon posing hypotheses and deducing logical relationships, it is often known as the *hypothetico-deductive method*.

Although these are the two polar approaches to theory building, there are various compromises and extensions. For example, many archaeologists use an essentially inductive form of reasoning to suggest those theories worth careful consideration. They may then analyse the theories, forming hypotheses to describe the nature of the relationship between the theory and the underlying data. At this point, the archaeologist may test these hypotheses against the evidence in a very similar way to the hypothetico-deductive method. If the hypotheses do not survive the test, they are amended until the formulation of the theory accords with the evidence in the most plausible way. Although in archaeology the data available may not allow very thorough testing, this method, sometimes called the *analytical inductive* approach, combines the practicality of the inductive approach with some of the rigour of the deductive approach.

In some circumstances, it may be possible to test an archaeological theory using statistical methodologies and probability analysis – particularly where those methods have themselves suggested an unusual and interesting relationship between variables in a sample. Essentially, these approaches demonstrate the likelihood of the relationship seen in the sample data having occurred by chance or by sampling error, and thus its significance in interpreting real-world relationships. When statistical tests are used to assess the plausibility of an inductive explanation, the conclusion is sometimes called an *inductive statistical* (or probabilistic) explanation. (Deductive statistical explanations also exist, but are rarely applicable in the discipline of archaeology.) It is important to stress that tests that prove a significant and strong relationship between variables do not themselves *prove* an inductive theory – they merely strengthen the argument that the particular correlations observed are unlikely to have happened by chance. For example, a careful statistical analysis of the 'ritual pottery' mentioned above might reveal whether the fact that the pottery was found only in the ritual contexts was a statistically significant association; but statistical analysis could never prove that the pottery was used for 'ritual' purposes.

The relationship between these modes of enquiry and the use of general or universal laws is discussed further in the entry on COVERING LAWS. *See also* THEORY AND THEORY BUILDING.

P.J. Watson et al.: *Explanation in archaeology: an explicitly scientific approach* (New York and London, 1971); G. Gibbon: *Explanation in archaeology* (Oxford, 1989).

RJA

inductively coupled plasma-atomic emission spectrometry (ICP-AES) Method of quantitative chemical analysis based on the measurement of the spectrum of atomic emission from a sample excited in an argon plasma. The technique is a development of OPTICAL EMISSION SPECTROMETRY using a high temperature plasma (6000–10,000°K), a more stable and efficient atomization source than an electric arc. It is applicable to metals, ceramics, glass and lithics and will quantify from major down to trace or ultratrace levels in some cases. Samples are required to be in solution and must be dissolved in high purity reagents, normally a mixture of concentrated acids. This operation must be carefully planned to ensure complete dissolution of the sample.

Samples are introduced into the plasma via a nebulizer which disperses the solution as an aerosol (see figure 24). The plasma temperature causes electron energy-level transitions within atoms of the elements in the sample which result in the emission of light at wavelengths characteristic of the individual elements present. It is necessary to measure the intensity of specific wavelengths corresponding to each element being quantified; this can be achieved by rapid scanning of the spectrum, measurement at preset wavelengths or a combination of both. The light intensities are proportional to the element concentrations in the plasma and hence in the solution. The instrument is calibrated using standard solutions containing known concentrations of the elements to be quantified.

The analysis is effectively simultaneous and typically 20 or more elements may be measured in one solution. The technique is applicable to the same range of materials as AAS (ATOMIC ABSORPTION SPECTROPHOTOMETRY) but has several advantages including speed, fewer interferences, linearity of calibration over wide concentration ranges and the ability to measure certain important elements such as sulphur and phosphorus. The earliest applications in archaeology have been on ceramics and glass.

M. Thompson, and J.N. Walsh: *Handbook of inductively coupled plasma spectrometry* (London, 1983); M.P. Heyworth et al.: 'The role of inductively coupled plasma spectrometry in glass provenance studies', *Archaeometry 1986* (Athens, 1988), 661–9.

MC

inductively coupled plasma-mass spectrometry (ICPMS) Method of quantitative chemical and isotopic analysis which combines the features of the two techniques of ICP-AES (INDUCTIVELY COUPLED PLASMA-ATOMIC EMISSION SPECTROMETRY) and mass spectrometry to produce a versatile trace and ultratrace. Samples, which must be in solution, are introduced into an argon plasma, similar to a conventional ICP, but

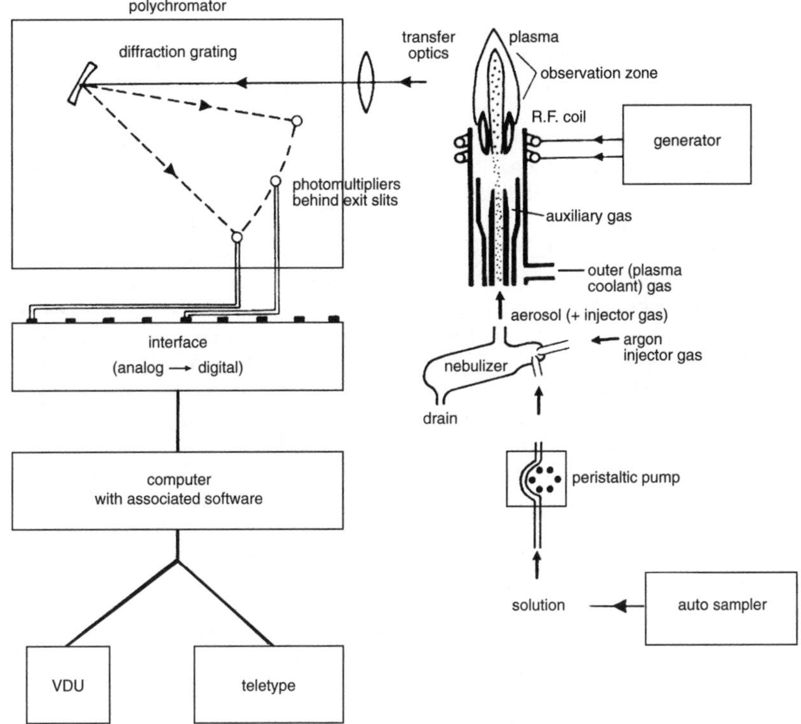

Figure 24 **inductively coupled plasma-atomic emission spectrometry (ICP–AES)** Schematic diagram of an inductively coupled plasma-atomic (ICP) system. *Source*: M. Thompson, and J.N. Walsh: *A handbook of inductively coupled plasma spectrometry* (London: Blackie, 1983), fig. 1.2.

this is used as an ion source for a quadrupole mass spectrometer. Thus, instead of measuring the atomic emission from the sample, the mass spectrum is recorded. The concentrations of elements are therefore determined by measurement of their individual isotopes after calibrating with standard solutions of known concentrations. Detection limits are uniformly lower than ICP-AES or flame AAS (ATOMIC ABSORPTION SPECTROPHOTOMETRY). The technique is also capable of determining isotope ratios. However, currently, the precision of these does not match the method of thermal ionisation mass spectrometry conventionally used, for example, for lead isotope ratios.

K.E. Jarvis et al.: *Handbook of inductively coupled plasma mass spectrometry* (Glasgow, 1992).

MC

inductive statistical explanation *see* INDUCTIVE AND DEDUCTIVE EXPLANATION

Indus civilization The earliest urban society of South Asia, the Indus (or Harappan) civilization emerged out of the local traditions of the early 3rd millennium BC focused on several small regional centres (e.g. AMRI and HARAPPA). It may be divided into three basic phases: Early Harappan (*c.*4000–2600 BC), Mature Harappan (*c.*2600–1900 BC) and Late Harappan (*c.*1900–1300 BC). The excavated remains at a number of Indus sites provide evidence of a complex and varied subsistence economy involving a wide range of methods of irrigation. Plant domesticates included wheat, barley, millets, pulses, vegetables and, in some areas, rice. Domesticated animals included cattle, water-buffalo, sheep and goat; wild animals and fish were also consumed (Meadow 1989; Weber 1991).

More than a thousand Indus-civilization sites have been found across a range of environmental zones in Pakistan, Afghanistan and northern India. The Indus period was characterized by the development of a complex 4- or 5-level hierarchy of settlements, concentrating on several major urban centres such as MOHENJO-DARO and Harappa. Other first-level cities were GANWERIWALA,

Rakhigari (80 ha in area) and possibly Dholavira; second-level towns of 10–50 ha include KALIBANGAN and Judeirjo Daro; and third-level towns in the 5–10 ha range include AMRI, LOTHAL AND CHANU-DARO. The smallest level of town, at 1–5 ha, comprised such settlements as KOT DIJI, Balakot, SUTKAGEN DOR and NAUSHARO. There were also many smaller sites, such as pastoral camps and specialized craft-production locales.

There has been much debate regarding the social and political organization of the Indus civilization; excavated remains at Mohenjo-Daro and other sites reveal complex urban plans, monumental constructions and a highly developed economic structure (Shaffer 1982; Malik 1984; Kenoyer 1991: 366–9). Indus sites, however, are still lacking in many of the traits characteristic of other early civilizations, such as warfare, royal burials and unambiguously identified palaces and temples. This may partly be a function of the poor quality of many of the early excavations conducted in the 1920s–1940s, which still provide most of the data on the Indus civilization. However, the situation may also reflect the fact that the archaeological models commonly applied to early states are perhaps unable to account for the full range of variability in ancient civilizations. For example, Kenoyer has suggested that Indus political structure may have been structured around several groups of semi-autonomous elites (1991:369), with an over-arching coherence in material culture and possibly ideology (Possehl 1991: 273–4), rather than being characterized by a well-integrated bureaucratic and administrative structure familiar to scholars of ancient Egypt and Mesopotamia.

During the Early Indus period (*c.*4000–2600 BC), the Indus Valley and surrounding highlands were characterized by the emergence of a number of localized regional traditions (e.g. AMRI, Nal, KOT DIJI, Kili Ghul Muhammad, Hakra). This was a period in which many of the traits that would characterize the succeeding urban period appeared, including specialized craft production, long-distance trade, intensification of agriculture and stock rearing, as well as the emergence of status differentiation and the development of large central settlements with monumental architecture.

The Mature Indus period emerged from this complex of localized traditions, but there is some disagreement as to whether this transition was sudden and dramatic (e.g. Possehl 1991) or the result of more gradual continuous transformations (Mughal 1990; Kenoyer 1991). The urban phase of the Indus civilization ended in *c.*2100–1900 BC: in some areas sites were abandoned completely, while in others, such as Harappa, occupation continued at a much smaller scale.

A variety of factors appear to have contributed to the decline of the Indus civilization, possibly including changing cultural and historical factors such as the overextension of economic and ritual networks (Kenoyer 1991; 370), as well as environmental changes that would have affected agricultural potential, such as the movement of the Indus river-course to the east and the drying up of the densely settled Ghaggar-Hakra region, where GANWERIWALA was located (Misra 1984). No evidence exists for extensive destruction or conflict at the end of the Indus period; instead there appear to have been localized patterns of depopulation or migration, and a return to more localized archaeological traditions.

I. Mahadevan: *The Indus script: texts, concordance and tables* (Delhi, 1977); G.L. Possehl, ed.: *Ancient cities of the Indus* (New Delhi, 1979); S. Ratnagar: *Encounters: the westerly trade of the Harappa Civilization* (Delhi, 1981); G.L. Possehl: *Harappan civilization* (New Delhi, 1982); J. Shaffer: 'Harappan culture: a reconsideration', *Harappan Civilization*, ed. by G.L. Possehl (Delhi, 1982), 41–50; S.C. Malik: 'Harappan social and political life', *Frontiers of the Indus Civilization*, ed. B.B. Lal and S.P. Gupta (Delhi, 1984), 201–10; V.N. Misra: 'Climate, a factor in the rise and fall of the Indus Civilization', *Frontiers of the Indus Civilization*, ed. by B.B. Lal and S.P. Gupta (Delhi, 1984), 461–90; R.H. Meadow: 'Continuity and change in the agriculture of the Greater Indus Valley: the palaeoethnobotanical and zooarchaeological evidence', *Old problems and new perspectives in the archaeology of South Asia*, ed. by J.M. Kenoyer (Madison, 1989), 61–74; D.K. Chakrabarti: *The external trade of the Indus Civilization* (Delhi 1990); M.R. Mughal: 'Further evidence of the Early Harappan culture in the Greater Indus Valley', *South Asian Studies* 6 (1990), 175–200; J.M. Kenoyer: 'The Indus Valley tradition of Pakistan and Western India', *JWP* 5 (1991), 331–85; G.L. Possehl: 'Revolution in the urban revolution: The emergence of Indus Civilization', *Annual Review of Anthropology* 19 (1991), 261–82; S.A. Weber: *Plants and Harappan subsistence* (New Delhi, 1991); W.A. Fairservis: *The Harappan civilization and its writings* (New Delhi, 1992).

CS

industrial archaeology Subdiscipline that developed in archaeology during the mid-20th century to investigate the tangible evidence of the social, economic and technological development of the industrial era. The period covered extends from the early 18th century to the first decades of the 20th, although some would include all of the 20th century. Industrial archaeology has also been defined as a thematic discipline dealing with the methods by which humankind have achieved their material civilization and modified the environment in which they live (Raistrick 1972), but the all-embracing nature of this definition is impossible to put into practice.

The discipline originated in the 1950s in Britain, after the post-war preoccupation with renewal had led to the destruction of much of the landscape associated with industrialization. Industrial archaeology was born out of an attempt to preserve selected relics of the period when Britain was the world leader in the process of industrialization – a process which probably had a more rapid and fundamental effect on material culture than any that had gone before.

Industrial archaeology, then, grew from concern about the future of standing structures rather than as an academic study concerned with deriving information from the tangible evidence of a period of the past. It was a spontaneous growth, resulting in volunteer activity on an immense scale in both preservation and recording. The CBA (Council for British Archeology) tried to give some shape to the latter by the introduction of record cards, which eventually grew into the NRIM (National Record of Industrial Monuments). The latter was based first at the University of Bath under R.A. Buchanan and later subsumed into the NMR (National Monuments Record) of the RCHME (Royal Commission on the Historical Monuments of England). The RCHME has come to play an important role in industrial archaeology, undertaking specific surveys and spearheading an attempt to ensure that sites and structures dating up to 1945 are included on both the NMR and Sites and Monuments Records. English Heritage has also taken due account of industrial archaeology in its Monuments Protection Programme by commissioning the first comprehensive surveys of a range of industries so that priorities can be assessed and more industrial monuments included in the Schedules.

The Association for Industrial Archaeology, which was set up in 1973 to represent the interests of industrial archaeology, attempts to hold a balance between the volunteers who have dominated industrial archaeology in the past and the professionals, as well as publishing the major British journal in the field, *Industrial Archaeology Review* (*IAR*). Industrial archaeology is no longer solely the province of Britain, and The International Committee for the Conversation of the Industrial Heritage (TICCIH) was set up in 1978. Many of its members have contributed to the Blackwell Encyclopedia of Industrial Archaeology, which sets the discipline in its world context (Trinder 1992). The volunteer preservation movement is responsible for hundreds of sites in Britain as well as overseas, and local and state authorities have also become aware of the heritage value of industrial archaeological sites. The most important of these in Great Britain is the IRONBRIDGE GORGE in Shropshire, which was designated in 1986 as a UNESCO World Heritage Site.

In the 1980s and early 1990s serious attempts were made to move beyond the early preoccupation with recording and preserving the monuments of the industrial period and to consider how the study of these can contribute to the understanding of society within that period. The dynamic force of industry has shaped human development and changed the landscape during the 19th and 20th centuries, and the monuments of industry must be considered in their cultural context.

It is possible to argue that the ample documentary evidence for the past two centuries renders any study of the monuments unnecessary, but until the 20th century the written word was the province of a minority, and the special value of industrial archaeology lies in illuminating the living and working conditions of the majority of people. Documentary evidence also gives a misleading impression of the pace and scope of change by concentrating on the innovative and spectacular, whereas the archaeological evidence of the industrial period illuminates the extent of technological inertia both in certain industries, such as textiles, leather and small metal wares, and also between regions in Britain and Europe. Industrial archaeology has played a major role in the interpretation of social and economic aspects of the industrial period under-represented in the documentary record such as workers' housing, pre-locomotive railways, food processing, mineral extraction and processing, and lime-burning.

However, the availability of documentary evidence for the industrial period means that many of the techniques of archaeology need to be re-examined to accommodate a wider range of evidence than is usual for other periods of archaeology. The use of documentary evidence in conjunction with field evidence can enable the sequence of development of both structures and sites to be determined by methods other than excavation. Anomalies in structural evidence can often be solved by reference to maps, drawings, photographic or even oral evidence. For example, the beam engine on the Glyn Pits colliery site near Pontypool, South Wales, ended its working life as a pumping engine in the 1920s, but it can be shown to have been first built as a pumping and winding engine in 1845 by relating site anomalies (such as redundant pits and the external gearing of the engine) with the surviving documentary evidence.

On the other hand, industrial archaeologists could make better use of other techniques of archaeology for the industrial period. Excavation has been little practised except on sites of non-ferrous mining and iron furnaces, especially those of the charcoal era. Environmental archaeology could illuminate vanished landscapes as well as patterns of consumption, while artefacts could be used to reveal patterns of distribution in relation to the transport networks which have hitherto only been considered on an historical basis. Post-excavation work lags sadly behind that for other periods of archaeology, partly because there are few reference collections of artefacts for the period.

Industrial archaeology has also tended to be particularly site specific, and there have been few national or international attempts to compare structures or even artefacts in such a way that they can be arranged into typological sequences that might illuminate technological development, with the exception of prime movers such as wind and water mills or steam engines. Structures concerned with non-ferrous metal mining and ore-dressing have been considered in the British context, while the surveys of textile mills undertaken by the RCHME provide the most comprehensive typological surveys of industrial buildings to date. A report, *Mills in the 80s*, commissioned by the county councils of Greater Manchester and West Yorkshire in 1984, quantified the decline of the traditional textile industries of these areas and drew attention to the large numbers of redundant textile mills. Since the demolition of many mills was inevitable, the RCHME undertook a pilot survey in a small area of West Yorkshire and followed this with an initial survey, using early 20th century, 25 inch Ordnance Survey maps as a basis. A standard report form was used on brief site visits to over 1800 sites, enabling comparisons to be made between mills which could be in the woollen, worsted, linen, silk, cotton, carpet, shoddy and mungo branches of the industry.

The sites for more detailed study were chosen to demonstrate the development of the factory system, the structural evolution of textile mills and the effect of mills on the landscape: this resulted in surveys of about a 10% sample. The Greater Manchester survey followed a similar methodology, but unlike West Yorkshire, the mills were mainly for cotton and comparisons were simpler, resulting in a chronologically-based typology in which size and layout, external details, methods of construction, internal organisation and power systems were considered for each period of mill building. Publication included detailed studies of the selected sites and gazetteers of all mill sites visited which can be followed up in the publicly accessible archive. Together with the forthcoming survey of East Cheshire, which has concentrated on the housing and factories associated with both silk and cotton mills, these surveys provide a model for other large-scale surveys of industrial structures (Giles and Goodall 1992; Williams and Farnie 1992; Calladine and Fricker 1993).

The impact of industrial activity on the landscape as a whole is little understood (*see* LANDSCAPE ARCHAEOLOGY), but landscape surveys are vital in elucidating the context of structures such as, for example, the relationship of transport and power systems to mines, quarries and ironworks as has been shown by Stephen Hughes of the RCAHMW (Royal Commission on Ancient and Historical Monuments in Wales). He has illuminated the relationship between the linear features of the Montgomeryshire and the Swansea Canal, together with a system of tramways which eventually extended the hinterland of the latter into the Brecon Beacons, and the trading patterns and settlements which they both served and generated. The canals and their feeders were also used as sources of power and both details and drawings are provided of the iron furnaces and foundries using water-wheels to drive bellows as well as a range of mills for corn-grinding, saw-milling and fulling.

Limestone was an important commodity and detailed investigation has been carried out on the limekilns to be found along the routes. The canals and tramways influenced settlement patterns, ranging from the isolated but complex depots at Sennybridge and Cnewr on the Brecon Forest Tramroad through the large warehouses at Newtown and Welshpool on the Montgomeryshire Canal to the many isolated houses at locks and wharves also to be found on the latter, many in a distinctive black and white patterned style. Detailed archaeological investigation has also been carried out on the engineering features of all the transport systems. Hughes demonstrates the importance of context, in its sense as the cultural environment of artefacts, in industrial archaeology.

Generally, PROCESSUAL ARCHAEOLOGY has had little impact on industrial archaeology, largely because the availability of evidence has led to fact replacing hypothesis in interpretations. Functionalism has dominated the study of structures and artefacts, and there has been little attention paid to their symbolic value within the material culture of the period, except where structures are regarded as 'flagships' in new technological developments. The use of CONTEXTUAL ARCHAEOLOGY might help to explain the often non-functional elaboration of both structures and artefacts of the industrial period.

A. Raistrick: *Industrial archaeology: an historical survey* (London, 1972); S.R. Hughes, 'The Swansea Canal: navigation and power supplier', *IAR* 4 (1979–80), 51–69; R.A. Buchanan: *Industrial archaeology in Britain*, 3rd edn (London, 1980); C. Giles and I.H. Goodall: 'Framing a survey of textile mills: RCHME's West Riding experience', *IAR* 9 (1986), 71–81; S.R. Hughes: *The archaeology of the Montgomeryshire Canal* (Aberystwyth, 1988); *IAR* 10 (1988): Textile mills special issue; S.R. Hughes: *The Brecon Forest tramroads* (London, 1990); M. Palmer: 'Industrial archaeology: working for the future', *IAR* 14 (1991), 17–32; C. Giles and I.H. Goodall: *Yorkshire textile mills, 1770–1930* (London, 1992); M. Williams and D.A. Farnie: *Cotton mills in Greater Manchester* (London, 1992); B. Trinder, ed.: *The Blackwell Encyclopedia of industrial archaeology* (Oxford, 1992); A. Calladine and J. Fricker: *East Cheshire textile mills* (London, 1993); N. Cossons: *The BP Book of industrial archaeology*, 3rd edn (Devon, 1993).

MP

industry Set of artefacts characterized by a particular technology, technological style or morphology, and drawn from a number of different, but contextually related, ASSEMBLAGES. The evolutionary history of an industry, or a related set of industries, is often referred to as a TRADITION.

RJA

information flow *see* SYSTEMS THEORY

infrastructure *see* MARXIST ARCHAEOLOGY

Ingombe Ilede Iron Age site near Churundu in Zambia which is famous for its rich burials and evidence for long-distance trade. Two cemeteries were found by the Zambian Water Department in the 1960s. A cemetery on the southern edge of the site yielded 31 burials, mostly consisting of infants, children and young adults with few grave goods. In contrast, the central cemetery contained adults richly adorned with gold beads, copper, bangles, sea shells, glass beads and, in some cases, cloth. Four burials were associated with metalworking implements such as iron tongs, wire-drawing plates, hammerheads and, in two of them, iron gongs. These links between wealth, status and metalworking are characteristic of Western Bantu speakers, and the ceramic style is related to the Naviundu complex (*see* DIVUYU *and* LUANGWA).

Later excavations by David Phillipson (1969) dated the burial zone to the 13th and 14th centuries AD. Other contemporaneous Ingombe Ilede sites are known near copper deposits in the Urungwe district of Zimbabwe, and Peter Garlake (1970) has identified them with the VaMbara mentioned in the 16th-century Portuguese documents.

B.M. Fagan et al.: *Iron Age cultures in Zambia* II (London, 1969); D.W. Phillipson and B.M. Fagan: 'The date of the Ingombe Ilede burials', *JAH* 10 (1969), 199–204; P.S. Garlake: 'Iron Age sites in the Urungwe district of Rhodesia', *SAAB* 25 (1970), 25–44.

TH

Ingharra, Tell *see* KISH

interval estimate *see* PARAMETER ESTIMATION

Inuit Term used to describe the Arctic-adapted populations (formerly described as Eskimos) who live in the region from eastern Siberia to Greenland. These communities are, and were, quite diverse, but they all follow a way of life that contrasts sharply with that of the Indian populations to the south of the tree line.

Perhaps the most characteristic Inuit settlement pattern (one found in the Canadian Arctic) involved spending winter, spring and summer in three different ecological niches. Thus, the winter was spent in temporary snowhouse communities out on the sea ice while hunting seals at their breathing holes; the spring was spent at the coast, hunting basking seals; and the late summer was spent further inland, hunting caribou. Biological, linguistic and archaeological evidence indicates that the Inuit (and the Aleuts of the Aleutian Islands) are distinct from all the other aboriginal populations of the Americas, and probably derive from a more recent population movement out of Asia. See also AMERICA 1 for discussion of the archaeology of Arctic North America.

D. Damas, ed.: *Handbook of North American Indians*, V: *Arctic* (Washington, D.C., 1984).

RP

inventories of tomb furnishings (China) Chinese custom of incorporating lists of artefacts that were placed alongside the occupants of burials. The use of such inventories seems to have begun in late Ch'un-ch'iu times (*c.*570–481 BC) but is principally characteristic of the CH'U culture. Although there is already a large corpus of inventories (the systematic survey of which would lead to the compilation of a very useful vocabulary of contemporary terms for an extensive variety of artefacts), only a small number of short individual studies have been made. Among the factors inhibiting such research are the occasionally poor quality of reproduction of the original brush-written tablets, the often incomplete presentation of individual inventories (in archaeological publications) and the difficulties encountered in gaining access to the original materials.

N. Barnard: 'The nature of the Ch'in "reform of the script" as reflected in archaeological documents excavated under conditions of control', *Ancient China: studies in early civilization*, ed. D.T. Roy and Tsuen-hsuin Tsien (Hong Kong, 1978), 181–213.

NB

Inyanga culture Located in the eastern highlands of Zimbabwe, the remains of the Inyanga culture include agricultural terraces, water furrows, pit structures (so-called 'slave pits') and hilltop forts. European settlers once thought that this area was the 'grain basket' for Great Zimbabwe, but radiocarbon dates have placed the Inyanga occupation in the 17th to 19th centuries, proving that the two cultures were independent of one another. Although extensive, the terraces are best explained by small-scale shifting agriculture. The pit structures comprise huts and grain-bins on a raised platform around a stone-lined pit, whose depth depends on the angle of slope. Cattle pens have been found outside these homesteads in large complexes, as exemplified by Ziwa (formerly Van Niekerk). The forts contain various European military features such as internal banquettes and loopholes for guns. The ceramic style and the oral traditions suggest that this culture was the product of Barwe-Hwesa people (Sena linguistic division of Bantu) who had been in close contact with the Portuguese in the Sena district of Mozambique. Barwe-Hwesa descendants living to the north today keep pigs, and the ancient pits may well have been pens for these animals.

R. Summers: *Inyanga prehistoric settlements in Southern Rhodesia* (Cambridge 1958); T.N. Huffman: 'Radiocarbon date from Zimbiti Ruin, Inyanga', *SAJS* 71 (1975), 247–8.

TH

Ipiutak culture Alaskan culture of the NORTON TRADITION, dating from the first through the ninth centuries AD. It takes its name from a site near Point Hope that contained over 60 semi-subterranean houses and a cemetery. Some of the elaborate ivory carvings from the graves suggest links to the Scytho-Siberian art style of Asia.

H. Larsen and F. Rainey: 'Ipiutak and the Arctic whale hunting culture', *Anthropological Papers of the American Museum of Natural History*, 42 (1948), 1–276.

RP

Ipswich Major Anglo-Saxon town in England, the origins of which lie in the 7th century AD. Its significance in terms of the archaeology of medieval Europe was indicated by rescue excavations in the 1950s. As with many other urban sites, the opportunity to investigate the town's origins was restricted by the vagaries of renewal of the present city. Conscious of this, Keith Wade devised a stratified sampling scheme in order to deploy rescue excavations to reconstruct the topography of the Anglo-Saxon town (Wade 1978). Small developments and watching-briefs were used in the 1970s to plot the extent of the settlement. Following this, as large developments occurred, middle-sized excavations were undertaken to chart the stratigraphic and detailed topographic characteristics of the Anglo-Saxon town.

Finally, in the 1980s, two large areas of the modern town were redeveloped, providing the means to test historical hypotheses devised from the preceding investigations. Excavations from 1974–90 show that Ipswich was founded as a small riverside trading site in the early 7th century. Its expansion to cover an area as large as 50 hectares occurred in the later 8th century, when a grid of gravelled streets was laid out. Parts of the town at this time were given over to industrial activities; at least one other part was occupied by a royal palace. Ipswich was thereafter developed in the Anglo-Scandinavian and Norman periods on this original grid. Only about 2% of the town has been fully excavated, but the innovative sampling programme permits a discussion of the site as a whole as opposed to its topographic elements.

K. Wade: 'Sampling at Ipswich: the origins and growth of the Anglo-Saxon town', *Sampling in contemporary British archaeology*, ed. J. Cherry et al. (Oxford, 1978), 279–84; ——: 'Ipswich', *The rebirth of towns in the West AD 700–1050*, ed. R. Hodges and B. Hobley (London, 1988), 93–100.

RH

Ironbridge Gorge Industrial archaeological site in Shropshire, England, which was designated as a UNESCO World Heritage site in 1986. A recognizable landscape of industries spanning more than two centuries grew up at a point where the River Severn cuts through the Coalbrookdale coalfield. By 1700 there were coal mines, potteries, saltworks, glasshouses and limeworks in the area. In 1709, Abraham Darby I (1678–1717) rebuilt a derelict charcoal blast furnace and was the first ironmaster to smelt iron successfully using coke. The world's first major iron bridge was built across the Severn between 1777 and 1781: a network of tub-boat canals with six inclined planes linked the coalfield and brickworks with the river; factories manufacturing porcelain and decorative tiles were established. New iron furnaces were built at Blists Hill in the mid-19th century, and the coal and iron companies constructed a variety of housing for their workforce, together with schools, churches and chapels.

Because later industrial development took place on more major coalfields, much of the early landscape, including the unique Darby Furnace and Iron Bridge, survived. In 1967, the Ironbridge Gorge Museum Trust was set up to preserve the area at a time when development was imminent with the construction of Telford New Town. A number of museums subsequently opened within the Gorge and the Ironbridge Institute is a centre for postgraduate work in INDUSTRIAL ARCHAEOLOGY.

N. Cossons and B.S. Trinder: *The Iron Bridge: symbol of the Industrial Revolution* (Bradford-on-Avon, 1979); C. Clark: *The Ironbridge Gorge* (London, 1993).

MP

Isanapura (Banteay Prei Nokor) *see* ZHENLA CULTURE

Isernia la Piretta *see* HOMO ERECTUS

Isfahan *see* MASJID AL-JAMI'

Ishango Midden site located on the Zaire side of Lake Edward in the Western Rift Valley, Ishango is of exceptional archaeological and palaeoenvironmental importance for the study of the Upper Pleistocene and Holocene of equatorial Africa, including among its finds probably the earliest bone harpoons in Africa, comprising a sequence from biserial to uniserial.

A.S. Brooks and C.C. Smith: 'Ishango revisited', *AAR* 5 (1987), 65–86.

JS

Ishchali (anc. Neribtum) *see* DIYALA REGION

Isimila Erosion gully in the southern highlands of Tanzania, containing one of the world's finest and densest collections of handaxes, cleavers and other tools of ACHEULEAN type. The artefacts have eroded from lake-beds, dated very approximately at 0.25–0.5 million years old. It appears that the lakeside situation recommended itself to bands of late *HOMO ERECTUS* hunter-gatherers. Acheulean deposits of roughly similar date have been excavated at KALAMBO FALLS, about 300 km to the west of Isimila, and somewhat earlier Acheulean remains were discovered at OLORGESAILIE in the Kenyan Rift Valley.

F.C. Howell et al.: 'Isimila, an Acheulean occupation site in the Iringa highlands, Tanganyika', *Actes du IVe congrès panafricain de préhistoire, Section III*, ed. G. Mortelmans and J. Nenquin (Tervuren, 1962), 43–111; C.L. Hansen and C.M. Keller: 'Environment and activity patterning at Isimila korongo, Tanzania', *American Anthropologist* 73 (1971), 1201–11.

JS

Isin-Larsa period After the fall of Ibbi-Sin, the last king of the Ur III dynasty in Mesopotamia, in *c.*2000 BC, there ensued a period of more than 200 years in which the regions of SUMER and AKKAD were fragmented into numerous city-states, with no single dynasty dominating the country as the rulers of Ur had done. Since the rival towns of Isin and Larsa were paramount among these states, the term 'Isin-Larsa' is usually applied to the period from *c.*2025 to 1763 BC. By the reign of Ishmedagan (*c.*1950 BC), the city of Isin was exacting tribute from many of the towns of southern Mesopotamia, including Ur and Nippur. The site of Isin (modern Ishan Bahriyat), located in southern Iraq 25 km south of NIPPUR, was excavated by a German expedition in the 1970s (Hrouda 1977–81). Even at its peak Isin was unable to control the cities of LAGASH and Larsa, and it was the latter that eventually supplanted Isin, gaining control of the holy city of Nippur. The site of Larsa, located at Senkera, about 48 km north of modern Nasriya, was excavated by French archaeologists from 1968 until the early 1980s (Huot 1983).

B. Hrouda: *Isin-Ishan Bahriyat*, 2 vols (Munich, 1977–81); J.-L. Huot, ed.: *Larsa et 'Oueili, travaux de 1978–1981* (Paris, 1983); J. Oates: *Babylon*, 2nd edn (London, 1986).

IS

Iskanwaya The largest site of the Mollo culture, situated in Bolivia and dating from *c.*AD 1000 to 1500. The material culture at Iskanwaya is essentially a local style of the southern highlands, comprising a planned town of stone masonry with rectangular houses grouped around patios, east–west streets, and running water available to the agglutinated house groups. Infants were buried in the houses, while adults were placed in *chullpas* (burial houses or towers).

H. Boero Rojo: *La incredible ciudad prehispanica de*

Iskanwaya (La Paz, 1977) [photographic documentation]; A.J. Arellano: *Mollo: investigaciones arqueológicas* (La Paz, 1985).

KB

Islamic archaeology Study of the material remains of the Islamic period and the excavation of Islamic sites, both of which have, until recently, been a relatively neglected field. This situation arises partly from the sheer quantity of standing Islamic monuments and material in museums, archives and libraries which have provided researchers with much to study without the need to embark on excavation. Furthermore, archaeological interest in the Near East has tended to stress the ancient, Biblical and classical pre-Islamic past. In the worst cases, the emphasis on periods predating Islam has led to the loss of Islamic occupation levels or they have been treated in a cursory manner. However, in recent years greater attention has been given to Islamic archaeology, and researchers have particularly studied the transition from the late antique to the early Islamic periods.

Islamic archaeology first received encouragement with the emergence of independent Arab states after the First World War, which led to growing interest in Islamic sites in Iraq and Egypt. In recent years, this concern with indigenous heritage has spread to other Arab and Islamic countries.

The continuing emphasis on monumental buildings in Islamic archaeology is partly a result of the importance of Islamic architecture within the art of the period, but it also reflects the influence of K.A.C. Creswell (1932–40; 1952–59), who virtually created the study of Islamic architecture. Creswell's legacy extends to Islamic archaeology where excavations have tended to concentrate on key monumental structures such as mosques or palaces. Only more recently has Islamic archaeology become concerned with issues of settlement and environment. This concern with the study of monuments rather than the use of excavation has contributed to the neglect of such areas as the Red Sea, central Arabia and Libya (where traditions of building in coral and clay have ensured relatively rapid collapse and disintegration of Islamic-period architecture), and has also discouraged research in areas where the remains are retrievable principally by excavation. It is only very recently that archaeologists have turned their attention to more ephemeral remains of occupation, such as ceramic scatters and shell middens (the latter marking the long tradition of pearling on the shores of the Arabian Gulf).

It is also only very recently that environmental issues have achieved any prominence in Islamic archaeology, and far less palaeobotanical material has been gathered from Islamic-period sites in the Near and Middle East than from sites of earlier date. In the past, bones, molluscs or material recovered by flotation have generally been neglected in Islamic-period excavations and much remains to be done in this area. The excavation at SIRAF was distinguished by the concern shown with flotation to recover environmental material and the effort made to study human remains. Particular issues in the history of cultivation are related to the Islamic period such as the introduction of coffee, and the mild narcotic *qat*. The study of palaeobotanical material from future fieldwork in Yemen will be a useful means to determine the antiquity of the use of these commodities.

The paucity of well-excavated and well-reported Islamic sites with reliable stratigraphy has affected the study of Islamic ceramics. A plethora of unstratified objects on the art market and in museums has contributed to a chronology that is sometimes based on stylistic analysis, while aesthetic interest in Islamic glazed ceramics contributed to the fact that unglazed wares were once virtually ignored. Only in the past 20 years or so have early Islamic and Ayyubid/Mamluk unglazed ceramics started to be understood on the basis of work in Jordan (*see* HISBAN), but the relevance of this work to the surrounding countries has still to be assessed. In Iraq and the Arabian Gulf, the glazed and unglazed ceramic traditions of the 4th–8th century AD are only now beginning to be distinguished, to allow the old but all-embracing label 'SASANIAN-Early Islamic' to be abandoned.

Islam has been an urban religion from its inception in the 7th century AD and the study of its archaeology has therefore necessarily often been concerned with sites which are still located in thriving cities. There are relatively few abandoned major urban sites, which is a reflection of the success of the key centres and newly founded towns of the early centuries of Islam. The excavation of settled Islamic towns presents problems of retrieval that are common to all urban archaeology. These have been exacerbated in many places by the fragility of building materials such as coral, seastone, sandbrick and clay, by the intensity of modern development and also sometimes by inadequately applied antiquities protection legislation.

There are certain problems that are peculiar to the Islamic context, such as the absolute religious embargo on the disturbance of Muslims' graves.

The study of human bones to assess age of death or disease is therefore unlikely to make much progress in Islamic archaeology, although the excavations at Siraf were remarkable in that they produced rare material concerning burial practices in the early Islamic period. Other factors of a religious nature also have an effect on archaeological retrieval. The Holy Cities of Mecca and Medina have never been accessible to archaeologists and their rebuilding in recent years has been so comprehensive that much – if not all – of their record is irremediably lost. Excavation in mosques is either difficult or impossible, and they are usually under the jurisdiction of the religious foundations (*Awqaf*), rather than antiquities authorities. The *Awqaf* naturally give priority to the maintenance of places of prayer as they stand, or to their renewal, rather than to the excavation of the past.

Early Baghdad, the Round City founded in AD 762 by the Abbasid Caliph al-Mansur, is lost under the modern city and the only extant buildings are associated with the 13th century AD or later. Understanding of Baghdad's urban plan has therefore largely been a matter of literary research correlated with topographical observations, rather than excavation (see Massignon 1912; Le Strange 1924; Adams 1965; Lassner 1970). By contrast, Damascus is more accessible, with its classical and Islamic city plan extant and well-recorded in the early years of this century (Watzinger and Wulzinger 1921–4; Sauvaget 1949). For archaeological retrieval, the problems that Damascus represents are those of any similar currently settled city with as much as four metres of later deposit covering the antique and early Islamic site. The eventual clarification of key archaeological issues (such as the location of the palace of Mu'wiya, the Qubbat al-Khadra') can only be solved when and if access to possible sites within the city becomes available, a standard problem of urban archaeology. The evolution of Damascus from a Roman and Byzantine city into an Islamic city is parallel to the process at the excavated sites of Jarash (Zayadine 1986), Pella (Smith 1973; Smith and Day 1989; Walmsley 1991, 1992), AMMAN, SCYTHOPOLIS or Tiberias (Stacey 1995) where flourishing Roman/Byzantine cities continued with an active life into the Umayyad period and beyond.

With so much urban archaeology from the early periods lost or inaccessible, the sites of al-FUSTAT, Caesaraea (Lenzen 1983), AMMAN, SAMARRA, NISHAPUR, AL-RAQQA and SUSA in Iran (Rosen-Ayalon 1974) provide the most important archaeological evidence available for the nature of early Islamic urban sites as well as for the development of ceramics and glass production. The excavations at Siraf give a detailed picture of the transition from the town's pre-Islamic origins through to its decline after the 12th century, and these are now complemented by the results from JULFAR on the Arabian coast of the Gulf which thrived from the 14th century through to Portuguese and late Islamic times. Less work has been undertaken on Islamic sites of the Saudi coast and Oman although important studies of ceramics have been accomplished (Whitcomb 1975, 1978). The later Islamic period is generally less well studied through archaeology.

Some areas that are likely to be important in terms of Islamic archaeology are relatively little known either because of their inaccessibility and insecurity or because of the language of publication. Thus, for instance, parts of northern Africa and Afghanistan or Kurdistan have received only limited attention in recent years, because of political instability, while the excavations at sites in the Islamic territories of the old Soviet Union are relatively little known because they have been published in Russian or central Asian languages. While such factors are not directly archaeological their practical consequences cannot be ignored.

The increasing costs of excavation in the Near East have been partly responsible for a growth in the use of cheaper forms of research instead, such as regional surveys, and a great deal of Islamic occupation has therefore been noted along with that of earlier periods. Surveys have been especially intensive in Jordan and this has contributed to our understanding of the settlement pattern in the Islamic period. Although surveys have taken place in the neighbouring countries they have not been conducted with the same intensity. Fieldwork on Islamic sites has only recently begun in Yemen, where the Islamic period has generally been neglected, and the same is true in the United Arab Emirates (UAE) at Abu Dhabi (see King et al. 1995). The surveys that were undertaken in the northern UAE by Beatrice de Cardi laid the foundations for the growing body of archaeology that has emerged there in recent years (de Cardi and Doe 1971; de Cardi 1972), while at Suhar in Oman, survey results remain the main information available on this major Indian Ocean site (Costa and Wilkinson 1987). In Saudi Arabia, apart from AL-RABADHA, the main body of information for Islamic archaeology is based on field survey.

The building of dams in northern Iraq led to intensive archaeological survey in an area where little work had previously been done on Islamic sites (Ball et al. 1989). However, many areas have still not been examined from the point of view of Islamic-period settlement patterns. The process of survey also breaks the tendency in earlier Islamic archaeological studies to concentrate on particular buildings rather than the entire site. Interpretations based on studies earlier in this century have often entered the literature and become authoritative. However, the reinvestigation of Samarra, like recent work in Jordan, has offered a very much more complex picture, arising from survey over large areas as much as excavation of specific sites. The methodology of the work carried out at Samarra is a model for future research on large sites, combining current approaches to ceramic retrieval and interpretation, and the use of AERIAL PHOTOGRAPHY. It is likely to prove especially useful when a large tract of land is involved and when rapid development, especially for agriculture, threatens site integrity.

L. Massignon: *Mission en Mésopotamie* II (Cairo, 1912); K. Watzinger and C. Wulzinger: *Damaskus*, 2 vols (Berlin, 1921–4); G. Le Strange: *Bagdad during the Abbasid Caliphate* (Oxford, 1924); J. Sauvaget: 'Le plan antique de Damas', *Syria* 26 (1949), 314–58; A.A. Duri: "Abbâsids', *Encyclopedia of Islam*, 2nd edn (Leiden, 1960); R.McC. Adams: *The land behind Baghdad: a history of settlement on the Diyala plains* (Chicago, 1965); J. Lassner: *The topography of Baghdad in the early Middle Ages* (Detroit, 1970); B. de Cardi and B. Doe: 'Archaeological survey in the northern Trucial states', *East and West* 21/3–4 (1971), 225–76; ——: 'Archaeological survey in Northern Oman, 1972', *East and West* 25 (1972), 9–75 [with sections by C. Vita-Finzi and A. Coles]; R.H. Smith: *Pella of the Decapolis* I (Wooster, 1973); M. Rosen-Ayalon: *La poterie Islamique* (Paris, 1974); D.S. Whitcomb: 'The archaeology of Oman: a preliminary discussion of the Islamic periods', *JOS* 1 (1975), 123–57; O. Grabar et al.: *City in the Desert: Qasr al-Hayr East*, 2 vols (Cambridge, 1978); D.S. Whitcomb: 'The archaeology of al-Hasâ' oasis in the Islamic period', *ATLAL* 2 (1978), 95–113; K.A.C. Creswell: *Early Muslim architecture* (Oxford, 1932–40; 1969; New York, 1979); ——: *The Muslim architecture of Egypt* (Oxford, 1952–9; New York, 1979); J.-P. Sodini and G. Tate et al.: 'Déhès (Syrie du Nord): campagnes I–III (1976–1978): recherches sur l'habitat rural', *Syria* 57 (1980), 1–304; D.L. Kennedy: *Archaeological explorations on the Roman frontier in north-east Jordan* (Oxford, 1982); G.W. Bowersock: *Roman Arabia* (Cambridge, MA, 1983); C.J. Lenzen: *The Byzantine/Islamic occupation at Caesaraea Maritima as evidenced through the pottery* (unpublished Ph.D. thesis, Drew University, 1983); J.-M. Dentzer: *Hauran I: recherches archéologiques sur la Syrie du sud à l'époque hellénistique et romaine*, 2 vols (Paris, 1985–6); H. Kennedy: 'From Polis to Madina: urban change in Late Antiquity and early Islamic Syria', *Past and present* 106 (1985), 3–27; M. Sartre: *Bostra des origines à l'islam* (Paris, 1985); S. Thomas Parker: *Romans and Saracens: a history of the Arabian frontier* (Winona Lake, 1986); F. Zayadine, ed.: *Jerash archaeological project I (1981–1983)* (Amman, 1986); P.M. Costa and T.J. Wilkinson: 'The hinterland of Sohar: archaeological surveys and excavations within the region of an Omani seafaring city', *JOS* 9 (1987), 1–238; S. Thomas Parker: *The Roman frontier in central Jordan: interim report of the Limes Arabicus Project, 1980–85* (Oxford, 1987); W. Ball, D. Tucker and T.J. Wilkinson: 'The Tell al-Hawa project: archaeological investigations in the north Jazira, 1986–87', *Iraq* 51 (1989), 1–66; R.H. Smith and L.P. Day: *Pella of the Decapolis* II (Wooster, 1989); T.J. Wilkinson: 'Extensive sherd scatters and land use intensity: some recent results', *JFA* 16 (1989), 31–46; F. Zayadine, ed.: *Jerash archaeological project II: 1984–1988* (Paris, 1989); A. Walmsley: 'Architecture and artefacts from Abbasid Fihl: implications for the cultural history of Jordan', *The fifth conference on the history of Bilâd al-Shâm during the Abbasid period* II, ed. M.A. Bakhit and R. Schick (Amman, 1991), 135–59; ——: 'Fihl (Pella) and the cities of North Jordan during the Umayyad and Abbasid periods', *Studies on the History and Archeology of Jordan* IV (Amman, 1992), 377–84; P.-L. Gatier: 'Villages du Proche-Orient protobyzantin (4ème–7ème siècles): étude régionale', *Land use and settlement patterns*, ed. G.R.D. King and A. Cameron (Princeton, 1994), 17–48 [for an overview of the literature]; H.I. Innes: 'Settlements and settlement patterns and central Transjordania, *c.*550–750', *Land use and settlement patterns*, ed. G.R.D. King and A. Cameron (Princeton, 1994), 49–93 [another overview]; M.G. Moroney: 'Late Sasanian and early Islamic Iraq', *Land use and settlement patterns*, ed. G.R.D. King and A. Cameron (Princeton, 1994), 221–9; G.R.D. King, D. Dunlop, J. Elders, S. Garfi, A. Stephenson and C. Tonghini: 'A report on the Abu Dhabi Islands archaeological survey (1993–4)', *PSAS* 25 (1995), 63–74; D. Stacey: *The archaeology of Early Islamic Tiberias* (unpublished Ph.D. thesis, University of London, 1995).

GK

isochron Method, usually graphical, used in a number of scientific dating techniques to determine the age of an archaeological level when not all necessary data are available. It requires a series of samples with different characteristics, but all of the same age and having the missing data in common. In ARGON-ARGON dating, for example, knowledge of the initial ^{40}Ar value is essential to the accuracy of the technique. It may be atmospheric in origin, in which case the ^{40}Ar/^{36}Ar ratio can be used to provide a correction, but it may also have a component from outgassing of nearby rocks during solidification. Using samples of different mineralogy, and therefore different ^{40}K content, an isochron plot of ^{40}Ar/^{36}/Ar vs.^{39}Ar/^{36}Ar has a slope related by known constants to the age of the samples and the intercept gives their initial ^{40}Ar/^{36}Ar value. In THERMOLUMINESCENCE (TL) dating, if the environmental dose-rate is unknown, TL measurements and radioactivity analysis of different types and size of grain can be used to produce an isochron and determine age.

The term may also be used to denote regions or markers of the same age, e.g. tephra layers from the same eruption found in different localities (*see* TEPHROCHRONOLOGY).

SB

Israel, Israelites The archaeological and historical definitions of the terms Hebrew and Israel have been obfuscated by the political struggles between modern Israelis and Arabs in the Middle East. The Biblical account of the origins of the people of Israel (principally recounted in Numbers, Joshua and Judges) often conflicts both with non-Biblical textual sources and with the archaeological evidence for the settlement of CANAAN in the late Bronze Age and early Iron Age.

Israel is first textually attested as a political entity in Egyptian texts of the late 13th century BC and the Egyptologist Donald Redford argues that the Israelites must have been emerging as a distinct group within the Canaanite culture during the century or so prior to this. It has been suggested that the early Israelites were an oppressed rural group of Canaanites who rebelled against the more urbanized coastal Canaanites (Gottwald 1979). Alternatively, it has been argued that the Israelites were survivors of the decline in the fortunes of Canaan who established themselves in the highlands at the end of the late Bronze Age (Ahlström 1986: 27). Redford, however, makes a good case for equating the very earliest Israelites with a semi-nomadic people in the highlands of central Palestine whom the Egyptians called Shasu (Redford 1992: 269–80; although see Stager 1985 for strong arguments against the identification with the Shasu). These Shasu were a persistent thorn in the side of the Ramessid pharaohs' empire in Syria-Palestine, well-attested in Egyptian texts, but their pastoral lifestyle has left scant traces in the archaeological record. By the end of the 13th century BC, however, the Shasu/Israelites were beginning to establish small settlements in the uplands, the architecture of which closely resembles contemporary Canaanite villages.

In the 10th century BC Solomon ruled over an Israelite kingdom that had overcome both Canaanites and PHILISTINES, emerging as the pre-eminent polity in the Levant. At Solomon's capital, JERUSALEM, only the bare foundations of his fabled temple and palace have survived. After his reign, the territory was split between the kingdoms of Israel (capital: Samaria) and Judah (capital: Jerusalem), which survived until attacks by the Assyrians in 722BC (Israel) and Babylonians in 587BC (Judah).

N.K. Gottwald: *The tribes of Yahweh* (New York, 1979); L.E. Stager: 'Merenptah, Israel and Sea Peoples: new light on an old relief', *Eretz-Israel* 18 (1985), 56–64; G.W. Ahlström: *Who were the Israelites?* (Winona Lake, 1986); I. Finkelstein: *The archaeology of the Israelite settlement* (Jerusalem, 1988); D.B. Redford: *Egypt, Canaan and Israel in ancient times* (Princeton, 1992), 257–82; K.W. Whitelam: *The invention of ancient Israel: the silencing of Palestinian history* (London, 1996).

IS

Isturitz Palaeolithic cave *c*.35 km south of Bayonne (Pyrénées-Atlantiques) which contains a fine group of low-relief carvings. The carvings, which were probably also painted originally, include a fine reindeer, a horse, a rough cave bear, and part of a mammoth. Excavations by Emmanuel Passemard (1913–22) and by Réne and Suzanne de Saint-Périer (1928–47) revealed evidence from the Mousterian, Aurignacian, Upper Périgordian, Solutrean, Magdalenian and Azilian; the carvings were sealed in Magdalenian levels and probably date from this phase. The mobiliary art recovered from Isturitz is spectacularly rich, including *bâtons* deeply carved with curvilinear designs, some engravings of bison wounded with arrows, and a rare 'scene' showing two human figures.

R. and S. de Saint-Périer: *La Grotte d'Isturitz*, Archives de L'institut de Paléontologie Humaine 7/17/25 (Paris, 1930, 1936, 1954); H. Delporte: *L'image de la femme dans l'art préhistorique* (Paris, 1979).

RJA

Itazuke Early Yayoi site (*c*.300–100 BC) in Fukuoka prefecture, Japan with an extensive paddy field system. Remains of fields, canals and embankments provided important evidence for the organisation of wet rice agriculture, and waterlogged conditions preserved many wooden tools, as at Toro. Palaeobotanical remains have proved that rice was grown in the preceding final Jomon period (*c*.1000–300 BC).

T. Mori and T. Okazaki: 'Fukuoka-ken Itatsuke iseki' [Itatsuke site, Fukuoka prefecture] *Nihon noko bunka no seisei*, ed. Nihon Kokogaku Kyokai (Tokyo, 1961); C.M. Aikens and T. Higuchi: *The prehistory of Japan* (London, 1982), 199–204.

SK

Itj-tawy *see* FAIYUM REGION; EL-LISHT

Iwajuku Late Palaeolithic site in Gunma prefecture, Japan which produced the first conclusive evidence for the Japanese Palaeolithic. During excavations in 1949 definite artefacts, including handaxes, scrapers and flakes, were recovered from the middle layers of the Kanto loam, dated to 20,000–14,000 BP.

S. Sugihara: 'The stone age remains found at Iwajuku, Gunma prefecture, Japan', *Meiji Daigaku Bungakubu kenkyu hokoku* 1 (Tokyo, 1956); C.M. Aikens and T. Higuchi: *The prehistory of Japan* (London, 1982), 42-6.

SK

Iwo Eleru Rockshelter situated 24 km northwest of Akure, southwest Nigeria, which was excavated by Thurstan Shaw and Steve Daniels over a four-month period in 1965. Located 25 km from the present northern boundary of the rain forest, it was deliberately chosen for investigation in order to test the conflicting hypotheses *either* that the forest could not have been occupied before the introduction of iron tools *or* that the occurrence of ground stone axes in presently forested areas implied that it had been so occupied. Excavations to a maximum depth of 1.5 m over an area of about 90 m^2 on the southward facing platform and talus produced an abundant Late Stone Age sequence with > 500,000 artefacts and a consistent block of radiocarbon dates, which allowed the excavators (despite the homogeneity of the deposits) to propose its division into four distinct periods (corresponding to eight 'time vector plane' groups according to Daniels on the basis of his analysis of the stone industry).

The Late Stone Age sequence at Iwo Eleru has been radiocarbon-dated to *c.*11,200–2000 BP. There is a surface layer of ash (whence the name of the site in Yoruba) and some recent and Iron Age potsherds. With regard to the original hypotheses, the stratigraphic sequence demonstrates that there was a Late Stone Age occupation in what is now a forested area, and tentative correlations can be made between its likely environmental history and the progression of material culture at the site. Iwo Eleru is the most extensively excavated, exhaustively analysed, and fully published site of its type in Nigeria to date.

D.R. Brothwell and T. Shaw: 'A late Upper Pleistocene Proto-West African negro from Nigeria', *Man* 6/2 (1971), 221–7; T. Shaw and S.G.H. Daniels: 'Excavations at Iwo Eleru, Ondo State, Nigeria', *WAJA* 14 (1984) [monograph comprising entire issue].

PA-J

Iximché Capital of the Cakchiquel Maya in the western highlands of Guatemala, established in the late 15th century after the Cakchiquels rebelled against their former allies, the Quiché. After the Spanish conquest of UTATLÁN, Cakchiquels of Iximché first allied with the Spaniards against the Quiché, then drove the Spaniards out and fought against them before falling in defeat.

J.F. Guillemin: 'The ancient Cakchiquel capital of Iximche', *Expedition* 9 (1967), 22–35; ——: 'Urbanism and hierarchy at Iximche', *Social process in Maya prehistory*, ed. N. Hammond (London, 1977), 227–64.

PRI

Izapa Located on the rich, CACAO-producing Pacific coastal plain of Chiapas, Mexico, Izapa is best known for its Middle and Late Preclassic (*c.*800 BC–AD 300) monumental art and architecture, which comprise some 80 structures arranged around plazas and roughly 250 sculptured stone monuments. The Late Preclassic Izapan art style on stelae (*see* STELE) and altars presents narrative and allegorical scenes showing elaborately clad humans together with birds, animals and vegetation. Long regarded as a direct stylistic link between earlier OLMEC art and later MAYA iconography, the Izapan style – which is also found at the highland site of KAMINALJUYÚ – is now viewed as a unique development.

V.G. Smith, 'Izapa relief carving', *Studies in Pre-Columbian art and archaeology* 27 (Washington, D.C., 1984).

PRI

J

Jaffa *see* PHILISTINES

Jainism Religion founded in the 6th century BC by Varadahaman Mahavira, a contemporary of the Buddha and a nobleman from Vaisali (a centre of the GANGES CIVILIZATION). Mahavira travelled throughout the Ganga-Yamuna region, preaching a faith of ascetism and a denial of the existence of a supreme deity. A major ethical principle of Jain belief is *ahimsa* (the practice of non-injury to any living thing). Mahavira is believed to be the last of the 24 Tirthankaras or Jain saviours.

Early Jain monuments date to the MAURYAN ruler Ashoka (273–232 BC) and the faith soon spread throughout India, with Jain temples and sculptures coexisting with Buddhist, and later Hindu constructions. A major Jain site of the 9th–10th century AD is Shravana Belgola in Karnataka, South India. Numerous stone shrines flank a stairway on a granite hill surmounted by a monolithic sculpture of the naked saint Bahubali, the son of the first Tirthankara; at 17.7 m tall this is the largest freestanding sculpture in India.

V.A. Smith: *The Oxford History of India*, 4th edn (Delhi, 1981), 76–80; G. Michell: *The Penguin guide to the monuments of India* I (Harmondsworth, 1989), 24–5, 466–8.

CS

Jamestown North American historic-period site, situated beside the James River in southeastern Virginia, which was the location of the first permanent English settlement in North America. Established in AD 1607, the town was the seat of the first legislative assembly in the English colonies, and was the scene of Bacon's Rebellion in 1676–7. Research at Jamestown has revealed much about the daily lives of colonial Virginia residents during the 17th and 18th centuries. Archaeological investigations conducted during the 1990s have focused on locating the settlement's original stockade, which until recently, was thought to have been destroyed by flooding and erosion.

W. Kelso: *Jamestown rediscovery* I (Richmond, 1995); C. Orser and B. Fagan: *Historical archaeology* (New York, 1995), 25–6; W. Kelso: *Jamestown rediscovery* II (Richmond, 1996).

RJE

Japan The Japanese archipelago lies off the west coast of the Asian continent. The main islands (Hokkaido, Honshu, Shikoku and Kyushu) are located mainly in the temperate zone, but the extreme northeast is subarctic and the far southwest is subtropical. The archipelago catches the edge of the monsoon and has great regional and seasonal differences in climate and vegetation. In general, cold dry winters contrast with hot humid summers. The Japan Sea coast of Hokkaido and northern

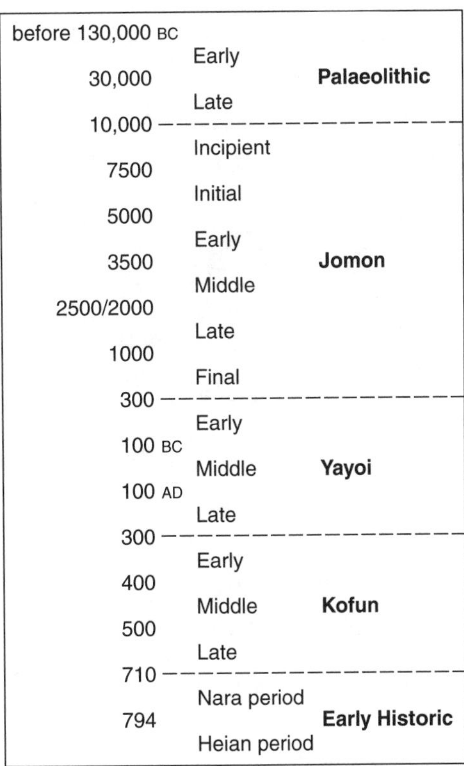

Date	Phase	Period
before 130,000 BC		
	Early	
30,000		**Palaeolithic**
	Late	
10,000		
	Incipient	
7500		
	Initial	
5000		
	Early	
3500		**Jomon**
	Middle	
2500/2000		
	Late	
1000		
	Final	
300		
	Early	
100 BC		
	Middle	**Yayoi**
100 AD		
	Late	
300		
	Early	
400		
	Middle	**Kofun**
500		
	Late	
710		
	Nara period	
794		**Early Historic**
	Heian period	

Table 13 **Japan** Chronology of Japanese prehistory.

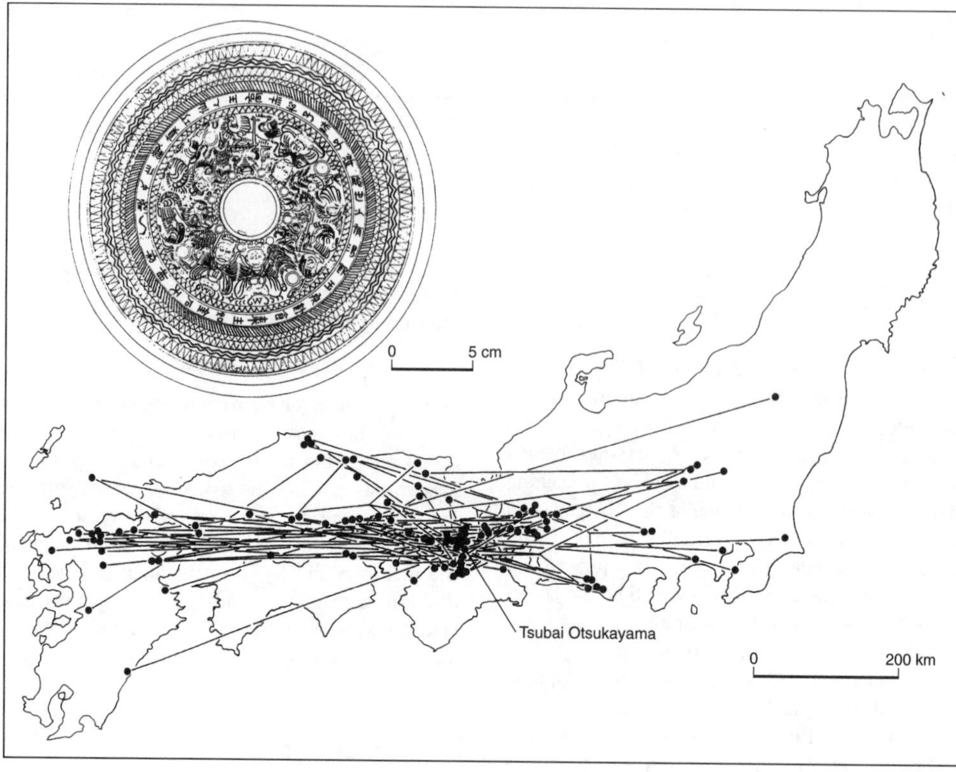

(a)

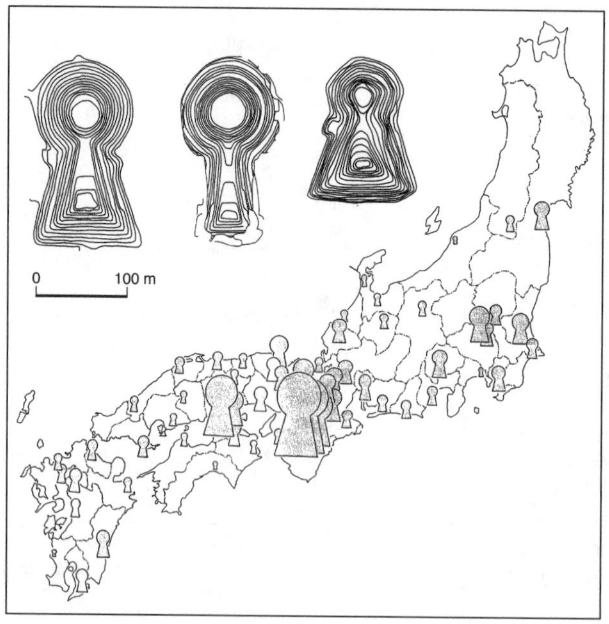

(b)

Figure 25 **Japan, 4** (a) Kofun-period bronze mirror found in the mounded tomb of Kannonyama No. 51, Hyogo prefecture, and map of mainland Japan showing the distribution of mirrors of the same type, as well as the location of Tsubai Otsukayama tomb which may well be the epicentre of the distribution, (b) contour plans of three typical examples of the characteristic 'keyhole shaped' tombs of the Kofun period in Japan, and map showing concentrations of keyhole-shaped tombs on the Japanese mainland. *Source*: A. Ono, H. Harunari and S. Oda (ed.): *Zukai: Nihon no Jinrui Iseki* (Tokyo University Press, 1992).

Honshu have heavy winter snows. The three predominant forest zones are, from north to south and with some altitudinal variation, coniferous, deciduous and broad-leaf evergreen, supporting diverse fauna and flora. Fish are abundant off the coasts of the archipelago, where warm and cold ocean currents meet. The islands have high interior mountains and less than 15% of the total land area of the archipelago consists of plains. Inland mountain basins and riverine terraces have attracted settlement throughout prehistory. Frequent volcanic activity and earthquakes make for an unstable environment but recently have provided useful archaeological marker horizons.

Sections: 1 Palaeolithic; 2 Jomon period; 3 Yayoi period; 4 Kofun period; 5 Early Historic periods

1 *Palaeolithic*. The Japanese archipelago was joined to the Asian continent by landbridges several times during the Pleistocene and was occupied by hominids prior to 200,000 BP. The Palaeolithic is divided into two main phases, Early (pre-30,000 BP) and Late (30,000 BP–10,000 BC). More than 3000 sites are now known, following the confirmation of the existence of a Palaeolithic period in 1949,

Map 23 **Japan** Major sites in the region mentioned in the main text or with individual entries in the Dictionary.

at IWAJUKU. Palaeolithic sites mainly consist of lithic scatters and piles of burnt cobbles within a cultural layer as at NOGAWA. The occupational histories of settlements are being extensively studied through the use of lithic refitting at sites such as SUNAGAWA in Tokyo. Most Palaeolithic artefacts in Japan are chipped stone tools which show morphological developments in tandem with the continent.

Although there is still considerable controversy over when humans first occupied Japan, sites such as BABADAN A suggest dates of at least 130,000 BP and probably considerably earlier. The earliest human remains are from Minatogawa and Mikkabe in Okinawa, and date to 18,000 BP. Early Palaeolithic technology comprised pebble tools, large flake tools and large blade flakes. The Late Palaeolithic began with the appearance of blade tools and is divided into four phases. Phase II (from 25,000 BP) was characterized by considerable regional variability of blade manufacturing techniques including the side-blow method, reflecting adaptation to locally available materials, some of which, notably obsidian and *sanukite*, were transported over long distances. Microlithic technology characterised Phase III, from 14,000 BP. Phase IV, synonymous with the Incipient Jomon (see below), included the earliest pottery associated with microcores (in western Japan) and with edge-polished axes and stemmed points (in eastern Japan).

2 *Jomon period*. At the beginning of the Holocene the landbridges which had connected Kyushu and Siberia to the continent at various times during the Pleistocene were finally submerged and Japan entered the Jomon period, during which many regional cultures of affluent foragers waxed and waned.

The six phases of the Jomon period are: Incipient (10,000–7500 BC), Initial (7500–5000 BC), Early (5000–3500 BC), Middle (3500–2500/2000 BC), Late (2500/2000–1000 BC) and Final (1000–300 BC). The oldest dated pottery is from the Incipient Jomon layers at FUKUI CAVE, but was associated with Late Palaeolithic lithics. The Initial Jomon was the formative stage in the Jomon tradition, while the archetypal Jomon way of life based around settled villages was established in the Early Jomon in a milieu of climatic warming and high sea-levels. Early Jomon settlements such as TORIHAMA had considerable impact on the surrounding environment, and present elaborate architecture as at SUGIZAWADAI. The Middle Jomon cultures in central Honshu represent a peak of cultural complexity seen at sites such as SHAKADO, TOGARI-ISHI AND YOSUKEONE. Long repeated occupations led to characteristic circular settlement plans as at Nishida. While the settlement of central Honshu suddenly declined at the end of the Middle Jomon, the appearance of large shell middens along the Pacific coast of eastern Honshu reflected the development of sophisticated fishing cultures in the Late Jomon. These continued into the Final Jomon, and resisted the advance of rice agriculture which had already appeared in Kyushu. There was widespread intensive ritual activity in the later part of the period, as at KINSEI, with the development of community cemeteries such as TSUKUMO and social differentiation as at KASHIWAGI B.

3 *Yayoi period (300 BC–AD 300)*. The cultivation of paddy rice began in Japan in the 1st millennium BC. Introduced from the continent, the arrival of this new subsistence strategy had a revolutionary effect on the course of Japanese prehistory and has provided the staple foodstuff of Japanese populations until the present. The spread of rice farming and associated sets of material culture derived from the continent constitute the Yayoi period (300 BC–AD 300), which is named after a location in Tokyo where Yayoi pottery was first discovered. Divided into Early, Middle and Late phases (Early: 300–100 BC, Middle: 100 BC–AD 100, and Late: AD 100–300), it was characterised by wet-rice agriculture at sites such as ITAZUKE, the use of bronze and iron, increasing social differentiation, and warfare and trade with the Asian continent.

Yayoi pottery comprises mainly utilitarian long-necked jars, wide-mouthed pots, deep basins and pedestalled bowls with simple geometric designs. Particularly in the Early Yayoi, there is considerable difference between assemblages from western Japan, where styles are close to Continental types, and eastern Japan, where there is much more continuity from Jomon styles.

Settlements such as TORO consist of small lowland communities of tightly packed pit houses with raised storehouses. They are often moated, as at YOSHINOGARI. In the Late Yayoi in some regions there was a shift to upland locations, probably for defensive purposes. Beliefs were largely related to rice agriculture and included divination. Ceremonial bronze swords and bell-shaped *dotaku* derived from more utilitarian Continental models. Inhumation was the main burial form, although there was considerable variation as at DOIGAHAMA. By the Late Yayoi, many small polities and some regional chiefdoms had arisen. Elite mound burials of the Late Yayoi such as TATETSUKI are ancestral to the mounded tombs of the succeeding Kofun period.

4 *Kofun period (AD 300–710).* By the 4th century AD the process of state formation was already underway in western Japan and by the 8th century the fully developed Ritsuryo state controlled much of the archipelago. This process dominated the Kofun period which is divided into three phases: Early (AD 250/300–400); Middle (AD 400–500) and Late (AD 500–600 in Kinai and AD 500–710 in other regions). During the Early phase, large keyhole-shaped mounded tombs, such as TSUBAI OTSUKAYAMA, appeared (see figure 25). These tombs, usually surrounded by earthenware *haniwa* funerary sculptures, derive in part from the mounded tombs of the preceding Yayoi period such as TATETSUKI, but also reflect Chinese influences seen in qualitative differences in scale, construction and grave goods. Pottery was the unglazed earthenware called Haji ware, which derived from Yayoi ceramic tradition.

The Middle Kofun saw the introduction of the Chinese writing system (seen in inscriptions as at SAKITAMA INARIYAMA), civil engineering projects, such as irrigation canals, and large scale land-clearance for agriculture, along with an increase in the importance of dry-field cultivation. These changes in land-use underlay the development of land reforms. The late 5th century AD was marked by the appearance of Sue pottery, a grey stoneware initially imported from the Korean peninsula and subsequently produced in Japan for funerary purposes.

Major social and political changes occurred in the Late Kofun. Burial in mounded tombs was no longer the preserve of chieftains, and many small round circular tombs appeared for lesser nobles and landowners. In the Kinai region the YAMATO state appeared, based at the capital at Fujiwara. Tombs such as TAKAMATSUZUKA show how the aristocracy were buried.

Throughout the Kofun period, status divisions between communities became marked within a predominantly dispersed settlement pattern. Major regional centres have been identified as at Narutaki in Wakayama Prefecture. Residences of local chiefs have been found at Mitsudera, along with commoners' settlements as at KUROIMINE.

5 *Early Historic periods (AD 710–1183).* The Early Historic periods in Japan began with the arrival of Buddhism in the middle of the 6th century AD. The 7th century AD is named after the political centre at ASUKA, and witnessed the first written law codes, the first centralised government and the first Chinese-style city plan at Fujiwara. In AD 710 the capital was moved to HEIJO, near present-day Nara city. The Nara period lasted until 794 when a new capital was established at Heian-kyo in modern Kyoto. The 8th century saw the consolidation of the Ritsuryo state, and military campaigns against the Ezo and Emishi from border garrisons such as TAGAJO.

The early chronicles, the KOJIKI and NIHON SHOKI provide many details of life in the Early Historic periods. Further written evidence has been provided by the discovery of large numbers of wooden tablets containing invaluable information about the movement of peoples and goods and the bureaucracy. Palaces, capital sites and local administrative centres have been excavated; these centres controlled the 58 provinces and three islands of the Yamato state. The provinces were further divided into 300–500 counties, which had their own administrative centres, often associated with a Buddhist temple.

T. Akazawa, S. Oda and I. Yamanaka: *The Japanese Palaeolithic: a techno-typological study* (Tokyo, 1980); T.E.G. Reynolds and G.L. Barnes: 'The Japanese Palaeolithic: a review', *PPS* 50 (1984), 49–61; T. Akazawa and C.M. Aikens, eds: *Prehistoric hunter-gatherers in Japan* (Tokyo, 1986); R.J. Pearson et al., eds: *Windows on the Japanese past: Studies in archaeology and prehistory* (Ann Arbor, 1986) [pp. 397–404, Early Historic period]; K. Tsuboi, ed. *Recent archaeological discoveries in Japan* (Paris and Tokyo, 1987); T.E.G. Reynolds and S.C. Kaner: 'Japan and Korea at 18,000 BP', *The world at 18,000 BP. Volume 1, High latitudes*, ed. O. Soffer and C. Gamble (London, 1989); S. Kaner: 'The Western-language Jomon', *Hoabinhian, Jomon, Yayoi, Early Korean States: bibliographic reviews of Far Eastern Archaeology 1990*, ed. G.L. Barnes (Oxford 1990), 31–62; H. Ishino: 'Rites and rituals of the Kofun period', *JJRS* 19/2–3 (1992), 191–216; R. Pearson: *Ancient Japan* (Washington, D.C., 1992); K. Tsuboi, ed.: *Archaeological studies of Japan*. Acta Asiatica 63 (Paris, 1992); D. Denoon et al., eds: *Multicultural Japan: Palaeolithic to postmodern* (Cambridge, 1996).

SK

Jarmo Typical small Neolithic tell-site in northern Iraq, consisting of 16 strata of occupation, 11 dating to the ACERAMIC NEOLITHIC phase. Between 1948 and 1955 the site was excavated by R.J. Braidwood, revealing square houses made of pisé, containing ovens and sunken clay basins. The characteristic artefacts include microliths as well as flint sickles, saddle querns, rubbers and mortars and pestles. These tools, along with the carbonized remains of cultivated grains and the bones of domesticated cattle, sheep and pigs, clearly indicate a highly developed agriculturally-based economy, the aceramic phase of which has been assigned by radiocarbon dating to as early as *c.*6750BC. The term

'Jarmoan' is used by Braidwood et al. (1983: 13) to describe the Mesopotamian 'early village farming community' exemplified not only at Jarmo but also at such sites as ALI KOSH, Ganj Dareh and Tepe Guran (*see* LURISTAN).

R.J. Braidwood: 'Jarmo: a village of early farmers in Iraq', *Antiquity* 24 (1950), 189–95; J. Mellaart: *The Neolithic of the Near East* (London, 1975), 80–2; L.S. Braidwood et al., eds: *Prehistoric archaeology along the Zagros flanks* (Chicago, 1983).

IS

Java The Javan sites of Trinil, Sangiran and Ngandong (Solo) provide some of the earliest evidence of hominid occupation in Asia. Found by Eugene Dubois in 1890, the Trinil beds yielded fossil teeth and cranial bones ('Java Man') later attributed to *HOMO ERECTUS*. The site is now thought to date from *c.*700,000 BP. The Sangiran site, discovered by von Koenigswald, produced fossil crania of a similar date. Ngandong, previously called Solo, has produced fossils of EARLY *HOMO SAPIENS* which resemble those from Africa (e.g. Broken Hill/Kabwe, *see* SANGOAN), Europe (e.g. Petralona) and also the Dali skull from Shaanxi province in China. The Ngandong fossils are said to be dated to between 200,000 and 150,000 years BP. A very early potassium-argon date of 1.8 million years has recently been proposed for the site of Mojokerto, with dates of 1.66 million years for the Sangiran material. However, the relationship between the tested materials and the fossils is very dubious.

PG-B

Jebel Mesolithic cave in southwestern Turkmenistan, in the southern fringe of the Greater Balkan ridge, the northern off-shoot of the Kopet Dag, 3 km north of the dry Uzboi valley. The cave was discovered and excavated by Okladnikov, who distinguished ten levels. Charcoal from level 4 suggests an approximate calendar date of 5100–5000 BC. Lithic materials include microliths (triangles, trapezes, segments), as well as small end-scrapers and retouched blades. Faunal remains include numerous desert species (tortoise, agama, lizard), and numerous fish bones. Similar assemblages have been identified in neighbouring caves (Dam-Dam-Cheshma 1 and 2), as well as in the Kaylyu cave off the Caspian coast, south of Krasnovodsk.

A.P. Okladnikov: 'Peshchera Djebel–pamjatnik drevnei kul'tury prikaspiiskih plemjon Turkmenii', *Trudy Yutake* 7 (1955), 11–219; ——: 'Paleolit i mezolit Srednei Azii', *Srednjaja Azija v epohu kamnja i bronzy*, ed. V.M. Masson (Moscow and Leningrad, 1966).

PD

Jebel Barkal *see* GEBEL BARKAL

Jebel Irhoud Site in southern Morocco where LEVALLOIS-MOUSTERIAN artefacts have been found in association with early hominid remains. It consists of a 'solution cavity' filled with 8 m of Pleistocene deposits on the eastern side of a karstic limestone outcrop 55 km southeast of modern Safi. It was discovered in 1960, in the course of mining operations for barytes, and was investigated from 1961 onwards by Emile Ennouchi. The faunal remains that he recovered include about 30 mammalian species, some of which have Middle Pleistocene affinities, but their exact stratigraphic provenance is unknown. A small excavation was conducted by Jacques Tixier in 1967 and 1969, as a result of which 22 layers were identified, the lower ones (8–21) revealing traces of human occupation and an industry classified as a Mousterian of Levallois facies.

Five hominid fossils have been found in the cave: two adult crania (Irhoud 1 and 2), one juvenile and one adult mandible (Irhoud 3 and 5), and one juvenile humerus (Irhoud 4). Only the last specimen, excavated by Tixier in 1969, has a precise stratigraphic position, at the base of his layer 18. Five ELECTRON SPIN RESONANCE dates have been obtained on horse teeth from just above it, but as Jean-Jacques Hublin remarks, their very wide range (90–125 or 105–190,000 years ago, depending on the assumptions employed) seems inconsistent with the 'close stratigraphic origin' of the samples employed. On faunal grounds it is considered likely that the site may be up to 150,000 years old. The hominids, as at HAUA FTEAH, were at first considered to be Neanderthal, but more recently Hublin and his colleagues have thrown doubt on this interpretation. They are now considered to be archaic *Homo sapiens* (lacking distinctive Neanderthal apomorphies) somewhat similar to if slightly more primitive than QAFZEH and SKHUL. They are the probable forerunners of the anatomically modern hominids associated with the ATERIAN in Morocco, as at DAR ES-SOLTANE II.

E. Ennouchi: 'Un néandertalien: l'homme du Jebel Irhoud (Maroc)', *L'Anthropologie* 66 (1962), 279–99; M.H. Day: *Guide to fossil man*, 3rd edn (London, 1977); J.J. Hublin, A.M. Tillier and J. Tixier: 'L'humérus d'enfant moustérien (Homo 4) du Jebel Irhoud (Maroc) dans son contexte archéologique', *Bulletins et Mémoires de la Société d'Anthropologie de Paris*, 4 (1987), 115–42; ——: 'Recent human evolution in northwestern Africa', *Philosophical Transactions of the Royal Society of London*, series B, 337/1280 (1992), 185–91; F. Amani and D. Geraads: 'Le gisement moustérien du Djebel Irhoud, Maroc: précisions sur la faune et la biochronologie, et description d'un nouveau reste humain', *CRASP*, série II, 31 (1993), 847–52.

PA-J

Jebel Moya Occupation site in the central Nile Basin of Sudan, the earliest phases of which date to the KHARTOUM MESOLITHIC. Purely on the basis of estimations of the rate of stratigraphic sedimentation Addison tentatively estimated the date of the initial occupation of Jebel Moya at *c.*1000 BC, but radiocarbon dates taken by J.D. Clark in the early 1970s suggest that the earliest occupation in Jebel Moya and the surrounding region dated to *c.*8000–7000 BP, while the main phase dated to *c.*4300 BP. The pottery from the earliest deposits at the site, decorated with 'dotted and wavy-line' impressed patterns, is of a similar type to that of Central Saharan cultures dating back to *c.*9000 BP. Caneva (1991) therefore suggests that the original settlement at Jebel Moya may have been one of the first parts of the Nile valley to come into contact with groups of pastoralists from the Central Sahara in *c.*8000 BP.

F. Addison: *Jebel Moya* (Oxford, 1949); I. Caneva: 'Jebel Moya revisited: a settlement of the 5th millennium BC in the middle Nile Basin', *Antiquity* 65 (1991), 262–8.

IS

Jebel Sahaba *see* QADAN

Jebel Uweinat Neolithic settlement and rock-art site in southeastern Libya, first examined by Hasanein Bey (1925) and Kemal el-Din (el-Din and Breuil 1928). The Uweinat rock carvings, similar to those in the Gilf Kebir, include depictions of giraffes, elephants, ostriches, wild asses and gazelle. After Myers' 1937–8 survey of the region, Winkler (1939) made the first serious attempt to divide the drawings into different chronological phases and to reconstruct the social systems and subsistence patterns of the artists. However, McHugh (1975) has reanalysed the results of Myers' expedition. Whereas Winkler had argued that the engraved drawings, dealing mainly with hunting, were executed by male artists and the paintings, mainly of pastoral scenes, were by women, McHugh's revised chronology shows that the engraved drawings simply predate the paintings, the change in subject-matter probably reflecting changes in subsistence practices as in other examples of SAHARA ROCK ART.

A.M. Hasanein Bey: *The lost oases* (New York, 1925), 228–9; K. el-Din and H. Breuil: 'Les gravures rupestres du Djebel Ouenat', *Revue Scientifique* 66 (1928), 105–17; H.A. Winkler: *Rock drawings of southern Upper Egypt* (London, 1939); W.P. McHugh: 'Some archaeological results of the Bagnold-Mond expedition to the Gilf Kebir and Gebel Uweinat, southern Libyan Desert', *JNES* 34 (1975), 31–62.

IS

Jeitun (Jeitun-depe) Early farming site in Turkmenistan, Central Asia, located at the margin of the alluvial fan of a small stream, Kara-su, within the southern sand ridge of the Kara-Kum desert, north of Ashgabad. A series of AMS radiocarbon measurements suggest an age of *c.*6000 BC; this and related sites represent the earliest farming economy in Central Asia (see also ASIA 1.1).

The site at Jeitun consisted of several rectangular one-roomed houses, 20–30 sq.m each, made of clay bricks, with hearths and adjacent courtyards. Domestic einkorn wheat formed 90% of the cereals identified. Stock-breeding was as important as agriculture, with domesticated goats and sheep predominant. Hunting remained an important source of meat, gazelle and onager being the most commonly exploited wild animals. In the early period about 12% of the pottery corpus consisted of distinctive hand-made cylindrical or conic bowls decorated by simple red painted patterns on a yellow background. Several figurines of humans and animals were also found. The lithic technology is dominated by microliths reminiscent of the Caspian Mesolithic.

The largest cluster of Jeitunian sites is found in Ahala, or the central Kopet Dag oasis. Jeitun-related sites are also found in the southern foothills of the Khorassan Mountains, in northern and eastern Iran, while an eastern cluster of sites is located in the interfluve of the Meana and Chaacha rivers.

V.M. Masson: *Poselenie Djeitun* (Leningrad, 1971); D.R. Harris, V.M. Masson et al.: 'Investigating early agriculture in Central Asia: new research at Jeitun, Turkmenistan', *Antiquity* 67 (1993), 324–38.

PD

Jemdet Nasr Type-site of the transitional phase between the late Uruk period and the Early Dynastic I period in southern Iraq. The Jemdet Nasr period (*c.*3100–2900 BC) was initially defined by a distinctive style of painted pottery (buff-coloured jars painted with red and black designs), first excavated in strata between the Uruk and Early Dynastic phases at Jemdet Nasr in 1925, as well as by the apparent proliferation of a deeply drilled style of cylinder seal.

Most other aspects of Jemdet Nasr material culture (including the majority of the pottery) are virtually indistinguishable from the preceding Uruk period (*c*.4300–3100 BC), and few sites have yielded sufficiently continuous stratigraphy from Uruk to Early Dynastic I to allow Jemdet Nasr material to be properly characterized. Finkbeiner and Röllig (1986) have therefore suggested that the Jemdet Nasr ware – which is relatively rare compared with other ceramics of the same period – might be better interpreted as a geographical variant of the Uruk culture rather than an indication of post-Uruk date. The balance of opinion, however, still favours the retention of a Jemdet Nasr period, on the grounds that there are other ceramics peculiar to the period (Killick in Finkbeiner and Röllig 1986), as well as a distinctive type of semi-pictographic CUNEIFORM tablet (Nissen 1986). Jemdet Nasr pottery was excavated not only at other sites in Mesopotamia but also at sites in Oman and along the Gulf coast (e.g. Hafit, *see* ARABIA, PRE-ISLAMIC), clearly indicating a wide trading network like that of the Uruk period.

Jemdet Nasr itself, located in southern Iraq about 30 km northeast of Babylon, consists of several tells covering a total area of about 15 ha, which were first excavated by Steven Langdon and Christian Watelin in 1925–8. A substantial mud-brick structure of the Jemdet Nasr period, identified by Langdon as a temple and by Watelin as a palace, is likely to have been an administrative structure, particularly in view of the tablets inscribed with 'Uruk III' texts that were found inside it.

E. Mackay: *Report on excavations at Jemdet Nasr, Iraq* (Chicago, 1931); H. Field and R.A. Martin: 'Painted pottery from Jemdet Nasr', *AJA* 39 (1935), 310–20; U. Finkbeiner and W. Röllig, eds: *Gamdat Nasr: period or regional style?* (Wiesbaden, 1986); H.J. Nissen: 'The Archaic texts from Uruk', *WA* 17 (1986), 317–34; R.J. Matthews: 'Excavations at Jemdet Nasr, 1989', *Iraq* 52 (1990), 25–40 [preliminary report on the excavations of the late 1980s].

IS

Jenne-jeno Tell located 3 km southeast of modern Jenne, between the Niger and Bani rivers, in the southwestern part of the Inland Niger Delta of Mali; excavated by Susan and Roderick McIntosh in 1977 and 1981. The mound measures 760 × 550 m and rises to a height of 8 m above the floodplain. A total of 22 radiocarbon dates were obtained, in good stratigraphic sequence, in the range from 2160 to 550 BP, supported by three others from the adjacent tells of Hambarketolo and Kaniana. The settlement shrank prior to the abandonment of the site, which was complete by AD 1468. The exclusively Iron Age cultural sequence is used by the McIntoshes to argue against an Islamic 'external stimulus' model for the development of trade and urbanism in the Western Sudan, since the archaeological sequence revealed at Jenne-jeno is 'too big, too early, too far south' to fit (McIntosh and McIntosh 1980: II, 448). Instead they propose a model based on indigenous trade networks and the PULSE THEORY.

S.K. and R.J. McIntosh: *Prehistoric investigations in the region of Jenne, Mali: a study in the development of urbanism in the Sahel* (Oxford, 1980); R.J. and S.K. McIntosh: 'The 1981 field season at Jenne-jeno: preliminary results', *NA* 20 (1982), 28–32; S.K. and R.J. McIntosh: 'Recent archaeological research and dates from West Africa', *JAH* 27 (1986), 413–42.

PA-J

Jericho (Tell es-Sultan) Tell site in the Jordan valley which dates back to at least as early as the NATUFIAN period (*c*.11000–9300 BC), presumably deriving its early prosperity from the proximity of the Ain es-Sultan, an abundant source of water for irrigation purposes. The subsequent phases at Jericho provide a good basis for the study of the early ACERAMIC NEOLITHIC (Pre-Pottery Neolithic A), when Jericho was an unusually substantial settlement, as well as the later Aceramic Neolithic (Pre-Pottery Neolithic B), the Pottery Neolithic and the Bronze Age. The Natufian and Proto-Neolithic levels provide crucial evidence of the gradual development of agriculture, although there was poor recovery of environmental data compared with more recently investigated sites such as AIN GHAZAL. In common with the rest of the Levant, the stratigraphy indicates a gap of about 500 years between the end of the Aceramic Neolithic and the emergence of the Pottery Neolithic in the 6th millennium BC, presumably as a result of the impact of a drastic climatic change disrupting the subsistence and settlement pattern. By the Late Bronze Age the city had regained its prosperity and became an important CANAANITE city. Little evidence has survived to cast and direct light on the well-known Biblical siege of the city when it was captured from the Canaanites by Joshua and the Israelites.

E. Sellin and C. Watzinger: *Jericho* (Leipzig, 1913); Preliminary excavation reports by J. Garstang in *LAAA* 19–23 (1932–6) and by K. Kenyon in *PEQ* 84–92

(1952–60); K. Kenyon: *Excavations at Jericho*, 2 vols (London, 1960–5); J.R. Bartlett: *Jericho* (Cambridge, 1982).
IS

Jerusalem Situated in the ancient Judaean region of ISRAEL, Jerusalem dates back to the Early Bronze Age (*c.*3000 BC), when it was probably founded by an AMORITE tribe, the Jebusites, who called it the 'Foundation of Salem' (Salem being an Amorite deity). It was captured by the ISRAELITES under David in *c.*1000 BC, and the 'City of David' became the capital of the Israelite kingdom, and subsequently the capital of the Kingdom of Judah. In AD 70 the city was destroyed by the Roman emperor Titus as a result of a Jewish revolt, but a new city (Aelia Capitolina) was founded by Hadrian in 135. In 638 an Arab army led by Caliph Omar Ibn al-Khattab conquered the city, but it was captured by Crusaders in 1099, eventually falling to Saladin in 1187 and becoming part of the Ottoman empire in 1516.

The site of the ancient city was first excavated by Lieutenant Charles Warren in the late 1860s, although his work was dogged by political and logistical problems. Warren's unorthodox methods involved the digging of deep shafts with long passages leading away from the foot of each, but he nevertheless produced a fairly comprehensive overview of the site. Since then, it has been excavated by a steady stream of different excavators, including Frederick Bliss and Kathleen Kenyon. The principal surviving features are a rock-cut water tunnel dating to the 8th century BC, remains of the Herodian palace and temple (*c.*AD 40–44), the Church of the Holy Sepulchre (built by Constantine in AD 335), the Mamluk–Ottoman city-walls and the late 7th-century Dome of the Rock (built over the site of King Solomon's temple).
M. Avi-Yonah et al.: *Jerusalem* (Jerusalem, 1973); K.M. Kenyon: *Digging up Jerusalem* (London, 1974); J. Perrot, ed.: 'Jerusalem: 5000 years of history', *DA* (special issue, March 1992); G.J. Wightman: *The walls of Jerusalem from the Canaanites to the Mamluks* (Sydney, 1993).
IS

Jin *see* CH'IN

Jomon period (10,000–300BC) *see* JAPAN 2

Jorwe Type-site of the Jorwe period, a phase of the Indian Deccan Chalcolithic divided into Early Jorwe (*c.*1400–1000BC) and the more spatially restricted Late Jorwe (*c.*1000–700 BC), found only in the Bhima River Valley (Dhavalikar 1988:13). Early Jorwe sites are distributed across much of modern Mahrashtra; a few, such as DAIMABAD, INAMGAON and Prakash, are about 20 ha in area, but most are comparatively small sites covering about 2–3 ha.

The site of Jorwe itself was excavated by Hasmukh Dhirajlal Sankalia and Shantaram Bhalchandra Deo in the early 1950s. Typical Jorwe ceramic ware has red or orange surface colour, sometimes painted with black geometric designs. Jorwe sites are also characterized by the presence of groundstone axes, copper tools and ornaments, and a distinctive blade and microlith industry.
H.D. Sankalia and S.B. Deo: *The excavations at Nasik and Jorwe, 1950–51* (Pune, 1955); M.K. Dhavalikar: *The first farmers of the Deccan* (Pune, 1988).
CS

Jui-ch'ang-shih (Ruichangshi) Ancient mining complex near the city of Jui-ch'ang, Chiang-hsi, China, on the eastern slopes of T'ung-ling ('Copper Ridge'). The earliest sector of the mines has been dated to the Middle Shang period (*c.*1650–1400 BC) on the basis of calibrated radiocarbon assessments clustering around 1400 BC (*see* T'UNG-LING MINES). These dates suggest that metallurgy not only appeared somewhat earlier in China than was previously thought but was also probably an independent discovery. The development of metallurgy in the CHUNG-YÜAN area relied on the procurement of copper from such sources as Jui-ch'ang-shih.
Yang Li-hsin: 'Wan-nan ku-tai t'ung-k'uang ch'u-pu k'ao-ch'a yu yen-chiu' [Preliminary researches into the ancient mines of the Wan-nan region], *WWYY* 3 (1988), 181–90; Hua Chüeh-ming, Liu Shih-chung, J. Head and N. Barnard: 'The ancient mines of T'ung-ling, Jui-ch'ang, Chiang-hsi' (in preparation).
NB

Julfar Town in the United Arab Emirates, which was the immediate predecessor of the city of Raʿs al-Khaimah, and the main town on the eastern side of the Arabian Gulf in the later Islamic period. It is the only site of this date to have been excavated in the area. Although Julfar is mentioned in texts of the 7th century AD, no remains earlier than the 14th century have yet been excavated. When the Portuguese dominated the Gulf in the 16th century, Julfar enjoyed great prosperity as the regional trading entrepôt, with its commercial network reflected in the quantities of Chinese, Vietnamese and Thai ceramics recovered, along with Indian glass bangles and Iranian pottery. These ceramics were major contributors to the dating of the local ceramics which came from the nearby kilns in Wadi Haqil.

Julfar underwent a great expansion, whereby a 14th century settlement consisting of huts was replaced by large sand-brick houses arranged in a grid-like pattern of streets. Its first small sand-brick mosque was reconstructed to accommodate a growing congregation, and a series of five mosques was eventually built one above the other as the congregation expanded. Mosques are a useful register of demographics as all adult males are required to attend Friday prayers, therefore any congregational mosque can be expected to be large enough to accommodate at least the maximum adult male population. The Julfar excavation was unique in Arabian archaeology in the opportunity that it offered to trace the changing plan of a mosque on the same site over time.

Around Julfar, the landscape is very mobile with wadi gravels descending from the mountains to the coastal fan, sandbars forming offshore, and the siltation of creeks. The process is very rapid, and geomorphological study was a major feature of the field research at the site. Although geomorphology is rarely brought to bear in ISLAMIC ARCHAEOLOGY, the unstable and evolving nature of the east Arabian coast makes it an important aspect of fieldwork in the area.

B. de Cardi and B. Doe: 'Archaeological survey in the northern Trucial states', *East and West* 21 (1971), 225–76; J. Hansman: *Julfar: an Arabian port* (London, 1985); G.R.D. King: 'Excavations of the British team at Julfar, Ras-al-Khaimah, United Arab Emirates', *PSAS* 20–2 (1990–2) [interim reports on the 1989–1992 seasons]; C. Hardy-Guilbert: 'Julfar, cité portuaire du Golfe arabo-persique à la periode islamique', *Archéologie islamique* 2 (1991), 162–203; T. and H. Sasaki: 'Japanese excavations at Julfar – 1988, 1989, 1990 and 1991 seasons', *PSAS* 22 (1992), 105–20; D. Kennet and G.R.D. King: 'Jazirat al-Hulayla – early Julfar', *JRAS*, 3rd series, 4/2 (1994), 163–212; R. Stocks: 'Wadi Haqîl survey, November 1992', *PSAS* 26 (1996), 145–63.

GK

K

K2 *see* BAMBANDYALANO

Kabáh *see* PUUC

Kabuye One of several areas of Rwanda and adjacent countries of interlacustrine East Africa which has yielded spectacular evidence of early iron-working, including furnace shafts built of hand-moulded clay coils ('decorated bricks'), and fine specimens of Urewe pottery (*see* EARLY IRON AGE), mostly dating to *c.*1500–2200 years ago. *See also* KATURUKA in the nearby Buhaya region of Tanzania.

F. Van Noten et al: *Histoire archéologique du Rwanda* (Tervuren, 1983).

JS

Kabwe *see* SANGOAN

Kachemak *see* KODIAK TRADITION

Kadero KHARTOUM NEOLITHIC site in the central Nile basin of central Sudan, about 20 km north of Khartoum. The settlement middens and cemeteries of Kadero show evidence of the domestication of cattle and the cultivation of cereal crops as early as *c.*4000 BC. By the end of the 3rd millennium, however, it appears that Kadero and the rest of the central Nile region were virtually deserted, as the focus of Neolithic settlement shifted northwards into Lower Nubia.

L. Krzyzaniak: 'The Neolithic habitation at Kadero (Central Sudan)', *Origin and early development of food-producing cultures in northeastern Africa*, ed. L. Krzyzaniak and M. Kobusiewicz (Poznan, 1984), 309–15; ——: 'Early farming in the Middle Nile Basin: recent discoveries at Kadero (Central Sudan)', *Antiquity* 65 (1991), 515–32.

IS

Kadesh *see* QADESH

Kahun *see* EL-LAHUN

Kalambo Falls Site in Zambia, at the south end of Lake Tanganyika, of a small basin in which sands, clays and rubble beds have accumulated, together with archaeological deposits in various degrees of disturbance, from ACHEULEAN times down to the Early Iron Age (excavated by J.D. Clark 1956–66). Several Acheulean floors dated to at least 110,000 BP by AMINO ACID RACEMIZATION, are important not only for the completeness of their assemblages, but also for their association with well preserved plant remains (logs, twigs, nuts, fruits, seeds, leaves, reeds and pollen). Several pieces of wood and bark are believed to be artefacts, and there is clear evidence of fire, possibly man-made. An arc of stones may mark the site of a hut or windbreak. The succession includes Acheulean, SANGOAN, LUPEMBAN, Later Stone Age and Early Iron Age material, including a good suite of radiocarbon dates. The Iron Age village was occupied from the 4th to the 11th centuries AD and later, and has yielded objects of iron, a copper bangle and several deep pits of uncertain use.

J.D. Clark: *The Kalambo Falls prehistoric site* I (Cambridge, 1969); G.L. Isaac: 'The earliest archaeological traces', *The Cambridge history of Africa* I, ed. J.D. Clark (Cambridge, 1982), 202–4.

RI

Kalhu *see* NIMRUD, TELL

Kalibangan Large Harappan site (*see* INDUS CIVILIZATION) located on the southern bank of the Ghaggar River in Rajasthan, India, which was excavated by Braj Basi Lal and Bal Krishen Thapar (1961–9). It consists of two main mounds (KLB 1 and 2), a third smaller mound and a Harappan cemetery. Two chronological phases have been defined through a series of nearly 40 calibrated radiocarbon dates (Lal 1979: 94): Early Harappan (*c.*2920–2550 BC) and Mature Harappan (*c.*2600–1990 BC). Five Early Harappan building phases from Mound KLB 1 provide evidence of dense mud-brick architecture (including standardized brick sizes) and massive enclosure walls. Typical artefacts of the period include terracotta figurines, ground stone and flaked stone implements, ornaments including copper, shell, and ceramic bangles, and agate, carnelian, shell, and copper beads, and six different ceramic wares, including black and white painted red wares, large storage jars with a textured (sandy slip) surface, and buff or grey wares decorated with black and white floral, faunal, and curvilinear motifs (Lal 1979: 70–4). A nearby field has revealed evidence for Early Harappan PLOUGHMARKS.

B.K. Thapar: 'Synthesis of the multiple data as obtained from Kalibangan', *Radiocarbon and Indian archaeology*, ed. D.P. Agrawal and A. Ghosh (Bombay, 1973), 264–71; B.B. Lal: 'Kalibangan and the Indus civilization', *Essays in Indian protohistory*, ed. D.P. Agrawal and D.K. Chakrabarti (Delhi, 1979), 65–97; ——: 'Some reflections on the structural remains at Kalibangan', *Frontiers of the Indus Civilization*, ed. B.B. Lal and S.P. Gupta (New Delhi, 1985), 55–62.

CS

Kalina Point *see* GOMBE POINT

Kalomo culture Central African Iron Age culture, first identified by Ray Inskeep as a result of excavations at Kalundu mound about 5 km southeast of Kalomo. Bryan Fagan later excavated Isamu Pati 16 km to the west, and the long stratigraphic succession at the two sites was virtually the same. As research progressed, however, the cultural affinities of the ceramic units were reassessed. Inskeep originally placed the entire sequence in the Kalomo culture, but David Phillipson excluded the lower unit, renaming it the Kalundu Early Iron Age (EIA) group. Based on excavations at Kumadzulo and other sites, Joseph Vogel excluded the upper unit at Isamu Pati, restricted the concept to Fagan's 11th–12th century mid-Kalomo, and derived it from the Shongwe EIA Tradition (Situmpa-Kumadzulo-Dambwe) in the Victoria Falls area. The MULTIDIMENSIONAL ANALYSIS of material from Gundu, 90 km northeast of Kalomo, prompted Huffman to separate Shongwe and reinstate the late Kalomo pottery at Isamu Pati. Thus in the 13th–14th centuries AD, Kalomo was contemporaneous with Kangila and INGOMBE ILEDE.

R. Inskeep: 'Some Iron Age sites in northern Rhodesia', *SAAB* 17 (1962), 136–80; B.M. Fagan: *Iron Age cultures in Zambia* I (London, 1967); D.W. Phillipson: 'The Early Iron Age in Zambia: regional variants and some tentative conclusions', *JAH* 9 (1968), 191–211; J.O. Vogel: *Kumadzulo: an Early Iron Age village site in southern Zambia* (Lusaka, 1971); T.N. Huffman: *Iron Age migrations: the ceramic sequence in southern Zambia* (Johannesburg 1989).

TH

Kaminaljuyú Large centre in the northern valley of Guatemala that flourished from the Middle Preclassic to the Classic period (i.e. *c.*800 BC–AD 900). Kaminaljuyú is believed to have controlled the large El Chayal OBSIDIAN quarry as well as the trade network that distributed it throughout the Maya highlands and lowlands. Strong influences from TEOTIHUACAN in the Early Classic period (*c.*AD 300–600), seen in the architecture, pottery and burials, were uncovered by early excavations (Kidder et al. 1946) and interpreted in terms of conquest of this site by the central Mexicans. Later work at other sites elsewhere in the valley suggests that a 'PORT OF TRADE' existed in the region and involved complex three-way trading relationships between Teotihuacán, Kaminaljuyú and the lowland Maya.

A.V. Kidder et al.: *Excavations at Kaminaljuyu, Guatemala*, C.I.W. Pub. 561 (Washington, D.C., 1946); K.L. Brown: 'The valley of Guatemala: a highland port of trade', *Teotihuacan and Kaminaljuyu: a study in prehistoric cultural contact*, eds W. T. Sanders and J.W. Michels (University Park, 1977), 205–395.

PRI

Kanesh *see* KÜLTEPE

Kansyore Type of East African pottery, named after an island in the Kagera river which flows into the west side of Lake Victoria. Kansyore pottery illustrates pre-Iron Age cultural and economic developments in the Lake region and perhaps over a broader area of East Africa. In view of its texture, open shapes and profuse indented decoration, a derivation from the early Holocene pottery of the Nile Valley 'Aqualithic' or 'Khartoum horizon' has been surmised; this theory is supported by the lakeside, riverbank and island situations of many Kansyore sites (*see* AQUATIC CIVILIZATION; Sutton 1977). Other archaeologists consider such comparisons superficial and deceptive, regarding Kansyore pottery as a late development in the final two millennia BC, that is shortly before the Iron Age. Radiocarbon results (Robertshaw 1991) tend to support this dating, but they are not entirely unambiguous, and the possibility of these late manifestations emerging from a much more ancient eastern African tradition is not ruled out. The fishing element is pronounced at the more typical Kansyore sites on rivers flowing into Lake Victoria (Kansyore Island itself and, on the eastern side, Ugunja and GOGO FALLS), all of which are situated above rapids where preferred species of fish can be caught.

S. Chapman: 'Kansyore Island', *Azania* 2 (1967), 165–91; J.E.G. Sutton: 'The African aqualithic', *Antiquity* 51 (1977), 25–34; P.T. Robertshaw: 'Gogo Falls: a complex site east of Lake Victoria', *Azania* 26 (1991), 63–195.

JS

Kao-ch'eng-hsien (Gaochengxian) *see* T'AI-HSI-TS'UN

Kapova Cave (Kapovaya, Shulgan Tash) Upper Palaeolithic cave with rock paintings, situated in the southern Urals in the valley of the Belaya River, 200 km south of the town of Ufa, Bashkirstan, Russia. The cave, a rare example of Upper Palaeolithic rock art in eastern Europe, was discovered by A.V. Ryumin in 1959 and investigated by O.N. Bader in the 1960s and 1970s. Since 1982 the site has been excavated by V.E. Shchelinsky. The paintings, in four separate galleries, represent animals (mammoth, horse, rhinoceros) and signs and geometric symbols (trapezes, triangles, a truncated cone, a square with loops). Two radiocarbon dates obtained from samples of charcoal indicate dates of around 14680±150 (LE-3443) and 13390±300 (GIN-4853) BP.

O.N. Bader: *Kapovaya peščra* [Kapova Cave] (Moscow, 1965); V.E. Shchelinsky: 'Some results of new investigations at the Kapova Cave in the southern Urals', *PPS* 55 (1989), 181–91.

PD

Kapwirimbwe Early Iron Age facies (cultural subdivision) in Zambia, named after a site on the outskirts of Lusaka. Along with Chondwe and Kalundu it formed the original core of David Phillipson's Western Stream. The cluster of styles has been renamed the Kalundu Tradition to avoid confusion with the historical classification of Bantu languages. Multidimensional stylistic analyses show that Kapwirimbwe is related to the 'LYDENBURG Tradition' (*see also* BAMBATA POTTERY) and other similar facies in South Africa and that it was the product of Eastern Bantu speaking people. The full settlement organization is not yet known, but the excavation of the type-site yielded storage pits, cattle bones and metal-working debris.

D.W. Phillipson: 'The Early Iron Age site at Kapwirimbwe, Lusaka', *Azania* 3 (1968), 87–105; ——: *The later prehistory of eastern and southern Africa* (London, 1977); T.N. Huffman: *Iron Age migrations: the ceramic sequence in southern Zambia* (Johannesburg, 1989).

TH

K-Ar *see* POTASSIUM-ARGON DATING

Karanog MEROITIC settlement-site and cemetery (*c*.300 BC–AD 350), located in Lower Nubia about 60 km south of Aswan. By the 3rd century AD, it had become a major town. Unlike other Meroitic centres (e.g. Faras or Qasr Ibrim) it was protected by a huge three-storey mud-brick 'castle' rather than a surrounding enclosure wall. Adams (1976) has suggested that Lower Nubian towns such as Karanog may have been controlled by local feudal rulers rather than being part of the Upper Nubian Meroitic kingdom itself.

C.L. Woolley and D. Randall-MacIver: *Karanog, the Romano-Nubian cemetery* (Pennsylvania, 1910); ——: *Karanog, the town* (Pennsylvania, 1911); W.Y. Adams: 'Meroitic north and south: a study in cultural contrasts', *Meroitica* 2 (1976), 11–26.

IS

Karanovo Large tell near Nova Zagora in the Tundza valley of central Bulgaria that has provided an important cultural and pottery sequence from the earliest Neolithic, in perhaps the 7th millennium BC, through the Copper Age to the Bronze Age. Karanovo levels I–IV are Neolithic; V–VI are Chalcolithic; VII is Early Bronze Age. Karanovo I is important as the type site of an early farming culture – very roughly contemporary with other early farming cultures in eastern Europe such as STARČEVO – which appears at other sites in central and southern Bulgaria (notably AZMAK tell). It is characterized by white bowls painted in red with geometric designs (with some instances of incised and plastic decoration), including a distinctive vessel form – the pedestalled bowl. The first phase of the settlement may already have comprised over 50 small (*c*.7 m square) houses – although some estimates suggest no more than 15 or so – set closely together in rows. The houses were simple and timber framed, with hearths and ovens. Level II continues the cultural tradition established in level I, although the ceramic decoration is relatively less rich. Karanovo III is Middle Neolithic, while IV and V are Late Neolithic. Level VI represents a rich Gumelniţa culture phase, with distinctive bowls painted with graphite and a rich copper industry with copper axes exhibiting carefully cast-in shaftholes; by Karanovo VI, the size of houses had increased substantially.

V. Mikov: 'The prehistoric mound of Karanovo', *Archaeology* 12 (1959), 88–97; S. Hiller and G. Georgiev: *Tell Karanovo* (Salzburg, 1984, 1986, 1987).

RJA

Karatepe *see* HITTITES

Karbuna (Corbuna) Hoard and settlement related to the early phases of the TRIPOLYE culture, located near the village of the same name in Central Moldova. The hoard was secreted in an anthropomorphic vessel, which had been placed in a storage pit dug between the dwellings of the Tripolye settlement. The vessel contained 852 artefacts, of which 444 were copper implements such as spiral bracelets, cylindrical beads, various plates (including anthropomorphic examples) and various types of copper celts. The tools were forged, and the copper ore originated from the Balkan-Carpathian region.

G.P. Sergeev: 'Rannetripol'skii klad u sela Karbuna' [An early Tripolye hoard near the village of Karbuna], *Sovetskaya arheologija* 1 (1963), 135–51; N.V. Ryndina: *Drevneišee metalloobrabatyvaješčee proizvodstvo Vostočnoi Evropy* [The most ancient metal-working industry of Eastern Europe] (Moscow, 1971).

PD

Kariandusi ACHEULEAN site of Middle Pleistocene age in an area of diatomite beds in the Kenya Rift Valley, overlooking Lake Elmenteita. It was examined by Louis Leakey in the 1920s and more recently by Gowlett. Kariandusi's cleavers, handaxes and other tools are remarkable for being made of obsidian, available from nearby Mount Eburru and the Naivasha basin. The dating is unclear, but some layers could be as much as 0.75 million years old. The site and its surrounds have been affected by rift faulting as well as gully erosion and lake-level changes, rendering them instructive for geological and geomorphological demonstration.

L.S.B. Leakey: *The Stone Age cultures of Kenya colony* (Cambridge, 1931); J.A.J. Gowlett: 'Acheulian sites in the Central Rift valley, Kenya', *Proceedings of the 8th Panafrican Congress of Prehistory 1977* (Nairobi, 1980), 213–7.

JS

Karmir Blur *see* URARTU

Karnak (anc. Ipet-sut) Massive collection of Egyptian temples and shrines, covering over a hundred hectares in the northeastern area of modern Luxor and dating from at least as early as the Middle Kingdom (*c.*2040–1640 BC) until the end of the Roman period (*c.*AD 395). It comprises three major sacred 'precincts' dedicated to the deities Amon-Re, Mut and Monthu, each of which was surrounded by trapezoidal mud-brick enclosure walls. The enclosures also included a number of smaller temples dedicated to Ptah, Opet and Khonsu respectively. The earliest axis of the temple of Amon-Re extended from west to east, incorporating the Great Hypostyle Hall of Ramesses II (*c.*1290–1224 BC), which is over 5 ha in area. The second axis extended the temple southwards and included the so-called 'cachette court', where thousands of royal and private statues were discovered hidden under the floor. Karnak lay at the heart of the city of Thebes (anc. Waset), which served as one of the most important Egyptian administrative centres for much of the pharaonic period.

G. Legrain: *Les Temples du Karnak* (Brussels, 1929); Centre Franco-égyptien d'étude des temples de Karnak: *Cahiers de Karnak*, 6 vols (1943–82); P. Barguet: *Le temple d'Amon-Re à Karnak: essai d'exégèse* (Cairo, 1962).

IS

Kartan culture Tool assemblage consisting of steep-edged scrapers and HORSE HOOF CORES, found mainly around Kangaroo Island and the adjacent mainland of South Australia. The tools have been picked up largely from surface scatters, but are thought to be Pleistocene in age. The predominant distribution is around lagoons, streams and swamps.

R.J. Lampert: *The great Kartan mystery* (Canberra, 1981).

CG

karum *see* ASSYRIA, KÜLTEPE

Kashiwagi B A series of five Late Jomon bank-enclosed cemeteries in Hokkaido, Japan (*c.*2500–1000 BC). One contained 21 burials within the central enclosure, 18 in the surrounding bank and a further five outside the bank. This spatial organization, along with the varied burial forms and grave goods, indicates complex social relations at a time of ecological change.

F. Ikawa-Smith and F. Kanjodori: 'Communal cemeteries of the late Jomon in Hokkaido', *Pacific Northeast Asia in prehistory*, ed. C.M. Aikens and S.N. Rhee (Pullman, 1992), 83–90.

SK

Kassites (Akkadian: *Kashshu*) Ancient Near Eastern non-Semitic people who were originally based in the central ZAGROS (roughly corresponding to the Luristan area of modern Iran), to the south of the homeland of the GUTIANS and Lullubi. They emerged from obscurity in the early 2nd millennium BC, achieving political control of Mesopotamia, during the 16th–13th centuries BC at roughly the same time as the rise of the HURRIANS and HITTITES in Anatolia. Like most other new arrivals in Mesopotamia, the Kassites are initially visible only through their unusual personal names, which began to appear in cuneiform texts in Babylonia during the 17th century BC, indicating their gradual peaceful influx into the population, usually as agricultural workers. Although no texts written exclusively in the Kassite language have survived, their language was clearly agglutinative and possibly related to Elamite.

In terms of material culture the most important surviving site of the Kassite period is Aqar Quf, west of modern Baghdad, where the city of Dur Kurigalzu was founded by Kurigalzu I (*c.*1400BC). Much of the art and architecture at Aqar Quf – including an unusually well-preserved ziggurat and the painted palace of the 12th-century Kassite ruler Marduk-apla-iddin – is distinctly Babylonian in appearance, indicating the degree to which the Kassite rulers of Babylon had simply assimilated the indigenous material culture. However, there are a number of Kassite innovations, such as the use of moulded baked bricks for the external decoration of buildings, the introduction of the *KUDURRU* (a ceremonial stele recording land transfers), and the increased use of horses in warfare. The CYLINDER SEALS of the Kassite period included a number of innovative geometrical and figurative motifs as well as the archaizing use of lengthy cuneiform texts in the Sumerian language. There are also a number of surviving buildings which appear to be Kassite rather than Babylonian in style, and the earliest surviving Kassite temple is the shrine constructed by Karaindash (*c.*1465 BC) at URUK.

Although the Kassite dynasty in Babylonia is regarded as a comparative 'dark age', this is partly a result of the neglect of archaeologists, since thousands of surviving Kassite-period documents (including an extensive archive from NIPPUR) remain unpublished. Oates (1986: 101–2) argues that the Kassite administration was not only unusually stable but also characterized by a move towards a more 'feudal' form of society, in which the concept of the king as sole 'law-giver' was gradually eroded by the transfer of land into communal and tribal ownership.

K. Balkan: *Kassitenstudien* I (New Haven, 1954); K. Jaritz: 'Quellen zur Geschichte der Kassu-Dynastie', *Mitteilungen des Instituts für Orientforschung* 6 (1958), 187–265; U. Seidl: 'Die babylonischen *Kudurru*-reliefs', *Baghdader Mitteilungen* 4 (1968), 7–220; J.A. Brinkman: *Materials and studies for Kassite history* I (Chicago, 1976); J. Oates: *Babylon*, 2nd edn (London, 1986), 83–104.

IS

Katelai *see* GANDHARA GRAVE CULTURE

Kathu Pan Shallow 3 ha basin in the northwest Cape region, South Africa, which has yielded significant evidence of the African Stone Age. The site is seasonally flooded and the floor is formed of variable strata of peat, silty sand, gravel, and calcified sand, to a depth of up to 11 m below the modern surface, overlying 40 m of calcrete and 30 m of sands, clays and gravels. The massive calcrete and subjacent deposits are of Tertiary age. Excavations by P. Beaumont (1979–90) revealed mainly shallow deposits of Holocene age. However, where there has been collapse, into solution cavities in the Tertiary calcretes, longer sequences are exposed. At KP1 two Acheulean horizons (one designated 'FAURESMITH') are overlain by Middle Stone Age and Later Stone Age occurrences. Pollen and faunal remains enhance the significance of the site.

P.B. Beaumont: 'Kathu Pan', *Guide to archaeological sites in the northern Cape*, ed. P.B. Beaumont and D. Morris (Kimberley, 1990), 75–100.

RI

Katuruka Located near the western shore of Lake Victoria in north-western Tanzania, this site, together with other sites excavated by Peter Schmidt, has stimulated discussion about the nature and dating of the East African EARLY IRON AGE. In local tradition Katuruka is associated with a king, Rugamora Mahe, who is thought to have ruled in the 18th century AD. The main archaeological materials however, including plentiful remains of iron-working, both here and at other sites associated with the same ruler or culture-hero, belong to the Early Iron Age. They include fine examples of Urewe pottery, and have been dated to about 2000 years ago. Certain of the radiocarbon results from Katuruka suggested at first that the origins of this Early Iron Age between the great lakes might be considerably older. On the basis of these dates and results obtained at Katuruka, Kemondo Bay and other sites nearby, as well as experiments in furnace building and smelting and the use of ethnographic analogies, Schmidt (1978) argued that the local early iron technology was remarkably sophisticated and original, obtaining exceptionally high temperatures through preheated air; this proved to be a source of considerable controversy in African archaeology from the 1960s to 1980s (e.g. Rehder 1986).

P.R. Schmidt: *Historical archaeology: a structural approach to an African culture* (Westport, 1978); S.T. Childs and P.R. Schmidt: 'Experimental iron smelting', *African iron working: ancient and traditional*, ed. R. Haaland and P. Shinnie (Oslo and Oxford, 1985); J.E. Rehder: 'Use of preheated air in primitive furnaces: comment on views of Avery and Schmidt', *JFA* 13 (1986), 351–3.

JS

Kausambi City of the early Historic period, located by the Yamuna River, about 50 km west of modern Allahabad, India. Excavations conducted by Govardhan Rhaj Sharma (1949–50) exposed remains dating from the PAINTED GREY WARE period (*c.*1300–600 BC) to the 6th century AD. Massive earth (and later brick) fortifications, cut by 11 gateways, enclose the northern, western and eastern edges of the settlement. Architectural remains include a standing column of the MAURYAN PERIOD, and Sharma's excavations revealed brick residential and defensive structures, altars, a Buddhist monastery and *STUPA* foundation, and a large building tentatively interpreted as a palace. Surviving artefacts include terracotta figurines, iron tools and weapons, and many types of coins and seals.

K.K. Sinha: 'Stratigraphy and chronology of early Kausambi – a reappraisal', *Radiocarbon and Indian archaeology*, ed. D.P. Agrawal and A. Ghosh (Bombay, 1973), 231–8; G.R. Sharma: *Excavations at Kausambi, 1949–1950* (New Delhi, 1974).

CS

Keatley Creek Village site consisting of 115 house-pits on the Fraser River near Lillooet in western North America, which was excavated by Brian Hayden from 1986 to 1994. The excavation of 21 housepits and 13 smaller pits revealed a sequence of occupations from 2000 BC to AD 1000 belonging to the PLATEAU PITHOUSE TRADITION. Occupation at the site ended with the failure of the salmon runs because of catastrophic landslides on the Fraser River.

B. Hayden and J. Ryder: 'Prehistoric cultural collapse in the Lillooet area', *AA* 56 (1991), 50–65; B. Hayden and J. Spafford: *The Keatley Creek Site and Corporate Group Archaeology* (Vancouver, 1993).

RC

Kebara, Kebaran The recently excavated materials from Kebara, one of the caves in the MOUNT CARMEL region of Israel, are important in the story of HUMAN EVOLUTION for a number of reasons. Firstly, thermoluminescence dates for the site indicate occupation by NEANDERTHALS around 60,000 years ago – much later than the ANATOMICALLY MODERN HUMAN occupation of the Qafzeh cave (*see* QAFZEH AND SKHUL). Similar datings for the Tabun site (*see* MOUNT CARMEL) seem to confirm that 'modern' humans were in the Levant *before* the Neanderthals. The skeletal material is also of some significance, since Neanderthal burials at the site have provided the most complete Neanderthal pelvis yet known. This fossil seems to indicate differences from modern humans in locomotion, due to the wider separation of the hip joints. (It had earlier been believed that the wider Neanderthal pelvis was associated with longer pregnancies and hence larger foetus size.) Finally, the fossil material includes a Neanderthal hyoid bone. This laryngeal bone appears the same as that of modern people, apparently contradicting claims that the Neanderthals were incapable of speech.

In 1931 Francis Turville-Petre found the first remains of the 'Kebaran complex' in Kebara cave. Dating to *c.*18,000–11,000 BC, this is the earliest group of Levantine EPIPALAEOLITHIC industries, roughly contemporary with the Mushabian complex and eventually evolving into (or superseded by) the 'Geometric Kebaran' and the NATUFIAN. Some Kebaran sites were only small seasonal encampments, but others were larger settlements occupied throughout the winter months and showing evidence of the exploitation of fish and cereals such as wheat and barley. Kebaran toolkits typical include groundstone mortars and pestles as well as bladelets and microliths.

B. Arensberg et al.: 'A Middle Palaeolithic human hyoid bone', *Nature* 338 (1989), 758–60; D.O. Henry: *From foraging to agriculture: the Levant at the end of the Ice Age* (Philadelphia, 1989), 151–77; O. Bar-Yosef et al.: 'The excavations in Kebara Cave, Mount Carmel', *CA* 33/5 (1992), 497–550.

PG-B/IS

Kechi Beg *see* QUETTA

Kefkalesi *see* URARTU

Kelteminar Early cultural tradition of Central Asia named after a site located in the Amu-Darya Syr-Darya interfluve in Khoresmia, Central Asia. The Kelteminar 'culture' is often described as 'Neolithic' in the literature because of technological developments (particularly the adoption of pottery); however, the economy was entirely based on hunting and gathering. The type site was first identified by Tolstov in 1939, and later intensively explored by Gulyamov, Islamov, Vonogradov, Mamedov and others.

Kelteminar as a hybrid Neolithic/Mesolithic culture. The development of the Kelteminar complex coincided with the wet climatic phase (the Lyavlyakan pluvial), which became noticeable in the Turanian lowland *c.*6000 BC. At that time, the Amu Darya river was flowing directly to the Caspian Sea, via Sarykamysh lake and Uzboi. A great number of sites emerged along this waterway. A large cluster of sites is located in the ancient deltas of Amu-Darya, notably Akcha-Darya, and along the Zerafshan further south.

Numerous sites were found in the Amu-Darya Syr-Darya interfluve, notably in the Lyavlyakan area in the present-day Kyzyl-Kum desert. This clustering is due to the large number of fresh-water lakes that formed in the area during the climactic optimum (Vinogradov and Mamedov 1975; Vinogradov 1981). Pollen analysis shows that the river floors were covered by *tugai* forests of fir, pine, birch, alder, oak, hornbeam and hazel. The faunal remains found at Kelteminar sites consist of wild animals adapted to *tugai* forests, open steppes and desert mountains (red deer, fallow, deer, boar, kulan, saiga, gazelle, mouflon, camel etc.). Hunting of water fowl (mallard, teal, grebe, cormorant, golden eye etc.) and fishing (pike, carp, catfish, pike-perch) were also important. Food-gathering included a wide spectrum of edible plants (pomegranate, apricots, wild olives), small animals (tortoise, agama) and molluscs (Vinogradov 1981). The lithic technology included grinding stones, mortars and pestles as well as blades with sickle gloss. However, the absence of domesticated cereals suggest that subsistence was based entirely on foraging strategies, and Vinogradov (1981) suggests that these tools were used for harvesting and processing wild plants. The pottery style reveals contacts with truly agricultural groups to the south (e.g. ANAU, JEITUN *and* NAMAZGA).

A.V. Vinogradov and E.D. Mamedov: *Pervobytnyi Ljavljakan* (Moscow, 1975); A.V. Vinogradov: *Drevnie ohotniki i rybolovy Sredneaziatskogo Mezhdurech'ja* (Moscow, 1981).

PD

Kemondo Bay *see* KATURUKA

Kempen project Survey of the archaeology of an area of the southern Netherlands organized by the University of Amsterdam since 1981 adopting 'a historico-anthropological perspective'. The major objective was to analyse the ways in which early medieval society in the area changed in response to intensified contacts with the core regions of Austrasia (the heart of the Frankish kingdom). This has involved intensive field survey, excavations of villages and cemeteries, notably at Dommelen, an analysis of the written sources and the place-name evidence. The data showed dramatic changes in the later 7th and the early 8th centuries AD, as the area became dependent upon Austrasia.

F. Theuws: 'Landed property and manorial organisation in Northern Austrasia: some considerations and a case study', *Images of the past: studies on ancient societies in northwestern Europe*, ed. N. Roymans and F. Theuws (Amsterdam, 1991), 299–407.

RH

Kenniff Cave This sandstone cave in southern Queensland produced the first evidence for the Pleistocene occupation of Australia, with a date of 19,000 BP from the lowest levels. The site was also important in distinguishing the AUSTRALIAN CORE TOOL AND SCRAPER TRADITION found in the lower layers, from the AUSTRALIAN SMALL TOOL TRADITION in the upper part. The cave was rich in artefacts and contains rock art.

D.J. Mulvaney and E.B. Joyce: 'Archaeological and geomorphological investigations on the Mt Moffatt Station, Queensland, Australia', *PPS* 31 (1965), 147–212.

CG

Kenya Aurignacian *see* KENYA CAPSIAN

Kenya Capsian Term used to encompass most of the Late Stone Age industries of the Eastern Rift Valley and flanking highlands of Kenya, although their stages or facies have been better defined recently (Ambrose 1984). Essentially the same as Louis Leakey's 'Kenya Aurignacian', they are typically blade industries made of obsidian obtained from Mount Eburru and other nearby sources in the Lake Naivasha basin; most archaeological occurrences are within 100 km of these sources and the term 'Eburran' is therefore preferred by some recent workers. The industries range in date from early in the Holocene (if not the terminal Pleistocene) through perhaps as much as 10,000 years, with some late derivations in the final millennia BC. Although later manifestations of this tradition contain increasing numbers of crescents, small tools and flakes, the Kenya Capsian rarely became truly microlithic; backed blades, *outils écaillés*, various scrapers and blade-derived tools remained distinctive.

L.S.B. Leakey: *The Stone Age cultures of Kenya colony* (Cambridge, 1931); S.H. Ambrose: 'The introduction of pastoral adaptations to the highlands of East Africa', *From hunters to farmers; the causes and consequences of food production in Africa*, ed. J.D. Clark and S.A. Brandt (Berkeley, 1984), 212–39.

JS

Kephala Settlement and cemetery on the island of Kea, dated to about 4000 BC, revealing some of the earliest evidence for copper-working in the Cyclades. The cemetery of built stone tombs or cists is also the earliest known in the islands, and was found to contain finely worked marble vessels and terracotta figurines. The site is seen as a precursor of the classic CYCLADIC CULTURE.

J.E. Coleman: *Keos I: Kephala, a Late Neolithic settlement and cemetery* (Princeton, 1974).

RJA

Kerma Settlement site of the early 2nd millennium BC, near the third Nile cataract in Upper Nubia, which is among the earliest surviving towns in tropical Africa. It appears to have been the capital of the kingdom of Kush during the Egyptian Old and Middle Kingdoms; it is therefore the type-site for the Kerma culture (*c.*2500–1500 BC). The site of Kerma incorporates a large settlement, a cemetery of tumulus-graves and two enigmatic mud-brick structures – known as the *deffufa* – dating to the 17th century BC. The L-shaped western *deffufa*, perhaps a fortress or temple (Bonnet 1981), is in the centre of the town, while the eastern *deffufa*, perhaps a funerary chapel, is part of the cemetery at the southern end of the site; each of them was originally an almost solid block of mud bricks covering an area of roughly 1500 sq.m.

The people of the Kerma (or Kushite) culture were located largely in Upper Nubia and were roughly contemporary with the Lower Nubian C GROUP. The archaeological remains at Kerma-culture sites are characterized by a rich variety of craftwork, including fine metalwork, faience tiles, mica and ivory ornamentation, and the distinctive handmade, tulip-shaped Kerma pottery vessels (the latter primarily discovered in funerary contexts). Kerma-cultures graves usually consisted of an earth tumulus covering a burial pit in which the deceased, clothed in leather and decorated with jewellery, was frequently laid on a bed. The accompanying funerary equipment typically included weaponry, ox-hides and ox-skulls, suggesting that large numbers of oxen may have been slaughtered as part of the funeral ceremony. This ceremony may also have involved large-scale human sacrifice, to judge from the substructures of the main tumuli at Kerma itself, where George Reisner (1923) excavated subdivided corridors containing hundreds of human skeletons which may be the remains of retainers buried alive at the time of the ruler's burial.

G.A. Reisner: *Excavations at Kerma I–V*, 2 vols (Cambridge, MA, 1923); B. Gratien: *Les cultures Kerma: essai de classification* (Lille, 1978); D. O'Connor: 'Kerma and Egypt: the significance of the monumental buildings Kerma I, II and XI', *JARCE* 21 (1984), 65–108; C. Bonnet et al.: *Kerma: royaume de Nubie* (Geneva, 1990); C. Bonnet: 'Excavations at the Nubian royal town of Kerma: 1975–91', *Antiquity* 66 (1992), 611–25.

IS

Kernonen Early Bronze Age tumulus in Finistère, France, that belongs to a rich group of graves known as the Armorican First Series (*see* ARMORICAN FIRST AND SECOND SERIES). The round mound, about 50 m in diameter and 6 m high, covered a rectangular dry-stone chamber about 5 m long; on the wooden floor of this chamber and within three wooden boxes laid upon it were bronze axes, daggers, flint arrowheads and an amber pendant. The daggers (one of which is long enough to be termed a 'sword') originally had hilts of wood studded with gold pins, and this and the general form and richness of the grave have encouraged comparison with the BUSH BARROW grave of the WESSEX CULTURE in southern Britain.

J. Briard: 'Un tumulus du bronze ancien Kernonen en Plouvorn (Finestère)', *L'Anthropologie* 74 (1970), 5–56; ——: *Les tumulus d'Armorique* (Paris, 1984); D.V. Clarke et al.: *Symbols of power at the time of Stonehenge* (Edinburgh, 1985), 129–35.

RJA

Keros-Syros culture Alternative name for the Early Cycladic II phase (*c.*2700–2300 BC) of the CYCLADIC CULTURE, defined by the large Chalandriani cemetery on Syros and the site of

Dhaskaleio Kavos on Keros. The Keros-Syros culture produced the classic series of Cycladic figurines.
RJA

Khabur The term 'Khabur pottery' is applied to a style of painted ceramic vessel found at sites in northern Mesopotamia during the early 2nd millennium BC.

Khafajeh (anc. Tutub) Early town-site in eastern Iraq consisting of three large mounds on the east bank of the Diyala river, about 20 km above its present confluence with the Tigris. The settlement of Tutub was established in the Protoliterate period and flourished throughout the Early Dynastic period. In the 1930s, the site was carefully excavated by Pinhas Delougaz, who discovered three temples in 'Tell A', including one ground-level complex dedicated to the moon-god Sin, which was larger than the Square Temple at ESHNUNNA and dated from the JEMDET NASR period (*c.*3200 BC) to Early Dynastic III (*c.*2350 BC). A number of ritual vessels and artefacts were discovered *in situ* in the earliest strata both of the temple of Sin and in three single-shrine temples among the adjacent domestic buildings. Elsewhere in the city, a platform-temple dating to Early Dynastic II and III (*c.*2750–2350 BC), the so-called 'Temple Oval', was surrounded by an oval enclosure but the whole complex was denuded almost down to pavement level. Between the walls was an annexe apparently serving as a residential area for priests. A set of three elaborate copper supports in the form of nude male figures were found buried beneath pavement level.

P. Delougaz: *The Temple Oval at Khafajah* (Chicago, 1940); H. Frankfort: *Sculpture of the 3rd millennium BC from Tell Asmar and Khafajeh* (Chicago, 1942); H.D. Hill et al.: *Old Babylonian public buildings in the Diyala region* (Chicago, 1990).
IS

Khami *see* GREAT ZIMBABWE

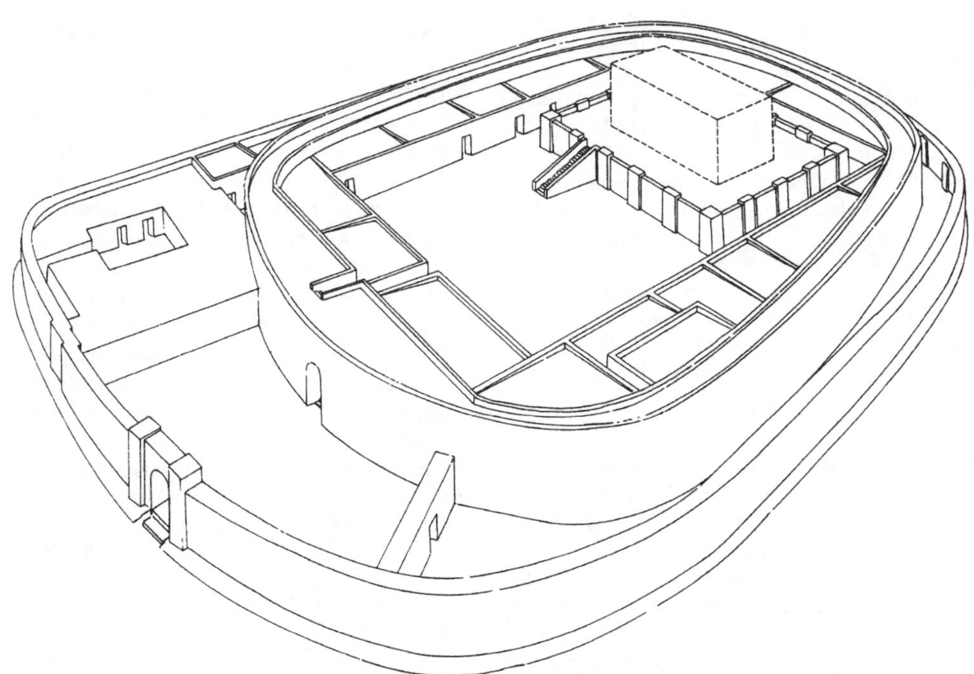

Figure 26 **Khafajeh** Reconstruction of the Temple Oval at Khafajeh (*c.*2750–2350), consisting of two concentric oval enclosure walls surrounding a platform approached by a flight of steps and surmounted by an inner sanctuary of an unknown deity (tentatively indicated here by the inner rectangular structure). *Source*: H. Crawford: Sumer and the Sumerians (Cambridge University Press, 1991), fig. 4.16.

Khao Chang Ngam Rock-art site in northeast Thailand which includes a well-known scene of a row of men, women and children with a dog, with one man firing an arrow. These painted scenes are related to a series of rock-art sites in the region. No dating evidence has yet been obtained, but a prehistoric context is highly likely.

P. Charoenwongsa et al.: *An inventory of rock art sites in northeast Thailand* (Bangkok, 1985).

CH

Khao Wong Prachan Valley Region of central Thailand that was the focus of intensive mining, smelting and casting of copper ore from 1500 to 300 BC. The ore was extracted from mines, crushed and sorted, and smelted in bowl crucibles. Ingots, projectile points and socketed axe heads were among the objects cast, the metal being a naturally high-arsenic copper. No evidence for alloying with tin has been found. There is also early evidence for iron forging, dating to *c.*600 BC.

A. Bennet: 'The contribution of metallurgical studies to Southeast Asian archaeology', *WA* 20/3 (1989), 329–51.

CH

Kharga Oasis The southernmost and largest of the major Egyptian oases, located in the Libyan Desert about 175 km west of Luxor. Traces of Middle Palaeolithic (MOUSTERIAN) occupation were discovered by Gertrude Caton-Thompson (1952). In the pharaonic period, strong links appear to have been established with the Egyptian culture in the Nile valley, but most of the surviving architectural remains of settlements, temples and cemeteries date from the Ptolemaic period onwards.

G. Caton-Thompson: *Kharga Oasis in prehistory* (London, 1952); L. Giddy: *Egyptian oases: Bahariya, Dakhla, Farafra and Kharga during pharaonic times* (Warminster, 1987), *passim.*

IS

Khartoum Mesolithic The Khartoum Mesolithic (initially known as the Early Khartoum culture, after its typesite) was widespread in the Khartoum and Shendi areas of the Nile Valley from *c.*6000 to 3500 BC. First recognized by A.J. Arkell, it is characterized by evidence for a hunting and fishing subsistence pattern highly adapted to the riverine environment. The material culture includes microlithic tools and hand-made 'wavy-line' globular ceramics (decorated with fish-bones or rocker-stamps), but there is no indication of plant or animal domestication. The semi-permanent encampments of the Khartoum Mesolithic are often described as 'midden settlements', due to the accumulation of human debris but lack of permanent dwellings. The ready availability of game and fish appears to have facilitated a sedentary lifestyle without agriculture. Apart from the burials within the Early Khartoum settlement-site no Khartoum Mesolithic cemeteries have yet been found. Adams (1984: 112) has pointed out that the precocious appearance of pottery-production seems to be a typical instance of North African cultures' tendency to absorb technological innovations without accepting their ecological concomitants. The development of the Khartoum Mesolithic is effectively the reverse process to that of the Levantine PRE-POTTERY NEOLITHIC, in which domestication preceded ceramics.

A.J. Arkell: *Early Khartoum* (London, 1949); W.Y. Adams: *Nubia: corridor to Africa*, 2nd edn (Princeton, 1984), 110–12.

IS

Khartoum Neolithic By the early 4th millennium BC the KHARTOUM MESOLITHIC of Central Sudan was gradually being superseded by the Khartoum Neolithic (*c.*4000–3000 BC), initially described by A.J. Arkell as the Shaheinab culture, after its original type-site el-Shaheinab. There are similarities between the Khartoum Neolithic material remains and those of the 'Khartoum Variant' sites in southern Lower Nubia (Shiner 1968). The pottery of the Khartoum Neolithic was closely related to that of the Mesolithic (being decorated with 'dotted wavy-line' motifs rather than the simple wavy lines of the Mesolithic). The Khartoum Neolithic communities also continued to employ a similar repertoire of microlithic tools for fishing and hunting, but their subsistence pattern was characterized by one major development: faunal evidence of the domestication of animals (usually goat). *See also* KADERO.

A.J. Arkell: *Shaheinab* (London, 1953); C.M. McBurney: *The Stone Age of northern Africa* (Harmondsworth, 1960), 244; J. Shiner: 'The Khartoum Variant industry', *The prehistory of Nubia* II, ed. F. Wendorf (Dallas, 1968), 768–90; H. Nordström: *Neolithic and A-Group sites* (Stockholm, 1972), 136–9, 212–20; F. Hassan, 'Chronology of the Khartoum "Mesolithic" and "Neolithic" and related sites in the Sudan: statistical analysis and comparisons with Egypt', *AAR* 4 (1986), 83–102.

IS

Khartoum Variant (*c.*4000–3000 BC) *see* KHARTOUM NEOLITHIC

Khirbet Kerak (Beth Yerah) One of the largest tell-sites in the Levant, situated immediately to the southwest of Lake Tiberias, 35 km east of Haifa. It was excavated between 1944 and 1964, revealing 23 strata dating from the end of the Chalcolithic period (*c.*3200 BC) to the 5th century AD, when it became the site of a Byzantine church. Khirbet Kerak gave its name to an important Early Bronze Age culture of the 3rd millennium BC in Syria-Palestine which appears to have been a Levantine version of the EARLY TRANSCAUCASIAN CULTURE in Anatolia. The Khirbet Kerak culture, roughly contemporary with the Early Dynastic phase in SUMER, is particularly characterized by red and red-and-black burnished pottery often decorated with geometrical motifs. Extensive traces of Khirbet Kerak ware have survived at other sites in the Levant, including JERICHO, BETH SHAN, Tell Judeida and UGARIT.

R.B.K. Amiran: 'Connections between Anatolia and Palestine in the Early Bronze Age', *IEJ* 2 (1952), 89–103; B. Maisler, M. Stekelis and M. Avi-Jonah: 'The excavations at Beth Yerah (Khirbet el-Kerak)', *IEJ* 2 (1952), 165–73, 218–29.

IS

Khmer *see* ANGKOR; BAN TAMYAE; KOH KER; LOPBURI; PHIMAI

Khoisan *see* AFRICA 4

Khok Charoen Cemetery of 44 extended inhumation buria ls, located in the Pa Sak valley, a tributary of the Chao Phraya River in central Thailand. When excavated by Watson and Loofs-Wissowa in 1966–7, the site yielded grave-goods such as pottery vessels, marine shell jewellery and stone adzeheads; no copper-based artefacts were found. The considerable variation in the quantity of goods deposited with individual burials may indicate some ranking, or at least differential personal achievement. Two thermoluminescence dates of 1180 and 1080 BC have been derived from the mortuary pottery, but when compared to the pottery typology these seem too late by 500–1000 years.

W. Watson: 'Khok Charoen and the early metal age of Central Thailand', *Early South East Asia*, ed. R.B. Smith and W. Watson (Oxford 1979), 53–62.

CH

Khok Phanom Di Large settlement (5 ha) and cemetery site dated to *c.*2000–1500 BC, located on a former shoreline now about 24 km from the Gulf of Siam in Thailand. After several small excavations, a major research programme took place in 1985 under the direction of Charles Higham and Rachanie Thosarat Bannanurag. This included excavation, flotation of a sample of all contexts and coring for sediment and pollen analysis. It was found that the site had been occupied between 2000 and 1500 BC. The excavations of 1985 encountered a sequence which began with industrial and occupation remains, then involved a cemetery, and finally reverted to a pottery-making area.

A remarkable feature of the cemetery was the pace with which the deposits accumulated. Within four centuries, the mound rose by 6 m. The cemetery pattern reveals that groups of individuals were laid out in clusters on a chequer-board pattern; as time went by, the dead were eventually buried above their ancestors. Two such groups have been traced through about 20 generations.

C.F.W. Higham et al.: 'Human biology, environment and ritual at Khok Phanom Di', *WA* 24/1 (1992), 35–54; C.F.W. Higham and R. Bannanurag: *The excavation of Khok Phanom Di, a prehistoric site in central Thailand* I: *The excavation, chronology and human burials* (London, 1990).

CH

Khok Phlap Cemetery site located west of the Chao Phraya River in central Thailand. The site was formerly located on or near the coast. Excavations there by Sod Daeng-iet encountered a cemetery in which people were inhumed in association with pottery vessels, shellfish remains and stone, bronze and turtleshell jewellery. Although not scientifically dated, the typology of the artefacts suggest that the site belongs to the 1st century BC.

S. Daeng-iet: 'Khok Phlap: a newly discovered prehistoric site', *Muang Boran* 4/4 (1978) 17–26.

CH

Khor Musa *see* KHORMUSAN

Khormusan Final Lower Nubian and Upper Egyptian lithic tradition of the Middle Palaeolithic period, named after Khor Musa (near Wadi Halfa in the northern Sudan) where the first Khormusan assemblage was identified at site 1017. Dating from about 45,000 to 15,000 BC, it is roughly contemporary with the Dabban industry (*see* HAUA FTEAH). The typical Khormusan site comprises an area of debris close to the Nile, covering several thousand square metres and consisting of numerous clusters of artefacts around hearths (i.e. small encampments rather than continuous stretches of settlement). The toolkit virtually always consists of LEVALLOIS flakes and cores, burins and denticulates, with a wide diversity of tool-sizes, while the surviving organic remains suggest that food-sources ranged from catfish to wild cattle, gazelles, antelopes and hippopotami.

A.E. Marks: 'The Khormusan: an Upper Pleistocene industry in Sudanese Nubia', *The Prehistory of Nubia* I, ed. F. Wendorf (Dallas, 1968), 315–91; M.A. Hoffman: *Egypt before the pharaohs* (New York, 1979), 70–7.

IS

Khorsabad (anc. Dur-Sharrukin) Tell-site of one of the most important cities of the Assyrian empire, located in northern Iraq, 24 km northeast of Mosul. It was a new capital founded by Sargon II (*c*.721–705 BC) on a virgin site, apparently built in less than ten years. But its duration as capital was even briefer than that of its Egyptian counterpart, the city of Akhetaten at EL-AMARNA; in 704 BC Sargon's city was abandoned in favour of NINEVEH by his successor Sennacherib after Sargon had been killed in battle. Unlike el-Amarna, however, the settlement continued to be occupied for almost a century after it had fallen out of royal favour, until its destruction at the end of the Assyrian empire in 612 BC. The principal elements of the main citadel at Dur-Sharrukin, constructed on a terrace about 16 m in height at the northern corner of the city, were a seven-stage ziggurat with each storey originally painted a different colour, the palace of Sargon (decorated with frescoes, painted reliefs and glazed bricks), the palace of his brother Sinahusur, and the temple of Nabu (linked to the main palace by a stone viaduct). 'Palace F', in the southwestern corner of the city, incorporates a form of BIT-HILANI (a type of pillared building), perhaps deliberately borrowing from Aramaean architecture in Syria; it was used as an arsenal for storage of weapons and booty, as at Nineveh and NIMRUD.

The site was excavated in 1843–4 by Paul-Emile Botta, who transported some of the *LAMASSU* (colossal statues of winged bulls) from the palace gateways to Paris, where they were the first substantial Mesopotamian sculptures to be displayed in a European museum. Unfortunately many other statuary and reliefs from Khorsabad were lost in the Tigris while in transit for France. The site was also excavated by Victor Place in 1851–5, and in 1930–5 Gordon Loud discovered a new king-list (Poebel 1942) and uncovered large areas of temples and houses which had escaped Botta's notice.

P.E. Botta and E. Flandin: *Les monuments de Ninive*, 5 vols (Paris, 1849–50); M. Pillet: *Khorsabad: les découvertes de Victor Place en Assyrie* (Paris, 1918); G. Loud, H. Frankfort, T. Jacobsen and C.B. Altmann: *Khorsabad*, 2 vols (Chicago, 1936–8); A. Poebel: 'The Assyrian king list from Khorsabad', *JNES* 1 (1942), 247–306; T.A. Busink: 'La Zikkurat de Dur-Sarukin', *Comptes rendus de la troisième rencontre Assyriologique internationale* (Leiden, 1954), 105–22; H. Frankfort: *The art and architecture of the ancient Orient*, 4th edn (Harmondsworth, 1970), 143–54, 170–4, Figs 196–9.

IS

Kiet Siel *see* ANASAZI

Kiik-Koba Oldest Palaeolithic cave-site in the Crimea (Ukraine), situated in the valley of the river Zuya, 25 km east of Simferopol. The sequence, discovered and excavated in the 1930s by G.A. Bonch-Osmolovsky, included two MOUSTERIAN occupation levels. the upper level included an artificial enclosure made of large cobbles, and two burials of NEANDERTHALS – one adult and one child (5–8 months old). The bodies had been laid close to each other in contracted postures.

G.A. Bonch-Osmolovsky: 'Itogi izhučcenija krymskogo paleolita' [Results of studies of the Crimean Palaeolithic], *Transactions of the INQUA Conference*, vol. vi (Moscow, 1934), 114–83.

PD

Kili Ghul Muhammad *see* QUETTA

Kilwa *see* SWAHILI HARBOUR TOWNS

Kinsei Late/Final Jomon settlement in Yamanashi prefecture, Japan (*c*.2500–300 BC). Thirty-five buildings including a row of Final Jomon stone-paved houses were associated with a series of adjoining circular and rectangular stone burial cists interspersed with phallic standing stones and ritual deposits of juvenile wild boar and religious artefacts.

T. Niitsu and Y. Yamaki: *Kinsei iseki II* [The Kinsei site II] (Kofu, 1989).

SK

Kintampo Village in Central Ghana which has given its name to the 'Kintampo culture', first identified by Oliver Davies. The culture is known from both open-air and rockshelter sites, as at Ntereso and Kintampo respectively, and it is characterized by the following elements: stone rasps (described by Davies as 'terracotta cigars'), polished stone axes and arm rings, grooved abrading stones and grinding stones, comb-stamped pottery, and burnt daub with wooden pole and/or thatch impressions. Kintampo 6 rockshelter, excavated by Colin Flight in 1967–8 (60 sq. m) and by Ann B. Stahl in 1982 (3 sq. m), has provided a particularly important stratigraphic sequence, in which the Kintampo culture was preceded by a so-called 'Punpun phase'. Flight emphasized the distinction between the two. In his view, the Kintampo culture alone was characterized by a food producing economy, and he regarded it as intrusive to the area. By contrast, Stahl points out that in the portion of the site excavated by her there was a stratigraphic overlap between Punpun and Kintampo pottery, and she also believes that there was no decisive economic break between the two cultures. The Kintampo culture alone had domestic goats and/or sheep, but in Stahl's view the bones earlier identified as domestic cattle may have belonged to forest buffalo. *Elaeis guineensis*, *Canarium schweinfurthii*, and *Celtis* sp. occur throughout the sequence, as do legume-like seeds earlier identified by Flight as cultivated cowpeas (*Vigna unguiculata*).

Stahl therefore proposes an alternative model for the origins of food production in the area and the Kintampo culture, whereby an indigenous Late Stone Age population interacted with an incoming one to produce a distinctive local adaptation based on a fusion of autochthonous and exotic traits. There was a progressive introduction of diagnostically Kintampo elements, and the development of a 'garden hunting' economy. A set of 18 radiocarbon dates from six sites with Kintampo and/or Punpun occupations span the period from 3700 to 2770 BP.

C. Flight: 'The Kintampo culture and its place in the economic prehistory of West Africa', *Origins of African plant domestication*, ed. J.R. Harlan et al. (The Hague/Paris, 1976), 211–21; A.B. Stahl: 'Reinvestigation of Kintampo 6 rock shelter, Ghana: implications for the nature of culture change', *AAR* 3 (1985), 117–50.

PA-J

Kisalian *see* AFRICA 5

Kish (Tell el-Uhaimir, Tell Ingharra, Tell el-Khazna and Tell el-Bender) One of the most important SUMERIAN cities, surviving in the form of a group of mounds covering an area of some four square kilometres in southern Iraq, about 20 km to the east of BABYLON. The rulers appear to have exercised some kind of hegemony over the other towns of the Early Dynastic period (*c*.2900–2350 BC); according to the Sumerian King List, the kingship was lowered down from heaven to Kish after the Flood. First identified in 1873, the site was excavated by Henri de Genouillac in 1912 and by an Anglo-American expedition between 1923 and 1933. There are strata dating to the UBAID and URUK periods, but the main occupation dates to the JEMDET NASR and Early Dynastic periods (*c*.3200–2350 BC).

The site includes one of the earliest known Mesopotamian 'palaces' (Moorey 1964) as well as a number of cemeteries of the Early Dynastic period. Cemetery Y includes several 'cart burials', which were at first identified as the 'chariot burials' of Sumerian 'princes' (Langdon and Watelin 1934). There are probably seven such graves, each originally containing several human bodies in association with a large wheeled vehicle drawn by a bovid. The dating and significance of the cemetery are both subjects of some debate, but the latest evidence suggests that they are the burials of non-royal individuals of the ED II phase (Moorey 1978). There are also substantial neo-Babylonian and Sasanian remains.

S. Langdon and C. Watelin: *Excavations at Kish*, 3 vols (Paris, 1924–34); P.R.S. Moorey: 'The "plano-convex building" at Kish and early Mesopotamian palaces', *Iraq* 26 (1964), 83–98; McG. Gibson: *City and area of Kish* (Miami, 1972); ——: *The Oxford–Chicago excavations at Kish (1923–33)* (Oxford, 1978).

IS

kitchen midden, shell midden Term used in a general sense to describe an archaeological deposit formed largely of refuse from food preparation and, in a more particular sense, to describe large mounds of shells (with associated cultural debris) found at some coastal sites. Examples of the latter include the ASTURIAN complex in northern Spain and the ERTEBØLLE culture in Denmark and Scandinavia. Another group is located at the mouth of the Tagus in Portugal. While shell middens are a particular feature of Mesolithic Atlantic economies, they also exist in the Mediterranean – for example, Île de Riou in the bay of Marseilles has impressive limpet middens perhaps dating from 6000–5000 BC. The site is associated with very early Neolithic pottery and querns, which suggests that shellfish remained part of some local economies even after elements of farming systems were adopted.

Recent studies of shell middens have tended to stress that although they often form the most impressive physical evidence of a hunting-gathering economy, in overall nutritional terms they may only form a minor or seasonal part of a much more complicated foraging strategy. Even where marine resources underpinned a hunter-gatherer economy, sea-bird catching, egg-collecting and fishing may have been more important components in terms of their nutritional value. At the same time, at some sites shellfish may have represented a crucial 'stand-by' resource at times of the year when other resources were very limited (*see also* FORAGING THEORY *and* NAMU).

C. Bonsall, ed.: *The Mesolithic in Europe* (Edinburgh, 1985).

RJA

kiva Type of ceremonial structure found at PUEBLO sites in the southwestern region of North America, *c.*AD 1–1540. Kivas are usually at least partly subterranean and shapes vary, with curvilinear forms (e.g. circular, D-shaped and keyhole-shaped) being particularly characteristic of ANASAZI settlements (e.g. PUEBLO BONITO). The largest kivas (known as 'great kivas') probably served as the ceremonial centres for whole communities; these can be up to 10 m in diameter.

IS

Kivik The reconstructed rectangular chamber under this round tumulus of the late 2nd millennium BC, located in Skåne in Sweden, is lined with a unique corpus of Bronze Age decorated slabs. The slabs present a series of scenes and motifs (boats, axes, spoked wheels) related to contemporary rock art, but more carefully arranged into horizontal zones. The most striking scenes show a charioteer – the earliest depiction of such in northern European art – moving behind four warriors, and a scene in which eight robed figures stand on either side of what may be an altar. The engravings may relate to the funerary rites of the entombed. The tomb was in a poor condition before its investigation, and the small amount of associated material does not allow for a precise dating.

C.-A. Moberg: *Kiviksgraven* (Stockholm, 1975); K. Barup et al.: *Kivik* (1977); N. Sandars: *Prehistoric art in Europe* (London, 1985; 1st edn 1968), 286–8.

RJA

Klasies River Mouth Caves A number of caves and rockshelters with evidence of prehistoric occupation, situated along a short stretch of coast, close to the mouth of the Klasies River, 84 km west of Port Elizabeth, South Africa. Five of these form a cluster referred to as the main site. Cave 1 is a sea-cut cave at about 6–8 m above sea level. Cave 2 is situated in the cliff above, at 18–20 m above sea level and was made accessible by a huge accumulation of deposits to the right of Cave 1, including human occupational debris, against the cliff, in what is referred to as Shelter 1A. Cave 1C is a small cavern devoid of human occupation, to the right of Cave 1, and buried by the deposits of Shelter 1A. Shelter 1B lies to the left of Cave 1, separated by a spur of rock.

The sites were first excavated by Singer and Wymer in 1967 and 1968, and subsequently in 1984–6 by H.J. Deacon, for the purpose of recovering environmental data and samples for a range of dating techniques. The combined main site sediments (16 m) contain a long sequence of MSA (Middle Stone Age) occupations designated MSA I, MSA II, HOWIESON'S POORT, and MSA III, which has become the standard reference for the MSA in the southern part of South Africa. On a combination of dating techniques and environmental data the MSA I material dates to before 110,000 uncal BP and MSA II material to *c.*90,000–*c.*70,000 uncal BP. Howieson's Poort is less clearly dated to a span of several thousand years around 70,000 uncal BP. ANATOMICALLY MODERN HUMAN remains are associated with MSA I and MSA II in cave 1, shelter 1A, and shelter 1B.

R. Singer and J. Wymer: *The Middle Stone Age at Klasies River Mouth in South Africa* (Chicago, 1982); H.J. Deacon: 'Late Pleistocene palaeoecology and archaeology in the southern Cape, South Africa', *The human revolution*, ed. P. Mellars and C. Stringer (Edinburgh, 1989), 547–64.

RI

Kleinaspergle (Klein Aspergle, Kleiner Asperg) Massive rounded tumulus (8 m high and 60 m in diameter) covering the richest of the Iron Age 'princely graves' that lie at the foot of the hillfort of Hohenasperg in Baden-Württemberg, Germany. Unlike most of the princely tumuli associated with major hillforts, Kleinaspergle is dated to the La Tène A period, rather than the earlier Hallstatt D period. (The settlement at Hohenasperg has never been properly excavated because it is overlain by a medieval castle, but was presumably still in use at the time of the Kleinaspergle interment.) When the tomb was partially excavated in 1879 the main chamber was found to have been robbed in antiquity, but a secondary chamber contained a series of exotic imports and artefacts of Celtic manufacture in a fully developed 'Early La Tène' style (*see* LA TÈNE). The imports, an Etruscan *stamnos* and Attic red-figure ware with locally added gold mounts, securely date the tomb to the second half of the 5th century BC (perhaps 430/20 BC). The Celtic items reveal the influence of the Mediterranean world, and include a flagon in the Etruscan-influenced high-shouldered beaked form – paralleled in the classic flagons from Basse-Yutz – as well a series of gold mountings and a plaque; two drinking horn ends strongly suggest Scythian influence.

W. Kimmig: 'Klein Aspergle', *Trésors des princes Celtes*, eds. J.P. Mohen et al., exh. cat. (Paris, 1987), 255–64; ——: *Das Kleinaspergle* (Stuttgart, 1988).

RJA

k-means *see* CLUSTER ANALYSIS

Knossos Foremost palace complex of the MINOAN culture of Crete, excavated by Arthur Evans in (principally) 1921–35. The material from Knossos allowed Evans to divide the Minoan chronology into three main phases: Early, Middle and Late. The site was first occupied during the Neolithic period, from the 7th millennium BC onwards. After a little-understood formative Early Minoan period, a substantial palace was built around 2000 BC; this was surrounded by a town but excavations of this and later phases have concentrated on the palace and only a few Knossos townhouses have been excavated. This first palace seems to have been destroyed by an earthquake in around 1700 BC. The grandest palace was then constructed, and continued in use until the 14th century BC – significantly *after* the massive volcanic explosion on the island of Santorini once thought to have precipitated Knossos's destruction (*see* THERA). It seems clear that from 1700 BC, at least, Knossos was the pre-eminent settlement on Crete, but the nature of its relations with other palace sites is still debated. In the final years before its destruction Knossos may have been controlled by princes of the MYCENAEAN civilization that had arisen on the Greek mainland.

The palace consists of a central court surrounded by suites of ceremonial rooms and storage and work rooms. The complex was built on two (or even three) storeys; the upper floors were of mud-brick laced with timber, possibly to strengthen them against tremors and earthquakes. The design displays sophisticated architectural features such as light wells, stone-lined drainage channels and clay piping, dressed stone colonnades and plastered interior walls. The rooms included storage magazines, royal reception rooms and shrines. Certain rooms are decorated with elaborate wall-paintings, the surviving examples of which mostly date from about 1550 BC onwards. Knossos and Thera provide the principal examples of Minoan painting. Themes include formal processions and religious festivals, athletes somersaulting over bulls, dancing girls, pictures of animals (monkeys, cats, deer) within landscapes, marine scenes (flying fish etc) and decorative schemes based around banding and floral motifs. The style is flexible, naturalistic and full of life; later examples are more monumental and rigid and betray Mycenaean influence.

A.J. Evans: *Palace of Minos at Knossos* (London, 1921–36); M. Ventris and J. Chadwick: *Documents in Mycenaean Greek* (Cambridge, 1973); G. Cadogan: *Palaces of Minoan Crete* (London, 1976); M.S.F. Hood and D. Smyth: *Archaeological survey of the Knossos area* (London, 1981); J.W. Graham: *The palaces of Crete* (Princeton, 1987); R. Hägg and N. Marinatos: *The function of the Minoan palaces* (Stockholm, 1987); P. Halstead: 'On redistribution and the origin of the Minoan-Mycenaean palatial economies' *Problems in Greek prehistory*, ed. E.B. Frence and K.A. Wardle (Bristol, 1988), 519–30; J.W. Myers et al.: *The aerial atlas of ancient Crete* (London, 1992).

RJA

Knowth One of three giant Neolithic PASSAGE GRAVES in the famous BOYNE VALLEY group, Knowth was excavated from 1960 by George Eogan and probably dates from the end of the 4th millennium BC. The conical mound has an oval groundplan (80 × 90 m) and covers two opposed megalithic passage-graves: Knowth East (40 m long with an elaborate cruciform and corbelled chamber) and West (24 m long). Like nearby NEWGRANGE, the external perimeter of the mound was lined with kerbstones (127). Knowth also produced one of the finest examples of Neolithic decorative art: a flint macehead delicately carved with spirals and faceted lozenges.

G. Eogan: *Knowth and the passage-tombs of Ireland* (London, 1986)

RJA

Kobadi *see* AFRICA 2

Kobystan *see* CIS AND THE BALTIC STATES

Kodiak tradition Tradition known from the Pacific Eskimo region around Kodiak Island in southwestern Alaska, where it replaced the Ocean Bay tradition around 2500 BC. It is characterized by a wide variety of polished slate implements. The period from 1500 BC to AD 1000 is known as the Kachemak stage of the Kodiak tradition, and is distinguished by an increasingly elaborate material culture. The introduction of aspects of

THULE culture from northern Alaska by AD 1000 marked the end of the Kodiak tradition.

D.E. Dumond: *The Eskimos and Aleuts* (London, 1987).

RP

Kofun period (AD 300–710) *see* JAPAN 4

Koh Ker Court centre of Jayavarman IV (AD 928–942), located 80 km northeast of ANGKOR. Founded as a rival to Angkor, then under the control of Harsavarman I and Isanavarman II, Jayavarman IV was responsible for the construction of Prasat Thom, one of the largest temple mausolea known from the Angkorean period. It was associated with a large reservoir and a range of secular buildings, which matches the usual configuration of a cult centre of this period. The art style, particularly on the stone lintels, represents a number of innovations giving rise to the so-called Koh-Ker style.

L.P. Briggs: 'The ancient Khmer empire', *TAPS* 4/1 (1951), 1–295.

CH

Kojiki One of the two earliest surviving chronicles of Japan, compiled under the Ritsuryo state as part of the legitimization of the ruling dynasty (the other being the Nihon Shoki). The Kojiki was compiled in AD 712 and consists primarily of a brief mythology and genealogical lists. Both the Kojiki and the Nihon Shoki were based on earlier, non-extant texts, the Teiki and Kyuji, and supplemented by four later works (together with which they comprised the Six Ancient Histories). They provide important documentary evidence for the Kofun period (*see* JAPAN 4).

D.L. Philippi, trans.: *Kojiki* (Tokyo and Princeton, 1968).

SK

Kolmogorov-Smirnov test *see* GOODNESS-OF-FIT

Kolomiishchina (Kolomiiscina) *see* TRIPOLYE

Kolomoki North American site, covering some 150 ha in the Chattahoochee River valley of southwestern Georgia, at which the primary occupation is characteristic of the Weeden Island culture (found along the Gulf Coastal Plain in the Late WOODLAND period). Kolomoki consists of a large, rectangular PLATFORM-MOUND (Mound A) at the east end of a plaza, an arc-shaped village surrounding the plaza, and a number of smaller mounds located both inside and outside the village. Mound A measures 60 × 100 m at the base and is 17 m high. Several of the smaller mounds contained evidence of elaborate mortuary events involving the burial of high status individuals. The village occupation and most mound construction date to between AD 300 and 500.

W. Sears: *Excavations at Kolomoki: final report* (Athens, GA, 1956); J. Bense: *Archaeology of the Southeastern United States: Paleoindian to World War I* (New York, 1994), 170–5.

RJE

Kolo rock paintings The most important collection of hunter-gatherer art in eastern Africa, located in the Kondoa district of north-central Tanzania. While the finest concentration is on a series of rock-shelters around Kolo (on the escarpment overlooking the Maasai Steppe), their distribution is much broader, extending from Kondoa into districts to west and northwest. Most of the painted rock-shelters were occupied on several occasions, and some of them possess deep sequences of Late Stone Age deposits spread over several millennia. Rarely however is it possible to correlate individual layers with particular paintings, therefore archaeologists' aspirations of employing the evidence of the paintings, alongside the excavated bones and lithics, to illustrate the succession of cultures and economies of Late Stone Age hunter-gatherers have been frustrated except in a general way. Attempts have been made to reconstruct a sequence of painting styles, especially by noting superpositions; but the results seem to be of limited validity.

H.A. Fosbrooke, L.S.B. Leakey et al.: *Tanganyika Notes and Records* 29 (1950), 1–61; M.D. Leakey: *Africa's vanishing art* (London, 1983).

JS

kom *see* TELL

Kom el-Ahmar *see* HIERAKONPOLIS

Kom Medinet Ghurob *see* GUROB

Kom Ombo (anc. Ombos) Egyptian stone-built temple and settlement site located 40 km north of Aswan, with surviving structural remains dating from at least as early as the 18th dynasty (*c.*1550–1070 BC). There are also a number of

Upper Palaeolithic sites scattered over the surrounding region (*see* SEBILIAN). The Ptolemaic and Roman temple, cleared by Jacques de Morgan in 1893, is an unusual structure divided into two halves, with one dedicated to the crocodile-god Sobek and the other to the hawk-god Haroeris.

J. de Morgan et al.: *Kom Ombos*, 2 vols (Vienna, 1909).

IS

Kom el-Shuqafa *see* ALEXANDRIA

Kondoa *see* KOLO ROCK PAINTINGS

Koobi Fora *see* EAST TURKANA

Koptos (Qift, anc. Kebet) Egyptian site located on the east bank of the Nile about 40 km north of Luxor. The surviving settlement remains at Koptos date back to the beginning of the historical period (*c*.3000 BC), including three colossal limestone statues of the local fertility god Min and various other items of 'preformal' sculpture, which were excavated by Flinders Petrie in an Early Dynastic context at the temple of Min. The upstanding remains of the temple date mainly to the New Kingdom and later (for a description of preformal art at Koptos and other Early Dynastic Egyptian sites see Kemp 1989: 64–91). To the east of the main city site there are cemeteries dating to the late predynastic period (*c*.3300–3000 BC), when NAQADA, situated almost opposite Koptos on the west bank, was the dominant town in the region. The Greek and Roman remains at Koptos have been studied by Claude Traunecker and Laure Pantalacci (1989).

W.M.F. Petrie: *Koptos* (London, 1896). A.J. Reinach: *Rapports sur les fouilles de Koptos* (Paris, 1910); B.J. Kemp: *Ancient Egypt: anatomy of a civilization* (London, 1989); C. Traunecker and L. Pantalacci: 'Le temple d'Isi à El Qual'a près de Coptos', *Akten München 1985* 3, ed.: S. Schoske (Hamburg, 1989), 201–10.

IS

Korolevo Stratified Palaeolithic site, situated on the high terrace of the Tisza river, in the Transcarpathian region of the Western Ukraine near the Hungarian border. The site was discovered in 1974 by V.N. Gladilin and comprises 14 levels, including seven ACHEULEAN and six MOUSTERIAN strata; the upper stratum allegedly belongs to an early stage of the Upper Palaeolithic. The archaeological deposits range in date from the Günz-Mindel interglacial to the Early Würm. The five Acheulean levels at Korolevo show considerable cultural continuity, and seem quite different to the other Acheulean assemblages of central and western Europe: choppers are common, handaxes are atypical, and there is an early development of the LEVALLOIS TECHNIQUE.

V.N. Gladilin: *Problemy rannego paleolita vostočnoi Evropy* [The problems of the early Palaeolithic in Eastern Europe] (Kiev 1976).

PD

Körös culture *see* STARČEVO (STARČEVO-KÖRÖS-CRIŞ) CULTURE

Kostenki-Borshevo Group of Upper Palaeolithic open-air sites situated in the valley of the River Don, 40 km south of the town of Voronezh, in central Russia. Discovered by I.S. Polyakov in 1879, the sites have been excavated since the 1920s by P.P. Efimenko, and later by N.D. Praslov and others. There are 24 sites in the group, 10 of which are multi-layered. At the oldest sites, two distinct cultural traditions are recognizable: the Streletzkian and Spitzinian. The Streletskian, characterized by archaic MOUSTERIAN-like tools, side-scrapers and laurel-leaf points, is represented at sites such as Kostenki 1, stratum 5; Kostenki 6, stratum 5; Kostenki 12, stratum 3. In the latter case, charcoal from stratum 1a (i.e. the layer considerably above the Streletskian level) has been radiocarbon dated to 34700 ± 700 BP (GrN 7758). The fauna included horse, mammoth, reindeer, wolf, red deer, rhinoceros and polar fox.

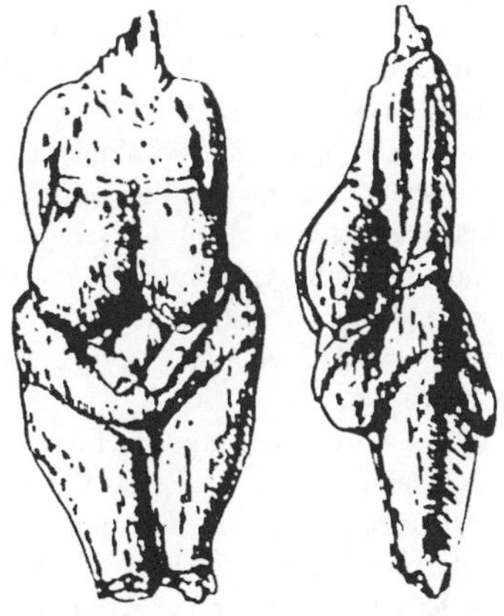

Figure 27 **Kostenki-Borshevo** Upper Palaeolithic 'Venus figurine' from Kostenki-Borshevo, central Russia. *Source*: A. Velichko (ed.): *Arheolojia i paleogeografija pozdnego paleolita russkoi rauniny* (Moscow: Nauka, 1981).

The lithic inventory of the Spitzinian lacks any archaic elements and is characterized by a high proportion of end-scrapers, a variety of burins, and scaled pieces. It has been investigated at two sites: Kostenki 12 (stratum 2) and Kostenki 17 (stratum 2). The latter site was radiocarbon dated to 32000 +2000/–1600 BP (GrN-10512). The faunal remains consist of wolf, horse, bison, reindeer, mammoth, polar fox, hare and antelope-saiga.

A later industry known as the 'Gorodtsovian' is also present at the sites (eg Kostenki 14, stratum 2). It presents a developed Upper Palaeolithic technology with a variety of small end-scrapers, scaled pieces, knives and a peculiar bone industry which includes spatulae. Radiocarbon dating at Kostenki produced several dates; the oldest are 32700 ± 700 BP (GrN-7758) and 25100±150 BP (LE-1437). The fauna includes horse, hare, red deer, rhinoceros, reindeer, mammoth, wolf, antelope-saiga, bison and polar fox. Another distinct industry, of uncertain age but with characteristic points, end-scrapers and scaled pieces (Telmanian), has been identified in the upper stratum of Kostenki 8. The fauna consists of wolf, hare, mammoth, horse, polar fox, cave lion and bison. A sample of charcoal from the underlying stratum 2 has been radiocarbon dated to 27700 ±750 BP (GrN-10509).

A fully developed Upper Palaeolithic tradition (Kostenkian) is represented at the site of Kostenki 1, stratum 1. A series of radiocarbon measurements range from 24100±500 to 21300±400 BP. The fauna consists of mammoth (more than 100 individuals), wolf, hare, polar fox, fox, horse, reindeer, brown bear and musk ox. The lithic inventory includes burins (the most common type), end-scrapers and a characteristic type of shouldered point (the 'Kostenki-type'). Stratum 1 of Kostenki 1 contained over 150 specimen of 'mobiliary art': anthropomorphic and zoomorphic figurines. The female figurines made of mammoth ivory and marl are the most common type. Amongst the zoomorphic types, mammoths, lionesses and brown bears may be recognized; *see also* GRAVETTIAN *and* 'VENUS' FIGURINES.

One of the most outstanding achievements of Soviet archaeology in the 1930s was the discovery of structures consisting of mammoth bones – usually interpreted as dwellings. Two such structures were located in stratum 1 of Kostenki 1. They are oval-shaped (36 by 14–15 m), oriented southeast to northwest, and have a row of hearths along one of the axes. The structures are surrounded by 10–12 storage pits.

N.D. Praslov and A.N. Rogachev, eds: *Paleolit Kostenki-Borševskogo raiona na Donu* [The Palaeolithic of the Kostenki-Borshevo area on the Don] (Leningrad, 1982).

PD

Koster North American prehistoric site located on thick alluvial and colluvial deposits along the eastern edge of the lower Illinois River in Greene County, Illinois. Large-scale excavations conducted during the 1970s revealed that these deposits contained at least 23 stratigraphically distinct cultural horizons dating from the Early Archaic to the Late Prehistoric periods (8000 BC–AD 1000). Investigation of these deposits yielded a continuous record of Holocene soil formation, deposition, and human occupation in west central Illinois. Of particular importance is the late Middle Archaic Helton phase dating from *c.*3800 to 2900 BC. Analysis of cultural materials from the Helton-phase occupation zones has provided important new insights on trends toward sedentism during the mid-Holocene.

T. Cook: *Koster: an artifact analysis of two Archaic phases in West Central Illinois* (Evanston, 1976); J. Brown and R. Vierra: 'What happened in the Middle Archaic? Introduction to an ecological approach to Koster Site archaeology', *Archaic hunters and gatherers in the American Midwest*, ed. J. Phillips and J. Brown (New York, 1983), 165–95; E. Hajic: *Koster Site archaeology I: stratigraphy and landscape evolution* (Kampsville, 1990).

RJE

Kot Diji Type-site of the Kot Dijian, a local culture which preceded the emergence of the INDUS CIVILIZATION. The site is located on an ancient flood channel of the Indus River, about 40 km east of MOHENJO-DARO, and was excavated by F.A. Khan in 1955–7. Sixteen main occupation levels have been identified at Kot Diji; the three uppermost levels date to the Mature Indus period (*c.*2600–1900 BC), including the remains of mud-brick structures containing typical HARAPPAN ceramic forms, steatite seals, terracotta figurines and copper implements. The 13 earlier levels belong to the 'Kot Dijian' period (roughly equivalent to the pre- and early Harappan phases elsewhere in the Indus region), which is dated by three calibrated radiocarbon dates to the first half of the 3rd millennium BC. A thick layer of charred materials separates Kot Dijian from Harappan materials, but it is uncertain whether this apparent disaster was natural or caused by human activity. A large stone and mud-brick perimeter wall was constructed early in the Kot Dijian period, enclosing 5 m thick deposits of superimposed structures.

Typical Kot Dijian artefacts include terracotta figurines, ground stone tools and chert sickle-blades and projectile points, as well as wheel-made ceramics, buff or red in surface colour and decorated with black or brown paint. Distinctive decorative motifs on Kot Diji ceramics include bands of wavy lines and fish-scale patterns. Ceramics in the Kot Diji style occur at a number of contemporaneous sites in the lower Indus area and beyond, including HARAPPA, AMRI, Gumla and Rahmen Dehri (Agrawal 1982).

F.A. Khan: 'Excavations at Kot Diji', *PA* 5 (1965), 11–85; D.P. Agrawal: *The archaeology of India* (Copenhagen, 1982), 129–35.

CS

kouros and kore (pl. *kouroi, korai*) Life-size marble sculptures of nude young men (*kouroi*) and dressed maidens (*korai*) produced in archaic Greece from the early 6th century BC until the early 5th century BC. The early *kouroi* reveal the strong influence of Egyptian conventions for standing male statues – stiff upright posture, strongly symmetrical except for one foot placed in front of the other – but the canon develops to form the basis of classical Greek sculpture. Some of the *kouroi* seem to have been offerings to the Gods Apollo and Poseidon, while the *korai* were strongly associated with the cult of Athena at Athens.

RJA

Kuang-han *see* SAN-HSING-TUI

Ku Bua *see* DVARAVATI CULTURE

Kudaro Group of stratified cave-sites on the southern slopes of the Greater Caucasus, in Southern Ossetia, Georgia. The faunal remains at each of the Kudaro sites are dominated by cave bear. The lower levels contain an ACHEULEAN-type assemblage, recently dated by means of THERMOLUMINESCENCE to 360,000–350,000 BP (Lyubin 1993). The upper levels yielded typical LEVALLOIS-MOUSTERIAN assemblages, radiocarbon dated to 44150±2400/1850 BP (GrN-6079).

Kudaro 3 is situated in the same valley at 1564 m above sea-level. The lower layers contained Acheulean-type industries, overlain by Mousterian deposits. The low concentration of finds suggests that the cave acted as a temporary camp-site.

Tsona Cave is situated on the southern slope of Mount Bub, at an altitude of 2100 m, near the sources of the Kvirila river in Southern Ossetia. Two lower levels contain Acheulean-type industries, while the upper levels produced Levallois-Mousterian assemblages.

V.P. Lyubin: *Moust'erskie kul'tury Kavkaza* [The Mousterian cultures of the Caucasus] (Leningrad, 1977); ——: 'Paleolit Kavkaza' [The Palaeolithic of the Caucasus], *Paleolit Kavkaza i Severnoi Aziii* [The Palaeolithic of the Caucasus and Northern Asia], ed.P.I. Boriskovsky (Leningrad, 1988), 9–142; V.P. Lyubin: 'Hronostratigrafija paleolita Kavkaza' [The chronostratigraphy of the Caucasian Palaeolithic], *Rossijskaja arheologija 1* (1993), 5–14.

PD

kudurru (Akkadian: 'frontier/limit') Type of Mesopotamian boundary stone in the form of a cone, oval or cylinder, decorated with reliefs depicting human figures and religious symbols, and often carved with cuneiform decrees or real estate contracts, as well as lists of threats to those who transgressed them. Textual references indicate that boundary stones were already in use in SUMERIAN times but they became particularly common in northern Mesopotamia during the KASSITE dynasty (*c.*1600–1100 BC) when the AKKADIAN term *kudurru* was introduced. Their inscriptions were often copied onto clay tablets and placed in temples, while the stones themselves served as physical tokens of land ownership, perhaps deriving originally from the rough boulders used to denote the edges of plots of agricultural land.

U. Seidl: 'Die babylonischen *Kudurru*-reliefs', *Baghdader Mitteilungen* 4 (1968), 7–220; I.J. Gelb, P. Steinkeller and R.M. Whiting: *Earliest land tenure systems in the Near East: ancient kudurrus* (Chicago, 1991).

IS

al-Kufa Islamic-period site in Iraq, which includes the only Umayyad period palace studied in the eastern Islamic world. The excavations carried out at al-Kufa in 1938, 1953 and 1956 were limited to the palace, which reflects the strong influence of SASANIAN architecture on early Islamic building. Its construction (in *c.*AD 670) is attributed very specifically to ʿUbayd b. Abihi, the Umayyad governor of Iraq. This interpretation connects the textual evidence on ʿUbayd's well-known career in Iraq as governor with the earliest palace on the site. While plausible, the association of structures and sites with specific individuals and events means that the earlier or subsequent life of a site tends to be ignored. The same process has occurred to some extent at AL-WASIT and to a degree is the result of excavating so that archaeology fills out the historical gaps, rather than allowing the archaeology to lead the interpretation of the site.

M.A. Mustafâr: 'Taqrîr awwalî ʿan at-tanqîb fi'l Kûfa l'l-mawsim al-thâlith', *Sumer* 12 (1956), 2–32. [translated into English by C. Kessler, *Sumer* 19 (1957), 36–65]; K.A.C. Creswell: *Early Muslim architecture* I/1 (Oxford, 1969), 46–58; H. Djait: 'Al-Kûfa', *Encyclopedia of Islam*, 2nd edn (Leiden, 1971); ——: *Al-Kufa: naissance de la ville islamique* (Paris, 1986).

GK

Kujavian barrows Polish earthen barrows of the late 5th and early 4th millennium BC, named after the region of Kujavia (in which they are concentrated). They consist of a trapezoidal or almost triangular mound that is higher and wider at the end oriented to the east. The eastern part of the mound usually covers an individual (occasionally paired or multiple) extended inhumation, which may be accompanied by a simple range of grave goods (collared jars, scrapers, arrowheads, amber beads etc.). The Kujavian graves are thus interesting exceptions to the – apparently – collective burials that are found in most monumental tombs in the Neolithic in Europe. Some of the Kujavian mounds may have contained a wooden chamber, or been built over the site of a wooden structure.

R. Joussaume: *Dolmens for the Dead*, trans. A. and C. Chippindale (London, 1988), 27–30.

RJA

Kuk swamp Situated near Mount Hagen in the Western Highlands of Papua New Guinea, and dating from after about 9000 years BP, this site offers the earliest evidence for agriculture in Oceania. Kuk has provided insight into changing forms of subsistence and the mutual relationship between food production, exchange and social hierarchy.

Around 9000 years ago a clay fan was laid down in the swamp, possibly as a result of erosion on the slopes around the swamp caused by human clearance. This clay fan was drained artificially, providing the first evidence of a tradition of ditch digging in the Highlands which has continued until today (Bayliss-Smith and Golson 1992). The exact use of the swamp at this period is unknown, but it may well have been used for growing root crops such as taro, which respond well to wet conditions. Swamp cultivation is itself just one element in Pleistocene land management in the Highlands: there is also evidence in various areas of tree clearance through burning (Swadling and Hope 1992). Burning may have been carried out in order to sustain areas of grassland useful for hunting, which were threatened by a rising tree-line after the glacial maximum.

The swamp was cultivated in a series of discontinuous phases, with major episodes of use around 6000 and 2000 years ago. These are associated with a complex system of mounds and drains, which together created a mosaic of wet and dry environments, good for growing root crops adapted to both sets of conditions. The discontinuous use of the swamp can be linked with farming practices in the region as a whole: the swamp was used at times of crisis in the dry-land farming system, and was abandoned when innovations (such as soil tillage or tree fallowing) extended the range and increased the yields from the dry-land sector.

Coincident with the first ditches at Kuk is the earliest evidence of the 'wealth economies' of the Highlands, in the form of polished axes and coastal sea shells. The link between production and exchange further explains the history of swamp use. The root crops grown in the swamp may have been used to support pig herds rather than people, at least from 6000 years ago onwards. In the Highlands today, the pig provides the point of articulation between subsistence on the one hand, and exchange and social standing on the other. Pigs are basic to all forms of exchange, and individuals wishing for success in exchange networks must intensify subsistence production to support more pigs. Those with access to swamp lands in the past (and present) could grow large amounts of root crops even when areas outside the swamp were degraded through over-exploitation.

It follows that the history of this early site cannot be explained simplistically in terms of nutritional requirements. Rather, the Kuk evidence shows that throughout the Holocene there has been a dynamic relationship between elements of the farming system and the demands of the social system that it was designed to provision.

J. Friedman and M. Rowlands, eds: *The evolution of social systems* (London, 1977), 419–55; J. Golson: 'No room at the top: agricultural intensification in the New Guinea Highlands', *Sunda and Sahul*, etc. J. Allen et al. (London, 1977); T. Bayliss-Smith and J. Golson: 'A Colocasian revolution in the New Guinea Highlands', *Archaeology in Oceania* 27 (1992), 1–21; P. Swadling and G. Hope: 'Environmental change in New Guinea since human settlement', *The naive lands*, ed. J. Dodson (Melbourne, 1992).

CG

Kuldura Site in the Southern Tadjikistan depression offering the earliest evidence for hominid presence in Central Asia. Discovered and studied by Ranov and Dodonov, the principal evidence consists of a small number of artefacts (including typical choppers and chopping tools) within the 11th and 12th (LOESS) levels of a sequence of fossil soils. Palaeomagnetic measurements revealed a reversed polarity compatible with the Matuyama epoch (i.e. older than 0.7 million years). Artefacts were also found in the upper levels of the fossil soils, the ages of which range from 500,000 to 300,000 BP.

V.A. Ranov: 'Tout commence au Paléolithique', *DA* 185 (1993), 4–13.

PD

Kulli Complex The large mound-site of Kulli, in southern Baluchistan, Pakistan (excavated by Auriel Stein in 1928) forms the type-site of the poorly dated Kulli Complex of the 3rd millennium BC, which includes more than 80 sites widely distributed throughout the Baluchistan highlands. The largest Kulli Complex site is the *c.*50 hectare site of Nindowari, about 15 km south of Kulli, where the excavations of Jean-Marie Casal have revealed HARAPPAN occupation levels preceded by evidence for Kulli Complex remains of a substantial urban settlement, including monumental architecture and an enclosure wall. The roughly contemporary Kulli settlements at Mehi and SHAHI TUMP have cemeteries associated with them. Mehi is a circular mound (about 100 m in diameter) in southern Pakistan, where Auriel Stein, Stuart Piggot and Walter Fairservis excavated a settlement with traces of stone architecture, and an adjacent cemetery in which the cremated bodies were placed in painted ceramic vessels.

Typical Kulli Complex artefacts include painted ceramics decorated in black or black and red, with geometric and naturalistic motifs, such as rows of caprids, fish or bulls, on a variety of bowl- and jar-forms. The sites are also characterized by perforated vessels (identical to those from sites of the INDUS CIVILIZATION), ceramic figurines of bulls and women, triangular cakes of terracotta (which are thought to have been used for the retention of heat in cooking fires), copper tools and carnelian beads, many having close parallels with coeval lowland sites of the INDUS CIVILIZATION. In addition, two Indus stamp seals were recovered in excavations at Nindowari, suggesting intensive interaction between upland Kulli and lowland Indus societies of the 3rd millennium BC. Gregory L. Possehl has therefore suggested that the Kulli complex is best viewed as the highland form of the Indus Civilization (1986:61).

M.A. Stein: 'An archaeological tour in Gedrosia', *Bulletin of the Archaeological Survey of India* 43 (1931), 155–63; S. Piggott: *Prehistoric India* (Harmondsworth, 1950), 96–9, 110–3; J.M. Casal: 'Nindowari: a chalcolithic site in south Baluchistan', *PA* 5 (1966), 51–5; W.A. Fairservis: *The roots of ancient India* (Chicago, 1971), 205–7; G.L. Possehl: *Kulli: an exploration of ancient civilization in Asia* (Durham, CA, 1986).

CS

Kültepe (anc. Kanesh) Tell-site near Kayseri in the Cappadocian plain of central Turkey, which was first identified as Kanesh, an important Bronze Age capital city, when it was excavated by the Czech archaeologist Bedrich Hrozny between 1925 and 1926. The main settlement, dating back to the mid-3rd millennium BC, was already an impressive town of substantial mud-brick buildings and is probably to be equated with the Early Bronze Age city of Nesa mentioned in Mesopotamian texts of the late 3rd millennium BC. The Indo-European inhabitants of Nesa and the surrounding kingdom – the Nesites – gradually took control of the Anatolian plateau and by the 2nd millennium BC had become known as the HITTITES. The archaeological significance of Kültepe derives mainly from Hrozny's discovery of an archive of thousands of Old Assyrian cuneiform tablets in an area of extra-mural settlement dating to the 19th and 20th centuries BC. Out of about a hundred excavated houses, more than seventy have yielded caches of tablets, mainly consisting of business documents.

The archive indicates that although this village at the edge of Kanesh was ostensibly identical to the main city in terms of its material culture, it was in fact a *karum* – a colony of merchants from the Mesopotamian city of Assur about 1600 km to the south, who were exchanging tin and textiles for Anatolian gold, silver and copper. The *karum* was occupied from *c.*1950 to 1850 BC, when it appears to have been destroyed by fire. Surviving texts indicate that there were also Old Assyrian trading colonies at other Hittite cities, including Burushattum (probably AÇEMHÖYÜK), Boghazköy (see HITTITES), and ALISAR HÜYÜK.

B. Hrozny: 'Rapport préliminaire sur les fouilles tchécoslovaques du Kültepe', *Syria* 8 (1927), 1–12; T. Özgüç: *Kültepe-Kanis* (Ankara, 1959); P. Garelli: *Les Assyriens en Cappadoce* (Paris, 1963); L.L. Orlin: *Assyrian colonies in Cappadocia* (The Hague, 1970); M.T. Larsen: *The Old Assyrian city-state and its colonies* (Copenhagen, 1976); M. Ichisar: *Les archives cappadociens du marchand Imdilum* (Paris, 1981); J.N. Postgate: *Early Mesopotamia: society and economy at the dawn of history* (London, 1992), 211–6.

IS

Kumadzulo *see* AFRICA 4.3

Kumma *see* SEMNA

Kunda Mesolithic site in northern Estonia, 110 km east of the city of Tallinn, in the coastal area of the Finnish Gulf. Mesolithic remains were found upon a hill (Lammäsmgi) in the middle of the peat bog, and in the bog itself, in a layer of marl. The bones of elk form 96% of the faunal remains; the rest is brown bear, wild pig, wild horse and seal. Flint and quartz implements include tanged arrowheads of Swiderian type, burins, scrapers, backed bladelets and microliths. The numerous bone and antler tools included a 'Lyngby' antler axe, fishhooks and picks. Radiocarbon dating suggests a calendar date of *c.*7200–4900BC.

The term 'Kunda' is also used to denote a Mesolithic cultural tradition (the 'Kunda culture') that spread across Estonia, northern Latvia and neighbouring regions of northwestern Russia. The earliest site, Pulli, is situated on the bank of the Pärmu river, in southwestern Estonia, in the stratified deposits of a lagoon of the Yoldia Sea. The fauna includes elk, brown bear and beaver. The Kunda-type industry comprises tanged points, points and adzes, and radiocarbon measurements suggest a calender date of *c.*8000 BC.

The stratified site of Narva was originally located on the southern shore of an inshore lagoon, 110 km east of Kunda. The faunal remains were dominated by elk (37–55%) and also included red deer, wild pig, roe deer, brown bear and seal. Radiocarbon dating of charcoal and wood suggests calendar dates of 6650–4900 BC.

The Mesolithic site of Osa, in the depression of Lubana Lake in eastern Latvia, has yielded bones of wild pig (40.5%) and elk (24.5%), and radiocarbon dating of wood from the cultural stratum suggests calendar dates of 6650–4900 BC.

Sites attributed to the Kunda culture have also been found near the town of Luga (130 km south of St Petersburg), and near the town of Velizh, in the upper stretches of the Western Dvina (Smolensk oblast', Russia).

R. Indreko: *Die mittlere Steinzeit in Estland* (Uppsala, 1948); L. and K. Jaanits: 'Frühmesolithische Siedlung von Pulli', *Izvestija AN Estonskoi SSR* 24 (1975), 64–70.

PD

Kura-Araxian Bronze-Age culture spread largely through Transcaucasia and dating from the 4th to 3rd millennium BC. The settlements, both fortified and unfortified, were located mainly in the intermontane depressions of the Greater and Little Caucasus (the Kura, Kura-Araxes and Ararat plain), penetrating into the surrounding mountains. Several local variants are distinguishable (Sagona 1984): rectangular wattle-and-daub houses reinforced with posts are characteristic for Georgia, while in Armenia, mud-brick circular buildings with adjoining non-residential structures are more typical. In the more mountainous areas, settlements tend to be fortified.

The economy was agricultural and well-developed, with draught animals commonly employed and a wide spectrum of crops including bread, spelt, club and emmer wheats; hulled and naked barley; Italian millet; flax, grape-wine and various fruits. Transhumant stock-breeding was practised, and sheep and goat were the principal domesticates. A key feature of the Kura-Araxian tradition was the developed metallurgy and metal-working of arsenic bronze and other copper alloys, based on the local ores. Workshops in Transcaucasia produced large quantities of armaments and working tools (various types of axes, knives, daggers, spearheads, sickles, awls, chisels) and ornaments (spirals, bracelets, pendants, pins, bears, ear-rings etc.). Another peculiarity of the Kura-Araxian assemblage is its pottery: silvery, lustrous black-burnished cups and jars, decorated with spirals.

Kura-Araxian sites are known in northwestern Iran (Geoy Tepe, Yanik Tepe, Godin Tepe) and in the upper Euphrates basin in eastern Turkey (Karaz, Putlur, Guzelova etc.). Assemblages similar to the Kura-Araxian are attested at KHIRBET KERAK-type sites near the Sea of Galilee and on the Plain of Antioch. Radiocarbon dating of samples from the Transcaucasian sites suggests calendar dates in the range 4000–2500 BC; in Anatolia of around 4400–2000 BC; and in Syria and Palestine of about 3600–2200 BC.

A.G. Sagona: *The Caucasian region in the Early Bronze Age*, BAR IS 214 (Oxford, 1984); K.Kh. Kushnareva: *Južnyi kavkaz v IX–II tys. do n.e.* [The Southern Caucasus in the 8th–2nd millennium BC] (St. Petersburg, 1993); P.M. Dolukhanov: *Environment and ethnicity in the Ancient Middle East* (Aldershot, 1994).

PD

kurgan cultures *see* CATACOMB GRAVE CULTURE; PIT-GRAVE CULTURE; SCYTHIANS; TIMBER-GRAVE CULTURE

Kurnub *see* NABATAEANS

Kuroimine A Late Kofun village site in Gunma prefecture, Japan, part of a landscape buried in the mid-6th century AD by a violent eruption of Mount Haruna. Roads, fields and habitation enclosures containing storage facilities, cattle sheds and houses have been recovered providing detailed information about the lives of ordinary people of the period.

H. Tsude: 'Kuroimine', *Ancient Japan*, ed. R. Pearson (Washington, D.C., 1992), 223–5.

SK

el-Kurru Napatan funerary site on the Dongola reach of the Nile in Upper Nubia. The earliest part of the cemetery at el-Kurru (*c.*1000–751 BC) consists of the tumuli of the rulers of the kingdom of Kush, the political centre of which was the district of NAPATA (which also incorporates Sanam, Gebel Barkal and NURI). The tombs of later Napatan rulers at el-Kurru (*c.*751–653 BC) consisted of small Egyptian-style pyramidal superstructures, each with an undecorated rectangular funerary chapel built against its east face. The subterranean burial chambers, all of which have been plundered, were reached by long flights of steps from an entrance at ground-level to the east of the pyramid. There is also a group of 24 horse burials dating to the same period as the pyramidal tombs. In about 653 BC the Napatan royal cemetery transferred to Nuri, about 15 km to the north.

D. Dunham: *The royal cemeteries of Kush*, I: *El-Kurru* (Boston, 1950); R. Morkot: 'The empty years of Nubian history', *Centuries of darkness*, ed. P. James et al. (London, 1991), 204–19.

IS

Kush *see* KERMA; EL-KURRU; NAPATA; NUBIA; NURI

Kuyunjik, Tell *see* NINEVEH

Kwale *see* EARLY IRON AGE

Kwatna Locality on the central coast of British Columbia halfway between Bella Bella and Bella Coola, incorporating a group of sites which provide evidence of the last 2000 years of local prehistory to *c.*AD 1840. The sites illustrate the value of the direct ethnographic approach to survey in that they were identified from Bella Coola oral tradition (McIlwraith 1948: 19–20) and then located by archaeological survey (Hobler 1990).

T.F. McIlwraith: *The Bella Coola Indians* (Toronto, 1948); P.M. Hobler: 'Prehistory of the Central Coast of British Columbia', *Handbook of North American Indians* VII, ed. W. Suttles (Washington, D.C. 1990), 298–305.

RC

L

Laang Spean Cave located in the valley of the Stung Sangker in western Cambodia. Excavations there by Mourer revealed five cultural layers; the intermittent occupation has been dated by radiocarbon from 7000 BC to about AD 900. During the second occupation phase (4000 BC), there was a rich stone industry matching in many respects that described in northern Vietnam as HOABINHIAN, together with cord-marked and impressed potsherds. The occupants exploited aquatic resources, for the remains of crabs, turtles and shellfish were recovered. The foragers of Laang Spean also hunted rhinoceros, deer, cattle and monkey.

C. and R. Mourer: 'Laang Spean and the prehistory of Cambodia', *MQRISA* 3 (1977), 29–56.

CH

Labná *see* PUUC

Lachish (Tell ed-Duweir) Palestinian city located about 45 km southwest of JERUSALEM, which was first occupied by troglodites in the late Chalcolithic period (*c.*3500 BC), but particularly flourished during the Bronze Age and early Iron Age (*c.*1450–587 BC). In the 18th century BC the settlement was transformed into a HYKSOS fortress, but by the early 16th century BC it was in the hands of the Egyptians. Subsequent phases were characterized by Canaanite, Israelite, Persian and Hellenistic material.

H. Torczyner et al.: *Lachish* I (London, 1938); O. Tufnell, C.H. Inge and L. Harding: *Lachish* II–IV (London, 1940–58); Y. Aharoni: *Investigations at Lachish (Lachish V)* (Tel Aviv and Tokyo, 1975).

IS

lacquer (*chi'i*, *qi*) Coloured varnish made from the sap of the *rhus verniciflua* tree (indigenous to China and Japan) and applied to such materials as wood, bamboo, bronze and silk. Remnants of lacquered wood have been excavated from burials as early as Shang times (*c.*2000–1122 BC) in China. Although offering the artist a medium for practically complete freedom of expression, there is little suggestion of such aesthetic use of lacquer in the MIDDLE STATES prior to EASTERN CHOU times (771–255 BC). In these earlier periods the art-forms of lacquer-ware were as restricted and conventionalized as the contemporary bronze decoration.

In the Eastern Chou period there was extensive use of lacquer-ware; CHU'U sites have yielded large quantities and varieties of vessels and other artefacts with exquisite paintings in lacquer depicting mythical beings and intricate interlacery with a marked freedom of artistic expression. Bronze vessels with cast-in recesses, filled with a paste of powdered silica, natural copper ores, and other materials (*see* TSENG HOU YI TOMB), were usually covered with a layer of lacquer. Occasionally the entire surface of a bronze vessel was painted with lacquer, as in finds from such sites as the Western Han Lo-po-wan tombs near Kuei-hsien, Kwang-hsi (Anon. 1988: pls iv–vii). In Han times (206 BC–AD 220) even greater artistic attainments are to be seen as, for example, the coffin lid in Tomb 1 of the MA-WANG-TUI site, Ch'ang-sha.

Shang Ch'eng-tso: *Ch'ang-sha ch'u-t'u Ch'u ch'i-ch'i t'u-lu* [Illustrations of Ch'u lacquerware unearthed in Ch'ang-sha] (Peking, 1957); Li Cheng-kuang, ed.: *Han-tai ch'i-chi'i yi-shu* [The art of lacquer of the Han Period] (Peking, 1987); Anon.: *Kuang-hsi Kuei-hsien Lo-po-wan Han-mu* [The Han tombs of Lo-po-wan, Kuei-hsien, Kuang-hsi] (Peking, 1988).

NB

'lacustrine tradition' *see* AQUATIC CIVILIZATION

Laetoli Early hominid site in Tanzania, located on the edge of the Serengeti plain very close to OLDUVAI gorge, where Mary Leakey excavated a sequence of Pleistocene and Pliocene aeolian tuffs with a date of 3.5–4 million years ago. She discovered remains of gracile Australopithecine jaws and teeth (either *AUSTRALOPITHECUS afarensis* or *africanus*), which are probably of similar date and species to the fossil remains excavated at HADAR in

Ethiopia. A number of footprints left by hominids and other animals in associated deposits of ashy mud have also provided crucial evidence of *Australopithecus*' bipedalism. The Laetoli deposits contained no artefacts, unlike the Hadar deposits, where a few stone tools – of a somewhat later date than the Australopithecine remains – were found.

M.D. Leakey and R.L. Hay: 'Pliocene footprints in the Laetolil beds at Laetoli, northern Tanzania', *Nature* 278 (1979), 317–23; M.P. Leakey and J.M. Harris, eds: *Laetoli: a Pliocene site in northern Tanzania* (Oxford, 1987).

JS

Laga Oda Site of two painted rock-shelters in the Dire Dawa region of Ethiopia, dating to at least 16,000 BP. The paintings include depictions of many different types of animals, such as cattle, giraffes, antelopes, elephants and buffalo. One of these incorporates a sequence of almost a thousand painted figures stretching for about 50 m along the top of the wall. The occupation debris excavated inside the shelters comprises artefacts of the WILTON INDUSTRY.

S. Cole: *The prehistory of East Africa* (London, 1964), 242; J.D. Clark and M.A.J. Williams: 'Recent archaeological research in southeastern Ethiopia, 1974–5', *AE* 11 (1978), 19–42.

IS

Lagash (Tell el-Hiba) Large tell-site in southern Iraq, consisting of the remains of the SUMERIAN capital city of the Lagash Dynasty (*c.*2570–2342 BC). It was first excavated by Robert Koldewey in 1887, who suggested that it was only a cemetery-site, but American excavations since 1968 have produced firm evidence that this site, rather than TELLOH (actually ancient Girsu), was the location of the capital of the city-state of Lagash. The excavated structures include a temple of Ningirsu (named Bagara) and an oval sanctuary dedicated to the goddess Innana (named Ibgal).

V.E. Crawford: 'Lagash', *Iraq* 36 (1974), 29–35; D.P. Hansen: 'Al Hiba, 1968/76', *Sumer* 34 (1978), 72–85.

IS

Lagreich *see* AFRICA 2

el-Lahun Located at the eastern edge of the FAIYUM REGION, about 100 km southeast of Cairo, el-Lahun is the site of the pyramid complex of Senusret II (*c.*1897–1878 BC) and, beside its valley temple, the remains of ancient Hetep-Senusret, a rectangular, planned town, measuring about 384 by 335 m. This settlement is thought to have initially housed the officials responsible for the royal mortuary cult but eventually appears to have developed into a town with its own *haty-ʿ* (mayor). The site has also yielded a large number of HIERATIC papyri, dating to the late Middle Kingdom (*c.*1850–1750 BC) and ranging from religious documents to private correspondence.

W.M.F. Petrie: *Kahun, Gurob and Hawara* (London, 1890); ——: *Illahun, Kahun and Gurob* (London, 1891); ——, G. Brunton and M.A. Murray: *Lahun* II (London, 1923); B.J. Kemp: *Ancient Egypt: anatomy of a civilization* (London, 1989), 149–57.

IS

Lake Eyasi *see* AFRICA 5

Lake Mojave Complex *see* STEMMED POINT TRADITION

Lake Mungo One of a series of relict Pleistocene lakes in western New South Wales, Australia, last full around 15,000 years ago. A dune system formed to the northeast of the lake on which people camped, and these deposits contain prehistoric remains dating back to 35,000 years ago. The remains include a human burial (with ochre) and a cremation, as well as large numbers of stone tools. Fish, shellfish and birds (derived from the lake) are found, as well as terrestrial fauna; some remains are deposited as single episodes, others as longer term deposits which may represent base camps. The main species of fish to be found, golden perch, are mostly of a similar size, suggesting the use of nets; a number of bone points have been found which may have been netting needles. After the lakes dried up, human activity declined markedly, and represents a major shift in the human exploitation of western New South Wales.

J. Bowler et al.: 'Pleistocene human remains from Australia', *WA* 2 (1970), 39–60; A. Ross et al.: 'The peopling of the arid zone: human-environment interactions', *The naive lands*, ed. J. Dodson (Melbourne, 1992), 76–114.

CG

Lake Nasser In 1902 the construction of the first Aswan Dam at the 1st Nile cataract in Upper Egypt led to the creation of the vast reservoir of Lake Nasser, threatening to engulf many of the archaeological sites of Lower Nubia. The American archaeologist George Reisner was therefore appointed as the director of the first international 'salvage campaign' in the history of archaeology. It was this 'Archaeological Survey of Nubia' that produced the first evidence for several phases of indigenous Nubian culture (the so-called A, B, C and X Groups), thus effectively refuting the commonly held belief that ancient Nubia was culturally dependent on Egypt.

From 1929 to 1934 there was a second Survey of Nubia, as a result of the enlargement of the Aswan Dam in 1932, but the most impressive campaign – necessitated by the construction of the much larger High Dam at Aswan (the Sadd al-ʿAli) which was completed in 1971 – took place during the 1960s and early 1970s. The new dam, over 4 km wide and about 100 m high, transformed Lake Nasser into a much larger reservoir, over 500 km in length. Whereas the two previous major phases of Nubian exploration had concentrated on the simple recording of threatened sites by mapping and excavation, the UNESCO-sponsored Nubian Salvage Campaign also included the ambitious dismantling of 14 entire stone temple complexes (including ABU SIMBEL, Aksha, Amada, Beit el-Wali, Derr, Kalabsha and PHILAE) so that they could be moved and rebuilt in new locations outside the area to be covered by the expanded Lake Nasser.

Apart from the accumulation of new data concerning the early history of Nubia, the Campaign acted as an important catalyst by focusing the attentions of archaeologists in the Nile valley on the hitherto-neglected study of towns and cities, thus also ensuring that many Egyptologists were trained in the more exacting scientific methods and approaches required by settlement archaeology.

A.E. Weigall: *Report on the antiquities of Lower Nubia* (Cairo, 1907); W.Y. Adams: *Nubia: corridor to Africa*, 2nd edn (Princeton, 1984), 81–90; T. Säve-Söderbergh, ed.: *Temples and tombs of ancient Nubia* (London, 1987).

IS

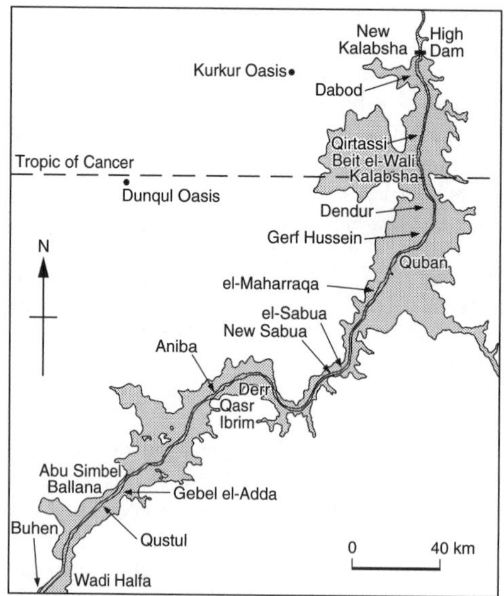

Map 24 **Lake Nasser** The principal archaeological sites in the area flooded by Lake Nasser, Egypt.

Lake Turkana *see* EAST TURKANA

Lalibela Medieval religious and urban site, located to the east of Lake Tana in the Ethiopian highlands, which was the capital of the Zagwe dynasty during the 12th and 13th centuries AD. The twelve distinctive rock-cut churches of the Lalibela region, first described by the Portuguese explorer Alvares in the early 16th century, owe a great deal to the architecture of the preceding Axumite period (*see* AXUM). All of the churches are basilican in plan, apart from the cruciform church of St George, a spectacular 10.6-metre-high structure hewn from one block of stone and located in a deep pit.

M. della Corte: *Lalibela* (Rome, 1940); I. Bidder: *Lalibela* (Cologne, 1959); G. Gerster: *Churches in rock* (London and New York, 1970).

IS

Lalibela Cave Neolithic rock-shelter located to the east of Lake Tana in the Ethiopian highlands, where material dating to the mid-1st millennium BC was excavated by Joanne Dombrowski. The inhabitants of the shelter appear to have had a subsistence base including cattle herding and the cultivation of barley, chickpea and certain legumes.

J. Dombrowski: 'Preliminary report on excavations in Lalibela and Natchabiet Caves, Begemeder', *AE* 8 (1970), 21–9.

IS

lamassu Akkadian term used to refer to the colossal sculptures of human-headed winged bulls or lions which were erected as guardian figures in the entrances to temples and palaces at late ASSYRIAN sites such as KHORSABAD and TELL NIMRUD, as well as at later Achaemenid sites such as PERSEPOLIS.

IS

Lamoka North American prehistoric site located in Schuler County in central New York state. Archaeological investigations conducted at Lamoka

Lake Site by William Ritchie in the 1920s and 1930s led to the definition of the 'Lamoka Complex', characterized by choppers, narrow-bladed, small projectile points, bevelled adzes and antler pendants. Radiocarbon dates indicate that the Lamoka Lake phase dates to 2500–2000 BC. In 1932, Ritchie used his Lamoka Lake data to define the Archaic Stage, denoting an early level of cultural development based on hunting, fishing and gathering of wild plant foods, and lacking pottery, agriculture and the smoking pipe.

W. Ritchie: 'The Lamoka Lake Site', *Researches and Transactions of the New York State Archaeological Association* (New York, 1932); ——: *The archaeology of New York State* (New York, 1969).

RJE

landscape archaeology School of archaeology which lays particular emphasis on the wider geographical and topographical surroundings of archaeological sites. Even in the early 19th century, the Swedish prehistorian Jens Worsaae was insisting that archaeological remains could only be understood in relation to the ancient environment. This kind of wide-focused environmental FUNCTIONALISM exemplified by Robert Gradmann's study of the links between LOESS soils and Neolithic settlements, was undoubtedly the forerunner of landscape archaeology. Although there has been a tendency, for much of the 20th century, to regard single, isolated sites as the real focal points of archaeology, this view has been gradually weakened by such methodological developments as AERIAL PHOTOGRAPHY, SPATIAL ANALYSIS and, more recently, GIS and 'space syntax' (*see* FORMAL ANALYSIS). On a methodological level, by the late 1960s Claudio Vita-Finzi and Eric Higgs (1970) had introduced the concept of 'SITE CATCHMENT ANALYSIS', involving the quantitative analysis of the economic potential of territory surrounding a settlement site. The later development of foraging theory attempts to apply similar decision analysis to the procurement strategies of hunter-gatherers. In the 1970s, landscape archaeology was established as a full subdiscipline, when Aston and Rowley (1974) applied landscape-oriented methodology to the study of boundaries and field systems in the English Middle Ages, and when Bowen and Fowler (1978) analysed Iron Age patterns of land-use.

In the 1990s, the influence of such theoretical approaches as STRUCTURALISM, POST-STRUCTURALISM and PHENOMENOLOGY has led many archaeologists and anthropologists to adopt less economic and functional views of the archaeological landscape, concentrating instead on attempts to understand the ways in which natural and architectural features were experienced by humans in the past, and how the ancient modification of the landscape can be interpreted as a reflection of ancient cognitive processes (see Bender 1993; Hirsch and O'Hanlon 1995).

C. Vita-Finzi and E.S. Higgs: 'Prehistoric economy in the Mount Carmel area of Palestine: site catchment analysis', *PPS* 36 (1970), 1–37; M. Aston and T. Rowley: *Landscape archaeology: an introduction to fieldwork techniques on post-Roman landscapes* (Newton Abbot, 1974); C. Bowen and P. Fowler: *Prehistoric land allotment* (Oxford, 1978); M. Aston: *Interpreting the landscape: landscape archaeology in local studies* (London, 1985); B. Bender, ed.: *Landscape: politics and perspectives* (Oxford and Providence, 1993); P. Hirsch and M. O'Hanlon, eds: *The anthropology of landscape: between place and space* (Oxford, 1995).

IS

Lanet *see* SIRIKWA HOLES

Langi tombs *see* TONGA

Lang Rongrien Cave located in Krabi Province, southern Thailand, with deposits from the Pleistocene and Holocene. The excavator, Douglas Anderson, identified four stratigraphic units. The uppermost included four burials with a material culture similar to that from BAN KAO to the north. These overlay a series of lenses incorporating HOABINHIAN material, dated 7500–8300 BP, that contained faunal remains indicating access to the sea. Below these, there was a 1.5 m deposit of rockfall which concealed a series of layers that included hearths and stone tools dating as far back as 37,000 BP. It is most unusual to find a sequence which covers the end of the Pleistocene through to the Holocene in Southeast Asia, and Anderson has been able to relate the material culture to the changing climate and sea level during that period.

D. Anderson: *Lang Rongrien rockshelter* (Philadelphia, 1990).

CH

L'Anse aux Meadows Site at the northern tip of Newfoundland, where Norse colonists from Greenland constructed and briefly occupied a small settlement approximately 1000 years ago. Eight turf-walled structures, similar to examples known from Greenland and Iceland, were found to contain a small number of Norse artefacts. The only site in the Americas with evidence of a Norse occupation, L'Anse aux Meadows is often cited as proof that

Newfoundland was the 'Vinland' of the Norse sagas.
R. McGhee: *Canada rediscovered* (Hull, 1991).
RP

Lapita cultural complex Pacific archaeological assemblages characterized by distinctive pottery decorated by fine-toothed stamps, shell artefacts, obsidian and polished stone axes found from the Bismarck Archipelago to Tonga and Samoa. Dating from 3500 to 2000 BP, Lapita represents the first colonization of many areas of the western Pacific, and is regarded as one of the principal sources of Polynesian culture. At the same time, opinions differ as to whether the complex constitutes evidence for a specialized trade item, a single widespread (Austronesian-speaking?) group or even 'some entity which is archaeologically recognizable, without having any clear social equivalent' (Chippendale 1996: 733). *See also* MUSSAU ISLANDS, OCEANIA 2, TALASEA.
R.C. Green: 'Lapita', *The prehistory of Polynesia*, ed. J. Jennings (Canberra, 1979), 27–60; P.V. Kirch and T. Hunt: *Archaeology of the Lapita cultural complex* (Seattle, 1988); M. Spriggs, ed.: *Lapita design, form and composition* (Canberra, 1990); J.C. Galipaud, ed.: *Poterie Lapita et peuplement* (Nouméa, 1992); C. Chippendale: Editorial, *Antiquity* 70 (1996), 729–39; W.R. Ambrose: 'Contradictions in Lapita pottery, a composite clone', *Antiquity* 71 (1997), 525–38.
IS/CG

Larsa *see* ISIN-LARSA PERIOD

Lascaux Most famous of France's decorated caves of the Upper Palaeolithic, situated near Montignac in the Dordogne. Discovered in 1940, the parietal art consists of more than 600 paintings and 1500 engravings, many of which may date from the same period (according with Leroi-Gourhan's style III). The 'Hall of the Bulls' is covered with paintings, including four massive black aurochs over 5 m in length, and an unidentified or 'mythological' animal with two very straight horns. The 'Axial Gallery' includes the famous image of a leaping cow and some very elegant horses. Deeper into the cave is a scene, possibly with narrative meaning – highly unusual in Upper Palaeolithic art – showing a bird-headed man associated with a bison (which he appears to have speared), with a bird-symbol on a 'stick' nearby. In another apparent 'scene' in the 'Nave' area of the cave, the heads of a group of deer are shown; although the interpretation is uncertain, they seem to be in the act of lifting their heads above the water as they swim across a river.

At Lascaux the animals tend to have disproportionately large bodies, and small heads and legs – sometimes referred to as the 'Lascaux style'. The artists may have used scaffolding to make some depictions that are high up on the cave walls, and they left behind them numerous pieces of pigment mineral (ochre, manganese dioxide), simple lamps and tools that may have been used for engraving. Unfortunately the archaeological layers in the cave were never fully excavated and are now largely lost, but evidence of radiocarbon dating, pollen analysis and tool typology suggest that some (not necessarily all) of the paintings may date to around 15,000 BC.

Lascaux is now closed to the public, but Lascaux II, a replica of the Hall of the Bulls and the Painted Gallery, has been created nearby. Lascaux II offers an example of a radical solution to a common dilemma in the management of ancient monuments – how to balance the demands of site conservation with those of public access and education.
A. Leroi-Gourhan et al.: *Lascaux inconnu,* XIIe supplément à Gallia Préhistoire (Paris, 1979); —— and ——: *Lascaux: art et archéologie* (Perigueux, 1984); B. and D. Delluc: 'Lascaux II: a faithful copy', *Antiquity* 58 (1984), 194–6; M. Ruspoli et al.: *The case of Lascaux: the final photographic record* (London, 1987).
RJA

laser microprobe Generic term for analytical techniques which incorporate a power laser to excite or sample small areas on a material. The laser excitation may be coupled with a variety of techniques including optical emission spectroscopy (OES) and INDUCTIVELY COUPLED PLASMA-ATOMIC EMISSION SPECTROMETRY (ICPAES).
MC

lashkari Bazar Islamic palace in Afghanistan dated to the 10th–12th centuries AD, which constitutes an important link back to Abbasid and central Asian traditions of architecture and painting (*see* ASIA 1). Lashkari Bazar characterizes the cultural milieu of the Ghaznavid rulers of eastern Iran and modern Afghanistan and the context in which the Seljuk Turks were Islamicized before going on to dominate Iran, Iraq and Anatolia in the 11th and 12th centuries. The Ghaznavid palace shows the impact of Abbasid influence from Baghdad and SAMARRA on the courts of these aspiring Muslim princes. For example, its axial symmetry is a recurrent characteristic of the Islamic palace tradition represented at AL-KUFA and Samarra, and ultimately derives from SASANIAN models. One of the most important discoveries at the palace was the group of wall-paintings that were excavated in the throne room, representing military figures standing in formal attendance on the prince. Their dress provides a good indication of textile decoration for the period and the frontality of their pose links them with pre-Islamic murals from central Asia.

D. Schlumberger et al.: *Lashkari Bazar: une résidence royale ghaznide et ghoride* (Paris, 1978).

GK

Las Vegas Semi-sedentary culture in coastal Ecuador from *c.*7000 to 4500 BC, which was gathering or beginning to cultivate corn (*Zea mays*) and which had elaborate burial customs including the combination of past secondary burials with new ones and, in one case, the burial of a pair of lovers in an intimate position.

K.E. Stothert: *La prehistoria temprana de la península de Santa Elena, Ecuador: cultura Las Vegas* (Guayaquil, 1988).

KB

La Tène Archaeological site on the shore of Lake Neuchâtel, Switzerland, that has lent its name to the second part of the Iron Age in central and western Europe. The La Tène period begins after the HALLSTATT period ends in the 5th century BC and continues until the Roman Conquest; it is usually divided into La Tène I (*c.*480–220 BC), La Tène II (*c.*220–120 BC), and La Tène III (120 BC – Roman Conquest).

From at least the 1850s, the inundated site of La Tène was well known to antiquarians as a source of interesting objects. The lowering of water levels in Lake Neuchâtel in the 1870s allowed Emil Vouga to make a series of excavations, followed by his son Paul Vouga in 1907–17. The thousands of objects recovered included decorated and undecorated weaponry (especially swords, decorated scabbards), other iron implements, pottery etc. Although there is evidence at the site of what may be two small bridges, wooden walkways, and several buildings, it is still not entirely clear what kind of site La Tène was – settlement, trading harbour, or (most probably) a place where votive objects were ritually deposited into the shallow waters of the lake. Most of the objects date from the middle of the La Tène period in the 3rd century BC, so the site of La Tène is not representative of the La Tène period as a whole.

The distinctively decorated objects found at La Tène came to form the typesite for a distinctive La Tène art-style (*see* CELTIC ART) found throughout much of Europe – from north Italy to south Poland, from Britain to Romania – from the early 5th century BC (conventionally, after 480 BC). While some elements of this style, and material culture generally, is related to that of the preceding HALLSTATT phase D, three major socio-economic changes help to define the La Tène period. Firstly, the upper Danube region ceases to be the epicentre of rich burials and exotic objects; instead the region notable for wealthy objects is in the Hunsrück-Eifel area of Germany, straddling the lower Mosel river. Hallstatt D burials are also known in this area, but it is only from the early 5th century BC that burials in this region start to be accompanied by exceptionally rich objects. Other rich areas during the La Tène include the central Rhine region, Champagne in eastern France, Belgium and the Thames valley in England.

Secondly, while strikingly rich objects, such as gold torcs and bronze vessels, mark out certain elite burials, even the Hunsrück-Eifel La Tène inhumations do not exhibit the huge tumuli and massive clusters of rich objects so characteristic of the classic Hallstatt D burials; in the La Tène period, the impression is of wealth spread more consistently and evenly across the regional elites. Although barrow burial does persist in the Hunsrück-Eifel, in most areas La Tène burials are simpler extended inhumations in small cemeteries. Of the burials accompanied by grave goods, the men have weapons (sword, spear, shield) and/or jewellery usually in the form of a brooch. The women tend to have multiple brooches and other female-specific jewellery such as bracelets, torcs and finger-rings.

Thirdly, while objects continued to be imported from Greek and Etruscan cities of the Mediterranean, they seem to have been accessed from northern Italy, via the Alps, rather than from the Greek trading entrepot of Massalia. In the Hallstatt period, the impression is of a small number of individually powerful chieftains dealing directly with traders from Massalia – and thus occasionally being offered extraordinary gifts such as the Vix krater. In the La Tène period, the impression is of an elite with a less dependent trading relationship with the Mediterranean world.

Studies indicate that the richest burials of the Hunsrück-Eifel area seem related to distributions of haematite iron ore, indicating one possible source of wealth through control of an increasingly important raw material. As in the Hallstatt period, salt extraction proved a source of wealth, as evidenced by the objects from Dürrnberg bei Hallein near Salzburg. Iron and salt were probably more important in local trade, while gold and slaves and fine weaponry perhaps contributed to the trade south of the Alps.

Hillforts continued to be a feature of the settlement hierarchy, along with smaller villages and single homesteads. However, in the 3rd and 2nd centuries BC, some settlements such as MANCHING in Bavaria (over 380 ha) developed to an unprecedented size and were apparently permanently and densely occupied. These characteristics, sometimes described as 'proto-urban', seem to have been driven by trade (Manching is close to the Danube and controlled an important crossing point) and to a lesser extent by a growth in craft production and specialisation. Whether such OPPIDA qualify as 'proto-urban' depends largely on how that term is defined: there is some evidence to suggest specialised craft production (metal-working, glass-making, amber-working etc), the minting of coins, dedicated craft areas, dedicated 'shops' or trading and storage spaces, and semi-organized planning of the settlement layout; there is no evidence to suggest strict planning, public buildings, carefully thought out drainage systems, properly surfaced roads etc.

P. Vouga: *La Tène: monographie de la station* (Leipzig, 1923); J.M. De Navarro: *The finds from the site of La Tène I: Scabbards and the swords found in them* (London, 1972); B. Cunliffe: *Greeks, Romans and Barbarians: spheres of interaction* (London, 1988); P. Nicholson: *Iron Age pottery production in the Hunsrück-Eifel-Kultur*, BAR IS 501 (Oxford, 1989); N. Roymans: *Tribal societies in northern Gaul* (Amsterdam, 1990).

RJA

Laugerie Haute/Basse Laugerie Haute and Laugerie Basse are two rockshelters of the Upper Palaeolithic near Les Eyzies in the Dordogne, France. Laugerie Basse provided its 19th century excavators with a number of superb art objects, apparently from the later Magdalenian. The 'Venus impudique,' an ivory figurine lacking the usual exaggerated breasts but with a carefully detailed pubic region, was one of the earliest pieces of *art mobilier* to be discovered (1864). A particularly interesting antler plaque is engraved with a swollen-bellied woman lying beneath the legs of a deer. Laugerie Haute yielded a much longer archaeological sequence from late Aurignacian, GRAVETTIAN and SOLUTREAN through into the early MAGDALENIAN.

H. Delporte: *L'image de la femme dans l'art prèhistorique* (Paris, 1979), 32–6.

RJA

Laussel Upper Palaeolithic rock shelter near Les Eyzies in the Dordogne, France, famed for a series of carved blocks uncovered during the site's excavation (1908–14). The blocks were found partly covered by a GRAVETTIAN deposit, but they could conceivably have been produced in an earlier period. The carvings form a frieze, consisting of a few engravings of animals, three low-relief 'Venuses', one male and an enigmatic double figure. The most striking 'Venus' stands plump and nude, holding up a bison or ibex horn.

G. Lalanne and J. Bouyssonie: 'Le gisement paléolithique de Laussel', *L'Anthropologie* 50 (1946); H. Delporte: *L'image de la femme dans l'art préhistorique* (Paris, 1979), 60–6.

RJA

La Venta Gulf coast OLMEC site in Tabasco, Mexico, with primarily late Middle Formative occupation (*c.*1000–600 BC). The site is best known from early excavations in Complex A, a group of earthen mounds arranged around a plaza on a north-south axis of symmetry. Particularly notable are La Venta's numerous caches and 'massive offerings' of deeply buried deposits of jade and serpentine, including mosaic jaguar masks and an elaborate stone sculptural tradition. Another distinctive feature of the site are the four 'colossal heads' carved from massive boulders of basalt, each weighing many tons. These heads wear helmet-like head-dresses with distinctive motifs (e.g. a jaguar paw or eagle talons) and have such highly individualized features as to be considered portraits, probably of rulers (see Clewlow et al. 1967; Grove 1981).

C.W. Clewlow, Jr., R.A. Cowan, J.F. O'Connell and C. Benemann: *Colossal heads of the Olmec culture*, Contributions of the University of California Archaeological Research Facility 4 (Berkeley, 1967); R.F. Heizer, P. Drucker and J.A. Graham: *Investigations at La Venta, 1967*, Contributions of the University of California Archaeological Research Facility 520 (Berkeley, 1968), 1–34; D.C. Grove: 'Olmec monuments; mutilation as a clue to meaning', *The Olmec and their neighbors, essays in memory of Matthew W. Stirling*, ed. E.P. Benson (Washington, D.C., 1981), 49–68; W.F. Rust and R.J. Sharer: 'Olmec settlement data from La Venta, Tabasco, Mexico', *Science* 242 (1988) 102–4.

PRI

LBK *see* LINEARBANDKERAMIK

lead-210 (^{210}Pb) dating (1) Scientific dating technique applicable to lead and lead white pigment and based on isotopes in the ^{238}U decay series (see also URANIUM SERIES DATING). When in equilibrium, ^{226}Ra and ^{210}Pb have equal activities (decay rate per gramme). The smelting of lead ores leaves little ^{226}Ra in the lead. The decay of the ^{210}Pb is then dominated by its 22-year HALF-LIFE as it returns to equilibrium with the new ^{226}Ra activity level. The smaller the ^{226}Ra to ^{210}Pb activity ratio, the more recent the sample. The age limit of the method is about 150 years; it has been successfully applied to authenticity testing of lead white in oil paintings.

B. Keisch: 'Art and atom: two dating methods based on measurements of radioactivity', *Application of science in examination of works of art*, ed. W.J. Young (Boston, 1970), 193–8.

SB

lead-210 (^{210}Pb) dating (2) Disequilibrium between ^{222}Rn and ^{210}Pb can also be caused by emanation of the former, which is a gas; this has been used for dating ground waters and peat (age range as above).

F. el-Daoushy: 'The value of ^{210}Pb in dating Scandinavian aquatic and peat deposits', *Radiocarbon* 28 (1986), 1031–40.

SB

lead isotope analysis Scientific technique consisting of the measurement of proportions of lead isotopes in an artefact, which is used primarily in provenance studies. Naturally occurring lead contains four stable isotopes of which three, ^{206}Pb, ^{207}Pb and ^{208}Pb, are formed in part from the decay of associated radio-isotopes (i.e. radioactive isotopes) of uranium and thorium whilst the fourth, ^{204}Pb, is not of radiogenic origin. Once separated from their parent radio-isotopes, as in the formation of an ore deposit, the proportions of the lead isotopes are fixed and are partly dependent on the geological age of the deposit and the mechanism of its formation. Different ore bodies tend to have different isotopic ratios and this provides the basis for the use of lead isotope analysis in provenance studies. The differences are nevertheless small and need to be measured with high precision and accuracy, usually by thermal ionization mass spectrometry which will routinely determine ratios to within ±0.1%. By comparison, the variation within a single ore body is rarely greater than ±0.3%. The three ratios $^{207}Pb/^{206}Pb$, $^{208}Pb/^{206}Pb$ and $^{206}Pb/^{204}Pb$ are normally used and all need to be taken into account to maximise the differentiation of sources. MULTIVARIATE STATISTICAL methods have been used for characterization.

The method is of course only applicable to artefacts containing lead, either in metallic form or as a compound. However, because of the association of lead with other metalliferous ores, it is more usual to provenance artefacts of other metals such as silver and copper which contain small amounts of lead derived from their respective ore sources. This assumes that no additional lead, from a potentially different source, has been subsequently introduced by alloying, since lead from different sources in the same artefact cannot be distinguished.

As a method of provenancing smelted metals, it is superior to the use of TRACE ELEMENT ANALYSIS because the concentrations of trace elements are usually modified by the processes of smelting and refining. The lead isotope ratios, on the other hand, are not significantly altered by chemical factors. The fractionation due to physical and chemical effects, of primary consideration for light element isotopic ratios, is insignificant for lead because the relative differences in mass between the isotopes is small compared with other elements, such as oxygen.

N.H. Gale and Z.A. Stos-Gale: 'Lead isotope studies in the Aegean', *New developments in archaeological science*, ed. A.M. Pollard (Oxford, 1992), 63–108.

MC

Lébous *see* FONTBOUISSE CULTURE

Lehner Kill site of the CLOVIS culture located in the San Pedro Valley, southern Arizona, where remains of mammoth, bison, horse and possibly camel have been excavated. The site has been RADIOCARBON dated to *c.*11,000 BP.

E.W. Haury, E.B. Sayles and W.W. Wasley: 'The Lehner mammoth site, southeastern Arizona', *AA* 25 (1959), 2–34.

JJR

Lei-ku-tun (Leigudun) *see* TSENG HOU YI TOMB

Lemek *see* NGAMURIAK

Lengyel culture Farming culture of the Neolithic (*c.*4500–3800 BC) that developed in Hungary and spread into the Czech Republic, Slovakia (especially southern Moravia) and southern Poland. The Lengyel culture postdates the earliest farming culture in the region (the LBK) and seems to have emerged from the Vinča cultural complex; it is closely related to the Tisza culture to the south. A characteristic pottery form is a bowl with a high hollow pedestal. Copper was used in the

Lengyel culture, but for ornaments only. The Lengyel culture is associated with a series of distinctive enclosures consisting of roughly circular interrupted ditches and palisade-ditches; the evidence from Slovakian Lengyel I and Lengyel II sites suggests that these were surrounded by rectangular post-built houses (Pavúk 1991). The function of the enclosures is still debated, but at certain sites they seem to represent non-utilitarian ritual areas.

J. Pavúk and S. Sistra: 'The Neolithic and Eneolithic', *Archaeological research in Slovakia*, Xth International Congress of Prehistoric and Protohistoric Sciences, (Nitra, 1981); J. Pavúk: 'Lengyel-culture fortified settlements in Slovakia', *Antiquity* 65 (1991), 348–57.

RJA

Lepcis *see* AFRICA 1

Lepenski Vir Mesolithic to Neolithic settlement on the banks of the Danube in Serbia. The most interesting phases of the site, dating from *c.*6000BC for perhaps 800 years (Phases I and II), exhibit the unusual combination of a pre-ceramic fishing, hunting and gathering economy with permanent settlement and monumental art. The huts are trapezoidal with mortar and stone-paved floors and hearths with spits, apparently for grilling fish from the nearby river. The art takes the form of boulders carved to represent the heads of 'fish-men'. Closely associated with the huts, these perhaps represent some deity or ancestor, and are arguably the earliest monumental figurative art in Europe. Fish were an important part of the economy of Lepenski Vir, but there is also evidence for pig, deer and wild ox; the rich stone industry includes artefacts that may have been used for grinding seeds or nuts. There was also a developed bone and antler industry. Over 80 burials have been excavated in and around the houses. There has been some controversy over radiocarbon dates which suggest that Phases I and II are contemporary with the introduction of farming into the area by the STARČEVO-CRIŞ culture, and their implications. It seems possible that the unusual settlement and sculptural activity at the site was a response by the indigenous hunting and gathering community to the proximity of the first farming culture of the region.

D. Srejovic: *Lepenski Vir* (London, 1972); B. Prinz: *Mesolithic adaptions on the Lower Danube* (Oxford, 1987), BAR IS 330, 32–43; B. Voytek and R. Tringham: 'Rethinking the Mesolithic: the case of south-east Europe', *The Mesolithic in Europe*, ed. C. Bonsall (Edinburgh, 1985), 492–9.

RJA

Le Petit-Chasseur Situated in the Rhône Valley in Switzerland, this Neolithic complex of the 4th millennium BC includes a settlement, a cist cemetery and an alignment built at the end, as well as a series of cists and chamber tombs of the Chalcolithic. The latter are especially interesting as they reutilize a series of earlier anthropomorphic slabs. These slabs, probably produced in the later 3rd millennium BC, depict precisely carved jewellery (double-spiral pendants) and weapons (copper daggers that resemble the Italian 'Remedello' type) as well as finely executed sunburst and geometrical motifs. Different authorities trace this style of art and the motifs to the Caucasus (Gimbutas) or the Mediterranean region (Gallay); many of the motifs are repeated in the art of Val Camonica.

A. Gallay: 'Recherches préhistoriques au Petit-Chasseur à Sion', *Helvetica Archaeologia* 10–22 (1972), 35–61; O.J. Bocksberger: *Le site préhistorique du Petit-Chasseur (Sion, Valais)*, 4, *Horizon supérieur secteur accidental et tombes Bronze ancien*, Cahiers d'archéologie Romande, 13/14 (Lausanne, 1978); A. Gallay: 'Stèles néolithiques et problématique archéologique', *Archives Suisses d'Anthropologie Génerale* xlii (1978), 75–103.

RJA

Leptolithic ('light stone') Term used (infrequently, nowadays) to describe industries characterized by thin blade lithic technology (i.e. industries of the Upper Palaeolithic onwards), as opposed to cruder flake technology (i.e. mainly industries of the Middle Palaeolithic).

RJA

Lerna Site of an Early Helladic fortified town near the sea and the village of Myloi, in the Argolid, Greece. The most prominent building in the settlement was an apparent palace or administrative complex known as the 'House of Tiles' – notable for its early use of stone and terracotta tiles as roofing materials. There are also fragmentary Middle Helladic and Mycenaean remains, including two shaft graves.

J.L. Angel: *Lerna II: The people* (Princeton 1971); J.L. Caskey: *A guide to Lerna* (1977).

RJA

Les Combarelles Decorated cave of the Upper Palaeolithic, situated 4 km west of Les Eyzies, France. The cave, in effect a long narrow gallery about 240 m in length, is renowned for its collection of engravings, which are executed in both fine and deeply-cut styles; a few drawings in black are also present. The art includes well over 100 horses, and 37 bison, as well as bears, lions, reindeer, mammoths, ibex and deer. A fox, fish and snake (all unusual subjects in cave art) have also been identified. The engravings are densely grouped and superimposed; Leroi-Gourhan regarded the cave as one of the clearest examples of his theory of 'topographic organization'. The art seems to date from the MAGDALENIAN, perhaps from 15,000 BC to around 12,000 BC.

L. Capitan, H. Breuil and D. Peyrony: *Les Combarelles aux Eyzies (Dordogne)* (Paris, 1924); C. Barrière: 'L'art parietal de la Grotte des Combarelles', *Travaux de l'institut d'art préhistorique de Toulouse* 23/25/27/29 (1981, 1983, 1985, 1987); A. Leroi-Gourhan: *The dawn of European art* (Cambridge, 1982).

RJA

Lespugue Series of shallow caves in Haute-Garonne, France, which yielded an extraordinary ivory 'Venus' figurine. The figurine is featureless and has greatly exaggerated breasts, buttocks and upper legs treated in such a balanced and geometrical manner that the piece verges on the abstract. An area of incised lines running down from the buttocks may represent clothing. The figurine has been assigned by some scholars to the Aurignacian, but seems more likely to belong the Upper Périgordian or GRAVETTIAN.

H. Delporte: *L'image de la femme dans l'art préhistorique* (Paris, 1979), 32–6.

RJA

Les Trois Frères Cave in Ariège, France, with one of the richest collections of CAVE ART in the French Pyrenees. Les Trois-Frères is decorated with many fine engravings of horses and bison, as well as certain famous engravings of a bird, an outline of a bear with circles inside it, and a lioness. There are also a few paintings, and some of the engravings are part painted. The area known as 'The Sanctuary' contains a series of famous panels of engravings of bison, horses and reindeer. Unusually for Palaeolithic art, this area also contains an anthropomorphic figure, depicted with phallus; known as the 'Sorcerer', the stance is human, while the antlered head and limbs show animal characteristics (especially deer). Les Trois Frères is one of the best-preserved of Upper Palaeolithic caves, and recent researchers have discovered bones, artefacts and bear's teeth stuffed into crevices in its walls. The style and occupation evidence suggest a date in the Magadalenian for the art. The engraved art of Les Trois Frères can be compared to the three-dimensional sculptures of nearby TUC D'AUDOUBERT, and its passages physically connect to the cave of Enlène with its abundance of finely incised PLAQUETTES.

R. Bégouën and H. Breuil: *Les cavernes du Volp: Trois-Frères – Tuc D'Audoubert* (Paris, 1958); D. Vialou: *L'art des grottes en Ariège Magdalénian*, XXIIe supplément a Gallia préhistoire (Paris, 1986), 99–188; R. Bégouën and J. Clottes: 'Le Trois Frères after Breuil', *Antiquity* 61 (1987), 180—7.

RJA

Le Tuc d'Audoubert Cave in Ariège region of France (next to the Trois Frères cave system) within which a unique Upper Palaeolithic clay sculpture of two bison was found in 1912. The bison (one female, one presumably male) are about 60 cm in length and modelled in high relief from clay dug from the floor of the cave; the outlines and the details of hair and eyes are carefully executed. The footprints of children apparently walking on their heels, surround the bison, and have led to speculation that the work formed part of some initiation ceremony. The cave also contains engravings of bison, horses etc. and signs; archaeological layers, dated by radiocarbon to about 14,000 BC in the MAGDALENIAN, suggest (but do not prove) a date for the sculpted bison.

R. Bégouën and H. Breuil: *Les cavernes du Volp: Trois-Frères – Tuc d'Audoubert* (Paris, 1958); R. Bégouën and J. Clottes: 'Grotte du Tuc d'Audoubert', *L'art des cavernes* (Paris, 1984), 410–15.

RJA

Leubingen *see* ÚNETICE

Levallois technique (method) Term used to describe the production of large standardized flint flakes from cores that have been prepared in such a way that the shape of the flake to be struck off is predetermined. Levallois tool production, named after the Seine valley site of Levallois-Peret in France, is characteristic of the Middle Palaeolithic and certain MOUSTERIAN industries (*c.*100,000–35,000). However, the technique was also used to a limited extent in the Lower Palaeolithic and in the (Levantine) Upper Palaeolithic; this range of use means that the Levallois method must be thought of as a distinctive technique rather than as a specific industry. Flint knappers using the Levallois method controlled the eventual shape of the flake by carefully preparing a flint nodule, roughing it out to give a flattened face and a carefully designed striking platform. It has been argued that the steps needed to produce the final tool, and the forethought this implies, demand considerably more skills of the knapper than later blade-based industries (this is not to imply that it is superior as a technology). The residual cores from which Levallois flakes have been struck are often known as 'tortoise cores' due to their regularly facetted appearance; sometimes more flakes were struck off in a more continuous manner so as to leave an especially regular and round core, often called a 'disc core'.

A. Berthelet and J. Chavaillon, eds: *The use of tools by human and non-human primates* (Oxford, 1993); E. Boëda: *Le concept Levallois* (Paris, 1994); N. Schlanger: 'Understanding Levallois', *CAJ* 6/2 (1996), 231–54.

RJA

Levant *see* SYRIA-PALESTINE

Levantine art *see* SPANISH LEVANTINE ROCK ART

Levanzo The small island of Levanzo off the western end of Sicily, possess a cave ('Cala dei Genovesi') decorated with a series of elegantly incised bovines, deer and horse outlines, as well as a rough sketch of figures. The figures, apparently costumed and wearing some sort of headdress, including in one instance a bird-bill like mask, show similarities with the more developed scene at ADDAURA. An incised sketch of a bovine was found detached from the wall and within an Epigravettian deposit, suggesting that the art may be dated to about the 9th millennium BC.

RJA

Liang-chu (Liangzhu) Neolithic culture named after the type-site near Hang-chou, Che-chiang, China. It is known from excavations as early as 1930, being an offshoot of the earlier Ma-chia-pang culture, which it replaced. Liang-chu is a manifestation of the LUNG-SHAN culture of the lower Yangtze Valley, dated *c.*3500–2250 BC on the basis of calibrated radiocarbon assessments. In Che-chiang and Chiang-hsi are several other sites belonging to this culture, such as Ch'ien-shan-yang and Shui-t'ien-pan, where rectangular buildings (each 5–20 sq.m in area) were built on flat ground, with walls originally made up of timber frames and wattle-and-daub. Agricultural implements included flat perforated spades, sickles and rectangular and semi-lunar knives with holes, as well as remains of rice grains, certain species of peach, melon, water chestnut, and a variety of peanut (including a well known early American variety). A high level of agriculture is indicated by the survival of the bones of domestic animals such as water-buffalo, pig, dog and sheep, although the discovery of net sinkers, wooden floats, boat remains, paddles of wood, and the remains of molluscs, turtle and fish, suggest that there was also an aquatic subsistence-base. This diet was evidently supplemented by hunting, judging from the presence of bones of such wild animals as deer, boar and fox. Black pottery of fine, soft paste, turned on the wheel, and finally polished to a high surface lustre, is characteristic of the culture. A certain amount of evidence has emerged to suggest that human sacrifice accompanied some of the burials.

Chang Kwang-chih: *The archaeology of ancient China*, 4th edn (New Haven, 1986), 253–61.

NB

Lind Coulee Camp site in eastern Washington state, western North America, which dates to *c.*7000–6600 BC. Research at this site had the effect of initiating interdisciplinary research in archaeology, geology, zoology and pedology in the Columbia Plateau (Daugherty 1956). Further work with refined techniques of microstratigraphy integrated with paleoecology, geochronology, TEPHROCHRONOLOGY and zooarchaeology was undertaken in the 1970s (Moody 1978). Granulometric and chemical analyses of four monolithic sections showed that the site deposits were floodplain sediments deposited within a period of 50–200 years. Spatial and associational analyses of artefacts and fauna demonstrated that the site was occupied during the spring season on at least seven different occasions. The artefactual remains belong to the intermontane STEMMED POINT TRADITION.

R.D. Daugherty: 'Archaeology of the Lind Coulee site, Washington', *Proceedings of the American Philosophical Society* 100, (1956), 223–278; U.L. Moody: *Microstratigraphy, paleoecology, and tephrochronology of the Lind Coulee Site, Central Washington* (Ph.D. thesis, Department of Anthropology, Washington State University, 1978).

RC

Lindow Man (Lindow 2) Well-preserved 'bog body' recovered from Lindow Moss in Cheshire, England, which has been subjected to a uniquely thorough scientific examination (Stead et al.). Before his body was dumped in the bog pool, the man had apparently been the victim of a ritual killing: he had been struck on the head, garrotted, and his neck had been cut. The body, probably dating from the 1st century AD, has proved to be an object lesson in the potential complications of the radiocarbon dating process (see Gowlett et al. 1989).

I.M. Stead et al.: *Lindow Man: the body in the bog* (London, 1986); J.A.J. Gowlett et al.: 'Radiocarbon accelerator (AMS) dating of Lindow Man', *Antiquity* 63 (1989), 71–9.

RJA

Linear A/B *see* MINOAN; MYCENAEAN

Linearbandkeramik (LBK, Linear Pottery, Danubian I) culture Early agricultural culture distributed across much of central and western Europe, named after its distinctive pottery with incised linear decoration. From the later 6th millennium BC, the LBK sites spread from northern Hungary in the east to the Paris Basin in the west, clustering in fertile valley and loess soil areas near water; in many areas, such as Germany and the Netherlands, the LBK provides the first evidence of the introduction of farming, pottery and settlements. The uniformity of the culture in its earliest stages suggests that this involved a movement of people rather than acculturation of the indigenous Mesolithic population. In most regions, it is not necessary to envisage long-distance migrations: the budding-off of settlements and small-scale movements of farmers in search of new land seems more probable in what has been termed a WAVE OF ADVANCE. In some of the eastern distribution (Romania) and again to the west (Dutch Limburg) elements of the lithic industry associated with the LBK seem to indicate that there was a limited degree of acculturation with the existing Mesolithic hunting and gathering population (Clark 1980).

The LBK does not spring from any obvious cultural precursor, although elements may be derived from the Körös culture in Hungary. Apart from its pottery – most characteristically rounded bowls decorated with incised curvilinear lines – it is defined by settlements of impressive free-standing long-houses built of posts (commonly 6–30 m long), with walls filled in using woven branches plastered with mud; a dispersed or 'hamlet' settlement distribution (occasionally loosely organised villages as at Bylany on the Bohemian plain, in the Czech Republic, and ELSLOO in southern Holland); cultivation of emmer and einkorn wheat, barley and legumes; a restricted range of domesticated animals (cattle mainly, some sheep/goat and pig); groundstone tools and, in some areas,

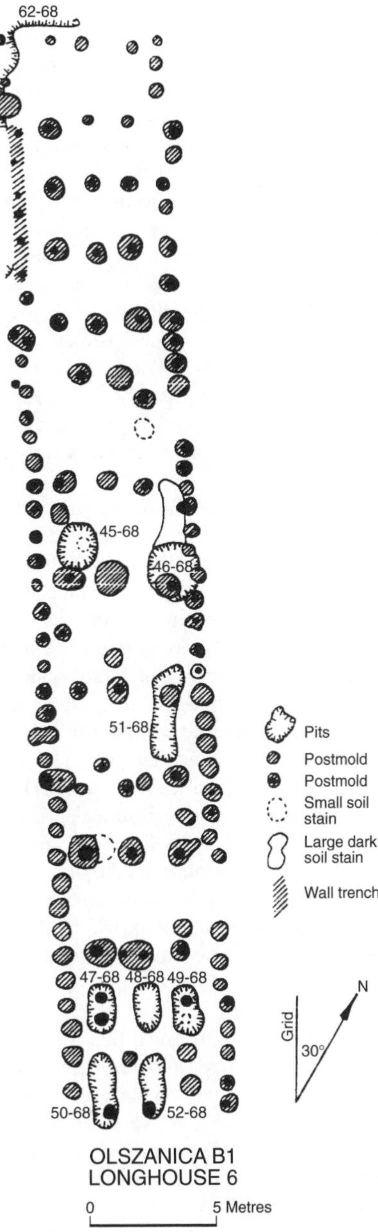

Figure 28 **Linearbandkeramik** Longhouse 6 of the LBK culture at Olszanica, Poland. *Source*: S. Milisauskas and J. Kruk: 'Archaeological investigations on Neolithic and Bronze Age sites in south-eastern Poland', *Cave studies in European prehistory*, ed. D. Bogucki (Boca Raton, 1993), p.73, fig. 3.

obsidian. The houses are flanked by linear pits (from which soil was extracted for daubing the walls) and by storage pits. Some settlements are associated with small cemeteries, inhumation being the dominant rite, with cremations at exceptional sites such as Elsloo; pottery, stone tools and ornaments accompanied some burials, but there is little evidence of any social stratification. The *Spondylus* shells (*see* SPONDYLUS) often found with burials indicate extensive exchange, as do many of the polished stone and flint artefacts – for example, a distinctive fine 'chocolate' flint naturally occurring in southern Poland is found in LBK sites in northern Poland and Slovakia. The early homogeneity of the LBK culture eventually fractures, giving rise to regionally distinctive successor cultures such as the RÖSSEN and STROKE-ORNAMENTED WARE.

LBK and shifting agriculture. Many early archaeologists describing the early agriculture of Europe implicitly assumed a model of agricultural technique and field organisation in which extensive agriculture gave way over time to intensive agriculture. The assumption was first made explicit by Boserup (1965). The work of Soudsky at Bylany supported this hypothesis, by seeming to establish that the LBK employed an extensive SWIDDEN AGRICULTURE involving the rotation of sites (*Brandwirtschaft*) and manual cultivation. However, it was soon pointed out that swidden agriculture in Europe in historical times has been confined to marginal soils that are quite unlike the rich LOESS soils associated with LBK sites. In addition, the LBK material culture seems to lack the technology necessary to continually clear large tracts of virgin forest, and there is anyway little evidence in the pollen record for this.

Instead, Kruk (1980) argued that the LBK sites in Poland were of a fixed-plot character. His argument was based essentially on the fertility of the soil, and the distribution of sites, which seemed to show that the first LBK farmers strongly favoured sites on terraces and lower levels of river valleys (i.e. dry and flooded alluvial soils). Experimental archaeology has demonstrated that high-fertility soils can retain a high level of fertility over many years. It had also never been quite clear in the earlier theory why LBK sites themselves should have shifted, as opposed to only the fields.

At present, the agricultural evidence from the Polish LBK is dominated by wheat, which is not a crop particularly suited to fixed-plot agriculture, but this is very probably the result of differential preservation: the food processing associated with wheat means that it has far more chance of being carbonized and entering the archaeological record than, say, pulses. A fuller picture of the LBK economy might be of intensive garden-plot cultivation near the settlements, including lentils and peas, with a more extensive and possibly rotational field system cultivation of wheat rather further away. Ethnographic and ethno-historical accounts support the possibility of this more complex model: economies can be a mix of fixed plot, simple swidden, complex swidden and so on. Intensive agriculture is not necessarily synonymous with fixed plot agriculture: some riverine sites with very fertile or annually flooded soils can be cultivated permanently without employing intensive techniques; by contrast, in shifting cultivation intensive techniques are sometimes used to temporarily offset a progressive deterioration in productivity caused by a growth in weeds and a lowering of fertility.

E. Boserup: *The conditions of agricultural growth: the economics of agrarian change under population pressure* (London, 1965); B. Soudsky: *Bylany* (Prague, 1966); J. Kruk: *Neolithic settlement of southern Poland*, BAR IS93, ed. and trans. by J.M. Howell and N.J. Starling (Oxford, 1980); P.J.R. Modderman: *Linearbandkeramik aus Elsloo und Stein*, 3 vols (Leiden, 1970); G. Clark: *Mesolithic prelude* (Edinburgh, 1980), 74; A. Whittle: *Neolithic Europe: A survey* (Cambridge, 1985), 73–95; M. Ilett: 'The Early Neolithic of north-eastern France', *Ancient France 6000–2000*, ed. C. Scarre (Edinburgh, 1987), 6–33; I. Hodder: *The domestication of Europe* (Oxford, 1990); A. Whittle: 'Radiocarbon dating of the Linear Pottery culture: the contribution of cereal and bone samples', *Antiquity* 64 (1990), 297–302; P. Bogucki and R. Grygiel: 'The first farmers of Central Europe: a survey article, *JFA* 20 (1993), 399–426.

RJA

el-Lisht Egyptian Middle Kingdom necropolis which includes the pyramid complexes of the two earliest 12th-dynasty rulers, Amenemhat I and his son Senusret I (*c*.1991–1926 BC, located on the west bank of the Nile about 50 km south of Cairo. The pyramids were built at this site as a result of the creation of the new royal city, Itj-tawy, the remains of which have not been found (probably lying beneath the cultivated land to the east of el-Lisht). Amenemhat I's pyramid was originally about 58 m high, with an internal rubble core including limestone blocks taken from Old Kingdom buildings at SAQQARA and its mortuary temple was located on the east side; the valley temple has not yet been located. Senusret I's complex, at the southern end of the site, is also of limestone and originally 61 m high.

W.K. Simpson, 'The residence of It-towy', *JARCE* 2

(1963), 53–64; D. and F. Arnold: *The south cemeteries of Lisht*, 3 vols (New York, 1988–92).
IS

Llano PALEOINDIAN tradition which is without known cultural antecedents. The period is divided into the Llano (9,500–9,000 BC), FOLSOM (9,000–8,000 BC), and PLANO cultures (8,000–5,000 BC). The diagnostic artefact of the Llano culture is the fluted CLOVIS projectile point. Other artefacts include prismatic blades, flake scrapers, bone foreshafts, bone wrenches, chopping tools, and hammer stones, and grinding stones. The culture occurs across the United States east of the Rocky Mountains and into northern Mexico. It is primarily known from sites, such as BLACKWATER DRAW, where solitary large mammals including mammoths, mastodons, camelids, bison, and horse, were killed and butchered by small bands of hunter-gatherers. Mortuary and camp sites are less well known and the population was sparse and transient. Subsistence is thought to have focused on the hunting of large mammals, but there is some evidence of the use of small animals and plant foods.

E.H. Sellards: *Early man in America* (Austin, 1952); H. Irwin and M. Wormington: 'Paleo-Indian tool types in the Great Plains', *AA* 25 (1970), 24–34.
WB

Loebanr *see* GANDHARA GRAVE CULTURE

loess Wind-blown yellowish dust which covers about a tenth of the land surface of the earth and is particularly extensive in northwest and central Europe, China, Alaska and the Mississippi and Ohio valleys of the USA. It serves as a useful indicator of climate change, in that it tends to be redeposited only in cold, dry conditions, therefore it usually alternates with the forest soils characteristic of warmer, wetter climate, as in the Paris basin, where François Bordes (1953) identified a sequence of loess and forest soils, each associated with different Palaeolithic industries.

Loess provided the basis for the fertile soils that facilitated the emergence of agriculture in early Neolithic Europe. As early as 1898, the geologist Robert Gradmann noted a close correlation between the occurrence of loess deposits and the patterning of LINEARBANDKERAMIK (LBK) sites in Europe (Gradmann 1906). It was at first assumed that the attraction of loess to early farmers was the relative lack of trees (see Hellmich 1923), but from the 1940s onwards pollen analysis showed that loess had actually been forested, leading to the conclusion that its real benefit, compared with other soils, was the fact that it was more easily tilled (Clark 1974).

R. Gradmann: 'Beziehung zwischen pflanzengeographie und Siedlungsgeschichte', *Geographische Zeitschrift* 12 (1906), 305–25; M. Hellmich: *Die Besiedlung Schlesiens in vor- und frühgeschichtlicher Zeit* (Breslau, 1923); F. Bordes: *Recherches sur les limons quaternaires du bassin de la Seine* (Paris, 1953). J.G.D. Clark; 'Prehistoric Europe: the economic basis', *Archaeological researches in retrospect*, ed. G.R. Willey (Cambridge, 1974), 31–57; D.N. Eden and R.J. Furkert: *Loess: its distribution, geology and soils* (Rotterdam, 1988).
IS

logical positivism As a philosophy of science, POSITIVISM reached its most extreme form in the logical positivist (or logical empiricist) movement that centred on the University of Vienna in the 1920s and 1930s, and which was further developed as a philosophy of science in the 1940s and 1950s. This movement, which included mathematicians, philosophers and social scientists, denied the usefulness of any statement that could not be proved empirically – a stance sometimes labelled as 'verificationism'.

Logical positivists endorsed the hypothetico-deductive approach to theory building (*see* INDUCTIVE AND DEDUCTIVE EXPLANATION), and regarded the use of COVERING LAWS as the most useful way of discovering truths about the world. As a philosophy of science it was largely defunct by the 1960s, although elements of the positivist approach continued to influence leading philosophers of science (e.g. Karl Popper). The key weaknesses of the approach might be summarized as: the problem of developing a value-free observational language; the impossibility of ever proving that any law was truly universal and true (since the discovery of a single exception to the law at some future time would render the law invalid); the difficulty of making any direct connection between empirical observations and useful (i.e. higher levels of) theory; the complementary difficulty of truly separating 'theory' from 'fact' in the way that the rigorous methodology demanded; the impossibility of impartially testing hypotheses. There had always been doubts over whether a method of enquiry based essentially on mathematical physics could usefully inform methods of enquiry in other areas, particularly the social sciences. There was also the test of time: logical positivism could not be shown to have advanced scientific methodology in any meaningful way, while other veins of philosophical enquiry began to highlight the usefulness of inductive reasoning in the history of scientific advance, and to examine the importance of the contexts within which scientific thought was formulated.

Although some strands of positivist thought remain influential, logical positivism in its more extreme form had become unfashionable among philosophers of science well before some of its central ideas were advanced by archaeological theorists. Despite the fact that many of the weaknesses in the logical positivist project identified above apply with particular force to the discipline of archaeology, certain concepts and approaches – particularly regarding the importance of linking arguments logically where possible, the importance of formulating general laws, and the testing of these against observable data – influenced the rhetoric and practice of the PROCESSUAL ARCHAEOLOGY of the 1960s. In part, this may have been because archaeology had remained an essentially historical discipline in terms of its explanation of cultures, if not in terms of technique: positivism provided a counterpoint, and a means of critique. Some elements of debate – for example, the usefulness of general laws and how they can be legitimately applied – are perennial concerns in the discipline and continue to be discussed, often using concepts and language borrowed from the positivists.

see EMPIRICISM; FALSIFICATION; NOMOTHETIC APPROACHES; POSITIVISM; VERIFICATION.

P.J. Watson, S.A. LeBlanc and C.L. Redman: *Explanation in archaeology: an explicitly scientific approach* (New York and London, 1971); G. Gibbon: *Explanation in archaeology* (Oxford 1989), 8–34, 35–60

RJA

logicism, logicist archaeology An approach in archaeological theory that embraces several distinct concepts put forward by Francophone archaeologists during the 1970s and 1980s. Logicist archaeologists have attempted to remedy the problems of conventional and post-modern archaeological theory by concentrating on the underlying structure of archaeological publications and interpretations rather than on the nature of the archaeological remains themselves. This dissection of the process of archaeological explanation itself is not as destructive as it may seem, since the essential aim of logicism in archaeology is to reveal the foundations of proposed interpretations as well as their flaws.

The use of a self-conscious logicist approach is particularly evident in the work of Jean-Claude Gardin and Alain Gallay. In *Archaeological constructs* (1980), Gardin discusses a number of different texts describing archaeological activities (e.g. catalogues of artefacts or syntheses of prehistoric culture-histories), analysing the assumptions made by archaeologists when categorizing, describing or interpreting archaeological data. He makes the point that archaeological interpretation is not served well by the predominantly narrative form of most publications and site reports, suggesting that such dynamics are better encapsulated in flow charts. Logicist approaches have been applied to such diverse topics as the SPATIAL ANALYSIS of Tuareg campsites (Gallay 1988) and the interpretation of Greco-Bactrian coinage (Guillaume 1990).

J.-C. Gardin: *Archaeological constructs: an aspect of theoretical archaeology* (Cambridge, 1980); A. Gallay: 'Vivre autour d'un feu: analyse ethnoarchéologique de campements Touaregs du Hoggar', *Bulletin du Centre Gene vois d'Anthropologie* 1 (1988); ——: 'Logicism: French archaeological theory', *Antiquity* 63 (1989), 27–39; O. Guillaume: *Analysis of reasonings in archaeology: the case of Graeco-Bactrian and Indo-Greek numismatics* (Oxford, 1990).

IS

log-linear analysis *see* CONTINGENCY TABLE

Long Count *see* CALENDARS (MESOAMERICAN)

Lopburi In the environs of this regional centre in central Thailand are a series of diverse archaeological monuments. The Lopburi artillery site is the location of an important late prehistoric cemetery dating to the late 1st millennium BC and containing graves accompanied by bronze artefacts and local evidence for bronze casting. Later, a centre of the DVARAVATI CULTURE was located at Lopburi; a rendition of the Buddhist wheel of the law, inscribed in Pali (the court language), was found within the precinct of the town. Lopburi was also a local centre of the expansive Khmer civilization, and the centre of the modern town is still dominated by the sandstone lotus towers of a Khmer sanctuary.

P. Wheatley: *Nagara and Commandery* (Chicago, 1983), 208.

CH

Los Millares Fortified Copper Age settlement and cemetery situated on a promontory about 20 km from Almería in southeast Spain. The largest prehistoric settlement and funerary complex in the region, it was excavated primarily by Almagro and

Arribas in the 1950s. It is the principal example of a group of about 20 sites with related evidence (the 'Millaran' culture), and parallels the VILA NOVA DE SÃO PEDRO (VNSP) culture of Portugal. Among the most interesting features of the Los Millares site are its elaborate defences: the spur on which the main settlement is situated is cut across by a wall over 300 m long that is strengthened by a fortified gateway and 19 semi-circular and square bastions, and behind this main wall are lesser walls. Numerous other dry-stone 'forts' – the most elaborate consisting of a tower surrounded by bastioned walls – defend the approaches; excavations in 1982 revealed that these are contemporary with the main settlement. The settlement inside the main defence, which has yielded Beaker pottery including early comb-decorated vessels and later incised examples (see BEAKER PHENOMENON), was supplied with water by means of a simple 'aqueduct'. The wall and one of the cemetery tombs have been dated using radiocarbon to a calendar date of before 3000 BC, but the site probably represents several phases of construction during the whole of the 3rd millennium BC.

Los Millares cemetery and social stratification. Outside the defences of the settlement is a cemetery of more than 85 tombs. The commonest form of tomb is a PASSAGE GRAVE with a circular or sub-circular chamber under a circular mound. The chambers, which may once have been painted with gypsum and which often have paved floors, have corbelled roofs and may be lined with stone slabs; the mounds often have several concentric circles of revetment walls, and the perimeter may be similarly edged with slabs. One characteristic feature of the Los Millares cemetery is that the passages, chambers, and sometimes side-chambers tend to be entered via port-hole slabs; another is the presence of settings of small plain 'stelae' or *baetyls* immediately outside some of the tombs. Other tombs in the cemetery lack passages, or have megalithic chambers of a rectangular or sub-triangular shape. The tombs yielded a range of 'prestige' goods and materials, including ostrich egg-shell and ivory from North Africa – cited by Renfrew (1972) as examples of directional trade – amber, jet, fine flint daggers, copper daggers, and stone plaques; a common decorative motif is a design resembling two eyes – the ocular motif – which also appears on a series of schematic carved bone 'idols'. The grave-goods are not distributed evenly (Chapman 1981), and together with the elaborate architecture of many of the tombs, and the relative complexity of the settlement architecture, this suggests the existence of social ranking.

Stylistic links. Apart from developments in the Aegean, the closest parallels for the Millaran defensive architecture are the fortified VNSP sites in Portugal and the bastioned fortification of Lébous at Hérault in southern France. The circular chamber-tombs are often termed *tholoi*, after the (much later and therefore unrelated) beehive-shaped tombs of the Greek mainland; the possibility of a link with the rather less similar but roughly contemporary *tholos*-style tombs of Crete is discussed in Joussaume (1988), but in all probability the tombs are a local development.

M. Almagro and A. Arribas: *Poblado y la necrópolis megalíticas de Los Millares* (Madrid, 1963); C. Renfrew: *The emergence of civilization: the Cyclades and the Aegean in the third millennium BC* (London, 1972); A. Arribas et al.: 'Excavaciones en Los Millares (Santa Fe, Almería): Campanas de 1978 y 1979', *Cuadernos de Prehistoria Granadina* 4 (1979), 61–109; R. Chapman: 'The megalithic tombs of Iberia', *Antiquity and Man: essays in honour of Glyn Daniel*, ed. B. Cunliffe et al. (London, 1981), 93–106; A. Arribas and F. Molina: 'Bell Beakers in Los Millares', *Bell Beakers of the Western Mediterranean*, ed. W.H. Waldren and R.E. Kennard, BAR IS 331(1), (Oxford, 1987), 133–46; R. Joussaume: *Dolmens for the dead*, trans. A. and C. Chippindale (London, 1988), 182–8; R. Chapman: *Emerging complexity: the later prehistory of south-east Spain, Iberia and the West Mediterranean* (Cambridge, 1990).

RJA

Lothagam The most important of several 'Aqualithic' sites in the Lake Turkana region of Kenya (*see* AQUATIC CIVILIZATION), which was investigated by L.H. Robbins. Other Aqualithic sites in this basin are known in the OMO valley (in Ethiopia) to the north and at Lowasera to the east of the lake. The carved bone harpoons relate to those of lake and riverside sites of the Middle Nile and Sahara 6–9 millennia ago. The Lothagam area has also yielded fossil remains of early hominids, possibly AUSTRALOPITHECUS, which has been dated to about five million years BP (*see* WEST TURKANA).

L.H. Robbins: 'A recent archaeological discovery in the Turkana district', *Azania* 2 (1967), 69–73; D.W. Phillipson: 'Lowasera', *Azania* 12 (1977), 1–32.

JS

Lothal Harappan (INDUS CIVILIZATION) settlement and extramural cemetery located at the head of the Gulf of Cambay in Gujarat, India, excavated by Shikaripur Ranganatha Rao of the Archaeological Survey of India. Five chronological phases were defined at Lothal: I–IV date to the Mature

Indus period, with calibrated radiocarbon dates from *c.*2460 to 2140 BC (Possehl 1989: 32), while phase V contains material from the Late Harappan period (calibrated radiocarbon dates, *c.*2000 BC and 1700 BC; Possehl 1990: 32). The settlement was initially enclosed within a rectilinear mud-brick wall measuring 400 × 300m, but it later expanded beyond this enclosure. Rao defined several discrete areas at Lothal, including a southern 'acropolis' and northern 'lower town'. Rao also excavated a large trapezoidal fired-brick-lined basin (214 × 36m), which he interpreted as a Harappan harbour, although Leshnik (1968) has suggested that it may actually have been an irrigation basin.

L.S. Leshnik: 'The Harappan port at Lothal: another view', *American Anthropologist* 70 (1968), 911–22; S.R. Rao: 'Lothal, le port de l'empire de l'Indus', *Archaeologia* 29 (1969), 64–73; ——: *Lothal: 1955–62* (New Delhi, 1979); G.L. Possehl: *Radiocarbon dates for South Asian archaeology* (Philadelphia, 1989); S.R. Rao: *Dawn and devolution of the Indus civilization* (New Delhi, 1991).

CS

Lowasera *see* LOTHAGAM

Lower Palaeolithic *see* PALAEOLITHIC

Lowland Maya The Lowland Maya area, heartland of development of Classic Maya civilization, is centred on the Yucatán peninsula, comprising the modern political regions of northern Guatemala (the Department of El Petén), Belize and the states of Yucatán, Quintana Roo, Campeche and part of Tabasco and Chiapas in Mexico. The inhabitants of the lowlands speak a number of Mayan languages. By far the most widespread is Yucatecan, including Yucatec, Lacandon, Itza and Mopan; Yucatec is spoken throughout the northern Yucatán peninsula, whereas the others are spoken only in small isolated pockets. The Classic Maya may have spoken Cholan Mayan, including Chorti, Chol and Chontal, which are now found on the southeastern and western peripheries of the lowlands; a fourth Cholan language, Cholti, is now extinct.

The lowlands are customarily discussed by archaeologists in terms of several subregions. These may be based on gross geographical criteria: for example, the northern lowlands (the northern Yucatán peninsula), the southern lowlands (Petén and Belize), the southeastern periphery (southeastern Guatemala and northern Honduras, i.e. the region of COPAN AND QUIRIGUÁ) and the western periphery (e.g. the Usumacinta [river] region, including PALENQUE, Piedras Negras and Yaxchilán). Subdivisions of lowland Maya culture may also be distinguished on the basis of distinctive architectural criteria, as, for example, the RIO BEC/CHENES and PUUC regions in the northern lowlands of the peninsula.

There is little evidence for occupation of the region during the Early Preclassic period (*c.*2500–800 BC; see MacNeish 1983 and COPAN) and it is not until the Middle Preclassic period, beginning around 900 BC or later, that small scattered settlements have been identified. Because these are located primarily along the major river courses draining the southern lowlands, it has been concluded that the early settlers moved into the region by following rivers and streams. These first villagers, as seen at sites like CUELLO, seem to have settled on well-drained terrain, where they lived in perishable houses on low platforms built near the plots where they grew corn, beans and squash; they also made pottery in a variety of colours and shapes and seem to have had access to highland goods such as OBSIDIAN. Through the next centuries the numbers of people living in the lowlands grew and began filling into interior regions. By the end of the Middle Preclassic, *c.*300 BC, they were constructing large stone temple-pyramids, as for example at the site of NAKBE in northern Petén.

The Late Preclassic period (*c.*300 BC–AD 200) was a period of dramatic population growth and expansion in the lowlands. By the end of this period (sometimes called the Terminal Preclassic or Protoclassic) many of the characteristics of the Classic period had developed, including complex masks and other decoration on building facades, the CORBELLED ARCH, erection of stelae, HIEROGLYPHIC WRITING, elaborate elite burials and the use of polychrome pottery. Multiple factors seem to have been operating to bring about the transition to the complex Maya civilization seen in later centuries. Population growth and the demands of feeding large numbers of people on a primarily slash-and-burn farming system could have led to agricultural intensification in some areas, including reduced fallow cycles or agro-engineering efforts such as terracing or raised fields. Competition for scarce resources may have led to increased conflict, as evidenced by the presence of defensive walls around a few sites. Trade in exotic goods, including obsidian, jade, marine shells, feathers and other items was an increasingly important elite activity. Far from being simply a prelude to Classic period greatness, the Late Preclassic period was a period of expansion and dynamic achievement and several large sites with impressive architectural construction, such as EL MIRADOR, Uaxactún and Cerros, date to this interval.

The Classic period is customarily divided into Early (AD 200–600) and Late (AD 600–900) intervals. The Early Classic period is the time of expansion of the STELE cult throughout the lowlands from its apparent centre of development in the region of TIKAL and many sites are 'named' in inscriptions by reference to a particular EMBLEM GLYPH. The period is also marked by contacts with TEOTIHUACAN, as evidenced by architectural details (TALUD-TABLERO-style buildings), motifs on buildings and stelae (e.g. images of the rain-god Tlaloc), cylinder tripod pottery and distinctive green obsidian. The end of the Classic period in parts of the southern lowlands, especially near Tikal, is marked by a 'hiatus' a perplexing interval of 60 or so years during which very few stelae were erected and elite burials were accompanied by grave goods of lesser quality and quantity.

The Late Classic period is best known in the southern lowlands, where large cities surrounded by dense rural settlement (see Ashmore 1981) covered the landscape. Cities consisted of complexes of stone and masonry buildings, including temple-pyramids and elite residential and administrative structures (such as palaces and acropolises); many of these were decorated with paint, mosaics and stuccoed and modelled reliefs. Other architectural forms found at large lowland centres included courts for playing the BALLGAME, causeways or SACBES joining complexes at the site, and reservoirs. The lowlands were heavily settled during this time, with total population estimates running into the millions. The size and distribution of archaeological sites suggests that population densities might have strained the ability of the agricultural technologies to meet the needs for food. Hieroglyphic texts speak of increased military activity, alliances between sites and frequent battles with the attendant capture of rival kings.

In the southern lowlands, the end of the Classic period is marked by the events of the 'collapse', which signalled a dramatic finale to elite culture (see Culbert 1973). Population declined precipitously and early Postclassic remains are found primarily at smaller site centres, in rural areas and around the peripheries of the former Classic core.

The collapse, beginning about AD 800, is marked by the cessation, over a century or longer, of most of the distinctive features of elite culture, such as STELAE, sumptuary burials, monumental construction and polychrome pottery manufacture. Most of the largest centres were also abandoned, leading to the traditional view that the entire southern lowlands was devoid of settlement by about AD 1000. Populations did indeed decline dramatically, but in some smaller centres and especially in rural regions occupation continued into Postclassic times. Possible causes of the collapse have been heavily debated and include environmental factors (drought, crop failure, soil exhaustion; see Rice and Rice 1984), disease, internal social disruptions (uprisings, continual elite warfare) and external conflicts. Most archaeologists agree that the collapse was an elite phenomenon and was multi-causal, with different factors operating more or less simultaneously in different places (*see* COPAN *for further discussion of the collapse).*

During the period of the collapse, however, the northern lowlands experienced an unparalleled cultural florescence during the Terminal Classic and Early Postclassic periods (see Sabloff and Andrews 1986). From about AD 700–1000 the sites of the PUUC region, such as SAYIL and Uxmal, Cobá to the east and also Chichén Itzá in the north-central peninsula, grew and prospered. According to Maya myth and history, Chichén Itzá fell to an alliance between MAYAPAN and Izamal around AD 1200 and its inhabitants fled after the city was sacked.

The Late Postclassic period in the lowlands dates from roughly AD 1200 to the time of European contact/conquest in the early 16th century (although conquest of some remote regions, such as Petén, Guatemala, did not take place until 1697). In the northern lowlands the Late Postclassic period is known from sites such as Tulum, a small port and trading/pilgrimage centre perched on the edge of the peninsula overlooking the Caribbean Sea and MAYAPAN, in the northwest part of the peninsula. The region was integrated politically into a confederacy or 'league' of 16 provinces or states, centred in Mayapán.

In the southern lowlands, the Late Postclassic period has been poorly known until recently. Only a few sites, such as Lamanai in Belize and Topoxté in Petén, provide evidence of continuity of occupation from the time of the Classic 'collapse' until European contact. At the time of the coming of the Spaniards there was a series of small Maya chiefdoms or kingdoms scattered throughout the area. In central Petén four lineages with separate capitals were integrated by a kind of confederacy centred on Late Petén-Itzá, similar to that of MAYAPAN. However, the antiquity of this arrangement is unknown.

T.P. Culbert, ed.: *The classic Maya collapse* (Albuquerque, 1973); S. Garza T. and E.B. Kurjack: *Atlas arqueológico del estado de Yucatán*, 2 vols (Mexico, 1980); W. Ashmore: *Lowland Maya settlement patterns* (Albuquerque, 1981);

R.S. MacNeish: 'Mesoamerica', *Early man in the New World*, ed. R. Shutler, Jr. (Beverly Hills, 1983), 125–35; S.G. Morley, G.W. Brainerd and R.S. Sharer: *The ancient Maya*, 4th edn (Stanford, 1983); D.S. and P.M. Rice: 'Lessons from the Maya', *Latin American Research Review* 19 (1984), 7–34; J.A. Sabloff and E.W. Andrews V, eds: *Late lowland Maya civilization: classic to postclassic* (Albuquerque, 1986); J.A. Sabloff: *The new archaeology and the ancient Maya* (New York, 1990).
PRI

Lo-yang (Luoyang) *see* EASTERN CHOU; WESTERN CHOU

Lu Ancient Chinese state which was enfeoffed to Po-ch'in, son of Chou-kung, the Duke of Chou, early in the WESTERN CHOU period (*c.*1115 BC). Its capital was situated in the vicinity of present day CHU'Ü-FU, Shan-tung, China. Chou-kung, brother of Wu-wang, the conqueror of SHANG and first king of the Chou dynasty, was 'regent' during the minority of Ch'eng-wang, the second king of Chou. These historical personages have been verified in contemporary and later inscribed bronzes.

Lu was also the home state of Confucius (fl.*c.*500 BC), whose existence has, however, yet to be archaeologically demonstrated. In the traditional literature, so strongly flavoured with Confucian concepts, there is, not unexpectedly, a wealth of detail but it is often of dubious validity. A vast literature, largely of Western Han and later compilation, has built up around the figure of Confucius. The indirect rôle of Confucian concepts, through the traditional literature, on interpretational matters requires constant review (*see* CHINA 2). A large number of works on Confucianism have been published by the Committee on Chinese thought (Chicago and Stanford, 1953–62), mainly under the editorship of A.F. Wright.

H.G. Creel: *Confucius, the man and the myth* (London, 1951); Shigeki Kaizuka: *Confucius*, trans. G. Bownas (London, 1956); Anon.: *Ch'ü-fu Lu-kuo ku-ch'eng* [The ancient city of Ch'ü-fu of the state of Lu] Ch'i-nan, 1982).
NB

Luangwa Central African Late Iron Age ceramic tradition found at sites such as Twickenham Road in Zambia. As part of his 'Two Stream' hypothesis, David Phillipson thought that the Luangwa Tradition developed north of the Copperbelt out of a Western Stream (i.e. Kalundu) unit similar to the Chondwe culture. According to this scheme, cattle-based societies with Luangwa pottery spread throughout the subcontinent, establishing the present distribution of Bantu languages. New linguistic research, along with settlement studies and ceramic analyses, have modified this interpretation. Rather than being related to Kalundu (see KALOMO CULTURE), the ceramic style is linked with the Naviundu complex (*see* DIVUYU), and associated with Western Bantu. At a general level Western Bantu speakers differ from Eastern Bantu in that they trace biological descent through the mother; they also own few, if any, cattle, emphasize brideservice, and traditionally have non-hereditary leaders. The distribution of Luangwa pottery does not extend far south of the Zambezi River, and its patterning reflects the formation of the 'matrilineal belt' across Central Africa.

D.W. Phillipson: 'Iron Age history and archaeology in Zambia', *JAH* 15 (1974), 1–25; T.N. Huffman: 'Ceramics, settlements and Late Iron Age migrations', *AAR* 7 (1989), 155–82.
TH

Luba *see* AFRICA 5.4

Lucy *see* AUSTRALOPITHECUS; HADAR; OLDUVAI

Lumbini Religious site located in the Himalayan foothills of Nepal, believed to be the birthplace of the Buddha. The remains include an inscribed sandstone column of the MAURYAN ruler Asoka (273–232 BC), several *STUPAS* (many now largely destroyed), temples, monastic complexes and an artificial pond enclosed by brick terraces. Evidence of construction at the site ranges in date from the 3rd century BC to the 10th century AD.

D. Mitra: *Buddhist monuments* (Calcutta, 1971), 58–60; B.L. Pradhan: *Lumbini-Kapilwastu-Dewadaha* (Kathmandu, 1979).
CS

luminescence dating *see* THERMOLUMINESCENCE; OPTICALLY STIMULATED LUMINESCENCE DATING.

Lung-shan (Lungshan) Neolithic culture in China (*c.*4000–2000 BC), out of which many of the essential aspects of Chinese civilization began to emerge, including the production of wheel-turned pottery and *li*-style ceramics; the building of *hang-t'u* structures, walled settlements and large buildings on raised *hang-t'u* platforms; the emergence of early writing and SCAPULIMANCY (*see* CHINA 3); an increase in differential burials and marked variations of mortuary wealth; more efficient kiln design; a greater variety of domesticated animals; the placement of human sacrifices under building foundations; signs of violence indicative of warfare; and evidence for the killing of captives.

The Lung-shan period was once described as the 'Black Pottery Culture' and viewed as the successor of the 'Painted Pottery Culture' (*see* YANG-SHAO), thus resulting in a 'two culture theory' of the Chinese Neolithic. These earlier interpretations of its significance, however, have undergone appreciable revision since the 1950s. The concept of a 'Lungshanoid expansion' was advanced and maintained until the late 1970s, then more or less discarded in favour of a 'Lungshanoid horizon' (Chang 1986a: 234). Following the course of archaeological discovery over the ensuing decades, the formulation of 'spheres of interaction' is now favoured as a more suitable basis for interpretation of the growing corpus of archaeological data.

In China, however, much of the study of archaeological assemblages may, perhaps, be classed as SERIATION (*see* CHINA 4). Accordingly, the Lung-shan has been compartmentalized into such general regions as the Shan-tung Lung-shan culture, the Middle Yellow River Valley Lung-shan cultures (Eastern, Northern, and Western Ho-nan Lungshan), Shan-hsi Lung-shan, and Shan-hsi Lung-shan, and the related LIANG-CHU, CH'I-CHIA and Ch'ing-lung-ch'üan III cultures. It has also been subdivided into phases, and it is likely that future research will concentrate on the interplay between the different geographical and chronological sections.

In the Shen-hsi and Ho-nan phases of the Lung-shan, especially the latter, the earliest signs of metal production appeared, although this evidence is somewhat complicated by the arguments relating to the existence of HSIA and the beginnings of the Shang period (*see* CHINA 2). Nevertheless, towards the close of the Lung-shan period, the development of metallurgy and writing clearly heralds the rise of civilization in China and the concept of a nuclear area from which influences began to spread centrifugally throughout the 'barbarian' peripheral regions.

Chang Kwang-chih: *Shang China* (New Haven, 1980); ——: *The archaeology of ancient China*, 4th edn (New Haven, 1986a); ——, ed.: *Studies of Shang archaeology* (New Haven, 1986b).

NB

Luni industries Middle Palaeolithic stone tool industry first identified by V.N. Misra from surface sites in the Luni River Valley of southern Rajasthan, India. Common tool types include concave and convex scrapers, carinated scrapers, burins, points, handaxes, cleavers and adze blades. Luni artefacts have been found in two main contexts: working floors near ancient lake beds and in association with river gravels. Rhyolite is the most common raw material, but quartzite and quartz were also used.

L.S. Leshnik: 'Prehistoric explorations in North Gujarat and parts of Rajasthan', *East and West* 118 (1968), 295–310; B. Allchin, A. Goudie and K. Hegde: *The prehistory and palaeogeography of the Great Indian Desert* (London, 1978), 166–96.

CS

lunulae Crescent-shaped chest ornaments manufactured from sheet gold in the 2nd millennium BC. Lunulae are the most magnificent of a range of beaten and incised goldwork associated with the 'food vessel' and BEAKER cultures of the British Isles. Their distribution is concentrated in Ireland, and they were probably hammered out of gold plucked from the streams of western Britain. Many lunulae are decorated with repeated geometric (often triangular) motifs and parallel lines, particularly around their rims and near their terminals. Unlike most contemporary prestige items, lunulae occur mainly as isolated finds and never as burial goods; this suggests they were used as votive offerings, and perhaps also that they were not owned by individuals.

J. Taylor: *Bronze Age goldwork of the British Isles* (Cambridge, 1980).

RJA

Luoyang (Lo-yang) *see* EASTERN CHOU; WESTERN CHOU

Lupemban industry *see* SANGOAN

Luristan Mountainous region of western Iran in which a number of early agricultural sites have been excavated, including Tepe Asiab, Tepe Guran, Tepe Giyan and Tepe Sarab. The earliest of these is Asiab, located in the Kermanshah region, where pit-like circular depressions and the surviving bones of goats indicate an early 7th-millennium semi-nomadic herding community living in tents or reed huts. Tepe Guran dates to a slightly later stage in the Neolithic of western Iran; its eight-metre-deep stratigraphy dates from *c.*6500 to 5500 BC, showing a gradual transition from an aceramic culture and ephemeral clusters of huts to more permanent Neolithic settlement characterized by pottery and domed ovens which are similar to those excavated at JARMO in Iraq. Tepe Sarab, like Asiab, appears to have been a seasonally occupied settlement; the earliest levels at Sarab are contemporary with the upper strata at Guran, according to calibrated radiocarbon dates ranging from 6006 ± 98 to 5655 ± 96 BC (see *Radiocarbon* 1963).

Luristan is best known for the unprovenanced 'bronzes' that began to appear on the antiquities market in large quantities in 1928–30 (although some examples had already been acquired by the British Museum in the 19th century). These distinctive bronze artefacts, mainly from late Bronze Age and early Iron Age tombs in the Zagros region, include ritual buckets, pinheads, horse-gear, daggers, axes, shields, pole-tops and standards. Some have reliable provenances, such as those excavated at Baba Jan, Kuh-i Dast, Pusht-i Kuh and Surkh Dum (see Vanden Berghe 1971), permitting the formulation of a basic chronology placing them mainly in the first half of the 1st millennium BC (Moorey 1974). In general, however, their interpretation is hampered by the fact that 'objects deriving from other places are given the fashionable label by dealers' Frankfort 1970: 340).

There appears to have been a sharp decline in Luristan metalworking after the emergence of the Achaemenian empire in the late 6th century BC, perhaps as a result of the centralization of craftworkers in the vicinity of such cities as Pasargadae and Persepolis (*see* PERSIA). The debate over the origins and development of the bronzes has centred on the question of whether they can be directly associated with a particular cultural group, such as the KASSITES or the ancestors of the Medes.

The excavations at such seasonally occupied Neolithic sites as Tepe Asiab and Tepe Sarab have been complemented by ethnographic work undertaken by Frank Hole and Sekandar Amanolahi-Baharvand among the modern pastoral nomads of Luristan (Hole 1979). Through a combination of interviews and observation they found that the fundamental differences between the settled agriculturalists and the nomads related to forms of accommodation and quantity of equipment. They also noted that the nomads' seasonal movements were surprisingly short, wherever possible exploiting regions where summer and winter pastures are only a few kilometres apart. The modern nomads were almost entirely independent of the settlements, leading Hole to suggest that the raising of animal stock in the early Neolithic might profitably be examined in complete isolation from contemporaneous developments in cereal cultivation.

P. Calmeyer: *Datierbare Bronzen aus Luristan und Kirmanshah* (Berlin, 1969); H. Frankfort: *The art and architecture of the ancient Orient*, 4th edn (Harmondsworth, 1970); C.L. Goff: 'Excavations at Baba Jan, 1968: third preliminary report', *Iran* 8 (1970), 141–56; H. Thrane: 'Tepe Guran and the Luristan bronzes', *Archaeology* 23 (1970), 27–35; C.L. Goff: 'Luristan before the Iron Age', *Iran* 9 (1971), 131–52; L. Vanden Berghe: 'Excavations in Push-i Kuh, tombs provide evidence in dating typical Luristan bronzes', *Archaeology* 24 (1971), 263–70; P.R.S. Moorey: *Ancient bronzes from Luristan* (Oxford, 1974); F. Hole: 'Rediscovering the past in the present: ethnoarchaeology in Luristan, Iran', *Ethnoarchaeology: implications of ethnography for archaeology*, ed. C. Kramer (New York, 1979), 192–218.

IS

Luwians Indo-European-speaking people who appear to have established themselves in southwestern Anatolia by the late 3rd millennium BC; they were perhaps responsible for violent destruction levels in settlements such as Alaça Hüyük and Hisarlik. It has been suggested that these invaders in fact constituted the earliest wave of 'HITTITES' (in the broadest sense of the term). The Luwian language at least seems to have survived well into the neo-Hittite phase (early 1st millennium BC), when one of its dialects was transcribed into the so-called Hittite hieroglyphs.

J.D. Hawkins: 'Some historical problems of the hieroglyphic Luwian inscriptions', *AS* 29 (1979), 153–67.

IS

Luxor Theban religious site dedicated to the cult of the fertility god, Amun Kamutef. Known as the *ipet resyt* ('southern harem'), the first major parts of Luxor temple were constructed in the reign of Amenhotep III (*c.*1391–1353 BC) and it was augmented by successive pharaohs (including Ramesses II and Alexander the Great). It was constructed largely as a suitable architectural setting for the culmination of the Festival of Opet, which comprised a ritual procession of divine images from KARNAK. The main purpose of this festival was to allow the reigning king annually to reinforce his power by uniting with his royal *ka* (spiritual essence or double) in the temple sanctuary. It was transformed into a shrine of the imperial cult in the Roman period and eventually partially overbuilt by the mosque of Abu Haggag. In 1989 a cachette of exquisitely carved and well-preserved 18th-dynasty stone statuary was excavated from beneath the floor of the court of Amenhotep III.

A. Gayet: *Le temple de Louxor* (Cairo, 1894); L. Bell, 'Luxor temple and the cult of the royal *ka*', *JNES* 44 (1985), 251–94; M. El-Saghir, *The discovery of the statuary cachette of Luxor temple* (Mainz, 1991).

IS

L'yalova culture *see* PIT-AND-COMB

Lydenburg (Heads site) Village site of the Early Iron Age just east of the town of Lydenburg in the eastern Transvaal, South Africa. The site, on sloping ground above a small stream, is heavily eroded, and the only structural features so far revealed by excavation are a dozen shallow pits containing variable quantities of bone, iron slag, charcoal, pottery, stone, and *daga* (puddled clay) from pole and *daga* huts. The most notable finds are the remains of seven terracotta heads, unique in the Early Iron Age of eastern and southern Africa (although a fragment, unassociated, has been recorded 50 km to the east). Small finds include beads of iron, copper, and shell, and pieces of worked bone and ivory. The site is securely dated to the early 6th century AD. Opinion is divided as to whether the ceramics owe their origin to movements from the north, or from the east coast.

R.R. Inskeep and T.M. Maggs: 'Unique art objects in the Iron Age of the Transvaal', *SAAB*, 30 (1975), 114–38; T.M. Evers: 'Excavations at the Lydenburg heads site, eastern Transvaal, South Africa', *SAAB* 37 (1982), 16–33.

RI

lynchet ('cultivation terrace') 'Positive lynchets' are formed by the build up of slopewash deposits along the edge of field boundaries as a result of ploughing. Erosion on the downslope side of the boundary creates 'negative lynchets'. They are well documented in the so-called CELTIC FIELDS, while long strip lynchets are characteristic of post-Roman agriculture.

Ordnance Survey: *Field archaeology in Great Britain* (Southampton, 1973), 141.

PTN

M

Ma'adi Late predynastic/protodynastic settlement and cemeteries located about 5 km south of Cairo, dating to *c.*3600–2900 BC. Ma'adi is the type-site of the final culture in the Lower Egyptian predynastic sequence, roughly equivalent to the late Gerzean (Naqada III) phases at such Upper Egyptian sites at HIERAKONPOLIS and ABYDOS (*see* EGYPT: PREHISTORIC). The settlement at Ma'adi, consisting mainly of wattle and daub oval huts, is thought to have acted as an important entrepôt, controlling trade between Upper Egypt and the Levant and probably also exploiting the copper reserves of the Sinai peninsula (Rizkana and Seeher 1984). Cemetery South at Ma'adi is the earliest of the three cemeteries, and the 468 graves shallow round pits sometimes covered with rough stone blocks – are among the first Lower Egyptian funerary contexts to show pronounced variations in quality of funerary equipment, thus suggesting the appearance of social stratification.

M. Amer: 'Annual report of the Maadi excavations, 1935', *CdE* 11 (1936), 54–7; M.A. Hoffman: *Egypt after the pharaohs* (New York, 1979), 200–14; I. Rizkana and J. Seeher: 'New light on the relation of Maadi to the Upper Egyptian cultural sequence', *MDAIK* 40 (1984), 237–52; ——: *Maadi*, 4 vols (Mainz, 1987–90).

IS

Mabveni Earliest cultural 'package' of the Central African Early Iron Age (EIA), dating to the 2nd–6th centuries AD. Mabveni was the first site to show that EIA people were newcomers with a new way of life and set of beliefs. Keith Robinson uncovered raised grain-bin supports, an underground storage pit, remains of domestic cattle, sheep/goat teeth, metal slag and characteristic pottery of the Gokomere facies of NKOPE. The pottery differs somewhat from that of Ziwa, the next Nkope facies to the north, and this may be due to a merge with an earlier Kulundu Tradition occupation such as BAMBATA.

K.R. Robinson: 'An early Iron Age site from the Chibi District, southern Rhodesia', *SAAB* 16 (1961), 75–102; T.N. Huffman: 'Cattle from Mabveni', *SAAB* 30 (1975), 23–4.

TH

Macassans Sailors from the southern Celebes port of Macassar in present-day Indonesia, who visited northern Australia to collect and process *bêche-de-mer* (sea-cucumber). These visits may date back over a thousand years.

C.C. Macknight: *The voyage to Marege* (Melbourne, 1976).

CG

Ma-chia-pang (Majiabang) *see* HO-MU-TU; LIANG-CHU; YANG-SHAO

Machu Picchu The fabled 'lost city' of the INCA – located in the Urubamba Valley, Peru – was in reality the country residence of Pachacuti Inca Yupanki, the founder of the Inca empire. It is remarkable for its preservation, for the numbers of shrines and religious edifices (Pachacuti was extremely interested in religious matters, having founded the state religion), and for its setting in a precipitous, forest-covered landscape with views of various snow-capped (and hence sacred) mountains. In modern times, Machu Picchu and related ruins are in danger because of their popularity with tourists.

H. Bingham: *Machu Picchu, a citadel of the Incas: report of the explorations and excavations made in 1911, 1912, and 1915 under the auspices of Yale University and the National Geographic Society* (Oxford, 1930); L. Meisch: 'Machu Picchu: conserving an Inca treasure', *Archaeology* 38/6 (1986), 18–25; J.H. Rowe: 'Machu Picchu a la luz de documentos del siglo XVI', *Histórica* 14/1 (1990), 139–45.

KB

Macon Plateau *see* OCMULGEE

Madrague de Giens Site near Toulon in southern France where a Roman wreck of *c*.70–50 BC was discovered in 1967 at a depth of 18 m. It was excavated in 1971–83 by Patrice Pomey and André Tchernia. The main cargo consisted of wine stored in about 6000–7000 amphorae, with a filled weight of some 350–400 tonnes; there were also consignments of black-gloss table ware and red coarseware. The forty-metre hull was magnificently preserved, and is a fine example of shell-first mortise-and-tenon construction (*see* MARITIME ARCHAEOLOGY). The excavation at Madrague de Giens has improved understanding of exchange mechanisms in pre-conquest Gaul, the economic behaviour of the Roman elite, and the organization of wine production. Alongside luxury commerce, the coarseware is one of many instances of wrecks providing evidence on long-distance trade in mundane, utilitarian goods, a possibility previously denied by primitivist models of the ancient economy.

A. Tchernia, P. Pomey and A. Hesnard: *L'épave romaine de la Madrague de Giens* (Paris, 1978); A. Tchernia: *Le vin de l'Italie Romaine* (Paris, 1986); A.J. Parker: 'The wines of Roman Italy', *Journal of Roman Archaeology* 3 (1990), 325–31; ——: *Ancient shipwrecks of the Mediterranean and the Roman provinces* (Oxford, 1992), 249–50.

DG

Maes Howe Neolithic PASSAGE GRAVE on Mainland in the Orkney Islands, Scotland – one of the most finely built examples of the chamber tomb tradition. Constructed in about 2750 BC, it consists of a passage 12 m long, lined with huge but thin megaliths and built in two sections of different height, leading into a vaulted chamber of about 4.5 metres square. This chamber has small square cells set into three of its walls above the floor-level, internal buttresses in each of the corners, and a corbelled roof. The impression given by the interior is almost 'architectural' – the builders have used the thin and regularly fractured local slabs of flagstone to great symmetrical effect. The chamber is surrounded by a stepped stone cairn, heaped over with earth and rubble to form a round mound, the whole now measuring about 35 m in diameter and 7.3 m high. The tomb was excavated by Gordon Childe (1954–5) and Colin Renfrew (1973–4), but the chamber had been largely empty for centuries: runic inscriptions on the chamber walls reveal that the tomb was entered during the medieval period by Vikings.

V.G. Childe: 'Maes Howe', *Proceedings of the Society of Antiquaries of Scotland* 88 (1954–6); C. Renfrew: *Investigations in Orkney*, Society of Antiquaries of London Research Report 38 (London, 1979); ——, ed.: *The prehistory of Orkney* (Edinburgh, 1985).

RJA

Magan *see* UMM AN-NAR

Magdalenian Final industry of the Upper Palaeolithic of Western Europe, centred on southwest France and northern Spain in the period between about 15,000 and 10,000 BC. The Magdalenian, named after the type-site of La Madeleine, is traditionally divided into Magdalenian I–VI (Breuil 1912) by means of the typology of the rich bone, ivory and antler industry (including spearthrowers, harpoons and BÂTONS PERCÉ (i.e. *bâtons-de-commandement*); this series has been extended backwards to include the primitive 'Magdalenian 0' uncovered at LAUGERIE HAUTE. However, the validity of the series is now doubted, and Abbé Breuil's strict evolutionary sequence from the various bone points and *bâtons* of the Lower Magdalenian (I–III) through to the increasingly complex prototype, single-row and double-row harpoons of the Upper Magdalenian (Magdalenian IV–VI) has largely been abandoned. The bone typology has never been satisfactorily tied to a stone tool typology; indeed Laville et al. (1980: 295) suggest that Magdalenian stone assemblages are best divided simply in two, equating with Magdalenian 0–I and Magdalenian II–VI. In this scheme, the earliest lithic assemblage is characterized by certain AURIGNACIAN traits (e.g. carinate scrapers) and later by raclettes. The later assemblage is rich in burins and backed bladelets.

Although the classic Magdalenian is concentrated around southern France and northern Spain, certain features of the complex are present in other parts of western Europe (Britain, Germany) and in Poland; Praslov et al. (1989) cite assemblages from Russia (e.g. Yudinovo on the Sudost River) that seem related to the Magdalenian lithic assemblages.

H. Breuil: *Les subdivisions du Paléolithique supérieur et leur signification*, Comptes Rendus de 14e Congrès International d'Antropologie et d'Archéologie Préhistorique (Geneve, 1912); H. Laville et al.: *Rockshelters of the Perigord* (New York, 1980); N.D. Praslov et al.: 'The steppes in the late Palaeolithic', *Antiquity* 63 (1989), 784–92.

RJA

Maghzalya, Tell Aceramic Neolithic settlement site on the Sinjar plain to the west of Mosul in northwestern Iraq. The village covered one hectare and, with its curving buttressed enclosure wall, is the earliest known fortified settlement in Mesopotamia. An area of about 4,500 sq. m was excavated by Soviet archaeologists in 1977–80, revealing a series of rectangular clay houses with stone-built foundations and stone-paved, plastered floors. The 15 occupation strata contained flint arrowheads and obsidian sickle blades, as well as stone rubbing stones, querns and pestles. The presence of wild and domesticated barley and emmer wheat, alongside faunal remains suggesting the hunting of wild bulls, indicates that the assemblage at Maghzalya was essentially characteristic of the 'Jarmoan' culture (*c.*7000–6000 BC; *see* JARMO). The site has been compared with ACERAMIC NEOLITHIC (Pre-Pottery Neolithic B) settlements in Syria and Anatolia, such as TELL ABU HUREYRA, ÇAYÖNÜ TEPESI and MUREYBET (Merpert et al. 1981: 62).

N.Y. Merpert, R.M. Munchaev and N.O. Bader: 'Investigations of the Soviet expedition in northern Iraq, 1976', *Sumer* 37 (1981), 22–54; N. Yoffee and J.J. Clark, ed.: *Early stages in the evolution of Mesopotamian civilization: Soviet excavations in northern Iraq* (Tucson, 1993).

IS

Maglemosian (Maglemosean) Widespread family of early Mesolithic industries, extending from Britain across the North European Plain, defined in the Magle Mose bogland area of Zealand, Holland. The lithic industry is characterized by the presence of axes obliquely blunted points and flints in the shape of large isoceles triangles. The presence of microliths (tiny worked flints) and axes (presumed to represent evidence of increased wood-working in the more thickly forested Holocene environment) differentiate the assemblages from those of the Upper Palaeolithic.

The Maglemosian is often contrasted with the other two main assemblage types of the Mesolithic, the SAUVETERRIAN and the TARDENOISIAN. However, the exact distribution of the Maglemosian really depends on how loosely or tightly the characteristics of the industry are defined – modern researchers tend to stress that variation between assemblages can arise from different environmental contexts and different preservation as much as from 'cultural' differences. It is now felt unwise, for example, to assume that the sites of northern Britain with 'Maglemosian' characteristics (most famously, STAR CARR) are culturally distinct from the non-Maglemosian lowland sites. Rowley-Conwy suggests that rather than debating how to assign each site, it might be better to break the Mesolithic of France, the United Kingdom and the North European Plain into the following broad chronological scheme (1) broad-blade assemblages with obliquely blunted points (roughly equivalent to the Maglemosian) (2) narrow-blade assemblages with a more varied range of microlith shape, especially in the scalene triangle shape (this phase seems to originate in southern France) (3) blade and trapeze industries across Europe, but not the United Kingdom.

S.K. Kozłowski, ed.: *The Mesolithic in Europe* (Warsaw, 1973); P. Rowley-Conwy: 'Between cavepainters and crop planters: aspects of the temperate European Mesolithic' *Hunters in transition*, ed. M. Zvelebil (Cambridge, 1986), 17–29.

RJA

magnetic survey Common geophysical survey technique that makes use of a magnetometer to measure minor fluctuations in the earth's magnetic field at specific points on an archaeological site. Anomalies in the magnetic field suggest that the underlying area has been disturbed in some way, possibly by ancient buried structures. In particular, magnetic surveys can be helpful in locating rubbish-filled ditches and pits, kilns, hearths, and features lined with fired clay. Like the other main geophysical survey technique, the soil RESISTIVITY SURVEY, magnetometer surveys are a form of relative measurement and the results have to be carefully interpreted. Unlike resistivity surveys, they are not affected by the amount of moisture retained in the soil, but care has to be taken to allow for natural fluctuations in the earth's magnetic field and, sometimes, to make sure that metal objects that may affect the results are removed from the surface of the site before the survey. Furthermore, many natural features and modern features also produce magnetic anomalies. Typically, the survey procedure might involve taking readings at one metre intervals across a grid laid out over the site using the most common type of magnetometer, a proton magnetometer. After correcting the readings for any general fluctuations in the magnetic field during the course of the survey, the data can be plotted out to reveal features of potential interest.

A. Clark: *Seeing beneath the soil: prospecting methods in archaeology* (London, 1990).

RJA

magnetometer *see* ARCHAEOMAGNETIC DATING; MAGNETIC SURVEY

Magosi, Magosian Stone Age rock-shelter located beside natural cisterns in a dry part of north-eastern Uganda, which was once thought to illustrate the 'intermediate' stage between the African Middle and Late Stone Ages, that is essentially the transition from LEVALLOIS flake industries towards a microlithic one ('WILTON' type), around the end of the Pleistocene. Such conclusions were based on E.J. Wayland's excavations in the 1920s. Re-examination in the 1960s (Posnansky and Cole 1963) indicated that much of the supposedly 'transitional' materials in the Magosi stratigraphy resulted from mixing of those from higher and lower levels. 'Magosian' levels elsewhere (notably at APIS ROCK in Tanzania) have been similarly reinterpreted, just as the concept of a linear progression of stone-age cultures defined by tool types and lithic technology has become less fashionable.

M. Posnansky and G.H. Cole: 'Recent excavations at Magosi, Uganda', *Man* (O.S.) 1963 [article no.133].

JS

Maiden Castle *see* HILLFORT

Maikop Famously rich series of Bronze Age burial mounds (kurgans), located in the North Caucasus (Russia) and discovered and excavated in 1897 by N.I. Veselovsky. The largest of the mounds was 11 m high; burial chambers contained pottery, metal tools and ornaments, and two golden and 14 silver vessels. Among the remarkable finds were gold figurines of bulls and lions, originally sewn onto garments; gold and silver bull-figurines adorning canopies; gold beads and rings; gold, silver, turquoise and carnelian beads; copper axes, tanged axes and spearheads. Some of these prestige items were of Middle Eastern origin.

By comparing the Maikop finds to similar assemblages from a number of sites, Russian archaeologists (Iessen 1950; Munchaev 1970) have identified a 'Maikopian culture', which is concentrated in the northwestern Caucasus, but which influenced the northeastern Caucasus and Transcaucasia. A.A. Iessen (1963) has distinguished two stages in the development of the Maikopian tradition: the Maikop proper and the Novosvobodnaya. The former is characterized by large rectangular burial chambers beneath kurgans, while the Novosvobodnaya-type kurgans contained dolmens. Iessen (1950) dates the Maikop culture to the middle/second half of the 3rd millennium BC, while a more recent series of radiocarbon measurements for the Ust'-Jegutinsky cemetery, near the town of Cherkessk, suggest calendar dates of *c*.2500–2400 BC. However, the detailed chronology of the culture, and its relationships with the (broadly contemporary) north-Caucasian variant of CATACOMB-GRAVE CULTURE and the KURA-ARAXIAN in Transcaucasia, remain unclear.

A.A. Iessen: 'Khronologii bol'ših kubanskih kurganov' [The chronology of the Great Kuban kurgans], *Sovetskaja arheologija* 12 (1950), 157–202; ——: 'Kavkaz i Drevnii Vostok v IV–III tysjačeletii do n.e.' [The Caucasus and the Ancient East in the 4th–3rd millennium BC], *KSIA* 93 (1963), 3–14; R.M. Munchaev: *Kavkaz na zare bronzovogo veka* [The Caucasus on the eve of the Bronze Age] (Moscow, 1970).

PD

Majiabang *see* MA-CHIA-PANG

Figure 29 **Maikop** Early 'landscape' design incised on a silver bowl of the 3rd millennium BC found at Maikop (now in the Hermitage, St Petersburg). *Source*: H. Frankfort: *The art and architecture of the ancient Orient*, 4th edn (Harmondsworth: Pelican, 1970), fig. 243.

Makapansgat Oldest of the South African sites that have yielded remains of AUSTRALOPITHECUS AFRICANUS, located in the ancient Limeworks cavern system, containing bone-rich breccia, ten miles east–northeast of Potgietersrus, central Transvaal, South Africa. On faunal grounds the site is thought to be around three million years old. Raymond Dart's osteodontokeratic (bone, tooth and horn) 'culture' proposed on the basis of finds from this site is now explained in terms of the natural factors affecting bone accumulation and preservation in ancient limestone caverns.

C.K. Brain: *The Transvaal ape-man-bearing cave deposits* (Pretoria, 1958); J.M. Maguire: 'Recent geological, stratigraphic and palaeontological studies at Makapansgat Limeworks', *Hominid evolution: past, present and future*, ed. P.V. Tobias (New York, 1985).

RI

Makouria *see* NUBIA

Malatya (Arslantepe; anc. Melitene) The modern Turkish town of Malatya is built over the ruins of a Hellenistic/Roman town but the adjacent tell-mound of Arslantepe dates back to the Bronze Age and early Iron Age. This earlier settlement flourished during the late Hittite and Syro-Hittite periods (*c.*1300–700 BC), but there are also strata dating back to the 4th millennium BC, which contain ceramic material comparable with URUK and TEPE GAWRA, as well as numerical tablets and Uruk-style CYLINDER SEALS, suggesting that the Sumerians had established extensive trading links as far north as the Anatolian plateau.

L. Delaporte: *Malatya Arslantepe* (Paris, 1940); S.M. Puglisi and P. Meriggi: *Malatya* I (Rome, 1964).

IS

Malkata Egyptian settlement and palace site of the early 14th century BC, situated at the southern end of western Thebes, opposite modern Luxor, which was excavated in 1888–1918 (Tytus 1903; Hayes 1951) and the early 1970s (Kemp and O'Connor 1974). It comprises several large official buildings (including four probable palaces) built by the 18th-dynasty ruler Amenhotep III (*c.*1391–1353 BC), as well as kitchens, store-rooms, residential areas and a temple dedicated to the god Amun. To the east of Malkata are the remains of a large artificial lake evidently created at the same time as Amenhotep III's palaces (Kemp and O'Connor 1974).

R. de P. Tytus: *A preliminary report on the pre-excavation of the palace of Amenhotep III* (New York, 1903); W. Hayes: 'Inscriptions from the palace of Amenophis III', *JNES* 10 (1951), 35–40; B.J. Kemp and D. O'Connor: 'An ancient Nile harbour: University Museum excavations at the Birket Habu', *International Journal of Nautical Archaeology and Underwater Exploration* 3/1 (1974), 101–36.

IS

Maltai *see* ASSYRIA

Maltese temples Group of around 24 architecturally similar ritual buildings erected on the Mediterranean islands of Malta and Gozo *c.*3500–2500 BC, representing some of the earliest sophisticated stone architecture in the world. The islands' first inhabitants, who may have arrived from Sicily in the 5th millennium BC, built simple stone and mud-brick ritual structures, exemplified by a small oval-roomed 'shrine' at Skorba. These structures, together with rock-cut tombs created in the 4th millennium BC, provide possible antecedents for the temples. Even so, the temples were a precocious development, unparalleled elsewhere in the Mediterranean. Their typological evolution remains unclear, but the most complicated designs appear to be elaborations of an early 'three-leaf clover' shaped groundplan (e.g. Ggantija South). Nearly all the temples have monumental concave facades, in front of which rituals were probably performed; the later examples are built entirely of large, well-tooled blocks. Trilithons form imposing temple entrances and the upper courses of walls are

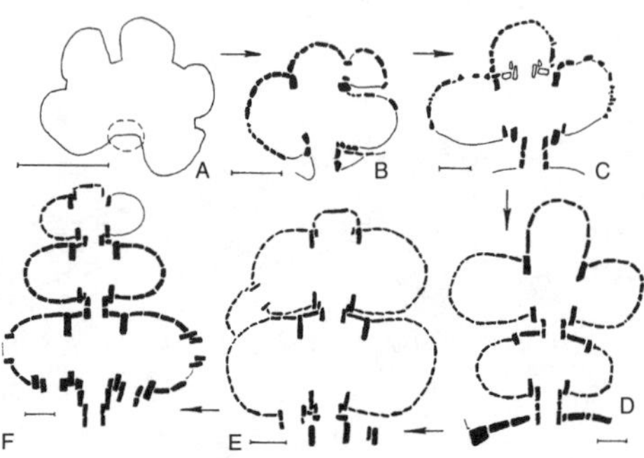

Figure 30 **Maltese temples** The evolution of the 'Maltese temples': (A) a rock-cut tomb, Xemxija, (B) lobed temple, Mgarr East, (C) trefoil temple, with later cross-wall, Skorba West, (D) 5-apse temple, Ggantija South, (E) 4-apse temple, Mnajdra Central, (F) 6-apse temple, Tarxien Central; the scale measures 3 m. *Source*: D. Trump: 'Megalithic architecture in Malta', *The megalithic monuments of western Europe*, ed. C. Renfrew (London, 1981), p. 65.

skilfully curved inwards to facilitate roofing (probably of timber and thatch). The use of large blocks of stone has led many authorities to describe the temples as MEGALITHIC, even though the stones are carefully dressed and there seems to be no connection with the megalithic tradition of the Atlantic seaboard. The care taken over temple design is revealed by the possible architectural models discovered at Tarxien (limestone carving) and Hagar Qim (terracotta). A love of architectural detail is also apparent in the underground complex of the Hypogeum. Here, a rock-cut temple connected to tombs reproduces in high-relief carving the lintels and orthostats of the surface temples; the monument performed a funerary role in its final phases but may not have been constructed with that intention. The Hypogeum has preserved wall decoration in the form of painted spirals. Many of the surface temples must also have been plastered and painted, while others are still adorned with simple 'area pitting' and low-relief carvings. The most striking carvings are of beautifully balanced spiral designs; at the late temple of Tarxien there are also simple animal friezes. The Maltese monuments are believed to have been temples partly because they contain no evidence of burials and partly because interior features (such as decorated stone 'altars') suggest repeated ceremonies. This theory is corroborated by the surviving half of a giant statue at Tarxien, which seems to represent a hugely corpulent, skirted deity; smaller examples have been found at other temples.

J.D. Evans: *The prehistoric antiquities of the Maltese Islands* (London, 1971); D. Trump: 'Megalithic architecture in Malta' *The megalithic monuments of Western Europe*, ed. C. Renfrew (London, 1981), 64–76.

RJA

Malwa Cultural phase in the Indian Deccan region (*c.*1800–1400 BC), named after the Chalcolithic sites on the Malwa plateau, to the east of the BANAS valley. The Malwa culture is defined by buff or orange-slipped pottery painted in black and dark brown. Painted motifs are typically found on the upper section of vessels, and include linear and triangular geometric designs, along with naturalistic motifs including plants, animals and human figures (Dhavalikar 1979: 238). Settlements were small, consisting of wattle and daub houses, and the inhabitants exploited a range of domesticated plant and animal resources including domestic wheat, barley, lentils and peas, as well as wild deer, fish and domestic cattle and pig. Small quantities of copper tools are known from several Malwa sites, including INAMGAON and NAVDATOLI.

H.D. Sankalia, S.B. Deo and Z.D. Ansari: *Chalcolithic Navdatoli* (Pune, 1971); M.K. Dhavalikar: 'Early Farming Cultures of Central India', *Essays in Indian protohistory*, ed. D.P. Agrawal and D.K. Chakrabarti (Delhi, 1979), 229–45 (relevant pages of article, 236–43); ——: 'The Malwa Culture in Maharashtra', *Srinidhih: perspectives in Indian archaeology, art, and culture*, ed. K.V. Raman (Madras, 1983), 17–21; ——: *The first farmers of the Deccan* (Pune, 1988).

CS

Malyan, Tal-i (anc. Anshan) Largest surviving PROTO-ELAMITE site, located in southern Iran to the north of modern Shiraz, which was excavated by William Sumner in the 1970s. The lower strata include the remains of 'Banesh'-period houses with wall-paintings (Nickerson 1977), dating to the 4th millennium BC. After the 3rd millennium BC it became known as Anshan, and, together with the city of SUSA, it formed the nucleus of the kingdom of ELAM. In the early 7th century BC, after a short period of relative obscurity, the city of Anshan was conquered by Teispes, the son of Achaemenes (the founder of the Achaemenid dynasty) and became an important city of the PERSIAN empire, along with PERSEPOLIS and PASARGADAE.

J. Hansman: 'Elamites, Achaemenians and Anshan', *Iran* 10 (1972), 101–26; Preliminary reports on the Tal-i Malyan excavations by W. Sumner published in *Iran* 12–14 (1975–6); J.W. Nickerson: 'Malyan wall paintings', *Expedition* 19 (1977), 2–6.

IS

mammisi (birth-house) Invented Coptic term, literally meaning 'place of birth', which was first used by the Egyptologist Jean-François Champollion to refer to the buildings in several Late Period, Ptolemaic and Roman temples (e.g. EDFU and DENDERA), in which the birth of the god was celebrated. It may have its origins in the reliefs concerning the divine birth of the king in temples dating at least as early as the 18th dynasty (*c.*1550–1307 BC), such as LUXOR and the temple of Hatshepsut at DEIR EL-BAHARI.

E. Chassinat: *Le mammisi d'Edfou*, 2 vols (Cairo, 1939); F. Daumas: *Les mammisi des temples égyptiens* (Paris, 1958); J. Junker and E. Winter: *Das Geburtshaus des Tempels der Isis in Philä* (Vienna, 1965).

IS

Man-ch'eng (Mancheng) Han-Dynasty site in the province of Ho-pei, China, where two tombs (M1 and M2), each hewn from the solid rock in a hillside 1.5 km southwest of Man-ch'eng-hsien, were excavated in 1968. M1 was the tomb of Liu Sheng, Prince Ching of Chung-shan-kuo (d. 113 BC), and M2, contained his concubine, Tou-Wan (named Chun Hsu). Tomb M1 measured 51.7 m long, 37.5 m wide and 6.8 m high, with an overall volume of 2,700 cubic metres, while the equivalent dimensions in M2 are 49.7 m, 65 m, 7.9 m and 3000 cubic metres. It has been estimated that it would have taken about a year to hollow out M1 with present-day excavation facilities, using a labour-force of 100 men.

The two tombs yielded more than 4000 artefacts, including chariots and horses, a suit of 'fish-scale armour' (*yü-lin-chia*) comprising 2859 lames of perforated wrought iron, jade, pottery, lacquer, bronze vessels, complex bronze articulated joinery, bronze (and some iron) chariot and equine equipment, gold and silver medical implements (for acupuncture?), textile fragments and coins. The bodies were both clothed in jade suits, the larger comprising about 2500 individually shaped pieces, each piece being interlocked with the next by means of gold wire-like thread.

Anon: *Man-ch'eng Han-mu fa-chüeh pao-kao* [Report on the excavation of the Han tombs at Man-ch'eng] (Peking, 1980); Hua Chüeh-ming: *Chung-kuo ye-chu-shih lun-chi* [Collected essays on the history of Chinese metallurgy] (Peking, 1986), 65–70.

NB

Manching One of the largest of the OPPIDA of the late Iron Age, in the vicinity of the Danube in Bavaria, south Germany, which flourished in the 2nd and 1st centuries BC. The earliest stage of the site is known only through a small inhumation cemetery, but it probably began as a small cluster of farmsteads during the middle part of the La Tène (La Tène B). Favoured by its location on a major trade route (attested, for example, by the presence of Mediterranean ceramics from the south and raw amber from the north). Manching developed into a trade and manufacturing centre. By the end of La Tène C it had become one of the most populous centres in western and central Europe. Extensive excavations have revealed streets laid out from east to west, lined with small houses; other structures include longer buildings and buildings enclosed in palisades. Whether Manching qualifies as being 'proto-urban' depends largely on how that term is defined: there is some evidence to suggest specialised craft production (high-quality pottery, metal-working, glass-making, amber-working etc), the minting of coins, dedicated craft areas, dedicated 'shops' or trading and storage spaces, and semi-organized planning of the settlement layout; there is no evidence to suggest strict planning, public buildings, carefully thought out drainage systems, properly surfaced roads etc. Interestingly, the site is not in an easily defensible location and as late as the end of La Tène C Manching was still an open settlement – though ramparts of the murus gallicus type enclosing *c.*380 ha were added in La Tène D.

Die Ausgrabungen in Manching, various volumes (Stuttgart, n.d.) [no author cited].

RJA

Manda *see* SWAHILI HARBOUR TOWNS

mandala Term used by I.W. Mabbett and O.W. Wolters to describe the indigenous states of Southeast Asia. In Indian political philosophy, the *mandala* was perceived as a circle or polity, surrounded by other such circles. Adjacent circles were seen as enemies, but other mandalas might be fostered as allies. The resultant polities were based more on the notion of the centre manifested by its leader, but with fluid boundaries, than a state with fixed territorial limits. The durability of a mandala depended on the charisma of its leader, and the concept becomes less useful following the establishment of ANGKOR, when a degree of permanence based on a dynastic succession was achieved.

Several variables can be identified in any attempt to understand how such complex centralized polities developed. The first and critical point is that Southeast Asian societies had reached a considerable level of sophistication by the end of the 1st millennium BC. The craft specialization seen in the field of pottery at KHOK PHANOM DI (2000–1500 BC) is further attested at BAN DON TA PHET in the expertise associated with bronze working. Iron forging was also widespread, and some communities, as at NON CHAI, had grown in size to the point that we can easily envisage regional centres of political and economic power. The leaders within such networks encountered new opportunities when both Chinese and Indian contact quickened towards the end of the 1st millennium BC. Those which commanded strategic locations, as on a frequented coast or riverine exchange node, were able to control the flow of a new range of exotic goods and ideas. Glass and etched carnelian beads are the physical evidence, but of equal importance was the selective adoption of political, legal and, above all, religious ideas originating in India.

Saivism, the worship of Siva, was prominent in providing emerging leaders with the means whereby semi-divine status could be obtained. The temples to Siva, and other members of the Hindu pantheon, are prominent in the archaeological record in the middle Mekong polities of the ZHENLA CULTURE, while Buddhism was favoured among the polities of the DVARAVATI CULTURE in the Chao Phraya valley. Leaders also adopted the Sanskrit language in taking exotic names and having commemorative stelae erected to advertise their achievements and status.

The critical role of attracting followers to the court centres provided the challenge of sustaining them with food and water. The drought of the long dry season was overcome by digging large reservoirs and moats around the centres, and these served a dual purpose, since, apart from supplying water and aquatic food, they also symbolized the lakes around Mount Meru, the home of the Hindu gods. If the moats represented the lakes, then the temples within were stone representations of the sacred mount. As the rulers assumed the aura of divinity, so their temples were transformed into personal mausolea, where they were worshipped in life as in death.

The identification of agricultural intensification, quickening exchange, the provision of food for specialist craftsmen and soldiers, religious legitimization and establishment of both a legal code and rights of accumulating tribute allow us some insight into the interrelationships between key variables. The archaeological manifestation of this trend is seen in the many court centres, as at Isnapura, MI SON, MUANG FA DAET, MUANG SIMA and U Thong. Archaeology has tended to concentrate on the more visible central temples and sacred precincts at the expense of secular remains. We can therefore not be sure of the extent to which a permanent populace would qualify such centres as urban rather than cermonial centres. Excavations away from the large and obvious surviving remains would contribute to this important issue, but at present we can be assured from surviving Chinese accounts that Isanapura, at least, included a substantial royal palace and population measured in thousands rather than hundreds.

I.W. Mabbett: 'Kingship at Angkor', *JSS* 66/2 (1978), 1–58; O.W. Wolters: *History, culture and religion in Southeast Asian perspectives* (Singapore 1982).

CH

Manekweni Royal settlement of the Zimbabwe period (*see* GREAT ZIMBABWE), situated a few kilometres inland from the Mozambique coastal town of Vilanculos. Paul Sinclair's work at nearby Chibuene shows that this coastal stretch was the source of glass beads found at Schroda, K2 and MAPUNGUBWE. An occupation of the 12th–13th centuries AD, predating the stone enclosure at Manekweni, may be associated with this trade; the main occupation encompasses both the Zimbabwe and Khami periods. Barker's faunal analyses showed that cattle made up 40–50% and small stock 30–35% of the bone sample associated with the enclosure, while a commoner midden contained only 16% cattle and 50% small stock. Besides this status difference, no calves and few old beasts were present. Barker's environmental study suggests that cattle had to be kept some distance away during the dry season because of the tsetse fly and poor surface water. As a result of these findings, Peter Garlake proposed that most Zimbabwe-period sites were temporary pastoral nodes on a transhumance cycle; his interpretation, however, is not supported by Portuguese records, by Shona and Venda traditions or by archaeological data pertaining to settlement organization and political hierarchies.

P.S. Garlake: 'An investigation of Manekweni, Mozambique', *Azania* 11 (1976), 25–47; G. Barker: 'Economic models for the Manekweni Zimbabwe, Mozambique', *Azania* 13 (1978), 71–100; P.S. Garlake: 'Pastoralism and Zimbabwe', *JAH* 19 (1978), 479–93; P.J.J. Sinclair: 'Chibuene: an early trading site in southern Mozambique', *Paideuma* 28 (1982), 150–64.

TH

Mangaasi Pacific pottery style with incised and applied-relief decoration which dates from 2700 BP until about 700 years ago; it is thus contemporary with, and post-dates, the LAPITA CULTURAL COMPLEX. It is best known from Vanuatu, but is also known from the Solomon islands, New Caledonia and Fiji. Some of the later assemblages from the Bismarck Archipelago bear some resemblance to this style.

J. Garanger: *Archéologie des Nouvelles-Hebrides* (Paris, 1972).

CG

Manneans *see* HASANLU

mano *see* METATE

Mapuche Modern indigenous group of people in southern central Chile. Ethnoarchaeological studies of the Mapuche have yielded important information concerning the delineation and utilization of ritual space, including ceremonial plazas and elite burial mounds and the iconography of material goods in a series of interconnected small chiefdoms. The mechanics of social evolution and change among the Mapuche have considerable bearing on archaeological theory concerning cultural change and the development of complex societies.

T.D. Dillehay: 'Mapuche ceremonial landscape, social recruitment, and resources rights', *WA* 22/2 (1990), 225–41; ——: 'Keeping outsiders out: public ceremony, resource rights, and hierarchy in historic and contemporary Mapuche society', *Wealth and hierarchy in the Intermediate area*, ed. F.W. Lange (Washington, D.C., 1992).

KB

Mapungubwe Hill Part of a complex of Iron Age sites on the farm Greefswald, N. Transvaal, South Africa (*see* BAMBANDYALANO). This site is particularly notable for the rich haul of gold objects from a grave on the summit of the hill. Subsequent excavations show that it was occupied initially from the late 10th century AD. The original population was replaced about AD 1100 when earlier structures were burned, Bambandyanalo was abandoned, and new settlement was restricted to Mapungubwe summit and the southern terrace slopes. Stone walling is associated with the hilltop settlement. The 'gold burial' evidently belongs to a late stage of the occupation, prior to final abandonment of the site about AD 1200. The economy was based on livestock supported by cultivation of millet, sorghum and beans; iron, copper and gold were smelted on the site, and fine ceramics produced. The site was probably the political centre of a group of dependent settlements engaged in trading networks extending to the east coast. It is probably no coincidence that the decline of Mapungubwe is accompanied by the rise of the Zimbabwe state (see GREAT ZIMBABWE) and a new Arab dynasty at Kilwa on the coast (*see* SWAHILI HARBOUR TOWNS).

L. Fouché, ed.: *Mapungubwe: ancient Bantu civilization on the Limpopo* (Cambridge, 1937); G.A. Gardner: *Mapungubwe* II (Pretoria, 1963); J.F. Eloff and A. Meyer: 'The Greefswald sites', *Guide to archaeological sites in the northern and eastern Transvaal*, ed. E. Voigt (Pretoria, 1981), 7–22.

RI

Maputo Matola *see* SILVER LEAVES

marae A combination of rectangular court and raised platform used for ritual purposes in central Polynesia (southern Marquesas, Tuamotus, Societies, Australs and Cooks). There are variations from island to island, but most *marae* seem to be late prehistoric, dating from the last few hundred years.

K.P. Emory: 'A re-examination of the east Polynesian *marae*', *Studies in Oceanic culture history*, ed. R.C. Green and M. Kelly (Auckland, 1970), 73–92; P. Bellwood: *Man's conquest of the Pacific* (New York, 1978), 329–30.

CG

Marajó Large island at the mouth of the Amazon in Brazil, where remains of villages on high artificial platforms, groups of ovens, and large cemeteries of urn burials with elaborate polychrome ceramics have been found, all dating to the Marajoara phase (*c*.AD 1000–1500). Marajó is currently the focus of an argument concerning the ability of the relatively poor and often seasonally inundated lands to support large sedentary populations. This argument has considerable bearing not only on the reconstruction of Amazon prehistory, but upon political rhetoric and development schemes in the Amazon today.

A.C. Roosevelt: *Mound builders of the Amazon: geophysical archaeology at Marajo Island, Brazil* (Orlando, 1991); B.J. Meggers: 'Amazonia: real or counterfeit paradise?', *The Review of Archaeology* 13/2 (1992), 25–40.

KB

Marana Platform-mound community of the Hohokam culture, dating to the early Classic period (AD 1100–1300), located in the northern Tucson Basin, southern Arizona. Full-coverage survey directed by Paul and Suzanne Fish of the Arizona State Museum has revealed multiple agricultural technologies and underlined the importance of agave as a food and fibre crop.

S.K. and P.R. Fish and J.H. Madsen: *The Marana community in the Hohokam world* (Tucson, 1992).

JJR

Marden Massive HENGE monument in Wiltshire, England, radiocarbon dated to 2000 BC. The bank and internal ditch form a 14 ha incomplete oval, punctured by two entrances. The henge encloses the remains of at least one circular timber structure (10.5 m in diameter) and, like nearby Avebury and comparable ceremonial structures at Durrington Walls and Mount Pleasant, it is associated with GROOVED WARE.

G.J. Wainwright: 'The excavation of a later Neolithic enclosure at Marden, Wiltshire', *AJ*, 51 (1971).

RJA

Mardikh, Tell *see* EBLA

Mari (Tell Hariri) Mesopotamian city site, located beside the River Euphrates on the border between modern Syria and Iraq, which was occupied continuously from the Jemdet Nasr period (*c.*3200–2900 BC) to the Seleucid dynasty (*c.*305–64 BC). Mari was the principal commercial centre on the trade route between Syria and Babylonia; the Early Dynastic remains include a number of substantial mud-brick buildings identified as temples and palaces, although Margueron (1982: 86) argues that the buildings identified as royal residences by the excavator, André Parrot, may have actually been sanctuaries.

The settlement flourished during the Old Babylonian period (*c.*1894–1595 BC) and it is to the early part of this phase that the extensive palace complex of Zimri-Lim has been dated. The complex comprises over three hundred rooms, including stables, storerooms, archives and bitumen-lined bathrooms, covering a total area of over two and a half hectares. It was never rebuilt after its destruction at the hands of the Babylonian ruler Hammurabi in *c.*1759 BC, although ironically this has ensured unusually good preservation, with some of the mud-brick walls still standing to a height of five metres and often bearing fragments of plaster and paintings. One surviving mural depicts the ruler of Mari in the presence of various deities, including Ishtar in the form of the goddess of war. An unusual FUNCTIONALIST architectural interpretation has been applied to the palace and its most important courtyard (al-Khalesi 1978).

Figure 31 **Mari** Wall-painting from Mari known as 'The investiture of Zimri-Lim', showing the King before the goddess Ishtar and other deities. *Source*: J. Oates: *Babylon*, 2nd ed. (Thames and Hudson, 1986), fig. 42.

Undoubtedly the most important discovery in the palace at Mari is the archive of some 23,000 Old Babylonian cuneiform tablets dating from *c.*1810 to 1760 BC (Dossin et al. 1946–). The cache includes scientific and economic texts, as well as several thousand items of diplomatic correspondence, including a vital set of letters between the ruler of northern Mesopotamia, Shamshi-Adad, and his son, Yasmah-Adad, the ruler of Mari. This archive, still incompletely published, provides enormously detailed information on the society and history of the northern Mesopotamian cities in the 18th century BC.

G. Dossin, J.R. Kupper, J. Bottéro, M. Birot et al: *Archives royales de Mari* (Paris, 1946–). [ongoing series, currently nearly thirty volumes consisting of transliterations and translations of the cuneiform texts from Mari]; A. Parrot: *Mission archéologique à Mari II: le palais*, 3 vols (Paris, 1958–9); ——: *Mari, capitale fabuleuse* (Paris, 1974); Y. al-Khalesi: *The court of the palms: a functional interpretation of the Mari palace* (Malibu, 1978); J. Margueron: *Recherches sur les palais mésopotamiens de l'âge due bronze* (Paris, 1982).

IS

Marib *see* ARABIA, PRE-ISLAMIC

Marietta Earthworks and mound complex located along the Muskingum River in southeastern Ohio (USA), near the confluence of the Muskingum and Ohio rivers (*c.*200 BC–AD 400). The site consists of two large square earthworks enclosing 20 and 11 ha, respectively. A graded 'roadway' extends about 180 m from the west side of the larger earthwork. Several large flat-topped mounds are located inside the larger earthwork, while the smaller one contains four conical mounds. A large conical mound surrounded by a ditch and exterior wall is located just to the east of the smaller square earthwork. The Marietta Works are associated with the Middle WOODLAND (HOPEWELL) cultural manifestation.

J. Maclean: 'Ancient works at Marietta, Ohio', *OAHSP* 12 (1903), 37–66; G.E. Squier and W.H. Davis: *Ancient monuments of the Mississippi Valley* (Washington, D.C., 1848 reprinted 1973).

RJE

marine archaeology *see* MARITIME ARCHAEOLOGY

maritime archaeology Study of the material evidence for human activity on the seas and inland waterways. The main concern of maritime archaeology is shipwrecks; other aspects include boat ethnography and experimentation, the recording of submerged coastal structures (such as harbours), and the anthropology of seafaring communities. One specialization, nautical archaeology, primarily concerns ship and boat technology. The term underwater (or at sea marine) archaeology refers to the package of techniques necessary to carry out underwater investigations to the standards of land archaeology.

As well as being complex artefacts of great intrinsic interest, wrecked hulls often contain assemblages of artefacts that offer unique information about seaborne transport. One strength is the typical nature of a wreck as a contemporaneous assemblage that was not consciously pre-selected for discard. It has unusually fine grain, or high resolution and integrity as a body of evidence, owing to the relative homogeneity, respectively, of the events or conditions whose by-products are present in the deposit, and of the agents responsible for those materials. A wreck cargo allows the pottery typologist to establish contemporaneous form variability, and a close date can be obtained from associated finds such as coins. The archaeologist of trade has an unparalleled opportunity to study packaged consumables in transit. In addition to their inferential advantages, wrecks are waterlogged sites that commonly preserve organic materials ranging from timbers to foodstuffs.

Underwater archaeology is conventionally dated from 1960, when George Bass excavated a wreck of the late 2nd millennium BC at GELIDONYA, southwestern Turkey, and demonstrated that scientific wreck investigation was possible (Bass 1966). The major technical breakthrough occurred 18 years earlier, however, when Jacques Cousteau and Emile Gagnan perfected the 'aqualung' (or SCUBA: 'self-contained underwater breathing apparatus'), a regulated compressed-air device that allows untethered access to the maximum safe airdiving depth of about 50 m. The archaeological significance of the first ancient wrecks reported by sport divers, off the south coast of France in the late 1940s, was swiftly recognized, but many sites were looted, and some excavations amounted to little more than salvage. Since 1960, matters have improved, with more diving archaeologists, many high-quality underwater projects world-wide, better protective legislation, and specialist institutes and journals.

Underwater and land techniques of excavation are fundamentally similar, with adaptations such as air-bags for raising artefacts and air-lifts for removing spoil (Dean et al. 1992). The treatment of waterlogged wreck materials has been at the forefront of archaeological conservation (e.g. Pearson 1987). Underwater fieldwork, however, is typically 8–15 times more expensive than that on land, and time and performance on-site are constrained by depth and conditions. The situation has been improved to some extent by the provision of timesaving survey equipment, such as SHARPS (sonic high accuracy ranging and positioning system), and the use of mixed-gas SCUBA, substituting a different inert gas for nitrogen, which in air-diving becomes dangerously toxic below 50 m and must also be allowed to dissipate from the bloodstream as the diver surfaces. Excavation in abyssal depth may eventually be possible using robots and manned submersibles (Gibbins 1991). Most work, however, will doubtless continue to take place in shallow water, at depths of less than 30 m, where sites are easier to investigate and often provide information comparable with that obtained from deeper wrecks.

The evolution of nautical technology has dominated maritime scholarship, with over a hundred well-preserved hulls excavated worldwide (Steffy 1994). In the Mediterranean, the Ulu Burun wreck (*see* GELIDONYA), dating to the 14th century BC, demonstrates the early foundation of mortise-and-tenon construction, in which planks were edge-joined and the frames added later. This construction technique is best exemplified by ships of the late Roman Republic (*c.*150–27 BC), such as MADRAGUE DE GIENS, and it may only have been replaced by wholly frame-first construction a few centuries before the appearance in the Mediterranean of sturdy northwestern European ships such as the cog (13th-century AD). Many wrecks of the Roman Imperial period (*c.*27 BC–AD 476) are below the minimum acceptable size for seagoing ships inferred from ancient authors, underlining the unreliability of historical evidence for the study of ancient economics and technology (Houston 1988). The socio-economic implications of ship size and shell-first construction – requiring more artistry and labour than frame-first – are now being explored. Also of interest are the sewn hulls of the Archaic Greek period (*c.*750–480 BC); this technique, easier but less durable, may reflect the scarcity of specialist shipwrights in the 'Dark Age' following the collapse of Bronze Age Aegean civilization (Mark 1991).

Ethnography and experimentation (*see* ARCHAEOETHNOGRAPHY *and* EXPERIMENTAL ARCHAEOLOGY) have improved understanding of ship construction and performance, for instance among prehistoric craft of northwestern Europe (McGrail 1987). Omani dhows and Sri Lankan outriggers are among traditional craft that have been recorded (e.g. Kapitän 1991). Full-scale sailing replicas have included a 4th century BC Hellenistic Greek merchantman and a 9th century AD Norse boat ('Kyrenia 2' and 'Gokstad faering' respectively; see McGrail 1977; Gould 1983: 189–206); other reconstructions have been more conjectural, based on written accounts and artistic depictions, although some cases, such as the reconstruction of a Greek trireme (Morrison and Coates 1986), are very convincing.

Theorists have predominantly addressed the bridge between wreck and ship, part of the maritime variant of MIDDLE-RANGE THEORY (Gibbins 1990). The need for site formation and assemblage analysis is heightened by the 'fine grain' of wrecks, their unfamiliarity, and the prevalence of sites in which material is missing or disordered. Pioneering research was carried out by Keith Muckelroy, who developed a methodology based on the 'scrambling' and 'extracting' effects of the wreck process (Muckelroy 1978). His primary case study for these methods was the *Kennemerland*, a wreck dating to the 17th century AD for which manifests had survived, making it an excellent example of historical archaeology. At undocumented wrecks, the likely components of shipboard material may be inferred from similar but better-preserved assemblages (e.g. Parker 1992).

Muckelroy's preservational categories of British wrecks, correlated with variables such as depth, slope and current, have a Mediterranean counterpart (Parker 1980), and have led to work on environmental transforms (e.g. Ferrari and Adams 1990), artefactual contamination (Parker 1981), and the distinction between a scattered wreck and other sites of similar appearance, such as an anchorage or eroded shore deposit (Muckelroy 1979).

Research is increasingly concentrating on the study of trade and the anthropology of seafaring. A particular challenge is the integration of maritime data into a wider archaeological or historical context, and the development of appropriate research strategies. Thus, in the study of Roman amphorae, a cargo is a reflection not only of transport but also of production, packaging and consumption (MADRAGUE DE GIENS). Questions to be asked of wreck data may arise from the complementary investigation of kiln or wharf-side deposits. A recent example is a programme of ceramic NEUTRON ACTIVATION ANALYSIS in which the wreck results highlight the organisation of production. Similarly, the material culture of shipboard life may be seen to reflect societal norms of behaviour and expression, as well as the constraints and adaptations of that life-style (e.g. Gould 1983: 37–64).

Another aspect of maritime middle-range theory is the quantification of actual sailings which may be suggested by wrecks, an acute problem if wreck data are to provide a 'statistics' of transport. The proportion of known to actual wrecks is a function of the extent of exploration, taking into account sea-routes, the relative likelihood of wrecks in shallow waters, and the visibility of different types of cargo in different preservational circumstances. Wreck incidence among unrecorded sailings may be estimated from comparative historical data, if the parameters appear similar; an example is the use of medieval maritime assurance records to gauge wreck incidence.

The most influential theorist in maritime archaeology has been Muckelroy, a Cambridge proponent of NEW ARCHAEOLOGY, whose achievements included a rigorous approach to site evaluation (see above), the application of spatial and statistical analysis, and a systemic model of shipboard dynamics. A group of American anthropologists more explicitly advocated HYPOTHETICO-DEDUCTIVE methods which seek behavioural regularities and underline the cross-cultural similarities of maritime data (Gould 1983). Various attempts have been made to adopt post-processual approaches, including CONTEXTUAL ARCHAEOLOGY and FEMINIST ARCHAEOLOGY (Spencer-Wood 1990) The most important recent development has been the notion of the 'maritime cultural landscape' (Westerdahl 1992), stressing the cellular nature and interrelationships of maritime regions, and encompassing the totality of evidence for seafaring, coastal settlement and inland influences; this has given a new focus for general accounts of ships and shipping (e.g. Hutchinson 1994), and a wider context for the study of regional traditions in ship and boat technology (e.g. Westerdahl 1994). The impetus to these developments continues to be the archaeological characterization and publication of sites, including ports and their wrecks (e.g. Marsden 1994), 'treasure' wrecks (Marken 1994), recent historic wrecks in the Americas and elsewhere (Bass 1988), and ancient Mediterranean wrecks, which now amount to over 1300 known sites (Parker 1992).

For case-studies see GELIDONYA, MADRAGUE DE GIENS, *and* SERÇE LIMAN.

G.F. Bass: *Archaeology underwater* (London, 1966); S. McGrail: 'Aspects of experimental boat archaeology',

Sources and techniques in boat archaeology, ed. S. McGrail (London, 1977), 23–45; K.W. Muckelroy: *Maritime archaeology* (Cambridge, 1978); ——: 'The Bronze Age site off Moor Sand, near Salcombe, Devon. An interim report on the 1978 season', *IJNA* 8 (1979), 189–210; A.J. Parker: 'The preservation of ships and artefacts in ancient Mediterranean wreck sites', *Progress in Underwater Science* 5 (1980), 41–70; ——: 'Stratification and contamination in ancient Mediterranean shipwrecks', *IJNA* 10 (1981), 309–35; R.A. Gould, ed.: *Shipwreck anthropology* (Albuquerque, 1983); J.S. Morrison and J.F. Coates: *The Athenian trireme* (Cambridge, 1986); S. McGrail: *Ancient boats in northwestern Europe* (London, 1987); C. Pearson, ed.: *Conservation of marine archaeological objects* (London, 1987); G.F. Bass: *Ships and shipwrecks of the Americas* (London 1988); G.W. Houston: 'Ports in perspective: some comparative materials on Roman merchant ships and ports', *AJA* 92 (1988), 553–64; B.J. Ferrari and J. Adams: 'Biogenic modifications of marine sediments and their influence on archaeological material', *IJNA* 19 (1990), 139–51; D.J.L. Gibbins: 'Analytical approaches in maritime archaeology: a Mediterranean perspective', *Antiquity* 64 (1990), 376–89; S. Spencer-Wood, ed.: 'Stretching the envelope in theory and method', *Underwater Archaeology: Proceedings from the Society for Historical Archaeology Conference*, ed. T.L. Carrell (Tucson, 1990), 20–45; D.J.L. Gibbins: 'Archaeology in deep water – a preliminary view', *IJNA* 20 (1991), 163–8; G. Kapitän: 'Records of native craft in Sri Lanka', *IJNA* 20 (1991), 23–32; S.E. Mark: 'Odyssey 5.234–53 and Homeric ship construction: a reappraisal', *AJA* 95 (1991), 441–5; M. Dean, B. Ferrari, I. Oxley, M. Redknap and K. Watson: *Archaeology underwater: the NAS guide to principles and practice* (London, 1992); A.J. Parker: *Ancient shipwrecks of the Mediterranean and the Roman provinces* (Oxford, 1992); C. Westerdahl: 'The maritime cultural landscape', *IJNA* 21 (1992), 5–14; G. Hutchinson: *Medieval ships and shipping* (London, 1994); M.W. Marken: *Pottery from Spanish shipwrecks 1500–1800* (Gainesville, 1994); P. Marsden: *Ships of the port of London, first to eleventh centuries AD* (London, 1994); J.R. Steffy: *Wooden ship building and the interpretation of shipwrecks* (College Station, 1994); C. Westerdahl, ed.: *Crossroads in ancient shipbuilding* (Oxford, 1994); D.J.L. Gibbins: 'The Roman wreck of *c.*AD 200 at Plemmirio, near Siracusa (Sicily): fifth interim report', *IJNA* 24 (1995); J.P. Delgado, ed.: *The British Museum encyclopedia of underwater and maritime archaeology* (London, 1997).
DG

Marlik Tepe Early Iron-Age cemetery-site near the Caspian Sea in northwestern Iran, consisting of rich CHAMBER-TOMB burials in which the deceased were often laid on stone slabs. About 20 of the tombs (varying between 2 and 5 m in length) were excavated by an Iranian expedition in 1961–2. The Marlik culture – also known as the Amlash culture after the nearby site of that name – dates to the late 2nd/early 1st millennium BC, and is particularly characterized by gold and silver vessels and jewellery. The grave goods bear certain resemblances to items at contemporaneous ASSYRIAN, Mannean and SCYTHIAN sites.

E.O. Negahban: *A preliminary report on Marlik excavation: Gohar Rud expedition: Rudbar 1961–1962* (Tehran, 1964); C.K. Wilkinson: 'Art of the Marlik culture', *BMMA* 24 (1965), 101–9; E.O. Negahban: *Metal vessels from Marlik* (Munich, 1983); ——: *Marlik: the complete excavation report*, 2 vols (Philadelphia, 1996).
IS

Marpole Type-site of the Marpole culture in the Strait of Georgia region of the northwest coast of North America. This large, deep habitation site, consisting mostly of a SHELL MIDDEN situated at the mouth of the Fraser river in British Columbia, was first investigated around the turn of the century by archaeologists H.I. Smith and Charles Hill-Tout, and then again in the 1950s by Charles E. Borden. The major monograph which defines the Marpole phase and culture by comparison with other sites in the Strait of Georgia region was written by David Burley in 1980.

The eighteen components of the Marpole phase were dated to between 400 BC and AD 400 using a combination of three approaches: MULTIDIMENSIONAL SCALING and Manhattan city block metric distances, SPATIAL ANALYSIS based on a two-dimensional plot of scaled distances, and a set of chronologically-ordered radiocarbon dates. SYSTEMS THEORY has also been used to create a model of the development of the Marpole cultural subsystems (Burley 1980).

D.V. Burley: *Marpole: anthropological reconstructions of a prehistoric Northwest Coast culture type* Burnaby, 1980); C.E. Borden: 'Prehistoric art of the Lower Fraser Region', *Indian art traditions of the Northwest Coast*, ed. R.L. Carlson (Burnaby, 1983), 131–66.
RC

Marquis of Tsai *see* TS'AI HOU LUAN TOMB

Marxist archaeology Marxists regard each human society as defined and shaped by its MODE OF PRODUCTION, which comprises both 'forces of production' (i.e. science, technology and all other human and natural resources) and 'relations of production' (i.e. the ways in which people relate to one another in order to facilitate the production and distribution of goods).

Among Western archaeologists, Gordon Childe was famously influenced by Marxist theory, particularly in the emphasis he placed on the forces of production as the most fundamental influences on prehistoric economies, societies and ideologies. However, his promotion of DIFFUSIONISM as a motor of social advance ran counter to Russian Marxist belief at the time. Childe's ambivalence prefigured the significant divide that came to exist between 'Soviet-style' Marxism and the 'neo-Marxist' theory employed by some Western archaeologists in the late 20th century (e.g. Spriggs 1984).

Neo-Marxists employ Marxist analysis and concepts without necessarily accepting orthodox Marxist explanations and research priorities. They form a heterogeneous group, although recurring themes in their work include: contradictions between social groups with different relations to the mode of production; contradictions as a motor for social change – often put forward as an antidote to the homeostatic (stabilizing) mechanisms assumed in a purely SYSTEMS THEORY approach to social dynamics; and concern with ideology and symbolism and its relation to economic exploitation and political power. Perhaps the key difference between orthodox and neo-Marxist analysis, mirrored in modern archaeological writing, is the discussion over whether the 'base' of any social structure (in essence, the way in which the relations of production are organized) determines, or is simply in dialogue with, the legal and political 'superstructure'. A central concern of neo-Marxist analysis is the exploration of the latter proposition.

At the same time, the explicitly political content of modern Marxist archaeology is often low, and in the case of many studies the label 'Marxist' says more about the intellectual stance of the writer than the content of the research, or even the nature of the interpretation. Furthermore, useful Marxist concepts have been absorbed into a whole range of enquiries that are not explicitly Marxist – notably economic theory, structure, relations between social entities, ideology and symbolism. For example, a combination of Marxism, STRUCTURALISM and anti-positivism is said to have at least partially inspired the emergence of 'SYMBOLIC ARCHAEOLOGY' in the 1980s. The idea that symbolic ideologies mask realities, but also actively transform social relations, is one of the more obvious neo-Marxist influences. Similarly, archaeological discussions of pre-state social systems often reveal a creative mix of concepts and non-exclusive approaches ranging from neo-Marxism to economic FUNCTIONALISM and SYSTEMS THEORY. As a final example, Marxist theorists are keenly aware of the effect of dominant world-views on the shaping of our views of past peoples; in a more self-critical sense, this has proved to be a key strand of enquiry in POST-PROCESSUAL ARCHAEOLOGY.

See CHINA 2 *for a discussion of the application of Marxist theory to the* SHANG *culture, and see also* CRITICAL THEORY.

M. Bloch, ed.: *Marxist analyses and social anthropology* (London, 1975); S. Frankenstein and M. Rowlands: 'The internal structure and regional context of Early Iron Age society in south-western Germany', *Bulletin of the Institute of Archaeology*, 15 (1978), 73–112; J. Friedman and M. Rowlands, ed.: *The evolution of social systems* (London, 1978); J. Gledhill: 'Time's arrow: anthropology, history, social evolution and Marxist theory', *Critique of Anthropology* 16 (1981), 3–30; M. Spriggs, ed.: *Marxist perspectives in archaeology* (Cambridge, 1984); M. Bloch: *Marxism and anthropology* (Oxford, 1985); B.G. Trigger: *A history of archaeological thought* (Cambridge, 1989), 212–43, 251–63, 340–7; I.M. Diakonoff and P.L. Kohl, eds: *Early Antiquity* (Chicago, 1991); I. Hodder: *Reading the past*, 2nd edn (Cambridge, 1991), 57–79; R.H. McGuire: *A Marxist archaeology* (New York, 1992).

IS

Masada (Aramaic; *mezad*, 'fortress') Naturally fortified settlement located on a plateau at the edge of the Judaean desert, beside the Dead Sea. It was occupied from at least the Chalcolithic period (*c*.4000 BC) onwards but it flourished particularly during the Iron Age. Most of the surviving ceremonial buildings and fortifications date to the Hasmonean Dynasty and the period of Roman domination of Syria-Palestine; Herod the Great (*c*.37–4 BC) constructed a palace complex, like that at the fortress of Herodium, as well as granaries, baths and water cisterns. In AD 73 the site achieved lasting fame as the stronghold in which almost a thousand Zealots committed mass suicide rather than surrender to the 10th Roman Legion; there is good archaeological evidence for the Zealots' re-use of the Herodian palace, including the construction of a synagogue and a pair of ritual baths (*mikvah*). The discovery of a cache comprising an ostracon and two Biblical scrolls suggests connections with the Essenes at QUMRAN.

M. Avi-Yonah et al.: 'Masada, survey and excavations, 1955– 1956', *Israel Exploration Journal* 7 (1957), 1–60; Y. Yadin: *Masada* (London, 1966).

IS

Masjid al-Jamiʿ (Isfahan) Mosque in the Iranian city of Isfahan, the underlying foundations of which were examined during restoration, thus presenting an unusual archaeological opportunity, since Islamic religious concerns tend to prevent excavation when such buildings are still in use. The core of the standing mosque is Seljuk (11th century AD) and its innovative domed plan was the inspiration of numerous other Seljuk and post-Seljuk mosques in Iran, Anatolia, Egypt and elsewhere. However, excavation revealed the foundations of the 9th- and 10th-century Buyid mosque, a period for which monuments in Iran are extremely rare. The excavation showed the proximity of the mosque's design to those of Iraq and elsewhere in the 9th century and the continuing impact of SASANIAN building techniques in southwestern Iran.

E. Galdieri: *Isfahan: Masgid-i Guma* 2 vols (Rome, 1972–3).

GK

Masjid-i Suleiman *see* PERSIA, MAP 28

Maskhuta, Tell el- (anc. Per-Temu Tjeku) Town-site and capital of the 8th nome of Lower Egypt during the Late Period (*c*.712–332 BC), located at the eastern edge of the Delta, 15 km west of modern Ismailiya and the Suez Canal. On the basis of its ancient name, Per-Temu, the site was identified with the Biblical city of Pithom, but more recent excavations (Holladay 1982) have disproved this theory, demonstrating that there was a HYKSOS level below the remains of the city. The late period town was founded by Necho II (*c*.610–595 BC), and it was still flourishing in the Roman period. The fluctuating importance of the site appears to have been closely linked to the fortunes of the Wadi Tumilat, through which an ancient canal connected the apex of the delta with the Red Sea.

H.E. Naville: *The store-city of Pithom and the route of the Exodus* (London, 1885); J.S. Holladay, Jr.: *Cities of the Delta III: Tell el-Maskhuta* (Malibu, 1982).

IS

Mask site Modern Eskimo site in north-central Alaska, studied by Lewis Binford (1978) as part of his ethnoarchaeological work concerning the material culture of prehistoric hunter-gatherers. The site is a hunting stand, where men congregated

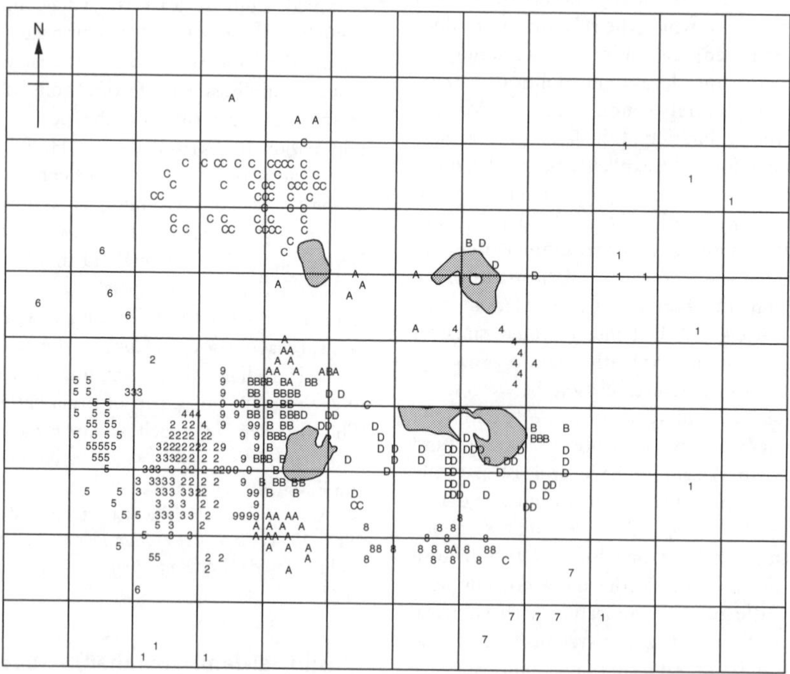

Figure 32 **Mask site** Spatial distribution of all item points over the Mask site, identified by cluster assignment in the 13-cluster solution (the shaded areas are hearths). *Source*: R. Whallon: 'Unconstrained clustering for the analysis of spatial distributions in archaeology', *Intrasite spatial analysis in archaeology*, ed. H. Hietala (Cambridge University Press, 1984), fig. 15.

to watch for game and plan hunting strategies. Binford studied the activities that took place, such as watching for game, eating and talking, crafts, target shooting, how much time was spent on each, and the related discard or placement of items that took place.

Robert Whallon (1984) used Binford's study of the Mask site as the basis for the first application his technique of UNCONSTRAINED CLUSTERING. The data consisted of the exact locations of objects of five types across the site: large bones, bone scraps, wood scraps, tools and projectiles, as well as the positions of hearths and large stones. The first step in the analysis was to smooth the spatial distribution of each type to give a smooth contoured surface the height of which represented the density of objects of that type (*see* TREND SURFACE ANALYSIS). At each point where an object was located, the height of each surface was calculated and expressed as a percentage of the total of all the heights at that location.

A data matrix consisting of the percentages of all the types at all the locations, measured in this way, was subjected to CLUSTER ANALYSIS. The 'best' number of clusters was not clear, so both the 7--cluster and the 13-cluster solutions were plotted (see Fig. 32). Some of the clusters defined in this way formed single contiguous groups of locations, while others formed small numbers of such groups. Finally, Whallon interpreted these clusters in terms of activities that had taken place on the site, such as eating, wood-carving, target practice.

Despite being acclaimed as a major advance in SPATIAL ANALYSIS, Whallon's approach seems to have serious defects. It seems to complicate rather than simplify or elucidate: from five object types, some with very simple distribution patterns, it derived either 7 or 13 clusters, most of which had two or more sub-clusters. Several spurious clusters were caused by the smoothing technique spreading the density of object types well beyond the area that they actually occupy. Thus a cluster described as comprising 25% of a particular type may have had none of that type within its borders. The root cause seems to be a mismatch between the attempt to define edges of areas, with the use of smoothing techniques which blur any such distinctions. It seems unlikely that this technique would perform well on a real archaeological site of any complexity.

L.R. Binford: 'Dimensional analysis of behaviour and site structure: learning from an Eskimo hunting stand' *AA* 43 (1978), 330–61; R. Whallon: 'Unconstrained clustering for the analysis of spatial distributions in archaeology', *Intrasite spatial analysis in archaeology*, ed. H. Hietala (Cambridge, 1984), 242–77; H.P. Blankholm: *Intrasite spatial analysis in theory and practice* (Aarhus, 1991), 75–90.

CO

mastaba-tomb (Arabic: *mastaba*, 'bench') Type of Egyptian tomb with a rectangular block-shaped superstructure, used from the 1st dynasty (*c*.3000 BC) until the end of the Old Kingdom (*c*.2150 BC) primarily in the vicinity of Cairo and the Faiyum. The most basic form of *mastaba* consisted of a subterranean burial chamber surmounted by a rectangular superstructure made of mud-bricks or stone masonry, usually incorporating offering niches or chapels.

A.J. Spencer: *Death in ancient Egypt* (Harmondsworth, 1982), 45–111; N. Cherpion: *Mastabas et hypogées d'Ancien Empire: le problème de la datation* (Brussels, 1989).

IS

Matara Settlement site of the pre-Axumite and Axumite periods, located in the Ethiopian highlands. The earliest occupation levels (dated to *c*.500–300 BC) include artefacts showing considerable South Arabian influence (as at YEHA); the stratigraphy of this phase has also helped to corroborate the pre-Axumite ceramic sequence, which was previously based primarily on typologies and seriation. By the 8th century AD Matara had acquired a new importance as an Axumite town, perhaps as a result of its geographical position roughly midway between AXUM and ADULIS. The prosperity of the town at this time has been demonstrated by the discovery of a hoard of Roman and Byzantine goldwork, as well as the excavation of several large, multi-room houses similar to those of the elite at Axum.

F. Anfray: 'Matara', *AE* 7 (1967), 33–88.

IS

Matenkupkum Limestone cave on New Ireland, Papua New Guinea (see OCEANIA 2), inhabited between 35,000 and 10,000 years ago. It demonstrates that humans had settled the western Pacific islands by the late Pleistocene, and it is the earliest evidence of island occupation in the world outside southeast Asia. There were low levels of occupation until around 20,000 years ago, with a limited range of animals and stone tools derived from the local rivers; after that date, there is evidence of the introduction of animals, obsidian from New Britain, and structural evidence such as hearths.

J. Allen et al.: 'Human Pleistocene adaptations in the tropical island Pacific: recent evidence from New Ireland,

a Greater Australian outlier', *Antiquity* 63 (1989), 548–61; C. Gosden and N. Robertson: 'Models for Matenkupkum: interpreting a late Pleistocene site from southern New Ireland, Papua New Guinea', *Report of the Lapita Homeland Project*, ed. J. Allen and C. Gosden (Canberra, 1991), 20–45.
CG

material culture studies *see* ACTUALISM; CONTEXTUAL ARCHAEOLOGY; ETHNOARCHAEOLOGY; FORMAL ANALYSIS

Matola Early Iron Age site on the outskirts of Maputo, Mozambique, dated to the 2nd–5th centuries AD. This single-component site was the subject of excavations in 1975 and 1982. No structural features have been found, and little in the way of organic remains. The chief interest of the site lies in its early date, and the clear affinities of the pottery with ceramics of the Early Iron Age (KWALE ware) in the coastal hinterland of Kenya, dated to the 2nd and 3rd centuries AD: a key element in the argument for a coastwise spread of early farming communities from the north.

T. Cruz e Silva: 'First indications of Early Iron Age in southern Mozambique: Matola IV 1/68', *Proceedings of the 8th Panafrican Congress of Prehistory and Quaternary Studies Nairobi, 5 to 10 September 1977*, ed. R.E. Leakey and B.A. Ogot (Nairobi, 1980); J. Morais: *The early farming communities of southern Mozambique*, Studies in African Archaeology 3 (Stockholm 1988).
RI

Matupi Later Stone Age (LSA) cave in the Ituri Forest, Zaïre, excavated in 1974. The site is important for its indication that LSA microlithic industries were present from 30,000 uncal BP and possibly much earlier. Also, there is evidence that during the late Paleistocene, at least from the Last Glacial Maximum and through most of the Holocene, the site was in savannah country, with the forest margin an estimated 10 km to the west. The encroachment of the forest is thus a very recent phenomenon. The earliest industries contain few shaped tools; later assemblages contain more retouched pieces, but few geometrics. Reamers and a bored stone are present at levels dating to 20,000 uncal BP.

F. Van Noten: 'Excavations at Matupi Cave', *Antiquity* 51 (1977), 35–40.
RI

Mauryan period First unified state of the Indian subcontinent as a whole. The Mauryan empire (*c*.324–184 BC) extended from its core region of Magadha in the Ganges Valley to cover most of South Asia. Prominent rulers include Chandragupta (324–301 BC) and Asoka (273–232 BC). Most knowledge of the Mauryan period derives from such historical sources as the reports of the Seleucid ambassador (*c*.302 BC) and the *Arthashastra*, a political exegesis on the nature of kingship attributed to Kautilya, a Mauryan government official (324–301 BC), the preserved text of which was probably written down at some unknown time after the Mauryan period itself. Wooden architecture was prevalent at the Mauryan capital of Pataliputra (modern Patna), leaving little archaeological trace.

See also KAUSAMBI *and* TAXILA.

R. Thapar: *Asoka and the decline of the Mauryas* (Oxford, 1961); V.A. Smith: *The Oxford history of India*, 4th edn (Delhi, 1981), 94–163.
CS

Mawaki Early to Final Jomon site in Ishikawa prefecture, Japan (5000–300 BC; *see* JAPAN 2 *for discussion of Jomon period*). Fish remains suggest year-round occupation. The bones from hundreds of dolphins were recovered form the Early–Middle Jomon layers suggesting large-scale communal exploitation. A Late Jomon clay mask and rebuilt circular arrangements of large wooden posts from the Final Jomon point to increased ritual activity in the later phases of the site.

T. Hiraguchi: 'Catching dolphins at the Mawaki site, central Japan, and its contribution to Jomon society',

Figure 33 **Mawaki** Late Jomon clay mask from the Mawaki site, Ishikawa prefecture, Japan (h. 128 mm). *Source*: K. Suzuki (ed.): *Jomonjin no seikatsu to bunka. Kodaishi Fukugen* (Tokyo: Kodansha, 1988), fig. 222.

Pacific Northeast Asia in prehistory, ed. C.M. Aikens and S.N. Rhee (Pullman, 1992), 35–46.
SK

Ma-wang-tui (Mawangdui) Earthen mound, 16 m in height, located 4 km from Ch'ang-sha city, in the province of Hu-nan, China. The central part was excavated early in 1972 and revealed a tomb of the Han period (206 BC–AD 220). This tomb (M1) is remarkable for the excellent preservation of the body and internal organs of the occupant, a 50-year-old female of short stature. Details from the autopsy of the cadaver showed a variety of ills leading up to her death, including coronary arteriosclerosis, pulmonary tuberculosis and gall-stones. Another tomb (M3), excavated in 1973 and precisely dated to 168 BC, is especially noted for the preservation of a large quantity of writings on silk, amounting to well over 10,000 characters. There are some 20 varieties of writings (several illustrated) dealing with such subjects as contemporary philosophical themes, early historical events, military information, astronomical and calendrical matters, geography and medicine.

Anon.: *Ch'ang-sha Ma-wang-tui yi-hao Han-mu* [The Han period tomb No. 1, Ma-wang-tui, Ch'ang-sha] (Peking, 1973); ——: *Ch'ang-sha Ma-wang-tui yi-hao Han-mu ku-shih yen-chiu* [Examination of the ancient cadaver from Tomb No. 1 Ma-wang-tui, Ch'ang-sha] (Peking, 1980); ——: *Ma-wang-tui Han-mu po-shu* [Silk manuscripts from the Han tomb at Ma-wang-tui], vols 1/3/4 (Peking, 1980–85); Ho Chien-chün and Chang Wei-min: *Ma-wang-tui Han-mu* [The Han period tomb of Ma-wang-tui] (Peking, 1982).
NB

Maya *see* LOWLAND MAYA

Mayapán Small walled settlement in the northern LOWLAND MAYA area of Mexico. Mayapán, incorporating an area of 4 sq. km, with a population of approximately 12,000 people, was the centre of a confederacy of 16 states during the Late Postclassic period. Headed by the Cocom family, this confederacy broke down, however, and after a revolt against the Cocoms sometime around AD 1450 the city was burned and its inhabitants fled. The site's main ceremonial complex, said to be a smaller and poorly constructed copy of CHICHÉN ITZÁ, is known for distinctive temple structures and human-figure INCENSARIOS. Structures and ceramics similar to those of the Mayapán are found at Late Postclassic sites throughout the Maya lowlands.

H.E.D. Pollock, R.L. Roys, T. Proskouriakoff and A.L. Smith: *Mayapan, Yucatan, Mexico* (Washington, D.C., 1962).
PRI

Figure 34 **Maya** Intricate Maya carving on the side of Stele 31, Tikal, Guatemala. *Source*: W. Coe, Tikal Project, University Museum, University of Pennsylvania, Philadephia.

Maysar *see* ARABIA, PRE-ISLAMIC

Meadowcroft Rockshelter Deeply stratified rockshelter in southwestern Pennsylvania which has yielded some of the earliest evidence of human occupation in eastern North America. A series of more than fifty radiocarbon dates indicates that human occupation of the site extended from *c.*12,500 BC to AD 1000. Flaked stone artefacts associated with the earlier occupation zones include an unfluted, lanceolate projectile point, prismatic blades, retouched unifacial (Mungai) knives and gravers. Despite the early dates, all of the faunal material associated with the early components is essentially modern. Some archaeologists have challenged the early dates because of the possibility of contamination from coal. Meadowcroft has also yielded information about the ways in which subsequent Archaic, WOODLAND and Late Prehistoric peoples adapted to changing Holocene environmental conditions.

J. Adovasio and R. Carlisle: 'Pennsylvania pioneers'. *Natural History* 95 (1986), 20–7; J. Adovasio, J. Donahue and R. Stuckenrath: 'The Meadowcroft Rockshelter radiocarbon chronology: 1975–1990', *AA* 55 (1990), 348–54; K. Tankersley and C. Munson; 'Comments on the Meadowcroft Rockshelter radiocarbon chronology and the recognition of coal contaminants', *AA* 57 (1992), 321–6.

RJE

mean (arithmetic) Statistical term used to describe one of many 'measures of central tendency' of a VARIABLE, indicating a 'typical' value. It is the sum of the values of the variables, divided by the number of values, often referred to as the 'average'. For instance, the mean length of 20 flint flakes would be the sum of their lengths divided by 20.

J.E. Doran and R.F. Hodson: *Mathematics and computers in archaeology* (Edinburgh, 1975), 38; S. Shennan: *Quantifying archaeology* (Edinburgh, 1988, 35–8; M. Fletcher and G.R. Lock: *Digging numbers* (Oxford, 1991), 34–8.

CO

Mecca *see* ISLAMIC ARCHAEOLOGY

Mechta-Afalou Population type or 'race', defined by Marcellin Boule and Henri V. Vallois in 1934, on the basis of skeletal material from two sites in eastern Algeria: Mechta el-Arbi, excavated by Gustave Mercier and Albert Debruge in 1907–23, and Afalou bou Rhummel, excavated by Camille Arambourg in 1928–30. The first site is a CAPSIAN 'escargotière' and the second an IBEROMAURUSIAN rock shelter, hence the type was from the beginning associated with at least two different 'EPIPALAEOLITHIC' industries in the Maghreb.

Classically, the Mechta-Afalou population, which is regarded as 'Cromagnoid', is said to be characterized by considerable robustness of form, with marked sexual dimorphism. The average height was 1.72–1.74 m for men and 1.62–1.64 m for women. The cranium was usually elongated with a protruding glabella and the face short and broad with low rectangular orbits and a wide interorbital region. The mandible was massive with a short vertical ramus and gonial eversion. Evulsion of the upper incisors, and sometimes the lower ones as well, was a common cultural practice among the members of this group.

According to Marie-Claude Chamla, a 'gracilization' process can be observed among the 114 'Mechtoids' found in the cemetery of Columnata, but nonetheless the type persisted in the Maghreb through the Capsian and Neolithic periods until Protohistoric times, when it was finally overwhelmed by an incoming 'Proto-Mediterranean' population. The type is sufficiently well characterized to have been recognised in areas far from the Maghreb, particularly at Wadi Halfa and Jebel Sahaba in the Nile valley and at Hassi el Abiod in the TAOUDENNI BASIN, in various archaeological contexts. Lubell et al. (1984) take objection to the typological approach employed in earlier studies. Their MULTIVARIATE ANALYSIS of 6 cranial and facial measurements on 68 individuals from 4 groups in the Maghreb (Iberomaurusian, Columnatian, Capsian and Neolithic) showed in their view that these populations constituted 'an almost indistinguishable mass', and they used this as an argument in favour of population continuity in the area and against any 'Proto-Mediterranean' incursion. Nevertheless, they were obliged to concede that Iberomaurusian males did still form 'a distinct, relatively homogeneous and identifiable group'. With regard to the origins of the Mechta-Afalou population, an apparent contradiction has been found to exist between the palaeontological and the archaeological data. There is a technological and typological contrast, and a chronological hiatus, between the Iberomaurusian and the preceding ATERIAN industrial complex; yet, as Denise Ferembach (1986) has shown, the specimens associated with the Aterian at DAR ES-SOLTANE II and other Moroccan sites can well be regarded as ancestral to those of Mechta-Afalou type. She proposes to bridge the gap by postulating a hypothetical migration of the Aterian people to Europe and their return in the guise of Iberomaurusian culture, a 'tragic adventure' which Gabriel Camps rejects as 'incredible.' Olivier Dutour, on the other hand, points out that anatomically modern populations did exist at this time in the Nile valley, at WADI KUBBANIYA and Nazlet Khater 4 (the latter dated to 33,470 ± 360 BP), and that this is relevant when considering the origins of the 'Cromagnoids' in North Africa as a whole.

G. Camps: *Les civilizations préhistoriques de l'Afrique du Nord et du Sahara* (Paris, 1974); K.P. Oakley, B.G. Campbell and T.I. Molleson: *Catalogue of fossil hominids, Part 1: Africa*, 2nd edn (London, 1977); M.C. Chamla: 'Le peuplement de l'Afrique du Nord de l'épipaléolithique à l'époque actuelle', *L'Anthropologie* 82 (1978), 385–430; D. Lubell, P. Sheppard and M. Jackes: 'Continuity in the Epipaleolithic of Northern Africa with emphasis on the Maghreb', *AWA* 3 (1984), 143–91; P.M. Vermeersch, E. Paulissen, G. Gijselings, M. Otte, A. Thoma, P. van Peer and R. Lauwers: '33,000 yr old chert mining site and related *Homo* in the Egyptian Nile Valley', *Nature* 309 (1984), 342–4; D. Ferembach: 'Les hommes du paléolithique supérieur autour du Bassin Méditerranéen', *L'Anthropologie* 90 (1986), 579–87; G. Camps: 'Un Scénario de "préhistoire catastrophe", l'odysée des Atériens et le retour des Ibéromaurusiens', *Bulletin de la Société Préhistorique Française* 84/3 (1987), 67–8; O. Dutour: 'Les Cro-Magnons sont-ils originaires de Nord de l'Afrique?', *DA* 161 (1991) 68–73.

PA-J

Medes Indo-Iranian people who are first mentioned in cuneiform texts in the early 1st millennium BC, although they probably settled in northern and western Iran as early as the 14th century BC. Possible early Median sites are Tell Gubba, in the Hamrin Basin, and Tille Höyük in southern Anatolia. The Medes were at first dominated by the late ASSYRIAN rulers of the 9th–8th centuries BC, but by *c.*700 BC – benefitting from the political vacuum left by the collapse of ELAM – they had begun to create their own empire, covering large areas of Iran, northern Mesoptamia and eastern and central Asia Minor (where they inherited much of the kingdom of URARTU). Between 614 and 612 BC they conquered the Assyrian cities of Assur, Nineveh and Kalhu, although it was their allies the Babylonians who eventually inherited the principal Assyrian territories. The capital of Media was the western Iranian city of Ecbatana (modern Hamadan), which later became an important PERSIAN city under the Achaemenid dynasty. In the mid-6th century BC Cyrus the Great defeated the Medes, thus effectively absorbing Media into the empire of the Persians, their former vassals.

The material culture of the Medes is still relatively undocumented, and few Median textual records have survived; although their palace at Ecbatana has not yet been excavated, the fortified sites of Godin Tepe and Tepe Nush-i Jan, both situated close to Ecbatana, were investigated during the 1960s and 1970s. The Central Temple at Tepe Nush-i Jan appears to have incorporated a FIRE ALTAR dating to the 8th century BC, while the excavations of the main fortress revealed a cache of 321 silver items buried in a bronze vessel in *c.*600 BC.

W. Culican: *The Medes and Persians* (London and New York, 1965); D. Stronach: 'Tepe Nush-i Jan, a mound in Media', *BMMA* 27 (1968); J. Curtis: *Nush-i Jan III: The small finds* (London, 1984).

IS

median Statistical term referring to the 'middle' one of a set of values of a VARIABLE, or the midpoint of the middle two if there is an even number of them. Thus the median diameter of three pots, the diameters of which are 15 cm, 20 cm and 40 cm, would be 20 cm, whereas the MEAN diameter would be 25 cm. Sometimes this value is used as an alternative to the mean, especially in NON-PARAMETRIC STATISTICS.

J.E. Doran and F.R. Hodson: *Mathematics and computers in archaeology* (Edinburgh, 1975), 39; S. Shennan: *Quantifying archaeology* (Edinburgh, 1988), 38–40; M. Fletcher and G.R. Lock: *Digging numbers* (Oxford, 1991), 33–4.

CO

medieval archaeology *see* EUROPE, MEDIEVAL AND POST-MEDIEVAL 1

Medina *see* ISLAMIC ARCHAEOLOGY

Medinet Habu (anc. Djamet; Jeme) Egyptian temple complex of the New Kingdom (*c.*1550–1070 BC) at the southern end of the Theban west bank, opposite modern Luxor. Most of the archaeological and epigraphic work at the site was undertaken by the Chicago Epigraphic Survey in the 1920s and 1930s. The earliest section of the complex was a small temple built by Hatshepsut and Thutmose III in the early 15th century BC, but this was eclipsed about 300 years later by the construction of the mortuary temple of Ramesses III (*c.*1198–1166 BC). Murnane (1980) discusses the significance of New Kingdom mortuary temples. *See also* RAMESSEUM *(on which the basic plan of Ramesses III's mortuary temple was modelled)*.

Epigraphic Survey, Chicago: *Medinet Habu*, 8 vols (Chicago, 1930–70); U. Hilscher: *The excavation of Medinet Habu*, 5 vols (Chicago, 1934–54); W.J. Murnane: *United with eternity: a concise guide to the monuments of Medinet Habu* (Chicago and Cairo, 1980).

IS

megalithic From the early Neolithic onwards, megalithic (literally, 'large stone') architecture formed one of the most distinctive and enduring features of prehistoric European architecture. The term megalithic is applied to any prehistoric monument or building that makes use of very large, unshaped blocks of stone as a principal component – although earth, rubble, drystone and timber often form subsidiary materials. By contrast, when blocks are carefully shaped and fitted – in Mycenaean architecture, for example – the term CYCLOPEAN is preferred. (STONEHENGE and the MALTESE TEMPLES, built of carefully shaped stones but conventionally regarded as prime examples of megalithic design, are among the exceptions that prove this rule.)

There are two key expressions of megalithic building: tomb-building in the Neolithic (discussed in this article), and the erection of ceremonial monuments in the Neolithic and the Bronze Age (*see* STONE CIRCLES). Megalithic tombs are known throughout much of northwestern and western Europe, particularly along the Atlantic seaboard. They are commonly grouped into key architectural forms such as PASSAGE GRAVES, GALLERY GRAVES and ALLÉES COUVERTES, with many regional variants such as the BOYNE VALLEY passage graves and SEVERN-COTSWOLD gallery graves (Joussaume 1988 provides a regional survey). Until the advent of radiocarbon dating, there were many attempts to trace the evolution of these regional styles through an inter-linked evolutionary tree, sometimes taken to begin in Iberia, Egypt or the Near East (*see also* DIFFUSIONISM). However, during the 1960s radiocarbon dates led archaeologists such as Colin Renfrew to suggest that the Breton tombs were among the earliest examples: the chronological sequences suggested by the diffusionary schemes thus became untenable, and it was suggested that megalithic construction might have been invented independently in several regions. The emphasis shifted to trying to understand *why* groups building megalithic structures were receptive to the idea of monumental architecture, rather than the construction of elaborate stylistic family trees.

Such explanations have stressed the collective and (supposedly) egalitarian nature of many of the burials; the monumental effect of the building within the natural landscape; and the 'legitimizing' symbolism of maintaining contact with dead ancestors. This suggests to many researchers that megalithic tombs were linked to concerns about establishing rights over agricultural land, and the reinforcement of social cohesion – perhaps in answer to pressure from neighbouring groups. Other analyses have thrown doubt on the egalitarian nature of burial in megalithic tombs (e.g. Bradley 1984), suggesting that some more elaborate tombs reveal signs of internal social competition. Various studies have also tried to link megalithic monuments to territories and to calculate local populations (notably Renfrew 1976).

Another long-running theme within megalithic studies has been the attempt to identify ALIGNMENTS in the orientation of the covering barrows and architectural elements of the tombs. The roof-box of NEWGRANGE is the most dramatic example of this, apparently aligned to allow winter sun to fill the chamber around the time of the winter solstice. More recently, studies (e.g. Hodder, 1992) have attempted to reveal the symbolism of Neolithic tombs as 'houses for the dead', while there have been renewed attempts to understand the ritual breaking of pottery, feasting and other activities that seem often to have taken place in the tomb forecourt. There have been suggestions, too, that the symbols and curvilinear designs of megalithic art found most notably on Breton and Irish passage tombs (surveyed by Shee Twohig, 1981) may be related to SHAMANISTIC practices (Lewis-Williams, 1993).

C. Renfrew: 'Megaliths, territories and populations', *Acculturation and continuity in Atlantic Europe*, ed. S. De Laet (Bruges, 1976), 198–220; C. Renfrew, ed.: *The megalithic monuments of western Europe* (London, 1981); E. Shee Twohig: *The megalithic art of Western Europe* (1981); R. Bradley: *The social foundations of prehistoric Britain* (London, 1984); R. Joussaume: *Dolmens for the dead; megalith building throughout the world* (London, 1988); I. Hodder: 'Burials, houses, women and men in the European Neolithic', *Theory and practice in archaeology*, ed. I. Hodder (London, 1992), 45–83; J.D. Lewis-Williams and T.A. Dawson: 'On vision and power in the Neolithic: evidence from the decorated monuments', *CA* 34 (1993), 55–65.

RJA

megalithic yard Since at least the time of the antiquary William Stukeley in the mid-18th century, researchers into the megalithic stone circles of the British Isles have suggested that the structures were laid out using a standard unit of measurement. The strongest exponent of the idea in recent years was Professor Alexander Thom, who in 1955 analysed the diameters of 46 megalithic rings and found that they tended to be set at multiples of about 1.657 m. Heggie (1981) summarizes the evidence, concluding that there is a case for a regular unit of measurement, but that it need not have been as precise or as standardized as Thom has claimed.

A. Thom: 'A statistical examination of the megalithic sites in Britain', *J.R. Stat. Soc*, A118 (1955), 275–95; A. and

A.S. Thom: 'The megalithic yard', *Measurement and control* 10 (1977), 488–92; D. Heggie: *Megalithic science* (London, 1981), 32–60.
RJA

megaron Distinctive architectural form employed in the Aegean Bronze Age, and typically consisting of a large hall with a central hearth, one or more anterooms, and a porch. The most famous examples form key elements of the great MYCENAEAN palaces such as PYLOS, built in the second half of the 2nd millennium BC.
RJA

Megiddo (Tell el-Mutesellim) CANAANITE – and later ISRAELITE – settlement in the southern Jezreel valley of Israel, about 35 km southeast of Haifa. Megiddo was the setting for the Egyptian king Thutmose III's victory over MITANNI in *c.*1503 BC, and it was subsequently transformed into an Egyptian garrison during the 15th and 14th centuries BC. Tell el-Mutesellim was identified with Megiddo when it was first excavated by J. Schumacher in 1903–5. The subsequent excavations of Clarence Fisher and Yigael Yadin revealed approximately twenty-five major phases of occupation from the Chalcolithic period (*c.*3300 BC) to the Persian domination (*c.*4th century AD).

C.S. Fisher: *Excavations of Armageddon* (Chicago, 1929); C. Watzinger: *Tell el-Mutesellim* II (Leipzig, 1929); R.S. Lamon and G.M. Shipton: *Megiddo* I (Chicago, 1939); G. Loud: *The Megiddo ivories* (Chicago, 1939); ——: *Megiddo* II (Chicago, 1948); G.I. Davies: *Megiddo* (Cambridge, 1986).
IS

Mehi *see* KULLI COMPLEX

Mehrgarh Early agricultural settlement dating back to the 7th millennium BC, located in the Kacchi plain in western Pakistan. The site of Mehrgarh, comprising a series of mounds spread along the banks of the Bolan River, was excavated from 1974 to 1986 by Jean-François Jarrige. The stratigraphy at Mehrgarh has been divided into seven periods, of which the earliest three belong to the Neolithic period, when agriculture was first developing in South Asia.

B. and R. Allchin: *The rise of civilization in India and Pakistan* (Cambridge, 1982), 105–8; J.-F. Jarrige: 'Chronology of the earlier periods of the greater Indus as seen from Mehrgarh, Pakistan', *South Asian archaeology, 1981*, ed. B. Allchin (Cambridge, 1984), 21–8.
CS

Meidum Egyptian funerary site, located at the entrance to the Faiyum basin, where one of the earliest pyramid complexes was constructed. The stone-built pyramid at Meidum is thought to have been built by Sneferu (*c.*2575–2551 BC) for the burial of his father Huni. Since Sneferu also constructed two pyramids for himself at DAHSHUR, in the southern part of the Memphite necropolis, he is generally regarded as the first Egyptian ruler to experiment with the engineering techniques necessary to accomplish the transition from the 'step-pyramids' of the 3rd-dynasty rulers (*see* SAQQARA) to the 'true pyramids' of the 4th dynasty at GIZA. The Meidum pyramid is surrounded by the rubble of its outer masonry, evidently indicating a dramatic collapse perhaps resulting from unsatisfactory methods of construction – opinions differ, however, as to whether the collapse took place before the completion of the monument (Mendelsson 1973) or as late as the 14th century BC (Edwards 1974). The pyramid is surrounded by a number of MASTABA-TOMBS of similar date, including those of Nefermaat and Ity, which contained surviving decoration in the form of inlaid pigments and paintings depicting scenes of daily life (including the famous 'Meidum geese').

W.M.F. Petrie: *Meydum* (London, 1892); ——, E. Mackay and G.A. Wainwright: *Meydum and Memphis III* (London, 1910); K. Mendelsson: 'A building disaster at the Meidum pyramid', *JEA* 59 (1973), 60–71; I.E.S. Edwards: 'The collapse of the Meidum pyramid', *JEA* 60 (1974), 251–2.
IS

Meir Group of decorated rock-cut tombs in Middle Egypt (about 50 km northwest of modern Asyut) dating to the 6th and 12th dynasties (*c.*2323–2150 and 1991–1783 BC respectively). The tombs, badly pillaged during the 19th century, were excavated and recorded by Aylward Blackman over the course of several seasons between 1912 and 1950. They contained the funerary remains of the governors of Cusae, as well as members of their families. There are few remaining traces of the town of Cusae itself, about 7 km to the east, which was the capital of the 14th province of Upper Egypt.

A.M. Blackman: *The rock tombs of Meir*, 6 vols (London, 1914–53).
IS

Melanesia *see* OCEANIA 2

Melka-Kunture Site in Ethiopia where very deep ACHEULEAN/OLDOWAN stratigraphy (stretching back to over 1.5 million years ago) was excavated. Finds have included lithics as well as the remains of hominids, but the excavations themselves have not yet been fully published.

F. Hours: 'Le Middle Stone Age de Melka-Kunturé: résultats acquis en 1971', *Documents pour Servir à l'Histoire des Civilizations Ethiopiennes* 4 (1973), 19–29; J. Chavaillon: 'Mission archéologique Franco-Ethiopienne de Melka-Kontouré', *L'Ethiopie avant l'Histoire* 1 (1976), 1–22.

IS

Melos *see* PHYLAKOPI

Meluhha Akkadian word referring to an unidentified geographical zone that is frequently mentioned in cuneiform texts from SUMER. Along with Magan (*see* UMM ANN-NAR), it was part of an extensive trading network centred on the Persian Gulf during the Akkadian and Ur III periods (*c*.2317–2000 BC) (see Tosi 1984). A seal from the Akkadian period apparently bears a depiction showing a Meluhhan acting as interpreter on behalf of a group of foreigners (Lamberg-Karlovsky 1981). In the 2nd and 3rd millennia BC the term probably refers to the INDUS CIVILIZATION, but by the 1st millennium BC it may have designated NUBIA.

C.C. Lamberg-Karlovsky: 'Afterword', *Bronze Age civilization of Central Asia*, ed. P. Kohl (New York, 1981), 386–7; M. Roaf: 'Weights on the Dilmun standard', *Iraq* 44 (1982), 137–42; M. Tosi: 'Early maritime cultures of the Arabian Gulf and the Indian Ocean', *Bahrain through the ages*, ed. Shaikha Haya al Khalifa and M. Rice (London, 1984), 94–107; K. Kitchen: *Documentation for ancient Arabia* I (Liverpool, 1994), 153–62.

IS

Memphis (anc. Mn-nfr) Located only 30 km from the head of the Egyptian Delta, the ancient city of Memphis occupied a crucial geographical position at the junction between Upper and Lower Egypt. It was the principal city of Egypt from *c*.3000 BC to the Arab conquest of AD 641, and the Memphite necropolis extended from ABU ROASH in the north, through SAQQARA to DAHSHUR in the south. The remains of the city of Memphis have suffered greatly from the proximity of the suburbs of modern Cairo, but archaeologists from the early 1800s to the present day have gradually pieced together parts of the network of temples, palaces and private houses, including the palaces of Merenptah (1213–1203 BC) and Apries (589–570 BC), and a large temple complex dedicated to the local god Ptah. Most of the recorded buildings tend to date from the New Kingdom onwards, although a survey of the entire site undertaken by the Egypt Exploration Society in the 1980's (Jeffreys 1985) has begun to reveal aspects of the earlier phases of the city.

W.M.F. Petrie: *Memphis* I (London, 1909); R. Anthes: *Mitrahina 1956* (Philadelphia, 1965); D.G. Jeffreys: *The survey of Memphis* (London, 1985); —— and A. Tavares: 'The historic landscape of Early Dynastic Memphis', *MDAIK* 50 (1994), 143–74.

IS

Mendes (anc. Per-banebdjedet) Egyptian settlement site consisting of two mounds (Tell el-Rub'a and Tell Timai) in the central Nile Delta, about 95 km north of Cairo. At the northwestern edge of Tell el-Rub'a is a cemetery of rams sacred to the local ram-god Banebdjedet. The site was already occupied in the late predynastic period and by the 26th dynasty it had developed into one of the principal Lower Egyptian cities.

H. De Meulenaere and P. Mackay: *Mends* II (Warminster, 1976); D.J. Brewer and R.J. Wenke: 'Transitional late predynastic-Early Dynastic occupations at Mendes: a preliminary report', *The Nile Delta in transition: 4th–3rd millennium BC*, ed. E.C.M. van den Brink (Tel Aviv, 1992), 191–7.

IS

Merimda Beni Salama Egyptian prehistoric site (*c*.4880 to 4200 BC), about 25 km northwest of Cairo, which is the earliest surviving predynastic village in Lower Egypt, preceded only by the less substantial FAIYUM A encampments along the northern shores of Lake Qarun. It is the type-site of the Merimda phase of the Lower Egyptian predynastic (Neolithic) sequence, roughly corresponding to the late BADARIAN and AMRATIAN periods in Upper Egypt. The principal features of the Merimda assemblage were decorated pottery, pear-shaped stone maceheads, chipped stone axes, saw-edged sickle-blades, spindlewhorls, bone harpoons, fish-hooks and diorite vases. It used to be suggested that the contrast with the microlithic technology of the preceding EPIPALAEOLITHIC period was so great that the Merimda population must have been an intrusive non-Egyptian group. However, earlier Egyptian sites in the eastern Sahara, such as NABTA PLAYA, show strong evidence of continuous cultural development from the Epipaleolithic toolkit to that of the Neolithic.

H. Junker: *Vorläufer Bericht über die Grabung der Akademie der Wissenschaften in Wien auf der neolitischen Siedlung von Merimde-Beni Salâme*, 6 vols (Vienna, 1929–40); B.J. Kemp: 'Merimda and the theory of house burial in prehistoric Egypt', *CdE* 43 (1968), 22–33; M.A. Hoffman: *Egypt after the pharaohs* (New York, 1979), 167–81; J. Eiwanger: *Merimde-Benisalâme*, 2 vols (Mainz, 1984–8).

IS

Meroe, Meroitic Town in the Butana region of Sudan, excavated by John Garstang (1911), George Reisner (Dunham and Chapman 1952–63) and Peter Shinnie (1967), which became the centre of the Kushite kingdom in the Meroitic period (*c*.300 BC–AD 350). Near the town is the site of Begarawiya, a cemetery of small pyramidal royal tombs of the Meroitic period, the earliest of which were located in the south. The settlement includes a number of two-storeyed palaces, a temple of Isis dating to the Napatan period (*c*.1000–300 BC) and a temple of Amun which was established in the 7th century BC and elaborated in the 1st century AD. To the east of the town there was also a temple of Apedemak, the Nubian lion-god, dating to the 3rd century BC. The presence of large slag heaps once led to the suggestion that iron-smelting was an important part of the city's economy, which perhaps involved the supply of iron to the rest of Africa. More recently, however, it has been pointed out that the quantities of iron artefacts found either in the settlement or in the cemetery are by no means unusually high – it is therefore likely that iron did not become an important economic factor until the post-Meroitic period.

The Meroitic period was roughly contemporary with the Ptolemaic and Roman periods in Egypt. The archaeological traces of commerce with Greco-Roman Egypt have survived both in the form of a cache of ebony and ivory, excavated at the trading centre of Wad Ban Naga, and the numerous imported grave goods which are found alongside the distinctive Meroitic pottery and metalwork at sites such as FARAS, GEBEL ADDA and KARANOG.

The material culture and political structure of the Meroitic period do not seem to have differed greatly from their NAPATAN counterparts, the main indication of the transferral of power from Napata to MEROE being the appearance of royal cemeteries at Begarawiya near Meroe in the early 3rd century BC. This was the first truly literate phase of indigenous Nubian culture. There were two forms of script used to write the Meroitic language; one comprised 23 signs derived from the Egyptian hieroglyphic system and the other was a more cursive script similar to DEMOTIC. Although Francis Griffith succeeded in deciphering the script in 1909, the lack of any surviving languages derived from the ancient Meroitic tongue has hindered most attempts at actually translating the surviving texts.

J. Garstang et al.: *Meroe: city of the Ethiopians* (Oxford, 1911); D. Dunham and S. Chapman: *The royal cemeteries of Kush*, III–V (Boston, 1952–63); P.L. Shinnie: *Meroe: a civilization of the Sudan* (London, 1967); —— and F.J. Kense: 'Meroitic iron working', *Meroitic Studies*, ed. N.B. Millet and A.L. Kelley (Berlin, 1982), 17–28; L. Török: *Meroe city: an ancient African capital* (London, 1997); D. Wildung, ed.: *Sudan: ancient kingdoms of the Nile* (Paris, 1997), 204–417.

IS

Mersa Matruh (anc. Paraetonium) Site of a lagoon and harbour on the Egyptian Mediterranean coast, about 200 km west of Alexandria, which was the Ptolemaic city of Paraetonium. A small settlement of the Late Bronze Age (*c*.1400–1150 BC), situated on an island in the lagoon to the east of the Ptolemaic town, appears to have been occupied by colonists from the Eastern Mediterranean. The material excavated on the island includes large quantities of Cypriot, Syro-Palestinian, Minoan and Mycenaean potsherds, indicating extensive trading contacts between the Aegean region and the north African coast at the time of the Egyptian New Kingdom (*c*.1505–1070 BC). The earliest traces of Egyptian occupation in the area are the remains of a fortress built by Ramesses II (*c*.1290–1224 BC) at Zawiyat Umm el-Rakham, about 20 km to the west of Paraetonium.

D. White: 'The 1985 excavations on Bates' Island, Marsa Matruh', *JARCE* 23 (1986), 51–84; ——: 'Provisional evidence for the seasonal occupation of the Marsa Matruh area by Late Bronze Age Libyans', *Libya and Egypt*, ed. M.A. Leahy (London, 1990), 1–14.

IS

Mersin (Yümüktepe) Neolithic and Chalcolithic tell-site near the southern coast of Turkey, at the western edge of the plain of Adana, which was excavated by John Garstang (1953). The presence of HASSUNA, HALAF and UBAID ceramics in the Chalcolithic levels has enabled the site's chronological sequence to be synchronized with sites in Mesopotamia. The stratum dating to the mid-5th millennium BC (level XVI) contained the remains of a mud-brick fortress surrounded by a thick enclosure wall complete with towered gateway and slit windows. Although the fortress was somewhat smaller than the earlier citadel at HAÇILAR, its defensibility was greatly enhanced by its location at the summit of the Neolithic settlement mound; the surviving piles of sling-pellets indicate the principal weapon used by its defenders. Each of the houses consisted of a single room and a walled courtyard.

A larger multi-roomed building to the south of the gate was perhaps occupied by the ruler of the settlement. The fortress was destroyed by fire in the late Chalclithic but the site was re-settled in the Middle Bronze Age and subsequent occupation continued until the Islamic period.

J. Garstang: *Prehistoric Mersin* (Oxford, 1953); I.E.S. Edwards, C.J. Gadd and N.G.L. Hammond, eds.: *Cambridge Ancient History* I/1, 3rd edn (Cambridge, 1970), 317–26.

IS

Mesolithic (Middle Stone Age) Period sandwiched between the Palaeolithic (Old Stone Age) and Neolithic (New Stone Age), and often taken to begin with the onset of the Holocene at the end of the last Würm glaciation and to end, at various times in various regions, with the advent of food production. This rather awkward definition reflects the retarded interest shown in the period by early archaeologists: for a long time the term Mesolithic was simply a catch-all for the uninteresting time between the glories of Palaeolithic art and the economic and social 'revolution' of the Neolithic. Graham Clark (1980) records the reasons why the term Mesolithic tended to be avoided by archaeologists (e.g. Childe) earlier this century, and charts the first uses of the term.

A more positive definition of the period is that it begins with the invention of geometric microliths; the interval between the MAGDALENIAN and this shortened Mesolithic is then reclassified as the EPIPALAEOLITHIC. This can confuse the wide-ranging reader, however, as the term Mesolithic is rarely employed in the archaeology of southeast Europe, north Africa and south-west Asia. Instead 'Epipalaeolithic' is generally used to describe any assemblages after the main Würm glaciation that have a microlithic component. Furthermore microliths can occur in non-Mesolithic contexts (*see* MICROLITH).

Mesolithic cultural adaptions. Like the other major divisions of prehistory, the Mesolithic is associated with fundamental socio-economic (as well as technological) changes. Some authorities (e.g. Kozłowki 1973, p.332) have regarded the term Mesolithic as synonymous with the particular type of hunting, fishing and gathering economy that evolved as a response to post-glacial environmental changes such as afforestation. This adaption is most marked in northern and western Europe, where from *c.*8000 BC to *c.*6000 BC a rise in temperature led to the end of dry, open cold environments in favour of dense woodlands, especially of hazel. The great herd animals died away in favour of forest-loving fauna such as boar and roe deer. The flooding of the North Sea and the creation of the English Channel, separating Britain from Europe, were only the most dramatic events in a general flooding of low-lying coastal areas and river valleys.

In early accounts of the Mesolithic, the disappearance of the specialized herd-animal hunting economy as a result of this climatic change seemed to explain the period's 'cultural impoverishment' – i.e. the absence of rich naturalistic art and impressive stone and bone industries. This change in material culture is now seen in a more positive light, as a gradual and successful adaptation to a more broadly based economy and more varied diet. The economic and material culture advances made during the Mesolithic include extensive forest clearance and an associated technology of mattocks, and tree-felling axes; elaborate seasonal scheduling of resource exploitation; domestication of the dog; the use of the bow and the development of microlithic technology; the development of river canoes and sea-going craft together with sophisticated fishing gear including the first evidence for nets and hooks; skis; and long-range exchange networks evidenced by the spread of Mediterranean obsidian and Polish chocolate-coloured flint. Furthermore, while Mesolithic assemblages are rarely visually impressive, microliths originally formed the cutting edge of a sophisticated and adaptable composite tool-type that made a far more efficient use of flint resources than its Palaeolithic predecessors. An important point is the proportion of arrowheads in Mesolithic assemblages (up to 60% in Tardenoisian assemblages), which is distinctly higher than in the Magdalenian and has led to the characterisation of the Mesolithic as 'essentially the era of hunting with a bow'.

The components of the diversifying Mesolithic economy show great variation from region to region, and the new methodological approach of FORAGING THEORY is increasingly applied to try to explain these complex strategies. In the Pyrenees and in many areas of northern and western Europe, red deer (e.g. STARR CARR) and wild pigs became a principal prey, while at sites in both northern and southern Europe (e.g. FRANCHTHI) there is evidence for specialized marine fishing. The impressive shellfish middens of the ASTURIAN and ERTEBØLLE economies attest to intense, but probably seasonal, exploitation of coastal resources. There is general agreement that the Mesolithic economy made increasing use of plant foods, although, hazelnuts aside, the direct evidence for this remains relatively puny. Some scholars have been tempted to see 'pre-adaptations' to the coming agricultural revolution in the intensifying use of plant resources, suggesting that a primitive form of animal husbandry developed in the Mesolithic. They also point to the domestication of the dog, the development of storage facilities and associated semi-sedentism, and the social developments reflected in the advent of 'cemeteries' in some regions and the increasing deposition of grave goods. *See also discussion in* CIS AND THE BALTIC STATES 1.

J.G.D. Clark: *The Mesolithic settlement of northern Europe* (Cambridge, 1936); S.K. Kozłowski, ed.: *The Mesolithic in Europe* (Warsaw, 1973); G. Clark: *Mesolithic prelude* (Edinburgh, 1980, 3–5; M. Zvelebil, ed.: *Hunters in transition: Mesolithic societies of temperate Eurasia and their transition to farming* (Cambridge, 1986); C. Bonsall, ed.: *The Mesolithic in Europe* (Edinburgh, 1989); G.L. Peterkin et al. eds: *Hunting and animal exploitation in the Later Palaeolithic and Mesolithic of Eurasia*, Archaelogical Papers of the American Anthropological Association 4. (1993).

RJA

Map 25 **Mesopotamia** Major sites in Mesopotamia which are mentioned in the main text or have individual entries in the Dictionary.

Prehistory	
Palaeolithic period	70,000 – 12,000 BC
Epipalaeolithic period	12,000 – 9300 BC
Mesolithic period	9300 – 7500 BC
Aceramic Neolithic period	7500 – 6000 BC
Pottery Neolithic (Proto-Hassuna)	6000 – 5800 BC
Hassuna period	5800 – 5500 BC
Samarra period	5600 – 5000 BC
Halaf period	5500 – 4500 BC
Ubaid period	5000 – 3800 BC
History	
Uruk period	4300 – 3100 BC
Jemdet Nasr period	3100 – 2900 BC
Early Dynastic I	2900 – 2750 BC
Early Dynastic II	2750 – 2600 BC
Early Dynastic III	2600 – 2350 BC
Lagash Dynasty	2570 – 2342 BC
Akkadian Dynasty	2317 – 2150 BC
Ur III period	2150 – 2000 BC
Isin-Larsa period	2025 – 1763 BC
First Dynasty of Babylon	1894 – 1595 BC
Old and Middle Assyrian periods	1800 – 884 BC
Mitannian empire	1480 – 1300 BC
Second Dynasty of Isin	1157 – 1026 BC
Second Dynasty of the Sealand	1026 – 1005 BC
Assyrian empire	883 – 612 BC
Ninth Dynasty of Babylon	713 – 626 BC
Neo-Babylonian (Chaldaean) Dynasty	625 – 539 BC
Achaemenid period	538 – 331 BC
Macedonian period	330 – 307 BC
Seleucid period	305 – 64 BC
Parthian (Arsacid) period	250 BC – AD 224
Sasanian Dynasty	AD 224 – 651

Table 14 **Mesopotamia** Chronology of Mesopotamia.

Mesopotamia Region of western Asia roughly corresponding to modern Iraq. The name Mesopotamia ('between the two rivers') refers to the dependence of this large area on the rivers Euphrates and Tigris, both of which flow from Anatolia down to the Persian Gulf.

See AKKAD, ASSYRIA, BABYLON, CHALDAEANS, DIYALA REGION *and* SUMER.

H. Frankfort: *The art and architecture of the ancient Orient*, 4th edn (Harmondsworth, 1970), 20–2, 138–40; M. Roaf: *Cultural atlas of Mesopotamia and the Ancient Near East* (New York and Oxford, 1990); H. Crawford: *Sumer and the Sumerians* (Cambridge, 1991), 73–6; J.N. Postgate: *Early Mesopotamia: society and economy at the dawn of history* (London, 1992).

meta-decision making *see* DECISION THEORY

metate A flat or trough-like stone slab, used with a handstone (*mano*) to grind softened corn kernels into a flour.
PRI

meteoritic iron (China) *see* T'AI-HSI-TS'UN

Mexica *see* AZTECS

Miamisburg Large conical earthen mound in southern Ohio, which is the largest ADENA (Early WOODLAND *c*.1000–200 BC) burial mound in the state, measuring at least 90 m in diameter and over 24 m high when first investigated during the mid-19th century. Archaeological investigation of the site is so far limited to the excavations undertaken by local citizens in 1869, consisting of a shaft descending from the top of the mound to 0.6 m below its base. This effort located a human burial 2.5 m below the mound top and a feature consisting of overlapping flat stones situated about 7 m below the mound summit.

Anon.: 'The Indian Mound, Miamisburg, Ohio', *OAHSP* 14 (1905), 346–7.
RJE

Michelsberg-Pfyn *see* PFYN

Microblade Tradition Early cultural tradition of the northern Northwest Coast of North America, dating to *c*.7500–2500 BC, which was typified by the presence of microblade technology and the near absence of bifacial tools. It probably derived from the PALEO-ARCTIC TRADITION of interior Alaska, which appears to have emerged several hundred years earlier. The Microblade Tradition is found in the territory occupied by speakers of Tlingit, Haida, and Athabascan-Eyak languages, and may constitute the material culture of the ancestors of these peoples, who introduced microblade technology into northern North America from Siberia. Microblade technology spread south from this region to already occupied sites such as NAMU. The earliest known Microblade Tradition sites are Hidden Falls (Davis, 1989) and Ground Hog Bay, while the remains at Chuck Lake (Ackerman et. al 1985) and the Queen Charlotte Islands are slightly later; their locations are indicative of a maritime tradition.

R.L. Carlson: 'The far west', *Early man in the New World*, ed. R.S. Shutler (Beverly Hills, 1983), 73–96; R.E. Ackerman, K.C. Reid, J.D. Gallison and M.E. Roe: *Archaeology of Heceta Island: A survey of 16 timber harvest units in the Tongass National Forest, Southeastern Alaska* (Pullman, 1985); S.D. Davis: *The Hidden Falls site, Baranof Island*, Alaska Anthropological Association Monograph (Fairbanks, 1989).
RC

microburin *see* MICROLITH

microlith Small flint blade, or fraction of blade, often defined as less than 5 mm long and 4 mm thick. Microliths are regarded as the archetypal tool technology of the MESOLITHIC. However, it is now recognized that some industries in the Upper Palaeolithic also manufactured microliths – although they form a much smaller fraction of the lithic assemblages. For example, microliths occur to a limited extent in the MAGDALENIAN, and quite substantially in other Upper Palaeolithic tool-kits (e.g. the Zarzian assemblages in the Zagros, for instance at SHANIDAR, and the CAPSIAN of North Africa). Microliths can be made by striking a very small core (just like making a normal flint blade), or by taking a larger blade, notching it, and then snapping a small portion off. This latter process produces tiny waste chips known as microburins and is known as the 'microburin method'. Single microliths were sometimes used as the tip of an implement, weapon or arrow. However, multiple microliths also seem to have been hafted together to form composite cutting edges on tools.
RJA

Micronesia *see* OCEANIA 2

microwear *see* USE-WEAR TRACES

midden settlement *see* KHARTOUM MESOLITHIC

Middle Missouri Tradition Tradition of the Plains Village period which begins in about AD 1000 and has direct cultural continuity with the Mandan Indians. Compact villages of earthlodges where a duel subsistence strategy of corn agriculture and bison hunting was practiced are found along the Missouri River and its tributaries from Iowa to North Dakota. The villages were fortified and occasionally show evidence of conflict. Settlements shifted through time several hundred miles up the Missouri River, apparently because of warfare with the Arikara Indians. The area vacated by the villages was occupied by Coalescent Tradition sites attributed to the Arikara.

W. Wood: *An interpretation of Mandan culture history*. River Basin Survey Papers 39, Bulletin 198, Bureau of American Ethnology, Smithsonian Institution (Washington, D.C., 1967); D. Lehmer: *Introduction to Middle Missouri archeology*. Anthropological Papers 1, National Park Service (Washington, D.C., 1971); R. Windham and E. Lueck: 'Cultures of the Middle Missouri', *Plains Indians*, AD 500–1500, ed. K.S. Schlesier (Norman, 1994) 149–75.

WB

middle-range theory Theoretical and methodological development introduced by the American archaeologists Lewis Binford (1968, 1977, 1981) and Michael Schiffer (1972) as a possible means of bridging the gap between archaeological data and general theory (i.e. the establishment of testable hypotheses and COVERING LAWS). The term 'middle-range theory' was first coined by Binford, who argued that in order to make robust inferences, archaeology 'must develop an appropriate language and instruments for measuring variables . . . in the archaeological record'. Such a language and instruments – or middle-range theory – would be devised and tested in a range of intellectual contexts. It could then be applied to justify inferences in other instances, helping archaeologists to avoid simply building up 'post hoc accommodative arguments' (Binford 1981). Moreover, the inferential techniques comprising middle-range theory would be specifically archaeological, and suited to linking observations of archaeological data to interpretation. They would provide a tested and certain platform on which more general theories (for example, about social dynamics) could be postulated and tested. During the 1970s and 1980s, the attempt to build and apply a body of middle-range theory was a significant part of the broader movement towards a PROCESSUAL ARCHAEOLOGY.

A key example of middle-range theory – and perhaps its most lasting endeavour – was the attempt to build a body of theory that explained SITE FORMATION PROCESSES. In building these theories, it became clear that most middle-range theory depended on ACTUALISM or ETHNOARCHAEOLOGY to elucidate the logical links between human behaviour and the found archaeological site. Binford (1984), for instance, has used middle-range theory to explore the possibility that many of the supposedly cultural aspects of the archaeological record in the Lower Palaeolithic (such as big-game hunting by early hominids) are actually the result of natural site formation processes. However, it has been suggested (e.g. Wylie 1989) that ethnoarchaeological studies characteristically rely too heavily on the biases and research agenda of the individual investigator. It has also been pointed out that present-day analogies can only be applied to the past if sufficient aspects of culture or nature are assumed to have been constant over the course of time.

Since the early 1980s, and especially in Europe, proponents of POST-PROCESSUAL ARCHAEOLOGY have either abandoned middle-range theory on the grounds of its supposed excessive scientism (Shanks and Tilley 1987) or transformed it into a set of approaches geared to the complexities and particularities of a specific set of archaeological remains (rather than attempting to identify a set of broadly applicable dynamics). There have also been attempts to argue that middle-range theory was doomed to failure for formal reasons; Joseph Kovacik (1993: 31–2), for instance, uses the arguments of the French philosopher J.F. Lyotard to suggest that middle-range theory is a 'translation device, yet translation is only operable between two genres of discourse within a single phrase universe, and not between two phrase universes'.

In assessing the contribution of middle range theory, it is important to be remember the dual objective of its original proponents. Even critics acknowledge that there has been some success in terms of amassing a body of theory of use to archaeologists when making 'low level' interpretations of archaeological evidence, especially concerning non-cultural site formation processes. Attempts to build a body of theory dealing with how archaeological data relates to cultural processes have not proved successful in terms of building secure COVERING LAWS; however, the original project aimed only to produce a body of theory that was applicable beyond the particular, and most critics concede that attempts to test middle-range theory have proved useful in forging a more explicit and disciplined approach to building ethnographic analogies.

In the second important aim – to link the growing body of middle range theory to general theory in a way that would allow grander economic and social theories to be tested – even many processual archaeologists admit that the project is incomplete. The debate centres around whether the incompleteness is inevitable: outside the natural sciences, general theories gain plausibility through such a complex relationship with data and other theory sets that, some argue, middle-range theory in its strictest sense will only ever prove to be a small part of the process of verifying (or refuting) them.

L.R. Binford: 'Some comments on historical versus processual archaeology', *SJA* 24/3 (1968), 267–75. M.B. Schiffer: 'Archaeological context and systemic context', *AA* 37/2 (1972), 156–65; L.R. Binford, ed.: *For theory building in archaeology* (New York, 1977); L.R. Binford: *Nunamiut ethnoarchaeology* (New York, 1978); ——, ed.: *Bones: ancient men and modern myths* (New York, 1981); ——: *Faunal remains from Klasies River Mouth* (New York, 1984); L.M. Raab and A.C. Goodyear: 'Middle range theory in archaeology: a critical review of origins and applications', *AA* 49 (1984), 255–68; M. Shanks and C. Tilley: *Social theory and archaeology* (Cambridge, 1987); M.A. Wylie: 'The dilemma of interpretation', *Critical traditions in contemporary archaeology*, ed. V. Pinsky and A. Wylie (Cambridge, 1989); I. Hodder: *Reading the past: Current approaches to interpretation in archaeology*, 2nd edn (Cambridge, 1991); P. Kosso: 'Method in archaeology: middle range theory as hermeneutics', *AA* 56/4 (1991), 621 ff; J.J. Kovacik: 'Archaeology as dialogue: Middle Range Theory and Lyotard's concept of phrase', *ARC* 12/1 (1993), 29–38; B.G. Trigger: 'Expanding middle-range theory', *Antiquity* 60/264 (1995), 449–58.

IS

Middle States (Chung-kuo, Zhongguo) Chinese geographical term which is most usefully applied to those 'princely states' (*chu-hou*) that were under Chou feudal suzereignty along with the ROYAL DOMAIN in the 1st millennium BC (*see* CHINA 2, EASTERN CHOU *and* WESTERN CHOU). The identification of the geographical locations of the 'states' themselves has proved difficult. In the philosophical works *Meng-tzu* and *Hsün-tzu*, the term is used in a similar way, but in the *Ta-hsüeh* [The great learning] and the *Shi-chi* [Memoirs of the historian] – particularly the latter – the Middle States are defined in direct contrast to the 'barbarian' regions lying outside the borders of the 'states'. There is only one instance of the phrase in contemporary inscribed bronzes; it suggests the ROYAL DOMAIN and adjacent states, but there is no further detail.

H.G. Creel: *The origins of statecraft in China* (Chicago, 1970), 196, note 1.

NB

migration period Chronological term used in Medieval Archaeology to describe the period between the 5th and 7th centuries when the Roman empire was gradually displaced by 'barbarians'. The material culture of the phase is reminiscent of that of the late Roman period in Asia and eastern Europe.

Martin Carver, ed.: *The age of Sutton Hoo* (Woodbridge, 1992).

IS

Millaran culture *see* LOS MILLARES

Milogradian Iron Age culture of the 7th to 3rd centuries BC, situated in the catchment area of the upper Dniepr river (i.e. northern/central Belarus and the neighbouring area of western Russia and northern Ukraine). The settlements usually take the form of hillforts (*gorodišče*) and are located on the upper river terraces, and on hills in the wetland areas. They are of considerable size (15,000–20,000 sq. m) and often include two rows of fortifications (turf walls and ditches). The inner enclosures are often densely packed with rectangular (4 × 4 m) houses, built of wooden posts and with hearths. The outer enclosure tends to have few houses and was probably intended for corralling animals. Several types of spearhead, iron belt and bronze bracelet have direct analogies in the LA TÈNE assemblages of Central Europe. A hoard near the village of Gorshkovo (near Mozyr, southern Belarus) contained 11 bronze and silver bracelets of La Tène-type dated to the 5th–3rd centuries BC. Contact with SCYTHIAN groups further south is documented by numerous finds of Scythian-style arrowheads, ear-rings and hammer-headed pins.

All the sites include slag, fragments of crucibles and blacksmith's instruments, denoting the local smelting and forging of iron. The rate of domesticates (mainly cattle and horse) in the faunal remains varies between 70 and 90%. Numerous finds of sickles and querns, as well as the impressions of grains (wheats, barley, millet) reveal a highly developed agricultural economy. Both surface graves and kurgan barrows are known; the burial rites included cremation and inhumation. No less than 10 cemeteries have been found: one of the largest, Gorshkovo, included 70 shallow oval-shaped graves with cremated human remains, fragments of ceramics and iron implements (arrowheads, rings and pins). Cemeteries with kurgan barrows are also known, e.g. Duboi, near Brest. One of the barrows contained a grave with the remains of two adults and one child; the grave goods included a golden ear-ring, an iron arrowhead and fragments of a hand-made vessel, suggesting that this was an elite burial.

P.N. Tretyakov: *Finno-urgy, balty i slavjane* [The Finno-Ugrians, Balts and Slavs] (Moscow and Leningrad, 1966); V.F. Isaenko et al.: *Očerki po arheologii Belorussi* (Essays on the archaeology of Belarus] (Minsk, 1970).

PD

Mimbres *see* MOGOLLON

Minaeans *see* ARABIA, PRE-ISLAMIC

mindalá Corporate, mainly hereditary, group of professional traders specializing in long distance trade of gold, cotton and luxury goods of late pre-hispanic northern Ecuador.

F. Salomon: 'Pochteca and mindalá: a comparison of long-distance traders in Mesoamerica and Ecuador', *Journal of the Steward Anthropological Society* 9: 1–2 (1977–8), 231–46.

KB

Minoan civilization Civilization of Bronze Age Crete, identified by Sir Arthur Evans after a series of excavations between 1921 and 1935 at the palace and city site of KNOSSOS. Based on the ceramic material from Knossos, Evans divided the Minoan chronology into three main phases: Early (*c.*3000–2000 BC), Middle (2000–1550 BC) and Late (1550–1100 BC); the phases are defined in stylistic terms and the precise chronology remains contentious.

During the Early phase, before 2000 BC, Minoan culture is believed to have developed independently, perhaps with influence from the Troad, though the archaeological evidence for this period is scant aside from some impressive THOLOI and rectangular tombs that housed increasingly elaborate grave goods (including cult figurines and gold jewellery). From 2000 BC, palaces developed in association with towns, and Crete began to develop the first true civilization of Europe. Substantial fragments of the first major palaces (2000–1600 BC) have been discovered at Knossos, Mallia and Phaistos. Like the later palaces, each is defined by extensive storage rooms often with massive storage jars or *pithoi* filled with oil, corn and wine; paved 'public' areas; finely built or decorated 'reception' rooms; and concentrations of luxury materials and craft items. Sealings (clay impressed using carved seal-stones) and inscribed tablets, apparently used for administration, are also present. Although the architectural complexes such as Knossos are called 'palaces', it is by no means certain that they were ruled by secular kings; it is equally possible to imagine political or religious oligarchies, or some more subtle political mechanism. With the development of these early palaces, however, Crete is clearly divided up into centralized palace economies (see below); in the early stages, and perhaps throughout most of the following centuries, the palaces seem to have been politically independent of each other while culturally and economically interlinked.

Around 1600 BC, these first palaces were destroyed – apparently by earthquakes. They were almost immediately rebuilt, and the visible remains today at sites such as Knossos, Phaistos, Mallia and Zakros are largely those of the post-1600 BC complexes. At Knossos, the rebuilding included extensive use of ashlar masonry, stone and wooden pillars, and elegant doorways. The new palace included impressive architectural features such as the paved and colonnaded 'Grand Staircase', leading up through three storeys. The palace walls were carefully engineered with foundations of large stone blocks and walls with timber lacing to minimize the effect of tremors, while light wells and verandahs kept the palace airy and open; there is evidence for drains and fresh-water piping. Walls were plastered or finished with gypsum, and the reception and (possibly) cult rooms were decorated with wall-paintings.

Writing seems to have been devised locally by the Minoans, developing from a stylized pictographic script with linear symbols. Linear A script was widely used in Crete, at Phylakopi, Ayia Irini, THERA etc; although it has not been deciphered, the signs show some similarities with Linear B and it was probably used for much the same purposes. Linear B, which probably developed from Linear A, perhaps at Knossos, seems mainly to have been used to record ownership of goods and for administrative purposes – there is no evidence of religious or diplomatic use (Ventris and Chadwick 1973).

Minoan religion is still largely mysterious. The presence of lustral basins and the quasi-religious ritual depicted in many Minoan murals has led some to consider the ceremonial rooms of the palaces as shrines or ritual centres rather than as secular 'reception rooms'. Outside the palaces, from the earliest period hilltops and caves seem to have sometimes become special places for making votive offerings (including clay figurines). Some sites have yielded numerous figurines of animals and humans in worship poses. Evans believed Minoan religion centred around a single goddess of fertility, but this is now discounted – a pantheon of more or less local deities seems more likely.

Perhaps the most remarkable of the Minoan arts was that of wall-painting. There is fragmentary evidence from the late Neolithic period on, but the finest examples are from the Middle Minoan period at KNOSSOS and THERA. There is a wide variety of themes, from monkeys and birds depicted at Knossos, and the many human and divine scenes, to the famous scenes of youths 'bull-leaping'. The style is essentially naturalistic, graceful and fluid; it inspired, but is distinct from, the more static and formal MYCENAEAN style of mural painting. Other Minoan artforms include elaborate carved stone vessels, and figurines cast in bronze and other materials, for example the bare-breasted 'goddesses' wreathed in snakes made from faience from the temple repositories in Knossos. Hard-stone seals were also manufactured; used for ornament as well as sealing, the drilled designs include mythical beasts such as the griffin, and divinities.

The widespread influence of Minoan civilization is apparent at sites such as THERA. Minoan art and the concept of the 'palace economy' fundamentally influenced the development of the MYCENAEAN civilization of the Greek mainland, which developed from about 1550 BC. From the mid-15th century BC (Late Minoan period) the Mycenaeans came to dominate Crete and the Aegean. The Mycenaean influence is manifest in a growing Mycenaean-style of wall-painting at Knossos – for example, the 'throne-room' design – and the use of Linear B (which is related to ancient Greek). While it is often assumed that the Mycenaeans exerted political and economic control over some of the palace economies, the nature of their hegemony is still debated.

In around 1425 BC, virtually all the known sites on Crete were destroyed by fire and were then abandoned. The volcanic eruption on Santorini (Thera) was once believed to have caused this wave of destruction, but the eruption is now dated to at least a century or so too early and this theory has been abandoned. The only palace to survive was Knossos, which seems to have been occupied for a further generation or two, arguably by an elite that shows a marked increase in Mycenaean influence – particularly in the adoption of Linear B script, deciphered by Michael Ventris as Mycenaean Greek.

The palace economies as 'redistributive centres'. It seems clear from the evidence of archives and the massive storage rooms that palaces such as Knossos gathered together and controlled much of the agricultural and craft produce of the economy. It is often assumed that the palaces therefore functioned as the nodal point of a 'redistributive economy', with a political or quasi-religious elite bringing together surpluses which could be redistributed to ameliorate the uncertainties of agricultural production. To keep control of the surpluses and to keep a tally of the work and reward of craftsmen, a more sophisticated writing system – Linear A – replaced the earlier hieroglyphic system. If the 'redistributive' model of the palace economy is accepted, one implication is that storage centres might have become vulnerable to control by an elite – who perhaps institutionalized and exaggerated the process for their own benefit. The further implication is that this elite subverted a part of this surplus to support an increasingly specialized, and dependent, 'service' economy of administrators and craftsmen. There is relatively little evidence of Minoan society outside the major centres, but a limited number of excavations suggest that smaller Minoan settlements may have had distinctly larger ashlar buildings at their centre which may have controlled the settlements for the benefit of larger centres; 'villa' type buildings without associated settlements may also have dotted the countryside, organizing and controlling the pressing of olives and grapes. THERA, although Minoan-influenced rather than strictly Minoan, provides the most detailed evidence for how a street in a Minoan settlement might have looked. The importance of international trade to the palace system is increasingly clear. The workshops depended upon imported tin and copper – various stores of ox-hide ingots have been discovered. Recent discoveries at TELL EL-DABʿA (ancient Avaris) in the Nile delta, including an apparent Minoan sanctuary with wall-paintings of bull-leapers, suggest that a distinct colony of Cretan merchants may have existed there in the 16th century BC. Minoan pottery is known from as far south as Aswan, and Cretans ('Keftiu') are pictured in a few Egyptian wall paintings.

A.J.Evans: *Palace of Minos at Knossos* (London, 1921–36); J.D.S. Pendlebury: *The archaeology of Crete* (London, 1939); M. Ventris and J. Chadwick: *Documents in Mycenaean Greek* (Cambridge, 1973); G. Cadogan: *Palaces of Minoan Crete* (London, 1976); H. Van Effenterre: *Le palais de Mallia* et al *cité minoenne* (Rome, 1980); M.S.F. Hood and D. Smyth: *Archaological survey of the Knossos area* (London, 1981); P.P. Betancourt: *The history of Minoan pottery* (Princeton, 1985); J.W. Graham: *The palaces of Crete* (Princeton, 1987); R. Hägg and N. Marinatos: *The function of the Minoan palaces* (Stockholm, 1987); P. Halstead: 'On redistribution and the origin of the Minoan – Mycenaean palatial economies', *Problems in Greek prehistory*, ed. E.B. French and K.A. Wardle (Bristol, 1988), 519–30; M. Bietak: 'Minoan wall-paintings unearthed at ancient Avaris' *Egyptian Archaeology: Bulletin of the EES* 2 (1992), 26–8; J.W. Myers et al.: *The aerial atlas of ancient Crete* (London, 1992); K.A. Wardle: 'The palace civilizations of Minoan Crete and Mycenaean Greece, 2000–1200 BC', *The Oxford illustrated prehistory of Europe*, ed. B. Cunliffe (Oxford, 1994) 202–43.

RJA

Minyan ware Distinctive ware characteristic of the Middle Helladic period (2000–1400 BC) in Greece. The first wheel-made ware in Greece, and closely related to wares found in Asia Minor in the same period, it is very finely produced with a polished surface and elegantly angular forms including 'wine goblet' and two-handled bowls. Minyan ware was named by Schliemann following his excavations at ORCHOMENOS in Boeotia, Greece – the seat of the legendary King Minyas. The earliest and most common Minyan ware, produced from the end of the 3rd millennium BC until around 1500 BC, is fired so as to be uniformly grey (Grey Minyan); a rarer variant (Yellow Minyan) appeared around 1700–1600 BC and continued to be produced into the 15th century BC. Minyan ware was used contemporaneously with other forms including painted, handmade forms – Minyan itself is undecorated aside from wheel-turned ridging – and in its latest stages it is found associated with Mycenaean ware.

RJA

Mirgissa (anc. Iken?) Egyptian site of the 2nd and 1st millennia BC, located in Lower Nubia, immediately to the west of the southern end of the 2nd Nile cataract, 350 km south of modern Aswan (now submerged under LAKE NASSER). The site was dominated by a large rectangular Middle Kingdom fortress surrounded by a ditch and inner and outer enclosure walls. Covering a total area of some 4 ha, it was the largest of 11 fortresses built in the reign of the Egyptian Middle Kingdom pharaoh Senusret III (*c.*1878–1841 BC) between the 2nd and 3rd cataracts, protecting the royal monopoly on trade from the south. On the island of Dabenarti, about 1 km east of Mirgissa, are the remains of a small unfinished fortified mud-brick garrison, apparently of similar date.

D. Dunham: *Second cataract forts* II: *Uronarti, Shalfak, Mirgissa* (Boston, 1967), 141–76; J. Vercoutter: *Mirgissa*, 3 vols (Paris and Lille, 1970–6); S.T. Smith: *Askut in Nubia* (London, 1995).

IS

Mi Son (Mi-son'n) The greatest of all CHAM religious centres, situated in the province of Quangnam in central Vietnam. Building commenced in the 7th century AD under Vikrantavarman I; numerous sanctuaries, characterized by single-chambered structures surrounded by rectangular walls, were added until the reign of Jayaindravarman in the 11th century AD.

M.H. Parmentier: *Inventaire descriptif de monuments Cams de l'Annam* (Paris, 1918).

CH

Mississippian Term used to describe archaeological complexes distributed across the southern Midwest and Southeast in North America that share certain similarities in artefact inventories, architectural features, subsistence practices and sociopolitical organization. Although dates vary from one region to another, Mississippian societies had developed in many places by AD 1000. Some of them were contacted by mid-16th century Spanish expeditions. These were sedentary agricultural peoples who grew maize and other cultigens, hunted game, fished, and collected wild plants. They lived in ranked societies known as chiefdoms, although some were more populous and powerful than others. Principal sites were marked by mounds which served as platforms for important buildings, including residences for highly ranked people, charnel houses for the bones of their ancestors, and community-related structures.

B.D. Smith, ed.: *Mississippian settlement patterns* (New York, 1978); D.G. Anderson: *The Savannah River chiefdoms: political change in the late prehistoric Southeast* (Tuscaloosa, 1994); J. Muller: *Mississippian political economy* (New York, 1991).

GM

Mitanni HURRIAN kingdom in northern Mesopotamia and the Levant which flourished during the 14th and 15th centuries BC. The heartland of Mitanni appears to have been the fertile area between the upper Tigris and Euphrates now known as the plain of el-Jazira, which forms a natural link between northern Iraq and Syria. Although Mitanni was at first assumed to be a separate entity from the land of the Hurrians (see Contenau 1934), the two are now generally agreed to have been virtually synonymous by the mid-2nd millennium BC at least (Liverani 1962).

At its height, the empire of Mitanni severely curbed Egyptian ambitions in Syria (*see* MEGIDDO) and also checked the resurgence of ASSYRIA and BABYLONIA in Mesopotamia. However, by the late 14th century BC, when the rulers of Mitanni were in correspondence with the Egyptian pharaohs of the 18th dynasty (*see* EL-AMARNA), the Mitannian sphere of influence had begun to diminish, probably in direct response to the growth of the Hittite empire.

Although much of the general population of Mitanni was clearly Hurrian, there is some controversy regarding the ethnic origins of their ruling elite. Many of the names of the rulers and deities are Indo-Aryan rather than Hurrian, and the term applied to the aristocracy as a whole, *maryannu* ('young warriors') may derive from an Indo-Aryan word. However, it has been argued that such Indo-Aryan connections were already characteristic of the areas occupied by the Mitannians rather than their elite in particular (Diakonoff 1972). In archaeological terms, Mitannian sites are characterized by fine white-painted pottery ('Nuzi ware') and objects made from frit. A small Hurrian temple has been excavated at the Syrian site of TELL BRAK, which was evidently a Mitannian town of some importance.

Neutron activation analysis and the search for Washshukanni. The location of the capital of Mitanni, Washshukanni, may be Tell Fakhariya, but this is a matter of some debate, and the two best-documented Mitannian sites (TELL ATCHANA and NUZI) lie at the western and eastern edges of the kingdom respectively. In the 1940s and 1950s, three archaeological expeditions were launched specifically in order to find Washshukanni (McEwan and Moortgat working at Tell Fakhariya, and Lauffray at Tell Chuera), but none produced any conclusive evidence.

In the 1970s, the problem was instead approached with the use of NEUTRON ACTIVATION ANALYSIS. This method is most commonly applied to pottery, but in this case it was used to attempt to determine the geographical origins of a set of 13 clay cuneiform letters sent from Tushratta, king of Mitanni, to the Egyptian king Akhenaten in the mid-14th century BC (Dobel et al. 1977). It was hoped by this means to arrive at an approximate idea of the location of Washshukanni, where the letters (found at EL-AMARNA in the Middle Egypt) might be assumed to have originated. The distinctive 'Tushratta fingerprint' resulting from the analysis of the 13 tablets could therefore be compared with a number of different locations in the region. There were marked differences between the 'Tushratta' and Tell Fakhariya profiles, particularly with regard to the proportions of nickel, thorium and hafnium, thus suggesting that this site should perhaps be finally abandoned as a possible location of Washshukanni. Although there was evidence to suggest a reasonable amount of diversity in terms of the chemical composition of clays in different parts of the Khabur triangle, none of the sampled clays within this region could be matched up with the 'Tushratta' profile. The geographical position of Washshukanni therefore remains something of an enigma, until clay samples are sampled from other areas associated with Mitanni, such as the Middle Khabur valley.

G. Contenau: *La Civilization des Hittites et des Mitannienes* (Paris, 1934); M. Liverani: 'Hurri e Mitanni', *Oriens Antiquus* 1 (1962), 253–7; I.M. Diakonoff: 'Die Arier im Vorderen Orient: Ende eines Mythos', *Orientalia* 41 (1972), 91–120; A. Dobel, F. Asaro and H.V. Michel: 'Neutron activation analysis and the location of Wassukanni', *Orientalia* 46 (1977), 375–82; H. Klengel: 'Mitanni: Probleme seiner Expansion und politische Struktur', *Revue hittite et asianique* 36 (1978), 94–5; G. Wilhelm: *The Hurrians* (Warminster, 1989);

For further bibliography see HURRIANS.

IS

Mitla *see* ZAPOTEC

Mixtecs One of two major cultural and linguistic groups in the Oaxaca region of Mesoamerica (the other group being the ZAPOTECS), the Mixtecs occupied the western portions of the state during the Late Postclassic period (*c.*AD 1200–1521). Known for exquisite metal and lapidary work and their CODICES that tell of the genealogies of their kings, the Mixtecs also used parts of MONTE ALBAN at times in the Late Postclassic.

R. Spores: *The Mixtec kings and their people* (Norman, 1967); K.V. Flannery and J. Marcus, eds: *The cloud people: divergent evolution of the Zapotec and Mixtec civilizations* (New York, 1983); 'Special section: rethinking Mixtec codices', *AM* 1/1 (1990) [whole journal]; J. Monaghan: *The covenants with earth and rain: exchange, sacrifice and revelation in Mixtec sociality* (Norman, 1995).

PRI

moa Large flightless bird of the ratite family found only in New Zealand and hunted to extinction by the 18th century (at the latest). Large moa hunting and butchery sites are common in the South Island of New Zealand.

A. Anderson: *Prodigious birds: moas and moa hunting in prehistoric New Zealand* (Cambridge, 1989).

CG

mobiliary art (*art mobilier*, portable art) Generic term used to describe smaller movable art objects. In the Upper Palaeolithic, it contrasts with the parietal or cave art of the same period. The term itself implies no particular style or period within the Upper Palaeolithic: it embraces the smaller sculptures, such as the 'VENUS FIGURINES', clay objects, the engraved and sculpted bone and antler tools, and other decorated objects such as PLAQUETTES. Although mobiliary art is defined as art that is portable, it should not be assumed that all these different types of objects (especially the plaquettes) *were* actually moved from site to site. Mobiliary art has been found in various regions across the whole Euroasian land mass, from western France to Siberia, and thus has a far wider distribution than parietal art; as it is generally recovered from an archaeological context, and is often made of organic material, it is usually also easier to date.

J. Clottes, ed.: *L'art des objets au paléolithique* 2 vols (Paris, 1990).

RJA

model (mathematical) A simplified representation of a complex reality, ranging from small 'tactical' issues such as the break-up of pottery, to large 'strategic' problems such as the spread of agriculture. The nature of the simplification depends on the uses of the model. Consisting of one or more mathematical statements and/or equations describing chosen aspects of a topic, it may range from a simple descriptive statement about a single VARIABLE (e.g. the size of pottery fragments) to a large interrelated set of equations which are intended to reproduce the workings of some system or process (e.g. a foraging system, *see* SIMULATION). Models form an essential link between archaeological THEORY and DATA (*see* STATISTICAL CYCLE); the extent to which they are made explicit depends on the complexity of the situation and the numeracy of the archaeologist. Many methods of statistical analysis are based on a model in which a certain VARIABLE has a certain STATISTICAL DISTRIBUTION; if this condition is not met (i.e. the model is incorrect), the use of the technique may not be valid. Techniques for examining whether a DATASET is adequately described by a particular model are known as GOODNESS-OF-FIT tests. If no model (distribution) can be found which appears to fit a particular dataset, it can be studied by the use of NON-PARAMETRIC STATISTICS, which do not rely on such assumptions.

D.L. Clarke: *Models in archaeology* (Cambridge, 1972); A.J. Ammerman and L.L. Cavalli-Sforza: 'A population model for the diffusion of early farming in Europe' *The explanation of culture change*, ed. C. Renfrew (London, 1973), 343–57 [spread of farming]; C. Renfrew, ed.: *The explanation of culture change* (London, 1973); J.E. Doran and F.R. Hodson: *Mathematics and computers in archaeology* (Edinburgh, 1975), 26–8; C.R. Orton: *Mathematics in archaeology* (Glasgow, 1980), 20–1 [general].

CO

mode of production Marxist term used to describe the various socioeconomic stages through which different cultures are thought to pass, i.e. tribal, ancient, asiatic, slave, feudal, capitalist and socialist (Marx and Engels 1962: 43–56). According to Marx himself, writing in 1859, 'The mode of production in material life determines the general character of the social, political and intellectual processes of life' (Marx and Engels 1962: 362). Some archaeologists (particularly Soviet and neo-Marxist researchers, *See* RUSSIA 3 *and* MARXIST ARCHAEOLOGY) have used this concept to describe the means by which cultural transformations occur. Thus Dean Saitta and Art Keene (1990) have studied prehistoric village formation in the PUEBLO culture of north America, identifying a communal mode of production which does not lead to egalitarianism (as traditional Marxism might have suggested).

K. Marx and F. Engels: *Selected works* I (Moscow, 1962); J. Friedman: 'Tribes, states and transformations', *Marxist analyses and social anthropology*, ed. M. Bloch (London, 1975); J. Friedman and M. Rowlands, eds: *The evolution of social systems* (London, 1978); D. Saitta and A. Keene: 'Politics and surplus flow in prehistoric communal societies', *The evolution of political systems: sociopolitics in small-scale sedentary societies*, ed. S. Upham (Cambridge, 1990), 203–24.

IS

Mogador *see* AFRICA 1

Mogollon Major prehistoric culture of the American Southwest, which lasted from the end of the Archaic period to the arrival of the Spanish in AD 1540. It was defined in 1936 by Emil W. Haury on the basis of extensive surveys of the mountains of east-central Arizona and west-central New Mexico in 1931. In 1933 Haury also excavated Mogollon Village along the San Francisco River and, in 1934, Harris Village in the Mimbres Valley. Haury's original definition was of a Mogollon culture characterized by true pithouses and coil-and-scraped, brown pottery – polished plain (Alma Plain), red-slipped (San Francisco Red), and decorated red-on-brown (Mogollon Red-on-brown). After AD 1000 Haury felt that the Mogollon lost their identity through assimilation with the ANASAZI. Current researches subscribe to Erik Reed's interpretation that a separate Mogollon identity can be traced after AD 1000 and in some regions up to the abandonment of the Arizona mountains around AD 1400. These distinctive characteristics include: PUEBLO village layout focusing inward on a plaza; rectangular KIVAS within room blocks; primary extended inhumation of the deceased; vertical-occipital head deformation; the three-quarter groove axe; and brown corrugated pottery often with patterned, incised or painted designs.

The Mogollon developmental sequence is most simply divided into three periods. The Early Pithouse period began around AD 200, with the addition of plain brown pottery to a late Archaic artefact assemblage and ended in the AD 600s around the time that red-on-brown decorated pottery appeared. The Late Pithouse period ends with construction of masonry pueblos around AD 1000 in the Mimbres Valley of New Mexico and from 100 to 200 years later, as pueblo architecture moved westward into the Arizona mountains. The Mogollon Pueblo period ends with the abandonment of the mountains by AD 1400. The latest tree-ring dates attributable to the Mogollon are in the 1380s.

The Mogollon were a hunting, gathering and sometimes gardening people, adapted primarily to the mountain uplands and secondarily to the adjacent desert lowlands of Arizona and New Mexico. A southern boundary in the present-day Mexican states of Sonora and Chihuahua is undefined. Loosely defined regional subdivisions or branches are a product of archaeologists working within the paradigm of CULTURE-HISTORICAL THEORY in exploring isolated areas with long, continuous occupations. These areas include New Mexico: the Mimbres Valley (Mimbres branch), San Francisco Valley (Pine Lawn Branch); Arizona: Point of Pines (Black River branch), San Simon Valley (San Simon branch) and Forestdale Valley (Forestdale branch). The hemispherical ceramic bowls of the Mimbres branch (often used as funerary offerings), bearing depictions of people, animals naturalistic scenes and geometric forms, are unique among prehistoric North American cultures.

The Jornada branch defined in the El Paso area seems to have been a distant relative of the mountain-adapted Mogollon. By abandoning the mountains to take up full-time farming, the Mogollon merged archaeologically with the other pueblo farmers of the northern Southwest. The Mogollon cannot be linked positively to a historical group. The major Mogollon sites in Arizona are Bear, Bluff, Crooked Ridge, Turkey Creek and GRASSHOPPER; and those in New Mexico are Harris, Mogollon Village, Cameron Creek, Galaz, Mattocks and Swarts.

J.J. Brody: *Mimbres painted pottery* (Santa Fe, 1977); S.A. LeBlanc: *The Mimbres people* (London, 1983); E.W. Haury: *Mogollon culture in the Forestdale Valley, east-central Arizona* (Tucson, 1985); J.J. Reid and D.E. Doyel, eds: *Emil W. Haury's prehistory of the American Southwest* (Tucson, 1986); J.J. Reid: 'A Grasshopper perspective on the Mogollon of the Arizona Mountains', *Dynamics of southwest prehistory*, ed. L.S. Cordell and G.J. Gumerman (Washington, D.C., 1989), 65–97.

JJR

Mohenjo-Daro Large multi-mound urban centre of the INDUS CIVILIZATION, dating to the 3rd millennium BC and located beside the Indus River in southern Pakistan. Excavators since the 1920s have included John Marshall (1921–2), Ernest Mackay (1927–31), Mortimer Wheeler (1950) and George Dales (1964–6). The total area of the site is about 200 ha, and the two principal mounds (a smaller 'citadel' to the west and a larger, lower eastern mound) cover an area of about 85 ha. This dual mound plan is found at other sites of the INDUS CIVILIZATION, including HARAPPA and KALIBANGAN and is often taken as evidence of rigid and highly formalized town planning. While

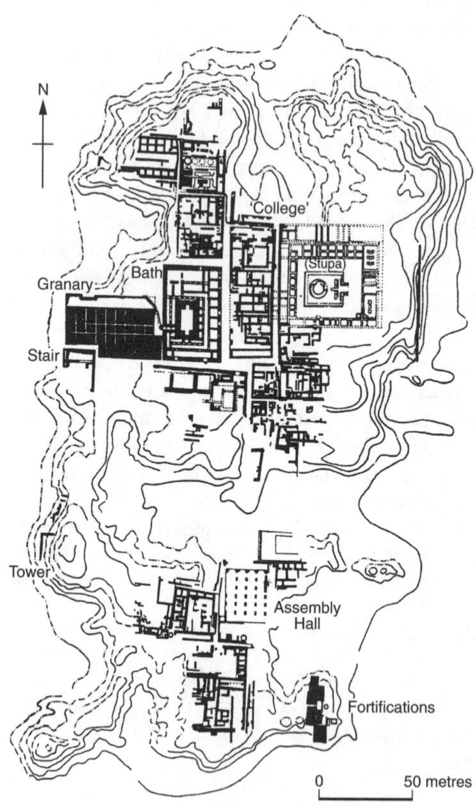

Figure 35 **Mohenjo-Daro** Plan of the citadel of Mohenjo-Daro. *Source*: B. and R. Allchin: *The rise of civilization in India and Pakistan* (Cambridge University Press, 1982), fig. 7.10.

planning is evident within urban sites, with their formal road and drainage systems, it is important to note that large Indus sites typically consist of multiple mounds, and research during the 1990s has increasingly demonstrated considerable inter-site variability in site plan (Kenoyer 1991: 352).

Several monumental structures have been found on the western mound of Mohenjo-Daro, including three identified as a 'granary', 'college' and 'assembly hall' respectively, as well as the 'great bath': a large basin lined with brick and plaster and surrounded by a portico and a series of rooms, often interpreted as a ritual structure. The precise functions of these structures are unknown, but they clearly represent a considerable investment of human labour and planning (Kenoyer 1991: 353).

The eastern mound is characterized by dense blocks of domestic architecture arranged into a gridiron pattern of streets equipped with brick drains. A project of mapping and surface survey during the 1980s–1990s (Jansen 1989) has revealed artefactual patterns characteristic of specialized craft production areas, but no cemetery has yet been located. Mohenjo-Daro is threatened by a rising water-table and a UNESCO project is currently attempting to save the site from destruction.

S.J. Marshall: *Mohenjo-daro and the Indus civilization* (London, 1931); E.J.H. Mackay: *Further excavations at Mohenjodaro* (New Delhi, 1938); M. Jansen: 'Some problems regarding the Forma Urbis Mohenjo-Daro', *South Asian archaeology 1985*, ed. K. Frifelt and P. Sorensen (London, 1989), 247–54. J.M. Kenoyer: 'The Indus Valley tradition of Pakistan and Western India', *JWP* 5 (1991), 331–85.

CS

Mohs scale A scratch (scelerometric) test for hardness, named after Friedrich Mohs (1773–1839). Hardness is determined using a set of standard minerals, the steps between which are unequal. In order of increasing hardness these are:

Mineral	*Equivalent Item for Field Tests*
1 Talc	Can be scratched with fingernail
2 Gypsum	Can be scratched with fingernail
3 Calcite	Can be scratched with copper coin
4 Fluorite	Easily scratched with knife
5 Apatite	Can be scratched with knife
6 Orthoclase	Can be scratched with steel file
7 Quartz	Can be scratched with window glass
8 Topaz	
9 Corundum	
10 Diamond	

The test is commonly used in archaeology for describing ceramic or lithic objects. Though other types of hardness test are available, they are mainly applied to other material, and the Mohs scale remains a useful and widely used field test in both geology and archaeology.

F. Mohs: *Treatise on mineralogy*, trans. W. Haidinger (London, 1825).

PTN

Mollo *see* ISKANWAYA

Molokwane (Selonskraal) Extremely large Sotho-Tswana town in the Transvaal dated to the end of the 18th century AD. A series of homesteads and wards each based on the 'CENTRAL CATTLE PATTERN', forms the town, and virtually every level of administration was present. At this time the Sotho-Tswana lived in anomalously large settlements compared to others with political stratification of equal (or even greater) complexity. This concentrated settlement pattern at Molokwane has usually been attributed to the comparatively dry environment, traditional cultural preferences or greater social stratification. However, archaeological data show not only that this urbanization only began after AD 1750 but also that the climate was wetter.

Large towns such as Molokwane were probably formed by the aggregation of small settlements with the chief's capital for mutual protection during the unprecedented military stress of the 18th and 19th centuries AD. Urbanism continued throughout most of the 19th century and is now an important element of Sotho-Tswana culture.

T.N. Huffman: 'Archaeological evidence and conventional explanations of Southern Bantu settlement patterns', *Africa* 56 (1986), 280–98; R.J. Mason: *Origins of black people of Johannesburg and the Southern Western Central Transvaal AD 350–1880* (Johannesburg, 1986); J.C.C. Pistorius: *Molokwane, an Iron Age Bakwena village: early Tswana settlement in the western Transvaal* (Johannesburg, 1992).

TH

Mombasa *see* SWAHILI HARBOUR TOWNS

Monks Mount *see* CAHOKIA

monothetic culture *see* POLYTHETIC CULTURE

Monsú *see* PUERTO HORMIGA, MONSÚ AND SAN JACINTO

Montagu Cave Cave in the Cape Folded Mountain Range, in the SW Cape, South Africa, 160 km east of Cape Town. Rich ACHEULEAN horizons occur, but with no organics, and no dating. An MSA (Middle Stone Age) layer is assigned to the HOWIESON'S POORT industry, with radiocarbon dates (five ranging from 19,100 to 50,000, and >38,000 uncal BP LSA (Later Stone Age) occupations at the site are undated but fall typologically within the range of the WILTON industry.

C.M. Keller: *Montagu Cave in prehistory: a descriptive analysis* (Berkeley, 1973).

RI

Monte Albán *see* ZAPOTECS

Monte Verde Cold-forest/tundra settlement in southern Chile, which is currently the earliest well-dated PALEO-INDIAN site in the Americas. The remains of wood and skin huts are associated with a larger y-shaped structure, a hafted stone tool, *BOLAS*, and abundant plant remains, including non-local species such as potato.

T.D. Dillehay: *Monte Verde: a late Pleistocene settlement in Chile* (Washington, D.C., 1989).

KB

Mont Lassois Natural outcrop commanding the Seine valley in the eastern France, 6 km north of Châtillon-sur-Seine, which was crowned with massive fortifications (2.7 km perimeter) in the 6th century BC. Mont Lassois was the means by which the local Celtic chieftans exerted control over a river valleys trade route that led eventually to the Mediterranean; the great wealth and contact with the civilized world that this control afforded are vividly demonstrated by the contents of the princely tomb of VIX nearby.

R. Joffroy: *L'Oppidum de Vix* (Paris, 1960); ——: *Vix et ses trésors* (Paris, 1979).

RJA

mortuary temple *see* MEDINET HABU; PYRAMID; RAMESSEUM

Moshebi's Shelter Stone Age rockshelter in southeastern Lesotho excavated in 1969 by P. Carter. An earlier and a later MSA (Middle Stone Age) level are overlain by LSA (Later Stone Age) material. The MSA industries contain interesting blade elements, those in the later industry being notably smaller. Backed pieces in the later industry invite comparison with the HOWIESON'S POORT industry. The LSA material post-dates 218 uncal BP and contains delicate backed blades and bifacially flaked barbed and tanged arrowheads.

P.L. Carter: 'Moshebi's shelter', *Lesotho Notes and Records*, 8 (1969), 13–23; —— and J. Vogel: 'The dating of industrial assemblages from stratified sites in eastern Lesotho', *Man* n.s. 9 (1974), 557–70.

RI

Motupore An island near Port Moresby, the capital of Papua New Guinea (*see* OCEANIA 2), which is the traditional home of the Motu people. Excavations uncovered evidence of pottery production, shell bead manufacturing and domestic debris dating back to 800 BP. In oral historical traditions the island is connected with the production of pottery for *hiri* trading expeditions to the Gulf of Papua, where the pottery was exchanged for sago. Archaeological evidence demonstrates a rise in intensity of both production and trade over eight centuries, as well as the extensive nature of local trading interactions.

J. Allen: 'Fishing for wallabies: trade as a mechanism for social interaction, integration and elaboration on the central Papuan coast', *The evolution of social systems*, ed. J. Friedman and M. Rowlands (London, 1977), 419–55; ——: 'Pots and poor princes: a multidimensional approach to the role of pottery trading in central Papua', *The many dimensions of pottery*, ed. S.E. van der Leeuw and A Pritchard (Amsterdam, 1984).

CG

mound center *see* AZTALAN; CAHOKIA; ETOWAH; MISSISSIPPIAN; MOUNDVILLE

Mound City Earthwork and mound complex dating to the Middle WOODLAND period (*c.*200 BC–AD 400, *see* HOPEWELL) and situated in the Scioto River valley, Ross County, Ohio (USA). When first reported in 1848, the site consisted of a large square earthwork enclosing *c.*5 ha and containing at least 24 earthen mounds. Excavation of several of the mounds in the 1920s revealed a variety of Hopewell mortuary features, including the 'Great Mica Grave' found in Mound 13. Many of the mortuary features contained Hopewell-series pottery and exotic artefacts, such as animal-effigy and plain-platform pipes, obsidian projectile points, copper effigies of animals and humans, plates, beads, axes and marine-shell cups.

W. Mills: 'Exploration of the Mound City Group', *OAHSP* 31 (1922), 422–584.

RJE

Mound Velarde Site in Bolivia dating from *c.*AD 100 to the early 20th century, which is still one of the very few stratified lowland sites in this part of the world to have been investigated. An earthen 'island', one of a large number of artificial living platforms connected by long causeways and surrounded by drained field systems on the seasonally inundated Llanos de Mojos. The upper stratum contained urn burials and painted tripod bowls, while the ceramics from the lower stratum show stylistic ties with both the Andes and the Amazon.

E. von Nordenskiold: 'Urnengräber und Mounds im Bolivienischen Flachlande', *Baessler Archiv* 3/1 (1912), 210–56.

KB

Moundville Large 'mound center' in the valley of the Black Warrior River, Alabama, USA, which is one of the largest MISSISSIPPIAN sites in the south-eastern United States, and the focus of an important regional group. Mound construction began by the late 11th century AD, and Moundville came to dominate neighbouring smaller mound centers by the 13th century. This control, however, had faded by the 16th century. The site extends over 120 ha, and contains at least 20 large earthen mounds, most of which are distributed around a large rectangular plaza. Other sites in the settlement system are smaller, but include 10 minor centres each with a single mound. Elite burials are found at these centres, with the highest ranking at Moundville itself.

The well defined settlement cluster and the presence of the single large site at Moundville suggests that this is a case of a unified chiefdom society. The Moundville settlement system has been used to test theories of settlement location in chiefdom societies, in particular a version of CENTRAL PLACE THEORY modified to recognize labour service and tribute payment, whether in staple commodities or luxury goods, as the dominant modes of economic activity rather than retail marketing as in Walter Christaller's original model. In such a system the costs of providing labour or tribute would require that the subordinate centres be located significantly nearer to the main central place than would otherwise be the case. The actual settlement system fits the expectations of such a model, although other factors such as local exchange, political rivalry or even warfare may also have been important factors.

V. Steponaitis, 'Location theory and complex chiefdoms', *Mississippian settlement patterns*, ed. B.D. Smith (London and New York, 1978), 417–53; C.S. Peebles: 'The rise and fall of the Mississippian in western Alabama: the Moundville and Summerville phases, AD 1000 to 1600, *Mississippi Archaeology* 22 (1987), 1–31; V.P. Steponaitis: 'Contrasting patterns of Mississippian development', *Chiefdoms: power, economy, and ideology*, ed. T. Earle (Cambridge, 1991), 193–228; P.D. Welch, *Moundville's economy* (Tuscaloosa, 1991).

TC

Mount Carmel Group of Middle and Upper Palaeolithic cave-sites to the east of Haifa in Israel, which were excavated by Dorothy Garrod in 1927–35. At Tabun cave she found a series of MOUSTERIAN levels of occupation, including a NEANDERTHAL burial. In the Tabun and (Mugharet) el-Wad caves Garrod found remains spanning the crucial period of transition between the Middle and Upper Palaeolithic, as well as later strata dating to the Mesolithic and NATUFIAN periods (Garrod and Bate 1937). In 1931–2 the excavations of Ted McCown at the nearby Skhul rock-shelter revealed 10 human burials (including the skull of a child) in association with Lower Mousterian artefacts similar to those at Tabun. René Neuville excavated similar human remains at the Qafzeh cave, and it was suggested that the remains from QAFZEH AND SKHUL represented different elements within a Levantine population which was evolving from Neanderthals into anatomically modern humans in about 40,000 BP (McCown and Keith 1939), although uncertainty remained as to whether this population was 'evolutionary' or 'hybrid'. This speculation, however, was superseded by Arthur Jelinek's re-examination of Tabun, revealing 85 strata, as opposed to Garrod's six layers, which suggested that this Mousterian occupation site probably dated back to 90,000 BP (Jelinek 1981). In 1988, the TL DATING of burnt stone flakes from the Qafzeh burials produced a date of 92,000 ± 5000 BP, thus indicating that anatomically modern humans had arrived in the Levant 50,000 years earlier than previously thought (Vandermeersch 1989).

The Mount Carmel region also includes Nahal Oren, an important stratified occupation site which, like the upper strata at el-Wad, dated from the Kebaran (*c.*16,000–14,000 BC) to the ACERAMIC NEOLITHIC (*c.*8000–5500 BC). The NATUFIAN levels at Nahal Oren (*c.*11000–9300 BC) included a small cemetery alongside a settlement consisting of circular drystone huts.

D.A.E. Garrod and D.M.A. Bate: *The Stone Age of Mount Carmel* I (Oxford 1937); T.D. McCown and A. Keith: *The Stone Age of Mount Carmel* II (Oxford, 1939); D.R. Brothwell: 'The people of Mount Carmel: a reconsideration of their position in human evolution', *PPS* 27 (1961),

155–9; A. Jelinek: 'The Middle Palaeolithic of the Levant: synthesis', *Préhistoire du Levant*, ed. J. Cauvin and P. Sanlaville (Paris, 1981); B. Vandermeersch: 'The evolution of modern humans: recent evidence from south-west Asia', *The human revolution*, ed. P. Mellars and C. Stringer (Edinburgh, 1989), 155–64.

IS

Mousa Scottish Iron Age broch (defensive stone tower) on the islet of Mousa off mainland Shetland, probably built largely in the 1st century BC and occupied and internally modified up to the 3rd century AD. Although Mousa has not been properly excavated, it is important as the finest surviving example of the BROCH class of monuments in Scotland. (It survived almost intact because there were no subsequent settlements nearby, and thus no stone robbing.) It consists of a massive drystone tower over 13 m high and 15 m in external diameter, tapering towards the top. After a single solid dry-stone wall to a height of nearly 4 m, the wall becomes a hollow double-skinned structure bounded by stone lintels at regular intervals to preserve its strength. The most architecturally striking feature of Mousa is a stairway with stone steps that runs up through this hollow wall from the first-floor height to the top of the building. The tower wall also contained several intramural cells, while its internal face is ledged so as to support a timber framework (gallery or floor) of some kind. It is uncertain whether the tower was ever roofed.

Inventory of Shetland, *Royal Commission on the Ancient Monuments of Scotland* (Edinburgh, 1946), 48–55.

RJA

Mousterian One of the key industries of the Early (or 'Middle') PALAEOLITHIC, it succeeded the ACHEULEAN and related industries and preceded the first industries of the Upper Palaeolithic. The Mousterian differs from earlier industries in that it is based on flakes produced from carefully prepared cores using the LEVALLOIS TECHNIQUE; as these smaller flake-based implements become dominant in assemblages, heavier handaxes tend to disappear. It was first identified at the French site of Le Moustier in the Dordogne, although variants are recognised across Europe, the Near East and parts of Asia; in western Europe, the relationship between the industries of the Palaeolithic has been clarified at sites such as PECH DE L'AZÉ in the Dordogne valley, which in the 1950s yielded a sequence of Acheulean and Mousterian deposits. Industries based on flakes had begun to emerge before 200,000 BP, while the classic Mousterian can be identified after perhaps 160,000 BP and lasts until *c*.40,000 BP in Europe.

Traditionally, this technological shift was thought to be very closely associated with the early forms of *homo sapiens* and especially with the emergence of NEANDERTHAL MAN – the Mousterian date range roughly coincides with that of skeletal evidence for the Neanderthals. However, the relationship between Mousterian technology and human evolution is now recognised to be significantly more complex: at some sites ANATOMICALLY MODERN HUMANS have been found in levels that yield 'Mousterian' technology – for example, at the site of STAROSEL'YE. Like the evidence from QAFZEH AND SKHUL caves in the Near East, this suggests that 'modern' humans made 'Mousterian' tools. Furthermore, towards the end of the Neanderthal date range, around 40,000 to 35,000 BP, the remains of Neanderthals seem to be associated with early variants of Upper Palaeolithic (ie non-Mousterian) blade-based technology, such as the CHÂTELPERRONIAN in France, the SZELETIAN of central Europe and the ULUZZIAN of Italy. At St Césaire, for example, a cave site in the Charente region of France, a Neanderthal burial has been found in apparent association with Upper Palaeolithic Châtelperronian tools.

Parts of eastern Europe, and particularly the Caucasus, were intensively settled during the Mousterian epoch as is clear from the cave-sites of Azykh, KUDARO and many others. Mousterian sites are also located near Volgograd (Sukhaya Mechetka), near Kursk (Khotylevo) and in a few other areas of European Russia, as well as in Moldovia and in the Ukraine (the Crimean cave sites of KIIK-KOBA, AK-KAYA and others). Many sites reveal sequences of Acheulean and later Mousterian levels, including KUDARO in Georgia; the five Acheulean levels at KOROLEVO seem different to the other Acheulean assemblages of central and western Europe: choppers are common, hand-axes are atypical, and there is an early development of the Levallois technique.

Whatever the precise relationship between tool industry and anatomical evolution, some archaeologists associate the more advanced Mousterian tool assemblages with a shift in human capabilities, notably in terms of conceptualisation and tool design. Steven Mithen (1996: 119), for example, notes that considerable skills were needed to envisage and knap flint tools using this new 'prepared core technology'. It is less certain whether this advance was essentially limited to the technological sphere, or whether it signified a more general advance in social and environmental intelligence reflected in hunting strategy, shelter construction and burial of the dead. At AK-KAYA (Zaskal'naya) in the Crimea, Zaskal'naya 5 comprises eight Mousterian levels with abundant faunal remains, numerous hearths and a rich flint inventory. Nearby, Zaskal'naya 6 contained the remains of burials of five children, aged 8–12 years old, and classed as *Homo sapiens neanderthalensis*; the skeletal evidence is morphologically similar to that from KIIK-KOBA in Crimea, TESHIK TASH in Uzbekistan and some Palestinian Neanderthals (*see* WADI AMUD, MOUNT CARMEL). At Kiik-Koba, the two Mousterian occupation levels included an upper level with an artificial enclosure made of large cobbles, and two burials of Neanderthals – one adult and one child (5–8 months old) laid close to each other in contracted postures. *For further discussion and bibliography, see* PALAEOLITHIC.

S. Mithen: *The prehistory of the mind* (London, 1996).

RJA

MSA (=Middle Stone Age) *See* AFRICA 4

Muang Fa Daet Large moated site located in the Chi valley, northeast Thailand. In its final form, the defences enclosed 171 ha, and a large rectangular reservoir lay outside the moats. It is possible to define three possible enclosures, suggesting that the site was progressively enlarged. The interior contains numerous decorated sema stones, Buddhist markers of sacred precincts. These are decorated with scenes from the life of the Buddha, but one also depicts city walls manned by defenders, an image of the defences that once surrounded such sites. Muang Fa Daet has not been dated archaeologically and was probably occupied for a lengthy period, for a mound in the northern part of the site is covered by prehistoric pottery. The main building period, however, belongs to the later 1st millennium AD and corresponds to the central Thai sites of the DVARAVATI CULTURE.

H. Quaritch-Wales: *Dvaravati: the earliest kingdom of Siam* (London, 1969), 105–13.

CH

Muang Sima One of a handful of large moated settlements of the late 1st millennium AD in northeast Thailand, this site is strategically situated in the upper Mun Valley so as to control traffic between the Central Plain and Khorat Plateau. The site has not been extensively excavated, but an inscription records a gift of cattle, water buffalo and slaves to the temple by the overlord of Sri Canasa, probably a small independent polity contemporary with those of the DVARAVATI CULTURE. Muang Sima was probably the centre of a polity which, to judge from the Khmer as well as Sanskrit text, was orientated towards the polities of the middle Mekong in Cambodia.

H. Quaritch-Wales: *Dvaravati: the earliest kingdom of Siam* (London 1969), 100–5.

CH

Mubende Hill Hilltop shrine in west-central Uganda, dating from the mid-Iron Age to modern times, which contains ritual objects of various ages (up to the present). Like other shrines in the interlacustrine region, that of Mubende Hill stands on an archaeological site of the mid-Iron Age, dating approximately to the 14th century AD. With its tall and ancient 'witch tree', it is renowned as a centre of religion, healing and traditional lore; some scholars (e.g. Lanning 1966, Sutton 1993) consider that it was also an ancient royal capital. The pottery from Robertshaw's excavations of 1987 (see Sutton 1993) relates Mubende to the same cultural complex as NTUSI and BIGO.

E.C. Lanning: 'Excavations at Mubende Hill', *UJ* 30 (1966), 153–63; J.E.G. Sutton: 'The antecedents of the interlacustrine kingdoms', *JAH* 34 (1993), 33–64.

JS

Muguruk *see* SANGOAN

multidimensional scaling (mdscal) A way of reducing the dimension of a MULTIVARIATE DATASET such as the shapes of artefacts as expressed by a set of measurements made on each one. For example, it enabled the shapes of a set of Iron Age fibulae to be plotted as points on a two-dimensional SCATTERGRAM, although it took many dimensions to accurately describe the shapes. The number of dimensions is reduced one at a time to the required number (usually two). At each step the distances between each pair of objects are calculated and ranked in size order; the aim is to preserve this order, as far as possible, as the pattern is squeezed down to one fewer dimension, so as to preserve the overall pattern of the objects in the space. The extent to which the order has to be distorted is called the strain. Mdscal can produce very good results on a small dataset, but it is very demanding of computer time, and it is difficult to tell whether the 'best' result has been achieved. It has been relatively little used since a period of experimentation in the 1970s.

J.B. Kruskal: 'Multidimensional scaling in archaeology:

time is not the only dimension', *Mathematics in the archaeological and historical sciences*, ed. F.R. Hodson, D.G. Kendall and P. Tautu (Edinburgh, 1971), 119–32; J.E. Doran and F.R. Hodson: *Mathematics and computers in archaeology* (Edinburgh, 1975), 213–7.
CO

multiplier effect *see* SYSTEMS THEORY

multivariate dataset, multivariate statistics Branch of statistics concerned with the simultaneous behaviour of two or (usually) more VARIABLES. The approaches used are often EXPLORATORY, rather than concerned with PARAMETER ESTIMATION or HYPOTHESIS TESTING, and the VISUAL DISPLAY of data is an important tool. The starting point of such analyses is frequently the presentation of a DATASET (such as a set of chemical analyses made on a series of artefacts) as points in a multidimensional space, each point representing an object and each dimension a VARIABLE. The distribution of the points in the multidimensional space may be analysed (*see* CLUSTER ANALYSIS), or the number of variables/ dimensions may be reduced (*using techniques such as* CORRESPONDENCE ANALYSIS, DISCRIMINANT ANALYSIS, MULTIDIMENSIONAL SCALING, *and* PRINCIPAL COMPONENTS ANALYSIS) so that the results may be reproduced graphically or analysed using conventional statistical processes.
J.E. Doran and F.R. Hodson: *Mathematics and computers in archaeology* (Edinburgh, 1975), 132–264; S. Shennan: *Quantifying archaeology* (Edinburgh, 1988), 166–297; M.J. Baxter: *Exploratory multivariate analysis in archaeology* (Edinburgh, 1993).
CO

mummification (Arabic: *Mummiya*, 'bitumen') The flesh and skin of humans and animals have sometimes been inadvertently preserved in particularly waterlogged, arid or frozen contexts (*see* BEECHEY ISLAND, LINDOW MAN, mammoth *and* Tollund man. However, the term 'mummification' is more properly applied to instances of deliberate, artificial preservation. The concept of the physical survival of the body after death was fundamental to the funerary practices of many ancient cultures, and a wide range of methods of artificial mummification were practised in Egypt, America, Libya, Siberia, China, Japan, Australia and Melanesia. Not unexpectedly, mummification has invariably been adopted in those extreme geographical locations (such as the Sahara, the Andes and the Siberian steppes, *see* PAZYRYK) where extreme climatic conditions no doubt produced the first instances accidentally. Grafton Elliot Smith (1923) argued that the apparent spread of mummification was an example of DIFFUSIONISM, but there is now little support for this theory that the process was invented in Egypt and then disseminated throughout the world, along with other innovative aspects of the pharaonic culture.
1. *Egypt*. Burials of the predynastic period in Egypt (*c*.5500–3000 BC) were spontaneously mummified by the desiccating effect of the desert sand in which they were buried. The earliest Egyptian technique of artificial mummification, involving only linen wrappings and resin, was developed at least as early as the 2nd dynasty (*c*.2770–2649 BC), but by the 4th dynasty more elaborate methods of embalming had been developed. At first only the heart, liver, lungs and intestines were removed and preserved separately in four CANOPIC JARS. In later times the brain tissue was extracted through the nostrils and the torso itself was dehydrated by covering with powdered natron. There are no surviving descriptions of mummification from the pharaonic period, but the later accounts of Greek writers such as Herodotus (*c*.450 BC) indicate that the entire process took about 70 days, including the precise placing of numerous prophylactic amulets among the linen wrappings.

Most surviving Egyptian mummies date to the New Kingdom (*c*.1550–1070 BC) or later, although the earliest surviving example is the body of a man called Waty dating to the 5th dynasty (*c*.2400 BC), from a tomb at Saqqara. The mummified bodies of many of the New Kingdom pharaohs were discovered at Western Thebes, having been reinterred in two caches, one in the tomb of Amenhotep II (in the VALLEY OF THE KINGS) and the other in a shaft-tomb at DEIR EL-BAHARI. From the Late Period onwards millions of mummified animals, such as falcons, ibises and cats, were dedicated at the temples of such deities as the cat-goddess Bastet and the crocodile-god Sobek, resulting in the creation of vast mummy-filled catacombs, such as the sacred animal necropolises at Saqqara and Tuna el-Gebel.
2. *Americas*. In Peru, the earliest surviving mummies are the four eviscerated and desiccated bodies found at Tres Ventanas Cave and dated at between 4000 and 2000 BC. The funerary rites of the PARACAS and INCA cultures of Peru, dating to *c*.900–200 BC and AD 1200–1534 respectively, involved the burial of desiccated bodies wrapped in a variety of materials, including cotton, cactus-fibre net, matting and basketry. Among the ANASAZI people of North America (*c*.AD 1–1300) desiccated bodies were placed in pits, stone-lined cists and

caves along with funerary offerings such as baskets and weapons. See also CHINCHORRO *and* MUMMY BUNDLE. *For mummification in Siberia see* PAZYRYK.

G.E. Smith: *The ancient Egyptians and the origin of civilization* (London, 1923); J.E. Harris and K.E. Weeks: *X-raying the pharaohs* (New York, 1973); K.E. Stothert: 'Unwrapping an Inca mummy bundle', *Archaeology* 32/4, (1979), 8–17; A. Cockburn and E. Cockburn, eds: *Mummies, disease and ancient cultures* (Cambridge, 1980); C.A. Andrews: *Egyptian mummies* (London, 1984); A.R. David: 'Mummification', *Ancient Egyptian materials and technology*, ed. P.T. Nicholson and I. Shaw (Cambridge, 1999).

IS

mummy bundle Term used to describe the form often taken by cadavers in Andean South America. The seated or flexed body is wrapped in layers of clothing and other textiles as well as artefacts and plant offerings, forming a large bundle. *See also* MUMMIFICATION 2.

K.E. Stothert: 'Unwrapping an Inca mummy bundle', *Archaeology* 32/4, (1979), 8–17.

KB

Munhata *see* ACERAMIC NEOLITHIC

Munsell colour charts Set of eight charts, comprising 251 standard colours, derived from a Soil Survey Manual which forms part of Handbook 18 of the U.S. Department of Agriculture (based on a system devised between 1900 and 1912 by an American artist, Alfred Munsell). The so-called 'Munsell Book of Color' (or, more usually, the smaller version known as the 'Munsell Soil Color Charts') is commonly used by archaeologists as a standard means of identifying and naming colours of such features as soils, sediments, pigments and pottery fabrics.

With use of the Munsell charts, soils or fabrics can be labelled with an alphanumeric defining three variables: *hue* (e.g. R = red, GY = green--yellow), *value* (lightness or darkness measured from 0 to 10) and *chroma* (i.e. saturation or purity). Each sheet of the book is perforated with holes so that both the archaeological sample and the Munsell colour chip can be viewed simultaneously. Thus, a yellowish-brown sample from a given layer at a site might correspond to a colour chip defined in the Munsell Book as 10YR 3/4. Munsell books usually also include a chart facilitating the distinction between deposits according to different 'granular and crumb structures', i.e. variation in texture from 'very fine' (comprising grains less than 1 mm in diameter) to 'very coarse' (more than 10 mm diameter).

There are several colour charts other than the Munsell Book, such as the Ostwald Colour Album, which was used to describe the colours of ceramics at the Egyptian site of ARMANT in the 1930s, the Schwaneberger chart (designed for philatelists), and the charts produced by the Japanese Colour Research Institute in Tokyo (see Coles 1972: 204).

In some instances, such as the accurate recording of the colours of ancient wall paintings, electronic measuring systems have been adopted. The Minolta CR–221, for instance, employs silicon photocells and a data processor to store and analyse colour measurements, displaying the results in the form of five different methods of colour notation, including the Munsell system (see Billmeyer, Jr. and Saltzman 1981; Strudwick 1991).

J. Coles: *Field archaeology in Britain* (London, 1972); Munsell Color Company: *Munsell soil color charts* (Baltimore, 1975); F.W. Billmeyer, Jr. and M. Saltzman: *Principles of colour technology* (New York, 1981); N. Strudwick: 'An objective colour-measuring system for the recording of Egyptian tomb paintings', *JEA* 77 (1991), 43–56.

IS

Muqayyar, Tell el- *see* UR

Mureybet Tell site comprising deposits dating to the NATUFIAN and ACERAMIC NEOLITHIC periods (*c*.9000–7000 BC), located next to the Euphrates in Syria. There were three major phases: a Natufian hunters' camp, a Proto-Neolithic cluster of circular mud huts and an Aceramic Neolithic village consisting of large, rectangular stone-built structures, some incorporating the bones and horned skulls of wild oxen, as in the later settlement at ÇATAL HÜYÜK. Although the animals and cereal crops on which the inhabitants of Mureybet relied for their subsistence were apparently undomesticated, it has been suggested that the wild barley may have been brought to the area from the Anatolian region of Gaziantep, almost 150 km away.

M. Van Loon: 'The Oriental Institute excavations at Mureybet, Syria', *JNES* 27 (1968), 264–90; J.C. Cauvin: 'Nouvelles fouilles à Tell Mureybet (Syrie) 1971–72. Rapport préliminaire', *Les Annales Archéologiques Arabes Syriennes* 22 (1972), 105–15; ——: *Les premiers villages de Syrie-Palestine du IXe au VIIe millénaire avant J.C.* (Lyons, 1978).

IS

Murray Springs Kill site of the CLOVIS culture, located in the San Pedro Valley, southeastern Arizona, 20 km north of the LEHNER site. Both the main site, including the remains of mammoth, bison and possibly horse, and an associated temporary camp site have been dated to 11,000 BP.

C.V. Haynes and E.T. Hemmings: 'Mammoth-bone shaft wrench from Murray Springs, Arizona', *Science* 159 (1968), 186–7.

JJR

Murzak-Koba Mesolithic cave site in the valley of the river Chernaya, Balaklava region, Crimea (Ukraine). The site was discovered and excavated by S.N. Bibikov in 1936–8. The faunal remains include wild goat, wild pig, red deer, wild cat, brown bear and dog. The stone industry includes geometric microliths (trapezes, lunates and triangles). The bone industry consisted of harpoons, awls, arrowheads, needles and pendants. The cultural stratum included burials of a female, 20–25 years of age, and a male 40–50 years old. Finger bones in both of the female's hands had been amputated during her life-time.

S.N. Bibikov: 'Grot Murzak-Koba – navaja pozdnepaleolitičeskaja stojanka v Krymu' [Murzak-Koba cave – a new Late Palaeolithic site in the Crimea], *Sovetskaja arheologija* 3 (1940), 159–78; E.A. Vekilova: 'Kamennyi vek Kryma: nekotorye itogi' [The Crimean Stone Age: some conclusions], *MIAS* 173 (Leningrad, 1971), 117–62.

PD

Mushabian complex Term applied in the late 1970s to a set of EPIPALAEOLITHIC assemblages from sites in Wadi Mushabi and the surrounding region of northeastern Sinai. As a result of the discovery of similar sites in the Negev and southern Jordan, the Mushabian has been identified as a 'complex' of different microlithic assemblages spread throughout the arid parts of the southern Levant, all dated by radiocarbon to *c.*14,170–11,700 BP. The Mushabian material culture typically consists of chipped stone tools, occasionally accompanied by groundstone, bone or shell artefacts.

D.O. Henry: *From foraging to agriculture: the Levant at the end of the Ice Age* (Philadelphia, 1989), 124–49.

IS

Mussau Islands Extensive excavations on these Pacific islands by Kirch have uncovered a series of sites from the LAPITA CULTURAL COMPLEX and later periods. Some sites, such as those on Eloaua Island, are waterlogged and have preserved wooden posts and plant remains (which demonstrate that all the tree crops in use in Melanesia today were exploited 3000 years ago), as well as large samples of pottery, obsidian, worked shell and faunal remains. Pottery at the sites may have been traded during the Lapita period, as was obsidian during all periods.

P.V. Kirch; 'Lapita and Oceanic cultural origins: excavations in the Mussau Islands, Bismarck Archipelago, 1985', *JFA* 14 (1987), 163–80; P.V. Kirch et al.: 'Mussau Islands prehistory: results of the 1985–6 excavations', *Report of the Lapita Homeland Project*, ed. J. Allen and C. Gosden (Canberra, 1991), 144–63.

CG

Mwitu tradition *see* EARLY IRON AGE

Mycenae, Mycenaeans Mycenae is the principal surviving site of the Mycenaean civilization of late Bronze Age Greece, comprising a citadel palace and concentric rings of richly furnished shaft graves. The site began as a substantial but unremarkable Middle HELLADIC settlement until, around 1650 BC, a richer culture developed, based on the local Helladic but adopting many MINOAN artistic and cultural conventions. The earliest evidence for this culture is a circle of shaft graves on the citadel excavated in the 1950s, known as 'Circle B'. These graves contained local Helladic material culture, pottery that reveals influences from the CYCLADIC CULTURE, stone vases imported from Crete, and sword-types that are derived from Crete. This mix of material culture and the form of the earliest graves in Circle B – a simple, relatively shallow pit burial that is similar to other pit graves in southern Greece in this period – proves that the Mycenaean civilization developed locally rather than representing an intrusion.

A slightly later set of shaft graves (*c.*1550–1500 BC), excavated earlier by Heinrich Schliemann and thus rather confusingly called Circle A, had formed the type-site for the Mycenaean civilization. (It now seems clear that the latest Circle B graves may be almost contemporary with the earliest Circle A graves.) Like the earlier circle, stelae were set over these shafts, some plain and some decorated with carvings of spirals, warriors, chariots etc. Again like Circle B, the grave goods in Circle A are a heterogeneous mix, including simple implements and jewellery as well as extraordinary gold and silver works of art revealing both strong local traditions and connections with Crete and other Mediterranean regions. The most remarkable items from Circle A include a silver bullshead rhyton that is almost certainly the work of a Cretan artisan, and a series of five goldsheet 'death masks' that are Helladic and have no real Cretan parallels. There are also items made locally but showing Cretan stylistic influence.

The sudden efflorescence of material culture at Mycenae has been explained in the past in terms of an incursive Minoan aristocracy, or of Helladic plundering of Crete. In fact, the mix of relative continuity in pottery styles with the presence of striking imported goods and a wider adoption of exotic styles seems more likely to be the result of a local polity building power and wealth, perhaps through trade, and then adopting selected elements of the richest cultures in the wider region. (The process may even be comparable to the importing and adaption of classical artistic styles and motifs by the HALLSTATT chiefdoms of north and west Europe in the last few centuries BC.) Between its genesis soon after 1700 BC, until its height in around 1450 BC, Mycenaean cultural influence spread throughout the Aegean, directly influencing Minoan society.

Later Mycenaean civilization. There is only fragmentary evidence for defensive structures and palaces contemporary with the shaft graves at Mycenae – as at other sites, the earliest structures were obliterated by later building and landscaping. The earliest well-preserved monumental buildings are the various major THOLOS tombs and chamber tombs, the greatest of which began to be built in the early to mid-14th century BC. From the 14th century BC, roughly in the same period that Minoan society on Crete largely collapsed probably due to warfare or invasions, massive Cyclopean walls were erected at Mycenae, presumably replacing less impressive fortifications. Similar walls defend the citadels of TIRYNS, GLA, Athens and lesser sites, and many of these fortifications were extended or embellished in the 13th century; Mycenae and Tiryns were given extraordinary corbelled stone passageways leading out from the defences to their water supplies. The traditional, but arguably misplaced, association of Mycenaean culture with war and hero-culture is partly due to these impressive fortifications and partly due to Homer's descriptions of battles and heroic deeds which some scholars believe are based on narratives of events and myths passed down from the Mycenaean era.

The use of 'Cyclopean' architecture, which seems to have evolved in the Greek Argolid, is very notable in Mycenean architecture: structures and walling using massive, flat-surfaced but irregularly shaped ashlar stone. Cyclopean walling is best evidenced at Mycenae and Tiryns, where it is used for defensive walling, bastions and gateways – notably the massive post and lintel gates such as the Lion Gate with its unique sculpture of two lions either side of a relief column. However, the Cyclopean style was also used for a series of dams, bridges and culverts which reveal an extensive Mycenaean road system radiating from Mycenae.

Within the walls of Mycenae, as at Thebes and perhaps Orchomenos in Boetia, and the undefended site of PYLOS in Messenia, palace complexes have been identified that have parallels with, but are much smaller than, the palace complexes of Minoan Crete. Like the Minoan palaces, the Mycenaean examples have ceremonial areas (MEGARON units), administrative areas (the archive at Pylos is the clearest evidence of this), areas for storage of agricultural produce such as oil and textiles and sometimes luxury items; and evidence of specialist manufacture. With the rise of the palaces, a script (Linear B) came to be used for administration, derived from Minoan Linear A but recording a different language – Mycenaean Greek. However, the Mycenaean palaces are organized on quite different principles to those of Crete. Rather than centring on an open courtyard they focus on a ceremonial 'megaron': a long rectangular hall approached via a porch and (often) an anteroom, usually surrounded by subsidiary rooms. Judging from evidence at Pylos, the megaron rooms possessed galleries and central hearths. Mycenaean frescoes are heavily influenced by their Minoan predecessors, but evolved a distinct and less naturalistic (more static) style.

The Mycenaean palaces are often associated with groups of villas of enigmatic function: they may be housing for an elite, or have administrative functions like the West House group at Mycenae (which has a megaron element). Other houses, with the finer rooms on the second storey and storage areas beneath – rather like better-preserved counterparts on THERA – may have housed merchants (e.g. the House of the Oil Merchant near the citadel of Mycenae).

The evidence for Mycenaean religion is limited, although there was an apparent 'cult centre' at Mycenae itself with altars and large figurines of worshippers, clay snakes, and the famous Room of the Fresco which seems to depict two goddesses facing one another, one with a staff, the other with a sword. The megara themselves may have been at the centre of cult ceremonies. The Pylos archives suggest that there were localized pantheons of gods, rather than a single well-defined set of deities.

It is often assumed that the palaces acted as administrative and redistributive centres, for which there is archival evidence at Pylos; a few Linear B script tablets have also been recovered from Mycenae. It is also sometimes argued that they encouraged a specialization of local economies, for which there is less direct evidence. Although the wealth of the burials, the sculpture (e.g. Lion Gate) and myth suggest that Mycenae was pre-eminent among the Mycenaean fortresses, it is not clear whether it dominated the other sites economically or politically.

G. Karo: *Die Schactgräber von Mykenai* (Munich, 1930–3); A.J.B. Wace: *Mycenae: an archaeological history and guide* (Princeton, 1943); V.R. d'A. Desborough: *The last Mycenaeans and their successors* (Oxford, 1964); C. Blegen: *The palace of Nestor at Pylos* (Princeton, 1966); G. Mylonas: *Mycenae and the Mycenaean Age* (Princeton, 1966); M. Ventris and J. Chadwick: *Documents in Mycenaean Greek* (Cambridge, 1973) [contents of Linear B tablets from Pylos and Knossos]; J. Hooker: *Mycenaean Greece* (London, 1976); J. Chadwick: *The Mycenaean world* (Cambridge, 1977); A. Harding: *The Mycenaeans and Europe* (London, 1984); Th. Palaima and C. Shelmerdine, eds: *Pylos comes alive: industry and administration in a Mycenaean palace* (New York, 1984); K. Kilian: 'The Mycenaeans Up To Date', *Problems in Greek prehistory*, ed. E.B. French and K.A. Wardle (Bristol, 1988).

RJA

N

NAA *See* NEUTRON ACTIVATION ANALYSIS

Nabataea, Nabataeans Geographical area and people in northern Arabia, first attested in the annals of the Assyrian King Ashurbanipal (*c.*669–627 BC); at this date the Nabataeans were a nomadic group occupying the region of Tayma and Madain Salih (*see* ARABIA, PRE-ISLAMIC). In archaeological terms, Nabataean sites are characterized by the production of extremely fine eggshell-like painted ceramics. It is thought that the Nabataeans controlled the area through which the traders of incense and spices passed, on their way from Hadramaut in the south to the Levant and Egypt in the north. Undoubtedly the most celebrated Nabataean site is Petra, in western Jordan, which was initially an Edomite settlement. It became the Nabataean capital in the 5th century BC and rapidly developed into a powerful commercial centre, famous for its rock-cut tombs, temples, palaces and houses, surrounded by a complex system of channels and cisterns supplying water to the city. The Nabataeans widened the narrow approach to Petra, via the gorge known as the Sik, and paved the surface with limestone slabs.

The Nabataean settlement of Kurnub (perhaps ancient Mampsis), 35 km southeast of Beersheba, was probably founded in the 1st century AD, reaching a peak of prosperity under the Roman emperors Trajan and Hadrian. It was spread over three small hills, with the major phase consisting of a set of fortified buildings arranged around an internal courtyard. Some of the houses were decorated with elaborate frescoes, and one contained a cache of silver tetradrachms hidden in about AD 220. It was eventually sacked by the Arabs in *c.*635.

The typical Nabataean architecture at Petra and Madain Salih combines elements of Assyrian, Babylonian and Hellenistic styles, as well as some distinctive indigenous motifs, such as the 'crow-step' surmounting many of the monuments. The Nabataean script, representing a mixture of Aramaic and early Arabic, is similar to the contemporary alphabets of the Levant, and its cursive form closely resembles the Qufic script.

M.A. Murray: *Petra: the rock-city of Edom* (London, 1939); P.C. Hammond: *The Nabataeans* (Gothenburg, 1973); J.I. Lawlor: *The Nabataeans in historical porportion* (Grand Rapid, 1974); J.S. McKenzie: *The architecture of Petra* (Oxford, 1990); 'Petra et la royaume des Nabatéens', *DA* 163 (1991) [entire issue devoted to Petra and the Nabataeans].

IS

Nabta Playa Prehistoric settlement in the Libyan Desert, about 100 km west of Abu Simbel. The Nabta Playa depression incorporates a continuous sequence of deposits from the terminal Palaeolithic (*c.*7300 BC) to the early Neolithic (*c.*4000 BC). Several areas of the site were excavated by Wendorf and Schild in 1974–7 as part of the Combined Prehistoric Expedition to the Western Desert of Egypt. The findings at Nabta Playa – as well as other sites in the Western Desert, such as el-Kortein Playa and el-Gebel el-Beid Playa – suggest that groups inhabiting the desert and savannah regions of northeast Africa must have played an important role in the introduction of cattle pastoralism, farming and trading practices into the Nile valley.

F. Wendorf and R. Schild: *Prehistory of the Eastern Sahara* (New York, 1980), 84–97, 144–65, 389–98; B. Midant-Reynes: *Préhistoire de l'Egypte* (Paris, 1992), 76–9.

IS

Nahal Hemar *see* ACERAMIC NEOLITHIC

Nahal Mishmar Cave-site in Israel where a cache of more than 600 copper artefacts relating to the Ghassulian culture (*see* GHASSUL, TELEILAT EL-) was discovered in 1960. Among the objects were intricately worked maces, crowns and sceptres, the appearance of which is remarkably ornate and sophisticated for the Chalcolithic period. It has been argued that the hoard may have derived from the ENGEDI sanctuary.

P. Bard-Adon: *The cave of the treasure: the finds from the caves in Nahal Mishmar* (Jerusalem, 1980).
IS

Nahal Oren *see* MOUNT CARMEL

Nahuatl A Nahua language of the Uto-Aztecan family, spoken by the AZTECS and perhaps also the TOLTECS; a related language, Nahuat, was spoken in Veracruz, Mexico.

Nakbe LOWLAND MAYA centre of the Middle Preclassic period (*c.*800–300 BC) in northern Petén, Guatemala. It is distinguished by its substantial public architecture, including a large temple-pyramid. Like nearby EL MIRADOR, Nakbe has little evidence of Classic period occupation.
R.D. Hansen: 'The road to Nakbe', *Natural History* (May 1991), 8–14.
PRI

Nakhon Pathom *see* DVARAVATI CULTURE

Namazga (Namazga-depe) Situated near the town of Kaakhka, this is the largest stratified tell in south Turkmenistan. Discovered in 1916 by D.D. Bukinich, and excavated by Kuftin, I.N. Khlopin and others since 1949, the site provides a framework for the Eneolithic (early Neolithic) and Bronze Age in Central Asia.

The settled area at the site dramatically increased during the Namazga II and III stages, reaching respectively 25 and 30 ha. The process of urbanization continued during the Early and Middle Bronze Age when the settled area reached *c.*50 ha. The transition to the Namazga VI stage, around 2170–2050 BC, corresponded with a collapse of proto-urban settlement, the settled area being reduced to *c.*2 ha. At the same time a number of small settlements appeared in the locality. This crisis of urbanization, which coincided with an increased reliance on stock-breeding and, particularly, the appearance of horse-breeding, is usually attributed to an increased aridity (*see also* ASIA 1).
P.L. Kohl: *Central Asia: Palaeolithic beginnings to the Iron Age* (Paris, 1984); V.M. Masson: *Pervye civilizacii* (Leningrad, 1989).
PD

Namazga I	Early Eneolithic	5800 – 4000 BC
Namazga II	Middle Eneolithic	4000 – 3500 BC
Namazga III	Late Eneolithic	3500 – 3000 BC
Namazga IV	Early Bronze Age	3000 – 2500 BC
Namazga V	Middle Bronze Age	2500 – 2100 BC
Namazga VI	Late Bronze Age	2100 – 1800(?) BC

Table 15 **Namazga** The cultural sequence at Namazga.

Nambillo Series of deeply buried village sites in the jungles of the western Andean slope (Northwest Ecuador), dating from the Formative to the Colonial period (*c.*3000 BC–AD 1500). Radial sampling through soil coring permitted access to the PALAEOSOLS with minimal damage to cultural levels and has resulted in a detailed knowledge of the stratigraphy prior to excavation, topographic mapping of the various occupations and, through phosphate analyses, identification of activity areas within the sequential occupations of the ridge top.
R.D. Lippi: 'Paleotopography and phosphate analysis of a buried jungle site in Ecuador', *JFA* 15/1 (1988), 85–97.
KB

Namu Shell-midden site on the central coast of British Columbia which is the longest continuously occupied site in Canada. Initial excavation took place in 1969–70 directed by J.J. Hester (Hester and Nelson 1978). Hester used ecological factors to establish a 9000-year sequence of separate phases at the site from 7000 BC to AD 1800. Further fieldwork directed by Roy Carlson in 1977–8 (Carlson 1979; Cannon 1991) and again in 1994 was directed at refining the chronology and increasing the sample size. This work resulted in the extension of the chronology back to 7700 BC. The earliest components (*c.*7000–4500 BC) are dominated by flaked stone technology and represent an interface between the PEBBLE TOOL and MICROBLADE traditions. After 3000 BC flaked stone is rare, extensive shell-midden deposits developed, and artefact assemblages became dominated by bone artefacts associated with fishing. Stable-CARBON ISOTOPE ANALYSIS of bone from 13 adult skeletons dating between 2500 and 800 BC indicated that marine resources accounted for 93–100% of total dietary protein intake.

The site chronology is supported by 39 radiocarbon dates. Samples were selected from features during excavation, from specific burials, and from particular places in the stratigraphic profile rather than from random charcoal. The dating in 1977–8 altered the earlier chronology by establishing that no faunal remains pre-dated 4500 BC. The overall result of the dating is a stratigraphically defined chronology of six periods, ranging from 7770–140 BC to AD 1460–80 (Cannon 1991: Table B–1). The site continued to be occupied with little evidence of culture change until the time of European contact.

X-RAY FLUORESCENCE analysis was undertaken on 194 obsidian artefacts from Namu in order to determine their source and infer trade patterns (Carlson 1995). This study showed that by 7000 BC obsidian was reaching NAMU through trade with sources 100 miles away. This trade in obsidian occurred throughout the occupation span, with most obsidian deriving from sources 100–200 miles distant, although a small amount during the 3rd millennium BC came from as far away as Oregon, 600 miles distant.

J. Hester and S. Nelson, eds: *Studies in Bella Bella prehistory* (Burnaby, 1978); R.L. Carlson: 'The early period on the Central Coast of British Columbia', *Canadian Journal of Archaeology* 3 (1979), 211–28; A. Cannon: 'Radiographic age determination of Pacific salmon: species and seasonal inferences', *JFA* 15 (1988), 103–8; A. Cannon: *The economic prehistory of Namu* (Burnaby, 1991); R.L. Carlson: 'Trade and exchange in prehistoric British Columbia', *Prehistoric exchange systems in North America* II, ed. T.G. Baugh and J.E. Ericson (New York, 1995).

RC

Nan Madol On the island of Ponape in eastern Micronesia, Nan Madol is a series of artificial platforms in a shallow lagoon. Many of the basalt platforms supported dwelling houses; however, there were also tomb and temple structures, some of which are amongst the largest stone structures in the Pacific. Much of the construction may well have taken place in the last few hundred years, although the origins of the artificial islands may be much older.

P. Bellwood: *Man's conquest of the Pacific* (New York, 1979), 289–92.

CG

Nan-Yüeh (Nanyue) *see* YÜEH

naos Type of Egyptian shrine used to house the cult-image or sacred bark of the god in the innermost rooms of temples. Usually taking the form of rectangular chests or boxes of wood or stone, naoi were also used as containers for funerary statues and mummified animals. Egyptian 'naophorous' statues portray the subject holding a shrine, sometimes containing a divine image.

G. Roeder: *Naos*, 2 vols (Leipzig, 1914).

IS

Napata, Napatan District of Sudan on the Dongola Reach of the Nile, about 30 km southwest of the 4th cataract, which was settled in the mid-15th century BC as a southern outpost of the Egyptian empire in Nubia. The site incorporates funerary remains, possible palace buildings and

Figure 36 **Nan Madol** Plan showing extent of platform structures at Nan Madol, Ponape, which supported houses, tombs and temples. *Source*: P. Bellwood: *Man's conquest of the Pacific* (New York: Oxford University Press, 1979).

an unusual temple of Amun at Gebel Barkal ('Pure Mountain', see Kendall 1986), a partially excavated settlement at the southern end of the site, and probably also a settlement on the opposite bank, although this has not yet been satisfactorily examined. The wider region of Napata includes three other sites: the extensive settlement and funerary remains at Sanam (see Griffith 1922) and the royal cemeteries at EL-KURRU and NURI. By the early 10th century BC, Napata had emerged as the political centre of the kingdom of Kush, which had previously been centred on the city of KERMA. The Kushite kings of the Napatan period controlled trade along the northern road through the desert to the town of Kawa and the southern route towards MEROE. Although Meroe eventually became the new Kushite capital from the early 6th century BC onwards, Napata continued to be of some importance throughout the MEROITIC period (*c*.300 BC–AD 350).

F. Ll. Griffith: 'Oxford excavations in Nubia', *LAAA* 9 (1922), 67–124; B.G. Haycock: 'Towards a better understanding of the kingdom of Cush (Napata-Meroê)', *Sudan Notes and Records* 49 (1968), 1–16; D. Dunham: *The royal cemeteries of Kush,* 4 vols (Boston, 1950–7); ——: *The Barkal temples* (Boston, 1970); J. Leclant: Preliminary reports on excavations at Gebel Barkal, *Orientalia* 43– (1974–); T. Kendall: *Gebel Barkal epigraphic survey 1986: preliminary report to the Visiting Committee of the Department of Egyptian Art* (Boston 1986); J.H. Taylor: *Egypt and Nubia* (London, 1991), 38–45.

IS

Naqada (anc. Nubt, Ombos) Egyptian site consisting of a number of areas of cemeteries and settlements of the predynastic and pharaonic periods, located about 26 km north of Luxor on the west bank of the Nile. When Flinders Petrie excavated two of the predynastic cemeteries (Tukh and el-Ballas) in 1895, he initially identified the contents of the graves as the remains of foreigners (the so-called 'New Race'), dating them to the 1st Intermediate Period (*c*.2180 BC). Soon afterwards, however, he realized that the material was prehistoric, and the grave goods from Naqada (as well as HIW-SEMAINA) formed the basis for his SEQUENCE DATING system. Cemetery T at Naqada is a collection of 57 brick-built and richly equipped graves which are thought to have belonged to the ruling elite of the late Naqada II (or Gerzean) period.

The site also includes the remains of a predynastic walled town (the 'South Town') founded at least as early as 3600 BC. By the Early Dynastic period, this settlement had probably been eclipsed by HIERAKONPOLIS and ABYDOS. About 3 km northwest of modern Naqada is a large MASTABA-TOMB which perhaps belonged to Neithhotep, a female relative of the 1st-dynasty ruler Aha. A small stone step-pyramid of unknown purpose, located near the village of Tukh, is one of seven small pyramids of unknown function erected at different sites from Seila down to Aswan, possibly in the reign of the 3rd-dynasty ruler Huni (*c*.2599–2575 BC). For the Naqada period *see* EGYPT 1.

W.M.F. Petrie and J.E. Quibell: *Naqada and Ballas* (London, 1896); J. De Morgan: *Recherches sur les origines de l'Egypte* 2 vols (Paris, 1896–7); J.J. Castillos: 'An analysis of the tombs in the predynastic cemeteries at Nagada', *JSSEA* 10 (1981), 97–106; W. Davis: 'Cemetery T at Naqada', *MDAIK* 39 (1983), 17–28; K. Bard: 'The evolution of social complexity in predynastic Egypt: an analysis of the Nagada cemeteries', *JMA* 2/2 (1989), 223–48.

IS

Naqsh-i Rustam *see* PERSIA

Narosura *see* PASTORAL NEOLITHIC

Narva Neolithic cultural tradition named after a cluster of three sites (Narva-Riigikula 1, 2 and 3) located on the lower stretches of the Narova River, on the border between Estonia and Russia. Discovered and excavated by N.N. Gurina between the 1950s and the 1980s, the sites are situated on a ridge of sand-dunes and include the remains of oval-shaped semi-subterranean dwellings (6–7 m in diameter). The faunal remains – practically identical at all three sites – include elk (which predominates), wild boar, aurochs, red deer, brown bear, waterfowl (ducks and swans), and many seals. The bones of a medium-sized whale were found at one of the sites. Pike, perch, salmon and catfish were identified among the numerous fish bones. The chipped stone inventory consists of numerous arrow- and spearheads, large scrapers, axes and adzes. The prolific bone and antler industry includes arrow- and spearheads, harpoons, axes, adzes, 'hoe-like' tools and fish-hooks. The so-called Narva-type pottery includes pots with either rounded or pointed bases, decorated with comb impressions, notches, strokes, and small pits which formed horizontal rows and zigzag patterns. Similar assemblages have now been identified in Latvia (Lubana), south of St. Petersburg, on the upper Western Dvina, northwest of Smolensk (Rudnya-Serteya) and, a later variety, in Lithuania (ŠVENTOJI).

N.N. Gurina: 'Iz istorii drevnih plemjon zapadnyh oblastei SSSR' [A history of the ancient tribes in the western area of the USSR], *MIAS* 114, (Moscow and Leningrad, 1970).
PD

Nasik Large settlement-mound located about 18 km north of Bombay, on the Godavari River in Maharashtra, India. It dates from the late 2nd millennium BC to the 18th century AD and was excavated by H.D. Sankalia and S.B. Deo in 1950–51. The earliest Chalcolithic occupation levels, including microliths, ochre-slipped pottery (sometimes decorated with red or black paint) and domestic pig, date to the JORWE period. A gap of about 500 years separates Chalcolithic levels from the later historic occupations. Small huts with earth and post walls, ceramic ring wells, and NORTHERN BLACK POLISHED WARE ceramics and copper coins are found in the earliest historic level (*c.*400–50 BC); no structures were excavated from later periods (Sankalia and Deo 1955).

H.D. Sankalia and S.B. Deo: *The excavations at Nasik and Jorwe, 1950–51* (Pune, 1955), 1–146; M.K. Dhavalikar: *The first farmers of the Deccan* (Pune, 1988), 71.
CS

Natufian Term applied to the latest of the Levantine 'EPIPALAEOLITIC' periods, which lasted from *c.*11000 to 9300 BC and was named after the Wadi el-Natuf in Israel. Most excavated Natufian sites are in the region of Syria-Palestine, although the nature of the remains at BELDIBI suggest that the culture probably reached parts of southern Anatolia. The Natufian constituted a transitional stage in Palestine between the exploitation of wild cereals in the KEBARAN period (*c.*18000–11000 BC) and the emergence of recognizable methods of plant and animal domestication in the Pre-Pottery Neolithic period (*c.*9300–5500 BC; *see* ACERAMIC NEOLITHIC). Natufian sites are characterized by distinctive flint assemblages as well as grindstones, storage pits and hearths. The botanical evidence clearly indicates a subsistence base combining hunting, gathering and early agriculture.

At Ain Mallaha, near Lake Huleh, nine Natufian stone-paved round huts have been excavated, each measuring about 3.5–5 m in diameter. Debate concerning the Natufian centres primarily on the degree to which wild or domesticated species of cereals and animals were being exploited.

G.A. Wright: 'Social differentiation in the early Natufian', *Social archaeology: beyond subsistence and dating*, ed. C. Redman et al. (New York 1978), 201–23; D.O. Henry: *From foraging to agriculture: the Levant at the end of the Ice Age* (Philadelphia, 1989), 179–228; O. Bar-Yosef and F.R. Valla, eds: *The Natufian culture in the Levant* (Ann Arbor, 1991).
IS

Naukratis (anc. Pi-meryet) City in the Egyptian Western Delta which is best known for the period during the 7th century BC when it was officially established by Psamtek I as the first Greek trading colony within Egypt. By the 4th century BC it had become a *polis*; many of the surviving buildings – including temples dedicated to Apollo, Aphrodite, Hera and the Dioskouroi – are Greek establishments dating from this period onwards, but there are also remains of an Egyptian temple of Amun and Thoth.

W.M.F. Petrie and E.A. Gardner: *Naukratis I: 1884–5* (London, 1886); J. Boardman: *The Greeks overseas* (Harmondsworth, 1964), 117–35; W.D.E. Coulson and A. Leonard, Jr.: *Cities of the Delta*, I: *Naukratis: preliminary report on the 1977–1978 and 1980 seasons* (Malibu, 1981); —— and ——: 'The Naukratis project 1983', *Muse* 17 (1983), 64–71.
IS

Nausharo Mound site near the Neolithic site of MEHRGARH in the Kachi Plain of Pakistan. The recent excavations of Jean-François Jarrige (1989) have revealed a continuous archaeological sequence spanning four phases (Samzun 1992: 245) from the Late Mehrgarh Period to the Early and Mature Indus periods (*c.*2900–2000 BC; *see* INDUS CIVILIZATION). The early occupations at Nausharo are contemporaneous with the latest levels at Mehrgarh (Mehrgarh VII), and many features of the ceramic styles and architecture show continuous development leading up to the Mature Indus, with local styles persisting alongside Indus styles. The architectural remains in the Mature Indus levels include large mud-brick platforms and multi-room structures. Although the precise relations between Early and Mature Indus levels are uncertain at present, Samzun (1992: 252) has suggested that Nausharo was characterized by a formative transition that reflects strong links between Baluchistan and the Indus Valley. These kinds of active interactions between upland and lowland regional traditions may have played a seminal role in the rise of the urban Mature Indus civilization.

J.-F Jarrige: 'Excavations at Nausharo, 1987–88', *PA* 24 (1989), 21–68; A. Samzun: 'Observations on the characteristics of the Pre-Harappan remains, pottery, and

artefacts at Nausharo, Pakistan (2700–2500 BC)', *South Asian archaeology 1989*, ed. J.-F Jarrige (Madison, 1992), 245–52.
CS

nautical archaeology *see* MARITIME ARCHAEOLOGY

Navdatoli Large Chalcolithic settlement-mound located on the southern bank of the Narbada River in Madhya Pradesh, India, which was excavated in the mid-1950s. The earliest levels were assigned to the MALWA period, stretching from *c.*2100 to 1600 BC, according to a series of eight calibrated radiocarbon dates (Sankalia et al. 1971), while later levels have been dated to the JORWE period. House form is consistent throughout the sequence and consists of circular and rectangular earthen and wattle-and-daub dwellings. M.K. Dhavalikar has suggested that Navdatoli was a centre of trade in copper and shell artefacts during the Chalcolithic period (1988: 53).

H.D. Sankalia, S.B. Deo and Z.D. Ansari: *Chalcolithic Navdatoli* (Pune, 1971); M.K. Dhavalikar: *The first farmers of the Deccan* (Pune, 1988), 44, 53.
CS

Naviundu *see* DIVUYU

Nazca Lines Geoglyphs formed by clearing the loose gravel from the sandy/stony substrate in the Pampa de Nazca and the nearby deserts in southern Peru, dating mainly to the Early Intermediate Period (*c.*400 BC–AD 500). The geoglyphs, which are associated with the Nazca culture (best known for its elaborate polychrome ceramics), consist of lines, rectangles, spirals and rare representational forms. Interpretations of these forms include astronomical markers, clan insignia, and ceremonial pathways to family or ethnic *huacas*, especially those of origin or of fertility. Recent studies have put them in their temporal and cultural context and indicate that they were an integral part of a distinctive Andean means of defining sacred space.

E. Hadingham: *Lines to the mountain gods: Nazca and the mysteries of Peru* (New York, 1987); A. Aveni: *The lines of Nazca* (Philadelphia, 1990); H. Silverman: 'New evidence for the date of the Nazca Lines', *Antiquity* 65 (1991), 208–20.
KB

Nderit Type of Neolithic pottery found in parts of the Eastern Rift Valley in Kenya. Nderit ware is highly distinctive because of its soft texture, open basket shapes, profuse or overall decoration in patterns of incised lines or indentations (further to imitate basketry) and internal decoration (the result apparently of pressing grass into the clay before firing). It was first identified by Louis Leakey in 1931 at sites in the Nakuru-ELMENTEITA basin under the 'Gumban A' variant of the 'Neolithic'.

Both in the Nakuru-Elmenteita and Lake Turkana basins, Nderit pottery frequently occurs on or close to shore-lines of mid-Holocene date; a lacustrine and fishing (late 'Aqualithic') association has therefore been argued (*see* AQUATIC CIVILIZATION). However, the economic and cultural orientations may be more complex, since the remains of domesticated livestock (cattle, goats and sheep) dating to the 3rd millennium BC have been found in association with Nderit pottery beside Lake Turkana (notably at Dongodien). In the elevated Nakuru-Elmenteita basin neither the dating nor the associations are so secure. Not infrequently this pottery occurs with or close to cairn burials with stone bowls, which are loosely classified as 'Neolithic'.

L.S.B. Leakey: *The Stone Age cultures of Kenya colony* (Cambridge, 1931), 198–9; F. Marshall et al.: 'Early domestic stock at Dongodien, northern Kenya', *Azania* 19 (1984), 120–7.
JS

Neanderthals Type of hominid named after a site in the Neander valley in Germany. The place of Neanderthals in human evolution has always been controversial. Early reconstructions presented them as ape-like primitives, but more recent evidence has rehabilitated both their anatomy and intelligence. Although more stocky than ANATOMICALLY MODERN HUMANS, and with a different pelvic and cranial structure (*see* KEBARA), Neanderthals may have been as intelligent as 'moderns,' and were capable of making Upper Palaeolithic stone tools and possibly bone tools also (*see* ARCY-SUR-CURE). At St Césaire, a cave site in the Charente region of France, a Neanderthal burial has been found in apparent association with Upper Palaeolithic CHÂTELPERRONIAN tools. Much as the QAFZEH AND SKHUL caves demonstrated that 'modern' humans did make MOUSTERIAN tools, St Césaire is the first indication that 'archaic' humans such as Neanderthals made the technological transition to the Upper Palaeolithic. Although it now seems likely that Neanderthals became extinct around 30–32,000 years ago, rather than forming one of our direct ancestors, the exact causes of this extinction may not be as simple as 'replacement' by more intelligent 'modern' humans. See also TESHIK-TASH.

M. Shackley: *Neanderthal man* (Hampden, 1980); C.B. Stringer and C. Gamble: *In search of the Neanderthals* (London, 1993); P. Mellars: *The Neanderthal legacy: an archaeological perspective from western Europe* (Princeton, 1996).

PG-B

Nea Nikomedia Tell on the Macedonian Plain of northern Greece, with later Neolithic layers overlying an important early Neolithic settlement dated to the 8th millennium BC – one of the earliest farming sites in Europe. Partial excavation by Robert Rodden and Graham Clark (1961–3) revealed individual rectangular houses with mud and reed walls reinforced by wooden poles, and an economy based on growing wheat, barley and lentils, and on herding sheep and goats (with some pigs and cattle). Obsidian was imported from the Cyclades (Melos). The earliest pottery is relatively thin-walled and is sometimes decorated with finger impressions; wares were often painted with triangles, wavy lines etc. in red on a cream ground. The early settlers also moulded schematic clay figurines of men and, especially, of women with exaggerated thighs. There are occasional animal sculptures (with amphibian features) in serpentine stone; one building, which seemed to be at the centre of a cluster of smaller buildings, contained three of these animal figures and a concentration of five female figurines and has been interpreted as having a special, possibly religious, function.

R. Rodden: 'Excavations at the Early Neolithic site of Nea Nikomedeia, Greek Macedonia,' *PPS* 28 (1962), 267–88; R. Rodden: 'An Early Neolithic village in Greece', *SA* 212/4 (1965), 82–92.

RJA

nearest-neighbour analysis Branch of SPATIAL ANALYSIS which uses as data the distance from each object in the study to the one nearest to it (its 'nearest-neighbour'). Some techniques use the distance to second- or third-nearest-neighbour. Such techniques are most suited to the study of local (small-scale) spatial patterns (such as the distribution of artefacts of a certain type on a site), and require the location of each object to be accurately plotted. They are mainly used in intra-site SPATIAL ANALYSIS. The average nearest-neighbour distance can be compared with a theoretical value to ascertain whether the distribution of the objects of a single class is aggregated, random or uniform, or whether the distributions of two (or more) classes of objects are associated. Its main drawbacks are that it can only deal with small-scale patterns, and that it suffers from 'edge-effects': since the true nearest-neighbour of an object near the edge of a site may lie outside the site, the wrong object may be called its nearest-neighbour, leading to over-statement of the nearest-neighbour distance.

P.J. Clark and F.C. Evans: 'Distance to nearest neighbour as a measure of spatial relationships in populations' *Ecology* 35 (1954) 445–53; I.R. Hodder and C.R. Orton: *Spatial analysis in archaeology* (Cambridge, 1976), 38–51.

CO

negative feedback *see* SYSTEMS THEORY

negative painting Type of black on red/white decoration found on pottery vessels throughout the Americas. A fired vessel was dipped in a plant resin solution, those parts which were to remain the base color were painted with clay solution and the vessel was exposed to the fire, charring the resin. When cool, the dry masking clay was brushed off revealing the 'negative' design.

KB

Nelson Bay Cave Large Middle/Later Stone Age coastal cave at Plettenberg Bay, 450 km east of Cape Town, South Africa. Excavations have revealed MSA (Middle Stone Age) occupation, followed by an hiatus until around 19,000 uncal BP, after which there is a fairly continuous sequence embracing the Robberg microblade industry (*c.*19,000–11,000 uncal BP), Albany non-microlithic industry (*c.*11,000–?6000 uncal BP), WILTON microlithic industry (? 6,000–3300 uncal BP), concluding with a macrolithic industry (3300–500 uncal BP) reminiscent of the earlier ALBANY INDUSTRY. It has been argued that the Wilton occurrences reflect sporadic seasonal visits to the coast by makers of those artefacts during a protracted hot dry period inland. The rich faunal remains reflect shifts in the coastline, drowning rich grazing land (Robberg). Marine resources are abundantly exploited from around 11,000 uncal BP, and fishing was highly specialized during the Holocene. A rich bone and shell industry is associated with the post-Wilton industry.

J. Deacon: *The Later Stone Age of southernmost Africa* (Oxford, 1984). R.R. Inskeep: *Nelson Bay Cave, Cape Province, South Africa; the Holocene levels* (Oxford, 1987).

RI

Nemrik (Nemrik 9) Large settlement of the Pre-pottery Neolithic period (*see* ACERAMIC NEOLITHIC) in northern Iraq (*c*.7500–6500 uncal BC), covering about 2 ha and comprising three or four phases. In its latest phase, it consisted primarily of round houses (and occasional rectangular structures) built with the *tauf* or *pisé* technique. The rich surrounding environments (including forests and steppes) facilitated the development of a stable sedentary community relying for subsistence on domesticated sheep, goats, cattle and pigs as well as cereals. The inhabitants had clearly reached a transitional stage between hunting and gathering and a combination of animal husbandry and agriculture (the latter attested by groundstones and mortars). QERMEZ DERE and TELL MAGHZALYA are the nearest similar sites in terms of subsistence and craftwork. S.K. Kozłowski argues that the strong similarities between the chipped stone industries of Nemrik and of proto-Hassuna sites may indicate that the origins of the HASSUNA culture are to be found at Nemrik.

S.K. Kozłowski: *Nemrik 9: a pre-pottery Neolithic site in Iraq* (Warsaw, 1990).

IS

Nemrut Dagh Mountain-top sanctuary of the 1st century BC, situated 250 km northeast of Gaziantep, in the Taurus range of eastern Turkey. One of a number of 'dynastic shrines' built by the rulers of Commagene, which was the last independent kingdom in Asia Minor in the 1st century BC (and was eventually absorbed into the Roman empire in AD 72). The principal features of Nemrut Dagh are the colossal stone sculptures and mausoleum (50 m high and 150m in diameter) erected by Antiochus I (*c*.69–34 BC). The fragmentary Greek inscriptions indicate that the statuary represented the Achaemenid and Seleucid rulers whom Antiochus claimed as his ancestors, as well as a variety of syncretic gods, such as Apollo-Mithras and Zeus-Oromasdes. The site was examined by Karl Humann and Otto Puchstein in 1890 and Friedrich-Karl Dörner between 1939 and 1963, but the burial chamber of Antiochus has not been located.

T. Fischer: 'Zum Kult des Antiochos I von Kommagene für seine Seleukidischen Ahnen', *Mitteilungen des Deutschen Archäologischen Instituts (Istanbul)* 22 (1972), 141–50; D.H. Sanders, ed.: *Nemrut Dagi: the hierothesion of Antiochus I of Commagene* (Winona Lake, 1995).

IS

neo-evolutionism School of archaeological thought which is based on the idea that human behaviour and cultural change are characterized by distinct patterns and mechanisms that can be explained in terms of processes of evolutionary change. Neo-evolutionist theories therefore include the well-known Childean concepts of the 'Neolithic revolution' and 'urban revolution' (see Childe 1951). Whereas 19th century evolutionists were prepared to accept that cultural change might have resulted from deliberate human attempts to change their environment for the better, neo-evolutionists are fundamentally deterministic, arguing that humans have always sought to maintain traditional ways of life, with the dominant roles in cultural change being played by such uncontrollable factors as economics, demography or technology. From the 1940s onwards, neo-evolutionary ethnologists such as Leslie White (1959) and Julian Steward (1955) argued that the effect of the environment could mean that very different cultures might arise from identical social processes, and by the 1960s, a number of American archaeologists were adopting similar neo-evolutionary approaches (e.g. Meggers 1960). However, after the emergence of the mature processual archaeology of the 1970s and 1980s, many neo-evolutionary approaches began to appear somewhat simplistic. Trigger (1989: 374), for instance, argues that 'it has become clear that cultural change is far more diversified than any neo-evolutionary view of parallel or even multilinear evolution has countenanced'. *See also* SOCIAL DARWINISM.

V.G. Childe: *Social evolution* (New York, 1951); J. Steward: *Theory of culture change* (Urbara, 1955); L.A. White: *The evolution of culture* (New York, 1959); B.J. Meggers: 'The law of cultural evolution as a practical research tool', *Essays in the science of culture*, ed. G.E. Dole and R.L. Carneiro (New York, 1960, 302–16; E.R. Service: *Primitive social organization* (New York, 1962); ——: *Origins of the state and civilization* (New York, 1975); B.G. Trigger: *A history of archaeological thought* (Cambridge, 1989), 289–94, 373–4.

IS

neo-Hittites *see* HITTITES

Neolithic Term used to describe the final phase of the Stone Age, following the MESOLITHIC. The Neolithic begins at widely differing dates in different regions of the world. For example, in the Middle East the period starts as early as the 10th millennium BC, while the onset of the Neolithic is identified across much of northern and central Europe with the arrival of the farming LINEARBANDKERAMIK (LBK) culture between the 6th millennium BC (Hungary) and the 4th millennium BC (northwest Europe). Although the Neolithic was originally defined with reference to presence of ground and polished stone tools in lithic assemblages, it quickly became associated with a major set of cultural and economic changes including the use of pottery, the domestication of animals, agriculture and sedentary living. Up until the 1950s, and the widespread use of radiocarbon dating, it tended to be assumed that, in each region, these changes occurred together as a package. In some regions, it has become apparent that this is an over-simplification. In the Near East, the slightly cumbersome term pre-pottery Neolithic (*see* ACERAMIC NEOLITHIC) had to be adopted to describe the early agricultural villages of the Levant before they started making pottery. Conversely, in some coastal Mediterranean areas pottery (*see* CARDIAL WARE) and perhaps, animal domestication seems to have arrived *before* the full adoption of cereal agriculture. In other areas, hunters and gatherers seem to have evolved sedentary or semi-sedentary settlements before the advent of farming (e.g. LEPENSKI VIR), or to have adopted the use of pottery and apparent Neolithic stone industries without developing a farming economy. An example of the latter is the Central Asian KELTEMINAR 'culture', often described as 'Neolithic' in the literature because of technological developments (particularly the adoption of pottery), though the economy was entirely based on hunting and gathering.

Western European definitions of the Neolithic answer this question by focusing on subsistence economy as the defining criterion. For example, Ammerman and Cavalli-Sforza (1984: 35) state explicitly that they 'adopt an economic approach to the classification of sites and cultures: the neolithic transition refers to the shift from hunting and gathering to food production,' (by which they mean food production based upon domesticated cereals and animals). However, in the literature of eastern Europe, the appearance of pottery at a site is normally enough to classify it as Neolithic. As a result, pottery-using hunting and gathering cultures of the Baltic tend to be called Neolithic in the eastern European literature, but Mesolithic in western European accounts.

As a further complication, it is becoming clearer that even where the key constituents of the food-producing revolution (domesticated animals, domesticated cereals, permanent settlement and storage) arrived contemporaneously, certain features of a developed farming economy emerged only much later (*see* SECONDARY PRODUCTS REVOLUTION).

C.M. McBurney: *The Stone Age of northern Africa* (Harmondsworth, 1960); J. Mellaart: *Çatal Hüyük: a Neolithic town in Anatolia* (London, 1967); H. Nordström: *Neolithic and A-Group sites* (Stockholm, 1972); J. Mellaart: *The Neolithic of the Near East* (London, 1975); J. Kruk: *The neolithic settlement of southern Poland*, BAR IS 93 (Oxford, 1980); D. Trump: *The prehistory of the Mediterranean* (1980); R. Mercer: *Farming practice in British prehistory* (Edinburgh, 1981); R.J. Ammerman and L.L. Cavalli-Sforza: *The Neolithic transition and the genetics of population in Europe* (Princeton, 1984); A. Whittle: *Neolithic Europe: a survey* (Cambridge, 1985); F. Hassan: 'Chronology of the Khartoum "Mesolithic" and "Neolithic" and related sites in the Sudan: statistical analysis and comparisons with Egypt', *AAR* 4 (1986), 83–102; M. Svelebil, ed.: *Hunters in transition* (Cambridge, 1986); T. Darvill: *Prehistoric Britain* (London, 1987); P. Bogucki: *Forest Farmers and stock-herders: early agriculture and its consequences in north-central Europe* (Cambridge, 1988); I. Hodder: *The domestication of Europe* (London, 1990); P. Vermeersch and P. van Peer, eds: *Contributions to the Mesolithic in Europe* (Leuven, 1990); B. Midant-Reynes: *Préhistoire de l'Egypt* (Paris, 1992), 118–22; P. Bogucki, ed.: *Case studies in European prehistory* (Boca Raton, 1993), chaps. 3, 4, 5; B. Cunliffe, ed.: *The Oxford illustrated prehistory of Europe* (Oxford, 1994), esp. 136–202.

RJA

Neribtum *see* ISCHALI

Nettilling Lake Locality in the interior of southern Baffin Island in the Canadian Arctic, with evidence of the Inuit and, particularly, THULE, cultures. A thorough study of the site by Douglas Stenton has greatly enhanced our understanding of the Thule economy.

For most of the 20th century, research on the Thule focused on sites that were occupied during the winter, and on maritime adaptations. The winter sites are usually located on the coast, and the faunal remains tend to derive from marine mammals. Sites occupied during other seasons of the year are found both on the coast and in the interior, but these often contain far fewer artefactual and faunal remains and have thus received far less archaeological attention. As a result, interpretations of Thule subsistence and settlement tended to stress the maritime element.

However, Stenton's surveys in the Nettilling Lake vicinity in the 1980s revealed the importance of terrestrial environments to the Thule. In a - multi-disciplinary project, Stenton explored the environmental and archaeological records of the Nettilling Lake region in order to understand the relationship between caribou population dynamics and Thule settlement and subsistence – particularly mobility patterns (Binford 1980) and predation strategies.

In addition to food, caribou provided skins for the warm winter clothes that allowed hunters to forage for other species through the extreme cold of winter. A survey of ethnographic sources revealed that adults required between five and seven caribou skins per year for winter clothing, plus additional skins for tents, blankets or kayaks. Thus, a family of five might need at least two dozen skins per year.

However, caribou are an unstable resource; the population fluctuates in a cyclic fashion – sometimes being reduced by up to 90%. Stenton demonstrated that documented, large-scale climatic changes do not adequately account for such fluctuations: they appear to be intrinsic to the species. Therefore, prehistoric Thule groups inhabiting the coast of southern Baffin Island must have devised ways of coping with the sporadic and unpredictable population crashes.

Based on the analysis of finds from 15 Thule sites at Nettilling Lake (including semi-subterranean houses, tent rings, burials, hearths, hunting blinds, kayak stands, caches and Inukshuk), Stenton concluded that when the caribou were numerous, the Thule hunted them from coastal settlements; the hunting tactics during these periods can be characterized as having 'logistical mobility'. However, when caribou were scarce, the Thule moved into the interior around Nettilling Lake, and relied to a greater extent on 'residential mobility' in order to obtain caribou. A detailed analysis of faunal remains from the Nettilling Lake sites – employing Binford's (1978) utility indices – suggests that most of the animals were hunted in close proximity to the residential camps. Further, most were female, indicating non-selective procurement. Thus, Stenton's research suggests that a flexible settlement system allowed the Thule to survive the fluctuations in caribou populations.

L.R. Binford: *Nunamiut ethnoarchaeology* (New York, 1978); ——: 'Willow smoke and dogs' tails: hunter-gatherer settlement systems and archaeological site formation', *AA* 45 (1980), 4–20; D.R. Stenton: 'Caribou population dynamics and Thule Culture adaptations on Southern Baffin Island, N.W.T.', *Arctic Anthropology* 28 (1991), 15–43; ——: 'The adaptive significance of caribou winter clothing for Arctic hunter-gatherers', *études/Inuit/Studies* 15 (1991), 3–28.

RP

neutron activation analysis (NAA) Radiometric method of quantitative chemical analysis particularly used for TRACE ANALYSIS and ultra-trace analysis of pottery and lithics but also applicable to metals. Although the technique is, in principle, non-destructive, it is normal to work with samples rather than complete artefacts because of the residual induced radioactivity. The samples (in solid form, and typically 100 mg for ceramics) are exposed to a suitable source of neutrons, usually in a reactor, which converts some stable isotopes into radio-isotopes (i.e. radioactive isotopes) of the same element by neutron capture. In the course of their decay, many of these radio-isotopes emit gamma-rays with characteristic energies. After irradiation, the spectrum of gamma-ray energies from each sample is measured, or counted, using a solid-state detector similar to that used for EDXRF (energy dispersive X-RAY FLUORESCENCE). Individual element isotopes are identified by their characteristic gamma-ray energies with intensities proportional to the amounts present. Comparison with the spectra of similarly irradiated standards, after correction for decay of the radio-isotopes, enables the element concentrations in the sample to be calculated.

Potentially, a large number of elements may be determined but the range partly depends on the irradiation time, the neutron flux and, particularly, the time elapsed between irradiation and spectrum counting. Elements with radio-isotopes of very short HALF-LIFE (e.g. Al and Mg) decay rapidly and must be measured at the reactor site. Normally counting begins a few days after irradiation and typically 30 elements are routinely detectable in ceramics. This includes the rare earth elements (e.g. lanthanum, cerium, samarium etc), with detection limits approaching 100 ppb, which are important for provenancing ceramics. The technique has some advantages for trace analysis of silicate-based materials because sample preparation is minimal and drillings can be analysed directly unlike for AAS (ATOMIC ABSORPTION SPECTROPHOTOMETRY) and ICP-AES (INDUCTIVELY COUPED PLASMA-ATOMIC EMISSION SPECTROMETRY) where the samples must be completely dissolved. Some elements are not quantifiable by conventional NAA, however, a notable example being lead which is not activated.

The technique has made a considerable contribution to provenance studies of pottery and other ceramics largely based on procedures devised by Perlman and Asaro (1969). There can be few pottery types which have not been analysed by NAA at some time. Work on metals has also included provenancing but usually only in support of other techniques such as lead isotope analysis.

I. Perlman and F. Asaro: 'Pottery analysis by neutron activation', *Archaeometry* 11 (1969), 21–52; S.J. Parry: *Activation spectrometry in chemical analysis* (New York, 1991).

MC

'New Archaeology' Term used to describe PROCESSUAL ARCHAEOLOGY when it was first emerging in the 1960s. *See also* ANALYTICAL ARCHAEOLOGY, BEHAVIORAL ARCHAEOLOGY, COVERING LAWS, FUNCTIONALISM *and* SYSTEMS THEORY.

Newark Large earthworks and mounds complex dating to the Middle WOODLAND period (*c.*200 BC–AD 400). Located in Licking County, Ohio (USA), it is associated with the HOPEWELL cultural manifestation. The site, covering about 5 sq. km, is located on an elevated plain near the junction of two forks of the Licking River. The site contains three major sections consisting of octagonal, square and circular earthworks, each enclosing 8–20 ha, and connected by corridors formed by pairs of parallel earthworks or roadways. Several smaller circular enclosures are located outside the major ones. Smaller conical and pyramidal mounds are constructed within some of the large earthworks.

G.E. Squier and W.H. Davis: *Ancient monuments of the Mississippi Valley* (Washington, D.C., 1848 repr.1973); C. Thomas: 'Report on the mound exploration of the Bureau of Ethnology', *Twelfth annual report of the Bureau of Ethnology* (Washington, D.C., 1894).

RJE

'new gastronomy' *see* AQUATIC CIVILIZATION

Newgrange The most famous example of the BOYNE VALLEY group of passage graves in Eire. It comprises a vast circular cairn *c.*80m across and 12 m high, retained by a drystone wall that is lined around its base with 97 megaliths – some of which are decorated with classic examples of MEGALITHIC ART. The monument was also encircled by a ring of free-standing monoliths, 12 of which survive. The orthostats of the passage (19 m long) support roof slabs; at the very front of the passage a unique 'window-box', made of slabs arranged so as to allow the beams of the winter solstice sunrise to enter the tomb and illuminate the rear wall of the chamber, forms one of the few certain examples of Neolithic astronomical ALIGNMENTS. The cruciform chamber has a false-corbelled roof that is nearly six metres high; the side-chambers were found to contain large stone basins. Newgrange was excavated and heavily restored by Michael O'Kelly, and has been dated by radiocarbon to about 3200 BC (e.g. 2465 ±40; 2250 ±45 BC).

M.J. O'Kelly: *Newgrange* (London, 1982).

RJA

Ngamuriak *see* PASTORAL NEOLITHIC

Niaux Decorated case of the Upper Palaeolithic, situated 4 km from Tarascon-sur-Ariège in the Pyrenees, France. One of the largest decorated cave systems, Niaux contains engravings scored on its clay floor, including a fish and a bison wounded by arrows. The walls of the famous 'Salon Noir' are dominated by bison, horses, ibex and deer boldly outlined in black (probably charcoal). Some of the depictions are carefully detailed – horses wearing winter coats, for example – and were probably drawn in the middle or later MAGDALENIAN.

L-R. Nougier and R. Robert: *Niaux* (Toulouse, 1954); A. Beltrán et al.: *La Cueva de Niaux* (Zaragoza, 1973); D. Vialou: *L'art des grottes an Ariège Magdalénian*, XXIIe supplément à Gallia préhistoire (Paris, 1986), 295–322 [detailed description; spatio-symbolic analysis].

RJA

Nicoya The region of northerwestern Costa Rica (and including southwestern Nicaragua in 'Greater Nicoya'), sometimes seen as an extreme southern 'sub-area' of Mesoamerica. The region is particularly known for its polychrome pottery manufactured after about AD 500.

F.W. Lange, ed.: *Costa Rican art and archaeology* (Boulder, 1988).

PRI

Nihon Shoki One of the two earliest surviving chronicles of Japan, compiled under the RITSURYO state as part of the legitimization of the ruling dynasty (the other being the KOJIKI). Compiled in the 8th century (a little later than the Kojiki), it provides a fuller account of imperial lineages, legendary events and reign chronicles up to the reign of Empress Jito (AD 696). Both the Kojiki and the Nihon Shoki were based on earlier, non-extant texts, the Teiki and Kyuji, and supplemented by four later works (together with which they comprised the Six Ancient Histories). The provide important documentary evidence for the Kofun period (*see* JAPAN 4).

W.G. Aston, trans.: *Nihongi: chronicles of Japan from the earliest times to AD* 697 (Tokyo, 1924).

SK

Nimrud, Tell (anc. Kalhu; Biblical Calah) City-site located between the Tigris and Zab rivers about 30 km south of Mosul in northern Iraq, which was the location of the second capital of the ASSYRIAN empire in the 9th–7th centuries BC. Kalhu was founded as a provincial city by Shalameser I in the 13th century BC, but in *c.*864 BC Ashurnasirpal II transformed it into a new royal capital, in place of Assur, and is said to have installed an ARAMAEAN population there. It was eventually replaced as capital by KHORSABAD and finally NINEVEH.

The main citadel of Kalhu, in the southwest corner of Tell Nimrud, was among the first archaeological sites to be excavated in Mesopotamia, when the ziggurat and temples of Ninurta, Ishtar and Kidmuru, as well as the magnificent southwestern palace of Ashurnasirpal were uncovered by Austen Henry Layard in 1845–7. There were also palaces belonging to Shalmaneser III, Tiglath-Pileser III and Esarhaddon, whose reigns spanned the period of *c.*858–680 BC. From the palace gateways Layard extracted colossal LAMASSU guardian figures in the form of winged bulls, which were laboriously conveyed back to his sponsors, the British Museum. He also sent back a selection of sculpted and inscribed stone slabs from the palace walls, the so-called Black Obelisk of Shalmaneser III (which provided one of the first concrete links with the Bible through its depiction of Jehu the King of Judah at the feet of the Assyrian ruler) and the famous 'Nimrud ivories'. The huge hoard of ivory sculptures and inlay, many of which were coated in gold leaf, almost certainly derive from the Levantine section of the empire, although there is still debate concerning their styles and provenance (Winter 1981).

Just over a century after Layard's work, the site was further excavated by Max Mallowan and David Oates between 1950 and 1963, resulting in the discovery of more ivories, clay cuneiform tablets and numerous stone reliefs, including Ashurnasirpal's inscription describing the re-founding of the city. The 1950s excavations also uncovered private houses and a richly equipped arsenal known as Fort Shalmaneser, including rooms stacked with military gear and stores of booty from foreign campaigns (some of which remain unexcavated).

A.H. Layard: *Nineveh and its remains* (London, 1849); R.D. Barnett: *A catalogue of the Nimrud ivories with other examples of Ancient Near Eastern ivories in the British Museum* (London, 1957); M.E.L. Mallowan: *Nimrud and its remains*, 2 vols (London, 1966); ——: *The Nimrud ivories* (London, 1978); I.J. Winter: 'Is there a southern style of ivory carving in the early 1st millennium BC?', *Iraq* 43 (1981), 101–30; G. Herrmann: *Ivories from Room SW37, Fort Shalmaneser*, 2 vols (London, 1986).

IS

Nindowari *see* KULLI COMPLEX

Nineveh (Tell Kuyunjik and Tell Nebi Yunus) City site in northern Iraq occupied continuously from the HASSUNA period (*c.*5800–5500 BC) until the Middle Ages. The enormous depth of prehistoric stratigraphy (constituting as much as 75% of the mound and including the NINEVITE 5 phase) has given the site an additional importance quite apart from its historical significance as one of the major cities of the ASSYRIAN empire (*c.*883–612 BC). Although, along with the rest of Assyria, it was destroyed by the Medes in 612 BC, it nevertheless survived into the Sasanian period and was finally supplanted by the town of Mosul, in the suburbs of which it now lies. The two principal mounds – Kuyunjik and Nebi Yunus – have yielded a great deal of evidence regarding the Assyrian empire. The city reached its peak in the reign of Sennacherib (*c.*704–781 BC, when it was the Assyrian capital, and its ruins include Sennacherib's stone palace and the 'arsenal' of his son Esarhaddon (*c.*680–669 BC). However, among the most crucial finds for Assyriologists was the North Palace of Ashurbanipal (*c.*669–627 BC), excavated by Rassam in 1853; this contained not only a series of exquisite stone-carved reliefs depicting the royal lion-hunt (Barnett 1976) but also the 'library' of Ashurbanipal, consisting of tens of thousands of cuneiform tablets. This library is probably the most important collection of texts from Mesopotamia, including versions of the Epic of Gilgamesh and the Epic of Creation, as well as vast numbers of religious and scientific documents.

P.-E. Botta and E. Flandin: *Monument de Ninive découvert et décrit par M.P.-E. Botta, mesuré et dessiné par M.E. Flandin*, 5 vols (Paris, 1849–50); V. Place: *Ninive et l'Assyrie*, 3 vols (Paris, 1867–80); A.H. Layard: *The monuments of Nineveh* (London, 1853); R.D. Barnett: *Sculptures from the North Palace of Ashurbanipal at Nineveh* (London, 1976); J.M. Russell: *Sennacherib's 'palace without rival' at Nineveh* (Chicago, 1991); J. Curtis

and J. Read, eds: *Art and empire: treasures from Assyria in the British Museum* (London, 1995).
IS

Ninevite 5 One of the three major styles of pottery in Mesopotamia in the early 3rd millennium BC. The 'Ninevite 5' ware is a style of pottery bearing painted and incised decoration which was first discovered in level 5 of a deep sounding at Nineveh. Ninevite 5 pottery dated to the period immediately after the URUK phase in northern Mesopotamia and was roughly contemporary with the EARLY TRANSCAUCASIAN ware of eastern Anatolia and the Levant, the 'scarlet ware' of the Diyala region and JEMDET NASR–Early Dynastic pottery in Sumer and Akkad. Unlike these phases in southern Mesopotamia, the Ninevite 5 sites so far excavated (e.g. CHAGAR BAZAR) show few signs of developing urbanism. Much of the recent archaeological information on this cultural phase derives from rescue excavations in northern Iraq (the Saddam Dam Salvage Project, including Tell Mohammed Arab) and northeastern Syria (including Tell Leilan).
G.M. Schwartz: 'The Ninevite 5 period and current research', *Paléorient* 11 (1985), 52–70; M. Roaf and R.G. Killick: 'A mysterious affair of style: the Ninevite V pottery of northern Mesopotamia', *Iraq* 49 (1987), 199–230.
IS

Nippur (Nuffar) Early Mesopotamian city-site and cult-centre of Enlil, the most important Sumerian deity, located in southern Iraq, about 150 km southeast of Baghdad. Although not politically powerful in itself (except for a period in the late 3rd millennium BC, when it may have been the seat of the Third Dynasty of UR), the approval of the city's priests of Enlil was generally regarded as essential for the legitimate rule of SUMER and AKKAD from the early 3rd millennium BC onwards. The settlement remains comprise one of the largest tells in Mesopotamia, about 1 km in diameter, up to 20 m in height, and ranging in date from the UBAID period (*c.*5000–3800 BC) until the Middle Ages. There is a distinct gap in the archaeological record at Nippur between the Old Babylonian and Kassite strata (i.e. *c.*1750–1550 BC), which mirrors the dearth of textual evidence from the cities of southern Iraq during the same period.
V. Crawford: 'Nippur, the Holy City', *Archaeology* 12 (1959), 74–83; G.F. Dales and D.P. Hansen: 'The temple of Innana, Queen of Heaven at Nippur', *Archaeology* 15 (1962), 75–84; D.E. McCown and R.C. Haines: *Nippur* 2 vols (Chicago, 1967–78); H.T. Wright: 'Problems of absolute dating in protohistoric Mesopotamia', *Paléorient* 6 (1980), 93–7; E.C. Stone: *Nippur neighbourhoods* (Chicago, 1987).
IS

Nishapur Site in northeastern Iran (Khurasan), which is one of the most extensively excavated Iranian Islamic sites. The finds, which included paintings, decorative plaster, metalwork and ceramics all bear witness to the importance of Khurasan as the prosperous industrial heartland of pre-Mongol Iran. The excavations of 1935–40 were halted by the Second World War and concluded afterwards, by which time the tells had been heavily looted by the local treasure hunters. The publication of the ceramics remains one of the most significant studies of excavated material from eastern Iran and provides an archaeological context for the large amount of unprovenanced material from Khurasan that appears on the art market and in museums.
C.K. Wilkinson: *Nishapur: pottery of the early Islamic Period* (New York, 1973); J.A. Allan: *Nishapur: metalwork of the early Islamic period* (New York, 1982); C.K. Wilkinson: *Nishapur: some early Islamic buildings and their decoration* (New York, 1986).
GK

nitrogen in bone Bone nitrogen content decreases *post mortem* with the breakdown of proteins. Fluorine and uranium contents increase with uptake from the burial environment (*see* FLUORINE UPTAKE *and* URANIUM SERIES DATING). In combination, these have been used as indicators of relative date and were instrumental in exposing the PILTDOWN MAN HOAX.
K.P. Oakley: 'Analytical methods of dating bones', *Science and archaeology*, ed. D. Brothwell and E. Higgs (London, 1969), 35–45.
SB

nitrogen profile dating Scientific dating technique, the principles of which are similar to those of OBSIDIAN HYDRATION dating. The extent of the diffusion of nitrogen into the carved surface of non-porous stones, such as jade, flint and possibly marble, is a function of the time that has elapsed since the carving of the stone (and is also temperature-dependent). An essential prerequisite is that there is no initial nitrogen in the stone. The technique, although suggested nearly 20 years ago, has only begun to be developed in the 1990s, using secondary ion mass spectrometry (SIMS) to determine the nitrogen profile.
K.V. Ettinger and E.L. Frey: 'Nitrogen profiling: a

proposed dating technique for difficult artefacts', *Proceedings of the 16th International Symposium on Archaeometry and Archaeological Prospection, Edinburgh 1976*, ed. E.A. Slater and J.O. Tate (Edinburgh, 1980), 293–311.

SB

Njoro River Cave Pre-Iron Age site in the elevated stretch of the Eastern Rift Valley in Kenya, famous for its numerous cremated burials excavated by Louis and Mary Leakey in 1938. The burials were accompanied by stone bowls, grind-stones and rubbing stones, several types of beads and ornaments as well as various carbonized organic objects, including basketry, string, ivory (perhaps pestles), a gourd and a wooden vessel (possibly for milk). Obsidian tools and pottery also buried there relate to the ELMENTEITAN, although the radiocarbon dating of Njoro River Cave to the end of the 2nd millennium BC (Merrick and Monaghan 1984) places it half a millennium earlier than Elmenteitan settlements dated so far. The site remains unique, although partly comparable pre-Iron Age burials are known from other caves along the same river and higher up the Mau escarpment.

M.D. and L.S.B. Leakey: *Excavations at the Njoro River Cave* (Oxford, 1950); H.V. Merrick and M.C. Monaghan: 'The date of the cremated burials in the Njoro River Cave', *Azania* 19 (1984), 7–11.

JS

Nkope Multi-component Iron Age site at the southern end of Lake Malawi, which is the type-site of a Central African cultural tradition. 'Nkope' material is stratified under Mawudzu and Nkudzi material at the site of Nkope itself. Similarities with KWALE on the East African coast and UREWE in the interior show that Nkope pottery is part of the Early Iron Age Urewe Tradition. The term Nkope formerly corresponded to David Phillipson's 'Highland Facies of Eastern Stream', but it now applies to a branch of the Urewe ceramic tradition that included Situmpa, Ziwa and Gokomere. The Ziwa sequence in northeast Zimbabwe (running from 6th-century Ziwa, via 8th-century Coronotion, to 10th-century Maxton) parallels the changes from Nkope to 10th-century Kapeni and from Kwale to the 10th-century ceramics at KILWA. This parallel process of cultural change in widely separated areas of Africa strengthens the argument that the Ziwa and Nkope sequences had common origins.

K.R. Robinson: *The Iron Age of the Southern Lake area of Malawi* (Zomba, 1970); T.N. Huffman: 'A guide to the Iron Age of Mashonaland', *Occasional Papers of the National Museums of Rhodesia A4* (1971), 20–44; K.R. Robinson: *Iron Age occupation north and east of the Mulanje Plateau* (Zomba, 1977).

TH

Nkudzi Bay Cemetery of late 18th- and 19th-century date located at the southwest corner of Lake Malawi. It is the type locality for a distinctive class of pottery (Nkudzi ware) of the recent end of the Later Iron Age of Malawi, and is thought to mark the arrival in the area of the people known as the Bisa (Wisa), described as 'great travellers and traders with the coast'.

R.R. Inskeep: *Preliminary investigation of a proto-historic cemetery at Nkudzi Bay, Malawi* (Livingstone, 1965); K.R. Robinson: *The Iron Age of the Southern Lake area of Malawi* (Zomba, 1970).

RI

Nobatae *see* BLEMMYES; MEROITIC

Nogawa Late Palaeolithic site in Tokyo, Japan, located in the Musashino Uplands of the Kanto loam, which has provided a clear stratigraphic sequence for the Japanese Palaeolithic (pre-30,000 BP–10,000 BC). One of many important Palaeolithic sites in the region excavated since the 1970s. Evidence for hearths and lithic clusters was recovered, suggesting a number of activity areas. The site is also important as an early example of a broad-area excavation of a Palaeolithic site. Obsidian tools have been dated using FISSION TRACK to a range between 21,600–9,500 BP. The obsidian was transported into the area from sources outside the Kanto Plain.

C.M. Aikens and T. Higuchi: *The prehistory of Japan* (London, 1982), 46–51.

SK

Nok Valley in the Chori hills southwest of the Jos Plateau, Central Nigeria, which has given its name to the 'Nok culture' or – as some scholars describe it – the Nok 'artistic tradition'. Characterized principally by dramatically stylized terracotta figurines, most of them recovered from alluvial deposits in the course of industrial mining operations, the 'Nok culture' extends over an area of about 480 × 160 km.

Three non-alluvial sites have been excavated: Samun Dukiya (in the Nok valley itself), Taruga, and Katsina Ala (south of the river Benue). At Taruga 13 iron smelting furnaces were found, as a result of which the 'Nok culture' has now been recognized as an exclusively Iron Age phenomenon. Ten radiocarbon dates at Taruga range from 2541 to 2042 BP, making it one of the earliest iron smelting sites in West Africa, and a number of TL dates on figurines from other sites (including Nok itself) are in agreement with this. It is suggested that the figurines (of which about 200 are now known) had most likely a magico-religious significance, whether as field altars or in connection with iron smelting.

B.E.B. Fagg: *Nok terracottas* (Lagos, 1977); D. Calvocoressi and N. David: 'A new survey of radiocarbon and thermoluminescence dates for West Africa', *JAH* 20/1 (1979), 1–29; T. Shaw: 'The Nok sculptures of Nigeria', *SA* 244/2 (1981) 114–23.

PA-J

nomads Mobile hunter-gatherers or pastoralists. According to Barth (1973), true pastoral nomads should be defined as an ethnic group among whom no subsistence activity other than pastoralism is practised (a modern example of which would be the Kababish, a nomadic tribe based in the semi-arid Kordofan region of western Sudan, see Asad 1970). In such a group, seasonal movement would be virtually inevitable as a result of the need for large areas of different types of pasture land.

Whereas some archaeologists have chosen to define 'nomads' simply as any mobile group (e.g. Taylor 1972), most would agree that the term generally refers to herding societies whose seasonal movements are primarily dependent on the search for fresh pastures (see Cribb 1991). This nomadic pastoralism is usually distinguished from other types that may be more sedentary or may combine herding with forms of cultivation. Various attempts have been made to assess how these different degrees of nomadism and pastoralism should be categorized. Goldschmidt (1979), for instance, distinguishes between (1) flat-land nomads herding large groups of livestock (either mounted or pedestrian, and including some who also cultivate crops to some extent) and (2) mountain-dwelling transhumants herding smaller numbers of stock. Khazanov (1984), on the other hand, suggests that there are six categories: (1) highly mobile pastoral nomads with no agriculture at all, (2) semi-nomadic pastoralists who practise some agriculture, (3) semi-sedentary pastoralists, among whom agriculture is more important than herding, (4) practisers of 'herdsman husbandry', most of whom are sedentary, with a small set of herdsmen looking after the livestock. (5) Yaylagh (or transhumant) pastoralists exploiting different ecological zones in highland regions, and (6) practisers of sedentary animal husbandry, for whom agriculture is their most important means of subsistence (i.e. farmers who each keep a small amount of livestock).

As far as the origins of nomadism are concerned, it was once widely believed that nomadic pastoralists were simply hunter-gatherers who had begun to domesticate the animals that they had previously hunted. However, this essentially evolutionary view of nomadism has been largely disproved by the discovery of numerous Near Eastern sites where hunting and gathering was immediately followed by agriculture (*see* ACERAMIC NEOLITHIC *and* NATUFIAN). The more recent consensus, therefore, is that nomads are almost invariably agriculturally-based groups who have been forced to give up cultivation through migration (or restriction) to more marginal land. This ecological approach to the emergence of nomadic life-styles, has, however, in its turn, also met with opposition, mainly in the form of anthropologists and archaeologists who believe that it is not usually environmental pressures but cultural ones (i.e. political, social or technological changes) that are responsible for the nomadic pastoralist adaptation. Thus R.B. Ekvall (1961) argues that the mobility of the Tibetan nomadic way of life served as a defensive response against the actions of an aggressive state. Some of the most recent case-studies and analyses of the problem (e.g. Lynch 1983) have argued that nomadism is invariably the result of both ecological and cultural pressures.

The archaeological study of nomads is still relatively underdeveloped, compared with the study of sedentary groups. Most substantial contributions to the subject have concentrated on north Africa and the Middle East. Karim Sadr (1991) has analysed the nature of nomadism in northeast Africa, while J.R. Kupper (1957) and Roger Cribb (1991) have both devoted monographs to the study of Ancient Near Eastern nomads.

Sadr uses such methods as the quantification of density of artefacts and the study of SITE FORMATION PROCESSES to distinguish between long, medium and short-term occupations in Egypt, Sudan and Ethiopia. He suggests that these north-eastern African nomads largely emerged through a process of symbiosis with developing states; thus, for instance, he argues that the appearance of nomadism in Upper Nubia in the late 3rd millennium BC was directly related to the emergence of a powerful late Predynastic agricultural economy in Upper Egypt and Lower Nubia, leading the Upper Nubian population to switch voluntarily from a mixed economy to the more specialized exploitation of the hinterland at the margins of the state.

Cribb's work (1991), concentrating particularly on the camps of modern Anatolian pastoralists, shows the ETHNOARCHAEOLOGICAL potential of the subject. Although he is very successful in demonstrating the great complexity of Near Eastern nomadic life, his case-studies have limited applications to the investigation of nomadism elsewhere in the world and arguably he does not go far enough towards establishing general archaeological criteria for the definition of non-sedentary settlement sites or camps.

See also AMORITES, ARAMAEANS, CHALDAEANS, CHICHIMECS, LURISTAN, PALEO-INDIAN, PAZYRYK, PIT-GRAVE CULTURE *and* SCYTHIANS.

E. Bacon: 'Types of pastoral nomadism in central and southwest Asia', *SJA* 10/1 (1954), 44–68; J.R. Kupper: *Les nomades en Mésopotamie au temps des rois de Mari* (Paris, 1957); R.B. Ekvall: 'The nomadic pattern of living among Tibetans as preparation for war,' *American Anthropologist* 63 (1961), 1250–63; T. Asad: *The Kababish Arabs: power, authority and consent in a nomadic tribe* (New York, 1970); W.W. Taylor: 'The hunter-gatherer nomads of northern Mexico: a comparison of the archival and archaeological records', *WA* 4/2 (1972), 167–79; W. Watson: 'The Chinese contribution to eastern nomad culture in the pre-Han and early Han periods', *WA* 4/2 (1972), 139–49; F. Barth: 'A general perspective on nomad-sedentary relations in the Middle East', *The desert and the sown*, ed. C.M. Nelson (Berkeley 1973), 11–21; W. Weissleder, ed.: *The nomadic alternative: modes and models of interaction in the African-Asian deserts and steppes* (The Hague, 1978); W. Goldschmidt: 'A general model for pastoral social systems', *Pastoral production and society*, Proceedings of the international meeting on nomadic pastoralism, Paris, 1–3 December 1976, ed. L'équipe écologie (Cambridge, 1979), 15–29; T.J. Barfield: *The Central Asian Arabs of Afghanistan: pastoral nomadism in transition* (Austin, 1981); T.F. Lynch: 'Camelid pastoralism and the emergence of Tiwanaku civilization in the south-central Andes', *WA* 15/1 (1983), 1–15; A.M. Khazanov: *Nomads and the outside world* (Cambridge, 1984); R. Cribb: *Nomads in archaeology* (Cambridge, 1991); K. Sadr: *The development of nomadism in ancient northeast Africa* (Philadelphia, 1991).

IS

nomothetic (generalizing) approaches Philosophers of the social sciences use the term 'nomothetic' to describe approaches that attempt to verify meaningful generalizations about human history and social organization, and to formulate these into law-like statements. The nomothetic approach contrasts with the more traditional 'individualizing' approach to history and sociology that explains social events and phenomena by reference to the particular.

A tension has existed (in explicit form) since the 19th century between these two approaches. Many of the early writings of Emile Durkheim, who attempted to found a 'science' of sociology (*see* FUNCTIONALISM), advocate adopting the nomothetic approach and a POSITIVIST methodology of truth-seeking (Durkheim 1895). On the other hand, Max Weber (1864–1920), who with Durkheim is often named as a co-founder of modern sociology, argued that the concept of universal laws was helpful in the natural sciences, but that the social sciences should remain focused on explaining the causes of social phenomena and events within a particular historical context. Weber's argument was not a rejection of positivist methodology per se, but a denial of its usefulness as an interpretative tool given the importance and complexity of context when seeking to understand *human* actions (i.e. within the *social* sciences).

In archaeology, the general concern in the social sciences over the relative value of nomothetic and individualizing approaches resurfaced as part of the debate between traditional and PROCESSUAL ARCHAEOLOGY in the 1960s. It continues to be a significant point of reference (and rhetoric) in the writings of post-processual and 'contextual' archaeologists.

See also CONTEXTUAL ARCHAEOLOGY, THEORY AND THEORY-BUILDING *and* COVERING LAWS.

E. Durkheim: *Les règles de la méthode sociologique* (Paris, 1895); M. Weber: *Economy and society* (1922; Berkeley, 1978).

RJA

Non Chai Late prehistoric settlement in the upper Chi Valley, northeast Thailand. Excavations by Pisit Charoenwongsa in 1978 revealed a deep stratigraphy dated to between 400 BC and AD 200, proving that substantial settlements had developed in Thailand by the beginning of the 1st millennium AD. The site has been destroyed through use as land fill and we have no information on domestic structures, layout, or whether it was once moated. Iron was present throughout the occupation, as were glass beads; clay moulds for casting bracelets and bells evidence a local bronze industry. The pottery is mainly red-slipped, offering a contrast to the contemporary layers at BAN CHIANG HIAN, where the ceramics bore red-painted designs, and to Non Dua, where the designs included red bands painted over a cord-marked surface. A series of such large central sites in the valley of the Chi, each with its own pottery styles, suggests that chiefdom centres (and small village communities in their orbit) were emerging during the late prehistoric period.

D.T. Bayard, P. Charoenwongsa and S. Rutnin: 'Excavations at Non Chai, northeastern Thailand', *Asian Perspectives* 25/1 (1986), 13–62.
CH

Non Dua Moated site first settled in the 1st millennium BC in the lower Chi Valley, which for at least the last two millennia has lain at the centre of a vigorous and continuing salt extraction industry. The site is adjacent to an extensive exposure of rock salt, round which deep mounds have accumulated. Excavations by Charles Higham and Hamilton Parker in 1969–70 in one of these have shown that early salt working did indeed take place during the occupation period of Non Dua. Using landsat images, John Parry has identified a canal linking moats at the site with the Lam Siao Yao stream. This suggests a development of water control and reticulation, as at the contemporary site of BAN CHIANG HIAN.

C.F.W. Higham: 'The prehistory of the southern Khorat Plateau, with particular reference to Roi Et Province'. *MQRSEA* 3 (1977), 103–42; J.T. Parry: 'The investigative role of Landsat-TM in the examination of pre- and protohistoric water management sites in northeast Thailand', *Geocarto International* 4 (1992), 5–24.
CH

Non Nok Tha Cemetery site of the 2nd millennium BC located in the Upper Chi valley of northeast Thailand. From 1965 to 1968, Down Bayard excavated over 200 burials with grave goods that included a small number of bronze axes and bracelets, sandstone casting moulds, many pottery vessels and some stone adzeheads. Due to a lack of well-provenanced dating material and the unclear stratigraphy, the chronological sequence at the site is difficult and controversial. There have been claims for a very long sequence, with bronze occurring as early as the 4th millennium BC, but it is more likely that the bronze phases at the site belong to the 2nd millennium BC. Bayard has controversially proposed that the burials represent two distinct affiliated groups on the basis of the differences in pottery forms found in the graves.

D.T. Bayard: *Non Nok Tha, the 1968 excavation: procedure, stratigraphy and a summary of the evidence* (Otago, 1972).
CH

Non Nong Chik Burial site located within Phu Wiang, a large sandstone monadnock about 10 km south of NON NOK THA in northeast Thailand. Limited excavations by Higham and Parker in 1970 revealed stratified inhumations, individuals being buried with pottery vessels resembling those from the later part of the sequence at Non Nok Tha.

R.A. Buchan: *The three-dimensional jig-saw puzzle: a ceramic sequence from NE Thailand* (MA thesis, University of Otago, 1973).
CH

non-parametric statistics A diverse collection of statistical techniques, with the common feature that they do not depend on an assumption that the DATA come from a particular STATISTICAL DISTRIBUTION (for example, it has been argued that the sizes of rim sherd fragments follow a distribution known as the log-normal distribution). For this reason they are sometimes called distribution-free statistics. They are often based on the order (RANK) of the observations rather than their values. For example, in comparing the length of flints from two assemblages, one would take account of the fact that one of the assemblages yielded the five smallest flints, rather than that the flints had lengths of 30 mm. Some well-known tests are the median test, runs test, sign test and Wilcoxon–Mann–Whitney test.

J.E. Doran and F.R. Hodson: *Mathematics and computers in archaeology* (Edinburgh, 1975), 54–6; M. Fletcher and G.R. Lock: *Digging numbers* (Oxford, 1991), 85–90.
CO

Non Pa Wai Prehistoric mound with evidence of early metallurgy, located in the copper-rich KHAO WONG PRACHAN VALLEY, central Thailand. The mound covers an area of 5 ha and contains three principal layers. The lowest comprises a cemetery dated to the 3rd millennium BC, in which inhumation burials were found associated with a range of pottery vessels and jewellery of shell and stone; no metal was found. There follow two further layers representing intensive copper-ore processing and smelting, followed by the casting of ingots and some artefacts. A burial cut from this layer yielded a socketed axe and associated bivalve clay moulds. The artefacts and ingots are made from a copper with significant quantities of arsenic, but no tin bronze. Vincent Pigott and Surapol Natapintu, the excavators, have obtained radiocarbon dates that chart the use of metals from 1500 BC. The huge quantity of copper-processing remains shows how the ore was smelted in bowl crucibles and cast into circular ingots.

V.C. Pigott: 'Pre-industrial mineral exploitation and metal production in Thailand', *Masca Journal* 3/5 (1986) 170–4.
CH

normal distribution The STATISTICAL DISTRIBUTION most commonly used by archaeologists. It is defined by a mathematical equation, but is colloquially known as the 'bell-shaped curve'. Its value to archaeologists lies not so much in the rare occasions on which it actually occurs in archaeology (e.g. uncalibrated RADIOCARBON DATES), but in the fact that the MEANS of many distributions which describe archaeological DATASETS have a normal distribution, even when the original distribution is far from normal.

S. Shennan: *Quantifying archaeology* (Edinburgh 1988), 101–12.

CO

normalization Statistical term that archaeologists often use to describe a process which is more properly called STANDARDIZATION. It is correctly used to denote the process of transforming a DATASET to make it fit a NORMAL DISTRIBUTION, for example by taking the logarithm of each value.

S. Shennan: *Quantifying archaeology* (Edinburgh, 1988), 108–12.

CO

normative explanations These explanations interpret individual cultural phenomena by relating them to cultural 'norms' or sets or shared beliefs and practices held in common with other members of the same cultural group. It might be argued that archaeology, as a discipline that is obliged to construct meaning from partial but complex assemblages of material culture, is inevitably drawn to normative explanation: it is often by this means that archaeologists find patterns and correlations in the archaeological record to begin with. At the same time, normative explanations can lead to simplistic assumptions: that a similarity in the material culture implies shared aims, or even shared mental templates and world-views. Normative explanations are therefore sometimes criticized on the grounds that they mask variability in the archaeological record, or mask variability in behaviour even where material culture is indeed similar. Normative explanations also tend not to offer a useful framework for explaining change over time, as they encourage archaeologists to look upon similarity, alone, as meaningful.

Traditional culture-historical archaeological narratives are often accused of normative bias (e.g. in assuming a homogeneous cultural identity); certain approaches in processual archaeology (e.g. the description of social dynamics in terms of systems theory) have been similarly criticized. By contrast, recent trends in archaeological explanation (e.g. CONTEXTUAL ARCHAEOLOGY) have tended to stress the diversity of ways in which material culture can be used and the importance of both the individual and the individual social context. Taken to the extreme, this reaction against 'normative' explanation can lead to a rather self-defeating form of archaeological introspection (*see* POST-PROCESSUAL ARCHAEOLOGY). In moderation, it encourages a useful sensitivity to the social mechanisms that lead to norms in culture, and to the particular contexts in which norms *may* be abandoned or even subverted.

RJA

Northern Black Polished Ware (NBPW) Widespread ceramic ware of the late 1st millennium BC (*c.*600–50 BC) which is primarily associated with the early historic cities of the Ganges and Yamuna river valleys (*see* GANGES CIVILIZATION), although NBPW sherds have also been found at sites in Nepal, Gujarat and the Deccan plateau. It is possible that the start of the NBPW period may have overlapped with the PAINTED GREY WARE phase (*c.*1300–600 BC) at some sites.

The NBPW ceramics were wheel-made and expertly fired; common forms included bowls, dishes, lids and carinated jars. The vessels were slipped with highly polished and burnished black or grey surfaces, some bearing painted decorations in yellow and light red consisting of simple linear bands, wavy lines and circular motifs. Usually found in association with other ceramics, their low frequencies suggest that they may have been used for specialized functions or restricted to an elite.

M.R. Bannerjee: *The Iron Age in India* (New Delhi, 1965), 240–3; H.C. Bhardwaj: 'Some technical observations on NBPW', *Potteries in ancient India*, ed. B.P. Sinha (Patna, 1969), 174–84; V. Tripathi: *The Painted Grey Ware: an Iron Age culture of northern India* (Delhi, 1976), 47–50.

CS

Norton tradition Alaskan tradition comprising the Choris, Norton and IPIUTAK cultures, which persisted from 1000 BC until AD 800 in some areas. Assemblages typically contain flaked stone tools similar to the Denbigh Flint complex (*see* ARCTIC SMALL TOOL TRADITION), but most also include pottery and oil lamps.

D.E. Dumond: *The Eskimos and Aleuts* (London, 1987).

RP

Noyen-sur-Seine Extensively excavated middle Neolithic enclosure in the Seine valley, France, close to an earlier site of the Mesolithic with remarkably well-preserved organic evidence. The Neolithic site (*c.*3 ha) consists of a series of ditches and interrupted pallisades of more than one phase. It yielded evidence of hearths and storage pits, and the excavators recognized areas of cereal processing and stock control. The pottery represents a mix of CHASSÉEN and MICHELSBERG styles. The Mesolithic site preserved the organic remains of large fish traps, a basket and a pine dug-out canoe dating from *c.*7000 BC; faunal evidence included red deer, boar, waterfowl, pike and eel.

C. and D. Mordant: 'Noyen-sur-Seine, habitat néolithique de fond de vallée alluviale', *Gallia Préhistoire*, 20 (1977), 229; D. and C. Mordant: 'Noyen-sur-Seine: a Mesolithic waterside settlement' *The Wetland Revolution in Prehistory*, ed. B. Coles (Exeter, 1992), 55–64.

RJA

Nsongezi Stone Age occupation site on the Ugandan side of the Kagera valley (the Tanzanian border), which contains an array of materials of the Middle and Upper Pleistocene. The artefacts range from ACHEULEAN to 'SANGOAN' (regarded as intermediate between Early and Middle Stone Age) and probably Middle Stone Age itself. After Wayland's pioneer work early in the 20th century, the site was examined in detail by Glen Cole (1967). Since all the deposits are in secondary alluvial situations with complex stratification lacking fossils, dating is very unclear. While the Sangoan (cum-Middle Stone Age?) could be less than a quarter of a million years old, the Acheulean could stretch back for twice that period or more, although at the time that Cole worked at Nsongezi a much later and more constricted dating of the African upper Acheulean and transition to the Middle Stone Age was assumed.

The nearby Nsongezi rock-shelter contains Late Stone Age materials of Holocene date. The upper deposits, although confused, have been dated to recent millennia, with pottery of KANSYORE and EARLY IRON AGE (Urewe) types. These are better represented on Kansyore itself, an island in the Kagera below the rock-shelter.

S. Pearce and M. Posnansky: 'The re-excavation of Nsongezi rock-shelter', *UJ* 27 (1963), 85–94; G.H. Cole: 'The Later Acheulean and Sangoan of southern Uganda', *Background to evolution in Africa* ed. W.W. Bishop and J.D. Clark (Chicago and London, 1967), 481–528.

JS

Ntereso *see* AFRICA 2

n-transforms Abbreviation for 'non-cultural formation processes', a term coined by the American archaeologist Michael Schiffer to describe the ways in which natural activities (such as wind, rain or frost) affect archaeological remains. N-transforms and C-TRANSFORMS (*cultural* formation processes) are the two fundamental types of Schiffer's SITE FORMATION PROCESSES, whereby the 'systemic context' is transformed into the archaeological context' (*see* BEHAVIOURAL ARCHAEOLOGY). Whereas c-transforms would include such cultural events as the discarding of rubbish, the demolition of buildings or the burial of a corpse, n-transforms involve purely environmental change, such as the effects of erosion, weathering, earthquakes or the activities of animals.

N-transforms have been further subdivided by Wood and Johnson (1976) into various categories of natural 'disturbance processes', including pedoturbation (soil formation), faunalturbation (disturbance by animals), floralturbation (disturbance by plants), cryoturbation (freeze-thaw action), graviturbation (mixing and movement of debris under the influence of gravity), argilliturbation (the expansion and contraction of clays), aeroturbation (effects of wind and soil-gas), aquaturbation (effects of water under pressure), crystalturbation (growth and deterioration of crystals) and seismiturbation (earthquakes).

Karl Butzer (1982: 101–2), for instance, has demonstrated the effects of running water (aquaturbation) on the horizontal patterning of Middle Stone Age lithics at Alexandersfontein, near Kimberley, South Africa, and the tendency of 'soil-frost sorting' (cryoturbation) at Torralba, a Pleistocene site in central Spain, to produce rings of stones that appeared man-made but were actually entirely natural. The artificially constructed earthworks at OVERTON DOWN and Wareham Down are practical, experimental attempts to understand n-transforms (*see* EXPERIMENTAL ARCHAEOLOGY). *See also* TAPHONOMY.

M.B. Schiffer: *Behavioral archaeology* (New York, 1976), 15–6; R. Wood and D.L. Johnson: 'A survey of disturbance processes in archaeological site formation', *Advances in archaeological method and theory* 1, ed. M.B. Schiffer (New York 1978), 315–81; K.W. Butzer: *Archaeology as human ecology* (Cambridge, 1982), 100–22; M.B. Schiffer: *Formation processes of the archaeological record* (Albuquerque, 1987); P.J. Fowler, 'The experimental earthworks 1958–88', *Annual Report of the Council for British Archaeology* 39 (1988–9), 83–98.

IS

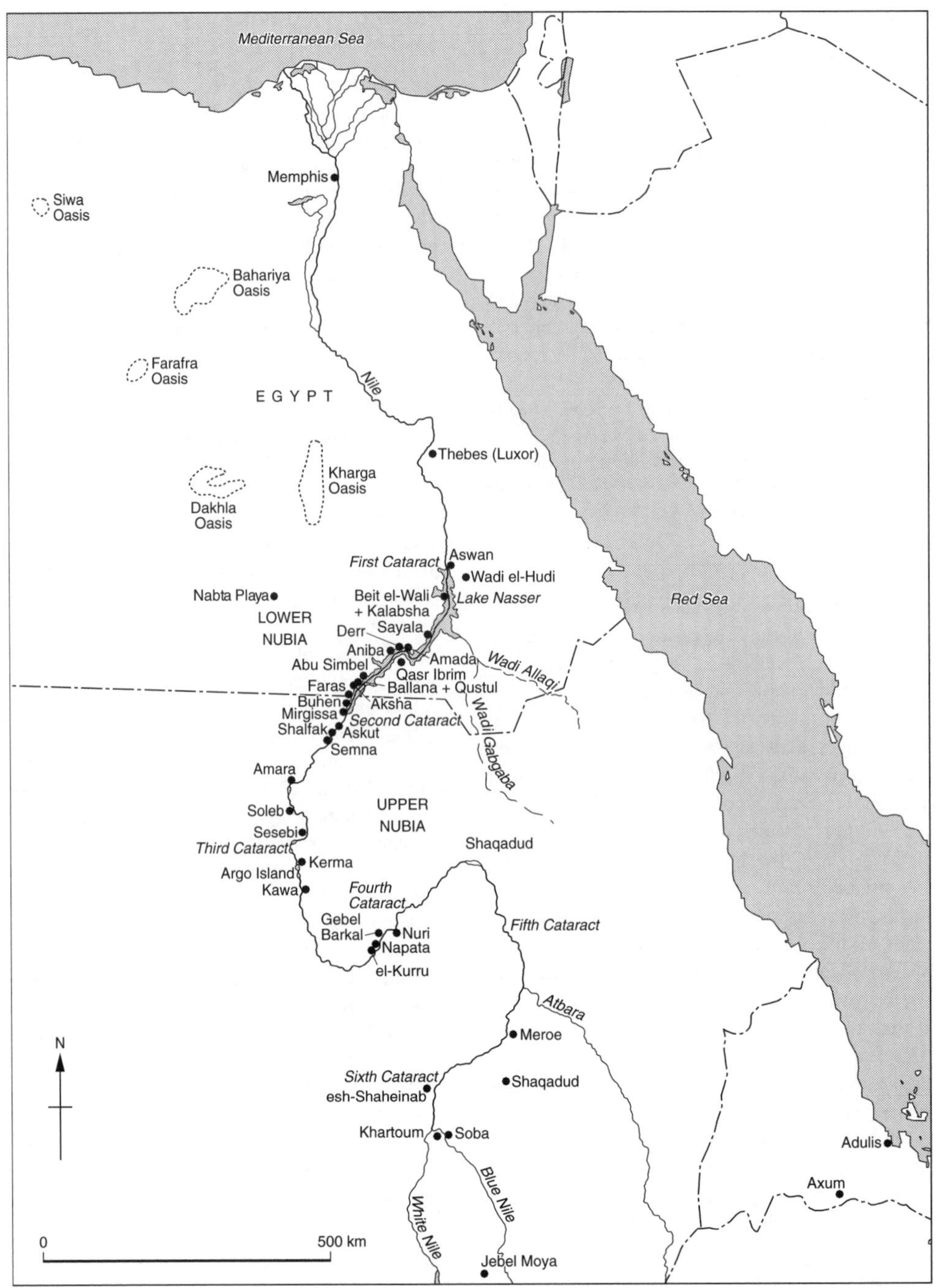

Map 26 **Nubia** Major sites in Nubia which are mentioned in the main text or have individual entries in the Dictionary.

Lower Palaeolithic	700,000 – 100,000 BC
Middle Palaeolithic	100,000 – 26,000 BC
Upper Palaeolithic	26,000 – 10,000 BC
Final Palaeolithic (Arkinian)	10,000 – 6000 BC
Khartoum Mesolithic	6000 – 3500 BC
Khartoum Neolithic/Cataract Tradition (Gemaian, Qadan and Abkan industries)	4000 – 3000 BC
A Group (A Horizon)	3500 – 2800 BC
C Group (C Horizon)	2300 – 1500 BC
Kerma culture	2500 – 1500 BC
New Kingdom (Egyptian occupation)	1540 – 1070 BC
Napatan period	1000 – 300 BC
25th dynasty (Nubian rule over Egypt)	712 – 664 BC
Meroitic period	300 BC – AD 350
X Group (X Horizon, Noba, Ballana)	AD 350 – 550
Christian period	AD 550 – 1500
Islamic period	AD 1500 –

Table 16 **Nubia** Chronology of Nubia.

Nubia Ancient geographical area which corresponds to the zone between modern Aswan and Khartoum, i.e. northern Sudan and southernmost Egypt. From at least as early as the 4th millennium BC until the Middle Ages Nubia has served as a crucial conduit, through which the raw materials of tropical Africa passed northwards en route for the civilizations of the Mediterranean and Western Asia. The region is punctuated by six Nile 'cataracts', a series of rocky areas of rapids marking the abrupt geological changes characterizing this section of the Nile valley. In terms of modern political boundaries, Nubia encompasses both northern Sudan and the southern end of Egypt, although most of the Egyptian section of Nubia has been submerged since the completion of the High Dam at Aswan in 1971 (*see* LAKE NASSER).

The material culture of the Palaeolithic period is broadly similar throughout the lower Nile valley, but the industries and 'traditions' of the Final Palaeolithic, Mesolithic and Neolithic periods are the first real indications of the existence of a number of culturally distinct groups in the Nubian section of the valley (*see* ABKAN, ARKINIAN, EPIPALAEOLITHIC, KHARTOUM MESOLITHIC *and* KHARTOUM NEOLITHIC). The subsequent history of Nubia was barely known until the survey and excavation undertaken by George Reisner in the first few decades of the 20th century, which enabled the various phases of indigenous Nubian culture to be delineated: the A GROUP, the C GROUP, the kingdom of Kush (divided chronologically into the KERMA culture and the NAPATAN and MEROITIC periods, the X Group or Ballana period (*see* BALLANA *and* BLEMMYES) and the Christian and Islamic periods. For discussion of the history of the archaeological exploration of Nubia *see* LAKE NASSER.

B.G. Trigger: *Nubia under the pharaohs* (London, 1976); D. O'Connor: *Ancient Nubia: Egypt's rival in Africa* (Philadelphia, 1983); W.Y. Adams: *Nubia: corridor to Africa*, 2nd edn (Princeton, 1984); T. Säve Söderbergh: *Temples and tombs of ancient Nubia* (London, 1987); P.L. Shinnie: *Ancient Nubia* (London, 1996); D.A. Welsby: *The kingdom of Kush: the Napatan and Meroitic empires* (London, 1996).

IS

Nuffar *see* NIPPUR

null hypothesis *see* HYPOTHESIS TESTING

nuraghi (nuragi) Defensive fortifications of the Sardinian Bronze Age, composed of massive stone-block (CYCLOPEAN) towers. The towers, which are shaped like truncated cones and may be 10–20 m high, enclose one or more floors of, generally, corbel-vaulted rooms; frequently a spiral staircase leads to the upper floor. Reliable absolute dates and associated pottery sequences are only slowly becoming available, but the nuraghi may have developed during the early to mid-2nd millennium BC, with complex nuraghi being built from about 1200 BC; many nuraghi were used and adapted until or beyond the Roman invasion of 238 BC. Mycenaean pottery has been found at some sites, and in the past Mycenaean architecture has been suggested as a prototype for nuraghic corbelled vaulting – though the early dates now suggested make a local origin more likely. The majority of the *c*.7000 nuraghic structures on Sardinia are single towers, and are presumed to have been the strongholds of the most powerful local families, while perhaps also acting as refuges and storehouses for the general community. The idea of the nuraghi as aristocratic centres of a 'clientage' system is developed in Webster (1996). The later complex nuraghi exhibit multiple subsidiary towers or bastions, curtain walls, and associated villages of predominantly round houses (e.g. BARUMINI). These complex nuraghi are sometimes presumed to have been 'proto-castles', acting as centres for a regional power in an essentially feudal system (Lilliu 1982) or, less dramatically, as the seats of petty chieftains (Webster 1991).

Nuraghic civilization. The builders of the nuraghi also constructed enclosed votive wells and 'tomba di giganti' – elongated stone-corridor tombs with curving façades and carved 'sunken panel' portals. Their most charming cultural product is an abundance of lively bronze figurines and models that were cast using the lost-wax method. Common subjects are archers and warriors, and these are also portrayed, together with less common portrayals of boxers and architectural models of nuraghi, among the large stone sculptures excavated at Monte Prama, Cabras.

G. Lilliu: *La civiltà nuragica* (Milan, 1982); M.S. Balmuth et al.: *Studies in Sardinian archaeology*, 2 vols (Ann Arbor, 1984–6); E.A. Arslan et al.: *Civiltà nuragica* (Milan, 1985); G. Webster: 'Monuments, mobilization and Nuragic organization', *Antiquity* 65 (1991), 840–56; ——: *The prehistory of Sardinia* (Sheffield, 1996).

RJA

Nuri NAPATAN funerary site located in Upper Nubia, about 25 km southwest of the 4th Nile cataract. Only a few kilometres to the northeast of Napata, the political centre of the kingdom of Kush, it was the burial site of the Kushite royal family from the early 7th to the early 3rd century BC (i.e. later than the tombs at EL-KURRU and earlier than those at southern MEROE). George Reisner identified at least 19 Kushite kings' burials at Nuri, each covered by a small pyramidal sandstone superstructure. Stylistic changes in the architecture of the royal tombs were used by Reisner as the basis for this relative chronology of Kushite kings. More than 50 of the female members of the Napatan royal family were buried in a separate section of the cemetery.

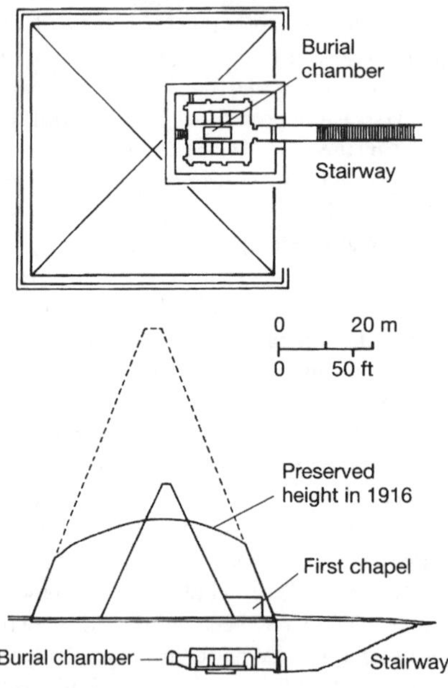

Figure 37 **Nuri** Plan and cross-section drawing of the tomb of the 25th-dynasty ruler Taharqo, the earliest pyramid at Nuri, Nubia. *Source*: M. Lehner: *The complete pyramids* (London, 1997), p. 196.

D. Dunham: *The royal cemeteries of Kush*, II: *Nuri* (Boston, 1955); W.Y. Adams: *Nubia: corridor to Africa*, 2nd edn (Princeton, 1984), 278–85.

IS

Nush-i Jan, Tepe *see* MEDES

Nuzi (Yorgan Tepe) Small north Mesopotamian settlement located about 13 km from Kirkuk in northern Iraq, where the excavations of Edward Chiera and R.F.S. Starr during the 1920s and 1930s revealed extensive remains of a HURRIAN community dating to the mid-2nd millennium BC. The mound of Yorgan Tepe comprises 12 principal phases of occupation dating from the UBAID period (*c*.5000–3800 BC) to at least the 14th century BC. The town was initially called Gasur during the Early Dynastic Period (*c*.2900–2350 BC), but when it was occupied by Hurrians, from the early 2nd millennium BC onwards, it became known as Nuzi and was ruled by a governor subservient to the king of MITANNI. 'Nuzi ware', a particular style of painted ceramics found in Mitannian strata at Nuzi, has also been excavated at other Mitannian sites. The site was extensively reoccupied in the PARTHIAN and SASANIAN periods (*c*.250 BC–AD 651). In 1896 a cache of cuneiform tablets were discovered at Nuzi; combined with later finds, this collection of almost 4000 tablets documents the history of the city during the 2nd and 3rd millennia BC, with a particular concentration of texts in the Mitannian strata (see Contenau 1926; Cassin 1958).

G. Contenau: *Les tablettes de Kerkouk et les origines de la civilization assyrienne* (Paris, 1926); E. Chiera: *Joint expedition with the Iraq Museum at Nuzi*, I–V (Paris and Philadelphia, 1927–31); R.F.S. Starr: *Nuzi*, 2 vols (Cambridge, MA, 1937–9); E. Cassin: 'Quelques remarques à propos des archives administratives à Nuzi', *Revue d'Assyriologie et d'Archéologie Orientale* 52 (1958), 16–28; M.A. Morrison and D.I. Owen et al., eds.: *Studies on the civilization and culture of Nuzi and the Hurrians*, 6 vols (Winona Lake, 1981–94).

IS

Nyarunazi Site in Burundi which has one of the fullest sequences of lithic industries in the East

African interlacustrine region, dating from the latter part of the Early Stone Age (Late ACHEULEAN and SANGOAN) to the Middle and Later Stone Age. All the deposits are riverine; the archaeological materials (brought to light during alluvial tin-mining, followed by Nenquin's excavations of 1960) are therefore in secondary situations and do not lend themselves to site-activity analyses as attempted on other East African sites.

J. Nenquin: *Contributions to the study of the prehistoric cultures of Rwanda and Burundi* (Tervuren, 1967).

JS

O

Oakhurst LSA (Later Stone Age) large rock-shelter located 22 miles east of George, Cape Province, South Africa. Excavated in the 1930s, the shelter provided the first direct stratigraphical evidence for the relationship between the entities known then as Smithfield and WILTON, currently seen as ALBANY and Wilton. The site is notable for the 31 burials recorded, often with various grave goods. Basal levels may contain MSA (Middle Stone Age) material.

A.J.H. Goodwin: 'Archaeology of the Oakhurst Shelter, George', *Transactions of the Royal Society of South Africa*, 25/3 (1938), 230–324; J. Deacon: *Guide to archaeological sites in the southern Cape*. (Stellenbosch, 1979).

RI

Oakhurst Industry *see* ALBANY INDUSTRY

obelisk (Gk *obeliskos*) Ancient Egyptian upright vertical shaft, generally of stone or wood, tapering gradually from top to bottom and surmounted by a pyramidion (miniature pyramid). Obelisks were first erected as part of the worship of the sun-god, with the pyramidion representing the sacred *benben*-stone (perhaps originally a symbol of the primeval mound of creation). In later periods pairs of obelisks were placed in front of the entrances to tombs and temples, as at Karnak and Luxor. An unfinished granite obelisk, probably dating to the 18th dynasty (*c.*1450 BC), is still *in situ* at the Aswan quarries.

E. Iversen: *Obelisks in exile* (Copenhagen, 1972); L. Habachi: *The obelisks of Egypt* (London, 1978); R. Hayward: *Cleopatra's needles* (Buxton, 1978).

IS

oblique photographs *see* AERIAL ARCHAEOLOGY

Obobogo Village site near Yaoundé, Cameroon, excavated by Pierre de Maret in 1980–3, where traces of Late Stone Age occupation have been dated to 6020 ± 505 BP. The main 'Neolithic' settlement has been dated to between 3625 and 2635 BP, with reliable radiocarbon age determinations for the first occurrence of iron slag at 2310 ± 100 and 2120 ± 70 or 150 BP. A number of pits (also known from about 10 other comparable sites in the area) may have been used for storage, construction or rubbish disposal purposes. Excavated materials include flat-bottomed pottery vessels and polished axes of dolerite, as well as organic remains including nuts of *Elaeis guineensis* and *Canarium schweinfurthii*, and charcoal indicative of forest species. De Maret suggests that there is a good parallel between developments at Obobogo and those at sites attributed to the 'KINTAMPO culture' in Ghana.

P. de Maret: 'Le contexte archéologique de l'expansion Bantu en Afrique centrale', *Les peuples Bantu, migrations, expansion et identité culturelle* I, ed. Th. Obenga (Libreville and Paris, 1989), 118–44; A. Holl: 'Néolithique: Cameroun'; 'L'âge du fer ancien: Cameroun', *Aux origines de l'Afrique Centrale*, ed. R. Lanfranchi and B. Clist (Paris, 1991), 148–54, 192–6.

PA-J

obsidian Natural glass formed by the cooling of siliceous magmas from volcanic eruptions and an important resource for stone tool-making. Obsidian was highly valued and widely traded because of its sharp edges, although its brittleness somewhat limits its usefulness in certain activities. Because the chemical composition of obsidian sources varies sensitively, artefacts can be 'fingerprinted' by archaeologists and traced to their original source flows, allowing reconstruction of ancient trade networks. Artefacts can also be dated by the OBSIDIAN HYDRATION method (*see* COPAN), in which age is determined from the degree of alteration of the surface since flaking of the tool, as measured with a special microscope. *For Japanese use of obsidian see* NOGAWA; *for Mesoamerican use see* TEOTIHUACÁN *and* TOLTECS; *for North American use see* NAMU; *for Ancient Near Eastern use see* ACERAMIC NEOLITHIC; *for East Africa see* KARIANDUSI; *for Europe see* CYCLADIC CULTURE; and for Oceania see TALASEA.

A. Lucas: 'Obsidian', *ASAE* 47 (1947) 113–23; R.S.

Santley: 'Obsidian trade and Teotihuacan influence in Mesoamerica', *Highland-Lowland interaction in Mesoamerica: interdisciplinary approaches*, ed. A.G. Miller (Washington, D.C., 1980), 69–124; R.L. Carlson: 'Trade and exchange in prehistoric British Columbia', *Prehistoric exchange systems in North America* II, ed. T.G. Baugh and J.E. Ericson (New York, 1995).
PRI

obsidian hydration dating Scientific dating technique based on the thickness of the hydration layer on a struck surface of obsidian; the layer is the result of the diffusion of water and its thickness depends not only on the time since exposure of the surface, but also on temperature and the type of obsidian (i.e. its source). It does not, however, depend on humidity, as the water uptake is small and there is sufficient in any environment. For a given temperature, the layer thickness increases according to the square root of the age.

Typical layer thicknesses are 1–50 μm (1 μ = 0.001 mm) and can be measured by optical microscopy of a polished section prepared from a V-shaped section at right angles to the surface. The measurement precision is about ±0.1 μm but it may be possible to improve this to ±0.02 by using new techniques. An error of 10% in the thickness measurement produces an error of 20% in the age estimate. The diffusion rate constant for a particular type (source) of obsidian can be determined by measurements at elevated temperature that induce a hydration layer in a short period. Deducing the effective burial temperature is less straightforward, particularly over long periods with significant climatic change (a similar problem is encountered in AMINO ACID DATING). Large systematic errors in age estimate could result, since the rate constant increases exponentially with temperature. The age range depends, at the lower end, on having a layer thickness that is measurable and thus on the rate constant and therefore temperature and, at the upper end, it largely depends on the preservation of the original surface. Published dates range from 200 to 100,000 years.

See also NITROGEN PROFILE DATING *and* SODIUM PROFILE DATING.

R.E. Taylor, ed.: *Advances in obsidian glass studies – archaeological and geochemical perspectives* (New Jersey, 1976).
SB

Oceania Oceania stretches from Papua New Guinea and Australia in the west, to EASTER ISLAND and the Hawaiian Islands in the east. It offers a huge diversity of environment, from the central Australian deserts to the small atolls of the remote Pacific. The region was settled progressively over a period of at least 60,000 years, with human groups moving into Australia at that date but not reaching New Zealand, the last major landmass on earth to be settled, until around AD 800. As far as we know, even the earliest of these groups were fully modern humans, and Oceania provides a series of case studies in the colonizing abilities of human beings.

Oceania can be divided in a number of ways, depending on the criteria used. Flora and fauna provide a unifying factor: the vast majority of the plants and the animals of the region derived from Gondwanaland, a super-continent comprising South America, southern Africa, India, Antarctica, Sahul (Australia and Papua New Guinea) and New Zealand. The most famous descendants of the Gondwanaland faunas are the marsupials of Sahul and the flightless birds, such as the emu and the extinct MOA. When people first entered the Oceanic region from southeast Asia, they left behind the familiar placental mammals of that region and encountered a whole new range of marsupial species. The only placental mammals found in Oceania today are humans and those species (such as pig, dog and chicken) introduced by humans. Plant species show more continuity than animals, with the rainforests of Papua New Guinea and the western Pacific sharing many plants in common with southeast Asia. However, many of the plants of Papua New Guinea and especially Australia would have been unfamiliar, such as the eucalypts, desert faunas and southern Australian rainforests.

Over the last century it has been established that the main source of species for the island Pacific is Sahul and island southeast Asia rather than the Americas. There is, however, a major biogeographic divide at the eastern end of the Solomon Island chain: east of that point there were no endemic animal species and the structure of plant communities is far simpler (except in New Zealand). The lack of plants and animals may have proved a major barrier to colonizing humans: human groups reached the Solomon chain by almost 30,000 years ago, but do not seem to have moved east of this until around 3500 BP. The Chatham Islands, to the east of New Zealand, were possibly the last part of the Pacific to be settled in prehistoric times – probably by a group known as the Moriori, from the South Island of New Zealand, about 300 years ago.

Sections: 1 Australia and Tasmania; 2 Melanesia, Polynesia and Micronesia

1 *Australia and Tasmania*. An example of one of the

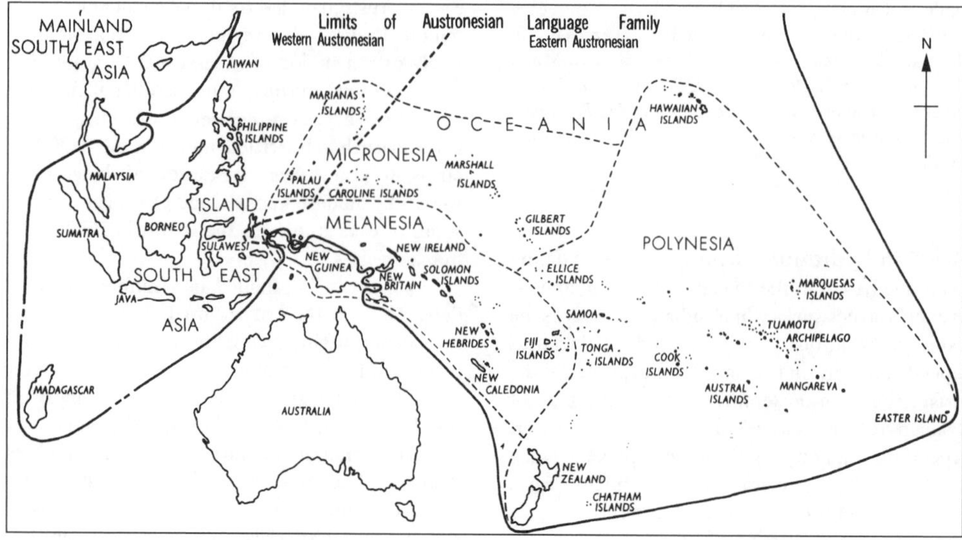

Map 27 **Oceania** The distribution of Austronesian languages in Oceania.

most ancient Australian sites is Malakunanja, a large rockshelter near the Arnhem Land escarpment in northern Australia. The shelter contained 4 m of deposit, the upper 2.6 m of which yielded stone tools. The lowest artefact-bearing layers have been dated using thermoluminescence to around 50,000 years ago, which would make Malakunanja one of the oldest inhabited sites in Australia – but the dating has aroused controversy. Other early sites include DEVIL'S LAIR, where artefact-bearing layers date from before 33,000 years ago. Sites such as Burrill Lake rock shelter, a large sandstone rock shelter on the south coast of New South Wales, first occupied *c.*20,000 years ago, preserve HORSE-HOOF CORES and other elements of the early AUSTRALIAN CORE TOOL AND SCRAPER TRADITION in the lower layers, while around 5000 BP there was a change to backed blades and tool types of the later AUSTRALIAN SMALL TOOL TRADITION (Lampert 1971). KENNIFF CAVE helped archaeologists to distinguish these two generic tool traditions, while CLOGG'S CAVE provides another example.

A.R. Radcliffe-Brown, the eminent anthropologist, famously described Australian Aborigines as 'an unchanging people in an unchanging landscape'. Archaeology has given the lie to this statement across the continent (e.g. the LAKE MUNGO in New South Wales), but perhaps nowhere more so than in Tasmania, where evidence from the Pleistocene has demonstrated the great range of environments to which humans were obliged to adapt during the last glaciation. Modern humans first entered Tasmania 35,000 years ago, at which time they were the most southerly people on Earth. During the height of the last glaciation, they lived in a sub-antarctic landscape close to upland glaciers. In the southwest of Tasmania, in an area today covered by temperate rainforest, seven limestone caves have been excavated which show that people inhabited this region from 35,000 years ago to the end of the Pleistocene. Glaciers existed at the upper end of mountain valleys in the region, reaching their maximum extent 18,000 years ago. At lower altitudes, grasslands and herbfields attracted wallabies and emus. These species were preyed upon by humans, who left huge amounts of bone in the caves. For instance, in Nunamira cave in the Florentine valley 200,000 pieces of bone were recovered from a cubic metre of soil, and 90% of this bone was from one species: the red-necked wallaby. The presence of emu eggshell shows that these sites were occupied in late winter and early spring, the most difficult period of the year in this subantarctic landscape. It is likely that people were moved through these areas seasonally. Bone points dating back to 26,000 years ago indicate the working of hides and other pliable materials, perhaps to make clothing.

By contrast, at the other end of the Sahulian continent, from about 35,000 years ago, humans occupied the limestone caves of New Ireland, just south of the equator. Here the temperature and rainfall throughout the last glaciation were little different from today, creating a fully tropical environment. The fact that people adapted to such diverse environments in different parts of the Greater Australian continent soon after the first colonization of that continent testifies to an extraordinary flexibility of response.

2 *Melanesia, Polynesia and Micronesia.* Outside Australia, the rest of the Pacific is conventionally divided into Melanesia, Ploynesia and Micronesia. Melanesia encompasses the area from Papua New Guinea to Fiji; it thus includes the large islands of the western Pacific and those which were settled first, although, as noted above, Papua New Guinea has a mixed history, having been joined to Australia until 8000 years ago and first settled as early as *c.*40,000 years ago. Ancient sites in the region include the New Ireland site of MATENKUPKUM. The later site of BALOF CAVE, again on New Ireland, provides evidence for the translocation of animals, while KUK SWAMP, in the Western Highlands of Papua New Guinea, offers some of the earliest evidence for farming in the world, going back to 9000 BP. The evidence from Kuk also illuminates the link between Oceanic economic production and social relations, as does the much later evidence from MOTUPORE. New Britain, the largest island in the western Pacific, is tectonically active, with a ring of volcanoes on the north coast that produced the widely-traded obsidian at TALASEA. New Britain's prehistory goes back 35,000 years, and open sites such as Yombon have been preserved by volcanic ashes (Pavlides 1993). Extensive excavations in the Arawe Islands on the south coast have revealed many sites with evidence of the LAPITA CULTURAL COMPLEX – a key cultural phenomenon in early Western Pacific prehistory – as well as providing a full picture of the island's later prehistory (Gosden et al. 1989).

TIKOPIA, a small island (4.6 sq. km) first settled in the Lapita period, lies 200 km north of Vanuatu and 200 km southeast of the Santa Cruz Islands in the Pacific. Recent in-depth studies of the island provide a classic example of the interdependence between landscape, society and subsistence – a recurring theme in Pacific archaeology. Tikopia also exemplifies the way in which the natural flora and fauna of many Pacific islands has been substantially replaced by introduced species – the notion of 'TRANSPORTED LANDSCAPES'.

Fiji, on the eastern border of Melanesia, was again settled at the time of the Lapita complex. Fiji's prehistory is mainly distinguished by changing pottery styles: Lapita styles last until around 2000 BP, when Navatu impressed pottery takes over, to be superseded by the incised wares of the Vuda (900–400 BP) and Ra (400 BP–present) phases. In the Lapita period, settlement is all coastal; from the Vuda and Ra phases thousands of forts are known, which vary in size and layout from one part of Fiji to another.

Polynesia is often thought of as a triangle, with the Hawaiian group, Easter Island and New Zealand as its three points. In contrast to the diversity of the Melanesian populations, Polynesians all speak closely-related Austronesian languages (see map 27 opposite), and are linked by material culture (e.g. the AHU) and social structure (Kirch 1984). Much of the prehistory of Polynesia has been written in culture-historical terms, with many scholars identifying Polynesian origins in southeast Asia, where the Austronesian languages are thought to have originated. The Polynesian islands range in size from New Zealand (501,776 sq. km) to tiny islands with relatively huge populations, such as Anuta (0.4 sq. km), and are distributed from the equator to sub-antarctic climes. Their cultural history thus provides a good example of how diverse environments can effect change upon one related cultural group; here, the anthropological work of Sahlins (1958) has considerably influenced the practice of archaeology.

Maoris, the indigenous inhabitants of New Zealand (probably east Polynesian in origin), arrived in New Zealand between 800 and 1000 years ago. As recorded in oral histories and the archaeological evidence, there may well have been settlement by more than one group: the north and south islands of New Zealand demonstrate different histories, with agriculture based around sweet potato mainly restricted to the north island, and the fortified PA (earthworks) and the largest MOA hunting sites known from the south island. TONGA represents another Polynesian island with a complex cultural history, while HALAWA VALLEY is an example of a number of alleys in the Hawaiian islands that have now been surveyed archaeologically.

Micronesia, which lies to the east of island southeast Asia and to the north of both Melanesia and western Polynesia, is the area of the Pacific least researched by archaeologists. The earliest dated entry of humans into Micronesia is roughly contemporary with the first moves into Polynesia, at around 3500 BP. The colonists possessed a broadly similar material culture, especially in the form of red-slipped pottery. As in Polynesia, anthropological investigations have heavily influenced archaeology, and one focus of interest has been the growth of stratified societies, such as the Yapese 'empire', over the last few hundred years.

Anthropological knowledge about recent social forms has tended to influence archaeologists. Thus Australia is seen as the 'hunter-gatherer' continent, settled by egalitarian groups with few of the social divisions found amongst farmers. Melanesia has provided anthropological studies of 'BIG MAN' social forms in which personal standing is achieved through manipulating subsistence and trade, rather than through inheritance. (The history of trading systems and their social consequences is central to much of the archaeology undertaken in Papua New Guinea.) In both Micronesia and Polynesia, the growth of chiefdom societies, in places such as Yap, Tonga and Hawaii, has formed the central issue. Much archaeological work in Oceania has been by American scholars, influenced by the NEO-EVOLUTIONARY school of anthropologists who worked in the area from the 1950s to the 1970s.

M. Sahlins: *Social stratification in Polynesia* (Seattle, 1958); R.J. Lampert: *Burrill Lake and Currarong* (Canberra, 1971); E.L. Frost: 'Fiji,' *The prehistory of Polynesia*, ed. J. Jennings (Canberra, 1979), 61–81; J. Davidson: *The prehistory of New Zealand* (Auckland, 1984); P.V. Kirch: *The evolution of Polynesian chiefdoms* (Cambridge, 1984); Gosden et al.: 'The Lapita sites of the Bismarck Archipelago', *Antiquity* 63 (1989), 561–86; A. Anderson and M. McGlone: 'Living on the edge: prehistoric land and people in New Zealand', *The naive lands*, ed. J. Dodson (Melbourne, 1992), 199–241; C. Pavlides: 'Archaeological research at Yombon, West New Britain, Papua New Guinea', *Archaeology in Oceania* 28 (1993), 55–9; J. Allen and J.F. O'Connell, eds: *Transitions: Pleistocene to Holocene in Australia and Papua New Guinea* [published as special number of the journal *Antiquity*, 69: (1995) 265].

CG

Oc Eo Rectangular site enclosed by five ramparts and four moats, and covering 450 ha, located in the transbassac region of southern Vietnam. Oc Eo is the key site for appreciating the timing and manner of the entry of Southeast Asia into the great trading network which linked China with India and Rome in the early centuries of the Christian era.

Aerial photographs reveal that Oc Eo was linked by canals to other sites in this flat, low-lying deltaic terrain. Excavations in 1944 by Mallaret uncovered large stone and brick structures in the central area and the remains of industrial activity, such as glass and metal working. A wealth of material items, excavated or purchased from local looters, shows that the site was occupied from the 2nd century AD. Malleret recovered two Roman medallions minted during the reigns of Antoninus Pius (AD 138–161) and Marcus Aurelius (AD 161–180), Iranian coinage, and jewellery engraved in the Brahmi script of India dated to the late 1st or early 2nd century AD. Further examples of Indian scripts suggest that the site was still occupied three centuries later. A great deal of gold jewellery was found, incorporating a variety of precious and semi-precious stones comprising virtually the entire available range. Pottery was also locally manufactured, and sandstone moulds for casting bronze and tin jewellery were recovered.

The date, monumentality and location of Oc Eo make it highly likely that it was a site of the FUNAN polity, which was described by two chinese emissaries of the Wu emperor, Kang Dai and Zhu Ying, in about AD 250. They reported a country with cities, kings, palaces and a taxation system. There was evidently also contact with India, since the same Chinese emissaries mention that they met a representative of the Murunda king in India.

L. Malleret: *L'archéologie du Delta du Mekong* (Paris 1959–63).

CH

Ochre Coloured Pottery (OCP) Ceramics associated with the early occupants of the Ganges–Yamuna river basin of northern India *c.*1800–1400 BC. The OCP ceramics include a wide variety of vessel forms including jars and bowls, pedestalled bowls, and miniature forms (Dikshit 1979: 291), typically wheel-made, poorly fired and coated with a red or orange slip or wash, sometimes with incised or painted decoration.

Remains of the OCP period are known from a number of sites, including Ahichchatra, ATRANJIKHERA and HASTINAPURA. OCP sites have sometimes been grouped into a single cultural tradition, associated with the similarly defined 'copper hoard culture' (*see* GANGETIC HOARDS), but several specialists have cautioned against this, citing regional variations in vessel forms and surface treatment, and poor chronological and stratigraphic control at many sites. In 1971, the Archaeological Survey of India organized a conference on the OCP in which it was acknowledged that OCP sites should be divided into a western and eastern geographic zone, each with distinctive forms (Gupta 1971–2).

The association of OCP ware with copper hoards is also unclear; both have been found in a number of different contexts, but provenance data is poor and D.P. Agrawal (1982: 208) has suggested that their association is at present only circumstantial, therefore much more research needs to be done to evaluate their relations.

S.P. Gupta, ed.: 'Proceedings of the seminar on OCP and NBP', *Puratattva* 5 (1971–72):1–104; K.N. Dikshit: 'The Ochre Coloured Ware settlements in Ganga-Yamuna

Doab', *Essays in Indian protohistory*, ed. D.P. Agrawal and D.K. Chakrabarti (Delhi, 1979), 285–99; D.P. Agrawal: *The archaeology of India* (Copenhagen, 1982), 198–210.
CS

Ocmulgee (Macon Plateau) Early MISSISSIPPIAN site in central Georgia (USA) that is thought to intrude into the area from about AD 950–1150, but there is also recent consideration of the role of indigenous cultures in its development. The site contains several large mounds, fortifications, household areas and extensive sets of ridges and furrows for agricultural fields. The most famous structure is a subterranean building 13 m in diameter that has been interpreted as a council chamber. It contains 47 niches (thought to be seats) around the perimeter of the structure, and a raised clay platform 'throne' in the shape of a bird with three seats.
C.H. Fairbanks: 'The Macon earth lodge', *AA* 12 (1946), 94–108; D.J. Hally, ed.: *Ocmulgee archaeology, 1936–1986* (University of Georgia Press, Athens, 1994).
WB

Ogooué Basin *see* AFRICA 5

Ohemir, Tel el- *see* KISH

Okhotsk Marine-oriented culture found around the coast of the Okhotsk Sea in the islands of Hokkaido, Japan and Sakhalin (Russia), as well as in the southern Kuriles between the 8th and 14th centuries AD. Characterized by large hexagonal houses, elaborate bone working and bear ritualism, it is contemporary with the SATSUMON culture.
C.M. Aikens and D.E. Dumond: 'Convergence and common heritage: some parallels in the archaeology of Japan and western north America', *Windows on the Japanese past*, ed. R. Pearson, K. Hutterer and G.L. Barnes (Ann Arbor, 1986), 163–78.
SK

Okvik culture *see* OLD BERING SEA CULTURE

Olbia Important Greek (Ionian) colony, later a city-state, situated on the Bug-Dniestr *Liman* (estuary), near the town of Ochakov in the Ukraine. The site has been excavated by Russian and Ukrainian archaeologists since the 1850s. The earliest Greek settlement emerged on the island of Berezan in the Bug-Dniestr estuary in the late 7th century BC. The Olbia township appeared in the mid-6th century and flourished especially in the 5th–4th centuries BC, when a network of agricultural settlements appeared in the hinterland. The density of Greek settlement declined in the late 3rd century BC. The city further declined in the 2nd–1st centuries BC, when it was controlled by the SCYTHIAN kings. There was a substantial development in the 1st–3rd centuries AD, and in the middle of the 2nd century AD, a Roman garrison was stationed in Olbia. The city ceased to exist in the 4th century AD.
E.I Levi, ed.: *Olvia: temenos i hora* (Leningrad, 1964); S.D. Kryzhytsky: *Olvia* (Kiev, 1985).
PD

Old Bering Sea culture This, and the closely related Okvik culture, represent the earliest phase of the THULE TRADITION (1st–6th century AD). Sites are found primarily on islands in the Bering Strait, but are also known on the adjacent Siberian shores. The economy is based primarily on the exploitation of sea mammals. The complex and intricate carving styles found on most implements – not seen on similar items from later in the Thule tradition – have been interpreted as having magical significance, and may indicate close cultural ties with societies in east Asia.
O.W. Geist and F.G. Rainey: 'Archaeological excavations at Kukulik, St Lawrence Island, Alaska', *Miscellaneous Publications of the University of Alaska* 2 (1936); H.B. Collins: 'Archaeology of St Lawrence Island, Alaska', *Smithsonian Miscellaneous Collections* 96 (1937).
RP

Old Copper Term used in North American archaeology to refer to the copper artefacts of the Late Archaic period (*c*.3000–1000 BC) found throughout the Lake Superior Basin, particularly in eastern Wisconsin. Once thought to represent the remains of a specific culture (Old Copper Culture),

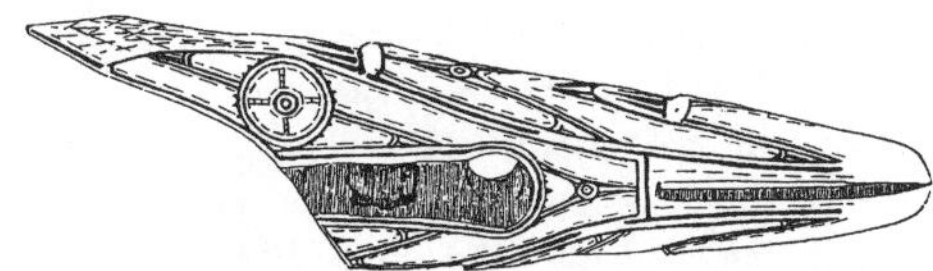

Figure 38 **Old Bering Sea culture** Intricately carved harpoon head, Old Bering Sea culture, Alaska. *Source*: O.W. Geist and F.G. Rainey: *Archaeological excavations at Kukulik, St Lawrence Island, Alaska* (Washington D.C.: University of Alaska Publications, 1936), fig. 41.

these artefacts are now recognized as having been manufactured by a variety of Late Archaic groups that lived throughout the Great Lakes region. Much that is known about Old Copper derives from vandalized cemeteries such as the Oconto, Osceola and Reigh sites in Wisconsin, providing a rather biased view of the cultures that produced these artefacts. The native copper used to manufacture the artefacts came from sources in Wisconsin and Michigan, of which Isle Royale (Michigan) is the best known. The most common Old Copper artefacts are awls, tanged knives, projectile points, semi-lunar objects or crescents, gouges and axes.

T. Ritzenthaler, ed.: 'The Old Copper culture of Wisconsin', *The Wisconsin Archaeologist* 38 (1957), 185–329; R. Mason: *Great Lakes archaeology* (New York, 1981), 181–99; J. Stoltman: 'The Archaic tradition', *Wisconsin archaeology: background for cultural resource planning*, ed. W. Green, J. Stoltman and A. Kehoe (Madison, 1986), 207–38.

RJE

Old Crow Flats Locality in Yukon, Canada, that has provided controversially early radiocarbon dates for the arrival of humans in the Americas. The redeposited river deposits produced quantities of modified bone from extinct animals, and a small number of undoubted artefacts. A caribou-tibia fleshing tool produced the early date of *c.*27,000 ± 3000 BP; however, a recent AMS date on the flesher produced an age of only 1350 ± 150 BP. In fact, all the undisputed artefacts have been shown to be less than 3000 years old. While, many of the modified bones do appear to be Pleistocene in age, their status as artefacts remains in doubt.

R. Morlan et al.: 'Accelerator Mass Spectrometry dates on bones from Old Crow Basin, Northern Yukon Territory', *Canadian Journal of Archaeology*, 14 (1990), 75–92.

RP

Old Minster (Winchester) West Saxon Cathedral, which was excavated in 1962–9 by Martin Biddle and Birthe Kjølbye-Biddle, where they developed OPEN-AREA EXCAVATION techniques that have been subsequently adopted throughout western Europe. The Biddles unravelled the complex of robber trenches left after the building was demolished in AD 1093–4, to illustrate how the cathedral evolved. The Old Minster was founded in AD 648 by King Cenwalh, then enlarged in the 9th and 10th centuries. The painstaking excavations showed that the architectural development of a great basilica could be documented archaeologically if excavated following scientific principles. The Biddles subsequently employed the same methods at two other medieval sites in England: Repton minster church and St Albans cathedral.

M. Biddle: 'Archaeology, architecture, and the cult of saints in Anglo-Saxon England', *The Anglo-Saxon church*, ed. L. Butler and R. Morris (London, 1986), 1–31; B. Kjølbye-Biddle: 'The seventh-century minster at Winchester interpreted', *The Anglo-Saxon Church*, ed. L. Butler and R. Morris (London, 1986), 196–209.

RH

Olduvai, Oldowan Gorge in Tanzania which has become almost synonymous with the quest for human origins, following the discoveries of the remains of early humans and near-humans made by Mary and Louis Leakey from 1959 onwards. The massive erosion gully – about 100 m deep – cuts through the southern edge of Serengeti plain, facing Ngorongoro and the Crater Highlands. It reveals a succession of Pleistocene lake-beds, the lowest nearly two million years old. The obvious geochronological and palaeo-environmental importance of this unparalleled sequence of exposed deposits is enhanced by their containing fossilized bones of numerous animals (in most cases extinct species of modern African genera). Equally important is the stratified succession of Early Stone Age tools and flakes, mostly of the ACHEULEAN (hand-axe) tradition, but in the lower beds, dating before 1.5 million years, belonging to the Oldowan (sometimes called 'pebble-tool') tradition.

The geological and palaeontological importance of Olduvai was recognised by Hans Reck, who worked there in 1913, but unfortunately his materials were lost during the First World War. In 1931 he returned to Olduvai with Louis Leakey, who quickly appreciated the site's archaeological potential, although it was not until 1959, after several subsequent expeditions, that significant fossils of early man and near-man were discovered at the site. That year the find of the *Zinjanthropus* skull (nicknamed 'Nutcracker Man' because of its massive jaw and teeth) set the scene for much more intense research effort and international funding. At the time it was believed that the low bed containing *Zinjanthropus* was only 0.5 million years old, and that this specimen might represent the makers of the associated tools. Both views were rapidly overturned in a flurry of scientific activity and debate. It was established by POTASSIUM-ARGON tests that this bed with the skull and tools was about 1.75 million years old: this more than tripled the chronology of the whole Olduvai sequence, and by extension the Pleistocene worldwide – let alone human history and the Stone Age succession in Africa. At the same time Leakey denied that *Zinjanthropus* was the toolmaker or even an early form of human, but assigned it to the genus of near-humans, AUSTRALOPITHECUS, already recognised in South Africa. By designating this species *Australopithecus* (*Zinjanthropus*) *boisei*, Leakey further argued that another bipedal species was represented among the Olduvai fossils in the same geological beds, one with a bigger brain and more adept hands. This one, which he regarded as human and the early stone toolmaker, he named HOMO HABILIS. Despite initial doubts about Leakey's 'juggling' of the pieces of skulls and limb-bones and criticisms of the sensational manner of announcing scientific discoveries, this view of the earliest tool-making humans existing alongside australopithecine hominids in eastern Africa about two million years ago has prevailed in outline.

Further important fossils, of both Lower and Middle Pleistocene age, were found at Olduvai in the early 1960s, and Mary Leakey continued working there long after, concentrating on the lithic sequence and interpretation of site-activities, while Richard Hay completed a parallel study of the complex volcanic and lacustrine geology. With further fossil discoveries in the region and also in northern Kenya and Ethiopia, the Olduvai discoveries came to be viewed in fuller context. This showed that earliest mankind, *Homo habilis*, extended back beyond the Olduvai sequence to perhaps 2.5 million years; while australopithecines, from which earliest Homo would have emerged in time, stretch back to twice that age. The matching of the australopithecine skeleton (nicknamed 'Lucy') found at HADAR in the eastern Ethiopian Rift Valley with the footprints unearthed by Mary Leakey at LAETOLI, near Olduvai, under volcanic ash dating to 3–4 million years ago, demonstrates, despite notorious academic rivalries and scientific disputes, the essentially collaborative and accumulative nature of the advancement of knowledge of human evolutionary history in the changing African environment of the whole Pleistocene span.

L.S.B. Leakey et al.: *Olduvai Gorge* I–V (Cambridge, 1965–94); R.L. Hay: *The geology of Olduvai Gorge* (Berkeley, 1976); J. Reader: *Missing links: the hunt for earliest man* 2nd edn (London, 1988).

JS

Oleneostrovski mogil'nik ('Oleneostrovski cemetery') The largest MESOLITHIC cemetery in Europe is on the Oleni (Reindeer) island in Onega Lake, in Russian Karelia. Excavated by A.I. Ravdonikas in 1936–8 and N.N. Gurina in the 1950s, the total number of graves is estimated at more than 400 (170 were excavated). The burials were 0.60–1.20 m below the ground surface, usually singly (16 double burials and three triple burials), in an extended posture facing east; after inhumation, the bodies had been sprinkled with red ochre. Four individuals in the northern part of the cemetery were interred in funnel-shaped shafts 1.3–1.8 m deep, in a standing posture facing west.

Hunting equipment (such as bone and stone points, bone daggers, slate knives, harpoons, fish-hooks and quivers) prevails in male graves. Female graves, in general poorer than the male examples, contained household artefacts, flint blades, awls, polishers, burins and scrapers, as well as perforated beaver incisors and snake-effigy figures. One of the shaft graves contained six beaver mandibles. The grave goods included 42 sculptured or ornamented objects, including representations of elk, snakes and humans carved in stone, wood and bone. After a multivariate analysis of the grave goods, O'Shea and Zvelebil (1984) concluded that the cemetery belonged to a relatively large and stable population with considerable internal social differentiation. It also seems that there was an active regional exchange network which included a wide variety of raw materials and exotic goods (e.g. arrowheads and knives made of grey flint). A recent series of radiocarbon dates suggests a time-span of 6500 to 6300 BC in calendar years.

N.N. Gurina: *Oleneostrovskii Mogil'nik*, *MIAS* 47 (Moscow and Leningrad, 1956); J. O'Shea and M. Zvelebil: 'Oleneostrovski Mogilnik: reconstructing social and economic organization of prehistoric forages in northern Russia', *JAA* 3 (1984), 1–40.

PD

Ollantaytambo *see* INCA

Olmec Name given to the Middle Formative society that flourished on the Gulf coastal plain of Veracruz and Tabasco, Mexico, *c*.1400–400 BC. The term 'Olmec' also refers to an unrelated group of 16th-century peoples in highland Puebla, Mexico, but when used by archaeologists 'Olmec' almost invariably refers to the Formative period culture.

The Gulf coast Olmec were one of several complex societies to develop out of late Preceramic and Early Formative village traditions in Mesoamerica and during the Middle Formative these groups maintained extensive contacts with each other. The precise origins of Olmec culture are still being debated, as there is little evidence for large Early Formative populations in the region. Many archaeologists see evidence of ties to Pacific coastal regions of Chiapas and Guatemala and the trans-isthmian zone. The Gulf coast's broad rivers and fertile floodplains would have been attractive to early farmers.

Most sites in the Olmec area are relatively poorly known archaeologically, the exceptions being SAN LORENZO TENOCHTITLAN (see Coe and Diehl 1980) and LA VENTA. These and other Olmec sites provide evidence for the early development of some of the characteristics of public architecture in Mesoamerica, chiefly the construction of pyramidal mounds and their arrangement around open plazas. Mounds at Olmec sites are constructed of earth, with floors and surfaces of different coloured clays and sands. Olmec culture traditionally has been best known through its art style, which featured monumental basalt stone sculptures in the form of human heads, possibly representing Olmec rulers, and 'altars', perhaps serving as thrones. Portable art included carved objects of green stone (jadeite, serpentine, or other minerals), often depicting a 'WERE-JAGUAR'.

Objects in the Olmec style have been found widely throughout Mesoamerica during the Middle Formative period at sites such as CHALCATZINGO and Oxtotitlán (a cave in Guerrero, best known for its Olmec-related painting of a costumed figure in a green bird suit, seated atop an altar or throne). Olmec objects include pottery with 'Olmec-like' motifs, carvings and paintings in the 'Olmec style' and other 'Olmecoid' artefacts. They are usually found together with objects of local manufacture and local stylistic traditions. It is clear from these distributions that much of what is distinctively Gulf coast Olmec was transmitted to other groups in Mesoamerica, but the meaning and mechanisms of this transmission are uncertain. Interpretations have generally been polarized into two camps. One view of the Olmec sees them as Mesoamerica's first civilization, the *cultura madre*, and the Olmec are credited with bringing civilization to the rest of the region through trade, religious proselytization or political unification (see Coe 1968). Another view sees the Olmec as one of many Middle Formative societies in Mesoamerica (*see* PASO DE LA AMADA; SAN JOSE MOGOTE) in which elite groups were emerging and competing for resources (see papers in Sharer and Grove 1989); the widespread stylistic features are interpreted as part of shared ideology, kin identification, and/or systems of status symbols.

M.S. Coe: *America's first civilization* (New York, 1968); M.D. Coe and R.A. Diehl: *In the land of the Olmec*, 2 vols (Austin, 1980); E.P. Benson, ed.: *The Olmec and their neighbors* (Washington, D.C., 1981); R.J. Sharer and D.C. Grove, eds: *Regional perspectives on the Olmec* (Cambridge, 1989).

PRI

Olorgesailie One of the best studied ACHEULEAN sites of between 0.5 and 1 million years ago, situated low in the Eastern Rift Valley in southern Kenya. Olorgesailie was from time to time a favoured lake- or waterside site at which groups of HOMO ERECTUS hunter-gatherers camped, perhaps seasonally. The concentrations of handaxes, cleavers and other tools and debitage result from erosion and mixing in small gullies; nevertheless, working from their spatial distribution and associations, as well as the environmental pointers provided by the deposits themselves and fossil bones of various animals, Glynn Isaac produced a classic study of site-use, activity patterns and economic exploitation of local resources in the Early Stone Age. Together with work at other eastern African Acheulean sites (ISIMILA, NSONGEZI, OLDUVAI and KALAMBO FALLS) in the 1960s, Olorgesailie in Isaac's interpretation illustrated the employment within a single population of varied tool-kits for different activities – from butchering and skinning to woodworking and heavy-duty pounding and digging – as opposed to the traditional archaeological fashion of defining 'cultures' and their successions by specific diagnostic stone tools.

G.Ll. Isaac: *Olorgesailie* (Chicago, 1977).

JS

Olsen-Chubbuck PALEO-INDIAN kill site in Colorado, dated to 8200 BC, containing Planview projectile points of the PLANO Culture associated with the remains of extinct species of bison. A herd of bison was driven into a gully and about 200 animals of all ages and both sexes were killed. The first animals in the gully were trampled by the stampeding herd behind them and the later animals were killed by hunters. Only a few of the animals were butchered. Disarticulation patterns revealed that the animals were systematically butchered and that animal parts varied in value.

J. Wheat: 'A Paleo-Indian bison kill', *Scientific American* 216/1 (1967), 44–53.

WB

el-Omari Group of Egyptian Neolithic sites about 12 km south of Cairo, consisting of three settlements and two associated cemeteries, which form the basis for the el-Omari phase of the Lower Egyptian predynastic. Despite some dispute over the radiocarbon dates from the el-Omari sites, the two main settlements (el-Omari A and B) are now thought to have been occupied throughout the 4th millennium BC, making them roughly contemporary with the late Amratian and Gerzean phases in Upper Egypt (*see* EGYPT: PREHISTORIC). Both el-Omari A and B comprised numerous circular wattle and daub huts, as well as storage pits, with tools and organic remains showing that they cultivated emmer wheat and barley. They buried their dead within the confines of the village, equipping them with relatively few grave-goods. The fact that the slightly later el-Omari C settlement (with which at least two separate cemeteries are associated) included chisel-shaped arrowheads suggests that it was still inhabited in Early Dynastic times (*c*.3000–2649 BC).

F. Debono: 'La civilization prédynastique d'El Omari (nord d'Hélouan)', *BIE* 37 (1956), 329–39; F. Debono and B. Mortensen: *El Omari: a Neolithic settlement and other sites in the vicinity of Wadi Hof, Helwan* (Mainz, 1990); B. Midant-Reynes: *Préhistoire de l'Egypte* (Paris, 1992), 118–22.

IS

Omo Early hominid site in the lower basin of the Omo river, southwest Ethiopia. The long sequence of Pliocene and Pleistocene deposits – the thickest fossiliferous stratigraphy in east Africa – have yielded many thousands of fossil remains both of early hominids and mammals such as elephants, pigs and hippopotami. The hominid remains in the earlier deposits, dated by POTASSIUM ARGON DATING, PALAEOMAGNETISM and faunal analysis to about 3 million years ago (Brown et al. 1985), have been identified as *Australopithecus africanus* and *boisei* (*see* AUSTRALOPITHECUS). The upper levels contain remains of *HOMO HABILIS* and *HOMO ERECTUS* dated to about 1.4 million years ago.

M.H. Day: 'Omo human skeletal remains', *Nature* 222 (1969), 1135–8; G.E. Kennedy: 'The emergence of Homo sapiens: the post-cranial evidence', *Man* 19 (1984), 94–100; F.H. Brown et al. 'An integrated Plio-Pleistocene chronology for the Turkana basin', *Ancestors*, ed. E. Delson (New York, 1985), 82–90.

IS

Ongbah Large cave containing rich burials of the 1st millennium BC, located in the upper reaches of the Khwae Yai River in central Thailand. Per Sørensen's research, although limited by the activities of looters, revealed that the dead were interred in wooden boat coffins, one of which has been dated to the last four centuries BC. Apart from iron implements, Sørensen has described five bronze drums of clear DONG SON affinities decorated with flying birds, human figures and geometric motifs. Bronze earrings, bracelets and a high-tin bronze bowl were also present. These rich graves contrast with ten burials without boat coffins, but containing a similar range of iron artefacts. Sørensen has suggested that the differences between these and the coffin burials reflect social status rather than chronology. The presence of such rich interments might well be explained by exchange up and down the river valley and the wealth generated from access to the local lead ores.

P. Sørensen: 'The Ongbah cave and its fifth drum', *Early South East Asia*, ed. R.B. Smith and W. Watson (Oxford, 1979), 443–56.

CH

Onion Portage Deeply stratified inland site located on the Kobuk River, Alaska. The earliest levels include remains from the Akmak and Kobuk complexes of the PALEO-ARCTIC TRADITION. The site appears to have functioned as a hunting station to intercept caribou crossing the river here; alternatively, it may have been used for fishing.

D.D. Anderson: 'A Stone Age campsite at the gateway to America', *SA* 218/6 (1968), 24–33.

RP

open-area excavation Style of excavation, also known as 'open excavation' or 'stripping' whereby large areas of an archaeological site are exposed, without the use of permanent BAULKS or sections, which can often have the effect of obscuring the excavator's full view of each cultural horizon. The technique was introduced from the 1940s onwards (see, for instance, Bersu 1940) as a replacement for the earlier GRID system of excavation favoured by Mortimer Wheeler, which is unsuitable for many types of site, especially those which have little vertical stratigraphy but cover very wide areas. The open-area system was used to great effect in the influential OLD MINSTER excavations at Winchester in the 1960s. It has been found to be particularly appropriate for sites incorporating timber buildings, where it is often essential to be able to see the whole plan (e.g. the post-Roman settlement at Cheddar, see Rahtz 1979). Even highly stratified sites, such as the Romano-British settlement of Wroxeter, which would previously have been regarded as prime candidates for the grid system, have been successfully excavated with the open-area method. The grid, block or trench systems are however still sometimes preferred for certain types of site, such as BARROWS or rock shelters, where it is essential to be able to see all of the stratigraphic phases at once.

G. Bersu: 'Excavations at Little Woodbury', *PPS* 6 (1940), 30–111; A. Steensburg: *Farms and water mills in Denmark* (Copenhagen, 1952); P.A. Rahtz: *The Saxon and Medieval palaces at Cheddar* (Oxford, 1979).

IS

Opone *see* HAFUN

oppidum (pl. oppida; *Lat*: 'defended administrative centre or town') During the later La Tène period in Gaul, from the 2nd century BC, there developed a series of large regional centres, some of which Julius Caesar in his reports of campaigns in the region, referred to as 'oppida' – a label that has stuck. Many of these oppida were defended, but unlike earlier hillforts of the 2nd and early 1st millennium BC, most seem to have been permanently and densely occupied. The more complex examples seem to have acted as tribal capitals, trade and distribution centres, and are often located near significant trade routes. Caesar mentions the presence of Italian merchants in some oppida. There is also considerable evidence at sites such as MANCHING in Bavaria, Germany, for a planned street lay-out, directional trade and specialized industries. Oppida probably also functioned as centres of political power, although this is difficult to prove, and they sometimes provide evidence of the minting of coinage. Because of these different functions, oppida are often held to be in some sense 'proto-urban', although there is little evidence of the public buildings, monumental temples and memorials that Caesar would have associated with a truly urban centre.

There is a concentration of large and apparently complex sites in France and southern Germany, but a similar phenomenon is represented by sites in eastern Europe such as Staré Hradisko in Moravia and to a much lesser extent in southern Britain – the internal evidence from massively defended sites such as DANEBURY is not as impressively complex as that from Manching. It should be noted that the term oppidum has rather different meanings to different writers: for some it should only be used when there is proof that the oppidum acted as a seat of regional power, or had a mint, while others use the term in a relative sense, to indicate a larger and more complex than average settlement. Bradley (1984) provides a short critique of the use of the term in Britain.

R. Bradley: *The social foundations of prehistoric Britain* (London, 1984), 150–2; J.R. Collis: *Oppida: earliest towns north of the Alps* (Sheffield, 1991).

RJA

optical emission spectrometry (OES) Analytical technique which was one of the first to become established as a means of analysing the trace elements in artefacts made from metal, glass and pottery. Originally it required a small amount of material to be dissolved in acid, but more recently lasers have been used to vaporize small parts of the sample, making the technique essentially non-destructive. Atoms in a sample are excited by a laser beam or electrical charge. The near-ultra-violet and visible light released from them at the end of this excitation is dispersed by a quartz prism or diffraction grating and can then be analysed as a pattern of black lines on photographic film. Each element has its own characteristic wavelength, while its concentration can be estimated by the intensity of the line (measured using a densitometer). The technique can be used in provenance studies, although recent work has favoured other techniques, such as X-RAY FLUORESCENCE SPECTROMETRY above OES.

J.S. Tite: *Methods of physical examination in archaeology* (London, 1972), 260–4.

PTN

optically stimulated luminescence (OSL) Scientific dating technique, the principles of which are the same as for THERMOLUMINESCENCE DATING, but light, rather than heat, is used to stimulate the emission of the luminescence signal. OSL has been developed for use on unheated sediments exposed to sunlight prior to deposition. The disadvantage of TL for such materials is uncertainty about the degree to which the geological TL signal was removed (bleached) prior to deposition. Laboratory bleaching to determine the residual signal may over- or under-bleach relative to what actually happened in the past and thus lead to systematic error in the age estimate. Light stimulation on the other hand empties only the most bleachable traps and does so rapidly; it therefore mimics the natural exposure more closely, and samples that have received only a short natural exposure should nevertheless be datable.

Green laser light is most often used for quartz-rich sediments and it has been found that infrared can be used for feldspars. In both cases, the luminescence emission is at shorter wavelength which enables the detection system to be designed to discriminate against the stimulating wavelengths.

Because of the sensitivity of the OSL signal to light, samples must not be inadvertently exposed to light either during collection or laboratory preparation. For collection, either blocks can be cut from a sediment section or a container can be driven in; surfaces exposed to light are removed in the laboratory. The range of sediments to which OSL has been applied include LOESS, river channel and lacustrine silts, dune, beach and cover sands. The lower age limit is typically a few thousand years to provide a measurable signal and, in quartz, for the effect of recuperation (a non-radiation signal that grows in after bleaching) to be negligible. Upper age limits are determined by signal stability, saturation of the signal (i.e. no further growth with radiation dose) and radiation dose-rate (*see* THERMOLUMINESCENCE DATING). For the most common feldspar signal in fine-grained sediments, the possibility of mean life of the order of 100,000 years for the stability of the luminescence centre is still a matter of some debate.

A.G. Wintle: 'Luminescence dating of aeolian sands: an overview', *The dynamics and environmental context of aeolian sedimentary systems*, ed. K. Pye (London, 1993) 49–58; ——: 'Recent developments in optical dating of sediments', *Radiation Protection Dosimetry* 47 (1993), 627–35.

SB

oracle bones (*chia-ku(wen)*; *jiaguwen*) Term used in the archaeology of China to refer to the divinatory queries and assessed divine responses recorded on animal scapulae (SCAPULIMANCY) and turtle plastrons (PLASTROMANCY) by means of incised characters. Most texts were incised directly into the surface of the bone or carapace, but in some cases tracings with styli are applied on top of prior writings with brush and ink. Pyro-scapulimancy significantly pre-dates the SHANG era (i.e. before 2000 BC) and was practiced by the Neolithic peoples of China on the bones of various animals, consisting of the incising of actual legible text.

'Writing', in the form of isolated symbols of probably associable meanings, exists in the incised marks on ceramics of YANG-SHAO, LUNG-SHAN, CHI'I-CHIA, and other Neolithic cultures; however, it is only in Late Shang times that the earliest instances of incised divinatory queries and answers appear in pyro-scapulimancy. The queries to the ancestors and the gods cover a multitude of subjects from harvest and rainfall to hunting expeditions and

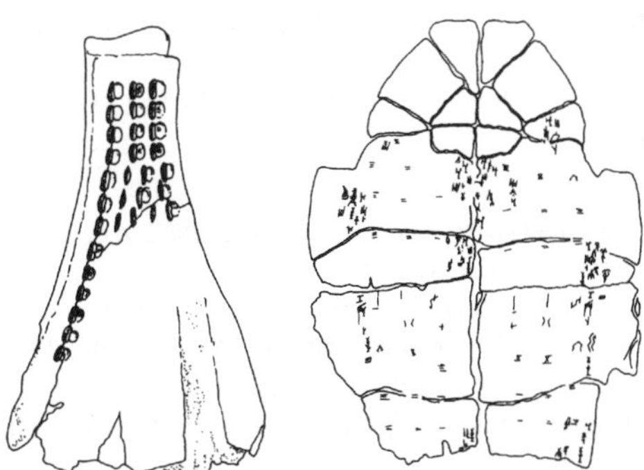

Figure 39 **'oracle bones'** A bovid shoulder blade (scapula) and a freshwater turtle under-shell (plastron) from ancient China, both incised with the queries of diviners. *Source*: G.L. Barnes: *China, Korea and Japan* (Thames and Hudson, 1993).

warfare. Even so mundane a matter as a royal toothache was the subject of oracular query, which generally manifested an appreciably advanced form of written expression. Since 1899, when inscribed oracle bones (then described as 'dragon bones') were first discovered, a vast corpus of literature has accumulated (see Serruys 1974 and Keightley 1978).

P.L.-M. Serruys: 'The language of the Shang oracle bone inscriptions', *TP* 60/1–3 (1974), 12–120; D.N. Keightley: *Sources of Shang history: The oracle-bone inscriptions of Bronze Age China* (Berkeley, 1978); Takashima-Ken'ichi: 'An evaluation of the theories concerning the Shang oracle-bone inscriptions', *Journal of International Studies* 15/16 (1988–9), 11–54.

NB

Oranian *see* IBEROMAURUSIAN

Orchomenos Mycenaean THOLOS tomb and fragmentary ruins of a Mycenaean acropolis in Boeotia, Greece. The tholos tomb, known as the 'Treasury of Minyas', is the finest outside MYCENAE. It has a diameter of *c.* 14 m, and is closely related in design to the Treasury of Atreus at Mycenae; it is probably of about the same date, soon after 1400 BC. A side-chamber preserves some of the finest Mycenaean carved stone reliefs, consisting of curvilinear and floral motifs. The nearby acropolis has yielded evidence for frescoes and large rooms – possibly indicating a Mycenaean palace complex. Heinrich Schliemann excavated at Orchomenos, and found here a distinctive wheel-made ware that he named MINYAN WARE (after the legendary King Minyas who is associated with the site).

R. Hope Simpson: *Mycenaean Greece* (New Jersey, 1981).

RJA

orientalizing Term sometimes used to describe artefacts, particularly art objects, produced outside the Ancient Near East but showing the influence of eastern civilizations or cultures. An example of an 'orientalizing' tradition is the SITULA ART produced in the sub-Alpine region in the later 1st millennium BC.

RJA

OSL *see* OPTICALLY STIMULATED LUMINESCENCE

'osteodontokeratic culture' *see* MAKAPANSGAT

otolith Minute calcareous concretion found in the inner ear of some vertebrates, especially fish. Otoliths can be recovered by fine wet sieving of archaeological deposits and are useful indicators of fish species, size of fish and even the season in which the fish were caught.

P.A. Mellars and M.R. Wilkinson: 'Fish otoliths as indicators of seasonality in prehistoric shell middens: the evidence from Oronsay (Inner Hebrides)', *PPS* 46 (1980), 19–44.

RJA

Otsuka Middle Yayoi moated settlement and associated cemetery in Yamanashi prefecture, Japan (*c*.100 BC–AD 100; *see* JAPAN 3). An area of 130 × 200 m was enclosed by a 2 m deep and up to 4 m wide fortification ditch, probably with an outer bank. Over 90 buildings were excavated, of which up to 30 were occupied contemporaneously. These were clustered into groups of a couple of large buildings and a raised floor storehouse. The 25 ditch-and-mounded graves from the associated Saikachido cemetery, 100 m southeast of the settlement, represent the burials of an elite class who resided at Otsuka.

C.M. Aikens and T. Higuchi: *The prehistory of Japan* (London, 1982), 240–1.

SK

'Oueili, Tell el- *see* UBAID

Overton Down Experimental earthwork in Wiltshire, constructed by a group of British archaeologists in 1962 as an exercise in EXPERIMENTAL ARCHAEOLOGY. Their aim was both to obtain a better understanding of the process of creating an earthwork and to find out what happened to such a monument (and various materials buried within it) through the passage of time. This was the first archaeological experiment that was designed to outlive its progenitors. The proposal was that the ditch and bank would be regularly sectioned after one year, then two years, then four years, and thereafter on a binomial progression until 128 years had passed.

The Overton Down earthwork was constructed on upper chalk on the open downs. In 1963 a second earthwork, of exactly the same proportions and design, was built on sandy acidic soil at Wareham Down. Both are linear earthworks, intended to simulate prehistoric boundaries, where the bank was set at some distance from the ditch, creating two elements rather than an integrated unit. With the advances made in scientific archaeology during the 1980s and 1990s, especially with regard to soil sciences, these earthworks have provided a wealth of invaluable data to enhance the understanding of the archaeological evidence from actual sites. The 32-year report on Overton (Bell et al. 1996) included SEM (SCANNING ELECTRON MICROSCOPE) analyses of buried materials such as wood, textiles and bone, as well as studies of soil micromorphology and chemistry.

P.A. Jewell and G.W. Dimbleby: 'The experimental earthwork on Overton Down, Wiltshire, England', *PPS* 32 (1966), 313–42; M. Bell, P.J. Fowler and S.W. Hillson: *The experimental earthwork project 1960–1992* (London, 1996).

PRE

Oxtotitlán *see* OLMEC

Oxus treasure Celebrated hoard of about 150 complete and fragmentary gold and silver objects (including figurines, bracelets and model chariots) and 1500 coins of uncertain provenance and mixed date, which appeared on the art market in about 1880, although they are said to have been discovered a few years earlier at or near Takht-i Kuwad by the Oxus river (Curtis 1989). Most of the objects have been identified stylistically as Achaemenid (4th–5th century BC), but many of the coins date as late as the 3rd century BC. Since the 'treasure' was simply sold to a British collector at Rawalpindi (now in Pakistan), its original archaeological context can now only be conjectured. It is considered likely that the dealers in Rawalpindi attempted to enhance the value of the hoard by adding other objects of different dates and provenances (such as SCYTHIAN and Egyptian). The original assemblage was perhaps part of a temple treasury (and/or a hoard valued for its precious weight) in an Achaemenian city.

O.M. Dalton: *The treasure of the Oxus* (London, 1964); J. Curtis: *Ancient Persia* (London, 1989).

IS

oxygen isotope analysis Oxygen exists in three isotopes, two of which are important in archaeology: ^{16}O and ^{18}O. The latter has a natural abundance of about 0.2%. Variations in the abundances of these isotopes can arise through physical and chemical factors which fractionate between the lighter and heavier isotopes leading to changes in their isotopic ratio. The ratio ($^{18}O/^{16}O$) is usually measured by gas source mass spectrometry on samples converted to carbon dioxide. Results are expressed in the form $\delta^{18}O$ which is the difference in the ratio in 'parts per mil' (parts per thousand) from a reference material. This is usually 'standard mean ocean water' (SMOW) with a $^{18}O/^{16}O$ ratio of 0.0020052. The $\delta^{18}O$ value may be positive, enriched in ^{18}O relative to the reference, or negative, depleted in ^{18}O. The $\delta^{18}O$ value of water is temperature-dependent and is used as a palaeotemperature indicator. Another major application of oxygen isotope measurements is in provenance studies. It has been successfully applied to Classical marble where the $\delta^{18}O$ value, in conjunction with that of CARBON ISOTOPE ANALYSIS, has been used to characterize raw material sources and provenance sculpture and building stone.

N. Herz and M. Waelkens: *Classical marble; geochemistry, technology, trade* (Dordrecht, 1988); P.J. Potts: *A handbook of silicate rock analysis* (Glasgow, 1992).

MC

oxygen isotope chronostratigraphy Method for correlating, and hence dating, deep sea sediments based on climate variations recorded in the ^{18}O values (*see* OXYGEN ISOTOPE ANALYSIS) of foraminifera with depth. Because the ocean-sedimentary record is continuous, the climatic stages identified within it are used as a global reference for terrestrial sites of the Quaternary and earlier, replacing the old Ice Age system (e.g. Mindel-Riss-Würm previously used in the Alpine regions of Europe).

The ^{18}O values of the carbonate tests of foraminifera reflect that of the surrounding waters. Fractionation (a temperature-dependent process) occurs on uptake of the oxygen, however, the greatest effect on the ^{18}O value of the foraminifera is ice volume. Temperature-dependent fractionation also occurs on evaporation and precipitation of water; the net result is that in a glacial period, because of the quantity of water locked up in the large ice masses, ocean waters have higher ^{18}O values than during interglacial periods: the difference is about 1‰. The ^{18}O value of foraminifera is therefore a climate indicator. Sediments are sampled by coring: with depth through a core, there are alternating periods of high and low ^{18}O values. Warm stages are labelled with odd numbers and cold ones with even numbers. Smaller fluctuations within these are usually given letters (e.g. 5a, 5c and 5e are warm peaks in Stage 5, while 5b and 5d are the cold troughs).

The dating of oxygen isotope records was initially achieved by the use of RADIOCARBON DATING on organic material in the top 30,000 years of the sediment core and by identification of the Brunhes-Matuyama polarity reversal at 730,000 years (*see* PALAEOMAGNETIC DATING); prior to the development of URANIUM SERIES DATING, interpolation between these assumed a constant sedimentation rate.

The timescale is now based on *orbital forcing* of climate, i.e. calculation of the effect on climate of changes in the earth's orbit with time, in turn caused by changes in gravitational pull with changing configuration of the planets. The orbital parameters are *eccentricity* (the degree to which the orbit is ellipsoidal, the period of relevance being 100,000 years), *tilt* (the angle between the equatorial plane and the orbital plane, the period of relevance being approximately 41,000 years) and *precession* (the wobble in the rotation about the earth's axis, the average period being 22,000 years). The recognition of all of these periods in the oxygen isotope record was the key factor in the acceptance that climate is controlled by changes in the earth's orbit.

Correlation with the terrestrial climatic record has been clearly demonstrated for the long LOESS sequences of China where alternating warm and cold periods are represented by PALAEOSOLS and loess layers respectively; pollen sequences in coastal sediments have also been used. For other sites, where the record is discontinuous, correlation is assumed and assignment of a particular series of layers to isotope stages depends on the particular combination of climatic indicators and age indicators found in those layers (e.g. flora, fauna, geomorphology, absolute dates).

N.J. Shackleton: 'Oxygen isotope analyses and Pleistocene temperatures re-assessed', *Nature* 215 (1967), 15–17;

—— and N.D. Opdyke: 'Oxygen isotope and palaeomagnetic stratigraphy of equatorial Pacific core V28–238: oxygen isotope temperatures and ice volumes on a 10^5 year and 10^6 year scale', *Quaternary Research* 3 (1973), 39–55; J.D. Hayes, J. Imbrie and N.J. Shackleton: 'Variations in the earth's orbit: pacemaker of the ice ages', *Science* 194 (1976) 1121–32; J. and J.Z. Imbrie: 'Modeling the climatic response of orbital variations', *Science* 207 (1980), 943–53; F.C. Bassinot et al.: 'The astronomical theory of climate change and the age of the Brunhes-Matuyama magnetic reversal', *Earth and Planetary Science Letters* 126 (1994), 91–108.

SB

Ozette Village site of the Makah Indians, situated on the Washington coast of western North America, dating to *c.* AD 1450–1950. The village was covered by catastrophic mud slides while still occupied, resulting in the preservation of wooden tools, baskets, blankets and sculpture. David Huelsbeck (1988) quantified food resources, on the basis of ethnographic analogy and actual faunal remains, in an attempt to determine whether the surpluses attested ethnographically are detectable archaeologically. Detailed spatial analyses of variations in shellfish assemblages within, between and outside houses have provided data from which inferences can be made regarding social status and resource ownership (Wessen 1988).

R.D. Daugherty and J. Friedman: 'An introduction to Ozette art', *Indian art traditions of the Northwest Coast*, ed. R.L. Carlson (Burnaby, 1983), 183–98; D.R. Huelsbeck: 'The surplus economy of the Central Northwest Coast', *Research in economic anthropology* (London, 1988), 149–78; G.C. Wessen: 'The use of shellfish resources on the Northwest Coast: the view from Ozette', *Research in economic anthropology*, ed. B.L. Isaac (London, 1988), 179–210; S.R. Samuels, ed.: *House structure and floor midden: Ozette Archaeological Research Reports 1* (Pullman, 1991).

RC

Ozieri culture Farming culture of the Late Neolithic and Eneolithic of Sardinia, identified from excavations at the cave of San Michele near Ozieri. The pottery is finely made, often slipped or burnished, and is typically decorated with impressed or incised, and sometimes filled or hatched, concentric curvilinear or geometric designs. The Ozieri culture produced schematic marble figurines (e.g. that from Senorbí) which have been compared to the famous CYCLADIC examples, as well as figurines (e.g. that from Macomer) in a contrasting 'naturalistic' style. Perhaps the most distinctive late Ozieri creations are the multi-roomed, decorated rock-cut tombs, found singly or in cemeteries, such as ANGHELU RUJU, where Ozieri pottery is found in association with bell BEAKERS.

M. Guido: *Sardinia* (London, 1963); D.H. Trump: 'The Bonu Ighinu Project and the Sardinian Neolithic', *Studies in Sardinian Archaeology* I, eds. M.S. Balmuth and R.J. Rowland, Jr. (Ann Arbor, 1984), 1–22.

RJA

P

pa Earthwork forts of varying size and complexity mainly found in the North Island of New Zealand. Some were defended food stores, whereas others have convincing evidence of intensive occupation. There are estimated to have been 6000 *pa*, most of which were constructed in the last 600 years.

G. Irwin: *Land, pa and polity* (Auckland, 1985). J. Davidson: *The prehistory of New Zealand* (Auckland, 1984).

CG

Pachacamac Site of an important oracle and centre of a major variant of the HUARI religion and art style in central coastal Peru from the Middle Horizon period to the Conquest (*c.*AD 550–1500). It became a large urban centre in the Middle Horizon (*c.*AD 550–900), dwindled to a ceremonial centre with the Huari collapse, but remained important enough for the Inca to consult the oracle and to build an *ACCLLAHUASI* and a major temple to the sun at the site.

M. Uhle: *Pachacamac* (Philadelphia, 1991) [reprint of the 1903 edition of the book with a new introduction by Izumi Shimada].

KB

Paiján The earliest cultural group identified in Peru and one of the few PALEO-INDIAN traditions to have direct association with extinct fauna (La Cumbre site). A series of inland workshop sites (about 15 km from the northern coast of Peru) show the process of fabrication of the characteristic tool, the 'Paiján point' (a long, narrow tanged point apparently used for fishing), from a block to a bifacial blank to the point itself. Other tools and faunal remains show a mixed economy based upon fishing large species, shore-line collecting and fishing, and land hunting.

C. Chauchat: *Préhistoire de la côte nord du Pérou: le Paijanien de Cupisnique* (Paris, 1993).

KB

Painted Grey Ware (PGW) Widespread ceramic type in southern Asia, found at over 450 early Iron Age sites in the Indo-Gangetic Basin between *c.*1300 and 600 BC (although the chronology is controversial, see Lal 1980). The wheel-made ceramics (mainly bowl and dish forms) are thin, extremely well-made and uniformly fired, with a variety of black-painted motifs, including swastikas, spirals, lines and circles. PGW vessels typically comprise only 7–10% of a site's total ceramics; they are associated with the appearance of iron in the Ganges basin (Lal 1984: 61) and Makhan Lal, Bal Krishen Thapar and others have suggested that the introduction of iron and PGW ceramics resulted from movement of population into the Ganges region from Iran and Central Asia (Lal 1984: 66). The inhabitants of PGW sites were small-scale agriculturalists and herders, living in riverside settlements (about 1.7–3.4 ha in size) such as Ahichhatra, ATRANJIKHERA, HASTINAPURA, Mathura and Noh. See figure 40 overleaf.

V. Tripathi: *The Painted Grey ware: an Iron Age culture of northern India* (Delhi, 1976); M. Lal: 'Date of Painted Grey Ware culture: a review' *Bulletin of the Deccan College Research Institute* 39 (1980), 65–77; ——: *Settlement history and rise of civilization in the Ganga-Yamuna Doab* (Delhi, 1984), 55–66; ——: 'The early settlement pattern of the Painted Grey Ware culture of the Ganga Valley', *Recent advances in Indo-Pacific prehistory*, ed. V.N. Misra and P. Bellwood (New Delhi, 1985), 373–81.

CS

Pai-Yüeh *see* YÜEH

Pakistan *see* ASIA, SOUTH

palaeofaeces *see* COPROLITES

Palaeolithic ('Old Stone Age') The first and longest division of the Stone Age, the Palaeolithic is essentially a technological classification starting with the products of the earliest toolmaking hominids, perhaps 2.5 million years ago, and ending with the onset of the Holocene in the 9th millennium BC and the technological changes that

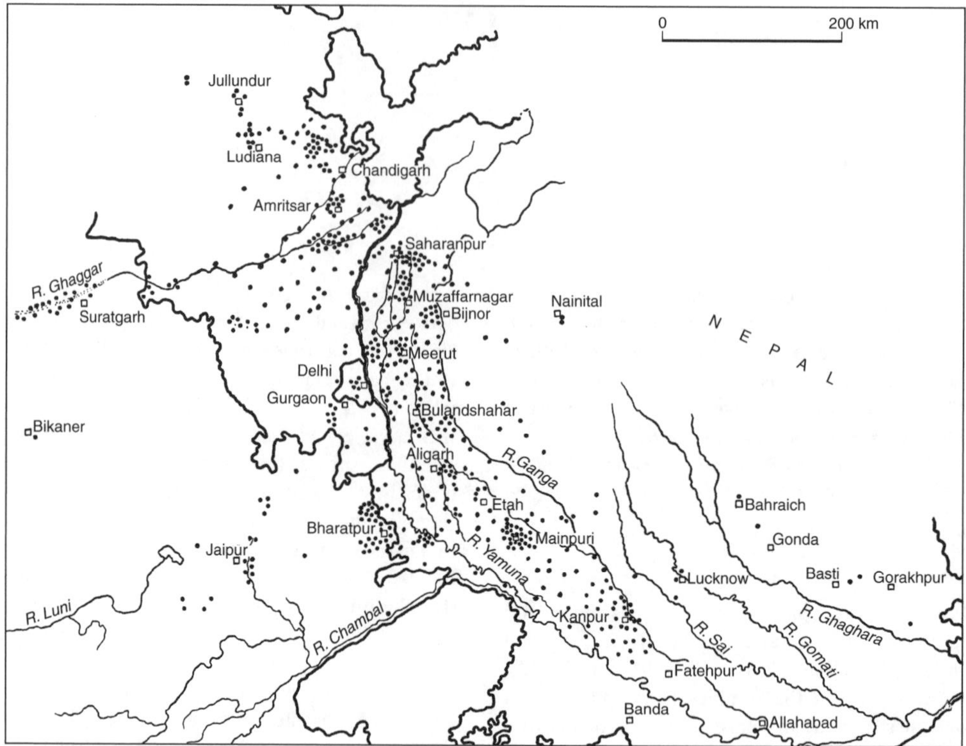

Figure 40 **Painted Grey Ware** Map showing the distribution of Painted Grey Ware in the Ganga Valley region of India. *Source*: M. Lal: 'The settlement pattern of the Painted Grey Ware culture of the Ganga valley', *Recent advances in Indo-Pacific prehistory*, ed. V.N. Misra and P. Bellwood (New Delhi, 1985), fig. 1.

characterize the succeeding MESOLITHIC period. Although originally defined with reference to stone industries alone, the term Palaeolithic came to imply a hunting and gathering economy and various cultural characteristics. Traditionally, it is divided into the Lower and Middle Palaeolithic (treated here), and the UPPER PALAEOLITHIC.

The Lower Palaeolithic begins with the first stone tools produced by hominids (found in layers classified by geologists as Early to Middle Pleistocene), from the simplest flake tools of the Oldowan industries around 2.5 million years ago to the relatively crude bifacial handaxes made from perhaps 1.5 million years ago until about 250,000 years ago. The Oldowan flake industries are associated first with *HOMO HABILIS*, and then with various early hominids that make up the story of HUMAN EVOLUTION. The later tool industries of the Lower Palaeolithic, characterized by roughly symmetrical bifacial handaxes and cleavers, seem to be linked to the appearance of *HOMO ERECTUS* and are also associated with later *Homo Sapiens*. These later industries are often grouped together and termed 'ACHEULEAN' – the term is a badge for industries of the same general level of technology, and does not imply cultural connections.

From perhaps 250,000 years ago, and particularly from after 150,000 years ago, the more advanced tool-making that involved preparation of cores and greater skills in design appeared – notably the use of the LEVALLOIS TECHNIQUE. At the same time, heavier handaxes tend to disappear from assemblages. According to traditional terminology, this technological change marks the beginning of the Middle Palaeolithic, and is closely associated with the early forms of *Homo sapiens* and especially with NEANDERTHALS (rather before 100,000 BP to 35,000 BP). A key industry of this type is the MOUSTERIAN tradition, first recognized at the French site of Le Moustier. Some archaeologists associate these more advanced tool assemblages with a shift in human capabilities, notably in terms of conceptualization (tool design, hunting strategy, perhaps shelter construction, burial of the dead). Increasingly, however, the distinction between the Middle and Lower Palaeolithic is not thought to be very clear or useful, and archaeologists have begun to refer instead to an Early Palaeolithic (i.e. Lower and Middle Palaeolithic combined).

In most accounts, a sharp distinction is still drawn between this Early Palaeolithic and the Later or UPPER PALAEOLITHIC – a period in which a much wider range of cultural artefacts, including complex CAVE ART, began to be produced. This exponential growth in human culture, and the emergence and proliferation of distinct cultural assemblages expressed through tools and other cultural artefacts, has been linked by some scholars to the final and most significant step in the evolution of the human mind (Mithen 1996).

C. Gamble: *The Palaeolithic settlement of Europe* (Cambridge, 1986); P. Allsworth-Jones: *The Szeletian and the transition from Middle to Upper Palaeolithic in Central Europe* (Oxford, 1986); J.K. Kozłowski: 'The transition from the Middle to the early Upper Palaeolithic in Central Europe and the Balkans', *The early Upper Palaeolithic*, ed. J.F. Hoffecker and C.A. Wolf, BAR IS 437 (Oxford, 1988), 193–237; P. Mellars and C. Stringer, eds: *The human revolution* (Edinburgh, 1989); E. Trinkhaus, ed.: *The emergence of modern humans* (Cambridge, 1989); N. Barton et al., eds: *The Late Glacial in North-west Europe: human adaption and environmental change at the end of the Pleistocene* (London, 1992); T. Akazawa et al., eds: *The evolution and dispersal of modern humans in Asia* (Tokyo, 1992); H.L. Dibble and P. Mellars: *The middle Palaeolithic: adaption, behaviour and variability* (Philadelphia, 1992); C. Gamble: *Timewalkers: the prehistory of global colonisation* (Stroud, 1993); K.R. Gibson and T. Ingold: *Tools, language and cognition in human evolution* (Cambridge, 1993); B. Hayden: 'The cultural capacities of Neanderthals: a review and re-evaluation', *Journal of Human Evolution* 24 (1993), 113–46; C. Stringer and C. Gamble: *In search of the Neanderthals* (London, 1993); H. Knecht et al., eds: *Before Lascaux: the complex record of the early Upper Palaeolithic* (Boca Raton, 1993); M.H. Nitecki and C.V. Nitecki: *Origins of anatomically modern humans* (New York, 1994); S. Kuhn: *Mousterian lithic technology* (Princeton, 1995); S. Mithen: *The prehistory of the mind: a search for the origins of art, religion and science* (London, 1996).

RJA

palaeomagnetic dating Scientific dating technique based on changes in the intensity and direction of the earth's magnetic field with time; changes that are recorded in a range of materials (e.g. lava flows, lake sediments etc.). The physical principles of palaeomagnetic dating and ARCHAEOMAGNETIC DATING are the same: the difference lies only in the types of material studied and time scale of application. Key areas of interaction are the establishment of regional reference curves of directional measurements versus time and the global applicability of polarity changes resulting from a reversal in the main dipole of the earth's magnetic field.

In periods of normal polarity, a compass needle points northwards; in periods of reversed polarity it points southwards. The major 'recent' periods, or 'chrons', are Brunhes (normal polarity, from the present back to about 0.78 million years), Matuyama (reversed polarity, 0.78 to 2.48 million years) and Gauss (normal polarity, 2.48 to 3.40 million years). Within these phases are shorter 'subchrons': Blake (reversed, 104–7 thousand years), Jaramillo (normal 0.90–0.97 million years), Olduvai (normal, 1.67–1.87 million years, (normal, 2.01–2.04 million years) and Réunion II (normal 2.12–2.14 million years). All of these chrons and subchrons are global events, in contrast to localized polarity reversals such as Laschamp-Olby (30–45,000 years). The time-scale for the boundaries between these is largely based on POTASSIUM-ARGON dating of volcanic minerals which record the field direction on cooling.

D.H. Tarling: *Palaeomagnetism* (London and New York, 1983); F.C. Bassinot et al.: 'The astronomical theory of climate change and the age of the Brunhes-Matuyama magnetic reversal', *Earth and Planetary Science Letters* 126 (1994), 91–108.

SB

palaeosols Type of buried or fossil soil which can yield chronological and palaeoenvironmental information. The study of the formation and nature of palaeosols is known as palaeopedology.

Palenque LOWLAND MAYA site of the Classic period (*c.* AD 300–900) in Chiapas, Mexico, known for its beautiful buildings and sculpture. Dynastic histories and portraits of rulers were carved on stone panels on temples and palaces, rather than on stelae as elsewhere in the lowlands. The tomb of the ruler Pacal, who died in AD 683, underlies the Temple of the Inscriptions and is entered through a stairway that descends through the centre of the pyramid construction, a rare feature in Maya construction.

M.G. Robertson: *The sculpture of Palenque I: The Temple of the Inscriptions* (Princeton, 1983); L. Schele: 'Architectural development and political history of Palenque'. *City-states of the Maya: art and architecture*, ed. E.P. Benson (Denver, 1986) 110–38.

PRI

Paleo-Arctic tradition Lithic tradition of the earliest well-documented human occupation of the North American Arctic, between 8000 and 5000 BC. The culture is only known from lithic artefacts, especially microblades and small bifaces, and the most diagnostic artefacts are wedge-shaped microcores. The sites with evidence of the tradition, such as ONION PORTAGE, are found in Alaska; they are all terrestrial (as opposed to marine) sites, but this may simply be a result of rising sea levels drowning the coastal sites. There is presently little evidence to link the Paleo-Arctic tradition to later occupations in the Arctic, although it seems possible that manifestations in southwestern Alaska, especially the KODIAK TRADITION, may be derived from the Paleo-Arctic tradition.

D.E. Dumond: *The Eskimos and Aleuts* (London, 1987).

RP

Paleoindian Term used to describe the earliest period of prehistoric settlement in the Americas, extending from the arrival of the first inhabitants (before 10,000 BC) to the beginning of the Archaic period (*c.*8000 BC). The Paleoindians were nomadic and semi-nomadic hunting and gathering peoples who entered North America via the Bering Straits and moved south through the many different environments of the Americas, reaching southern Chile by *c.*12,000 BC (*see* MONTE VERDE). The North American Paleoindian period comprises three successive cultural traditions: LLANO, FOLSOM and PLANO. Paleoindian cultures are extremely varied, although all initially depended upon hunting of now-extinct species, such as mammoth, giant sloth and bison. There has in the past been over-emphasis by scholars upon big-game hunting, given that contemporary studies show foraging for plants and shoreline gathering and fishing to have been just as important among many of these earliest Americans, leading to an early invention of agriculture in areas where sedentism and foraging economies were earliest established (LAS VEGAS). Many Early Paleoindian groups manufactured fluted Clovis or Folsom projectile points, while lanceolate forms like Agate Basin and Eden were made by later groups on the Great Plains.

T.D. Dillehay and D.J. Meltzer: *The first Americans: search and research* (Ann Arbor, Boston and London, 1991); B. Lepper and D. Meltzer: 'Late Pleistocene human occupations of the Eastern United States', *Clovis: origins and adaptations*, ed. R. Bonnichsen and K. Turnmire (Corvallis, 1991), 175–84; D. Stanford: 'Clovis origins and adaptations: an introductory perspective', *Clovis: origins and adaptations*, ed. R. Bonnichsen and K. Turnmire (Corvallis, 1991), 1–13; T.D. Dillehay et al.: 'Earliest hunters and gatherers of South America', *JWP* 6/2 (1992), 145–204.

KB/RJE

Palliser Bay Situated at the south end of the North Island of New Zealand, the bay contains a series of sites ranging from early settlements (*c.*800 BP), with gardens attached, to burials at Washpool that reveal signs of dietary stress. A further feature of the sites is evidence for environmental degradation of both land and marine environments, caused by soil erosion through vegetation clearance.

B.F. and H.M. Leach, eds: *Prehistoric man in Palliser Bay* (Wellington, 1979); J. Davidson: *The prehistory of New Zealand* (Auckland, 1984), 39–41, 53–55, 166–7.

CG

pan-grave culture The term 'pan-grave' refers to an unusual type of shallow circular inhumation found at a number of small cemetery sites (typically consisting of up to a hundred burials) between Deir Rifeh in Upper Egypt and Tushka in Lower Nubia during the late Middle Kingdom and 2nd Intermediate Period (*c.*1800–1550 BC). The human remains and assemblages excavated at pan-grave cemeteries such as Balabish and Mostagedda – including distinctive black-topped or incised pottery bowls, mother of pearl bracelets, the skulls and horns of sheep, ox and gazelle, and various weapons – comprise a material culture clearly distinct from the two more widespread Nubian cultures of the period, C GROUP and KERMA. In addition pottery apparently of a pan-grave style has been found at Egyptian settlements in the north (e.g. EL-LAHUN and ABYDOS) and at forts further to the south (e.g. MIRGISSA and Quban). These finds perhaps lend support to suggestions that the pan-grave people, if they are indeed a distinct ethnic group, are to be identified with the 'Medjay', a people of the Eastern Desert, known only from texts, who often served as mercenaries in the Egyptian army.

M. Bietak: *Ausgrabungen in Sayala-Nubien 1961–1965. Denkmäler der C-Gruppe und der Pan-Gräber-Kultur* (Vienna, 1966); E. Strouhal and J. Jungwirth: 'Anthropological problems of the Middle Empire and Late Roman Sayala', *Mitteilungen der Anthropologischen Gesellschaft in Wien* 101 (1971), 10–23; B.J. Kemp: 'Old Kingdom, Middle Kingdom and Second Intermediate Period', *Ancient Egypt: a social history*, ed. B.G. Trigger et al. (Cambridge, 1983), 71–182 (169–71); K. Sadr: 'The Medjay in southern Atbai', *Archéologie du Nil Moyen* 4 (1990), 63–86.

IS

P'an-lung-ch'eng (Panlongcheng) Important site of the SHANG period (*c.*2000–1122 BC) located near the village, She-k'ou, Huang-p'i-hsien in the province of Hu-pei, China. It comprises a walled enclosure 290 × 260 m with cemeteries on three sides (Lou-tzu-wan, Yang-chia-wan, and Li-chia-tsui). The enclosure walls are built of *hang-t'u* layers and the moat surrounding the site was apparently 10 m wide. Within the walls was a large *hang-t'u* platform (60 × 10 m) upon which large rectangular houses were built. One of the houses consisted of a hall 34 × 6 m in area, with four inner divisions surrounded by a long verandah at the edges of which were found 43 postholes probably indicating the supports of a lean-to roof. Of the three cemetery areas, the richest burials excavated are those in the Li-chia-tsui locus, comprising pit tombs with wooden chambers (elaborately carved and painted in lacquer on the exterior) and coffins. Among the several burials reported to date, were bronze, jade, wooden and ceramic artefacts.

R.W. Bagley: 'P'an-lung-ch'eng: a Shang city in Hupei', *Artibus Asiae* 39 (1977), 165–219; Chang Kwang-chih; *Shang civilization* (New Haven, 1980), 298–305; An Chih-huai: 'The Shang city at Cheng-chou and related problems', *Studies of Shang archaeology*, ed. Chang Kwang-chih (New Haven, 1986), 28, 35–8, 71.

NB

Pan-p'o (Banpo) *see* YANG-SHAO

Papua New Guinea *see* OCEANIA 2

papyrus Material manufactured from the pith of the papyrus plant (*Papyrus cyperus*) in ancient Egypt, which was used as a writing surface from at least as early as the 1st dynasty (*c.*3000–2770 BC). Until the widespread adoption of parchment (4th century AD) and linen paper (7th century AD), Egyptian papyrus was employed throughout the Roman empire.

M.L. Bierbrier, ed.: *Papyrus: structure and usage* (London, 1986); R. Parkinson and S. Quirke: *Papyrus* (London, 1995).

IS

Paracas Important early culture of the Andes region. The burials found on the Paracas Peninsula of southern Peru are justly famous for the elaborately embroidered textiles which envelop the dead. Despite their fame, however, there has been relatively little scientific study of the burials since the initial excavations of Tello and Mejia Xesspe in the 1920s. That the burials pertain to the very end of the Early Horizon (*c.*400 BC) has been fixed by other investigations, but knowledge regarding most aspects of the burials and the societies that made them is very incomplete.

Paracas mummies and textiles have been known since 1911, but most studies regarding them have been concerned with unlineal stylistic chronologies and/or considerations of textile iconography. These investigations have generally ignored context, save for the general provenance of south coast, Paracas culture. Studies by Anne Paul, using each excavated MUMMY BUNDLE itself as a single analytical unit have added immeasurably to our knowledge of Paracas culture. Her studies show that the very different Linear and Block Colour styles – the former depicting a human/feline/bird deity (the so-called 'Oculate Being') in a geometric manner, and the latter depicting realistic figures of supernatural figures, humans dressed as supernaturals, animals and objects – are contemporary and, presumably, intended for different uses. Experimental studies of how long embroideries take to produce (using a skilled embroideress), comparing these data to the amounts of clothing and the quantities of decoration represented in the textiles of each bundle, have resulted in a considerably more sophisticated understanding of wealth in this ancient society (since the bundles vary immensely in the number and quality of textiles). Paul's work also bolsters ideas that in Peru time equalled wealth (i.e. the more time spent on fabrication of an object, the more value it had).

A. Paul and S. Niles: 'Identifying hands at work on a Paracas mantle', *Textile Museum Journal* 25 (1985), 5–15; A. Paul: *Paracas ritual attire: symbols of authority in ancient Peru* (Norman, 1990); ——: *Paracas: art and architecture: object and context in South Coastal Peru* (Ames, 1991).

KB

paradigm Conceptual framework or canon of scientific practice, forming the context for a particular set of theoretical conditions and objectives, examples of which in archaeology arguably include the CULTURE-HISTORICAL and the various POST-PROCESSUAL approaches. The view of science set out by Thomas Kuhn (1962) suggests that different 'research paradigms', e.g. STRUCTURALIST or MARXIST ARCHAEOLOGY, are each sustained and controlled by a 'research community'. Kuhn argues, however, that these paradigms cannot be compared with one another, since they are each characterized by a completely different vocabulary, frame of reference and viewpoint. He not only makes a clear distinction between paradigm and theory, the latter being a subset of the former, but also proposes that all theories are affected by the subjective paradigm (or 'world-view') within which they were created, therefore no theory can claim to be truly objective.

In 1968, David Clarke described archaeological theory before New Archaeology as 'pre-paradigmatic' in that it was too undisciplined and incoherent to constitute any sequence of Kuhnian research paradigms. Preucel and Hodder (1996: 4) take this a stage further by making the point that: 'While we . . . agree that our understanding of the archaeological past has dramatically increased after over a century of research, we are concerned that this seems to imply that all of our theories have been equally progressive and that culture history has somehow been superseded or that processual is being replaced by post-processual archaeology'.

E.L. Sterud (1973), on the other hand, views the various phases in the history of archaeology as an evolutionary sequence of 'scientific revolutions' created by innovative scholars such as Oscar Montelius, Gordon Childe and Lewis Binford. Bruce Trigger (1989: 5) suggests that there *was* a sequence of major paradigms between the mid-18th and mid-20th centuries (e.g. ANTIQUARIAN, CULTURE-HISTORICAL and FUNCTIONALIST) but that these were implicit and unconsciously held positions, as opposed to the more self-conscious and polemical paradigms of the late 20th century (e.g. CONTEXTUAL ARCHAEOLOGY or POST-STRUCTURALIST ARCHAEOLOGY).

T.S. Kuhn: *The structure of scientific revolutions*, (Chicago, 1962) [2nd edn 1970]; D.L. Clarke: *Analytical archaeology* (London, 1968); E.L. Sterud: 'A paradigmatic view of prehistory', *The explanation of cultural change: models in prehistory*, ed. A.C. Renfrew (Cambridge, 1973), 3–17; D.J. Meltzer: 'Paradigms and the nature of change in American archaeology', *AA* 44 (1979), 644–57; L.R. Binford and J.A. Sabloff: 'Paradigms, systematics and archaeology', *JAR* 38 (1982), 137–53; B.G. Trigger: *A history of archaeological thought* (Cambridge, 1989) 4–12; R.W. Preucel and I. Hodder, eds: *Contemporary archaeology in theory: a reader* (Oxford, 1996).

IS

parameter estimation Branch of statistics concerned with making the best possible estimates of the parameters of a STATISTICAL DISTRIBUTION, e.g. the mean date of a RADIOCARBON determination, on the basis of DATA from a SAMPLE. Such estimates may be given in the form of a single value (point estimates, e.g. 2000 BP) or ranges (interval estimates, e.g. 2000 ± 80 BP). The latter are usually given as CONFIDENCE INTERVALS; for point estimates their PRECISION is of key importance.

J.E. Doran and F.R. Hodson: *Mathematics and computers in archaeology* (Edinburgh, 1975), 42–51; C.R. Orton: *Mathematics in archaeology* (Glasgow, 1980), 90–4; S. Shennan: *Quantifying archaeology* (Edinburgh, 1988), 301–13.

CO

parchmarks *see* AERIAL ARCHAEOLOGY; CROPMARKS

parietal art Term used to describe art executed on rock walls, usually within caves or rockshelters (from the French *pariétal*, itself derived from the Latin *paries* or wall), and especially Palaeolithic CAVE ART.

Parthians (Parthava: 'mounted warrior') From *c*.250 BC to AD 224, a large area of the ancient Near East was dominated by the Parthians. They first appear in the mid-1st millennium BC as the inhabitants of a province of the Seleucid empire to the east of the Caspian Sea. In the mid-3rd century BC the Parthian rulers Arsaces and Tiridates conquered large areas to the north of the modern Iranian border, establishing the first of a series of capitals at Nysa (in Turkmenistan), but it was Mithridates I who took advantage of the ailing fortunes of the Seleucid empire to push southwards in the mid-2nd century BC, establishing a military camp on the opposite side of the Tigris from Seleucia; this camp was to be the site of the final Parthian capital, Ctesiphon. The Parthian (or Arsacid) dynasty established cities at HATRA, Dura-Europus, Firuzabad and Takht-i Sulaiman, using a style of architecture featuring the *iwan* and employing paintings and relief decoration characterized principally by their 'frontality'.

Many aspects of Parthian material culture (e.g. styles of pottery, small objects and burial practices) vary widely from one region to another. The tendency for 19th-century excavators to focus on Mesopotamia and Susiana resulted in the accidental discovery of many Parthian and Sasanian remains in the process. Much is therefore known about the Parthians from such Mesopotamian sites as NINEVEH and URUK, rather than from sites in the original Parthian heartland.

O. Reuther: *Die Ausgrabungen der Deutschen Ktesiphon-*

Expedition (Berlin, 1930); R. Ghirshman: *Parthes et Sassanides* (Paris, 1962); M.A. Colledge: *The Parthians* (London, 1968); N.C. Debevoise: *A political history of Parthia* (Chicago, 1938, repr. 1969); E. Mathiesen: *Sculpture in the Parthian empire*, 2 vols (Aarhus, 1992).
IS

particle induced gamma-ray emission (PIGME) Non-destructive prompt nuclear analysis technique using a particle beam, usually of protons, to excite gamma-ray emission in materials. The technique, which is useful for light element analysis, is often used in conjunction with PARTICLE INDUCED X-RAY EMISSION (PIXE) since both require similar particle sources.

J.R. Bird, P. Duerden and D.J. Wilson: 'Ion beam techniques in archaeology and the arts', *Nuclear Science Applications* 1 (1983) 357–526.
MC

particle induced X-ray emission (PIXE) Non-destructive technique for multi-element chemical analysis related to X-RAY FLUORESCENCE which makes use of a particle beam. Instead of using an X-ray source to stimulate fluorescence, a beam of particles is used, usually protons, generated by a cyclotron or similar source and directed at the specimen. The fluorescent X-rays produced are detected using an energy dispersive spectrometer. The technique can be used to analyse artefacts *in situ* but, like XRF, only of the surface. Detection limits are lower than conventional EDXRF and the beam may be focused to analyse small areas (about 1 μm). The technique has been applied to metals, ceramics and lithics.

S.J. Fleming and C.P. Swann: 'The application of PIXE spectrometry to bronze analysis', *Masca Journal* 3 (1985), 142–9.
MC

Pasargadae *see* PERSIA

Pa-Shu (Ba-Shu) Two ancient states of the 1st millennium BC on the western periphery of China, in and around present-day Ssu-ch'uan but also extending into parts of Hu-pei and Kuei-chou. Shu and Pa only rarely occur in the traditional texts, and they are generally mentioned together; there does not seem to be any marked cultural distinction between them. Like many other leaders in these peripheral 'barbarian' regions, the rulers of Shu adopted the Chinese title of 'king' and ascribed to themselves an appropriate lineage (*see* CHINA 2). The two states were extinguished by CH'IN in 316 BC.

N. Barnard and Satö Tamotsu: *Metallurgical remains of ancient China* (Tokyo, 1975); Li Hsueh-ch'in: *Eastern Zhou and Qin civilizations*, trans. Chang Kwang-chih (New Haven, 1985); N. Barnard: 'Bronze casting technology in the peripheral "barbarian" regions', *BMM* 12 (1987), 3–37.
NB

Paso de la Amada Early Formative village on the Pacific coastal plain of Chiapas, Mexico, dating to *c.*1700–1200 BC. It has provided evidence of early sedentism and social ranking that predates the OLMEC florescence.

J.F. Ceja Tenorio: *Paso de la Amada: an early Preclassic site in the Soconusco, Chiapas, Mexico*, Papers of the New World Archaeological Foundation 49 (Provo, 1985).
PRI

passage grave One of the two main types of Neolithic chambered tomb (the other being the GALLERY GRAVE), defined by a well-differentiated passage – typically about one metre wide and just under a metre tall – leading through a covering mound or cairn to a taller and broader chamber. The chamber, which sometimes has side-chambers, may be constructed of megaliths, drystone, or both; the tomb is usually covered by a circular mound, which may be ringed with kerbstones. Passage graves occur particularly in the Iberian Peninsula, Brittany (where the earliest radiocarbon dates, of before 4500 BC, have been recorded), Wales (e.g. BRYN CELLI DDU), Scotland (notably the MAES HOWE group in the Orkneys) and Ireland. Perhaps the most impressive examples are those of the BOYNE VALLEY, which are decorated with of the megalithic art that tends to be associated with passage graves.
RJA

pastoralism Mode of subsistence consisting of the rearing of livestock (usually cattle, sheep or goats) and a process of constant movement between two or more different areas of pasture. In some cases, pastoralism is adopted as only one part of an agriculturally-based, semi-sedentary culture, while in other, more extreme cases, a wholly nomadic lifestyle is adopted. *For further discussion and bibliography see* NOMADS *and* PASTORAL NEOLITHIC.

W. Goldschmidt: 'A general model for pastoral social systems', *Pastoral production and society*, Proceedings of the international meeting on nomadic pastoralism, Paris, 1–3 December 1976, ed. L'équpe écologie (Cambridge,

1979), 15–29; R. Cribb: 'Greener pastures: mobility, migration and the pastoral mode of subsistence', *Production Pastorale et Société* 14 (1984), 11–46.
IS

Pastoral Neolithic Currently fashionable term used to summarize the pre-Iron Age East African cultures with pottery and other advanced technological features of the final millennia BC in the Eastern Rift Valley, flanking highlands and adjacent plains of Kenya and northern Tanzania. The Pastoral Neolithic comprises the former 'Gumban' and 'stone bowl' cultures (names now redundant), as well as the ELMENTEITAN (late in the sequence and restricted geographically) and later facies of the 'KENYA CAPSIAN' (or 'EBURRAN'). It should be noted, however, that the criteria for using the term 'Neolithic' – whether technological or economic – have not been clearly agreed in sub-Saharan Africa, and some archaeologists prefer to avoid the label altogether.

Narosura, a Pastoral Neolithic site in the Kenyan highlands, west of the Rift Valley on the Loita plains, is situated beside a small river where cattle-keepers camped or congregated seasonally. Radiocarbon dating and the study of comparative archaeological evidence (such as the types of ceramics and stone bowls) suggest that Narosura was occupied by *c.*3000 BP, a full millennium before the inception of the local Iron Age. Together with Tunnel Rockshelter further north, it has produced the best dated evidence for early pastoralism in the East African highlands. The lithic industry seems to derive from the KENYA CAPSIAN tradition.

The most revealing of several 'PASTORAL NEOLITHIC' sites in the Lemek valley on the high grasslands of the eastern Mara plains in south-western Kenya is Ngamuriak, which was excavated by Peter Robertshaw and the British Institute in Eastern Africa in the 1980s, and is assigned to the ELMENTEITAN tradition of about 2000 years ago more or less, shortly before the Iron Age. Ngamuriak's importance lies in the discovery of structural remains, which are very rare for this period in East Africa. Attempts have been made to understand the nature of the settlement, its pastoral economy and herding strategy, by spatial analytical methods and detailed finds studies, including Fiona Marshall's faunal analyses (Robertshaw 1990).

S. Cole: *The Prehistory of East Africa* (New York, 1963), 274–5; K. Odner: 'Excavations at Narosura, a stone bowl site', *Azania* 7 (1972), 25–92; J.R.F. Bower et al.: 'Later Stone Age/Pastoral "Neolithic" in Central Kenya,' *Azania* 11 (1977), 119–46; D.W. Phillipson: *The later prehistory of Eastern and Southern Africa* (London, 1977); D.P. Collett and P.T. Robertshaw: 'Dating the Pastoral Neolithic of East Africa', *AAR* 1 (1983), 57–74; S.H. Ambrose: 'The introduction of pastoral adaptations to the highlands of East Africa', *From hunters to farmers; the causes and consequences of food production in Africa*, ed. J.D. Clark and S.A. Brandt (Berkeley, 1984), 212–39; P.T. Robertshaw: *Early pastoralists in south-western Kenya* (Nairobi, 1990).
JS

Pataliputra *see* MAURYAN PERIOD

Patayan Poorly known prehistoric culture of the American Southwest dating to *c.*AD 800–1540. The Patayan practised floodwater farming along the lower Colorado River and hunting and gathering in the surrounding desert. They are thought to have been ancestral to Yuman-speaking groups.

R.H. McGuire and M.B. Schiffer, eds: *Hohokam and Patayan* (New York, 1982).
JJR

patch/patch-use model *see* FORAGING THEORY

Paviland Site of a cave known as the Goat's Hole on the Gower Peninsula of Wales, which has yielded an Upper Palaeolithic (possibly AURIGNACIAN) burial and an important collection of tools. The original excavator, William Buckland in 1823, believed the ruddle-stained partial skeleton to be that of a woman, and it became famous as the 'Red Lady of Paviland'. In fact, the remains are those of a young man, who was buried with ivory rods, ivory arm rings and, possibly, the skull of a mammoth. Although the dating is uncertain, it is probably the earliest known formal burial in Britain, dating to before 20,000 and 25,000 years ago. The tool typology suggests the cave was occupied as early as the MOUSTERIAN.

R.M. Jacobi: 'The upper Palaeolithic in Britain, with special reference to Wales', *Culture and environment in prehistoric Wales*, ed. J.A. Taylor, BAR BS 76 (Oxford, 1980), 15–99.
RJA

Pazyryk Group of five large barrows in the eastern Altai Mountains, Gorno-Altai Republic (southern Siberia), constructed for the elite of the local SCYTHIAN-related nomadic group in the 5th–4th centuries BC. Discovered by S.I. Rudenko in 1924, and excavated by him in 1929 and 1947–9, the earthern mounds were covered by cairns of rocks, under which a lens of frozen soil formed soon after the interments. Due to this permanent refrigeration, organic matter such as objects of wood, leather, fur and textiles – as well as the mummified bodies of humans and horses – were uniquely preserved. The rectangular tomb-shafts under the barrows, oriented east-west, contained human burials in a log chamber, with horse burials in the northern part of the shaft. The finds include a four-wheeled carriage, a large felt carpet, and various art objects.

S.I. Rudenko: *Frozen tombs of Siberia* (London, 1970).

PD

PCA *see* PRINCIPAL COMPONENTS ANALYSIS

Pebble Tool Tradition The basal cultural tradition of the Northwest Coast of North America north of the Strait of Juan de Fuca, which is defined on the basis of the co-occurrence of unifacial pebble tools, leaf-shaped bifaces, and simple flaked stone tools (Carlson 1983). The earliest dated component (7700 BC) was excavated in the lowest 30 cm of stratigraphy at NAMU. At one time it was thought that assemblages of pebble tools without bifaces constituted an early part of the tradition pre-dating the Wisconsin glaciation (Borden 1969), but pedological work and radiocarbon dating have proved this incorrect (Haley 1987). The Pebble Tool Tradition is centred on the territory occupied by Salishan and Wakashan speakers and may represent the material culture of their ancestors.

C.E. Borden: 'Early population movements from Asia into western North America', *Syesis* 2/1–2 (1969), 1–13; S.D. Haley: *The Pasika Complex cobble reduction strategies on the Northwest Coast*, Ph.D. thesis, Department of Archaeology, Simon Fraser University (Burnaby, 1987); R.L. Carlson: 'The Far West', *Early man in the New World*, ed. R.S. Shutler (Beverley Hills, 1983), 73–96; ——: 'Cultural antecedents', *Handbook of North American Indians* VII, ed. W. Suttles (Washington DC, 1990), 60–9.

RC

Pech de l'Azé Palaeolithic cave and shelter sites situated 2 km north of the Dordogne valley in France, which, when excavated by François Bordes in the 1950s, yielded a classic sequence of ACHEULEAN and MOUSTERIAN deposits. The careful study of sediments and pollen allowed the evidence of the lithic industries (Acheulean type, Typical Mousterian, Denticulate Mousterian and Ferrassie Mousterian) to be associated with a sequence of climatic changes.

F. Bordes: *A tale of two caves* (New York, 1972); Laville et al.: *Rock shelters of the Périgord: geological stratigraphy and archaeological succession* (New York, 1980); R. Grün et al.: 'ESR chronology of a 100,000-year archaeological sequence at Pech de I'Azé II, France', *Antiquity* 65 (1991), 544–51.

RJA

Pech-Merle Large and beautifully preserved Upper Palaeolithic painted cave in Lot, France. The paintings and engravings include mammoth, bison, horses, aurochs and deer, and some quite schematic representations of humans, as well as complicated patterns of dots and hand stencils. The main gallery contains a famous frieze of black outline drawings of mammoth, bison, horses and aurochs which seem to form a composition, and which could conceivably have been executed in a single painting session by one artist. There is also a collection of finger-tracings; these are largely indecipherable but include mammoth and a few female outlines. The most striking frieze at Pech-Merle shows two spotted horses with disproportionately small heads, bordered by stencilled hands. Dating the art is difficult, but it may have been created in three or four main phases between perhaps 20,000 BC and 14,000 BC; the spotted horses are thought to be relatively early.

A. Lemozi: *La grotte-temple du Pech-Merle: un nouveau sanctuaire préhistorique* (Paris, 1929); M. Lorblanchet: 'Les dessins noirs du Pech-Merle', *XXIe Congrés Préhistorique de France* (Montauban, 1981), I, 178–207.

RJA

Pedra Furada One of many PALEOINDIAN rockshelter sites in the Minas Gerais region of Brazil, it is distinguished by a claim of extreme antiquity (30,000+ years ago). However, the lithics and the remains of wall paintings seem to pertain to a considerably later period (*c*.6000–5000 BC, and there remain unresolved problems with the context of the radiocarbon dates.

N. Guidon and G. Delibrias: 'C-14 dates point to man in the Americas 32,000 years ago', *Nature* 321 (1986), 769–71; T.D. Dillehay et al.: 'Earliest hunters and gatherers of South America', *JWP* 6/2 (1992), 145–204.

KB

peer polity interaction Term coined by the British archaeologist Colin Renfrew to refer to the tendency for regional groups of polities (small-scale, independent cultural entities) to experience similar organizational and cultural transformations roughly simultaneously, as a result of the polities' interaction with one another. This interaction might take numerous forms, ranging from comparatively overt practices such as trade and warfare to the less concrete processes of information exchange and competition. The concept of peer polity interaction has been applied to a number of different case-studies, such as Aegean city-states and islands (Renfrew and Wagstaff 1982; Renfrew and Cherry 1986), HOPEWELLIAN settlements and Iron-Age chiefdoms. Shanks and Tilly (1987), however, argue that – like other strands of the area of theory that they call 'FUNCTIONALIST social archaeology' – studies of peer polity interaction have tended to be concerned with social *systems* (i.e. patterning and organization) without reaching any real understanding of social *structures* (the 'rules and concepts which give meaning to the system').

C. Renfrew and M. Wagstaff, eds: *An island polity: the archaeology of exploitation in Melos* (Cambridge, 1982), 264–90; A.C. Renfrew and J. Cherry, eds: *Peer polity interaction and socio-political change* (Cambridge, 1986); M. Shanks and C. Tilley: *Social theory and archaeology* (Cambridge, 1987), 41–2, 51–3.

IS

Peiligang *see* P'EI-LI-KANG

P'ei-li-kang (Peiligang) Neolithic culture dating to *c*.6500–5000 BC and related to the TZ'U-SHAN culture. Named after the type-site, in Hsin-cheng-hsien, province of Ho-nan, China, it is the most extensively excavated of a growing number of pre-YANG-SHAO sites of this recently recognized cultural horizon, and P'ei-li-kang is perhaps the term that should be applied to several other cultures (including Tz'u-shan), all datable, on the basis of calibrated radiocarbon assessments, to the range 6500–5000 BC, and with distinctive ceramic types and many features in common. The pottery was entirely hand-made, mostly of a coarse, sandy paste, with firing temperatures ranging from 700 to 960°C. The surfaces of the vessels were mainly plain, with some decoration (cord-marks, comb-marks, appliqués, incisions, and press-and-pick designs).

Chang Kwang-chih: *The archaeology of ancient China*, 4th edn (New Haven, 1986), 87–95.

NB

'Peking man' *see* CHOUKOUTIEN

Pemba *see* SWAHILI HARBOUR TOWNS

Pender Canal Multi-component village site (*c*.3000 BC–AD 1500) on Pender Island off the mouth of the Fraser River in British Columbia. Excavation was undertaken to test Kroeber's (1939) model that Northwest Coast culture developed in the protected Gulf Islands. The project showed that complex culture with woodworking, sophisticated art, social ranking, memorial 'potlatch', use of masks, and SHAMANISM developed there from extant maritime-based culture between 2000 and 1500 BC. Since the art at Pender Canal is intellectually appealing, complicated and cultured, it probably constitutes evidence (through ETHNOGRAPHIC ANALOGY) for the existence of beliefs in spirit power, shamanism and social ranking. Stable CARBON ISOTOPE ANALYSIS (Chisholm 1986) demonstrated an overwhelmingly marine diet throughout the sequence, the chronological phases of which are supported by 45 radiocarbon dates, including 27 using ACCELERATOR MASS SPECTROMETRY. Faunal analysis has shown the seasonal nature of the later part of the occupation.

A.L. Kroeber: *Cultural and natural areas of native North America* (Berkeley, 1939); B.S. Chisholm: *Reconstruction of prehistoric diet in British Columbia using stable-carbon isotopic analysis*, Ph.D. thesis, Department of Archaeology, Simon Fraser University (Burnaby, 1986); R.L. Carlson: 'Northwest Coast culture before AD 1600', *The North Pacific to 1600*, ed. E.A. Crownhart-Vaughn (Portland, 1991), 109–36; D. Hanson: *Late prehistoric subsistence in the Strait of Georgia region of the Northwest Coast*, Ph.D. thesis, Department of Archaeology, Simon Fraser University (Burnaby, 1991); R.L. Carlson and P.M. Hobler: *The Pender Canal excavations and the development of Coast Salish culture* (Vancouver, 1993).

RC

periodization *see* CHINA 2

Persepolis *see* PERSIA

Persia The Persians, like their neighbours the MEDES, were an Indo-Iranian group whose heartland lay in the region of modern Iran during the 1st millennium BC. The land of 'Parsua', apparently situated next to URARTU and to the south of Lake Urmia, is first mentioned in the annals of the ASSYRIAN king, Shalmaneser III (*c*.858–824 BC). In the first half of the 1st millennium there appear to have been two separate regions occupied by Persians, one next to the Medes' territory in the central Zagros and the other in the area surrounding the Elamite city of Anshan, modern TAL-I MALAYAN, in southern Iran. In the early 7th-century BC Anshan was captured by the Persian king Teispes or perhaps by his father Achaemenes, the founder of the Achaemenid dynasty which was

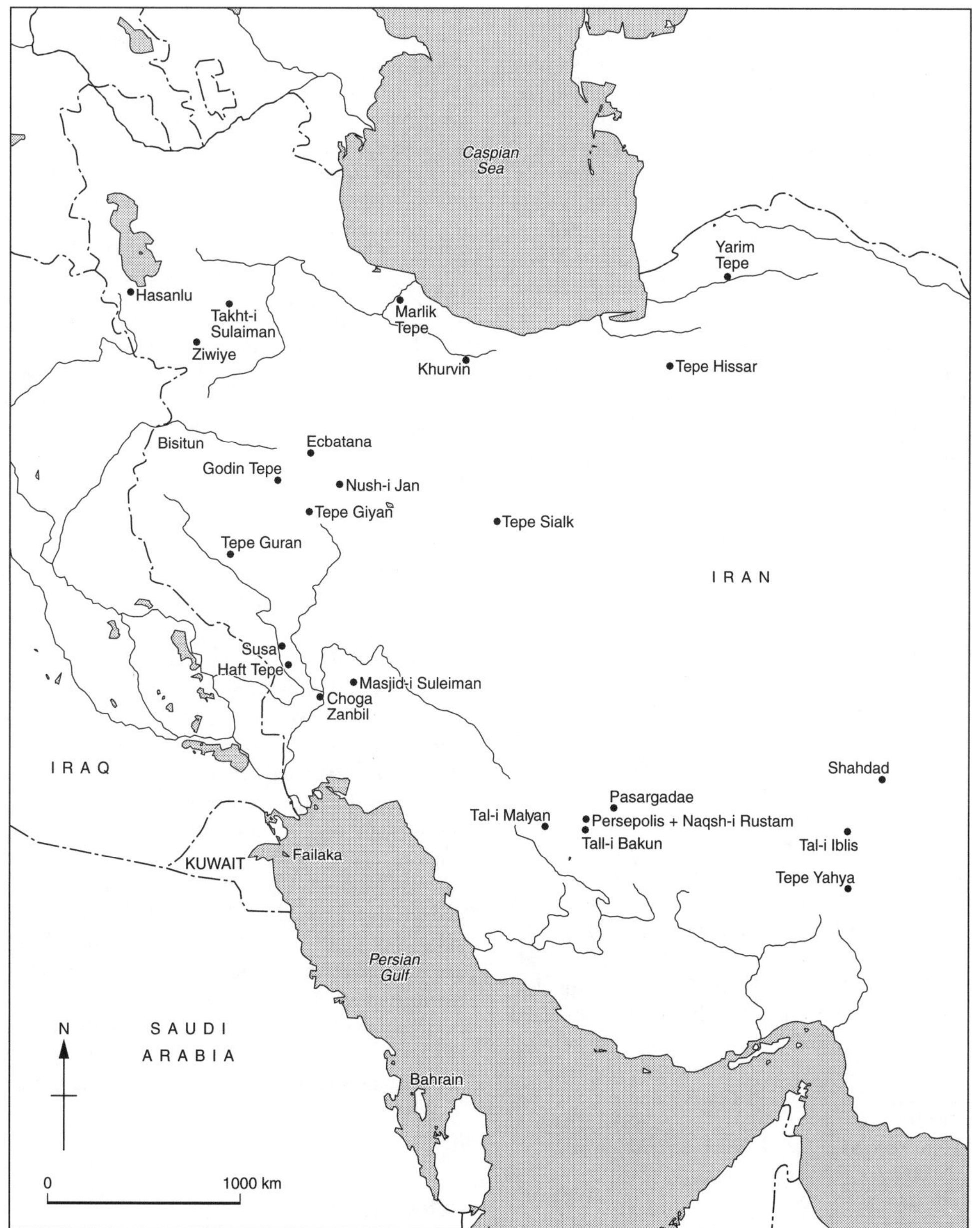

Map 28 **Persia, Persians** The major sites in ancient Persia.

ultimately to mould the Persian empire. At this time the royal capital may have been at Anshan itself (Hansman 1972).

The two principal cities of the Persian heartland in the 5th and 6th centuries BC were Pasargadae and Persepolis (Takshi-i Jamshid), the latter comprising a succession of palaces built by Darius I and his successors, each of which incorporated elements derived from Egyptian, Median, Babylonian and Greek architecture. Although the city was destroyed by Alexander the Great in 330 BC, it is one of the best surviving settlement sites in the ancient Near East. The tombs of four of the Persian kings (Darius I, Xerxes, Artaxerxes and Darius II) were carved out of the cliffs of Naqsh-i Rustam, 6 km north of Persepolis. Pasargadae was founded by Cyrus the Great (*c.*559–350 BC) soon after his conquest of Media and Lycia, and he is said to have employed Lydian masons in the construction and embellishment of the buildings within the fortified citadel, including palaces guarded by winged bulls in the Assyrian tradition, a sacred precinct with fire altars on stone platforms, and the megalithic tomb of Cyrus. In the late 6th century BC Darius transformed the former Elamite city of SUSA into the administrative capital of the empire, constructing an immense palace that incorporated both Babylonian-style courtyards and typically Persian columned halls and porticoes. One of the most distinctive features of Persian cities was the widespread use of the APADANA, a square columned chamber flanked by porticoes and functioning primarily as an audience hall.

At its height in *c.*500 BC, the Persian empire extended from Libya to the Indus region and from Babylonia to western Turkey, comprising about 20 'satrapies', each contributing regular tax and tribute to the Persian king. Although a great deal of the characteristic material culture of the Persian empire was drawn from conquered territories, it has been pointed out that their art and architecture are unified by the tendency towards an essentially decorative style. Henri Frankfort (1970: 377–8) draws attention to the close iconographic connections between Achaemenian monumental and applied art: 'The oddities of the architecture – the scattering of buildings over platforms, the elongated columns, their number, the bizarre capitals – all this betrays the direction of people foreign to the tradition, the practice and the potentialities of Near Eastern architecture . . . it would seem that the Persians drew on the traditions of their native crafts when they directed the hosts of foreign craftsmen collected at Persepolis and Susa'.

Cyrus the Great	559 – 530 BC
Cambyses II	529 – 522
Smerdis	552
Darius I	521 – 486
Xerxes I	485 – 465
Artaxerxes I	464 – 425
Xerxes II	424
Sogdianus	424
Darius II	423 – 405
Artaxerxes II	404 – 359
Artaxerxes III	358 – 338
Arses	337 – 336
Darius III	335 – 330

Table 17 **Persia, Persians** Chronology of the Achaemenid Dynasty.

E. Schmidt: *Persepolis*, 3 vols (Chicago, 1953–70); R. Ghirshman: *Iran from the earliest times to the Islamic conquest* (Harmondsworth, 1962); W. Culican: *The Medes and Persians* (London and New York, 1965); ——: *Imperial cities of Persia: Persepolis, Susa and Pasargadae* (London, 1970); H. Frankfort: *The art and architecture of the ancient Orient*, 4th edn (Harmondsworth, 1970); A. Bausoni: *The Persians* (London, 1971); J. Hansman: 'Elamites, Achaemenians and Anshan', *Iran* 10 (1972), 101–26; D.B. Stronach: *Pasargadae* (London, 1978); L. Vanden Berghe: *Bibliographie analytique de l'archéologie de I'Iran ancient* (Leiden, 1979); J.E. Curtis: *Ancient Persia* (London, 1989).

IS

Peterborough ware Later Neolithic impressed ware of southern and eastern England, dating to perhaps 3000–2500 BC. Defined by R.A. Smith, Peterborough ware has a distinctive carination and is often heavily decorated. Now recognized as an important regional style within a wider late Neolithic impressed ware tradition, it was once regarded as the principal ware across late Neolithic Britain. Peterborough ware can be broken down into three distinct styles: Ebbsfleet, round-based bowls with wide necks and undeveloped rims, cross-hatching and herring-bone decoration; Mortlake, round based with heavy developed rim and profuse and varied decoration; Fengate, with sides that taper down to a tiny flat base, heavy accentuated collar, and decoration that is a development from Mortlake. Although Ebbsfleet seems to be the earliest substyle of Peterborough ware, all three variants seem to have been in contemporary use at some sites (e.g. WEST KENNET long barrow in Wiltshire).

RJA

Petra *see* NABATAEANS

petrography *see* PETROLOGICAL ANALYSIS

petrological analysis Term referring, strictly speaking, to the study of all aspects of rocks, notably their origin, mineralogy, texture and structure. In recent years, however, archaeologists have made much use of ceramic petrology, the application of these geologically derived methods to pottery. The main techniques used are macroscopic examination,

THIN SECTIONING, HEAVY MINERAL ANALYSIS and chemical analyses. These analyses can be used in provenance studies, or for the simple description of the characteristics of a stone or ceramic artefact, in which case it is more properly called petrography.
D.R.C. Kempe and A.P. Harvey, eds: *The petrology of archaeological artefacts* (Oxford, 1983).
PTN

Peukolaotis *see* CHARSADA

Peu Richardien pottery Heavily decorated pottery style of the Late Neolithic in France, named after an enclosure site in Charente, that makes use of incised and relief decoration in bold motifs – notably *oculi* (eye motifs). Originally regarded as defining an intrusive culture – many authorities believed the *oculi* signified an Iberian origin – the style is now interpreted as having evolved locally in the mid-4th millennium BC, adopting selected 'Mediterranean' motifs. The lithic material associated with Peu Richardien pottery is not distinctive, but the ware is associated with a series of sites that are the most strongly fortified settlements in the French Neolithic. Champs Durand (Vendée), for example, is surrounded by three concentric ditches-and-banks (the rock-cut ditches are up to 2.5 m deep), one of the entrances being gated and flanked by a drystone 'tower'. Entrances at other Peu Richardien sites (e.g. Peu-Richard itself) are protected by elaborately curved banks (entrance works). As at all surviving Peu Richardien sites, there is little evidence for domestic structures inside the banks of Champs Durand, but this is probably because of poor preservation – the pottery and refuse etc. suggests that this was a defended settlement.
R. Joussaume: *Champ Durand à Nieul-sur-l'Autize (Vendée): Site préhistorique fortifié* (La Roche-sur-Yon, 1980); C. Scarre, ed.: *Ancient France* (Edinburgh, 1983).
RJA

Pfyn (Michelsberg-Pfyn) Regional Swiss Neolithic culture, known from lake-side settlements and other sites in the Lake Zurich and Lake Constance region, and distinguished from the related Michelsberg cultural complex in 1959 by J. Driehaus. Dating from the first half of the 3rd millennium BC, it is the earliest major Neolithic culture over much of northeast Switzerland, and is securely stratified below the succeeding late Neolithic HORGEN culture at a number of sites. Pfyn pottery is characterized by flat-bottomed vessels and a unique assemblage of decorative elements drawn from other Neolithic ceramic styles (including some RÖSSEN decorative elements). Likewise, while the lithic equipment is closest to Swiss CORTAILLOD assemblages, the perforated axe hammers resemble those found in MICHELSBERG contexts. A limited range of metal objects are known and – unlike the Cortaillod – crucibles and other evidence suggest local metalworking.
J. Winiger: *Das Fundmaterial von Thayngen-Weier im Rahmen der Pfyner Kultur* (Basle, 1971); M. Sakellarides: *The economic exploitation of the Swiss area in the Mesolithic and Neolithic periods*, BAR IS 67 (Oxford, 1979), 48–50, J. Winiger: *Das Neolithikum der Schweiz* (Basle, 1981).
RJA

Phalaborwa Important centre for iron and copper smelting from the 8th century AD onwards, located in the eastern Transvaal, South Africa. Small villages occupied flat ground at the foot of volcanic hills, and in the harsh environment of the Transvaal Lowveld the economy was probably dependent on trade in metal products rather than on locally produced foodstuffs. The site has particularly yielded detail on mining and smelting technology and logistics. Pottery production undergoes no change in technology or style from the 11th to the 19th century, and provides clear links with the modern northeastern Sotho people.
N.J. van der Merwe and T.K. Scully: 'The Phalaborwa story: archaeological and ethnographic investigation of a South African Iron Age group', *WA* 3/2 (1971), 178–96; N.J. Van der Merwe and D.J. Killick: 'Square: an iron smelting site near Phalaborwa', *South African Archaeological Society Goodwin Series 3* (1979), 86–93.
RI

phenomenology The science of phenomena (i.e. anything that can be apprehended via the senses), a philosophical approach formulated by Edmund Husserl (1931), was based on the idea of the experiences of the self, in contrast to the empirical approach of POSITIVISM inaugurated by Auguste Comte in the early 19th century. Husserl's ideas found their way into psychology and sociology via the work of Martin Heidegger (1962) and Alfred Schütz, eventually exerting some influence on geography (e.g. Taun 1977; Relph 1985), anthropology and archaeology. Most of the applications of phenomenology have so far been restricted to European sites dating from the Mesolithic to the early Bronze Age.

Chris Tilley (1994) takes a phenomenological approach to the archaeological landscapes of the Mesolithic and Neolithic in Wales and Dorset, asking the question: 'why were particular locations chosen for habitation and the erection of monuments as opposed to others?'. The aspects of the archaeological record which would traditionally be used to answer this question (e.g. climate, soils, availability of resources, demography, technology and territoriality) are characterized by Tilley (1994:2) as 'the function of a contemporary myth-making in which an exclusively modernist Western logic has simply been superimposed on the past'. He therefore concentrates primarily on 'the symbolics of landscape perception and the role of social memory in choice of site location', arguing that these need to be taken into account alongside conventional factors of the type listed above.

Archaeologists have made numerous attempts to understand the function(s) performed by Early Neolithic CAUSEWAYED CAMPS (large circular monuments enclosed by concentric ditches), producing such suggestions as meeting places, animal enclosures, trading areas or sanctuaries. Whereas the landscapes within and around the 'camps' are often studied only in terms of two-dimensional maps and plans, Mark Edmonds (1993) uses practical observations and first-hand experience of the monuments in an attempt to appreciate their impact on the individuals who built them and who were no doubt buried in the closely associated earthen long BARROWS.

Julian Thomas (1993) presents a similarly phenomenological perspective on the development of the Neolithic and early Bronze Age landscapes around AVEBURY in north Wiltshire, stressing that 'the emergence of the monumental complex cannot be understood entirely from plans and distribution maps, but requires a consideration of the positioning of persons in relation to the monuments'. By walking through and around the site and experiencing at first hand the spatial constraints and visual particularities of the archaeological and natural features, Thomas gains a sense of Avebury as a complex in which the various elements were arranged in such a way as to reflect different individuals' access to power and knowledge. Thus, for instance, 'The Obelisk . . . stood at the centre of a series of nested spaces, separated by barriers which impeded rather than totally closed off access, and which rendered activities at the centre obscure and partial rather than totally invisible', while, the Avebury henge, on the other hand, 'serves to draw in far more people than the chambered tombs through its sheer size, but as the same time its architecture functions to classify them more rigorously through their movements and access to knowledge and performance'.

E. Husserl: *Phenomenological philosophy*, trans. W.R.B. Gibson (London, 1931); M. Heidegger: *Being and time* (Oxford, 1962); Y.-F. Taun: *Space and place: the perspective of experience* (London, 1977); E. Relph: 'Geographical experiences and being-in-the-world: the phenomenological origins of geography', *Dwelling, place and environment*, ed. D. Seamon and R. Mugerauer (New York, 1985), 15–32; M. Edmonds: 'Interpreting causeway enclosures in the past and in the present', *Interpretive archaeology*, ed. C. Tilley (Oxford, 1993), 99–142; J. Thomas: 'The politics of vision and the archaeologies of landscape', *Landscape: politics and perspectives*, ed. B. Bender (Oxford and Providence, 1993), 19–44; C. Tilley: *A phenomenology of landscape: places, paths and monuments* (Oxford and Providence, 1994).

IS

Philae The original island site of a temple of the goddess Isis, located about 7 km south of Aswan. The surviving elements of the sandstone temple, dating from the 30th dynasty to the late Roman period, was transferred to the nearby island of Agilqiyya during the early 1970s in order to save it from the rising waters of LAKE NASSER. The worship of Isis at Philae appears to have survived well into the Christian era, and it was not until the reign of Justinian (*c.*AD 535) that the temple was finally closed down.

H. Junker: *Der grosse Pylon des Tempels der Isis in Philä* (Vienna, 1958); —— and E. Winter: *Das geburtshaus des Tempels der Isis in Philä* (Vienna, 1965); E. Vassilika: *Ptolemaic Philae* (Leuven, 1989).

IS

Philistines People in Iron Age Palestine who were probably the descendants of the Late Bronze Age Peleset, identified as one of the invading SEA PEOPLES in the annals of the eighth year of the reign of the Egyptian pharaoh Ramesses III (*c.*1194–1163 BC). Later in the same king's reign, Papyrus Harris states that Peleset troops were employed as mercenaries in the Egyptian army. The Biblical Philistines, however, are not attested until the 10th century BC by which time they appear to have established themselves in the Pentapolis, a group of five cities along the Palestinian coastal plain: Gaza, Ashkelon, Ashdod, Ekron and Gath. Moshe Dothan's excavations at Ashdod in 1962–9 revealed a burnt layer dating to the 13th century BC, corresponding perhaps to the Levantine campaign of the pharaoh Merenptah or, alternatively, to the arrival of the Sea Peoples in Palestine.

During the early Iron Age, Ashdod, Ashkelon and Gezer (the three cities of the Pentapolis that have been excavated) were characterized by a distinctive material culture, although opinions differ as to whether these settlements can be described as 'Philistine' (Dothan and Freedman 1967–71). Several other sites in northern Palestine (including Jaffa and Tell el-Far'ah) are characterized by sherds of 'Philistine pottery', a painted ware combining Aegean, Canaanite and Egyptian shapes and decoration (Dothan 1982), as well as unusual forms of religious and funerary architecture thought to be influenced by the Philistines' Aegean origins.

Jonathan Tubb (1990: 80) considers that the correlation between the archaeological remains and the textually-attested Philistines is unequivocal: 'There are very few cases in which archaeologists are able to tie pots to people with any degree of certainty. In the case of Philistine pottery, however, the relationship is secure, and indeed this has provided the means by which it has been possible to chart the progress and expansion of the Philistines subsequent to their initial settlement'. Nancy Sandars (1985: 169) prefers to regard the Biblical Philistines, the Peleset and the Iron Age settlements with 'Philistine pottery' as three separate entities, although she agrees that 'a linguistic connection between Egyptian *plst* (Peleset) and Philistine must be conceded' (Sandars 1985: 164).

M. Dothan and D.N. Freedman: *Ashdod*, 3 vols (Tel Aviv, 1967–71); K.A. Kitchen: 'The Philistines', *Peoples of Old Testament times*, ed. D.J. Wiseman (Oxford, 1973), 53–78; T. Dothan: *The Philistines and their material culture* (Yale and London, 1982); N. Sandars: *The Sea Peoples: warriors of the ancient Mediterranean*, 1250–1150 *BC* 2nd edn (London, 1985), 164–77; J.N. Tubb: 'Biblical archaeology: a synthesis and overview', *Archaeology and the Bible*, ed. J.N. Tubb and R.L. Chapman (London, 1990), 41–93; T. and M. Dothan: *Peoples of the Sea: the search for the Philistines* (New York, 1992); D.M. Howard, Jr.: 'Philistines', *Peoples of the Old Testament world*, ed. A.J. Hoerth et al. (Grand Rapid, 1994).

IS

Phimai Major religious and administrative Khmer centre located in a strategic position in the upper Mun Valley of northeast Thailand. The central enclosed precinct has been restored, the large central tower of the principal temple being 18 m high. Phimai was also an important site during the later prehistoric period, and excavations have revealed rich burials of the later 1st century BC in association with a lustrous black burnished style of pottery.

L.P. Briggs: 'The ancient Khmer empire', *TAPS* 4/1 (1951), 1–295.

CH

Phoenicians West-Semitic-speaking, maritime people of the east Mediterranean coast during the 1st millennium BC, who were perhaps the immediate descendants of the CANAANITES (although the identification of the Canaanites themselves is problematic); Donald Redford (1992: 299), for instance, describes them as 'coastal Canaanites', and D.R. ap Thomas (1973: 262) asserts that they were 'Canaanites, culturally, and indeed racially also'. It was the Greeks who referred to them as 'Phoenicians', but they described themselves simply in terms of their individual cities of origin. These towns along the Syro-Palestinian coastal strip ranged from Arvad and Amrit in the north, via Byblos and Sidon, to Tyre and Ushu in the south. There were also Phoenician settlements in Cyprus, Sicily, Sardinia, Crete and north Africa, but the best-known Phoenician colony - Carthage - was to gain control of large areas of the Mediterranean region during the late 1st millennium BC, at a time when the Levantine Phoenicians were absorbed into the Assyrian and Persian empires.

Phoenician material culture, like that of the Canaanites, is characterized primarily by its eclecticism and tendency to draw ideas and technology from surrounding peoples – their pottery is essentially Aegean in nature whereas their styles of ivory-carving and cylinder-seals owe a great deal to Egypt and Mesopotamia respectively (the alphabetic fitter's marks on the backs of the 'NIMRUD ivories' probably indicate a Phoenician origin). The Phoenician alphabetic script is closely related to that of the Canaanites, from which it appears to have developed, although the signs also show indications of the influence of cuneiform. Bernal (1987: 317–438) discusses the gradual changes in modern western attitudes to the Phoenicians; he argues that the growth of anti-Semitism between the 1880s and World War II caused many scholars to belittle the Phoenicians' role in the emergence of Greek civilization.

D. Harden: *The Phoenicians* (Harmondsworth, 1971); D.R. ap Thomas: 'The Phoenicians', *Peoples of Old Testament times*, ed. D.J. Wiseman (Oxford, 1973), 259–86; P.M. Bikau: 'The late Phoenician pottery complex and chronology', *Basor* 229 (1978), 47–56; M. Bernal: *Black Athena: the Afro-Asiatic roots of Classical civilization* (London, 1987); D. Redford: *Egypt, Canaan and Israel in ancient times* (Princeton, 1992).

IS

photomicrograph Photograph of an object, or part of an object, taken through a microscope. Such photographs can be made using any type of microscope, from the simple optical microscope to polarizing or scanning electron microscopes. The photographs may be required for record purposes or as a stage in further examination such as image analysis.

Kodak Ltd: *Photography through the microscope* (New York, 1974).

PTN

Phrygia, Phrygians The Phrygians were not a single cultural group but a 'federation' or 'coalition' of tribal peoples from eastern Europe who invaded Anatolia in the late 2nd millennium BC, effectively displacing the HITTITES. The Phrygian kingdom comprised most of central Anatolia, bordered to the west by the independent cities along the Aegean coast, to the south by Cilicia and to the east by Assyria. The history of Phrygia is derived mainly from Mesopotamian and Greek textual sources, starting with the Assyrian annals of the mid-12th century BC, when they are described as 'Mushki and Tabal'.

Many early Phrygian settlements were built on the ruins of Hittite towns such as Alaça Hüyük and Boghazköy, but the 8th century capital was Gordium (the modern mound of Yasi Hüyük, 90 km west of Ankara). Despite its massive stone and timber fortifications Gordium was eventually pillaged by the CIMMERIANS in *c*.685 BC, but continued in use until at least the 6th century BC. The adjacent cemetery consisted of about 80 tumulus-graves, including the 50 m high 'tomb of Midas', containing the skeleton of an unknown 60-year-old ruler, along with wooden furniture, 169 bronze vessels and a bag containing 165 fibulae. Elsewhere, primarily in isolated mountain-top locations, the Phrygians of the 8th century BC erected stone sculptures, many carved with inscriptions in their own distinctive alphabet which is still undeciphered (Barnett 1953).

R.D. Barnett: 'The Phrygian rock-façades and the Hittite monuments', *BO* 10 (1953), 77–82; E. Akurgal: *Phrygische Kunst* (Ankara, 1955); C.H.E. Haspels: *The highlands of Phrygia: sites and monuments*, 2 vols (Princeton, 1971); R.S. Young: *Gordion* (Ankara, 1975); S. Lloyd: *Ancient Turkey: a traveller's history of Anatolia* (London, 1989), 61–7.

IS

Phu Lon Southeast Asian copper source on the southern bank of the Mekong River, northeast Thailand, which was exploited from the mid-2nd millennium to the end of the 1st millennium BC. The mine shafts and the deep deposits of ore processing, smelting and casting residue probably represent seasonal activity. Sites on the adjacent Khorat Plateau, such as NON NOK THA and BAN NA DI, have yielded sandstone and clay moulds, suggesting that casting was often undertaken away from the mines.

V.C. Pigott and S. Natapintu: 'Archaeological investigations into prehistoric copper production: the Thailand archaeometallurgy project', *The beginnings and uses of metals and alloys*, ed. R. Maddin (Boston 1986), 156–62.

CH

Phung Nguyen Prehistoric settlement, located above the confluence of the Red and Black rivers in northern Vietnam, that has given its name to the earliest metal-using culture of the region. Extensive excavations (1959–68) uncovered a rich material culture in which polished stone adzeheads, chisels and stone bracelets were particularly well represented, together with pottery vessels bearing ornate parallel-incised designs infilled with impressions. Over 50 similar sites have now been identified and ascribed to the Phung Nguyen culture; 11 of these have yielded fragments of bronze, but no complete artefacts. There is no corpus of radiocarbon dates, but the culture probably belongs to the period 2500–1500 BC.

Nguyen Ba Khoach: 'Phung Nguyen', *Asian Perspectives* 23/1 (1980), 23–54.

CH

Phylakopi Principal prehistoric settlement on the obsidian-producing island of Melos in the Cyclades. Excavations conducted between 1896 and 1899 at Phylakopi (see Atkinson et al.) helped to establish the framework of Cycladic prehistory, and revealed the successive influence of the Minoan and Mycenaean civilizations on the island; these early investigations have recently been supplemented by the work of Colin Renfrew and others. From 1600 BC Phylakopi was impressively fortified, and possessed at least one major building of probable administrative function. A Linear A clay tablet has been recovered, as have fragments of graceful Minoan-inspired frescoes. Renfrew's detailed description of a later (1360–1100 BC) shrine at Phylakopi has elucidated our understanding of MYCENAEAN religion, and is interesting as an unusually systematic attempt to relate archaeological evidence to ritual.

T.D. Atkinson et al.: *Excavations at Phylakopi in Melos*, Society for the Promotion of Hellenic Studies Supplementary Paper No. 4 (London, 1904); C. Renfrew and M. Wagstaff, eds: *An island polity* (Cambridge, 1982); ——: *The archaeology of cult: the sanctuary at Phylakopi* (London, 1985).

RJA

phytoliths (Gk. 'plant stones') Microscopic deposits of silica formed in the epidermal cells of plants. The silica, absorbed from groundwater, resists decay and the differently shaped phytoliths it forms within the plant cells have a restricted but useful taxonomic value. A very few plants, notably certain forms of maize, produce sets of phytoliths that can be distinguished at species level after careful size and morphological analysis (Piperno 1984). However, most phytoliths are family specific or non-specific. A crude form of phytolith analysis uses the density of silica within soils as an indicator of past grass cover; the future of more subtle means of analysis depends on the success of basic research in the variability of phytolith morphology and the effect upon phytolith sets of PRE- and POST-DEPOSITIONAL PROCESSES.

D.M. Pearsall; 'Phytolith analysis: applications of a new paleoethnobotanical technique in archaeology', *American Anthropologist* 84/4 (1982), 862–71; D.R. Piperno: 'A comparison and differentiation of phytoliths from maize and wild grasses: use of morphological criteria', *AA* 49/2 (1984), 361–83; A. Powers: 'Phytoliths: animal, vegetable and mineral?', *Science and archaeology*, ed. E.A. Slater and J.O. Tate, BAR BS 196, ii (Oxford, 1988), 459–72.

RJA

Piklihal Neolithic settlement in the Raichur District of southern India, consisting of two Neolithic phases dating from the late 3rd to the early 2nd millennium BC, and later Iron Age and early Historic levels (Allchin 1960). Domestic cattle are common in both Neolithic phases, along with remains of sheep, goats, tortoises and shellfish. Artefacts include hand-made ceramics, ground stone axes, blade tools and terracotta cattle-figurines. Cattle, gazelle, sheep and goat are depicted in rock-drawings on nearby boulders and cave-walls.

F.R. Allchin: *Piklihal excavations* (Hyderabad, 1960); ——: *Neolithic cattle keepers of South India* (Cambridge, 1963), 59.

CS

Pikunda-Munda Group *see* AFRICA 5.3

Piltdown Man hoax Palaeontological forgery which was widely accepted as fact for the first half of the 20th century. Fragments of a skull, a mandible and various EOLITHS and animal bones were found in 1912 by Charles Dawson (a solicitor with an interest in geology and archaeology) and Arthur Smith Woodward (a palaeontologist) at the site of Barkham Manor near Piltdown Common, about 13 km north of Lewes, in the English county of Sussex. At the time they were thought to be evidence of the so-called 'missing link', a hominid which was halfway between ape and man, dated to *c.*75,000 BP. In the second edition of his *Outline of history* (1925), H.G. Wells confidently described the so-called 'dawn man' (Eoanthropus) as 'an intermediate form between the Heidelberg man and the Neanderthal man . . . a member of a number of species of sub-human running apes of more than ape-like intelligence'. By the 1950s, however, such analyses as FLUORINE UPTAKE demonstrated conclusively that the find was an elaborate hoax, involving the deliberate juxtaposition of a modern cranium and the mandible of an orang-utan. Since then, the controversy has centred not so much on the find itself as the identity of the perpetrator of the hoax, who was at first thought to be Charles Dawson. It now, however, seems likely that the major culprit was Arthur Keith, an anatomist whose enthusiasm for the concept of 'tertiary man' (i.e. a Tertiary date for *HOMO SAPIENS*) seems to have led him to fabricate the evidence to support his theories.

C. Dawson: 'The Piltdown skull', *Hastings and East Sussex Nature* 2 (1913), 73–82; H.G. Wells: *The outline of history*, 2nd edn (London, 1925); J.S. Weiner: *The Piltdown forgery* (Oxford, 1955); R. Millar: *The Piltdown men* (London, 1974); C. Blinderman: *The Piltdown inquest* (Buffalo, 1986); F. Spencer: *Piltdown: a scientific forgery* (London, 1990).

IS

Pirak Post-Harappan settlement-mound located on the Kachi Plain near the foot of the strategic Bolan Pass, Pakistan. Pirak is about 9 ha in area and there is a great deal of continuity in material culture and settlement-plan, which spans three chronological phases from the late 2nd to the early 1st millennium BC. Architectural remains include rectangular multi-room houses with rows of small rectangular wall niches, and complexes of larger interconnected buildings with evidence for specialized craft production activities, including flaked flint blades, bone and ivory tools. Rice was evidently the most important crop at Pirak, but traces of millet, sorghum, wheat, barley (and other wild and domesticated plants), as well as the domesticated horse, Bactrian camel and cattle have also been found.

Contact between the occupants of Pirak and contemporary communities in Central Asia, Afghanistan and Iran, such as ANAU, Yaz, Tillya Tepe, TEPE YAHYA, and SHAHR-I SOKHTA (Jarrige 1985), is demonstrated by similarities in technology, and the presence of certain artefacts, especially compartmented bronze seals, copper strainers, flint points and ceramic figurines. The faunal remains and figurines representing horses have been linked by Jean François Jarrige to the increasing importance of the horse and pastoral nomads throughout the Eurasian steppes at this time, and he suggests that they may represent direct evidence of the emergence of a complex and dynamic inter-regional interaction network (1985: 58).

J.F. Jarrige: *Fouilles de Pirak*, 2 vols (Paris, 1979); ——: 'Continuity and change in the north Kachi Plain', *South Asian Archaeology, 1983*, ed. J. Schotsmans and M. Taddei (Naples, 1985), 35–68.

CS

Piramesse *see* QANTIR; TELL EL-DABʿA

pit-and-comb Style of pottery characteristic of Middle Neolithic sites on the East European Plain, consisting of conic-bottomed vessels of various sizes decorated with comb impressions and small pits that form horizontal bands. During the later phases, more complicated patterns appear. In several cases stylized waterfowl (usually duck) may be recognized. By extension, the term is used to denote the Middle Neolithic cultural tradition in the same area. The earliest pit-and-comb sites are located in the catchment of the Upper Volga and Oka (central Russia) and are often considered as an independent cultural entity (the 'L'yalovo culture'). Sites such as Sakhtysh (see below), Yazykovo 1 and Ivanovskoye 3 (*see also* UPPER VOLGA) have yielded calibrated dates of around 4000–3500 BC. In all these cases, the pit-and-comb levels are stratified above those of the 'Upper Volga' cultural complex.

At a later stage, the pit-and-comb tradition expanded over a wide area of the East European Plain: up to the White Sea and Kola peninsula in the north, Latvia and Belarus in the west, the Urals in the east, the northern Ukraine and the middle stretches of River Don in the south. Several local variants are recognizable: Ryazanian, Belevian, Karelian, the White Sea etc. Pit-and-comb sites are usually situated on the flood-plains of small rivers, and on the shores of lakes, and in central Russia they have often been discovered in large peat-bogs. In many cases, the remains of oval-shaped, semi-subterranean dwellings have been revealed, and, at the site of Sakhtysh, a rectangular dwelling with a total floor area of 200 sq. m was identified. The economy of pit-and-comb sites was based entirely on foraging. The following species were identified at the Ust'-Rybezhna site south of the Ladoga Lake (St Petersburg district): elk, aurochs, wild boar, brown bear, reindeer, seal, numerous birds, catfish and perch.

Rock carvings (PETROGLYPHS) concentrated on granite outcrops along the shores of Lake Onega offer one of the most outstanding features of the Karelian pit-and-comb culture. One of the most impressive assemblages, Besov Nos (Devil's Cap), comprises 116 compositions including birds, fish, elk, red deer, seals, beaver, human figures, and three boats with oarsmen. Another group of petroglyphs is situated in the mouth of the River Vyg, in the coastal area of the White Sea; boats and hunting scenes are the most common motifs. Based on their height above the water-level, the rock carvings have been dated to between 2800 and 1800 BC.

V.P. Tret'yakov: *Kul'tura jamočno-grebenčatoi keramiki v lesnoi polose evropeiskoi časti SSSR* [The pit-and comb culture in the European part of the USSR] (Leningrad, 1972); S.V. Oshibkina et al.: *Iskusstvo kamennogo veko* [Art of the Stone Age] (Moscow, 1992).

PD

Figure 41 **pit-and-comb** Rock carvings of (A) hunting and (B) fishing scenes, Karelian pit-and-comb culture, Lake Onega region, Russia.

pit-grave culture (Russ. *yámnaya*). Bronze Age cultural tradition which spread over a vast area of Russia, from the Urals in the east to the low Danube in the west, in the course of the late 3rd and early 2nd millennia BC; it was first identified by V.A. Gorotsov in 1901–3. The most characteristic feature of the pit-grave culture are burial pits (*'yama'* in Russian) of rectangular or, rarely, oval shape, covered by burial mounds (kurgans). For this reason it is sometimes called the first 'kurgan culture' of the Bronze Age, preceding the

CATACOMB GRAVE culture and the TIMBER-GRAVE culture. In the case of the pit-grave culture, the kurgans are of various sizes, and in some cases several stages in their construction may be distinguished. The pits were often covered with wooden slabs. Reed, grass and/or red ochre lined the bottom of the pits. The red ochre also covered the body of the dead, and may have been an essential element of the mortuary rites. In some cases, wheels or even the remains of complete wheeled carts were found inside the pits (e.g. Storozhevaya Mogila, near Dnepropetrovsk on the Dniepr). The position of the skeletons – mostly on the back or on the side with legs contracted – finds an obvious antecedent in the SREDNI STOG tradition. Other Sredni Stog features may be seen in the stone cairns, cromlechs and anthropomorphic stelae incorporated in the kurgan constructions.

The economy of the pit-grave culture was based on stock breeding. In the upper layer of Mikhailovka (Shaposhnikova 1985) nearly 90% of the determined faunal remains belonged to the domesticates such as cattle (38%), sheep/goat (32.5%) and horse (17.6%). It is assumed that oxen were used as draught animals. At the same time, there is evidence that crops were grown at some sites; this is true of the middle layer at Mikhailovka where the impressions of emmer wheat, hulled barley and millet have been identified (Pashkevich 1991). In its final stage, this settlement grew to a size of 1.5 ha, and was surrounded by fortifications which included stone ramparts and ditches.

The western outposts of the pit-grave culture stretch to northern Bulgaria, Hungary and Romania, where so called 'ochre graves' are found (e.g. Hamangia-Baia tumuli in Dobruja, the area between the Lower Danube and the Black Sea). The mortuary rite includes kurgans with stone cairns and cromlechs and all the usual elements of pit-grave mortuary practice.

According to N.Ya. Merpert (1968), the pit-grave sites formed a distinct 'cultural-historic entity' based on a common subsistence economy (predominantly nomadic stock-breeding) and common ideology (the kurgan mortuary rite, primarily). According to Merpert, this entity came about from the integration of numerous local traditions over a vast area: from the Urals in the east, to the Lower Danube in the west. Basing her analysis on some formal elements of the burial ritual, and the cord ornamentation of the pottery, Gimbutas (1973) expands the 'kurgan culture' to a still wider area: to the Balkans, central and northern Europe, the Caucasus and even to the Near East. According to Gimbutas, between 4000 and 2500 BC, three consecutive waves of 'kurgan people' (identified with speakers of Indo-European), beginning with the pit-grave culture, pushed to the west, to the north, and later expanded southwards through the Caucasus to occupy Asia Minor. Some groups moved on towards India, while the others remained in the steppe, and pressed into the Iranian plateau and Central Asia. Variations of this hypothesis have been accepted by many scholars, including Merpert (1968) and Mallory (1989).

The main deficiency of the hypothesis resides in the direct indentification of archaeological entities (ie the pit-grave or kurgan 'culture') with linguistic and/or ethnic groups. It seems more likely that the emergence of pit-grave assemblages was related to the social development of various local Bronze Age communities. It represents an expression of social stratification, and the emergence of chiefdom-type nomadic social structures. The development of nomadic chiefdoms was accompanied by the intensification of inter-group information exchange between what were essentially *heterogeneous* social groups. These processes, which might be compared to the social dynamics underlying the later BEAKER PHENOMENON of western Europe, need not imply any large-scale migration; neither are they related to the spread of the Indo-European language.

N.Ya. Merpert: *Drevneišaja istorija naselenija stepnoi polosy Vostočnoi Evropy* [The most ancient history of the population of the steppe belt of Eastern Europe] (Moscow, 1968); M. Gimbutas: 'The beginning of the Bronze Age in Europe and the Indo-Europeans: 3500–2500 BC', *Journal of Indo-European Studies* 1 (1973), 163–214; O.G. Shaposhnikova: 'Jamnaja kul'turno-istoričeskaja obščnost,' *Arheologija Ukrainskoi SSR* [Archaeology of the Ukrainian SSR], col. 1, ed. D. Ya. Telegin (Kiev, 1985), 325–36; J.P. Mallory: *In search of Indo-Europeans: language, archaeology and myth* (London, 1989); G.A. Pashkevich: *Paleoetnobotaničeski nahodki na territorii (Neolit-bronza): Katalog* [Palaeothnobotanical finds in the territory of Ukraine (Neolithic-Bronze Age): catalogue] (Kiev, 1991).

PD

Plains Village Period Period from *c.* AD 1000 to 1850, which developed out of (or replaced) the PLAINS WOODLAND PERIOD in the Great Plains of the United States. It is made up of the Middle Missouri, Central Plains, and Coalescent traditions. Tribes with long residence in the Plains that derive from these traditions are the Mandan, Hidatsa, Arikara, Pawnee and Wichita. Sedentary settlements consisting of a few to several hundred earthlodges were situated along major rivers during this period. Historically the inhabitants of these villages practised a duel subsistence strategy of agriculture and bison hunting. They lived in the permanent earthlodge villages in the spring, when corn, beans, and squash were planted in the river bottomlands, and returned to the villages in the autumn, for harvest. The summer and part of the winter were spent in tipis away from the villages on an extended buffalo hunt. Contact with Spanish, French, English and American traders, explorers and naturalists began in the 16th century AD, but continuous contact did not occur until the 18th century.

W. Wood: *An interpretation of Mandan culture history*. River Basin Survey Papers 39, Bulletin 198, Bureau of American Ethnology, Smithsonian Institution (Washington, D.C., 1967); D. Lehmer: *Introduction to Middle Missouri archeology*. Anthropological Papers 1, National Park Service (Washington, D.C., 1971); S. Ahler, T. Thiessen and M. Trimble: *People of the willows: the prehistory and early history of the Hidatsa indians* (Grand Forks, 1991).

WB

Plains Woodland Period Beginning about 500 BC and continuing to about AD 1000, the cultures in the level-to-rolling Great Plains of the United States show evidence of general relationships with peoples to the east of the area inhabited by the people of the WOODLAND period. This eastern orientation is designated the Plains Woodland period. Diagnostic features of the Plains Woodland that are derived from the eastern woodlands are conoidal-shaped ceramic vessels, projectile point styles, and linear and conical burial mounds.

Plains Woodland sites occur from Canada to Texas, but are concentrated in the eastern Great Plains, along major rivers, such as the Missouri, and their tributaries. Subsistence was predominantly based on hunting, fishing and gathering of wild plants, but incipient horticulture of local plants and imported cultigens, such as corn, became increasingly important through time. There is variation geographically and temporally across the Great Plains in the importance of cultivation and in the types of animals hunted. It is only the later Plains Woodland sites, and then those in the eastern Plains, that cultivation becomes an important factor. Bison was a major food source in the northern and western Plains, while deer was more important on the eastern Plains. Habitations consisted of small villages and camps that are often deeply buried; they were usually situated in the river valleys, while burials, often accompanied by shell beads and stone tools, were placed in burial mounds on the overlooking bluffs.

M. Adair: *Prehistoric agriculture in the Central Plains*, Publications in Anthropology 16, University of Kansas, (Lawrence, 1988); D. Benn: *Woodland cultures on the western prairies: the Rainbow Site investigations*, Report 18, Office of the State Archaeologist, (Iowa City, 1990).

WB

plane-table levelling/survey Method of surveying – now rarely used – whereby a map is drawn on a carefully levelled, centred and orientated table, using an alidade to sight on various points.

Plano The last of three PALEOINDIAN cultures that are found east of the Rocky Mountains in the United States and Canada. The period extends from *c*.8000 to 5000 BC, and artefacts include a gradually changing sequence of types of lanceolate projectile points, scraping tools and knives. Several regional and temporal complexes have been identified. In the Great Plains, small bands of hunter-gatherers attacked solitary bison, or killed herds of bison by driving them into gullies, as at OLSEN-CHUBBUCK, or over jumps, as at BONFIRE SHELTER. Habitation sites, such as HELL GAP, are poorly known. In the eastern United States, sites of this period are placed in the early ARCHAIC period.

H. Irwin and M. Wormington: 'Paleo-Indian tool types in the Great Plains', *AA* 25 (1970), 24–34; D. Stanford: 'The Jones-Miller site: an example of Hell Gap bison procurement strategy', *PAnth, Memoir* 14 (1978), 90–7.

WB

plano-convex brick Type of rectangular mud brick (usually unbaked) with a distinctive domed upper surface often retaining the maker's thumbmarks, which was employed in southern Mesopotamia during the Early Dynastic and Akkadian periods (*c*.2900–2150 BC).

planum method Style of excavation involving the removal of successive layers of arbitrary depth ('spits') across an entire site (or, more often, the whole of a feature within a site). After the removal of each spit the whole surface is recorded, with all find-spots being recorded in three dimensions. The method is particularly suitable in dealing with deposits where there are comparatively few solid features such as walls or floors.

plaquettes Small stone, bone, antler or ivory blocks, flattened on one side and often decorated, which were manufactured by the hunters and gatherers of the Western European Upper Palaeolithic. They are often found in groups, such as the numerous examples recovered from Montastruc, France (now held in the British Museum). The decorated examples commonly depict animals – such as horses, deer and bison – but also present are occasional human figures, schematized designs and repeated simple motifs. Their subject inventory is thus comparable to Palaeolithic mural art. The designs are either incised (possibly originally filled with ochre) or in very low relief. The maximum dimension of plaquettes is nearly always below 30 cm, and they are usually classed as MOBILIARY or portable art. However, Sieveking points out that there is little evidence of curation, and it seems likely that the creation and display of plaquettes formed part of repeated ceremonies at particular habitation sites and that they were then simply discarded.

A. Sieveking: *Engraved Magdalenian plaquettes*, Bar IS 369 (Oxford, 1987).

RJA

plastromancy Chinese method of divination by the turtle shell (*plastron*) to seek the advice of the gods and ancestors regarding projected activities. During the Late SHANG period (*c.*1400–1123 BC), the practice was accompanied by the incising of texts and has thus provided valuable information on many aspects of Shang life. Although it seems possible that turtles were reared in captivity to ensure a supply of shells for the daily ritual of divination, marginal notations incised in the *plastrons* indicate that non-Shang sources apparently contributed up to as many as 1000 shells at a time, suggesting that a considerable proportion came from outlying regions (Keightley 1978: 11–12). The preparation of the shells and bones for divination was a painstaking process, in which hollows were drilled into the rear surfaces to receive an application of heat – the nature of the heat source is uncertain (*see* CHINA 3 *and* SCAPULIMANCY).

D.N. Keightley: *Sources of Shang history: The oracle-bone inscriptions of Bronze Age China* (Berkeley, 1978).

NB

Plateau Pithouse Tradition Cultural tradition in the Fraser-Thompson drainage system of the interior plateau of south central British Columbia, dating to *c.*2000 BC–AD 1850. The tradition was formulated on the basis of detailed comparative analysis of the cultural content and ecological context of components from 78 excavated sites, supported by 244 radiocarbon dates. It shows continuity throughout but is divisible on stylistic grounds into three successive cultural horizons, each correlated with environmental changes. The bow and arrow appears in the latest horizon, dating to *c.*AD 500.

T.H. Richards and M.K. Rousseau: *Late prehistoric cultural horizons on the Canadian Plateau* (Burnaby, 1987).

RC

platform-mound Term used in the archaeology of North America to describe flat-topped mounds of earth usually serving as platforms for domestic or ceremonial buildings. The alternative term 'temple mound' is sometimes employed in eastern North America.

plumbate ware A widely traded type of pottery found throughout Mesoamerica during the Early Postclassic period (*c.*AD 900–1200), believed to have been manufactured on the Pacific coastal plain of Mexico and Guatemala. Its name derives from the distinctive hard, iridescent, lead-gray surface that was initially thought to have been a true lead glaze. Technological analyses (including spectography and wet chemistry) have shown that it is a slip made of fine iron-rich clay, fired (often to vitrification) in a reducing atmosphere.

A.O. Shepard: *Plumbate: a Mesoamerican trade ware* (Washington, D.C., 1948); H. Neff: 'The theoretical and methodological lessons of Shepard's research on Plumbate ware', *The ceramic legacy of Anna O. Shepard*, ed. R.L. Bishop and F.W. Lange (Boulder, 1991), 177–204.

PRI

Pluvial Lakes Tradition *see* STEMMED POINT TRADITION

point estimate *see* PARAMETER ESTIMATION

Polonnaruva Historic capital of Sri Lanka in the 6th–13th centuries AD, although occasionally secondary to the alternative capital of ANURADHAPURA. The site was enclosed within fortification walls and associated with massive irrigation reservoirs. The surviving architecture includes residential remains, administrative buildings, royal palaces and reception halls, as well as a Buddhist *STUPA* and monasteries.

Ministry of Cultural Affairs, Sri Lanka: *A guide to Polonnaruwa* (Colombo, 1982). P.L. Prematilleke: *Alanana Parivena Polonnaruva: archaeological excavation report, April–September 1981* (Sri Lanka, 1982).

CS

Polynesia *see* OCEANIA 2

polythetic culture Cultures are often defined in terms of recurrent patterns and similarities in the material culture evidence within a specific geographical and chronological area. A *monothetic* culture would be a grouping of traits where *each trait* is distinctive to that culture. A *polythetic* culture is a cultural grouping defined by a *distinctive mix* of cultural traits, though each individual trait may be identifiable in the surrounding cultural environment. A polythetic culture may therefore arise as a particular set of overlappings of cultural influences, undermining the idea of cultures as an exclusive and absolute ethnic definition. In the real world, most cultures possess both unique and shared traits, but it can be useful to classify cultures as *relatively* mono- or polythetic.
RJA

'Pompeii premise' *see* BEHAVIORAL ARCHAEOLOGY

Po Nagar *see* CHAM

Pong Tuk The first major site in Thailand containing evidence for the adoption of Buddhism, it was originally thought to date to the 2nd century AD, but P. Dupont now dates a bronze statue of the Buddha to the 6th century AD at the earliest. Located in the western edge of the Central Plain, it incorporates the foundations of a series of religious structures, including a *STUPA*, a *CAITYA* and what is probably a *VIHARA* (meeting hall). A bronze Roman lamp of the 1st–2nd centuries AD has also been found there, providing an index of the widespread trading network within which sites such as Pong Tuk operated.

G. Coedes: 'The excavations of Pong Tuk and their importance for the ancient history of Siam', *JSS* 21 (1928), 195–209; R.H. Robinson: *The Buddhist religion: a historical introduction* (Belmont, 1970).
CH

population In statistical analysis a 'population' is the aggregate of objects about which a researcher wishes to make statements, often on the basis of DATA taken from a SAMPLE. Archaeologists often distinguish between a target population (e.g. the total original set of stone tools in use at a particular Palaeolithic site) and the corresponding sampled population (e.g. the tools which have actually survived in the archaeological record). The sampled population is therefore that part of the target population which is actually available for study, because other parts (such as urban land in a field survey) are inaccessible.

J.E. Doran and F.R. Hodson: *Mathematics and computers in archaeology* (Edinburgh, 1975), 94–9; J.F. Cherry, C. Gamble and S. Shennan: 'General introduction: attitudes to sampling in British archaeology', *Sampling in contemporary British archaeology*, ed. J.F. Cherry, C. Gamble and S. Shennan (Oxford, 1978), 1–8; S. Shennan: *Quantifying archaeology* (Edinburgh, 1988), 298–328.
CO

portable art *see* MOBILIARY ART

port of trade Term used in Mesoamerican archaeology to refer to a politically neutral area, where representatives of political entities (often rivals) met for purposes of conducting carefully regulated commercial transactions.

Portuguese trading *feiras* Trading stations established by the Portuguese in Central Africa during the mid-16th century AD. The Portuguese encountered the Zimbabwe culture (*see* GREAT ZIMBABWE) while searching for a sea route to India. Recognizing the potential profit in capturing the Indian Ocean gold and ivory trade from the Swahili (*see* SWAHILI HARBOUR-TOWNS), they established a fort in 1505 AD at Sofala, near present-day Beira in Mozambique. In the 1560s they established a number of *feiras*, or trading stations, in the Mutapa (or Monomatapa) kingdom in northeastern Zimbabwe, where they traded glass beads and cloth for gold and ivory. The best known *feiras* were Luanze, Dambarare near Mazoe, Ongoe, and Massapa at the base of Mount Fura (modern Mt Darwin). Commonly, the *feira* comprised a number of individual trading stores owned by merchants living in Sena and Tete on the Zambezi. The stores were rectangular structures made with sun-dried bricks, surrounded by a rectangular ditch and pallisade. Each store was separated from its neighbours by a few hundred metres, the whole settlement stretching along a river or watershed for a kilometre or more. Large and important settlements included a chapel and garrison.

D.P. Abraham: 'Maramuca: an exercise in the combined use of Portuguese records and oral tradition', *JAH* 2 (1961), 211–25; P.S. Garlake: 'Seventeenth-century Portuguese earthworks in Rhodesia', *SAAB* 21 (1966), 157–70; ——: 'Excavations at the seventeenth-century

Portuguese site of Dambarare, Rhodesia'. *Proceeding and Transactions Rhodesia Scientific Association* 54 (1969), 23–61.
TH

positive feedback *see* SYSTEMS THEORY

positivism Philosophy of science developed from the early 19th century that influenced the 'New Archaeologists' of the 1960s (*see* PROCESSUAL ARCHAEOLOGY). Set in train by the early French social scientist and thinker, Auguste Comte (1798–1857), positivism described an approach to truth-seeking that set aside simple hypothesizing and metaphysical discussion of the 'inner essences' and motivations that gave rise to social phenomena, in favour of careful observation and experiment regarding how social phenomena manifested themselves and related to each other in the real world. This essentially EMPIRICAL approach to understanding society may originally have been a reaction against the intellectual anarchy of revolutionary and post-revolutionary France (and the resulting social and political chaos), which seemed inferior to the explanations of the natural world as revealed by the methodologies of the physical sciences in the 18th and early 19th century. Positivism informed the much more rigorously formulated LOGICAL POSITIVIST movement in the early 20th century, and it was partly through the aims and methodologies of this (now defunct) school of philosophy that it influenced processual archaeology.
C. Hempel: *Aspects of scientific explanation* (New York, 1965).
RJA

post-depositional theory One of the five bodies of theory postulated by David Clarke in 1973 (published as Clarke 1979: 83–103). Whereas pre-depositional and depositional theory are primarily concerned with the establishing of links between individual human activity, social practices and the environment, as well as the exploration of connections between these phenomena and the archaeological record, post-depositional theory is concerned with the many influences that are brought to bear on the archaeological record, such as the ploughing of fields, the looting of tombs or the effects on the soil of freezing and drought. It is therefore broadly similar to the 'N-TRANSFORMS' of Michael Schiffer's BEHAVIORAL ARCHAEOLOGY, while pre-depositional and depositional theory equate with his 'C-TRANSFORMS'.
D.L. Clarke: *Analytical archaeologist* (New York, 1979); D.T. Nash and M.D. Petraglia, eds: *Natural formation processes and the archaeological record*. BAR IS 352 (Oxford, 1987).
IS

posthole (American: 'postmold') Small man-made pit visible as a smudge on the surface of an archaeological deposit, where a wooden post has once been pushed into the ground surface. Usually the decayed remains of the wood enable the post-hole to be differentiated from the surrounding deposit. Several long-term experiments were carried out at the Princes Risborough Laboratory of the Building Research Establishment in the 1970s in order to determine the rates of decay of posts made from different types of wood (see Morgan 1975; Barker 1982: 89–91). At some sites, such as the Romano-British town of Wroxeter, large areas of settlement have been mapped almost entirely on the basis of postholes. *See also* STAKEHOLES.
J.W. Morgan: 'The preservation of timber', *Timber Grower* 55 (1975); P. Barker: *Techniques of archaeological excavation* 2nd edn (London, 1982), 77–94, 254–67, figs 23–5, 31.
IS

post-medieval archaeology *see* EUROPE, MEDIEVAL AND POST-MEDIEVAL 2

post-positivism *see* POST-PROCESSUAL ARCHAEOLOGY

post-processual archaeology Any attempt to reach a satisfactory definition of this body of archaeological theory is frustrated by the fact that, as its name implies, it is a disparate set of approaches united only by a sense of revolt against the domination of the subject by PROCESSUAL, FUNCTIONALIST and POSITIVIST theory. The term post-processual archaeology was coined by Ian Hodder in 1986 in the first edition of *Reading the past* (see Hodder 1991, the second edition), and is now usually taken to encompass approaches such as CONTEXTUAL ARCHAEOLOGY, CRITICAL ARCHAEOLOGY, CRITICAL THEORY, FEMINIST ARCHAEOLOGY, MARXISM, PHENOMENOLOGY and POST-STRUCTURALISM.

For many archaeologists, the movement is exemplified by two books published in 1987, in which Michael Shanks and Chris Tilley sought to overturn many of the sacred cows of a 'New Archaeology' that had ceased to be radical or revisionist and which, by the 1980s, had itself become very much the established approach in the discipline. Shanks and Tilley (1987b) argue that IDEOLOGY – consciously or unconsciously – informs virtually all archaeological description and interpretation, and that there is no truly objective set of data or conclusions, given that all approaches are inevitably coloured by ideological biases and constraints. Furthermore, not even the awareness of such self-limitations can relieve archaeologists of their ideological baggage – an argument that is founded in the concerns of POST-STRUCTURALISM. The solution put forward forcefully by Shanks and Tilley is the adoption of a combination of relativism and CRITICAL THEORY, whereby, instead of striving for an unattainable set of archaeological 'truths' or 'facts', archaeologists should pursue self-consciously ideologically informed approaches to their data, in other words: 'polemic and rhetoric should be an essential part of archaeological text production to stimulate the reader to be a producer of the text's meaning and its relation to the meaning of the past, not a passive consumer of a bland and smooth narrative . . . inviting acquiescence rather than critical reflection' (1987b: 207). One of the most recent manifestations of post-processual archaeology is 'interpretive archaeology' (see, for instance, Tilley 1994).

M. Shanks and C. Tilley: *Re-constructing archaeology* (London, 1987a); ——: *Social theory and archaeology* (Cambridge, 1987b); B.G. Trigger: *A history of archaeological thought* (Cambridge, 1989), 348–57; I. Hodder: *Reading the past*, 2nd edn (Cambridge, 1991), 156–81; N. Yoffee and A. Sherratt, eds: *Archaeological theory: who sets the agenda?* (Cambridge, 1993); C. Tilley, ed.: *Interpretative archaeology* (Oxford, 1994) [see review: I. Hodder, *CAJ* 5/2 (1995), 306–9]; I. Hodder et al., eds: *Interpreting archaeology; finding meaning in the past* (London, 1995); R.W. Preucel and I. Hodder, eds: *Contemporary archaeology in theory: a reader* (Oxford, 1996).

IS

post-Shamarkian *see* SHAMARKIAN

post-structuralism Intellectual movement that emerged in several disciplines during the 1960s as a reaction against – and development of – STRUCTURALISM. The essence of post-structuralism is that it stressed the 'significatory' nature of linguistic and cultural constructions. If, as the Swiss linguist Ferdinand de Saussure originally explained, words and other signs were linked in only an *arbitrary* way to the external world, and gained meaning largely through their relationship with other signs, then cultural 'texts' had to be analysed largely by reference to meanings within themselves (and, perhaps, within the mind of the reader of the text).

This contrasted with many structuralist analyses – for example, the work of Lévi-Strauss (*see* STRUCTURALISM) – which examined structures in cultural communications as a way of illuminating society itself, and which often searched for universal laws and truths. Post-structuralist critiques proclaimed the *autonomy* of the cultural text from the social context that had produced it, and focused instead on meaning relationships within the individual text and the mind of the reader. The autonomous text was no longer explained by, or important because of, its relationship with 'real' social phenomena.

Post-structuralists criticized the 'scientific' approach of structuralism, which had led to over-dependence on simplistic notions such as binary oppositions. Leading post-structuralist thinkers included the French theorist Jacques Derrida, who stressed for example that the meaning of a word arises from past uses in other texts and contexts, and cannot be understood simply by analysing its formal position within a system of structures. Derrida also insisted that the reader or speaker of a text played equal part in giving the text meaning: speech should not be privileged over writing, and writer should not be privileged over reader. Derrida denied that a 'final' meaning of any text could be discovered: instead the post-structuralist critic's deconstruction of the text offered only one account of (or interaction with) its possible meanings. Careful analysis of the meaning structures within a text could lead a text to deconstruct and thus 'subvert' itself. But there was no final objective truth, simply an ever-evolving set of insightful interpretations. The French philosopher-historian Michel Foucault (1926–84) hugely influenced post-structuralist thought in the 1970s, stressing that communicated knowledge is structured into 'discursive formations', and therefore helps to shape society and social institutions.

The intellectual currents summarized above can be seen as influences on various approaches in archaeology. In particular, the antagonism to positivism and the certainties of science, the stress placed on reflexive modes of thought, and the idea of the reader as active rather than passive, surface as powerful features of Ian Hodder's influential CONTEXTUAL ARCHAEOLOGY. This and other approaches that developed in archaeology in the late 1970s and early 1980s came to be bundled together as POST-PROCESSUALIST rather than post-structuralist, partly because the processual approach in archaeology (particularly North American archaeology) dominated the discipline much more than structuralist approaches – the intellectual reaction was thus overtly 'anti-positivist' rather than 'anti-structuralist' – but also because early post-processualist theorists in archaeology did not adopt a fully post-structuralist stance.

Just as post-structuralist approaches in literary criticism and sociology led some writers to conclude that finding objective truths about texts or social institutions was an impossible (or endless) task, so post-structuralist approaches in archaeology suggested to some that objective provable knowledge of past societies is also unattainable. The complexities of deconstruction were rarely attempted as a mode of analysis of archaeological evidence, but the intellectual rhetoric gave a powerful prop to those who sought to counter the bold attempts by processualist archaeologists to formulate and apply general laws.

For some time, the language of post-structuralism was clearly visible in the dialectic between processualists and post-processualists, but it seemed that the discipline would be spared a concerted attempt to build a 'post-structuralist' archaeology. In the early 1990s, however, a series of texts (e.g. Bapty and Yates 1990; Baker and Thomas 1990; Olsen 1990) adopted a much more radical post-structuralist stance. At the extreme, the idea that an archaeologist can or should attempt to reach the original meaning of an action that produced part of the archaeological text (i.e. the motive of the prehistoric 'author') is discounted. Archaeological data, like texts, are simply systems of structured differences, with arbitrarily assigned meanings that will be interpreted differently by different readers (even within the ancient society, let alone the modern society of the archaeologist). As a result, the possible interpretations of the archaeological text are endless, and it is impossible and, more importantly, fruitless, to attempt a single 'objective' interpretation of the past. It is the analysis of the subjective nature of the archaeological interpretation, rather than the ancient society itself, that is privileged.

Hodder (1992: 160–8), whose own work stresses the complexity of interpreting symbolism and material culture within past societies, rejects this extreme post-structuralist approach. He argues that in valuing the importance of present interpretation more highly than what it tells us about the past the archaeologist is in danger of undermining archaeology's special purpose and value – and of disappearing into a quagmire of relativism. Instead, faced with the extreme version of ideas that he had advanced more cautiously in his own CONTEXTUAL ARCHAEOLOGY, Hodder chooses to stress the 'objectivity of the data' – that is, inherent qualities within sets of archaeology data that help us to sort likelihoods from unlikelihoods (*see also* THEORY AND THEORY BUILDING).

Post-structuralism, as a self-conscious intellectual approach, has faded away in most disciplines in which it was identifiable as a moving force in the 1970s and 1980s. In archaeology, post-structuralism in its purest but least 'archaeological' form may continue to be of interest as a way of criticizing archaeological texts themselves – of analysing the ways in which they structure meaning, and as a useful technique within the subdiscipline of historiography. In shaping approaches to primary archaeological material, it has had an unintended but perhaps more important effect: by making clear the destructiveness of extreme relativism, it has forced post-processualist archaeologists to consider again the nature of objectivity and truth in the discipline, and to realize that these concerns remain, whether or not it is the ambition of the archaeologist to construct universal laws.

F. Baker and J. Thomas, eds: *Writing the past in the present* (Lampeter, 1990); I. Bapty and T. Yates, eds: *Archaeology after structuralism* (London, 1990); B. Olsen: 'Roland Barthes: from sign to text', *Reading material culture*, ed. C. Tilley (Oxford, 1990); C. Tilley, ed.: *Reading material culture* (Oxford, 1990); I. Hodder: *Theory and practice in archaeology* (London, 1992).

RJA

potassium-argon (K-Ar) dating Scientific dating technique, which, in archaeology, has mainly been used for dating volcanic deposits associated with early hominid remains in East Africa, notably at OLDUVAI GORGE and KOOBI FORA. It has also been the main technique used to establish the timescale of the geomagnetic reversal and oxygen isotope sequences (*see* PALAEOMAGNETIC DATING *and* OXYGEN ISOTOPE CHRONOSTRATIGRAPHY).

The principles of the technique lie in the decay of the ^{40}K isotope of potassium, comprising 0.00117% of naturally occurring potassium. The half-life of ^{40}K is 1250 million years. The decay product of interest is the stable ^{40}Ar isotope of the gas argon, the probability of formation for which is 11.2%. As a first approximation it is assumed that, being a gas, the amount of argon in a rock on formation from the molten state is zero, and from this time the ^{40}Ar builds up from decay of ^{40}K. Also from this initial time, it is assumed that the system is closed to ^{40}K and ^{40}Ar i.e. their concentrations change only due to radioactive decay and build-up respectively. The K-Ar age can then be determined by measurement of these concentrations. Total potassium can be readily determined by analytical techniques such as ATOMIC ABSORPTION SPECTROPHOTOMETRY. The ^{40}Ar is measured, relative to a known amount of ^{38}Ar, by mass spectrometry of the gas released on fusion by a separate sample.

If there has been reheating, recrystallization or weathering of the rock, or hydration or devitrification of glassy materials, the closed system assumption will be invalid. Another problem is incorporation of detrital material which can lead to high K-Ar ages. Dating of different mineral fractions will reveal these problems, as the ages will vary. The assumption of initial zero concentration of ^{40}Ar is also problematic because atmospheric argon (typically 1% of the atmosphere) is usually incorporated by minerals as they cool. Fortunately this can be detected and corrected for using ^{36}Ar which comprises about 0.34% of atmospheric argon. Incorporation during cooling of non-atmospheric ^{40}Ar from the outgassing of surrounding rocks is more of a problem, but can be detected by the ARGON-ARGON technique.

Given the long half-life of ^{40}K, the lower age limit of the technique is the constraint in archaeological applications. For minerals with a high potassium content, samples as young as 1000 years can be dated, but the error terms are high (typically ±100%). At 100,000 years, however, errors of ±5% are achievable, but these increase with decrease of the potassium content.

G. Faure: *Principles of isotope geology*, 2nd edn (New York, 1986); D.A. Richards and P.L. Smart: 'Potassium-argon and argon-argon dating', *Quaternary dating methods – user's guide*, ed. P.L. Smart and P.D. Fraces (Cambridge, 1991), 37–44.

SB

Poverty Point Prehistoric site in northeastern Louisiana, along the western edge of the Mississippi River valley, which is the type site for the Poverty Point culture (*c.*1500–1000 BC). It consists of six large concentric semicircular earthworks with a maximum diameter of about 1200 m, several large earthen mounds, and an associated habitation area. The excavated artefacts include evidence of a well-developed lapidary technology in which exotic raw materials (such as jasper, steatite, fluorite and galena) were used to manufacture beads, plummets and pendants. Distinctively-shaped baked clay objects are also common. The presence of such a wide array of exotic materials at the Poverty Point site has led some researchers to speculate that the site was a regional economic centre. More than 100 additional Poverty Point culture sites are known for the region.

J. Ford and C. Webb: *Poverty Point: a late Archaic site in Louisiana* (New York, 1956); R. Neuman: *An introduction to Louisiana archaeology* (Baton Rouge, 1984), 90–112.

RJE

Prasat Pram Loven (Plain of Reeds) Low-lying area near the Mekong Delta in Vietnam, where an important early Sanskrit inscription was found. It records that Gunavarman consecrated a footstep of Visnu, and also that this prince was sent to the area to reclaim marshland. G. Coedes has dated the text on stylistic grounds to the 6th century AD, and the reference to drainage recalls the extensive network of canals found in this area which provided not only transport and communication, but also the control by drainage of the annual Mekong floods.

G. Coedes, 'Deux inscriptions Sanskrites de Fou-nan', *BEFEO* 31 (1931) 1–23.

CH

precision In the statistical analysis of archaeological DATA, the precision of a PARAMETER ESTIMATE indicates how close it is likely to be to the true value, for example the ± of a RADIOCARBON DATE indicates how close to the quoted date the true date is likely to lie. The STANDARD DEVIATION of the estimate is often used to express this. It should not be confused with the *accuracy* of an estimate, which is the actual difference between it and the true mean, and is usually unknown.

CO

pre-depositional theory *see* BEHAVIORAL ARCHAEOLOGY; C-TRANSFORMS; POST-DEPOSITIONAL THEORY

prehistoric Term used since the mid-19th century to indicate the period of human history before writing was invented or (in most cases) introduced into a region. The complex etymology of the term is discussed by Clermont and Smith (1990).

N. Clermont and P. Smith: 'Prehistoric, prehistory, prehistorian . . . who invented the terms?', *Antiquity* 64 (1990), 97–102.

RJA

Pre-Pottery Neolithic *see* ACERAMIC NEOLITHIC

Pre-Sargonic period *see* EARLY DYNASTIC PERIOD (MESOPOTAMIA)

pressure flaking Technique for retouching flint by applying pressure to the edge of a flake, using a pressure flaking tool (often of bone, antler or wood), rather than by striking the flake. Pressure flaking allows a much greater degree of precision and enables skilled flint knappers to detach regular flat flakes. Experimental work suggests that some knappers in the Upper Palaeolithic were pre-heating flints in hearths to make the material more amenable to pressure flaking.
RJA

prey-choice model *see* FORAGING THEORY

primary silt, primary fill, rapid silt Term used to describe the debris (comprising silt, scree and fallen turf) which accumulates at the bottom of a freshly dug ditch, usually taking about a decade or two to form. Once the ditch has become somewhat wider and shallower, a 'secondary silt' forms over the top of the primary deposit.

principal components analysis (PCA) A branch of MULTIVARIATE STATISTICS which represents multivariate archaeological DATASETS (for example the results of analysing a set of artefacts for a series of chemical elements) by a SCATTERGRAM in two dimensions, accompanied by related useful statistics. The principal components are combinations of the original VARIABLES, and represent a rotation of the original space to better show the pattern of the points in it. The first axis of such a plot is the first principal component of the dataset, i.e. the axis which achieves the greatest possible dispersion of the points when they are plotted along it. The second axis is the one at right angles to the first which achieves the greatest possible dispersion not already accounted for by the first, and so on. It is a useful technique of EXPLORATORY DATA ANALYSIS (EDA), provided that the variables are all continuous and can be measured on the same scale. If the variables are measured on different scales, it may still be possible to use PCA, provided the data are first STANDARDIZED.
J.E. Doran and F.R. Hodson: *Mathematics and computers in archaeology* (Edinburgh, 1975), 190–7; C.R. Orton: *Mathematics in archaeology* (Glasgow, 1980), 56–62; S. Shennan: *Quantifying archaeology* (Edinburgh, 1988), 245–70; M.J. Baxter: *Exploratory multivariate analysis in archaeology* (Edinburgh, 1993).
CO

probabilistic approach *see* COVERING LAWS

probability In classical statistics, the probability that a VARIABLE takes certain values is the proportion of occasions in which it would take those values in a large number of repeated experiments or SAMPLES. For example, the probability that a single transect of a field survey would cross a certain site is the proportion of all the possible but hypothetical transects that would cross the site. Partly in response to the difficulty of applying this definition to situations in which repeated sampling is not possible, e.g. in taking RADIOCARBON DATES, BAYESIAN STATISTICS were developed, in which the interpretation of probability is subjective – a researcher's degree of belief that a variable will take certain values.
J.E. Doran and F.R. Hodson: *Mathematics and computers in archaeology* (Edinburgh, 1975), 30–71; C.R. Orton: *Mathematics in archaeology* (Glasgow, 1980), 219–20.
CO

processual archaeology Approach which was adopted by many American and some western European archaeologists during the 1960s and 1970s, formally beginning with the argument set out by Kent Flannery (1967) that 'culture process' (*rather than* 'CULTURE HISTORY') was the true aim of archaeological research. Whereas culture-historical archaeologists, such as Gordon Childe and Gordon Willey, had been concerned primarily with the transformation of archaeological data into prehistoric narratives, Flannery suggested that the archaeologist ought to be seeking out the basic systems or predictable sets of laws and mechanisms (e.g. geological, ecological or social) which brought into existence the constituents and patterns of the archaeological record.

The practitioners of archaeology since its beginnings had been mainly educated in classics and history, whereas the so-called 'New Archaeology' of the 1960s opened the field up to the methods and theory of geography, sociology and the information sciences. A key feature of processual archaeology as practised was the use of quantitative methods to analyse features and patterns within the archaeological record (*see, for instance*, SPATIAL ANALYSIS). Evidence was presented in a more 'scientific' style with much greater use of graphs, diagrams, flow charts, and schematic plans and maps. The focus of investigation shifted towards questions that involved 'harder' or more scientifically accessible data such as economy, settlement hierarchies, population densities, materials analysis etc., and away from attempts to understand the motivation of individuals or interpret evidence in 'non-functional' ways. Rather than simply presenting archaeological interpretation as self-evident, or as a plausible narrative full of insightful ideas, archaeological theses and reports were increasingly constructed so as to clarify the links between statement and evidence.

At a more philosophical level, the idea of the archaeological site as a means of obtaining one or more cultural 'snapshots' from within a long historical sequence, was to be replaced by the sense that every artefact or assemblage was part of some form of pattern that could be scientifically decoded if the archaeologist could only determine the universal laws governing site formation processes, cultural factors or ecological determinants. The nature and identity of such laws could be investigated not only by the traditional techniques of survey and excavation, but also by such methods as ETHNOARCHAEOLOGY, ACTUALISTIC STUDIES and EXPERIMENTAL ARCHAEOLOGY.

There were initially at least two strands of New Archaeology, consisting of the ANALYTICAL ARCHAEOLOGY of the British archaeologist David Clarke and the processual and FUNCTIONALIST approaches being set out by Lewis Binford. Whereas Clarke's approach was primarily concerned with the different ways of interpreting archaeological remains (particularly the use of statistics), Binford began to move gradually away from traditional archaeological data, pursuing instead the kinds of ethnographic information that could serve as links and analogues between ancient and modern material cultures. This project underlined the POSITIVIST nature of the New Archaeology, and drew on the COVERING LAW approach to knowledge gathering that characterized the LOGICAL POSITIVIST project. By making explicit and testing a body of theory (Binford's 'MIDDLE-RANGE THEORY') that linked archaeological data and low-level theorizing more securely to interpretation of human behaviour at archaeological sites, the New Archaeologists hoped to build a platform of secure statements about the past from which they could infer and test general theories about social dynamics. Although many processual archaeologists held that their ultimate aim was the construction of a body of general theory, the most characteristic and contentious part of the project turned out to be the creation of reliable and useful middle-range theory. Michael Schiffer's BEHAVIORAL ARCHAEOLOGY, conceived as a critique of simplistic interpretations of patterning in the archaeological record, was probably the most ambitious attempt to lay down a set of rules governing the processes of site formation and cultural development. The approaches adopted by Flannery, Clarke, Binford, Schiffer and many other processual archaeologists had much in common, but at the time there were many very public arguments concerning such issues as the validity or relevance of the approach. Perhaps the only real consensus among the most vocal proponents of processual archaeology was the sense that there could be no return to culture history.

Since the early 1980s, the cruder versions of processual archaeology have been increasingly criticized for their tendency towards determinism of various sorts as well as the occasional predilection for 'number-crunching' as an end in itself. Ian Hodder (1991: xiv) has pointed out that this propensity has, if anything, been accentuated by the methods of funding archaeology, in the 1990s, which have become increasingly geared towards science-based projects, thus threatening to 'nudge archaeology not towards a fruitful integration with science . . . but towards a narrow scientism'. It was primarily in reaction to this perception of processual archaeology as an attempt by archaeologists to ape 'real scientists' that the earliest exponents of POST-PROCESSUAL ARCHAEOLOGY (Shanks and Tilley 1987a; 1987b; Hodder 1991) set out their more humanistic, subjective and 'self-critical' approaches to the interpretation of the past.

Renfrew and Bahn (1991: 405) suggest that COGNITIVE ARCHAEOLOGY should be regarded as a further development of the processual school rather than a reaction against it. They thus make a distinction between the earlier 'functionalist processual' approaches characterized by the work of Schiffer and Binford in the 1970s and 1980s, contrasting these with the 'cognitive-processual' approaches of the late 1980s and 1990s (e.g. Renfrew and Zubrow 1994).

See CARTER RANCH PUEBLO *for a discussion of the emergence of processual archaeology in America, particularly with regard to the study of social organization.*

K.V. Flannery: 'Culture history v. culture process: a debate in American archaeology', *SA* 217 (1967), 119–22; L.R. Binford: 'Some comments on historical versus processual archaeology', *SJA* 24/3 (1968), 267–75; D.L.

Clarke: *Analytical archaeology* (London, 1968); P.J. Watson: 'Archaeological interpretation, 1985', *American archaeology: past and present*, ed. D.J. Meltzer, D.D. Fowler and J.A. Sabloff (Washington, D.C., 1986); T.K. Earle and R.M. Preucel: 'Processual archaeology and the radical critique', *CA* 28 (1987), 501–38; M. Shanks and C. Tilley: *Re-constructing archaeology* (London, 1987a); —— and ——: *Social theory and archaeology* (Cambridge, 1987b); R. Preucel, ed.: *Between past and present: issues in contemporary archaeological discourse* (Carbondale, 1990); I. Hodder: *Reading the past* 2nd edn (Cambridge, 1991); C. Renfrew and P. Bahn: *Archaeology: theories, methods and practice* (London, 1991); C. Renfrew and E.B. Zubrow, eds: *The ancient mind: elements of cognitive archaeology* (Cambridge, 1994).

IS

Proconsul *see* RUSINGA

profile Vertical section that can be used to view both the stratigraphy and the horizontal relationships of the various natural and cultural features making up an archaeological site. The term is also used to refer to drawings of such sections.

Prolonged Drift Waterside Late Stone Age site located in ELMENTEITA, in the elevated stretch of the Kenya Rift Valley; it lies on or adjacent to a site previously called 'Long's Drift' by Louis Leakey: hence the jocular nomenclature. Prolonged Drift was investigated by Glynn Isaac, Charles Nelson and colleagues in the late 1960s. The faunal remains, analysed by Diane Gifford-Gonzalez (Gifford et al. 1980), provide an important model for reconstructing the economy and ecology of later African hunter-gatherers and early ('Neolithic') pastoralists.

D.P. Gifford, G.Ll. Isaac and C.M. Nelson: 'Predation and pastoralism at Prolonged Drift: a Pastoral Neolithic site in Kenya', *Azania* 15 (1980), 57–108.

JS

Protogeometric *see* GEOMETRIC AND PROTOGEOMETRIC

Protoliterate period The earliest historical phase in the history of SUMER, defined by Frankfort (1970: 381) as comprising most of the URUK period and the whole of the JEMDET NASR period, when Sumerian writing and art were both emerging in Mesopotamia.

H. Frankfort: *The art and architecture of the ancient Orient*, 4th edn (Harmondsworth, 1970).

Protosinaitic Early alphabetic script of the mid-2nd millennium BC, discovered in the form of rock-carved inscriptions at Egyptian mining sites in the Sinai peninsula (particularly SERABIT EL-KHADIM).

W.F. Albright: *The Protosinaitic inscriptions and their decipherment* (Harvard, 1966); W.V. Davies: *Egyptian hieroglyphs* (London, 1987), 57–61.

IS

proxemics Study of the spatial aspects of human social interaction.

Pucara Large urban site in southern Peru, which was occupied for a single period from 100 BC to AD 100. The religious art features a female deity with a llama and a warrior with feline characteristics, trophy heads, incised polychrome ceramics with mythic figures, and full round stone sculptures of humans and deities; these artistic features were extremely influential on contemporary cultures of the *altiplano* and northern Chile. The settlement is built of adobe upon stone foundations, and the major structure is a U-shaped temple with stone cist tombs in the courtyard.

A.L. Kidder: *Some early sites in the northern Lake Titicaca Basin* (Washington, D.C., 1943); S.J. Chávez: 'Archaeological reconnaissance in the province of Chumbivilcas, South Highland Peru', *Expedition* 30/3 (1988), 27–38.

KB

pueblo (Spanish: 'village') Term used to describe the historic stone-masonry or adobe-built settlements of the American Southwest, such as the ANASAZI town, PUEBLO BONITO. Each pueblo consists of many rooms, often several storeys in height.

JJR

Pueblo Historical and present-day cultural group in the American Southwest, who are thought to be the descendants of the prehistoric ANASAZI, MOGOLLON and HOHOKAM groups. The term is also used to describe the five latest phases in the Anasazi chronological sequence, from *c.*AD 700 to the present.

E.P. Dozier: *The Pueblo Indians of North America* (New York, 1970).

JJR

Pueblo Bonito Located in Chaco Canyon, northwestern New Mexico, Pueblo Bonito is the most famous ANASAZI pueblo in the American

Southwest. Consisting of 800 rooms, 60 kivas, three great kivas and two platform mounds, it was inhabited throughout the Pueblo II period (AD 900–1150) and was the centrepiece of the CHACO culture.

S.H. Lekson: *Great Pueblo architecture of Chaco Canyon, New Mexico* (Albuquerque, 1986); S.H. Lekson, T.C. Windes, J.R. Stein and W.J. Judge: 'The Chaco Canyon community', *Science* 259 (1988), 100–109; R.G. Vivian: *The Chacoan prehistory of the San Juan Basin* (New York, 1990).

JJR

Puerto Hormiga, Monsú and San Jacinto Group of sites on the Caribbean littoral near Cartagena in northern Colombia, dating from 3800 to 3300 BC, which have yielded the earliest well-dated ceramics in the Americas. Puerto Hormiga and Monsú are shell mounds, and San Jacinto is a seasonal camp site where plants were roasted in pits. The ceramic assemblages from all three are technically and aesthetically complex, but bear little resemblance to each other. There is no evidence of either agriculture or the use of ceramics in cooking.

G. Reichel-Dolmatoff: 'The cultural context of early fiber tempered pottery in Colombia', *The Florida Anthropologist* 25/2 (1972), 1–2; ——: *Monsú: un sitio arqueológico* (Bogotá, 1985); C.A. Oyuela: 'Dos sitios arqueológicos con desgrasante de fibra vegetal en la Serranía de San Jacinto', *Boletín de Arqueología* 2/1 (1987), 5–26.

KB

pulse theory Model put forward by Roderick McIntosh to account for the origins of urbanism in the Inland Niger Delta (IND) of Mali in the 1st millennium AD. It is assumed that this was an indigenous development, not dependent on the stimulus of outside trade, representing an elaboration of existing trends, not a revolutionary event. The model presupposes the interaction of three local factors – climatic, geomorphological and social – which may have brought it about:

1 *Climate*. The climate of West Africa is in large part determined by the north–south movement (or 'pulse') of the InterTropical Convergence Zone (ITCZ). Annually, this causes the alternating dry and wet seasons which characterize the region; in addition, it is known that over millennia the position of the ITCZ has varied, periods of desiccation coinciding with its southerly displacement and vice versa. It was during a northern swing of the ITCZ that the IND will have been occupied, but the population will have been constrained by previous soil damage from following the pulse further north.

2 *Geomorphology*. The floodplain of the IND, however, constitutes a privileged area, a hydrological and landform labyrinth making up an 'unusual geomorphological anomaly', which provided a functionally advantageous setting for agricultural experimentation, population expansion, and the development of a clustered urbanism in which major settlements were surrounded by numerous satellites.

3 *Society*. This by itself was not sufficient, since the intensification of specialization demanded by a developing urbanism depended also on the elaboration of a shared ideology, which was achieved (and finds its echo today) in the pattern of settlement of the IND, where different ethnic groups pursue different subsistence occupations but are bound together by well recognized mutual obligations.

R.J. McIntosh: *The pulse theory: genesis and accommodation of specialization in the inland Niger Delta of Mali* (Houston, 1988).

PA-J

Punt East African region to which Egyptian trading missions were being sent from at least the early 3rd millennium BC. Scenes of Punt and its inhabitants are depicted on the second terrace of the Temple of Hatshepsut at DEIR EL-BAHARI (*c*.1460 BC). Many missions evident departed from the ports of Quseir or Mersa Gawasis on the west coast of the Red Sea, but there is still some dispute concerning the precise geographical location of Punt. It was once commonly considered to have been in the region of modern Somalia – Herzog (1968) even suggests an upper Nile location – but the fauna and flora depicted at Deir el-Bahari suggest that Punt was located in southern Sudan or the Eritrean region of Ethiopia (Kitchen 1971; 1993).

R. Herzog: *Punt* (Glückstadt, 1968); K.A. Kitchen: 'Punt and how to get there', *Orientalia* 40 (1971), 184–207; ——: 'The land of Punt', *The archaeology of Africa*, ed. T. Shaw et al. (London, 1993), 587–608.

IS

Pushkalavati *see* CHARSADA

Puuc A subregion of LOWLAND MAYA culture, centred on the low Puuc hills in northwestern Yucatán. The region has given its name to a Late-Terminal Classic (*c*.AD 800–1000) architectural style characterized by fine veneer masonry and elaborate mosaic facades. This is best seen on sites within the region, such as SAYIL, Labná and Kabáh, but also appears at CHICHÉN ITZÁ.

H.E.D. Pollock: *The Puuc: an architectural survey of the hill*

country of Yucatan and northern Campeche, Mexico (Cambridge, MA, 1980).
PRI

P'u-yang-shih (Puyangshi) Site of the YANG-SHAO Neolithic culture, which was excavated in March, 1987, at Hsi-shui-p'o near the southwest corner of the city of P'u-yang, province of Ho-nan, China. It is remarkable for three groups of animal representations laid out with molluscan shells, one in Tomb 45 and the other two to the south of the tomb. The group in Tomb 45 comprised a dragon and a tiger; the second group, a dragon with a spider near its head, and a tiger on the back of which is a deer; the third group, a dragon with a man riding on its back, and again a tiger. The excavators considered that there was a ritual significance attending these, thus suggesting the possibility of a connection with the much later Taoism: in the *Pao-p'u-tzu* of Ko Hung (*c.*AD 283–343) there are references to the *san ch'iao*: the dragon-*ch'iao*, the tiger-*ch'iao*, and the deer-*ch'iao*. Possibly the explanation of the frequently depicted 'man-beast' or *alter ego* motif throughout Chinese art from Shang times might also be sought here. Tomb 45 is therefore thought to have been that of a SHAMAN, together with his three travelling companions.

Anon.: 'Ho-nan P'u-yang Hsi'shui-p'o yi-chih fa-chüeh pao', *WW* 3 (1988), 1–6; D. Bulbeck, ed.: *Ancient Chinese and Southeast Asian bronze cultures* (Taipei, 1996).
NB

pylon (Greek: 'gate') Classical term for the Egyptian ceremonial gateway or *bekhenet* used in temples from at least the Middle Kingdom to the Roman period (*c.*2040 BC–AD 395), probably symbolizing the horizon. The basic structure of a pylon

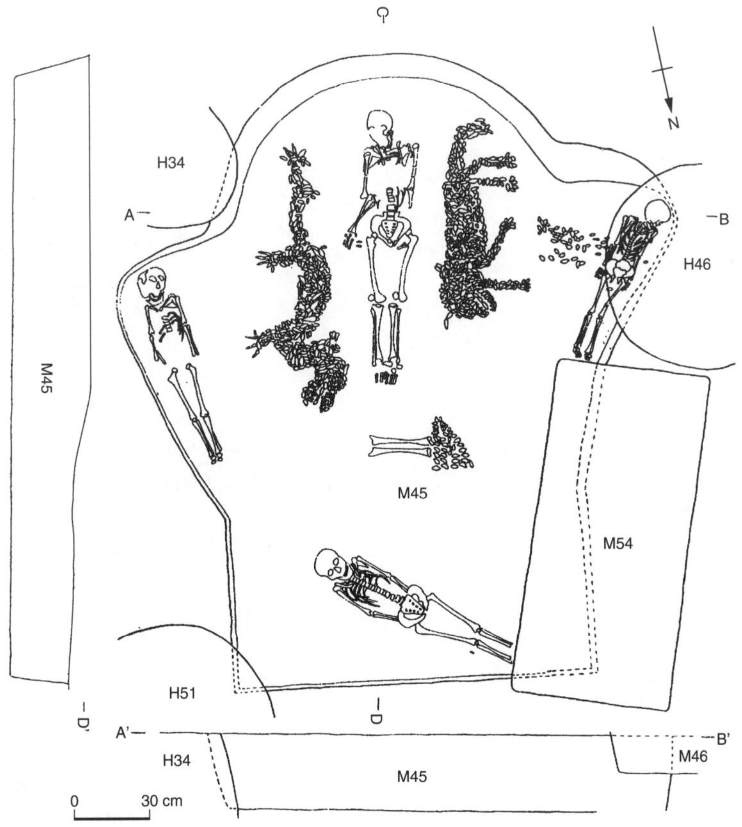

Figure 42 **P'u-yang-shih** P'u-yang 'shaman tomb' (no. 45), China, showing how concentrations of shells were arranged in the shapes of animals. *Source*: *WW* 3 (1988), fig. 5.

consists of two massive towers of rubble-filled masonry tapering upwards, surmounted by a cornice and linked in the centre by an elaborate doorway. Ancient depictions of pylons show that the deep vertical recesses visible along the facades of surviving examples were intended to hold flag staffs.

T. Dombardt: 'Der zweitürige Tempelpylon altägyptischer Baukunst und seine religiöse Symbolik', *Egyptian Religion* 1 (1933), 87–98; P.A. Spencer: *The Egyptian temple: a lexicographical study* (London, 1984), 193–4.

IS

Pylos Mycenaean palace located on the hill at Ano Englianos in the Messenian plain, Greece. Together with the sites of MYCENAE and TIRYNS, it offers the most impressive evidence of the Mycenaean culture of the Greek Bronze Age. In contrast to these other sites, Pylos is completely unfortified, and appears to have been the seat of a local chief or king. It was built during the Late Helladic IIIb pottery phase, indicating that it flourished during the 13th century BC, until being destroyed by fire. The complex centres on a MEGARON, consisting of a vestibule and portico leading in from a courtyard to a great 'throne-room' with hearth and frescoes, store-rooms (especially for olive oil), and a wine magazine. The walls are of rubble on the ground floor, with ashlar facades and fine plaster on the interiors. Other decoration includes painted and fluted columns, and fresco painting in the Mycenaean style (i.e. Minoan influenced, but conventionalized and less naturalistic). Upper stories are of mud brick, and the sophisticated design includes lightwells and a drainage system. Pylos is especially important because it contained an archive of Linear B script tablets; these represent a series of administrative records, naming 16 tributary localities in the Messenian plain.

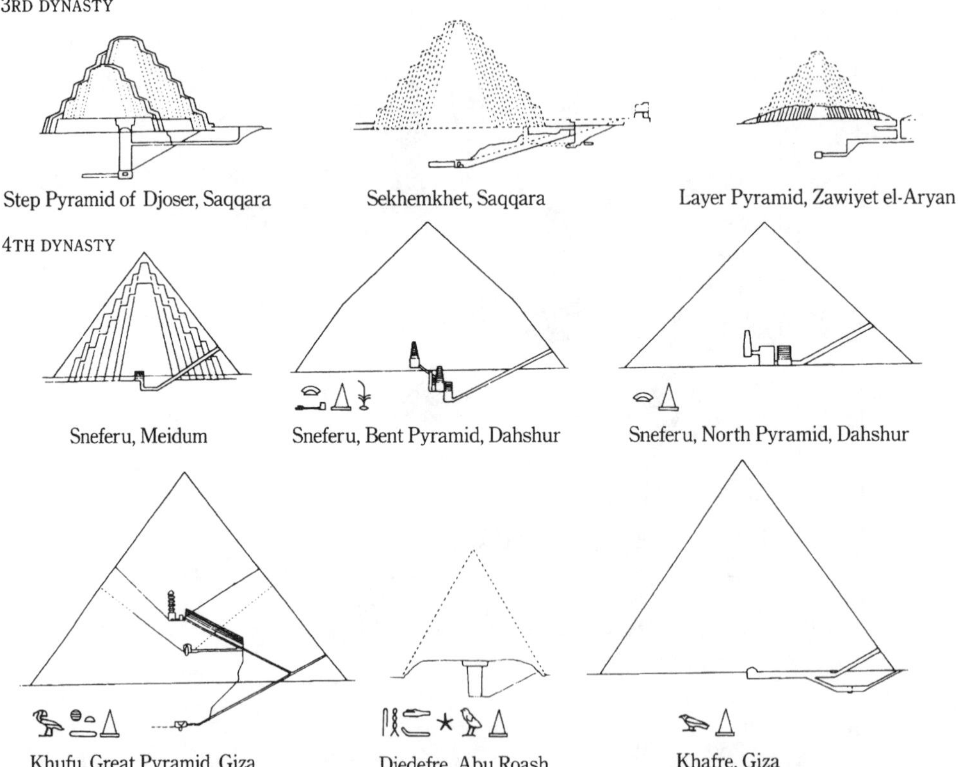

Figure 43 **pyramid** Cross-sections of the major pyramids built during the 3rd and 4th dynasties in Egypt, drawn to the same scale. *Source*: M. Lehner: *The complete pyramids* (Thames and Hudson, 1997), p. 16.

C. Blegen: *The palace of Nestor at Pylos* (Princeton, 1966); M. Ventris and J. Chadwick: *Documents in Mycenaean Greek* (Cambridge, 1973); J. Chadwick: *The Mycenaean world* (Cambridge, 1977); Th. Palaima and C. Shelmerdine, eds: *Pylos comes alive: industry and administration in a Mycenaean palace* (New York, 1984).

RJA

pyramid

1 *Egypt and Nubia*. Pyramid-shaped superstructures were used for Egyptian royal tombs from the 3rd dynasty to the end of the Middle Kingdom (*c*.2649–1640 BC); throughout the rest of the pharaonic period private tombs occasionally incorporated small-scale 'pyramidia'. The first 'step-pyramids' appear to have developed initially out of the rectangular royal and private MASTABATOMBS of the Early Dynastic period (*c*.3000–2649 BC), but by the end of the 3rd dynasty the first smooth-sided 'true pyramid' had been constructed at DAHSHUR. Over the next thousand years the pyramid gradually acquired a range of symbolic meanings. The full-scale 'pyramid complex', consisting of a pyramid with its mortuary and funerary temples (the two temples being linked by a long causeway), had evolved by the beginning of the 4th dynasty, but its origins can be discerned in the royal tombs and 'funerary palaces' at Early Dynastic ABYDOS and the Step Pyramid complex at SAQQARA. In the reign of the 5th-dynasty ruler Unas, the internal chambers began to be inscribed with funerary spells now known as the Pyramid Texts.

In the 18th dynasty, the pharaohs began to be buried in the subterranean rock-tombs of the VALLEY OF THE KINGS, instead of pyramids, and the royal mortuary temples were constructed some distance away from the royal burials themselves. Hundreds of years later the pyramid form was revived, albeit on a smaller scale, by the Napatan and Meroitic kings of Nubia (*see* MEROE, NAPATA *and* NURI).

See also ABU ROASH, GIZA, HAWARA, EL-LAHUN, EL-LISHT, MEIDUM *and* NAQADA.

2 *Mesoamerica*. The term 'pyramid' is sometimes applied to certain Mesoamerican religious buildings (see Kubler 1973): *see* LOWLAND MAYA, MESOAMERICA, PALENQUE *TALUD-TABLERO*, TEOTIHUACAN *and* TIKAL.

R.O. Faulkner: *The ancient Egyptian Pyramid Texts* (Oxford, 1969); G. Kubler: 'Iconographic aspects of architectural profiles at Teotihuacan and in Mesoamerica', *The iconography of Middle American sculpture* (New York 1973), 24–39; D. Arnold, *Building in Egypt: pharaonic stone masonry* (Oxford, 1991); I.E.S. Edwards, *The pyramids of Egypt*, 5th edn (Harmondsworth, 1993).

IS

Q

Qadan *see* CATARACT TRADITION

Qadesh (Tell Nebi Mend) Syro-Hittite Bronze Age city where the famous battle between the Egyptians and the Hittites was fought in *c*.1290 BC. In 1921 it was identified with the site of Tell Nebi Mend next to the River Orontes, which was excavated by Maurice Pézard in 1921–2 and by Peter Parr in the 1970s. The investigation of the massive tell, measuring about a kilometre in length and over 30 m in height, revealed strata dating back at least as early as the 2nd millennium BC, when it may have been an AMORITE settlement. After the Syro-Hittite period the site continued to be occupied in the early Iron Age, during which time a large wooden-columned palace was constructed.

M. Pézard: *Qadesh, mission archéologique à Tell Nebi Mend* (Paris, 1931); H. Goedicke: *Perspectives on the Battle of Kadesh* (Baltimore, 1985); S.J. Bourke: *The transition from the Middle to the Late Bronze Age in the northern Levant: the evidence from Tell Nebi Mend, Syria* (unpublished Ph.D. thesis, University of London, 1992).

IS

Qafzeh and Skhul Cave sites in the MOUNT CARMEL region of Israel which have yielded the earliest fossils of ANATOMICALLY MODERN HUMANS outside Africa. Thermoluminescence analyses of burnt flint indicate that the burials in these caves, including a child with grave goods, are dated to *c*.90–100,000 BP (Vandermeersch 1989). These dates are significantly earlier than those derived from the nearby caves of Tabun and KEBARA which produced NEANDERTHAL fossils, suggesting that 'modern' humans had colonized the Levant before the Neanderthals. Qafzeh and Skhul are also notable for the fact that 'modern' human remains are associated with MOUSTERIAN technology, thereby undermining the claim that 'anatomical' modernity is *necessarily* to be equated with superior technology (which itself is often rather dubiously equated with superior intelligence).

B. Vandermeersch: 'The evolution of modern humans: recent evidence from southwest Asia', *The human revolution*, ed. P. Mellars and C. Stringer (Edinburgh, 1989), 155–64.

PG-B

Qannas, Tell *see* HABUBA KEBIRA

Qantir (anc. Piramesse) Egyptian city-site in the eastern Delta near modern Khatana, which was established by Seti I (*c*.1306–1290 BC) and became an important centre of power during the Ramessid period. Excavations have revealed a mud-brick palace of Ramesses II (Hayes 1937) as well as Ramessid military barrack-rooms and workshops (Pusch 1996). By the beginning of the 3rd Intermediate Period (*c*.1070 BC) the city had diminished in importance and a great deal of its stonework was eventually transferred to the Late Period temples at TANIS and BUBASTIS.

W.C. Hayes: *Glazed tiles from a palace of Ramesses II at Kantir* (New York, 1937); E. Uphill: *The temples of Per Ramesses* (Warminster, 1984); E. Pusch: 'Pi-Ramesses-beloved-of-Amun, Headquarters of thy chariotry: Egyptians and Hittites in the Delta Residence of the Ramessides', *Pelizaeus Museum: the Egyptian collection*, ed. A. Eggebrecht (Mainz, 1996), 126–45.

IS

Qarnawu *see* ARABIA, PRE-ISLAMIC

Qasr al-Hayr al-Gharbi Extensive Islamic-period site in the desert southwest of Palmyra, Syria, which was founded as a monastery in the 6th century AD by Harith b. Jabala, a Ghassanid prince allied to the Byzantines. According to its foundation inscription, it was expanded by the Caliph Hisham in AD 727 – a rare case of precise dating and attribution among Umayyad palaces. Its ornate fortress-like doorway echoes Byzantine models in form but the ornamental plaster reflects SASANIAN influence and presages the dominant position of plaster in Islamic decoration. A similar synthesis of Mediterranean and eastern influences occurs in the floor paintings from the palace, one of which is a Sasanian-style hunting scene, while the other includes a representation of the Greek earth-goddess Gea. The palace stands at the centre of an extensive agricultural estate, equivalent to Roman *latifundia*. Such sites as Qasr al-Hayr al-Gharbi, Qasr al-Hayr al-Sharqi (northeast of Palmyra, see Grabar et al. 1978), and Khirbat al-Mafjar (between JERUSALEM and AMMAN) all reflect the Umayyads' heavy investment in agricultural development, and in recent years the diversity of roles served by these Umayyad ryural sites has been increasingly recognized.

D. Schlumberger: 'Deux fresques omeyyades', *Syria* 25 (1946), 86–102; K.A.C. Creswell: *Early Muslim architecture* 1/2 (Oxford, 1969), 506–18; O. Grabar et al.: *City in the desert: Qasr al-Hayr East*, 2 vols (Cambridge, 1978); D. Schlumberger: *Qasr el-Heir el-Gharbi* (Paris, 1986).

GK

Qasr al-Hayr al-Sharqi *see* QASR AL-HAYR AL-GHARBI

Qasr Ibrim (anc. Pedeme, Primis) Site of a fortified settlement in Lower Nubia, located on the edge of LAKE NASSER, about 240 km south of Aswan. The earliest evidence of occupation dates to the 11th dynasty (*c*.2000 BC), but the major surviving building is a Nubian cathedral dating to the 8th century AD. The other architectural remains include four New Kingdom rock-shrines (*c*.1640–1070 BC) and several temples dating from the 25th dynasty (*c*.700 BC) to the late MEROITIC period (*c*.AD 250). The cemeteries, situated to the north and south of the town-site, date principally to the Meroitic, BALLANA, Christian and Islamic phases of the site's history.

J. Plumley et al.: Preliminary reports on the EES excavations, *JEA* 50– (1964–); R.A. Caminos: *The shrines and rock inscriptions of Ibrim* (London, 1968); A.J. Mills: *The cemeteries of Qasr Ibrim* (London, 1982).

IS

Qatabaneans *see* ARABIA, PRE-ISLAMIC

Qau el-Kebir (Tjebu; Antaeopolis) Necropolis in Egypt, located about 55 km southeast of the modern city of Asyut. The site is known primarily for the massive funerary complexes of the 12th-dynasty governors and other officials of the 10th Upper Egyptian nome, which were probably the largest provincial tombs of their time. They were modelled on royal pyramid complexes, taking the form of rock tombs fronted by terraced courts and pillared rooms approached by sloping causeways. In the Ptolemaic period the site retained its importance and a temple was constructed by Ptolemy IV and VI (221–145 BC).

W.M.F. Petrie: *Antaeopolis* (London, 1930); H. Steckeweh: *Die Fürstengräber von Qâw* (Leipzig, 1936).

IS

Qau-Matmar *see* EL-BADARI

Qermez Dere EPIPALAEOLITHIC and ACERAMIC NEOLITHIC settlement in the northern plains of Iraq, excavated in the 1980s by Trevor Watkins. The proto-Neolithic levels, dating to about 8000 BC, include the remains of several circular mud huts with sunken floors. The contents of these structures included stone hearths, stone and plaster pillars and scattered human skulls, suggesting that, like the houses at ÇATAL HÜYÜK, they may have played a ritualistic role in the life of the community. The lithic remains are similar to those at MUREYBET in Syria as well as those at Karim Shahir, M'lefaat and NEMRIK in the eastern Zagros region.

T. Watkins and D. Baird: *Qermez Dere: the excavation of an Aceramic Neolithic settlement near Tel Afar, N. Iraq* (Edinburgh, 1987).

IS

Qijia *see* CH'I-CHIA

Qin *see* CH'IN

Qingliengang (Ch'ing-lien-kang) *see* TA-WEN-K'OU

Qinglongquan *see* CH'ING-LUNG-CH'UAN

Qishan (Ch'i-shan) *see* WESTERN CHOU

Qsar es-Seghir Medieval port midway between Tangier and Ceuta on the Moroccan shore, guarding the Strait of Gibraltar. The port was founded in the 12th century AD as an Islamic town, taken by the Portuguese as a colony in the 15th century, and finally abandoned in the 16th century. Between 1974 and 1981, about 5000 sq. m were excavated, following a sampling strategy (*see* SAMPLES, SAMPLING STRATEGIES) based upon a set of 19 excavation units each 9 × 9 m, designed by Charles Redman. As an illustration of probability and judgement sampling it represents an innovative project in medieval archaeology. Redman not only examined the topographic features of the two very different phases of the port's history, but also used the sampling scheme to evaluate the spatial patterning of material culture.

C.L. Redman: *Qsar es-Seghir, an archaeological view of medieval life* (Orlando, 1986).

RH

quadrant method Excavation technique, based on the grid or box system, which is used primarily on roughly circular sites such as round barrows. Four quadrants of the site are excavated, leaving baulks between them. On a smaller scale, the quadrant system may sometimes be used to excavate such features as POSTHOLES or pits (although in such cases no baulks are left).

quadrat analysis Branch of SPATIAL ANALYSIS which uses as DATA the counts of objects of one or more classes in cells of a grid imposed on the region or site being studied (e.g. the fragments of stone tools spread across prehistoric occupation floors). The size of the cells can be chosen to match the scale of the patterning being sought, provided that it is greater than the precision with which the locations of the objects have been measured. The technique is suited to both intra-site and inter-site SPATIAL ANALYSIS. The variation between counts in different cells can indicate whether the distribution of a class of objects is aggregated, random or uniform; associations between the distributions of two or more classes can also be studied. The main drawbacks of the approach are (i) it can only reliably detect square or rectangular patterns, and (ii) the choice of scale of patterning is arbitrary. The latter has been partly overcome by the dimensional analysis of variance used by Whallon (1973).

P. Grieg-Smith: *Quantitative plant ecology* (London, 1964); R. Whallon: 'Spatial analysis of occupation floors: the application of dimensional analysis of variance', *The explanation of culture change*, ed. C. Renfrew (London, 1973), 115–30; I.R. Hodder and C.R. Orton: *Spatial analysis in archaeology* (Cambridge, 1976), 33–8.

CO

quantification In a general sense, quantification is the process of choosing the VARIABLES (and their values) by which a set of archaeological objects can be described. This is not as easy as it sounds, and gives rise to theoretical and practical problems, sometimes known as the 'coding problem'. In a specific archaeological sense, it refers to the measuring of the amounts of different TYPES of pottery in assemblages (Orton 1993; Orton, Tyers and Vince 1993). Because pottery is almost always found broken, it cannot simply be counted like other classes of artefact. For many years (*c.*1916–60) the usual way was to count individual sherds; more recently, however, various other methods of quantifying pottery have been proposed, such as weight, number of vessels represented and 'eves' (estimated vessel-equivalents, in which each measurable fragment is recorded as the appropriate fraction of a whole vessel).

J.E. Doran and F.R. Hodson: *Mathematics and computers in archaeology* (Edinburgh, 1975), 99–114; S. Shennan: *Quantifying archaeology* (Edinburgh, 1988), 8–21; M. Fletcher and G.R. Lock: *Digging numbers* (Oxford, 1991), 5–8; C.R. Orton: 'How many pots make five?', *Archaeometry* 35 (1993), 169–84; ——, P.A. Tyers and A.G. Vince: *Pottery in archaeology* (Cambridge, 1993), 166–81.

CO

Quelccaya Ice Cap Glacier in the Peruvian southern Andes which has yielded cores providing a detailed precipitation record some 1500 years long. Highland precipitation feeds the oasis valleys of the coast where irrigation supported large, often urban, polities from the Early Horizon (1200–400 BC) onwards. In the 6th century AD major changes can be observed in the archaeological record as the Moche state collapsed and its population moved inland to the necks of the valleys. Similar events are noted to the north in the Lambayeque Valley and to the south in the Lima and NAZCA valleys. Although hampered by poor chronologies, these cataclysmic cultural events may well be connected to a detectable series of droughts in the 6th and 7th centuries AD, causing economic and political disruption and necessitating withdrawal inland to the heads of the irrigation systems.

L.G. Thompson, E. Moseley-Thompson, J.F. Bolzan and B.R. Koci: 'A 1500 year record of tropical precipitation in ice cores from the Quelccaya Ice Cap, Peru', *Science* 229 (1985), 971–3; I. Shimada, C. Barker-Schaaf, L.G. Thompson and E. Moseley-Thompson: 'Cultural impacts of severe draughts in the prehistoric Andes: application of a 1500 year ice core precipitation record', *WA* 22/3 (1991), 247–70.

KB

Quetta Valley in Baluchistan, Pakistan, incorporating several important pre-Harappan settlements, including Kili Ghul Muhammad, Kechi Beg and DAMB SADAAT. Quetta ceramics include plain ware and black-on-buff painted vessels, typically decorated with black painted motifs located between parallel rows of horizontal lines. Common Quetta motifs include curvilinear, zigzag and diagonal lines, along with crosses, leaves, a variety of geometric forms and occasional plant and animal motifs (bull, ibex or gazelle, fish and bird). Other Quetta decorated wares (Quetta Wet Ware) bore fabric impressions and plastic motifs such as ridges or stamped designs. Quetta ceramics have been found at numerous sites of the 4th millennium BC both within the Quetta valley itself and beyond (e.g. MEHRGARH and SUR JANGAL).

The archaeological remains at Kechi Beg cover an area measuring only 46 × 23 m, and a single 8 × 3 m trench was excavated by Walter Fairservis in the early 1950s. Although there were few surviving architectural remains, the site yielded several distinctive ceramic types, including Kechi Beg Polychrome and Kechi Beg Red Painted Ware, which have been found at other sites in the Quetta region.

Kili Ghul Muhammad is a small settlement mound (only about 0.5 ha in area) at which Walter Fairservis, on the basis of a single trench (excavated in 1950–1), defined four chronological periods, from the mid-5th to mid-4th millennium BC. The only absolute dates are from Period I, the rest of the sequence being dated within a relative sequence by ceramic wares. The earliest phase, dated by calibrated radiocarbon dates to the mid-late 5th millennium BC, included the remains of wattle-and-daub huts, domesticated animals (sheep, goat and cattle), bone points and flaked and ground stone lithics; mud-brick architecture appeared near the end of this period. The fourth phase at Kili Ghul Muhammad featured a new style of polychrome pottery of the Kechi Beg black-on-buff and white-on-dark painted styles.

W.A. Fairservis: 'Excavations in the Quetta Valley, West Pakistan', *APAMNH* 45 (1956), 169–492; S. Ashthana: *Pre-Harappan cultures of India and the Borderlands* (New Delhi, 1985), 70–3, 120–4.

CS

Quetzalcoatl The Mesoamerican feathered- or plumed-serpent deity of the Classic and Postclassic periods (*c.*AD 300–1521), known by the LOWLAND MAYA as Kukulcán and by the highland Maya as Gucumatz. Closely identified with Tollan (*see* TOLTECS), Quetzalcoatl is a complex concept, simultaneously a historical human figure (Topiltzin Quetzalcoatl), a deity and a symbol. Like most Mesoamerican gods, Quetzalcoatl the deity is a composite with many aspects, including god of learning, creator god and Venus as morning star and/or evening star. Quetzalcoatl was also a powerful symbol of city and legitimate royal authority for urban peoples throughout Postclassic Mesoamerica (*c.*AD 900–1521).

D. Carrasco: *Quetzalcoatl and the irony of empire. Myths and prophecies in the Aztec tradition* (Chicago, 1982).

PRI

quipu Mnemonic device used by the INCA people of South America for accounting by means of a series of knotted strings recording numerical information in a decimal system. A *quipu* generally consisted of a series of cords attached to a main cord; each string represented a single number in a series of overhand knots with a totals string attached to the other side so that numbers and totals could be read by running the thumb nail over the knots. The colour of the cords was also apparently important in encoding. *Quipu*s were used for keeping accounts of all kinds, and could also be used to preserve non-numerical information, although the means of encoding such data is now lost. *Quipu*s appeared in Peru in the Middle Horizon and were still used in some isolated communities.

M. Ascher and R. Ascher: *The code of the quipu: a study in media, mathematics, and Culture* (Ann Arbor, 1981); C. Mackey, ed.: *Quipu y yupana: colección de escritos* (Lima, 1990).

KB

Quiriguá A small (4 sq km) LOWLAND MAYA centre of the Classic period (*c.*AD 200–900) lying on the floodplain of the Motagua River in the lowlands of southeastern Guatemala. Famed for its beautiful STELAE the site's ceremonial architecture includes a ballcourt (*see* BALLGAME), an acropolis, and numerous temple-pyramids and palaces arranged in groups around plazas. Quiriguá is believed to have been founded during the Early Classic period (*c.*AD 300–600) by an elite group from Petén, perhaps to control riverine commerce that represented highland, lowland and Central American interests. Quiriguá's prosperity occurred during the reign of the ruler Cauac Sky (AD 724–784), who in AD 737 captured and executed the ruler of COPAN, 18 Rabbit. Much later, the arrival of a new ruling group may be signalled by the recovery of a CHACMOOL from the site, but Quiriguá seems to have been abandoned around AD 900.

R.J. Sharer: *Quiriguá, a classic Maya centre and its sculptures* (Durham, NC, 1990).

PRI

Qumran Cave site near the remains of Khirbet Qumran, to the northwest of the Dead Sea in Israel, about 13 km south of Jericho. It was here that the Dead Sea Scrolls, comprising fragments of leather inscribed with sections of the Old Testament and the Apocrypha, were discovered by a goatherd in 1947. Khirbet Qumran was the religious settlement of a group of Jews known as Essenes, which was destroyed by the Romans in *c.*AD 66–70. One of the rooms at Khirbet Qumran has been tentatively identified as the 'library' in which the Dead Sea Scrolls would have originally been stored, before being hidden away in the nearby caves when the community was first threatened by the Romans. Despite the appointment of an editorial team in 1953, the manuscripts are still only partially published.

J.P.M. van der Ploeg: *Excavations at Qumran* (London, 1958); J.M. Allegro: *The Dead Sea Scrolls: a reappraisal* (Harmondsworth, 1964); P.R. Davies: *Qumran* (Guildford, 1982); R.H. Eisenman and M. Wise: *The Dead Sea Scrolls uncovered* (Shaftesbury and Rockport, 1992).

IS

Qustul *see* BALLANA

Quynh Van *see* COASTAL NEOLITHIC

R

al-Rabadha Islamic settlement in Saudi Arabia, located to the west of Medina on the pilgrim road known as Darb Zubayda (after the consort of Harun al-Rashid, the fifth Abbasid Caliph of Baghdad, AD 786–809). Al-Rabadha was the first major Islamic-period site to be investigated in Saudi Arabia, and its occupation sequence may be of relevance to sites further west around Medina and elsewhere in the Hijaz.

The pilgrim road ran from AL-KUFA in Iraq to Mecca, with a branch to Medina, and although much older as a trans-Arabian caravan route, it was greatly developed in the late 9th century AD with numerous sites expanded with facilities to ease the passage of pilgrims to Mecca. There was a pre-Islamic settlement at al-Rabadha where copper was smelted in small quantities. The site was a major camel pasturage before Islam, and great quantities of camel bones were retrieved. Under the Muslims, al-Rabadha became a state pasturage for camels. The pre-Islamic levels produced ceramics that had affinities with the pre-Islamic Arabian traditions better known in the south, but with the Umayyad period, ceramics of the types known from Jordan begin to appear. In the Abbasid period the site went through a phase of massive expansion, with a large public water-tank and an extraordinarily large number of small water tanks under houses and other structures. In the 9th century, lustreware and other fine glazed ceramics were imported in quantities from Iraq, and this process of bringing in luxury wares probably holds true at the numerous stations all along the Darb Zubayda.

S.A. Al-Râshid: *Darb Zubaydah: the pilgrim road from Kufa to Mecca* (al-Riyâd, 1980); ——: *Al-Rabadhah: a portrait of early Islamic civilization in Saudi Arabia* (al-Riyâd, 1986).

GK

Rabita de Guardamar An Islamic settlement situated near Alicante in southeastern Spain, which was excavated in 1984–7. It comprises three separate long structures, possibly belonging to a caliph recorded in AD 944. Three phases of stone-built structures were identified, of a type now recognized as early Arabic in southern Spain and the Balearic islands. The excavations have special importance for the sequence of 9th- to 11th-century pottery, including jars, amphorae, lamps and red-painted tableware. A number of Arabic inscriptions and graffiti were found in the excavations.

R.A. Ruiz: *La Rabita Califal de las Dunas de Guardamar* (Alicante, 1989).

RH

racemization *see* AMINO ACID DATING

radiocalcium dating Scientific dating technique for bone based on the formation of ^{41}Ca by the interaction of cosmic-ray neutrons with ^{40}Ca in the top metre or so of soil. Calcium in the soil is taken up by plants and thus by animals to form bone. The HALF-LIFE of ^{41}Ca is about 100,000 years, and the method is theoretically applicable over the past 300,000 years. On death, however, the activity of the ^{41}Ca concentration does not simply decrease by radioactive decay, as is the case for ^{14}C (*see* RADIOCARBON DATING). Instead, cosmic rays can continue to form ^{41}Ca in the bone unless it is well shielded by an overburden of a few metres of soil or rock. Other problems are, firstly, that the initial activity of ^{41}Ca is not well known but depends on the local and variable soil make-up, and, secondly, that the activity is very low (typically 1 part ^{41}Ca to 10^{14} of ^{40}Ca).

M. Raisbeck and F. Fiou: 'Possible use of ^{41}Ca for radioactive dating', *Nature* 277 (1979), 42–4; R. Middleton, D. Fink, J. Kelin and P. Sharma: '^{41}Ca concentrations in modern bone and their implications for dating', *Radiocarbon* 31 (1989), 305–10.

SB

radiocarbon dating Scientific dating technique based on the amount of the radioactive isotope of carbon, ^{14}C, (relative to stable ^{12}C or ^{13}C) left in an organic sample. ^{14}C is formed in the upper atmosphere by the action of cosmogenic neutrons on ^{14}N. It forms carbon dioxide and rapidly mixes through the atmosphere; it enters plant life via photosynthesis and animal life via the food chain. Assuming a constant production rate, there is an equilibrium between formation and decay so that the biosphere has a known $^{14}C/^{12}C$ ratio. After death of a plant or animal, exchange with the biosphere ceases, and the ^{14}C level decreases by radioactive decay with a HALF-LIFE of 5730 years. Relative to a modern standard, the measured $^{14}C/^{12}C$ ratio will in principle yield the age of the sample. In practice, production varies because of varying cosmic ray flux caused by changes in the earth's magnetic field and sunspot activity. The radiocarbon age of a sample is therefore not the same as calendar age. A plot of radiocarbon dates on tree rings versus their DENDROCHRONOLOGICAL ages (a calibration curve) over the past 7000 years shows a broad, approximately sinusoidal variation superimposed on which are relatively short-term wiggles (due to magnetic field and sunspot effects respectively). Thus at about 5000 BC radiocarbon results are some 700 years too young, but at around 50 BC there is no major difference.

Datable samples are organic materials, such as bone and wood. Each type of sample must be appropriately pre-treated to remove possible carbon-containing contaminants, such as calcium carbonate, from the burial environment, and is then converted to whatever form needed for the particular measurement process used (*see* ACCELERATOR MASS SPECTROMETRY *and* CONVENTIONAL RADIOCARBON DATING). Modern reference standards ($^{14}C/^{12}C \sim 10^{-12}$), made from oxalic acid, are also measured, as are background samples having no ^{14}C activity left. A fractionation correction is applied to the measured $^{14}C/^{12}C$ ratio using the $\delta^{13}C$ value (*see* CARBON ISOTOPE ANALYSIS).

Apart from the problems of calibration (below), specific problems arise for particular types of sample and environment. Only the protein part of bone is accurately datable, this precludes cremated bone, as the protein has been lost. Tree-rings cease exchange with the biosphere shortly after formation, hence radiocarbon dating of wood or charcoal from a mature long-lived species does not date the time of felling or burning but formation of the specific rings dated, indeed the result can be in error by many centuries. Marine species also show radiocarbon ages that are too old because they take up carbon, directly or indirectly, from the oceans, and the upwelling of ^{14}C depleted deep water means that surface water has an apparent radiocarbon age relative to the atmosphere: this amounts to *about* 400 years, but the effect is variable. Freshwater molluscs and aquatic plants are subject to the *hard-water effect*: the uptake of carbon, of various sources and ages, from groundwater. This is often associated, but not directly correlated, with the presence of calcium ions resulting from dissolution of calcium carbonate which, in radiocarbon terms, is infinitely old.

The upper age limit is determined by the ability to detect very low ^{14}C levels above background; typically it is in the region of 40,000 years, but with isotopic enrichment on a large sample it has been possible to extend the method to 75,000 years. The lower limit is about 200 years because of the mutual interference of the *fossil fuel effect* (depletion of the atmospheric $^{14}C/^{12}C$ ratio by burning of large quantities of fuel such as coal which started in the 19th century) and the *bomb effect* (production of large quantities of ^{14}C by nuclear weapons testing). The error terms achievable on the radiocarbon result depend on the sample size, but are typically 50–100 radiocarbon years; high precision dating can achieve ± 20 radiocarbon years (but requires 3 to 4 times more sample than normal CONVENTIONAL RADIOCARBON DATING). The calibration of a radiocarbon result plus associated error, however, gives one or more age *ranges*, the length of which depends on the form of the calibration curve at that point. It may have a steep or shallow slope, or it may be wiggly, giving rise to several possible calendar dates corresponding to one radiocarbon result. Radiocarbon results cannot, therefore, be used to give a relative chronology other than in a crude way and where the events are separated by several centuries.

Calibration curves are constructed by high-precision radiocarbon dating of groups of tree rings (usually 10 or 20) for which there are dendrochronological dates. At present there is a continuous curve going back some 8000 years (a further 2000 are yet to be replicated). Calibrated dates can only be faithfully represented by probability distributions which fully take account of both the error term on the radiocarbon results and the effect of wiggles in the calibration curve. To generate probability distributions requires the use of a computer program. Such programs implicitly use Bayesian methodology with the eminently reasonable *a priori* assumption that, in the absence of any information to the contrary, all *calendar* ages for the event being dated are equally likely.

The established convention for quoting radiocarbon results gives them in uncalibrated years (uncal) BP, where 0 BP is 1950 AD. They are rounded to the nearest 10 years (5 if the error term is less than

50 years) and calculated on the 'Libby half-life' of 5568 years (named after the founder of the technique). Each result is ideally quoted with its error (±1 σ), and its laboratory reference e.g. 2020 ±50 BP (BM-2558). Calibration corrects to the more accurate 5370 year half-life. The accepted convention for quoting specific individual calibrated results is cal BC or cal AD with the confidence level and calibration method.

W.G. Mook and H.T. Waterbolk: *Handbook for archaeologists No. 3, European Science Foundation, Radiocarbon Dating* (Strasbourg, 1985); S. Bowman: *Radiocarbon dating* (London, 1990); C.E. Buck et al.: 'Combining archaeological and radiocarbon information: a Bayesian approach to calibration', *Antiquity* 65 (1991), 808–21; S. Bowman: 'Using radiocarbon: an update', *Antiquity* 68 (1994), 838–43; See also the journal *Radiocarbon*.

SB

radiometric dating Any scientific dating technique in which the age is directly determined by radioactive decay (or grow-in): *see* RADIOCARBON DATING, URANIUM SERIES DATING, POTASSIUM-ARGON DATING, RADIOCALCIUM DATING, FISSION TRACK DATING.

Rajghat Settlement site of the GANGES CIVILIZATION, consisting of several mounds located on a small plateau to the east of the sacred city of Varanasi (modern Banaras) in Uttar Pradesh, India. Excavations by the Banaras Hindu University (1957–69) documented occupation from the 8th century BC onwards, characterized by a local tradition of BLACK AND RED WARE ceramics, followed by NORTHERN BLACK POLISHED WARE (NBPW) levels of the 6th–3rd centuries BC. No PAINTED GREY WARE period is found at this site, and the NBPW appears to have been incorporated into a local ceramic tradition, in which Black and Red Ware and other local plain wares continued. The site attained urban status only near the end of the NBPW period, and reached its maximum extent in the 1st–3rd centuries AD, from which period the remains of mud- and fired-brick structures have survived. This latest phase was also characterized by mould-made human and animal terracotta figurines, seals, sealings and die-struck coins. The site was occupied until the 12th century AD.

A.K. Narain and T.N. Roy: *Excavations at Rajghat* (Varanasi, 1976); T.N. Roy: *The Ganges Civilization* (New Delhi, 1983), 50–3, 96–8.

CS

Ramesseum Mortuary temple of the Egyptian pharaoh Ramesses II (*c*.1290–1224 BC), located on the west bank of the Nile at Thebes (modern Luxor). The principal building – where the funerary cult of the king was celebrated – is a typical stone-built New Kingdom temple, consisting of two successive courtyards (each entered through a pylon), a hypostyle hall with surrounding annexes, leading to a room for the sacred 'bark' (a ritual boat containing a cult image) and the sanctuary. The complex includes the remains of a royal palace and large numbers of mud-brick granaries and storerooms. The Ramesseum is among the most prominent of the West Theban monuments. Its reliefs and architecture, as at other funerary complexes such as MEDINET HABU, provide a great deal of evidence regarding the rituals relating to the royal funerary cult.

J.E. Quibell: *The Ramesseum* (London, 1898); W. Helck: *Die Ritualdarstellungen des Ramesseums* I (Wiesbaden, 1972).

IS

ranch boundaries Term sometimes applied in Britain to linear earthworks constructed from the 2nd millennium BC that are assumed to mark out prehistoric land divisions and/or to have controlled livestock. They are most apparent on downland (e.g. the Berkshire Downs), perhaps simply for reasons of preservation. 'Ranch boundaries' are often associated with smaller rectangular enclosures of the later Bronze Age and with banjo-shaped enclosures of the later 1st millennium BC – both of which seem to have been used to corral livestock, although they might also have divided arable land.

RJA

rank If a certain VARIABLE, such as length or weight, is measured on a set of archaeological objects, the RANK of a chosen object is its position when the objects are arranged in order (either increasing or decreasing) of their values of that variable (e.g. 5th smallest, 3rd largest). *See* NON-PARAMETRIC STATISTICS.

CO

rapid silt *see* PRIMARY SILT

al-Raqqa Islamic-period site in Syria, at which excavations commenced in 1982, exposing a large area of the extensive ruins. Al-Raqqa is the most important Abbasid (AD 750–1258) palace and town to have been examined in recent years, its importance being on the level of SAMARRA. The recent excavations have defined both early Abbasid al-Raqqa and also Harun al-Rashid's town and palace at al-Rafiqa, exposing the walls and towers of the fortifications. Earlier assumptions regarding the date of the well-known Bab Baghdad have been overturned and it is now associated with the mediaeval rather than the early Abbasid period. The excavations have also clarified the nature of the town in the Ayyubid period when kilns producing fine glazed wares were established to the south of the Friday Mosque. The excavation at these kilns along with recent work at other north Syrian sites is likely to greatly improve the dating and spread of the so-called 'Raqqa-wares' in the 12th–13th century.

M. Meinecke: 'al-Rakka', *Encyclopedia of Islam*, 2nd edn (Leiden, 1971); V. Porter: *Medieval Syrian pottery (Raqqa ware)* (Oxford, 1981).

GK

Ras Mkumbuu *see* SWAHILI HARBOUR TOWNS

Ras Shamra *see* UGARIT

raster format *see* GIS

ratio variable *see* VARIABLE

recumbent-stone circles Regional group of Neolithic stone circles found in County Cork and County Kerry in Ireland, so-named because each ring contains a single horizontally placed stone. There are usually two orthostats, acting as 'portals', opposite the recumbent stone, while the rest of the megaliths are graded down in height toward the recumbent. Barber (1973) held that the axes of the circles were oriented in an astronomically significant manner; Heggie (1981) summarizes the arguments against this.

J. Barber: 'The orientation of the recumbent stone circles of the south-west of Ireland', *Journal of the Kerry archaeology and history society*, vi (1973), 26–39; D. Heggie: *Megalithic science* (London, 1981), 182–4.

RJA

'Red Lady of Paviland' Misnomer for a famous ruddle-stained skeleton of a young man found at PAVILAND CAVE on the Gower Peninsular, south Wales.

reduction of data An analytical approach to archaelogical DATA, advocated by Ehrenberg, which seeks to reduce large amounts of DATA to a much smaller number of 'summary statistics' which still give a good impression of the overall pattern of the data. This approach concentrates on producing tables of summary statistics in which any pattern is, hopefully, obvious to the reader. The most common summary statistics of a single VARIABLE are its MEAN and its STANDARD DEVIATION. The collective term 'descriptive statistics' is also used.

J.E. Doran and F.R. Hodson: *Mathematics and computers in archaeology* (Edinburgh, 1975), 38; A.S.C. Ehrenberg: *Data reduction* (London, 1975); S. Shennan: *Quantifying archaeology* (Edinburgh, 1988), 33–5.

CO

refuse deposition The study of refuse deposition has played an increasingly important role in archaeology, not only in terms of excavation but also in terms of ETHNOARCHAEOLOGY, EXPERIMENTAL ARCHAEOLOGY and other forms of ACTUALISM. For example, Lewis Binford (1983: 144–92) has studied the behavioral patterns among modern Nunamiut and Bushmen in order to obtain a better understanding of prehistoric hunter-gatherers' use of camp-space, including such depositional features as 'drop zones', 'toss zones' and 'aggregate dumping areas'. Since the 1970s, William Rathje's Garbage Project has used archaeological techniques to analyse patterns of refuse disposal in modern Tucson, Arizona (Rathje 1974).

According to the model of site formation processes put forward by Michael Schiffer (1976; *see* BEHAVIORAL ARCHAEOLOGY), there are three basic modes of refuse deposition: primary (i.e. material discarded at point of use), secondary (material moved away from point of use as a result of maintenance or cleaning) and de facto types of refuse (material deposited at the time of a site's abandonment). Some PROCESSUAL archaeologists have therefore argued that the understanding of the mechanisms of deposition relies largely on the ability to distinguish between these three modes of refuse disposal. By the early 1980s it was clear to many archaeologists that this was too simplistic an approach; Binford, for instance, argued that when Schiffer's model was applied to the Joint Site (Arizona), it was incapable of distinguishing between (a) the de facto refuse left behind by a sedentary community at the time of a site's abandonment, and (b) the primary refuse subsequently left by groups reusing the ruins as a camp-site (Binford 1981).

Trigger (1989: 360) argues, on the basis of ethnographic research, that 'artifacts and artifact debris are more likely to be abandoned in the localities where they were used in temporary hunter-gatherer sites than in larger and more sedentary ones, where the disposal of waste material was much more highly organized'. Nevertheless it has proved difficult to validate even very general cross-cultural observations about refuse disposal.

W. Rathje: 'The Garbage Project: a new way of looking at the problems of archaeology', *Archaeology* 27 (1974), 236–41; M.B. Schiffer: *Behavioral archaeology* (New York, 1976); L.R. Binford: 'Behavioral archaeology and the "Pompeii premise"', *JAR* 37/3 (1981), 195–208; G. Hammond and N. Hammond: 'Child's play: a distorting factor in archaeological distribution', *AA* (1981), 634–6; B. Hayden, and A. Cannon: 'The corporate group as an archaeological unit', *JAA* 1 (1982), 132–58; L.R. Binford: *In pursuit of the past* (London, 1983); M.B. Schiffer: *Formation processes of the archaeological record* (Albuquerque, 1987); B.G. Trigger: *A history of archaeological thought* (Cambridge, 1989).

IS

regression analysis Techniques for examining the relationship between two (or more) continuous VARIABLES, each measured on a set of objects from the archaeological record. The simplest linear regression, seeks the best straight-line relationship between two variables, and studies the differences (known as residuals) between the ideal and actual data. The extent to which the relationship can be described as a straight line (i.e. that one variable can be exactly predicted from the other) is measured by the correlation coefficient, which can vary from –1 for an exact negative relationship through 0 for no linear relationship to +1 for an exact positive relationship. The term correlation is also used more generally (but wrongly) to mean association (*see* CONTINGENCY TABLE). More complex types of regression are curvilinear regression (more complicated relationships between two variables) and multiple regression (relationship between one 'dependent' variable and several 'independent' ones).

Case-study: regression analysis and the distribution of Roman pottery. Regression has been used to good effect in SPATIAL ANALYSIS; for instance, Fulford and Hodder (1974) used regression analysis to study the distribution of late Roman pottery from the north Oxfordshire kilns. They calculated the

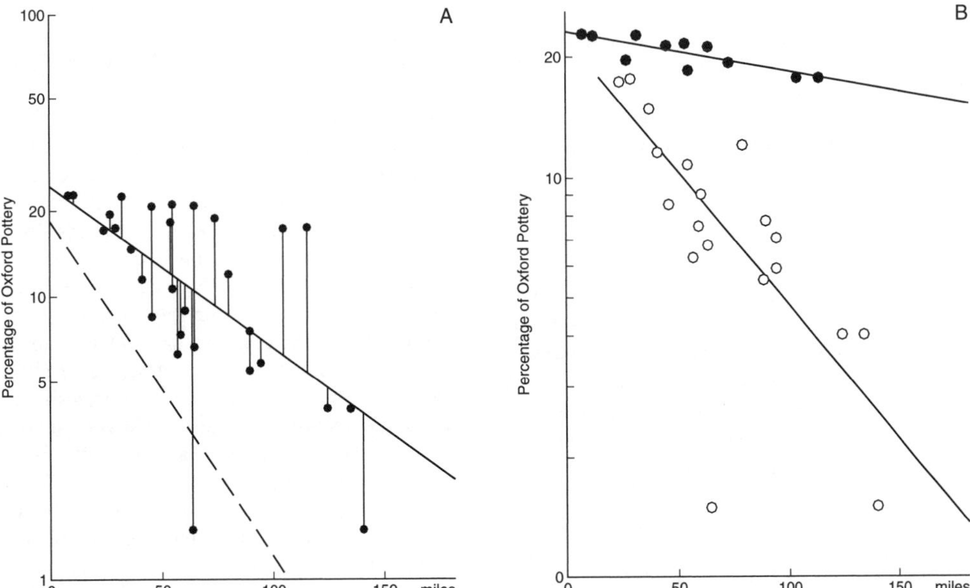

Figure 44 **regression analysis** Graphs showing (A) best-fit linear regression line for the decrease in Oxford pottery with increasing distance from the kilns (the dotted line shows the decrease in New Forest Pottery away from the New Forest kilns); (B) decrease in Oxford pottery away from the kilns (filled circles indicate sites which may have been reached using water transport; open circles indicate sites not easily reached by water). *Source*: M.G. Fulford and I.R. Hodder: 'A regression analysis of some late Romano-British fine pottery: a case study', *Oxoniensia* 39 (1974), figs 1 and 3.

proportions of this ware at contemporary sites in southern England, and plotted them against the distances of the sites from the kilns (Fig. 44A). Although, as expected, the proportion decreased as distance from the kilns increased, this pattern was not followed consistently, and there was much unexplained variation.

However, when the sites were divided into two groups – those with easy access by water from the kilns, and those without – the position became much clearer. Each group could be fitted closely by its own regression line, the two lines differing greatly. The sites with access by water had a very shallow regression line, showing that the proportion of the ware decreased only slowly with distance from the kilns, while the other sites had a much steeper regression line, with the proportion decreasing much faster with distance from the kilns (Fig. 44B).

Although this study could be criticized because (i) the proportions were based on counts of sherds, and (ii) the sites were not necessarily exactly contemporary, so chronological differences may have entered the picture, it clearly shows two distinct groups of sites, and suggests a reasonable interpretation of the difference between them – that the main form of transport of this ware was by water.

M.G. Fulford and I.R. Hodder: 'A regression analysis of some late Romano-British fine pottery: a case study', *Oxoniensia* 39 (1974), 26–33; J.E. Doran and F.R. Hodson: *Mathematics and computers in archaeology* (Edinburgh, 1975), 61–5; C.R. Orton: *Mathematics in archaeology* (Glasgow, 1980), 116–24; S. Shennan: *Quantifying archaeology* (Edinburgh, 1988), 114–89; M. Fletcher and G.R. Lock: *Digging numbers* (Oxford, 1991), 103–14.

CO

Remigia Rockshelter and cave site with one of the most striking concentrations of SPANISH LEVANTINE ROCK ART, in the Gasulla ravine, in Castellón, Spain. The figures, mainly of archers, vary from about 0.05 m to 0.5 m tall, and are painted in red and occasionally black. There are also animals such as deer, boars and goats (including herds of animals as well as single examples); other depictions have been interpreted as beehives, spiders etc. The most famous 'scene' at Remigia seems to show an execution: archers wave their bows above their heads as their victim lies in front of them, pierced with up to ten arrows.

A. Beltrán: *Rock art of the Spanish Levant* (Cambridge, 1982).

RJA

Reshnoe *see* SEIMA-TURBINO

residues Term used to describe material surviving on the surfaces of artefacts. For example, residues of such organic substances as blood, hair, bone or cartilage on butchery tools may be identified and characterized (and, more recently, subjected to DNA ANALYSIS). Useful evidence survives only in a small number of depositional conditions and environments. Blood residues, for instance, tend to survive primarily in such protected areas of artefacts as step fractures at the edge of undetached stone flakes.

J. Eisele: *Survival and detection of blood residues on stone tools* (Reno, 1994); R. Fullagar, J. Furby and B. Hardy: 'Residues on stone artefacts: state of a scientific art', *Antiquity* 70 (1996), 740–4; N. Tuross, I. Barnes and R. Potts: 'Protein identification of blood residues on experimental stone tools', *JAS* 23 (1996), 289–96.

IS

resistivity survey Technique of non-destructive prospection which was first developed by Schlumberger in 1912, as a means of oil exploration. It relies on the principle that different deposits beneath the ground offer different resistance to the passage of an electric current, depending largely on the amount of water present. A damp pit will offer less resistance than the surrounding soil, while a brick wall will present more resistance. Unusual types of material give anomalous readings that can be plotted in terms of their depth and location.

If the soil conditions are right, and agricultural practice and modern digging has not confused the area too much, resistivity surveys can be an efficient way of locating major structural features across an extensive archaeological site. A typical resistivity survey comprises a linear array of copper rods laid out at regular intervals, with a source of electricity and a meter to measure the resistance at various depths. The resistance is measured along a number of different depths, thus being shown graphically as a set of lines showing the fluctuations in resistance at various depths. Because resistivity surveys measure *relative* values, they are more effective in some conditions than others. In very wet soils, for example, it may be difficult to distinguish features that reduce resistivity. Resistivity surveys are often used to plan excavation strategies, or to generate a sketch map of major features in the immediate vicinity of an excavation. They may be used in conjunction with another principal geophysical surveying technique, the MAGNETIC SURVEY. The technique has been used at many sites throughout the world (see, for instance, the work of Ian Mathieson at the ancient Egyptian sites of el-

Amarna, Memphis and Saqqara: Mathieson 1984; Mathieson and Tavares 1993).

C. Carr: *Handbook on soil resistivity surveying: interpretation of data from earthen archaeological sites* (Evaston, 1982); I. Mathieson: 'A resistivity survey at el-Amarna', *Amarna Reports* I, ed. B.J. Kemp (London, 1984), 99–123; —— and A. Tavares: 'Preliminary report of the National Museums of Scotland Saqqara Survey Project, 1990–91', *JEA* 79 (1993), 17–31.

IS

Rhapta The principal harbour of ancient Azania (East Africa), which is documented in an Alexandrine Greek text of the 1st century AD (*The Periplus of the Erythraean Sea*). The archaeological site of Rhapta has not yet been located, despite searches along the Tanzanian and Kenyan shores and estuaries (cf. the roughly contemporaneous port of HAFUN). Rhapta's exports were ivory, tortoise-shell, rhino-horn and pearly shells; the shipping was largely in South Arabian hands but connected with both India and Roman Egypt.

L. Casson: *The Periplus Maris Erythraei: text with introduction, translation and commentary* (Princeton, 1989).

JS

Rhohri industry Palaeolithic stone tool industry identified from the Rhohri hills located to the east of the Indus River near Sukkar in Sind Province, Pakistan. Numerous chert nodules are still visible on the hill tops and in 1975 a brief survey conducted by Bridget Allchin, Andrew Goudie and Karunarkara Hegde resulted in the identification of numerous lithic production sites, dating from the Middle Palaeolithic, Upper Palaeolithic and INDUS CIVILIZATION. These surface sites were dated according to typological variation in lithic forms; no absolute dates are available. The Middle Palaeolithic artefacts include scrapers, cleavers, chopping tools, flakes, blades and cores, while those from the Upper Palaeolithic sites are characterized by higher frequencies of blades and blade cores. The Indus period sites provide evidence for large-scale blade production at discrete working floors or activity areas.

B. Allchin, A. Goudie and K. Hegde: *The prehistory and palaeogeography of the Great Indian Desert* (London, 1978), 273–94.

CS

Rillaton Round barrow in Cornwall, England, which yielded the Rillaton gold cup – perhaps the single most famous object produced by the 'WESSEX CULTURE'. The piece is made of corrugated sheet gold and has a single riveted handle. It is related in design to a series of small cups made out of gold, silver, amber and shale which have been recovered from roughly contemporary Early Bronze Age contexts across Western Europe. Joan Taylor (in D.V. Clarke et al. 1985) suggests that the piece may even have been made in the same workshop as the plainer gold cup from Fritzdorf, Germany; the similarities between these finely crafted objects highlights the emergence of a series of regional but connected elites, choosing to define themselves by their possession of supra-regional 'prestige objects'.

A.F. Harding: *The Mycenaeans and Europe* (London, 1984), 108; D.V. Clarke et al.: *Symbols of power at the time of Stonehenge* (Edinburgh, 1985), 115–19, 191–2, ill. 4.44.

RJA

Rimah, Tell el- Site in Mesopotamia dating from the Old Assyrian to the Middle Assyrian period (*c*.1726–1206 BC) which was excavated by David Oates in the 1960s in order to gain better understanding of events in Assyria in the early 2nd millennium BC. The site included a temple and ziggurat complex which were in use throughout most of the 2nd millennium. These buildings were initially axial and symmetrical, with the use of sophisticated vaulting and decoration comprising half-columns and niches.

D. Oates: 'The excavations at Tell al-Rimah, 1964, 1965, 1966', *Iraq* 27–9 (1965–7); S.M. Dalley, C.B.F. Walker and J.D. Hawkins: *The Old Babylonian tablets from Tell el-Rimah* (London, 1976); S.M. Dalley: *Mari and Karana: two Old Babylonian cities* (London, 1984).

IS

Río Bec/Chenes Regional architectural styles of the Classic period LOWLAND MAYA (*c*.AD 300–900), found in the area of the Yucatán peninsula just north of Petén, Guatemala. Both styles feature elaborate mosaic façades similar to the PUUC style, but Río Bec is distinguished by the use of false-terraced pyramid towers, while the closely related Chenes style has monster-mask doorways.

D.F. Potter: 'Prehispanic architecture and sculpture in central Yucatán', *AA* 41/4 (1976), 430–48; P. Gendrop: 'Dragon-mouth entrances: zoomorphic portals in the architecture of central Yucatan', *Third Palenque Round Table 1978, Part 2*, ed. M.G. Robertson (Austin, 1980), 138–50.

PRI

Riwat Palaeolithic site (Site 55) in the SOAN Valley, southeast of Rawalpindi, Pakistan, which has been thermoluminescence dated to a minimum age of 45,000 BP. Along with numerous quartzite flakes, blades and cores, the remains at the site include a linear boulder alignment, a stone-lined pit, and possible post-holes. It has been interpreted as a lithic procurement site or hide processing location.

R.W. Dennell, H.M. Rendell, M. Halim and E. Moth: 'A 45,000-year-old open-air Palaeolithic site at Riwat, Northern Pakistan', *JFA* 19 (1992), 17–33.

CS

robust A statistical technique is said to be robust if it performs well even when the MODEL on which it is based does not hold for the DATA being considered. For example, although Wenban-Smith's use of DISCRIMINANT ANALYSIS at BOXGROVE was based on assumptions about the VARIABLES which did not hold in practice, it performed well and gave useful results. Discriminant analysis can be said to be robust in this respect. Robustness is a desirable property, but difficult to study because there are many different ways in which data can depart from a model.

CO

Rocca San Silvestro Situated in a hill overlooking the coastal plain of western Tuscany near the town of Campiglia Marittima, Rocca San Silvestro is a remarkably well-preserved 11th- to 13th-century mining village. The greater part of the village was excavated between 1984 and 1993, and a systematic survey was made of mines in its environs. The excavations revealed a highly controlled feudal operation, managed for the Pisans by a local family occupying the small *rocca* (fortified tower). A romanesque church with a compact graveyard containing hundreds of burials was situated beside a piazza on the north side of the *rocca*. Well-built, two-floor dwellings gathered within the walls, around the contours on the east side of the hill. The communal olive press was found at the northern extent of the dwellings. Copper, lead and bronze were worked on the western side of the hill, each within its own enclosure. Silver for coinage was extracted here too. Iron, by contrast, was worked in a forge immediately outside the south gate of the village. Twenty-metre-deep shafts for the extraction of the minerals were excavated in the valley below. By AD 1350 the large village had been deserted, as the Pisans sought new, richer mineral sources in Sardinia.

R. Francovich: *Rocca San Silvestro* (Rome, 1992).

RH

Roc de Combe Sited on a tributary of the Dordogne, the cave/shelter of Roc de Combe is probably the only known site with reliable interstratification of CHÂTELPERRONIAN and AURIGNACIAN deposits. In a sequence from the MOUSTERIAN through to GRAVETTIAN/Upper Périgordian, the basal layer dating to the Upper Palaeolithic (layer 10) is fragmentary, but layers 9 and 7 are clearly Early Aurignacian, while layer 8 is clearly Châtelperronian. Given the now prevailing view that the Châtelperronian was the indigenous product of NEANDERTHALS, whereas the Aurignacian is intrusive, this site gives conclusive evidence that ANATOMICALLY MODERN HUMANS and Neanderthals coexisted in Western Europe for some time. Unfortunately, it is difficult to tell exactly how long this coexistence lasted.

PG-B

Roc de Sers Upper Palaeolithic rockshelter in Charente, France, in which blocks of carved limestone depicting animals such as ibex, horses and bison (0.30–0.70 m tall) were found during the 1920s. The most famous block depicts two ibexes facing each other, their body outlines and curved horns boldly delineated in deep relief. Like the reliefs at the comparable site of ANGLES-SUR-L'ANGLIN the sculptures were originally painted; unlike the works found at that site, they were carved on blocks already detached from the cave wall, and were apparently set up to run as a single decorated frieze around the walls of the shelter. The Solutrean archaeological material found in the cave suggests that the sculptures may date from some time after 20,000 BC.

H. Martin: *La frise sculptée et l'atelier solutréen du Roc de Sers* (Paris, 1928); H. Delporte: 'La frise sculptée du Roc de Sers', *DA* 131 (1988), 38–9.

RJA

Rollright Stones Middle to Late Neolithic monument near Chipping Norton, England, which consists of a stone circle (the King's Men), an earlier portal dolmen (the Whispering Knights) and a monolith (the King Stone). The King's Men are the remnants of what was possibly a continuous and almost perfectly round (33 ± 1 m) lightly embanked stone circle with a portal entrance to the southeast.

G. Lambrick: *The Rollright Stones* (London, 1988).

RJA

Romanelli Vast cave on the Mediterranean coast, *c*.15 km from Otrante in southern Italy, which has given its name to a distinctive late Upper Palaeolithic industry of *c*.10,000 BC. This industry, which is stratified over an earlier but meagre MOUSTERIAN or Upper Palaeolithic cultural layer, comprises points and burins similar to the GRAVETTIAN/Upper Périgordian tradition but scrapers and microburins that parallel later industries such as the AZILIAN. The Romanellian industry, often described as 'EpiGravettian', is associated at Romanelli with concentrations of wall engravings and engraved *art mobilier*.

RJA

rongorongo Undeciphered Easter Island script, which some have interpreted as a copy of European writing, but using indigenous symbols, whereas others have seen it as an indigenous mnemonic device connected with rituals.

A. Metraux: *Ethnology of Easter Island* (Honolulu, 1940); P. McCoy: 'Easter Island', *The prehistory of Polynesia*, ed. J. Jennings (Canberra, 1979), 135–66.

CG

Rose Cottage Cave MSA (Middle Stone Age) cave site in the Orange Free State, South Africa, located a few kilometres east of Ladybrand. First excavated between 1943 and 1946 by B.D. Malan, the 7 m deep succession of deposits has been a matter of controversy for most of the intervening time. New excavations and reassessment of Malan's records and material by L. Wadley have done much to clarify the situation. The succession commences with a pre-HOWIESON'S POORT expression of the MSA, followed by classic Howieson's Poort, possibly divisible for the first time into two or three phases, followed by a variant MSA persisting to between 27,000 and 20,000 uncal BP, and anticipating, in its later stages, the ensuing Robberg industry (13,360–9250 uncal BP). The succession concludes with Oakhurst/Albany levels (9250–8380 uncal BP) and typical WILTON material. Associated charcoals indicate a shift from grass and heathland in the Late Pleistocene to grass, scrub and woodland in the Holocene.

L. Wadley and P. Harper: 'Rose Cottage Cave revisited: Malan's Middle Stone Age collection', *SAAB* 44 (1989), 23–32; ——: 'Rose Cottage Cave: background and a preliminary report on the recent excavations', *SAAB* 46 (1991), 125–30.

RI

Rosetta Stone Black granitic stele (British Museum EA24), which derives its name from the village of el-Rashid in the Egyptian Delta, where it was found in 1799. It was inscribed with the same text written three times over in different scripts (hieroglyphics, demotic and Greek), thus providing Jean-François Champollion with the key to the decipherment of Egyptian hieroglyphs. The text itself was actually a decree issued at Memphis and dated to 27 March, 196 BC, the anniversary of Ptolemy V Epiphanes' coronation.

C.A. Andrews: *The Rosetta Stone* (London, 1981); S. Quirke and C.A. Andrews: *The Rosetta Stone: a facsimile drawing* (London, 1988).

IS

Rössen Early Neolithic culture of central and southern Germany characterized by dark, highly polished pottery, some plain and some decorated with geometric motifs such as diamonds or zigzags, and a stone industry including shoe-last celts and disc bracelets. This stone industry is closely related to the earlier LINEARBANDKERAMIK culture, the first farming culture of the region. Rössen material succeeds the LBK, and may be partially contemporaneous with the *Stichbandkeramik* (SBK *see* STROKE-ORNAMENTED WARE), another LBK development, in south-west Germany. It persists longer than the SBK, and so is also a contemporary of early Michelsberg (the principal 'middle Neolithic' culture of the region). A notable difference between the Rössen and the LBK in most areas is the layout of the houses: the LBK houses are long rectangular/trapezoidal whereas Rössen examples have a less regular shape and tend to be squarish. At the late Rössen settlement of Berry-au-Bac, for example, a (probably defensive) ditch and inner palisade mark out an area of 2–3 ha, within which stand four timber buildings, the largest of which is 20 m long by 10 m wide, with deep postholes and foundation trenches. At a few Rössen sites in Germany, however, the longhouses are of a notably long, trapezoidal shape that is much more closely related to earlier LBK forms.

RJA

Rouffignac Deep cave apparently embellished with Magdalenian engravings and black-outline drawings, situated near Les Eyzies, France. Unusually, the cave is dominated by representations of mammoth (*c*.150) and there are no deer or oxen; it also has a unique frieze of large rhinoceros. The authenticity of some, or even all, of the works of art has been questioned; Barrière's well-illustrated but uncritical account was denounced in the editorial of *Antiquity* cited below, which usefully summarizes the arguments.

C. Barrière: *L'art parietal de Rouffignac* (Paris, 1982); Editorial of *Antiquity* 58 (1984), 167–8.
RJA

Royal Domain (*ch'i*, *chi*) Geographical area under the direct control of the kings of Chou, in the feudal-like administrative set-up which was established in China in WESTERN CHOU times (1122–771 BC; *see* CHINA 2). The exact nature and extent of the Royal Domain is a matter for debate: some rather fanciful views allege that the vast size of the 'royal domain', as compared to the 'princely states', arose towards the close of the EASTERN CHOU era (771–255 BC) and in the early centuries of Western HAN (206 BC–AD 24). These views still tend to temper most reconstructions of the past (see Creel 1970: 363–6), despite the increasing array of relevant archaeological evidence (*see* CHINA 3).
H.G. Creel: *The origins of statecraft in China* (Chicago, 1970), 363–6; Ch'en ch'uan-fang: *Chou-yuan yü Chou-wen-hua* [Chou-yüan and the culture of Chou] (Shanghai, 1988).
NB

Rudna Glava Copper mine of the 5th millennium BC in northeast Serbia. Rudna Glava is the most intensively investigated early mining site in the central Balkans – 30 or so shafts have been excavated – and the site has helped to prove the autonomy and scale of copper metallurgy in the region. The ore (malachite and azurite) was extracted from horizontal and vertical shafts (up to 20 m deep) using antler picks and stone pounds to break up deposits which may already have been weakened by fire-heating and sudden dowsing with water. The mines have only been dated indirectly by their association with VINČA ware (Vinča D). The site was also worked, as an iron ore mine, in the Roman period.
B. Jovanovic: 'The origins of copper mining in Europe', *SA* 242/5 (1980), 114–20; M. Gimbutas: 'Copper mining in Old Europe, 5000–4000 BC, *Quarterly Review of Archaeology* 4/1 (March 1983), 2.
RJA

Ruichangshi *see* JUI-CH'ANG-SHIH

'Ruins of Yin' (Yinxu) *see* AN-YANG

Rusahinili *see* URARTU

Rusinga Island on the eastern (Kenyan) side of Lake Victoria, where remains dating from some 15 to 20 million years ago, have been excavated. Rusinga is a relic of a collapsed Miocene volcano, and, together with other sites with volcanic deposits of this period, it has yielded valuable and varied fossils of early African fauna. Especially important for the study of the evolution of higher primates is the anthropoid-ape '*Proconsul*' skull, discovered at Rusinga by Louis and Mary Leakey in 1948. *Proconsul* is now generally regarded as a member of the Dryopithecine group, represented in both Asia and Africa.
S. Cole: *The prehistory of East Africa* (New York, 1963), 87–8.
JS

Russell Cave Multi-component prehistoric site in northeastern Alabama along the western edge of the Tennessee River valley. Archaeological investigations conducted during the 1950s and 1960s revealed seven stratigraphic zones. The bottom three strata contained cultural material dating from the Early to Late Archaic periods. Three radiocarbon dates calibrated between 4030 and 4360 BC were associated with a Middle Archaic 'Morrow Mountain' component (the Morrow Mountain phase (*c*.5300–3500 BC), identified by distinctive stemmed projectile points, was first defined at sites in the North Carolina piedmont). Late Archaic artefacts resembling those found at the well-known Tennessee River shell middens were found above the Middle Archaic stratum. The upper four strata contained ceramic and lithic artefacts dating to the WOODLAND and MISSISSIPPIAN periods.
J. Griffin: *Investigations at Russell Cave.* (Washington, D.C., 1974); J. Walthall: *Prehistoric Indians of the Southeast: achaeology of Alabama and the Middle South* (Tuscaloosa, 1980).
RJE

S

Sabaeans *see* ARABIA, PRE-ISLAMIC

Sab Champa One of two moated sites in central Thailand to exhibit a substantial prehistoric occupation prior to the development of the DVARAVATI CULTURE. Excavations have uncovered prehistoric inhumations associated with pottery vessels and with the moulds used for bronze casting.

M. Veerapan: 'The excavation of Sab Champa', *Early South East Asia*, ed. R.B. Smith and W. Watson (Oxford 1979), 337–41.

CH

Sabrières de Libreville *see* AFRICA 5.3

Sabz, Tepe Neolithic settlement site in the Kuzistan region of southwestern Iran that has given its name to the Sabz phase, dating to the late 6th millennium BC. The earliest Sabz assemblages show great continuity with the preceding Muhammad Jaffar phase, in terms of the ceramics and microlithic tools, as well as the remains of plastered mud-brick houses, built on stone foundations (with the addition, in the Sabz phase, of party-walls made of *tauf*). The painted buff Sabz ware is closely related to the Susiana A–D ceramic sequence defined at Neolithic SUSA. It has been suggested that the scale of flax production at Tepe Sabz may be an indication of the introduction of irrigation (Hole et al. 1965).

F. Hole, K.V. Flannery and J. Neely: 'Early agriculture and animal husbandry in Deh Luran, Iran', *CA* 6 (1965), 105–6; F. Hole and K.V. Flannery: 'The prehistory of southwestern Iran: a preliminary report', *PPS* 33 (1967), 147–206.

IS

sacbe (Mayan: 'white road') Mayan term for a causeway, perhaps ceremonial, constructed of stone and rubble and paved with plaster, traversing often rough terrain to join two sites or architectural complexes within a site. At the Classic Maya site of Coba (in the northeastern Yucatan peninsula), for example, at least ten *sacbeob* crisscross the site centre and extend out to satellite sites within Coba's orbit. One of these, joining Coba to Yaxuna (south of CHICHÉN ITZÁ) is 100 km long; one leading to Ixil is 20 km in length.

W.J. Folan, E.R. Kintz and L.A. Fletcher: Coba: a *Classic Maya metropolis* (New York, 1983).

PRI

***saff* tomb** Arabic term (meaning 'row') which is used to describe an unusual type of ancient Egyptian royal rock-tomb, fronted by a court lined on three sides with rows of pillars, built in the el-Tarif area of western Thebes during the 1st Intermediate Period (*c*.2150–2040 BC). A number of private *saff*-tombs have also been excavated at ARMANT and DENDERA.

D. Arnold: *Gräber des Alten und Mittleren Reiches in El-Tarif* (Mainz, 1976).

IS

Saharan rock art 'Rock art' (engravings and paintings on rock surfaces such as boulders, cliff faces and rock-shelter walls) is distributed across the whole of North Africa (*see* AFRICA 1), from western Mauretania to the Nile Valley, and from the Atlas mountains to the Ennedi hills of Chad, with another concentration further south in the mountains of Ethiopia. It is in the upland regions that Saharan rock art has been found: the Tassili-n-Ajjer/Hoggar region in southern Algeria (the Tassili covering the northern half of the upland massif, the Hoggar covering the southern half, *see* map 1) and its offshoot the Tadrart Acacus in western Libya. Other major sites include Adrar des Iforas (across the Mali/Algeria border), Air (in Niger), Tibesti and Ennedi (in Chad) and JEBEL UWEINAT (on the borders of Libya, Egypt and Sudan). There is also rock art in the lower-lying Fezzan area.

Several tens of thousands of paintings and engravings have now been registered, even though many regions are still poorly explored. Although many 19th-century European explorers reported seeing rock paintings and drawings in their travels across the Sahara, the first systematic studies by archaeologists were those of G.-B.-M. Flamand (1921) and Raymond Vaufrey (1939) in the western desert, and Leo Frobenius (1937) and Paolo Graziosi (1937; 1939; 1942) in the eastern desert. These studies indicated a broad chronological division between an earlier style (showing game and stock such as cattle), which is assumed to be prehistoric in date, and a later style (with scenes of horses, chariots and camels) which is presumed to reflect contact between the Saharan population and peoples such as the Egyptians, although no absolute dating evidence was available for either.

In the 1950s and 1960s, efforts were made by Henri Lhote (1958; 1965) and F. Mori (1965) to refine and date the development of the art. Developmental stages in the material were established by detailed typological studies, based on analyses of style and technique augmented by inferences from patina, overlay, and archaeological and historical correlations, and occupation deposits in decorated caves or rock shelters were excavated for material for radiocarbon dates: the latter could at least indicate a general date for the paintings by association or, better still, date them from the occurrence in the occupation deposits of objects decorated in the same style, or even pieces of the rock art that had flaked off the walls into the deposits.

These studies indicated five main styles/periods: (1) Big Game, with incised pictographs of animals such as elephant, buffalo, crocodile, hippopotamus, giraffe and rhinoceros, a savannah fauna indicating a period of much greater moisture in the Sahara than today; (2) Round Heads – paintings of round-headed humans; (3) Pastoral or Cattle – paintings and engravings of humans herding cattle; (4) Equid – incised and painted scenes with horses; and (5) Camel – incised and painted scenes with camels. Radiocarbon dates in the Libyan Tadrart Acacus indicated dates of *c*.7000 uncal BP for the Round Head style and *c*.5000 uncal BP for the Pastoral style (Mori 1965). The Big Game motifs were variously regarded as Palaeolithic or Mesolithic in date. The Horse and Camel styles also included depictions of chariots and other motifs indicating contact with the Egyptian and classical civilizations.

The validity of these typological sequences, however, is now very doubtful. Muzzolini, in particular, has argued in a series of studies, firstly, that the Big Game motifs (also termed 'Bubaline') form a style or school of designs, not an initial phase of rock art, secondly that they were in fact contemporary with the Pastoral or Cattle motif along with many of the 'Round Head' paintings, and thirdly, that the main corpus of early rock art in general was contemporary with the transition from hunting to herding in the Sahara (Muzzolini 1986, 1990, 1991, 1993). The most recent radiocarbon dates indicate that cattle and sheep herding had appeared in the Sahara by 5000 or 5500 BC. The Equid and Camel motifs are certainly late in the rock art tradition, but again there are many indications of contemporaneity, and there is general agreement that most of them probably date from about 1500 BC onwards, reflecting contact between the Saharan peoples with Egypt and later also with the Phoenicians and Greeks (Muzzolini 1982a, 1982b).

Detailed studies of the Fezzan material by Le Quellec (1987) support Muzzolini's arguments for regional diversity and stylistic mixing after about 4000 BC, rather than a long sequence of widespread styles beginning much earlier in the Holocene. In the Adrar des Ifroras in Mali, too, the Big Game and Pastoral motifs appear to be more or less contemporary, separated from a later set of pictographs indicative of horse and camel herding (Dupuy 1989, 1990). Dupuy (1992) links the two groups of material respectively with the ancestral peoples of present-day Fulani pastoralists and Tuareg conquerors.

The period of the transition from hunting to herding in the Sahara was characterized by significant climatic fluctuations, with increasing aridity over time. Rather than seeing the rock art as literal representations of hunting or herding, as before, therefore, Le Quellec (1987), Smith (1993) and Muzzolini (1995) have suggested that most of it is probably best understood in terms of the changing ideologies of Saharan peoples at a time of major transformations in life-styles in response to environmental change. They draw parallels with the role of rock art (both the art of making it, and the completed 'text') in the complex ideologies of the Kalahari San (Lewis-Williams 1981, 1982, 1983), in which it operates as encoded messages in activities such as initiation rites. Smith suggests that the animals drawn acted as metaphorical intermediaries between humans and the spirit world, interpreted by specialist SHAMANS. The analysis of the Saharan rock art in such terms promises to yield considerable insights into the social and cognitive transformations experienced by societies as they changed from hunting to herding. ACCELERATOR MASS SPECTROMETRY dating applied to pigments also offers the hope of considerable refinements in the chronology of the art.

G.-B.-M. Flamand: *Les pierres écrites* (Paris, 1921); L. Frobenius: *Ekade Ektab: die Felsbilder Fezzans* (Leipzig,

1937); P. Graziosi: 'Preistoria del Fezzan', *Reale Società Geografica Italiana* (1937), 243–74; ——: *L'Arte rupestre della Libia* (Naples, 1939); R. Vaufrey: *L'art rupestre Nord-Africain* (Paris, 1939); P. Graziosi: *L'arte rupestre della Sahara Libico* (Florence, 1942); H. Lhote: *A la découverte des fresques du Tassili* (Paris, 1958); ——: 'L'évolution de la faune dans les gravures et les peintures rupestres du Sahara et ses relations avec l'évolution climatique', *Miscelánea an Homenaje al Abate Henri Breuil, 1877–1961* (Barcelona, 1965), 83–118; F. Mori: *Tadart Acacus* (Turin, 1965); J.D. Lewis-Williams; *Believing and seeing: symbolic meanings in southern San rock art* (London, 1981); ——: 'The economic and social context of southern San rock art', *CA* 23 (1982), 476; A. Muzzolini: 'Les climats Sahariens durant I'Holocene et la fin du Pleistocene', *TLAPEPMO* (1982a), 1–38; ——: 'La 'periode des chars' au Sahara: l'hypothèse de l'origine égyptienne du cheval et du char', *Les chars préhistoriques du Sahara*, ed. G. Camps and M. Gast (Aix en Provence, 1982b), 45–56; J.D. Lewis-Williams: *The rock art of southern Africa* (Cambridge, 1983); A. Muzzolini: *L'art rupestre préhistorique des massifs centraux Sahariens* (Oxford, 1986); J.-L. Le Quellec: *L'art rupestre du Fezzan septentrional (Libye); Widyan Zreda et Tarut (Wadi esh-Shati)* (Oxford, 1987); C. Dupuy: 'Les gravures naturalistes de l'Adrar des Iforas (Mali) dans le contexte de l'art rupestre saharien', *TLAPEPMO* 9 (1989), 151–74; ——: 'Réalization et perception des gravures rupestres stylisées de l'Adrar des Iforas (Mali)' *TLAPEPMO* 10 (1990), 93–109; A. Muzzolini: 'The sheep in Saharan rock art', *Rock Art Research* 7 (1990), 93–109; ——: 'Proposals for up-dating the rock-drawing sequence of the Acacus', *LS* 22 (1991), 7–30; C. Dupuy: 'Trois milles ans d'histoire pastorale au sud du Sahara', *Préhistoire et Anthropologie Méditerranée* 1 (1992), 105–26; A. Muzzolini: 'The emergence of a food-producing economy in the Sahara', *The archaeology of Africa*, ed. T. Shaw et al. (London, 1993), 227–39; A.B. Smith: 'New approaches to Saharan rock art of the 'Bovidian period', *Environmental change and human culture in the Nile basin and northeast Africa*, ed. L. Krzyzaniak et al. (Poznan, 1993), 77–90; A. Muzzolini: *Les images rupestres du Sahara* (Toulouse, 1995).

GB

Sahul *see* OCEANIA

Sa Huynh Prehistoric urnfield cemetery in coastal Vietnam, discovered in 1909. Excavations led to the recovery of 120 large lidded jars, disposed in groups, which contained cremated human remains. Numerous other such sites have been found, all concentrated in the coastal tract of central and southern Vietnam (e.g. Tam My, where the cremated bones of the dead were placed in large lidded jars, and the grave goods included iron spearheads, knives and sickles, as well as bronzes). Calibrated radiocarbon dates fall within the second half of the 1st millennium BC, and the grave goods include iron spearheads, knives and sickles as well as bronze spearheads and bells and exotic stone jewellery. Double animal-headed stone pendants from this area are paralleled in DONG SON, Philippine and central Thai contexts. The mortuary ritual is so unlike any other in prehistoric Southeast Asia that there is a serious case for considering the Sa Huynh culture as intrusive. The sites are located in the same region as the later CHAM polities, and could well have been ancestral to the Austronesian-speaking Chams themselves.

W.G. Solheim II: 'Sa-Huynh related pottery in Southeast Asia', *Asian Perspectives* 3 (1959), 177–88; Trinh Can and Pham Van Kinh: 'Excavation of the urnfield of Tam My' *Khao Co Hoc* 23 (1977), 49–57 [in Vietnamese].

CH

Saikachido *see* OTSUKA

St Césaire *see* NEANDERTHALS

St Gall Abbey Abbey in Switzerland which was the first monastic site to be planned in detail. The plan comprised a schematic red-ink drawing composed of five separate pieces amounting to an overall size of 0.77 × 1.12 m., which is now in the Stiftsbibliothek (Ms. 1092) of the Abbey of St Gall. This drawing depicts the plan of a monastery at *c.*AD 820, and a dedication indicates that it was a specific building project made at the request of the Abbot Gozbert of St Gall.

The plan has been the subject of much debate because Walter Horn proposed that it was a paradigm for all early medieval monasteries (Horn and Born 1979); Jacobsen 1992). It depicts a medieval monastic lay-out, showing an abbey-church with an attached cloister, surrounded by a variety of service and other buildings. Excavations at St Gall indicate that the plan was never realized, whereas excavations at nearby Mittelzell, Reichenau suggest that the draughtsman was using local architectural ideas already developed there (Zettler 1990).

W. Horn and E. Born: *The Plan of St Gall* (Berkeley, 1979); W. Jacobsen: *Der Klosterplan von St Gallen und Die Karolingische Architektur* (Berlin, 1992); A. Zettler: 'Der St Galler Klosterplan: Überlegungen zuseiner Herkunft und Entstehung', *Charlemagne's heir, new perspectives on the reign of Louis the Pious (814–840)*, ed. P. Godman and R. Collins (Oxford, 1990), 655–90.

RH

Saint-Michel-du-Touch Settlement site in the suburbs of Toulouse, Haute-Garonne, south

France, of the Middle Neolothic CHASSÉEN complex. A palisade and a series of deep ditches mark off the promontory on which the site is located, and may form part of an interrupted ditch system. Like other Chasséen sites in the region (e.g. VILLENEUVE-TOLOSANE), the structural remains of the interior of Saint-Michel-du-Touch are dominated by multiple cobble structures, which were originally assumed to be hut bases but may represent large food-processing or cooking hearths. There are also pits and graves, most notably a double burial within a massive rectangular pit (7.4 m × 4 m) filled with cobbles and with pottery. The pottery includes two decorated VASE SUPPORTS (a pottery type diagnostic of the Chasséen complex), decorated with ladder and elongated triangle motifs. The honey-coloured flint and the obsidian blade found in the grave are also typical of the French Middle Neolithic, for it was in this period that trade or exchange systems first developed extensively and 'exotic' materials were introduced. The site was probably in use for over a millennium, perhaps between 4900 and 3200 BC.

G. Simmonnet: 'Le village chasséen de Saint-Michel-du-Touch à Toulouse', *IXe Congrès UISPP* (Nice, 1976), 16–34.

RJA

Sais (Sa el-Hagar) Town-site in the Egyptian western Delta, dating principally to the 8th–6th centuries BC, when it was the provincial capital of the 5th nome of Lower Egypt and the seat of the 24th- and 26th-dynasty rulers. The remains of the tell have been largely destroyed by local farmers removing archaeological deposits for use as agricultural fertilizer, and there appear to be no surviving remains earlier than the 11th century BC.

B. Porter and R. Moss: *Topographical bibliography of ancient Egyptian hieroglyphic texts, reliefs and paintings* IV (1934), 46–9; L. Habachi: 'Sais and its monuments', *ASAE* 42 (1942), 369–416; R. el-Sayed: *Documents relatifs à Saïs et ses divinités* (Cairo, 1975).

IS

Sai Yok Rockshelter in Kanchanaburi Province, central Thailand, which was the first site in this area to exhibit a flaked stone industry resembling the HOABINHIAN material from northern Vietnam. Subsequent research in the area has expanded the number of such sites; no radiocarbon dates have been reported from this site.

H.R. van Heekeren and E. Knuth: *Archaeological excavations in Thailand* I: *Sai Yok*' (Copenhagen, 1967).

CH

Sakitama Inariyama Keyhole-shaped mounded tomb in Saitama prefecture, Japan, which contained one of the few datable inscriptions from the Kofun period (*see* JAPAN 4). A sword was shown by X-ray analysis to bear an inscription of 115 Chinese characters referring to a date of AD 471 or 531, commemorating the service of a regional chief to the central YAMATO authority. (See figure 25.)

W. Anazawa and J. Manome: 'Two inscribed swords from Japanese tumuli: discoveries and research on finds from the 'Sakitama-Inariyama and Eta-Funayama tumuli', *Windows on the Japanese past*, ed. R. Pearson, K. Hutterer and G.L. Barnes (Ann Arbor, 1986), 375–96.

SK

Salado Late prehistoric culture in the American Southwest, primarily in southeastern Arizona and southern New Mexico. The geographical range and temporal span (*c*.AD 1280–1500) are defined by the occurrence of Roosevelt Red Ware ceramics (including Pinto, Gila and Tonto polychrome); associated cultural characteristics include adobe and rock-adobe construction of PUEBLOS, PLATFORM MOUNDS and walled compounds.

There are three models with which the Salado can be interpreted. The first and oldest model regards it as a distinct culture formed late in prehistory either by the merging of ANASAZI and MOGOLLON elements or by a specialized adaptation of the HOHOKAM. The second interprets Salado not as a culture but as a multi-ethnic phenomenon resulting from the demographic upheaval of the abandonment of the Colorado Plateau, rapid population increase in the central Arizona mountains, and expansion out of Chihuahua into southern New Mexico and Arizona. The Lake Roosevelt/Tonto Basin region, considered to be the Salado heartland in the first model, reflects the multi-ethnic use of the area. Ethnic co-residence during Salado times is to be seen in the mixture of architectural conventions: cliff dwellings with rectangular and T-shaped doors; rambling checkerboard-style, cobbled masonry pueblos; platform mounds; and walled compounds. The third model interprets the weak unity of Salado as indicative of a cult or ideological system, cross-cutting different ethnic groups.

B.A. Nelson and S.A. LeBlanc: *Short-term sedentism in the American Southwest* (Albuquerque, 1986); P.L. Crown: *Ceramics and ideology* (Albuquerque, 1994).

JJR

Saliagos On this tiny Greek island, a Neolithic settlement has yielded some of the earliest radiocarbon dates (*c.*5000 BC) in the Cyclades. The series was the first to prove that settlements existed in the Cyclades long before the development of the Cycladic culture (from *c.*3300 BC). The Saliagos farmers grew barley and wheat and kept sheep and goats and some pigs; fishing was also very important. The village produced pottery decorated with white paint, and some simple flat marble figurines that strongly resemble the later 'violin' figurines of the Early Cycladic I culture; there is also a rather different figurine with massive rounded buttocks, irreverently called the 'Fat Lady of Saliagos'.

J.D. Evans and C. Renfrew: *Excavations at Saliagos near Antiparos* (London, 1968).

RJA

Samarra Type-site of the prehistoric Samarra culture and major city-site of the early Islamic period.

1 *Prehistory.* The 'Samarra culture' appeared in the northern Mesopotamian plain and the ZAGROS region around the middle of the HASSUNA period (*c.*5600 BC), continuing until well after the onset of the HALAF phase (*c.*5000 BC). The first distinctive Samarra-culture assemblage was discovered by Herzfeld in 1912–14, during his excavation of the prehistoric cemeteries at the site. However, it was not until the excavation of the settlement and cemetery at TELL ES-SAWWAN (about 10 km south of Samarra itself) in the 1960s that the Samarra culture was identified as an important phase in the Neolithic of the Ancient Near East, particularly in the area of the Tigris valley. Its principal distinguishing features are pottery vessels decorated with skilfully painted geometrical and figurative motifs, female figurines made of terracotta and alabaster (similar to those of the UBAID period), and exquisitely carved marble vessels. Typical Samarra-culture settlements and assemblages have been excavated at Tell Songor (Matsumoto 1987), while imported Samarra pottery has been found at the Ubaid site of Tell Abada in the Hamrin Basin. The ceramics of the late Samarra period at CHOGA MAMI ('Choga Mami transitional pottery') appear to have developed their own regional characteristics.

2 *Islamic period.* Samarra is also the key site for the Abbasid period (AD 750–1258), having been founded in AD 836 by the Caliph al-Muʿtasim as a capital for himself and his Turkish military commanders and forces. It remained the capital until the Caliph Muʿtamid was forced to move back to Baghdad in 892, and even after this date it was still occupied. Because of its Shiʿa shrine, it eventually developed into a pilgrimage centre in the mid-10th century. The excavations of Viollet, Sarre and Herzfeld, in 1910–13, provided detailed knowledge of the ground-plan of the mosques and palaces, through large-scale clearance of the vast palace of al-Muʿtasim, the palace of Balkuwârra, the Great Mosque and the Mosque of Abu Dulaf. A corpus of Abbasid paintings found in al-Muʿtasim's palace have provided the basic repertoire on which our knowledge of the subject still largely depends. The problem of the origin of the Abbasid lustreware and other fine glazed wares was, for the first time, able to be studied via a large body of material as a result of the excavations at Samarra.

3. *Aerial photography and surface survey at Samarra.* The history of the excavation and survey of Samarra is an excellent example of the changing approach to sites since the beginning of the 20th century. The massive clearances achieved with large (and cheap) labour forces that marked the first investigations at Samarra are no longer possible or even desirable. The work undertaken by Alastair Northedge in the 1980s addressed the enormous scale of the site through survey, and underlined how much of it had not been addressed by earlier research. Northedge's work demonstrated the particular value of AERIAL PHOTOGRAPHY with the exploitation of a sequence of aerial photographs taken between 1924 and 1961. The process is applicable elsewhere and is especially effective where the landscape is undergoing rapid change as is the case in many parts of the Middle East.

In contrast to the earlier excavations, which had concentrated on the narrow period of the residence there of the Abbasid Caliphs, the new work recognized that the site was occupied both before and after its 9th century expansion and also that it was far larger than previously thought, extending for over 40 km along the River Tigris. The new study also included detailed examination of surface ceramics and their distribution, recognizing a far more complex picture, especially as a result of advances in ceramic analysis in recent years. An important new discovery is evidence of a glass production site in the southern part of Samarra. The industrial production of Samarra has always been a mystery, and it is often stressed that Sarre and Herzfeld discovered no pottery kilns at the site, leaving the source of lustreware and other glazed ceramics a matter for speculation.

H. Viollet: 'Description du palais de al-Moutasim fils d'Haroun-al-Raschid à Samara et de quelques monuments arabes peu connus de la Mésopotamie', *Mémoires présenté par divers savants de l'Academie des Inscriptions et Belles-Lettres* 12 (1909), 567–94; ——: 'Fouilles à Samara en Mésopotamie: un palais musulman du IXe siècle',

Mémoires présentés par divers savants à l'Academie des Inscriptions et Belles-Lettres 12 (1911), 685–717; E.E. Herzfeld: *Die Malereien von Samarra* (Berlin, 1927); ——: *Die vorgeschichtlichen Töpfereien von Samarra* (Berlin, 1930); ——: *Geschichte der Stadt Samarra* (Berlin, 1948); A. Northedge: 'Planning 'Sâmarrâ: a report for 1983–4', *Iraq* 47 (1985), 109–28; K. Matsumoto: 'The Samarra period at Tell Songor A', *Préhistoire de la Mésopotamie*, ed. J.L. Huot (Paris, 1987), 189–98; A. Northedge et al.: 'Survey and excavations at Samarra, 1989', *Iraq* 52 (1990), 121–47; M. Tampoe: *Maritime trade between China and the West: an archaeological study of the ceramics from Siraf (Persian Gulf), 8th to 15th centuries AD* (Oxford, 1989); A. Northedge: 'Archaeology and new urban settlement in early Islamic Syria and Iraq', *The Byzantine and early Islamic Near East II land use and settlement patterns*, ed. G.R.D. King and A. Cameron (Princeton, 1994), 231–65.

IS/GK

Samaria *see* ISRAELITES

sambaquís Immense shell mounds of partly natural and partly cultural origin found along the southern coast of Brazil. Although the first occupation of some *sambaquís* may have been as early as *c.*6500 BC, the main period of use was during the 1st millennium BC and later.

R.W. Hurt: *Maritime adaptations in Brazil* (Greeley, 1986).

KB

samples, sampling theory In statistical analysis, a sample is a set of objects drawn from a POPULATION; sampling theory consists of techniques, including HYPOTHESIS TESTING and PARAMETER ESTIMATION, for making inferences about the population on the basis of DATA from the sample. For inferences to be valid, the sample must be representative of the population, i.e. it should be chosen according to a random sampling process. In the simplest case, 'simple random sampling', each object in the population has the same chance of selection; in more complex schemes the chances vary from one object to another, but can always be specified in advance. One aim of sampling theory is to derive the most information (often meaning the highest PRECISION) from the smallest possible sample, or the one requiring the least effort. The term is also used in a more general sense to mean a small part of a larger whole, e.g. a soil sample.

See QSAR ES-SEGHIR.

W.G. Cochran: *Sampling techniques* (New York, 1963); J.E. Doran and F.R. Hodson: *Mathematics and computers in archaeology* (Edinburgh, 1975), 42–3, 94–9; J.F. Cherry, C. Gamble and S. Shennan, eds: *Sampling in contemporary British archaeology* (Oxford, 1978); C.R. Orton: *Mathematics in archaeology* (Glasgow, 1980), 162–7; S. Shennan: *Quantifying archaeology* (Edinburgh, 1988), 298–330.

CO

sampling strategies Statisticians make a crucial distinction between a *sampled* population and a *target* population (see, for instance, Krumbein and Graybill 1965: 149; Doran and Hodson 1975: 95), and archaeologists' sampling strategies are based on the assumption that there is a systematic relationship between samples of archaeological material (e.g. trenches excavated within a large site) and the entire set of archaeological material from a site, region or culture. Redman and Watson (1970) use systematic intensive surface collection of artefacts at two prehistoric mounds in southeastern Turkey (Çayönü and Girik-i-Haciyan) to explore the strengths and weaknesses of various sampling designs and analytical procedures. They argue that, providing such factors as weather, local topography, number of phases present and amount of human disturbance are taken into account, a multivariate model can be constructed of the relationship between surface and subsurface material at any particular site. At the INCA urban site of Huánuco Pampa, 275 km northeast of Lima, Morris (in Mueller 1975) uses the architectural plans (constituting an estimated 80% of the city's original buildings) to divide the city into eight basic zones, five of which are then subdivided to produce a total of 21 'spatially separated strata'.

For a case-study see EL-HIBA.

W.C. Krumbein and F.A. Graybill: *An introduction to statistical models in geology* (New York, 1965); C.L. Redman and P.J. Watson: 'Systematic intensive surface collection', *AA* 35 (1970), 279–91; J.E. Doran and F.R. Hodson: *Mathematics and computers in archaeology.* (Edinburgh, 1975); J.W. Mueller, ed.: *Sampling in archaeology* (Tucson, 1975); R.D. Drennan: *Statistics for archaeologists: a commonsense approach* (New York and London, 1996), 79–98 passim.

IS

San Agustín Region in southern Colombia, around the head waters of the Magdalena River, where the people occupying a series of agriculture villages of the Isnos phase (*c.*AD 100–1200) erected elaborate stone statues depicting supernatural figures, animals and humans as part of their mortuary practices. The statues were buried in stone cists or left in the barrow chambers or passages, probably serving protective functions for the dead.

L. Herrera, ed.: *San Agustín 2000 años 1790–1990:*

Seminario: La arqueología del Macizo y el suroccidente Colombianos (Bogotá, 1991); K.O. Bruhns: 'Monumental sculpture as evidence for hierarchical societies', *Wealth and hierarchy in the Intermediate area*, ed. F. Lange (Washington, D.C., 1992), 331–56.

KB

Sanchi Buddhist site located near Bhopal in central India, dating from the 3rd century BC to the 11th century AD. The site contains a number of significant Buddhist monuments enclosed within a massive stone wall which postdates most of the construction at the site. Structures within the walled area include *STUPAS*, shrines, temples and monasteries.

J. Marshall: *Excavations at Sanchi*, Archaeological Survey Reports II (Delhi, 1914); ——: *A guide to Sanchi* (Delhi, 1936); M.K. Dhavalikar: *Sanchi: a cultural study* (Pune, 1965); K.K. Murthy: *Material culture of Sanchi* (Delhi, 1983).

CS

Sanghao Cave Palaeolithic cave site in northwest Pakistan, which was excavated by Ahmad H. Dani in the 1960s. Twelve stratified levels were identified in 3 m of deposit; levels 12–5 date to the Palaeolithic period, disturbed levels 4–3 contain microliths, and Buddhist remains were found in the upper two levels. The lithic artefacts were made of quartz, while artefacts from the Palaeolithic levels included a small handaxe, scrapers, awls, and burins, as well as prepared cores and flakes produced by the LEVALLOIS technique. No absolute dates are available for Sanghao Cave.

A.H. Dani: 'Sanghao excavation: the first season, 1963', *AP* 1 (1965), 1–50; B. Allchin: 'Blade and burin industries of West Pakistan and Western India', *South Asian archaeology*, ed. N. Hammond (Cambridge, 1973), 39–50.

CS

Sangoan (Sangoan-Lupemban) 'Industry' in Central Africa, which was once thought to be part of a typological succession of post-ACHEULEAN macrolithic 'forest industries' but is now much more cautiously defined. First found by E.J. Wayland on the hills above Sango Bay on the west side of Lake Victoria, most finds of the Sangoan and related industries have been from surface collections along river terraces. Only a few *in situ* living floors are known, including KALAMBO FALLS (Zambia) and the Mwaganda Elephant Kill site (Malawi). Desmond Clark (1959) linked the first Sangoan finds to an adaptation to forest environment with picks being used for digging tubers and animal traps, chopping tools for bringing down trees, and push-planes for the working of wood. Indeed, the distribution of these Sangoan-Lupemban *fossiles directeurs* may still be shown to follow the modern Central and West-Central African forest and savanna-forest ecozones.

However, some of the initial suppositions about the Sangoan were shown to have been false as research progressed. Firstly, the Sangoan was thought to be dominated by heavy duty tools (e.g. crude picks, push planes and cleavers), while the Lupemban was thought to be a later variant distinguished by the presence of fine lanceolates. However, the excavated living floors of Kalambo Falls showed heavy duty tools to be in the minority (>30%) with flake scrapers and other 'light duty tools' comprising at least 60% of the lithic assemblage in most contexts (Clark 1970). Similar heavy-duty–light-duty ratios have since also been demonstrated at ASOKROCHONA (Ghana) and Muguruk (Kenya).

Additionally, the research of Daniel Cahen has cast doubt on the security and universality of the initial temporal ordering of Acheulean–Sangoan–Lupemban–Tshitolean. From a re-excavation of the important GOMBE POINT (Zaire) stratigraphic succession, Cahen (1976) was able to show that lithic conjoins cross-cut the sequence, with an additional tendency for artefacts of greater volume to be lower in the sequence than those of lesser volume. He subsequently suggested that millennia of river terrace re-working has hopelessly skewed most known sequences from Central African river basins, and that most so-called industries were only 'pseudo-industries'. Cahen thus suggested the abandonment of most of the post-Acheulean stone age sequence for Central Africa, with a re-start from scratch. In the meantime the broad terms Acheulean complex and post-Acheulean complex were suggested (Cahen 1978).

However, other researchers such as Sally McBrearty have called for the retention of the name 'Sangoan' at a TECHNOCOMPLEX level, since it still describes a broad macrolithic core tool adaptation which can be shown to have post-dated the Acheulean and pre-dated 'MOUSTERIAN' industries in central Africa. In Western Kenya at Muguruk, McBrearty has had the good fortune to find relatively rich deposits with their stratigraphic integrity intact. These deposits showed a succession from a local Ojolla industry (of Sangoan-Lupemban technocomplex) to a Pundo Makwar (of LEVALLOIS Mousterian technocomplex). The Sangoan can also be shown to underlie Levallois technology at Asokrochona (Ghana).

The age range of the Sangoan-Lupemban technocomplex remains uncertain. Dates include a *c.*200,000 BP ESR (electron spin resonance) determination on the Kabwe (Broken Hill, Zambia) archaic *Homo sapiens* remains (associated with supposed Sangoan light-duty components), and a date of greater than 130,000 BP at Lake Eyasi (Tanzania) where archaic *Homo sapiens* remains are also associated with a 'Sangoan' industry. Other dates are either minimum (40,000+ BP) ones, from several sites including Kalambo Falls, or seemingly aberrant dates for 'Lupemban' localities in the Lunda regions (Angola) which are as recent as *c.*15,000 BP.

J.D. Clark: *The prehistory of Southern Africa* (London, 1959); ——: *The prehistory of Africa* (London, 1970); D. Cahen: 'Nouvelles fouilles à la Pointe de la Gombe (ex-Pointe de Kalina), Kinshasa, Zaire', *L'Anthropologie* 80 (1976), 573–602; ——: 'Vers une revision de la nomenclature des industries préhistoriques de l'Afrique Centrale', *L'Anthropologie* 82 (1978), 5–36; P. Allsworth-Jones: 'The earliest human settlement in West Africa and the Sahara', *WAJA* 17 (1987), 87–129; S. McBrearty: 'The Sangoan-Lupemban and the Middle Stone Age sequence at the Muguruk site, western Kenya,' *WA* 19 (1988), 388–420; P. Allsworth-Jones: 'The archaeology of archaic and early modern *Homo sapiens*: an African perspective', *CAJ* 3 (1993), 21–39.

KM

San-hsing-tui (Sanxingdui) Chinese Neolithic site with cultural levels from LUNG-SHAN through to the SHANG and CHOU periods (*c.*2000–1000 BC) including the remains of a city wall. The site is situated 8 km from Kuang-han hsien (Guang-han) in the province of Ssu-ch'uan, China. In 1986, the excavations of two unusual pit burials containing a vast hoard of bronze artefacts, jade objects, elephant tusks and gold-foil ornaments, caused a considerable stir throughout China and the archaeological world. The bronze-using culture at San-hsing tui was of a kind that had not hitherto been found in China, and had no apparent affinities elsewhere: it appeared to be culturally isolated from the surrounding Neolithic environment.

Among the more curious artefacts are such items as a standing bronze statue (260 cm) of pre-Han date, several bronze masks (the largest having a width of 138.5 cm) with cylindrical pupils protruding from the eyes, a series of bronze heads with 'inverted' eyes and square chins – the latter feature reminiscent of wood sculpture – and various other bronze artefacts, including several vessels obviously deriving from other areas of China, some of the latter datable as early as Western Chou.

Although the cultural remains have been dated to the Late Shang period (*c.*1400–1122 BC) by the local excavators, there are significant parallels of ornamentation with that of the 6th-and 5th-century art of CH'U. The full significance and date of the find have yet to be acceptably determined, including any association it may have had with the PA-SHU cultures of Western China.

N. Barnard: 'Some preliminary thoughts on the significance of the Kuang-han pit-burial bronzes and other artifacts', *Beiträge zur Allgemeinen und Vergleichenden Archäologie* 9–10, (1990), 249–80.

NB

San Jacinto *see* PUERTO HORMIGA, MONSÚ AND SAN JACINTO

San José Mogote Small Formative-period village in an agriculturally highly productive portion of the valley of Oaxaca, Mexico, which came to prominence between 1100 and 800 BC, reaching its peak around 700–500 BC. The traditional idea of the primacy of the OLMEC culture in the genesis of Mesoamerican civilization has been challenged by the presence, at San José Mogote, of early public architecture and evidence of the use of status symbols. Investigators recognized residential neighbourhoods at the village, differentiated by distributions of motifs on pottery in burials and areas of specialized craft production. San José Mogote functioned as the major civic centre of the Etla (northern) arm of the Valley of Oaxaca until the founding of MONTE ALBAN.

Marcus and Flannery (1994) have used the 'direct historical approach' and COGNITIVE ARCHAEOLOGY to examine ZAPOTEC ritual and religion, demonstrating that many elements of ritual described in 16th century accounts have been preserved in the archaeological record at San José Mogote. The excavation of Structure 35, for instance, has revealed material evidence of the activities of the *bigaña* (priests), including blood-letting with prismatic obsidian blades and the use of obsidian daggers to sacrifice not only quails and turkeys but also human slaves and prisoners of war, all of which are described in 16th century texts. However, the archaeological work also goes beyond the documentary records to show that the Zapotec turned secular ground into sacred ground by including valuable offerings in the temple foundations (as in the case of 'Features 94–96'). Marcus and Flannery (1994: 71–2) therefore make the point that cognitive archaeology at such sites as San José Mogote lies at the interface between archaeology and history: 'First ethnohistory tells us what a temple should look like and accurately predicts that we should discover obsidian blades, sacrificial knives, incense burners and quail. Archaeology then reveals unpredicted offerings beneath the temples, but ethnohistory gives us some clues for interpreting them. In the case of Feature 96 at San José Mogote, it suggests that we are seeing metamorphosis, a major career transition of deceased royalty'.

K.V. Flannery, ed.: *The early Mesoamerican village* (New York, 1976); J. Marcus and K.V. Flannery: 'Ancient Zapotec ritual and religion: an application of the direct historical approach', *The ancient mind: elements of cognitive archaeology*, ed. C. Renfrew and E. Zubrow (Cambridge, 1994), 55–74.

PRI

San Lorenzo Tenochtitlán Complex of early OLMEC (Middle Formative) sites – San Lorenzo, Tenochtitlán (Río Chiquito) and Potrero Nuevo – in the Gulf coast region of Veracruz, Mexico. Best known is San Lorenzo proper, dating after 1500 BC, which was built by raising and enlarging a natural promontory, possibly in effigy form. Its primarily public/ceremonial architecture includes more than 20 earthen mounds, a series of ponds or lagoons with drainage troughs, and at least 75 sculptured monuments. The site is usually seen as a ceremonial centre because of the comparative lack of evidence for domestic occupation.

M.D. Coe and R.A. Diehl: *In the land of the Olmec, I: The archaeology of San Lorenzo Tenochtitlán* (Austin, 1980).

PRI

San Pedro de Atacama Major oasis in the Atacama desert of Chile, and the scene of human activity from the earliest PALEOINDIAN hunting groups through to the development of sedentary farming/herding communities increasingly under the influence of PUCARA and TIAHUANACO and finally falling to the INCAS. The site is especially important because the aridity of the desert has ensured excellent preservation of organic materials.

A.M. Barón Parra: 'Tulor: posibilidades y limitaciones de un ecosistema', *Revista Chungara* 16–17 (1986), 149–58; M. Rivera: 'The prehistory of Northern Chile: a summary', *JWP* 5/1 (1991), 1–47.

KB

Santorini *see* THERA

San Vincenzo al Volturno Major Benedictine monastery in the Appennines of Central Italy, which flourished between the 8th and 12th centuries AD. Excavations in 1980–94 brought to light many elements of an early medieval monastery, preserved thanks to an Arab sack of October 10, 881. The history of the monastery is well-established as a result of a 12th-century account, the *Chronicon Vulturnense*. The deserted site first came to notice with the discovery of a complete painted crypt in 1832, including one panel on which Abbot Epyphanius (AD 824–42) is depicted. Excavations commenced in 1980 to examine the layout of an early medieval monastery, following the publication of Walter Horn and Ernest Born's *The Plan of St Gall* (*see* ST GALL ABBEY), and a sequence of monastic plans has now been identified (Hodges 1993–5).

The builders of the first monastery effectively re-used a Late Roman villa, covering about half a hectare, which was possibly the seat of the bishop of Samnium. The 5th-century funerary church became the first early medieval abbey-church. Later in the 8th century a painted altar was made in its apse, and a fine ambulatory had by then been added, in order to provide visitors with a view of the altar.

In the early 9th century Abbot Joshua created a monastic city – the second lay-out – modelled upon Carolingian prototypes. A triple-apsed abbey-church, 63 m long and 28 m wide, was consecrated in 808. The old monastery was converted into quarters for distinguished guests. In between lay the cloisters with provision for over 300 monks. South of the abbey lay a collective workshop. Many other buildings have also been provisionally identified in a complex that now covered 6 ha. Most parts of the monastery were richly painted, while re-used Roman *spolia* were incorporated in most buildings. A rich material culture, including a prolific use of glass, distinguishes this phase. Abbot Joshua's plan was enlarged by Abbot Epyphanius when the abbey-church was aggrandized with an eastwork, and the distinguished guests' palace was enlarged with a new western apsidal end. In 848 an earthquake damaged several buildings.

Thereafter, until the comprehensive Arab sack in 881, the monastery fell slowly into decline. With the development of its territory in the later 10th century, San Vincenzo emulated its neighbour, Monte Cassino, by building a new romanesque monastery – a third lay-out – involving the demolition of the earlier ruins. Built between *c.*AD 1000 and 1060, this typical, compact settlement was subjected to attacks by local families. As a result the Romanesque monastery was dismantled and transposed to a new defensible site some 400 metres away. Here the

Chronicon Vulturnense was written soon after the move, recalling the colourful history of the earlier site. A monastery still exists at the site in modern times.

C. Wickham: *Il problema dell' Incastellamento nell' Italia Centrale: L'esempio di San Vincenzo al Volturno* (Florence, 1985); J. Mitchell: 'Literacy displayed: the use of inscriptions at the monastery of San Vincenzo al Volturno in the early ninth century', *The uses of literacy in early Medieval Europe*, ed. R. McKitterick (Cambridge, 1990), 186–225; R. Hodges, ed.: *San Vincenzo al Volturno*, 2 vols (London, 1993–5).

RH

Sanxingdui *see* SAN-HSING-TUI

Sapalli (Sapalli-tepe) Bronze Age fortified settlement located on the Amu-Darya plain, 70 km west of the town of Termez in southern Uzbekistan, Central Asia. Excavated by Askarov (1973), the site (*c*.4 ha) includes a central area fortified by a system of walls, and a 'lower area' where three construction levels were recognized. The earlier two phases belong to the 'Sapalli culture' of about 2200–1800 BC, and the later one to the 'Jarkutan culture' of about 2000 BC. The settled area in the first level of the lower area contained eight distinct large residential units, interpreted as separate 'patriarchal households'. Each of these had several domestic hearths and evidence for pottery production. The number of residences nearly doubled in the second level, but the structures were destroyed by fire at the end of the period. The later settlement, corresponding to the third level, was much smaller. A total of 138 graves had been studied, mostly in the central fortified area of the site (which was possibly occupied by the social elite): 29 burials contained metal and stone objects; 23 female graves included toilet articles; graves of infants and children had a poorer assortment of goods.

A. Askarov: *Sapallitepa* (Tashkent, 1973); ——: 'Southern Uzbekistan in the second millennium BC', *The Bronze age civilization of Central Asia*, ed. P. Kohl (Armonk, 1981); P. Kohl: *Central Asia: Palaeolithic beginnings to the Iron Age* (Paris, 1984), 154–8.

PD

Saqqara Necropolis associated with the Egyptian city of MEMPHIS, southwest of Cairo, with funerary and religious buildings dating from *c*.3000 BC to AD 950. It included the tombs of elite officials of the Early Dynastic period (*c*.3000–2649 BC); the Step Pyramid complex of King Djoser (*c*.2620 BC; the pyramids of the 5th- and 6th-dynasty rulers Unas, Userkaf, Teti, Pepi I and II, Merenra, Shepseskaf and Djedkara Isesi; the tombs of New Kingdom officials such as the 18th-dynasty general Horemheb (*c*.1310 BC); the Serapeum (*c*.1250–BC–AD 400), where the sacred Apis bulls were buried from at least the reign of Amenhotep III until the Ptolemaic period (*c*.1400–30 BC); the Sacred Animal Necropolis, and many other tombs, temples and shrines. Northern Saqqara also incorporates the ruins of the monastery of Appa Jeremias, founded around the end of the 5th century AD and abandoned by the late 9th century.

J.-P. Lauer: *Saqqara: the royal cemetery of Memphis* (London, 1976); G.T. Martin: *The sacred animal necropolis at north Saqqara* (London, 1981); ——: *The hidden tombs of Memphis* (London, 1991).

IS

Sarab, Tepe *see* LURISTAN

Saraçhane Site of the lost early Byzantine church of St. Polyeuktos, built by Anicia Juliana in AD 524–7 and excavated in 1964–9. This was one of the major churches of Constantinople in the early Byzantine period. The excavations (like those at the Cripta Balbi, Rome; Manacorda and Zanini 1989) provided the first sequence of archaeological deposits containing objects extending from the 6th century to the later Middle Ages. These include domestic pottery, glassware, and metalwork, making Saraçhane 'a type site' for early to middle Byzantine archaeology.

R.M. Harrison: *Excavations at Saraçhane* (Istanbul and Princeton, 1986); D. Manacorda and E. Zanini: 'The first millennium AD in Rome: from the Porticus Minucia to the Via delle Botteghe Oscure', *The birth of Europe*, ed. K. Randsborg (Rome, 1989), 25–32.

RH

Sarazm Eneolithic-Bronze Age site consisting of ten small mounds, situated in the Zerafshan Valley near the medieval town of Penjikent in Tadjikistan. The site has been excavated since 1977 by Isakov with the help of French archaeologists. Several radiocarbon measurements suggest a calender date of around 3250–2750 BC. A small cemetery belonging to the initial stage shows some elements of the burial rite typical of steppe groups to the north. The pottery corpus reveals elements of the GEOKSYUR style, in association with styles related to Sistan-Baluchistan and Northern Iran (Hissar III B). The typology of the locally produced copper tools, based

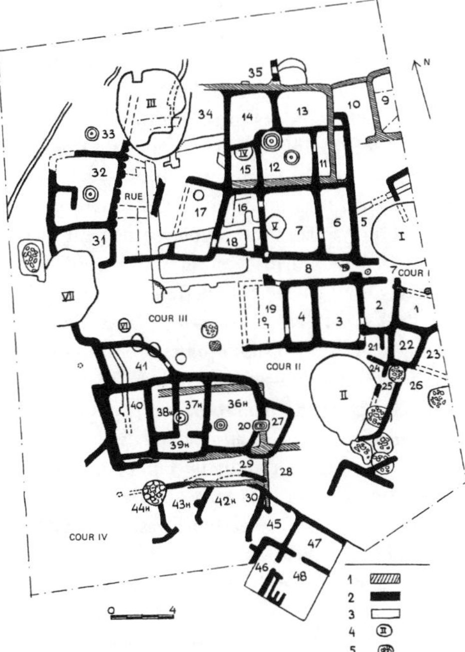

Figure 45 **Sarazm** Eneolithic–Bronze Age settlement at Sarazm, Tadjikistan: (1) walls of Sarazm III, (2) walls of Sarazm II, (3) walls of Sarazm I, (4) ditches, (5) hearths. *Source*: A. Isakov: 'Excavations of the Bronze Age settlement of Sarazm', *The Bronze Age civilization of Central Asia*, ed. P. Kohl (Armonk, 1981), fig. 3.

on local metallurgy, also reveals North Iranian affinities. The Sarazm tradition is usually interpreted as resulting from an interaction between Geoksyur-related agricultural groups (migrating from the 'northern foothills' of the Kopet Dag) and local social units.

A. Isakov: 'Excavations of the Bronze Age settlement of Sarazm', *The Bronze age civilization of Central Asia*, ed. P. Kohl (Armonk, 1981), 273–86.

PD

Sarnate Group of Neolithic settlements, dated to between about 3500 and 2900 BC in calendar years and situated in the marginal zone of a peat-bog in the coastal area of western Latvia (south of the town of Ventspils). The sites were discovered and excavated by L. Vankina in the 1960s. There were over 40 dwellings built on piles over sandy foundations, and varying in size from 3 to 15 sq. m. The faunal remains, although limited in quantity, included elk, beaver, wild boar and seal. One of the dwellings was completely filled with fish bones. Large amounts of water chestnut (*Trapa natans*) were found in all of the excavated dwellings. Several large fragments of boats (made of single tree-trunks), as well as numerous oars, were found. Amber ornaments – including disks, buttons, rings and pendants – were discovered within most of the structures. Several clay figurines and wooden anthropomorphic sculptures have also been recovered.

L.V. Vankina: *Torfjanikovaja stojanka Sarnate* [Sarnate peat site] (Riga, 1970).

PD

sarsen Natural boulder of silicified sandstone, probably formed during the Tertiary age, and shaped and deposited by glacial action. Large groups of sarsens appear at surface level in areas of the Marlborough Downs in Wiltshire, England, where they formed ideal material for the construction of monuments such as AVEBURY and the trilithons of STONEHENGE. Most of the natural sarsen fields have now been broken up for use in more recent constructions, but a preserved group can be seen at Fyfield Down, near Avebury in Wiltshire.

RJA

Sasanian Iranian dynasty, founded by Sasan in AD 208, which dominated most of the ancient Near East from the fall of the PARTHIAN empire in 224 until the assassination of Yezdegerd III in 651, followed by the gradual Islamicization of the local population. The Sasanian rulers considered themselves to be the true heirs of the Achaemenid empire (*see* PERSIA), regarding their Parthian predecessors as westernized usurpers of the throne. Typical Sasanian cities incorporated palaces and fire temples retaining some of the architectural styles that had characterized Parthian public buildings. There are surviving remains of typical Sasanian palaces at such sites as Firuzabad, Bishapur and Qasr-i Shirin, Ctesiphon and KISH. The sides of a deep gorge near the city of Bishapur in western Iran are decorated with six distinctive Sasanian rock-carved reliefs depicting Shapur I's victory over the Romans in AD 266.

R. Ghirshman: *Bichâpour*, 2 vols (Paris, 1956–72); ——: *Parthes et Sassanides* (Paris, 1962); P.O. Harper: *The royal hunter* (London, 1978); G. Herrmann: *The Iranian revival* (Oxford, 1977); B.J. Overlaet et al., eds.: *Splendeur des Sassanides* exh. cat. (Brussels, 1993).

IS

Satsumon Culture found in Hokkaido, Japan between the 4th and 14th centuries AD, partly associated with the Emishi ethnic group, contemporary with the Kofun and Early Historic periods further south in Japan (*see* JAPAN 4–5). Characterized by the use of iron, incised pottery similar to the Haji ware of Kofun period and the cultivation of cereals such as millet, it was partly contemporary with the OKHOTSK culture.

E. Yokoyama: *Satsumon bunka* (Tokyo, 1990); Y. Fukasawa: 'Emishi and the Ainu: from an archaeological point of view', Paper presented at *Japanese archaeology in protohistoric and early historic period: Yamato and its relations to surrounding populations*, International symposium at the University of Bonn, 1992.

SK

Sauveterrian Term applied to an ill-defined group of Mesolithic assemblages, characterized principally by the presence of small triangular points and narrow blades. First identified at Sauveterre-la Lemance, southwest France, the assemblages date from about 7000 BC onwards, being produced for perhaps a millennium. Kozłowski interprets the Sauveterrian as an assemblage type, originally including a specific tool-kit, that evolved in southern France and was then adopted to a greater or lesser extent through much of west and central Europe (including Britain). Sauveterrian assemblages are generally thought to post-date assemblages defined as MAGLEMOSIAN, or to be contemporary with the later Maglemosian, and to predate assemblages defined as TARDENOISIAN; however, the relationship with the Tardenoisian has been the subject of much debate since the 1950s, as summarized by Peter Rowley-Conwy (1986). It seems clear that in most regions the Sauveterrian does not represent a 'culture'; whether its spread represents some change in implement use and economy, or whether it is simply a stylistic phenomenon, is as yet undecided.

S.K. Kozłowski, ed.: *The Mesolithic in Europe* (1973); J.K. Kozłowski: 'Les industries à pointes à cran en Europe Centre-Est', *Ixe Congrès UISPP, Nice, Coll. XV* (Paris, 1976), 121–7; P. Rowley-Conwy: 'Between cavepainters and crop planters: aspects of the temperate European Mesolithic', *Hunters in transition*, ed. J. Zvelebil (Cambridge 1986), 17–29.

RJA

Sawwan, Tell es- The classic site of the SAMARRA culture (*c.*5600–5000 BC), located on the left bank of the Tigris north of Baghdad, in central Iraq. It incorporates several strata of settlement remains dating back to the HASSUNA phase (*c.*5800–5500 BC), providing the first clear evidence that the painted pottery originally discovered at the site of Samarra was not simply a specialized form of Hassuna ceramics but a cultural sequence in its own right. The earliest Samarra settlement at Sawwan consisted of large rectangular multi-room buildings, each constructed with long mud bricks and provided with external buttresses, the whole settlement being surrounded by a 3 m deep ditch. The individual buildings each covered about 150 sq. m and were initially interpreted as granaries (Roux 1992: 54) although all are probably domestic structures. In later phases the houses were much smaller (only about 70 sq. m) and the settlement plan as a whole was considerably looser and defended by an enclosure wall as well as the ditch. The people of Tell es-Sawwan, as at CHOGA MAMI further to the east, evidently relied on a subsistence base including the cultivation of wheat and barley as well as cattle herding and hunting; their use of irrigation agriculture and the construction of impressive mud-brick buildings all suggest that the Samarra culture represented a distinct prelude to the process of urbanization in Mesopotamia.

Preliminary reports by B. Abu es-Soof et al. in *Sumer* 21–26 (1965–70); H. Helbaek: 'Early Hassunan vegetables from Tell es-Sawwan, near Samarra', *Sumer* 20 (1964), 45–8; J. Oates: 'The baked clay figurines from Tell es-Sawwan', *Iraq* 28 (1966), 146–53; G. Roux: *Ancient Iraq*, 3rd edn: (Harmondsworth, 1992), 53–5; C. Breniquet: 'Tell es-Sawwan: réalités et problèmes', *Iraq* 53 (1991), 75–90.

IS

Sayala *see* A GROUP

Sayil One of several large Mesoamerican sites in the PUUC region of the northwestern Yucatán peninsula, Sayil recently the focus of mapping and excavations in the 1980s, designed to understand how and why this region flourished during the tumultuous Terminal Classic period (*c.*AD 800–1000), when sites further to the south were subject to the LOWLAND MAYA 'collapse'. The city was occupied by approximately 10,000 people, while another 7000 lived around the urban core. House platforms had garden plots in the vicinity and CHULTUNES served for storing water.

J.A. Sabloff and G. Tourtellot: *The ancient Maya city of Sayil: the mapping of a Puuc region center* (New Orleans, 1991).

PRI

scanning electron microscope (SEM) Type of microscope in which an extremely fine beam of electrons (5–100 kV) is used to scan an area of a gold- or carbon-coated specimen in a series of parallel lines. Secondary electrons emitted from the surface of the specimen along the lines can be used to reproduce an image of the specimen via a cathode ray tube. These high resolution three-dimensional images can then be magnified up to 100,000 times, providing considerably more depth of focus than conventional microscopes. The SEM can thus reveal details of morphologies and textures too small to be seen in thin sections, allowing it to be used for such archaeological purposes as the study of ancient food remains (Dronzek et al. 1972) and the provenancing of stone artefacts (Middleton and Bradley 1989). The 'electron microprobe' is a combination of a scanning electron microscope and multiple wavelength dispersive spectrometers; it can be used to perform fully quantitative elemental analyses of specimens. For further discussion *see* ELECTRON PROBE MICROANALYSIS (EPMA) *and* X-RAY FLUORESCENCE SPECTROMETERY (XRF).

B.L. Dronzek et al.: 'Scanning electron microscopy of starch from sprouted wheat', *Cereal Chemistry* 49/2 (1972), 232–9. A. Middleton and S.M. Bradley: 'Provenancing of Egyptian limestone sculpture', *JAS* 16 (1989), 475–88.

IS

scapulimancy Chinese method of divination, using the reading of features such as colourations and cracks in animal shoulder blades to predict future happenings or explore the advisability of carrying out some planned activity. In the related method of PLASTROMANCY, turtle plastrons were employed for the same purpose. A distinction should be made between *apyro*-scapulimancy, where the natural condition of the bone (after scraping away the flesh) is read, and *pyro*-scapulimancy, where the bone is heated in order to create 'omen cracks'. Pyro-scapulimancy was common in Neolithic China, while in the Late Shang period (*c.*1400–1123 BC) incised writings were added both before and after the heat-induced omen cracks were read. Due to the latter practice, a large corpus of archaeological documents, the ORACLE BONES, has accumulated since the beginning of the 20th century, providing invaluable insights into many aspects of Shang culture (*see* CHINA 3).

D.N. Keightley: *Sources of Shang history: the oracle-bone inscriptions of Bronze Age China* (Berkeley, 1978).

NB

scarab Type of seal found in Egypt, Nubia and Syria-Palestine from the 6th dynasty until the Ptolemaic period (*c.*2040–30 BC). It derives its name from the fact that it was carved or moulded in the form of the sacred scarab beetle Khepri. The flat base was usually decorated with designs or inscriptions, sometimes including a royal name.

P.E. Newberry: *Ancient Egyptian scarabs: an introduction to Egyptian seals and signet rings* (London, 1905; repr. Chicago, 1979); M. Malaise: *Les scarabées de coeur dans l'Egypte ancienne* (Brussels, 1978); C. Andrews: *Amulets of ancient Egypt* (London, 1994), 50–9.

IS

scattergram, scatterplot Graphical representation of archaeological DATA in which two variables are represented along two axes, and objects are plotted as points whose locations are fixed by the values taken by the variables on each object. Objects that are 'similar' to each other appear close to each other on the plot and 'dissimilar' objects are located away from each other. It is often used to give a visual impression of the outcome of a PRINCIPAL COMPONENTS ANALYSIS or a CORRESPONDENCE ANALYSIS, in which case the variables plotted are combinations of the original variables.

CO

Scythians Predominantly nomadic groups of the steppe regions of Ukraine and southern Russia, mid-to late 1st millennium BC. The first excavations of Scythian antiquities in Southern Russia and Ukraine date back to 1763, when General A.P. Melgunov opened a series of magnificent barrows near the town of Elizavetgrad (Kirovograd). In 1830, P. Dubrux discovered and excavated the stone burial chamber at Kul-Oba barrow, near the town of Kerch in eastern Crimea. Intensive excavations of Scythian barrows at the turn of the century were carried out by N.I. Veselovsky, while the settlements and hill-forts (*gorodišče*) in the forest-steppe zone were studied by A.A. Spitsyn and V.A. Gorodtsov.

In the Soviet era, large-scale excavations of both barrows and settlements were conducted by A.I. Terenozhkin, B.M. Mozolevsky, I.B. Brashinsky and others. The problems related to the origin, ethnicity and social pattern of Scythian groups were discussed by scholars such as M.I. Rostovtseff, V.I. Ravdonikas, M.I. Artamonov, P.D. Liberov, and A.M. Khazanov. Three main groups of Scythian sites are distinguished in the Pontic steppes: (1) Central steppe; (2) Lower Don; (3) Crimean steppe.

Scythian burials in the steppe areas mainly take the form of barrows (kurgans), which start to emerge at the turn of the 7th/6th centuries BC in a region stretching from the Danube to the Don. From the end of the 5th century BC, the barrows tend to cluster in the Low Dniepr, the Low Southern Bug and in the Dniestr-Danube interfluve. The number of 'rich' barrows increases from this period, though most of the so-called 'royal tombs' belong to the 4th century BC. In terms of physical size, the tallest barrows are: Alexandropol (21 m); Chertomlyk (19 m); Oguz (20 m); Bol'shaya Tsymbalka (15 m); Kozel (14 m). There is also a range of medium-sized monuments such as Melitopol (6 m); Tolstaya Mogila (8.6 m); and Gaimanova Mogila (8 m). By contrast, the barrows of common tribesmen are usually less than 2 m in height and less than 100 m in diameter; they form cemeteries consisting of 10–15 (occasionally up to 100) barrows.

The barrows usually cover either rectangular or oval-shaped graves; timber burial chambers and catacombs were also sometimes constructed. The latter become particularly complex in the case of the royal tombs. Inhumation was the predominant burial rite: the dead were usually laid on their backs, and more rarely in a contracted posture on the right or left side. The head was directed either to the west or northwest. About 80% of the burials are single graves, and multiple burials started to occur only after the 4th–3rd centuries BC. The body was often placed on a mat of reed, grass or bark, or more rarely on skin or fur. Coffins or sarcophagi were employed only in the richest tombs (Chertomlyk, Melitopol, Tolstaya Mogila, Oguz).

The burial inventory of common tribesmen usually included a quiver and arrowheads and, rarely, one or two spears; still more rarely, a sword, a dagger or armour were added or (in very exceptional cases) elements of horse gear. Female graves of the commoner sort tend to contain clay or plumb spindle-whorls and various ornaments, although perhaps 25–27% of common female graves contain weapons (arrows, spears, swords or daggers; more rarely a belt with gold plaques). Both male and female graves might contain a 'meal', as evidenced by the bones of sheep, cattle or horse. Cemeteries close to Greek colonies often contained Greek-made drinking vessels.

The rich burials reveal considerable social differentiation in Scythian society. From the 5th century BC, the richest tombs were often augmented by burials of horses and human attendants. In some cases (e.g. Strashnaya Mogila, mound 1), horse and human burials accompanied tombs that in other respects are not particularly rich. Horse burials are most often found associated with male tombs, but in some cases accompany rich female graves (Khomina Mogila, Gaimanova Mogila, Solokha, Alexandropol). In some examples (Chertomlyk), the graves of servants contained a rich series of grave goods (including gold and silver implements). At Chmyreva Mogila and Gaimanova Mogila, women apparently killed at the time of the funeral were buried in separate chambers that contained items comparable with those buried with the 'king'. All royal tombs contain numerous decorative gold 'plates' (up to 2000) which were sewn onto clothing. Both male and female tombs contained bracelets and gold pendants. The number of ritual vessels varied from 1–2 to 10; these were mostly Greek-made amphorae, kitchen vessels or bronze cauldrons containing the remains of a ritual meal (horse, goat or cattle). The tombs of rich warriors contained trimmed quivers with arrows, one or several swords, and hatchets. The graves of noble Scythian women usually contained mirrors, glass and gold beads, various ornaments of precious metals, bronze and ivory – predominantly of Greek workmanship.

Permanent settlements started to appear in the steppe area in the late 5th century BC. The largest settlement, Kamenskoe, on the river Dniepr, opposite Nikopol, reached the size of 12,000 sq. km. The settlement boasted a large citadel, and was protected by earthern walls and ditches. Bronze and iron tools and blacksmith's implements were found around many of the houses. The settlement of Elizavatovskaya was situated on one of the islands in the Don delta. The site emerged at the turn of the 6th/5th centuries BC as an important centre of maritime trade and crafts, and was encircled in the 4th century BC by a system of defensive walls and ditches.

The economy of most Scythian groups is thought to have been based on nomadic stock-breeding. The faunal remains reveal a predominance of cattle (which were also used as draught animals) and horse. At least in the Lower Dniepr and the Lower Don, there was also a fallow system of agriculture based on the cultivation of rye, Italian millet and emmer.

In the forest-steppe zone, a system of fortified settlements (*gorodišče*) emerged from the 7th century BC. Eight local groups are distinguished: the Middle Dniepr (Right Bank); the Southern Bug; West Podolian; Vorksla; Seima; North Donetsian; Sula; and the Middle Don. These groups are often identified with the 'Scythian cultivators', 'who grow corn not for their own use, but for sale' as described by Herodotus (*The Persian Wars*, book IV). Archaeological evidence reveals an economy based on intensive agriculture, including the cultivation of emmer, hulled barley and (to a lesser extent) bread wheat, club wheat, rye, Italian millet and pulses (pea, lentil). Numerous imported Greek goods (mostly pottery and metalware) attest to strong trading links with the Greek colonies. The ethnicity of the forest-steppe groups remain unclear. However, it is now generally accepted by the Russian scholars that the 'royal Scythians' spoke a northern dialect of the Iranian language. See also ARZHAN and PAZYRYK.

A.I. Terenožkin and V.A. Il'inskaya: 'Skifija' [Scythians], *Arheologija Ukrainskoi SSR* [The archaeology of the Ukrainian SSR], ed. S.D. Kryzhitsky (Kiev, 1986), vol. 2, 43–169; R. Rolle: *The World of the Scythians* (London, 1984); T. Taylor: 'Thracians, Scythians and Dacians', *The Oxford illustrated prehistory of Europe*, ed. B. Cunliffe (Oxford, 1994), 373–410.

PD

Scythopolis (Beth Shan, Tell el-Husn, Baysan) Settlement-site located at the eastern edge of the plain of Jezreel on the West Bank (Israel/Jordan), which was occupied from the Chalcolithic to the Islamic period. It was excavated between 1921 and 1933 as well as in the 1990s.

1 *Pre-Roman period (Beth Shan/Tell el-Husn)*. The site's location in the Jordan valley, on the most convenient route between the Nile valley and the Euphrates, made it a key site for trading and campaign routes, particularly from the point of view of New Kingdom pharaohs such as Thutmose III (*c.*1440 BC), during whose reign two sanctuaries were dedicated to the CANAANITE deity Mikal. From at least as early as the reign of Ramesses II (*c.*1290–1224 BC) an Egyptian garrison was established at Beth Shan, and it is possible that a group of clay anthropoid coffins in the 'north cemetery' may have contained the remains of foreign mercenaries drafted into the Egyptian army, since many of the coffins bear depictions of feathered headdresses similar to those worn by some of the SEA PEOPLES. In the early Iron Age the site was influenced by the PHILISTINES (judging from the presence of 'Philistine pottery') but by the 10th century BC it had been incorporated into the kingdom of ISRAEL.

2 *Roman/Islamic period (Scythopolis/Baysan)*. The excavation of the later town-site, dating primarily to the Roman, Byzantine and Islamic periods, is of great importance in terms of the process of change that was taking place in the period between the 4th century AD and the early Islamic period. The transformation of the urban space and fabric of Scythopolis that took place during this period is by no means peculiar to this site but it has been better studied than at most other places. The excavations show the evolution of a pagan Roman grid-plan town into a Christian Byzantine town which continued to be occupied into the early Islamic period. This evolution corresponds to what happened at Damascus, JERUSALEM, Jarash (in Jordan) and Tiberias (in Israel), and the model represented by Scythopolis is probably applicable throughout the region. Indeed, the same process has been recognized as far west as the Libyan coast.

A. Rowe and G.M. Fitzgerald: *Beth-Shean*, 3 vols (Philadelphia, 1930–40); F.W. James: *The Iron Age of Beth-Shan* (Philadelphia, 1966); E. Oren: *The northern cemetery at Beth Shean* (Leiden, 1973); F.W. James and P.E. McGovern: *The Late Bronze Egyptian garrison at Beth Shan: a study of levels VI and VIII*, 2 vols (Philadelphia, 1993); Y. Tsafrir and G. Foerster: 'From Scythopolis to Baysân – changing concepts of urbanism', *The Byzantine and early Islamic Near East II: land use and settlement patterns*, ed. G.R.D. King and A. Cameron (Princeton, 1994), 95–115.

GK/IS

Sealand Area of ancient southern Mesopotamia roughly corresponding to the region of modern Iraq now occupied by the Marsh Arabs and currently under severe threat both from political persecution and environmental change. The 'second dynasty' of Babylon (1026–1005 BC) is also known as the Sealand dynasty. According to the Babylonian Royal Lists, it consisted of 11 kings. Its capital city, Urukug, has not been located archaeologically.

G. Maxwell: *A reed shaken by the wind* (London, 1957); W. Thesiger: *The Marsh Arabs* (London, 1964; Harmondsworth, 1967).

IS

Sea Peoples Term used by the Egyptians to describe a large group of sea-going Indo-European migrants (including the Ekwesh, Shekelesh, Tjeker, Weshesh, Teresh, Sherden, Peleset Lukka and Denyen) of uncertain origins. A relief on the wall of Karnak temple records an unsuccessful invasion of Egypt by an alliance of Libyans and Sea Peoples in *c.*1207 BC. The attacks of the Sea Peoples appear to have been part of a general scenario of invasions and population movements in the Mediterranean region. In 1174 BC the Egyptian ruler Ramesses III defeated them again in a great naval battle, which was depicted on the outer wall of his mortuary temple at MEDINET HABU (in western Thebes). Although the 20th-dynasty pharaohs maintained control of Canaan, the Sea Peoples (particularly Peleset and Tjeker) were allowed to settle there and the Egyptian garrison at Beth-shan came to be manned by Peleset mercenaries. By the 11th century BC, Canaan seems to have been largely controlled by Sea Peoples. *See also* PHILISTINES.

G.A. Wainwright, 'Some Sea-Peoples and others in the Hittite archives', *JEA* 25 (2) (1939) 148–53; W. Helck, *Die Beziehungen Ägyptens und Vorderasiens zur Agäis bis ins 7.Jh. v.Chr.* (Darmstadt, 1979); N.K. Sandars, *Sea Peoples* (London, 1985).

IS

Sebekian *see* SEBILIAN

Sebilian Upper Palaeolithic industry found at sites in Upper Egypt, originally identified by Edmund Vignard in the KOM OMBO plain, about 40 km north of Aswan. Vignard (1923) divided the Sebilian into three basic phases (*c.* 13,000–10,000 BC), developing gradually from LEVALLOIS flakes in phase 1 to microblades in phase 3. According to more recent work in the Kom Ombo plain, however, the earliest Sebilian assemblages were contemporary with the Silsilian and the Sebekian microblade industries (Smith 1968), suggesting a much greater technological diversity for the Kom Ombo plain during the Upper Palaeolithic than Vignard's simple evolutionary model had implied. Whether the three industries can be interpreted as different ethnic groups or simply the remains of three roughly contemporaneous groups practising different combinations of hunting, fishing and gathering remains a matter for discussion.

E. Vignard: 'Une nouvelle industrie lithique: le "Sébilien"', *BIFAO* 22 (1923), 1–76; A.E. Marks: 'The Sebilian industry of the Second Cataract', *The prehistory of Nubia* I, ed. F. Wendorf (Dallas, 1968), 461–531; P.E.L. Smith: *A revised view of the later Paleolithic of Egypt* (Paris, 1968); F. Hassan and F. Wendorf: 'A Sebilian assemblage from El Kilh (Upper Egypt)', *CdE* 49 (1974), 211–21.

IS

secondary products revolution Hypothesis outlined by Andrew Sherratt in 1981, and refined by him in 1983, which suggested that the 'secondary' products of animal husbandry were intensively and connectedly exploited from the mid-4th millennium BC in temperate Europe in such a way as to promote significant and multiplying changes in farming and social systems. Secondary products, in contrast to primary animal products such as meat or hide, may be defined as those economic benefits that are produced *by*, rather than *from*, domestic animals: dairy foodstuffs; wool; traction for ploughs and wagons; riding and pack transport. Sherratt believed that the use of secondary products first developed, from the 5th millennium BC or earlier, in various areas of the Near East (the horse in the Steppes region), and that these innovations then spread as a distinct package into much of temperate Europe. The theory thus suggests that the development of Old World agriculture can be divided into two stages: 'an initial stage of hoe cultivation . . . in which animals were kept purely for meat; and a second stage in which both plough agriculture and pastoralism can be recognized.'

Sherratt regards the elements of this 'second wave' of farming as dependent upon one another, so that, for example, the deforestation encouraged by plough agriculture eventually also promoted pastoralism. The various elements of the secondary products revolution can be recognized archaeologically in various ways, for example age and sex differences in the culling of herds; representation of plough and traction animals in art; specialized pottery for the handling of milk products or artefacts for the processing of wool. Criticism of the hypothesis has centred on whether the archaeological manifestations of the secondary products revolution are indeed connected and contemporary (Chapman 1982: reply, Sherratt 1986). Greenfield attempted to test the theory with regard to a specific area, the Central Balkans; he concluded that there was evidence for a relatively rapid and significant adoption of the use of secondary products in the area, but questioned the idea of a distinct 'package' spreading from the Near East. Sherratt himself has increasingly stressed the complexity of local adoptions of secondary products, pointing to the importance of social symbolism and social prestige in the adoption of the secondary products revolution.

A. Sherratt: 'Plough and pastoralism: aspects of the secondary products revolution' *Pattern of the past: studies in honour of David Clarke*, ed. Ian Hodder et al. (Cambridge, 1981), 261–305; J. Chapman: 'The secondary products revolution', *Institute of Archaeology Bulletin* 19 (1982), 107–22; A. Sherratt: 'The secondary exploitation of animals in the Old World', *WA* 15/1 (1983), 90–104; ——: 'Wool, wheels and ploughmarks: local developments or outside introductions in Neolithic Europe?', *Institute of Archaeology Bulletin* 23 (1986), 1–15; H.J. Greenfield: 'The origins of milk and wool production in the Old World: a zoological perspective from the Central Balkans', *CA* 29/4 (1988), 573–94 [additional comments 743–8].

RJA

Second Series *see* ARMORICAN FIRST and SECOND SERIES

section Vertical face of a BAULK showing the changes in soil colour and texture comprising the stratigraphy of a site or feature, and allowing archaeologists to record the relative positions of those layers and features 'caught' in the section. Features as small as stakeholes are also often 'sectioned' so that their vertical profile can be accurately recorded. Section drawings are invariably made by setting up a horizontal piece of string across the face of the baulk and measuring offsets from this 'datum line'.

Sehonghong Middle/Later Stone Age rock-shelter in southeast Lesotho, South Africa. The explanation in symbolic terms of a painting on the wall of this shelter, given by a Bushman in 1874, has provided the key to understanding much of the art in southern Africa. The excavations of Pat Carter in 1971 and Peter Mitchell in 1992 have revealed a succession of industries including four stages of the Middle Stone Age: MSA 3 (oldest, with segments); and MSA 5, 6, and 9, without segments; a Late Pleistocene microblade industry (13,000–12,000 uncal BP); and Mid- and Late Holocene microlithic industries. This is one of only a few sites with occupations spanning the Middle Stone Age/Later Stone Age transition, and provides evidence of the survival of Middle Stone Age technique to almost 20,000 years ago, with indications of increasing emphasis on reduction in blade size over a period of thousands of years prior to the transition.

P.L. Carter, P.J. Mitchell and P. Vinnicombe: *Sehonghong: the Middle and Later Stone Age industrial sequence at a Lesotho rockshelter* (Oxford, 1988).

RI

Seima-Turbino Bronze Age metalworking tradition, and associated culture, identified at various sites in European Russia and Siberia. Typology and a single radiocarbon date from Yelupino cemetery in the Altai mountains suggest that the tradition dates to 1700–1600 BC. It was first recognized before the First World War by A.M. Tallgren and V.A. Gorodtsov, who noticed the similarities between certain types of bronze implements; it was later studied by O.N. Bader (1970) and others. Information regarding the Seima-Turbino culture comes from several cemeteries excavated over a prolonged period and with varying degrees of professionalism.

Seima (Sejma) cemetery is situated on a sand-dune ridge on the left bank of the River Oka, at its confluence with the Volga. The site was excavated in 1912–14 by a local military detachment, and judging from the incomplete records, no less than 50 graves were discovered. Out of the 112 metal objects found, no more than 70 have survived. Turbino-1 cemetery lies within the town of Perm. Excavated by A.V. Schmidt in 1924–7 and by O.N. Bader in 1958–60, the cemetery contained about 200 graves; no skeletal remains were found. Among 3128 metal implements were: 44 socketed celts, 40 daggers or knives, 13 spearheads, three shaft-hole axes, 23 temple rings, and 9 bracelets. At the neighbouring cemetery of Turbino-2, a knife with a terminal cast as a bull's head was found.

Reshnoe cemetery is located in Nizhni-Novgorod district, on a dune ridge, on the right bank of the River Oka. It was excavated in 1974–5 by Bader, who found 18 graves arranged in three rows, but no human remains. The metal objects included socketed celts, spearheads, knives-daggers, adzes and awls. The grave inventory comprises numerous flint implements, two nephrite rings and nine ceramic vessels.

Rostovka cemetery lies on the River Om, in the southern suburb of the city of Omsk. V.I. Matyushchenko excavated (1966–9) 38 shallow rectangular graves, in which the dominant burial rite was inhumation, in some cases combined with partial cremation. The remaining bodies were generally oriented to the west. Some bodies had been beheaded; there were also separate burials of skulls.

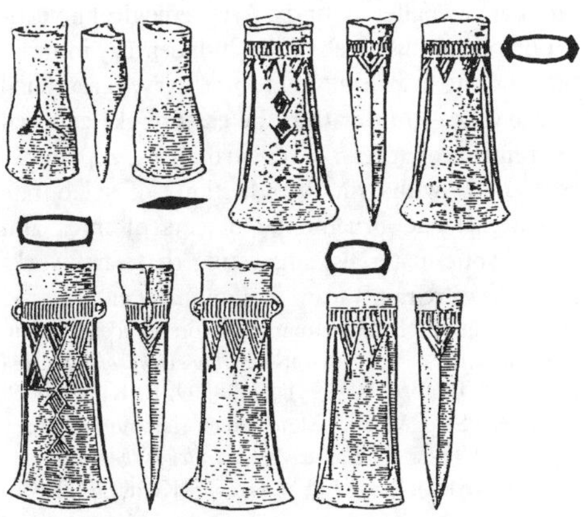

Figure 46 **Seima–Turbino** Bronze celts of the Seima–Turbino tradition. *Source*: E.N. Chernykh and S.V. Kuz'minykh: 'Pamyatniki seiminsko-turbinskogo tipa v Evrazii', *Epoha bronzy lesnoi polosy SSSR*, ed. O.N. Bader (Moscow, 1987), fig. 42.

The Seima-Turbino metal tools fall into three main categories: celts, spearheads and daggers-knives with numerous sub-types. Tin and tin-arsenic bronze alloys account for 41.4% of the analyzed objects. Tools made of these materials are spread over a wide area, from Finland to the Altai. E.N. Chernykh (1970) suggests that these tools were manufactured from ores originating in the Altai mines. Copper sandstone east of the Urals probably formed the source of the 'pure' copper. Metal artefacts showing Seima-Turbino characteristics are known from the numerous sites over a very wide area: from Finland in the west to the Baikal Lake in the east.

O.N. Bader: *Bassein Oki v epohu bronzy* [The Oka basin in the Bronze age] (Moscow, 1970); E.N. Chernykh: 'Drevneišaja metallurgija Urala i Povolž'ja' [The most ancient metallurgy of the Urals and Volga area], *MIAS* 172 (Moscow, 1970); E.N. Chernykh and S.V. Kuz'minykh: 'Pamyatniki seiminsko-turbinskogo tipa v Evrazii' [Sites of Seima-Turbino type in Eurasia], *Epoha bronzy lesnoi polosy SSSR* [The Bronze age in the forest zone of the USSR], eds. O.N. Bader et al., Arheologija SSSR (Moscow, 1987).

PD

Seine-Oise-Marne culture *see* SOM CULTURE

Seip Middle WOODLAND geometric earthwork in Ross County, Ohio (USA). Radiocarbon-dated to a calendar date of *c.*AD 200–300, it consists of two circles and a square enclosing more than 40 ha. Within the earthworks are a large loaf-shaped mound, three large conjoined mounds and a number of smaller mounds. Archaeological investigations spanning much of the 20th century indicate that the site is a HOPEWELL mortuary/ceremonial centre. Excavation within the earthworks exposed the remains of at least seven structures, apparently associated with the production of elaborate ceremonial and ornamental objects of mica and other exotic materials, suggesting that earthworks like Seip were not 'vacant' ceremonial centres.

H. Shetrone and E. Greenman: 'Explorations of the Seip group of prehistoric earthworks', *Ohio Archaeological and Historical Quarterly* 40 (1931), 343–509: R. Baby and S. Langlois: 'Seip Mound State Memorial: nonmortuary aspects of Hopewell', *Hopewell archaeology: the Chillicothe conference*, ed. D. Brose and N. Greber (Kent, OH, 1979), 16–18.

RJE

Seleucid The historical definition of the Seleucid period is relatively straightforward, stretching from 312 to 64 BC. After the death of Alexander the Great, his generals quarrelled and by 312 BC the Macedonian empire had been divided into two halves. The former Achaemenid areas of Western Asia were then ruled by Seleucus, a former satrap of Babylon, and his descendants, while North Africa and the Levant were ruled by Ptolemy and his successors. At the beginning of the period a new royal city, Seleucia-on-the-Tigris, was founded 90 km to the north of Babylon, but Esagila, the precinct of the god Marduk, at Babylon clearly retained its importance and cuneiform continued to be used until at least AD 75, particularly for reading astronomical observations. The 'Seleucid period' drew to a close when the territories of the Seleucid dynasty were effectively squeezed between the expanding empires of Rome and PARTHIA. A great deal of socio-economic information has survived in the form of texts on clay tablets, papyrus and parchment, as well as bullae (small clay balls inscribed with Greek or Aramaic texts and attached by string to papyrus or parchment documents).

A. Kuhrt and S. Sherwin-White, eds: *Hellenism in the East* (London, 1987); —— and ——: *From Samarkand to Sardis: a new approach to the Seleucid empire* (London, 1993).

IS

SEM *see* SCANNING ELECTRON MICROSCOPE

Semaina *see* HIW-SEMAINA REGION

Semainean culture Discredited term for the final protodynastic phase of the Upper Egyptian predynastic period, introduced by Flinders Petrie at the turn of the century.

Semna Egyptian fortified settlement site founded in *c.*1950 BC on the west bank of the Nile at the southern end of a chain of Egyptian fortresses established in the 2nd-cataract area of Lower Nubia during the 12th dynasty (*c.*1991–1783 BC). A cluster of four mud-brick fortresses (Semna, Kumma, Semna South and Uronarti, all now submerged under LAKE NASSER) were constructed in the strategically important area of the Semna gorge, the narrowest section of the entire Nile valley and the southern frontier of 12th-dynasty Egypt (for a detailed description and interpretation of the Semna forts see Kemp 1989: 172–8). Semna and Kumma also included the remains of temples, houses and cemeteries dating to the New Kingdom (*c.*1550–1070 BC), contemporary with such Lower

Nubian towns as AMARA West and SESEBI, when the 2nd cataracts region was no longer a frontier zone but effectively part of the Egyptian 'empire'.

G.A. Reisner: 'Excavations in Egypt and Ethiopia', *BMFA* 22 (1925), 18–28; D. Dunham and J.M.A. Janssen: *Second cataract forts* I: *Semna, Kumma* (Boston, 1960), 5–112; B.J. Kemp: *Ancient Egypt: anatomy of a civilization* (London, 1989), 172–8.

IS

Sepharvaim *see* SIPPAR

sequence dating Method of 'occurrence SERIATION' used by Flinders Petrie in the early 20th century to construct a relative chronology for the Egyptian predynastic period (*see* EGYPT 1). Since virtually all excavated Upper Egyptian predynastic material was from cemeteries rather than stratified settlement sites, only seriation could provide an adequate framework for a relative chronology. Petrie arranged the pottery that he had excavated from the cemeteries of Diospolis Parva (*see* HIW-SEMAINA REGION) into a set of more than 700 different pottery types. He then assigned the material from 900 different graves (each containing at least five different types of artefact) to 51 phases in a relative chronology, which he numbered from SD30 (i.e. sequence date 30) to SD80. The task of compiling this sequence was aided by Petrie's own intuitive observations, such as the apparent tendency for wavy-handled vessels to grow smaller and more cylindrical over time, while handles seemed to diminish in size. Confirmation of the reliability of sequence dating has since been provided by radiocarbon dating and by the excavation of stratified predynastic settlements such as Hammamiya (*see* EL-BADARI) and HIERAKONPOLIS. Whereas Petrie developed his sequence by the relatively crude technique of arranging strips of cardboard into lines, in 1963 the statistician David Kendall provided a more rapid and scientific method of seriation in the form of a computer program using a version of the Shepard-Kruskal MULTI-DIMENSIONAL SCALING routine (Kendall, 1963; see also Kemp 1982).

W.M.F. Petrie: 'Sequences in prehistoric remains', JAI, n.s. 29 (1899), 290–301; ——: *Diospolis Parva: the cemeteries of Abadiyeh and Hu, 1898–9* (London, 1901); D.G. Kendall: 'A statistical approach to Flinders Petrie's sequence-dating', *Bulletin of the International Statistics Institute* 40 (1963), 657–80; B.J. Kemp: 'Automatic analysis of Predynastic cemeteries: a new method for an old problem', *JEA* 68 (1982), 5–15.

IS

Serabit el-Khadim Group of Egyptian turquoise mines in central southern Sinai, with an unusual associated temple complex dating to the Middle and New Kingdoms (*c.*2040–1070 BC). In the temple precincts and the surrounding area there are numerous rock-cut and free-standing stelae dedicated by mining expeditions to the goddess Hathor 'Lady of Turquoise', as well as inscriptions in the PROTOSINAITIC script.

W.M.F. Petrie: *Researches in Sinai* (London, 1906); A. Gardiner and J. Cerny: *The inscriptions of Sinai II* (London, 1955), 32–51; D. Valbelle and C. Bonnet: '*Le sanctuarie d'Hathor, maîtresse de la turquoise*' (Paris, 1996).

IS

Serapeum *see* ALEXANDRIA; SAQQARA

Serçe Liman Site of the wreck of a deep-draughted cargo ship, 15 m long, 5.13 m across its beam, with a capacity of 30–40 tons, which sank off the coast of southwestern Turkey in *c.*AD 1025. Underwater excavations between 1977 and 1981 by Frederick Van Doorninck and George Bass brought to light the complex nature of its cargo. Its principal hold contained a large quantity of glass waste, probably brought from a Fatimid glass factory in Egypt. Several small cargoes included Fatimid ceramic lamps, and a collection of Byzantine maiolica dishes from southern Turkey. It is believed to have been bound for western Anatolia, or possibly Constantinople. The finds are now on display in the St Peter's Castle Museum at Bodrum, Turkey.

G. Bass and F.H. Van Doorninck, Jr.: 'An 11th-century shipwreck at Serçe Liman, Turkey', *IJNA* 7 (1978), 119–32; J.R. Stiffy: 'The reconstruction of the 11th century Serçe Liman vessel, a preliminary report', *IJNA* 11 (1982), 13–37.

RH

serdab (Arabic: 'cellar') Term used to describe the room in Egyptian MASTABA-TOMBS where statues of the deceased were usually placed. There were often eye-holes in the wall of the *serdab* to allow offerings to pass through to the statues from the tomb chapel.

A.M. Blackman: 'The ka-house and the serdab', *JEA* 3 (1916), 250–4; A.J. Spencer: *Death in ancient Egypt* (Harmondsworth, 1982), 60–1.

IS

seriation Method of arranging artefacts, sites or assemblages into a linear sequence on the basis of the degree of similarity between the various elements in the sequence. First scientifically applied in the early 19th century, seriation is still a common means of constructing relative chronologies for prehistoric cultures (on the basis of such criteria as developments in artefactual style, function or material), particularly when there is a lack of stratified material.

Christian Jurgensen Thomsen (1788–1865) was the earliest exponent of seriation. In 1816 he began to use the method to organize the collection of prehistoric artefacts in the National Museum of Antiquities at Copenhagen into a chronological order that corresponded to the Three Age System (i.e. a sequence of three culture-history stages distinguished by the use of Stone, Bronze and Iron respectively; see Gräslund 1981, 1987). Thomsen's seriation of artefacts from Neolithic and Bronze Age sites in Denmark laid the foundations for the chronology of European prehistory. By 1885 Gustav Oscar Montelius had produced a more refined artefactual seriation for the Bronze Age (Montelius, 1986), but it was the use of stratigraphic excavation by Jens Worsaae that eventually provided conclusive corroboration of the Three Age chronological sequence.

Thomsen and Montelius used seriation to construct simple evolutionary typologies of artefacts, but in 1899 Flinders Petrie became the first archaeologist to apply seriation methods to excavated assemblages from specific sites, with his development of 'SEQUENCE DATING' for the Egyptian predynastic period (Petrie, 1899). A distinction is usually made between Petrie's application of 'occurrence' or 'incidence' seriation (a sequence constructed on the basis of presence or absence in an assemblage of many different artefactual types) and the use of 'frequency' or 'abundance' seriation (which relied on observation of changing frequencies of a smaller number of artefacts), such as that applied by Kroeber and Spier to the ceramic sequence of the Zuni people of North America (Spier 1917). The essential techniques of frequency seriation are summarized by Brainerd (1951) and Robinson (1951).

Various computerized methods of seriation have been devised to analyse particular sets of data, such as Goldmann's seriation of about 4000 finds from various European Bronze Age sites, which utilized stratigraphic information in the interpretive stage of the analysis (Marquardt 1978) and Kendall and Kemp's reanalysis of Petrie's predynastic material (Kendall 1963; Kemp 1982).

The mathematical aspects of seriation itself have been considerably refined, but its validity in any individual instance still depends on the answers to numerous contextual questions. What types of attributes are the best chronological indicators and how can they be distinguished from other variants? What social situations are likely to encourage rapid technological or stylistic development? David Clarke has pointed out that there are various potential problems with the use of seriation, such as the assumption that all aspects of a material culture must have developed at a similar rate, and there is also a risk (especially when using data from more than one site) that spatial patterns may be confused with chronological trends, but he concludes that 'if the data is carefully controlled and if the interpretation is of the broad kind . . . then these techniques [of seriation] remain dangerous but invaluable, like all the most useful methodology'.

W.M.F. Petrie: 'Sequences in prehistoric remains', *JAI*, n.s. 29 (1899), 295–301; L. Spier: *An outline for a chronology of Zuni ruins* (New York, 1917); G.W. Brainerd: 'The place of chronological ordering in archaeological analysis', *AA* 16 (1951), 301–13; W.S. Robinson: 'A method for chronologically ordering archaeological deposits', *AA* 16 (1951), 293–301; D.G. Kendall: 'A statistical approach to Flinders Petrie's sequence-dating', *Bulletin of the International Statistics Institute* 40 (1963), 657–80; W.H. Marquardt: 'Advances in archaeological seriation', *Advances in archaeological method and theory*, I (1978), 257–314; B. Gräslund: 'The background to C.J. Thomsen's Three-Age system', *Towards a history of archaeology*, ed. G. Daniel (London, 1981), 45–50; B.J. Kemp: 'Automatic analysis of predynastic cemeteries: a new method for an old problem', *JEA* 68 (1982), 5–15; O. Montelius: *Dating in the Bronze Age with special reference to Scandinavia* (Stockholm, 1986); B. Gräslund: *The birth of prehistoric chronology* (Cambridge, 1987).

IS

Serpent Mound Prehistoric site in Adams County, Ohio (USA), consisting of an 'animal-effigy' mound built in the form of a serpent (*see* EFFIGY MOUND CULTURE). It was once considered to be of Early WOODLAND origin (*c.*1000–200 BC), but radiocarbon dates suggest that it was built during the Late Prehistoric period (*c.*AD 1070; see Fletcher et al. 1996). The serpent, which extends for more than 365 m along a low ridge overlooking Brush Creek, has a tightly coiled tail, an undulating body and a wide-opened mouth. The head and the neck are extended, pointing to the west, with the head resting on its right side. Immediately in front of the opened mouth is a large (18 × 36 m) oval-shaped mound resembling an egg or eye. At its midpoint, the serpent's body was about 6 m wide and 1.5 m high, gradually tapering toward the tail.

E. Randall: *The Serpent Mound, Adams County, Ohio*

(Columbus, 1905); C. Willoughby: 'The Serpent Mound of Adams County, Ohio', *American Anthropologist* 21 (1919), 153–63; R. Fletcher, T. Cameron, B. Lepper, D. Wymer and W. Pickard: 'Serpent Mound: a Fort Ancient icon?', *MJA* 21 (1996), 105–43.

RJE

Serra d'Alto Painted ware of the Neolithic in Southern Italy, named after a settlement site near Matero. Characterized by necked and flat-bottomed vessels, painted with a variety of motifs, typically painted in dark or purply pigment against a light brown background, Serra d'Alto vessels are most notable for their distinctive handles modelled into rolled spirals and volutes. Serra d'Alto ware may date from the mid-5th millennium to the first half of the 4th millennium BC; it seems to be earlier than, but overlapping with, DIANA WARE, which has a similar geographical distribution. Serra d'Alto ware is often found among grave goods, and occurs as a small percentage of the pottery corpus over a wide area of Sicily and central Italy. Together with the evidence for careful production, this suggests that it was created and traded as a prestige ware – perhaps playing a role analogous to that of GROOVED WARE in Britain.

RJA

Sesebi Egyptian walled settlement site in Nubia (northern Sudan), founded in *c.*1350 BC and excavated by Aylward Blackman and H.W. Fairman in the 1930s. The roughly contemporaneous Egyptian towns at BUHEN and MIRGISSA were essentially extensions of much earlier garrisons established in the Middle Kingdom (*c.*2040–1640 BC), but Sesebi was a newly created town forming part of the New Kingdom Egyptian policy of colonization of Nubia.

A.L. Blackman and H.W. Fairman: Preliminary reports in *JEA* 23–5, 34 (1937–9, 1948); R. Morkot: 'The excavations at Sesebi (Sudla) 1936–38', *Beiträge zur Sudanforschung* 3 (1988), 159–64.

IS

Sesklo Neolithic tell site on the plains of Thessaly, about 15 km southwest of Volos, Greece. Sesklo is particularly important in that it has yielded a succession of levels from the earliest agricultural phases until the proto-urbanism of the Sesklo culture proper. The tell was investigated in the early 1900s by Christos Tsountas, and again between 1956 and 1977 by Demetrios Theocharis, but it has not been fully published. The earliest level (*c.*7000 BC) is recorded as 'pre-ceramic', with evidence for domesticated cereals and animals and the scanty remains of huts – it may be compared to similar phases at FRANCHTHI CAVE and ARGISSA. This is followed by an Early Neolithic phase, characterized by largely monochrome and some simple painted ware. By the Middle Neolithic, the settlement had developed into a small, lightly fortified town with perhaps 3000 inhabitants. There are narrow, parallel streets, and a large central 'MEGARON' structure with a paved courtyard. In this period there developed a distinctive painted pottery tradition, with vessels typically adorned with a limited range of zig-zag triangular and saw-tooth motifs painted in red on a white slip. The style spread over much of Thessaly, and defines what has become known as the 'Sesklo culture'; some very accomplished schematic figurines are associated with this pottery.

D. Theocharis et al.: *Neolithic Greece* (Athens, 1973); M. Wijnen: 'The Early Neolithic I settlement at Sesklo: an early farming community in Thessaly, Greece', *Analecta Praehistorica Leidensia XIV* (Leiden, 1981).

RJA

Setouchi technique Lithic technique characteristic of the Late Palaeolithic of Japan, particularly adapted to the manufacture of tools from *sanukite* (a form of andesite). Large flakes were struck from a *sanukite* block to produce a dihydral striking platform from which a series of uniform trapezoidal long flakes could be removed for the manufacture of Kou knives.

C.M. Aikens and T. Higuchi: *The prehistory of Japan* (London, 1982), 52–3.

SK

Severn-Cotswold tombs *see* COTSWOLD-SEVERN TOMBS

SG *see* SPECIFIC GRAVITY ANALYSIS

shabti (*ushabti*, *shawabty*) Mummiform figurine which was introduced into the Egyptian funerary repertoire by the Middle Kingdom (*c.*2040–1640 BC). *Shabtis* were at first carved individually out of wood or stone but by the late New Kingdom they were being mass-produced in glazed composition, and often several hundred might accompany a single burial (frequently placed in *shabti*-boxes). Most New Kingdom *shabtis* were inscribed with at least a short extract from chapter 6 of the Book of the Dead (a collection of funerary spells), the text of which indicates that *shabtis* were intended to undertake specific agricultural tasks for the deceased in the afterworld.

H. Schneider: *Shabtis*, 3 vols (Leiden, 1977); H.M. Stewart: *Egyptian shabtis* (Princes Risborough, 1995).

IS

shadow sites *see* AERIAL ARCHAEOLOGY

Shaduppum *see* HARMAL, TELL

shaft-and-chamber tomb Tomb in South America consisting of a vertical, sloping or stepped shaft off the bottom of which open one or more chambers where burials are placed. The incredible variety of such tombs indicates their multiple origins and local evolutions.

Shahdad Group of sites in an oasis northeast of the Iranian city of Kirman, where the major archaeological remains are a set of three cemeteries of the late 4th and 3rd millennia BC. The extravagant funerary equipment, including baked clay statuary as well as artefacts of silver, bronze, steatite and lapis lazuli, combined with surface survey across the settlement, indicate that there were extensive areas of stone-carving and metalworking. The town was an important early trade centre in contact with the Sumerians of the EARLY DYNASTIC period in Mesopotamia. A large quantity of sherds from the earlier phases of Shahdad are incised with an unusual pictographic script, as well as one inscription using the rare Linear ELAMITE script, 17 examples of which were found at SUSA.

IS

el-Shaheinab *see* KHARTOUM NEOLITHIC

Shaheinab culture *see* KHARTOUM NEOLITHIC

Shahi Tump Site of a small settlement and cemetery of the KULLI COMPLEX of the late 3rd millennium BC in southwest Baluchistan, Pakistan. Small-scale excavations were carried out by Auriel Stein in the 1920s, revealing traces of stone and mud-brick architecture, grey-ware ceramics ('Anjira ware') and painted Kulli ceramics. The site also incorporated approximately 14 burials (including one adult male buried with a copper axe) and other disarticulated human remains, many associated with distinctive ceramic vessels. These vessels were highly uniform with extremely thin walls, and decorated with simple painted designs incorporating narrow bands, triangles and swastikas. Some of the forms, such as rimless bowls and cups, were found to be nested within each other. Other goods found in the burials included animal bones, copper beads and bangles and stone beads.

M.A. Stein: 'An archaeological tour in Gedrosia', *MASI* 43 (1931), 88–103.

CS

Shahr-i Sokhta Large tell-site in the Seistan region of the eastern Iranian plateau, dating mainly from the late 4th to the early 2nd millennium BC, which perhaps developed as a result of its important role in one of the lapis lazuli trade-routes from Afghanistan to SUSA and beyond. The site, excavated by Maurizio Tosi in the 1960s and 1970s, was found to be remarkably well-preserved as a result of an overlying saline deposit. The settlement covers about 100 ha, with an additional 40 ha taken up by its unusually large cemetery. The study of the patterning of activities within the settlement has produced interesting results concerning the state organization of craftwork, suggesting that certain crafts, such as stone-working, were practised by specialists, almost on an industrial scale, whereas others, such as weaving, were common throughout the residential parts of the town. The lapis lazuli workshops still contained large quantities of flint artefacts and unfinished stone beads. Tosi (1984) has interpreted the intra-settlement patterning from a MARXIST point of view, with the aim of assessing the 'variability in the spatial allocation of craft production', but this approach is open to the charge that it imposes politicized jargon on a comparatively straightforward socio-economic system. Philip Kohl, on the other hand, in an impressive example of ETHNOARCHAEOLOGY, analysed the chlorite carved vessels made at Shahr-i Sokhta and Tepe Yahya, comparing the methods of production and consumption with those employed at the modern chlorite-working centre of Meshed (Kohl 1975).

R. Biscione: Dynamics of an early southern Asian urbanization', *South Asian Archaeology*, ed. N. Hammond (London, 1973), 105–18; K. Fischer: 'Micro-drilling at Shahr i-Sokhta', *South Asian Archaeology*, ed. N. Hammond (London, 1973), 119–30; P.L. Kohl: 'Carved chlorite vessels', *Expedition* 18 (1975), 18–31; M. Tosi: 'The notion of craft specialization and its representation in the archaeological record of early states in the Turanian Basin', *Marxist perspectives in archaeology*, ed. M. Spriggs (Cambridge, 1984), 22–52.

IS

Shakado A series of five Early and Middle Jomon (*c.*5000–2000 BC) habitation sites in Yamanashi prefecture, Japan, where 1000+ fragments of ceramic anthropomorphic figurines were excavated in 1980–81. Refitting of the fragments has shown that the figurines were designed so as to be easily broken. Rituals involving the breakage and distribution of these figurines were important in the social relations of Jomon communities from the surrounding region.

M. Yamagata: 'The Shakado figurines and Middle Jomon ritual in the Kofu Basin', *JJRS* 19/2–3 (1992), 129–38.

SK

Shalfak Egyptian fortress located on the west bank of the Nile in the 2nd cataract region; one of a string of fortresses established by Senusret III in order to safeguard the economic and political interests in Nubia. The barracks and granary, together occupying an area of some 2250 sq. m, were protected by a 5 m thick mud-brick outer wall and three spur-walls.

D. Dunham: *Second cataract forts II: Uronarti, Shalfak, Mirgissa* (Boston, 1967), 115–40; B.J. Kemp: *Ancient Egypt: anatomy of a civilization* (London, 1989), 172–3.

IS

shaman, shamanism Shaman is the Tungusian word for a priest or priest-doctor. The term shamanism was therefore originally applied by anthropologists to the religion of the Ural-Altaic peoples of Siberia, according to which the good and evil elements in life were regarded as deriving from spirits over whom the shaman exercised some control. The word has since been applied to similar priestly figures in many different places and periods, from the magical man-beast figure of the Yang-Shao Neolithic culture of China (*see* P'U-YANG-SHIH) to the medicine-man of north-western America. A perception has also grown up that there may have been strong connections between shamanism and various forms of ancient art (see Schrire et al. 1986; Reichel-Dolmatoff 1988). The ceramics and jewellery from the site of CALIMA in Colombia and the rock art of CUEVA IGLESIA in Venezuela are regarded as possible expressions of shamanism.

A. Lommel: *Shamanism: the beginnings of art* (New York and Toronto, n.d.); H. Breuil: 'Partiques religieuses chez les humanités quarternaires', *Scienza e Civilita* (1951): 45–75; M. Eliade: *Shamanism: archaic techniques of ecstasy* (New York, 1964); P.T. Furst: 'The roots and continuities of shamanism', *Stone bones and skin*, ed. A.T. Brodzky et al. (Toronto, 1977), 1–28; C.J. Schrire, J. Deacon, M. Hall and D. Lewis-Williams: 'Burkitt's milestone', *Antiquity* 60 (1986): 123–31; G. Reichel-Dolmatoff: *Goldwork and shamanism* (Bogotá, 1988).

IS

Shamarkian Nubian microlithic industry found at a number of Nilotic sites in the region of Wadi Halfa, radiocarbon-dated to *c.*4500–4000 BC and therefore roughly synchronous with the KHARTOUM MESOLITHIC of Central Sudan. It is currently not clear whether the Shamarkian – the earliest Lower Nubian culture to produce pottery – was contemporary with the ARKINIAN industry or a later development. Both the Shamarkian and Arkinian lithic industries appear to have been subphases – or perhaps regional variants – of the EPIPALAEOLITHIC period in Lower Nubia. There are also a number of sites described as 'post-Shamarkian', which are larger than Shamarkian sites and incorporate stone tools imported from Upper Egypt. Post-Shamarkian sites date to *c.*4000-3000 BC (i.e. roughly contemporary with the ABKAN industry and KHARTOUM NEOLITHIC).

R. Schild et al.: 'The Arkinian and Shamarkian industries', *The Prehistory of Nubia* II, ed. F. Wendorf (Dallas, 1968), 651–767.

IS

Shancunling *see* SHANG-TS'UN-LING

Shang The earliest of the periods in Chinese history that are documented by contemporaneous written records (inscribed ORACLE BONES). *See* CHINA 2.

Shanga Early SWAHILI HARBOUR TOWN with international contacts from the 9th or late 8th century AD, situated on Pate island off the northern Kenyan coast. The lowest excavated levels (Horton 1996) corroborate the findings at nearby Manda and at Kilwa on the southern Swahili coast, and contribute to the reinterpretation of the conclusions and dating proposed there by Neville Chittick (1974, 1984). At the beginning of its sequence Shanga was occupied by people from the African mainland and by Muslims with Persian Gulf connections. The latter are attested by a series of wooden mosques, the first built about 800 AD or slightly before. In the 10th century the mosque was rebuilt in stone, and the extant ruin is that of the 11th century reconstruction. The houses were mostly constructed of wood until *c.*1300 when, as became the fashion in many Swahili settlements, richer townsmen had houses built of coral-rag. In the 15th century Shanga was sacked and deserted, most of the population moving to nearby towns.

H.N. Chittick: *Kilwa: an Islamic trading city on the East African coast* (Nairobi, 1974); ——: *Manda; excavations at an island port on the Kenya coast* (Nairobi, 1984); M.C. Horton: 'Early Muslim trading settlements on the East African coast: new evidence from Shanga', *AJ* 67 (1987), 290–323; ——: *Shanga* BIEA 13 (Nairobi, 1996).

JS

Shang-ts'un-ling (Shancunling) Cemetery of the Chinese state of Northern Kuo, which was in use for a period of 120 years between 771 BC, when the state was founded, and 655 BC, when it was annexed by the state of CH'IN. It was at Shang-ts'un-ling, 4.7 km from the city of San-men-hsia, in the province of Ho-nan, that the first major excavations relating to the state of Kuo were conducted, in 1956–7. The cemetery consisted of three chariot pit-burials and 234 tombs. The largest pit-burial held 10 chariots and 20 horses; structural details of the vehicles were well preserved and allowed reliable reconstructions. Several bronze vessels and weapons from the site bore inscriptions referring to scions of the state of Kuo.

Anon.: *Shang-ts'un-ling Kuo-kuo mu-ti* [The state of Kuo cemetery at Shang-ts'un-ling] (Peking, 1959); Kuo Mo-jo: 'San-men-hsia ch'u-t'u t'ung-ch'i erh-san-ssu' [Two or three bronze vessels unearthed at San-men-hsia], *WW* 1 (1959), 13–15.

NB

Shanidar Cave in Iraq where the excavations of Ralph Solecki in 1953 and 1960 uncovered the stratified remains of nine NEANDERTHAL skeletons dated by radiocarbon to the MOUSTERIAN period and the early Upper Palaeolithic (*c*.49,600 BP and *c*.32,300 BP respectively; Bar-Yosef 1989). This is the largest number of Neanderthal skeletons discovered at a single Middle Eastern site, and some were apparently deliberately buried rather than simply abandoned on the surface. One of the graves – Shanidar 4 – also contained a scattering of pollen grains around the body, which was interpreted by Solecki (1971) as a wreath of flowers laid over the body, implying that the Neanderthals were capable of cultural behaviour similar to that of early 'modern humans'. It has subsequently been suggested, however, that the pollen may have been brought

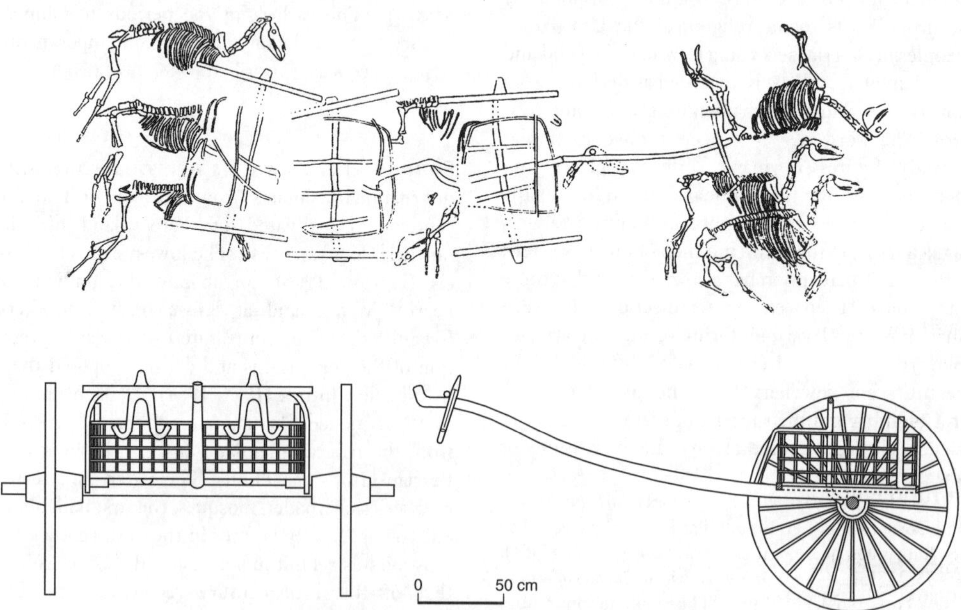

Figure 47 **Shang-ts'un-ling** Plan of one of the chariot burials from Shang-ts'un-ling and a reconstruction drawing of the chariot, 1st millennium BC. *Source*: Anon.: *Shang-ts'un-ling Kuo-kuo mu-ti* (Peking, 1959).

into association with the skeleton as a result of natural POST-DEPOSITIONAL activity such as soil movement or animal burrowing (Turner and Hannon 1988). Another of the bodies – Shanidar 1 – appears to have survived as a crippled old man for several years before his death, which may perhaps indicate that the Neanderthals looked after the older, less able members of their groups. The published pottery from later strata makes it clear that the cave had a long later history of use, including habitation in the Uruk period and late Islamic period. The nearby site of ZAWI CHEMI SHANIDAR was occupied both in the Epipalaeolithic period and the Sasanian period.

R. Solecki: *Shanidar – the first flower people* (New York, 1971); E. Trinkaus: *The Shanidar Neandertals* (New York, 1983); C. Turner and G.E. Hannon: 'Vegetational influence for late Quaternary climatic changes in southwest Europe in relation to the influence of the North Atlantic Ocean', *Philosophical Transactions of the Royal Society of London* B/318 (1988), 451–85; O. Bar-Yosef: 'Geochronology of the Levantine Middle Palaeolithic', *The human revolution*, ed. P. Mellars and C. Stringer (Edinburgh, 1989), 589–610.

IS

Shaqadud KHARTOUM NEOLITHIC site in Sudan, which was excavated by Anthony Marks over the course of several seasons in the 1960s. This large occupation site, covering some 2 ha, includes 3 m deep stratigraphy dating from the 4th millennium to the late 2nd millennium BC.

K.H. Otto: 'Shaqadud: a new Khartoum Neolithic site outside the Nile Valley', *Kush* 11 (1963), 108–15; A.E. Marks et al.: 'The prehistory of the Central Nile Valley as seen from its eastern hinterlands: excavations at Shaqadud, Sudan', *JFA* 12 (1985), 261–78.

IS

Sheba *see* ARABIA, PRE-ISLAMIC

shell midden *see* KITCHEN MIDDEN, SHELL MIDDEN

Shemshara, Tell *see* TELL HASSUNA

shifting cultivation *see* LINEARBANDKERAMIK

Shih-chai-shan (Shizhaishan) Cemetery site situated 50 km west of Chin-ning-hsien, in the Chinese province of Yun-nan; first excavated in 1955, it has shed light on the ancient Tien (Dian) culture of southwest China, which flourished between the 4th and 2nd centuries BC. The large quantity of bronze, gold and iron artefacts unearthed is significant from several viewpoints. On the one hand, the bas-relief scenes on many of the bronze drums and other vessels vividly portray the daily life of the time, including the buildings, dress, personal ornaments, domesticated animals, agriculture, ceremonial activities, implements and weapons employed. Particularly remarkable are the group scenes of small detailed figurines on cowrie-containers. On the other hand, technological study of the metallurgical attainments of these peoples throws valuable light on the appearance of such alien approaches as metal-working (e.g. the engraving of the metal surface, repoussé, pierced-work and splitting, wire-drawing, mechanical shaping, etc.), *cire-perdue*, and possibly gold amalgam applications.

M. Pirazzoli-t'Serstevens: *La civilization du royaume de Dian à l'époque Han* (Paris, 1974); Anon.: *The Chinese bronzes of Yünnan*, ed. J. Rawson (London, 1983); N. Barnard: 'Bronze casting technology in the peripheral 'barbarian' regions', *BMM* 12 (1987), 3–37; ——: 'The entry of *cire-perdue* investment casting, and certain other metallurgical techniques (mainly metalworking) into South China and their progress northwards', *Ancient Chinese and Southeast Asian bronze cultures* I, ed. D. Bulbeck (Taipei, 1996), 1–94; ——: 'Bronze vessels with copper inlaid décor and pseudo-copper inlay of Ch'un-ch'iu and Chan-kuo times II', *Ancient Chinese and Southeast Asian bronze cultures* I, ed. D. Bulbeck (Taipei, 1996), 176–272.

NB

Shih-huang-ti (Shihuangdi) *See* CH'IN

Shinto Literally 'the way of the gods', Shinto is the native religion of Japan, which took its traditional form after the introduction of rice cultivation. The core of beliefs is that spirits reside in numerous natural phenomena such as the sun, water, fire and mountains and that it is important to attain ritual purity from pollution through offerings and participation in festivals and rituals. Shrines share architectural details with the buildings represented on Yayoi-period bronze bells and by Kofun-period *haniwa* (unglazed pottery funerary sculptures).

I. Oba: *Shinto kokogaku koza* [A course in Shinto archaeology] (Tokyo, 1981).

SK

Shizaishan *see* SHIH-CHAI-SHAN

Shu *see* PA-SHU

Shum Laka Rockshelter 14 km southwest of Bamenda, western Cameroon, with a distinctive Late Stone Age sequence, which was excavated by Pierre de Maret in 1978–80, by Raymond Asombang in 1982, and then again by de Maret and his colleagues in 1991–4. De Maret's 1991–4 excavations were extensive (49 m^2 in the upper part and 34 m^2 in the lower), and have revealed a stratigraphy which is up to 3.3 m thick. This stratigraphy comprises three phases:

(1) An exclusively microlithic quartz industry in rockfall, sand and loam, at the base (which it is thought may go back some 30,000 years)
(2) an orange layer (dating from 8705 to 6070 uncal BP) in which macrolithic artefacts in basalt are also prominent. These include bifacially worked, waisted and partially polished axes or hoes, as well as some Levaliois flakes, points, and cores.
(3) The same type of industry (radiocarbon dated to 3810 ± 60 and 3140 ± 80 uncal BP) is accompanied by some pottery in a grey ashy deposit at the top.

A total of 15 human skeletons have been found at the site. The mammalian fauna recovered during the earlier excavations were exclusively wild, mainly giant forest hog (*Hylochoerus meinertzhageni*), forest buffalo (*Syncerus caffer nanus*), and cane rat (*Thryonomys swinderianus*). This suggested that the landscape in the upper layers was forested, and that the western Cameroon grasslands took on their present form subsequently due to human action, but there are now preliminary indications that a savanna environment may also have been characteristic of the basal deposits. Detailed analyses of the data gathered 'should provide us with the first evidence of the transition from the Pleistocene to the Holocene, as well as the change from Later Stone Age to food producing communities in West Central Africa' (de Maret et al. 1995: 3).

P. de Maret, B. Clist and W. van Neer: 'Résultats des premières fouilles dans les abris de Shum Laka et d'Abeke au Nord-ouest du Cameroun', *L'Anthropologie* 91 (1987), 559–84; R. Asombang: 'Age de la pierre récent: Cameroun', *Aux origines de l'Afrique Centrale*, ed. R. Lanfranchi and B. Clist (Paris, 1991), 99–101; P. de Maret: 'Pits, pots and far west streams', paper presented to the conference on *The growth of farming communities in Africa from the equator southwards*, British Institute in East Africa and African Studies Centre (Cambridge, 1994); ——, R. Asombang, E. Cornelissen, P. Lavachery and J. Moeyersons: 'Continuing research at Shum Laka rock shelter, Cameroon (1993–1994 field season)', *NA* 43 (1995), 2–3.

PA-J

Shuruppak *see* FARA, TELL

Sialk, Tepe Pair of settlement mounds (and associated cemeteries), collectively dating to the 6th–1st millennia BC, located on an ancient east–west trade route at the edge of the central Iranian desert, about 200 km to the south of modern Tehran. In 1933–7 Roman Ghirshman defined six major phases at the site, the earliest of which (Sialk I) was a small village, consisting initially of reed huts and later of pisé and mud-brick structures. The Sialk I occupation was found only on the northern mound and roughly corresponded to the HASSUNA and SAMARRA phases of Mesopotamia (*c*.5800–5000 BC). The Sialk II phase, comprising some seven metres of stratigraphy, includes buildings made of hand-made bricks bearing thumb-prints, closely resembling those of the early UBAID temple at ERIDU. This suggests that there was an Ubaid-related material culture in Iran during the 5th millennium BC, although the hand-made ceramics appear to be quite different to those of the Ubaid culture.

In assessing the material culture at Sialk, Max Mallowan (1970: 455) stresses the balance between local characteristics and external influences: 'The rich material . . . demonstrates a long and steady internal development of native styles which were never altogether out of touch with technological advances in Elburz, in Susiana, in Assyria, and, to a lesser extent perhaps, in Babylonia'. At the end of the 4th millennium BC the site appears to have been abandoned. The two final phases, Sialk V and VI, consist simply of a pair of Iron Age cemeteries at the edge of the site, dating to the late 2nd and early 1st millennia BC respectively and perhaps indicating the arrival of Indo-Europeans on the Iranian plateau.

R. Ghirshman: *Fouilles de Tepe Siyalk, près de Kashan*, 2 vols (Paris, 1938–9); M.E.L. Mallowan: 'The development of cities from al-'Ubaid to the end of Uruk 5', *Cambridge Ancient History* 1/1, ed. I.E.S. Edwards et al., 3rd edn (Cambridge, 1970), 327–462 [447–56].

IS

sickle sheen Polish or 'sheen' that develops on the blade of stone (especially flint) implements as they are used to cut grain, grasses etc. When there is no botanical evidence for cultivated cereals at a site, sickle sheen is often taken as strong evidence

that a group had started to harvest wild cereals – and is sometimes cited as circumstantial evidence of 'incipient agriculture' by gathering and hunting groups. However, the presence of sickle sheen does not prove that wild cereals formed part of the diet; ethnographic accounts indicate that hunter and gatherer groups may also collect grasses regularly for building purposes.
RJA

Sidi Abderrahman *see* AFRICA 1

sign and symbol In common parlance, a sign is taken to be something which communicates a particular meaning to an observer. However, the Genevan linguist Ferdinand de Saussure (1857–1913), who identified the sign as the most fundamental unit of communication, gave the term a more precise meaning: a sign is the *relationship* between the signifier, the signified and the particular context in which the sign is used. For example, in the written language, 'trowel' signifies a useful archaeological tool within a quite particular context. In this case, the relationship between the signifier (the written word 'trowel') and the signified (the concept of an archaeological trowel) is based on convention – any signifier *could* have been used. Furthermore, the same signifier (the written word 'trowel') may signify something else again in a different context (in the minutes of a Masonic meeting, for example). Thus the idea of the sign as a *relationship* between signifier, signified and context is of great importance.

Signs can be divided up into three main types, depending upon the nature of this relationship: index, icon and symbol. Writers in different fields concerned with semiotics (particularly linguistics and anthropology) have not always defined these different types of sign in the same way. However, usually an *index* is a sign that has an existential or natural relationship with the signified – for example, in most contexts the sound of thunder signifies (is an index for) lightning. An *icon* is a signifier that has a representational relationship with the signified. For example, in prehistoric art a wave-like pattern is often taken to be an icon of water. A sign such as a downward gesture has an iconic relationship to the signified action ('sit down'). Although icons are relatively unimportant in linguistic analysis, their interpretation is a prominent feature in discussions of ancient art and material culture.

By contrast to the index and the icon, the *symbol* is usually defined as a signifier that is entirely arbitrary in its connection to the signified – that is, the connection is formed by social convention (usage) only. However, in anthropology and archaeology many writers concentrate on symbols that have special emotional or cultural meanings. Confusingly, some anthropologists have argued that the word 'symbol' should be reserved for signs that have some special link to emotional meanings or some resonance from the physical or natural world – and which are therefore, in a sense, non-arbitrary (*see* SYMBOLIC ARCHAEOLOGY for further discussion).

Symbolic anthropology is a particularly rich field and has had great, if indirect, influence on archaeological interpretations of symbols in prehistoric material culture. It has also affected interpretations of religious and 'ritual' sites, and the analysis of prehistoric IDEOLOGY. Numerous strands can be traced in symbolic anthropology, but some of the most directly influential in archaeological writing are the works of Claude Lévi-Strauss, Victor Turner's writings on the relationship between ritual, symbol and social structure, and Mary Douglas' seminal work on the symbolism of purity and pollution and how this affects material culture, decoration amd ritual behaviour.

The study of the ways in which signs and symbols are organized is described in the entry on STRUCTURALISM. The symbolism of material culture, and the 'archaeology of the mind', are described respectively in SYMBOLIC ARCHAEOLOGY and COGNITIVE ARCHAEOLOGY, while the complications for the archaeologist arising from an active use of symbolic meaning are explored in CONTEXTUAL ARCHAEOLOGY.

M. Douglas: *Purity and danger* (London, 1966); V. Turner: The forest of symbols (London, 1967); ——: *The ritual process* (London, 1969); M. Douglas: *Natural symbols* (London, 1970); D. Sperber: *Rethinking symbolism* (Cambridge, 1974); I. Hodder: *Symbols in action* (Cambridge, 1982); ——, ed.: *Symbolic and structural archaeology* (Cambridge, 1982); ——: *The present past* (London, 1982); ——, ed.: *The archaeology of contextual meanings* (Cambridge, 1987).
RJA

significance In the analysis of archaeological DATA, the 'significance level' of a HYPOTHESIS TEST is the PROBABILITY of rejecting a null hypothesis, given that it is actually true. The level should be specified in advance of the test, taking into account the strength with which the null hypothesis is held, and the consequences of rejecting it. Significance testing says nothing about the chances of accepting or rejecting a false null hypothesis, and to that extent is a limited concept. The value of 5% is conventionally used but has no intrinsic validity; it means that there is a 1 in 20 chance of rejecting the null hypothesis when it is true.

J.E. Doran and F.R. Hodson: *Mathematics and computers in archaeology* (Edinburgh, 1975), 52–8; S. Shennan: *Quantifying archaeology* (Edinburgh, 1988), 53–63; M. Fletcher and G.R. Lock: *Digging numbers* (Oxford, 1991), 60–2.

CO

Silsilian *see* SEBILIAN

Silver Leaves Iron Age settlement near Tzaneen, South Africa, where road construction exposed a village horizon with storage pits containing metal slag and pottery decorated with flutes and bevels. Radiocarbon dates of the 3rd–4th centuries AD show that this pottery forms the first phase of the Early Iron Age in the eastern half of southern Africa. Some call the ceramic facies Silver Leaves while others name this cultural tradition after Matola, a site in Maputo, Mozambique. The style is clearly related to Kwale (*see* EARLY IRON AGE) further north, and belongs to David Phillipson's 'lowland facies of Eastern Stream'. Although preservation in Silver Leaves/ Matola sites is not good, Silver Leaves itself yielded pottery with seed impressions of domesticated millet (*Pennisetum* sp.), and another site in the northern Transvaal contained the bones of domestic small stock.

M. Klapwijk: 'A preliminary report on pottery from the northeastern Transvaal, South Africa', *SAAB* 29 (1974), 19–23; T. Maggs: 'Mzonjani and the beginning of the Iron Age in Natal', *Annals of the Natal Museum* 24 (1980), 71–96; J. Morais: *The early farming communities of southern Mocambique* (Maputo, 1988).

TH

similarity *see* CLUSTER ANALYSIS

simulation The imitation of the behaviour of one or more VARIABLES, in order to explore their STATISTICAL DISTRIBUTION or the overall pattern of their behaviour. Archaeological simulation ranges from the plotting of the distribution of a single variable, e.g. in order to carry out a HYPOTHESIS TEST (known as the 'monte carlo' approach), to the operation of a large complex model, e.g. of foraging or subsistence systems (*see* FORAGING THEORY). Predictably, small exercises have tended to have more success than large. The model is run with different values of its PARAMETERS, using a computer to repeat each 'run' several times (at least 100) with a randomly-selected starting point. Much depends on the reliability of the random number generator. There are often so many possible combinations of the different values of the parameters that the main result is a very large pile of computer print-out. A task not to be undertaken lightly, and, some would argue, only as a last resort.

J.E. Doran and F.R. Hodson: *Mathematics and computers in archaeology* (Edinburgh, 1975), 298–306; I.R. Hodder and C.R. Orton: *Spatial analysis in archaeology* (Cambridge, 1976), 126–54; ——, ed.: *Simulation studies in archaeology* (Cambridge, 1978); P. Freeman: 'How to simulate if you must', *Computer and quantitative methods in archaeology* 1987, ed. C.L.N. Ruggles and S.P.Q. Rahtz (Oxford, 1988), 139–46.

CO

Sinagua Prehistoric culture (*c*.AD 700–1450) of the American Southwest, located in the Arizona mountains from Flagstaff south along the Verde River Valley and its northeastern tributaries. Sinagua cultural development was punctuated by the eruption of Sunset Crater volcano, 25 km north of Flagstaff in AD 1064. Prior to this time, the material culture of the Sinagua resembled that of the mountain-adapted MOGOLLON with pithouses and brown pottery. After the eruption, the Flagstaff area exhibits a cultural picture which may be interpreted by three models with different causal emphases. Harold S. Colton, the founder of the Museum of Northern Arizona, who defined the Sinagua, proposed that the greatly improved agricultural productivity of the land after the eruption encouraged immigration by ANASAZI, Mogollon, HOHOKAM and Cohonina people. The second model interprets the admixture as the result of extensive trade managed by the Sinagua. The third model takes an ideological perspective, proposing that the Flagstaff region – with an active volcano and in the shadow of the historically sacred San Francisco peaks – came to have powerful religious significance to different people of the Southwest. The Sinagua are generally thought to be among the people ancestral to the HOPI. The major Sinagua sites are Chavez Pass, Ridge, Tuzigoot, Winona and Wupatki, all in Arizona.

H.S. Colton: *The Sinagua* (Flagstaff, 1946).

JJR

Sinai *see* SERABIT EL-KHADIM

Sintiou-Bara Site in the middle valley of the River Senegal, which was excavated by Guy

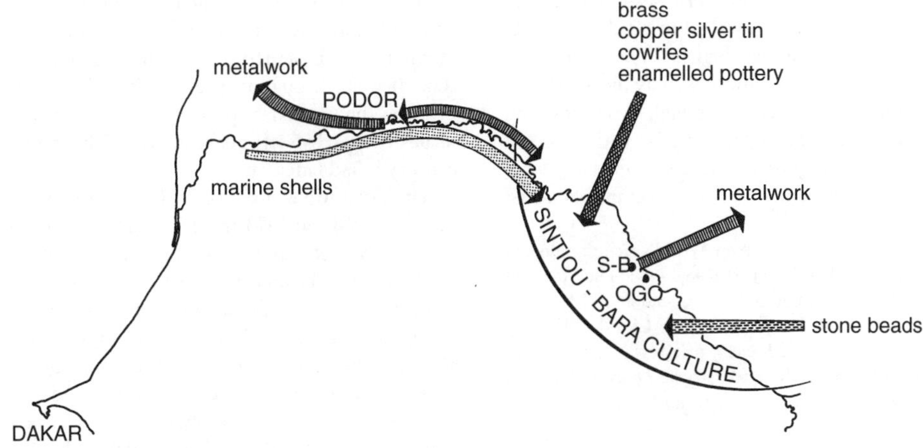

Figure 48 **Sintiou-Bara** Long-distance trade contacts indicated by finds at Sintiou-Bara and the extent of the 'culture area' (drawn by Philip Allsworth-Jones).

Thilmans and Annie Ravisé in 1973–8. These excavations yielded eight radiocarbon dates in the range AD 400–1050, and in Thilmans' view formed the centre of a 'culture area' defined largely on the basis of its distinctive pottery, slipped and burnished ware with channelled decoration, including geometric designs, which Susan and Roderick McIntosh consider to be comparable with similar motifs found on North African glass goblets at Tegdaoust. Long-distance trade contacts are indicated by several of the objects found at the site: cowries, glass beads, non-ferrous metals, and enamelled pottery of a type which may ultimately be traced back to Spain. Metalworking of a very high standard was carried out *in situ*, as demonstrated by the presence of numerous furnaces and at least 140 finished artefacts (not counting 7600 small brass 'collars' which probably served a decorative purpose). The majority of the larger artefacts, such as bells and discs, are interpreted as horse trappings, although no actual remains of horses have been found at the site. Other objects, such as rings and pendants, had a decorative function, and a conical 'mitre' of brass recalls the description given by al-Bakri in AD 1068 of headware used by the kings of Ghana. Traces of seven wattle and daub structures (two of which are interpreted as having had religious significance) and six burials were found over an excavated area of 153 m². This constitutes a relatively small part of the 67 ha settlement, which, according to Thilmans, probably corresponds to the historical city or state of Silla and its first Dia-ogo dynasty.

G. Thilmans and A. Ravisé: *Sintiou-Bara et les sites du fleuve* (Dakar, 1980).

PA-J

Sinú Style of gold work manufactured in northern Colombia for long-distance trade in the 7th to 12th centuries AD. Investigations along the Río San Jorge have placed this metal in a cultural context of large communities who created the most extensive system of drained fields known in South America. The earliest construction dates to a period of severe drought between 800 and 100 BC, and until the 9th century AD there was a gradual evolution of peoples making elaborate pottery, living in linear settlements along the waterways on artificial platforms, and burying their dead in tumuli associated with the settlements. Then strong fluctuations in flood levels apparently led to the gradual abandonment of the flood plains.

A. Legast: *La fauna en la orfebreria sinú* (Bogotá, 1980); C. Plazas et al.: *La sociedad hidraulica Zenu: estudio arqueológico de 2000 años de historia en las llanuras del Caribe Colombiano* (Bogotá, 1993).

KB

Sion *see* LE PETIT-CHASSEUR

Sipán Site of a series of burials dating to the Early Intermediate Period (*c*.400 BC–AD 500) in the

Lambayeque Valley of northern Peru. These were the first set of unlooted royal/elite Moche burials to be excavated by archaeologists. They show the wealth of the Moche elite as well as the artistry of their finest craftsmen in metal, ceramics and lapidary work. The Sipán burials, with those of neighbouring San José de Morro, show that people and scenes represented in Moche ceramics existed in reality.

W. Alva: 'Discovering the New World's richest unlooted tomb', *NGM* 174/4 (1988), 510–48; ——: 'The Moche of ancient Peru: new tomb of royal splendor' *NGM* 177/6 (1990), 2–15; C.B. Donnan and L.J. Castillo: 'Finding the tomb of a Moche priestess', *Archaeology* 45/6 (1992), 38–42; S. Kirkpatrick: *Lords of Sipán: a tale of pre-Inca tombs, archaeology, and crime* (New York, 1992).

KB

Sippar (Abu Habba and Tell ed-Der; Biblical Sepharvaim) Site in southern Iraq about 30 km southwest of Baghdad, adjacent to an ancient canal linking the Tigris and Euphrates. Sippar was one of the major cities of the Early Dynastic period (*c*.2900–2350 BC). When Hormuzd Rassam excavated the temple of the sun-god Shamash in 1880–2, he discovered the marble tablet of Nabu-apla-idinna (*c*.870 BC) decorated with a relief of the god in his shrine. During the same 18-month season he uncovered an archive of some 50,000 cuneiform cylinders and tablets from the rooms surrounding the ziggurat. One of these cylinders bears a text describing the excavations beneath the temple floor undertaken by Nabonidus (555–539 BC) which resulted in his discovery of the foundation stone laid by the Akkadian ruler Naram-Sin (2254–2218 BC) almost two millennia earlier. Despite the comparative fragility of the unbaked clay tablets from Sippar, a great deal of information has been obtained regarding the administration and liturgy of neo-Babylonian temples. The main settlement mound (Abu Habba) was also excavated by Scheil in 1894 and Andrae and Jordan in 1927, and the library was re-examined by Iraqi archaeologists in the 1980s. In the late 1960s and 1970s a team of Belgians worked on the neighbouring fortified town-site of Tell ed-Der (see de Meyer 1976).

V. Scheil: *Une saison de fouilles à Sippar* (Paris, 1902); W. Andrae and J. Jordan: 'Abu Habbah-Sippar', *Iraq* 1 (1934), 51–9; L. de Meyer: 'La sixième campagne de fouilles à Tell ed-Deir, 1974', *Sumer* 32 (1976), 161–5.

IS

Siraf Port on the southern coast of Iran, 200 km south of Shiraz, which was an important centre for international maritime commerce during the 9th and 10th centuries AD, with the origins of goods ranging from East Africa to China and Southeast Asia. It went through its great period of expansion between the SASANIAN period (*c*.AD 224–651) and its destruction by earthquake in AD 977; by the 13th century it had faded away.

The excavations directed by David Whitehouse between 1966 and 1973 are among the most important to have been undertaken on a major early site of the eastern Islamic territories in the late 20th century. The approach was comprehensive, investigating not only the main buildings and houses but also the subsistence economy of the town, addressing the geomorphology, the water supply and traces of land-use as well as retrieving seeds and other material as a part of the environmental study. At an Islamic site this approach was revolutionary, even if standard procedure in the archaeology of other periods. One of the most unusual and instructive studies involved excavation of a funerary site, rare information in Islamic archaeology. The results were remarkable, seeming to indicate the persistence of pre-Islamic burial practices into the Islamic period.

D. Whitehouse: 'Excavations at Siraf', *Iran* 6–11 (1968–74) [six interim reports]; ——: 'Siraf: a Sassanian port', *Antiquity* 45 (1971), 262–7; ——: *Siraf III: the Congregational Mosque* (Leiden, 1980); V.F. Piacentini: *Merchants – merchandise and military power in the Persian Gulf (Sûriânj/Shahriyâj–Sîrâf)* (Rome, 1992).

GK

Sirikwa holes Artificial depressions associated with the semi-legendary Sirikwa people, widely found in the western highlands of Kenya and the elevated stretch of the adjacent Eastern Rift Valley at sites such as Chemagel (see figure 11) and HYRAX HILL. Dating to the 13th–18th centuries AD, the Sirikwa holes comprise a range of regional and chronological variants.

Occurring in groups of between five and a hundred either on hillsides or around streams and springs, each 'hole' is a saucer-shaped hollow, usually about 10 m across, with signs of an entrance facing downhill and an earthen mound or pair of mounds below it. In rocky terrain, drystone walling was sometimes used to line the entrance and revet the interior of the hollow. Excavations in the 1960s and 1980s (Sutton 1973, 1987) showed that they were unroofed but stoutly protected by stockades and defensive gateways. They have been interpreted as stock-pens, particularly for cattle (but also for goats and sheep), and the external mounds are thought to have resulted from the dumps of mud and dung removed daily. Houses were not built inside the hollows, but were attached outside, either beside the gate – in order to guard the pen, as with the small houses at Hyrax Hill – or around the perimeter. These would have catered for the herdsmen. With later Sirikwa holes in the west, where cultivation was combined with the pastoral economy, more substantial round thatched houses were built for whole families.

Sirikwa pottery, often called 'Lanet ware' after a site near Hyrax Hill excavated by Posnansky in 1957, is a very distinctive pastoral ware of the late Iron Age, with bands of twisted-cord rouletted decoration and shapes imitating milk-gourds. The semi-legendary Sirikwa themselves, now vindicated archaeologically, are believed to have been linguistically ancestral to the Kalenjin population of this region. The Sirikwa way of life was phased out in the 17th–18th centuries AD, as its methods of grassland exploitation, herding and stock protection proved too vulnerable to large-scale raiding in the Maasai era. It is argued however that the recent success of the pastoral sections of the Maasai owes much to the Sirikwa experience and their pioneering of advanced pastoral strategies in these fine high equatorial grasslands.

J.E.G. Sutton: *The archaeology of the Western Highlands of Kenya* (Nairobi, 1973); ——: 'Hyrax Hill and the Sirikwa', *Azania* 22 (1987), 1–36.

JS

Sirkap *see* TAXILA

Sirsukh *see* TAXILA

Sisupalgarh Fortified Iron Age urban site (*c.*400 BC–AD 400) near Bhuvenshwar in Orissa, India, which was excavated by Braj Basi Lal in 1948–9. The walled core of the site is square in plan (1.2 × 1.2 km), with two gateways in each side, each gate being linked with the others by paved roads lined with structures and wells. Several monolithic columns stand in the centre of Sisupalgarh, perhaps marking the location of an elite residence. Ceramics dominate the artefact assemblage from the site and include BLACK AND RED WARE and red slipped wares in early levels, while red and ochre slipped wares dominate in later levels; other artefacts that span the entire occupation include ceramic ear ornaments, iron implements and gemstone beads. Copper, ceramic and gold coins appeared near the end of the occupation.

B.B. Lal: 'Sisupalgarh', *AI* 5 (1948), 62–105; ——: 'Sisupalgarh: some reflections on its layout', *Archaeology and art* II, ed. C.R.P. Sinha (Delhi, 1990), 589–96.

CS

Sitagroi Tell site on the Drama plain of northeastern Greece, occupied primarily from the Middle Neolithic to the Early Bronze Age (*c.*5500–2200 BC). The excavation of Sitagroi (1968–70) by Colin Renfrew and others greatly elucidated the relationship between the early metal-using cultures of the northern Aegean and their counterparts in the Balkans. Traditional DIFFUSIONIST explanations of cultural and technological change in the Balkans depended upon the notion that the significant innovations were all derived from the east (specifically, Anatolia). Renfrew knew that these explanations would be invalidated if it could be shown that early copper-using cultures in the Balkans (exemplified by the Vinča and Gumelniţa complexes) were older than their supposed progenitors in the Aegean (exemplified by Troy I etc.). At Sitagroi, Renfrew recovered material related to the Gumelniţa culture (Sitagroi phase III) at a markedly lower level than material which formed part of the Aegean Early Bronze Age (Sitagroi phase V). Thus the stratigraphic evidence at Sitagroi, confirmed by calibrated radiocarbon dates, strongly suggested the autonomy of metallurgical innovations in Central Europe.

C. Renfrew et al., eds: *Excavations at Sitagroi: a prehistoric village in northeast Greece*, vol. 1 (Los Angeles, 1986).

RJA

site catchment analysis Quantitative and qualitative evaluation of the natural resources within an easily exploitable distance of a given settlement or archaeological site. Although the approach was implicit in many traditional analyses of sites, Eric Higgs coined the term and explicitly employed the techniques of site catchment analysis. In the 1970s, formal site catchment analysis became a standard technique in the economic analysis of prehistoric sites, and seemed to complement the move toward a more quantitative approach to site description.

The catchment area can be defined according to various criteria, but it is often taken to be the resources within a day's walk of the site. This means that when a catchment area in a region of rugged relief is plotted onto a map, it is often far from circular. At its simplest, the approach gives only the roughest indication of the type of resources available to early communities – notably the percentage of land fit for certain types of cereal farming or animal husbandry. It does not in itself provide any proof that these resources were used, or even that they could have been used (given the limited technology available).

In order to increase the usefulness of the analysis it is therefore necessary to take into account economic variables such as technology (e.g. tool and seed types), climate change and seasonal effects, farming traditions and size of settlement; cultural variables such as taboos about land use, political factors, land distribution; land-sharing and resource-allocation relationships with neighbouring communities; the effect of any settlement hierarchy or regional trade and redistribution; and whether the settlement may have been located where it is for reasons that have little to do with land use (e.g. religious, historical or defensive reasons).

C. Vita-Finzi and E.S. Higgs: 'Prehistoric economy in the Mount Carmel area of Palestine: site catchment analysis', *PPS* 36 (1970), 1–37; F.J. Findlow and J.E. Ericsson, eds: *Catchment analysis: essays on prehistoric resource space* (Los Angeles, 1980).

IS

site formation processes Term used to describe the various natural and cultural processes which combine to create an archaeological site. The interpretation of any set of archaeological remains must involve some assessment of the ways in which they have been modified by such processes. *See* BEHAVIORAL ARCHAEOLOGY, C-TRANSFORMS, N-TRANSFORMS, POST-DEPOSITIONAL THEORY, REFUSE DEPOSITION *and* TAPHONOMY.

Si Thep Moated centre containing temples dedicated to Hindu and Buddhist deities, located in the upper Pasak Valley between the central Plain of Thailand and the Khorat Plateau. An inscription raised there by a certain Bhavavarman in the 6th or 7th century AD records that he established a temple to Siva on his accession (the ruins of which still survive). A man called Bhavavarman was overlord of a ZHENLA-CULTURE polity in Cambodia, and he might have exercized hegemony over this area. There is also evidence of Buddhism in the form of images carved on the walls of a nearby cavern on Thomarat Hill, while Hinduism is further evidenced by the discovery, in a nearby modern temple, of an image of Visnu that may possibly derive from the site. As with MUANG FA DAET and MUANG SIMA, Si Thep is an example of a small polity contemporary with those of the DVARAVATI CULTURE.

H.G. Quaritch-Wales: *Dvaravati: the earliest kingdom of Siam* (London, 1969), 81–5.

CH

Sitio Conte Ceremonial site of the COCLÉ culture of Panama, situated inland off the north-western Gulf of Panama, roughly in the centre of the country. Sitio Conte is well-known for its extraordinarily rich funerary complex dating to *c.*AD 300–900. Excavation of a series of graves with multiple burials yielded tools and weapons, textiles, cast gold and TUMBAGA ornaments, jewellery (such as necklaces, bracelets, rings, headbands, helmets and whistles) and gemstones. The pottery includes a variety of forms such as spouted effigy vessels, plates and dishes.

S.K. Lothrop: *Coclé, an archaeological study of central Panama: Part I*, Memoirs of the Peabody Museum, Harvard University 7 (Cambridge, MA, 1937).

PRI

situla (pl. situlae) Bronze, and occasionally ceramic, 'pail-shaped' vessels that were produced in prehistoric Europe from the late 2nd millennium BC onwards, and which seems to have been employed in drinking ceremonies. The name is used particularly for the decorated situlae produced in the sub-Alpine region, especially in north Italy around ESTE, from about 600 BC on (*see* SITULA ART).

RJA

situla art Style of art produced in north Italy and Slovenia in the later 1st millennium BC (especially the 5th and 4th centuries BC, and manifested largely on bronze or occasionally earthenware situlae and related bronzework such as belts and mirrors. The situlae are usually made from a single sheet of bronze that was beaten from the inside, and then chased on the outside to provide fine detail, before being rivetted and seamed together to form a vessel. The decoration consists of a series of horizontal ornamental bands and figurative friezes (shown in profile), for example, an assortment of animals, a feasting ceremony, or a military or religious procession. Specific scenes in situla art include men (women are usually shown only as attendants) sitting on thrones in hats with wide brims, men with musical instruments, men boxing, animals being led to slaughter and in processions, men with mixing and drinking vessels etc. – all perhaps relating to the same feasting ritual. The scenes seem to illustrate the life of the elite of the region, rather than depicting mythologies or simply copying more sophisticated Etruscan or Greek work, although key elements of the style (e.g. the use of figurative human and animal friezes), and many of the details, betray the direct influence of the former region at least. A minority of the animals are mythological, including gryphons and sphinxes, and reveal the indirect influence of the civilizations of the ancient Near East. The origin of the situla style seems to have been in northern Italy, especially around ESTE, where a tradition of beaten bronzework using largely animal motifs evolved from the 7th century BC; however, most of the situlae were manufactured in the 5th and 4th centuries in the wider southeast Alpine region of north Italy and Slovenia.

W. Lucke and O.H. Frey: *Die Situla in Providence, Rhode Island* (Berlin, 1962); O.H Frey: *Die Entstehung der Situlenkunst* (Berlin, 1969); N. Sandars: *Prehistoric art in Europe* (London, 1985), 337–40.

RJA

Siwa Oasis (anc. Sekhet-imit; Ammonium) Natural depression in the Libyan Desert about 560 km west of Cairo, where the earliest remains date to the Egyptian 26th dynasty (664–525 BC). The site includes the cemetery of Gebel el-Mawta, dating from the 26th dynasty to the Roman period, and two temples dedicated to the god Amun, dating to the reigns of Amasis (570–526 BC) and Nectanebo II (360–343 BC) respectively; in 331 BC the famous oracle of Amun is said to have been visited by Alexander the Great soon after his conquest of Egypt. The caravan route from northwest Africa passed through Siwa in medieval times.

A. Fakhry: *The oases of Egypt I: Siwa Oasis* (Cairo, 1973); K.P. Kuhlmann: *Das Ammoneion: Archäologie, Geschichte und Kultpraxis des Orakels von Siwa* (Mainz, 1988).

IS

Skara Brae One of the best-preserved Neolithic villages in Europe, this small collection of drystone houses was preserved under sand-dunes on the coast of mainland Orkney. Discovered in the mid-19th century after storms disturbed the dunes, the village was excavated principally by Gordon Childe in the 1930s and D.V. Clarke in the 1970s. The houses, only about half a dozen of which were in use at any one time, were joined by passages and contain furniture built of drystone and slabs including a 'dresser', stone 'beds', storage alcoves and tanks and benches around hearths. As well as GROOVED WARE pottery, a number of 'prestige' items, such as a finely carved ground stone ball and decorated bone and ivory pins and pendants, have been recovered from the site (see Clarke et al. 1985).

V.G. Childe: *Skara Brae* (London, 1931); D.V. Clarke: 'Excavations at Skara Brae: a summary account', *Settlement and economy in the third and second millennia BC*, BAR BS 33 (Oxford, 1976), 233–50; —— et al.: *Symbols of power at the time of Stonehenge* (Edinburgh, 1985), 245–6.

RJA

Skhul *see* MOUNT CARMEL

slash and burn agriculture *see* SWIDDEN AGRICULTURE

SMA (Stone to Metal Age) *see* AFRICA 5.3

small tool tradition *see* AUSTRALIAN SMALL TOOL TRADITION

Snaketown *see* HOHOKAM

Snettisham Site in Norfolk, England, which in 1948–50 yielded a remarkable group of hoards of Iron Age metalwork; metal-detecting and excavation revealed a further six deposits in 1990. In total the hoards contained 75 complete and *c.*100 incomplete torcs, over 100 ingot rings/bracelets, and 170 coins; the metals used were electrum, gold, silver and bronze. An electrum torc from Hoard E, the terminals of which are intricately decorated with raised circular motifs filled in with a basketry pattern, is often quoted as one of the finest examples of insular (i.e. British) Celtic art. To judge from the numismatic evidence, the hoards date from the first half of the 1st century BC. They were almost certainly deposited for the purpose of safe-keeping: the excavation proved that the site is not part of a settlement, and Stead (1991) points out that there is no evidence that torcs were ever ritually deposited in the Iron Age.

R.R. Clarke: 'The Early Iron Age treasure from Snettisham, Norfolk', *PPS* 20 (1954), 27–86; I.M. Stead: 'The Snettisham Treasure: excavations in 1990', *Antiquity* 65 (1991), 447–65.

RJA

snowmarks *see* AERIAL ARCHAEOLOGY; FROSTMARKS

Soan Palaeolithic sequence of the Potwar Plateau region of northern Pakistan, defined by Helmut de

Terra and Thomas T. Paterson (1939). Their work was significant in locating several South Asian Palaeolithic sites, but was flawed by a lack of understanding of the geological complexity of the region and exclusive dependence on surface finds, with no *in situ* remains. As a result, the archaeological sequence that they defined (pre-, early and late Soan flake tools) is no longer widely accepted (Allchin and Dennell 1989: 2; Dennell and Hurcomber 1992: 71). A reexamination of the region was initiated by the British Archaeological Mission in 1980. Through a program of systematic geological, paleontological, and archaeological documentation, coupled with the use of THERMOLUMINESCENCE and PALEOMAGNETISM dating techniques, this research is reappraising the sequence of early human settlement in South Asia. Artefacts from dated contexts include flaked tools that may date as early as 2 million years ago (Allchin and Dennell 1989: 12) as well as lithic and structural remains from a *c.*45,000 year old lithic procurement or hide processing site near RIWAT.

H. de Terra and T.T. Paterson: *Studies on the Ice Age of India* (Washington, D.C., 1939); R.W. Dennell: 'The importance of the Potwar Plateau, Pakistan, to studies of early man', *South Asian archaeology*, 1981, ed. B. Allchin (Cambridge, 1984), 10–19; H. Rendell: 'The Pleistocene sequence in the Soan Valley, northern Pakistan', *South Asian archaeology*, 1981, ed. B. Allchin (Cambridge, 1984), 3–9; B. Allchin and R.W. Dennell: 'Palaeolithic survey in Potwar Region – 1980: History and Result', PA (1989), 1–19; R.W. Dennell and L. Hurcombe: 'Paterson, the British Clactonian, and the Soan flake industry: a re-evaluation of the early Palaeolithic of Northern Pakistan', *South Asian archaeology*, 1989, ed. C. Jarrige (Madison, 1992), 69–72.

CS

Soba Early medieval settlement site covering an area of about a square mile on the east bank of the Nile in central Sudan, 22 km from Khartoum. It was the capital city of the Christian Nubian state of Alwa (*c.*AD 550-1500). Peter Shinnie's excavations at Soba in the early 1950s, involved the pioneering use of ETHNOARCHAEOLOGY, including the documentation of local pottery manufacture and the analysis of mud-brick buildings, as well as the first published stratigraphic drawings from a Nile Valley site (Shinnie 1955). Shinnie recovered large quantities of imported glass of the 6th–12th centuries AD, which helped to establish the site's chronology, now confirmed by radiocarbon dates obtained during the excavations of the 1980s (Welsby and Daniels 1991).

P. Shinnie: *Excavations at Soba* (Khartoum, 1955); D.A. Welsby and C.M. Daniels: *Soba: archaeological research at a medieval capital on the Blue Nile* (London, 1991).

IS

social Darwinism Just as Darwinism is the theory of biological evolution by means of natural selection, social Darwinism is the belief that a similar principle helps to explain the success and evolutionary trajectory of social groups and societies. A few years before the publication of Darwin's *Origin of species by means of natural selection* in 1859, the journalist and thinker Herbert Spencer had invented the phrase 'survival of the fittest' to describe competition for resources among societies. Spencer believed that if this competition were given free rein, it would lead to the optimal form of society. His ideas, and those of related social thinkers, later drew metaphorical power from the much more rigorously formulated and observed Darwinian theory of natural selection.

Social Darwinism offered social theorists of the later 19th century a powerful template to explain the way in which societies interact and social history unfolds. Unlike Darwinism, social Darwinism developed a strong prescriptive flavour: it became associated both with the political arguments for economic libertarianism and, from the early 20th century, with the arguments by the Eugenic Society for artificially manipulating biological reproduction to improve the gene pool. As a simple concept – the survival of the fittest social group – it could be argued that social Darwinism lies behind many modern explanations of the dominance of particular cultures in the archaeological record. However, the confusing political and eugenic connotations mean that the phrase 'social Darwinism' needs to be carefully defined if used outside its particular historical context.

H. Spencer: *On social evolution*, ed. J. Peel (Chicago, 1972).

RJA

social status analysis Technique devised by Roy Hodson (1977) to analyse the Iron Age cemetery of HALLSTATT, later used on cemeteries of other periods, such as the early Saxon cemetery at Sleaford (Brenan 1985). Starting from a table of the presence or absence of each functional type of artefact in each grave, it assigns a score to each type according to the average number of other types with which it is found. The graves are then ordered according to the total score of the types found in each (alternatively, the score of the highest-scoring type found in a grave is used as the score of the grave). This creates a ranking of graves, from those with many different types through those with few types to those with one or none. The interpretation of the ranking is then up to the archaeologist. It is often necessary to analyse male and female graves separately (*see* GENDER ARCHAEOLOGY). The main drawback of social status analysis is that large samples (about 100+ graves) are needed for the technique to work well.

F.R. Hodson: 'Quantifying Hallstatt', *AA* 42 (1977), 394–411; J. Brenan: 'Assessing social status in the Anglo-Saxon cemetery at Sleaford', *Institute of Archaeology Bulletin* 21/22 (1985), 125–31.

CO

sodium profile dating Scientific dating technique similar to NITROGEN PROFILE DATING, which has been used on OBSIDIAN but has not yet been fully developed (*see also* OBSIDIAN HYDRATION DATING).

G. Coote and P. Nistor: 'Depth profiles of sodium in obsidian by the resonant nuclear reaction method: a potential dating technique', *Archaeometry: an Australian perspective*, ed. W. Ambrose and P. Duerden (Canberra, 1982), 243–50.

SB

Sofala *see* MANEKWENI

soilmarks Term used in AERIAL ARCHAEOLOGY to refer to a type of marking by which the presence of ancient features may be recognized in the bare soil. In some regions, soilmarks have been of great importance in the recognition of archaeological sites in heavily plough-levelled areas – for example the identification of ploughed-out CELTIC FIELDS on the Wessex chalkland by Crawford and Keiller (1928), the discovery of numerous Roman villas in Picardy by Agache (1978) or the identification of prehistoric sites under arable cultivation in the American mid-west (Baker and Gumerman 1981: 16–20, pl.1).

Soilmarks appear as changes in the basic colour of the soil or as apparent changes due to differing soil moisture. Direct soilmarks are due to the exposure of actual archaeological deposits as a result of their partial destruction through cultivation. Examples include the Roman villas recorded in northern France (Agache 1978), seen as masonry where the walls have been freshly clipped by the plough, or the black markings in ploughsoil where charcoal-burning sites have been disturbed. Indirect soilmarks, often dampmarks, derive from the same class of below-ground features as do cropmarks. The variation in the moisture-retaining or evaporation capacities of the buried feature and its surrounding matrix may give rise to variation in the colour of the ploughsoil above. A buried ditch with humic fill will retain moisture after a free-draining subsoil may have dried out (see CROPMARKS). Moisture will evaporate at different rates from materials of different specific heat, producing either positive or negative dampmarks. The use of false-colour infra-red film (see AIRBORNE REMOTE SENSING) can be helpful in enhancing the visibility of marks in bare soil.

O.G.S. Crawford and A. Keiller: *Wessex from the air* (Oxford, 1928); D.R. Wilson: *Aerial reconnaissance for archaeology* (London, 1975), 53–69; R. Agache: *La Somme pre-Romaine et Romaine* (Amiens, 1978); C. Baker and G.J. Gumerman: *Remote sensing: archaeological applications of remote sensing in the north central lowlands* (Washington, 1981); O. Braasch: *Luftbildarchäologie in Süddeutschland* (Stuttgart, 1983).

FG

soil phosphorus analysis The determination of the phosphorus (more specifically, the phosphate) content of soils for site location and interpretation. First applied in the 1930s, the method relies on the fact that there is an enhancement in soil phosphorus concentration at sites of human settlement due to the accumulation of waste products and also the presence of burials. Phosphorus is mainly present in soils as the phosphate anion in both organic and inorganic compounds, the latter including calcium and iron phosphates. Most methods of analysis applied to large surveys have determined only the inorganic content since simpler extraction techniques are required. The phosphorus is usually extracted with dilute acids and determined by COLORIMETRIC ANALYSIS, for example by conversion to a blue complex with ammonium molybdate (molybdenum blue method).

Apart from the potential as a prospecting tool, at a particular site the distribution of phosphate can be used as an aid to the interpretation of features and to determine the limits of occupation. When applied as a surveying technique it is necessary to take samples at regular recorded intervals over the area to be investigated from a consistent soil horizon or excavation context. The spacing of samples may be less than 1 m for intra-site studies or 100 m or more for site location. In both cases large numbers of samples are often involved and consequently rapid methods of analysis have been developed.

D. Gurney: *Phosphate analysis of soils: a guide for the field*

archaeologist (Birmingham, 1985); P. Bethell and I. Máté: 'The use of soil phosphate analysis in archaeology, a critique', *Scientific analysis in archaeology*, ed. J. Henderson (Oxford, 1989), 1–29.
MC

Soleb Religious and funerary site in the 3rd cataract region of Upper Nubia. The site consists primarily of an Egyptian temple dating to the reign of Amenhotep III (*c.*1391–1353 BC) and a cemetery of the Meroitic period (*c.*300 BC–AD 350).
M. Schiff Giorgini: *Soleb*, 2 vols (Florence, 1965–71).
IS

Solutrean (Solutrian) Upper Palaeolithic tool tradition or industry of *c.*21,000 16,000 BC, characterized by leaf-shaped or 'foliate' points. Often superbly finished using pressure retouch or delicate percussion retouch, Solutrean points are among the finest examples of Upper Palaeolithic stone tool technology. The tradition is named after the site of Solutré (Saône and Loire), but largely understood from the phases identified at LAUGERIE-HAUTE rockshelter; the earlier Solutrean is concentrated in southwest France but later Solutrean assemblages appear throughout much of western Europe. The points may be fairly clearly divided into: Proto-Solutrean, marked by the emergence of flat-faced (unifacial) points; Early Solutrean with developed flat-faced points; Middle Solutrean with classic bifacial finely flaked laurel-leaf points (during this phase the Solutrean industry increased its geographical range considerably); and final or Late Solutrean with shouldered or notched foliate (or willow-leaf shaped) points. The bone industry is not as varied and developed as in the succeeding MAGDALENIAN, although the later Solutrean is marked by the invention of the perforated needle. The distinction between the latest 'Solutrean' and the early 'Magdalenian' is a rather artificial construct; the assemblages are often rather similar and increasingly the radiocarbon dates from sites classified into one or the other seem to overlap.
P. Smith: 'The solutrean culture', *SA* 211 (1964), 86–94; R.R. Larick: 'Circulation of Solutrean foliate points within the Périgord, S.W. France', *The human uses of flint and chert*, ed. G. de G. Sieveking and M.H. Newcomer (Cambridge, 1987), 217–30.
RJA

SOM (Seine-Oise-Marne) culture Late Neolithic to Early Bronze Age cultural complex of northern France, defined in 1950 by Gordon Childe and Nancy Sandars. Centred on the rivers Seine, Oise and Marne, the group extends into north France generally and has close parallels with the HORGEN CULTURE of Switzerland. It dates from the 3rd millennium BC, and in northern France it succeeds the CHASSÉEN cultural complex of the middle Neolithic. The SOM is defined by the following features: pottery of poor quality – markedly poorer than the undecorated but finely finished Chasséen ceramics – and often in the form of 'flower-pot' shaped vessels without lugs or handles; the presence of GRAND PRESSIGNY FLINT; fine flint daggers and barbed and tanged arrowheads; a particular form of notched flint sickleblade (*scies-à-encoche*); an increase in the number of flint axes; and a range of distinctive jewellery including axe-amulets, horn and bone pendants and schist bracelets.

The SOM is associated with distinctive funerary practices. For the first time in the Paris basin, collective burial was practised – with formal funerary monuments such as ALLÉES COUVERTES (megalithic gallery graves), pits and hypogees cut into the chalk. The tombs are sometimes decorated with distinctive anthropomorphic figures.

Although very few SOM settlement sites have been identified (but see Watté 1976), SOM culture sites generally have a more expansive distribution pattern than the Chasséen or earlier Neolithic sites, and the use of more varied soil types and rainfall dependent plateau areas may indicate that the SOM coincides with the introduction of the plough and the use of animals for traction. A limited range of metal objects (copper beads etc.) begin to appear during the SOM period, but these were probably obtained through exchange as there is no evidence of local metallurgy. A few *allées couvertes* contain early forms of beaker, indicating acceptance of elements of the BEAKER PHENOMENON.
V.G. Childe and N. Sandars: 'La civilization de Seine-Oise-Marne', *L'Anthropologie* 54 (1950); J-P Watté: 'L'habitat Seine-Oise-Marne du Grand-Epauville à Montvilliers (Seine-Maritime), *BSPF* 73 (1976), 196.
RJA

Somerset Levels Area of peat bog in Somerset, England, that has provided the most extensive 'wetland' evidence in British archaeology. Although the area is affected by drainage schemes and peat extraction, the waterlogged conditions have helped preserve features such as Neolithic wooden tracks, notably the 'Sweet Track'. Quickly built of planks and rails raised over the bog to provide a dry walkway about 1800 m long, this track seems to have been used for about a decade, during which time axe-heads (one of Sussex flint, the other probably from the Alpine region), leaf-shaped arrowheads, and uniquely preserved wooden artefacts (a possible mattock and spades, bows, spoon, paddles etc.) were deposited around the structure. Analysis of the wood used to build the track suggests that, even at this early date, Neolithic farmers were beginning to manage woodlands. A significant attribute of this wetland evidence is that it has begun to yield absolute dates of an extraordinary precision through the use of DENDROCHRONOLOGY – the construction of the Sweet Track has been dated to 3807/3806 BC – for itself and the associated range of Early Neolithic artefacts.

B. Coles and J. Coles: *Sweet Track to Glastonbury: The Somerset Levels in prehistory* (London, 1986); J.M. Coles: 'Precision, purpose and priorities in wetland archaeology', *AJ* 66/2, 227–47; J. Hillam et al.: 'Dendrochronology of the English Neolithic', *Antiquity* 64 (1990), 210–20.

RJA

Songo Mnara *see* SWAHILI HARBOUR TOWNS

Son Vi culture Late Pleistocene gathering and hunting culture of northern Vietnam, dated to 18,000–9000 BC. Most of the 60 or so sites identified are found in uplands surrounding the Red River valley, but at CON MOONG cave the 'Sonviian' remains were clearly stratified under the HOABINHIAN. Several stone-tool types have been defined, including cobbles with a flaked transverse cutting edge, scrapers, and side choppers where the flaking is found on the lateral side. Since most of the sites were open (as opposed to caves), no biological finds have survived, but at Con Moong cave there is evidence for a broad spectrum of gathering and foraging subsistence within a forested habitat.

Ha Van Tan: 'The Hoabinhian in the context of Viet Nam', *Vietnamese Studies* 46 (1976), 127–97.

CH

Sources de la Seine The source of the river Seine is the find-spot of a rarely preserved series of wooden *ex-voto* carvings. The 200 or so carvings, of variable but generally rather low quality, represent both whole figures and parts of the body – such as specific organs, limbs and especially heads. The carvings were probably a means of gaining divine help in the healing of ailments. Associated pottery and dendrochronological evidence suggest that the pieces date from the early 1st century BC.

S. Deyts: *Les bois sculptés des sources de la Seine*, Éditions du centre national de la recherche scientifique, XLIIe supplément à 'Gallia' (Paris, 1983).

RJA

South Arabian civilization *see* ARABIA, PRE-ISLAMIC

Southern Cult (or Southeastern Ceremonial Complex) Term used to refer to the distinctive motifs and artefacts found at some MISSISSIPPIAN sites in eastern North America. Elements of the Southern Cult can be identified over an extended period, although its classic expression occurred in the 13th century AD. The objects were closely associated with high social positions, and were often buried with important people. Many were fashioned from valued non-local materials, including engraved whelk shells and thin copper plates with raised designs. Images such as men in falcon costumes indicated boldness and prowess in war. Skull and bone designs underscored close connections with illustrious ancestors and therefore bolstered claims to leading positions in these societies.

J.A. Brown: 'The southern cult revisited', *MJA* 1 (1976), 115–35; P. Galloway, ed.: *The southeastern ceremonial complex* (Lincoln, NE, 1989).

GM

Soviet Union *see* CENTRAL ASIA; CIS AND THE BALTIC STATES

Spanish Levantine rock art Rock art of eastern Spain (i.e. 'Levantine' Spain) of the Epipalaeolithic, Mesolithic and early Neolithic. Painted in shallow rockshelters, the art contrasts with the cave art of the Upper Palaeolithic in that it represents complex scenes (including narrative scenes) of men and animals. It is nearly always executed in shades of red or black (but never both together), with occasional paintings in white and some engravings. As a rule, the different techniques seem to represent different bodies, and probably periods, of art.

The style and content of the paintings varies, from archetypal complex scenes of tiny figures (for example, engaged in battle at the rockshelter at Civil, Valltorta, or the detail of a group of hunters apparently executing a man by firing arrows at him at REMIGIA, Castellón) to single animals (the great bull, 1.10 m long at Cuevas de la Araña). In most paintings, figures are nude and are often equipped with bows and arrows. Most often they are shown hunting, running, dancing in a stylized but lively manner that is quite distinct from the static and schematic art of the Spanish farming Neolithic. Abbé Breuil maintained that part of Spanish Levantine art was Palaeolithic, though this is now discounted by most authorities. It seems more probable that it represents a complex succession of styles from the Epipalaeolithic through a later period in which hunting and gathering peoples existed contemporaneously with agricultural and herding communities on adjacent plains. This would explain why some of the scenes in the art depict the economic activities of hunting and gathering peoples, while others seem to show domesticated animals and digging implements.

A. Beltrán: *Rock art of the Spanish Levant* (Cambridge, 1982).

RJA

spatial analysis Wide range of statistical techniques applied to a variety of archaeological problems, sharing the need to study the spatial distribution of archaeological objects. The techniques can be divided archaeologically into inter-site and intra-site analyses, and statistically by the nature of the DATA (*see* NEAREST-NEIGHBOUR ANALYSIS *and* QUADRAT ANALYSIS). The term was introduced into archaeology by Ian Hodder; recent trends have begun to subsume it into GEOGRAPHICAL INFORMATION SYSTEMS (GIS), but it remains a body of theory and methodology in its own right. *See also* REGRESSION ANALYSIS, SPATIAL AUTOCORRELATION, THIESSEN POLYGONS, TREND SURFACE ANALYSIS. *For a critical description of a technique of spatial analysis called* UNCONSTRAINED CLUSTERING *see* MASK SITE.

I.R. Hodder and C.R. Orton: *Spatial analysis in archaeology* (Cambridge, 1976); H. Hietala, ed.: *Intrasite spatial analysis in archaeology* (Cambridge, 1984); H.P. Blankholm: *Intrasite spatial analysis in theory and practice* (Aarhus, 1991).

CO

spatial autocorrelation A situation which occurs in statistical analysis when values of a spatial VARIABLE at nearby locations are correlated with each other; this correlation usually decreases as the distance between locations increases. It can cause complications; for example, when using QUADRAT ANALYSIS to study the relationship between two variables, SIGNIFICANCE levels will be adversely affected if either is spatially autocorrelated. It can also be studied in its own right as a simple method of spatial analysis.

A.D. Cliff and J.K. Ord: *Spatial autocorrelation* (London, 1973); I.R. Hodder and C.R. Orton: *Spatial analysis in archaeology* (Cambridge, 1976), 174–83.

CO

specific gravity analysis (SG) Method of analysis based on the measurement of the density of a material relative to that of water at 4°C. The measurement is usually made by 'Archimedes' principle' and involves weighing the artefact in air and then in a liquid (usually a high density organic compound). It has been applied to the analysis of gold artefacts such as coins and depends on the higher density of gold compared with the alloying metal e.g. silver. The method is strictly only applicable to binary alloys, i.e. gold-silver or gold-copper.

M.J. Hughes and W.A. Oddy: 'A reappraisal of the specific gravity method for the analysis of gold alloys', *Archaeometry* 12 (1970), 1–11.

MC

speos Type of rock-cut temple or shrine in Egypt and Nubia (*see* ABU SIMBEL, BENI HASAN *and* GEBEL EL-SILSILA).

Speos Artemidos *see* BENI HASAN

sphinx (Egyptian: *shesep ankh*, 'living image') Imaginary beast, usually combining the body of a lion with the head of a human being, frequently found in the art and myths of Egypt, the Ancient Near East and Greece. The earliest sphinxes appeared in the iconography of Egypt and Mesopotamia in the early 3rd millennium BC, primarily taking the form of guardian figures. The Great Sphinx at GIZA, regarded as a personification of the god 'Horus in the horizon', is the most significant surviving archaeological example.

A. Dessene: *Le sphinx: étude iconographique* (Paris, 1957); H. Demisch: *Die Sphinx* (Stuttgart, 1977); M. Lehner: 'Reconstructing the Sphinx', *CAJ* 2/1 (1992), 3–26.

IS

Spirit Cave Small rockshelter with a sequence of deposits dated 11,000–5500 BC, located at an altitude of 650 m on a steep hillside overlooking the Khong Stream in northern Thailand. Excavations by C.F. Gorman from 1966 uncovered a material culture which parallels that from the HOABINHIAN sites in Vietnam, including the late development of polished stone adzes and pottery. Spirit Cave was the first such site to be subjected to rigorous screening, resulting in a sample of plant remains and microfauna. The former included canarium nuts, butternut, almonds and fruits of a species now used for poisoning arrowheads; animal bones covered a wide spectrum including fish, squirrel, badger, porcupine, deer and a few pig bones. The site thus seems to have been used as a base for broad spectrum foraging.

C.F. Gorman: 'Excavations at Spirit Cave, North Thailand: some interim impressions', *Asian Perspectives* 13 (1972), 79–107.

CH

Spiro Eastern North American site encompassing 11 mounds, located along the Arkansas River in eastern Oklahoma. This Caddoan site is best known for an impressive mortuary deposit in the Craig Mound that contained the remains of many high-ranking people. Disarticulated bones were found arranged in several ways, such as on litters or in cane baskets. They were accompanied by numerous finely crafted artefacts often made from imported raw materials, including engraved marine shell cups and copper cut-out figures. The site was occupied for many centuries, although the mortuary feature dates to the 14th century AD.

J.A. Brown: 'Spiro art and its mortuary contexts', *Death and the afterlife in pre-Columbian America*, ed. E.P. Benson (Washington, D.C., 1975), 1–32; ——: *The Spiro ceremonial center* (Ann Arbor, 1996).

GM

***spondylus* shell** Type of marine bivalve shell with long spines on its exterior which appears in archaeological deposits both in Europe and South America. Ornaments made from the *S. gaederopus* species frequently appear in Neolithic contexts around the Mediterranean (e.g. SITAGROI in Greece) and central and southeastern Europe (e.g. VARNA in Bulgaria). They are often taken as evidence of trade or exchange networks, particularly in central Europe, since the Mediterranean is the only possible source of the living shellfish. Although this assumption is probably correct, fossil varieties of *spondylus* can be obtained locally; once these have been worked into an ornament, the difference between fossil shell and Mediterranean shell may only become apparent after geochemical analysis, which excavators in the past have rarely applied.

Two species (*S. princeps* and *S. calcifer*) are native to the deep warm waters of the Gulf of Guayaquil and northwards to the Gulf of California. These were much prized by the people of Peru, who traded to Ecuador for them from the Initial period (2300–1200 BC) onwards.

A. Paulsen: 'The thorny oyster and the voice of God: Spondylus and Stromus in Andean prehistory', *AA* 39 (1974), 597–606; J. Shackleton and H. Elderfield: 'Strontium isotope dating of the source of Neolithic European Spondylus shell artefacts', *Antiquity* 64 (1990), 312–15.

KB/RJA

Sredni Stog Neolithic/Copper Age cultural tradition that existed largely in the forest-steppe interfluve between the Dniepr and the Don. The settlements (unfortified) were located on low river terraces – which were intensely forested at that time. The outstanding feature of the Sredni Stog settlements is that their economy, unusually for the period, included horse-breeding as an important component. In some cases (Dereivka, Molyukov Bogor, Alexandria) the bones of horses make up over 50% of the total faunal remains. The situation of Dereivka (Telegin 1986) is typical. The site is situated on a low terrace of river Omelnik, a tributary of the Dniepr, and covers an area of the *c*.3000 sq. m. The single cultural layer includes at least three subterranean dwelling structures, and a ritual emplacement comprising a horse skull, a foot and foreparts of two dogs. In all, the faunal assemblage from the site includes the remains of at least 52 horses. Four radiocarbon measurements date the site – attributed by Telegin to the middle stage of the Sredni Stog sequence – to between 3380 and 4570 calendar years BC. Cemeteries were found at Dereivka and at some other Sredni Stog sites; the ochre-covered dead were placed on their backs in a contracted posture in oval-shaped flat graves. In several cases (Yama near Donetsk and Koisug on the lower Don), Stredni Stog burials were placed under burial mounds.

D.Ya. Telegin: *Sredn'ostogis'ka kul'tura epohi midi* [The Sredni Stog culture of the Copper Age] (Kiev, 1973); ——: *Dereivka, a settlement and cemetery of Copper Age horse keepers on the Middle Dniepr*, BAR IS, S267 (Oxford, 1986). M.A. Levine: 'Dereivka and the problem of horse domestication', *Antiquity* 64 (1990), 727–40.

PD

Sri Lanka *see* ASIA 2; ANURADHAPURA; POLONNARUVA

stable isotope analysis Measurement of the abundance ratios of stable (i.e. non-radioactive) isotopes of certain elements with applications in provenance, dietary studies and dating.

See CARBON ISOTOPE ANALYSIS, LEADISOTOPE ANALYSIS *and* OXYGEN ISOTOPE ANALYSIS.
MC

stakehole Feature produced by the act of driving a wooden stake into the ground. Whereas POSTHOLES are larger and usually consist of a prepared hole, the remains of the post itself (the post pipe') and sometimes also 'post packing', stakeholes simply comprise the hole and fill formed by the point of the stake.

standard deviation In statistical analysis, the term 'standard deviation' is one of several 'measures of dispersion' of a VARIABLE about its MEAN. In mathematical terms it can be expressed by the equation s^2=i(xi – x) 2/n, i.e. it is the square root of the variance, which is the mean of the squared differences between the data values and their mean. The '±' term of an uncalibrated RADIOCARBON DATE is the standard deviation of the estimated date.

J.E. Doran and F.R. Hodson: *Mathematics and computers in archaeology* (Edinburgh, 1975), 39; C.R. Orton: *Mathematics in archaeology* (Glasgow, 1980), 90–4; S. Shennan: *Quantifying archaeology* (Edinburgh, 1988), 42–4; M. Fletcher and G.R. Lock: *Digging numbers* (Oxford, 1991), 44–6.
CO

standardized, standardization In statistical analysis, a VARIABLE is said to be standardized if it has been transformed so that it has a zero MEAN and STANDARD DEVIATION of one. Standardization is used in order to compare STATISTICAL DISTRIBUTIONS with standard distributions given in statistical tables, and to reduce multivariate data to a common scale (*see* PRINCIPAL COMPONENTS ANALYSIS). The transformation is sometimes (incorrectly) called NORMALIZATION.

J.E. Doran and F.R. Hodson: *Mathematics and computers in archaeology* (Edinburgh, 1975), 39; S. Shennan: *Quantifying archaeology* (Edinburgh, 1988), 105–7, 246; M. Fletcher and G.R. Lock: *Digging numbers* (Oxford, 1991), 47.
CO

Star Carr Early Mesolithic site, dated to the earlier 9th millennium BC (*c*.7300 uncalibrated years BC), and used intermittently for perhaps three centuries. It is located about 8 km west of Scarborough in Yorkshire, England. The excavation of the site by Grahame Clark (1949–51) greatly illuminated our understanding of the British and European Mesolithic; although certain of his interpretations have now been questioned, Clark's work at Star Carr is regarded as a pioneering example of a multidisciplinary investigation, or, to use Clark's term, 'bioarchaeology'.

The main feature of the site was a rough birchwood platform on the edge of a now extinct lake; Clark (1954) believed that this platform formed a living area, although it has been controversially reinterpreted as a mixture of driftwood and debris thrown from the actual (supposedly largely unexcavated) living area (Price 1989). Clark believed the site to have been occupied only in the winter and spring by migratory deer hunters. However, this conclusion was based upon the original faunal analysis (included in Clark's 1954 excavation report), which has been endlessly reviewed. A comprehensive revision by Legge and Rowley-Conwy (1988), who usefully summarize earlier arguments, concluded that Star Carr was indeed seasonally occupied, but in the late spring and summer, and that the site may have acted as a hunting station from which meat (red and roe deer, elk and aurochs) was transported to a base camp elsewhere.

Star Carr has a particularly rich and well-preserved antler and bone industry, with many barbed spearheads and digging tools. This and the character of the flint industry (microliths, burins, scrapers etc.) led Clark to suggest that the site was an early variant of the MAGLEMOSIAN complex. However, he also noted a number of idiosyncracies, especially the preference for barbed points made from antler, rather than bone. The most evocative finds were 21 perforated stag frontlets with carefully pared down antlers, which may have been worn as head-dresses during ceremonies (or possibly as disguises during hunts).

J.G.D. Clark: *Excavations at Star Carr* (Cambridge, 1954); W.F. Libby: *Radiocarbon dating*, 353 (Chicago, 1955, 2nd edn), 1988; A.K. Legge and P.A. Rowley-Conwy: *Star Carr revisited* (London, 1988); T.D. Price: 'Willow tales and dog smoke', *The interpretation of prehistory: essays from the pages of the Quarterly Review of Archaeology*, vol. 10/1 (1989), 107–14.
RJA

Starčevo (Starčevo–Körös–Criş) culture Earliest farming culture of Serbia, named after a site beside the Danube near Belgrade that was partially excavated in the 1930s. Although Starčevo farmers cultivated early forms of wheat (especially emmer) and raised sheep, cattle and pig, hunting continued to play a significant part in their economy; faunal remains include red deer, roe deer, wild cattle, horse and boar, game and fish. Incomplete stratigraphies at Starčevo sites (most of the material from Starčevo itself came from pits rather than deep stratigraphies) mean that the pottery sequence is not entirely clear. The decoration is relatively crude in comparison to the succeeding VINČA culture, but is sometimes impressed, incised or, especially in Starčevo II, painted. The painted designs are predominantly black motifs on a red slip, in contrast to early Neolithic wares further south in the Balkans and Greece which tend to be white and red. During the Starčevo II phase the culture expanded and began to be influenced by other early farming cultures of southeast Europe, such as KARANOVO I and SESKLO. Like other early farming groups, Starčevo villages manufactured a range of anthropomorphic and animal figurines.

The neighbouring early farming cultural groupings of Körös in Hungary and Criş in Romania are closely related to the Starčevo culture, and are often treated as one complex in the literature (Starčevo–Körös–Criş culture). In the case of the Körös culture, the exploitation of marine resources seems to have been even more pronounced, and bones of catfish and pike are often preserved; one site, Röszke-Ludvár, preserved dense layers of fish scales a few centimetres thick, suggesting large-scale fish drying and processing. Sheep also seem to form a larger proportion of the faunal assemblages than cattle and pigs – over 50%, like the early farming groups in Greece and the southern Balkans such as Anza – in contrast to the main Starčevo–Criş grouping. The Körös culture is often cited as a probable cultural predecessor of the LINEARBANDKERAMIK culture. The lithic technology of the Criş culture includes microliths, which are assumed to be a carry-over from the local Mesolithic toolkit. Criş pottery sherds have been found at sites of the BUG-DNIESTRIAN culture to the east, providing interesting evidence of contact between an early farming economy and a late hunting and gathering economy.

V. Fewkes et al.: 'Excavations at Starčevo, Yugoslavia, seasons of 1931 and 1932: a preliminary report', *Bulletin of the American School of Prehistoric Research* 9 (1933), 33–54; D. Garašanin *Starcevacka kultura* (Lljubljana, 1954); R. Tringham: *Hunters, fishers and farmers in eastern Europe 6000–3000 BC* (London, 1971); M. Garašanin: 'The Stone Age in the central Balkan area; the Eneolithic period in the central Balkan area', *Cambridge Ancient History III* part 1 (Cambridge, 1982), 75–162; A. Whittle: *Neolithic Europe: A survey* (Cambridge, 1985), 45–6.

RJA

Starosel'ye Palaeolithic cave-site in the Crimea, Ukraine, situated in the valley of Kandy-Dere near the town of Bakhchisarai. The site was discovered and excavated (1952–6) by A.A. Formozov, and includes a MOUSTERIAN lithic industry. The extended skeleton of a child, 18–20 months old, was found buried in the middle part of one of the lower levels. Several writers (Yakimov and Kharitonov 1979) classify the specimen as an ANATOMICALLY MODERN HUMAN.

V.P. Yakimov and V.M. Kharitonov: 'K probleme krymskih neandertal'cev' [The problem of the Crimean Neanderthals], *Issledovanie paleolita v Krymu* [Palaeolithic studies in the Crimea], ed. Yu.G. Kolosov (Kiev, 1979), 60–2.

PD

statistical cycle A model of the way in which archaeologists interact with their material in a research setting. It formalizes the stages by which archaeologists relate their ideas to evidence from excavations and other fieldwork, by contrasting the world of THEORY with the real world represented by DATA (see Fig.49). It sees the relationship between the two as mediated through MODELS, which vary considerably in their complexity and expression. It does not constrain an archaeologist to any particular paradigm of research, e.g. HYPOTHETICO-DEDUCTIVE or INDUCTIVE, since the cycle may be entered at any point. It encompasses the four main ways in which archaeologists use statistics – EXPLORATORY DATA ANALYSIS, DATA REDUCTION, PARAMETER ESTIMATION and

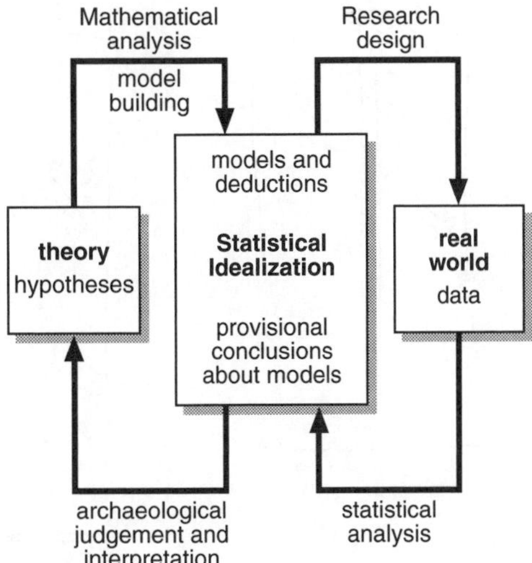

Figure 49 **statistical cycle** Flow chart illustrating the concept of the statistical cycle (drawn by Clive Orton).

HYPOTHESIS TESTING. It can also accommodate subjective (BAYESIAN) approaches as well as the more common objective approaches.

J.E. Doran and F.R. Hodson: *Mathematics and computers in archaeology* (Edinburgh, 1975), 343–6; C.R. Orton: *Mathematics in archaeology* (Glasgow, 1980), 19–24.

CO

statistical distribution In statistical analysis of archaeological DATA, a 'distribution' is a mathematical model of the behaviour of one (or more) VARIABLE(S), e.g. how frequently its value is likely to exceed certain limits. For example, it is believed that an uncalibrated RADIOCARBON DATE has a NORMAL DISTRIBUTION. A distribution may be based on observations (empirical distribution) or theoretical consideration. The form of a distribution depends on its PARAMETERS, of which there may be one, two or more (e.g. MEAN, STANDARD DEVIATION). One object of statistical analysis is to estimate the parameters of such distributions; another is to test whether a particular distribution is an appropriate description of a particular DATASET (*see* GOODNESS-OF-FIT). When a distribution cannot be found to fit a dataset, NON-PARAMETRIC STATISTICS must be used.

J.E. Doran and F.R. Hodson: *Mathematics and computers in archaeology* (Edinburgh, 1975), 39–50; S. Shennan: *Quantifying archaeology* (Edinburgh, 1988), 33–44.

CO

statue-menhir Term applied in European prehistory to any standing stone or 'menhir' that has been carved into a simple anthropomorphic form. Statue-menhirs are concentrated in southern France and Corsica, Sardinia and Italy, with some examples in northwest Europe, notably western France and the Channel Islands; they were largely erected from the later 3rd millennium BC into the 2nd millennium BC. Corsica has the most impressive concentrations, notably at FILITOSA and Pagliaiu. Here, the more elaborate examples may be 2–3 m high, with a distinct head and simplified facial features, and daggers and swords in bas-relief; a few may once have had horns attached to their heads, and all appear to be male (see Whitehouse 1981 for typological summary).

The statue-menhirs of the Alpine region of north Italy, for instance at Val Camonica, are very

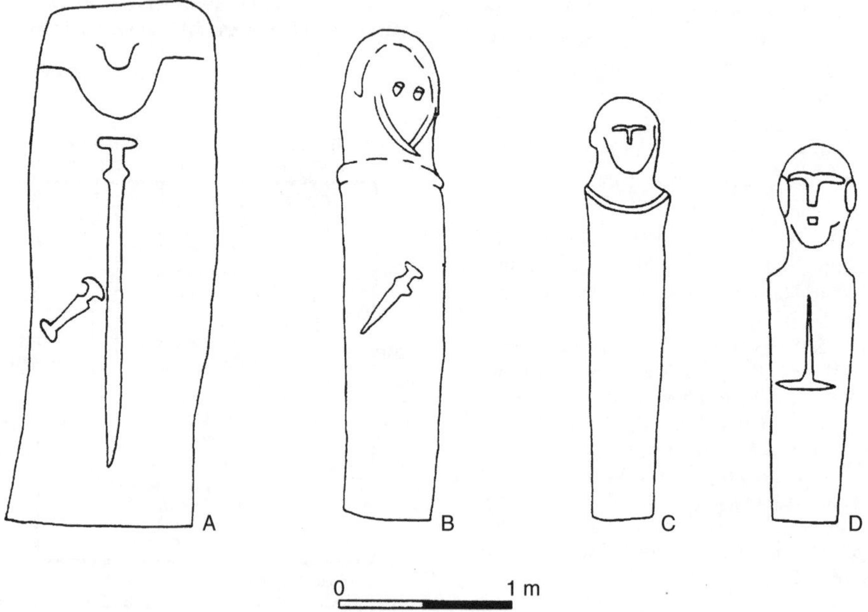

Figure 50 **statue-menhir** Corsican statue-menhirs: (A) Filitosa V, (B) Nativu, (C) Barbaggiu, (D) Filitosa IV (drawn by Philip Howard). *Source*: R. Whitehouse: 'Megaliths of the Central Mediterranean', *The megalithic monuments of Western Europe*, ed. C. Renfrew (London, 1981), fig. 9.

schematic, and often anthropomorphized simply by the addition of a belt or collar and sometimes a weapon. The group is related to the statue-menhirs found in Switzerland at Petit Chasseur. Some of the statue-menhirs from the group in northwest Tuscany are similar, although more examples depict breasts; here there is also a later, more elaborate and exclusively male group, displaying a larger array of weapons. A few low slabs carved with breasts and necklaces etc., occur in southern Italy on the edge of the Tavoliere plain.

Some early MEGALITHIC art associated with the Neolithic chamber tombs of France is similar to the later corpus of statue menhirs, in that it depicts schematic human figures and weapon motifs on megaliths; there is also evidence from Gavrinis that the builders may have used re-used earlier carved menhirs in the building of the tomb. Representations of pairs of breasts, often with necklaces, also occur frequently on megaliths that form part of the *allées couvertes* of western and north-central France.

J. Armal: *Les statues-menhirs, hommes et dieux* (Toulouse, 1976); R. Whitehouse: 'Megaliths of the central Mediterranean', *The megalithic monuments of Western Europe*, ed. C. Renfrew (London, 1981), 42–63; R. Joussaume: *Dolmens for the Dead*, trans. A. and C. Chippindale (London, 1988), 116–23, 141–2.

RJA

Steep Cliff Cave Rockshelter in the limestone uplands of northern Thailand, which contained a thick midden of animal bones and other deposits, dated to 5500–3500 BC. The material culture includes many of the unifacial discoids typical of the Vietnamese HOABINHIAN stone industry. The shelter is on a precipitous slope, some distance from the nearest water source. A forested habitat is evidenced by the bones of macaques, langur monkeys and the Himalayan striped squirrel, but most bones come from large bovids and deer, and the remains of tiger and leopard are also present. It has been suggested that the site was a location for the drying and processing of animal carcases, because the bones have been subjected to much battering, and many have been burned. Screening during excavation led to the recovery of canarium and almond shells, pepper vine seeds and bamboo remains.

CH

stela. stele Slab of stone or wood bearing inscriptions or depictions, usually of a funerary, votive, commemorative or liminal nature, although these four categories may often overlap. Stelae are generally roughly rectangular in shape, with plain, painted, inscribed and/or sculpted surfaces.

In Mesopotamia, there were many different forms of stelae: from at least the Uruk period (c.4300–3100 BC) onwards, rulers placed votive stelae in temples in order to inform the gods of their achievements. In later times (particularly in the Kassite period, c.1600–1100 BC) the KUDURRU, or boundary stone, was used to record land transfers. In pharaonic Egypt, the so-called 'false-door stele', often incorporating lists of funerary offerings and relief depictions of the deceased, was a focal point of the private tombs of the elite from the 3rd Dynasty (c.2686–2613 BC) onwards.

The Mesoamerican stele, dating from Preclassic to Postclassic times (2500 BC–AD 1521), was most typically associated with the Classic period LOWLAND MAYA. Sometimes decorated with human figures, glyphs and 'long count' dates, the Mesoamerican stele was erected in a plaza, usually in front of a pyramidal structure (and often paired with an accompanying altar).

I. Graham and E. Von Euw: *Corpus of Maya hieroglyphic inscriptions* (Cambridge, MA, 1975–) [ongoing multi-volume series]; S. Wiebach: *Die ägyptische Scheintür* (Hamburg, 1981) [the Egyptian false-door stele]; I.J. Gelb, P. Steinkeller and R.M. Whiting: *Earliest land tenure systems in the Near East: ancient kudurrus* (Chicago, 1991).

IS/PRI

Stemmed Point Tradition Early cultural tradition (*c.*8500–6000 BC) found in many sites between the Rocky Mountains and the Coast-Cascade-Cordilleran range in Western North America (Carlson 1983: 75–83). This tradition is based on the distribution of similar stemmed projectile points and chipped stone crescents in sites extending southwards from southeast British Columbia to interior Oregon, Nevada, and California, which co-occur with older landforms. Regional variations are the LIND COULEE and Windust phases of Washington, the Pluvial Lakes Tradition of Oregon, and the Lake Mojave Complex of Nevada and California. Binary comparisons were used by Rice (1972) to demonstrate the validity of the Windust phase. The functional groupings of artefact categories, based on their association with occupational features, indicated that most assemblages were associated with hunting. This tradition occupies the same territory as the western FLUTED POINT TRADITION and is probably a derivative of it (Carlson 1988). *See* map 8 (p. 44).

D.G. Rice: *The Windust phase in Lower Snake River prehistory* (Pullman, 1972); R.L. Carlson: 'The far west', Early man in the New World, ed. R.S. Shutler (Beverly

Hills, 1983), 73–96; ——: 'The view from the North', *Early human occupation in far western North America: the Clovis-Archaic interface*, ed. J.A. Willig, C.M. Aikens and J.L. Fagan (Carson City, 1988), 319–24; ——: 'Cultural antecedents', *Handbook of North American Indians VII*, ed. W. Suttles (Washington, 1990), 60–9.
RC

Stentinello Settlement site on Sicily near Syracuse which has given its name to an elaborate early pottery tradition and associated cultural assemblage that spread over Sicily and Calabria in the late 6th and early 5th millennium BC (Middle Neolithic). The site of Stentinello itself is known mainly from the excavation of the rich deposits in its defensive rock-cut ditch – a common feature of 'Stentinello' villages; the internal layout of the village is not clear. The pottery differs from the pre-Stentinello wares in the relatively fine texture of its dark-coloured fabric, the range of forms (gourd-shaped vessels with necks of varying length, cups and large lipped bowls), and especially in its fine decoration. Like many early Neolithic decorated wares, the repeated geometric patterns (zig-zags, circles) seem to be inspired by textiles, although there is also a double motif resembling a pair of eyes; the decoration is usually impressed or incised with occasional white inlay. Stentinello pottery is often regarded as part of the early impressed ware family of pottery styles, although it is perhaps better regarded as having *developed* from this group.
RJA

Sterkfontein One of several localities close to Krugersdorp, Transvaal, South Africa, to have yielded fossil remains of *AUSTRALOPITHECUS AFRICANUS*, and, additionally, *HOMO HABILIS*, the latter associated with ACHEULEAN artefacts. The fossils and artefacts are contained in breccia deposits filling solution cavities developed along ancient fracture lines in pre-Cambrian dolomite. More than 500 australopithecine specimens are recorded from Member 4, estimated, on faunal grounds, to be between 2.8 and 2.4 million years old. The overlying Member 5, with *Homo habilis* and Acheulean artefacts is faunally dated to between 2 million years (lower levels) and 1 million years ago. Deeper Members (1, 2, and 3) contain fossils which could be as old as 3.6 to 6.5 million years: these still await detailed investigation.
E.S. Vrba: 'Early hominids in southern Africa: updated observations on chronological and ecological background', *Hominid evolution, past, present and future*. ed. P.V. Tobias (New York, 1985), 195–200; M.J. Wilkinson: 'Lower lying and possibly older fossiliferous deposits at Sterkfontein', *Hominid evolution, past, present and future*. ed. P.V. Tobias (New York, 1985), 165–70; R.J. Clarke: 'Habiline handaxes and paranthropine pedigree at Sterkfontein', *WA* 20 (1988), 1–12.
RI

Stichbandkeramik *see* STROKE-ORNAMENTED WARE

Stiftmosaik (cone mosaic) Type of wall decoration used in Mesopotamian temples during the URUK and JEMDET NASR periods (*c.*4000–2900 BC); it consisted of colourful geometrical (and later figurative) designs produced by covering walls and columns with thousands of painted clay or stone cones, perhaps imitating textile wall-hangings.
H. Frankfort: *The art and architecture of the ancient Orient*, 4th edn (Harmondsworth, 1970), 24–5, figs 8–9.
IS

Stillbay Small holiday resort located 270 km east of Cape Town, which was designated the type-site of the Stillbay MSA (Middle Stone Age) industry in 1929. The artefacts were surface finds on high ground overlooking the sea. The site is undated but may equate with Middle Stone Age II at KLASIES RIVER MOUTH CAVES.
A.J.H. Goodwin and C. van R. Lowe: 'The Stone Age cultures of South Africa', *Annals of the South African Museum* 27 (1929) 127–9.
RI

stirrup bottle Very common ceramic form in northern Peru, which is also found sporadically in most Native American and one Zaire/Congolese culture. It consists of a closed body with a tubular handle in the form of an up-ended U with a spout in the middle, thus forming handle and spout in one.

stomion *see* THOLOS

stone-bowl cultures *see* PASTORAL NEOLITHIC

stone circles Circular or subcircular arrangements of MEGALITHS, usually free-standing, built from the later 4th millennium BC. The most famous examples are from the Neolithic and Bronze Age in Britain – although there are significant examples of the same periods in Ireland, France (Brittany) and

Portugal, as well as later traditions in various regions around the world (see below). In the case of the British tradition, both the size of the stones and the diameter of the ring vary enormously, from the massive AVEBURY (330 m diameter) to small examples such as Little Meg in Cumbria (5 m diameter). A few examples have more than one ring of stones, arranged internally (the great circle at Avebury contains two smaller stone circles), concentrically (Oddendale, Westmoreland) or adjacently (The Hurlers, Cornwall). Other megalithic features often augment the circle, for example outlying standing stones or occasionally processional avenues of stones or a CURSUS. Circles are often associated with other types of ritual monument, for example they may form part of a massive HENGE construction (Avebury), or be associated with cairns or burials. Occasionally the megaliths are not free-standing: at Lough Gur (Ireland) they line the inner perimeter of a wide bank. Sometimes stone circles form the subsidiary part of a construction, for example the huge round burial mound of NEWGRANGE is edged with a circle of megaliths.

The stone circles of the British Isles often seem to contain within them astronomical sight-lines and markers. This seems highly probable in the case of the midwinter-midsummer solstice alignment at STONEHENGE, whereby a key alignment in the design of the whole circle centres on an easily observable astonomical event of great symbolic significance. However, as even a small stone circle can create a large number of possible sight-lines to an equally large number of conceivably significant astronomical events, alignments must often be proven statistically (i.e. it must be shown that they are highly unlikely to have occurred by chance). Heggie (1981) describes the problems involved in such proofs, and concludes that few stone circles in Britain have yet been shown to contain deliberate alignments.

Outside Britain, the most notable examples of free-standing rings of megaliths are the contemporary monuments of the CARNAC REGION of Brittany and the Evora region of Portugal. Traditions of stone-circle building occur sporadically outside Europe in later periods. For example, West Africa contains some fine multiple circles of standing stones dating perhaps from 200 BC until as late as AD 1000: the monuments at Sine-Ngayene in Senegal apparently mark collective graves of up to 60 individuals. The Bouar region of the Central African Republic also contains prehistoric megalithic structures (see AFRICA 5.3). Stone circles are associated with the early megalithic cemeteries of the Jordan Valley (e.g. the 12 stone circles beside the tombs of Ala-Safat may have been used to cremate bodies before interment). Stone cairns enclosed by large boulders are quite common in peninsular India, covering pit or urn or sarcophagus burials – often the circle is the only remaining visible element, giving the misleading impression of a free-standing monument. Similarly, the Hokkaido region of Japan exhibits circular cairns of stones with occasional orthostats that can appear rather like stone circles. All these examples, however, seem much more closely related to commemorating the dead than is the earlier European tradition.

A. Thom, A.S. Thom and A. Burl: *Megalithic rings*, BAR BS 81 (Oxford, 1980); D.C. Heggie: *Megalithic science* (London, 1981); R. Bradley: *The social foundations of prehistoric Britain* (London, 1984); R. Joussaume: *Dolmens for the dead: megalith building throughout the world* (London, 1984); C. Ruggles: *Megalithic astronomy*, BAR BS 123 (Oxford, 1984); J. Barnatt: *Stone circles of Britain*, 2 vols, BAR BS 215 (Oxford, 1989); A. Ghosh: *An encyclopedia of Indian archaeology* 2 vols, (New Delhi, 1989); C. Malone: *Avebury* (London, 1989).

RJA

Stonehenge Neolithic and Bronze Age HENGE monument and ceremonial complex on Salisbury Plain, Wiltshire, England. The monument visible today represents a complex series of construction phases, beginning with a relatively simple henge monument in the later 4th millennium BC (*c.*3200 BC), known as Stonehenge I. This consisted of a circular ditch and bank about 90 m in diameter with a single entrance; two standing stones were placed to mark the entrance to the henge, with a larger stone, now known as the 'Heel stone', some metres outside the entrance. Four stones, the 'Station Stones', were carefully set up inside the perimeter of the henge as if to mark the four corners of a rectangle (the dating of the Station Stones to the first main construction phase is not quite secure).

The entrance and design axis of this first monument is roughly, but deliberately, aligned on the point of the horizon above which the sun rises at the midsummer solstice. The rectangle formed by the Station Stones lies about this axis (as do later elements of the monument, notably the massive trilithon horseshoe). It also seems possible that the Heel stone was deliberately placed slightly off-centre of the sunrise axis so that, for observers watching the sun rise in the weeks leading up to the solstice, it acted as a marker of a sacred period within which festivities could take place. Less convincingly, some prehistorians have claimed that 56 pits about 1m deep which were dug around the inner circumference in the earliest phase of the monument (the so-called 'Aubrey Holes'), were used as part of an elaborate calculation of lunar events. This and other claims for the existence of sophisticated solar and lunar astronomical alignments in Stonehenge are critically examined by Heggie (1981), who offers a bibliography of the extensive literature.

About 900 years after this first phase, during Stonehenge II, the entrance to the monument was widened in the first of many reconstructions; the new entrance was aligned much more precisely on the rising of the sun in midsummer (a feature still obvious to visitors on that day). A formal ditch and bank avenue was constructed leading away from the monument; this was lengthened many centuries later, and can still be easily traced in parts. The famous 'bluestones', weighing up to 4 tonnes, may have been imported to the site from the Prescelly Mountains in southwest Wales, although some authorities believe that they may have been moved to the locality naturally by glacial action. Abandoned postholes suggest that these stones were first intended to form a double circle/horseshoe arrangement on their own in the centre of the henge. When this idea was discontinued in favour of a much more ambitious plan involving the huge sarsen trilithons that dominate the site today, there seem to have been a succession of attempts to make use of the bluestones before they were integrated (not entirely happily) into the design as it now exists.

During the most impressive phase of construction (Stonehenge III), perhaps a century or so later at the end of the 3rd millennium BC, large sarsen blocks weighing up to about 50 tonnes were brought to the site from perhaps 20–30 km away. Carefully dressed using stone pounders into smooth regular uprights and lintels, the sarsens were erected to form a complete lintelled circle, surrounding five more massive free-standing trilithons (and it is the latter that dominate the modern visitor's first impressions of the site). Mortice and tenon joints were used to secure the lintels to the uprights; this technique, perhaps adapted from woodworking, suggests that while Stonehenge is quite unique as a stone circle in its use of trilithons and extensive stone dressing, it may have been closely related to contemporary wooden structures. Some centuries later, the bluestones were rearranged around the trilithon centrepiece.

In the final phase (IV), the avenue was lengthened to a total of 2.5 km in a direction quite different to that of its original construction. This final construction, dated to about 1100 BC, brought to a close the complex constructional history of what appears today to be a single monument. It is increasingly realized that the monument itself forms the centrepiece to a complex ritual landscape. This was particularly so during the early Bronze Age when the rich WESSEX CULTURE burials in the locality included that of BUSH BARROW.

R.J.C. Atkinson et al.: *Excavations at Dorchester*, Oxon (Oxford, 1951); R.J.C. Atkinson: *Stonehenge and neighbouring monuments* (London, 1978); ——: *Stonehenge* (London, 1979); D.C. Heggie: *Megalithic science* (London, 1981), 145–52, 195–205; C. Chippindale: *Stonehenge complete* (London, 1983); J. Richards: 'The development of the neolithic landscape in the environs of Stonehenge', *Neolithic studies: a review of some current research*, ed. R. Bradley and J. Gardiner (Oxford, 1984), 177–87; D.V. Clarke et al.: *Symbols of power at the time of Stonehenge* (Edinburgh, 1985), 71–80.

RJA

Stone to Metal Age (SMA) *see* AFRICA 5.3

strain *see* MULTIDIMENSIONAL SCALING (MDSCAL)

Strathalan Cave B Stone Age cave-site situated at 1340 m above sea level in the eastern Cape foothills of the Drakensberg Mountains, South Africa. It was occupied just prior to the Last Glacial Maximum (at around 23,000 uncal BP) and just prior to an environmental shift to colder and drier conditions. Stone artefacts are of MSA (Middle Stone Age) technology with an important flake-blade component. The site is remarkable for well-preserved grass and food-plant remains in patches on three sides of a large elongate hearth. Food remains include geophytes, and these and the general patterning of the occupation are strongly reminiscent of LSA (Late Stone Age) sites in the Holocene.

H. Opperman and B. Heydenrych: 'A 22,000 year-old Middle Stone Age camp site with plant food remains from the north-eastern Cape', *SAAB* 45 (1990), 93–9.

RI

Strettweg Earlier Iron Age (i.e. HALLSTATT period) barrow near Graz in Austria which in 1851 yielded a remarkable model 'cult wagon' in bronze. Other grave goods, which include a large bronze urn and iron spear-heads, suggest that the barrow was constructed in the first half of the 6th century BC, but the wagon may be a century or so older. The four-wheeled wagon (48 × 32.5 cm; ht. 22.6 cm) has an open-work platform pierced with a wheel design, on top of which is the giant figure of a nude but belted woman wearing ear-rings who supports a large shallow basin on her head. On the wagon in front of this figure is a tableaux of smaller figures, in which a woman with ear-rings and man with an axe, flanked by two horsemen wearing pointed helmets, stand behind two further attendants who lead a deer by its antlers; the same tableaux is repeated behind the giant figure. The wagon is usually interpreted as depicting a religious procession, and may itself have been used as part of the associated rituals. The style of the figures seems to be related to that of the Greek GEOMETRIC bronzes.

W. Modrijan: *Der Kultwagen von Strettweg* (1977), 91ff; W. Kramer: 'Strettweg', *Trésors des princes celtes*, ed. J.-P. Mohen et al., exh. cat. (Paris, 1987), 60–1.

RJA

strip method, stripping *see* OPEN-AREA EXCAVATION

Stroke-ornamented ware (*Stichbandkeramik*) Early to Middle Neolithic ceramic tradition in central Europe (Bohemia, south and central Germany, western Poland), characterized by rounded and pear-shaped vessels ornamented with short strokes/stabs or indentations within defined zones. The style dates to the early 5th millennium BC and is a successor to the LINEARBANDKERAMIK (LBK) culture, the first farming culture of much of temparate Europe, which by contrast produced pottery decorated with continuous lines. In stroke-ornamented ware, the strokes are typically used to form either horizontal borders, between which zigzag patterns run, or repeated bands of triangular motifs. The settlement pattern and architecture is quite similar to the LBK (some of the longhouses take on a more trapezoidal shape), and the little evidence available suggests the economy and burial rites (Zápatocká 1981) remained fundamentally the same. The lithic technology is a development of LBK technology, and includes shafthole adzes and hammer-axes.

M. Zápatocká: 'Bi-ritual cemetery of the Stroked-pottery culture at Miskovice, district of Kutna Hora', *Nouvelles archéologiques dans la république socialiste tchèque*, ed. J. Hrala (Prague, 1981), 26–31.

RJA

Stroked-pottery culture Iron Age culture which spread over central and northern Belarus and southeast Lithuania from about the 7th to the 1st century BC, with a ceramic tradition characterized by flat-bottomed pots decorated using strokes. Settlements, usually located on top of morainic hills or on high river terraces, were at first unfortified, but from the 4th and 3rd centuries BC tended to be enclosed within turf walls and timber fences. Still later, in the 3rd–1st centuries BC, the fortifications were elaborated to include outer ramparts and one or several inner walls. Within the walls, in flattened areas, were longhouses (20–25 sq. m) built of wooden posts and consisting of several square rooms.

The central area of the forts was reserved for animal corrals and workshops. Numerous storage pits contained pottery, slag, animal bones and charred grains. Domesticates comprise 55–56% of the faunal remains (cattle, followed by pig, horse and sheep/goat); wild animals included boar, elk, red deer and brown bear. Finds of loom weights indicate the importance of weaving (wool, flax). Crops included Italian millet, wheats, pulses and lentils; stone querns are common finds at the sites. Iron implements were numerous, and included sickles, axes, arrow- and spearheads, daggers, awls, needles and fishhooks; ornaments such as iron pins, bronze brooches, plaques, rings and bracelets are also known. At a number of sites, blacksmith's shops have been recognised from the presence of furnaces, lumps of smelted iron and blacksmith's instruments such as hammers, anvils and tongs; local bog-ores were the main source of iron. However, some metal objects (e.g. brooches) are of Scandinavian origin, while various goods from the later periods reveal contacts with the LA TÈNE sites in Central Europe and with Greek colonies on the Black Sea.

V.F. Isaenko et al.: *Očerki po arheologii Belorussii* [Essays on the Archaeology of Belarus] (Minsk, 1970); A.G. Mitrofanov: *Železnyi vek srednei Belorussii, VII–VI vv.do n.e.–VI v.n.e.* [The Iron Age of central Belarus, 7th–6th centuries BC – 6th century AD] (Minsk, 1978).

PD

structural history *see* ANNALES

structuralism Structuralism is an approach to complex products of human culture such as language, literature, myth and decoration, that seeks to explain their superficial form by identifying and analysing more fundamental underlying structures and structural relationships. During the 1950s and 1960s, structuralism became a leading method of enquiry in linguistics, literature, sociology and anthropology – and influenced many other fields. Its effect on archaeology, in the sense of explicitly structuralist analyses of archaeological material, has been quite limited and lies mainly in the field of prehistoric art, decoration, and analysis of the design of monuments and settlements (see below). In part, this may be because structuralism evolved as a science of the spoken and written word: neither of these rich sets of data is accessible in prehistoric archaeology. However, the concepts, language and assumptions of structuralist approaches in linguistics and anthropology have had a pervasive effect on the discipline, and both structuralist and POST-STRUCTURALIST approaches (the reaction against, and development of, structuralist thought) have heavily influenced CONTEXTUAL ARCHAEOLOGY and other recent theoretical approaches to archaeology.

Structuralism – unlike, for example, MARXISM – is really a label given to a number of similar approaches rather than the name of a closely defined theoretical or academic programme. Most authorities agree, however, that the structuralist approach originated in the work of the founder of modern linguistics, Ferdinand de Saussure (1857–1913). In his teachings (published posthumously as *The course in general linguistics*), Saussure identified an underlying structure in language that can be summarized as 'a system of differences'. In Saussure's structural linguistics, the important analysis was no longer the history of, and relationships between, individual alphabets, or syllables, or words, or grammars. Instead, he focused on how these ways of communicating gained meaning through the systems of contrast embedded within them. In describing his thoughts about language structure, Saussure himself often paired up key concepts. For example, he talked about the 'synchronic' study of language (the study of language at one moment in time) and the less fundamental 'diachronic' study of change in language through time. Another of Saussure's dual concepts identified the *significant* or signifier (i.e. the thing that signifies, which in language may be a particular sound) and the *signifié* or the signified (the original concept in the mind of the speaker; for further discussion see SIGN AND SYMBOL). Together, the signifier and the signified comprise a sign which – usually by convention alone, rather than any essential link – relates to a referent or object in the outside world. The study of the nature and use of signs developed into a sub-discipline from the late 1950s, known as semiotics.

Fundamental to Saussure's idea of language as a system are the *syntagmatic* and asociative (or *paradigmatic*) – concepts which describe the relationship between words. For example, in the sentence 'I will dig now', the relationship between 'I' 'will' 'dig' and 'now' in building up the meaning of the sentence is syntagmatic. By contrast, if we relate this sentence to another sentence, 'You must think first', the relationship between the 'I' and the 'You' in both sentences is paradigmatic, as is the relationship between each of the other words ('now' and 'first' etc.). Using these and other concepts, all centred on the belief that elements within language only gain meaning through their relationship with other elements, Saussure founded the modern conception of language as a complex interdependent system. Indeed, structuralism has some similarities to SYSTEMS THEORY as an approach to understanding complex cultural constructs.

Saussure's approach was hugely elaborated in succeeding decades, notably by Leonard Bloomfield, who developed a range of techniques for objectively analysing sentence structure. From the late 1950s, this developed structuralist approach was challenged by the work of Noam Chomsky who, while working from Saussurian structuralist principles, developed the idea of a 'surface' and a 'deep' grammatical structure. According to Chomsky, whose approach is often labelled as the 'transformational grammar' approach, language is governed by generative grammar. At the heart of Chomsky's work is an attempt to discover the universal rules that govern the production of structure in all human languages, and which must be related to the fundamental nature of the human mind. The investigation of universal laws of cognition within the field of prehistory forms one strand of COGNITIVE ARCHAEOLOGY.

The ideas developed in linguistics profoundly influenced the way researchers in other fields approached complex cultural products. For archaeologists, one of the most influential conduits was the work of the French anthropologist Claude Lévi-Strauss, who took the fundamental idea of a hidden structure beneath a cultural construct dependent for its form on contrasts, and used this approach to explore the ways that, for example, myths, eating habits and etiquette, and kinship structures are generated. In Lévi-Strauss's work, the idea that meaning is constructed through using contrasting units – or 'binary opposition' – was elaborated. For example, in *Mythologiques* he described how myth is formed from, and acts as a continuing expression of, sequences of fundamental oppositions (such as death/creation, nature/culture, maternal/paternal). Although the myth narrative sometimes acts to explain (and justify) particular social structures, the emphasis in *Mythologiques* is on the universal structures of meaning behind myth and – by extension – human cognition. Even so, in relating structure to social relations and to symbolic power, Lévi-Strauss created a less formalistic, more subjective form of structuralist analysis.

The most notable early attempt to use this new strand in structuralist analysis to interpret prehistoric material was the work of André Leroi-Gourhan (e.g., 1965, 1982) whose approach relates closely to Lévi-Strauss. Leroi-Gourhan used structural concepts to examine and interpret the spatial arrangement and use of symbols in the CAVE ART of prehistoric Europe. The different animal species were accorded specific roles in a complex system of sexual symbolism, and the location in the caves of the individual works and the frequency of associations between the different animals were used to form hypotheses about the function of cave art and the nature of Palaeolithic society. The tenuous arguments justifying this complex symbolic system, and the difficulty of treating the works in any one cave as a consistently related and contemporary corpus of art, were brushed over by Leroi-Gourhan; instead, he offered detailed analyses of cave topography and statistical treatments. Leroi-Gourhan's work, though immensely influential, was never entirely accepted by prehistorians – especially outside France.

Of later attempts, the work of Washburn (e.g., 1983) stands out as a concerted attempt to use structural analysis as a tool for interpreting archaeological material. Unlike Leroi-Gourhan's work, Washburn's formal structural analysis of pottery decoration remains quite close in approach to structural linguistics. That is, it tried to discover the rules (of symmetry etc) that lay behind complex pottery designs, rather than leaping from structure to underlying social meaning and complex communication. Washburn's methodology involved close analysis of the way decoration was structured from the smallest assymetrical unit of design upwards. This kind of analysis can to some extent be tested: the rules it claims to identify governing decorative structure can be compared to new samples of pottery, and to pottery from unrelated cultures, to see if they remain useful.

The approach also seems to offer a detailed and objective way of describing and comparing decorative traditions. If decorative traditions were closely related to other aspects of culture, the structural analysis of pottery decoration seemed also to offer an objective way of measuring the cultural closeness and 'relatedness' of different groups. The degree to which this kind of analysis is truly 'objective' has been questioned by Ian Hodder (1986: 39–40), who argues that even in defining the decoration that is to be the subject of analysis a level of interpretation, or subjectivity, is unavoidable. However, it certainly offers a more testable approach than analysis of decoration relying on subjective evaluation of the similarities of style or motif.

The main difficulty with this kind of carefully conducted FORMAL ANALYSIS lies in connecting the results to the questions that most prehistorians actually want to ask. Most prehistorians want to know how, and to what extent, any structural similarities in pottery decoration in a given culture are related to other aspects of cultural production and self-conscious ethnic identity, and can thus be taken as reliable material culture indicators of more ephemeral human activities and relationships. Most also want to know whether formal analyses can provide clues to 'deeper' social realities, of a kind attempted prematurely by Leroi-Gourhan.

A well-trodden route to applying structuralist analytical tools to archaeological analysis is to identify a series of inter-linked binary oppositions in a set of material culture and to use these to 'explain' some social dynamic within the culture under examination. Hodder (1982) provides ethnographic examples, Jameson (1987) an historical material culture example, and Shanks and Tilley (1987: 155–71) an archaeological example. This kind of analysis can be revealing in terms of identifying patterns within the material culture record, but it is difficult to verify the links between symbolic communications in different areas of material culture, and even more difficult to relate these securely to behavioural and social dynamics. The challenge of establishing such sound links is in some ways similar to establishing valid ETHNOGRAPHIC ANALOGIES. It is often dependent upon a tenacious web of similarities across different facets of culture that are not easily accessible to the archaeologist, and the process can quickly lead to circular arguments. It may be better in many circumstances to recognize that a structuralist hypothesis is simply suggestive and interesting, or to use it to bolster or elaborate evidence gained from other approaches.

N. Chomsky: *Syntactic structures* (The Hague, 1957); C. Lévi-Strauss: *Mythologiques* (Paris, 1964–72); A. Leroi-Gourhan: *Préhistoire de l'art occidental* (Paris 1965); C. Lévi-Strauss: *Structural anthropology* (London, 1968); F. de Saussure: *Course in general linguistics* (London 1978); A. Leroi-Gourhan: *The dawn of European art* (Cambridge, 1982); I. Hodder: *Symbols in action* (Cambridge, 1982); ——, ed.: *Symbolic and structural archaeology* (Cambridge, 1982); D. Washburn: *Structure and cognition in art* (Cambridge 1983); I. Hodder: 'Burials, houses, women and men in the European Neolithic', *Ideology, power and prehistory*, ed. D. Miller and C. Tilley (Cambridge, 1984); ——: 'Structuralist archaeology', *Reading the past* (Cambridge, 1987), 34–54; R. Jameson: 'Purity and power

at the Victorian dinner party', *The archaeology of contextual meanings*, ed. I. Hodder (Cambridge 1987), 55–66; M. Shanks and C. Tilley: *Re-Constructing archaeology* (Cambridge, 1987); I. Hodder: *Theory and practice in archaeology* (London 1992), 24–80.
RJA

stupa Stone-faced cylindrical Buddhist structure with a hemispherical dome enclosing earthen and rubble fill and a relic casket. *Stupas* were constructed to enshrine the cremated remains of Buddha and his disciples as well as Mahavira, the founder of the JAIN faith, gradually coming to symbolize the teachings of these two indigenous Indian religious traditions. The earliest surviving *stupas* date to the reign of the MAURYAN emperor Asoka (273–232 BC). Worship involves the circumnambulation of the monument, and a paved path typically encircles the structure.
D. Mitra: *Buddhist monuments* (Calcutta, 1971), 21–30; G.A. Michell: *The Penguin guide to the monuments of India* (Harmondsworth, 1989), 64–6.
CS

Suberde *see* ACERAMIC NEOLITHIC

Sugizawadai Large Early JOMON settlement in Akita prefecture, Japan (*c.*5000–3500 BC). A central plaza contained four large buildings, the largest of which was over 220 sq. m in area – one of the largest Jomon buildings yet discovered. The largest building had six hearths aligned along the central axis and had been rebuilt three times; 40 smaller buildings and 100 storage pits were located around the edge of the plaza. The function of these large buildings remains contentious, possibly being community gathering places or workplaces for winter tasks in the snowy region.
Akita Prefectural Board of Education: *Sugizawadai and Takei sites* (Akita, 1981).
SK

Sui-chou-shih (Suizhoushi) *see* TSENG HOU YI TOMB

Suizhoushi (Sui-chou-shih) *see* TSENG HOU YI TOMB

Sultan, Tell es- *see* JERICHO

Sumbar River in the Kopet-Dag Mountains of southern Turkmenistan, a tributary of the Atrek river, in the valley of which were located several Iron Age settlements and famous Bronze Age cemeteries. The Iron Age sites (the 'archaic Dakhistan') were excavated by V.M. Masson and others in the 1940s and 1950s. The sites range in age between 1500 BC and AD 700, and include four-cornered citadels, 'manors' and separate houses, as well as complicated irrigation works in the presently desertified region of western Turkmenistan.

Later, in the late 1960s to early 1990s, a group of Bronze Age cemeteries and settlements were found in the middle stretches of Sumbar, near the town of Kara-Qala, and studied by I.N. Khlopin. Khlopin believes that the cemeteries of Parkhai I, and Sumbar I–III belong to the Late Bronze Age, and are equivalent to the periods Namazga V–VI (see NAMAZGA, roughly 2500–1800 BC). They consist of catacomb graves with a horizontal or a vertical entrance; the dead were buried in a contracted posture. The grave goods include a grey ware, bronze arrowheads and spearheads, knives, awls, rings as well as stone mace-heads in (presumed) elite graves. The grey ware is similar to that known in northern Iran (e.g., SIALK, TEPE), however Khlopin convincingly argues for the continuity of a local tradition known as the 'Sumbar culture'; the appearance of 'grey ware' is therefore simply a technological innovation in pottery-making and does not imply a cultural relationship.
I.N. Khlopin: *Jugo-zapadnaja Turkmenija v epohu pozdnei bronzy* (Leningrad, 1983).
PD

Sumer, Sumerian The word 'Sumer' is used in early CUNEIFORM texts to describe the geographical region of southern Iraq, however the term is also applied by archaeologists to the earliest civilization in this region of Mesopotamia, the formative phase of which was the UBAID period (*c.*5000–3800 BC). An ethnic distinction is usually made between the Semites in central Mesopotamia and the Sumerians further to the south, although in fact the material culture and social systems of these two groups are virtually identical, the only real differences being linguistic. Georges Roux therefore argues that '*Stricto sensu*, the appelation 'Sumerians' should be taken as meaning 'Sumerian-speaking people' and nothing else . . . This incidentally explains why all efforts to define and to assess the relations between Sumerians and Semites in other fields than philology are doomed to failure.' (Roux 1992: 81).

It seems likely that the Sumerian population actually included both Sumerian and Semitic

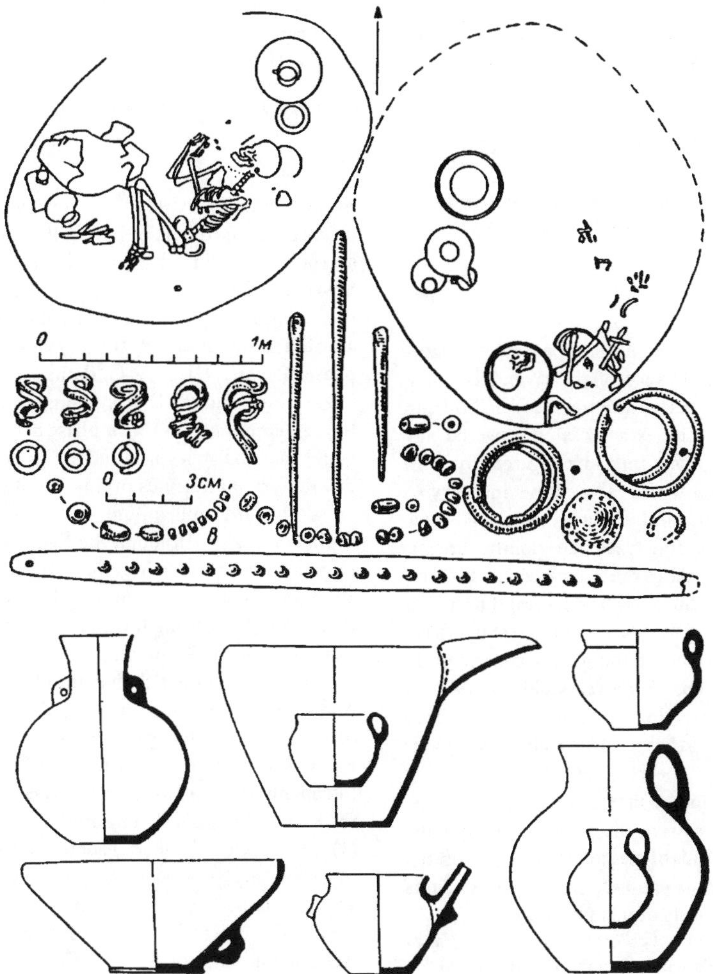

Figure 51 **Sumbar** Grave goods from the Sumbar cemetery. *Source*: I.N. Khlopin: *Jugo-zapadnaja Turkmenija v epohu pozdnei bronzy* (Leningrad, 1983).

linguistic/ethnic elements, although all may have shared the same Sumerian material culture, thus making them difficult to distinguish in archaeological terms – this quandary is usually described as the 'Sumerian problem'. As Harriet Crawford (1991: 20) points out, 'It is not possible to tell how much of this culture should be attributed to the Sumerian speakers and how much to those speaking a Semitic language, but the question hardly matters as it seems to have been the fusion of all the elements in the population which produced the distinctive [Sumerian] civilization . . .'. It is clear, however, that the term Sumerian can be comfortably applied, in a general sense, to the culture that dominated Mesopotamia for two millennia, from the Uruk period to the end of the Early Dynastic phase (*c*.3800–2010 BC). During the 3rd millennium BC the great Sumerian cities, such as UR, ERIDU, KISH and NIPPUR, flourished in the region between the Tigris and Euphrates.

S.N. Kramer: *The Sumerians* (Chicago, 1963); T. Jones, ed.: *The Sumerian problem* (New York, 1969); F.R. Kraus: *Sumerer und Akkader* (Amsterdam, 1970); J. Oates: *Babylon*, 2nd edn (London, 1986), 19–23; H. Crawford: *Sumer and the Sumerians* (Cambridge, 1991); N. Postgate: *Early Mesopotamia: society and economy at the dawn of history* (London, 1992); G. Roux: *Ancient Iraq*, 3rd edn (Harmondsworth, 1992), 80–4 [including discussion of the so-called Sumerian Problem].

IS

Sunagawa Late Palaeolithic site in Saitama prefecture, Japan. Two locations, each containing three artefact units and one burned cobble cluster, were discovered some 10 m apart. The site was one of the first where extensive refitting of lithics was achieved, the results suggesting occupation by at least two small bands.

T. Inada: 'The Palaeolithic age', *Recent archaeological discoveries in Japan*, ed. K. Tsuboi (Paris and Tokyo, 1987), 5–23.

SK

Sunghir Upper Palaeolithic open-air site situated on the upper terrace of the river Klyaz'ma, several kilometres east of the town of Vladimir, in central Russia. The site was discovered by O.N. Bader in 1955 and investigated by him between 1956 and 1975. The stone industry is Upper Palaeolithic and includes Kostenki-style shouldered knives and Szeletian points; uncalibrated radiocarbon dates range between 26,000 and 20,000 years BP. Since 1964, several burials of ANATOMICALLY MODERN HUMANS (AMH) have been discovered. One of the graves contained an AMH male skeleton, 55–65 years old, interred on his back in an extended posture, with the head directed to the northeast. The rich grave-goods include two large spears (1.66 and 2.24 m) of straightened mammoth task, spearheads, javelins, and knives. There were also various ornaments: 3500 perforated beads of mammoth tusk; perforated pendants of polar fox canines; perforated pendants of schist; and bracelets of mammoth tusk.

O.N. Bader: *Sungir: Verhnepaleolitičeskaja stojanka* [Sungir: an Upper Palaeolithic site], (Moscow, 1978).

PD

Su Nuraxi *see* BARUMINI

superstructure *see* MARXIST ARCHAEOLOGY

Sur Jangal Small prehistoric village of the 4th and 3rd millennia BC, located in the Baghnao Valley of northern Baluchistan, Pakistan. The remains of mud-brick architecture and domesticated cattle were found throughout the three phases of occupation. Artefacts include painted ceramics, with a variety of geometric and naturalistic designs, including humped cattle motifs, as well as flint and ground stone tools, clay bangles and large numbers of female terracotta figurines. The material culture at Sur Jangal shows similarities to several contemporary Baluchistan sites, such as Kechi Beg, DAMB SADAAT and Kili Ghul Muhammad (*see* QUETTA).

A. Stein: 'An archaeological tour in Waziristan and Northern Baluchistan', *MASI* 37 (1929); W.A. Fairservis: 'Archaeological surveys in the Zhob and Loralai District, West Pakistan', *APAMNH* 47 (1959), 277–448

CS

Susa (Shush) City in southwestern Iran originating in the late 5th millennium BC; the surrounding alluvial plains became known as Susiana and the earliest phases of urbanization in the region are expressed in terms of the stratigraphy at Susa, consisting of three major post-UBAID phases (Susa I–III or A–C) dating to the 4th millennium BC. Susa I–II was strongly influenced by the contemporaneous URUK phase in Mesopotamia, while Susa III was characterized by a much more distinctively indigenous proto-Elamite culture.

By the 3rd millennium BC Susa became the capital of ELAM. Although the Elamite rulers were initially subject to the hegemony of the AKKADIAN and UR III rulers, they eventually became a power in their own right during the 2nd millennium BC, and many plundered Mesopotamian objects (including the Law Code of the Babylonian ruler Hammurabi) have been excavated from the palace buildings at Suva. The archaeological remains of Susa, first excavated by William Loftus in 1851–3, comprise four main areas, of which the earliest is the site of the Elamite 'acropolis'. The other three mounds are (1) the palace of the Achaemenid ruler Darius, incorporating an APADANA (palace reception hall) and a columned hall, (2) the 'royal city', and (3) the 'city of the artisans' which consists mainly of post-Achaemenid housing.

A. Le Breton: 'Susa, the early periods', *Iraq* 19 (1957), 79–124; M.J. Stève and H. *Gasche: L'acropole de Suse: nouvelles fouilles* (Leiden and Paris, 1971); E. Carter: 'The Susa sequence 3000–2000 BC', *AJA* 83 (1979), 451–4; F. Vallat: *Suse et l'Elam, études élamites* (Paris, 1980); P.O. Harpur, J. Aruz and F. Tallon, eds: *The royal city of Susa* (New York, 1992).

IS

Sutkagen Dor Small fortified settlement of the INDUS CIVILIZATION located on sandstone ridges near the Makran coast, western Pakistan. The westernmost Harappan site in Pakistan, it was excavated by Auriel Stein in 1931 and George Dales in 1962. The site was enclosed within a massive stone and earth wall, with its main entrance flanked by two towers. Dales identified three phases of occupation and a bipartite spatial division of the site into 'citadel' and 'lower town' areas. Material remains from Sutkagen Dor are exclusively

Harappan, with no affinities to contemporary SHAHI TUMP or KULLI COMPLEX traditions of the Makran region (Besenval 1992: 27). Because of its location, the site is often interpreted as a Harappan port, the occupants of which were engaged in maritime trade, although direct evidence for such activities (e.g. seals, sealings or trade goods) has not been found (Ratnagar 1981: 48–51).

G.F. Dales: 'Harappan outposts in the Makran Coast', *Antiquity* 36 (1962), 86–92; S. Ratnagar: *Encounters: the westerly trade of the Harappa Civilization* (New Delhi, 1981), 48–51; R. Besenval: 'Recent archaeological surveys in Pakistani Makran', *South Asian archaeology, 1989*, ed. C. Jarrige (Madison, 1992), 25–35.

CS

Sutton Hoo The cemetery of burial mounds at Sutton Hoo (Suffolk) is presently the most systematically investigated funerary monument of the MIGRATION PERIOD. An early 7th century boat-burial with an extraordinarily rich array of grave goods was excavated in 1939. In 1983–92, Martin Carver led a new programme of investigations including a rigorous evaluation of the previous excavations and a modern field strategy, involving the use of SAMPLES: the cemetery was sampled by means of the excavation of two wide, intersecting transects. The results revealed not only the character of other burial mounds, but the existence of a cemetery of 'sand-men', poorly preserved burials of individuals associated with the mound graves. As a result, Carver was able to trace the complex evolution of the 6th- to 8th-century burial ground of the Wuffingas family.

Martin Carver, ed.: *The age of Sutton Hoo* (Woodbridge, 1992).

RH

Šventoji Group of 42 Neolithic sites, situated in the coastal peat-bog of Pajuris, in the mouth of the Šventoji river in Lithuania – formerly a lagoon of the Baltic Sea. The sites were discovered and excavated in the 1970s by R. Rimantiene. The earlier sites, dated by radiocarbon to calendar years 3500–2600 BC, belong to the local variant of the later phase of the NARVA tradition. The later sites belong to the so-called 'coastal tradition' of the CORDED WARE culture. The economy of the Narva-related sites was based mostly on hunting, fishing and food-collecting. The occupants of the 'coastal tradition' sites relied predominantly on seal hunting, and six nets made of lime bast thread were discovered at Site 2B. The bones of cattle and sheep/goat were also found in limited numbers.

R. Rimantiene: *Šventoji I/II*, 2 vols (Vilnius, 1979–1980).

PD

Swahili harbour towns Settlements of the Swahili-speaking East African maritime civilization of the 9th–19th centuries AD, centred on the coasts of Tanzania and Kenya, and involved in trade with the lands around the Indian Ocean. Swahili is a Bantu language spoken on the coast and islands of Tanzania and Kenya, as well as in some areas to the south (Comores, Mozambique and northern Madagascar) and north (the southern Somali coast). Notable sites include Bur Gavo, GEDI, Kilwa, Manda, Mombasa and SHANGA, as well as the islands of ZANZIBAR and Pemba. There is no thorough description of Bur Gavo, the northernmost of the harbour towns, but Neville Chittick, who visited briefly in 1968, left valuable notes on, inter alia, a walled enclosure, a curious domed building and various tombs, some with pillars.

In the 9th and 10th centuries the focus of Swahili commerce was with the Persian Gulf and the Islamic heartlands of the Abbasid empire. Later, however, the overseas contacts – not only commercial but also cultural and Islamic – diversified,

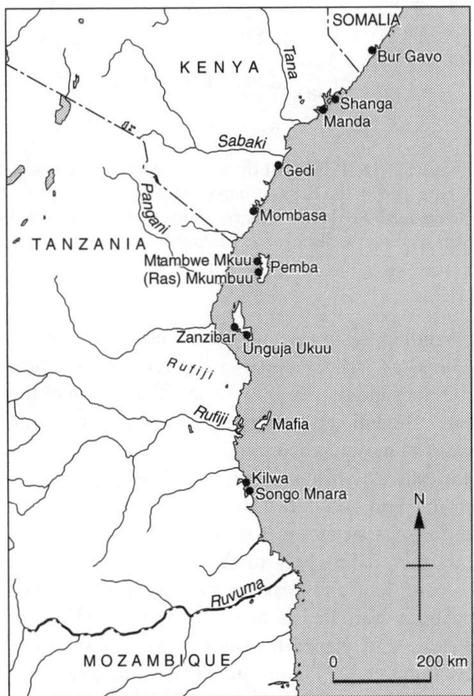

Map 29 **Swahili harbour towns** The locations of the Swahili harbour towns.

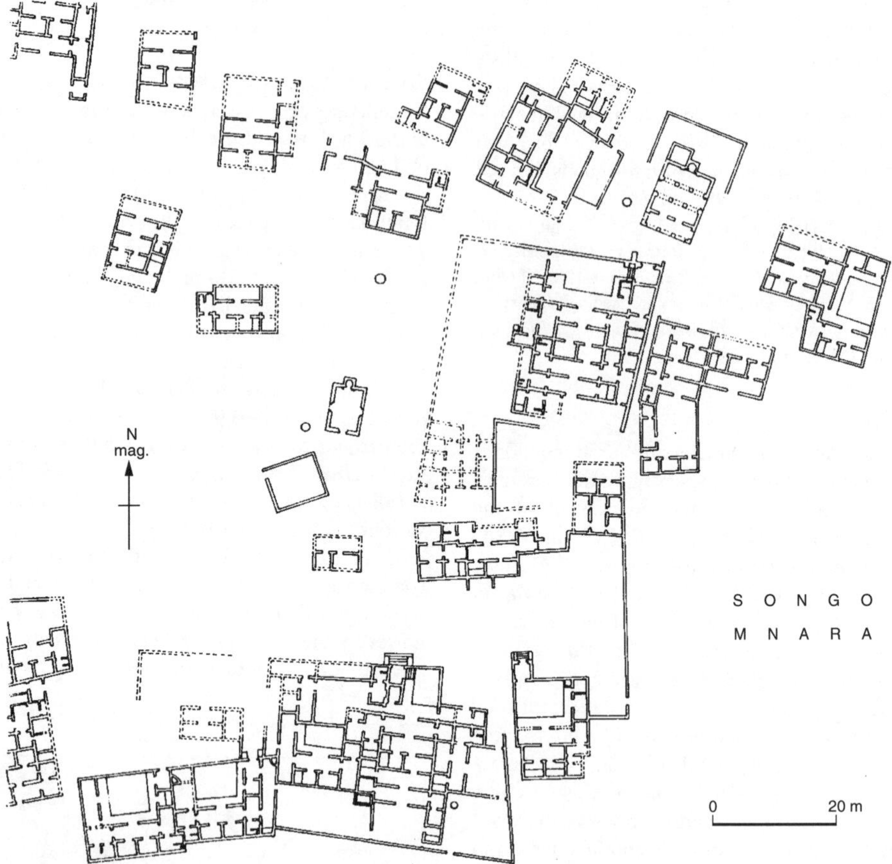

Figure 52 **Swahili harbour towns** Stone buildings of the 14th- and 15th-century Swahili harbour town of Songo Mnara, part of the Kilwa group complex. The mosques can be identified by their *mihrâb* projections in the *qibla* wall facing north to Mecca; the larger houses on the plan can be seen to contain interior courtyards; the small circles on the plan represent wells. *Source*: J.E.G. Sutton: *A thousand years of East Africa* (BIEA, 1990).

extending eastwards to India and indirectly to China, as well as northwards, via the Red Sea, to Egypt and the Mediterranean. The wealth of the early Swahili settlements is reflected in the stone ruins of mosques and tombs as well as rich houses and palaces. Most of the stone architecture belongs to the 14th and 15th centuries, although the tradition of stone mosques is much older. The earliest mosques, dating back to about AD 800 at Shanga, were of wood and earth construction with thatched roofs, as were houses generally. On the islands of Pemba and Zanzibar, there were several early Swahili sites. Those on Pemba included Ras Mkumbuu (probably the 'Qanbalu' documented in 9th- and 10th-century Arab writings) and Mtambe Mkuu (where a hoard of locally minted 11th-century silver coins was discovered). Those on Zanzibar included the early 9th-century site of Unguja Ukuu ('old' or 'great Zanzibar'), with plentiful 'SASANIAN-Islamic' pottery. The 13th-century remains on Tumbatu, a separate islet off the north end of Zanzibar, have yielded a connection with Yemen, perhaps foreshadowing the architectural feats of Kilwa (to the south) in the early 14th century AD.

Until the 15th century the larger Swahili harbour towns of the coast and islands thrived on the sale of African products, notably ivory and gold from Zimbabwe, to the wider world. There is a good chronological correspondence between Kilwa, the most southerly of the Swahili sultanates, and GREAT ZIMBABWE in the gold-producing zone, and there are indications of specific commercial connections between them in the 14th century, although culturally and architecturally the two sites seem unrelated.

The site of Kilwa, situated on an island in a sunken estuary of the southern Tanzanian coast, was excavated in the 1960s by Neville Chittick (1974). With its lowest levels dating to the early 9th century AD – as at SHANGA and Manda in the north, Mkumbu on Pemba and Unguja Ukuu on Zanzibar – it rose to prominence in the 11th century when a sultanate was established, copper coinage minted and the first stone mosque built. The domed, arched and barrel-vaulted extension to Kilwa's Great Mosque, as well as the magnificent palace and trade emporium called Husuni Kubwa, date to that period. There followed a severe slump during which Husuni Kubwa was abandoned and much of the Great Mosque collapsed. Early in the 15th century the trade of gold and other items revived, and Kilwa with it; it is to this period that most of the stone domestic architecture of Kilwa town (and the adjacent island of Songo Mnara) belongs.

Mombasa overtook Kilwa in the 15th century to become the biggest such settlement on the East African coast. Together with its fine harbour, in the creek between Mombasa island and the mainland, Mombasa's central position on the coast gave it an advantage, especially for the bulk commerce with India. Because of the continued occupation and growth of the town till the present, nothing is visible of the pre-1500 period and little systematic archaeological investigation has been attempted. The most impressive monument at Mombasa is Fort Jesus, which was built in the 1590s by the Portuguese (employing an Italian military architect) to command the harbour approach and to serve as their headquarters on the Swahili coast.

Following Vasco da Gama's voyage of 1498–9 and the Portuguese invasion of the Indian Ocean from the south, the commerce and wealth of the Swahili coast declined sharply (see PORTUGUESE TRADING FEIRAS). After the ending of Portuguese control there was a revival in the late 18th century, fuelled by renewed international demands, for ivory and slaves especially. This is illustrated at several sites by renewed stone buildings, which included forts.

J.S. Kirkman: *Men and monuments on the East African coast* (London, 1964); P.S. Garlake: *The early Islamic architecture of the East African coast* (Nairobi and London, 1966); H.N. Chittick: 'An archaeological reconnaissance of the southern Somali coast', *Azania* 4 (1969), 125–30; ——: *Kilwa: an Islamic trading city on the East African coast* (Nairobi, 1974); J.S. Kirkman: *Fort Jesus*, BIEA 4 (Oxford, 1974); H.N. Chittick: *Manda: excavations at an island port on the Kenya coast* (Nairobi, 1984); M.C. Horton, H. Brown and W.A. Oddy: 'The Mtambwe hoard', *Azania* 21 (1986), 115–23; M.C. Horton: 'Early Muslim trading settlements on the East African coast: new evidence from Shanga', AJ 67 (1987), 290–323; J.E.G. Sutton: *A thousand years of East Africa* (Nairobi, 1990), 57–88.

JS

Swartkrans Ancient fissure with breccias of various ages, close to Krugersdorp, Transvaal, South Africa. Four stratigraphic Members are identified and dated on the basis of contained fossils. Member 1, rich in *Australopithecus robustus* specimens, is around 1.6–1.8 million years old and contains bone 'digging-tools' in the upper part (*see* AUSTRALOPITHECUS). Member 2 (>1.0 my, <1.6 my) contains *A. robustus* and *Homo* (sp.indet.), a few stone artefacts of ACHEULEAN aspect, bone tools, and abundant mammal bones, many with cutmarks and some showing signs of burning.

C.K. Brain: *The hunters or the hunted?: an introduction to African cave taphonomy* (Chicago, 1981); ——: 'New information from the Swartkrans cave of relevance to "Robust" australopithecines', *Evolutionary history of the "robust" australopithecines*, ed. F.E. Grine (New York, 1988), 311–16.

RI

Swasey-phase pottery *see* CUELLO

swidden agriculture Method of farming in which a swidden (strip of agricultural land) is obtained by cutting down, drying and burning the existing natural vegetation, thus clearing the area for cultivation. The system therefore includes the use of the 'slash-and-burn' technique (or *Brandwirtschaft*), whereby the ash from the wild vegetation can be employed as a fertilizer in the soil. The swidden land, however, can be cultivated successfully for only a few years, therefore farmers using this method are obliged to move on periodically to exploit new areas of land. The swidden system was used by many prehistoric groups, such as the people of Preclassic Mesoamerica (*see* LOWLAND MAYA) and some of the Neolithic inhabitants of central and northern Europe (although see LINEARBANDKERAMIK for a discussion of the possible limitations on the use of swidden agriculture in prehistoric Europe).

P. Bogucki: *Forest farmers and stockherders* (Cambridge, 1988).

IS

symbol *see* SIGN

symbolic archaeology Study of the use and importance of symbolism in material culture, and how this can be recognized and recovered from the archaeological record. Symbolic archaeology forms one of the most fruitful parts of a general movement in archaeology towards an 'archaeology of the mind' – and towards a more sophisticated understanding of how material culture was perceived and manipulated in ancient societies. In part a reaction against the more materialist and functionalist aspects of PROCESSUAL ARCHAEOLOGY, this general movement encompasses the work of Ian Hodder's CONTEXTUAL ARCHAEOLOGY, Colin Renfrew's COGNITIVE ARCHAEOLOGY (which he describes as developing out of processual archaeology, rather than contradicting it), and STRUCTURALISM, as well as an increasing volume of diverse individual studies.

In this still-developing field, four key areas of interest can be defined. Firstly, how do we define the terms sign and symbol and relate them to their social context? Ian Hodder (1987: 11–12) defines the symbol as 'an object or situation in which a direct, primary or literal meaning also designates another indirect, secondary and figurative meaning' and argues that 'symbols do not "reflect" but . . . play an active part in forming and giving meaning to social behaviour'. Most archaeologists in this area have turned to the key works in social anthropology, which in turn inherited many key concepts (see SIGN AND SYMBOL) from linguistic analysis. However, a key confusion in social anthropology over the question of whether the signified and signifier of a symbol are truly arbitrary seemed likely to pose a particular problem when interpreting material culture. The more arbitrary the link, the more difficult the task of interpreting symbols in the archaeological record. Hodder (1992: 207) suggests that they are indeed arbitrary, but with an important qualification: 'Blood, for example, has qualities which constrain its symbolic meaning but a range of specific meanings (from danger and death to the source of life) can be given . . . The ideological implications of this duality are that the meanings of objects, while imposed by convention, appear based on necessity'. In other words, the particular meaning of symbols arises out of social convention (i.e. is arbitrary in the sense that the signified is not linked to the signifier by any existential or representational link), but symbols often gain power and a sense of inevitability from innate references to the wider world.

Secondly, and given this, how can archaeologists define and recognise the conventional meaning of individual symbols in material culture, without the help of the written records or living witnesses available to ethnographers and historians? A central problem here is the verification of any interpretation of a symbolic meaning. Simply testing our interpretation of symbols by seeking out further instances in the material culture record inevitably leads to charges of circularity and subjectivity.

Thirdly, and moving on from the problem of interpreting individual symbols, archaeologists have tried to understand the relationship between different signs and symbols, to identify underlying rules that govern the generation of symbolic and decorative patterning. This line of enquiry can be divided up into FORMAL ANALYSIS, where the meaning (content) of signs and symbols tends to take second place to their patterning, and structuralist analysis (see STRUCTURALISM), where in many analyses the meaning of symbols is both important and directly related to their structuration (e.g. Leroi-Gourhan's structuralist analysis of the symbolic meaning of CAVE ART).

Lastly, and perhaps most interestingly, there has been an increasing understanding of the ways in which symbols are actively manipulated by social players. Here, Marxist archaeologists have investigated how individuals use symbols as tools within a wider cultural ideology or world view – the 'social production of reality'. Aside from Marxist analyses, there has also been a strong tendency to stress the active role of the individual and of subordinate groups within society in manipulating and using symbols to promote their social ambitions. In part, these analyses (e.g. Hodder 1982a) have been used to warn against simplistic functionalist or materialist interpretations of material culture in the archaeological record. Symbols have come to be seen as powerful 'tools' for individual and group strategies as much as expressions of the NORMATIVE beliefs (shared world-views) of whole societies. While significantly complicating interpretation, such studies also hint at the potential richness of material culture studies in revealing the true complexity of social groups and their symbolic interactions.

M. Douglas: *Purity and danger* (London, 1966); V. Turner: The forest of symbols (London, 1967); ——: *The ritual process* (London, 1969); M. Douglas: *Natural symbols* (London, 1970); D. Sperber: *Rethinking symbolism* (Cambridge, 1974); I. Hodder: *Symbols in action: ethnoarchaeological studies of material culture* (Cambridge, 1982a); ——, ed.: *Symbolic and structural archaeology* (Cambridge, 1982b); ——: *The present past* (London,

1982c); A.C. Renfrew: *Towards an archaeology of mind* (Cambridge, 1982); I. Hodder: 'The contextual analysis of symbolic meanings', *The archaeology of contextual meanings*, ed. I. Hodder (Cambridge, 1987), 1–10; C. Tilley, ed.: *Reading material culture* (Oxford, 1990); I. Hodder: Material practice, symbolism and ideology, in *Theory and practice in archaeology* (London, 1992), 201–12; K.A. Hays: 'When is a symbol archaeologically meaningful? Meaning, function and prehistoric visual arts', *Archaeological theory: who sets the agenda?*, ed. N. Yoffee and A. Sherratt (Cambridge, 1993), 81–92.
RJA

Syria-Palestine Part of Western Asia bordering the Mediterranean, situated between Anatolia in the north, and the Arabian desert and Mesopotamia to the south and east. It comprises two basic topographical zones: a long coastal strip to the east, and an area of uplands to the west, the latter broken by a north–south geological fault incorporating the Sea of Galilee, the Dead Sea and the Wadi Arabah. For discussion of some of the ancient cultures and peoples, *see* AMORITES, ARAMAEANS, CANAANITES, ISRAEL, KEBARAN, NATUFIAN, PHILISTINES *and* PHOENICIANS. (See map 30.)

Kebaran period	18,000 – 11,000 BC
Natufian period	11,000 – 9300 BC
Pre-pottery Neolithic period A	9300 – 7000 BC
Pre-pottery Neolithic period B	7000 – 5500 BC
Pottery Neolithic A	5500 – 4500 BC
Pottery Neolithic B	4500 – 3500 BC
Ghassul-Beersheba culture	4200 – 3500 BC
Proto-urban period	3500 – 3100 BC
Early Bronze Age I	3100 – 2800 BC
Early Bronze Age II	2800 – 2600 BC
Early Bronze Age III & IV	2600 – 2180 BC
Middle Bronze Age I & II	2180 – 1550 BC
Late Bronze Age I	1550 – 1400 BC
Late Bronze Age II	1400 – 1200 BC
Late Bronze Age III	1200 – 1150 BC
Iron Age I	1150 – 1000 BC
Saul	1030 – 1000 BC
David	1000 – 960 BC
Solomon	960 – 931 BC
Rehoboam (King of Judah)	931 – 913 BC
Jeroboam I (King of Israel)	931 – 910 BC
Iron Age II	1000 – 587 BC
Neo-Babylonian Empire	587 – 538 BC
Achaemenid Empire	538 – 331 BC
Alexander the Great	332 – 323 BC
Ptolemaic Empire	323 – 198 BC
Seleucid Empire	198 – 142 BC
Hasmonean Dynasty	142 – 63 BC
Roman Empire	63 BC – AD 395
Herod the Great	40 – 4 BC
Pontius Pilate	AD 27 – 30
Herod Agrippa I	AD 40 – 44

Table 18 **Syria-Palestine** Chronology of Syria–Palestine.

Y. Aharoni: *The land of the Bible: a historical geography*, 2nd edn (Philadelphia, 1979); K.M. Kenyon: *Archaeology in the Holy Land*, 4th edn (London, 1979); M. Roaf: *Cultural atlas of Mesopotamia and the Ancient Near East* (New York and Oxford, 1990).

systems theory Approach to understanding complex phenomena by characterizing them as bounded 'systems' within which distinguishable interdependent elements (subsystems) or units interact to form the whole. In archaeological analysis, subsystems often include 'economy', 'politics', 'kinship' etc. The interactions are often characterized as information flows, set in motion by flows from the outside environment. In essence, systems theory attempts to facilitate the identification of systems, subsystems and system elements, as well as the nature and level of their information flows. It has been self-consciously used in archaeological explanation since the mid-1960s and the advent of PROCESSUAL ARCHAEOLOGY, notably in the writings of David Clarke (1968) and Kent Flannery (1968).

While systems theory, in its widest sense, developed in the natural sciences and especially in biology, the concepts and terms used to describe the nature of natural systems were adopted by the social sciences from an early date. The founder of modern sociology, Emile Durkheim, used the analogy of the bodily system to explain his essentially FUNCTIONALIST views of how society was organized and remained in equilibrium. (Poets and philosophers had employed the analogy in a less systematic manner since the dawn of history.) In later sociological writings, Herbert Spencer (1820–1903), who believed that society must learn to consciously control key social mechanisms, and Vilfredo Pareto (1848–1923), an Italian mathematical economist who helped to develop equilibrium theory (see below), developed and formalized the concept of a social 'system'. In the work of Talcott Parsons (1902–79), sociological systems theory was used to hugely elaborate a functionalist view of social institutions. Parsons' 'structural-functionalism' was based on the premise that systems functioned in various ways to achieve four things: adaptation to the physical environment; goal attainment; integration (i.e. social cohesion and orderliness); and latency (i.e. system stability). Parsons believed that four subsystems could be identified in society that accorded with these aims: the economic system, political system, community

Map 30 **Syria–Palestine** Major sites in ancient Syria–Palestine.

system, and the system of socialization (i.e. social education in its widest sense). Information flowed to and from the subsystems in the form of money, power, influence etc.

The details and over-elaborate nature of Parsons' scheme, hugely influential in the 1960s, are now largely set aside in anthropology and have only tentatively been applied in archaeology. However, there have been numerous attempts by archaeologists to use the basic concepts and language of systems theory to describe how they believe prehistoric societies may have been structured.

Key concepts in systems theory. The core concepts are information media and information flow: boundary maintenance; feedback; and equilibrium. Information media describe the form in which information flows through a system (e.g. money might be regarded as information within an economic system). Information flow describes the mechanisms of information storage, control and output. Boundary maintenance describes the mechanisms within systems that define the elements that comprise the system itself, and separate it off from other systems and its wider environment. Within social systems, for example, it is often claimed that system boundary concern is manifested in concentrated symbolic and ritual activity.

Feedback, a concept borrowed from the physical sciences, describes how the output of a system or subsystem continually feeds back into the system to control the level or character of subsequent output. Positive feedback leads to a continual increase in output, and thus to instability or change. For example, in an agricultural system in which the harvester gathers the most productive stands of cereal to preserve for next year's planting, each crop will contain successively more wheat with that beneficial characteristic – and this may happen quite *quickly* because of the nature of the system (i.e. grain is selected for planting). Colin Renfrew used a form of positive feedback which he called the 'multiplier effect' to explain the emergence of Aegean civilization: 'changes or innovations occurring in one field of human activity (in one subsystem of a culture) sometimes act so as to favour changes in other fields (in other subsystems). The multiplier effect is said to operate when these induced changes in one or more subsystems themselves act so as to enhance the original changes in the first subsystem' (Renfrew 1972; 37).

Negative feedback describes a subsystem relationship which tends to dampen down the effects of any change in system output and thus promote system stability. In the agricultural system described above, if harvesters had the habit of *consuming* the most productive stands of cereal then this might slow down the evolution of productive agricultural systems – and associated changes in other subsystems. Note that the harvesting actions in this example are essentially the same – it is the effect on the next cycle of the subsystem that determines whether the feedback is positive or negative, relatively strong or relatively weak.

In common speech, equilibrium is a term used to describe a state of balance. One of the more questionable (and tautological) assumptions of the elaborated form of systems theory in sociology was that all systems tended toward either a 'steady state' of equilibrium with regard to the environment in which they existed, or changed only according to an 'orderly process'. This assumption, implicit or explicit, is one of the principal weaknesses of the approach. It underlines the ahistorical character of many interpretations of social systems relying on systems theory. However, it is only really through the notion of equilibrium that systems theory appears to have explanatory and predictive power when applied to real-world situations. Without it, systems theory becomes (and is now often recognized as) a simplifying *descriptive* framework (see Shanks and Tilley 1987: 31–6, 138–43).

In more developed discussions of systems qualities, notions such as 'hypercoherence' can help us to understand complex system behaviour that would otherwise be difficult to grasp. Hypercoherence is simply the label given to a system that is both closely integrated and very delicately balanced: a crisis in one subsystem quickly leads to massive change or disruption in the other subsystems and the system as a whole. However, like other concepts in systems theory, it is largely helpful as a means of conceptualizing and making more *plausible* a sequence of interactions between social entities. Because interactions between social subsystems are not, and never will be, quantifiable, systems theory cannot itself offer *proof* of any argument in the social sciences. *See also* WORLD SYSTEMS THEORY.

D.L. Clarke: *Analytical archaeology* (London, 1968); K. Flannery: 'Archaeological systems theory and early Mesoamerica', *Anthropology and archaeology in the Americas*, ed. B. Meggers (Washington, D.C., 1968); J.E. Doran: 'Systems theory, computer simulations and archaeology', *WA* 1 (1970), 289–98; C. Renfrew: *The emergence of civilization: the Cyclades and the Aegean in the third millennium* BC (London, 1972); F. Plog: 'Systems theory in archaeological research', *ARA* 4 (1975), 207–24; C. Renfrew: *Approaches to social archaeology* (Edinburgh, 1984); B.G. Trigger: *A history of archaeological thought* (Cambridge, 1989), 303–12; M. Shanks and C. Tilley: *Social theory and archaeology* (Cambridge, 1987).

RJA

Szeletian Intermediate Middle to Upper Palaeolithic industry of Moravia and western Slovakia and northeast Hungary, named after the Szeleta Cave in the Bükk Mountains of Hungary. The Szeletian may have developed out of the Middle Palaeolithic Central European Micoquian, but it presents blades and core-preparation techniques of a distinctly Upper Palaeolithic type. As well as 'Middle Palaeolithic' side scrapers, the tools produced include end-scrapers and burins. The most striking artefacts are the finely made bifacial leaf-shaped points, which grew larger and more elongated as the Szeletian progressed. In the past these leaf points have led archaeologists to construe some link with the much later SOLUTREAN industries, although this is now usually discounted. Split-based bone points have also been found at Szeleta Cave. At Szeleta Cave the 'Early' Szeletian is dated to *c*.41,000 uncal BP and the 'Developed' to *c*.32,000 uncal BP. These dates suggest that even the 'Early' Szeletian may be contemporaneous with the early Aurignacian, a variant of which is dated to 39,700 ± 900 uncal BP at the other Hungarian site of Istállóskö. This contemporaneity has led Philip Allsworth-Jones and others to suggest that the Szeletian is an acculturated version of the AURIGNACIAN produced by NEANDERTHALS. The Szeletian in Central Europe would therefore occupy the same position as the CHÂTELPERRONIAN or Lower PERIGORDIAN in Western Europe. This theory assumes that the Neanderthals were replaced by ANATOMICALLY MODERN HUMANS, a premise not universally accepted.

P. Allsworth-Jones: *The Szeletian and the transition from Middle to Upper Palaeolithic in Central Europe* (Oxford, 1986); J.K. Kozłowski: 'The transition from the Middle to the early Upper Palaeolithic in Central Europe and the Balkans', *The early Upper Palaeolithic*, eds. J.F. Hoffecker and C.A. Wolf, BAR IS 437 (Oxford, 1988), 193–237; M. Oliva: 'The Szeletian in Czechoslovakia', *Antiquity* 65 (1991), 318–25.

RJA

T

Tabun *see* MOUNT CARMEL

Tadrart Acacus *see* AFRICA 1

Taforalt *see* AFRICA 1

Tagajo Garrison of the 8th and 9th centuries AD in Miyagi prefecture, northern Japan, which was one of several centres for frontier administration mentioned in historical records in connection with attempts by the central state to subdue groups such as the Emishi. Excavations since 1961 have revealed extensive earthworks and wooden slips bearing ink inscriptions.
Tohoku Historical Museum and the Miyagi Prefectural Tagajo Research Institute: *Tagajo to kodai Tohoku* [Tagajo and ancient Tohoku] (Sendai, 1985).
SK

T'ai-hsi-ts'un (Taixicun) Site of the SHANG period (2000–1122 BC), near the village of T'ai-hsi-ts'un, in the central Ho-pei province of China. It is one of three large earth mounds in the area, which was excavated in 1973–6; bringing to light the remains of 14 houses, two wells, over 100 burials and many pits. Building remnants include some parts of the roofs which indicate the method of gabling employed; the overall structures comprise wooden posts and beams with wall fillings of rammed earth, or sun-dried brick. Wooden frames supported the well bottom, and, significantly, they were found to have been laid out in the shape of the character *ching* ('well').

Over two thousand artefacts were recovered, including pottery, stone and bone implements, ORACLE BONES (uninscribed), turtle shells, LACQUER remnants, hemp fabric, gold foil, bronze vessels, bronze knives and weapons. A bronze *yüeh*-axe with an iron blade has become the basis of controversy as to the antiquity of iron manufacture in China. The iron in this axe, and two others like it, is apparently of meteoritic origin; as it would necessarily require smithing in its manufacture, such a worked material would be more likely to have been a cultural intrusion.
Anon.: *Kao-ch'eng T'ai-hsi Shang-tai yi-chih* [The Shang period remains at Kao-ch'eng, T'ai-hsi] (Peking, 1985).
NB

Taixicun *see* T'AI-HSI-TS'UN

Takamatsuzuka Late Kofun-period (AD 300–710) mounded tomb in Nara prefecture, Japan, famous for its painted murals depicting the Chinese directional symbols on the plastered walls of the tomb. The stone chamber is in a small round mound. Recent opinions suggest artistic influence from the Chinese Tang dynasty (AD 618-907) on this tomb of an aristocrat from the YAMATO state.
C.M. Aikens and T. Higuchi: *The prehistory of Japan* (London, 1982), 284–5.
SK

Takht-i Sulaiman *see* PARTHIANS; SASANIANS

Talasea Series of obsidian sources deriving from volcanoes on the north coast of West New Britain, Papua New Guinea. Obsidian from Talasea has been used continuously from 20,000 years ago, the earliest examples deriving from New Ireland cave sites such as BALOF CAVE. During the time of the LAPITA CULTURAL COMPLEX, Talasea obsidian was distributed widely, ending up in Sabah, Malaysia to the west and Fiji to the east. *See also* OCEANIA 2.
R. Torrence 'What is Lapita about obsidian? A view from the Talasea sources', *Poterie, Lapita et peuplement*, ed. J.C. Galipaud (Nouméa, 1992), 111–26; C. Gosden et al.: 'The Lapita sites of the Bismarck Archipelago', *Antiquity* 63 (1989), 561–86.
CG

talayots (talaiots; 'watchtowers') Monumental round or rectangular drystone tower-like structures characteristic of the full Bronze Age – or Talayotic Period – in the Mediterranean Balearic islands (Majorca and Minorca). The absolute dates of the talayot phenomenon are unclear, but may run from *c.*1500 BC to *c.*800 BC or later. Talayots, which occur singly and in groups, are often compared to the NURAGHI of Sardinia, although they are smaller and simpler in form and lack a sophisticated corbelling technique. They may have acted as places of refuge or as central strongpoints for local powers.

G. Rossello-Bordoy: *La cultura talayotica en Mallorca* (Palma, 1979); R. Chapman and A. Grant: 'The Talayotic monuments of Mallorca, formation processes and function', *Oxford Journal of Archaeology* 8 (1989), 55–72.

RJA

talud-tablero Mesoamerican style of temple-pyramid construction associated with the site of TEOTIHUACAN, in which each tier or terrace of the substructure was composed of two parts: a sloping apron (*talud*) topped by a flat, rectangular panel (*tablero*).

G. Kubler: 'Iconographic aspects of architectural profiles at Teotihuacán and in Mesoamerica', *The iconography of Middle American sculpture* (New York, 1973), 24–39.

PRI

Tamaya Mellet *see* AFRICA 1.1

tambo Groups of storehouses and shelters located at intervals along roads by the INCA.

Tam My *see* SA HUYNH

Tanis (anc. Djaʿnet; San el-Hagar) Egyptian town, temple and royal cemetery located in the Nile delta about 130 km northeast of Cairo. It was capital of Egypt for much of the 3rd Intermediate Period (*c.*1070–712) and continued to flourish until the early Roman period (*c.*30 BC). The preservation of Tanis, a typical tell-site covering some 180 ha, has been greatly assisted by its location in one of Egypt's poorest areas of agricultural land, which has tended to protect it from the depredations of farmers digging for fertilizer (the so-called *sabakhin*), unlike other post-New Kingdom sites such as SAIS and MENDES. Because of the large number of Ramessid monuments at Tanis, both Auguste Mariette and Flinders Petrie mistakenly identified the site with Piramesse, the city said to have been founded by Ramesses II in the Delta (which is now known to have been located at QANTIR and TELL EL-DABʿA). From 1929 to 1952 Pierre Montet excavated the site, concentrating on the precincts of the temple of Amun, which was founded by Psusennes I (*c.*1020 BC). In 1939–40 he discovered the relatively undisturbed tombs of some of the rulers of the 3rd Intermediate Period, complete with much of the original funerary equipment, a discovery which would perhaps have brought Montet the same fame as Howard Carter had it not coincided with the outbreak of the Second World War.

W.M.F. Petrie: *Tanis*, 2 vols (London, 1885–8); P. Montet: *La nécropole royale de Tanis*, 2 vols (Paris, 1947–60); H. Stierlin and C. Ziegler: *Tanis: trésors des pharaons* (Paris, 1987); J. Yoyotte et al.: *Gold of the pharaohs* (Edinburgh, 1988); P. Brissaud: 'Tanis: the golden cemetery', *Royal cities of the biblical world*, ed. J. Goodnick Westenholz (Jerusalem, 1996), 113–70.

IS

T'ao-ssu (Taosi) Extensive site of the Neolithic LUNG-SHAN culture (*c.*4000–2000 BC), near the village of T'ao-ssu-ts'un, Hsiang-fen-hsien, Shanhsi, China. Still only partly excavated, it primarily consists of a cemetery area that is estimated to cover an area of 30,000 sq.m, containing several thousand burials, about a thousand of which have been excavated. Calibrated radiocarbon dates range from *c.*2875 to 1905 BC.

Chang Kwang-chih: *The archaeology of ancient China*, 4th edn (New Haven, 1986), 275–9; N. Barnard: 'Thoughts on the emergence of metallurgy in pre-Shang and Early Shang China and a technical appraisal of relevant bronze artifacts of the time', *BMM, Sendai*, 19 (1993), 3–48.

NB

Taoudenni Basin The southeastern part of the Taoudenni basin, within the Republic of Mali, has been investigated by N. Petit-Maire and her colleagues since 1980. This area, lying between 17° and 24° N, presently forms part of the Sahara and has an annual precipitation of 50–55 mm, but the investigation has demonstrated that during the early Holocene rainfall is likely to have reached 400–250 mm, and there were several freshwater lakes, as well as an extensive Neolithic occupation of this region. Dates obtained on molluscs suggest that there were two main humid phases, a major one from 9500 to 6000 BP and a minor one from 5000 to 4000 BP. After 3000 BP the region was deserted. The early phase of occupation is dated to 6970 ± 130 BP at Hassi el-Abiod and 6340 ± 130 BP at Erg Ine Sakane. At both localities, large middens contained an abundant fauna, with fish, crocodiles, turtles, snakes, bovids, hippos and antelopes, as well as artefacts and human burials. The tools, apart from geometric microliths, also include polished stone axes, fish hooks and grinding equipment, taken to indicate the exploitation of wild grasses. There are numerous bone harpoons (>100 at one site) similar to those found at ADRAR BOUS and Shaheinab (KHARTOUM NEOLITHIC), and pottery which at Erg Ine Sakane includes wavy-line and dotted wavy-line motifs. At Hassi el-Abiod 89 skeletons were recovered from 16 sites. These according to O. Dutour form a homogeneous 'Cromagnoid' population, which in terms of metrical characteristics is very close to the 'Mechtoids' from the North African IBEROMAURUSIAN sites of Afalou and Taforalt. As Petit-Maire says, this similarity 'may be a result of early Holocene trans-Saharan migrations or a common Aterian ancestry'. ATERIAN stone tools were found *in situ* beneath thick deposits of sand and silt at Sbeita northwest of Taoudenni, and stratigraphically they may correspond to palaeolake deposits 130 km away dated to 21,000 ± 300 BP.

N. Petit-Maire et al.: 'The Sahara in northern Mali: man and his environment between 10,000 and 3500 years BP (Preliminary results)', *AAR* 1 (1983), 105–25; N. Petit-Maire: 'Palaeoclimates in the Sahara of Mali: a multidisciplinary study', *Episodes* 9/1 (1986), 7–16; —— and O. Dutour: 'Holocene populations of the Western and Southern Sahara: Mechtoids and paleoclimates', *Prehistory of arid North Africa*, ed. A.E. Close (Dallas, 1987), 259–85.

PA-J

Ta-p'en-k'eng (Dapenkeng) Neolithic site near Taipei, which is one of the best-studied prehistoric sites on the island of Taiwan (see Chang et al. 1969) and is also the type-site for the Ta-p'en-k'eng culture. This culture is characterized by cord-marked pottery (the cord-marks demonstrating the existence of highly sophisticated cordage techniques), stone net-sinkers, shell-mounds, woodworking implements such as stone adzes and chisels (illustrating the possibility of boat building), and bark-beaters (for the production of fibres for rope-making). Some form of agriculture may have been practised but the obvious means of subsistence was hunting, fishing and collecting. The culture, along with others related to it, is represented in sites on the Chinese mainland, a few of which are located directly opposite, in Fu-chien, but many have been recognized in Kuang-tung and coastal Kuang-hsi. Calibrated radiocarbon datings indicate a span of 5000–3000 BC, thus making it contemporary with such cultures as Ma-chia-pang and HO-MU-TU to the north, in Chiang-su and Che-chiang, TA-WEN-K'OU in Shan-tung, and YANG-SHAO in the Huang-ho River Basin.

Chang Kwang-chih et al.: *Fengpitou, Tapenkeng, and the Prehistory of Taiwan* (New Haven, 1969); Chang Kwang-chih: *The archaeology of ancient China*, 4th edn (New Haven, 1986), 228–33.

NB

taphonomy Palaeontological term coined by I.A. Efremov in 1940 to describe the study of the transformation of organic remains into fossil deposits as a result of spatial, temporal and biological factors. The term has been used by archaeologists since at least the early 1980s to describe the transformation of bone (and sometimes other material) in the archaeological record, i.e. the organic aspects of SITE FORMATION PROCESSES. The most useful applications of taphonomy include the work of C.K. Brain (1981), studying faunal remains associated with australopithecine hominids at the South African site of SWARTKRANS, and the ethnoarchaeological researches of Lewis Binford (1981), distinguishing between patterns of faunal remains created by dogs, wolves and humans at various sites in North America.

I.A. Efremov: 'Taphonomy: a new branch of paleontology', *Pan-American Geologist* 74 (1940), 81–93; A.K. Behrensmeyer and A.P. Hill: *Fossils in the making: vertebrate taphonomy and paleoecology* (Chicago, 1980); L.R. Binford: *Bones: ancient men and modern myths* (New York, 1981); C.K. Brain: *The hunters or the hunted? An introduction to African cave taphonomy* (Chicago, 1981); D.P. Gifford: 'Taphonomy and paleoecology: a critical review of archaeology's sister disciplines', *Advances in archaeological method and theory* 4, ed. M.B. Schiffer (New York, 1981), 365–438.

IS

Tarascans Late Postclassic state in the state of Michoacán in western Mexico, with its capital at Tzintzuntzan, on the shores of Lake Pátzcuaro. Claiming CHICHIMEC ancestry, the Tarascans maintained an uneasy frontier with the AZTECS to the south and were known for their fine metalworking, especially in copper.

D.D. Brand: 'An historical sketch of geography and anthropology in the Tarascan region, Part 1', *New Mexico Anthropologist* 6 (1943) 37–108.

PRI

Tardenoisian Term applied to an ill-defined group of Mesolithic assemblages, characterized principally by the presence of asymmetrical trapezes (*pointe tardenoisienne*) and long blades. First identified at Fère-en-Tardois in southwest France, the assemblages date from about 6000 BC into the 5th millennium. Assemblages with Tardenoisian characteristics can be identified across

Europe from Iberia to Sweden (excluding Britain, presumably because eustatic changes had recently created the English Channel), centring on northern France. Tardenoisian assemblages are generally thought to post-date assemblages defined as MAGLEMOSIAN and those defined as SAUVETERRIAN; however, the relationship with the Sauveterrian has been the subject of much debate since the 1950s, as summarized by Peter Rowley-Conwy (1986). There is some limited evidence that hunters and gatherers using lithic industries of Tardenoisian character existed at the same time as early farming groups in northern France, that the two economies occupied different landscape zones, and that there was a (limited, except perhaps in Brittany) degree of contact and cultural interchange.

C. Barrière: *Les civilizations Tardenoisiennes en Europe Occidentale* (Paris, 1956); R. Parent: 'Le peuplement préhistorique entre le Marne et l'Aisne', *Travaux de l'institut d'art préhistorique de l'Université de Toulouse* 13 (1971); S.K. Kozłowski, ed.: *The Mesolithic in Europe* (1973); P. Rowley-Conwy: 'Between cavepainters and crop planters: aspects of the temperate European Mesolithic', *Hunters in transition*, ed. M. Zvelebil (Cambridge, 1986), 17–29.

RJA

el-Tarif *see SAFF-TOMB*

Tarkhan Religious and funerary site in the Nile valley, about 60 km south of Cairo, excavated by Flinders Petrie in 1912–13. The main components of the site comprise a temple dating to the 9th–7th centuries BC and a number of cemeteries ranging in date from the late predynastic to the Roman period (*c*.3200 BC–AD 395).

W.M.F. Petrie et al.: *Tarkhan and Memphis V* (London, 1913); W.M.F. Petrie: *Tarkhan II* (London, 1914);

IS

Tărtăria Romanian Neolithic site of the Vinča-Tordos culture, famous for the discovery in a pit of three clay tablets bearing signs that were once claimed to be related to the pictographs used in the JEMDET NASR period in Mesopotamia – an interpretation that clashes with the accepted VINČA chronology and is now discounted. The signs may represent some simple form of notation, or religious symbolism, but researchers no longer regard them as 'proto-writing'.

RJA

Tasian *see* BADARIAN

Figure 53 **Tărtăria** Inscribed clay tablets from Tărtăria, Transylvania, Romania. *Source*: A. Whittle: *Neolithic Europe: a survey* (Cambridge, 1985), fig. 3.15.

Tasmania *see* OCEANIA 1

Tassili-n-Ajjer *see* AFRICA 1

Tatetsuki Very large Late Yayoi (AD 100–300) burial mound in Okayama prefecture, Japan which has provided good evidence for the burial customs of regional chiefs and insight into the extent of indigenous Japanese origins of the keyhole-shaped mounded tombs of the succeeding Kofun period (*see* JAPAN 3–4).

Y. Kondo, ed.: *Tatetsuki mound of the Yayoi period* (Okayama, 1992) [in Japanese with English summary].

SK

Taung Site of the discovery of the type specimen of *AUSTRALOPITHECUS AFRICANUS* in 1924, close to the town of Taung, N. Cape Province, South Africa. The site consists of four superimposed travertine aprons (with associated breccia and conglomerate deposits) banked against the Gaap escarpment. The Taung skull and associated fossils came from sediments filling a cavern system eroded in the oldest (Thabaseek) travertine, probably contemporaneous with the next younger (Norlim) travertine. Attempts to derive radiometric dates for the Taung skull are considered inconclusive, and estimates based on faunal remains vary between 2.3 and 1.8 million years.

K.W. Butzer: 'Palaeoecology of South African australopithecines: Taung revisited', *CA* 15 (1974), 367–82; P.V. Tobias, ed.: *Hominid evolution: past, present and future* (New York, 1985), 25–40, 189–200.

RI

Ta-wen-k'ou (Dawenkou) Neolithic culture named after the type-site near T'ai-an, in the Shan-tung region of China, which is sometimes referred to as the Ch'ing-lien-kang culture (a red pottery culture investigated in 1951 at the type-site of this name, in Huai-an-hsien, in northern Chiang-su). Over a hundred Ta-wen-k'ou culture sites are known, mainly distributed in central and southern Shan-tung and northern Chiang-su; clusters of radiocarbon datings range from 5500 to 3500 BC. The culture is more or less contemporary with YANG-SHAO to the west in the Huang-ho River Basin, Ma-chia-pang and HO-MU-TU to the south in Chiang-su and Che-chiang, and TA-PEN-K'ENG in the southern coastal region of Fu-chien, Kuang-tung, Kuang-hsi and western Taiwan.

For the most part the Ta-wen-k'ou predates the LUNG-SHAN culture. Agriculture was practised, as suggested by millet grains found in several sites and the presence of sickles of bone, tooth and shell. A large variety of animal bones including the domestic pig, cattle, deer, alligator, turtles, chickens, fish, molluscs and snails bear witness to the diet and hunting and fishing activities, as well as providing an indication of the more humid and warmer lacustrine environment of the time. Houses were of the round semi-subterranean type, some square, and with postholes, but only a few have been found.

Anon.: *Ta-wen-k'ou* (Peking, 1974); Chang Kwang-chih: *The archaeology of ancient China*, 4th edn (New Haven, 1986), 156–69.

NB

Taxila Large urban site located near modern Rawalpindi in northern Pakistan alongside a major

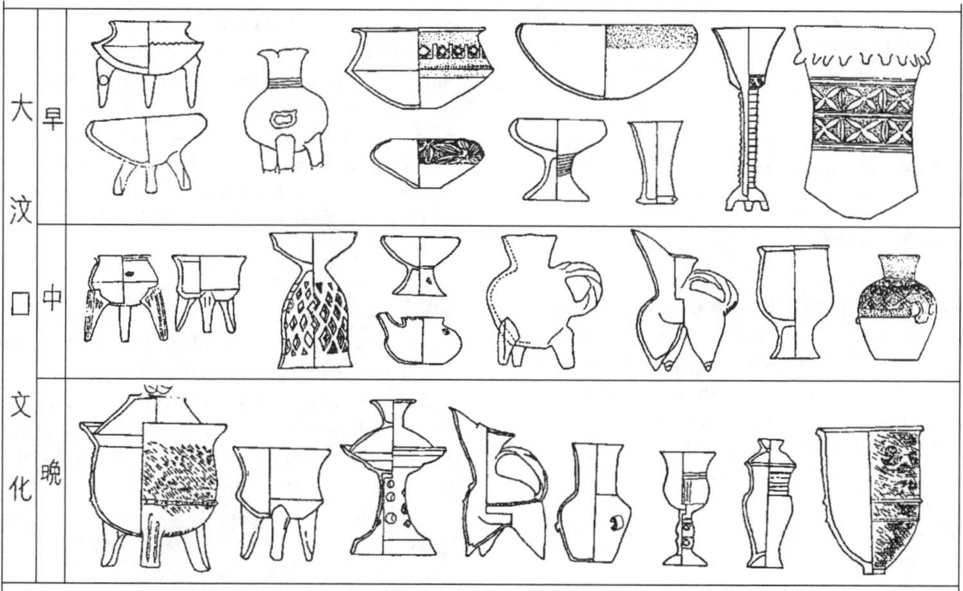

Figure 54 **Ta-wen-k'ou** Division of the Ta-wen-k'ou culture into three phases as reflected in the pottery styles. *Source*: Anon.: Ta-wen-k'ou (Peking, 1974), fig. 91.

route between Central Asia and the Indian subcontinent. First excavated by A. Cunningham in the 1860s, it consists of several mounds (Hathial, Bhir, Sirkap and Sirsukh), not all of which were occupied at the same time. The occupation levels, dated primarily by numismatic evidence, stretch from the ACHAEMENID period (*c.*516 BC) to the 3rd century AD. Although Greek textual sources document the arrival of Alexander the Great at Taxila in 326 BC, definitive archaeological evidence of his brief occupation has yet to be identified.

During the MAURYAN PERIOD (*c.*321–189 BC) the city of Taxila was a major political centre, first under the Mauryan empire and later under autonomous rulers. Indo-Greek occupation of the city began in the early 2nd century BC, and it was during this period that the construction of the walled city of Sirkap was initiated (but see Erdosy 1990 for a different perspective). The next occupants of Taxila were the Sakas (SCYTHIANS) and PARTHIANS (*c.*90 BC–AD 60; Erdosy 1990: 668). The mound of Sirsukh is associated with subsequent Kushana occupation of the city (*c.*AD 60–230), during which many of the Buddhist monasteries were expanded and GANDHARAN-style sculpture flourished. Excavations have revealed dense architectural remains, including Buddhist STUPAS and monasteries, and a wide array of ceramic, copper and iron goods, as well as sculptures and ornaments of gold, silver and other precious materials.

J. Marshall: *Taxila*, 3 vols (Cambridge, 1951); A.H. Dani: *The historic city of Taxila* (Paris, 1986); G. Erdosy: 'Taxila: political history and urban structure', *South Asian archaeology 1987*, ed. M. Taddei (Naples, 1990), 657–75.

CS

Tayma *see* ARABIA, PRE-ISLAMIC

tazunu *see* AFRICA 5.3

technocomplex Term used to describe a group of cultures which are characterized by assemblages sharing a polythetic range. Each of the cultures in the group has different specific types of the same general family of artefacts, but they all share a widely diffused and interlinked response to common factors in environment, economy and technology.

D.L. Clarke: *Analytical archaeology* (London, 1968).

KM

Tehuacán Arid highland valley in Puebla, south-central Mexico, where a series of caves and open-air sites provided evidence for the history of domestication and the beginnings of sedentism in Mesoamerica between *c.*7000 and 2300 BC. The valley continued to be occupied during Classic and Postclassic periods (*c.*AD 300–1521).

D.S. Byers, ed.: *The prehistory of the Tehuacán Valley, I: environment and subsistence* (Andover, 1967).

PRI

Teishebaina *see* URARTU

Tekkalakota Neolithic site located in an area of granitic hills in modern Karnataka, southern India. The excavations of M.S. Nagaraja Rao in 1963–4 defined two chronological periods (Phase I, 1700–1600 BC and Phase II, 1600–1500 BC) and revealed well-preserved foundations of circular huts as well as large quantities of faunal remains, including domestic cattle, sheep, deer and rodents. The botanical remains indicate that horse gram (*Dolichos biflorus*) was being cultivated.

Artefacts excavated at Tekkalakota include hand- and wheel-made ceramics, beads, copper implements and gold ear ornaments. Seven burials were excavated: six from phase I and one from Phase II. In Phase I partially disarticulated adult skeletons were buried in shallow pits covered with stones, while children were buried in ceramic urns. The Phase II burial comprised the extended body of an adult associated with BLACK AND RED WARE and plain red ceramic vessels. Nearby rock-shelters contain petroglyphs and wall paintings depicting bulls, dogs, and humans, interpreted by Nagaraja Rao and M.C. Malhotra (1965: 98) as dating to the Neolithic period.

M.S. Nagaraja Rao and M.C. Malhotra: *The Stone Age hill dwellers of Tekkalakota* (Pune, 1965); B.P. Sahu: *From hunters to breeders* (Delhi, 1988), 189–91, 225–6.

CS

tell Arabic term used to describe the distinctive stratified mounds of archaeological deposits which formed on the sites of early settlements, particularly in Western Asia, southeastern Europe and North Africa. Tell sites accumulate vertically because of the repeated demolition and re-levelling of mud-brick houses over the course of long periods of time. Probably the earliest examples are to be found in the Jordan valley, including the town of JERICHO, where the Proto-Neolithic strata form a 10-metre high mound. The word 'tell' can be traced back to *tilu*, the AKKADIAN word for mound. The equivalent words used to describe such town-mounds in

Egypt, Persia and Turkey are *kom*, *tepe* and *hüyük* respectively.

Despite the growth of interest in GEOARCHAEOLOGY and LANDSCAPE STUDIES during the 1980s and 1990s, only a small number of specific tell sites, e.g. SITAGROI (Davidson 1976), LACHISH (Rosen Miller 1986) and AXUM (Butzer 1982: 93–7, 142–5), have been studied explicitly in terms of their SITE FORMATION PROCESSES. Arlene Miller Rosen (1986: 1) points out that there is still 'only a vague understanding of the processes by which tells form and why tells develop from some urban sites and not others', but her own research, involving a combination of MICROARCHAEOLOGY, mud-brick analyses and the study of the processes of erosion, has provided a good scientific basis for future work. Wendy Matthews' use of micromorphology at ABU SALABIKH has proved to be a promising means of determining the original functions of specific rooms within a tell site (see Matthews and Postgate 1994).

D.A. Davidson: 'Particle size and phosphate analysis: evidence for the evolution of a tell', *Archaeometry* 15 (1973), 143–52; ——: 'Processes of tell formation and erosion', *Geoarchaeology: earth science and the past*, ed. D.A. Davidson and M.L. Shackley (London, 1976), 255–66; K.W. Butzer: *Archaeology as human ecology: method and theory for a contextual approach* (Cambridge, 1982); A. Miller Rosen: *Cities of clay: the geoarchaeology of tells* (Chicago, 1986); W. Matthews and J.N. Postgate: 'The imprint of living in an early Mesopotamian city: questions and answers', *Whither environmental archaeology?*, ed. R. Luff and P. Rowley-Conwy (Oxford, 1994).

IS

Tell (el-) For the purposes of alphabetization, the word 'Tell' is disregarded, e.g. see HASSUNA, TELL.

Telloh (anc. Girsu) City site in southern Iraq, 48 km north of Nasriya, which was the first Sumerian site to be scientifically excavated (*see* SUMER). Although initially misidentified as the city of LAGASH, it is now known to be Girsu, an important cult centre of the god Ningirsu during the Lagash Dynasty (*c*.2570–2342 BC), located about 20 km from the site of Lagash itself (Tell el-Hiba). It was first investigated in 1877–1900 by Ernest de Sarzec, who discovered thousands of cuneiform tablets bearing important texts regarding the history and socio-economic structure of the Lagash Dynasty but succeeded in destroying much of the architecture through failing to identify unbaked brick structures.

The later excavations of Georges Cros (1903–9), Henri de Genouillac (1928–31) and André Parrot (1931–3) were more fruitful. One of the most important monuments from Telloh is the so-called Stele of the Vultures (now in the Louvre), which records a series of disputes over water between the states of Lagash and Umma in the reign of Eanatum of Lagash (*c*.2440 BC). The earliest settlement at the site dates to the late Ubaid period (*c*.3800 BC) but it reached its peak during the 3rd millennium BC. Temporarily subdued by the Akkadians in the late 3rd millennium BC, the state of Lagash underwent a brief renaissance under Ur-Bau and his successor Gudea, during the late Gutian period, *c*.2200–2150 BC. Apart from the huge brick mausoleum of Urningirsu (Gudea's son) there are few surviving buildings from this period, but the renewed prosperity at Girsu is best indicated by the magnificent diorite statues of Gudea, more than twenty of which have been excavated at Telloh. The city maintained a certain degree of importance during the early 2nd millennium, but it was eventually abandoned in the late 18th century BC and there was no further occupation until the Parthian period (*c*.250 BC–AD224).

L. Heuzey: *Découvertes en Chaldée*, 2 vols (Paris, 1884–1912); G. Cros, L. Heuzey and F. Thureau-Dangin: *Nouvelles fouilles de Tello*, 2 vols (Paris, 1910–14); H. de Genouillac: *Fouilles de Tello*, 2 vols (Paris, 1934–6); A. Parrot: *Tello, vingt campagnes de fouilles (1877–1933)* (Paris, 1948).

IS

Temple Mound Period Rarely-used term pertaining to the MISSISSIPPIAN period. It refers to the presence of flat-topped, rectangular earthen mounds at large Mississippian sites distributed throughout the southern Midwest and Southeast of North America. These mounds served as platforms for buildings, including so-called temples or mortuary houses that contained the bones of the ancestors of highly ranked people.

G.R. Willey: *An introduction to American archaeology I: North and Middle America* (Englewood Cliffs, 1966).

GM

temple mountain Architectural term used in southeast Asian archaeology to refer to structures built to house the god-king's cremated remains and to serve as a temple to him after his death. The tallest surviving examples are at ANGKOR Wat in Cambodia.

Tenochtitlán *see* AZTECS

Teotihuacán Located in an arid valley northeast of the BASIN OF MEXICO, near modern Mexico city, this massive Late Formative and Classic city

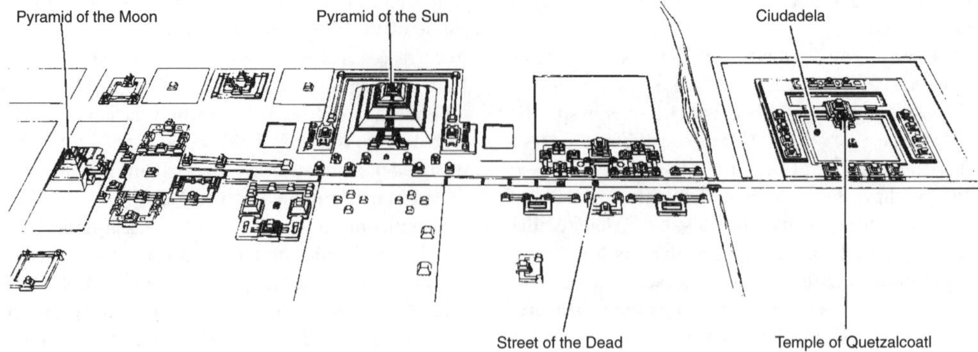

Figure 55 **Teotihuacán** Isometric view of the ceremonial structures lining the main north-south axis of Teotihuacán, known as the Street of the Dead. *Source*: M.E. Miller: *The art of ancient Mesoamerica* (Thames and Hudson, 1986), fig. 41.

exerted a profound influence on the development of many of the later cultures in Mesoamerica. Teotihuacán covers an area of about 20 sq. km; its total population has been estimated at about 125,000 people or more during its Classic peak around AD 300–500. The principal centre of a powerful highland state, Teotihuacán began its dramatic growth in the Late Formative period, with most major construction in the city completed by *c.* AD 150. The city's enormous size and the difficulty of understanding the complex factors leading to its rise and fall have posed enormous challenges to archaeological research; these have been exacerbated by modern occupation and disturbance of the site. Two ambitious projects of survey and settlement pattern analysis combined mapping and surface collection of artefacts in an investigation of the site's history. One project was directed toward the processes of urbanization and growth of the city itself (Millon 1973) and the other addressed Teotihuacán's role in the larger basin context (Sanders et al. 1979). More recent work has explored the social and ideological factors underlying the site's structure (Sugiyama 1993).

Teotihuacán exhibits a strikingly integrated site plan laid out on a regular grid of streets. Major civic-ceremonial architecture is arranged along a broad avenue stretching some 2 km north-south, known as the Street of the Dead. At the north end is a large terraced pyramid known as the Temple of the Moon; on the east side is another terraced pyramid known as the Temple of the Sun. The Sun temple sits above a natural cave in the bedrock, believed to have been a sacred location that probably determined the temple's siting. South of the Sun Temple is a huge square enclosure, the Ciudadela, with a large temple on its east side; across the avenue is another enormous enclosure that might have served as a market. Recent work around the Temple of Quetzalcoatl in the Ciudadela (Cabrera et al. 1991) has shown that the structure was built in a single phase of construction accompanied by the sacrifice and burial of perhaps 200 individuals. The temple-pyramids at Teotihuacán were built in characteristic TALUD-TABLERO style.

All around this civic-ceremonial core is a dense arrangement of buildings, including perhaps as many as 2000 multi-family apartment compounds. Residents of these compounds may have been linked by family (lineage) ties, and may have shared occupational specialities, as particular compounds seem to have concentrations of artefacts associated with pottery making, for example, or woodworking. Compounds associated with wealthier families were decorated with beautiful, brightly-coloured murals showing religious scenes.

There is abundant evidence for obsidian working at the Teotihuacán apartment compounds. One of the explanations offered for the dramatic size and influence of Teotihuacán throughout Classic period Mesoamerica is that the city controlled the exploitation and distribution of two or more valued sources of obsidian for tool-making. Other explanations focus on the many springs in the otherwise dry Teotihuacán valley: these were incorporated into irrigation systems, which increased agricultural yields by permitting water to be delivered to crops before the normal rainy (planting) season and by allowing crops to mature before the first frosts in this relatively cold, high-altitude region.

The language spoken by Teotihuacános is unknown, although it may have been Totonacan. Unlike other contemporaneous areas of 'prehistoric' Mesoamerica, no written texts have been found at Teotihuacán; the city's art – known primarily from murals – is ahistorical and lacks reference to dates and events. Similarly little is known about Teotihuacán's political organization: it is uncertain whether the city and state were governed by a divine king or secular leaders.

Teotihuacán engaged in widespread trade with other areas of Mesoamerica, obsidian and CACAO being two of the principal goods involved. Teotihuacán influence is seen as far away as the LOWLAND MAYA area in architectural styles, sculptural motifs (e.g. representations of the rain-god Tlaloc) and pottery vessels such as cylinder tripods.

Between AD 550 and 650 Teotihuacán began to experience disruptions in its architectural and population growth, as well as a retraction of its ties to other areas of Mesoamerica. Toward the end of this period archaeological investigations have revealed signs of conflict at the city, including destruction of temples and extensive conflagrations. The reasons for these disruptions are unclear, but Teotihuacán apparently underwent a major 'collapse' or decline around AD 750. The population of the city is estimated to have dropped to approximately 30,000 persons. At about the same time that Teotihuacán was experiencing difficulties, sites around the periphery of the basin of Mexico, such as Tula (*see* TOLTECS) and CHOLULA, began to flourish. Teotihuacán was never completely abandoned, however, and during Late Postclassic times the city had a population of approximately 80,000 persons; some AZTEC legends claimed that Teotihuacán was the place of creation of the sun and moon gods and the names of its principal temples are those used by the Aztecs.

R. Millon: *Urbanization at Teotihuacán, Mexico, I: The Teotihuacán map* (Austin, 1973); W.T. Sanders et al.: *The basin of Mexico: ecological processes in the evolution of a civilization* (New York, 1979); R. Cabrera et al.: 'The templo de Quetzalcoatl project at Teotihuacan', *AM* 2 (1991), 77–92; S. Sugiyama: 'Worldview materialized in Teotihuacán, Mexico', *LAA* 4 (1993), 103–29.

PRI

tepe *see* TELL

tephrochronology The use of chemically characterized layers of volcanic glass particles (tephra) as stratigraphic markers for correlating one location with another: historical dating of the eruption or other dating evidence (e.g. RADIOCARBON DATING on associated peat layers) provides a reference chronology. The technique has been used in northwestern Europe, the United States of America and the Far East.

In northwestern Europe, for example, the tephra layers are largely from Icelandic eruptions; in Britain no other source has been identified. The tephra are air-borne particles (typically 200 μm) that are most heavily deposited by rainfall over high ground; thus the incidence of tephra layers in Scotland is high, but peters out further south in Britain. The deposition of these layers is rapid and their distribution is wide (up to 2000 km); each provides a synchronous marker over a potentially large area (northern Britain, northern Germany, central and southern Scandinavia for the Icelandic tephra). Not all eruptions will necessarily be represented at each locality, however, depending on the size of the eruption and meteorological conditions (nearly 80 layers have been identified in Iceland for the Holocene period compared to some 20 in Scotland and about 12 in Northern Ireland).

It has been shown that tephra from volcanoes in a relatively restricted locality have distinct petrological and chemical characteristics, definable by optical microscopy (e.g. refractive index and birefringence) and analysis in the electron microprobe respectively: many are characterized by analysis alone. The study of tephra layers generally concentrates on those in peat bogs and lake sediment where the record is more continuous than for other terrestrial sediments. Their presence is identified by X-radiography of columns or cores. The direct association of these marker layers with pollen sequences provides the opportunity to study environmental change on both a regional and broader basis.

Apart from a small number of historically recorded eruptions (e.g. Hekla 1 in AD 1104), the dating of tephra layers has largely been by radiocarbon dating of associated organic material: high-precision radiocarbon dating and WIGGLE-MATCHING have provided calendar dates to within a decade or two. Large eruptions have an effect on tree-ring size, but there is no direct means of correlating a specific eruption with the particular episode of reduced growth. The occurrence of tephra in ICE CORES, however, has the potential to provide another dating source. Research has been undertaken in the 1990s to identify Icelandic tephra in the Swedish VARVE sequence which would provide dates to the nearest year for those eruptions represented.

A.J. Dugmore: 'Tephrochronology and UK archaeology', *Archaeological sciences*, ed. P. Budd (Oxford, 1991), 242–50.

SB

terminus ante quem (Latin: 'end before which') Phrase used to describe a situation where it can be assumed that a piece of archaeological evidence dates to a period earlier than a certain date. In terms of stratigraphy, it is possible to assign a terminus ante quem when the deposit in question is sealed by, or cut through by, one or more datable features. If a building can be assigned a secure date, e.g. AD 1300, then it can be assumed that any layers through which its foundation trenches cut must have a terminus ante quem of AD 1300. *See also* CROSS DATING.

P. Barker: *Techniques of archaeological excavation*, 2nd edn (London, 1982), 197–200.

IS

terminus post quem (Latin: 'end after which') Phrase used to describe a situation where it can be assumed that an archaeological feature or deposit was formed on or after a certain date. Thus, the presence of a coin of the emperor Augustus in the lowest stratum of a Romano-British settlement would suggest a terminus post quem of the 1st century AD for the foundation of the town (i.e. the deposit could not have been formed earlier than that date but it could be later). *See also* CROSS DATING.

P. Barker: *Techniques of archaeological excavation*, 2nd end (London, 1982), 197–200.

IS

Ternifine Pleistocene artesian lake site (now known as Tighénif) 20 km east of Mascara, northwestern Algeria, discovered in 1872 when a sand pit was opened by the side of a Muslim cemetery; the floor of the sand pit was excavated to a depth of 7 m beneath the water table by Camille Arambourg and R. Hoffstetter in 1931 and 1954–6, and, after a considerable lowering of the water table, again by a Franco-Algerian team in 1981–3. Faunal remains and ACHEULEAN artefacts were found at the base of the sands and in a greyish clay layer with carbonate nodules, above sterile varicoloured clay which formed the bed of the lake. On faunal grounds (supported by PALAEOMAGNETIC measurements) the site is considered to belong to the beginning of the Middle Pleistocene, about 700,000 years ago. Three adult human mandibles and one parietal found together with the other remains (as well as a number of isolated teeth, four of which are now thought to have belonged to a child) were attributed by Arambourg to *Atlanthropus mauritanicus*, but he recognized their similarity to the hominids from CHOUKOUTIEN, and they are now generally classified as *HOMO ERECTUS*. As such they still constitute the earliest hominid remains known from North Africa.

C. Arambourg and R. Hoffstetter: *Le gisement de Ternifine* (Paris, 1963); M.H. Day: *Guide to fossil man*, 4th edn (London, 1986); D. Geraads, J.J. Hublin, J.J. Jaeger, H. Tong, S. Sen and P. Toubeau: 'The Pleistocene hominid site of Ternifine, Algeria: new results on the environment, age, and human industries', *Quaternary Research* 25 (1986), 380–6.

PA-J

'terracotta army' *see* CH'IN

terra preta South American form of 'black earth' consisting of the dark fertile soils of anthropic origin found along the Amazon and its tributaries.

M.J. Eden, W. Bray, L. Herrera, and C. McEwan: '*Terra preta* soils and their archaeological context in the Caquetá Basin of Southeast Colombia', *AA* 49/1 (1984), 125–40.

KB

Teshik-Tash Palaeolithic (MOUSTERIAN) cave site in southern Uzbekistan, in the Baisuntau Mountains, in the valley of Turgan-Darya. Discovered in 1937 by A.P. Okladnikov, who

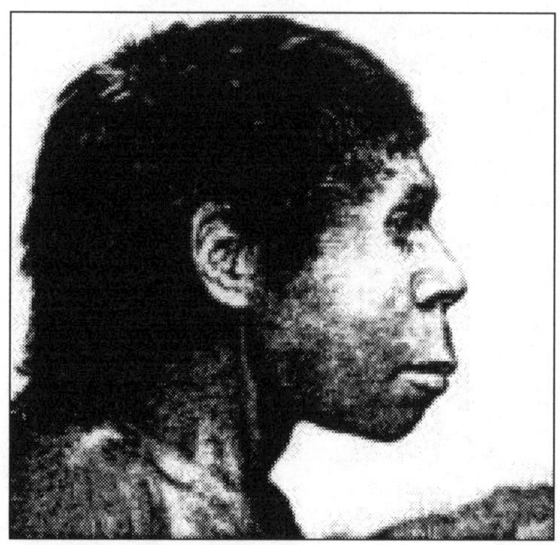

Figure 56 **Teshik-Tash** Reconstruction drawing of the head of a Neanderthal, based on the skull found at Teshik-Tash. *Source*: V.A. Ranov: *DA* 185 (1993).

identified five archaeological levels, the faunal record is dominated by Siberian ibex and also includes red deer, wild horse, brown bear etc. The lithic inventory includes discoid cores and typical Mousterian points. The most remarkable discovery was that of a NEANDERTHAL child, eight or nine years of age, found beneath the deposits of the first level. The skeleton was found in a shallow niche on top of which horns of ibex had been set vertically to form a regular circle, suggesting a deliberate burial.

A.P. Okladnikov: 'Paleolit i mezolit Srednei Azii', *Srednjaja Azija v epohu kamnja i bronzy* ed. V.M. Masson (Moscow and Leningrad, 1966).

PD

Thac Lac culture *see* COASTAL NEOLITHIC

Thailand *see* ASIA 3

Thala Borivat *see* ZHENLA CULTURE

Thapsos Situated on the Magnisi peninsula near Syracuse, this settlement of the later 2nd millennium BC is the type-site of the Sicilian Bronze Age culture that existed in between the CASTELLUCCIO and Pantalica cultural phases, and offers unique evidence of an intrusive trading depot. The original settlement consists of round, oval and rectangular huts, with roofs supported by internal posts. The elaborate grey pottery includes distinctive pedestal vases – some supporting shallow bowl forms – which may have been used as part of eating or drinking rituals.

Soon after 1400 BC the earlier village gained a series of buildings of a quite different style: rectangular structures about 20 m long placed around the four sides of a paved courtyard, with associated paved streets. These unusual structures are usually interpreted as warehouses or as part of a palace/storage complex, and it is assumed that at this stage Thapsos effectively became a small trading 'port'. It is not yet agreed whether the builders of the complex were local or intrusive – there is little material culture directly associated with the structure. However, it can only be understood in terms of the complex trading networks that developed in the Mediterranean at this period, evidenced by the Mycenaen and Cypriot ware found in the associated tombs.

The 400 or so rock-cut tombs associated with this settlement were excavated by Paolo Orsi in the 1890s and exhibit carved portals, often approached via a ramp, beyond which are single and multiple chambers with niches. The tombs contained multiple inhumations, and grave-goods including pottery, paste beads and bronze weaponry.

P. Orsi: 'Thapsos, necropoli sicula con vasi e bronzi miceni', *Monumenti Antichi* vi (1895); G. Voza: 'Thapsos, primi resultati delle piu recenti ricerche', *Atti XIV Riunione Scientifica Istituto Italiana Preistoria e Protostoria* (Florence, 1972), 175–205.

RJA

Thebes (anc. Waset; modern Luxor) Extensive Egyptian site situated on both sides of the Nile, about 500 km south of Cairo, consisting primarily of temples and tombs dating from at least as early as the 3rd millennium BC until the Roman period. For the archaeological remains on the east bank see KARNAK and LUXOR; for the west bank *see* DEIR EL-BAHARI, DEIR EL-MEDINA, MALKATA, MEDINET HABU, RAMESSEUM, *SAFF*-TOMB, VALLEY OF THE KINGS *and* VALLEY OF THE QUEENS.

H.E. Winlock: *The rise and fall of the Middle Kingdom in Thebes* (New York, 1947); E. Riefstahl: *Thebes in the time of Amunhotep III* (Norman, 1964); L. Manniche: *City of the dead: Thebes in Egypt* (London, 1987).

IS

theory and theory building At the most fundamental level, abstract thinking about archaeology tries to make explicit the purposes of archaeology and to relate these aims directly to an efficient and defensible archaeological methodology. It may try to link these aims to the place, or function, that archaeologists are deemed to hold within society generally. It may try to analyse how archaeologists select areas of inquiry, and identify and prioritize research goals.

However, while all of this is 'theoretical archaeology' in the widest sense of the term, most archaeologists have a much narrower conception of archaeological theory. Despite some radical thinking within the POST-PROCESSUAL movement, in practice, most archaeological theorizing attempts to accomplish one of two interrelated objectives:

1 To explain in a general sense how archaeologists can move from a knowledge of the available data on a subject – e.g. material culture from particular sites, or distributions of sites within a region – to making some useful statement about the past or past behaviours. Archaeological theory is, in this sense, an explicit discussion of the link between data and different levels of interpretation or meaning.

2 To devise, apply or test a conceptual, social or economic model (e.g., FORAGING THEORY) in

relation to a particular aspect of the archaeological record.

Since many of the individual entries in this dictionary discuss the latter, we will concentrate here on the different ways archaeologists have discovered of linking data to meaning. Often the archaeologist gives meaning to primary evidence by making some commonsensical analogy with the way modern humans behave, or by using a clearly argued historical or ETHNOGRAPHIC ANALOGY. Alternatively, the archaeologist might make a wholly imaginative leap or, at the other extreme, attempt to construct a strictly logical argument. Either way, the process by which the statement is made and linked to the data, how it is verified or assessed for plausibility (*see also* VERIFICATION *and* FALSIFICATION), and how it is related to existing assumptions and theories about past cultures is of interest to the theorist. Here we can add one further quality of archaeological theorizing: it is the *self-conscious* statement and analysis of assumptions, accepted principles, rules of procedure and methodologies that have been devised to describe, predict or explain the relationship between archaeological data and social phenomena. To be a theory, rather than simply a way of doing things, an approach to the data/meaning problem must be *explicit*.

Like other aspects of the discipline, archaeological theory borrows heavily from social and natural sciences. Archaeological theorists have repeatedly turned to leading philosophies of science (e.g. Popper 1934, 1963; Hempel 1965, 1966; Kuhn 1962), and in doing so they have also had to ask whether the nature of archaeological data is different to the nature of data in other areas of human enquiry. Occasionally a philosopher of science has returned the favour (Salmon, 1982). In the philosophy of science, the principal approaches to theory building are often divided into those that build meaning up from looking at individual instances, and those that formulate laws and then deduce hypotheses from them that are testable in the real world – although in practice few research programmes are purely one or the other. These two approaches are discussed in the entry on INDUCTIVE AND DEDUCTIVE EXPLANATION. Many of the arguments between those expounding PROCESSUAL ARCHAEOLOGY and POST-PROCESSUAL ARCHAEOLOGY, centre around the relative *truthfulness* and *usefulness* – not quite the same thing – of these different explanatory approaches.

Explicitly or otherwise, and like other scientists, archaeologists tend to classify different kinds of statement into a sort of hierarchy of interest and (more contentiously) reliability. For example, some archaeological statements such as 'All large pottery vessels found at site X are decorated with a wave design' are simple generalizations that can be quite easily proved or disproved (tested) by further research or experiment. These 'low-level' theories – essential to much archaeological *description* – are usually just summaries of repeated associations which suggest a strongly positive correlation between two sets of data. The link between data and statement is often straightforward – even if at a philosophical level it is contentious to identify correlation with causality. However, although such statements are a building block of archaeology, they rarely add much to our knowledge of the culture at an *explanatory* level.

The link between data and other kinds of statements is much more complex. For example, 'All pottery decorated with a wave design was used to hold ritual water' is much more difficult to prove or disprove. As a statement, it may have been prompted by the archaeologist making a simplistic link between the motif and the area of the site where the pottery was found, or by a statistically significant link noted at a hundred other better-understood sites. Either way, the difficulty in the link between the data and the statement is that both the validity *and the usefulness* of the statement no longer reside in a simple description of correlations between data sets, but depend upon a presumed understanding of an element of human behaviour. We might try to break the statement down into a series of carefully worded definitions linked by logical rules, and test it in various ways. But this would not offer us proof that the statement was true in any general sense. Setting aside the problem of devising convincing tests, and the problem of sampling, those tests would only suggest that the statement was true for as long as the rules about human behaviour, as stated in our argument, obtained. The problem remains when examining any open system – human behaviour is not the only indefinable variable.

This hints at some of the problems encountered in processual archaeology, and at one of the reasons for the limited success of archaeologists in discovering useful and widely accepted MIDDLE-RANGE THEORY. This was the name the New Archaeology of the 1960s and 1970s gave to a concerted attempt to identify and test a body of theories which consistently explained distinctive characteristics of the archaeological record, whatever context they might be applied to. By developing a platform of verified theories, often linking human behaviour to archaeological evidence, archaeologists would be able to make secure inferences. This emphasis on testing hypotheses against data gave theory building in processual archaeology a strongly POSITIVIST flavour (*see for example*, IWO ELERU). Michael Schiffer's BEHAVIORAL ARCHAEOLOGY also attempted to build testable laws with regard to the dialogue between human behaviour and the archaeological record. His C-TRANSFORMS and N-TRANSFORMS described and codified the cultural and natural processes which formed the archaeological record (Schiffer 1976). Gibbon (1989) provides a thorough examination of the LOGICAL POSITIVIST assumptions underlying the New Archaeology and argues that the movement failed to construct and verify a useful body of theory.

Other theorists, from both CONTEXTUAL ARCHAEOLOGY and the broad POST-PROCESSUAL ARCHAEOLOGY, have attacked the processualist approach for a number of reasons. They argue that the kinds of theories that can be stated in such a way as to make them verifiable tend to be extremely simple, mechanistic theories. In other words, the processual archaeologists are doomed only to succeed with the trivial. The interesting questions asked by archaeologists concern social phenomena that cannot be isolated, and are often unique in any particular manifestation. This means that essential elements of the verification obtained by experimentation in the natural sciences, notably the notion of closed systems and repeatability, are absent. They accuse processual archaeologists of dressing up their arguments in scientific language, illustrations and paraphernalia, which far from making arguments explicit and challengable, act to cover up archaeology's unavoidable platform of assumptions, its obscure and broken sets of data.

Gibbon (1989: 144–80) also describes what he terms the 'realist' approach to knowledge gathering, formulated by various philosophers of science since the demise of logical positivism. This approach is much more self-conscious about the effect of preconceptions on theory building, and better adapted to dealing with complex open systems and hidden causes. Logical positivism's insistence on absolutes – specifically the equivalence of causality and correlation – meant that it could not offer useful ways of analysing relationships between phenomena in most of the circumstances scientists faced. By contrast, 'statements of laws in realist science make a claim about the activity of a tendency', so that rather than attempting to formulate universal truths or laws 'the task of the applied scientist is to untangle the web of interlocking influences' in each empirical manifestation.

A related approach to the ways in which theory is actually constructed in archaeology has also been outlined by Ian Hodder (1992: 213–40). This takes as its inspiration a close analysis of what Hodder, as an archaeologist, believes that archaeologists actually *do* when they approach an archaeological problem. As an example, Hodder describes his process of thought when investigating a particular site, showing how the assumptions and hypotheses he initially held went through a series of radical revision and refinements as excavation progressed. In this process, many of the ideas are not stated formally or closely defined in a strictly logical or 'scientific' manner – as they would have been in a more processual approach. Instead, they informed the decisions made on where and how to excavate in a sort of continuous dialectic. Hodder characterizes this as a *hermeneutic* (interpretative or explanatory) *circle*. According to this idea, rather than setting out to construct theories with testable propositions to arrive at some objective verified statement, archaeologists should acknowledge that they build most archaeological theories from a whole set of earlier assumptions and theories, some carefully considered and others half baked. The important part of the process is not the theory building, or even the theory testing in any formal sense, but continually setting the theory against the evidence in a particular context. Even as the theory is readjusted, the evidence grows and alters in character and complexity, inviting a continual reworking and re-presentation of the theory – a sort of truth-seeking spiral. It is this continual reshifting of knowledge that prevents theory from becoming circular, even though it is to some extent both generated by and tested against the archaeological evidence.

An interesting feature of this argument is that its *description* of the central motor of theory building – the generation of ideas, their formulation into statements, their setting against the evidence, their repeated revision – is not dissimilar to the actions *prescribed* in the New Archaeology of the 1960s and 1970s. The difference is that Hodder's approach focuses on a tightening oscillation around the 'truth', rather than a laborious but secure way of validating single statements. And the concern shifts from specifying the exact status and relationships of the components of the theory or model (in an effort to increase the universality of the theory and to tie it securely to other explanatory efforts) to an on-going pragmatic effort to find a 'best fit' model or theory for a particular circumstance.

The rhetoric of the various camps of archaeological theory suggests that their approaches to truth-seeking in archaeology are different in essence, whereas often differences seem to resolve themselves into style and communication. This is important because it suggests that practising archaeologists may *legitimately* choose between them on the basis of appropriateness and utility – make 'trade-offs' – when theory-building in different areas. In some areas, for example when attempting to justify analogies or create law-like generalizations, the usefulness of which can be leveraged by other archaeologists, it may be convenient to practise the truth-seeking methods and rhetoric of processual archaeology. In other circumstances, archaeologists may not want to invest time and effort in building (and expensively and laboriously justifying) a single theory of dubious value, when the alternative is to throw twenty specific but flimsy theories at a rich and evolving set of data knowing that only the fittest will survive.

As implied above, a distinguishing feature of middle-range theory in archaeology is that it not only attempts to build an explicit verified link between data and human action, but also attempts to generalize this link. That is, it attempts to state a defining rule or principle that will hold good beyond the specific cultural or archaeological context in which it was formulated. In this, it is similar to other theory-building approaches such as the attempt to build cross-cultural laws or use ETHNOGRAPHIC ANALOGIES. The tension between the formulation of theories about particular human behaviour based on particular evidence, and the formulation of generalizing theories about societies or human behaviour at a wider level, is a strong feature of the development of archaeological theory. In a discipline dependent upon the tenuous link between material culture and human behaviour, and with inherently patchy sets of evidence, the attraction of generalizing theories is undeniable. Whether such theorizing is framed as a law, or a formal or suggestive analogy, is perhaps simply a question of efficiency and clarity (*see also* COVERING LAW).

In the wider social sciences, 'general' or 'social' theory is the name given to the highest-level theories that explain how regularities in human societies are generated. MARXISM, for example, offers a series of statements about human social organization as an explanation for both regularities seen in human societies over time and the behaviour of key phenomena within every society of a certain kind. This kind of general theory is extremely difficult to prove or disprove within the social sciences, as it inevitably depends upon hypothesized links and relationships that cannot be observed in the real world. Marxism depends ultimately upon a belief in the linking concept of contradictions in the forces of production. Although most high-level theories are less general and less complex in application than Marxism, the large and disparate body of economic and social theory in archaeology includes older concepts such as DIFFUSIONISM or HYDRAULIC DESPOTISM as well as relative newcomers such as SYSTEMS THEORY and WORLD SYSTEMS THEORY.

Whether a particular general theory is accepted depends upon both plausibility (how well it seems to accord with the available evidence) and receptiveness (i.e. the social and academic environment in which the theory is put forward). Because of this dependence upon receptiveness, some archaeologists have argued that it is wrong to speak about archaeological theory without a self-conscious examination of how archaeology as a discipline, and particular approaches within archaeology, relate to wider concerns and beliefs within modern society. This concern with the social practice of disciplines such as archaeology, often termed *praxis* (Greek for 'practice'), is characteristic of post-processual archaeology. Just as David Clarke in 1973 described the loss of innocence of the New Archaeology, as a process whereby implicit thinking was replaced by explicit theory building and testing, so post-processual theorists came eventually to speak of the 'innocence' of thinkers such as Lewis Binford and other processual archaeologists, whose attempts to build bodies of tested theories of archaeology imply a belief in a scientific archaeology free from the wider influences of society. Post-processualists argued that even if such theories can be shown to be 'true', in the sense that they have a consistent relationship with the raw archaeological data, they can never be formulated 'objectively'. The selection of the theory to be tested, its exact formulation, the extent and the way in which it is applied to the evidence, and above all the importance it is accorded will all inevitably be informed by the research PARADIGM and the wider intellectual and social environment of the discipline. Perhaps the classic example of the importance of *praxis* to theory building in archaeology is GENDER ARCHAEOLOGY. Gender archaeology not only confronts many assumptions within archaeology, but also makes clear that many fundamental questions about human prehistory have simply never been posed: historically, because of the male-centred intellectual and social environment, they were not considered important.

K. Popper: *The logic of scientific discovery* (London, 1934/1959); T.S. Kuhn: *The structure of scientific revolutions* (Chicago, 1962); K. Popper: *Conjectures and refutations* (London, 1963/1972); C.G. Hempel: *Aspects of scientific explanation and other essays in the philosophy of science* (New York, 1965); ——: *Philosophy of natural science* (Princeton, 1966); I. Lakatos and A. Musgrave, eds: *Criticism and the growth of knowledge* (Cambridge, 1970); P.J. Watson, S.A. LeBlanc and C.L. Redman: *Explanation in archaeology: an explicitly scientific approach* (New York and London, 1971); D.L. Clarke: 'Archaeology: the loss of innocence', *Antiquity* 47 (1973), 6–18; M.H. Salmon: *Philosophy and archaeology* (New York, 1982); M.B. Schiffer: *Behavioural archaeology* (New York, 1976); L. Binford: *In pursuit of the past* (London 1983); G. Gibbon: *Explanation in archaeology* (Oxford, 1989); B. Trigger: *A history of archaeological thought* (Cambridge, 1989); I. Hodder: *Theory and practice in archaeology* (London, 1992); K.R. Dark: *Theoretical archaeology* (London, 1995).
RJA

Thera (mod. Santorini) Island in the Cyclades that was partly destroyed by a massive volcanic explosion in the mid 2nd millennium BC, the ash from which buried and uniquely preserved a major Cycladic port of the Middle Bronze Age. The ancient settlement, now often referred to as Akrotiri after the nearby modern village, began to develop during the Early Cycladic period, and by the Middle Bronze Age had developed into a major town. Theran material culture reflects its geographical position – the pottery retains a Cycladic character (*see* CYCLADIC CULTURE), while wall-paintings, architectural features and luxury craft items reveal the influence of the MINOAN civilization of Crete and the MYCENAEAN civilization of the Greek mainland. (It is possible that the town became prosperous as a nodal point in trade between the two civilizations.) The houses, which are often preserved up to their second storey, were built of unworked stone and clay with timber and ashlar reinforcements. There was no rigid town-plan, and instead the houses line winding alleys and irregularly shaped 'squares'. Only a small part of the town has been excavated, but it appears to have been a rich quarter, with a number of houses containing wall murals – the wall paintings of Akrotiri are second only to those of KNOSSOS. The most remarkable painting is the 'Flotilla' or 'Ship Procession' scene: the ships sail across a sea full of dolphins between two festive towns (one of which may be Akrotiri itself) in what seems to be a nautical procession or ritual.

Dating the explosion. The ancient town was first excavated in the 1960s by Spyridon Marinatos, who believed that the volcanic explosion which destroyed Thera (and preserved its archaeological remains) was also responsible for the destruction of the Minoan civilization on Crete. However, while most of the Cretan palaces were abandoned during the pottery phase known as Late Minoan IB, the evidence from Akrotiri suggests that the eruption happened at least two or three generations earlier during Late Minoan IA. Furthermore, the only ashy layers found on excavation sites on Crete that could have been caused by the volcano distinctly predate the end of Minoan civilization. Vulcanologists have also thrown doubt on the severity of the disturbances likely to have been caused so far away (Crete is about 110 km distant). The third international conference on Thera (Hardy et al. 1990) therefore dismissed the connection between the Theran eruption and the final wave of destruction on Crete. The eruption may have taken place around 1520 BC, but more probably occurred about a century earlier in 1620 BC.

C. Doumas: *Thera* (London, 1983); L. Morgan: *The miniature wall-paintings of Thera* (Cambridge, 1988); D.A. Hardy et al.: *Thera and the Aegean World III*, 3 vols (London, 1990); K.A. Wardle: 'The palace civilizations of Minoan Crete and Mycenaean Greece, 2000–1200 BC', *The Oxford illustrated prehistory of Europe*, ed. B. Cunliffe (Oxford, 1994), 202–43.
RJA

thermal analysis Blanket term which encompasses a range of firing temperature determination methods for ceramics. This includes thermal shrinkage and thermal expansion methods of re-firing, which examine the dimensional changes of pottery during re-firing. In these, once the original firing temperature is exceeded, sintering and densification of the ceramic body are resumed and shrinkage becomes marked. Other methods of thermal analysis include SEM (SCANNING ELECTRON MICROSCOPY) of sherds or clays re-fired to different temperatures, DTA (differential thermal analysis), which measures temperature changes in experimentally heated clays, and THERMOGRAVIMETRIC ANALYSIS.

M.S. Tite: 'Determination of the firing temperature of ancient ceramics by measurement of thermal expansion: a reassessment', *Archaeometry* 11 (1969), 131–43; R.B. Heimann: 'Firing technologies and their possible assessment by modern analytical methods', *Archaeological ceramics*, ed. J.S. Olin and A.D. Franklin (Washington, D.C., 1982), 89–96.
PTN

thermal colour test Technique of ceramic analysis based on the temperature-dependent colour changes of clays caused by their mineral content and impurities. Clay briquettes are fired at intervals and their hue, value and chroma recorded, using a MUNSELL COLOUR CHART, after each successive firing. The results are then plotted; similar clays should yield similar graphs. The clay briquettes can then be compared with sherds which have been similarly heated in stages, though here change will occur only above the original firing temperature. Where the latter stages of the graphs for the clay briquettes correspond to those for the sherds, a similar clay is indicated. The technique can also be used to estimate ancient firing temperatures, since if the clay can be ascertained then the temperature at which the original sherd colour is reached can be discovered from comparison with the relevant clay briquette.

B. Hulthén: 'On thermal colour test', *NAR* 9 (1976), 1–6.

PTN

thermal gradients *see* THERMAL STRESS

thermal prospection, thermal sensing Method of AIRBORNE REMOTE-SENSING which depends on slight temperature variations (comprising tenths of a degree centigrade) of deposits overlying buried structures, the thermal properties of which differ from the surrounding soil. Usually undertaken from an aeroplane (although ground-level measurements can also be made), this technique has mainly been applied to large structures such as prehistoric enclosures.

A. Clark: *Seeing beneath the soil* (London, 1990), 122.

IS

thermal stress The difference in temperature between the surfaces and interior of, for example, a ceramic vessel wall, which occur during firing, cooling and use. For example, heating over a cooking fire will lead to differences in temperature across the profile of a vessel wall which will lead to stresses in the material as the outer surface expands more rapidly than the inside. Such stresses can eventually break the vessel. Thermal gradients can be reduced by producing thin walled vessels and vessels with a non-angular profile.

P.M. Rice: *Pottery analysis: a sourcebook* (Chicago, 1987), 363–5.

PTN

thermogravimetric analysis Means of determining the weight-loss in ceramics while re-heating to 1000°C. A significant weight change accompanies the dehydroxylation of the clay, typically between 500 and 700°C, and if this loss is exhibited by a sample it indicates an original firing temperature below 700°C, insufficient for complete dehydration. Such low temperatures may either result from the potter's deliberate attempt to conserve fuel or from the fact that a higher temperature would have achieved no benefit for the particular type of vessel being produced. Coarse vessels to be used in cooking, and therefore subject to thermal stress, are often low fired. Problems from rehydration of fired pottery during burial may be encountered however, and this, along with the loss of organic material from some ceramic bodies, can make the results of this technique difficult to interpret with certainty.

P.M. Rice: *Pottery analysis: a sourcebook* (Chicago, 1987), 388.

PTN

thermoluminescence (TL) dating Scientific dating technique applicable to ceramics, burnt stone, calcite (particularly stalagmites and flow stones) and sediments. The decay of naturally occurring uranium, thorium and potassium (^{40}K) produce alpha, beta and gamma radiation; because of the long half-lives of these isotopes the radiation flux is constant over the periods of interest (there is also a small cosmic ray contribution). On passage through matter, this radiation produces electrons which can become 'trapped' at defects in the crystalline lattice of minerals in the sample (there is a net deposition of energy in the crystal – the 'radiation dose'). If the sample is heated, the electrons are released and some re-combine at so-called luminescence centres with the emission of light i.e. thermoluminescence. To a first approximation, this TL (known as the 'natural' TL) is proportional to the radiation dose-rate, the sample sensitivity to radiation (i.e. TL per unit of radiation dose) and the time elapsed since the 'traps' were last emptied.

In pottery, the elapsed time is the age of the ceramic, as the act of firing to a temperature in excess of about 400°C is sufficient to empty the traps. For calcite, the zero-time point is the formation of the crystal. For sediments, it is the exposure to light ('bleaching') prior to deposition and covering with other layers. Light bleaching of the TL signal is not very efficient and there may be a substantial, and unknown, residual signal on deposition: OPTICALLY STIMULATED LUMINESCENCE circumvents this problem. The age equation is often expressed in terms of the ratio of 'archaeological dose' (or palaeodose) relative to 'effective radiation dose-rate'. The archaeological dose is the amount of beta or gamma radiation required to produce the signal equal to the natural TL, while the 'effective annual radiation dose-rate' is all radiation contributions incorporating sensitivity relative to beta or gamma radiation.

Sample collection requires care. Because of the different ranges of the radiations involved, evaluation of the radiation dose-rate is simplified if the outer 2 mm of sample is removed. Sherds, for example, therefore need to be more than about 8 mm thick to be accurately datable. The gamma ray contribution is largely from the burial environment, which may be inhomogeneous; *in situ* measurement by the TL scientist is best. The radiation dose-rate internal to the sample is inferred by laboratory measurement of the uranium, thorium and potassium contents: U and Th contents are measured indirectly by counting alpha-particles emitted, for example, and K_2O by flame photometry, or NEUTRON ACTIVATION ANALYSIS for all three. The water content of the sample and soil is also important as this attenuates the radiation dose. Samples (sediment in particular) must not be exposed to light during collection.

TL dating has a number of variants depending on the grain type and size selected for measurement (e.g. *fine-grain polymineral*, *quartz inclusion*, *feldspar inclusion*). The effective radiation dose-rate received in each case varies largely because of the differing internal radioactivities of the grains and the short range of alpha particles (typically 25 µm). Measurement of the TL signal produces a 'glow curve' (TL versus temperature). The TL sensitivity of the sample to both alpha and beta radiation is measured by applying known radiation doses and determining the TL induced at a given temperature or over a temperature range; the growth of TL with dose is also plotted, and correction is made for any non-linearity. The traps used for dating must be deep enough for electrons to remain trapped for periods well in excess of the date of interest; such traps produce TL at temperatures greater than or about 300°C. Tests for trapped electron stability include the 'plateau test' (comparison of the shape of the natural TL signal with one induced by laboratory radiation) and tests for 'anomalous fading' (rapid and usually short-term loss of TL signal, which on kinetic grounds should be stable): feldspar minerals in volcanic lava flows are particularly prone to anomalous fading, but quartz is usually immune.

The precision on a TL age is typically between ± 5 and ± 10% of the age (i.e. ± 100–200 years for an object 2000 years old). This precision is usually achieved by averaging the TL dates for several samples from the same context. TL dating can be used for pottery samples ranging from a few hundred years old to the earliest ceramics, and for burnt flint the age range can be extended into the Lower Palaeolithic period. Precise definition of the age range is not possible, as it depends on the specific sample (signal stability and how many traps are available) and its radiation exposure (how rapidly the traps fill).

It is possible to use TL for authenticity testing of ceramics, despite not knowing their environmental radiation history. A TL authenticity test is not very accurate in the sense of determining the true age of a particular object, but it is usually sufficient to allow discrimination between modern and ancient manufacture. A sample (50–100 mg) is drilled from an inconspicuous area; because of the hardness of porcelain it must be cored.

M.J. Aitken: *Thermoluminescence dating* (London and Florida, 1985); S.J. Fleming: *Authenticity in art* (London and Bristol, 1985).

SB

thermoremnant magnetism *see* ARCHAEOMAGNETIC DATING

Thiessen polygons Branch of SPATIAL ANALYSIS which divides a region into areas, each associated with a site. It works by drawing a line at right angles through the mid-point of the join of each pair of sites. Each line is extended until it meets another line. The effect is to surround each site by a polygon, such that each point inside it is nearer to that site than to any other. The technique can be used to study settlement patterns, although the equation of polygons with catchment areas (*see* SITE CATCHMENT ANALYSIS), for instance, is not automatic.

I.R. Hodder and M. Hassall: 'The non-random spacing of Romano-British walled towns', *Man* 6 (1971), 391–407; I.R. Hodder and C.R. Orton: *Spatial analysis in archaeology* (Cambridge, 1976), 59–60.

CO

thin sectioning Technique used by archaeologists as a means of examining the provenance of stone or ceramic artefacts via their petrology. The technique of preparation is essentially that employed by geologists, and involves cutting and consolidating a section from the artefact which is then mounted on glass and ground to 0.03 mm. At this thickness the minerals will exhibit characteristic optical properties when viewed under the polarizing microscope. These properties facilitate the identification of the mineral. Thin sections can also be used to investigate the technology of pottery making, and to separate different ceramic fabrics from one another according to their inclusions and the size and shape of their grain. For ceramic objects the technique provides information on inclusions in the clay, not on the clay itself. In addition to rock and ceramic specimens, soils can also be examined in thin section, often under fluorescent light as well as with the conventional polarizing microscope.

D.R.C. Kempe and A.P. Harvey, eds: *The petrology of archaeological artefacts* (Oxford, 1983).

PTN

tholos (pl. tholoi) Form of tomb with beehive-shaped chambers and domed roofs, built using a fine CORBELLING technique. The classic tholoi are those of the MYCENAEAN culture of Bronze Age Greece (e.g., ORCHOMENOS). In their archetypal form, these consist of the tholos itself (ie the circular, dome-roofed burial chamber), a *dromos* (an open passageway leading to the tholos) and a *stomion* (a narrow doorway covered with a massive lintel slab). Mycenaean tholoi are usually sunk into a hill-slope or level ground up to the level of the lintel slabs; the dome may be covered with an earth mound. Remarkable examples include the Treasury of Atreus (*c.*1375) and the slightly later Tomb of Clytaemnestra, both robbed out during ancient times. By analogy, the term tholos is often applied to any Mediterranean ancient tomb with a carefully corbelled beehive-shaped chamber, for example the megalithic example at ANTEQUERA in Spain. The similarity of form between Neolithic tombs such as this and the much later Mycenaean examples is no longer taken to imply any cultural connection.

RJA

Three Age System *see* SERIATION

Thule tradition Arctic tradition which existed from about AD 1 to 1600, and included the OLD BERING SEA, Okvik, Punuk, Birnirk and Thule cultures. It is characterized by a novel foraging tactic, which involved the use of large skin boats and drag floats in the hunting of large sea mammals in open water. Another major Thule innovation was the use of dog traction.

Thule communities sometimes spent the winters in large communities of semi-subterranean houses, subsisting on a stored surplus that was typically obtained by hunting Bowhead whales. The earliest sites are on islands in Bering Strait, and exhibit an almost complete reliance on maritime resources. However, the later sites demonstrate a reliance on both maritime and terrestrial resources.

This kind of adaptation of the Thule tradition developed around Bering Strait; it spread, primarily through migration, to practically the entire Arctic region by AD 1000. After the 13th century AD, there seems to have been a climatic deterioration; this is generally credited with causing the Thule to modify their way of life into that of the various Historic INUIT groups. *See also* NETTILLING LAKE.

L.R. Binford: 'Willow smoke and dogs' tails: hunter-gatherer settlement systems and archaeological site formation', *AA* 45 (1980), 4–20; D. Damas, ed.: *Handbook of North American Indians* V: *Arctic* (Washington, D.C., 1984); J.M. Savelle: *Collectors and forages: subsistence-settlement system change in the Central Canadian Arctic, AD 1000–1960* (Oxford, 1987).

RP

Thunderbird PALEOINDIAN site in northwestern Virginia (USA) on the South Fork of the Shenandoah River, where the presence of CLOVIS fluted, later Paleoindian and Early Archaic projectile points indicates that occupation of Thunderbird started about 9000 BC and continued intermittently during the Early Archaic period (*c.*7000 BC). The Thunderbird Site is one of a series of sites (quarry, reduction station, base camp, maintenance site and hunting camps) comprising the so-called 'Flint Run Paleoindian complex'. Thunderbird is a base camp consisting of more than 20 artefact concentrations which have been interpreted as household activity areas. An important activity was the refurbishing of toolkits with new flaked stone tools manufactured from jasper collected from a nearby quarry.

W. Gardner: 'The flint run Paleo-Indian complex and its implications for eastern North American prehistory', *Annals of the New York Academy of Sciences* 288 (1977), 257–63; ——: *Lost arrowheads and broken pottery: traces of Indians in the Shenandoah Valley* (Front Royal, 1986).

RJE

Tiahuanaco (Tiwanaku) Site in the Bolivian Altiplano that flourished between *c.*AD 300 and 700. The cultural successor to PUCARA, Tiahuanaco formed a large political unit which politically and culturally dominated much of Bolivia, southern highland Peru, and northern Chile. Tiahuanaco itself was an urban centre with a ceremonial core featuring several huge temples, a pyramid, and many palace structures decorated with cut stone lintels and adorned with large statues in a distinctive style. The Tiahuanaco major deity (best known from reliefs on the monolithic 'Gateway of the Sun') was represented as a male with a rayed headdress and two staves, evidently derived from the Staff God of CHAVÍN.

Investigations in the Bolivian *altiplano*, centred on the site of Tiahuanaco and with its supporting hinterland, have shown that an important aspect of the economy of the ancient city, permitting the growth of a large sedentary population, was an immense (82,000+ ha) system of raised fields surrounding Lake Titicaca. These fields were formed by cutting deep canals in the low lying, often waterlogged, soils along the lake, throwing up the soils to form long low mounds which have improved drainage and which are warmer than the surrounding dry lands as the water in the canals acts as a solar sink, blanketing the fields in warmer air on freezing nights. Canal sediments were used to fertilize the fields, lessening soil alkalinity, which along with freezing is a major agricultural problem in the region. Pollen analysis has shown that these fields were used to grow potatoes and quinoa, still major crops among the indigenous Aymara and Quechua speaking peoples of the *altiplano*. Modern experiments, growing into full-scale projects involving local peoples, have demonstrated that greatly increased yields and even double cropping are still possible if these canals and raised field systems are used.

I.Z. Garaycochea: 'Agricultural experiments in raised fields in the Lake Titicaca Basin, Peru: preliminary considerations', *Pre-Hispanic agricultural fields in the Andean region*, ed. William M. Denevan et al. (London, 1987), 385–402; C. Erickson: 'Raised field agriculture in the Lake Titicaca Basin: putting ancient agriculture back to work', *Expedition* 30/3 (1988), 8–16; A. Kolata and C. Ortloff: 'Thermal analysis of Tiwanaku raised field systems in the Lake Titicaca basin of Bolivia', *JAS* 16 (1989), 233–63; J. Albarracín Jordan: *Asentamientos Prehispanicos del Valle de Tiwanaku* (La Paz, 1990); L.J. Arellano: 'The new cultural contexts of Tiahuanaco', *Huari administrative structure: prehistoric monumental architecture and state government*, ed. W. Isbell and G.F. McEwan (Washington, D.C., 1991), 259–80; A.L. Kolata: 'The technology and organization of labor production in the Tiwanaku state', *LAA* 2/2 (1991), 99–125.

KB

Tien culture (Dian) *see* SHIH-CHAI-SHAN

Tighénif *see* TERNIFINE

Tikal The largest known Maya centre of the Classic period (*c*.AD 300–900), located in north-central Petén, Guatemala. Tikal was the site of a massive mapping and excavation project carried out by the University Museum of the University of Pennsylvania from 1956 to 1967. Several years of mapping at the start of the project revealed that the site's civic-ceremonial architecture covers an area of some 16 sq. km and comprises more than 3000 constructions, including 3 acropolises, 5 SACBES, 9 reservoirs, a ballcourt (*see* BALLGAME), a sweathouse and countless temple-pyramids, plazas, complexes, residences and more than 200 stone monuments, including stelae.

The beginnings of settlement in Tikal date to the Middle Preclassic (Formative) period (*c*.600 BC), with recovery of refuse deposits and a few simple burials. Growth of ceremonial architecture at the site was underway by the beginning of the Late Preclassic. Recent excavations by Guatemalan archaeologists have been directed toward the Early Classic structures in the Mundo Perdido complex and the connections between Tikal and TEOTIHUACAN. Most of what is known about the site comes from the massive and abundant structural remains dating to the Late Classic period, including the elite residences of the Central and South Acropolises and the spectacular royal burials in the North Acropolis and under the largest temple-pyramids at Tikal. Although scattered Postclassic finds have been found, Tikal seems to have been largely abandoned during the 9th-century LOWLAND MAYA collapse.

Tikal's centre had an estimated population of 60,000 people, but residential settlement spreads over another 60 sq. km around the centre. This area of rural settlement was investigated by means of what was at the time an unusual survey and sampling technique in the Maya lowlands: transects. Four long trails were cut through the forest, extending out from the site centre to the cardinal directions. Four kilometres north of the centre a low wall and ditch – probably defensive – extended between the swampy areas (*bajos*) bordering the site on the east and west. The distribution of residential structures around the site suggests a rural population estimated at 30,000. The total population of the Tikal state, including secondary centres within its political orbit (such as Yaxhá and Naranjo), is estimated at 425,000 (Culbert et al. 1990: 117). (*See* figure 57.)

University of Pennsylvania: *Tikal Reports*, 22 vols (Philadelphia, 1958–); W.A. Haviland: 'Population and social dynamics: the dynasties and social structure of Tikal', *Expedition* 27 (1985), 34–41; P.D. Harrison: 'Tikal: selected topics', *City States of the Maya*, ed. E.P. Benson (Denver, 1986) 45–71; T.P. Culbert, L.J. Kosakowsky, R.E. Fry and W.A. Haviland; 'The population of Tikal,

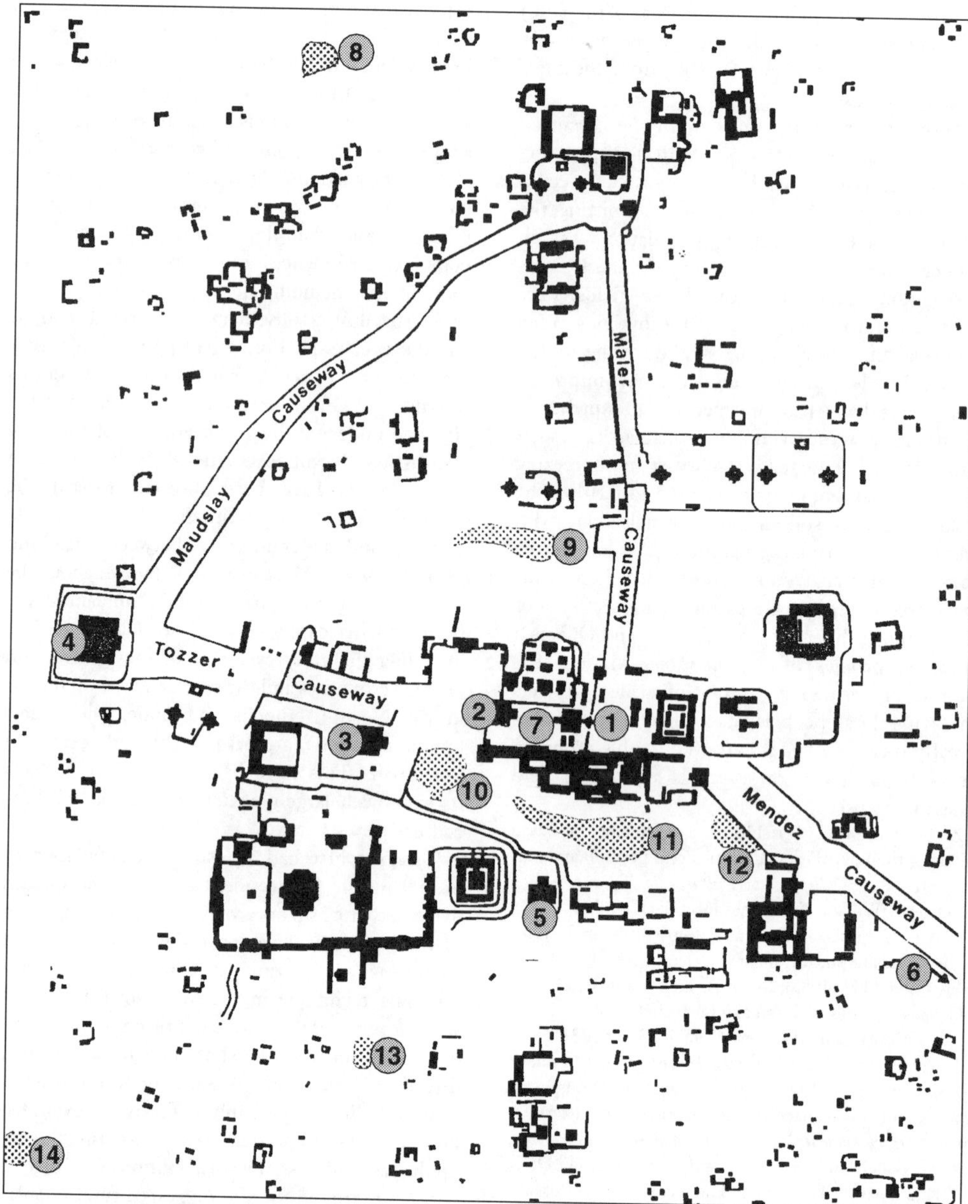

Figure 57 **Tikal** Map of the central part of the Mayan city of Tikal, Guatemala; (1–5) Temples I–V, (6) Temple of Inscriptions, (7) Great Plaza, (8–14) Reservoirs. *Source*: M.D. Coe: *The Maya*, 2nd ed. (Thames and Hudson, 1980), fig. 53.

Guatemala', *Precolumbian population history in the Maya lowlands*, ed. T.P. Culbert and D.S. Rice (Albuquerque, 1990) 103–21.

PRI

Tikopia Small island (4.6 sq. km) lying 200 km north of Vanuatu and 200 km southeast of the Santa Cruz Islands in the Pacific. A study of the island by Pat Kirch and Doug Yen (1982), based mainly on archaeological data but complemented by anthropological evidence, forms a classic example of the principal focus of archaeological work in the Pacific: the casual cycle linking landscape, society and subsistence.

Tikopia is formed mainly of a volcanic cone rising some 360 m above the sea, with reefal growth to the west in the lee of the volcano on which sands and volcanic debris have accumulated. The island was the subject of a long period of anthropological study by Raymond Firth, who looked at the clan structure, agricultural practices and religious beliefs of the Polynesian population (Firth 1936). In 1977 and 1978 Kirch and Yen undertook a joint study of the systems of settlement, agriculture and society that have evolved during the 3000-year occupation of the island. The present day land-use is a complex mixture of tree and root crops. Trees such as breadfruit, *canarium* (Pacific almond) and coconut are planted both for food and for soil conservation measures. The soil erosion has largely been caused by the (now total) clearance of natural forest in order to plant root crops such as taro and the introduced manioc. Tree cropping, common throughout the Pacific, is found in a particularly complex form in Tikopia: the planting of small and large trees together mirrors the upper- and under-storeys of the natural rainforest.

Many islands of the Pacific have been cleared of their natural vegetation, which has been replaced by species introduced by people, giving rise to the concept of 'transported landscapes'. Not only have people taken with them all the plant and animal (chiefly pig, dog and chicken) species on which they lived, but also bodies of knowledge on how to combine these species in a manner that is productive and appropriate for provisioning the social system. The Tikopia evidence shows that people went further, and transformed the physical structure of the landscape. When people arrived on Tikopia, roughly 3000 years ago, they found an island which looked very different from that of today. The cone was in its present form, but the lowlands to the west of the island, on which much present day agriculture takes place, were far smaller. The earliest colonists relied heavily on marine resources (fish, turtle and shellfish) and land birds – some of which they wiped out – while they established their agricultural systems. (This heavy reliance on wild resources is typical of the earliest phase of colonization across the Pacific.) The earliest material culture assemblages, particularly the pots, fit into the LAPITA CULTURAL COMPLEX found throughout the western Pacific.

Around 2000 years ago the pottery changed to that of the MANGAASI styles, also widespread throughout the Pacific region. In this phase, the agricultural system seems to have been well established, as evidenced by plant remains and bones, but there are also indications of soil erosion from the slopes of the volcano, presumably due to forest

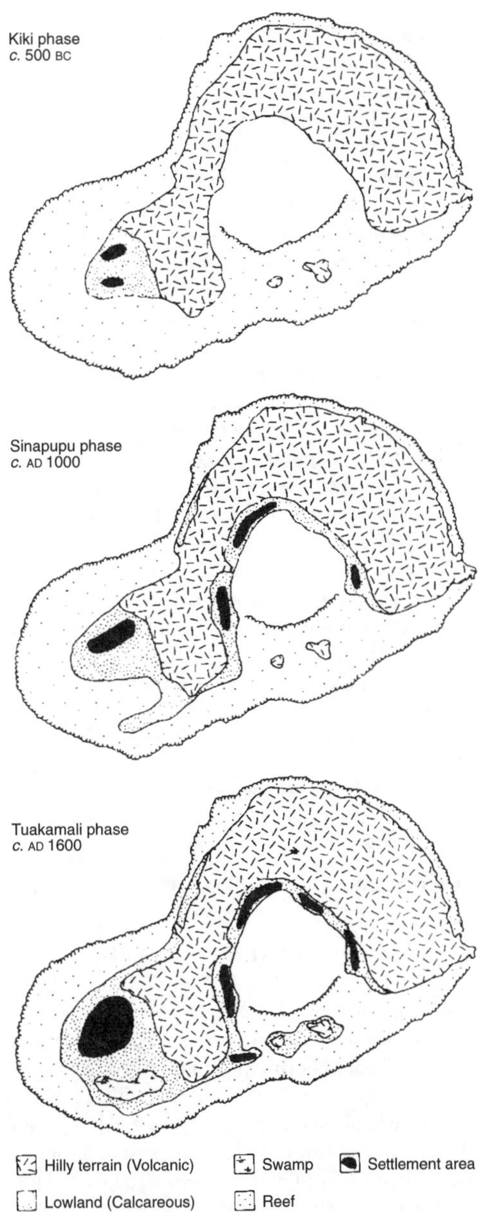

Figure 58 **Tikopia** Paleogeographic reconstruction of the Tikopia environment at three points in time *Source*: P. Kirch and D.E. Yen: Tikopia: *The prehistory and ecology of a Polynesian outlier* (BMP, 1982), fig. 124.

clearance. Soil from the slopes built up on the lowland areas to the west and formed new areas of cultivable land.

Between 2000 and 800 years ago there was a marked switch from wild to cultivated foods, a more intensive concentration on pigs, and the expansion of settlement. During the final phase of Tikopia's prehistory, after 800 years ago, there was further aggradation of the shoreline to the west and a much larger build-up of soil on the western flats. Agriculture seems to have taken on its modern form, with storage of breadfruit starch in pits. Pigs disappear from the faunal record, which fits in with oral historical evidence suggesting that the pig herd was deliberately wiped out because of its destructive effect on gardens. Monumental architectural forms, such as MARAE, appear during this phase.

Kirch and Yen estimate that around one million cubic tons of soil have been eroded from the volcano and deposited on the lowlands, much of it in the last 1000 years. This has increased the area of land useful for horticulture by about 40%. Thus Tikopia today represents an ecology in which humans have substantially introduced the communities of plants and animals, and have also altered the physical relief of the island.

R. Firth: *We, the Tikopia* (London, 1936); P.V. Kirch and D.E. Yen: *Tikopia: The prehistory and ecology of a Polynesian outlier* (Honolulu, 1982).

CG

Timargarha *see* GANDHARA GRAVE CULTURE

Timber-grave culture (*Srúbnaya*) Bronze Age culture first identified by V.A. Gorodtsov (1900 to 1903) in the Seveski Donets area. Later, sites belonging to this culture were studied by Russian and Ukrainian scholars, including N.Ya. Merpert, O.A. Krivtsova-Grakova, and A.I. Terenozhkin and were identified in a vast area, stretching from the Middle and Lower Volga in the east to the lower Danube in the west and dated to *c.*1600–1200 BC. The main characteristic of the culture is a rectangular timber burial chamber (or *'srub'*, in Russian), 1.8–2.2 m long, 1.2–1.4 m wide and 0.4–0.6 m high, beneath a kurgan or mound. Stone cists were also common. The dead were usually laid in a contracted posture on their left side, the head facing east. The grave-goods are usually restricted to one, rarely two, ceramic vessels. The few richer graves that are known contain bronze knives, and ornaments such as rings, and wooden vessels with bronze inlays. Animal bones are often found in the graves (e.g. six bull skulls in kurgan no. 5 at Kamushevakha, near the town of Bakhmut on the Severski Donets). The barrows form small groups (numbering 5–10), usually along the edges of the plateaux.

More than 100 settlements belonging to the Timber-grave culture are known in the Seveski Donets catchment alone; they are usually situated on dunes or on small hills along the river valley and consist of semi-subterranean houses of square or rectangular shape (e.g. 7 × 7 or 6 × 8 m) arranged in one or two rows. The remains of fortifications have been found in a few cases. The economy was based on stock-breeding, agriculture and metallurgy. The faunal remains consisted of the bones of cattle, sheep/goat, pig and horse. Flint and bronze sickles, pestles and quern stones are indicative of agriculture. At the site of Usovo Ozero (near Donetsk), G.A. Pashkevich (1991) has identified the grains of einkorn and club wheats, six-row barley, rye, oats and Italian millet. Metallurgy was particularly developed in the area close to the copper mines of the Donets Basin: near the villages of Klonovoe, Pilipchatino, Kalinovka and Pokrovskoe. These sites contained the remains of workshops, furnaces, slag, ingots, fragments of crucibles and clay moulds.

Many scholars, e.g. A.I. Terenozhkin (1976) and B.N. Grakov (1977), identify the Timber-grave culture with the historically-attested 'Cimmerians', who were said to live north of the Caucasus and the Black Sea in the period between 714 and *c.*500 BC.

S.S. Berezanskaya and N.N. Chernichenko: 'Srúbnaja kul'tura' [The Timber-grave culture], *Arheologiya Ukrainskoi SSR* [The archaeology of the Ukrainian SSR], ed. D. Ya. Telegin (Kiev, 1985), 462–72; B.N. Grakov: *Rannii železnyi vek* [The early Iron Age] (Moscow, 1977); A. Häusler: *Die Gräber der älteren Ockergrabkultur zwischen Ural and Dnepr* (Berlin, 1974); G.A. Pashkevich: *Paleoetnobotaničeski nohodki na territorii Ukrainy (neolit-bronza): Katalog* [Palaeoethnobotanic finds in the territory of the Ukraine (Neolithic – Bronze Age): catalogue] (Kiev, 1991); A.I. Terenozhkin: *Kimmeriicy* [The Cimmerians] (Kiev, 1976).

PD

Timna Copper-mining site in the Wadi Arabah (at the edge of the Sinai peninsula in southern Israel, about 30 km north of Eilat), which has been excavated by Beno Rothenberg since 1959. The earliest mines (at site F2) possibly constitute the earliest metallurgical workshop in the world, since they have been dated to the 5th or 6th millennium BC by associated pottery assigned to the 'Qatifian' Neolithic culture. Site F2, to the west of Mount Timna, consists of a small area of slag lumps and nodules of copper ore, scattered in the vicinity of a granite mortar with which the ore had been crushed. The method of copper extraction is described as 'a rather primitive, unsophisticated technology, which appears to be at a stage near the threshold of iron ore flux utilization' (Rothenberg and Merkel 1995:5), but it is uncertain whether iron ore was being added deliberately.

The Chalcolithic mining and metallurgical operations at the site were probably undertaken by the local inhabitants of southern Palestine, although the analysis of copper implements at the late Predynastic site of MAADI suggest that the Egyptians were already using copper obtained from Timna. By the Ramessid period (*c.*1307–1070 BC), the Egyptians had become heavily involved in the mining itself, and a chapel was constructed for the Egyptian goddess Hathor, who was regarded as a protectress of mining and quarrying areas. The Timna mines were later reutilized by the NABATAEANS, Romans and Arabs.

B. Rothenberg: *Timna: valley of the Biblical copper mines* (London, 1972); ——: *The Egyptian mining temple at Timna* I (London, 1988); ——: *The ancient metallurgy of copper* (London, 1990); —— and J. Merkel: 'Late Neolithic copper smelting in the Arabah', *Institute for Archaeo-Metallurgical Studies Newsletter* 19 (1995), 1–7.

IS

Timna' *see* ARABIA, PRE-ISLAMIC

Tintagel Spectacular headland on the north coast of Cornwall which was the subject of systematic excavations in 1933–4 by C.A. Ralegh Radford, who identified a sub-Roman monastery with Mediterranean trade connections. As a result, the distinctive Late Roman 'A' wares (tableware) and 'B' ware amphorae became diagnostic type fossils for identifying other sub-Roman/early christian settlements in the Irish Sea zone. The function of Tintagel itself has been the subject of much speculation. Having been associated with the Arthurian legend, it is not surprising that some scholars interpret the monastic site as a secular elite settlement engaged in long-distance trade. The site was later occupied by a 13th century castle, built by Richard of Cornwall, younger brother of King Henry III.

C. Thomas: *Tintagel* (London, 1991).

RH

tipline Stratigraphic layer formed by the gradual sliding of material (e.g. dumped refuse) down the side of a feature (e.g. a pit or mound).

Tiryns Mycenaean citadel and palace situated on a low-lying hill in the Argolid, Greece. Tiryns began as a palace in the Late Helladic IIIa period. Subsequently, the 'Middle Citadel' area was fortified with notably thick, strong walls, and a fortified gate added. In the final phase of construction the circuit walls were greatly extended to form the Lower Citadel. In the 1960s, excavation revealed two passages under the northwest section of the wall leading to a spring – presumably fulfilling the same function as the 'secret cistern' at Mycenae. Like that at Mycenae, the palace structure at Tiryns contains a large MEGARON with a central hearth, approached from a court via two anterooms. Houses outside the circuit walls included a large megaron-type structure with hearth. Like Mycenae, there are few stratified deposits that can be reliably associated with the main structures, so that the history of the site is rather tentative. The citadel seems to have ceased to be used after about 1200 BC.

K. Muller: *Die Architektur der Burg und des Palastes* (Tiryns III) (Augsburg, 1930).

RJA

TL *see* THERMOLUMINESCENCE DATING

Togari-ishi and Yosukeone Pair of Middle Jomon (*c.*3500–2000 BC) sites in Nagano prefecture, Japan, which form part of the classic settlement cluster located on the southwestern slopes of the Yatsugadake volcanic massif. Togari-ishi was excavated between 1930 and 1942 by Miyasaka Fusakazu. The remains of some 85 buildings have been recovered from the site. At Yosukeone, 27 buildings were excavated between 1946 and 1952. Togari-ishi was the first site in Japan to be interpreted and reconstructed as a primitive settlement, and Yosukeone was the first primitive settlement to be excavated on a broad scale. Important in the history of Japanese archaeology, these sites continue to be central to theories about Jomon period community organization. In 1952 they were granted the status of sites of national historical importance, and a number of reconstructed Jomon houses and a museum have now been built at the sites. The use of detailed ceramic, artefactual and architectural typologies in the attempted reconstruction of the occupational history of the sites are typical of the methods used in social and settlement archaeology in Japan.

Masayoshi Mizuno (1969) presented an analysis of Yosukeone as part of his seminal work on the nature of Jomon settlement. Mizuno suggested that the social structure of the settlement of Yosukeone could be reconstructed as two extended families of two or three nuclear families each occupying a pit house. This model has since become the norm for reconstructing Jomon community structure. Mizuno distinguished two phases of occupation from the overlapping of pit houses and the presence or absence of stones outlining the hearths. He assumed that the hearth stones had been taken from buildings of the first phase and re-used in those of the second. He divided the buildings of the second phase into two clusters, east and west, each of which were occupied by an extended family. These clusters were then divided into smaller groups of two or three buildings, which represented smaller family units. The whole settlement was taken to represent one community.

Mizuno went on to suggest that various classes of rituals were performed by different parts of the community on the basis of the spatial distribution of pottery figurines, stone bars and standing stone altars. These included non-funerary ceremonies performed in the central plaza (in which the whole community participated) and funerary rituals carried out both by the whole community and within the extended families. Gender-specific rituals associated with hunting, sexual potency, growth and ancestors (involving standing stones and stone bars) were male, while those associated with motherhood and gathering involved the pottery figurines and were female.

While Mizuno's work continues to be influential, he has been criticized for not taking into account details of pottery typology, which threw into doubt the contemporaneity of the buildings. Support for his ideas concerning community structure was, however, provided by the results of a Q-mode factor analysis of buildings at Yosukeone performed by Takeru Akazawa and Kazuro Hanihara in 1978. The buildings fell into three clusters on the basis of the analysis of 60 variables concerning the structure of the buildings and associated artefacts. This study received a mixed reception but remains one of the few applications of explicit statistical methods to Jomon archaeology.

E. Miyasaka: *Togari-ishi* (Chino, 1957) [in Japanese]; M. Mizuno: 'Basic guidance towards settlement research for the Jomon period', *Kodai Bunka* 21/3–4 (1969), 1–21 [in Japanese]; T. Akazawa and K. Hanihara: 'A statistical analysis of the Yosukeone site in Nagano prefecture', *Kikan Jinruigaku* 9/2 (1978), 76–100 [in Japanese].

SK

Tolita Series of estuarine-adapted local cultures on the coasts of southern Colombia and northern Ecuador, dating to the Formative and Regional Developmental Periods (*c.*3000 BC–AD 500). Their modelled ceramics, mainly found washing out of the fill of house platforms (*tolas*), depict an exuberant world of lovers, dancers, musicians, supernatural felines, dragons and folkloric figures. They are also noted for their use of gold and platinum, especially in small tools.

J.-F. Bouchard: *Recherches archéologiques dans la region de Tumaco, Colombie* (Paris, 1984); F. Váldez: *La Tolita: proyecto arqueológico* (Quito, 1987).

KB

Toltecs Early Postclassic culture that flourished in northcentral Mexico in AD 900–1200. The Toltec capital of Tollan is believed to be the archaeological site of Tula, located in Hidalgo, northwest of the BASIN OF MEXICO. The remains at Tula include several groups of civic-ceremonial architecture, including a temple-pyramid with serpent columns (Pyramid B), a COATEPANTLI ('serpent-wall'), two courts for the BALLGAME, a CHACMOOL sculpture and numerous apartment-like multi-family residential structures. Architectural similarities with CHICHÉN ITZÁ are noteworthy, but disputed (Kubler 1961; Lincoln 1986).

Much of what is known about the history of the Toltecs in Mesoamerica is filtered through later AZTEC myths and histories, which they wrote and rewrote to glorify their own accomplishments, and many contradictions complicate the picture. The Toltec heritage developed out of indigenous central Mexican – and particularly TEOTIHUACAN – elements, combined with those of the peoples known as CHICHIMECS, who are thought to have begun sporadic incursions into the basin sometime around AD 700.

The early history of the Toltecs is murky at best; the ending is recorded in more detail. According to myth, a Chichimec leader conquered the town of Culhuacan and married a local noblewoman. Their child, Ce Acatl (calendar name 'One Reed', the year of his birth) Topiltzin, became the priest-king Topiltzin Quetzalcoatl in Tollan/Tula, where he was head of the Quetzalcoatl cult. In these histories, as variously told, the downfall of Tula came soon after Topiltzin Quetzalcoatl lost a dispute with rival god/cult Tezcatlipoca and/or dynastic leader Huemac. Topiltzin Quetzalcoatl was forced to leave the city in disgrace, probably in the early 12th century and sometime later so did Huemac, who subsequently killed himself. Topiltzin Quetzalcoatl, however, journeyed to CHOLULA and thence to the sea, vowing to return to his people at some time in the future during a year One Reed.

There is much speculation that in the mind of the Aztec king Motecuhzoma ('Montezuma'), this anticipated return was linked with the arrival of the Spaniard Hernán Cortés in 1519, a year that corresponds to One Reed in the Aztec calendar (*see* CALENDARS, MESOAMERICAN).

The Toltecs were fabled throughout later Mesoamerica as the originators of civilization, as mythic heroes, larger than life, as expert craftsmen and skilled farmers. They seem to have assumed control of mining and distribution of the valuable OBSIDIAN mines previously dominated by Teotihuacán. They participated in widespread trading networks throughout Mesoamerica and into the southwestern United States. They may have been involved in the spread of metallurgy in Mesoamerica. Contacts with the Maya are suggested by the marked architectural similarities between Tula and the northern LOWLAND MAYA site of CHICHÉN ITZÁ. Yet there is little archaeological or historical evidence to suggest that the Toltecs maintained control of any vast territory that might be described as an 'empire'.

For the Aztecs, the Toltecs played a critical role as a great ancestral civilization. In order to legitimize their kings and establish their own noble lineages, the Mexica – likewise of Chichimec ancestry – contrived to marry into the descendants of Toltec nobility in the basin of Mexico. Indeed, throughout Late Postclassic Mesoamerica – including the highland Maya region – rulers attempted to claim dynastic ties to the earlier Toltecs in order to legitimize their claims to power.

G. Kubler: 'Chichén Itzá y Tula', *Estudios de cultura Maya* 1 (1961), 47–79; N. Davies: *The Toltecs until the fall of Tula* (Norman, 1977); R.A. Diehl: *Tula, the Toltec capital of ancient Mexico* (London, 1983); C.E. Lincoln: 'The chronology of Chichen Itza: a review of the literature', *Late lowland Maya civilization*, ed. J.A. Sabloff and E.W. Andrews (Albuquerque, 1986), 141–96; D.M. Healen, ed.: *Tula of the Toltecs: excavations and survey* (Iowa City, 1989).

PRI

tomba di giganti ('giant's grave') Local name for a type of megalithic collective tomb associated with the nuraghic civilization of Sardinia (*see* NURAGHI). The tombs have a long, narrow chamber (up to *c.*15 m long) made of megaliths and/or drystone and covered with a mound. Access to the chamber is usually through an arched opening in a tall entrance slab carved with relief moulding; these may be imitations of the entrances to earlier rock-cut tombs on the island. Many examples have approximately semi-circular or 'horned' forecourts in front of the tomb entrance. The first examples may have been built late in the 3rd millennium BC, and the tradition may have continued into the 1st millennium BC.

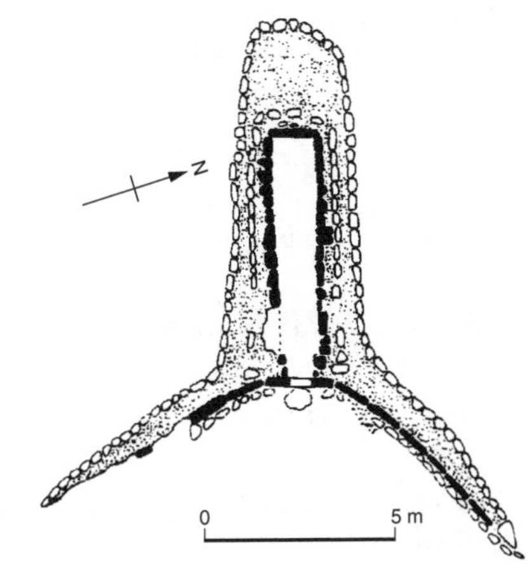

Figure 59 **tomba di giganti** Plan of tomba di giganti, Li-Mizzani, Palau, Sardinia. *Source*: R. Joussaume: *Dolmens for the dead* (London, 1987), fig. 53.

R. Whitehouse: 'Megaliths of the Central Mediterranean', *The megalithic monuments of Western Europe*, ed. C. Renfrew (London, 1981), 49–53; G. Lilliu: *La civiltà nuragica* (Milan, 1982).

RJA

Tondidarou *see* AFRICA 2

Tonga On the boundary of Polynesia, Tonga was first settled during the period of the LAPITA CULTURAL COMPLEX, just over 3000 years ago. There is widespread evidence for early settlement, but this is much sparser after 2000 BP; after this date, pottery was apparently no longer made. About 1000 years ago, the first stone-built monuments appear, but the developments in the previous thousand years are little known. Monumental architecture, connected with the rise of the Tongan 'empire', known from both archaeological and oral historical evidence, dominates the last 500 years. During this period Tongatapu became the centre of a polity encompassing the more northerly Tongan islands, and extensive trade relations developed with Fiji and Samoa. 'Langi' tombs, rectangular stone-faced mounds believed to be the burial places of the Tui Tonga (the royal line in Tonga), are most numerous around Tongatapu.

J. Davidson: 'Samoa and Tonga', *The prehistory of Polynesia*, ed. J. Jennings (Canberra, 1979), 82–109; P.V. Kirch: *The evolution of Polynesian chiefdoms* (Cambridge, 1984), 215–42.
CG

Tongling *see* T'UNG-LING MINES

Tonglushan *see* T'UNG-LÜ-SHAN

Toprakkale *see* URARTU

Torihama Incipient and Early Jomon site in Fukui prefecture, Japan where waterlogging has preserved evidence of horticultural practices as well as many bone and wooden artefacts such as dugout canoes, paddles, bows, tool hafts, wooden bowls and lacquer combs. Remains of gourds and beans from 5000 to 3000 BC suggest mid-Holocene extension of control over plant foods in Western Japan well before the adoption of rice agriculture (*see* ITAZUKE) and disturbance of the environment encouraged new human-plant relationships. SITE CATCHMENT ANALYSIS showed that the great range of food resources available in the area was being exploited.
T. Akazawa: 'Maritime adaptation of prehistoric hunter-gatherer and their transition to agriculture in Japan', *Senri Ethnological Studies* 9 (1981), 213–60 [site catchment analysis]; M. Nishida: 'The emergence of food production in neolithic Japan', *JAA* 2 (1983), 305–22.
SK

Toro Late Yayoi (AD 100–300) village site in Shizuoka prefecture, Japan, considered typical of a wet rice-growing community since its excavation in 1948 by the Japanese Archaeologists' Association. Excavated pit houses and granaries with raised floors have been reconstructed, along with paddy fields that were found adjoining the habitation area. Many wooden agricultural tools were also preserved.
Nihon Kokogaku Kyokai Kenkyukai: *Toro*, 2 vols (Tokyo, 1949–54) [in Japanese with English summaries]; C.M. Aikens and T. Higuchi: *The prehistory of Japan* (London, 1982), 226–38; G.L. Barnes: 'Toro', *Atlas of archaeology*, ed. K. Branigan (London, 1982), 198–201.
SK

torre Drystone circular towers of the Corsican Bronze Age, probably built from the 3rd millennium to mid-2nd millennium BC. Comparable to the Sardinian NURAGHI and the talayots of the Balearic Islands, *torre* are often part of, or occur near to, fortified settlement sites (known locally as *castelli*). The material culture associated with *torre* is not well known, although graves thought to be broadly contemporary have yielded assemblages similar to Beaker assemblages (but without beakers) found elsewhere in the Early Bronze Age Mediterranean (see 'BEAKER PHENOMENON').
J. Lewthwaite: 'The Neolithic of Corsica', *Ancient France 6000–2000 BC*, ed. C. Scarre (Edinburgh, 1987), 168–71.
RJA

'tortoise' core *see* LEVALLOIS TECHNIQUE

Toteng *see* BAMBATA POTTERY

Toumbian *see* CAP MANUEL

Toutswemogala Large flat-topped hill near Palapye in eastern Botswana, where excavations have revealed ceramics from the third phase of the Gokomere tradition (Gokomere-Zhizo-Toutswe; *c*.AD 1000–1300). The thick deposit of vitrified cattle dung, middens and village debris is covered by a specific grass (*Cenchrus ciliaris*) which is adapted to enriched soils. Denbow's detailed aerial and ground survey of similar sites shows that Toutswemogala was the capital of a chiefdom consisting of at least three hierarchical levels. Large-scale excavations with an earth-moving machine at a small site, corresponding to level one in the hierarchy, uncovered an almost complete example of the 'CENTRAL CATTLE PATTERN', including males buried on their right-hand side in the cattle byre and women buried on their left side behind huts. Two other large hilltop capitals lay 100 km south and west. Other than a unique cache of glass beads, trade imports were conspicuously absent, and these political hierarchies arose through the control of cattle wealth. Toutswemogala was contemporaneous with K2 and MAPUNGUBWE, and its hilltop location may have been defensive.
J. Denbow: '*Cenchrus ciliaris*: an ecological indicator of Iron Age middens using aerial photography in eastern Botswana', *SAJS* 76 (1979), 405–8; ——: 'The Toutswe Tradition: a study in socio-economic change', *Settlement in Botswana*, ed. R. Hitchcock and M. Smith (Johannesburg, 1982), 73–86; ——: 'A new look at the later prehistory of the Kalahari', *JAH* 27 (1986), 3–29.
TH

Town Creek Short-lived centre of the Southern Appalachian Mississippian tradition of the Pee Dee culture that dates to about AD 1300–1400, consisting of a temple mound surrounded by a palisade. Several nearby farmsteads may be outliers of this ceremonial, political and social centre. The site is thought to be affiliated with Muskhogean-speaking Indians and represents the northernmost extension of Mississippian peoples into North Carolina.

M.A. Mathis and J.J. Crow: *The prehistory of North Carolina: an archaeological symposium* (Raleigh, 1983); J. Coe: *Town Creek Indian mound: a Native American legacy* (Chapel Hill, 1995).

WB

trace elements Elements present in mineral crystals in very low concentrations, less than 0.1%. Trace elements are usually measured as parts per million (ppm) or parts per billion (ppb). Where the concentration is less than 1 ppm the term 'ultra-trace' may be used. Trace elements, if accurately measured, are often a key to the source of the mineral or rock, and their analysis is therefore one of the methods of certain provenance studies. Since the elements are present in such small amounts, they are obviously not deliberate additions to alloys, pottery fabrics etc. – this makes them especially valuable to the archaeologist. They can be detected by many techniques including OPTICAL EMISSION SPECTROMETRY and X-RAY FLUORESCENCE.

P.M. Rice: *Pottery analysis: a sourcebook* (Chicago, 1987), 314, 325.

PTN

tradition Term used to describe a set of industries that are technologically or aesthetically similar enough to imply an underlying cultural or historical connection. The term is often used to describe a set of industries related across time, so that, in effect, a tradition forms the 'genealogy' of any given industry. The recognition of a group of traditions in different technological areas (flint knapping, bone carving) which occur together repeatedly may lead to the identification of a CULTURE. Sometimes, the term is used more loosely to describe a sequence of related cultures, or cultural trait, over time.

RJA

Tra Kieu *see* CHAM

'transported landscapes' Term used in the archaeology of Oceania to describe the way in which the natural flora and fauna of many Pacific islands has been substantially replaced by introduced species. Migrants took with them not only all the plant and animal (chiefly pig, dog and chicken) species on which they lived, but also the knowledge of how to combine these species so as to provision their social systems. *See* TIKOPIA *for extended example and discussion.*

CG

TRB (Funnel Beaker culture) Prominent regional material culture complex of the Early and Middle Neolithic in Northern Europe and parts of Central Europe, from the Czech republic through Poland and Germany into south Scandinavia and Holland. In the central and southern areas of this distribution, it succeeds the Early Neolithic LBK and post-LBK cultures, while in south Scandinavia it represents the first farming culture. The culture dates from *c.*3500 to 3000 and so is roughly contemporary with the other key cultural complexes of the Middle Neolithic in Europe, the Chassey (France), Michelsberg (Rhineland) and the Cortaillod (Switzerland). The TRB is characterised by the *Trichterrandbecher*, a highly distinctive globular vessel with a long, funnel-like neck. There are many local and chronological variants of the assemblages as a whole, but they tend to contain bowls, amphorae-like vessels, and in some regions pedestalled vessels; tools include ground-stone axes, some with perforated holes for the shafts. The TRB assemblage is closely associated with early examples of megalithic and earthern graves in many regions, notably the early KUJAVIAN BARROWS and passage graves such as the HUNEBEDDEN.

In the later stages, copper artefacts begin to be found among TRB assemblages, particularly in the southeast region. The TRB was succeeded by the more widely spread CORDED WARE complex of the 3rd millennium BC in northern Europe and by the Baden culture in southeast Europe. Many researches now believe that the TRB is ancestral to the Corded Ware complex, although the sequences seem to overlap in part and the dating is unclear.

A. Whittle: *Neolithic Europe: a survey* (Cambridge 1985), 204–6, 241; J.A. Bakker: *The TRB West Group: studies in the chronology and geography of the makers of Hunebeds and Tiefstich pottery* (Amsterdam, 1979); K. Randsborg: 'Resource distribution and the function of copper tools in early Neolithic Denmark', *The origins of metallurgy in Atlantic Europe*, ed. M. Ryan (Dublin 1980), 303–18.

RJA

tree ring dating *see* DENDROCHRONOLOGY

trend surface analysis Branch of SPATIAL ANALYSIS which represents the spatial behaviour of a VARIABLE by a smooth surface, the height of which gives the value of the variable at each location, for example, the proportions of a certain type of pottery at sites in a region (*see* REGRESSION). The surface may be formed by local smoothing (grid generalization) or by attempting to fit a mathematical equation to the data values. The latter approach has rarely been successful in archaeology, although examination of the reasons for its failure may be fruitful (*compare* GOODNESS-OF-FIT). *For case-study see* MASK SITE.

I.R. Hodder and C.R. Orton: *Spatial analysis in archaeology* (Cambridge, 1976), 155–74

CO

trepanation Surgical procedure involving the removal of a small piece (strictly, a disk) of the cranium. Surprisingly, trepanation is known from prehistoric cultures, although the motivation behind the operation is unknown. The regrowth of bone indicates that many individuals survived the procedure.

Triple alliance *see* AZTECS

Tripolye (Cucuteni; Cucuteni-Tripolye) Distinctive Eneolithic (Neolithic to Copper Age) farming culture which developed in the Ukraine, Moldova and eastern Romania between perhaps 4600 BC and 3000 BC. The culture was named after the type sites of Cucuteni (Romanian Moldovia) and Tripolye (Dniepr valley, Ukraine) by Romanian and Russian scholars respectively. Both Cucuteni and Tripolye make up a single entity, but two separate chronologies based upon local pottery styles and other elements of culture have been established (these are correlated in the table below). In its developed stage (Tripolye B), the cultural assemblage included vessels painted boldly in red, black and white, the spiral and its derivative being the main decorative motifs. Tripolye pottery is technologically precocious and on some sites there is evidence for the use of updraught kilns and specialized manufactories (large ground-floor workshops with drying lofts above). Anthropomorphic and zoomorphic clay figurines are another important element of the culture; female figurines were particularly common.

Chronology and early Tripolye. The culture was first distinguished by V.V. Khvoiko (Chvoika) in the 1890s, after the excavation of sites in the Middle Dniepr area, including the site of Tripolye (Tripil'ye) near Kiev in the Ukraine. At about the same time, the first excavations of Cucuteni sites were conducted in Romania by N. Belduceanu, Gr. Buţureanu, D. Butulescu and H. Schmidt. A large number of important Tripolye sites were excavated by T.S. Passek and by S.N. Bibikov from the 1930s to the 1960s. Passek was the first to suggest the conventional chronological division of Tripolye, which comprises three stages: early (A), middle (B) and late (C) with subdivisions. At the same time, Bibikov put forward a socioeconomic interpretation of the Tripolye sites.

An independent chronological division was suggested for the Cucuteni sites by Romanian archaeologists, including Vl. Dumitrescu, and M. Petrescu-Dîmovita. According to the latest radiocarbon measurements, a unified chronology may be suggested; as set out in table 19.

Early Tripolye sites tend to cluster on the low terraces of the rivers Prut, Dniestr and Southern Bug and their tributaries. The settlements were rather small; they included large plaster platforms ('ploščadka') which are now recognized as the foundations of rectangular houses. Each house was flanked by a storage pit. At the site of Luka-

Age C-14 BP uncal	Age C-14 BC cal	Ukraine, Moldova	Romania
6000	5250		Precucuteni I
6000	4750	Tripolye AI	Precucuteni II
5700	4500	Tripolye AII	Precucuteni III
5000	4370	Tripolye BI	Cucuteni A 1-3
5200	4250	Tripolye BII	Cucuteni A–B 1-2
5000	3750	Tripolye CI	Cucuteni B1-3
4500	3250	Tripolye CII	Gorodiste,
4200	2750	Tr.CII-'Symbol' II	Floresti I

Table 19 **Tripolye** Correlation and dating of Tripolye and Cucuteni phases.

rublevetskaya, the houses were semi-subterranean and formed a row (over 200 m) along the bank of the Dniestr. A child was buried under the hearth of one of the houses, while in an another house a bull's skull was found. The ceramics included bowls, beakers, biconical and other vessels with covers; anthropomorphic vessels also occurred, as did female figurines made of clay to which grains of wheat had been added. The lithic inventory retained a Mesolithic character, and wild animals made up 50% of the total faunal remains. However, towards the end of the Early Tripolye stage, evidence for metallurgy and metal-working begins to emerge (e.g. the KARBUNA hoard).

Middle to Late Tripolye. In the Middle Tripolye, the culture expanded east of the Dniestr, penetrating to the valley of the Southern Bug and reaching the Dniepr. The settlements are located either on the floodplain or on the promontories of higher terraces. In several cases, settlements occupy an area of 10–40 ha. In the Middle Dniepr area, the houses tend to form circles, and often number 30–40; the largest rectangular houses at Kolomiiščina reach a size of 30 × 6–7 m.

West of Dniestr, two-storied dwellings appeared, and furnaces began to be used for firing pottery; painting the pottery before firing also became more common. Female figurines were still the dominant form of sculpture, but the number of male representations increased. Copper-working became more developed, and ornaments and at least two types of celt were produced. Two large hoards containing metal implements (axes and ornaments) have been found in western Ukraine (Gorodnicy II near Ivano-Frankovsk, and Ryngach near Chernovitsi). Copper-silver alloys came into use by the end of the Middle Tripolye.

The Middle Tripolye economy developed a predominantly agricultural character. Hulled wheats (emmer, einkorn and spelt) and hulled barley were the dominant crops; garden pea and vetch were the most common pulses. The bones of domesticates – cattle, sheep/goat and pig, in that order of importance – constituted more than 80% of the total faunal remains.

During the Late Tripolye, there was a gradual fragmentation, and a wider dispersal of the cultural tradition. One of the local groups (the Vykhvatiuntsy-type sites) gradually spread from the Middle Dniestr to the south, to the steppe areas of the northwestern Pontic Lowland. Later, this group developed into the Usatovo variant of the Late Tripolye. Subsequently, the Usatovo sites spread over a vast area of the Prut-Dniestr-Southern Bug interfluve, and further west into the lower Danube valley and into Romanian Moldova. Simultaneously, another Tipolye group, Brynzeny, spread to the north, to eastern Volhynia, where the Troyan variant emerged, and then the Sofievka variant in the Middle Dniepr area.

The economy of Usatovo was largely dependent on stock-breeding, especially of horse and sheep/goat. Cattle-breeding was more important among the groups that settled in the Middle Prut and Dniestr area (the Brynzeny type). This type of mixed agriculture was equally typical of Volhynia and the Middle Dniepr region.

In the late Tripolye culture, metallurgy and metalworking acquired the status of an independent craft. E.N. Chernykh (1970) distinguishes two main centres of metalworking in the Late Tripolye: the Usatovo and Sofievka. Usatovo metallurgy used ores that mostly came from the Carpathians and from the Balkan peninsula; as for Sofievka, its metal tools were manufactured mostly from the Caucasian ores.

The settlements and cemeteries of Usatovo are usually located on high terraces, on the edges of watershed plateaux high above the Black Sea. The most important sites, Usatovo and Majaki, lie on the edge of a high cliff of the Dniestr *liman* (estuary), west of Odessa. Two groups of kurgan barrows and two cemeteries with flat graves were located near the settlement of Usatovo; only the graves under the kurgans contained rich inventories. The central graves in kurgan cemetery I contained ornaments made of Baltic amber and Near Eastern antimony, numerous rings and beads of silver and copper, arsenic-copper daggers, copper flat-axes and chisels (Zbenovich 1976). All of this evidence suggests marked social stratification in Late Tripolye society. It seems clear that the common people buried their dead in simple flat graves, while the social elite were interred in impressive tombs with exotic prestige goods.

H. Schmidt: *Cucuteni* (Berlin, 1932); T.S. Passek: *Periodizacija tripol'skih poselenii* [The periodization of the Tripolye settlements] (Moscow, 1949); S.N. Bibikov: *Rannetripol'skoe poselenie Luka-Vrubleveckaja na Dnestre* [The early Tripolye site of Luka Vrublevetskaya on the Dniestr] (Moscow, 1953); M. Petrescu-Dîmovita: *Cucuteni* (Bucharest, 1966); E.N. Chernykh: *O drevneiših očagah metalloobrabotki jugo-zapada SSSR* [On the most ancient centres of metal-working in the southwest of the USSR] *KSIA* 123 (1970), 23–31; T. Sulimirski: *Prehistoric Russia: an outline* (London, 1970); V.G. Zbenovich: *Pozdnetripol'skie plemena Severnogo Pričernimor'ja* [The Late Tripolye tribes of the North Pontic area] (Kiev, 1976); S. Milisauskas: *European prehistory* (New York, 1978), 133–41, 161–5; S. Marinescu-Bîlcu: *Tîpesti* BAR IS 107 (Oxford, 1981); L. Ellis: *The Cucuteni-*

Tripolye culture: a study in technology and the origins of complex society. BAR IS 217 (Oxford, 1984).
PD

TRM *see* ARCHAEOMAGNETIC DATING

Troy *see* HISARLIK

Ts'ai Hou Luan tomb (Caihouluanmu) Tomb of the Marquis (*hou*) of Ts'ai in China, probably dating to the 5th century BC, which came to light unexpectedly in May 1955, during the excavation of earth inside the Western Gate of Shou-hsien, Anhui, China. The workmen had unearthed some 30 bronze *yung-chung*-bells, *ting*-cauldrons, *chien*-basins and other artefacts before the importance of the site was realized by the municipal authorities, and qualified personnel were able to take over. Thus few of the original non-metal objects from the tomb were recovered, and although the coffin and coffin-chamber were apparently painted with lacquer designs and gold leaf, only jade ornaments and a sword survived to indicate the position of the tomb's occupant. Altogether, 486 bronze ritual vessels and numerous other bronze artefacts were unearthed. Three long inscriptions identify the tomb occupant as the Marquis Luan of Ts'ai, an ancient state which was engulfed by Ch'u in 447 BC. The tomb was probably constructed in the Early Chan-kuo period (*c*.450 BC).
Anon.: *Shou-hsien Ts'ai-hou-mu ch'u-t'u yi-wu* [Relics unearthed from the Marquise of Ts'ai tomb, Shou-hsien] (Peking, 1956); Kuo Mo-jo: 'Yu Shou-hsien Ts'ai-ch'i lun-tao Ts'ai-mu ti nien-tai' [On the date of the Ts'ai tomb of Shou-hsien with reference to the inscribed bronzes therein], *KKHP* 1 (1956), 1–5; N. Barnard: *The Ch'u silk manuscript – translation and commentary* (Canberra, 1973).
NB

Tseng Hou Yi tomb (Zenghouyimu) Undisturbed burial dating to the late 1st millennium BC (*c*.433–400BC), which was excavated in 1978 at Lei-ku-tun, near Sui-chou, in the northern part of the Hu-pei province, China. Its total of 105 tonnes of bronze artefacts is an unsurpassed illustration of the immensity of bronze production in ancient China. The outer sarcophagus of the main occupant of the tomb contained no less than 6 tonnes of bronze. The finds included a carillon of 75 *chung*-bells (some consisting of up to 100 characters) bearing inscriptions which have thrown extremely valuable light on the musicological terms employed in the period.
Anon.: *Tseng-hou Yi mu*, 2 vols (Peking, 1989); N. Barnard: 'The entry of *cire-perdue* investment casting, and certain other metallurgical techniques (mainly metal-working) into South China and their progress northwards', *Ancient Chinese and Southeast Asian bronze cultures*, ed. D.N. Bulbeck (Taipei, 1996), 1–94.
NB

Tsubai Otsukayama Large mounded tomb of the Early Kofun period (AD 250–400) in Kyoto prefecture, Japan, containing nearly 40 bronze mirrors which were probably cast from the same mould. As the same type of mirror has been discovered in mounded tombs from north Kyushu to eastern Honshu, the person interred here is thought to have been at the centre of an elite prestige network, the mirrors being a symbol of political alliance. See figure 25 (p. 316).
C.M. Aikens and T. Higuchi: *The prehistory of Japan* (London, 1982), 255–63.
SK

Tsukumo Shell midden and cemetery in Okayama prefecture, Japan, dating mainly to the Late Jomon period (2500–1000 BC). It was discovered in 1867, and over 170 bodies were excavated between 1918 and 1924. Most of the skeletons showed evidence of tooth mutilation, patterns in which are interpreted as reflecting post-marital residential patterns. The burials were both flexed and extended, and many were adorned by body ornaments.
H. Harunari: 'Rules of residence in the Jomon period, based on the analysis of tooth extraction', *Windows on the Japanese past*, ed. R. Pearson, K. Hutterer and G.L. Barnes (Ann Arbor, 1986), 293–315.
SK

Tuc d'Audoubert *see* LE TUC D'AUDOUBERT

Tula *see* TOLTECS

tumbaga Alloy of gold, in which either silver or copper may be added or occur as natural impurities. Copper lowers the temperature at which the material can be melted and easily cast. Artefacts of tumbaga, such as bells and ornaments, were manufactured in Costa Rica and Panama (at sites such as SITIO CONTE) and traded throughout the region, including into Mesoamerica.
W. Bray: 'Maya metalwork and its external connections', *Social process in Maya prehistory*, ed. N. Hammond (New York, 1977), 365–403; D. Hosler: 'Ancient west Mexican

metallurgy: South and Central American origins and west Mexican transformations', *American Anthropologist* 90 (1988), 832–55.
PRI

Tumulus complex (tumulus culture) Central European complex of the Middle Bronze age, defined by a custom of burial under round barrows and dating to perhaps *c.*1800–1500 BC. It succeeds, and seems to have developed from, the flat-grave Unětice tradition (which itself is occasionally associated with rich barrows, see UNĚTICE) of the Early Bronze Age, and precedes the URNFIELD CULTURE of the later Bronze Age. Centred on the Czech Republic, Slovakia, Austria and southern Germany, the period of the Tumulus complex is an era of increasing trade and craftsmanship: amber from the Baltic flowed south through the Tumulus complex region, while bronze-working (e.g. casting) and decoration became more complex and gave rise to numerous regional styles; bronze hoards also become more numerous.
RJA

Tuna el-Gebel Egyptian religious and funerary site which includes a rock-cut 'boundary stele' of Akhenaten (*see* EL-AMARNA), an unusual free-standing Greek-influenced tomb-chapel belonging to a priest of Thoth, Petosiris, and his family (*c.*320 BC), as well as a temple of Thoth and extensive catacombs of ibis and baboon mummies dating mainly to the Persian, Ptolemaic and Roman periods (*c.*525 BC–AD 395).
G. Lefèbvre: *Petosiris*, 3 vols (Cairo, 1923–4); D. Kessler: *Die heiligen Tiere und der König* (Wiesbaden, 1989).
IS

T'ung-ling mines (Tongling) Area on the eastern slopes of the T'ung-ling 'Copper Ridge', JUI-CH'ANG-SHIH, in the Chinese province of Chiang-hsi, where a mining complex of the Middle Shang period (1650–1400 BC) was discovered in late 1988. The excavations have revealed mining structures and associated equipment of a standard comparable with those at the T'UNG-LÜ-SHAN and Kang-hsia-ts'un mines. It is now evident that standards of mining practice in this area, in about 1500 BC or earlier, were comparatively advanced. Moreover, the study of the T'ung-ling mines should provide a better understanding of the probable sources of copper for bronze production in the vicinity of the Shang city-state of AN-YANG. The mining complex is almost exactly comparable, in principle and construction, with those described and depicted in Georgius Agricola's *De re metallica* (AD 1556) and Lazarus Ercker's *Treatise on ores and assaying* (AD 1574).
Anon.: 'Chiang-hsi Jui-ch'ang T'ung-ling Shang-Chou ku'ang-ye yi-chih ti-yi-chi'i fa-chüeh chien-pao' [Brief report on the first season of excavation of the Shang and Chou mining and smelting remains at T'ung-ling, Jui-ch'ang, Chiang-hsi], *CHWW* 3 (1990), 1–12; Hua Chüeh-ming, Liu Shih-chung, J. Head and N. Barnard: 'The ancient mines of T'ung-ling, Jui-ch'ang, Chiang-hsi' (in preparation).
NB

T'ung-lü-shan (Tonglushan; 'copper verdigris mountain') Early mining complex covering an area of 2 sq. km near Ta-yeh-hsien, in the Hu-pei province of China. The workings date from the WESTERN CHOU period to the Han dynasty (*c.*1122–200 BC) and the scale of production was immense, producing an accumulation of slag totalling some 400,000 tonnes. The amount of copper produced over the period of operation is assessed to have been in excess of 80,000 tonnes, and more than 50 smelting sites had been surveyed by 1980. Comparison with ancient Western mining activities, such as the Laurion mines of *c.*600 BC, suggests that the overall technical standards attained at T'ung-lü-shan were certainly no less advanced, and in many respects the illustrations and descriptions in Agricola's *De re metallica* (published in 1556) can be seen to fit the T'ung-lü-shan reconstructions of shaft and gallery structures, including such features as the drainage troughs, windlasses, and stone, wood and metal implements employed (see Barnard 1989).
D.B. Wagner: 'Ancient Chinese copper smelting, sixth century BC: recent excavations and simulation experiments', *Journal of the Historical Metallurgy Society, London* 20 (1986), 1–16; N. Barnard: 'From ore to ingot – mining, ore-processing, and smelting in ancient China', *Proceedings of the Second international Conference on Sinology, 1986* (Taipei, 1989), 141–205.
NB

tupu Long straight pins with a flattened or decorative head used by Andean women to hold their dresses and shoulder cloths together.

Turner Middle WOODLAND mound and earthworks complex (*c.*200 BC–AD 400) located on the banks of the Little Miami River in Hamilton Country, Ohio (USA). The primary earthwork consists of an oval enclosure measuring 455 m long and 290 m wide that is connected to a smaller elevated circular earthwork by means of a graded roadway. Within these earthworks are two smaller earthen circles and fourteen mounds. Additional mounds and earthworks are located outside. Excavations conducted during the 19th and early 20th centuries recovered hundreds of artefacts associated with the HOPEWELL cultural manifestation including copper bracelets, beads, and cones, clay figurines, mica cut into zoomorphic designs, and Hopewell-series ceramics.

C. Willoughby and E. Hooton: *Turner group of earthworks, Hamilton County, Ohio* (Cambridge, MA, 1922).

RJE

Tushka *see* ESNA; QADAN

Tushpa *see* URARTU

Tutankhamun *see* VALLEY OF THE KINGS

Tutub *see* KHAFAJEH

Tyre *see* PHOENICIANS

tzompantli (Mayan: 'skull-rack') Mesoamerican ceremonial structure of the Postclassic period (*c.*AD 900–1521), usually comprising a low platform near a temple. The heads of sacrificial victims were displayed on a wooden rack on the platform, either suspended or strung on horizontal poles. Tzompantlis are found at sites in northwestern Mexico, at Tula and TENOCHTITLAN, and at CHICHÉN ITZÁ, in the MAYA area.

O.P. Salazar: 'Eltzompantli de Chichén Itzá, Yucatan', *Tlatoani* 1 (1952), 5–6.

PRI

Tz'u-shan (Cishan) Neolithic culture dating to the period of 6500–5000 BC, which was named after its type-site located in Wu-an-hsien, in the southern region of the Chinese province of Hu-pei. Material of this type (typically including stone grinders and rounded three-legged bowls) was first excavated in 1976–7 and recognized as evidence of a culture pre-dating the YANG-SHAO phase (*c.*6000–4500 BC). Further Tz'u-shan-culture sites have since been reported in central Ho-nan province, including P'EI-LI-KANG, where the most extensive excavations have been undertaken.

Chang Kwang-chih: *The archaeology of ancient China*, 4th edn (New Haven, 1986), 87–95.

NB

U

Ubaid Type-site for the major Neolithic culture originating in southern Mesopotamia (*c*.5000–3800 BC), which was first identified by Henry Hall and Leonard Woolley in the 1920s. The most diagnostic feature of the Ubaid period was the pottery, often over-fired and usually decorated with brown or black geometrical motifs, which were probably related to Hajji Muhammed ware. The most extensive Ubaid stratigraphic sequence was excavated at ERIDU, where platform temples (antecedents of the ZIGGURAT) have been found in strata dated to Ubaid 4. Two shrines of the Ubaid period have also been found near the 'White Temple' at URUK.

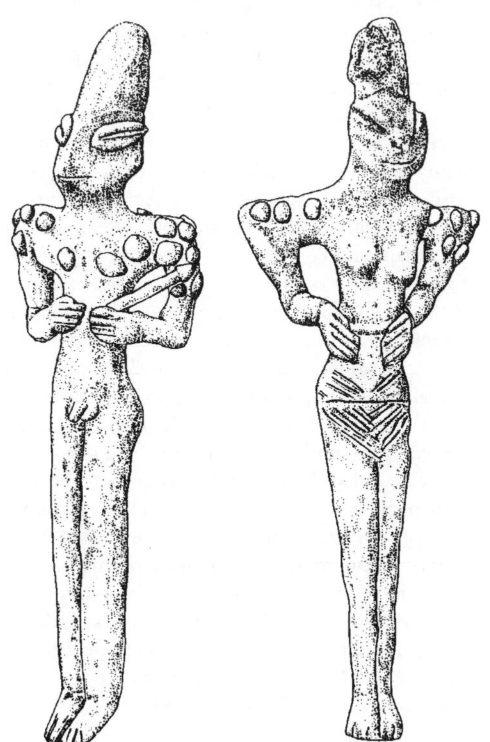

Figure 60 **Ubaid** Male and female baked clay figurines of the Ubaid period (5th millennium BC) from Eridu and Ur (drawn by Tessa Rickards). *Source*: J. Black and A. Green: *Gods, demons and symbols of ancient Mesopotamia: an illustrated dictionary* (BMP, 1992), fig. 64.

The excavations at Tell el-Awayli (Tell el-'Oueili) (Huot 1983) revealed eleven upper strata dating to the four phases of the Ubaid period, as well as nine lower levels containing very early ceramic material (similar to SAMARRA ware) which the excavators describe as pre- or earlier Ubaid (i.e. 'Ubaid 0'). Ubaid domestic architecture has been excavated at a number of sites, including Tell Madhhur in the Hamrin Basin and TEPE GAWRA in northern Mesopotamia. Although there are certain differences between the Ubaid remains of northern and southern Mesopotamia (particularly in terms of burial customs), it is a relatively homogeneous culture, and its widespread influence in the Near East as a whole is indicated by the presence of imported Ubaid ceramics at sites such as UGARIT in the Levant and BAHRAIN in the Persian Gulf.

H.R. Hall and C.L. Woolly: *Al-'Ubaid* (London, 1927); T.E. Davidson and H. McKerrell: 'The neutron activation analysis of Halaf and 'Ubaid pottery from Tell Arpachiyah and Tepe Gawra', *Iraq* 42 (1980), 155–67; F. Safar, M.A. Mustafa and S. Lloyd: *Eridu* (Baghdad, 1982); J. Huot, ed.: *Larsa et 'Oueili: travaux de 1978–1981* (Paris, 1983); E.F. Henrickson and I. Thueson, eds: *Upon this foundation: the Ubaid reconsidered* (Copenhagen, 1989).

IS

Ugarit (Ras Shamra and Minet el-Beida) One of the most important CANAANITE sites on the Levantine coast during the Bronze Age, with traces of previous settlements stretching back as early as the ACERAMIC NEOLITHIC (*c*.8500–7000 BC). The tell site at Ras Shamra has been excavated by French archaeologists since 1928, revealing numerous large ceremonial buildings, including one of the largest surviving royal palaces in the Near East, at the west end of the site, and temples of Baal and Dagan on an acropolis at the eastern end. A number of extensive archives of cuneiform tablets have been discovered, including some written in the 'Ugaritic' script, which is the earliest known alphabetic version of CUNEIFORM. The city of Ugarit appears to have been destroyed in *c*.1200 BC, at the time of the SEA PEOPLES, but the nearby harbour site of Minet el-Beida continued to be occupied until at least the Hellenistic period.

C.F.A. Schaeffer et al.: *Ugaritica* I–VI (Paris, 1939–69); C. Virolleaud and J. Nougayrol: *Le palais royal d'Ugarit*, II–VI (Paris, 1949–70); G. Saadé: *Ougarit, métropole Canaanéenne* (Beirut, 1979); A. Curtis: *Ugarit: Ras Shamra* (Cambridge, 1985).

IS

Ugwuele-Uturu Stone workshop site near Okigwe in southern Nigeria, excavated by F.N. Anozie and his colleagues in 1977–8 and 1981. The site comprised a dolerite ridge, the northern end of which took the form of a virtual scree, a massive accumulation of artefacts up to 6 m deep. The site contained no pottery and no fragments of polished stone tools were found. Among the artefacts, according to Anozie, there were distinctive triangular preforms or roughouts for bifacial tools, as well as large numbers of flakes and some cores. He classified the site as ACHEULEAN, since in his view handaxes – most of them broken – constituted 80% of the tools, plus cleavers, picks, sidescrapers and other miscellaneous items. An alternative view expressed is that the bifacial artefacts themselves may be no more than preforms for ground stone axes, the more successful examples of which were removed for further working elsewhere.

F.N. Anozie, V.E. Chikwendu and A.C. Umeji: 'Discovery of a major prehistoric site at Ugwuele-Uturu, Okigwe', *WAJA* 8 (1978), 171–6; J.D. Clark: 'The 9th Panafrican Congress on prehistory and related studies, Jos, Nigeria, 11–17th December 1983', *NA* 23 (1983), 1–4; P. Allsworth-Jones: 'The earliest human settlement in West Africa and the Sahara', *WAJA* 17 (1987), 87–128.

PA-J

ultratrace *see* TRACE ELEMENTS

Ulu Burun *see* GELIDONYA

Uluzzian Early Upper Palaeolithic culture found in southeast Italy which, like the CHÂTELPERRONIAN identified in France, and the SZELETIAN identified in eastern Europe, differs markedly from the classic culture of the period, the ubiquitous (and apparently intrusive) AURIGNACIAN culture. Moreover, all three 'indigenous' assemblages are markedly different from one another – while the Châtelperronian, for example, is dominated by projectile points, the Uluzzian is characterized by the manufacture of crescent-shaped bladelets. The Uluzzian also runs parallel to the Aurignacian in Italy for much longer than the Châtelperronian coexists with the Aurignacian in France. Although there is, as yet, only one hominid associated with such 'indigenous' assemblages, the NEANDERTHAL from St Césaire, it appears that these three cultures represent a parallel development of Upper Palaeolithic blade technology, perhaps in response to the appearance of the Aurignacian. Identified in 1965 (di Cesnola, 1965–6), Uluzzian assemblages consist of lithics diagnostic of the MOUSTERIAN (side-scrapers, Mousterian points, flake technology) which gradually disappear in favour of Upper Palaeolithic type artefacts appear (endscrapers, burins, blade technology).

P. di Cesnola: 'Il paleolitico superiore arcaaico (facies Uluzziana) della Grotta del Cavallo, Lecce', *Revista di Scienze Preistoriche* 20 and 21 (1965–6), 33–62, 3–59; C. Farizy, ed: *Paléolithique moyen récent et paléolithique supérieur ancien en europe* (Nemours, 1990).

PG-B

Umm an-Nar Island in Abu Dhabi, near the southeastern coast of the Arabian peninsula, which was occupied during the 3rd millennium BC. The site was at first identified with Magan, a foreign toponym in texts from Mesopotamia, but this term is now considered to refer to the entire Oman peninsula in the 3rd millennium BC (although, confusingly, it is later used to refer to Egypt in neo-Assyrian texts). The area of Magan was an important source of timber, stone and copper for the Second LAGASH and UR III dynasties of Mesopotamia. Two seasons of survey and excavation at Umm an-Nar in 1959–60 revealed a cemetery consisting of tumuli dated to *c.*2800–2400 BC, each containing multiple burials (36 in one instance). The surviving artefacts include Early Dynastic pottery from southern Mesopotamia and it has been suggested that Umm an-Nar may have been a settlement through which the SUMERIANS' copper and chlorite trade-routes passed, en route from quarrying and mining sites in the Arabian interior. Since the site also includes artefacts from the INDUS CIVILIZATION (Potts 1990: 150), it is likely that a down-the-line form of trading was in operation in the Persian Gulf. The excavations suggest that Umm an-Nar was deserted by 2000 BC, when trade probably transferred to BAHRAIN.

K. Thorvildsen: 'Gravrøser pä Umm en-Nar' [Burial cairns on Umm an-Nar], *Kuml: Journal of the Archaeological Society of Jutland* (1963), 190–219; D.T. Potts: *The Arabian Gulf in antiquity* I (Oxford, 1990), 93–150.

IS

Umm Dabaghiyah Small settlement interpreted as a trading post of the early or proto-HASSUNA culture (i.e. early Pottery Neolithic, 6th millennium BC), situated in the southern Jazira desert of Iraq, some distance south of the edge of the modern dry-farming region. The site was excavated in 1971–3 by Diana Kirkbridge, who identified it as a community of hunters rather than farmers. The subsistence pattern combined consumption of domesticated cereals (perhaps imported from the north) alongside a dependence on the meat of onager, wild asses and gazelles. Her excavations not only uncovered houses which were apparently entered via the roof, but also three blocks of small structures where the skins of onagers and gazelles may have been stored. One of the houses was decorated with a red and white wall-painting apparently depicting an onager hunt using a form of 'hunting' kite, a type of funnel-shaped trap used in Middle Eastern deserts as late as the 20th century AD. Kirkbridge therefore interprets the village as a specialized trading community, and it has been hypothesized that there may have been similar settlements elsewhere in Neolithic Mesopotamia, trading in materials such as salt or bitumen. Such communities – essentially benefiting from the accumulation of surpluses in raw materials – would have been early prototypes for the first cities in Mesopotamia.

Preliminary reports by D. Kirkbridge in *Iraq* 34–7 (1972–5); D. Kirkbridge: 'Umm Dabaghiyah', *Fifty years of Mesopotamian discovery*, ed. J. Curtis (London, 1982), 11–21.

IS

unconstrained clustering Technique of intra-site SPATIAL ANALYSIS, developed by Robert Whallon (*see* MASK SITE), following suggestions that CLUSTER ANALYSIS could be useful in such studies. It divides a site into zones or clusters in which the proportions of different artefact types are broadly consistent. It is claimed to avoid the need for assumptions about the number and shape of clusters, but suffers from a tendency to create spurious clusters.

R. Whallon: 'Unconstrained clustering for the analysis of spatial distributions in archaeology', *Intrasite spatial analysis in archaeology*, ed. H. Hietala (Cambridge, 1984), 242–77.

CO

underwater archaeology *see* MARITIME ARCHAEOLOGY

Unětice Bronze Age cemetery site near Prague which lends its name to a wider cultural complex of the Early Bronze Age in the Czech Republic, southwest Poland and south Germany. Small, flat inhumation cemeteries are characteristic, in contrast to the succeeding TUMULUS COMPLEX. Grave-goods include pottery, flint arrowheads and a limited range of metal objects such as pins, simple torcs, spiral pendants, with daggers and more developed bracelets becoming more common as the period goes on. There are also limited numbers of barrow burials, with a few outstandingly large and rich burial mounds, notably Helmsdorf and Leubingen in Saxo-Thuringia, Germany. The latter barrow (34 m in diameter and 8.5 high) covered an elaborately constructed wooden mortuary chamber containing two skeletons, one probably of an older man, presumably a chieftain, the other probably of an adolescent girl. Grave-goods included wood-working implements, small daggers, and gold ornaments (large pins, a spiral bead, bracelet).

I. Billig: *Die Ausjetitzer Kultur in Sachsen* (Dresden, 1958); M. Gimbutas: *Bronze Age cultures in Central and Eastern Europe* (The Hague, 1965), 245–75.

RJA

Upper Palaeolithic The final division of the PALAEOLITHIC, dated in Europe to between about 40,000 BP and 10,000 BP, and preceding the MESOLITHIC. The border between the Middle and Upper Palaeolithic industries is usually defined by the common use of blade, as opposed to flake, technology. It should be noted, however, that, outside Europe, the presence of blade-orientated assemblages stratified between Middle Palaeolithic layers at sites such as KLASIES RIVER MOUTH in Africa and Mount Carmel in the Near East slightly complicates this definition.

Although the Upper Palaeolithic was originally defined with reference to its stone typology, it became closely associated with a series of changes that are still generally assumed to be interconnected: the appearance of ANATOMICALLY MODERN HUMANS; the introduction of all or part of the AURIGNACIAN stone tool typology and a developed bone industry; the development of specialized, co-operative hunting strategies; alterations in settlement patterns, including the construction of relatively permanent houses or huts in some areas; the development of a multiplicity of distinct 'cultures'; a growing population; and, most famously of all, the advent of CAVE ART.

Complicating this analysis is the fact that, in the

Near East, anatomically modern populations seem to have established themselves during what is traditionally known as the Middle Palaeolithic (the Skhul burials were found in a Mousterian context, *see* MOUNT CARMEL); they then developed a blade technology during an 'Initial Palaeolithic', and only at a relatively late stage adopted a strongly Aurignacian (classic Upper Palaeolithic) tool typology. To some, this suggests that key features of the Upper Palaeolithic developed in the Near East.

Further complicating the division between the Upper and Middle Palaeolithic, the CHÂTELPERRONIAN, SZELETIAN and related industries, which many authorities now accept are some of the first fully fledged 'Upper Palaeolithic' technologies apparent in Europe, may have been produced by a NEANDERTHAL population – possibly after contact with modern humans. The debate has become caught up in a wider controversy over whether Neanderthal populations were part of the population that evolved into modern humans, or formed a separate line that simply died away.

Culture sequence. The Upper Palaeolithic in Europe is often divided into two according to climatic change. During the Early Upper Palaeolithic (40,000–20,000 BP) the climate deteriorated, with gathering speed, towards the period of maximum continental glaciation (20,000–18,000 BP). Human populations retreated south to areas such as southern France. As the glaciation receded during the second half of the Late Upper Palaeolithic (20,000–10,000 BP) humans were able to recolonize the continent.

This aside, the main divisions are based on tool typology (i.e. industries), although these have sometimes become associated with other changes, such as styles of art; in the past, tool typologies have often been treated implicitly in the literature as if they were cultural classifications. To the extent that the industries can be regarded as successive, they appear in the following order and are described in the following entries: the transitional or acculturated industries of the CHÂTELPERRONIAN (Lower Périgordian) of France, ULUZZIAN of Italy and SZELETIAN of central Europe; the first fully Upper Palaeolithic assemblages of the AURIGNACIAN; the GRAVETTIAN (Upper Périgordian); the SOLUTREAN; and the MAGDALENIAN. The AZILIAN industries are usually regarded as transitional between the Upper Palaeolithic and the MESOLITHIC proper.

P. Ucko and A. Rosenfeld: *Palaeolithic cave art* (London, 1967); H. Laville et al.: *Rockshelters of the Périgord* (New York, 1980); O. Soffer: *The Upper Palaeolithic of the Central Russian Plain* (New York, 1985); D. Collins: *Palaeolithic Europe* (Tiverton, 1986); C. Gamble: *The Palaeolithic settlement of Europe* (Cambridge, 1986); P. Bahn and J. Vertut: *Images of the Ice Age* (London, 1988); J.F. Hoffecker and C.A. Wolf, eds: *The Early Upper Palaeolithic*, BAR IS 437 (Oxford, 1988); N. Barton et al., eds: *The Late Glacial in North-West Europe: Human adaptation and environmental change at the end of the Pleistocene* (London, 1992); L.G. Strauss: *Iberia before the Iberians: the Stone Age prehistory of Cantabrian Spain* (Albuquerque, 1992); C. Gamble: *Timewalkers: The prehistory of global colonisation* (Stroud, 1993); H. Knecht et al., eds: *Before Lascaux: the complex record of the early Upper Palaeolithic* (Boca Raton, 1993); C. Stringer and C. Gamble: *In search of the Neanderthals* (London, 1993); M.H. Nitecki and C.V. Nitecki: *Origins of anatomically modern humans* (New York, 1994); S. Mithen: *The prehistory of the mind: a search for the origins of art, religion and science* (London, 1996).

RJA

Upper Volga Early Neolithic tradition represented at a number of sites in the Upper Volga area of central Russia (Yaroslavl, Ivanovo, Tver districts), which was identified and studied by D.A. Krainov and N.A. Khotinsky in the 1970s. In some areas it forms the predecessor to the PIT-AND-COMB culture of the Middle Neolithic. The main feature of the 'Upper Volga' complex is the ceramic assemblage: wide-mouthed vessels with straight walls, and with pointed or rounded bases. The ornamentation consists of strokes, stamp impressions and incised lines which form horizontal and diagonal lines, as well as simple geometric motifs (triangles, rhombi and intersecting lines). The stone inventory is of MESOLITHIC character: burins, end-scrapers, arrowheads of post-Swiderian type, and knives made from blades. Furthermore, all the faunal remains at Upper Volga sites belong to wild animals.

Many of the sites have been discovered within peat bogs. The peat-bog of Ivanovskoye contained the remains of eight camp-sites; one of the stratified sites, Ivanovskoye 3, was located on an island in the western part of a huge peat-bog. The 'Upper Volga' stratum at the latter site overlay Mesolithic deposits and was itself overlain by deposits containing a late Lyalovo assemblage (*see* PIT-AND-COMB). An impressive series of radiocarbon dates suggests that the Upper Volga stratum was deposited between 5500 and 4800 BC (calendar years). Four sites with Upper Volga material of *c*.5200 BC were discovered within the peat-bog of Yazykovo, below the stratum bearing pit-and-comb pottery.

D.A. Krainov and N.A. Khotinsky: 'Verhnevolžskaja arheologičeskaja kul'tura' [The Upper Volga archaeological culture], *Sovetskaja arheologija* 3 (1977), 42–68; —— et al.: 'Stratigrafija i absoljutnaua hronologija stojanki Ivanovskoe III' [Stratigraphy and absolute chronology of the Ivanovkoye 3 site], *Sovetskaja arheologija* 3 (1990), 25–31.

PD

Ur (Tell el-Muqayyar) Mesopotamian city covering an area of some 55 ha in southern Iraq, which was first occupied in the Ubaid period (*c*.5000–3800 BC) but flourished during the Early Dynastic and Ur III periods (*c*.2900–2350 and 2150–2000 BC respectively). Ur was a commercial port reliant on maritime trade with the Gulf countries and the Indus region (although there has been some considerable debate on this point, see Oppenheim 1954; Oates et al. 1977; Roaf and Galbraith 1994). It was therefore probably the change in the course of the Euphrates that eventually precipitated its abandonment in the 4th century BC. First identified by Pietro della Valle in 1625, the site was excavated from 1922 to 1934 by Leonard Woolley, who initially claimed to have discovered traces of the original Biblical Flood in one sounding at the site, but this stratum is now generally considered to have been a purely local phenomenon.

The Early Dynastic elite were buried along with rich burial equipment (including gold and silver jewellery, chariots and numerous bodies of retainers) in 17 of the 1,850 burials in the so-called 'Royal Cemetery' (see below). As the dynastic seat of power during the Ur III period the city was essentially rebuilt, including the construction of a ZIGGURAT (probably over the remains of an earlier temple), temples of the moon-god Nanna and his consort Ningal, a new palace, and the 'mortuary chapels' of Shulgi and his successor Bur-Sin. The design of these mortuary chapels apparently represents a return to the early Sumerian house-plan temples such as the Square Temple at KHAFAJEH. Although the city's political and economic importance diminished in the 1st and 2nd millennia BC, the temples were still being restored and embellished as late as the Neo-Babylonian period (*c*.625–539 BC).

The 'Royal Cemetery', dug into refuse tips at the edge of the citadel, appears to represent a good cross-section of the population, unlike most other cemeteries of the period (Woolley 1934). Debate has centred primarily on the identification and social ranking of the owners of the richest graves (only three of whom have been named: Queen Puabi, Akalamdug and Meskalamdug) and the question of why their retainers were sacrificed en masse (Moorey 1977; Pollock 1991).

C.L. Woolley: *Ur excavations*: II *The Royal Cemetery*, 2 vols (London, 1934); A.L. Oppenheim: 'The seafaring merchants of Ur', *JAOS* 74 (1954), 6–17; J. Oates: 'Ur and Eridu: the prehistory', *Iraq* 22 (1960), 32–50; ——, T.E. David, D. Kamilli and H. Mckerrell: 'Seafaring merchants of Ur?', *Antiquity* 51 (1977), 221–34; P.R.S. Moorey: 'What do we know about the people buried in the Royal Cemetery?', *Expedition* 20 (1977), 24–40; C.L. Woolley and P.R.S. Moorey: *Ur of the Chaldees: the final account*, 3rd edn (London, 1982); S. Pollock: 'Of priestesses, princes and poor relations: the dead in the Royal Cemetery of Ur', *CAJ* 1 (1991), 171–89; M. Roaf and J. Galbraith: 'Pottery and p-values: "Seafaring merchants of Ur" re-examined', *Antiquity* 68 (1994), 770–82.

IS

uranium series dating (U-series) Family of scientific dating techniques based on the decay chains of uranium i.e. ^{238}U and ^{235}U, the latter having an abundance of 0.72% of total natural uranium. These isotopes each decay radioactively to a daughter isotope which in turn decays, and via a series of such decays, each chain ends with a stable lead isotope. Disruption to the chains, resulting from differences in the geochemistry of the different elements involved, and useful differences in half-lives of daughter products within each series, form the basis of the U-series methods. The isotopes of relevance in the ^{238}U chain are ^{234}U and its daughter ^{230}Th, with half-lives of 248 thousand years and 75.2 thousand years respectively. In the ^{235}U chain the only long-lived isotope in the chain is ^{231}Pa (half-life 34.3 thousand years). The key geochemical difference between uranium and thorium (Th) is that uranium forms water-soluble compounds whereas thorium does not; geochemically, protactinium (Pa) behaves like thorium and is insoluble.

In archaeology, the two U-series methods used are ^{230}Th/^{230}U and ^{231}Pa/^{235}U, the latter largely to demonstrate concordance of dates for the time period over which the two methods overlap. The principles of the two methods are the same and are therefore outlined for ^{230}Th/^{234}U. Their most reliable application is to the dating of calcitic speleothems, in particular stalagtites and flowstones. Uranium from the ground water precipitates with the calcite, but ^{230}Th is missing because of its insolubility. By the decay of ^{234}U, which has a considerably longer half-life than ^{230}Th, ^{230}Th will grow back at a rate determined by its 75.2 thousand year HALF-LIFE. The form of the growth with time is a saturating exponential: initially linear, then sublinear and ultimately reaching an equilibrium level which determines the maximum age limit of the technique (approximately 350,000 years for $^{230}Th/^{234}U$; 150,000 years for $^{231}Pa/^{235}U$). The form of the growth of $^{230}Th/^{234}U$ also leads to asymmetric error terms on the age. The minimum age limit is typically 5000 years, depending on the uranium concentration (but higher for $^{231}Pa/^{235}U$ because of the low natural abundance of ^{235}U). If the ^{234}U and ^{238}U are not in equilibrium on crystallization, a correction must be made.

Key assumptions in uranium series dating are (1) that there is zero concentration of ^{230}Th on crystal formation and (2) that the system is closed (i.e. no uranium or thorium migrates out of or into the calcite after formation). In practice, detrital material containing thorium can be incorporated in the calcite. This can be detected by the presence of ^{232}Th (the half-life of which is 1.39×10^{10} years, i.e. very long relative to the time scales of interest). If the $^{230}Th/^{232}Th$ ratio is less than 20, the contamination can be considered to have a negligible effect on the age. The closed system assumption for calcite is generally good, but for other archaeological materials this is less often the case.

Application of U-series dating to bone and teeth is based on the uptake of uranium from ground water after death (living bone, for example, typically contains 0.1 ppm of uranium whereas fossil bone can contain up to 1000 ppm). As for calcite dating, the assumption is that no ^{230}Th is present initially. The problem lies in whether the uranium remains fixed and when it was taken up: immediately after death (known as 'early uptake'), gradually with time ('linear uptake'), or indeed more variably. Results on bone have been mixed, but there is evidence to suggest that tooth enamel may act as a closed system and provide more reliable dates; the model for initial uptake of the uranium is, however, still problematic.

Measurement of isotope ratios has until recently been achieved mainly by alpha spectrometry: counting the alpha particles of a particular energy associated with the decay of a specific isotope. Mass spectrometry, on the other hand, directly measures the number of atoms of a given isotope present, or a proportion of them. This is a more efficient technique, if considerably more costly, but it also allows much smaller samples to be dated (typically milligrams rather than grams). In the case of $^{230}Th/^{234}U$ dating it also widens the date range of the method, taking it as low as 50 years and up to about 500,000 years. *See also* LEAD-210 DATING.

H.P. Schwarcz: 'Absolute age determination of archaeological sites by uranium series dating of travertines', *Archaeometry* 22 (1980), 3–24; P.L. Smart: 'Uranium series dating', *Quaternary dating methods – a user's guide*, ed. P.L. Smart and P.D. Fraces (Cambridge, 1991), 45–83.

SB

Urartu (Biblical Ararat) Anatolian kingdom centred on Lake Van and covering a large area at the junction of eastern Turkey, Iran, Armenia and Azerbaijan. The Urartians dominated this region in the 9th–7th centuries BC while the ASSYRIAN empire (*c*.883–612 BC) was flourishing to the south. The first historical references to the HURRIAN-speaking tribes of Urartu appear in the Assyrian annals of the mid-13th century BC, but it is not until the early 9th century BC that they become clearly recognizable as a political and archaeological entity. Many Urartian sites include rock-inscriptions written in the 'Vannic' script (a form of cuneiform used to record the Urartian language), which was first studied by F.E. Schultz in 1827 but was not deciphered until the turn of the century.

Seven of the principal Urartian fortress-towns have been excavated, including the main capital Tushpa (near modern Van) and the sites of Altintepe, Erebuni (Yerevan), Kefkalesi, Teishebaina (Karmir Blur), Rusaurutur (Bastam) and Rusahinili (Toprakkale). The Toprakkale citadel, which was excavated by Hormuzd Rassam in 1877 and 1879, was the first Urartian site to be scientifically investigated, but it was the exploration of the rich site of Erebuni by Soviet archaeologists in 1938 that initiated the most productive phase in Urartian archaeology.

Altintepe, located 20 km from Erzincan, includes the best-preserved Urartian temple, dedicated to the god Haldi, comprising a cella, or inner shrine (originally painted and still containing a number of ritual implements), set in a large courtyard surrounded by wooden colonnades. In the south-eastern section of the site a set of subterranean royal tombs have been excavated, each containing one or two bodies placed in wooden or stone sarcophagi and accompanied by typical Urartian gold, silver and bronze funerary equipment.

Apart from their distinctive ceramics, the archaeological remains of the Urartians (including the celebrated metalwork) have been traditionally interpreted as provincial versions of Assyrian material culture (Frankfort 1970: 194, n. 55). Seton Lloyd, however, argues that the ambitious stone-built, turreted fortresses and tower-like bastioned temples suggests an Urartian society in radical contrast to the Mesopotamian civilizations, with their mud-brick flat-roofed houses and platform temples (Lloyd 1989: 99–100).

C.A. Burney: 'Urartian fortresses and towns in the Van region', *AS* 7 (1957), 37–53; T. Özgüç: *Altin Tepe, architectural monuments and wall paintings*, 2 vols (Ankara, 1966–9); B. Piotrovski: *The ancient civilization of Urartu* (London, 1969); H. Frankfort: *The art and architecture of the ancient Orient*, 4th edn (Harmondsworth, 1970), 194–6; T.B. Forbes: *Urartian architecture* (Oxford, 1983); S. Lloyd: *Ancient Turkey: a traveller's history of Anatolia* (London, 1989), 94–109; R. Merhav, ed.: *Urartu: a metalworking centre in the 1st millennium BCE* (Jerusalem, 1991).

IS

Urewe *see* EARLY IRON AGE

urnfield culture (urnfield complex) Late Bronze Age to early Iron Age complex of cemetery sites, characterized by cremation burials in urns of various kinds. The complex is focused in central Europe, notably the Lusation or Lausitz culture of East Germany and Poland, but extends westwards into France and eastwards into the Ukraine, and south to Italy and even Spain. Beginning towards the end of the 14th century BC, the rite continued into the Hallstatt A/B periods in the 8th century BC. The urnfields are flat cemeteries – in contrast to the earlier inhumation burials, often under barrows, that are so characteristic of the Middle Bronze Age in Central Europe (*see* TUMULUS COMPLEX). They vary from a few tens of urns to substantial clusters of hundreds or even thousands of burials (e.g. the Kiertrz cemetery of southwest Poland), and the sheer numbers are sometimes taken to indicate a growth in population in central Europe in the later Bronze Age. Grave-goods accompanying the urns include bronze ornaments, tools and weapons; just as the cremation rite itself suggests a broadly homogeneous Late Bronze Age culture in the region, so the items deposited are broadly similar in the technological skills and main typologies. The number of items varies considerably from grave to grave in most cemeteries (and from region to region); this is normally taken to indicate social status differences, but at the same time it is difficult to identify clear social hierarchies. BISKUPIN is one of the most carefully excavated settlement sites closely associated with the urnfield complex. During the urnfield period, hillforts began to be constructed, another feature that continues into the Iron Age.

RJA

Uronarti *see* SEMNA

Uruk (Warka) Tell-site of the Biblical city of Erech, located midway between Baghdad and Basra in southern Iraq, which is the type-site of the Uruk period (*c*.4000–3200 BC). The city of Uruk, known to the Sumerians as Unu, was occupied from early in the UBAID period (*c*.5000–3800 BC), when it was perhaps initially two separate settlements (Kullaba and Eanna), but it was in the mid-4th millennium BC that it became the most important settlement in SUMER and probably the first true city in the world. The site, with virtually continuous stratigraphy stretching from the 5th millennium BC to the 3rd century AD, therefore provides crucial evidence for the process of early state formation. There was also a settlement of the SASANIAN period (AD 224–651) located immediately outside the city walls. Surveys have shown that urbanization in Mesopotamia accelerated at the beginning of the Uruk period (see Adams and Nissen 1972). At its height the city was more than 400 hectares in area, and one of the city's earliest rulers appears to have been the historical counterpart of Gilgamesh – hero of the Sumerian epic – thus providing an unexpectedly strong link between the archaeology and mythology of early Mesopotamia.

The earliest excavations at Uruk were undertaken by William Kennet Loftus in 1850–2, revealing a Parthian cemetery of slipper-coffins, part of a complex that later proved to be a Parthian temple, as well as a section of Uruk-period wall decorated with *STIFTMOSAIK*. In the heart of the city were Kullaba and Eanna, the cult centres of the gods Anu and Inanna (later Ishtar), where most of the German excavations have taken place from 1924 until the present day (Heinrich 1941; Lenzen 1964; Boehmer 1991). The precinct of Eanna included the so-called Mosaic and Limestone temples, dating to the Uruk period, as well as the White Temple, dating to the late Uruk or early Jemdet Nasr period (*c*.3200 BC) and perhaps showing an early stage in the development of the ZIGGURAT. It was about a thousand years later that one of the first known ziggurats was constructed by Ur-Nammu in the precinct of Kullaba. The city appears to have retained some importance even in the Seleucid and Parthian periods (*c*.305 BC – AD 244), when many of the older temples were restored and a new sanctuary was constructed for Gareus, a Parthian deity.

During the Uruk period – 'arguably the most innovative and important of any in the history of Mesopotamia' (Crawford 1991: 13) – most of the salient features of Sumerian civilization emerged. There were a large number of technological innovations, including the introduction of the potter's wheel and the initial stages in the development of the CUNEIFORM script; in addition, the stamp-seal was superseded by the CYLINDER SEAL (a small stone cylinder bearing engraved designs), which is one of the most diagnostic features of the Uruk and JEMDET NASR periods. Towards the end of the period, the influence of the Uruk civilization spread northwards and eastwards, strongly affecting the material culture of sites on the Mesopotamian fringes, such as HABUBA KEBIRA in Syria and SUSA in Iran.

W.K. Loftus: *Travels and researches in Chaldaea and Susiana* (London 1857); Preliminary reports of German excavations published as *Uruk Vorläufiger Berichte* since 1928; E. Heinrich: *Topographie von Uruk* (Leipzig, 1941); H.J. Lenzen: 'New discoveries in Warka, S. Iraq', *Archaeology*, 17 (1964), 122–31; R.McC. Adams and H.J. Nissen: *The Uruk countryside* (Chicago, 1972); R.M. Boehmer: 'Uruk 1980–1990: a progress report', *Antiquity* 65 (1991), 465–78; H. Crawford: *Sumer and the Sumerians* (Cambridge, 1991), 13–14, 57–62 [discussion of the material culture of the Uruk period]; G. Roux: *Ancient Iraq*, 3rd edn (Harmondsworth, 1992), 68–76.

IS

Urukug *see* SEALAND

Usatovo *see* TRIPOLYE

U-series *see* URANIUM SERIES DATING

use-wear traces (microwear traces) Term used to refer to the pattern of wear on the surfaces and edges of stone artefacts, the analysis of which was pioneered by the early 19th-century Swedish zoologist Sven Nilsson (1868). Nilsson studied the use-wear traces on artefacts in order to gain a better understanding of the functions of tools, thus enabling him to deduce a cultural-evolutionist sequence of prehistoric subsistence patterns. Little further study of use-wear traces was undertaken until the early 20th century, when a number of different researchers (e.g. Warren 1905) began to apply similar techniques of analysis to EOLITHS (naturally formed fragments of flint) in order to determine whether they were natural or artefactual in origin.

In the late 1950s, the Soviet archaeologist S.A. Semenov found that he was able to deduce the functions of many stone and bone tools by means of a combination of experimental use-wear studies and the examination of the polishes and striations on lithics through a binocular microscope. When his work was translated into English (Semenov 1964), a new generation of archaeologists (e.g. Tringham et al. 1974) began to analyse the use-wear traces on stone tools. Some, such as Laurence Keeley (1980), improved the accuracy of microwear analyses by using an SEM (scanning electron microscope). Most use-wear studies have involved experimental work, since it would otherwise be difficult to know precisely which activities might produce particular types of wear on lithics. Thus Binneman and Deacon (1986), for instance, created replica stone adzes in order to prove that early woodworking was practised at the Later Stone Age site of BOOMPLAAS CAVE in South Africa.

S. Nilsson: *The primitive inhabitants of Scandinavia*, 3rd edn, trans. J. Lubbock (London, 1868); S.H. Warren: 'On the origin of "eolithic" flints by natural causes', *JRAI* 35 (1905), 337–64; S.A. Semenov: *Prehistoric technology* (London, 1964); R. Tringham et al.: 'Experimentation in the formation of edge damage; a new approach to lithic analysis', *JFA* 1 (1974), 171–96; B. Hayden: *Lithic use-wear analysis* (New York, 1979); L.H. Keeley: *Experimental determination of stone tool uses: a microwear analysis* (Chicago, 1980); J. Binneman and H.J. Deacon: 'Experimental determination of use wear on stone adzes from Boomplaas Cave, South Africa', *JAS* 13 (1986), 219–28.

IS

USSR *see* CENTRAL ASIA; CIS AND THE BALTIC STATES

Usvyaty Group of sites dating from the Late Palaeolithic, Mesolithic, Neolithic and Bronze Ages, situated in and around lakes on the upper stretches of the Western Dvina and Lovat rivers, in the Pskov and Smolensk districts, in northwestern Russia. The sites were discovered and excavated by A.M. Miklyayev from the 1960s into the 1990s.

The earliest sites are Epipalaeolithic (tanged points are present) and were discovered on the dunes that developed on terraces in the Late Glacial period (*c*.12,000–10,000 BP). Industry complexes of a Mesolithic character, with blades and axes, were found on the terraces at lower levels. A group of Neolithic sites was found near Rudnya. The earliest stratum at the site of Rudnya-Serteya contained blades and axe-like tools, and fragments of coarse conical vessels decorated with a combination of horizontal, vertical and diagonal rows of triangular impressions. The upper stratum of the same site (*c*.5100–4900 BC) corresponds to the NARVA tradition.

In about 3300–3100 BC, as lake levels rose during the Early Sub-Boreal, pile-dwellings were constructed in the coastal areas of the Usvyaty and Sennitsa lakes. A third village of pile-dwellings,

Naumovo, emerged around 2500 BC in the off-shore area of Lake Zhizhitsa. All three settlements belonged to the same cultural tradition: Usvyaty (*c*.3300–2500 BC). The faunal assemblages from these sites included elk, brown bear, wild bear and fur-bearing animals (such as the otter and squirrel), pike and perch. Judging from the age groups, elk was hunted throughout the year. The tradition of pile dwellings resumed after a break caused by a change in the size of the lakes. The later settlements belonged to the North Bielorussian tradition – the local variant of the CORDED WARE culture (*c*.2500–2100 BC). At this stage, domesticates (sheep, goat, pig, cattle) appear among the faunal remains, but represent less than 15% of the assemblages.

A.M. Miklyayev: 'O svajnyh poselenijah III–II tys. do n.e. v Pskovskoi i Smolenski oblastjah' [On the pile-dwellings of the 3rd–2nd millennia BC in the Pskov and Smolensk districts], *Drevnie pamjatniki kul'tury na territorii SSSR* [The ancient cultural sites in the territory of USSR], ed. B.B. Piotrovsky (Leningrad, 1977); P.M. Dolukhanov et al.: 'Rudnya-Serteya, a stratified dwelling-site in the Upper Duna basin (a multidisciplinary research)', *Fennoscandia archaeologica* 6 (1989), 23–7.

PD

Utatlán Late Postclassic capital of the Quiché Maya, in western highland Guatemala. Also known as Gumarcaaj, Utatlán was established in the early 15th century AD and destroyed by the Spaniards in 1523. The site is defensively located on a plateau surrounded by deep ravines. Architectural features include a dense arrangement of temples set around a plaza, colonnaded halls (possibly lineage palaces) and at least one ballcourt (*see* BALLGAME). Utatlán has been surveyed and excavated but the remains are now poorly preserved and recorded.

D.T. Wallace: 'An intra-site locational analysis of Utatlán: the structure of an urban site', *Archaeology and ethnohistory of the central Quiché*, ed. D.T. Wallace and R.M. Carmack (Albany, 1977), 20–54; R.M. Carmack: *The Quiché Mayas of Utatlán* (Norman, 1981); J.W. Fox: *Maya Postclassic state formation* (Cambridge, 1987), 158–75.

PRI

U Thong *see* DVARAVATI CULTURE

Utnur ASH-MOUND site of the 3rd millennium BC, in Raichur Doab, southern India, which was excavated by Raymond Allchin in 1957. Calibrated radiocarbon dates from the site indicate that it was in use between *c*.2700 and 2200 BC (Possehl and Rissman 1992: I, 489; II, 466). The ashy matrix that makes up the Utnur ash mound is largely composed of carbonized cow dung. Large quantities of cattle bones were recovered in excavations, along with hand-made ceramics, chipped stone blades and cores, ground stone axes, handstones and grindstones.

F.R. Allchin: *Neolithic cattle keepers of the Deccan* (Cambridge, 1963), 6–46, 143–52; G.L. Possehl and P.C. Rissman: 'The chronology of prehistoric India: from earliest times to the Iron Age', *Chronologies in Old World archaeology*, ed. R.W. Ehrich, 2 vols (Chicago, 1992), I, 465–90; II, 447–74.

CS

Utqiagvik Site at Barrow, Alaska, where, at some point between the 16th and 18th centuries AD, pack ice was driven up onto the shore overnight and overran a semi-subterranean log-house, crushing it and killing its occupants (whose cultural affinities are uncertain). During building construction in 1982, the house was uncovered and found to contain the well-preserved bodies of two women and three children. Some items were removed from accessible parts of the house soon after the disaster; but the house, its contents and the bodies of its inhabitants provide a fascinating picture with which to compare houses that have gone through more typical processes of abandonment and re-use.

E.S. Hall, Jr., and L. Fullerton, eds: *The Utqiagvik excavations* (Barrow, 1990).

RP

Uvinza Collection of several sites in western Tanzania in an area celebrated for its salt, obtained from a series of springs (or 'salt-wells') whose plentiful brine is boiled to produce exceptionally pure salt. Before the 20th century the brine was evaporated in earthenware pots over wood fires. Oral accounts and 19th century travellers' reports describe Uvinza as a centre of seasonal industrial activity and a market for the caravan trade. In 1967 John Sutton's excavations in the vicinity of selected brine-springs revealed layers documenting activity back to the EARLY IRON AGE (mid-1st millennium AD) below the plentiful 19th-century debris. The earliest pottery at the site has affinities with the well-known Urewe tradition of the Early Iron Age. Uvinza's archaeological sequence is thus among the most valuable yet obtained through the East African Iron Age to modern times.

J.E.G. Sutton and A.D. Roberts: 'Uvinza and its salt industry', *Azania* 3 (1968), 45–86.

JS

V

vacuum airlift *see* GELIDONYA

Valdivia Village site on the central coast of Ecuador, dating to the Early Formative period (*c*.3000–2000 BC). The complexity of the Valdivia ceramics, despite being the earliest yet found in Ecuador, led the excavators to propose an origin in the JOMON culture of Japan, hypothesizing that fisherman on rafts brought the art of ceramics to Ecuador sometime in the later 4th millennium BC. This hypothesis has not been accepted, as it can be shown that Valdivia ceramics are not the oldest in South America nor was it possible, given available technology, wind, and current conditions for such a diffusion to have taken place.

E. Estrada and B.J. Meggers: 'A complex of traits of probable transpacific origin on the Coast of Ecuador', *American Anthropologist* 63/5 (1961), 913–39; G.F. McEwan and D.B. Dickson: 'Valdivia, Jomon fisherman, and the nature of the North Pacific: some nautical problems with Meggers, Evans, and Estrada's (1965) transoceanic contact hypothesis', *AA* 43/3 (1978), 362–71; E. Salazar: *Entre mitos y fabulas: el Ecuador aborigen* (Quito, 1995).

KB

Valley of the Kings (Biban el-Muluk) Egyptian royal necropolis of the New Kingdom, situated in the cliffs about 5 km to the west of modern Luxor, which actually comprises two separate valleys. There are 62 tombs altogether, the earliest probably being KV38, which has been identified as that of Thutmose I (1504–1492 BC) and the latest being KV18, which was built for Ramesses XI (1100–1070 BC), although it is doubtful whether he was ever buried there. Each of the tombs consisted of a long succession of rock-cut corridors and chambers, sloping downwards into the cliffs. Until the time of Horemheb (1323–1295 BC), the main corridor had a bent-axis and their decoration consisted primarily of scenes of the Amduat (one of the 'books of the netherworld'), whereas the Ramessid tombs had relatively straight main corridors and were decorated with a scenes from the Book of Gates and other funerary texts. The most famous tomb in the valley is that of Tutankhamun (1333–1323 BC; KV62), which was discovered almost intact by Howard Carter in 1922, thus providing some indication of the funerary equipment which must have been plundered over the centuries from the other tombs in the valley. The bodies of virtually all of the New Kingdom pharaohs were moved in the 21st–2nd Dynasties (1070–945 BC) and placed in two caches, one in the tomb of Amenhotep II (KV35) and the other in the family tomb of Pinudjem II at Deir el-Bahari (DB320), where they were discovered in 1871 and 1898 respectively.

J. Romer: *Valley of the Kings* (London, 1981); E. Hornung: *Valley of the Kings* (New York, 1990); C.N. Reeves: *Valley of the Kings: the decline of a royal necropolis* (London, 1990); ——, ed.: *After Tutankhamun* (London, 1991); —— and R.H. Wilkinson: *The complete Valley of the Kings* (London, 1996).

IS

Valley of the Queens (Biban el-Harim) Egyptian necropolis of the royal wives and sons of some of the pharaohs of the 19th–20th dynasties, situated on the west bank at Thebes, about a kilometre to the northwest of MEDINET HABU. Although most of the 18th-dynasty rulers' wives were buried in the same tombs as their husbands in the VALLEY OF THE KINGS, many of the 19th- and 20th-dynasty royal women and children were buried in the Valley of the Queens, which includes about 75 rock-cut tombs, the earliest inscribed tomb being that of Satra, the wife of Ramesses I (1307–1306 BC). The best-known tomb, however, is that of Nefertari, the principal wife of Ramesses II (1290–1224 BC), the painted decoration of which was restored at great expense in the 1980s (*see* McDonald 1996).

E. Schiaparelli: *Esplorazione della 'Valle delle Regine'* (Turin, 1923); G. Thuasing and H. Goedicke: *Nofretari: eine Dokumentation der Wandgemälde ihres Grab* (Graz, 1971); J.H. McDonald: *House of eternity: the tomb of Nefertari* (London, 1996).

IS

valley temple *see* PYRAMID

Van, Lake *see* URARTU

Vannic texts *see* URARTU

variable In statistical analysis of archaeological DATA, a variable is a characteristic shared by a set of objects, whether a measurement, a count or an assignment to a category. A variable takes a distinct value on each object; collectively these values are known as DATA. The term 'attribute' is sometimes used for variable and 'attribute state' for value. There is a hierarchy of different types of variables – ratio, interval, ordinal and nominal. The lowest type, nominal, are simply names or 'labels' which can be applied to objects, e.g. colour or type. If there is, in addition, a natural order to these categories, e.g. a developmental sequence of types, the variable is said to be ordinal. Interval variables differ in that meaning can be assigned to the differences between values as well as to the values themselves; a good example is date (in years BC/AD). Ratio variables possess the additional feature that ratios of two values also have a meaning, e.g. 10 is twice 5 in a way that AD 10 is not twice AD 5; good examples of ratio variables are length and weight. Variables can also be described as continuous (capable of taking any value within a range) or discrete (taking only certain values); continuous variables are either ratio or interval, but discrete ones can belong to any of the four types. The type of a variable determines the statistical techniques which can be applied to it.

J.E. Doran and F.R. Hodson: *Mathematics and computers in archaeology* (Edinburgh, 1975), 99–104; S. Shennan: *Quantifying archaeology* (Edinburgh, 1988), 10–13; M. Fletcher and G.R. Lock: *Digging numbers* (Oxford, 1991), 2–5.

CO

variance *see* STANDARD DEVIATION

Varna Cemetery near the Black Sea coast of Bulgaria, dated to approximately 4600–4200 BC, which has yielded a unique collection of early gold artefacts. When excavated between 1972 and 1976 the inhumations and CENOTAPH burials were found to contain GLUMELNIŢA pottery, stone and copper tools and over 2000 hammered gold objects (largely jewellery and simple animal silhouettes). Three cenotaph burials yielded clay masks variously adorned with gold diadems, discs, 'mouth-plates', and earrings, while other graves contained gold 'sceptres'. The presence of the shells of *SPONDYLUS gaederopus* indicates trade of at least an indirect kind with the Aegean region. Colin Renfrew has argued that the richness of certain graves at Varna indicates a chiefdom society, as opposed to the more egalitarian models usually proposed for early agricultural communities.

I. Ivanov: *Sukrovishtata na Varnenskija Chalkoliten Nekropol* [Treasures of the Varna necropolis; English translation, colour plates] (Sofia, 1978); ——: 'Les fouilles archéologiques de la nécropole chalcolithique à Varna (1972–75)', *Studia Praehistorica*, 1–2 (1978), 13–26; C. Renfrew: 'Varna and the social context of early metallurgy', *Antiquity* 52 (1978), 199–203; I. Ivanov: 'Le Chalcolithique en Bulgaria et dans la nécropole de Varna', *Ancient Bulgaria*, ed. A. Poulter (Nottingham, 1983), 154–63.

RJA

varves Layers in lake sediments usually caused by the annual melt of glaciers. The sediment carried by the melt waters is deposited on the lake bottom, the coarser fractions settling first: the change in texture from the end of one year to the start of the next is therefore clearly visible in sections through dried lake beds. The thickness of each layer depends on the prevailing climatic conditions: warmer weather causes more melting and more sediment build-up. The resulting pattern of thick and thin layers allows the CROSS-DATING of sections, provided that they were formed under the same climatic conditions. Thus long sequences analogous to the master chronologies of DENDROCHRONOLOGY can be built up for a given region. Significant errors can arise if discontinuous sequences are not recognized or if mismatching occurs.

The best known varve chronology is that for Scandinavia, particularly Sweden. Because the glacial retreat was simple, and not complicated by re-incursions, it has been possible to extend this chronology back for a period of some 13,000 years; it has been linked by layer-counting to the present. The sequence is used to provide an absolute chronology for pollen sections. Its use as the absolute timescale for calibration in RADIOCARBON DATING is problematic, since there are many possible sources of the carbon within varves. Research on identification of tephra within varves could, however, provide an accurate timescale for TEPHROCHRONOLOGY.

Non-glacial lake sediments may also show varves as a result of seasonal variations in the deposition of organic debris, combined with variation in sedimentation rate.

D.J. Schove and R.W. Fairbridge: 'Swedish chronology revisted', *Nature* 304 (1983), 583; —— and ——: *Ice-cores, varves and tree-rings* (Rotterdam, 1984); I. Cato: 'The definitive connection of the Swedish geochronological time scale with the present, and the new date of the zero year in Döviken, northern Sweden', *Boreas* 14 (1985), 117–22; B. Strömberg: 'Revision of the late glacial Swedish varve chronology, *Boreas* 14 (1985), 101–5.

SB

vase supports Distinctive decorated pottery objects found within CHASSÉEN assemblages of the French middle Neolithic, and regarded as one of the diagnostics of that culture (although they are not evenly distributed within the Chasséen region). The earliest examples seem to be from the Midi, and there are concentrations in Languedoc and Brittany. They are called 'vase supports' because they typically consist of a shallow dished surface on top of a hollow cylinder or squarish support – and it was originally thought that they were used to support the bases of jars. Their function continues to be debated, but many authorities now believe they were perfume burners (*brûle-parfums*). In the Paris basin, vase supports tend to be found at high camps such as the site of Chassey-le-Camp (the Chasséen type-site), while in Brittany they are associated with funerary and ceremonial sites. The stone circle site of Er Lannic in Brittany yielded one of the greatest concentrations (160 examples) decorated in a distinctive style. This association, and the fact that they are the only heavily decorated items in the plain Chasséen ceramic repertoire, supports a ritual, rather than domestic, function.

RJA

vector format *see* GIS

Ventana Cave Rockshelter in southern Arizona which was excavated in 1941–2 by Emil W. Haury and Julian Hayden. The deeply stratified deposits contained the terminal Pleistocene Ventana Complex, which has been radiocarbon-dated to 11,300 BP, as well as a thick Archaic-period midden, HOHOKAM occupation and historical Tohono O'odham (Papago) material. The cave stratigraphy at Ventana led Haury to argue that there was cultural continuity between the Archaic COCHISE culture and the Hohokam, a position he later changed, in 1976, in favour of a movement of the Hohokam people out of Mexico.

E.W. Haury: *The stratigraphy and archaeology of Ventana Cave* (Tucson, 1950); ——: *The Hohokam* (Tucson, 1976).

JJR

'Venus' figurines Name given to the female figurines produced during the Upper Palaeolithic, most being found in GRAVETTIAN and MAGDALENIAN contexts. In contrast to CAVE ART, they were produced across a wide area of the continent, including France, Germany, Italy, central Europe, Russia and Siberia. They vary from 3 to 23 cm in height and were made from ivory, schist, steatite and calcite. The corpulent, fat-bottomed and full-breasted examples are often taken as typical, and the figurine discovered at the site of Willendorf in Lower Austria in 1908, carved of limestone, with wide hips and large breasts, has become something of an archetype. The sculptor provided no facial details, but the head, limbs, plump stomach and pubic region are all carefully delineated and the figurine was originally coloured red. Dated very approximately to around 30,000 BC, the figurine is often assumed to embody female fertility. The baked clay examples from Dolní Věstonice in Slovakia are also full-bodied, but in fact Palaeolithic figurines include elegantly stylized versions (LESPUGUE in France) and thin, graceful figurines (Ostrava Petřkovice in Slovakia). The figurines are often quite schematic – in some, only the breasts and buttocks are discernible – although a minority present facial details and even indicate hairstyles (Brassempouy, France). Where there is any detail, the bodies all appear to be nude except in some Siberian examples, which seem to wear fur coats. *See also* GRIMALDI, and figure 27 (p. 341).

H. Delporte: *L'image de la femme dans l'art préhistorique* (Paris, 1979); ——: *Brassempouy* (1980); P. Rice: 'Prehistoric Venuses: symbols of motherhood or womenhood?, *JAR* 37 (1981), 402–14; P. Bahn and J. Vertut: *Images of the Ice Age* (Leicester, 1988); M.D. Gvozdover: 'The typology of female figurines of the Kostenki Palaeolithic culture', *Soviet Anthropology and Archaeology* 27 (1989), 32–94; H. Delporte: 'Gravettian female figurines: a regional survey', *Before Lascaux: The complex record of the early Upper Palaeolithic*, ed. H. Knecht et al. (Boca Raton, 1993), 243–57; N. Hamilton et al.: 'Can we interpret figurines?', *CAJ* 6/2 (1996), 281–307.

RJA

verification Process of proving a theory or hypothesis by testing it against the empirical evidence (via observation or experiment) and presenting these instances as supporting evidence of the general truthfulness of the statement. Philosophers of science differ in the degree to which the hypothesis and observation are linked, the extent to which a hypothesis is tested before being accepted as verified, and in the question of whether unverified statements may form a useful part of the scientific process. In its most extreme and limiting form, the POSITIVIST approach to truth-seeking recognizes only verified theories, closely tied to observations from the real world, as useful modes of explanation (*see* LOGICAL POSITIVISM). Many philosophers of science believe that FALSIFICATION better describes the process of assessing claims of 'truth'. Arguably, neither concept is directly applicable. In the case of archaeology as a social science, where even the simplest statements are definitionally complex and dependent upon other untested (and untestable) premises. Instead, archaeologists use a variety of strategies to increase the *plausibility* and *acceptability* of the theories that they put forward.

See also MIDDLE-RANGE THEORY, NEW ARCHAEOLOGY, THEORY AND THEORY BUILDING *and* INDUCTIVE AND DEDUCTIVE EXPLANATION.

RJA

vertical photographs *see* AERIAL ARCHAEOLOGY

Victoria West Small town in the central Karoo, Cape Province, South Africa, which gave its name to two types of core (Victoria West I and II) associated with the manufacture of ACHEULEAN handaxes. They are a type of prepared core and generally restricted to areas of dolerite in South Africa.

C. van R. Lowe: 'The evolution of the Levallois technique in South Africa', *Man*, 37 (1945), 49–59.

RI

Viet Khe *see* DONG SON CULTURE

Vietnam *see* ASIA 3

vihara Meeting hall within a Buddhist temple area.

Viking *see* BIRKA; COPPERGATE

Vila Nova de São Pedro (VNSP culture) Fortified settlement site in the Tagus River valley in central Portugal which has given its name to a developed Copper Age culture in the region that flourished from the very late 4th or early 3rd millennium BC until about 2000 BC. The VNSP culture is characterized by fortified settlements and the importation and production of 'prestige' goods. At the type-site a sub-rectangular thick-walled enclosure (externally *c*.30–40 m across), strengthened with ten semi-circular bastions, contains limited evidence of huts and pits; the structure is enclosed by two further defensive walls. Like the site of LOS MILLARES in Spain, Vila Nova de São Pedro has produced evidence of imported goods, including indications of directional trade in the form of ostrich egg-shell and ivory from North Africa; other items found at the site include BELL BEAKERS (from the later 3rd millennium), clay and stone plaques decorated with motifs such as rayed suns, various copper daggers and other artefacts made from copper.

H.N. Savory: 'The cultural sequence at Vila Nova de São Pedro', *Madrider Mitteilungen* 13 (1972), 23–37.

RJA

Villanovan culture Defined largely by the contents of the urnfields it produced, this early Italian Iron Age culture of the first half of the 1st millennium BC is recognized as a precursor of the Etruscan civilization. The culture was identified in the mid-19th century from a cemetery of urns with cremations and inhumations dug up at Villanova, near Bologna, and similar urnfields have since been excavated from Bologna itself. The cemeteries are from various periods and have been divided into Villanovan I–IV. The urns are often simply placed in the earth, with or without a covering slab, but may also be contained within rough slab cists or, rarely, within a larger clay vessel. Elaborately decorated, the urns were often covered with a bowl or a pottery version of a helmet. The grave goods (including many items of beaten decorated bronze such as helmets, and fibulae) reveal connections with HALLSTATT Central Europe as well as other regions of Italy. Villanovan urnfields are found both north and south of the Apennines. The southern – and probably earlier – distribution approximates to the region of Etruria (Tuscany) and disappears with the emergence of the early Etruscan culture in the 8th century BC; the northern distribution remains distinct until the 6th century BC.

H. Hencken: *Tarquinia, Villanovans and early Etruscans* (Cambridge, MA, 1968); L.H. Barfield: *Northern Italy before Rome* (London, 1971).

RJA

Villeneuve-Tolosane Large and complex Middle Neolithic site in Haute-Garonne, France, associated with the CHASSÉEN complex. The site, over 30 ha in area, is linked with a series of interrupted ditches. Like the other major Chasséen site in the region, SAINT-MICHEL-DU-TOUCH, the site interior presents a rich array of Chasséen material and pits, but the most important structures are over 700–800 enigmatic cobbled areas. These fall into two distinct classes: round areas (typically 2 m diameter) or narrow sub-rectangular areas (typically 10 m × 2 m). They seem to have been created by first digging a pit, then layering it with wood and placing cobbles on top. The wood was then fired, leaving a layer of charcoal (in the case of the rectangular structures this is dense, with unburnt chunks of wood), and a layer of burnt cobbles perhaps 20 cm thick. The excavator, Méroc, interpreted these as the bases of huts (or *fonds de cabanes*). However, other possible functions include food processing or cooking. The site also has a well-pit, and a pit containing an estimated 50,000 snailshells.

J. Clottes et al.: 'Le village chasséen de Villeneuve-Tolosane (Haute-Garonne), Fouilles 1978', *La Préhistoire du Quercy dans la contexte de Midi-Pyrénées* (Montauban–Cahors, 1979), 116–28; P. Bahn: 'The Neolithic of the French Pyrenees', *Ancient France 6000–2000* ed. C. Scarre (Edinburgh, 1987), 116–28.

RJA

Vinča culture One of the principal Middle Neolithic to Eneolithic cultures of eastern Europe (east Yugoslavia, south Hungary, west Romania), characterized by a rich ceramic tradition of dark burnished, knobbed and fluted ware. The Vinča culture offers some of the earliest evidence in Europe of copper metallurgy. Vinča pottery is distinct from other major Neolithic pottery traditions in southeast Europe in being unpainted. Vinča potters also produced an abundance of striking anthropomorphic and zoomorphic figurines and vessel lids; literally thousands of these figures were discovered at the type site of Vinča-Belo Brdo itself, on the banks of the Danube near Belgrade, Serbia. The tell comprised at least nine stratified layers of Vinča material, lying over an earlier layer of STARCEVO material (later layers included evidence of Bronze Age BADEN and later Iron Age LA TÈNE occupations). The excavations of the tell by Miloje Vasic from 1908 remain central to any understanding of Vinča culture, although the lack of precise stratigraphic control has greatly complicated the definition of the cultural phases (new excavations by M. Garaşanin and D. Srejovic began in 1978).

The common division of the Vinča material into stages A–E is based largely on the typology of pottery from Vinča–Belo Brdo; the chronological significance of this scheme and the extent to which it can be applied to other Vinča sites is only slowly becoming clear. (For a selection of Vinča radiocarbon dates and a map of principal sites, see Srejovic 1988, 45–9 and discussion in Chapman 1981, p.18 ff). The earlier Vinča sequence, in which copper is very rare, is often called the Vinča-Tordos phase (*c*.5400–4800 BC), after the Transylvanian site of Tordos; the later sequence, marked by taller forms of pottery, heavy production of anthropomorphic lids and four-legged vases, and the substantial development of metallurgy, is called the Vanča-Pločnik (*c*.4800–4500 BC), after the settlement of Pločnik in Serbia – which yielded a fine early hoard of 13 chisels or axes.

There have been attempts in the past to link the Vinča to Troy 1, now set aside for chronological reasons; the link with Mesopotamia (*see* TĂRTĂRIA) is also now discounted, although some recent researchers look to Anatolia for the genesis of certain elements of the culture. Others, however, have begun to stress the possibility of a local origin, and even an evolution from the preceding Starčevo culture.

M. Vasic: *Preistoriska Vinča I–IV*, 4 vols (Belgrade, 1932, 1936); N. Tasic: *Neolitska Plastika* (Belgrade, 1973); V. Dumitrescu: *The Neolithic settlement at Rast*, BAR IS 72 (Oxford, 1980) [site report on Vinča settlement; short discussion of Vinča chronology, p.107]; J.C. Chapman: *The Vinča culture of south-east Europe: studies in chronology, economy and society*, BAR IS 117, 2 vols (Oxford, 1981); D. Srejovic, ed.: *The Neolithic of Serbia: archaeological research 1948–88* (Belgrade, 1988).

RJA

visual display of data The visual display of archaeological data is often recommended, especially in EXPLORATORY DATA ANALYSIS, on the grounds that 'one picture is worth a thousand words'. However, there is a danger, in that while the human eye is probably better at seeing patterns in graphics than in tables, it is also good at creating patterns where none exist. Common techniques for displaying the values of a single variable are bar and pie charts, historgrams, and frequency polygons and curves. For two variables, SCATTERGRAMS and bivariate histograms can be used. There are pitfalls in producing such displays; rules for avoiding them are given by Tufte (1983). *See also* GIS.

J.E. Doran and F.R. Hodson: *Mathematics and computers in archaeology* (Edinburgh, 1975), 115–34; E.R. Tufte: *The visual display of quantitative information* (Cheshire, CT, 1983); S. Shennan: *Quantifying archaeology* (Edinburgh,

1988), 22–31, 45–6; M. Fletcher and G.R. Lock: *Digging numbers* (Oxford, 1991), 13–30.
CO

Vix Celtic princely tomb in the Seine Valley, just below the contemporary hillfort of MONT LASSOIS in eastern France. Dated to *c*.480 BC (Hallstatt D), the massive cairn, originally *c*.42 m in diameter, contained an inhumation with an extraordinary series of imported and locally manufactured grave goods. Among these were a giant (1.64 m high) crater and Black Figure ware of Greek manufacture, a gold 'diadem' decorated with winged horses, bronze vessels and a dismantled four-wheeled chariot. Vix is one of the richest of a group of graves in eastern France, Switzerland and southern Germany (e.g. Eberdingen-HOCHDORF), many of which occur near fortified sites controlling trade routes south to the Mediterranean or east to the Alpine passes. Imported items such as those found at Vix influenced CELTIC ART of the subsequent LA TÈNE period.

R. Joffroy: *Vix et ses trésors* (Paris, 1979); J.-P. Mohen et al.: *Trésors des Princes Celtes*, exh. cat. (Paris, 1987).
RJA

VNSP culture *see* VILA NOVA DE SÃO PEDRO

Voloshski-Vassil'evka Group of Mesolithic cemeteries on the bank of the River Dniepr south of the town of Dniepropetrovsk (Ukraine). Voloshski cemetery was excavated by O.V. Bodyanski and V.N. Danilenko. In the western part (13 graves), the dead were buried in a contracted posture on their right sides, with their heads directed to the south. The eastern part (6 graves) reveals no distinct pattern; the dead were buried in a contracted posture on their backs, or stomachs, or in an extended posture on their backs. The burial inventory consisted of numerous flint implements, including backed bladelets, end-scrapers, burins, points and flakes. An arrowhead was found embedded in the cervical vertebra of one skeleton. Many of the graves in Vasil'evka-3 cemetery, excavated by D.Ya. Telgin, also contained flint implements (mostly arrowheads), and again arrowheads were found in the bones of the dead – one in a rib and another in a spine.

V.N. Danilenko: 'Vološskii epipalaeolithičeskii mogilnik' [The Voloshkski epipalaeolithic cemetery], *Sovetskaja etnografija* 3 (1955), 56–61; D.Ya. Telegin: *Mezolitichni pam'jatki Ukrainy* [Mesolithic sites of the Ukraine] (Kiev, 1981).
PD

Vorbasse Medieval site in central Jutland, the excavations of which – like those of Feddersen Wierde in West Germany (Haarnagel 1979) or Wijster (van Es 1967) – aimed to expose the entire settlement, using machinery. In this case an area of 260,000 m² was uncovered, showing how a village founded in the 1st century BC passed through eight stages before being deserted in the 11th century AD. Of special interest is the process by which the 20 dwellings of the later Roman period were transformed into fenced magnate farms with subsidiary buildings in the Viking age. In the 11th century the site of the village was transferred to the place that it presently occupies.

W.A. van Es: 'Wijster: a native village beyond the imperial frontier', *Palaeohistoria* 11 (1967); W. Haarnagel: *Die Grabung Feddersen Wierde: Methode, Hausbau, Siedlungs – und Wirtschaftsformen sowie Sozialstruktur* (Wiesbaden, 1979); S. Hvass: 'Rural settlements in Denmark in the first millennium AD', *The birth of Europe*, ed. K. Randsborg (Rome, 1989), 91–9.
RH

Vučedol culture Central European culture of *c*.3000 to 2200 BC, defined by the Croatian type-site of Vučedol on the Danube. Vučedol tell settlements typically contain tightly packed wood-lattice and clay houses with large storage/refuse pits. Copper-working is well-developed, and two-piece moulds were used extensively for tools and axes (often fan-shaped). The fine Vučedol pottery is heavily decorated, typically with white encrusted geometric patterns and motifs (sun, cross etc.) on a black ground. One of the most famous Vučedol artefacts is a decorated dove-shaped ritual vessel recovered from Vučedol itself. Many small clay female figurines were also produced, as well as certain horn-shaped 'altars'. While based on raising cattle and growing cereal, the economy retained a strong hunting and fishing component.

R.R. Schmidt: *Die Burg Vučedol* (Zagreb, 1945); *Vučedol: trece tisucljece p.n.e.* [Vučedol: three thousand years BC] (Zagreb, 1988) [exh. cat. with full English trans.].
RJA

Vumba Commoner settlement of the early Khami period (*c*.AD1450–1830) near Francistown in northeast Botswana. The settlement followed the 'CENTRAL CATTLE PATTERN', but Van Waarden found a surprising number of grain-bin supports – 108 in all. Using k-means CLUSTER ANALYSIS, she was able to distinguish subdivisions corresponding to compounds of polygamous family units, such as a senior man and his wives and children, and his brothers or sons with their families. Smaller subdivisions suggest that each adult owned their own set of granaries. According to Van Waarden's reconstruction, the settlement faced west, and the senior man lived at the back with junior households to his left and right. Some 50 head of cattle and 40 small stock could have been kept in the two central byres, while the grain-bins had a storage capacity of 200 m^3. These dual subsistence spheres characterized Eastern Bantu speaking societies throughout the Iron Age.

C. Van Waarden: 'The granaries of Vumba: structural interpretation of a Khami period commoner site', *JAA* 8 (1989), 131–57.

TH

W

Wadi Amud Valley near the Sea of Galilee in Israel, where several cave sites of the MOUSTERIAN and Emiran periods have been excavated. The Upper Palaeolithic material from Emireh Cave provided the basis for the Emiran period, while Amud Cave itself (the typesite for the Amudian, or pre-Aurignacian, blade industry) contained several NEANDERTHAL skeletons and the nearby Zuttiya Cave included a fragment of a skull which perhaps also derived from a Neanderthal.

M. Suzuki and F. Takai: *The Amud man and his cave* (Tokyo, 1970).

IS

Wadi el-Hudi A cluster of Egyptian amethyst quarrying and gold mining sites located 35 km southeast of Aswan and dating from the early Middle Kingdom (*c.*2100 BC) to the Roman period. The surviving traces of the Middle Kingdom phase of exploitation include a pair of amethyst quarries associated with a hill-top settlement and an unusual rectangular drystone fortress, as well as a large number of rock-drawings and stelae bearing commemorative hieroglyphic inscriptions left behind by the various quarrying expeditions.

A. Fakhry: *The inscriptions of the amethyst quarries at Wadi el-Hudi* (Cairo, 1952); A.I. Sadek: *Wadi el-Hudi: the amethyst mining inscriptions*, 2 vols (Warminster, 1980–5); I. Shaw and R. Jameson: 'Amethyst mining in the Eastern Desert: a preliminary survey at Wadi el-Hudi', *JEA* 79 (1993), 81–97.

IS

Wadi Kubbaniya Group of Palaeolithic sites near Aswan where many grindstones have been discovered, suggesting that cereal cultivation was taking place at a very early period in Egyptian prehistory (*c.*18,000 BP). The subsistence pattern at Wadi Kubbaniya appears to have combined plant cultivation with hunting and gathering, judging from the fact that the rest of the lithics are similar to those employed at HALFAN and late EDFUAN encampments of roughly the same period.

F. Wendorf et al.: *Loaves and fishes: the prehistory of Wadi Kubbaniya* (Dallas, 1980).

IS

Wadi el-Natuf *see* NATUFIAN

Wang-ch'eng-kang (Wangchenggang) The first site in China at which the remains of a walled city datable as early as the Middle–Late LUNG-SHAN period (*c.*2500–1700 BC) were discovered. The ruins in fact comprise two cities, one to the east (which is the better preserved) and remnants of the western wall of a second to the west. The name of the site is the one that was given to the mound itself, which was situated close to the village of Pa-fang-ts'un, about 11 km from Teng-feng-hsien, in western Ho-nan province.

The area is rich in archaeological remains, mainly of the Ho-nan Lung-shan culture, which in places is underlaid by a P'EL-LI-KANG horizon, while a large YANG-SHAO site is also located in the vicinity. Only parts of the western wall, and small parts of the northern and southern walls have survived, owing to changes of the river Wu-tu-ho. In most cases, the existence of the walls is indicated simply by the preservation of rammed earth foundation ditches: the four walls of the city originally formed a square which enclosed an area of approximately 10,000 sq. m, with sides of about 90 cm. The rammed earth (*hang-t'u*) foundations of a large building within the walled enclosure have been assigned to Period II of the site and radiocarbon-dated to *c.*2455 BC, while the strata relating to Periods III and IV have yielded radiocarbon dates of *c.*2280 and 1900 BC respectively. A bronze fragment of part of a container found in an ash-pit of Period IV level is presently the earliest example of a bronze container reported to date in China. Whether actual indications of foundry activities in this pre-Shang Bronze Age site will come to light is uncertain in view of the highly eroded nature of the general site-area.

Anon.: *Teng-feng Wang-ch'eng-kang yu Yang-ch'eng* [Wang-ch'eng-kang and Yank-ch'eng of Teng-feng]

(Peking, 1992); N. Barnard: 'Thoughts on the emergence of metallurgy in pre-Shang and Early Shang China and a technical appraisal of relevant bronze artefacts of the time', *BMM, Sendai* 19 (1993), 3–48.
NB

Wareham Down *see* OVERTON DOWN

Warka *see* URUK

Washshukanni *see* MITANNI

al-Wasit Islamic-period city in southeastern Iraq which was founded in *c.*AD 702–5 by al-Hajjaj, the Umayyads' governor of the East (*al-Mashriq*), to serve as the centre of administration for the entire Islamic east. It is an extensive area of low mounds, dominated by an ornate Seljuq-period gateway in baked brick. It is unusual among the earliest Islamic urban foundations in Iraq in that it is free of present occupation, in contrast to AL-KUFA and al-Basra. Excavations began in 1936 and parts of the mosque were cleared, the first version of which proved to be the original mosque of al-Hajjaj with two later mosques built on top of it. These later mosques had their *qibla* walls on a different orientation to that of the first, so that they faced Mecca. The first mosque at al-Wasit lacked a *mihrâb* (prayer niche), thus confirming the textual evidence that recessed *mihrâb*s were not introduced until 707–9. The first mosque was also excellent evidence that the *qibla* (direction of Mecca) in early mosques was not calculated in the same manner as in later mosques. Emphasis on the mosque and the early period by the excavators overshadows the equally interesting issue of the subsequent evolution of al-Wasit and its longevity as a town down to the 13th century when Iraq was devastated by the Mongols.

F. Safar: *Wâsit: the sixth season's excavation* (Cairo, 1945); K.A.C. Creswell: *Early Muslim architecture* I/1 (Oxford, 1969), 132–8.
GK

wavelength dispersive X-ray fluorescence (WDXRF) *see* X-RAY FLUORESCENCE SPECTROMETRY

wave of advance Theoretical model that attempted to describe the spread of agriculture across Europe. The model was first proposed by Ammerman (an archaeologist) and Cavalli-Sforza (a geneticist) in 1971, after they discovered that a consistent 'rate of spread' measurement could be obtained by plotting radiocarbon dates from the earliest known cereal farming sites across a map of Europe. This 'rate spread' analysis has since been much refined (1973, 1984), but the basic finding, that agriculture advanced at a rate of approximately one kilometre per year (25 km per generation) remains.

Ammerman and Cavalli-Sforza sought to explain this discovery by stating that *if* early agriculture led to a growth in population, and *if* this population growth led to small-scale migratory activity on the agricultural frontier, then it could be shown mathematically that a 'wave of population expansion will ensue and progress at a constant radial rate' (1984: 61). In an 'initial test' Ammerman and Cavalli-Sforza have compared their observed rate of spread against this 'wave of advance model', with the all-important variables of the model calculated according to ethnographic data on likely rates of population growth and types of migratory activity. The results suggested that the model is a feasible explanation for the observed data, but, as with so many other archaeological models, the variables are such that it is impossible to prove that it is *the* answer.

The authors of the 'wave of advance' model do not insist that it provides a universal explanation for the spread of agriculture. As they admit, the observed rate of spread is much patchier than the model allows, particularly in the western Mediterranean; the idea of a single mechanism of spread simply does not fit all the regional archaeological evidence, as summarized in Whittle (1994). Instead, the model seems most likely to be a useful description of the spread of agriculture during certain phases of the Linearbandkeramik expansion in some areas of temperate Europe.

A.J. Ammerman and L.L. Cavalli-Sforza, 'A population model for the diffusion of early farming in Europe', *The explanation of culture change* (London, 1973), 343–57; ——: *The Neolithic transition and the genetics of population in Europe* (Princeton, 1984); A. Whittle: 'The First Farmers', *The Oxford illustrated prehistory of Europe*, ed. B. Cunliffe (Oxford, 1994), 136–66.
RJA

WDXRF *see* X-RAY FLUORESCENCE SPECTROMETRY

were-jaguar Anthropomorphic creature depicted in the OLMEC art of Mesoamerica, which has an infantile human face combined with animal characteristics such as fangs and paws. The animal represented is usually thought to be a jaguar, although crocodilian creatures (e.g. caimans) and toads have also been suggested.

P.T. Furst: 'The Olmec were-jaguar motif in the light of ethnographic reality', *Dumbarton Oaks conference on the Olmec*, ed. E.P. Benson (Washington, D.C., 1968), 143–78.

PRI

Wessex culture Bronze Age cultural complex defined by a regional group of round barrow burials in southern Britain, as described by Stuart Piggott in his classic account of 1938. The 'Wessex culture' is characterized by a series of burials equipped with finely made gold, jet and amber ornaments, copper and bronze daggers, polished maceheads etc. – though these rich burials form only a small minority of the whole set of barrows. Many of the richest burials occur in Wiltshire, but 'Wessex-type' graves are scattered over southern Britain (e.g. the gold cup found at Rillaton, Cornwall, or the amber cup from Hove, Sussex).

The Wessex burials are often divided into two types. In the earlier and richer group, termed Wessex I or the Bush Barrow group, burials tend to be inhumations, with some cremations, and the daggers are the Armorico-British style; in the later Wessex II period cremation is predominant and the daggers are of the Camerton-Snowhill type.

The 'Wessex culture' continues to fascinate prehistorians for two major reasons. Firstly, it is the most dramatic manifestation of the fundamental change in burial rites that took place between the late 3rd and early 2nd millennium BC, in which the earlier, supposedly communal, burial tradition of the Neolithic gave way to richly equipped individual burials – a development which is often assumed to mirror a change in social organization. Secondly, certain of the grave-goods suggest that the Wessex elite maintained direct or indirect links with other elite groups on the continent. There is little doubt over the links with Brittany – demonstrated by the use of minute gold pins to decorate the pommels of daggers from KERNONEN, Brittany, and BUSH BARROW, Wiltshire, for instance – and perhaps Central Europe. However, there has been a continuing controversy over whether such artefacts as the 'staff' mounts found at Bush Barrow (paralleled by examples from the Shaft Graves of MYCENAE) and the faience beads (or at least, their technique of manufacture) prove a link with the Mycenaean civilization of Greece; in one of the more dramatic revisions prompted by radiocarbon dating, Renfrew (1968) attempted to prove that Wessex pre-dated Mycenae, although his argument that stylistic links are anyway of little relevance in *explaining* the genesis of the 'Wessex culture' is perhaps more significant.

S. Piggot, 'The Early Bronze Age in Wessex', *PPS* 4 (1938), 52–106; C. Renfrew: 'Wessex without Mycenae', *Annual of the British School at Athens* 63 (1968), 277–85' C. Burgess, *The Age of Stonehenge* (London, 1980); A.F. Harding: *The Mycenaeans and Europe* (London, 1984).

RJA

Western Chou (Hsi-Chou; Xizhou) Name applied to the first half of the Chinese Chou dynasty comprising a dozen rulers. Originally Chou was located in the present-day CHOU-YÜAN area, but in 1122 BC (according to the traditional literature) Wu Wang of Chou subjugated the SHANG city-state and established Chou's hegemony over most of the then 'civilized' area (as contrasted to the 'barbarian' regions). The traditional literature also suggests that the Western Chou administrative system operated from its inception very much along the lines of Western feudalism, allowing the more or less centrally situated Chou (the ROYAL DOMAIN) to maintain an effective but often uneasy hold over the rulers of the surrounding princely states (i.e. the *Chu-hou*). The latter were required to undergo formal investiture by the Chou kings upon their hereditary assumption to the feudal title and associated territories: this was an elaborate ceremony, regarding which many details are recorded among scores of contemporary bronze inscriptions, marking the investitures along with details of the royal commands issued to the Chou-hou.

There were continual incursions from 'barbarian' peoples, such as the Ti, Jung and YI, who were scattered in the surrounding regions. Military expeditions were frequently launched against these 'tribes' to whom reference is often found both in the traditional literature and in the inscriptions on bronze vessels. Traditionally, it is considered that the shift of the Royal Domain to the east, near Lo-yang, was due to the increasing severity of barbarian attacks. The large number of storage-pit burials of bronze vessels and other artefacts in the Fu-feng and Ch'i-shan sites excavated in recent decades would surely seem to confirm this.

Ch'i Ssu-ho: 'Chou-tai hsi-ming-li k'ao' [Researches into the investure ceremony of the Chou period], *YCHP* 23 (1947), 197–226; ——: 'A comparison between Chinese and European feudal institutions', *YJSS* 4 (1948), 1–13; H.G. Creel: *The origins of statecraft in China* (Chicago, 1970); N. Barnard: 'The Nieh Ling Yi', *JICS* 9 (1978), 585–628; E.L. Shaughnessy: *Sources of Western Zhou history: inscribed bronze vessels* (Berkeley, 1991).

NB

West Kennet Early Neolithic drystone and megalithic tomb of the SEVERN-COTSWOLD type located near the later stone circle of AVEBURY in Wiltshire, England. The trapezoidal earth and chalk mound is over 100 m long, heaped up from flanking ditches. The large gallery, giving access to four transept chambers and a terminal chamber, is entered through an unusually impressive concave blocking facade. The tomb was used for collective burial over many centuries: the skeletons found within the tomb were largely disarticulated and had been much rearranged, for example with longbones stacked together and fingerbones placed in the crevices of the walling. The fact that fewer skulls were found in the tomb than is suggested by the count of other types of bones led researchers to speculate that they may have been removed as part of ancestor rituals. The tomb was probably built around 3300 BC in roughly the same period that the causewayed camp of WINDMILL HILL was in use, and finally backfilled with rubble after a last burial some time after 2500 BC; the final deposits contained BEAKER pottery.

S. Piggot: *The West Kennet Long Barrow: excavations 1955–6* (London, 1962).

RJA

West Turkana Region to the west of Lake Turkana (Rudolf) in northern Kenya where important remains of early hominids have been discovered. Although West Turkana has produced less Stone Age fossils and artefacts than sites to the east and north of the lake, such as KOOBI FORA and OMO, an important example of the robust australopithecine (*AUSTRALOPITHECUS boisei*) was discovered by Kamoya Kimeu, Alan Walker and Richard Leakey. This hominid has been dated to about 2.5 million years ago, i.e. rather earlier than the '*Zinjanthropus*' type-specimen from OLDUVAI in Tanzania. The most spectacular find in the region, however, is the most complete specimen of *HOMO ERECTUS* yet discovered, dating to some 1.5 million years ago. The West Turkana example is unusually revealing with regard to the body, limbs, locomotion and manipulatory potential of *Homo erectus*, which was previously represented largely by skulls in isolation. Pliocene and Miocene fossils are also being recovered from the region, as at RUSINGA.

Y. Coppens et al., eds: *Earliest man and environments in the Lake Rudolf basin* (Chicago, 1976); J. Reader: *Missing links: the hunt for earliest man*, 2nd edn (London, 1988).

JS

Wharram Percy Deserted English medieval village in the North Yorkshire Wolds with evidence of continuous settlement from Roman times until the 20th century. Excavations began in 1952 and continued until 1990. The excavators, Maurice Beresford and John Hurst, experimented with open-area investigations of the earthworks as opposed to trenches, setting a methodological standard for the archaeology of medieval sites. The reconstruction of the village topography, shifting around within the narrow confines of the valley, from Early Anglo-Saxon times, has made Wharram the type-site for post-Roman village formation in England, and a model for such approaches in Europe.

J.G. Hurst: *Wharram, a study of settlement on the Yorkshire Wolds* 1 (London, 1979); ——: 'The Wharram research project: results to 1983', *Medieval Archaeology* 28 (1984), 77–111.

RH

White Temple *see* URUK; ZIGGURAT

wiggle matching Technique based on high-precision RADIOCARBON DATING of a set of samples, the time intervals between which are known (e.g. adjacent groups of 10–20 tree rings): typically five dates are needed. The idea is to replicate a part of the radiocarbon calibration curve which can be fixed in calendar time by matching it to the master calibration curve. Statistical techniques are used to determine the best fit. If the master curve is sufficiently detailed at the time in question, the sample can be dated to within about ten 'calendar years'. Tree rings are ideal for wiggle matching (but the relationship of the rings dated to the bark and thus to the time of felling must be known: *see* RADIOCARBON DATING *and* DENDROCHRONOLOGY). The technique has also been used on peat and lake sediments, where the deposition rate can be estimated.

G.W. Pearson: 'Precise calendrical dating of known growth period samples using a 'curve fitting' technique', *Radiocarbon* 28 (1986) 292–9.

SB

Willendorf *see* 'VENUS' FIGURINES

Wilton Somewhat outmoded term applied (from the 1920s onwards) to Late Stone Age industries with microlithic tendencies in the savanna regions of eastern and southern Africa during the Holocene. The name Wilton derives from the South African typesite, the WILTON LARGE ROCK SHELTER. In recent decades, following the appreciation of greater regional and environmental diversity and the application of more sophisticated archaeological analyses (as well as the reaction against classification based on particular tool-types or sets), the term has lost much of its currency. Some of the late occurrences broadly labelled 'Wilton' in the East African highlands may overlap in time with the beginnings of pastoralism and even the use of iron, perhaps representing a late continuation of 'archaic' hunter-gatherer ways of living.

J.D. Clark: *The prehistory of Africa* (London, 1970), ch 5; J. Deacon: 'Wilton – a re-assessment after fifty years', *SAAB* 27 (1972), 10–48.

JS

Wilton Large Rockshelter Stone Age site near Alicedale in the eastern Cape, South Africa. This is the type-site of the WILTON industry (see above), which was adopted in 1929 to replace the term 'pygmy culture' (on account of small convex scrapers and small backed pieces). In 1966–7, the site was re-excavated by J. Deacon, who, following D.L. Clarke's ontogenetic model, identified Formative, Climax, Post-Climax, and Death/Birth phases in the succession, with higher frequencies of small backed pieces (segments and backed blades) characterizing the Climax phase. A 'pre-Wilton' industry at the base of the succession is attributed to the ALBANY INDUSTRY. Interestingly, while the industry was named after this site (in the Albany District) the industry actually received its definition at Nelson Bay Cave, 300 km to the southeast.

J. Deacon: 'Wilton: an assessment after fifty years', *SAAB* 27 (1972), 10–48.

RI

Winchester *see* OLD MINSTER

Windmill Hill Neolithic site in Wiltshire, southern England, situated close to the later henge monument of AVEBURY. It is important as the archetypal CAUSEWAYED ENCLOSURE, an enigmatic class of monuments built in the early Neolithic in Britain that consist of concentric circuits of interrupted ditches. At Windmill Hill, a substantial portion of the three concentric ditch circuits and interior (covering 9.6 ha in total) have been excavated. The outermost ditch is the largest (up to 3 m deep originally), and seems to have been in use longest – radiocarbon dating provides a calendar date of the end of the 4th millennium BC, but this may be relatively late in the history of the site. The two inner ditches contain some evidence for the ceremonial disposal of food, and the site as a whole yielded evidence for well over 1000 pottery vessels. Some of the pottery came originally from some distance away (Somerset and Cornwall), while the stone used in tools found at the site originated from an unusually wide range of sources (including material from Cornwall, from GREAT LANGDALE in Cumbria, and from Craig Lwyd in Wales). There is some evidence that animal bones and pottery were deliberately placed in the ditches, rather than being discarded; the faunal remains are dominated by domestic cattle bones, with sheep and some pig, but also include a few wild animals. All this has led to suggestions that the site acted as a ceremonial centre for rituals, and perhaps as a node for exchange systems across Neolithic Britain.

I.F. Smith: *Windmill Hill and Avebury – excavations by Alexander Keiller 1925–39* (Cambridge, 1965).

RJA

Wittfogel, Karl *see* HYDRAULIC DESPOTISM

Wonderwerk Cave Very large cave 40 km south of Kuruman, northern Cape, South Africa, which was the subject of several investigations from 1943 onwards. The cave contains a very full sequence from ACHEULEAN of Middle Pleistocene age to Late Holocene, including the historical period. The large size of the cave (140 m deep, 17 m wide, 3.7–7.0 m high), and an early history of disturbance from guano digging have influenced the placing of cuttings, such that there are horizontal gaps in a demonstrably complex stratigraphy. Fauna is well preserved throughout, and plant remains variably so. There is compelling evidence of controlled use of fire from the Middle Pleistocene, and there are indications of LEVALLOIS technique in the later Acheulean. Engraved stone tablets occur from around 12,500 uncal BP. Environmental evidence points to changes in both temperature and rainfall within the past 12 millennia.

K.W. Butzer: 'Archaeology and Quaternary environment in the interior of southern Africa', *Southern African prehistory and palaeoenvironments*, ed. R.G. Klein (Rotterdam, 1984), 1–64; P.B. Beaumont: 'Wonderwerk Cave', *Guide to archaeological sites in the northern Cape*, ed. P.B. Beaumont and D. Morris (Kimberley, 1990), 101–36.

RI

Woodland Term referring to both a time period and a tradition in eastern North American prehistory. The Woodland period extends from *c.*1000 BC to AD 900, preceded by the Archaic and followed by the Late Prehistoric; it is commonly subdivided into Early (*c.*1000–200 BC), Middle (*c.*200 BC–AD 400) and Late (*c.*AD 400–900) subperiods, however the dates assigned to these phases vary considerably. The Woodland tradition includes a wide variety of prehistoric cultures that share a number of traits including the construction of burial mounds, the production of ceramic vessels, and the cultivation of native and tropical plants. In the southeastern and midwestern United States, the Woodland tradition is replaced by the MISSISSIPPIAN tradition (*c.*AD 900–1600). In the northeast, the Woodland tradition continues up to the time of European contact.

J. Griffin: 'Eastern North American archaeology: a summary', *Science* 156 (1967), 175–91; J. Stoltman: 'Temporal models in prehistory: an example from Eastern North America', *Current Anthropology* 19 (1978), 703–46.

RJE

world systems theory Theoretical approach involving the FUNCTIONALIST study of spatial systems across the entire world, with the aim of understanding the ways in which different cultural entities in the past and present were/are linked via processes of interaction and exchange. It makes use of subsidiary concepts such as 'CORE-PERIPHERY MODELS', whereby dominant cultures at the core or centre of regions are supplied with goods and labour by more peripheral cultures (see Rowlands et al. 1987).

The approach was first developed by Immanuel Wallerstein in the early 1970s, as an attempt to understand the origins and rise of capitalism. He argued that world economies are intrinsically ephemeral and unstable, but the capitalist system, which has lasted for about half a millennium, is an outstanding exception. Wallerstein's ideas emerged partly from the ideas of the Belgian economist Ernst Mandel regarding the essentially boom-bust nature of capitalist economies, partly from the ANNALES SCHOOL (with its emphasis on the observation of social change over long periods of time), and partly from MARXISM (particularly the so-called 'dependence theory', i.e. the two-way economic links between first-, second- and third-world nations).

The great benefit of the world systems approach, compared with other versions of SYSTEMS THEORY is the fact that it avoids falling into the trap of treating a single culture or region as if it were an isolated or closed system, emphasizing instead that all cultures are affected not only by their immediate environmental context but also by a wide network of cultural groupings.

Many American prehistorians adopted the world systems approach in the 1980s, but it has probably been used to best effect in the case of sites or cultures dating to the historical period (e.g. Paynter 1985, a study of the history of Connecticut Valley, Massachusetts). Philip Kohl, making use of the theory as a basis for the study of the process of state formation in western Asia, stresses that world systems in ancient times were not the same as those that have prevailed in more recent times. Whereas Wallerstein relies on economic factors, particularly the movement of labour, in his definitions of core or peripheral cultures, many prehistoric core-periphery systems may have been based on other factors such as religion or ideology. Another flaw in the approach is that it emphasizes the *units* within the system (i.e. the cores, peripheries etc.) but cannot satisfactorily explain or clarify the relations between them.

I. Wallerstein: *The modern world-system*, 2 vols (New York, 1974–80); R.E. Blanton, S.A. Kowalewski, G. Feinman and J. Appel: *Ancient Mesoamerica: a comparison of change in three regions* (Cambridge, 1981); R. Paynter: 'Surplus flow between frontiers and homelands', *Archaeology of frontiers and boundaries*, ed. S.W. Green and S. Perlman (Orlando, 1985), 125–37; P.L. Kohl: 'The ancient economy, transferable technologies, and the Bronze Age world system: a view from the northwestern frontier of the Ancient Near East', *Centre and periphery in the ancient world*, ed. M.J. Rowlands and M.T. Larsen (Cambridge, 1987), 13–24; M. Rowlands, M. Larsen and K. Kristiansen, eds: *Centre and periphery in the ancient world* (Cambridge, 1987).

IS

Wu Ancient state in China, which flourished during the first half of the 1st millennium BC; like YÜEH, it was regarded by the MIDDLE STATES as merely a barbarian region, although the rulers of both states used the Chinese title for 'king'. The site of the capital of Wu is located near modern Su-chou, Chiang-su. Despite the suggestion that Wu was a barbaric region, inscribed bronzes from the state of Ts'ai (excavated at Shou-hsien in 1995, *see* TS'AI HOU LUAN TOMB) indicate that there was intermarriage between the princely family of Ts'ai and the royal family of Wu *c.*457 BC. This was some 15 years following the traditional records of the fall of Wu and its subjection to Yüeh (472 BC). Yüeh itself eventually succumbed to the kingdom of CH'U in 334 BC. There is a growing amount of archaeological information that not only supplements the paucity of data in the traditional literature concerning Wu and Yüeh (the two not being easily distinguishable) but also indicates the comparatively advanced nature of the indigenous cultures.

The Wu walled city of Han, located near Yang-chou and dating to the Ch'un-ch'iu period (771–481 BC), was excavated sporadically from 1956 to 1972, revealing an almost square enclosure comprising inner and outer *hang-t'u* walls with a moat between the two and a further moat surrounding the outer wall (the lengths of the outer moat and inner wall being 6 km and 5 km respectively). Among the various reported finds were GEOMETRIC POTTERY, glazed pottery, stone plough-shares of rectangular shape, wooden boats and bronze artefacts.

N. Barnard: 'A recently excavated inscribed bronze of Western Chou date', *Monumenta Serica Nagoya* 17 (1958), 12–46; Li Hsüeh-ch'in: *Eastern Zhou and Qin civilizations*, trans. Chang Kwang-chih (New Haven, 1985); N. Barnard: 'Bronze casting technology in the peripheral "barbarian" regions', *BMM Sendai* 12 (1987), 3–37.

NB

Wu-kuan-ts'un (Wuguancun) *see* AN-YANG

Wu-wei (Wuwei) *see* HUANG-NIANG-NIANG-T'AI

X

X Group *see* AMARA; BALLANA; BLEMMYES; QASR IBRIM

Xia *see* HSIA

Xian *see* CH'IN

Xiaotun *see* AN-YANG

Xibeigang *see* AN-YANG

Xichuan, Xiasi *see* HSI-CH'UAN, HSIA-SSU

Xingan, Dayangzhou-xiang *see* HSIN-KAN, TA-YANG-CHOU-HSIANG

Xinyang *see* HSIN-YANG

Xiongnu *see* HSIUNG-NU

Xizhou (Hsi Chou) *see* WESTERN CHOU

X-ray diffraction analysis (XRD) Technique for mineralogical or structural chemical analysis, which identifies the crystalline compounds in a material. It is also possible to estimate the approximate quantity of major components. Applications include the identification of inorganic compounds or minerals such as corrosion products on metals, pigments and mineral phases of ceramics and slags. The technique relies on the diffraction, or angular reflectance, of monochromatic X-rays by the planes of atoms in the lattice of crystalline materials. For a given source of X-rays the reflectance angle is proportional to the spacing of the lattice plane. In most crystalline materials there are a number of planes with different but consistent spacings which produce a characteristic diffraction pattern from which the material may be identified.

In X-ray powder diffractometry, a small sample, in the microgramme range, is mounted on a support, such as a gelatine filament, in the centre of a cylindrical camera and then exposed to a narrow beam of X-rays. The diffraction pattern produced is recorded on a strip of photographic film, inside the camera, as a series of lines. The spacings of these enable the components of the material to be identified. This is the method usually used for the identification of CORROSION PRODUCTS, pigments, inlays, gemstones and CYLINDER SEALS (Sax and Middleton 1992), since the sample required is small.

M. Bimson: 'The examination of ceramics by X-ray powder diffractionary', *Studies in Conservation* 14 (1969), 83–9; M. Sax and A.P. Middleton: 'A system of nomenclature for quartz and its application to the material of cylinder seals', *Archaeometry* 34 (1992), 11–20.

MC

X-ray fluorescence spectrometry (XRF) Widely used technique for elemental chemical analysis utilizing the non-destructive phenomenon of X-ray emission from material subjected to a source of X-rays. The incident X-rays ionize atoms in the material and, in the subsequent electron rearrangement, energy is released as fluorescent X-rays with specific energies characteristic of the elements present. The X-ray emission is instantaneous and ceases when the source is removed: there is no residual activity. The intensity of emitted radiation is proportional to the quantity of each element and the technique is both qualitative and quantitative. Standards need to be measured under the same conditions for quantitative analysis.

All elements undergo XRF, but those with very low atomic numbers are difficult to detect and hence the technique is not generally suitable for organic materials but has been extensively applied to metals, ceramics and glass etc. However, unless equipped with a vacuum chamber enclosing the X-ray source, specimen and detector, light elements such as sodium and magnesium will not be detectable. An important limitation of XRF is that it provides only a surface analysis, typically probing not deeper than 100 μm (0.1 mm). The different methods of detecting and analysing the fluorescent X-rays have led to the development of two types of instrument: the EDXRF and the WDXRF.

The *energy dispersive X-ray fluorescence* (EDXRF) instrument uses a spectrometer with a solid state detector which registers the complete spectrum of fluorescent X-rays simultaneously. Particularly suited to rapid non-destructive *in situ* qualitative and quantitative analysis of complete artefacts or small areas on them and normally considered a technique for major and minor rather than trace element analysis. Since XRF is a surface method, and as artefact surfaces are rarely representative of the bulk, for *in situ* analysis the surface must be abraded to obtain accurate quantitative results unless the surface itself is of interest, as in the case of platings, EDXRF is the most commonly applied XRF technique to archaeological material.

The *wavelength dispersive X-ray fluorescence* (WDXRF) technique uses a spectrometer with a diffracting crystal and detector which scans sequentially over an X-ray wavelength range to measure individual element peaks. It is less suited to *in situ* analysis, compared with EDXRF, because of limitations governed by the geometry of the crystal and specimen but it has been used in this mode on coins for example. Samples are normally required although the technique is more precise than EDXRF and has better detection limits into the trace element range. It has therefore been used extensively for provenance studies on pottery and lithics.

E.T. Hall, F. Schweizer and P.A. Toller: 'X-ray fluorescence analysis of museum objects, a new instrument', *Archaeometry* 15 (1973), 53–78; E.P. Bertin: *Principles and practice of X-ray spectrometric analysis* (New York, 1975).

MC

X-ray powder diffractometry *see* X-RAY DIFFRACTION ANALYSIS

XRF *see* X-RAY FLUORESCENCE SPECTROMETRY

Y

Yahudiya Tell el- (anc. Naytahut, Leontopolis) Egyptian town-site in the eastern Delta, dating from at least as early as the Middle Kingdom until the Roman period (*c*.2000 BC–AD 200). It has given its name to a particular type of juglet found not only in Egypt but also in Cyprus, Syria-Palestine and Nubia (see Kaplan 1980). The site is dominated by a rectangular enclosure of uncertain date (probably late Middle Kingdom) and unknown function, which was first excavated by Edouard Naville and Flinders Petrie, and perhaps has some connection with the HYKSOS occupation. Among the other remains at Tell el-Yahudiya are a temple built by Ramesses III (*c*.1198–1166 BC) and a small settlement established by Onias, an exiled Jewish priest, which flourished between the early 2nd century BC and the late 1st century AD.

H.E. Naville: *The Mound of the Jew and the city of Onias* (London, 1890); G.R.H. Wright: 'Tell el-Yahudiya and the glacis', *Zeitschrift des Deutschen Palästina-Vereins* 84 (1968), 1–17; M.K. Kaplan: *The origin and distribution of Tell-el-Yahudijah-ware* (Gothenburg, 1980).

IS

Yamato Ancient name for the Nara prefecture in Japan, where the first Japanese state developed and which, in the 4th–8th centuries AD, was the centre of Japanese art and politics. The ruler of the Yamato court had, by the 5th century AD, established some degree of hegemony over a loose confederation of chiefdoms through a combination of warfare, diplomacy and marriage alliance.

G.L. Barnes: *Protohistoric Yamato: archaeology of the first Japanese state* (Ann Arbor, 1988).

SK

Yan Alternative (older) name for Peking.

Yang-shao (Yangshao) Term applied to several of the earliest Neolithic cultures in China (*c*.6000–4500 BC). The type-site, in the middle Huang-ho region, was discovered in the 1920s by peasants of the village of that name, near Mien-ch'i-hsien in the province of Ho-nan, and was first investigated by J.G. Andersson shortly afterwards. The villages of this prehistoric culture, among which the site of Pan-p'o is the best known, were located on the banks of rivers. Agriculture was the main source of subsistence, based on the cultivation of millet of various types supplemented by the hunting of such animals as deer, horse, bear, turtle and rhinoceros. Domesticated animals included dogs and pigs. Kilns of somewhat rudimentary structure, utilitarian and painted pottery of distinctive design, some with incised markings (which may be embryonic Chinese characters), spinning whorls, basketry, and a considerable variety of stone and bone implements, characterize the general culture.

Numerous Neolithic sites, datable on the basis of calibrated radiocarbon assessments falling within the time span of 6000–3000 BC, have been excavated in recent decades. At the beginning of this period, the Yang-shao coexisted with several other distinct cultures, including TA-WEN-K'OU, Ma-Chia-Pang, HO-MU-TU, TA-P'EN-K'ENG, and Ta-Hsi, and varying degrees of influences spread from one cultural area to another during the period between 4000 and 3000 BC (see Chang 1986).

Chang Kwang-chih: *The archaeology of ancient China*, 4th edn (New Haven, 1986), 107–56 and *passim*.

NB

Yarim Tepe Neolithic site of the HASSUNA culture (*c*.5800–5500 BC), consisting of several small mounds located 7 km southwest of Tell Afar in the Jebel Sinjar region of Iraq. Mound I at Yarim Tepe, about 100 m in diameter, is made up of 13 building strata. Since 1969 it has been excavated by archaeologists from the former Soviet republics; in the earliest levels there are the remains of both circular and rectangular houses built of pisé or of crude unmoulded blocks of mud. There are also sets of parallel low walls which may have served as the foundations for drying racks ('granaries'), a common feature of Neolithic societies as far as JEITUN in Turkmenistan. The evidence of subsistence at Yarim Tepe includes einkorn, emmer wheat, bread wheat, club wheat, barley, lentils, peas and flax, and the domesticated animals included cattle, sheep, goat, pig and dog (although wild species of sheep and goats as well as deer, gazelle and leopards were evidently still being exploited). The dead appear to have been buried in cemeteries outside the settlement, since few bodies have been found either at Yarim Tepe or Tell Hassuna itself.

N.Y. Merpert and R.M. Munchaev: 'The earliest levels at Yarim Tepe I and Yarim Tepe II in northern Iraq', *Iraq* 49 (1987), 1–36; N. Yoffee and J.J. Clark, eds: *Early stages in the evolution of Mesopotamian civilization: Soviet excavations in northern Iraq* (Tucson, 1993).

IS

Yayo *see* AFRICA 1

Yayoi period (300 BC–AD 300) Japanese protohistoric period following the JOMON, named after a location in Tokyo where Yayoi pottery was first discovered. *See* JAPAN 3.

Yazilikaya (1) *see* HITTITES; (2) *see* PHRYGIANS

Yeha Urban and cultic site of the pre-Axumite and Axumite periods (*c.*500 BC–AD 100 and *c.*AD 100–1000 respectively), located some 50 km northeast of AXUM in the Ethiopian highlands. It was excavated by Francis Anfray between 1960 and 1973. The pre-Axumite material – including temples, inhumations and settlement remains – shows evidence of strong South Arabian cultural influence. The principal surviving pre-Axumite monument is a rectangular stone-built temple dated to about the 5th century BC by the South Arabian inscriptions on a pair of stelae. Jospeh Michels undertook a stratified random sampling survey in a

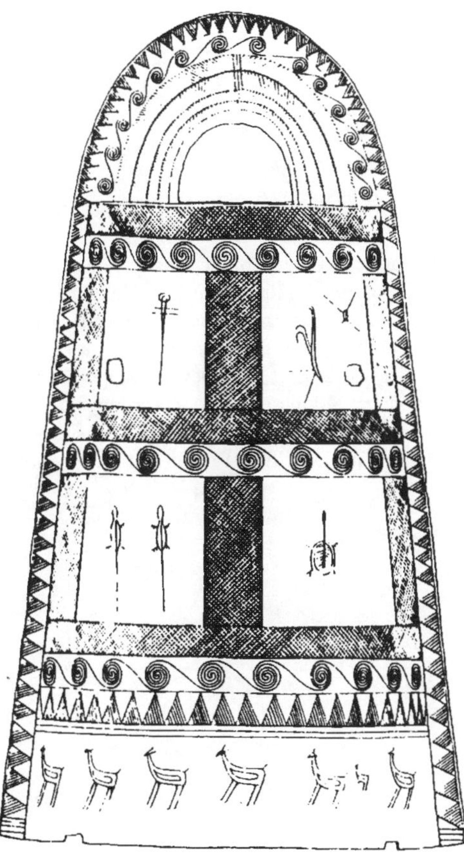

Figure 61 **Yayoi** Yayoi period bronze bell-shaped *dotaku* from Sakuragaoka, Hyogo prefecture, Japan. *Source*: M. Komoto and S. Yamasaki: *Yayoi Jidai no Chisiki* (Tokyo: Tokyo Bijustsu Kokogaku Shirizu, 1984), fig. 28-1.

500 sq. km area of the Axum-Yeha region, revealing new evidence for Axumite settlement patterns (Michels 1979; *see* AXUM *and* SAMPLING STRATEGIES).

F. Anfray: 'Les fouilles de Yeha (mai-juin 1973)', *Travaux de la Recherche Coopérative sur le Programme 230* 4 (1973), 35–8; J.W. Michels: 'Axumite archaeology: an introductory essay', *Aksum*, ed. Y.M. Kobishchanov (Philadelphia, 1979), 1–34; H. de Contenson: 'Pre-Aksumite culture', *General History of Africa* II, ed. G. Mokhtar (London, Berkeley and Paris, 1981), 341–61.

IS

Yerevan *see* URARTU

Yi General name given during Shang and Chou times (2000–771 BC) to the 'barbarian' peoples inhabiting regions in China outside the territory of the MIDDLE STATES.

Yin *see* AN-YANG; CHINA 2

Yin-hsü (Yinxu) *see* AN-YANG

Yorgan Tepe *see* NUZI

York *see* COPPERGATE

Yoshinogari Large double-moated village site of the Yayoi period (300 BC–AD 300) in Saga prefecture, Japan. Broad-area excavation since 1986 for the first time exposed a settlement with clear evidence for the social complexity suggested in contemporary Chinese texts describing Yayoi polities such as Yamatai, with which this site has been mistakenly identified. Five jar burials containing unusual grave-goods, including beads and a bronze sword, were discovered in the top of a large burial mound dating to the early 1st century BC. This is the largest and also one of the oldest burial mounds of the Yayoi period, and is probably the resting place of an powerful family or group. Over two thousand ordinary jar burials have been discovered in cemeteries near the settlement which consisted of pit houses, watchtowers and storage facilities.

M. Hudson and G.L. Barnes: 'Yoshinogari – a Yayoi settlement in northern Kyushu', *Monumenta Nipponica* 46/2 (1991), 211–35.

SK

Yosukeone *see* TOGARI-ISHI AND YOSUKEONE

Yüeh (Yue) Ancient name given to the various 'barbarian' peoples inhabiting the eastern coast and southern areas of China in the 1st millennium BC. The name Pai-Yüeh was applied to the Yueh along the eastern coast (Nan-Yüeh being used to describe those in southern China). Yüeh is also the name of the state in the Pai-Yüeh region, where the rulers used the Chinese title for 'king'. Both Yüeh and the neighbouring state of WU are best known for their intricately manufactured swords, often inscribed with 'bird-script' characters and inlaid with gold. In recent years many of these swords bearing inscriptions with the names of kings such as Kou-chien (496–465 BC) and Lu-ying (464–459 BC) have been unearthed.

Li Hsueh-ch'in: *Eastern Zhou and Qin civilizations*, trans. Chang Kwang-chih (New Haven, 1985).

NB

Yümüktepe *see* MERSIN

Z

Zaachila *see* ZAPOTECS

Zabid The first Islamic-period site to have been excavated in Yemen. Situated on the Red Sea coast, it provides good stratigraphy and chronology for local ceramics, thus providing a framework for much future work in Yemen. The excavations were initiated with the avowed intention of examining 'the dynamics of an Islamic city and its hinterland'. The programme of research also included the recording of the town's mosques; this was a particularly valuable contribution as it is now very much more difficult to enter them.

Later seasons' work included consideration of the significance of pipes and whether they indicated the use of hashish or the arrival of tobacco directly from the Portuguese via the Indian Ocean in the 16th century AD instead of via Europe in the 17th century. Other issues relate to the discovery of iron cannonballs and the question of whether they were manufactured in Yemen or abroad. In effect, the problems of (1) the date of introduction of tobacco and (2) the use of artillery ammunition as a dating tool are both part of the pre-modern area of archaeology to which later Islamic sites are connected, in much the same way as late European sites. These areas are significant and require further research, following on the questions raised at Zabid. The Zabid project has been distinguished by the degree to which petrographic analysis of pottery has been undertaken in post-excavation study, marking the future direction of ceramic studies and giving points of reference for other research in the area.

E.J. Keall: 'Zabîd and its hinterland: 1982 report', *PSAS* 13 (1983), 53–69; ——: 'The dynamics of Zabîd and its hinterland: the survey of a town on the Tihâmah plain of North Yemen', *WA* 14/3 (1983), 378–92; ——: 'A preliminary report on the architecture of Zabîd', *PSAS* 14 (1984), 51–65; J.R. Hallett, E.J. Keall, V. Vitali and R.G.V. Hancock: 'Chemical analysis of Yemeni archaeological ceramics and the Egyptian enigma', *Journal of Radio-nuclear Analytical Chemistry Articles* 110/1 (1987), 293–302; J.R. Hallett, M. Thompson, E.J. Keall and R.B. Mason: 'Archaeometry of medieval Islamic glazed ceramics from Yemen', *Canadian Journal of Chemistry* 66 (1988) 266–72; R.B. Mason and E.J. Keall: 'Provenance of local ceramic industry and the characterisation of imports: petrography of pottery from medieval Yemen', *Antiquity* 62 (1988), 452–63; E.J. Keall: 'A few facts about Zabîd', *PSAS* 16 (1989), 61–9; R.B. Mason, J.R. Hallett and E.J. Keall: 'Provenance of Islamic pottery from Yemen: INAA and petrographic analysis', *25th International Archaeometry Symposium, Proceedings* (Athens, 1989), 543–50; E.J. Keall: 'Drastic changes in 16th century Zabîd', *PSAS* 21 (1991), 79–96; ——: 'Smokers' pipes and the fine pottery tradition of Hays', *PSAS* 22 (1992), 29–46.

GK

Zagros Mountainous range in northeastern Iraq and northwestern Iran, roughly corresponding to the area now occupied by the Kurds. The sites in the Zagros range, a forested area intersected by four tributaries of the River Tigris, include SHANIDAR (a Middle Palaeolithic rock-shelter containing MOUSTERIAN artefacts and the remains of nine NEANDERTHAL skeletons) as well as several settlements of the EPIPALAEOLITHIC and Proto-Neolithic periods (*c*.18000–8500 BC) where some of the earliest evidence for agriculture in the Near East has been excavated (e.g. Karim Shahir and ZAWI CHEMI SHANIDAR). In later times the foothills of the Zagros formed the northern sector of the heartland of ASSYRIA (*c*.1800–612 BC).

J. Braidwood and B. Howe: *Prehistoric investigations in Iraqi Kurdistan* (Chicago, 1960); D. Oates: *Studies in the ancient history of northern Iraq* (London, 1986); P.E.L. Smith: *Palaeolithic archaeology in Iran* (Philadelphia, 1986); D. Olszewski and H. Dibble, eds: *The Palaeolithic prehistory of the Zagros-Taurus* (Philadelphia, 1993).

IS

Zanzibar *see* SWAHILI HARBOUR TOWNS

Zapotecs One of two major cultural and linguistic groups in Oaxaca, Mesoamerica (along with the sometimes-rivals, sometimes-allies MIXTECS), the Zapotecs are associated with the site of their capital at Monte Albán during the Late Classic period.

Zapotec royal families intermarried with Mixtec royalty as well as into distant Mexica dynasties after becoming a tributary state of the AZTECS. As known archaeologically from Monte Albán, Zapotec culture is most distinctively characterized by elaborate ceramic funerary urns with sculptured deity figures on the front, painted murals, stone sculpture and limited hieroglyphic texts.

Monte Albán, perched on a high ridge overlooking a confluence of rivers, was occupied from at least 500 BC to AD 1500, with its peak in *c.*AD 500–750. It was the focus of an intensive mapping and surface collection project carried out to obtain information on the foundation and collapse of the city, and about the characteristics of the social groups occupying it. Investigators (e.g. Blanton 1978) believe that it served throughout its history as a regional capital, and as the hub of a military confederacy uniting several centres in the Oaxaca valley. The low-relief Formative period carvings found on stone slabs at Monte Albán, and known as the Danzantes, are believed to represent prisoners or sacrificial victims.

By Postclassic times, the focus of Zapotec power and royal residence is believed to have been the small site of Zaachila to the south, while the larger site of Mitla (near Monte Albán) may have been a religious capital. Known particularly for its mosaic 'fret' or 'greca' designs on building facades, Mitla consists of several stone plazas and a defended fortress-like *mesa* (flat-topped hill).

I. Bernal: 'Architecture in Oaxaca after the end of Monte Alban', *Handbook of Middle American Indians* III/2, ed. G.R. Willey (Austin, 1965), 837–43; J.W. Whitecotton: *The Zapotecs: princes, priests and peasants* (Norman, 1977); R.E. Blanton: *Monte Albán: settlement patterns at the ancient Zapotec capital* (New York, 1978); J.F. Scott: *The Danzantes of Monte Albán*, 2 parts, Studies in Pre-Columbian art and archaeology 19 (Washington, D.C., 1978); K.V. Flannery and J. Marcus, eds: *The cloud people: divergent evolution of the Zapotec and Mixtec civilizations* (New York, 1983).

PR

Zaskal'naya

see AK-KAYA

Zawi Chemi Shanidar

Open-air EPIPALAEOLITHIC site in the ZAGROS region of northern Iraq, close to SHANIDAR Cave. It was excavated at the same time as the latter by Ralph and Ruth Solecki in the 1970s, and it has been suggested that Zawi Chemi may represent the summer encampment of the same group who were probably spending their winters at Shanidar Cave, where a number of human burials have also been found. The Epipalaeolithic deposits at Zawi Chemi, immediately underlying Iron Age strata, are about 1–2 metres deep, with refuse pits cut into 'natural' at the base. The remains of circular stone huts have survived, as well as huge quantities of animal bones, which have been used to demonstrate a gradual shift in subsistence from the hunting of red deer to the domestication of sheep. In the more recent levels there is also some evidence of artefacts used in the preparation of plant food (e.g. querns and sickle-hafts).

J. Mellaart: *The Neolithic of the Near East* (London, 1975), 70–3; R.L. Solecki: *An early village site at Zawi Chemi Shanidar* (Malibu, 1980).

IS

Zawiyat Umm el-Rakham

see MERSA MATRUH

Zendjirli

see ZINJIRLI

Zenghouyimu

see TSENG HOU YI TOMB

Zhenla culture

Polity in Southeast Asia between AD 550 and 800. It is known from Chinese sources to have succeeded the polity of FUNAN, but the meaning of the Chinese references is not clear, and the location of Zhenla is therefore debatable. Most agree that it was centred in Cambodia between the junction of the Mekong and the Bassac to the south, and the Dangraek range to the north. The archaeological sites identified with the Zhenla culture include Isanapura and Thala Borivat.

Isanapura, situated in the tributary valley of the Stung Sen, covers an area of 400 ha enclosed by double walls, outside which is a reservoir. Three walled precincts have been traced, each containing single-chamber brick temples which are dedicated to the worship of Siva and decorated with motifs of Indian origin. Associated inscriptions describe the military success of Isanavarman and record that he founded the temples. The site of Thala Borivat, near Stung Treng on the Mekong River (where the San and Srepok rivers give access from the Mekong valley to the territory of the CHAMS) incorporates several sanctuaries with impressive lintels stylistically slightly earlier than those from Isanapura.

M.H. Parmentier: '*L'art Khmer primitif*, 2 vols (Paris, 1927); P. Levy: 'Thala Borivat ou Stung Treng: sites de la capitale due souverein Khmer Bhavavarman 1 er', *JA* 257 (1970), 113–29; C. Jacques: '"Funan" "Zhenla". the reality concealed by these Chinese views of Indochina', *Early South East Asia*, ed. R.B. Smith and W. Watson (Oxford, 1979), 371–9; W.J. van Liere: 'Traditional water

management in the lower Mekong Basin', *WA* 11/3 (1980), 265–80; P. Wheatley: *Nagara and Commandery* (Chicago, 1983), 119–63.
CH

Zhongguo (Chung-kuo) *see* MIDDLE STATES

Zhongyuan *see* CHUNG-YÜAN

Zhou dynasty *see* EASTERN CHOU; WESTERN CHOU

Zhou-kou-dian *see* CHOUKOUTIEN

Zhouyuan *see* CHOU-YÜAN

ziggurat (Akkadian *ziqqurratu*) Type of Mesopotamian religious monument consisting of a series of stepped mud-brick platforms, which, according to the Greek historian Herodotus, were surmounted by a shrine (although there is no surviving archaeological evidence of this, since most surviving ziggurats are severely eroded). The ziggurat has its origins in the platform temples of the UBAID culture (*c*.5000–3800 BC), which were evidently designed to raise the shrine of the god nearer to heaven (Businck 1970). The White Temple at URUK, dating to the late Uruk period, *c*.3150 BC, appears to be part of an early predecessor of the ziggurat (Frankfort 1970: 20). Depictions on cylinder seals suggest that the earliest true ziggurats were probably constructed in the Early Dynastic period (*c*.2900–2350 BC). Although there are traces of Early Dynastic large stepped temples at Kish, Nippur and UR (Crawford 1991: 74), the first definite surviving ziggurat is the Temple of Sin built by Ur-Nammu at Ur in *c*.2100 BC, which consists of three platforms of unbaked brick (cased with outer layers of baked brick), the lowest stage covering an area of almost 3000 sq. m and reaching a height of 11 m at its centre. The uppermost stages and shrine were, however, eroded away.

The typical early ziggurat – found mainly in southern Mesopotamia – had a rectangular base, and built against one of its sides were three ascending staircases forming a T-shape. A later type, found at more northerly sites such as KHORSABAD, NIMRUD and Tell Rimah (the latter located in the Afar Sinjar plain) was directly attached to the rear of a larger temple complex. Perhaps the most famous ziggurat is the temple of Etemenanki at BABYLON, which is traditionally equated with the Biblical 'Tower of Babel', but ironically this is the worst preserved. There are remains of ziggurats at 16 sites in Mesopotamia, ranging in date from the Ur III period to the Assyrian empire (*c*.2112–612 BC). Examples of similar stepped temples have also been found at sites outside Mesopotamia, such as CHOGA ZANBIL in Iran and ALTINTEPE in Turkmenia, but these may well have been independent developments, bearing only a superficial resemblance to the Mesopotamian ziggurats.

H. Lenzen: *Die Entwicklung der Zikkurat* (Leipzig, 1941); T.A. Busink: 'L'origine et l'évolution de la ziggurat Babylonienne', *Jaarbericht Ex Oriente Lux* 21 (1970), 91–142; H. Frankfort: *The art and architecture of the ancient Orient*, 4th edn (Harmondsworth, 1970), 20–2, 138–40; M. Roaf: *Cultural atlas of Mesopotamia and the Ancient Near East* (New York and Oxford, 1990), 104–5 [distribution map of ziggurats]; H. Crawford: *Sumer and the Sumerians* (Cambridge, 1991), 71–6.
IS

Zimbabwe culture *see* GREAT ZIMBABWE

Zinchecra *see* AFRICA 1

Zinjanthropus *see* OLDUVAI

Zinjirli (Zendjirli; anc. Sam'al) Iron Age townsite located in southeastern Turkey (near the border with modern Syria), consisting of a hilltop citadel incorporating a number of neo-HITTITE palace buildings dating principally to the 8th century BC. Excavated by a German expedition in 1881–91, Zinjirli is the most complete surviving north Syrian city of its period. The citadel, probably founded as early as *c*.1500 BC, is surrounded by a 3.5 m thick mud-brick double wall, 800 m in diameter and incorporating a number of circular towers. It was entered through an inner and outer gateway, the latter protected by pairs of lions and bulls sculpted in relief on the orthostats. The five main palaces were built in the typical *BIT-HILANI* style, and one of them was probably occupied in the 7th century BC by an ASSYRIAN governor. Since the city appears to have been largely populated by ARAMAEANS, the art and architecture are essentially a synthesis of Aramaean and neo-Hittite styles. A series of Aramaic inscriptions found at the site have enabled the dynasty of local rulers to be reconstructed.

F. von Luschan: *Ausgrabungen in Sendschirli*, 5 vols (Berlin, 1893–1943).
IS

Zulla *see* ADULIS

Zvejnieki Extensive prehistoric cemetery located on a morainic hill in northern Latvia, 110 km northeast of the city of Riga. The earliest burials are late Mesolithic and contained bone spears with short blades, symmetrical barbs and long shafts, leaf-shaped spearheads, bone daggers, stone knives, scrapers, blades and pendants made of perforated animal teeth. In the Early Neolithic graves, the deceased were buried with spear- and arrowheads, while pendants made of animal teeth were the most common ornaments. In one grave, a female figurine made of bone was found. The largest group of graves, in the southeastern section of the cemetery, belong to the Middle and Late Neolithic and contained hunting and fishing equipment such as spear- and arrowheads, with some items deliberately broken, as well as flint scrapers, bone harpoons, chisels and awls. Ornaments included amber beads, pendants and discs. Ceramics included PIT-AND-COMB, NARVA and Piestina styles and, in the Late Neolithic, various styles of CORDED WARE pottery.

F. Zagorskis: *Zvejnieku Akmens Laikmeta Kapulauks* (Riga, 1987).

PD